ROGET'S THESAURUS

OF SYNONYMS AND ANTONYMS

1980 Edition

BY

PETER MARK ROGET, M.D., F.R.S.

ENLARGED BY
JOHN LEWIS ROGET, M.A.

NEW EDITION REVISED AND ENLARGED BY
SAMUEL ROMILLY ROGET, M.A.

PLAN OF CLASSIFICATION

TABULAR SYNOPSIS OF CATEGORIES

Class I. ABSTRACT RELATIONS

I. EXISTENCE

1°. ABSTRACT...........	1. Existence.	2. Inexistence.
2°. CONCRETE..........	3. Substantiality.	4. Unsubstantiality.
3°. FORMAL............	*Internal.*	*External.*
	5. Intrinsicality.	6. Extrinsicality.
4°. MODAL.............	*Absolute.*	*Relative.*
	7. State.	8. Circumstance.

II. RELATION

	9. Relation.	10. Irrelation.
	11. Consanguinity.	
1°. ABSOLUTE..........	12. Correlation.	
	13. Identity.	14. Contrariety.
	15. Difference.	
2°. CONTINUOUS........	16. Uniformity.	16a. Non-uniformity.
	17. Similarity.	18. Dissimilarity.
3°. PARTIAL...........	19. Imitation.	20. Non-imitation.
	20a. Variation.	
	21. Copy.	22. Prototype.
4°. GENERAL...........	23. Agreement.	24. Disagreement.

III. QUANTITY

1°. SIMPLE............	*Absolute.*	*Relative.*
	25. Quantity.	26. Degree.
	27. Equality.	28. Inequality.
	29. Mean.	
	30. Compensation.	
2°. COMPARATIVE.......	*By Comparison with a Standard.*	
	31. Greatness.	32. Smallness.
	By Comparison with a similar Object.	
	33. Superiority.	34. Inferiority.
	Changes in Quantity.	
	35. Increase.	36. Decrease.
	37. Addition.	38. { Non-addition. Subduction. }
	39. Adjunct.	40. Remainder.
3°. CONJUNCTIVE.......		40a. Decrement.
	41. Mixture.	42. Simpleness.
	43. Junction.	44. Disjunction.
	45. Vinculum.	
	46. Coherence.	47. Incoherence.
	48. Combination.	49. Decomposition.

2°. LINEAR—continued...

210. Summit.	211. Base.
212. Verticality.	213. Horizontality.
214. Pendency.	215. Support.
216. Parallelism.	217. Obliquity.
218. Inversion.	
219. Crossing.	

3°. CENTRICAL

1. General

220. Exteriority.	221. Interiority.
222. Centrality.	
223. Covering.	224. Lining.
225. Investment.	226. Divestment.
227. Circumjacence.	228. Interjacence.
229. Circumscription.	
230. Outline.	
231. Edge.	
232. Inclosure.	
233. Limit.	

2. Special

234. Front	235. Rear.
236. Laterality.	237. Contraposition.
238. Dextrality.	239. Sinistrality.

III. FORM

1°. GENERAL

240. Form.	241. Amorphism.
242. Symmetry.	243. Distortion.

2°. SPECIAL

244. Angularity.	
245. Curvature.	246. Straightness.
247. Circularity.	248. Convolution.
249. Rotundity.	
250. Convexity.	252. Concavity.

251. Flatness.

3°. SUPERFICIAL

253. Sharpness.	254. Bluntness.
255. Smoothness.	256. Roughness.
257. Notch.	
258. Fold.	
259. Furrow.	
260. Opening.	261. Closure.
262. Perforator.	263. Stopper.

IV. MOTION

1°. MOTION IN GENERAL

264. Motion.	265. Quiescence.
266. Journey.	267. Navigation.
268. Traveler.	269. Mariner.
270. Transference.	
271. Carrier.	
272. Vehicle.	273. Ship.

2°. DEGREES OF MOTION

274. Velocity.	275. Slowness.

3°. CONJOINED WITH FORCE...

276. Impulse.	277. Recoil.

4°. WITH REFERENCE TO DIRECTION.....

278. Direction.	279. Deviation.
280. Precession.	281. Sequence.
282. Progression.	283. Regression.
284. Propulsion.	285. Traction.
286. Approach.	287. Recession.
288. Attraction.	289. Repulsion.
290. Convergence.	291. Divergence.
292. Arrival.	293. Departure.
294. Ingress.	295. Egress.
296. Reception.	297. Ejection.
298. Food.	299. Excretion.
300. Insertion.	301. Extraction.
302. Passage.	
303. Overstep.	304. Shortcoming.

4°. **With Reference to Direction**—*cont*...

305. Ascent.	306. Descent.
307. Elevation.	308. Depression.
309. Leap.	310. Plunge.
311. Circuition.	
312. Rotation.	313. Evolution.
314. Oscillation.	
315. Agitation.	

Class III. MATTER

I. MATTER IN GENERAL.......

316. Materiality.	317. Immateriality.
318. World.	
319. Gravity.	320. Levity.

II. INORGANIC MATTER

1°. **Solids**.............

321. Density.	322. Rarity.
323. Hardness.	324. Softness.
325. Elasticity.	326. Inelasticity.
327. Tenacity.	328. Brittleness.
329. Texture.	
330. Pulverulence.	
331. Friction.	332. Lubrication.

2°. **Fluids**

1. *In General*

333. Fluidity.	334. Gaseity.
335. Liquefaction.	336. Vaporization.
337. Water.	338. Air.
339. Moisture.	340. Dryness.

2. *Specific*...

341. Ocean.	342. Land.
343. { Gulf. Lake. }	
	344. Plain.
345. Marsh.	346. Island.

3. *In motion*

347. Stream.	
348. River.	349. Wind.
350. Conduit.	351. Air-pipe.

3°. **Imperfect Fluids**...

352. Semiliquidity.	353. Bubble.
354. Pulpiness.	355. Unctuousness.
	356. Oil.
	356a. Resin.

III. ORGANIC MATTER

1°. **Vitality**

1. *In General*....

357. Organization.	358. Inorganization.
359. Life.	360. Death.
	361. Killing.
	362. Corpse.
	363. Interment.

2. *Special*

364. Animality.	365. Vegetability.
366. Animal.	367. Vegetable.
368. Zoology.	369. Botany.
370. Cicuration.	371. Agriculture.
372. Mankind.	
373. Man.	374. Woman.

2°. SENSATION

(1) General

375. Sensibility.	376. Insensibility.
377. Pleasure.	378. Pain.
379. Touch.	

(2) Special

1. Touch

380. { Sensations of Touch.	381. Numbness.

2. Heat

382. Heat.	383. Cold.
384. Calefaction.	385. Refrigeration.
386. Furnace.	387. Refrigeratory.
388. Fuel.	
389. Thermometer.	

3. Taste

390. Taste.	391. Insipidity.
392. Pungency.	
393. Condiment.	
394. Savouriness.	395. Unsavouriness.
396. Sweetness.	397. Sourness.

4. Odor

398. Odor.	399. Inodorousness.
400. Fragrance.	401. Fœtor.

5. Sound

(i.) Sound in General.

402. Sound.	403. Silence.
404. Loudness.	405. Faintness.

(ii.) Specific Sounds.

406. Snap.	407. Roll.
408. Resonance.	408a. Non-resonance.
	409. Sibilation.
410. Stridor.	
411. Cry.	412. Ululation.

(iii.) Musical Sounds.

413. { Melody. Concord.	414. Discord.
415. Music.	
416. Musician.	
417. Musical Instruments.	

(iv.) Perception of Sound.

418. Hearing.	419. Deafness.

6. Light

(i.) Light in General.

420. Light.	421. Darkness.
422. Dimness.	
423. Luminary.	424. Shade.
425. Transparency.	426. Opacity.
427. Semitransparency.	

(ii.) Specific Light.

428. Color.	429. Achromatism.
430. Whiteness.	431. Blackness.
432. Gray.	433. Brown.
434. Redness.	435. Greenness.
436. Yellowness.	437. Purple.
438. Blueness.	439. Orange.
440. Variegation.	

(iii.) Perceptions of Light.

441. Vision.	442. Blindness.
443. Dimsightedness.	
444. Spectator.	
445. Optical Instruments.	
446. Visibility.	447. Invisibility.
448. Appearance.	449. Disappearance.

SYNOPSIS OF CATEGORIES

Class IV. INTELLECT

Division (I.). Formation of Ideas

I. Operations of Intellect in General

450. Intellect.	450a. Absence of Intellect.
451. Thought.	452. Incogitancy.
453. Idea.	454. Topic.
455. Curiosity.	456. Incuriosity.
457. Attention.	458. Inattention.
459. Care.	460. Neglect.

II. Precursory Conditions and Operations

461. Inquiry.	462. Answer.
463. Experiment.	
464. Comparison.	
465. Discrimination.	465a. Indiscrimination.
466. Measurement.	
467. Evidence.	468. Counter-evidence.

469. Qualification.

III. Materials for Reasoning

Degrees of Evidence.

470. Possibility.	471. Impossibility.
472. Probability.	473. Improbability.
474. Certainty.	475. Uncertainty.

IV. Reasoning Processes

476. Reasoning.	477. { Intuition. Sophistry. }
478. Demonstration.	479. Confutation.
480. Judgement.	481. Misjudgement.
480a. Discovery.	
482. Over-estimation.	483. Under-estimation.

V. Results of Reasoning

484. Belief.	485. { Unbelief. Doubt. }
486. Credulity.	487. Incredulity.
488. Assent.	489. Dissent.
490. Knowledge.	491. Ignorance.
492. Scholar.	493. Ignoramus.
494. Truth.	495. Error.
496. Maxim.	497. Absurdity.

Faculties.

498. { Intelligence. Wisdom. }	499. { Imbecility. Folly. }
500. Sage.	501. Fool.
502. Sanity.	503. Insanity.
	504. Madman.

VI. Extension of Thought

1°. *To the Past.*

505. Memory.	506. Oblivion.
507. Expectation.	508. Inexpectation.
	509. Disappointment.

2°. *To the Future.*

510. Foresight.
511. Prediction.
512. Omen.
513. Oracle.

VII. Creative Thought

514. Supposition.
515. Imagination.

SYNOPSIS OF CATEGORIES

Division (II.). COMMUNICATION OF IDEAS

I. NATURE OF IDEAS COMMUNICATED......

516. Meaning.   517. Unmeaningness.
518. Intelligibility.   519. Unintelligibility.
520. Equivocalness.
521. Metaphor.
522. Interpretation.   523. Misinterpretation.
524. Interpreter.

II. MODES OF COMMUNICATION............

525. Manifestation.   526. Latency.
527. Information.   528. Concealment.
529. Disclosure.   530. Ambush.
531. Publication.
532. News.   533. Secret.
534. Messenger.
535. Affirmation.   536. Negation.
537. Teaching.   538. Misteaching.
               539. Learning.
540. Teacher.   541. Learner.
542. School.
543. Veracity.   544. Falsehood.
               545. Deception.
               546. Untruth.
547. Dupe.   548. Deceiver.
               549. Exaggeration.

III. MEANS OF COMMUNICATION

1°. *Natural Means*.......

550. Indication.
551. Record.   552. Obliteration.
553. Recorder.
554. Representation.   555. Misrepresentation.
556. Painting.
557. Sculpture.
558. Engraving.
559. Artist.

2°. *Conventional Means*

1. *Language generally*

560. Language.
561. Letter.
562. Word.   563. Neology.
564. Nomenclature.   565. Misnomer.
566. Phrase.
567. Grammar.   568. Solecism.
569. Style.

Qualities of Style.

570. Perspicuity.   571. Obscurity.
572. Conciseness.   573. Diffuseness.
574. Vigour.   575. Feebleness.
576. Plainness.   577. Ornament.
578. Elegance.   579. Inelegance.

2. *Spoken Language*

580. Voice.   581. Aphony.
582. Speech.   583. Stammering.
584. Loquacity.   585. Taciturnity.
586. Allocution.   587. Response.
588. Interlocution.   589. Soliloquy.

3. *Written Language*

590. Writing.   591. Printing.
592. Correspondence.   593. Book.
594. Description.
595. Dissertation.
596. Compendium.
597. Poetry.   598. Prose.
599. The Drama.

Class V. VOLITION

Division (I.). Individual Volition

I. Volition in General

1°. Acts....

600. Will.	601. Necessity.
602. Willingness.	603. Unwillingness.
604. Resolution.	605. Irresolution.
604a. Perseverance. }	
606. Obstinacy. }	607. Tergiversation.
	608. Caprice.
609. Choice.	609a. Absence of Choice.
	610. Rejection.
611. Predetermination.	612. Impulse.
613. Habit.	614. Desuetude.

2°. Causes..

615. Motive.	615a. Absence of Motive.
	616. Dissuasion.
617. Plea.	

3°. Objects..

618. Good.	619. Evil.
620. Intention.	621. Chance.
622. Pursuit.	623. Avoidance.
	624. Relinquishment.

II. Prospective Volition........

1°. Conceptional..

625. Business.	
626. Plan.	
627. Method.	
628. Mid-Course.	629. Circuit.
630. Requirement.	

2°. Subservience to Ends...

1. Actual Subservience.

631. Instrumentality.	
632. Means.	
633. Instrument.	
634. Substitute.	
635. Materials.	
636. Store.	
637. Provision.	638. Waste.
639. Sufficiency.	
641. Redundance.	640. Insufficiency.

2. Degree of Subservience.

642. Importance.	643. Unimportance.
644. Utility.	645. Inutility.
646. Expedience.	647. Inexpedience.
648. Goodness.	649. Badness.
650. Perfection.	651. Imperfection.
652. Cleanness.	653. Uncleanness.
654. Health.	655. Disease.
656. Salubrity.	657. Insalubrity.
658. Improvement.	659. Deterioration.
660. Restoration.	661. Relapse.
662. Remedy.	663. Bane.

3. Contingent Subservience.

664. Safety.	665. Danger.
666. Refuge.	667. Pitfall.
668. Warning.	
669. Alarm.	
670. Preservation.	
671. Escape.	
672. Deliverance.	

CLASS VI. AFFECTIONS

II. PERSONAL

1°. PASSIVE
- 827. Pleasure.
- 828. Pain.
- 829. Pleasureableness.
- 830. Painfulness.
- 831. Content.
- 832. Discontent.
- 833. Regret.
- 834. Relief.
- 835. Aggravation.
- 836. Cheerfulness.
- 837. Dejection.
- 838. Rejoicing.
- 839. Lamentation.
- 840. Amusement.
- 841. Weariness.
- 842. Wit.
- 843. Dulness.
- 844. Humorist.

2°. DISCRIMINATIVE
- 845. Beauty.
- 846. Ugliness.
- 847. Ornament.
- 848. Blemish.
- 849. Simplicity.
- 850. Taste.
- 851. Vulgarity.
- 852. Fashion.
- 853. Ridiculousness.
- 854. Fop.
- 855. Affection.
- 856. Ridicule.
- 857. Laughing-stock.

3°. PROSPECTIVE
- 858. Hope.
- 859. Hopelessness.
- 860. Fear.
- 861. Courage.
- 862. Cowardice.
- 863. Rashness.
- 864. Caution.
- 865. Desire.
- 867. Dislike.
- 866. Indifference.
- 868. Fastidiousness.
- 869. Satiety.

4°. CONTEMPLATIVE
- 870. Wonder.
- 871. Expectance.
- 872. Prodigy.

5°. EXTRINSIC
- 873. Repute.
- 874. Disrepute.
- 875. Nobility.
- 876. Commonalty.
- 877. Title.
- 878. Pride.
- 879. Humility.
- 880. Vanity.
- 881. Modesty.
- 882. Ostentation.
- 883. Celebration.
- 884. Boasting.
- 885. Insolence.
- 886. Servility.
- 887. Blusterer.

III. SYMPATHETIC

1°. SOCIAL
- 888. Friendship.
- 889. Enmity.
- 890. Friend.
- 891. Enemy.
- 892. Sociality.
- 893. Seclusion.
- 894. Courtesy.
- 895. Discourtesy.
- 896. Congratulation.
- 897. Love.
- 898. Hate.
- 899. Favorite.
- 900. Resentment.
- 901. Irascibility.
- 901a. Sullenness.
- 902. Endearment.
- 903. Marriage.
- 904. Celibacy.
- 905. Divorce.

SYNOPSIS OF CATEGORIES

ABBREVIATIONS, &c.

Adj.	*adj.*	Adjectives, Participles, and Words having the power of Adjectives.
Adv.	*adv.*	Adverbs and Adverbial Expressions.
Int.	*int.*	Interjections.
Phr.	*phr.*	Phrases.
V.	*v.*	Verbs.

The numbers are those of the headings, or Categories.

Words in italics within parentheses are not intended to explain the meanings of the words which precede them, but to indicate the nature of allied group of words under the numbers which follow them.

THESAURUS

OF

ENGLISH WORDS AND PHRASES

1. Existence.—N. existence, being, entity, *ens, esse,* subsistence, quiddity.

reality, realness, actuality; positiveness etc. *adj.*; fact, matter of fact, sober reality; truth etc. 494; actual existence.

presence etc. (*existence in space*) 186; coexistence etc. 120.

stubborn fact; not a -dream etc. 515; no joke.

substance, essence, prime constituent, hypostatis. [Science of existence], ontology.

V. exist, be; have -being etc. *n.*; subsist, live, breathe, stand, obtain, be the case; occur etc. (*event*) 151; have place, rank, prevail; find oneself, pass the time, vegetate.

consist in, lie in, reside in, inhere in.

come into -existence etc. *n.*; arise etc. (*begin*) 66; come forth etc. (*appear*) 446.

become etc. (*be converted*) 144; bring into existence etc. 161; coexist, preexist, endure etc. 141.

Adj. existing etc. *v.*; existent, subsistent, under the sun; in -existence etc, *n.*; extant; afloat, on foot, current, prevalent, rife, in force, -vogue; undestroyed.

real, actual, positive, absolute; true etc. 494; substan-tial, -tive; self-existing, -ent.

well-founded, -grounded; un-ideal, -imagined; not -potential etc. 2.

Adv. actually etc. *adj.*; in -fact, — point of fact, — reality; indeed; *de —, ipso-facto.*

2. Nonexistence.—N. nonexistence; inexistence, -subsistence; nonentity, *nil;* negativeness etc. *adj.*; nullity; nihil-ity, -ism; *tabula rasa,* blank; abeyance; absence etc. 187; no such thing etc. 4; nothingness, oblivion, *non esse.*

annihilation; extinction etc. (*destruction*) 162.

V. not -exist etc. 1; have no -existence etc. 1; be null and void; cease to -exist etc. 1; pass away, perish; be —, become-extinct etc. *adj.*; die out; disappear etc. 449; melt away, dissolve, leave not a rack behind, leave no trace; go, be no more; die etc. 360.

annihilate, render null, nullify; abrogate etc. 756; destroy etc. 162; take away; remove etc. (*displace*) 185.

Adj. inexistent, non-existent etc. 1; negative, blank, null and void; missing, omitted; absent etc. 187; visionary etc. 515.

unreal, potential, virtual; baseless, *in nubibus;* unsubstantial etc. 4; vain.

un-born, -created, -begotten, -conceived, produced, -made.

perished, annihilated etc. *v.*; extinct, exhausted, gone, lost, departed; defunct etc. (*dead*) 360; fabulous, ideal etc. (*imaginary*) 515; supposititious etc. 514.

Adv. negatively, virtually, etc. *adj.*

3. Substantiality.—N. substantiality, *hypostasis;* person, thing, object, article; something, a being, an existence; creature, body, substance, flesh and blood, stuff, *substratum;* matter etc. 316; physical nature.

[Totality of existences], world etc. 318; *plenum.*

Adj. substan-tive, -tial, concrete; hypostatic; personal, bodily; tangible etc. (*material*) 316; real, corporeal, evident.

Adv. substantially etc. *adj.*; bodily, essentially.

4. Unsubstantiality.—N. un-, in-substantiality; nothingness, nihility.

nothing, naught, *nil,* nullity, zero, cipher, no one, nobody; never —, ne'er -a one; no such thing, none in the world; nothing -whatever, — at all, — on earth; not a -particle etc. (*smallness*) 32; all - talk, — moonshine, — stuff and nonsense, matter of no import.

thing of naught, man of straw, John Doe and Richard Roe; *nominis umbra,* nonentity, figurehead, lay figure; flash in the pan, *vox et praeterea nihil.*

shadow; phantasm, phantom etc. (*fallacy of vision*) 443; dream etc. (*imagination*) 515; *ignis fatuus* etc. (*luminary*) 423; 'such stuff as dreams are made of;' air, thin air; bubble etc. 353; 'baseless fabric of a vision;' mockery.

hollowness, blank; vacuity, void etc. (*absence*) 187.

inanity, fool's paradise, fatuity, stupidity, emptiness of mind.

V. vanish, evaporate, fade, sink, fly —, die —, melt- away, dissolve, disappear etc. 449; become extinct, become invisible.

Adj. unsubstantial; fleeting; base-, ground-less; ungrounded; without —, having no- foundation.

visionary etc. (*imaginary*) 515; immaterial etc. 317; spectral etc. 980; dreamy; shadowy; ethereal, airy, imponderable, tenuous, vague.

vacant, vacuous; empty etc. 187; eviscerated; blank, hollow; nominal; null; inane.

Phr. there's nothing in it.

1

5. Intrinsicality.—N. intrinsicality, inbeing, inherence, inhesion, immanence; subjectiveness; *ego*; essence; essentialness etc. *adj.*; essential part, essential stuff, substance, quintessence, incarnation, quiddity, gist, pith, core, kernel, marrow, sap, lifeblood, backbone, heart, soul, life, flower; important part etc. (*importance*) 642.

principle, nature, constitution, character, ethos, type, quality, crasis, *diathesis*.

habit; temper, -ament; spirit, humor, grain, disposition, streak, tendency etc. 176.

endowment, capacity; capability etc. (*power*) 157; moods, declensions, features, aspects; peculiarities etc. (*specialty*) 79; idiosyncrasy; idiocrasy; diagnostics.

V. be – , run- in the blood; be born so; be - intrinsic etc. *adj.*

Adj. derived from within, subjective; idiocratic, idiosyncratic, intrin-sic, -sical; fundamental, cardinal, normal, inherent, essential, natural; in-nate, -born, -bred, -dwelling, -grained; -wrought; radical, incarnate, thoroughbred, hereditary, inherited, immanent; congen-ital, -ite; connate, running in the blood; coeval with birth, genetic, ingenerate, -genite; indigenous; in the -grain etc. *n.*; bred in the bone, instinctive; inward, internal etc. 221; to the manner born; virtual.

characteristic etc. (*special*) 79, (*indicative*) 550; invariable, incurable, ineradicable, fixed, settled, constant, unchanging.

Adv. intrinsically etc. *adj.*; at bottom, in the main, in effect, essentially, practically, virtually, substantially, *au fond*; fairly.

6. Extrinsicality.—N. extrinsicality, objectiveness, *non ego*; extraneousness etc. 57; accident; letter of the law.

Adj. derived from without; objective; extrinsic, -sical; extraneous etc. (*foreign*) 57; modal, adventitious, additional, supervenient, fortuitous; a-, ad-scititious; incidental, casual, accidental, unessential, non-essential, accessory.

implanted, ingrafted; instilled, inculcated.

outward etc. (*external*) 220.

Adv. extrinsically etc. *adj.*

7. State.—N. state, condition, category, estate, lot, case, trim, mood, pickle, plight etc. 704; temper; aspect etc. (*appearance*) 448.

constitution, habitude, *diathesis;* frame, fabric etc. 329; stamp, set, fit, mold.

mode, modality, schesis; fettle; form etc. (*shape*) 240.

tone, tenor, turn; trim, guise, fashion, light, complexion, style, character.

V. be in –, possess –, enjoy –, labor under- a -state etc. *n.;* be on a footing, do, fare; come to pass.

Adj. conditional, modal, formal; structural, organic.

Adv. conditionally etc. *adj.;* as -the matter stands, – things are; such being the case etc. 8.

8. Circumstance.—N. circumstance, situation, phase, position, posture, attitude, place, point; terms; *régime;* footing, standing, status.

occasion, juncture, conjuncture; contingency etc. (*event*) 151.

predicament; emergen-ce, -cy; exigency, crisis, pinch, pass, push; turning point; crossroads.

bearings, how the land lies.

Adj. circumstantial; given, conditional, provisional; critical; modal; contingent, incidental; adventitious etc. (*extrinsic*) 6.

Adv. in the circumstances etc. *n.,* under the conditions etc. 7; thus, in such wise.

accordingly; that –, such- being the case; that being so, since, seeing that.

as matters stand; as -things, – times- go.

conditionally, provided, if, in case; if -so, – so be, – it be so; if it so -happen, – turn out; in the event of; in such a -contingency, – case, – event; provisionally, unless, without.

according to -circumstances, – the occasion; as it may -happen, – turn out, – be; as the -case may be, – wind blows; *pro re natâ.*

9. Relation.—N. relation, bearing, reference, connection, apposition, interconnection, concern, cognation; applicability, appositeness; correlation etc. 12; analogy; similarity etc. 17; affinity, intimacy, friendship; homology, alliance, homogeneity, association, rapport; approximation etc. (*nearness*) 197; filiation etc. (*consanguinity*) 11; interest; relevancy etc. 23; relationship, relative position; relativity; interrelation etc. 12.

comparison etc. 464; ratio, proportion.

link, tie, bond, bond of union.

V. be-related etc. *adj.;* have a relation etc. *n.;* relate –, refer- to; bear upon, regard, concern, touch, affect, have to do with; pertain –, belong –, appertain- to; have respect to; answer to; interest.

bring -into relation with, – to bear upon; connect, associate, draw a parallel; link etc. 43.

Adj. relative; correlative etc. 12; cognate; relating to etc. *v.;* relative to, in relation with, referable *or* referrible to; belonging to etc. *v.;* appurtenant to, in common with.

related, connected; implicated, associated, affiliated, akin, allied to; collateral, cognate, congenial, kindred, affinitive, *en rapport*, in touch with.

approxima-tive, -ting; approaching; proportion-al, -ate, -able; allusive, comparable.

in the same -category etc. 75; like etc. 17; relevant etc. (*apt*) 23.

Adv. relatively etc. *adj.;* pertinently etc. 23.

thereof; as -to, – for, – respects, – re-gards; about; concerning etc. *v.;* anent; relating –, as relates- to; with -relation, – reference, – respect, – regard-to; in respect of; while speaking –, *à propos* -of; in connection with; by the -way, – by; whereas; for –, in -as much as; in point of, as far as; on the -part, – score- of; *quoad hoc; pro re natâ;* under the -head etc. (*class*) 75- of; in the matter of, *in re.*

Phr. 'thereby hangs a tale.'

10. Irrelation. [Want, or absence of relation.]—**N.** irrelation, dissociation; inapplicability; inconnection; multifariousness; disconnection etc. (*disjunction*) 44; inconsequence, independence; incommensurability; irreconcilableness etc. (*disagreement*) 24; heterogeneity;

unconformity etc. 83; irrelevancy, impertinence, *nihil ad rem;* intrusion etc. 24.

V. have no -relation etc. 9 to, − bearing upon, − concern etc. 9 with, − business with; not -concern etc. 9; have -nothing to do with, − no business there; intrude, etc. 24.

bring −, drag −, haul −, lug- in head and shoulders.

Adj. irrelative, irrespective, unrelated, irrelated; arbitrary; independent, unallied; un-, dis-connected; adrift, isolated, insular; extraneous, strange, alien, foreign, outlandish, exotic.

not comparable, incommensurable, heterogeneous; unconformable etc. 83.

irrelevant; rambling etc. 279; inapplicable; not -pertinent, − to the purpose; impertinent, inapposite, beside the mark, *à propos de bottes;* away from −, foreign to −, beside- the -purpose, − question, − transaction, − point; misplaced etc. (*intrusive*) 24.

remote, far fetched, out of the way, forced, neither here nor there, quite another thing; detached, segregated, segregate.

multifarious; discordant etc. 24.

incidental, parenthetical, *obiter dictum,* episodic.

Adv. parenthetically etc. *adj.;* by the -way, − by; *en passant,* incidentally; irrespecitively etc. *adj.;* without reference, − regard- to; in the abstract etc. 87; *a se.*

11. Consanguinity. [Relations of kindred.]

—N. consanguinity, relationship, kindred, blood; parentage etc. (*paternity*) 166; filiation, affiliation; lineage, agnation, connection, cognation, alliance; family -connection, − tie; ties of blood; blood relationship; nepotism.

kins-man, -folk; people; kith and kin; relation, -tive; connection; sib; next of kin; uncle, aunt, nephew, niece; cousin, -german; first −, second- cousin; cousin -once, − twice etc.- removed; near −, distant-relation; brother, sister, one's own flesh and blood.

family, patriarch, matriarch; fraternity; brother-, sister-, cousin-hood.

race, stock, generation; sept etc. 166 ; stirps, side; strain; breed, clan, tribe.

V. be -related etc. *adj.* − to; claim -relationship etc. *n.-* with.

Adj. related, akin, consanguineous, matrilinear, patrilineal, of the blood, family, allied, collateral; cog-, ag-, con-nate; kindred; affiliated, affine; fraternal, avuncular.

intimately −, nearly −, closely −, remotely −, distantly- related, − allied; german.

12. Correlation. [Double or reciprocal relation.]

—N. reciprocalness etc. *adj.;* recipro-city, -cality, -cation; mutuality, correlation, correspondence, interdependence; interchange etc. 148; exchange, barter; interrelation, interconnection; alternation, see-saw.

V. reciprocate, alternate; interchange etc. 148; exchange; counterchange; interact, correspond, mutualize, give and take.

Adj. reciprocal, mutual, commutual, correlative; alternate; interchangeable; international; correspondent, complementary, analogous.

Adv. *mutatis mutandis; vice versâ;* each other; by turns etc. 148; reciprocally etc. *adj.;* to and fro etc. 314.

13. Identity.

—N. identity, sameness, oneness, ditto, homogeneity; unity, coincidence, coalescence; convertibility; equality etc. 27; self-ness, self, oneself; identification.

monotony, tautology etc. (*repetition*) 104.

synonym.

fac-simile etc. (*copy*) 21; *alter ego* etc. (*similar*) 17; *ipsissima verba* etc. (*exactness*) 494; same; self − , very − , one and the same; very −, actual-thing, no other.

V. be -identical etc. *adj.;* match, coincide, coalesce.

treat as −, render--the same , −identical; identify; recognize the identity of.

Adj. identical; self, ilk; the -same etc. *n.;* self same; synonymous; one and the same.

coincid-, coalesc-ent, -ing; indistinguishable; one; equivalent etc. (*equal*) 27; much -the same, − of a muchness; unaltered.

Adv. identically etc. *adj.;* on all fours; ibid-, -em.

14. Contrariety. [Non-coincidence.]

—N. contrariety, contrast, foil, antithesis, oppositeness; counterpole; contradiction; antagonism etc. (*opposition*) 708; counteraction etc. 179.

inversion etc. 218; the -opposite, − reverse, − inverse, − converse, − antipodes, − other extreme etc. 237.

antonym.

V. be -contrary etc. *adj.;* contrast with, oppose; differ *toto coelo.*

invert, reverse, turn the tables etc. 218.

contra-dict, -vene; antagonize etc. 708.

Adj. contrar-y, -ious, -iant; opposite, counter, dead against; ad-, con-, reverse; opposed, antithetical, contrasted, antipodean, antagonistic, opposing; conflicting, inconsistent, contradictory, at cross purposes; negative; hostile etc. 708.

differing *toto coelo;* diametrically opposite; as opposite as -black and white, − light and darkness, − fire and water, − the poles, as different as chalk from cheese; 'Hyperion to a satyr;' quite the -contrary, − reverse; no such thing, just the other way, *tout au contraire.*

Adv. contrarily etc. *adj.; contra,* contrariwise, *per contra,* on the contrary, nay rather; topsyturvy; *vice versâ;* on the other hand etc. (*in compensation*) 30.

15. Difference.

—N. difference, unlikeness; heterogeneity; vari-ance, -ation, -ety; diversity, dissimilarity etc. 18; disagreement etc. 24; disparity etc. (*inequality*) 28; distinction, contradistinction; distinctness; discrepancy, divergence, contrast etc. 18; nonconformity, incompatibility, antithesis.

discord etc. 713.

modification, moods and tenses.

nice −, fine −, delicate −, subtle- distinction; shade of difference, *nuance;* discrimination etc. 465; *differentia.*

different thing, something else, variant, apple

off another tree, horse of another color, another pair of shoes; this that or the other.

V. be -different etc. *adj.;* differ, vary, ablude, mismatch, contrast; diverge −, depart −, deviate- -from; divaricate; differ -*toto coelo,* − *longo intervallo.*

disagree etc. 713.

vary, modify etc. (*change*) 140.

discriminate etc. 465.

Adj. differing etc. *v.;* different, diverse, divided, heterogeneous; distinguishable; varied, modified; divergent, incongruous, diversified, various; discrepant, dissentient, differential; divers, all manner of; variform etc. 81; discordant etc. 713.

other, another, not the same; unequal etc. 28; unmatched; widely apart.

distinctive, characteristic; discriminative; distinghishing.

Adv. differently etc. *adj.*

Phr. *il y a fagots et fagots; tot nomines tot sententiae;* one man's meat is another man's poison.

16. Uniformity.—N. uniformity; homogeneity, -ousness; continuity, stability, consistency; connatural-ity, -ness; homology; accordance; conformity etc. 82; agreement etc. 23.

regularity, constancy, even tenor, routine; monotony, evenness, sameness, dead level; steadiness, equability, unity.

V. be -uniform etc. *adj.;* accord with etc. 23; run through.

become -uniform etc. *adj.;* conform to etc. 82.

render uniform etc. *adj.;* assimilate, level, smooth, dress.

Adj. uniform; homo-geneous, -logous; of a piece, consistent, steady; connatural; monotonous, changeless, dreary, even, invariable, equable, level, regular, stereotyped, unchanged, unvarying; methodical etc. 60; habitual etc. 613.

Adv. uniformly etc. *adj.;* uniformly with etc. (*conformably*) 82; in harmony with etc. (*agreeing*) 23; in a -rut, − groove.

always, ever etc. 112; invariably, without exception, never otherwise; by clock-work; endlessly etc. 112.

Phr. *ab uno disce omnes.*

16a. Non-uniformity. [Absence or want of uniformity.]−N. diversity, irregularity, unevenness; multiformity etc. 81; unconformity etc. 83; roughness etc. 256; heterogeneity, heteromorphism.

Adj. diversified, varied, irregular, uneven, rough etc. 256; multifarious; multiform etc. 81; of various kinds; all -manner, − sorts, − kinds-of.

Adv. in all manner of ways, here there and everywhere.

17. Similarity.—N. similarity, resemblance, likeness, similitude, semblance; affinity, approximation, parallelism; parity; agreement etc. 23; ana-logy, -logicalness; correspondence, equality etc.

connatural-ness, -ity; brotherhood, family likeness.

alliteration, rhyme, pun.

repetition etc. 104; sameness etc. (*identity*) 13; uniformity etc. 16.

analogue; the like; match, *pendant,* fellow, companion, pair, mate, twin, double, counterpart, brother, sister; one's second self, *alter ego,* chip of the old block, *par nobile fratrum,* Arcades ambo, birds of a feather, *et hoc genus omne.*

parallel; simile; type etc. (*metaphor*) 521; image etc. (*representation*) 554; photograph; close −, striking −, speaking −, faithful etc *adj.* − likeness, − resemblance.

V. be -similar etc. *adj.;* look like, resemble, bear resemblance, favor; savor −, smack- of; approximate; parallel, match, rhyme with; take after; imitate etc. 19; run in pairs.

Adj. similar; resembling etc. *v.;* like, alike; twin.

analog-ous, -ical; parallel, of a piece; such as, so.

connatural, congeneric, allied to; corresponding, cognate; akin to etc. (*consanguineous*) 11.

approximate, much the same, near, close, something like, such like; a show of; mock, *pseudo,* simulating, representing.

exact etc. (*true*) 494; lifelike, faithful, realistic; true to -nature, − the life; the -very image − pic·ure- of; for all the world like, *comme deux gouttes d'eau;* as like as -two peas, − it can stare; *instar omnium,* case in the same mold, ridiculously like.

Adv. as if, so to speak; as −, as if- it were; *quasi,* just as, *veluti in speculum.*

18. Dissimilarity.—N. dissimil-arity, -itude; unlikeness, diversity, disparity, dissemblance; divergence, inequality, difference etc. 15; novelty; variation, variety, originality, disguise.

V. be -unlike etc. *adj.;* vary etc. (*differ*) 15; bear no resemblance to, differ *toto coelo.*

render -unlike etc. *adj.;* vary etc. (*diversify*) 140.

Adj. dissimilar, unlike, disparate; of a different kind etc. (*class*) 75; unmatched, unique; new, novel; unprecedented etc. 83; original.

nothing of the kind; no such −, quite anotherthing; far from it, other than, cast in a different mold, *tertium quid,* as like a dock as a daisy, 'very like a whale;' as different as -chalk from cheese, − Macedon and Monmouth; *lucus a non lucendo.*

diversified etc. 16a.

Adv. otherwise, *alias.*

19. Imitation.—N. imitation; copying etc. *v.;* transcription; repetition, mimeograph, mimeotype, duplication, reduplication; quotation; reproduction.

mockery, mimicry, mime, simulation, personation; representation etc. 554; semblance, pretence; copy etc. 21; assimilation.

paraphrase, parody etc. 21.

plagiarism; forgery etc. (*falsehood*) 544.

imitator; echo, cuckoo, parrot, ape, monkey, mocking-bird, mimic, impersonator, copyist.

V. imitate, copy, mirror, reflect, reproduce, repeat, borrow; do like, echo, re-echo, catch; transcribe; match, parallel.

mock, take off, mimic, ape, simulate, personate, impersonate; forge; act etc. (*drama*) 599; represent etc. 554; counterfeit, duplicate; portray, parody, travesty, caricature, burlesque.

follow −, tread- in the- -steps, − footsteps, − wake- of; pattern after, take pattern by; follow - suit, − the example of; walk in the shoes of, take a leaf out of another's book, strike in with; take −, model -after; emulate.

Adj. imitated etc. *v.;* mock, mimic; counterfeit, false, pseudo; modelled after, molded on, paraphrastic; literal; imitative, apish; second-hand; imitable; sham etc. 545.

Adv. literally, to the letter, strictly, precisely, *verbatim, literatim, sic, totidem verbis,* word for word, *mot à mot.*

Phr. like master like man.

20. Non-Imitation.—N. no imitation, genuineness, originality; creativeness.

Adj. unimitated, uncopied; unmatched, unparalleled; inimitable etc. 33; *unique,* original, primordial, primary, pristine, underived, first-hand, archetypal, prototypal.

20a. Variation.—N. variation; alteration etc. (*change*) 140. modification, moods and tenses; modulation.

divergency etc. 291; deviation etc. 279; aberration; innovation.

V. vary etc. (*change*) 140; deviate etc. 279; diverge etc. 291.

Adj. varied etc. *v.;* modified; dissimilar etc. 18; diversified etc. 16a.

21. Copy. [Result of imitation.]—N. copy, facsimile, counterpart, *effigies,* effigy, symbol, image, form, likeness, similitude, semblance, resemblance, cast, electrotype, stereotype, tracing, ectype; imitation etc. 19; model, representation, adumbration, study; counterfeit presentment, portrait etc. (*representment*) 554.

duplicate; transcript, -ion; reflex, -ion; shadow, echo; chip of the old block; reprint, reproduction, casting, engraving, replica; transfer; second edition etc. (*repetition*) 104; *réchauffé* apograph, fair copy; revise.

parody, caricature, cartoon, burlesque, travesty, paraphrase.

servile -copy, − imitation; counterfeit etc. (*deception*) 545; *pasticcio.*

Adj. faithful; lifelike etc. (*similar*) 17.

22. Prototype. [Thing copied.]—N. prototype, original, model, pattern, founding, precedent, standard, scantling, type, arche-, anti-type; protoplast, copy-book, module, exemplar, example, ensample, specimen; paradigm; guide; templet; lay-figure.

text, copy, manuscript, MS., design; fugleman, keynote.

die, mold; matrix, engraving, last, plasm; pro-, proto-plasm; mint; seal, punch, *intaglio,* negative, stamp.

V. be −, set- an example; set a copy; standardize.

23. Agreement.—N. agreement; ac-cord, -cordance; unison, harmony, concord etc. 714; concordance, concert, understanding, convention, *entente -cordiale, consortium,* consensus of opinion, pact, mutual understanding, unanimity.

conformity etc. 82; conformance; uniformity etc. 16; consonance, consentaneousness, consistency; congruity, -ence; keeping; congeniality; correspondence, concinnity, parallelism, apposition, union.

fitness, aptness etc. *adj.;* relevancy; pertinence, -cy; sortance; case in point; aptitude, propriety, applicability, admissibility, commensurability, compatibility, suitability; cognation etc (*relation*) 9.

adaptation, adjustment, arrangement, graduation, accommodation; reconcil-iation - ement; assimilation; attunement.

consent etc. (*assent*) 448; concurrence etc. 178; co-operation etc. 709.

right man in the right place, very thing; quite −, just- the thing.

V. be -accordant etc. *adj.;* agree, accord, harmonize; correspond, tally, respond; meet, suit, fit, befit, do, adapt itself to; fall in −, chime in −, square −, quadrate −, consort −, comport- with; dovetail, assimilate; fit like a glove; fit to a -tittle, − T; match etc. 17; become one.

consent etc. (*assent*) 488.

render -accordant etc. *adj.;* fit, suit, adapt, accommodate; graduate; adjust etc. (*render equal*) 27; dress, regulate, readjust; accord, harmonize, reconcile; fadge, dovetail, square.

Adj. agreeing, suiting etc. *v.;* in accord, accordant, concordant, consonant, congruous, consentaneous, correspondent, corresponding, homologous, congenial; becoming; harmonious, reconcilable, conformable; in -accordance, − harminy, − keeping, − unison, etc. *n.;*-with; at one with, of one mind, of a piece; consistent, compatible, proportionate, answerable; commensurate; on all fours.

apt, apposite, pertinent, pat; to the -point, −-purpose; happy, felicitous, germane, *ad rem,* in point, bearing upon, applicable, relevant, admissible.

fit, adapted, *in loco, à propos,* appropriate, seasonable, sortable, suitable, idoneous, deft; meet etc. (*expedient*) 646.

at home, in one's proper element.

Adv. *à propos of;* pertinently etc. *adj.; pro rata.*

Phr. *rem acu tetigisti,* the cap fits.

24. Disagreement.—N. disagreement, discord, -cordance; disunion, dissonance, dissidence, discrepancy; unconformity etc. 83; incongru-ity, -ence; discongruity, *mésalliance, oxymoron;* jarring etc. *v.;* clash, collision, dissension etc. 713; conflict etc. (*opposition*) 708; controversy etc. 720; falling out, wrangle, argument.

disparity, mismatch, misfit, disproportion; disproportionateness etc. *adj.;* variance, divergence, repugnance.

unfitness etc. *adj.;* inaptitude, impropriety; inapplicability etc. *adj.;* inconsistency, inconcinnity; irrelevancy etc. (*irrelation*) 10.

misjoin-ing, -der; syncretism, intrusion, interference; *concordia discors.*

fish out of water.

V. disagree; clash, quarrel, jar etc. *(discord)* 713; interfere, intrude, come amiss; not concern etc. 10; mismatch; *hymano capiti cervicem jungere equinam.*

Adj. disagreeing etc. *v.;* discordant, discrepant; at -variance, − war; hostile, antagonistic, repugnant, factious, contradictory, dissentious, incompatible, irreconcilable, inconsistent with; unconformable, exceptional etc. 83; intrusive, incongruous; disproportionate, -ed; unharmonious; unconsonant; divergent, repugnant to.

inapt, unapt, inappropriate, inept, infelicitous, improper; unsuit-ed, -able; inapplicable; un-fit, -fitting, -befitting; unbecoming; ill-timed, ill-adapted, unseasonable, *mal à propos,* inadmissible; inapposite etc. *(irrelevant)* 10.

uncongenial; ill-assorted, -sorted, -matched; mis-matched, -mated, -joined, -placed; unaccommodating, irreducible, uncommensurable, unsympathetic.

out of -character, − keeping, − proportion, − joint, − tune, − place, − season, − its element; at -odds, − variance with.

Adv. in -defiance, − contempt, − spite-of; discordantly etc. *adj.; à tort et à travers.*

25. Quantity. [Absolute quantity.]—**N.** quantity, magnitude; size etc. *((dimensions)* 192; amplitude, mass, amount, *quantum,* measure, measurement, substance, strength.

[Science of quantity.] Mathematics, Mathesis.

[Definite or finite quantity] arm-, hand-, mouth-, spoon-, thimble-, capful; stock, batch, lot, dose, ration, quotum, quota, pittance, driblet, part, portion etc. 51.

Adj. quantitative, some, any, more or less.

Adv. to the tune of.

26. Degree. [Relative quantity.]—**N.** degree, grade, extent, measure, proportion, amount, ratio, stint, standard, height, pitch; reach, amplitude, range, scope, size, caliber; gradation, shade; tenor, compass; sphere, station, rank, standing; rate, way, sort.

point, mark, step, stage etc. *(term)* 71; intensity, strength etc. *(greatness)* 31.

V. compare, graduate, calibrate, measure.

Adj. comparative; gradual, shading off, gradational; within the bounds etc. *(limit),* 233.

Adv. by degrees, gradually, inasmuch, *pro tanto;* how-ever, -soever; step by step, bit by bit, little by little, inch by inch, drop by drop, gradatim; by -inches, − slow degrees, − little and little; in some -degree, − measure; to some extent; just a bit.

27. Equality. [Sameness of quantity or degree.]—**N.** equality, parity, co-extension, symmetry, balance, poise; evenness, monotony, level.

equivalence; equi-pollence, -poise, -librium, -ponderance; par, quits; not a pin to choose; distinction without a difference, six of one and half a dozen of the other; identity etc. 13; similarity etc. 17; isotropism; coequality.

equalization, equation, equilibration, co-ordination, adjustment, readjustment.

drawn -game, -battle, draw, stalemate; neck and neck race; tie, dead heat.

match, peer, compeer, equal, mate, fellow, brother; equivalent.

V. be -equal etc. *adj.;* equal, match, reach, keep pace with, run abreast; come −, amount −, come upto; be −, lie- on a level with; balance; cope with; come to the same thing; level off.

render -equal etc. *adj.;* equalize, level, dress, balance, equate, handicap, give points, trim, adjust, poise; fit, accommodate; adapt etc. *(render accordant)* 23; strike a balance; establish −, restore- equality, − equilibrium; readjust; stretch on the bed of Procrustes.

Adj. equal, even, level, monotonous, coequal, symmetrical, coordinate; on a -par, − level, − footing- with; up to the mark; equiparent.

equivalent, tantamount; quits; homologous; synonymous etc. 522; resolvable into, convertible, much at one, as broad as long, neither more nor less; much the same −, the same thing −, as good- as; all -one, — the same; equi-pollent, -ponderant, -ponderous, -balanced; equalized etc. *v.;* drawn; half and half; isochronous; isoperimetrical.

Adv. equally etc. *adj.; pari passu, ad eundem, caeteris paribus; in equilibrio;* to all intents and purposes.

Phr. it -comes, -adds up, − amounts- to the same thing.

28. Inequality. [Difference of quantity or degree.]—**N.** inequality; dis-, im-parity; odds; difference etc. 15; ill-balanced; unevenness; inclination of the balance, partiality; shortcoming; casting −make- weight; superiority etc. 33; inferiority etc. 34.

V. be -unequal etc. *adj.;* countervail; have −, give- the advantage; turn the scale; kick the beam; topple, -over; over-match etc. 33; not come up to etc. 34.

Adj. unequal, uneven, disparate, partial; un-, over-balanced; top-heavy, lop-sided.

Adv. *haud passibus aequis.*

29. Mean.—**N.** mean, medium, intermedium, average, run of the mill, normal, balance; mediocrity, generality, rule, ordinary -run, -ruck; golden mean etc. *(mid-course)* 628; middle etc. 68; compromise etc. 774; neutrality; middle point, middle course.

V. split the difference; take the -average etc. *n.;* reduce to a -mean etc. *n.;* strike a balance, pair off.

Adj. mean, intermediate; medial; middle etc. 68; average, normal, standard, neutral; middling, moderate.

médiocre, middle-class; *bourgeois,* commonplace etc. *(unimportant)* 643.

Adv. on an average, in the long run; taking - one with another, − all things together, − it for all in all; *communibus annis,* in round numbers.

30. Compensation.—**N.** compensation, equation; commutation; indemnification; compromise etc. 774; neutralization, nullification; counteraction etc. 179; reaction; measure for measure; retaliation etc. 718; equalization etc. 27; redemption, recoupment, recompense.

set-off, offset; make- casting-weight; counterpoise, equipoise, ballast; indemnity, reparation etc. 790; equivalent, *quid pro quo;* bribe, hush-money, tribute etc. 784; amends etc. *(atonement)* 952; counterclaim, counterbalance, equiponderance, countervail, cross demand.

V. make -amends, − compensation; compensate, -pense; indemnify; counter-act, -vail, -poise; equiponderate; balance; out-, over-, counterbalance; set off, offset, cancel; hedge, square, give and take; make up -for, − lee way; cover, fill up, neutralize, nullify; equalize etc. 27; make good; redeem etc. *(atone)* 952; recoup, pay etc. 973.

Adj. compensat-ing, -ory; amendatory, reparative, countervailing etc. *v.;* in the opposite scale; equivalent etc. *(equal)* 27.

Adv. in -return, − consideration; but, however, yet, still, notwithstanding; neverthe-, nathless; although, though; al-, how-beit; in spite of, despite; mauger; at -all events, − any rate; be that as it may, for all that, even so, on the other hand, at the same time, *quoad minus, quand même,* however that may be; after all, − is said and done; taking one thing with another etc. *(average)* 29.

31. Greatness. − N. greatness etc. *adj.;*

magnitude; size etc. *(dimensions)* 192; multitude etc. *(number)* 102; immensity, enormity, infinity etc. 105; might, strength, intensity, fulness; importance etc. 642; fame etc. 873.

great quantity, quantity, deal, power, sight, pot, volume, world; mass, heap etc. *(assemblage)* 72; stock etc. *(store)* 636; peck, bushel, load, cargo; cart −, wagon −, car −, truck −, shipload; flood, spring tide; abundance etc. *(sufficiency)* 639.

principal −, chief −, main −, greater −, major −, best −, essential- part; bulk, mass etc. *(whole)* 50.

V. be -great etc. *adj.;* run high, soar, loom up, tower, bulk large, transcend; rise −, carry- to a great height; know no bounds; scale, overtop, ascend.

enlarge etc. *(increase)* 35, *(expand)* 194.

Adj. great; greater etc. 33; large, considerable, fair, above par; big, massive, huge etc. *(large in size)* 192; ample; abundant etc. *(enough)* 639; Herculean etc. 159; full, intense, strong, sound, passing, heavy, plenary, deep, high; signal, at its height, in the zenith.

world-wide, wide-spread, extensive; wholesale; many etc. 102.

goodly, noble, precious, mighty; sad, grave, serious; far gone, arrant, downright; utter, -most; crass, gross, arch, profound, intense, consummate; rank, unmitigated, red-hot, desperate; glaring, flagrant, stark staring; thorough-paced, - going; roaring, thumping, thundering, strapping, whacking; extraordinary; important etc. 642; unsurpassed etc. *(supreme)* 33; complete etc. 52.

vast, immense, enormous, extreme; inordinate, excessive, extravagant, exorbitant, outrageous, preposterous, unconscionable, swinging, monstrous, over-grown; towering, stupendous, prodigious, astonishing, incredible; terrific, frightful; marvelous etc. *(wonder)* 870; grand.

unlimited etc. *(infinite)* 105; unapproachable, unutterable, indescribable, ineffable, unspeakable, inexpressible, beyond expression, fabulous.

un-diminished, -abated, -reduced, -restricted.

absolute, positive, stark, decided, unequivocal, essential, perfect, finished.

remarkable, of mark, marked, pointed, veriest; noticeable, uncommon, noteworthy, eminent etc. 873.

Adv. [in a positive degree] truly etc. *(truth)* 494; decidedly, unequivocally, purely, absolutely, seriously, essentially, fundamentally, radically, downright, in all conscience; for the most part, in the main.

[in a complete degree] entirely etc. *(completely)* 52; abundantly, etc. *(sufficiently)* 639; widely, far and wide.

[in a great or high degree] greatly etc. *adj.;* much, muckle, well, indeed, very, very much, a deal, no end of, most not a little; pretty, − well; enough, in a great measure, passing richly; to a -large, − great, − gigantic- extent; on a large scale; so; never −, ever- so; ever so much; by wholesale; mightily, mighty, powerfully; with a witness, *ultra,* in the extreme, extremely, exceedingly, intensely, exquisitely, acutely, indefinitely, immeasurably; beyond -compare, − comparison, − measure, − all bounds; incalculably, infinitely.

[in a supreme degree] pre-eminently, superlatively etc. *(superiority)* 33.

[in a too great degree] immoderately, unduly, monstrously, grossly, preposterously, inordinately, exorbitantly, excessively, enormously, out of all proportion, with a vengeance.

[in a marked degree] particularly, remarkably, singularly, curiously, uncommonly, unusually, peculiarly, notably, signally, strikingly, pointedly, mainly, chiefly; famously, egregiously, prominently, glaringly, emphatically, strangely, wonderfully, amazingly, surprisingly, astonishingly, incredibly, marvelously, awfully, stupendously.

[in an exceptional degree] peculiarly etc. *(unconformity)* 83.

[in a violent degree] furiously etc. *(violence)* 173; severely, desperately, tremendously, extravagantly, confoundedly, deucedly, devilishly, with a vengeance; *à −, à toute- outrance.*

[in a painful degree] painfully, sadly, grossly, sorely, bitterly, piteously, grievously, miserably, cruelly, woefully, lamentably, shockingly, frightfully, dreadfully, fearfully, terribly, horribly, distressingly, balefully.

32. Smallness.—N. smallness etc. *adj.;* littleness etc. *(small size)* 193; tenuity; paucity; fewness etc. *(small number)* 103; meanness, insignificance etc. *(unimportance)* 643; mediocrity, moderation.

small quantity, *modicum, minimum;* vanishing point; material point, electron, atom, particle, molecule, corpuscle, point, dab, fleck, speck, dot, mote, jot, iota, ace; *minutiae,* details; look, thought, idea, *soupçon,* whit, tittle, shade, shadow; spark, *scintilla,* gleam; touch, cast; grain, scruple, granule, globule, minim, sup, sip, sop, spice, drop, droplet, sprinkling, dash, smack, tinge, tincture; inch, patch, scantling, dole; scrap, shred, tag, splinter, rag, tatter, cantlet, flitter, gobbet, mite, bit, morsel, crumb,

seed, fritter, shive; snip, -pet; snick, snack, snatch, slip, scrag; chip, -ping; shiver, sliver, driblet, clipping, paring, shaving, hair.

nutshell; thimble-, spoon-, hand-, cap-, mouthful; fragment; fraction etc. (*part*)51; drop in the ocean, drop in the bucket.

animalcule etc. 193.

trifle etc. (*unimportant thing*) 643; mere —, next to- nothing; hardly anything; just enough to swear by; the shadow of a shade.

finiteness, finite quantity.

V. be -shall etc. *adj.;* lie in a nutshell.

diminish etc. (*decrease*) 36, (*contract*) 195.

Adj. small, little, tiny, weeny; diminutive etc. (*small in size*) 193; minute; minikin, fine, inconsiderable, dribbling, paltry etc. (*unimportant*) 643; faint etc. (*weak*) 160; slender, light, slight, scanty, scant, limited; meager etc. (*insufficient*) 640; sparing; few etc. 103; low, so-so, middling, tolerable, no great shakes; below —, under-par, — the mark; at a low ebb; half-way; moderate, modest; tender, subtle; petty, shallow, skin-deep.

inappreciable, evanescent, infinite-simal, homeopathic, very small, atomic, molecular, ultra-, -microscopic.

petty, shallow etc. 499.

mere, simple, sheer, stark, bare; near run.

Adv. [in a small degree] to a small extent, on a small scale; a -little, — wee, — tiny bit; slightly etc. *adj.;* imperceptibly; miserably, wretchedly; insufficiently etc. 640; imperfectly; faintly etc. 160; passably, pretty well, well enough.

[in a certain or limited degree] partially, in part; in —, to a certain degree; to a certain extent; comparatively; some, rather; in some -degree, -measure; some-thing, -what; simply, only, purely, merely; at —, at the- -least, — most; ever so little, as little as may be, *tant soit peu,* in ever so small a degree; thus far, *pro tanto;* within bounds, in a manner, after a fashion.

almost, nearly, well nigh, short of, not quite, all but; near —, close- upon; *peu s'en faut,* near the mark; within an -ace, — inch- of; on the brink of; scarcely, hardly, barely, only just, no more than.

[in an uncertain degree] about, therabouts, somewhere about, nearly, say; be the same - more, — little more- or less.

[in no degree] no- ways, — wise; not -at all, — in the least, — a bit, — a bit of it, — a whit, — a jot, — a shadow; in no -wise, — respect; by no - means, — manner of means; on no account, at no hand.

33. Superiority.—N. superiority, supremacy, majority; greatness etc. 31; advantage, odds, pull; preponderance, -ation; predominance, vantage ground, coign of vantage, prevalence, partiality; personal superiority; sovereignty etc. 737; nobility etc. (*rank*) 875; Triton among the minnows, *primus inter pares, nulli secundus,* superman; captain etc. 475.

supremacy, pre-eminence; primacy, lead, *maximum;* record; climax, crest, top; culmination etc. (*summit*) 210; transcendence; *ne plus ultra;* lion's share, Benjamin's mess; excess; bisque, surplus etc. (*remainder*) 40, (*redundance*) 641.

V. be -superior etc. *adj.;* exceed, excel, transcend; out-do, -balance, -weigh, -rival, -Herod, outrank, pass, surpass, surmount, get ahead of; over-top, -ride, -pass, -balance, -weigh, -match; top, o'er-top, cap, beat, win out, cut out; beat hollow; outstrip etc. 303; eclipse, throw into the shade, take the shine out of, put one's nose out of joint; have the -upper hand, — whip hand of, — advantage; turn the scale, play first fiddle etc. (*importance*) 642; preponderate, predominate, prevail; precede, take .precedence, come first; come to a head, culminate; beat etc. all others, bear the palm; break the record, take the cake.

become —, render- -larger, etc. (*increase*) 35, (*expand*) 194.

Adj. superior, greater, major, higher; exceeding etc. *v.;* great etc. 31; distinguished, *ultra;* vaulting; more than a match for.

supreme, greatest, maximal, maximum, utmost, paramount, pre-eminent, foremost, crowning; first-rate etc. (*important*) 642, (*excellent*) 648; unrivalled; peer-, match-less; none such, second to none, *sans pareil;* un-paragoned, -paralleled, -equalled, -approached, -surpassed; superlative, inimitable, *facile princeps,* incomparable, sovereign, without parallel, *nulli secundus, ne plus ultra;* beyond -compare, — comparison; culminating etc. (*topmost*) 210; transcendent, -ental; *plus royaliste que le Roi.*

increased etc. (*added to*) 35; enlarged etc. (*expanded*) 194.

Adv. beyond, more, over; over —, above- the mark; above par; upwards —, in advance- of; over and above; at the top of the scale, on the crest, at it height.

[in a superior or supreme degree] eminently, egregiously, pre-eminently, surpassing, prominently, superlatively, supremely, above all, of all things, the most, to crown all, *par excellence,* principally, especially, particularly, peculiarly, *a fortiori,* even, yea, still more.

Phr. 'we shall not look upon his like again.'

34. Inferiority.—N. inferiority, minority, sub-ordinancy; shortcoming, deficiency; handicap; *minimum;* smallness etc. 32; imperfection, shabbiness.

[personal inferiority] commonalty etc. 876; subordinate, substitute, sub.

V. be -inferior etc. *adj.;* fall —, come- short of; not -pass, — come up to; want.

become —, render- smaller etc. (decrease) 36, (*contract*) 195; hide its diminished head, retire into the shade, yield the palm, play second fiddle, take a back seat; bow.

Adj. inferior, smaller; small etc. 32; minor, less, lesser, deficient, minus, lower, subordinate, secondary; second-rate etc. (*imperfect*) 651; sub, subaltern; thrown into the shade; weighed in the balance and found wanting; not fit to hold a candle to.

least, smallest etc. (*see* little, small etc. 193); lowest.

diminished etc. (*decreased*) 36; reduced etc. (*contracted*) 195; unimportant etc. 643.

Adv. less; under —, below- -the mark, — par; at -the bottom of the scale, — a low ebb, — a disadvantage; short of, under.

35. Increase.—N. increase; augmentation, addition, enlargement, extension; dilatation etc. (*expansion*) 194; multiplication; increment, accretion; accession etc. 37; production etc. 161; development, growth; aggrandizement, aggravation, intensification; rise; ascent etc. 305; anabasis; ex-aggeration, -acerbation; spread etc. (*dispersion*) 73; flood-, spring-, -tide; gain, produce, profit etc. 618; booty, plunder etc. 793.

V. increase, augment, add to, enlarge; dilate etc. (*expand*) 194; grow, wax, mount, swell, get ahead, gain strength; advance; run —, shoot- up; rise; ascend etc. 305; sprout etc. 194.

aggrandize; raise; exalt; deepen, heighten; lengthen; thicken; strengthen; intensify, enhance, inflate, magnify, double, redouble; multiply; aggravate, exaggerate; ex-asperate, -acerbate; add fuel to the flame, *oleum addere camino*, superadd etc. (*add*) 37; spread etc. (*disperse*) 73.

Adj. increased etc. *v.;* on the increase, undiminished, additional etc. (*added*) 37; increasing etc. *v.;* growing, crescent, intensive, cumulative.

Adv. *crescendo*, increasingly.

Phr. *vires acquirit eundo.*

36. Non-Increase. Decrease.—N. decrease, diminution, lessening etc. *v.;* subtraction etc. 38; reduction, abatement, declension; shrinkage etc. (*contraction*) 195; coarctation; abridgment etc. (*shortening*) 201; extenuation.

subsidence, catabasis, wane, ebb-, neap-tide, decline; descent etc. 306; decrement, reflux, depreciation; erosion, wear and tear, deterioration etc. 659; anticlimax; mitigation etc. (*moderation*) 174.

V. decrease, diminish, lessen; abridge etc. (*shorten*) 201; shrink etc. (*contract*) 195; drop —, fall —, tail- off; fall away, waste, wear, erode; wane, ebb, decline; descent etc. 306; subside; deliquesce, melt —, die -away; retire into the shade, hide its diminished head, fall to a low ebb, run low, languish, decay, crumble, consume away.

bate, abate, dequantitate; discount; depreciate; extenuate, lower, weaken, attenuate, fritter away; mitigate etc.(*moderate*) 174; belittle, minimize; dwarf, throw into the shade; keep down, reduce etc. 195; shorten etc. 201; subtract etc. 38.

Adj. unincreased etc. (*see* increase etc. 35); decreased etc. *v.;* decreasing etc. *v.;* on the -wane etc. *n.;* deliquescent.

Adv. *diminuendo, decrescendo,* decreasingly.

37. Addition.—N. addition, annexation, adjection; junction etc. 43; super-position, -addition, -junction, -fetation; accession, reinforcement; increase etc. 35; increment, supplement; accompaniment etc. 88; interposition etc. 228; insertion etc. 300; summation etc. 85; adjunct etc. 39.

V. add, annex, adject, affix, attach, superadd, subjoin, superpose; clap —, saddle- on; tack to, postfix, append, tag; ingraft; saddle with; sprinkle; introduce etc. (*interpose*) 228; insert etc. 300.

become added, accrue; ad-, supervene; add up etc. 85.

reinforce, strengthen, swell the ranks of; augment etc. 35.

Adj. added etc. *v.;* additional; supplement, -al, -ary; suppletory, subjunctive; adjec-, adsci-, ascititious; additive, extra, spare, further, fresh, more, new, ulterior, other, auxiliary, supernumerary, accessory.

Adv. in addition, more, plus, extra; and, also, likewise, too, furthermore, further, item; and -also, — eke; else, besides, to boot, *et cetera;* etc.; and so -on, — forth; into the bargain, *cum multis aliis,* over and above, moreover.

with, withal; including, inclusive, as well as, not to mention, let alone; together —, along —, coupled —, in conjunction- with; conjointly; jointly etc. 43.

38. Non-Addition. Subduction.—N. sub-traction, -duction; deduction, retrenchment; removal; ab-, sub-lation; abstraction etc. (*taking*) 789; garbling etc. *v.;* mutilation, detruncation; amputation, severance; abs-, ex-, re-cision; curtailment etc. 201; minuend, subtrahend; decrease etc. 36; abrasion.

V. sub-tract, -duct; rebate, de-duct, — duce; bate, retrench; remove, withdraw; take — from, — away; detract.

garble, mutilate, amputate, sever, detruncate; cut -off, — away, — out; expurgate; abscind, excise; pare, thin, prune, decimate; abrade, scrape, file; geld, castrate, emasculate, unman, spay, caponize; eliminate.

diminish etc. 36; curtail etc. (*shorten*) 201; deprive of etc. (*take*) 789; weaken.

Adj. subtracted etc. *v.;* subtractive.

tailless, acaudal.

Adv. in -deduction etc. *n.;* less; short of; minus, without, except, excepting, with the exception of, barring, bar, save, exclusive of, save and except, with a reservation.

39. Adjunct. [Thing added.]—N. adjunct, addit-ion, -ament; *additum,* affix, appendage, annex; augment, -ation; increment, reinforcement, supernumerary, accessory, item; garnish, sauce; accompaniment etc. 88; adjective, *addendum,* accession, complement, supplement; continuation; extension, subscript, tag, appendix, postscript, interlineation, interpolation, insertion.

rider, codicil, off-shoot, episode, side issue, corollary; piece; flap, lapel, label, tab, strip, fold, lappet, apron, skirt, embroidery, trappings, *cortège*; tail, suffix etc. (*sequel*) 65; wing.

Adj. additional etc. 37.

Adv. in addition etc. 37.

40. Remainder. [Thing remaining.]—N. remainder, residue; remains, *remanet,* remnant, rest, relic, relict; leavings, heel-tap, odds and ends, cheese-parings, candle ends, orts; *residuum;* dottle, dregs, etc. (*dirt*) 653; refuse etc. (*useless*) 645; stubble, result, educt; fag-end, stub; ruins, wreck, skeleton, stump; *alluvium.*

surplus, overplus, excess; balance, complement; superfluity etc. (*redundance*) 641; survival, -ance; afterglow.

V. remain; be -left etc. *adj.*; exceed, survive; leave.

Adj. remaining, left; left -behind, — over;

residu-al, -ary; over, odd; unconsumed, sedimentary; surviving; net; exceeding, over and above; outlying, -standing; cast off etc. 782; superfluous etc. (*redundant*) 641.

V. remain; be -left; left -behind, − over; redidual, -ary; over, odd; unconsumed, sedimentary; surviving; net; exceeding, over and above; outlying, -standing; cast off etc. 782; superfluous etc. (*redundant*) 641.

40a. Decrement. [Thing deducted.]—N. decrement, discount, rebate, defect, loss, deduction, eduction, tare; drawback; waste, wastage; reprise.

41. Mixture. [Forming a whole without coherence.]—N. mix-, admix-, commix-ture, -tion, mingling; commixion, immixture, interfusion, intermixture, alloyage, matrimony; junction etc. 43; combination etc. 48; entanglement, interlacing; miscegenation, interbreeding.

impregnation; in-, dif-, suf-, transfusion; infiltration; seasoning, sprinkling, interlarding; interpolation etc. 228; adulteration, sophistication.

[Thing mixed] tinge, tincture, touch, dash, smack, sprinkling, spice, seasoning, infusion, *soupçon*.

[Compound resulting from mixture] alloy, brass, bronze, pewter etc.; amalgam, *magma*, blend, half-and-half, *mélange, tertium, quid*, miscellany, *ambigu*, medley, mess, hash, hotchpotch, hodgepodge, *pasticcio*, patchwork, odds and ends, all sorts; jumble etc. (*disorder*) 59; salad, sauce, mash, *omnium gatherum*, gallimaufry, ragout, *olla podrida, olio*, salmagundi, *potpourri*, Noah's ark; texture, mingled yarn; mosaic etc. (*variegation*) 440.

half-blood, -caste, -breed, Eurasian; mulatto; terc-, quart-, quinteron etc.; quad-, octo-roon; *griffo, zambo*; cross, hybrid, mongrel etc. 83.

V. mix; join etc. 43; combine etc. 48; com-, im-, inter-mix; mix up with, mingle; com-, inter-, bemingle; shuffle etc. (*derange*) 61; pound together; hash −, stir- up; knead, brew; impregnate with; interlard etc. (*interpolate*) 228; intertwine, -weave etc. 219; associate with, miscegenate, interbreed.

be mixed etc.; get among, be entangled with.

instil, imbue; in-, suf-, trans-fuse; infiltrate, dash, tinge, tincture, season, sprinkle, besprinkle, attemper, medicate, blend, cross; alloy, amalgamate, compound, adulterate, sophisticate, infect.

Adj. mixed etc. *v.;* implex, composite, half-and-half, linsey-wolsey, hybrid, mongrel, heterogeneous; motley etc. (*variegated*) 440; miscellaneous, promiscuous, indiscriminate; miscible.

Adv. among, amongst, amid, amidst, with; in the midst of, in the crowd.

42. Simpleness [Freedom from mixture.]—N. simpleness etc. *adj.;* purity, homogeneity.

elimination; sifting etc. *v.;* purification etc. (*cleanness*) 652.

V. render -simple etc. *adj.;* simplify.

sift, winnow, bolt, eliminate; narrow down; get rid of, exclude etc. 55; clear; purify etc. (*clean*) 652; disentangle etc. (*disjoin*) 44.

Adj. simple, uniform, of a piece, homogeneous, single, pure, clear, sheer, neat; Attic.

un-mixed, -mingled, -blended, -combined, -compounded; elementary, undecomposed; unadulterated, -sophisticated, -alloyed, -tinged, -fortified; pure and simple.

free −, exempt- from; exclusive.

Adv. simply etc. *adj.;* only.

43. Junction.—N. junction; joining etc. *v.;* joinder, union; con-nection, -junction, -jugation, compendency, annex-ion, -ation, -ment; coalition; astriction, attachment, compagination, vincture, ligation, alligation; accouplement; marriage etc. (*wedlock*) 903; infibulation, inosculation, symphysis, anastomosis, confluence, communication, concatenation; concurrence, meeting, reunion; assemblage etc. 72.

copulation, coition, intercourse.

joint, joining, juncture, chiasma, pivot, hinge, articulation, commissure, seam, suture, gusset, stitch, splice; link etc. 45; miter, mortise.

closeness, tightness etc. *adj.;* coherence etc. 46; combination etc. 48.

V. join, unite; con-join, -nect; associate; put −, lay −, clap −, hang −, lump −, hold −, piece −, tack −, fix −, bind up- together; embody, re-embody; roll into one.

attach, fix, affix, saddle on, fasten, bind, secure, clinch, twist, make -fast etc. *adj.;* tie, pinion, string, strap, sew, lace, stitch, tack, paste, knit, button, buckle, hitch, lash, truss, bandage; braid, splice, swathe, gird, tether, moor, picket, harness, chain; fetter etc. (*restrain*) 751; lock, latch, belay, brace, hook, grapple, leash, couple, accouple, link, yoke, bracket; marry etc. (*wed*) 903; bridge over, span.

pin, nail, bolt, hasp, clasp, clamp, screw, rivet; impact, solder, braze, cement, set; weld −, fuse-together; wedge, rabbet, mortise, miter, jam, dovetail, enchase; graft, ingraft, inosculate; en-, in-twine; inter-link, -lace, -twine, -twist, -weave; entangle; twine round, belay; tighten; trice −, screw-up.

be -joined etc.; hang −, hold- together; cohere etc. 46.

Adj. joined etc. *v.;* joint; con-joint, -junct; corporate, compact; hand in hand.

firm, fast, close, tight, taut, taught, tense, secure, set, intervolved; in-separable, -dissoluble, -secable, -severable.

Adv. jointly etc. *adj.;* in conjunction with etc. (*in addition to*) 37; fast, firmly etc. *adj.;* intimately.

44. Disjunction.—N. dis-junction, -connection, -unity, -union, -association, -engagement, -sociation; discontinuity etc. 70; inconnection; abstraction, -edness; isolation; insul-arity, -ation; oasis; separateness etc. *adj.;* severalty; *disjecta membra;* dispersion etc. 73; apportionment etc. 786.

separation; parting etc. *v.;* detachment, segregation; divorce, sejunction, seposition, diduction, diremption, discerption; elision; *caesura*, division, subdivision, break, fracture, rupture; compartition; dis-memberment, -integration, -location; luxation; sever-, dis-severance; scission; re-, ab-scission; circumcision;

lacer-, dilacer-ation; dis-, ab-ruption; avulsion, divulsion; section, resection, cleavage; fission; separability; separatism.

fissure, breach, rent, split, rift, crack, slit, slot, incision.

dissection, anatomy; decomposition etc. 49; cutting instrument etc. (*sharpness*) 253; saw.

V. be -disjoined etc.; come −, fall- -off, − to pieces; peel off; get loose.

dis-join, -connect, -engage, -unite, -sociate, -pair; divorce, part, dispart, detach, uncouple, separate, cut off, rescind, segregate; set −, keep-apart; insulate, isolate; throw out of gear; cut adrift; loose; un-loose, -do, -bind, -tie, -hitch, -chain, -lock etc. (*fix*) 43, -pack, -ravel; disentangle; set free etc. (*liberate*) 750.

sunder, divide, subdivide, sectionalize, sever, dissever, abscind; cut; segment; in-cide, -cise; circumcise; saw, snip, nib, nip, cleave, rive, rend, slit, split, splinter, chip, crack, snap, break, tear, burst; rend etc. -asunder, − in twain; wrench, rupture, shatter, shiver, cranch, crunch, craunch, chop; rip up; hack, hew, slash; whittle; haggle, hackle, discind, lacerate, scamble, mangle, gash, hash, slice.

cut up, carve, quarter, dissect, anatomize; take −, pull −, pick −, tear- to pieces; tear to tatters, − piecemeal; divellicate; skin etc. 226; dis-integrate, -member, -branch, -band; disperse etc. 73; dis-locate, -joint; break up; mince; comminute etc. (*pulverize*) 330; distribute, apportion etc. 786.

part, − company; separate, leave; alienate, estrange.

Adj. disjoined etc. *v.;* discontinuous etc. 70; bipartite, multipartite, abstract; digitate; disjunctive; isolated etc. *v.;* insular, separate, disparate, discrete, apart, asunder, far between, loose, free; unattached, -annexed, -associated, -connected; distinct; adrift; straggling; rift, reft, cleft, split.

[capable of being divided] scissile, partible, divisible, separable, severable, detachable.

Adv. separately etc. *adj.;* one by one, severally, apart; adrift, asunder, in twain; in the abstract, abstractedly.

45. Vinculum. [Connecting medium.]—**N.** vinculum, link, *nexus*; connec-tive, -tion; junction etc. 43; bond of union, copula, intermedium, hyphen; bracket; bridge, stepping-stone, isthmus.

bond, tendon, tendril; fiber; cord, -age; riband, ribbon, rope, guy, cable, line, halser, hawser, painter, moorings, wire, chain; string etc. (*filament*) 205.

fastening, tie; liga-ment, -ture; strap; bowline, halliard, tackle, lanyard, rigging, shrouds; standing −, running- rigging; traces, harness; yoke; band, -age; brace, roller, fillet; inkle; with, withe, withy; thong, braid; girder, tie-beam; girt, cinch, girth, girdle, cestus, garter, braces, suspenders; halter, noose, lasso, lariat, surcingle, knot, hitch, running knot, frog.

pin, corking pin, nail, brad, tack, skewer, staple, cleat, clamp; cramp, screw, button, buckle, clasp, hasp, hinge; hank, catch, latch, bolt, ring, latchet, pawl, tag; tooth; stud; hook, − and eye; morse, lock, holdfast, padlock, rivet; anchor, grappling-iron, drawbar, coupler, draw-

head, coupling, treenail, trennel, stake, pale, pile, post, bollard.

cement, glue, gum, paste, size, wafer, solder, lute, putty, bird-lime, mortar, stucco, plaster, grout.

shackle, rein etc. (*means of restraint*) 752; suspender etc. 214; prop etc. (*support*) 215.

V. bridge over, span; connect etc. 43; hang etc. 214.

46. Coherence.—N. co-, ad-herence, -hesion, -hesiveness; concretion, accretion; con-, agglutination, -glomeration; aggregation; consolidation, set, cementation; sticking, soldering etc. *v.;* connection.

tenacity, toughness; stickiness etc. 352; insepara-bility, -bleness; hur, remora.

conglomerate, concrete etc. (*density*) 321.

V. cohere, adhere, stick, cling, cleave, hold, take hold of, hold fast, close with, embrace, clasp, hug; grow −, hang-together; twine round etc. (*join*) 43.

stick like -a leech, − wax; stick close; cling like -ivy, − a bur; adhere like -a remora, − Dejanira's shirt.

glue; ag-, con-glutinate; cement, lute, paste, gum; solder, weld; cake, coagulate, consolidate etc. (*solidify*) 321; agglomerate.

Adj. co-, ad-hesive, -hering etc. *v.;* tenacious, tough; sticky etc. 352.

united, unseparated, sessile, inseparable, inextricable, infrangible; compact etc. (*dense*) 321.

47. Incoherence. [Want of adhesion, non-adhesion, immiscibility.]—N. non-adhesion; immiscibility; incoherence; looseness etc. *adj.;* laxity; relaxation; loosening etc. *v.;* freedom; disjunction etc. 44; rope of sand.

V. make -loose etc. *adj.;* loosen, slacken, relax; un-glue etc. 46; detach etc. (*disjoin*) 44.

Adj. non-adhesive, immiscible; incoherent, detached, loose, slack, baggy, lax, relaxed, flapping, streaming; dishevelled; segregated, like grains of sand; un-consolidated etc. 321; -combined etc. 48; non-cohesive.

48. Combination.—N. combination; mixture etc. 41; alloy; junction etc. 43; union, unification, synthesis, incorporation, amalgamation, embodiment, coalescence, crasis, fusion, blend, blending, absorption, centralization, federation.

compound, amalgam, composition, *tertium quid;* resultant, impregnation.

V. combine, unite, incorporate, alloy, intertwine etc. 41; amalgamate, embody, absorb, re-embody, blend, merge, fuse, melt into one, consolidate, coalesce, centralize, impregnate; put −, lump- together; federate, associate; fraternize; cement a union, marry, wed, couple, pair, ally.

Adj. combined etc. *v.;* conjunctive, conjugate, conjoint, allied, confederate; impregnated with, ingrained, inoculated.

49. Decomposition.—N. decomposition, analysis, diaeresis dissection, resolution, catalysis, electrolysis, hydrolysis, photolysis, dissolution; dispersion etc. 73; disjunction etc. 44;

putrescence, caries, necrosis, corruption etc. (*uncleanness*) 653.

V. decom-pose, -pound; analyze, disembody, dissolve; resolve —, separate- into its elements; electrolyze; dissect, decentralize, break up; disintegrate; disperse etc. 73; unravel etc. (*unroll*) 313; crumble into dust; decay etc. *n.;* deteriorate etc. 659.

Adj. decomposed etc. *v.;* catalytic, analytical.

50. Whole. [Principal part.]—**N.** whole, totality, integrity; totalness etc. *adj.;* entirety, *ensemble,* collectiveness; unity etc. 87; completeness etc. 52; indivisibility, indiscerptibility; integration, embodiment; integer, integral.

all, the whole, total, aggregate, one and all, gross amount, sum, sum-total, *tout ensemble,* length and breadth of, Alpha and Omega, 'be all and end all,' lock, stock and barrel.

bulk, mass, lump, tissue, staple, body, torso, *compages;* truck, bole, hull, hulk, skeleton; greater —, major —, best —, principal —, mainpart; essential part etc. (*importance*) 642; lion's share, Benjamin's mess; the long and the short; nearly —, almost- all.

V. form —, constitute- a whole; integrate, embody, amass; aggregate etc. (*assemble*) 72; amount to, come to.

Adj. whole, total, integral, entire; complete etc. 52; one, individual.

un-broken, -cut, -divided, -severed, -clipped, -cropped, -shorn; seamless; undiminished; undemolished, -dissolved, -destroyed, -bruised.

in-divisible, -dissoluble, -dissolvable, -discerptible.

wholesale, sweeping, comprehensive.

Adv. wholly, altogether; totally etc. (*completely*) 52; entirely, all, all in all, considering all things, in a body, collectively, all put together; in the -aggregate, — lump; — mass, — gross, — main, — long run; *en masse,* on the whole, as a whole, bodily, *en bloc, in extenso,* throughout, every inch; substantially.

51. Part.—**N.** part, portion; dose; item, particular; aught, any; division, ward; subdivision, section; chapter, verse; article, clause, count, paragraph, passage; phrase; number, volume, book, fascicule; sector, segment; fraction, fragment; cantle, -t; frustum; detachment, parcel, unit, class etc. 75.

piece, lump, bit; cut, -ting; chip, chunk, collop, slice, scale, shard; lamina etc. 204; moiety; small part; morsel, scrap, crumb; particle etc. (*smallness*) 32; instalment, dividend; share etc. (*allotment*) 786.

débris, odds and ends, oddments, *detritus; excerpta;* member, limb, lobe, lobule, arm, wing, scion, branch, bough, joint, link, offshoot, ramification, twig, stipule, tendril, bush, spray, sprig; runner; leaf, -let; stump; constituent, ingredient, component part etc. 56.

compartment; department etc. (*class*) 75; county etc. (*region*) 181.

V. part, divide, break etc. (*disjoin*) 44; partition etc. (*apportion*) 786.

Adj. fractional, fragmentary; sectional, aliquot; divided etc. *v.;* in compartments, multifid, incomplete, partial, divided etc. 44.

Adv. partly, in part, partially; piecemeal, part by part; by -instalments, — snatches, — inches, — driblets; bit by bit, inch by inch, foot by foot, drop by drop; in -detail, — lots.

52. Completeness.—**N.** completeness etc. *adj.;* completion etc. 729; integration; integrality.

entirety; universality; totality; perfection etc. 650; solid-ity, -arity; unity; all; *ne plus ultra,* ideal, limit.

complement, supplement, make-weight; filling up etc. *v.*

impletion; satur-ation, -ity; high water; high —, flood —, spring- tide; fill, load, bumper, bellyful; brimmer; sufficiency etc. 639.

V. be -complete etc. *adj.;* come to a head.

render -complete etc. *adj.;* complete etc. (*accomplish*) 729; fill, charge, load, replenish; make-up, — good; piece —, eke- out; supply deficiencies; fill -up, — in, — to the brim, — the measure of; saturate etc. 869.

go the whole -hog, — length, go all lengths.

Adj. complete, entire;whole etc.50; perfect etc. 650; full, good, absolute, thorough, plenary; solid, undivided; with all its parts.

exhaustive, radical, sweeping, thorough-going; dead.

regular, consummate, unmitigated, sheer, unqualified, unconditional, free; abundant etc. (*sufficient*) 639.

brimming; brim-, top-ful; chock —, chokefull; as full as- an egg is of meat, — a vetch, — a tick; saturated, crammed; replete etc. (*redundant*) 641; fraught, laden; full-laden, -fraught, -charged; heavy laden.

completing etc. *v.;* supplement-al, -ary; ascititious.

Adv. completely etc. *adj.;* altogether, outright, wholly, totally, *in toto,* quite; over head and ears; effectually, for good and .all, nicely, fully, through thick and thin, head and shoulders; neck and -heel, — crop; all out; in -all respects, — every respect; at all points, out and out, to all intents and purposes; *toto coelo;* utterly, clean, — as a whistle; to the -full, — utmost, — backbone; hollow, stark; heart and soul, root and branch; down to the ground.

to the top of one's bent, as far as possible, *à outrance.*

throughout; from -first to last, — beginning to end, — end to end, — one end to the other, —Dan to Beersheba, — head to foot, — head to heels, — top to toe, — top to bottom; *de fond en comble; à fond, a capite ad calcem, ab ovo usque ad mala,* fore and aft; every -whit, — inch; *cap-à-pie,* to the end of the chapter; up to the -brim, — ears, — eyes; as ... as can be.

on all accounts; *sous tous les rapports;* with a -vengeance, — witness.

53. Incompleteness.—**N.** incompleteness etc. *adj.;* deficiency, short -measure, — wieght; shortcoming etc. 304; insufficiency etc. 640; imperfection etc. 651; immaturity etc. (*nonpreparation*) 674; half measures.

[part wanting] defect, deficit, shortage, ullage, defalcation, omission, *caret;* interval etc. 198; break etc. (*discontinuity*) 70; non-completion etc. 730; missing link.

V. be -incomplete etc. *adj.;* fall short of etc. 304; lack etc. (*be insufficient*) 640; neglect etc. 460.

Adj. incomplete; imperfect etc. 651; unfinished; uncompleted etc. (*see* complete etc. 729); defective, deficient, wanting; failing; in -default, − arrear; short, − of; hollow, meagre, lame, half-and-half, perfunctory, sketchy; crude etc. (*unprepared*) 674.

mutilated, garbled, mangled, docked, lopped, truncated; bobtailed, cropped, bobbed, shingled.

in -progress, − hand; going on, proceeding.

Adv. incompletely etc. *adj.;* by halves.

Phr. *caetera desunt; caret.*

54. Composition.—N. composition, constitution, crasis, synthesis; make-up; combination etc. 48; inclusion, admission, comprehension, reception; embodiment, formation, conformation, production.

compilation etc. 72. (*musical*) composition etc. 415; painting etc. 556; writing etc. 590; typography etc. 591.

V. be -composed, − made, − formed, − made up- of; consist of, be resolved into.

include etc. (*in a class*) 76; subsume; synthesize; contain, hold, comprehend, take in, admit, embrace, embody; involve; implicate, drag into.

compose, constitute, form, make; make −, fill −, build- up; weave, construct, fabricate; compile; write, draw; set up (*printing*); enter into the composition of etc. (*be a component*) 56.

Adj. containing, constituting etc. *v.*

55. Exclusion.—N. exclusion, non-admission, omission, exception, rejection, repudiation; exile etc. (*seclusion*) 893; preclusion, lock out, ostracism, prohibition; disbarment, expulsion, ban.

separation, segregation, seposition, elimination, coffer-dam.

V. be excluded from etc.

exclude, bar, ban; leave −, shut −, thrust −, bar- out; reject, repudiate, spurn, blackball; ostracize, boycott; lay −, put −, set-apart, − aside; relegate, segregate; throw overboard; strike -off, − out; neglect etc. 460; banish etc. (*seclude*) 893; separate etc. (*disjoin*) 44.

pass over, omit; garble; eliminate, weed, winnow.

Adj. excluding etc. *v.;* exclusive.

excluded etc. *v.;* unrecounted, not included in; inadmissible; preventive, interdictive.

Adv. exclusive of, barring, except; with the exception of, save, bating.

56. Component.—N. component; component −, integral −, integrant-part; element, constituent, ingredient, leaven; part and parcel; contents; appurtenance; feature; member etc. (*part*) 51; personnel.

V. enter into, − the composition of; be a- component etc. *n.;* be −, form- part of; merge −, be merged- in; be implicated in; share in etc. (*participate*) 778; belong −, appertain- to.

form, make, constitute, compose.

Adj. forming etc. *v.;* inclusive; inherent etc. 5.

57. Extraneousness.—N. extraneousness etc. *adj.;* extrinsicality etc. 6; exteriority etc. 220; alienism.

foreign -body, − substance, − element; alien, stranger, intruder, interloper, foreigner, tramontane, *novus homo,* new comer, immi-, emi-grant; creole, Afrikander; outsider, outlander, tenderfoot.

Adj. extraneous, foreign, alien, ulterior; exterior, external, outside, outlandish; oversea; tra-, ultra-montane.

excluded etc. 55; inadmissible; exceptional.

Adv. in foreign -parts, − lands; abroad, beyond seas, overseas.

58. Order.—N. order, regularity etc. 80; uniformity, symmetry, *lucidus ordo;* harmony, music of the spheres.

gradation, progression; series etc. (*continuity*) 69.

subordination; course, even tenor, routine; method, disposition, arrangement, array, system, economy, discipline; orderliness etc. *adj.*

rank, place etc. (*term*) 71.

V. be −, become- in order etc. *adj.;* form, fall in, draw up; arrange −, range −, place- itself; adjust; fall into −, take- -one's place, − rank; rally round; arrange etc. 60.

Adj. orderly, regular; in -order, − trim, − apple-pie order, according to Cocker, − its proper place, neat, neat as a pin, tidy, *en règle,* well regulated, correct, methodical, uniform, symmetrical, ship-shape, business-like, systematic; habitual; unconfused etc. (*see* confuse etc. 61) arranged etc. 60.

Adv. in order; methodically etc. *adj.;* in -turn, − its turn; step by step; by regular -steps, − gradations, − stages, − intervals; *seriatim,* systematically, by clockwork, *gradatim;* at stated periods etc. (*periodically*)138.

59. Disorder. [Absence, or want of Order, etc.]—N. disorder; derangement etc. 61; irregularity; anomaly etc. (*unconformity*) 83; anar-chy, -chism; want of method; dishevelment, untidiness etc. *adj.;* disunion; discord etc. 24.

confusion; confusedness etc. *adj.;* disarray, jumble, mix-up, huddle, litter, lumber; *cahotage;* farrago; mess, muss, mash, muddle, hash; hotchpotch; *imbroglio,* chaos, *omnium gatherum,* medley; mere -mixture etc. 41; fortuitous concourse of atoms, *disjecta membra, rudis indigestaque moles.*

complexity; complexness etc. *adj.;* com-, implication; intri-cacy, -cation; perplexity; network, maze, labyrinth, wilderness, jungle; involution, ravelling, entanglement; coil etc. (*convolution*) 248; sleave, tangled skein, knot, Gordian know, kink, web; wheels within wheels.

turmoil; ferment, etc. (*agitation*) 315; to do, trouble, pudder, pother, row, disturbance, convulsion, tumult, pandemonium; uproar, riot, rumpus, stour, scramble, *fracas,* embroilment, *mêleé,* spill and pelt, rough and tumble; whirlwind etc. 349; bear garden, Babel, Saturnalia, Donnybrook Fair, confusion worse confounded, most admired disorder, *concordia discors;* Bedlam −, hell- broke loose; bull in a china shop;

all the fat in the fire, *diable à quatre,* Devil to pay; pretty kettle of fish; pretty piece of -work, — business.

slattern, slut, sloven; draggle-tail.

V. be -disorderly etc. *adj.;* ferment, play at cross purposes.

put out of order; derange etc. 61; ravel etc. 219; ruffle, rumple; bungle, botch.

Adj. disorderly, orderless; out of -order; — place, — gear, — whack; irregular, desultory; anomalous etc. (*unconformable*) 83; acephalous, disorganized, straggling; un-, immethodical; unsymmetric; unsystematic; untidy, slovenly, bedraggled, messy; dislocated; out of sorts; promiscuous, indiscriminate; chaotic, anarchical, lawless; unarranged etc. 60; confused, tumultuous, turbulent, tempestuous; deranged etc. 61; topsy turvy etc. (*inverted*) 218; shapeless etc. 241; disjointed, out of joint.

com-plex, -plexed; intricate, complicated, perplexed, involved, ravelled, entangled, knotted, tangled, inextricable; irreducible.

troublous; riotous etc. (*violent*) 173.

Adv. irregularly etc. *adj.;* by fits and -snatches, — starts; pell-mell; higgledy-piggledy; helter-skelter, harum-scarum; in a ferment; at -sixes and sevens, — cross purposes; upside down etc. 218.

Phr. the cart before the horse, chaos is come again.

60. Arrangement. [Reduction to Order.]—N. arrangement; plan etc. 626; preparation etc. 673; dispos-al, -ition; col-, al-location; distribution; sorting etc. *v.;* assortment, allotment; grouping; apportionment, *taxis,* taxonomy, *syn-taxis,* graduation, organization, grading; re-organization, rationalization.

analysis, classification, division, digestion; systematism.

[Result of arrangement] order, orderliness, form, array; digest, synopsis etc. (compendi -um) 596; *syntagma,* table, atlas; register etc. (*record*) 551; score etc. 415; cosmos, organism, architecture.

[Instrument for sorting] sieve etc. 260; file, card index.

V. reduce to —, bring into- order; introduce order into; rally.

arrange, dispose, place, form; put —, set —, place- in order; straighten up, tidy up; set out, collocate, allocate, pack, marshal, range, size, rank, array, group, parcel out, allot, space, distribute, deal; cast —, assign- the parts; dispose of, assign places to; assort, sort; sift, riddle; put —, set- -to rights, — into shape, — in trim, — in array.

class, -ify; divide; file, string together, thread; register etc. (*record*) 551; list, catalogue, tabulate, index, alphabeticize, graduate, digest, grade, codify; orchestrate, score.

methodize, regulate, systematize, standardize, co-ordinate, organize, settle, fix.

unravel, disentangle, ravel, card; disembroil.

Adj. arranged etc. *v.;* embattled, in battle array; cut and dried; methodical, orderly, regular, systematic, tabular.

61. Derangement. [Subversion of Order: bringing into disorder.]—N. derangement etc. *v.;* dis-

order etc. 59; evection, discomposure, disturbance; dis-, de-organization; involvement; dislocation; perturbation, interruption; shuffling etc. *v.;* inversion etc. 218; corrugation etc. (*fold*) 258; insanity etc. 503.

V. derange; dis-, mis-arrange; dis-, mis-place; mislay, discompose, disorder, de-, dis-organize; embroil, unsettle, disturb, confuse, trouble, perturb, jumble, tumble; huddle, shuffle, muddle, toss, hustle, fumble, riot; bring —, put —, throw-into -disorder etc. 59; break the ranks, disconcert, convulse; break in upon.

unhinge, dislocate, put out of joint, throw out of gear.

turn topsy-turvy etc. (*invert*) 218; bedevil; complicate, involve, perplex, confound; im-, embrangle; tangle, en-tangle, ravel, tousle, dishevel, ruffle, rumple etc. (*fold*) 258; dement.

litter, scatter; mix etc. 41.

Adj. deranged etc. *v.;* syncre-tic, -tistic.

62. Precedence.—N. precedence; coming before etc. *v.;* the lead, *le pas;* superiority etc. 33; importance etc. 642; anteced-ence, -ency; anteriority etc. (*front*) 234; precursor etc. 64; priority etc. 116; precession etc. 280; anteposition, preference.

V. precede; come -before, — first; forerun, head, lead, take the lead; lead the -way, — dance; introduce, usher in; have the *pas;* set the fashion etc. (*influence*) 175; lead off, kick off, open the ball; take —, have- precedence; outrank; have the start etc. (*get before*) 280.

place before; prefix; premise, prelude, preface.

Adj. preceding etc. *v.;* pre-, antecedent; anterior, prior etc. 116; before; former, foregoing; before-, above-mentioned; aforesaid; said; precurs-ory, -ive; prevenient, preliminary, prefatory, introductory; prelus-ive, -ory; proemial, preparatory.

Adv. before; in advance etc. (*precession*) 280.

Phr. *seniores priores.*

63. Sequence.—N. sequence, coming after; going after etc. (*following*) 281; consecution, succession; posteriority etc. 117.

continuation; prolongation, order of succussion; successiveness; Elijah's mantle.

secondariness; subordinancy etc. (*inferiority*) 34.

V. succeed; come -after, — on, — next; follow, ensue, step into the shoes of; alternate.

place after, suffix, append.

Adj. succeeding etc. *v.;* sequent; sub-, consequent; sequacious, proximate, next; consecutive etc. (*continuity*) 69; alternate, amoebaean.

latter; posterior etc. 117.

Adv. after, subsequently; behind etc. (*rear*) 235.

64. Precursor.—N. precursor, antecedent, precedent, predecessor; forerunner, van-courier, *avant-coureur,* pioneer, prodrome, *prodromos,* outrider; leader, bell-wether; herald, harbinger; dawn.

prelude, preamble, preface, prologue, foreword, *avant-propos, protasis,* prolusion, proem, *prolepsis, prolegomena,* prefix, introduction;

lead, heading, frontispiece, groundwork; preparation etc. 673; overture, voluntary, *exordium*, symphony, *ritornello;* premises.

prefigurement etc. 511; omen etc. 512.

Adj. precursory; prelu-sive, -sory, -dious; proemial, introductory, prefatory, prodromous, inaugural, preliminary; precedent etc. (*prior*) 116.

65. Sequel.—N. sequel, suffix, successor; tail, *queue*, train, wake, trail, rear; retinue, suite; appendix, postscript, subscript; epilogue; conclusion; peroration; codicil; continuation, *sequela;* appendage etc. 39; tail –, heel-piece; tag, more last words; *colophon.*

follower, after-glow, -growth, -crop, -taste, - math.

after-part, -piece, -course, -thought, -game; *arrière pensée*, second thoughts.

66. Beginning.—N. beginning, commencement, opening, outset, incipience, inception, inchoation; introduction etc. (*precursor*) 64; *alpha;* initial; foundation; inauguration, *début, le premier pas,* embarcation, rising of the curtain; zero hour; exordium, curtain raiser; maiden speech; prelude; outbreak, onset, brunt; initiative, move, first move; gambit, narrow –, thin- end of the wedge; fresh start, new departure; forefront.

origin etc. (*cause*) 153; source, rise; bud, germ etc. 153; egg, rudiment; genesis, birth, nativity, cradle, infancy, incunabula; start, starting-point etc. 293; dawn etc. (*morning*) 125.

title-page; head, -ing, caption; van etc. (*front*) 234.

en-trance, -try; inlet, orifice, mouth, chops, lips, porch, portal, portico, *propylon,* door; gate, -way; postern, wicket, threshold, vestibule; skirts, border etc. (*edge*) 231; tee.

first -stage, – blush, – glance, – impression, – sight.

rudiments, elements, outlines, *principia*, grammar, *protasis;* alphabet, ABC.

V. begin, commence, inchoate. rise, arise, originate, institute, conceive, initiate, open. dawn, set in, take its rise, enter upon, start; enter; set out etc. (*depart*) 293; embark in.

usher in; lead -off, – the way; take the -lead, – initiative; inaugurate, head; stand -at the head, – first, – for; lay the foundations etc. (*prepare*) 673; found etc. (*cause*) 153; set -up, – on foot, – agoing, – abroach, – the ball in motion; apply the match to a train; launch, broach; open -up, – the door to; set -about, – to work; make a -beginning, – start; handsel; take the first step, lay the first stone, cut the first turf; break -ground, – the ice, – cover; pass –, cross- the Rubicon; open -fire, – the ball; ventilate, air; undertake etc. 676.

come into -existence, – the world; make one's *début*, take birth; burst forth, break out; spring –, crop- up.

begin -at the beginning, – *ab ovo,* – again, – *de novo;* start afresh, make a fresh start, shuffle the cards, resume, recommence.

Adj. beginning etc. *v.;* initi-al, -atory, -ative; inceptive, introductory, incipient; proemial, inaugural; incho-ate, -ative; embryonic, rudimental; primogenial; primeval etc. (*old*) 124; rudimentary, aboriginal; natal, nascent.

first, foremost, front, leading, head; maiden. begun etc. *v.;* just -begun etc. *v.*

Adv. at –, in- the beginning etc. *n.;* first, in the first place, *imprimis,* first and foremost; *in limine;* in -the bud, – embryo, – its infancy; from -the beginning, – its birth; *ab -initio, – ovo. – incunabilis,* primarily, originally.

67. End.—N. end, close, termination; desinence, conclusion, *finis, finale,* period, term, *terminus,* last, *omega;* extreme, -tremity; gable –, butt –, fagend; tip, nib, point; tail etc. (*rear*) 235; verge etc. (*edge*) 231; tag, epilogue, peroration; *bonne bouche*, bitter end, tail end; terminal; *apodosis;* appendix.

consummation, *dénouement;* finish etc. (*completion*) 729; fate; doom, -sday; crack of doom, day of Judgment, fall of the curtain, wind-up; goal, destination; limit, stoppage, end all, determination; expiration, expiry; death etc. 360; end of all things; finality; eschatology.

break up, *commencement de la fin,* last stage, turning point; *coup de grâce,* death-blow; knock-out.

V. end, close, finish, terminate, conclude, be all over; expire; die etc. 360; come –, draw- to a - close etc. *n.;* have run its course; run out, pass away.

bring to an -end etc. *n.;* put an end to, make an end of; determine; get through; achieve etc. (*complete*) 729; stop etc. (*make to cease*) 142; shut up shop.

Adj. ending etc. *v.;* final, terminal, definitive, conclusive; crowning etc. (*completing*) 729; last, ultimate; hindermost; rear etc. 235; caudal.

contermin-ate, -ous, -able.

ended etc. *v.;* at an end; settled, decided, over, played out, set at rest.

penultimate; last but -one, – two, etc.

unbegun, uncommenced; fresh.

Adv. finally etc. *adj.;* in fine; at the last; once for all.

68. Middle.—N. middle, midst, mediety; mean etc. 29; medium, middle term; center etc. 222; mid-course etc. 628; *mezzo termine; juste milieu* etc. 628; half-way house, nave, navel, omphalos; nucle-us, -olus.

equidistance, bisection, half-distance; equator, diaphragm, midriff; interjacence etc. 228.

Adj. middle, medial, mesial, mean, mid; middle-, mid-most; middling; mediate; intermediate etc. (*interjacent*) 228; equidistant; central etc. 222; mediterranean, equatorial.

Adv. in the middle; in the thick; mid-, halfway; midships, *in medias res.*

69. Continuity. [Uninterrupted sequence.]—N. continuity; consecu-tion,, -tiveness etc. *adj.;* succession, round, suite, progression, series, train, chain; cat-, concatenation; catena; scale; gradation, course, constant flow, perpetuity.

procession, column; retinue, *cortège*, cavalcade, rank and file, line of battle, array.

pedigree, genealogy, lineage, race etc. 166.

rank, file, line, row, range, tier, string, thread; team; suit; colonnade.

V. follow in –, form- a series etc. *n.;* fall in.

arrange in a -series etc. *n.;* string together, catenate, file, thread, graduate, tabulate.

Adj. continu-ous. -ed; consecutive; progressive, gradual; serial, successive; immediate, unbroken, entire; linear; in a -line, — row etc. *n.;* uninter-rupted, -mitting; unremitting; perennial, evergreen; constant.

Adv. continuously etc. *adj.; seriatim;* in a -line etc. *n.;* in -succession, — turn; running, gradually, step by step, *gradatim,* at a stretch; in -file, — column, — single file, — Indian file.

70. Discontinuity. [Interrupted sequence.]—**N.** discontinuity; disjunction etc. 44; anacoluthon; interruption, break, fracture, flaw, fault, split, crack, cut; gap etc. (*interval*) 198; solution of continuity, *caesura;* broken thread; parenthesis, episode; rhapsody, patchwork; intermission; alternation etc. (*periodicity*) 138; dropping fire.

V. be -discontinuous etc. *adj.;* alternate, intermit.

discontinue, pause, interrupt; intervene; break, — in upon; interpose etc. 228; break —, snap- the thread; disconnect etc. (*disjoin*) 44.

Adj. discontinuous, unsuccessive, broken, interrupted, *décousu;* dis-, un-connected, discrete, disjunctive; fitful etc. (*irregular*) 139; spasmodic, desultory, intermit-ting etc. *v.;* -tent; alternate; recurrent etc. (*periodic*) 138; few and far between.

Adv. at intervals; by -snatches, — jerks, — skips, — catches, — fits and starts; skippingly, *per saltum; longo intervallo.*

71. Term.—**N.** term, rank, station, stage, step; degree etc. 26; scale, remove, grade, link, peg, round —, rung- of the ladder, *status,* position, place, point, mark, *pas,* period, pitch; stand, -ing; footing, range.

V. hold —, occupy —, fall into- a place etc. *n.*

72. Assemblage.—**N.** assemblage; col-lection, location, -ligation; compilation, levy, gathering, ingathering, mobilization, meet, foregathering, muster, *attroupement;* con-course, -flux, - gregation, -tesseration. -vergence etc. 290; meeting, *levée, réunion,* drawing room, at home; conversazione etc. (*social gathering*) 892; assembly, congress, eisteddfod; conven-tion, -ticle; gemote; conclave, etc. (*council*) 696; posse, *posse comitatus;* Noah's ark.

miscellany, *collectanea,* symposium; museum, menagerie, etc. (*store*) 636.

crowd, throng, multitude; flood, rush, deluge; rout, rabble, mob, press, crush, *cohue,* jam, horde, body, tribe; crew, gang, knot, squad, band, party; swarm, shoal, school, covey, flock, herd, drove, kennel; array, bevy, galaxy; *corps,* company, troop, *troupe;* army, force, regiment, etc. (*combatants*) 726; host etc. (*multitude*) 102; populousness.

clan, brotherhood, association etc. (*party*) 712.

volley, shower, storm, cloud.

group, cluster, Pleiades, clump, pencil; set, batch, lot, pack; budget, *dossier,* assortment, bunch; parcel; pack-et, -age; bundle, *fasciculus,* fascine, bale; ser-on, oon; faggot, wisp, truss, tuft; shock, rick, fardel, stack, sheaf, swath, gavel, haycock, stook.

accumulation etc. (*store*) 636; congeries, heap, lump, pile, *rouleau,* tissue, mass, pyramid; drift; snow-ball, -drift; acervation, cumulation; amassment, glom-, agglom-eration; conglobation; conglomeration, -ate; coacervation, coagmentation, aggregation, concentration, congestion, *omnium gatherum, spicilegium,* black hole of Calcutta; quantity etc. (*greatness*) 31.

collector, gatherer; whip, -per in.

V. [be or come together] assemble, collect, muster; meet, unite, join, rejoin; cluster, flock, swarm, surge, stream, herd, crowd, throng, associate; con-gregate, -glomerate, -centrate; center round, *rendezvous,* resort; come —, flock —, get —, pig- together; forgather; huddle; reassemble.

[get or bring together] assemble, muster, mobilize; bring —, get —, put —, draw —, scrape —, lump- together; col-lect, -locate. -ligate; get —, whip- in; gather; hold a meeting; con-vene, -voke, -vocate; rake up, dredge; heap, mass, pile; pack, put up, truss, cram; acervate; ag-glomerate, -gregate; compile; group, aggroup, concentrate, unite; collect —, bring- into a focus; amass, accumulate etc. (*store*) 636; collect in a drag-net; heap Ossa upon Pelion.

Adj. assembled etc. *v.;* closely packed, dense, serried, crowded to suffocation, teeming, swarming, populous; as thick as hops; all of a heap, fasciculated; cumulative.

Phr. the plot thickens.

73. Non-assemblage. Dispersion.—**N.** dispersion; disjunction etc. 44; divergence etc. 291; scattering etc. *v.;* dissemination, broadcasting, diffusion, dissipation, distribution; apportionment etc. 786; spread, respersion, circumfusion, interspersion, spargefaction.

waifs and estrays, flotsam and jetsam, *disjecta membra.*

V. disperse, scatter, sow, disseminate, radiate, diffuse, shed, spread, ted, bestrew, overspread, dispense, disband, disembody, demobilize, dismember, distribute; apportion etc. 786; blow off, let out, dispel, cast forth, draught off; strew, straw, strow; spirtle, cast, sprinkle, shatter; issue, deal out, retail, utter; re-, inter-sperse; set abroach, circumfuse.

turn —, cast- adrift; scatter to the winds; sow broadcast.

spread like wildfire, disperse themselves.

Adj. unassembled etc. (*see* assemble etc. 72); dispersed etc. *v.;* sparse, dispread, broadcast, sporadic, widespread; far-flung; epidemic etc. (*general*) 78; adrift, stray; dishevelled, streaming.

Adv. *sparsim,* here and there, *passim.*

74. Focus. [Place of meeting.]—**N.** focus; point of- convergence etc. 290; corradiation; center etc. 222; gathering-place, resort; haunt; retreat; *venue, rendezvous;* rallying point, head-quarters, home, club; *dépôt* etc. (*store*) 636; tryst, trysting-place; place of -meeting, — resort, — assignation; *point de —, lieu de- réunion;* issue.

V. bring to- a point, — a focus, — an issue; focus.

75. Class.—N. class, category, *categorema*, head, order, section; division, subdivision; department, province, domain, sphere.

kind, sort, genus, species, variety, branch, family, race, tribe, caste, sept, clan, breed; *clique, coterie*; type, kit, sect, set; assortment; feather, kidney; suit; range; gender, sex, kin.

manner, description, denomination, persuasion, connection, designation, character, stamp; predicament; conviction etc. 484.

similarity etc. 17.

76. Inclusion. [Comprehension under, or reference to a class.]—N. inclusion, admission, incorporation, comprehension, reception.

composition etc. (*inclusion in a compound*) 54.

V. be -included in etc.; come −, fall −, range- under; belong −, pertain- to; range with; merge in.

include, compromise, comprehend, contain, admit, embrace, receive; enclose etc. (*circumscribe*) 229; incorporate, cover, embody, encircle.

reckon −, enumerate −, number- among; refer to; place −, arrange-under, − with; take into account.

Adj. includ-ed; -ing etc. *v.;* inclusive; comprehensive, all-embracing; congen-er, -erous; of the same -class etc. 75.

Phr. *et hoc genus omne,* etc.; *et caetera.*

77. Exclusion.*—N. exclusion etc. 55.

* The same set of words is used to express *Exclusion from a class* and *Exclusion from a compound*. Reference is therefore made to the former at 55. This identity does not occur with regard to *Inclusion,* which therefore constitutes a separate category.

78. Generality.—N. general-ity, -ization; universality; catholic-ity, -ism; miscel-lany, -laneousness; drag-net.

every-one, -body; all hands, all the world and his wife; any body, N or M, all sorts; *tout le monde.*

prevalence, run.

V. be -general etc. *adj.;* prevail, obtain, be going about, stalk abroad.

render -general etc. *adj.;* generalize; spread, broadcast.

Adj. general, usual, current, generic, collective; broad, comprehensive, sweeping; encyclopedical, panoramic, widespread etc. (*dispersed*) 73.

universal; catho-lic, -lical; common, world-wide; e-cumenical; transcendental; prevalent, prevailing, rife, epidemic, besetting; all over, covered with.

every, all; indeterminate, indefinite, unspecified, impersonal.

customary etc. (*habitual*) 613.

Adv. what-ever, -soever; to a man, one and all, without exception.

generally etc. *adj.;* always, for better for worse; in general, generally speaking; speaking generally; for the most part; in the long run etc. (*on an average*) 29.

79. Speciality.—N. speciality, *spécialité,* individ-uality, -uity; particularity, pecularity;

idiocrasy etc. (*tendency*) 176; personality, characteristic, mannerism, idiosyncrasy, attribute specificness etc. *adj.;* singularity etc. (*unconformity*) 83; reading, version, lection; state; *trait;* distinctive feature; technicality; *differentia.*

particulars, details, minutiae, items, counts.

I, self, I myself, *ego;* my-, him-, her-, it-self.

V. specify, particularize, individualize, realize, specialize, designate, differentiate, determine, define, denote, indicate, itemize, detail.

descend to particulars, enter into detail, come to the point.

Adj. special, particular, individual, specific, proper, personal, intimate, original, private, respective, definite, concrete, determinate, especial, certain, esoteric, endemic, partial, party, peculiar, marked, appropriate, several, characteristic, diagnistic, exact, exclusive; singular etc. (*exceptional*) 83; idiomatic; typical, representative, distinctive.

this, that; yon, -der.

Adv. specially etc. *adj.;* in particular, *in propriâ personâ; ad hominem;* for my part.

each, apiece, one by one; severally, respectively, each to each; *seriatim,* in detail, bit by bit; *pro hac vice,* − *re natâ.*

namely, that is to say, *videlicet,* viz.; to wit.

80. Rule.—N. regularity, uniformity etc. 16; clock-work precision; punctuality etc. (*exactness*) 494; routine etc. (*custom*) 613; formula; system; rut; canon, convention, maxim; rule etc. (*form, regulation*) 697; key-note, standard, model; precedent etc. (*prototype*) 22; conformity etc. 82.

nature, principle; law; order of things; normal −, natural −, ordinary −, model- -state, − condition; standing -dish, − order; normality; Procrustean law; law of the Medes and Persians; hard and fast rule.

Adj. regular, uniform, symmetrical, constant, steady; according to rule etc. (*conformable*) 82; customary etc. 613; orderly etc. 58.

81. Multiformity.—N. multi-, omniformity; variety, diversity; multifariousness etc. *adj.*

Adj. multi-form, -fold, -farious, -generous; multiplex, variform, manifold, many-sided, multiplicate; omni-form, -genous, -farious; polymorphic; protean; heterogeneous, motley, mosaic; epicene, indiscriminate, desultory, irregular, diversified, different, divers; all manner of; of -every description, − all sorts and kinds; *et hoc genus omne;* and what not? *de omnibus rebus et quibusdam aliis.*

82. Conformity.—N. conform-ity, -ance; observance.

naturalization; conventionality etc. (*custom*) 613; agreement etc. 23.

example, instance, specimen, sample, quotation; exemplification, illustration, case in point; object lesson.

conventionalist, formalist, Philistine.

pattern etc. (*prototype*) 22.

V. conform to, − rule; accommodate −, adapt- oneself to; rub off corners.

be -regular etc. *adj.;* move in a groove; follow —, observe —, go by —, bend to —, obey- -rules, — precedents; comply —, tally —, chime in —, fall in-with; be -guided, — regulated- by; fall into a -custom, — usage; follow the -fashion, — multitude; pass muster, do as others do, *hurler avec les loups;* do at Rome as the Romans do; go —, swim- with the -stream, — current, — tide; tread the beaten track etc. (*habit*) 613; rubber-stamp; keep one in countenance.

exemplify, illustrate, cite, quote, put a case; produce an- instance etc. *n.*

Adj. conformable to rule, adaptable, compliant, consistent, agreeable; regular etc. 80; according to -regulation, — rule, — Cocker; *en règle, selon les règles,* well regulated, orderly; symmetric etc. 242.

conventional commonplace etc. (*customary*) 613; of -daily, — every day- occurrence; in the natural order of things; ordinary, common, — or garden, prosaic, habitual, usual.

in the order of the day; naturalized.

typical, normal, formal; canonical, orthodox, sound, strict, rigid, positive, uncompromising, Procrustean; point device.

secundum artem, ship-shape, technical.

exemplary, illustrative, in point.

Adv. conformably etc. *adj.;* by rule; agreeably to; in -conformity, — accordance, — keepingwith; according to; consistently with; as usual, *ad instar, instar omnium; more -solito,* — *majorum.*

for the sake of conformity; of —, as a matter of- course; *pro formâ,* for form's sake, by the card; according to plan.

invariably etc. (*uniformly*) 16.

for -example, — instance; *exempli gratiâ; e.g.; inter alia.*

Phr. *cela va sans dire, ex pede Herculem, noscitur a sociis.*

83. Unconformity.—N. non-conformity etc. 82; un-, dis-conformity; unconventionality, informality, abnormity, anomaly; anomalousness etc. *adj.;* exception, peculiarity, etc. 79; infraction —, breach —, violation —, infringement- of -law, — custom, — usage; eccentricity, *bizarrerie,* oddity, *je ne sais quoi,* monstrosity, rarity; freak of Nature.

individuality, idiosyncrasy, singularity, oritinality, mannerism.

aberration; irregularity; variety; singularity; exemption; salvo etc. (*qualification*) 469.

nonconformist; nondescript, character, original, nonsuch, monster, prodigy, wonder, miracle, curiosity, missing link, flying fish, black swan, *lusus naturae, rara avis,* queer fish; mongrel; half-caste, -blood, -breed; *métis,* cross breed, hybrid, mule, mulatto, sacatra, marabou; *tertium quid,* hermaphrodite, gynander, androgyn.

phoenix, chimera, hydra, sphinx, minotaur; griff-in, -on; centaur; hippogriff, -centaur; sagittary; kraken; cockatrice, wyvern, roc, liver, dragon, sea-serpent; mermaid; unicorn; Cyclops, ·men whose heads do grown beneath their shoulders;. Teratolgy.

fish out of water; neither -one thing nor another, — fish flesh nor fowl nor good red her-

ring; one in a -way, — thousand; out-cast, -law; Ishmael, pariah; oasis.

V. be -unconformable etc. *adj.;* leave the beaten -track, — path; infringe —, break —, violate- a -law, — habit, — usage, — custom; drive a coach and six through; stretch a point; have no business there; baffle —, beggar- all description.

Adj. unconformable, exceptional; abnorm-al, -ous; anomal-ous, -istic; out of -order, — place, — keeping, — tune, — one's element; irregular, arbitrary; lawless, informal, aberrant, stray, wandering, wanton; peculiar, exclusive, unnatural, eccentric, crotchety, egregious; out of the -beaten track, — common, — common run, — pale of; misplaced; funny.

un-usual, -accustomed, -customary, -wonted, -common; rare, singular, *unique,* curious, odd, extraordinary, strange, monstrous; wonderful etc. 870; unexpected, unaccountable; *outré,* out of the way, remarkable, noteworthy; queer, quaint, nondescript, none such, *sui generis;* original, unconventional, Bohemian, unfashionable; un-described, -precedented, -paralleled, -exampled, -heard of, -familiar; fantastic, newfangled, grotesque, *bizarre;* outlandish, exotic, *tombé de nues,* preternatural; denaturalized.

heterogeneious, heteroclite, amorphous, mongrel, amphibious, epicene, half-blood, hybrid; androgyn-ous, -al; unsymmetric etc. 243.

qualified etc. 469.

Adv. unconformably etc. *adj.;* except, unless, save, barring, beside, without, save and except, let alone.

however, yet, but.

Int. what -on earth! — in the world!

Phr. never was -seen, — heard, — known- the like.

84. Number.—N. number, symbol, numeral, figure, cipher, digit, integer; counter; round number; formula; function; series.

sum, total, aggregate, difference, complement, subtrahend; product; multipli-cand, -er, -cator; coefficient, multiple; dividend, divisor, factor, quotient, sub-multiple, fraction; mixed number; numerator, denominator; decimal, circulating decimal, repetend; common measure, aliquot part; reciprocal; prime number; totitive, totient.

permutation, combination, variation; election. ratio, proportion; progression; arithmetical —, geometrical —, harmonical- progression; percentage.

figurate —, pyramidal —, polygonal- numbers.

power, root, exponent, index, logarithm, antilogarithm; modulus.

differential, integral, fluxion, fluent.

Adj. numeral, complementary, divisible, aliquot, reciprocal, prime, fractional, decimal, figurate, incommensurable.

proportional, exponential, logarithmic, logometric, differential, fluxional, integral.

positive, negative; rational, irrational; surd, radical, real, imaginary, impossible.

85. Numeration.—N. numeration, numbering etc. *v.;* pagination; tale, tally, recension, enumer-

ation, summation, reckoning, computation, supputation; calcu-lation, -lus; algorithm, rhabdology, dactylonomy; measurement etc. 466; statistics.

arithmetic, analysis, algebra, fluxions; differential —, integral —, infinitesimal-calculus; calculus of differences.

[Statistics] dead reckoning, muster, poll, census, capitation, roll-call, recapitulation; account etc. (list) 86.

[Operations] notation, addition, subtraction, multiplication, division, proportion, rule of three, practice, equations, extraction of roots, reduction, involution, evolution, approximation, interpolation, differentiation, integration.

[Instruments] abacus, swan-pan, logometer, sliding —, slide- rule, tallies, Napier's bones, calculating —, adding- machine, difference engine; cash register.

arithmetician, calculator, abacist; mathematician, actuary, statistician, surveyor, geodesist.

V. number, count, tell; call —, run- over, take an account of, enumerate, call the roll, muster, poll, recite, recapitulate; sum; sum —, cast- up; tell off, score, cipher, compute, calculate, set a price, reckon, — up, estimate; suppute, add, subtract, multiply, divide, extract roots.

check, prove, demonstrate, balance, audit, overhaul, take stock; affix numbers to, page, foliate, paginate.

amount —, come- to.

Adj. numer-al, -ical; arithmetical, analytic, algebraic, statistical, numerable, computable, calculable; commensur-able, -ate; incommensur-able, -ate.

86. List.—N. list, catalogue, enumeration, inventory, schedule; register etc. (record) 551; account; bill, — of costs, syllabus; terrier, tally, file; almanac, calendar, index, table, atlas, contents, card index; rota, ticket; book, ledger; synopsis, catalogue raisonné, tableau, scroll, manifest, invoice, bill of lading; prospectus, programme; bill of fare, menu, carte; score, census, statistics, returns; Red —, Blue —, Domesday- book; cadaster; directory, gazetteer, dictionary, glossary, lexicon, thesaurus, gradus.

roll; check —, chequer —, bead- roll, — of honor; muster -roll, — book; roster, panel; cartulary, diptych.

V. list, enrol, schedule, register etc. n.; indent, post, docket; matriculate.

Adj. cadastral, listed etc. v.

87. Unity.—N. unity; oneness etc. adj.; individuality; solitude etc. (seclusion) 893; isolation etc. (disjunction) 44; unification etc. 48.

one, unit, ace; item; individual; solo, none else, no other, naught beside.

V. be -one, — alone etc. adj.; dine with Duke Humphrey.

isolate etc. (disjoin) 44.

render one; unite etc. (join) 43, (combine) 48.

Adj. one, sole, single, solitary, only- begotten; individual, apart, alone; kithless.

un-accompanied, -attended; solus, singlehanded; singular, odd, unique, unrepeated, azygous, first and last; isolated etc. (disjoined) 44; insular; unitary.

lone; lone-ly, -some; desolate, dreary.

in-secable, -severable, -discerptible; compact, irresolvable.

Adv. singly etc. adj.; alone, by itself, per se, only, apart, in the singular number, in the abstract; one -by one, — at a time; simply; one and a half, sesqui-.

Phr. natura il fece, e poi roppe la stampa.

88. Accompaniment.—N. accompaniment; appurtenance, adjunct etc. 39; context.

coexistence, concomitance, company, association, companionship; part-, copart-nership; coefficiency.

concomitant, accessory, coefficient; companion, attendant, fellow, associate, consort, spouse, colleague, fidus Achates; part-, co-partner; satellite, hanger on, shadow; escort, entourage, suite, cortège; convoy, follower etc. 65; attribute.

V. accompany, coexist, attend, convoy, chaperon; hang —, wait- on; go hand in hand with; synchronize etc. 120; bear —, keep- company; row in the same boat; bring in its train, associate —, couple- with.

Adj. accompanying etc. v.; concomitant, fellow, twin, joint; associated —, coupled- with; accessory, attendant, obbligato.

Adv. with, withal; together —, along —, in company- with; hand in hand, side by side; cheek by -jowl, — jole; arm in arm; there-, here-with; and etc. (addition) 37.

together, in a body, collectively.

89. Duality.—N. dual-ity, -ism; duplicity; bi-plicity, -formity; span, polarity.

two, deuce, couple, couplet, doublet, brace, pair, cheeks, twins, Castor and Pollus, gemini, Siamese twins; fellows; yoke, conjugation, dyad, distich.

V. [unite in pairs] pair, couple, bracket, yoke; conduplicate, mate.

Adj. two, twain; dual, -istic; binary, binomial; twin, biparous; dyadic; conduplicate; duplex etc. 90; tête-à-tête; paired; dihedral.

coupled etc. v.; conjugate.

both, — the one and the other.

90. Duplication.—N. duplication, doubling etc. v.; gemi-, ingemi-nation; reduplication; iteration etc. (repetition) 104; renewal.

V. double; re-double, -duplicate; geminate; repeat etc. 104; renew etc. 660; duplicate, copy etc. 21.

Adj. double; doubled etc. v.; bicameral, bicapital, bi-fold, -form, -lateral, -farious, -facial; two-fold, -sided, -headed, -edged etc.; duplex; double-faced; twin, duplicate, ingeminate; second; dual etc. 29.

Adv. twice, once more; over again etc. (repeatedly) 104; as much again; twofold.

secondly, in the second place, again.

91. Bisection. [Division into two parts.]—N. bi-section, -partition; di-, subdi-chotomy; halving etc. v.; dimidiation; hendiadis.

bifurcation, forking, branching, furcation, ramification, divarication; fork, prong; fold.

half, moiety.

V. bisect, halve, divide, split, cut in two, cleave, dimidiate, dichotomize, divaricate.

go halves, divide with.

separate, fork, bifurcate; branch -off, − out; ramify.

Adj. bisected etc. v.; cloven, cleft; bipartite, biconjugate, bicuspid, bifid; bifur-cous, -cate, -cated; semi-, demi- hemi-.

92. Triality.—N. triality, trinity,* triplicity.

three, triad, triplet, trey, trio, ternion, tri-nomial, leash; tierce; triennium; trefoil, triangle, trident, tripod, triumvirate, troika.

third power, cube.

Adj. three; tri-form, -nal, -nomial; tertiary; triune.

*Trinity is hardly ever used except in a theological sense; see Deity 976.

93. Triplication.—N. tripli-cation, -city; trebleness, trine, trilogy.

V. treble, triple, triplicate, cube.

Adj. treble, triple; tern, -ary; triplex, triplicate, threefold, trilogistic; third; trinal; trihedral.

Adv. three -times, − fold; thrice, in the third place, thirdly; trebly etc. adj.

94. Trisection. [Division into three parts.]—N. tri-section, -partition, -chotomy; third, − part.

V. trisect, divide into three parts, trifurcate.

Adj. trifid; trisected etc. v.; tripartite, -chotomous, -sulcate.

95. Quaternity.—N. quaternity, four, tetrad, quartet, quaternion, square, quadrature, quarter, quadruplet; quadrilateral, quadrangle, quatre-foil; quadriga.

V. reduce to a square, square.

Adj. four; quat-ernary, -ernal; quadratic; quar-tile, quartic, tetractic, tetrad, tetrahedral; quad-rennial; quadrivalent.

96. Quadruplication.—N. quadruplication.

V. multiply by four, quadruplicate, bi-quadrate.

Adj. fourfold; quad-ruple, -ruplicate, -rible; quadruplex; fourth.

Adv. four times; in the fourth place, fourthly.

97. Quadrisection. [Division into four parts.]—N. quadri-section, -partition; quarter-ing etc. v.; fourth; quart, -er, -ern; farthing (i.e. fourthing); quarto.

V. quarter, divide into four parts, quadrisect.

Adj. quartered etc. v.; quadri-fid, -partite.

98. Five, etc.—N. five, cinque, quint, quin-cunx, quintuplet, quintet, pentagon, pentameter, Pentateuch; six, half-a-dozen; sextet, hexagon, hexameter; seven, Heptarchy; eight, octet, octa-gon, octave; nine, three times three; ten, decade; eleven; twelve, dozen; thirteen; long −, baker's-dozen.

twenty, score; twenty-four, four and twenty, two dozen; twenty-five, five and twenty, quarter of a hundred; forty, two score; fifty, half a hundred; sixty, three score, sexagenarian; seven-ty, three score and ten, septuagenarian; eighty, four score, octogenarian; ninety, four score and ten, nonagenarian.

hundred, centenary, hecatomb, century; hundredweight, cwt.; one hundred and forty-four, gross; bicentenary, tercentenary etc.

thousand, chiliad; myriad, millennium, ten thousand; lac, lakh, one hundred thousand, plum; million; thousand million, milliard.

billion, trillion etc.

V. centuriate.

Adj. five, quinary, quintuple; fifth; senary, sextuple; sixth; seventh; octuple; eighth; nine-fold, ninth; tenfold, decimal, denary, decuple; tenth; eleventh; duo-denary, -denal; twelfth; in one's 'teens, thirteenth.

vices-, viges-imal; twentieth; twenty-fourth etc. n.

cent-uple, -uplicate, -ennial, -enary, -urial; secular, hundredth; thousandth; millenary etc.

99. Quinquesection, etc.—N. division by -five etc. 98; quinquesection etc.; fifth etc.; decima-tion.

V. decimate, quinquesect.

Adj. quinque-fid, -partite; quinquarticular; octifid; decimal, tenth, tithe, teind; duodecimal, twelfth; sexagesimal, -genary; hundredth, centesimal; millesimal etc.

100. Plurality. [More than one.]—N. plurality; a -number, − certain number; one or two, two or three etc.; a few, several; multitude etc. 102.

Adj. plural, more than one, upwards of, some, certain; not -alone etc. 87.

Adv. et cetera, etc., etc.

Phr. non deficit alter.

100a. Fraction [Less than one.]—N. fraction, fractional part, fragment; part etc. 51.

Adj. fractional, fragmentary, partial.

101. Zero.—N. zero, nothing, naught, nought, duck's egg, goose egg; cipher, none, nobody; not a soul; âme qui vive; absence etc. 187; unsubstantiality etc. 4.

Adj. not -one, − any.

102. Multitude.—N. multitude; numerousness etc. adj.; numer-osity, -ality; multiplicity; profu-sion etc. (plenty) 639; legion; host; great −, large −, round −, enormous- number; a quantity, numbers, array, sight, army, sea, galaxy; scores, peck, bushel, school, shoal, swarm, draft, bevy, cloud, flock, herd, drove, flight, covey, hive, brood, litter, farrow, fry, nest; mob, crowd etc. (assemblage) 72; lots, loads, heaps; all the world and his wife.

[Increase of number] greater number, ma-jority; multiplication, multiple.

V. be -numerous etc. adj.; swarm −, teem −, crawl −, creep -with; crowd, swarm, come thick upon; outnumber, multiply; people; swarm like -locusts, − bees.

Adj. many, several, sundry, divers, various,

not a few; a -hundred, − thousand, − myriad, − million, − thousand and one; some -ten or a dozen, − forty or fifty etc.; half a -dozen, − hundred etc.; very −, full −, ever so- many; numer-ous, -ose; profuse, in profusion; manifold, multiplied, multitudinous, multiferous, multiple, multinomial, teeming, crawling, populous, peopled, crowded, thick, studded; galore.

thick coming, many more, more than one can tell, a world of; no end -of, − to; *cum multis aliis*; thick as -hops, − hail; plenty as blackberries; numerous as the -stars in the firmament, − sands on the sea-shore, − hairs on the head; and -what not, − heaven knows what; endless etc. (*infinite*) 105.

Phr. their name is 'Legion.'

103. Fewness.—N. fewness etc. *adj.*; paucity, small number; small quantity etc. 32; scarcity, sparsity; rarity; infrequency etc. 137; handfull; maniple; minority, exiguity.

[Diminution of number] reduction; weeding etc. *v.*; elimination, sarculation, decimation.

V. be -few etc. *adj.*

render -few etc. *adj.*; reduce, diminish the number, weed; eliminate, thin, decimate.

Adj. few; scarce; scant, -y; thin, rare, thinly scattered, few and far between; exiguous; infrequent etc. 137; *rari nantes*; hardly −, scarcely- any; to be counted on one's fingers; reduced etc. *v.*; unrepeated.

Adv. here and there.

104. Repetition.—N. repetition, iteration, reiteration, duplication, ding-dong, alliteration; *epistrophe;* harping, recurrence, succession, run; batto-, tauto-logy; monotony, tautophony; rhythm etc. 138; pleonasm, redundancy, diffuseness.

chimes, repetend, echo, *ritornello,* burden of a song, *refrain;* rehearsal; encore; *réchauffé, rifacimento,* recapitulation.

cuckoo etc. (*imitation*) 19; reverberation etc. 408; drumming etc. (*roll*) 407; renewal etc. (*restoration*) 660.

twice-told tale; old -story, − song, chestnut; second −, new- edition; reprint, new impression; return game, return match, reappearance, reproduction; periodicity etc. 138.

V. repeat, iterate, reiterate, reproduce, parrot, echo, re-echo, drum, harp upon, battologize, hammer, redouble.

recur, revert, return, reappear; renew etc. (*restore*) 660.

rehearse; do −, say- over again; ring the changes on; harp on the same string; din −, drum- in the ear; conjugate in all its moods, tenses and inflexions, begin again, go over the same ground, go the same round, never hear the last of; resume, return to, recapitulate, reword.

Adj. repeated etc. *v.*; repetition-al, -ary; recur-rent, -ring; ever recurring, thick coming; fre-quent, incessant, redundant, pleonastic, tautological.

monotonous, harping, iterative; mocking, chiming; retold; aforesaid, -named; above-mentioned, said; habitual etc. 613; another.

Adv. repeatedly, often, again, afresh, anew,

over again, once more; ditto, *encore, de novo, bis, da capo.*

again and again; over and over, − again; many times over; time- and again, − after time; year after year; day by day etc.; many −, several −, a number of- times; many −, full many- a time; times out of number, year in and year out, morning, noon and night; frequently etc. 136.

Phr. *ecce iterum Crispinus, toujours perdrix,* cut and come again; 'tomorrow and tomorrow.'

105. Infinity.—N. infini-ty, -tude, -teness etc. *adj.;* perpetuity etc. 112.

V. be -infinite etc. *adj.;* know −, have- no - limits, − bounds; go on for ever.

Adj. infinite, immense; number-, count-, sum-, measure-less; innumer-, immeasur-, incalcul-, illimit-, intermin-, unfathom-, unapproach-able; exhaustless, inexhaustible, indefinite; without - number, − measure, − limit, − end; incompre-hensible; limit-, end-, bound-, termless; un-told, - numbered, -measured, -bounded, -limited; il-limited; perpetual etc. 112.

Adv. infinitely etc. *adj.; ad infinitum.*

106. Time.—N. time, duration; period, term, stage, space, span, spell, season; the whole -time, − period; course etc. 109.

intermediate, time, while, *interim,* interval, bit, pendency; inter-vention, -mission, -mit-tence, -regnum, ⁌lude; respite.

era, epoch, eon, cycle; time of life, age, year, date; decade etc. (*period*) 108; moment, etc. (*in-stant*) 113; reign etc. 737.

glass −, ravages −, whirligig −, noiseless foot- of time; scythe.

V. continue, last, endure, go on, hold out, remain, stay, persist, abide, run; intervene; elapse etc. 109.

take −, take up −, fill −, occupy- time.

pass −, pass away −, spend −, while away −, consume −, talk against −, kill- time; take over; use −, employ- time; tarry etc. 110; seize an opportunity etc. 134; waste time etc. (*be in-active*) 683.

Adj. continuing etc. *v.;* on foot; permanent etc. (*durable*) 110.

Adv. while, whilst, during, pending; during the -time, − interval; in the course of; for the time being, day by day; in the time of, when; mean-time, -while; in the -meantime, − *interim; ad interim, pendente lite; de die in diem;* from -day to day, − hour to hour etc.; hourly, always; for a -time, − season; till, until, up to, yet; the whole −, all the- time; all along; throughout etc. (*com-pletely*) 52; for good etc. (*diuturnity*) 110.

here-, there-, where-upon; then; *anno, − Domini;* A.D.; *ante Christum;* A.C.; before Christ; B.C.; *anno urbis conditae;* A.U.C.; *anno regni,* A.R.; once upon a time, one fine morning.

Phr. time -runs, − runs against; *tempus fugit.*

107. Neverness.—N. 'neverness;' absence of time, no time; *dies non;* Tib's eve; Greek Kal-ends.

Adv. never; at no -time, − period; on no occa-sion, never in all one's born days, nevermore, *sine die.*

108. Period. [Definite duration, or portion of time.]—N. period; second, minute, hour, day, week, sennight, octave, month, moon, quarter, semester, year, *lustrum, quinquennium,* decade, *decennium,* indiction, lifetime, generation, epoch, era, cycle.

century, age, *millennium; annus magnus.*

Adj. horary; hourly, annual etc. (*periodical*) 138.

108a. Contingent Duration.—Adv. during - pleasure, → good behavior; *quamdiu se bene gesserit.*

109. Course. [Indefinite duration.]—N. course –, progress –, process –, succession –, lapse –, flow –, flux –, effluxion, stream –, tract –, current –, sweep –, tide –, march –, step –, flight- of time; duration etc. 106.

[Indefinite time] aorist.

V. elapse, lapse, flow, run, proceed, advance, pass; roll –, wear –, press –, drag- on; flit, fly, slip, slide, glide, crawl; run -its course.

out; expire; go –, pass- by; be -past etc. 122.

Adj. elapsing etc. *v.;* aoristic; progressive, transient etc. 111.

Adv. in due -time, – season; in -course, – process, – the fulness- of time; in time.

Phr. *labitur et labetur; truditur dies die; fugaces labuntur anni;* 'tomorrow and tomorrow and tomorrow creeps in this petty pace from day to day.'

110. Diuturnity. [Long duration.]—N. diuturnity; a -long –, length of -time; an age, a century. an eternity, aeons; slowness etc. 275; perpetuity etc. 112; blue moon.

dura-bleness, -bility; persistence, lastingness etc. *adj.;* continuance, assiduity, endurance, standing; permanence etc. (*stability*) 150; survival, -vance; longevity etc. (*age*) 128; distance of time.

protraction –, prolongation –, extension- of time; delay etc. (*lateness*) 133.

V. last, endure, stand, remain, abide, continue, brave a thousand years.

tarry etc. (*be late*) 133; drag -on, – its slow length along, – a lengthening chain; protract, prolong; spin –, eke –, draw –, lengthen- out; temporize; gain –, make –, talk against- time.

out-last, -live; survive; live to fight again.

Adj. durable; perdurable; lasting etc. *v.;* of long -duration, – standing; permanent, chronic, long-standing; intransi-ent, -tive; intransmutable, persistent; life-, live-long; longeval, long-lived, macrobiotic, diuturnal, sempervirent, evergreen, perennial; unin-, ter-, unremitting; perpetual etc. 112.

lingering, protracted, prolonged, spun out etc. *v.;* long-pending, -winded; slow etc. 275.

Adv. long; for -a long time, – an age, – ages, – ever so long, – many a long day; long ago etc. (*in a past time*) 122; *longo intervallo.*

all the -day long, – year round; the livelong day, as the day is long, morning, noon and night; hour after hour, day after day, etc.; for good; permanently etc. *adj.*

111. Transientness. [Short duration.]—N. transientness etc. *adj.*; evanescence, impermanence, fugacity, transitoriness, volatility, caducity, mortality, span; flash in the pan, nine days' wonder, bubble, May-fly; spurt; temporary arrangement, interregnum.

velocity etc. 274; suddenness etc. 113; changeableness etc. 149.

V. be -transient etc. *adj.;* flit, pass away, fly, gallop, vanish, fade, fleet, melt away, evaporate; pass away like a -cloud, – summer cloud, – shadow, – dream.

Adj. transi-ent, -tory; passing, evanescent, fleeting; flying etc. *v.;* fug-acious, -itive; shifting, slippery; spasmodic.

tempor-al, -ary; provis-ional, -ory; cursory, short-lived, ephemeral, deciduous; perishable, mortal, precarious; impermanent.

brief, quick, brisk; cometary, meteoric, extemporaneous, summary; pressed for time etc. (*haste*) 684; sudden, momentary etc. (*instantaneous*) 113.

Adv. temporarily etc. *adj.;* pro tempore; for - the moment, – a time; awhile, en passant, in transitu; in a short space; soon etc. (*early*) 132; briefly etc. *adj.;* at short notice; on the -point, – eve -of; *in articulo;* between cup and lip.

Phr. one's days are numbered; the time is up; her to-day and gone tomorrow; *non semper erit aestas; eheu! fugaces labuntur anni; sic transit gloria mundi.*

112. Perpetuity. [Endless duration.]—N. perpetuity, eternity, timelessness; everness, aye, sempiternity, immortality, athanasia; everlastingness etc. *adj.;* perpetuation; infinite duration.

V. last –, endure –, go on- for ever; have no end.

eternize, eternify, perpetuate, immortalize.

Adj. perpetual, eternal, eterne; everlasting, -living, -flowing; continual, constant, sempiternal; co-eternal; endless, unending; ceaseless, incessant, uninterrupted, indesinent, unceasing; interminable, having no end; unfading, evergreen, amaranthine; neverending, -dying, -fading; deathless, immortal, undying, imperishable.

Adv. perpetually etc. *adj.;* always, ever, evermore, aye; for -ever, – aye, – evermore, – ever and a day, – ever and ever; in all ages, from age to age; without end; world –, time- without end; *in saecula saeculorum;* to the -end of time, – crack of doom, – 'last syllable of recorded time;' till doomsday; constantly etc. (*very frequently*) 136.

Phr. *esto perpetuum; labitur et labetur in omne volubilis aevum.*

113. Instantaneity. [Point of time.]—N. instantane-ity, -ousness; sudden-, abrupt-ness.

moment, instant, second, minute; twinkling, trice, flash, breath, crack, jiffy, *coup,* burst, flash of lightning, stroke of time.

epoch, time; time of -day, – night; hour, minute; very -minute etc., – time, – hours; present –, right –, true –, exact –, correcttime.

V. be -instantaneous etc. *adj.;* twinkle, flash.

Adi. instantaneous, momentary, extempore, sudden, instant, abrupt; subitaneous, hasty; quick as- thought, * – lightning, – a flash; rapid as electricity.

Adv. instantaneously etc. *adj.*; in — in less than-no time; *presto, subito, instanter,* suddenly, at a stroke, like- a shot, — greased lightning; in a trice, in a moment etc. *n.*; eftsoons, in the twinkling of - an eye, — a bed post; at one jump, in the same breath, *per saltum, uno saltu;* at — , all at- once; in one's tracks; plump, slap; 'at one fell swoop,' at the same -instant etc. *n.*; immediately etc. (*early*) 132; *ex tempore,* on the -spot, — spur of the moment, — dot; just then; slap- dash etc. (*haste*) 684; before you could -turn round, — say -knife, — Jack Robinson.

Phr. touch and go; no sooner said than done.
*See note on 264.

114. Chronometry. [Estimation, meas-urement, and record of time.]—**N.** chrono-, horo-metry, -logy; date, epoch; style, era.

almanac, calendar, ephemeris; register, -try; chronicle, annals, journal, diary, chronogram.

[Instruments for the measurement of time] clock, watch; chrono-meter, -scope, -graph; repeater, alarum; time-keeper, -piece; dial, sun-dial, *gnomon, pendule,* horologe, pendulum, hourglass, water clock, clepsydra.

mean — , Greenwich — , solar — , sidereal — , local — , summer- time; daylight saving.

chrono-grapher, -loger, -logist; annalist.

V. fix — , mark- the time; date, register, chronicle; measure — , beat — , mark- time; bear date.

Adj. chrono-logical, -metrical, -grammatical; isochronal.

Adv. o'clock; *a.m., p.m.*

115. Anachronism. [False estimate of time.]—**N.** ana-, meta-, para-, prochronism; *prolepsis,* misdate; anticipation, antichronism.

disregard — , neglect — , oblivion- of time.

intempestivity etc. 135.

V. mis-, ante-, post-, over-date; anticipate; take no note of time.

Adj. misdated etc. *v.;* undated; overdue; out of date; anachronous etc. *n.*

116. Priority.—**N.** priority, antecedence, anteriority, pre-existence, precedence etc. 62; precession etc. 280; precursor etc. 64; the past etc. 122; premises.

V. precede, come before; forerun; antecede, go before etc. (*lead*) 280; pre-exist; dawn; premise, presage etc. 511.

be -beforehand etc. (*be early*) 132; steal a march upon, anticipate, forestall; have — , gain-the start.

Adj. prior, previous; preced-ing, -ent; anterior, antecedent; pre-existing, -existent; foresighted; former, foregoing; afore — , before-, above-men-tioned; aforesaid, said; introductory etc. (*precur-sory*) 64; pre-war.

Adv. before, prior to; earlier; previously etc. *adj.;* afore, ere, theretofore, erewhile, ere — , before- -then, — now; erewhile, already, yet, beforehand; aforetime; on the eve of, in anti-cipation.

117. Posteriority.—**N.** posteriority; succes-sion, sequence; following etc. 281; subsequence,

supervention; futurity etc. 121; successor; sequel etc. 65; remainder, reversion.

V. follow etc. 281 —, come —, go- after; ensue, result; succeed, supervene; step into the shoes of.

Adj. subsequent, posterior, following, after, later, succeeding, postliminious, postnate; successive etc. 63; postdiluvial, -an; *puisné;* posthumous; post-war, future etc. 121.

Adv. subsequently, after, afterwards, since, later; at a -subsequent, — later- period; next, in the sequel, close upon, thereafter, thereupon, upon which, eftsoons; from that -time, — mo-ment; after a -while, — time; in process of time.

postcenal, postcibal, postprandial, after-dinner.

118. The Present Time.—**N.** the present -time, — day, — moment, — juncture, — occasion; the times, existing time, time being; twentieth cen-tury; nonce, crisis, epoch, day, hour.

age, time of life.

Adj. present, actual, instant, current, latest, existing, that is.

Adv. at this -time, — moment etc. 113; at the -present time etc. *n.;* now, at present.

at this time of day, to-day, now-adays; al-ready; even — , but — , just-now; on the present occasion; for the -time being, — nonce; *pro hâc vice;* on the -nail, — spot; on the spur of the -mo-ment, — occasion.

until now; to -this, — the present day.

119. Different Time. [Time different from the present.]—**N.** different — , other- time.

[Indefinite time] aorist.

Adj. aoristic.

Adv. at that — , at which- -time, — moment, — instant; then, on that occasion, upon.

when; when-ever, -soever; upon which, on which occasion; at -another, — a different, — some other, — any - time; at various times; some — , one- -of these days, — fine morning, — day; sooner or later; some time or other; once upon a time, once.

120. Synchronism.—**N.** synchronism; coex-istence, coincidence; simultaneousness etc. *adj.;* concurrence, concomitance, unity of time, interim.

[Having equal times] isochronism, syntony.

contemporary, coetanian.

V. coexist, concur, accompany, go hand in hand, keep pace with; synchronize, isochronize.

Adj. synchron-ous, -al, -ical, -istical; simul-taneous, coexisting, coincident, concomitant, concurrent; coev-al, -ous; contempora-ry, -neous; coetaneous; coterminous, coeternal; isochronous.

Adv. at the same time; simultaneously etc. *adj.;* together, in concert, during the same time; in the same breath; *pari passu;* in the interim.

at the -very moment etc. 113; just as, as soon as; meanwhile etc. (*while*) 106.

121. Futurity. [Prospective time.]—**N.** futur-ity, -ition; future, hereafter, time to come; approaching — , coming — , after- -time, — age, — days, — hours, — years, — ages, — life;

morrow, to-morrow, bv and bv: millennium, doomsday, day of judgment, crack of doom, remote future.

approach of time, advent, time drawing on, womb of time; destiny etc. 152; eventuality.

heritage, heirs, posterity, descendants.

prospect etc. (*expectation*) 507; foresight etc. 510.

V. look forwards; anticipate etc. (*expect*) 507, (*foresee*) 510; forestall etc. (*be early*) 132.

come —, draw- on; draw near; approach, await, threaten; impend etc. (*be destined*) 152.

Adj. future, to come; coming etc. (*impending*) 152; next, near; near —, close- at hand; eventual, ulterior; expectant, prospective, in prospect etc. (*expectation*) 507.

Adv. prospectively, hereafter, on the knees of the gods, in future; to-morrow, the day after to-morrow; in -course, — process, — the fulness- of time; eventually, ultimately, sooner or later; *proximo; paulo post futurum*; in after time; one of these days; after a -time, — while.

from this time; hence-forth, -forwards; thence; thence-forth, -forward; whereupon, upon which.

soon etc. (*early*) 132; on the -eve, — point, — brink- of; about to; close upon.

122. Preterition. [Retrospective time.]—N. preterition, priority etc. 116; the past, past time; days —, times- -of yore, — of old, — past, — gone by; bygone days, good old days; old —, ancient —, former -times; fore time; yesterdays; the olden —, good old- time; auld lang syne; eld.

antiquity, antiqueness, *status quo*; time im-memorial; distance of time; remote -age, — time; ancient history; remote past; rust of antiquity; ancientness.

pale-ontology, -ography, -ology; palaetiol-ogy,* archaeology; archaism, antiquarianism, mediaevalism, pre- Raphaelitism; retrospection, looking back; memory etc. 505.

laudator temporis acti; mediaevalist, pre-Raphaelite; antiqu-ary, -arian; archaeologist etc.; Oldbuck, Dryasdust.

ancestry etc. (*paternity*) 166.

V. be -past etc. *adj.;* have -expired etc. *adj.;* — run its course, — had its day; pass; pass —, go- -by, — away, — off; lapse, blow over.

look —, trace —, cast the eyes- back; exhume.

Adj. past, gone, gone by, over, passed away, bygone, foregone; elapsed, lapsed, preterlapsed, expired, no more, run out, blown over, that has been, whilom, extinct, never to return, exploded, forgotten, irrecoverable; obsolete etc. (*old*) 124; extinct as the dodo.

former, pristine, *quondam, ci-devant,* late; ancestral.

foregoing; last, latter; recent, overnight; past, preterite, preter-perfect, -pluperfect, past perfect.

looking back etc. *v.;* retro-spective, -active; archaelogical etc. *n.*

Adv. formerly; of -old, —yore; erst, whilom, erewhile, time was, ago, over; in -the olden time etc. *n.;* anciently, long -ago, — since; a long - while, — time- ago; years —, ages-ago; some time -ago, — since, — back.

yesterday, the day before yesterday; last -year, — season, — month etc.; *ultimo,* lately etc. (*newly*) 123.

retrospectively; ere —, before —, till- now; hitherto, heretofore; no longer; once, — upon a time; from time immemorial; in the memory of man; time out of mind; already, yet, up to this time; *ex post facto.*

Phr. time was; the time -has, — hath- been. *Whewell.

123. Newness.—N. newness etc. *adj.;* neologism, neoterism; novelty, recency; im-maturity; youth etc. 127; gloss of novelty.

innovation; renovation etc. (*restoration*) 660.

modernist, neologist, neoteric.

modernism, modernity; mushroom; latest fashion, *dernier cri.*

upstart, *parvenu, nouveau riche.*

V. renew etc. (*restore*) 660; modernize.

Adj. new, novel, recent, fresh, green; young etc. 127; evergreen; raw, immature; virgin; un-tried, -handseled, -used, -trodden, -beaten; fledgling.

late, modern, neoteric; new-born, -fashioned, -fangled, -fledged; of yesterday; just out, brand —, span-new, up to date, topical; vernal, renovated; innovatory.

fresh as -a rose, — a daisy, — paint; spick and span.

Adv. newly etc. *adj.;* afresh, anew, lately, just now, only yesterday, the other day; latterly, of late.

not long —, a short time- ago.

124. Oldness.—N. oldness etc. *adj.;* age, antiq-uity; cobwebs of antiquity.

maturity, ripeness; decline, decay; senility etc. 128.

seniority, eldership, primogeniture.

archaism etc. (*the past*) 122; thing —, relic- of the past; megatherium.

tradition, prescription, custom, folklore, im-memorial usage, common law.

V. be -old etc. *adj.;* have -had, — seen- its day; become -old etc. *adj.;* age, fade.

Adj. old, olden, ancient, antique; of long standing, time-honored, venerable; eld-er, -est; first-born.

prime; prim-itive, -eval, -igenous; primordi-al, -nate; aboriginal etc. (*beginning*) 66; diluvian, antediluvian; pre-historic; patriarchal, preadamite; paleocrystic; fossil, paleozoic, pre-glacial, ante-mundane; archaic, classic, mediaeval, pre-Raphaelite, ancestral, black-letter.

immemorial, traditional, prescriptive, customary, whereof the memory of man runneth not to the contrary; inveterate, rooted.

antiquated, of other times, rococo, of the old school, after-age, obsolete; fusty, moth-eaten; out of -date, — fashion; stale, old-fashioned, behind the -age, — times; exploded; gone out, — by; *passé,* outworn, run out; disused; senile etc. 128; time-worn; crumbling etc. (*deteriorated*) 659; second-hand.

old as -the hills, — Methuselah, — Adam, — history.

Adv. since the -world was made, — year one, — days of Methuselah.

125. Morning. [Noon.]—N. morning, morn, matins, forenoon, *a.m.,* prime, dawn, daybreak, daylight, sun-up, peep —, break- of day; aurora,

Eos; first blush −, prime- of the morning; twilight, crepuscule, sunrise, cockcrow.

spring; vernal equinox.

noon; mid-, noon-day; noontide, meridian, prime.

summer, midsummer; summer solstice.

Adj. matin, matutinal; vernal, aestival.

Adv. at -sunrise etc. *n.*; with the lark, when the morning dawns.

126. Evening. [Midnight.]—N. evening, eve; decline −, fall −, close- of day; eventide, evensong, vespers; candlelight; nightfall, curfew, dusk, twilight, blind man's holiday; eleventh hour; sun-set, -down; going down of the sun, cock-shut, dewy eve, gloaming, bed-time.

afternoon, *post meridiem, p.m.*

autumn; fall, − of the leaf; autumnal equinox, Indian summer, harvest-time.

midnight; dead −, witching time- of night; winter, − solstice.

Adj. vespertine, autumnal, nocturnal, wintry, brumal, hiemal.

127. Youth.—N. youth; juven- -ility, -escence; juniority; infancy; baby-, child-, boy-, girl-, youth-hood; *incunabula;* minority, immaturity, nonage, teens, tender age, bloom.

cradle, nursery, leading-strings, pupilage, puberty, *pucelage.*

prime −, flower −, spring-tide −, seedtime −, golden season - of life; heyday of youth, school days; rising generation, younger generation.

Adj. young, youthful, juvenile, green, callow, budding, sappy, *puisné*, beardless, unfledged, unripe, under age, in one's teens; *in statu pupillari;* younger, junior.

128. Age.—N. age; oldness etc. *adj.;* old −, advanced- age; sen-ility, -escence; years, anility, grey hairs, climacteric, grand climacteric, declining years, decrepitude, hoary age, caducity, superannuation; second childhood, -ishness; dotage; vale of years, decline of life, 'sear and yellow leaf;' three-score years and ten; green old age, ripe old age; longevity; time of life.

seniority, eldership; elders etc. (*veteran*) 130; firstling; *doyen*, dean, father; primogeniture; nostology.

V. be -aged etc. *adj.;* grow −, get- old etc. *adj.;* age; decline, wane.

Adj. aged; old etc. 124; elderly, senile; matronly, anile; in years; ripe, mellow, run to seed, declining, waning, past one's prime; grey, - headed; hoar, -y; venerable, time-worn, antiquated, *passé*, effete, doddering, decrepit, superannuated; advanced in -life, − years; stricken in years; wrinkled, marked with the crow's feet; having one foot in the grave; doting etc. (*imbecile*) 499.

old-, eld-er, -est; senior; first-born.

turned of, years old; of a certain age, no chicken, old as Methuselah; gerontic; ancestral; patriarchal etc. (*ancient*) 124.

129. Infant.—N. infant, babe, baby; nurse-, suck-, year-, wean-ling; *papoose, bambino.*

child, bairn, little- one, − tot, − mite, chick, brat, chit, pickaninny, kid, urchin; bant-, bratling; elf.

youth, boy, lad, slip, sprig, stripling, youngster, cub, unlicked cub, younker, callant, whipster, whipper-snapper, schoolboy, hobbledehoy, hopeful, cadet, minor, master.

scion; sap-, seed-ling; tendril, olive branch, nestling, chicken, duckling; larva, caterpillar, chrysalis, cocoon; tadpole, whelp, cub, pullet, fry, callow; codlin, -g; *foetus*, calf, colt, pup, foal, kitten; lamb, -kin.

girl; lass, -ie; wench, miss, damsel, *demoiselle,* damozel; maid, -en; virgin; nymph; colleen; minx, baggage, school-girl; tomboy, flapper, hoyden.

Adj. infant-ine, -ile; puerile; boy-, girl-, child-, baby-, kitten-ish; baby; new-born, unfledged, new-fledged, callow.

in -the cradle, − swaddling clothes, − long clothes, − arms, − leading strings; at the breast; in one's teens; young etc. 127.

130. Veteran.—N. veteran, old man, seer, patriarch, greybeard, dugout, grand-father, -sire; grandam, beldam; gaffer, gammer; hag, crone; pantaloon; sexage-, octoge-, nonage-, cente-narian; old stager; dotard etc. 501.

preadamite, Methuselah, Nestor, Rip van Winkle, old Parr; elders; forefathers etc. (*paternity*) 166.

131. Adolescence.—N. adolescence, pubescence, majority; adultness etc. *adj.;* manhood, virility, maturity; flower of age; prime −, meridian- of life.

man etc. 373; woman etc. 374; adult, no chicken.

V. come -of age, − to man's estate, − to years of discretion; attain majority, assume the *toga virilis;* have -cut one's eye-teeth, − sown one's wild oats, settle down.

Adj. adolescent, pubescent, of age; of -full, − ripe- age; out of one's teens, grown up, mature, full- blown, − grown, in one's prime, in full bloom, manly, virile, adult; womanly, matronly; marriageable, nubile.

132. Earliness.—N. earliness etc. *adj.;* morning etc. 125.

punctuality; promptitude etc. (*activity*) 682; haste etc. (*velocity*) 274; suddenness etc. (*instantaneity*) 113.

prematurity, precocity, precipitation, anticipation; prevenience, a stitch in time.

V. be -early etc. *adj.;* − beforehand etc. *adv.;* keep time, take time by the forelock, anticipate, forestall; have −, gain- the start; steal a march upon; gain time, draw on futurity; bespeak, secure, engage, pre-engage.

accelerate; expedite etc. (*quicken*) 274; make haste etc. (*hurry*) 684.

Adj. early, prime, timely, in time, punctual, forward; prompt etc. (*active*) 682; summary.

premature, precipitate, precocious; prevenient, anticipatory; rathe.

sudden etc. (*instantaneous*) 113; unexpected etc. 508; impending, imminent; near, − at hand; immediate.

Adv. early, soon, anon, betimes, rathe; eft, -soons; ere −, before- long; punctually etc. *adj.*; to the minute; in time; in -good, − military, − pudding, − due- time; time enough.

beforehand; prematurely etc. *adj.*; precipitately etc. (*hastily*) 684; too soon; before -its, − one's- time; in anticipation; unexpectedly etc. 508.

suddenly etc. (*instantaneously*) 113; before one can say 'Jack Robinson,' at short notice, extempore; on the spur of the -moment, − occasion; at once; on the -spot, − instant; at sight; off −, out of- hand; *à vue d'oeil;* straight, -way, -forth; forthwith, incontinently, summarily, instanter, immediately, briefly, shortly, quickly, speedily, apace, before the ink is dry, almost immediately, presently, at the first opportunity, in no long time, by and by, in a while, directly.

Phr. touch and go, no sooner said than done.

133. Lateness.—**N.** lateness etc. *adj.*; tardiness etc. (*slowness*) 275.

de-lay, -lation; cunctation, procrastination; detention; deferring etc. *v.*; filibuster, postponement, adjournment, prorogation, retardation, respite, reprieve, stay; protraction, prolongation, moratorium; contango; demurrage; remand; Fabian policy, *médecine expectante,* chancery suit; leeway; high time.

V. be -late etc. *adj.*; tarry, wait, stay, bide, take time; dawdle etc. (*be inactive*) 683; linger, loiter, saunter, lag behind; bide −, take- one's time; hang -about, − around, − back, − in the balance; gain time; hang fire; stand −, lie-over.

put off, defer, delay, lay over, suspend; shift −, stave- off; waive, retard, remand, postpone, adjourn; procrastinate; dally; prolong, protract; spin −, draw −, lengthen- out; prorogue; keep back; tide over; push −, drive- to the last; let the matter stand over; reserve etc. (*store*) 636; temporize; consult one's pillow, sleep upon it.

shelve, table, lay on the table.

lose an opportunity etc. 135; be kept waiting, dance attendance; kick −, cool- one's heels; *faire antichambre;* wait impatiently; await etc. (*expect*) 507; sit up, − at night.

Adj. late, tardy, slow, behindhand, belated, postliminious, posthumous, backward, unpunctual; dilatory etc. (*slow*), overdue 275; delayed etc. *v.*; in abeyance.

Adv. late; late-, back-ward; late in the day; at -sunset, − the eleventh hour, − length, − last, − long; ultimately; after −, behind- time; too late; too late for etc. 135.

slowly, leisurely, deliberately, at one's leisure; *ex post facto; sine die.*

Phr. *nonum prematur in annum.*

134. Occasion.—**N.** occasion, opportunity, opening, room, scope, field; suitable −, proper- time, − season; high time; opportuneness etc. *adj.*; tempestivity.

crisis, turn, juncture, emergency, conjuncture; turning point; given time.

nick of time; golden −, well-timed −, fine −, favorable- opportunity; clear stage, fair field; *mollia tempora; fata Morgana;* spare time etc. (*leisure*) 685.

V. seize etc. (*take*) 789 −, use etc. 677 −, give etc. 784- an -opportunity, − occasion; improve the occasion.

suit the occasion etc. (*be expedient*) 646.

strike the iron while it is hot, *battre le fer sur l'enclume,* make hay while the sun shines, take time by the forelock, *prendre la balle au bond.*

Adj. opportune, timely, well-timed, timeous, timeful, seasonable.

providential, lucky, fortunate, happy, favorable, propitious, auspicious, critical; suitable etc. 23; *obiter dicta.*

Adv. opportunely etc. *adj.*; in -proper, − due- -time, − course, − season; for the nonce; in the -nick, − fulness- of time; all in good time; just in time, at the eleventh hour, now or never.

by the -way, − by; *en passant, à propos; pro re natâ,* − *hac vice; par parenthèse,* parenthetically, by way of parenthesis; while -speaking of, − on this subject; *ex tempore;* on the spur of the -moment, − occasion; on the spot etc. (*early*) 132.

Phr. *carpe diem; occasionem cognosce;* one's hour is come, the time is up; that reminds me.

135. Intempestivity.—**N.** intempestivity; unseasonableness; unsuitable −, improper-time; unreasonableness etc. *adj.*; evil hour; *contretemps;* intrusion; anachronism etc. 115.

V. be -ill timed etc. *adj.*; mistime, intrude, come amiss, break in upon; have other fish to fry; be -busy, − engaged, − tied up, − occupied.

lose −, throw away −, waste −, neglect etc. 460- an opportunity; allow −, suffer- the -opportunity, − occasion- to -pass, − slip, − go by, − escape, − lapse; waste time etc. (*be inactive*) 683; let slip through the fingers, lock the stable door when the steed is stolen.

Adj. ill-, mis-timed; untimely, intrusive, unseasonable; out of -date, − season; inopportune, timeless, untoward, *mal à propos,* unlucky, inauspicious, unpropitious, unfortunate, unfavorable; unsuited etc. 24; inexpedient etc. 647.

unpunctual etc. (*late*) 133; too late for; premature etc. (*early*) 132; too soon for; wise after the event.

Adv. inopportunely etc. *adj.*; as ill luck would have it, in an evil hour, the time having gone by, a day after the fair.

Phr. after meat mustard, after death the doctor.

136. Frequency.—**N.** frequency, oftness; repetition, etc. 104.

V. recur etc. 104; do nothing but; keep, − on.

Adj. frequent, many times, not rare, thickcoming, incessant, perpetual, continual, constant, recurrent, repeated etc. 104; habitual etc. 613; hourly, etc. 138.

Adv. often, often to be met with, oft; oft-, often-times; frequently; repeatedly etc. 104; un-seldom, not unfrequently; in -quick, − rapid-succession; many a time and oft; daily, hourly etc.; every -day, − hour, − moment etc.

perpetually, continually, constantly, incessantly, without ceasing, at all times, daily and hourly, night and day, day and night, day after day, morning, noon and night, ever and anon.

most often; commonly etc. (*habitually*) 613.

sometimes, occasionally, at times, now and then, from time to time, there being times when, *toties quoties,* often enough, again and again etc. 104.

137. Infrequency.—N. infrequency, infrequence, rareness, rarity; fewness etc. 103; seldomness, uncommonness.

V. be -rare etc. *adj.*

Adj. un-, in-frequent; uncommon, sporadic, rare, − as a blue diamond; few etc. 103; scarce; almost unheard of, unprecedented, which has not occurred within the memory of the oldest inhabitant, not within one's previous experience.

Adv. seldom, rarely, scarcely, hardly; not often, unfrequently, infrequently, unoften; scarcely −, hardly- ever; once in a blue moon.

once; once -for all, − in a way; *pro hac vice;* like angels' visits, few and far between.

138. Regularity of recurrence. **Periodicity.**—N. periodicity, intermittence; beat; oscillation etc. 314; pulse, pulsation; rhythm; alternation, -nateness, -nativeness, -nity.

bout, round, revolution, rotation, turn.

anniversary, birthday, jubilee, centenary, bi-, ter-centenary.

[Regularity of return] rota, cycle, period, stated time, routine; days of the week; Sunday, Monday etc.; months of the year; January etc.; feast, fast, saint's day etc.; Christmas, Easter, New Year's Day etc. 998; quarter-, Lady-, Midsummer-, Michaelmas-day; May Day, the King's Birthday; leap year, seasons.

punctuality, regularity, steadiness.

V. recur in regular -order, − succession; return, revolve, rotate; come -again, − in its turn; come round, − again; beat, pulsate; alternate; intermit.

Adj. periodic, -al; serial, recurrent, cyclic-, -al, rhythmic-, -al, even; recurring etc. *V.;* inter-, remittent; alternate, every other.

hourly; diurnal, daily; quotidian, tertian, weekly; hebdomad-al, -ary; bi-weekly, fortnightly; monthly, menstrual, catamenial; yearly, annual; biennial, triennial, etc.; bissextile; centennial, secular; paschal, lenten, etc.

regular, steady, punctual, constant, methodical, regular as clockwork.

Adv. periodically etc. *adj.;* at -regular intervals, − stated times; at -fixed, − established-periods; punctually etc. *adj.; de die in diem;* from day to day, day by day.

by turns, in -turn, − rotation; alternately, every other day, off and on, ride and tie, round and round.

139. Irregularity of recurrence.—N. irregularity, uncertainty, unpunctuality; fitfulness etc. *adj.*

Adj. irregular, uneven, uncertain, unpunctual, capricious, erratic, desultory, fitful, flickering; rambling, rhapsodical; spasmodic, unsystematic, unequal, variable, halting.

Adv. irregularly etc. *adj.;* by fits and starts etc. (*discontinuously*) 70.

140. Change. [Difference at different times.]—N. change, alteration, mutation, permutation, variation, modification, modulation, inflexion, mood, qualification, innovation, *metastasis,* deviation, shift, turn; diversion; break.

transformation, transfiguration; metamorphosis; metabolism; transmutation; transsubstantiation; metagenesis, transanimation, transmigration, metempsychosis; version, metathesis, transmogrification; catalysis; *avatar;* alterative.

conversion etc. (*gradual change*) 144; revolution etc. (*sudden or radical change*) 146; inversion etc. (*reversal*) 218; displacement etc. 185; transference etc. 270.

changeableness etc. 149; tergiversation etc. (*change of mind*) 607.

V. change, alter, vary, wax and wane; modulate, diversify, qualify, tamper with; turn, shift, veer, jibe, tack, chop, shuffle, swerve, dodge, warp, deviate, turn aside, evert, intervert; pass to, take a turn, turn the corner, resume.

work a change, modify, vamp, revamp, superinduce; trans-form, −mute, -ume, -figure etc. *n.;* metamorphose, ring the changes; convert, resolve; revolutionize; chop and change; patch, re-shape.

innovate, introduce new blood, shuffle the cards, spin the wheel; give a -turn, − color- to; influence, turn the scale; shift the scene, turn over a new leaf.

recast etc. 146; reverse etc. 218; disturb etc. 61; convert into etc. 144.

Adj. changed etc. *v.;* new-fangled; changeable etc. 149; transitional; modifiable; alterative.

Adv. *mutatis mutandis.*

Int. *quantum mutatus!*

Phr. 'a change came o'er the spirit of my dream;' *nous avons changé tout cela; tempora mutantur et nos mutamur in illis; non sum qualis eram.*

141. Permanence. [Absence of change.]—N. stability etc. 150; quiescence etc. 265; obstinacy etc. 606.

permanence, -cy, persistence, fixity, fixity of purpose, endurance, durability; standing, *status quo;* maintenance, preservation, conservation; conservatism; *laissez-faire;* law of the Medes and Persians; standing dish.

V. let -alone, − be; persist, remain, stay, tarry, rest; hold, − on; last, endure, bide, abide, aby, dwell, maintain, keep; stand, − still; − fast; subsist, live, outlive, survive; hold −, keep- one's ground, − footing; hold good.

Adj. stable etc. 150; persisting etc. *v.;* permanent; established, fixed; durable; unchanged etc. (change etc. 140); unrenewed; intact, inviolate; persistent; monotonous, uncheckered; unfailing.

un-destroyed, -repealed, -suppressed; conservative, *qualis ab incepto;* prescriptive etc. (*old*) 124; stationary etc. 265.

Adv. *in statu quo;* for good, finally; at a stand, -still; *uti possidetis;* without a shadow of turning.

Phr. as you were!; *j'y suis j'y reste; esto perpetua; nolumus leges Angliae mutari;* let sleeping dogs lie.

142. Cessation. [Change from action to

rest.]—N. cessation, discontinuance, desistance, desinence.

inter-, re-mission; sus-pense, -pension, interruption, hitch; hartal; stop; stopping etc. *v.*; closure, stoppage, halt; arrival etc. 292.

pause, rest, lull, respite, truce, armistice, drop; interregnum, abeyance.

closure etc. 261.

dead -stop, — stand, — lock; checkmate; comma, colon, semicolon, period, full stop; end etc. 67; death etc. 360; *caesura.*

V. cease, discontinue, desist, stay; break —, leave- off; hold, stop, pull up, stall, stop short, check; stick, deadlock, hand fire; halt; pause, rest.

have done with, give over, surcease, shut up shop; give up etc. (*relinquish*) 624.

hold —, stay- one's hand; rest on one's oars, repose on one's laurels.

come to a -stand, — standstill, — dead lock, — full stop; arrive etc. 292; go out, die away, peter out; wear -away, — off; pass away etc. (*be past*) 122; be at an end.

intromit, interrupt, suspend, interpel; inter-, re-mit; put -an end, — a stop, — a period- to; bring to a stand, -still; stop, cut out, cut short, arrest, avast; stem the -tide, — torrent; pull the check string; switch off.

Int. halt! hold! stop! enough! avast! have done! a truce to! soft! leave off! shut up! give over! chuck it!

143. Continuance in action.—N. continu-ance, -ation; run; extension, prolongation; maintenance, perpetuation; persistence etc. (*perseverance*) 604a; repetition etc. 104.

V. continue, persist; go —, jog —, keep —, carry —, run — hold- on; abide, keep, pursue, stick to; endure; take —, maintain- its course; keep up.

sustain, uphold, hold up, keep on foot; follow up, perpetuate, prolong; maintain; preserve etc. 604a; harp upon etc. (*repeat*) 104.

keep -going, — alive, — at it, — the pot boiling, — the ball rolling, — up the ball; plod-, plug-along; slog on; die in harness; hold on —, pursue- the even tenor of one's way.

let be; *stare super antiquas vias; quieta non movere;* let things take their course.

Adj. continuing etc. *v.*; uninterrupted, unintermitting, unremitting, unvarying, unshifting; unreversed, unstopped, unrevoked, unvaried; sustained; undying etc. (*perpetual*) 112; inconvertible.

follow-up.

Int. carry on! right away!

Phr. *vestigia nulla retrorsum, labitur et labetur.*

144. Conversion. [Gradual change to something different.]—N. conversion, reduction, transmutation, transformation, development, resolution, assimilation; assumption; naturalization.

chemistry, alchemy; progress, growth, lapse, flux.

passage; transit, -ion; transmigration, shifting etc. *v.*; conjugation; convertibility.

crucible, alembic, caldron, retort, test tube etc.

convert, neophyte, proselyte, pervert, renegade, deserter, apostate, turncoat.

V. be converted into; become, get, wax; come —, turn- -to, — into; turn out, lapse, shift; run —, fall —, pass —, slide —, glide —, grow —, ripen —, open —, resolve itself —, settle —, merge- into; melt, grow, come round to, mature, mellow; assume the -form, — shape, — state, — nature, — character- of; illapse; assume a new phase, undergo a change.

convert —, resolve- into; make, render; mold, form etc. 240; remodel, new model, refound, reform, reorganize; assimilate —, bring —, reduce- to; transform.

Adj. converted into etc. *v.*; convertible, resolvable into; transitional; naturalized.

Adv. gradually etc. (*slowly*) 275; *in transitu* etc. (*transference*) 270.

145. Reversion.—N. reversion, return; revulsion; reaction.

turning point, turn of the tide; *status quo ante bellum;* calm before a storm.

alternation etc. (*periodicity*) 138; inversion etc. 219; recoil etc. 277; regression etc. 283; restoration etc. 660; relapse etc. 661; vicinism, atavism, throwback.

V. revert, turn back, return; relapse etc. 661; recoil etc. 277; retreat etc. 283; restore etc. 660; undo, unmake; turn the -tide, — scale; escheat.

Adj. reverting etc. *v.*; revulsive, reactionary.

Adv. *à rebours,* wrong side out.

146. Revolution. [Sudden or violent change.]—N. revolution, *bouleversement,* subversion, break up; destruction etc. 162; sudden —, radical —, sweeping —, organic- change; clean sweep, *coup d'état,* overthrow, *débâcle;* counter-revolution, rebellion etc. 742.

transilience, jump, leap, plunge, jerk, start; explosion; spasm, convulsion, throe, revulsion; storm, earthquake, eruption, upheaval, cataclysm.

legerdemain etc. (*trick*) 545.

V. revolutionize; new model, remodel, recast; strike out something new, break with the past; change the face of, unsex; revert etc. 742.

Adj. unrecognizable.

Revolutionary, Bolshevik etc. 742.

147. Substitution. [Change of one thing for another.]—N. substitution, subrogation, commutation; supplanting etc. *v.*; supersession, metonymy etc. (*figure of speech*) 521.

[Thing substituted.] substitute, *succedaneum,* make-shift, temporary expedient, shift, *pis aller,* stop-gap, jury-mast, *locum tenens,* warming-pan, dummy, goat, scape-goat; double; change-ling; *quid pro quo,* alternative; remount; representative etc. (*deputy*) 759; palimpsest.

price, purchase-money, consideration, equivalent.

V. substitute, put in the place of, change for; make way for, give place to; supply —, take- the place of; supplant, supersede, replace, cut out, serve as a substitute; step into —, stand in- the shoes of; make a shift —, put up- with; borrow of Peter to pay Paul; commute, redeem, compound for.

Adj. substituted etc. *v.;* vicarious, subdititious; substitutional.

Adv. instead; in -place, − lieu, − the stead, − the room- of; *faute de mieux.*

148. Interchange. [Double or mutual change.]—**N.** inter-, ex-change; com-, per-, intermutation; reciprocation, transposal, transposition, shuffling; reciprocity, castling [at chess]; hocus-pocus.

interchange-ableness, -ability.

barter etc. 794; tit for tat etc. *(retaliation)* 718; cross fire, battledore and shuttlecock; *quid pro quo.*

V. inter-, ex-, counter-change; bandy, transpose, shuffle, change hands, swap, trade, permute, reciprocate, commute; give and take, return the compliment; play at -puss in the corner, − battledore and shuttlecock; retaliate etc. 718; barter etc. 794.

Adj. interchanged etc. *v.;* reciprocal, mutual, commutative, interchanged etc. *v.;* interchangeable, intercurrent.

Adv. in exchange, *vice versâ, mutatis mutandis,* backwards and forwards, by turns, turn and turn about, turn about; each −, every one- in his turn.

149. Changeableness.—**N.** changeableness etc. *adj.;* mutability, inconstancy; versatility, mobility; instability, unstable equilibrium; vacillation etc. *(irresolution)* 605; fluctuation, vicissitude; alternation etc. *(oscillation)* 314.

restlessness etc. *adj.;* fidgets, disquiet; dis-, inquietude; unrest; agitation etc. 315.

moon, Proteus, chameleon, kaleidoscope, quicksilver, shifting sands, weathercock, harlequin, Cynthia of the minute, April showers; wheel of Fortune; transientness etc. 111.

V. fluctuate, vary, waver, flounder, flicker, flitter, flit, flutter, shift, shuffle, shake, totter, tremble, vacillate, wamble, turn and turn about, ring the changes; sway −, shift- to and fro; change and change about; oscillate etc. 314; vibrate −, oscillate- between two extremes; alternate; have as many phases as the moon.

Adj. change-able, -ful; changing etc. 140; mutable, variable, checkered, ever changing, kaleidoscopic, prote-an, -iform; versatile.

unstaid, inconstant; un-steady, -stable, -fixed, -settled; fluctuating etc. *v.;* restless; mercurial; agitated etc. 315; erratic, fickle; irresolute etc. 605; capricious etc. 608; touch-and-go; inconsonant, fitful, spasmodic; vibratory; afloat; alternating; alterable, plastic, mobile; fleeting, transient etc. 111.

Adv. see-saw etc. *(oscillation)* 314; off and on.

150. Stability.—**N.** stability; immutability etc. *adj.;* unchangeableness etc. *adj.;* constancy; stable equilibrium, immobility, soundness, vitality, stabiliment, stabilization, stiffness, ankylosis, solidity, *aplomb.*

establishment, fixture; rock, pillar, tower, foundation, leopard's spots, Ethiopian's skin, law of the Medes and Persians.

stabilimeter, stabilizator.

permanence etc. 141; obstinacy etc. 606.

V. be -firm etc. *adj.;* stick fast; stand −, keep −, remain- firm; weather the storm.

settle, establish, stablish, ascertain, fix, set, stabilitate, stabilize; retain, stet, keep hold; make -good, − sure; fasten etc. *(join)* 43; set on its legs, float; perpetuate.

settle down; strike −, take- root; take up one's abode etc. 184; build one's house on a rock.

Adj. unchangeable, immutable; unalter-ed, -able; not to be changed, constant; permanent etc. 141; invariable, undeviating; stable, durable; perennial etc. *(diuturnal)* 110.

fixed, steadfast, firm, fast, steady, balanced; confirmed, valid, fiducial, immovable, irremovable, riveted, rooted; settled, established etc. *v.;* vested; incontrovertible, stereotyped, indeclinable.

tethered, anchored, moored, at anchor, on a rock, firm as a rock; firmly -seated, − established etc. *v.;* deep-rooted, ineradicable; inveterate; obstinate etc. 606.

transfixed, stuck fast, aground, high and dry, stranded.

indefeasible, irretrievable, intransmutable, incommutable, irresoluble, irrevocable, irreversible, reverseless, inextinguishable, irreducible; indissol-uble, -vable; indestructible, undying, imperishable, indelible, indeciduous; insusceptible, − of change.

Int. *stet.*

151. Eventuality.—**N.** eventuality, event, occurrence, incident, affair, transaction, proceeding, fact; matter of −, naked- fact; phenomenon; advent.

business, concern; circumstance, particular, casualty, happening, accident, adventure, passage, crisis, pass, emergency, contingency, consequence etc. 154.

the world, life, things, doings, affairs, matters; things −, affairs- in general; the times, state of affairs, order of the day; course −, tide −, stream −, current −, run −, march- of -things, − events; ups and downs of life; chapter of accidents etc. *(chance)* 156; situation etc. *(circumstances)* 8.

V. happen, occur; take -place, − effect; come, become of; come -off, − about, − round, − into existence, − forth, − to pass, − on; pass, present itself; fall; fall −, turn- out; run, be on foot, fall in; be-fall, -tide, -chance; prove, eventuate, draw on; turn −, crop −, spring −, cast- up; super-, sur-vene; issue, emanate, arrive, ensue, arise, start, hold, take its course; pass off etc. *(be past)* 122.

meet with; experience; fall to the lot of; be one's -chance, − fortune, − lot; find; encounter, undergo; pass −, go- through; endure etc. *(feel)* 821.

Adj. happening etc. *v.;* going on, doing, current; in the wind, afloat; on -foot, − the *tapis;* at issue, in question; incidental.

eventful, momentous, signal; stirring, bustling, full of incident.

Adv. eventually, ultimately, in -the event of, − case; in the course of things; in the -natural, − ordinary- course of things; as -things, − times- go; as the world -goes, − wags; as the -tree falls, − cat jumps; as it may -turn out, − happen.

Phr. the plot thickens.

152. Destiny.—N. destiny etc. (*necessity*) 601;
hereafter, future −, post- existence; future state,
next world, world to come, after life; futurity etc.
121; everlasting -life, − death; prospect etc. (*ex-pectation*) 507.

V. impend; hang −, lie −, hover- over;
threaten, loom, await, come on, approach, stare
one in the face; fore-, pre-ordain; predestine,
doom, foredoom, foreshadow, have in store for.

Adj. impending etc. *v.;* destined; about to -be,
− happen; coming, in store, to come, going to
happen, instant, at hand, near; near −, close- at
hand; overhanging, hanging over one's head, imminent; brewing, preparing, forthcoming; in the
wind, on the cards, in reserve; that -will, − is to-
be; in prospect etc. (*expected*) 507; looming in
the -distance, − horizon, − future; unborn, in
embryo; in the womb of -time; − futurity; on the
knees of the gods; pregnant etc. (*producing*) 161.

Adv. in -time, − the long run; all in good time;
eventually etc. 151; whatever may happen etc.
(*certainly*) 474; as -chance etc. 156- would have
it.

153. Cause. [Constant antecedent.]—N. cause,
origin, source, principle, element; occasioner,
prime mover, engine, turbine, motor, *primum
mobile; vera causa;* author etc. (*producer*) 164;
main-spring, agent; dynamo, generator, battery
(electric); leaven; groundwork, foundation etc.
(*support*) 215.

spring, fountain, well, font; fountain −,
spring- head; *fons et origo,* genesis; descent etc.
(*paternity*) 166; remote cause; influence.

pivot, hinge, turning-point, lever; key; kernel,
core; proximate cause, *causa causans;* last straw
that breaks the camel's back.

ground; reason, − why; why and wherefore,
rationale, occasion, derivation; final cause etc.
(*intention*) 620; *le dessous des cartes;* undercur-
rents.

rudiment, egg, germ, embryo, fetus, bud, root,
radix, radical, etymon, nucleus, seed, stem, stalk,
stock, *stirps,* trunk, tap-root; latent organism.

nest, cradle, nursery, womb, *nidus,* birth-,
breeding-place, hot-bed.

caus-ality, -ation; origination; production etc.
161.

V. be the -cause etc. *n.*- of; originate; give -
origin, − rise, − occasion- to; cause, occasion,
sow the seeds of, kindle, suscitate; bring -on, −
to pass, − about; produce; create etc. 161; set -
up, − afloat, − on foot; found, broach, institute,
lay the foundation of, inaugurate; lie at the root
of.

procure, induce, draw down, open the door to,
superinduce, evoke, entail, operate; elicit, provoke.

conduce to etc. (*tend to*) 176; contribute; promote; have a -hand in, − finger in- the pie; determine, decide, turn the scale, give the casting vote;
have a common origin; derive its origin etc.
(*effect*) 154.

Adj. caused etc. *v.;* causal, original; prim-ary, -
itive, -ordial; aboriginal; radical; inceptive,
embry-onic, -otic; *in -embryo, − ovo;* seminal,
germinal; formative, productive etc. 168; at the
bottom of; connate, having a common origin.

Adv. because etc. 155; behind the scenes.

154. Effect. [Constant sequent.]—N. effect,

consequence, sequela; derivative, -tion; result;
result-ant, -ance; upshot, issue, *dénouement;* out-
come; termination, end etc. 67; development,
outgrowth, fruit, crop, harvest, product, bud,
blossom, florescence, ear.

production, produce, product, finished product, work, handiwork, fabric, performance;
creature, creation; offspring, -shoot; first-fruits, -
lings; *prémices.*

V. be the -effect etc. *n.*- of; be -due, − owing-
to; originate -in, − from; rise −, arise −, take its
rise −, spring −, proceed −, emanate −, come
−, grow −, bud −, sprout −, germinate −, issue
−, flow −, result −, follow −, derive its origin
−, accrue- from; come :to, − of, − out of;
depend −, hand −, hinge −, turn- upon.

take the consequences, sow the wind and reap
the whirlwind.

Adj. owing to; resulting from etc. *v.;* resultant;
derivable from; due to; caused etc. by, 153;
dependent upon; derived −, evolved- from;
derivative; hereditary.

Adv. of course, it follows that, naturally, consequently; as a −, in- consequence; through all,
all along of, necessarily, eventually.

Phr. *cela va sans dire,* thereby hangs a tale.

155. Attribution. [Assignment of cause.]—N.
attribution, theory, etiology, ascription, reference to, rationale; accounting for etc. *v.;* imputation, derivation from.

fil-, affil-iation; pedigree etc. (*paternity*) 166.

explanation etc. (*interpretation*) 522; reason
why etc. (*cause*) 153.

V. attribute −, ascribe −, impute −, refer −,
lay −, point −, trace −, bring home- to; put −,
set- down- to; charge −, ground- on; invest with,
assign as cause, charge with, blame, lay at the
door of, father upon; saddle with; affiliate; account for, derive from, point out the -reason etc.
153; theorize; tell how it comes; put the saddle on
the right horse.

Adj. attributed etc. *v.;* attributable etc. *v.;*
refer-able, -rible; due to, derivable from; owing
to etc. (*effect*) 154; putative.

Adv. hence, thence, therefore, for, since, on
account of, because, owing to; on that account;
from -this, − that- cause; thanks to, forasmuch
as; whence, *propter hoc.*

why? wherefore? whence? how -comes, − is, −
happens- it? how does it happen?

in -some, − some such- way; somehow, − or
other.

Phr. that is why; *hinc illae lachrymae; cher-
chez la femme.*

156. Chance.† [Absence of assignable
cause.]—N. chance, indetermination, accident,
fortune, hazard, hap, haphazard, chance-med-
ley, random, luck, *raccroc,* casualty, fortuity, con-
tingence, coincidence, adventure, hit; fate etc.
(*necessity*) 601; equal chance; lottery, raffle, tombola, sweepstake; toss up etc. 621; turn of the -
table, − cards; hazard of the die, chapter of accidents; cast −, throw- of the dice; heads or tails,
wheel of Fortune, whirligig of chance; *sortes;* -
Virgilianae.

probability, possibility, contingency, odds,
long odds, run of luck; main- chance.

theory of -probabilities, − chances; book-making; assurance; speculation, gamble, gaming etc. 621.

V. chance, hap, turn up; fall to one's lot; be one's chance etc. 601; stumble on, light −, blunder −, hit- upon; take one's chance etc. 621.

Adj. casual, fortuitous, accidental, haphazard, random, stray, adventitious, adventive, causeless, incidental. contingent, uncaused, undetermined, indeterminate; possible etc. 470; unintentional etc. 621.

Adv. by -chance, − accident; casually; perchance etc. (*possibly*) 470; for aught one knows; as -good, − bad, − ill-luck etc. *n.*- would have it; as it may -be, − chance, − turn up, − happen; as the case may be.

†The word *Chance* has two distinct meanings: the first, the absence of assignable r*ause*, as above; and the second, the absence of *design*—for the latter see 621.

157. Power.—**N.** power; poten-cy, -tiality; puissance, might, force; energy etc. 171; dint; right -hand, − arm; ascendency, sway, control; pre-potency, -pollence; almightiness, omnipotence; authority etc. 737; strength etc. 159.

ability; ableness etc. *adj.*; competency; efficiency, -cacy; validity, cogency; enablement; vantage ground; influence etc. 175; horse power; dynamometer.

pressure; elasticity; gravity; attraction, repulsion; *vis -inertiae*, − *mortua*, − *viva*; friction, suction.

electricity, magnetism, galvanism, voltaic electricity, voltaism, electro-magnetism, electro-statics, electrification; electric − current, − power; potential −, dynamic −, kinetic −, electrical −, chemical −, atomic- energe; electric field, circuit, charge, discharge, shock, polarity, pole; amperage, voltage, wattage, resistance, conduction, induction, electrification, electrolysis.

electronics, radionics, electron physics, electrophysics, avionics, radiometry, photoelectronics; electron, negatron, positron; photoelectron, thermion, barytron; electronic effect; electron emission; electron −, cathode −, anode −, positive − ray; electron − current, − flow − stream, − beam, − volt; electronic circuit; conductance; electron tube, tube, vacuum tube, photoelectric tube, call; transistor.

capability, capacity; *quid valeant humeri quid ferre recusent;* faculty, quality, attribute, endowment, virtue, gift, property, qualification, susceptibility.

V. be -powerful etc. *adj.*; gain -power etc. *n.* belong −, pertain- to; lie −, be- in one's power; can.

electrify, generate, magnetize.

give −, confer −, exercise- power etc. *n.*; empower, enable, invest; in-, en-due; endow, arm; strengthen etc. 159; compel etc. 744.

Adj. powerful, puissant; potent, -ial; capable, able; equal −, up- to; cogent, valid; effect-ive, -ual; efficient, efficacious, adequate, competent; multi-, pleni-, omni-, armi- potent; mighty, ascendent; almighty.

electric, electrical, electronic etc.

forcible etc. *adj.* (*energetic*) 171; influential etc. 175; productive etc. 168.

Adv. powerfully etc. *adj.*; by -virtue, − dint-of.

158. Impotence.—**N.** impotence; in-, dis-ability; disablement, impuissance, imbecility, caducity; incapa-city, -bility; inapt-, inept-itude; indocility; invalidity, inefficiency, incompetence, disqualification.

telum imbelle, brutum fulmen, blank cartridge, flash in the pan, *vox et praeterea nihil,* dead letter, bit of waste paper, dummy; scrap of paper.

inefficacy etc. (*inutility*) 645; failure etc. 732.

helplessness etc. *adj.*; prostration, paralysis, palsy, ataxia, apoplexy, syncope, sideration, *deliquium,* collapse, exhaustion, softening of the brain, e nasculation, inanition, senility etc. 128; castrato, eunuch.

cripple, old woman, muff, molly-coddle, milksop.

V. be -impotent etc. *adj.*; not have a leg to stand on.

vouloir -rompre l'anguille au genou, − *prendre la lune avec les dents.*

collapse, faint, swoon, fall into a swoon, drop; go by the board; end in smoke etc. (*fail*) 732.

render -powerless etc. *adj.*; deprive of power; decontrol; dis-able, -enable; disarm, incapacitate, disqualify, unfit, invalidate, undermine, deaden, cramp, tie the hands; double up, prostrate, paralyze, muzzle, cripple, be-cripple, maim, lame, hamstring, draw the teeth of; throttle, strangle, *garrotte;* ratten, silence, sprain, clip the wings of, render *hors de combat,* spike the guns; take the wind out of one's sails, scotch the snake, put a spoke in one's wheel; break the -neck, − back; un-hinge, -fit; put out of gear.

unman, unnerve, devitalize, attenuate, enervate; emasculate, spay, caponize, castrate, geld; effeminize.

shatter, exhaust; weaken etc. 160.

Adj. powerless, impotent, unable, incapable, incompetent; ineff-icient, -ective; inept; un-fit, -fitted; un-, dis-qualified; unendowed; in-, un-apt; crippled, decrepit; disabled etc. *v.*; armless.

harmless, unarmed, weaponless, defenceless, *sine ictu,* unfortified, indefensible, vincible, pregnable, untenable.

para-lytic, -lyzed; palsied, imbecile; nerve-, sinew-, marrow-, pith-, lust-less; emasculate, disjointed, out of -joint, − gear; un-nerved, -hinged; water-logged, on one's beam ends, rudderless; laid on one's back; done up, dead beat, exhausted, shattered, demoralized; gravelled etc. (*in difficulty*) 704; helpless, unfriended, fatherless; without a leg to stand on, *hors de combat,* laid on the shelf.

null and void, nugatory, imoperative, good for nothing; dud; invertebrate; ineffectual etc. (*failing*) 732; inadequate etc. 640; inefficacious etc. (*useless*) 645.

159. Strength. [Degree of power.]—**N.** strength; power etc. 157; energy etc. 171; vigor, force; main −, physical −, brute- force; spring, elasticity, tone, tension, tonicity.

stoutness etc. *adj.*; lustihood, stamina, nerve,

muscle, sinew, thews and sinews, *physique;* pith, - iness; virility, vitality.

athlet-ics, -icism; gymnastics, feats of strength.

adamant, steel, iron, oak, heart of oak; iron grip; grit, bone.

athlete, gymnast, tumbler, acrobat; Atlas, Hercules, Antaeus, Samson, Cyclops, Goliath, Titan; tower of strength; giant refreshed.

strengthening etc. *v.;* invigoration, refresh- ment, refocillation.

[Science of forces] dynamics, statics.

V. be -strong etc. *adj.,* − stronger; overmatch.

render -strong etc. *adj.;* give -strength etc. *n.;* strengthen, invigorate, brace, nerve, fortify, buttress, sustain, harden, case-harden, steel; gird; screw −, wind −, set- up; gird −, brace- up one's loins; recruit, set on one's legs; vivify; re- fresh etc. 689; refect; reinforce etc. *(restore)* 660.

Adj. strong, mighty, vigorous, forcible, hard, adamantine, stout, robust, sturdy, hardy, power- ful, potent, puissant, valid.

resistless, irresistible, invincible, proof a- gainst, impregnable, unconquerable, indomit- able, inextinguishable, unquenchable; incontest- able; more than a match for; over-powering, - whelming; all-powerful; sovereign.

able-bodied; athletic, gymnastic; Herculean, Cyclopean, Atlantean; muscular, husky, brawny, wiry, well-knit, broad-shouldered, sinewy, strap- ping, stalwart, gigantic.

man-ly -like, -ful; masculine, male, virile, in the prime of manhood.

un-weakened, -allayed, -withered, -shaken, - worn, -exhausted; in full -force, − swing; in the plenitude of power.

stubborn, thick-ribbed, made of iron, deep- rooted; strong as -a lion, − a horse, − brandy; sound as a roach; in -fine, − high- feather; in fine fettle; like a giant refreshed.

Adv. strongly etc. *adj.;* by -force etc. *n.;* by main force etc. *(by compulsion)* 744.

Phr. 'our withers are unwrung.'

160. Weakness.—N. weakness etc. *adj.;* debility, atony, relaxation, languor, enervation; impotence etc. 158; infirmity; effeminacy, feminality; fragility, flaccidity; inactivity etc. 683.

declension −, loss −, failure- of strength; delicacy, invalidation, decrepitude, asthenia, adynamy, cachexy, *cachexia,* anemia, bloodlessness, sprain, strain.

reed, thread, rope of sand, broken reed, house -of cards, − built on sand.

soft-, weak-ling; infant etc. 129; youth etc. 127.

V. be -weak etc. *adj.;* drop, crumble, give way, totter, tremble, shake, halt, limp, fade, languish, decline, flag, fail, have one foot in the grave.

render -weak etc. *adj.;* weaken, enfeeble, debilitate, shake, deprive of strength, relax, enervate; un-brace, -nerve; cripple, unman, etc. *(render powerless)* 158; cramp, reduce, sprain, strain, blunt the edge of; dilute, impoverish; deci- mate; extenuate; reduce -in strength, − the strength of; invalidate; *mettre de l'eau dans son vin.*

Adj. weak, feeble, debile; impotent etc. 158; relaxed, unnerved etc. *v.;* sap-, strength-, power- less; weakly, unstrung, flaccid, adynamic, asthenic; nervous.

soft, effeminate, feminate, womanish.

frail, fragile, shattery, frangible, brittle etc. 328; flimsy, unsubstantial, gimcrack, ginger- bread; rickety, cranky; creachy; drooping, totter- ing etc. *v.;* broken, lame, halt, game, withered, shattered, shaken, crazy, shaky, tumble-down; palsied etc. 158; decrepit; C3.

lanquid, poor, poorly, infirm; faint, -ish; sickly etc. *(disease)* 655; dull, slack, evanid, spent, short-winded, effete; weatherbeaten; decayed, rotten, worn, seedy, languishing, wasted, washy, wishy-washy, laid low, pulled down, the worse for wear.

un-strengthened etc. 159, -supported, -aided, - assisted; aidless, defenceless etc. 158.

on its last legs; weak as a -child, − baby, − chicken, − cat, − rat; weak as -water, − water gruel, − gingerbread, − milk and water; color- less etc. 429.

Phr. *non sum qualis eram.*

161. Production.—N. production, creation, construction, formation, fabrication, manufac- ture; building, architecture, erection, edifica- tion; coinage; organization; *nisus formativus;* putting togeher etc. *v.;* establishment; work- manship, performance; achievement etc. *(com- pletion)* 729; effect etc. 154.

flowering, fructification fruition.

bringing forth etc. *v.;* parturition, birth, birth- throe, child-birth, delivery, confinement, *accouchement,* travail, labour, midwifery, obstetrics; geniture; gestation etc. *(maturation)* 673; evolution, development, growth; genesis, fertilization, breeding, conception, germination, generation, *epigenesis,* pro-creation, -genera- tion, -pagation; fecundation, impregnation; spontaneous generation; *arche-genesis,* -*biosis; bio-, abio-, homo-, xeno-genesis.*

authorship, publication; works, *oeuvre, opus.*

edifice, building, structure, fabric, erection, pile, tower, flower, fruit.

V. produce, perform, operate, do, make, gar, form, construct, fabricate, frame, contrive, manufacture; weave, forge, coin, carve, chisel; build, raise, edify, rear, erect, put together; set −, run- up; establish, constitute, compose, organize, institute, get up; achieve, accomplish etc. *(complete)* 729.

flower, sprout, blossom, burgeon, bear fruit, fructify, spawn, teem, ean, yean, farrow, drop, calf, pup, whelp, kitten, kindle; bear, lay, bring forth, give birth to, lie in, be brought to bed of, evolve, pullulate, usher into the world.

make productive etc. 168; create; beget, con- ceive, get, generate, fecundate, impregnate; pro- create, -generate, -pagate; engender; bring −, call- into -being, − existence; breed, hatch, de- velop, bring up.

induce, superinduce; suscitate; cause etc. 153; acquire etc. 775.

Adj. produc-ed, -ing etc. *v.;* productive of; prolific etc. 168; creative; formative; gen-etic, - ial, -ital; fertile; pregnant; *enceinte,* big −, fraught-with; with child, in the family way,

teeming, parturient, in the straw, brought to bed of; puerper-al, -ous.

architectonic; constructive.

162. Destruction. [Non-production.]—N. destruction; waste, dissolution, breaking up; di-, dis-ruption; consumption; disorganization.

fall, downfall, ruin, perdition, crash, smash, havoc, *délabrement, débâcle;* break -down, — up; prostration; desolation, *bouleversement,* wreck, crack-up, crash, wrack, shipwreck, cataclysm; Caudine Forks, Sedan.

extinction, annihilation; destruction of life etc. 361; knock-out, knock-down blow; doom, crack of doom.

destroying etc. *v.;* demo-lition, -lishment; biblioclasm; overthrow, subversion, suppression; abolition etc. (*abrogation*) 756; sacrifice; ravage, devastation, *sabotage, razzia;* incendiarism; revolution etc. 146; extirpation etc. (*extraction*) 301; *commencement de la fin,* road to ruin; dilapidation etc. (*deterioration*) 659.

V. be -destroyed etc.; perish; fall, — to the ground; tumble, topple; go —, fall- to pieces; break up; crumble, — to dust; go to -the dogs, — the wall, — smash, — shivers, — wreck, — pot, — wrack and ruin; go -by the board, — all to smash, — to pieces, — under; be all -over, — up- with; totter to its fall.

destroy; do —, make- away with; nullify; annul etc. 756; sacrifice, demolish; tear up; over-turn, -throw, -whelm; upset, subvert, put an end to; seal the doom of, do for, dish, undo; break -, cut- up; break —, cut —, pull —, mow —, blow —, beat-down; suppress, quash, put down; cut short, take off, blot out; dispel, dissipate, dissolve; consume.

smash, — to smithereens, quell, squash, squelch, crumple up, shatter, shiver; batter; tear —, crush —, cut —, shake —, pull —, pick- to pieces; nip; tear to -rags, — tatters; crush —, knock- to atoms; pulverize; ruin; strike out; throw —, knock- -down, — over; lay by the heels; fell, sink, swamp, scuttle, wreck, crash, ship-wreck, engulf, submerge; lay in -ashes, — ruins; sweep away, erase, expunge, strike out, delete, efface, raze; level, — with the -ground, — dust.

deal destruction, lay waste, ravage, gut; dis-organize; dismantle etc. (*render useless*) 645; devour, swallow up, desolate, devastate, sap, mine, blast, confound; exterminate, extinguish, quench, annihilate; snuff —, put —, stamp —, trample- out; lay —, trample- in the dust; prostrate; tread —, crush —, trample- under foot; lay the axe to the root of; make -short work, — a clean sweep, — mincemeat-of; cut up root and branch; fling —, scatter- to the winds; throw overboard; strike at the root of, sap the foundations of, spring a mine, blow up; ravage with fire and sword; cast to the dogs; eradicate etc. 301.

Adj. destroyed etc. *v.;* perishing etc. *v.;* trembling —, nodding —, tottering- to its fall; in course of destruction etc. *n.;* extinct.

destructive, subversive, ruinous, incendiary, deletory; destroying etc. *v.;* suicidal; deadly etc. (*killing*) 361.

Adv. with -crushing effect, — a sledge-hammer.

Phr. *delenda est Carthago.*

163. Reproduction.—N. reproduction, renova-tion; restoration etc. 660; renewal; new edition, reprint etc. 21; revival, regeneration, palin-genesia, revivification; apotheosis; resuscitation, reanimation, resurrection, resurgence, re-appearance, atavism; Phoenix; reincarnation.

generation etc. (*production*) 161; multiplica-tion.

V. reproduce; restore etc. 660; revive, renovate, renew, regenerate, revivify, resusci-tate, reanimate, refashion, stir the embers, put into the crucible; multiply, repeat, resurge.

crop up, spring up like mushrooms.

Adj. reproduced etc. *v.;* renascent, reappear-ing; reproductive; resurgent; progenitive; Hydra-headed.

164. Producer.—N. producer, creator, de-viser, designer, originator, inventor, author, founder, generator, mover, architect; grower, constructor, maker etc. (*agent*) 690.

165. Destroyer.—N. destroyer etc. (destroy etc. 162); cankerworm etc. (*bane*) 663; iconoclast; assassin etc. (*killer*) 361; executioner etc. (*punish*) 975; Hun, Vandal, nihilist, anarchist.

166. Paternity.—N. paternity; parentage; fatherhood; consanguinity etc. 11.

parent, father, sire, dad, daddy, papa, gover-nor, *pater, paterfamilias, abba;* genitor, pro-genitor, procreator, begetter; ancestor; grand-sire, -father; great-grandfather.

house, stem, truck, tree, stock, *stirps,* pedigree, lineage, line, family, tribe, sept, race, clan; genealogy, descent, extraction, birth, ancestry; forefathers, forbears, patriarchs.

motherhood, maternity; mother, dam, mam-ma, *materfamilias;* grand-mother; matriarch.

Adj. paternal, parental; maternal; family, ancestral, linear, matrilinear, patrilineal, patriarchal.

167. Posterity.—N. posterity, progeny, breed, issue, offspring, brood, litter, seed, farrow, spawn, spat; family, children, grandchildren, heirs; great-grandchild.

child, son, daughter; kid; infant etc. 129; bantling, scion; shoot, sprout, olive branch, sprit, branch; off-shoot, -set; ramification; descendant; heir, -ess; heir -apparent, — presumptive; chip of the old block; heredity; rising generation.

straight descent, sonship, line, lineage, filia-tion, promogeniture.

Adj. filial.

168. Productiveness.—N. productiveness etc. *adj.;* fecundity, fertility, luxuriance, uberty.

pregnancy, pullulation, fructification, mul-tiplication, propagation, procreation; superfeta-tion.

milch cow, rabbit, hydra, warren, seed-plot, land flowing with milk and honey; second crop, after-crop, -growth, -math; fertilization.

V. make -productive etc. *adj.;* fructify; pro-create, generate, fertilize, spermatize, impregnate; fecund-ate, -ify; teem, pullulate, multiply; produce etc. 161; conceive.

Adj. productive, prolific; teem-ing, -ful; fertile, fruitful, frugiferous, fruit-bearing; fructiferous; fecund, luxuriant; pregnant; uberous.

procre-ant, -ative; generative, life-giving, spermatic; originative; multiparous; omnific; propagable.

parturient etc. (*producing*) 161; profitable etc. (*useful*) 644.

169. Unproductiveness.—N. unproductiveness etc. *adj.;* infertility, steril; ity, infecundity; impotence etc. 158- unprofitableness etc. (*inutility*) 645.

waste, desert, Sahara, wild, wilderness, howling wilderness.

V. be -unproductive etc. *adj.;* hang fire, flash in the pan, come to nothing.

Adj. unproductive, inoperative, barren, addle, unfertile, unprolific, arid, sterile, unfruitful, acarpous, infecund; *sine prole;* fallow; teem-issue-, fruitless; unprofitable etc. (*useless*) 645; null and void, of no effect.

170. Agency.—N. agency, operation, force, working, strain, function, office, maintenance, exercise, work, swing, play; inter-working, -action, procuration, procurement.

causation etc. 153; instrumentality etc. 631; influence etc. 175; action etc. (*voluntary*) 680; *modus operandi* etc. 627.

quickening —, maintaining- power; home stroke.

V. be -in action etc. *adj.;* operate, work; act, — upon; perform, play, support, sustain, strain, maintain, take effect, quicken, strike.

come —, bring- into -operation, — play; have - play, — free play; bring to bear upon.

Adj. operative, efficient, efficacious, practical, effectual.

at work, on foot; acting etc. (*doing*) 680; in -operation, — force, — action, — play, — exercise; acted —, wrought- upon.

Adv. by the -agency etc. *n.-* of; through etc. (*instrumentality*) 631; by means of etc. 632.

171. Physical Energy.—N. energy, physical energy, force; keenness etc. *adj.;* intensity, vigor, strength, elasticity; 'go; pep, live wire, high pressure; backbone, mettle, fire, vim.

acri-mony, -tude, -dity; causticity, virulence, poignancy; harshness etc. *adj.;* severity, edge, point; pungency etc. 392.

cantharides; Spanish fly; seasoning etc. (*condiment*) 393; stimulant, excitant.

activity, agitation, effervescence; ferment, -ation; ebullition, splutter, perturbation, stir, bustle; voluntary energy etc. 682; quicksilver.

resolution etc. (*mental energy*) 604; exertion etc. (*effort*) 686; excitation etc. (*mental*) 824.

V. give -energy etc. *n.;* energize, stimulate, kindle, excite, activate, exert; sharpen, pep up, intensify; inflame etc. (*render violent*) 173; wind up etc. (*strengthen*) 159.

strike, — into, — hard, — home; make an impression.

Adj. strong, energetic, forcible, active; strenuous, forceful, mettlesome, enterprising, go ahead; intense, deep-dyed, severe, keen, vivid, sharp, acute, incisive, trenchant, brisk, vigorous, live.

rousing, irritating; poignant; virulent, caustic, corrosive, mordant, harsh, stringent; double-edged, — shotted, — distilled; drastic, escharotic; racy etc. (*pungent*) 392; sarcastic etc. 932.

potent etc. (*powerful*) 157; radio-active.

Adv. strongly etc. *adj.; fortiter in re;* with telling effect.

Phr. the steam is up; *vires acquirit eundo.*

172. Physical Inertness.—N. inertness, dulness etc. *adj.;* inertia, *vis inertiae,* inertion, inactivity, torpor, languor; dormancy, quiescence etc. 265; latency, inaction, passivity.

mental inertness; sloth etc. (*inactivity*) 683; inexcitability etc. 826; irresolution etc. 605; obstinacy etc. 606; permanence etc. 141.

V. be -inert etc. *adj.;* hang fire, smoulder.

Adj. inert, inactive, passive, pacific; torpid etc. 683; sluggish, stagnant, dull, heavy, flat, slack, tame, slow, blunt; lifeless, dead, uninfluential.

latent, dormant, smouldering, unexerted.

Adv. inactively etc. *adj.;* in -suspense, -abeyance.

173. Violence.—N. violence, inclemency, vehemence, might, impetuosity; boisterousness etc.; *adj.;* effervescence, ebullition; turbulence, bluster; uproar, riot, row, rumpus, *le diable à quatre,* devil to pay, all the fat in the fire.

severity etc. 739; ferocity, rage, berserk, fury; exacerbation, exasperation, malignity; fit, paroxysm, orgasm; force, brute force; outrage; *coup de main;* strain, shock, shog; spasm, convulsion, throe; hysterics, passion etc. (*state of excitability*) 825.

out-break, -burst; burst, bounce, dissilience, discharge, volley, explosion, blow up, blast, detonation, rush, eruption, displosion, torrent.

turmoil etc. (*disorder*) 59; ferment etc. (*agitation*) 315; storm, tempest, rough weather; squall etc. (*wind*) 349; earthquake, volcano, thunderstorm.

fury, dragon, demon, tiger, beldame, Tisiphone, Megaera, Alecto, madcap, wild beast; fire-eater etc. (*blusterer*) 887.

V. be -violent etc. *adj.;* run high; ferment, effervesce; romp, rampage; run -wild, — riot; break the peace; rush, tear; rush head-long, -foremost; run amuck, raise a storm, make a riot; make —, kick up- a row, — a fuss; bluster, rage, roar, riot, storm; boil, — over; fume, foam, come in like a lion, wreak, bear down, ride roughshod, out-Herod Herod; spread like wildfire.

break —, fly —, burst- out; bounce, shock, strain; break-, pry-, force-, prize- open.

render -violent etc. *adj.;* sharpen, stir up, quicken, excite, incite, urge, lash, stimulate; irritate, inflame, exacerbate, kindle, suscitate; foment; accelerate, aggravate, exasperate, convulse, infuriate, madden, lash into fury; fan —; add fuel to- the flame; *oleum addere camino.*

explode, go off, displode, fly, detonate, thunder, blow up, flash, flare, erupt, burst; let - off, − fly; discharge, detonize, fulminate.

Adj. violent, vehement, forcible; warm; acute, sharp; rough, rude, ungentle, bluff, boisterous, wild, vicious; brusque, abrupt, waspish; impetuous; rampant.

turbulent; disorderly; blustering, raging etc. *v.;* troublous, riotous; tumultu-ary, -ous; obstreperous, uproarious; extravagant; unmitigated; ravening, tameless; frenzied etc. *(insane)* 503; desperate etc. *(rash)* 863; infuriate, towering, furious, outrageous, frantic, hysteric, in hysterics.

fiery, flaming, scorching, hot, red-hot, ebullient.

savage, fierce, ferocious, fierce as a tiger.

excited etc. *v.;* un-quelled, -quenched, -extinguished, -repressed, -bridled, -ruly; headstrong; un-governable, -appeasable, -mitigable; un-, in-controllable; insup-, irre-pressible.

spasmodic, convulsive, explosive; detonating etc. *v.;* volcanic, meteoric; stormy etc. *(wind)* 349.

Adv. violently etc. *adj.;* amain; by -storm, − force, − main force; with might and main; tooth and nail, *vi et armis,* at the point of the -sword, − bayonet; at one fell swoop; with a high hand, through thick and thin; in desperation, with a vengeance; *à −, à touteoutrance;* head-long, -foremost, -first; like a bull at a gate.

174. Moderation.—N. moderation; lenity etc. 740; temperance, temperateness, gentleness etc. *adj.;* sobriety; quiet; mental calmness etc. *(inexcitability)* 826.

moderating etc. *v.;* relaxation, remission, mitigation etc. 834; tranquilization, alleviation, assuagement, appeasement, contemporation, pacification.

measure, *juste milieu,* golden mean etc. 29.

moderator; lullaby, sedative, lenitive, demulcent, rose-water, balm, soothing syrup, poppy, opiate, anodyne, milk, opium, laudanum, 'poppy or mandragora;' wet blanket; palliative, calmative.

V. be -moderate etc. *adj.;* keep within -bounds, − compass; sober −, settle- down; keep the pease, remit, relent; take in sail.

moderate, soften, mitigate, temper, accoy; at-, con-temper; mollify, lenify, dull, take off the edge, blunt, obtund, sheathe, subdue, chasten; sober −, tone −, smooth- down; censor, blue-pencil, weaken etc. 160; lessen etc. *(decrease)* 36; check; palliate.

tranquilize, assuage, appease, dulcify, swage, lull, soothe, compose, still, calm, cool, quiet, hush, quell, sober, pacify, tame, damp, lay, allay, rebate, slacken, smooth, alleviate, rock to sleep, deaden, smother; throw -cold water on, − a wet blanket over; slake; curb etc. *(restrain)* 751; tame etc. *(subjugate)* 749; smooth over; pour oil on the -waves, − troubled waters; pour balm into, *mettre de l'eau dans son vin.*

go out like a lamb, 'roar you as gently as any sucking dove.'

Adj. moderate; lenient etc. 740; gentle, mild; cool, sober, temperate, reasonable, measured; tempered etc. *v.;* calm, unruffled, quiet, tranquil,

still; slow, smooth, untroubled; tame; peaceful, -able; pacific, halcyon.

un-exciting, -irritating; soft, bland, oily, demulcent, lenitive, anodyne; hypnotic etc. 683; sedative; assuaging.

mild as mother's milk; milk and water; gentle as a lamb.

Adv. moderately etc. *adj.;* gingerly; *piano;* under easy sail, at half speed; within -bounds, − compass; in reason.

Phr. *est modus in rebus.*

175. Influence.—N. influence; importance etc. 642; weight, pressure, preponderance, prevalence, sway, pull; predomi-nance, -nancy; ascendency; control, dominance, reign; authority etc. 737; capability etc. *(power)* 157; interest; spell, magic, magnetism.

footing; purchase etc. *(support)* 215; play, leverage, vantage ground.

tower of strength, host in himself; protection, patronage, auspices.

V. have -influence etc. *n.;* be -influential etc. *adj.;* carry weight, actuate, sway, bias, weigh, tell; have a hold upon, magnetize, bear upon, gain a footing, work upon; take -root, − hold; strike root in.

run through, pervade, prevail, dominate, predominate, subject; out-, over-weigh; over-ride, - bear, − come; gain head; rage; be -rife etc. *adj.;* spread like wildfire; have −, get −, gain- -the upper hand, − full play.

be -recognized, − listened to; make one's voice heard, gain a hearing; play a -part, − leading part- in; lead, control, rule, master; get the mastery over; make one's influence felt, cut ice with; take the lead, pull the strings; turn −, throw one's weight into- the scale; set the fashion, lead the dance.

Adj. influential; important etc. 642; weighty; prevailing etc. *v.;* prevalent, rife, rampant; dominant, regnant, predominant, in the ascendant, hegemonical; authoritative, recognized, telling, with authority.

Adv. with telling effect.

175a. Absence of Influence.—N. impotence etc. 158; inertness etc. 172; irrelevancy etc. 10.

V. have no -influence etc. 175.

Adj. uninfluential; unconduc-ing, -ive, -ting to; powerless etc. 158; irrelevant etc. 10.

176. Tendency.—N. tendency; apt-ness, -itude; proneness, proclivity, bent, turn, tone, bias, set, warp, leaning to, predisposition, inclination, conatus, propensity, susceptibility; liability etc. 177; quality, nature, temperament; characteristic, idio-crasy, -syncrasy; cast, vein, grain; humor, mood; drift etc. *(direction)* 278; conduciveness, -ducement; applicability etc. *(utility)* 644; subservience etc. *(instrumentality)* 631.

V. tend, contribute, conduce, lead, dispose, incline, verge, bend to, warp, turn, trend, affect, carry, redound to, bid fair to, gravitate towards; promote etc. *(aid)* 707.

Adj. tending etc. *v.;* conducive, working to-

wards, in a fair way to, calculated to; liable etc. 177; subservient etc. (*instrumental*) 631; useful etc. 644; subsidiary etc. (*helping*) 707.

Adv. for, whither.

177. Liability.—N. lia-bility, -bleness; possibility, contingency; suscepti-vity, -bility.

V. be -liable etc. *adj.;* incur, lay oneself open to; run the —, stand a- chance; lie under, expose oneself to, open a door to.

Adj. liable, subject; in danger etc. 665; open —, exposed —, obnoxious- to; answerable, responsible, accountable, amenable; unexempt from; apt to; dependent on; incident to.

contingent, incidental, possible, on the cards, within range of, at the mercy of.

178. Concurrence.—N. concurrence, co-operation, coagency; coincidence, consilience; union; agreement etc. 23; consent etc. (*assent*) 488; alliance; concert etc. 709; partnership etc. 712; collaboration, conformity.

V. con-cur, -duce, -spire, -tribute; agree, unite, harmonize; hang —, pull- together etc. (*co-operate*) 709; help to etc. (*aid*) 707.

keep pace with, run parallel to; go —, go along —, go hand in hand- with.

Adj. concurring etc. *v.;* concurrent, conformable, joint, co-operative, concordant, coincident, concomitant, harmonious; in alliance with, banded together, of one mind, at one with; parallel.

Adv. with one consent.

179. Counteraction.—N. counteraction, opposition; contrariety etc. 14; antagonism, polarity; clashing etc. *v.;* collision, interference, resistance, renitency, friction; reaction; retroaction; repercussion etc. (*recoil*) 277; counterblast; neutralization etc. (*compensation*) 30; *vis inertiae;* check etc. (*hindrance*) 706.

voluntary -opposition etc. 708, — resistance etc. 719; repression etc. (*restraint*) 751.

V. counteract; run counter, clash, cross; interfere —, conflict- with; jostle; go —, run —, beat —, militate- against; stultify; antagonize, frustrate, oppose etc. 708; withstand etc. (*resist*) 719; hinder etc. 706; repress etc. (*restrain*) 751; react etc. (*recoil*) 277.

undo, neutralize, cancel; counterpoise etc. (*compensate*) 30; overpoise.

Adj. counteracting etc. *v.;* antagonistic, conflicting, retroactive, renitent, reactionary; contrary etc. 14.

Adv. although etc. 30; in spite of etc. 708; *malgré;* against.

180. Space. [Indefinite space.]—N. space, extension, extent, superficial extent, expanse, stretch; capacity, volume, room, accommodation, scope, range, latitude, field, way, expansion, compass, sweep, play, swing, spread.

dimension, fourth dimension; relativity, geometry.

spare —, elbow —, house- room; stowage, roomage, margin; opening, sphere, arena; lee-, sea-, head-way.

open —, free- space; wide open spaces, void etc. (*absence*) 187; waste; wild-, wilder-ness; up-, bottom-, moor -land; *campagna, veldt,* prairie, steppe.

abyss etc. (*interval*) 198; unlimited space; infinity etc. 105; world, wide world; ubiquity etc. (*presence*) 186; length and breadth of the land.

proportions, acreage; acres, — roods and perches; square -inches, — yards etc.

V. reach, extend, stretch, sweep, spread, range, cover, thrust out, reach forth.

Adj. spacious, roomy, extensive, expansive, capacious, ample; wide-spread, vast, world-wide, uncircumscribed; boundless etc. (*infinite*) 105; shore-, track-, path-less; large etc. 192.

spatial, dimensional, proportional; two-, three-, four-dimensional; stereoscopic.

Adv. extensively etc. *adj.;* wherever; everywhere; far and -near, — wide; right and left, all over, all the world over; throughout the -world, — length and breadth of the land; under the sun, in every quarter; in all -quarters, — lands; here, there and everywhere; from -pole to pole, — China to Peru, — Indus to the pole, — Dan to Beersheba, — end to end; on the face of the earth, in the wide world, from all points of the compass; to the -four winds, — uttermost parts of the earth.

180a. Inextension.—N. in-, non-extension; point; atom etc. (*smallness*) 32; pinprick; limitation etc. 229.

181. Region. [Definite space.]—N. region, sphere, sphere of influence, corridor, ground, soil, area, realm, hemisphere, quarter district, beat, orb, orbit, zone, belt, circuit, circle; pale etc. (*limit*) 233; com-, department; domain, tract, territory, terrain, country, canton, county, shire, province, *arrondissement,* diocese, parish, township, borough, constituency, *commune,* ward, wapentake, hundred, riding, lathe, garth, soke, tithing, bailiwick; empire, kingdom, principality, duchy, grand —, arch- duchy, palatinate, republic, commonwealth, dominion, colony, state, island.

arena, precincts, *enceinte,* walk, march; patch, plot, -enclosure, etc. 232; close, *enclave,* field, court; street etc. (*abode*) 189.

clime, climate, zone, meridian, latitude.

Adj. territorial, local, parochial, provincial, insular.

182. Place. [Limited space.]—N. place, lieu, spot, point, dot; niche, nook, etc. (*corner*) 244; hole; pigeonhole etc. (*receptacle*) 191; compartment; premises, precinct, station, confine; area, court, yard, quadrangle, square, compound; abode etc. 189; locality etc. (*situation*) 183.

ins and outs; every hole and corner.

Adv. somewhere, in some place, wherever it may be, here and there, in various places, *passim.*

183. Situation.—N. situation, position, locality, *locale, status,* latitude and longitude; footing, standing, standpoint, post; stage, aspect, attitude, posture, *pose.*

place, site, base, station, seat, *venue,* whereabouts, environment, neighborhood; bearings etc. (*direction*) 278; spot etc. (*limited space*) 182.

top-, ge-, chor-ography; map etc. 554.

V. be -situated, — situate; lie; have its seat in.

Adj. situ-ate, -ated; local, topical, topographical etc. *n.*

Adv. in -situ, — loco; here and there, *passim;* here-, there-, whereabouts; in place, here, there.

in —, amidst- such and such -surroundings, — *environs,* — *entourage.*

184. Location.—N. loca-tion, -lization; lodgement; de-, re-position; stow-, pack-age; collocation; packing, lading; establishment, settlement, installation; fixation; insertion etc. 300.

anchorage, roadstead, mooring, mooring mast, encampment, camp, bivouac.

plantation, colony, settlement, cantonment, encampment, reservation; colonization, domestication, situation; habitation etc. (*abode*) 189; cohabitation; 'a local habitation and a name;' indenization, naturalization.

V. place, situate, locate, localize, make a place for, put, lay, set, scat, station, lodge, quarter, post, install; storehouse, stow; extablish, fix, pin, root; graft; plant etc. (*insert*) 300; shelve, pitch, camp, lay down, deposit, reposit; cradle; moor, tether, picket; pack, tuck in; embed; vest, invest in.

billet on, quarter upon, saddle with; load, lade, freight; pocket, put up, bag.

inhabit etc. (*be present*) 186; domesticate, colonize, populate, people; take —, strike-root; anchor; cast —, come to an- anchor; sit —, settle-down; settle; take up one's -abode, — quarters; plant —, establish —, locate- oneself; squat, perch, hive, *se nicher,* bivouac, burrow, get a footing; encamp, pitch one's tent; put up -at, — one's horses at; keep house.

indenizen, naturalize, adopt.

put back, replace etc. (*restore*) 660.

Adj. placed etc. *v.;* situate, posited, ensconced, embedded, embosomed, rooted; domesticated; vested in unremoved; settled, stationed, established.

moored etc. *v.;* at anchor.

185. Displacement.—N. displacement, elocation, transposition.

ejectment etc. 297; exile etc. (*banishment*) 893; removal etc. (*transference*) 270; unshipment.

misplacement, dislocation etc. 61; fish out of water.

V. dis-place, -plant, -lodge, -nest, -establish; misplace, unseat, disturb; exile etc. (*seclude*) 893; ablegate, set aside, remove; take —, cart- away; take —, draft- off; lade etc. 184, unship.

unload, empty etc. (*eject*) 297; transfer etc. 270; dispel.

vacate; depart etc. 293.

Adj. displaced etc. *v.;* un-placed, -housed, -harbored, -established, -settled; house-, home-less; out of -place, — a situation.

misplaced, out of its element.

186. Presence.—N. presence; occupancy, -ation; attendance; whereness.

permeation, pervasion; diffusion etc. (*dispersion*) 73.

ubi-ety, -quity, -quitariness; omnipresence.

bystander etc. (*spectator*) 444.

V. exist in space, be -present etc. *adj.;* assist at; make one -of, — at; look on, attend, remain; find —, present- oneself; show one's face; fall in the way of, occur in a place; lie, stand; occupy.

people; inhabit, dwell, reside, stay, sojourn, live, room, abide, bunk, lodge, nestle, roost, perch; take up one's abode etc. (*be located*) 184; tenant, occupy.

resort to, frequent, haunt; revisit.

fill, pervade, permeate; be -diffused, — disseminated- through; over-spread, -run; run through; meet one at every turn.

Adj. present; occupying, inhabiting etc. *v.;* moored etc. 184; residential, resi-ant, -dent, -dentiary; domiciled.

ubiquit-ous, -ary; omnipresent.

peopled, populous, full of people, inhabited.

Adv. here; there, where, everywhere, aboard, on board, at home, afield; on the spot; here, there and everywhere etc. (*space*) 180; in presence of, before; under the -eyes, —nose- of; in the face of; *in propriâ personâ.*

187. Absence. [Nullibiety.]—N. absence; inexistence etc. 2; non-residence, absenteeism; non-attendance, *alibi.*

emptiness etc. *adj.;* void, *vacuum;* vac-uity, -ancy; *tabula rasa;* exemption; *hiatus* etc. (*interval*) 198; no man's land.

truant, absentee.

nobody; nobody -present, — on earth; no one; not a soul; *âme qui vive.*

V. be -absent etc. *adj.;* keep -away, — out of the way; play truant, absent oneself, stay away. withdraw, make oneself scarce, vacate; go away, slip out, slip away, retreat etc. 293.

Adj. absent, not present, away, nonresident, gone, from home; missing; lost; wanted, wanting; omitted; nowhere to be found; inexistent etc. 2. empty, void; blank, vac-ant, -uous; unten-anted, -occupied, -inhabited; tenantless; desert, -ed; devoid; un-, uninhabitable.

exempt from, not having.

Adv. without, *minus,* nowhere; elsewhere; neither here nor there; in default of; *sans;* behind one's back.

Phr. the bird has flown, *non est inventus.*

188. Inhabitant.—N. inhabitant; habitant, resident, -iary; dweller, in-dweller; occup-ier, -ant, farmer, planter; householder, lodger, boarder, paying guest; inmate, tenant, renter, incumbent, sojourner, *locum tenens,* commorant; settler, squatter, backwoodsman, colonist; islander; denizen, citizen; burgher, oppidan, cockney, cit, townsman, burgess; villager; cottager, -tier, -ter; compatriot.

native, indigene, aboriginal, aborigines, autochthones; Briton, Englishman, John Bull; new comer etc. (*stranger*) 57.

garrison, crew; population; people etc. (*mankind*) 372; colony, settlement; household.

V. inhabit etc. (*be present*) 186; indenizen etc. (*locate oneself*) 184.

Adj. indigenous; enchorial; national, nat-ive, -al; autochthonous; British, English; colonial; domestic, domiciliated, -ed; naturalized, vernacular, domesticated; domiciliary.

in the occupation of; garrisoned —, occupied-by.

189. Abode. [Place of habitation, or resort.]—N. abode, dwelling, lodging, -s; diggings, domicile, residence, address, habitation, where one's lot is cast, local habitation, berth, seat, lap, sojourn, housing, quarters, headquarters, resiance, tabernacle, throne, ark.

home, fatherland, mother country, country etc. 181; home-stead, -stall; fireside, chimney corner; hearth, — stone; household gods, *lares et penates*, roof, household, housing, *dulce domum*, paternal domicile; native -soil, — land, blighty.

nest, *nidus*, snuggery; arbor, bower etc. 191; lair, den, cave, hole, hidingplace, cell, *sanctum sanctorum*, aerie, eyry, rookery, hive; *habitat*, haunt, covert, resort, retreat, perch, roost; nidification.

bivouac, camp, encampment, cantonment, castrametation; barrack, casemate, casern.

tent etc. (*covering*) 223; building etc. (*construction*) 161; chamber etc. (*receptacle*) 191.

tenement, messuage, farm, farmhouse, grange, *hacienda*.

cot, cabin, log cabin, shack, hut, *châlet*, croft, shed, booth, stall, hovel, bothy, shanty, igloo, tepee, wigwam; pen etc. (*inclosure*) 232; barn, bawn; kennel, sty, dog-hole, cote, coop, hutch, byre; cowhouse, -shed; stable, dove-cote, shippen.

house, mansion, place, villa, cottage, box, lodge, hermitage, *rus in urbe*, folly, rotunda, tower, *château*, castle, pavilion, hotel, court, manor-house, capital messuage, hall, palace, alcazar; country seat; kiosk, bungalow; temple etc. 1000; home of rest, alms-, poor-, work-house, asylum; boarding-, lodging-house; flat, maisonette, duplex, penthouse, suite of rooms, apartments, rooms, room building etc. 161; Mansion House, town hall, Capitol.

assembly-room, auditorium, coliseum, meeting-house, pump-room, spa, health resort, watering-place; club; theatre etc. 840; drill hall, gymnasium, church etc. 1000; Houses of Parliament etc. 696; school etc. 542; inn; hostel, -ry; hotel, tavern, caravansary, khan, hospice; public-, ale-, pot-, mug-house; gin-palace, gin mill; coffee-, eating-house; canteen, *restaurant*, *rotisserie*, cafeteria, grill-room, *buffet*, *café*, *estaminet*, *posada*, *bodega*; bar; saloon, speakeasy, shebeen.

hamlet, village, thorp, dorp, ham, kraal; borough, burgh, town, county-seat, — town, city, capital, metropolis; suburb, quarter, parish etc. 181; ghetto; province, country.

street, place, terrace, parade, esplanade, promenade, pier, embankment, road, villas, row, walk, lane, alley, court, quadrangle, quad, wynd, close, yard, passage, rents, mansions, buildings, mews.

square, polygon, circus, crescent, mall, *piazza*, arcade, colonnade, peristyle, cloister; gardens, grove, residences; block of buildings, market-place, *place*.

anchorage, roadstead, roads; dock, basin, wharf, quay, port, harbor; dry-, graving-, floating-dock.

garden, park, pleasure-ground, pleasance, demesne.

V. take up one's abode etc. (*locate oneself*) 184; inhabit etc. (*be present*) 186.

Adj. urban, oppidan, metropolitan; suburban; provincial, rural, rustic; countrified; regional, parochial, domestic; cosmopolitan; palatial.

190. Contents. [Things contained.]—N. contents; cargo, lading, freight, shipment, load, bale, burden; cart-, ship-load; cup —, basket —, etc. (*receptacle*) 191 - of; inside etc. 221; stuffing, ullage.

V. load, lade, ship, charge, fill, stuff.

191. Receptacle.—N. receptacle, container; inclosure etc. 232; recipient, receiver, reservatory.

compartment; cell, -ule: follicle; hole, corner, niche, recess, nook; crypt, stall, pigeon-hole, cove, oriel; cave etc. (*concavity*) 252.

capsule, vesicle, cyst, pod, calyx, *cancelli*, utricle, bladder, udder.

stomach, paunch, *venter*, abdomen, ventricle, crop, craw, ingluvies, maw, gizzard, bread-basket, belly, little Mary; mouth.

pocket, pouch, fob, sheath, scabbard, socket, bag, vanity bag, compact, sac, sack, saccule, despatch —, attaché-, tachy- case, wallet, scrip, card-, note-, case, billfold, poke, knit, knap-, haver-, ruck-sack, sachel, satchel, reticule, budget, net; ditty-, -box, -bag, kitbag; portfolio; saddlebags, holster; quiver etc. (*magazine*) 636.

chest, box, coffer, caddy, case, casket, pyx, pix, *caisson*, desk, *bureau*, reliquary, shrine; trunk, portmanteau, band-box, *valise*, suitcase, hand-, traveling-, overnight-, Gladstone-, carpet-bag, brief case; boot, imperial; *vache*; cage, manger, rack.

vessel, vase, bushel, barrel; canister, jar; pottle, basket, punnet, pannier, buck-basket, hopper, maund, creel, cran, crate, cradle, bassinet, wisket, whisket, *jardinière*, *corbeille*, hamper, wastepaper basket, dosser, dorser, tray, hod, scuttle, utensil, spittoon, cuspidor.

[For liquids] cistern etc. (*store*) 636; vat, caldron, barrel, cask, puncheon, keg, rundlet, tun, butt, firkin, hogshead, kilderkin, carboy, amphora, ampulla, bottle, jar, leather bottle, decanter, ewer, cruse, carafe, crock, kit, canteen, flagon; demijohn; flask, -et; stoup, noggin, vial, phial, ampoulé, cruet, caster; gourd; urn, *épergne*, salver, *patella*, *tazza*, *patera*; pig-, big-gin; tea-, coffee-pot, percolator, *samovar*; tyg, nipperkin, pocket-pistol; tub, bucket, pail, skeel, pot, tankard, jug, pitcher, toby, mug, pipkin; gal-, gall-ipot, pannikin; matrass, receiver, retort, alembic, bolthead, can, kettle; bowl, basin, jorum, punch-bowl, cup, goblet, chalice, tumbler, glass, wineglass, rummer, beaker, tass, horn, saucepan, skillet, posnet, tureen, terrine, *casserole*, sauce-, gravy-boat.

plate, platter, paten, dish, vegetable —, *entrée*-dish, trencher, calabash, porringer, potager, saucer, pan, crucible.

shovel, trowel, spoon; table-, dessert-, tea-, egg-

salt-spoon; spatula, ladle; dipper; baler; watch-glass, thimble.

closet, commode, cupboard, cellaret, *chiffonnière*, locker, bin, bunker, *buffet*, press, safe, sideboard, drawer, chest of drawers, till, *scrutoire*, *secrétaire*, *écritoire*, davenport, book-case, cabinet, canterbury; corner cupboard, wardrobe.

chamber, apartment, room, cabin; office, court, hall, atrium; suite of rooms, flat, story; saloon, *salon*, parlor; presence-chamber; sitting-, drawing-, reception-, state-, living-, work-room; gallery, cabinet, closet, cubicle; pew, box; *boudoir*; *adytum*, *sanctum*; bed-room, dormitory, dressing-room; refectory, dining-room, *salle-à-manger*; nursery, schoolroom; library, study; *studio*; billiard-, bath-, smoking-room; den, canteen, mess, officers' mess; gun-, ward-, mess-room.

attic, loft, garret, cockloft, clerestory; cellar, vault, hold, cockpit; *entre-sol*; mezzanine floor; ground-floor, *rez-de-chaussée*; basement, kitchen, cook-house, galley, pantry, scullery, offices; store-room etc. (*depository*) 636; lumber-room; dust-hole, -bin; dairy, laundry, coachhouse; *garage*; *hangar*; out-, pent-house; lean-to.

portico, porch, piazza, verandah, lobby, court, hall, vestibule, corridor, passage; ante-room, chamber; lounge; *foyer*, *loggia*.

conservatory, green-house, glass-house, vinery, bower, arbor, summer-house, alcove, grotto, hermitage, pergola.

lodging etc. (*abode*) 189; bed etc. (*support*) 215; carriage etc. (*vehicle*) 272.

Adj. capsular; saccu-lar, -lated; recipient; ventricular, cystic, vascular, vesicular, cellular, camerated, locular, multilocular, poly-gastric; marsupial; siliqu-ose, -ous.

192. Size.—N. size, magnitude, dimension, bulk, volume; largeness etc. adj.; greatness etc. (*of quantity*) 31; expanse etc. (*space*) 180; amplitude, mass; proportions.

capacity; ton-, tun-nage; caliber, scantling.

turgidity etc. (*expansion*) 194; corpulence, obesity; plumpness, etc. adj.; *embonpoint*, corporation, flesh and blood, lustihood.

hugeness etc. adj.; enormity, immensity, monstrosity.

giant, Brobdingnagian, Antaeus, Goliath, Gog and Magog, Gargantua, monster, mammoth, Cyclops; whale, porpoise, behemoth, leviathan, elephant, hippopotamus; colossus; tun, lump, bulk, block, loaf, mass, clod, nugget, bushel, thumper, whopper, spanker, strapper; Triton among the minnows.

mountain, mound; heap etc. (*assemblage*) 72. largest portion etc. 50; full-, life-size.

V. ve- large etc. adj.; become -large etc. (*expand*) 194.

Adj. large, big; great etc. (*in quantity*) 31; considerable, bulky, voluminous, ample, massive, massy; capacious, comprehensive; spacious etc. 180; mighty, towering, fine, magnificent.

corpulent, stout, fat, plump, squab, full, lusty, strapping, bouncing; portly, burly, well-fed, full-grown; stalwart, brawny, fleshy; goodly; in good -case, - condition; in condition; chopping, jolly; chub-, chubby-faced.

lubberly, hulky, unwieldy, lumpish, gaunt, spanking, whacking, whopping, thumping, thundering, hulking; overgrown; puffy etc. (*swollen*) 194.

huge, immense, enormous, mighty; vast, -y; amplitudinous, stupendous; monst-er, -rous; gigantic, elephantine; giant, -like; colossal, Cyclopean, Brobdingnagian, Garguantuan, Titanic; infinite etc. 105.

large as life; plump as a dumpling, – partridge; fat as -a pig, – a quail, – butter, – brawn, – bacon.

193. Littleness.—N. littleness etc. adj.; smallness etc. (*of quantity*) 32; exiguity, inextension; parvi-tude, -ty; duodecimo; Elzevir edition, epitome, microcosm; rudiment; vanishing point; thinness etc. 203.

dwarf, pigmy, atomy, Liliputian, midget, chit, pigwidgeon, urchin, elf; doll, puppet; Tom Thumb, Hop-o'-my thumb, Humpty-dumpty; man-, mannikin; *homunculus*, dapperling, fingerling, dandiprat, cock-sparrow, scalawag.

animalcule, monad, mite, insect, emmet, fly, midge, gnat, shrimp, minnow, worm, maggot, entozoon; *bacillus*, microbe, micro-organism, *bacteria*; *infusoria*; microbe; grub; tit, tomtit, runt, mouse, small fry; millet-, mustard-seed; barleycorn; pebble, grain of sand; mole-hill, button, bubble.

point; atom etc. (*small quantity*) 32; fragment etc. (*small part*) 51; powder etc. 330; point of a pin, mathematical point; *minutiae* etc. (*unimportance*) 643.

micro-graphy, -meter, -scope; vernier; scale.

V. be -little etc. adj.; lie in a nutshell; become small etc. (*decrease*) 36, (*contract*) 195.

Adj. little; small etc. (*in quantity*) 32; minute, diminutive, microscopic; inconsiderable etc. (*unimportant*) 643; exiguous, puny, tiny, wee, petty, minikin, miniature, pigmy, elfin; under sized; dwarf, -ed, -ish; spare, stunted, limited; cramp, -ed; pollard, Liliputian, dapper, pocket; port-ative, -able; duodecimo; dumpy, squat; compact, handy; short etc. 201.

impalpable, intangible, evanescent, imperceptible, invisible, inappreciable, infinitesimal, homeopathic; atomic, corpuscular, molecular; rudiment-ary, -al; embryonic.

weazen, scant, scraggy, scrubby; thin etc. (*narrow*) 203; granular etc. (*powdery*) 330; shrunk etc. 195.

Adv. in a -small compass, – nutshell; on a small scale.

194. Expansion.—N. expansion; increase etc. 35 -of size; enlargement, extension, augmentation; ampli-fication, -ation; aggrandizement, spread, increment, growth, development, pullulation, swell, dilation, dilatation, rarefaction; turg-escence, -idness, -idity; obesity etc. (*size*) 192; dropsy, tumefaction, intumescence, swelling, tumor, *diastole*, distension; puff-ing, -iness; inflation; pandiculation.

dilatability, expansibility.

germination, growth, upgrowth; accretion etc. 35.

over-growth, -distension; hypertrophy, tympany.

bulb etc. (*convexity*) 250; plumper; superiority of size.

V. become -larger etc. (large etc. 192); expand, widen, enlarge, extend, grow, increase, incrassate, swell, gather; fill out; deploy, take open order, dilate, stretch, spread; mantle, was; grow −, spring- up; bud, bourgeon, shoot, sprout, germinate, put forth, vegetate, pullulate, open, burst forth, flower, blow etc. 734; gain −, gather- flesh; outgrow; spread like wildfire, overrun.

be larger than; surpass etc. (*be superior*) 33.

render -larger etc. (large etc. 192); expand, spread, extend, aggrandize, distend, develop, amplify, spread out, widen, magnify, rarefy, inflate, puff, puff out, blow up, stuff, pad, cram; exaggerate; fatten.

Adj. expanded etc. *v.*; larger etc. (large etc. 192); swollen; expansive; wide-open, -spread; fan-shaped; flabelliform; overgrown, exaggerated, bloated, fat, turgid, tumid, hypertrophied, dropsical; pot-, swag-bellied; edematous, obese, puffy, pursy, blowzy, distended; patulous; bulbous etc. (*convex*) 250; full-blown, -grown, -formed; big etc. 192.

195. Contraction.—N. contraction, reduction, diminution; decrease etc. 36- of size; defalcation, decrement; lessening, shrinkage; collapse, emaciation, attenuation, tabefaction, comsumption, marasmus, atrophy; systole, neck, hourglass.

condensation, compression, constraint, compactness; compendium etc. 596; squeezing etc. *v.* ; strangulation; corrugation; astringency, constringency; astringents, sclerotics; contractility, compressibility; coarctation.

inferiority in size.

V. become -small, − smaller; lessen, decrease etc. 36; grow less, dwindle, shrink, contract, narrow, shrivel, collapse, wither, lose flesh, wizen, fall away, waste, wane, ebb; decat etc. (*deteriorate*) 659.

be smaller than, fall short of; not come up to etc. (*be inferior*) 34.

render smaller, lessen, diminish, contract, draw in, shrink, shrivel, narrow, coarctate; constrict, constringe; condense, compress, boil down, deflate, exhaust, empty; squeeze, corrugate, crush, crumple up, warp, purse up, pack, stow; pinch, tighten, strangle; cramp; dwarf, bedwarf; shorten etc. 201; circumscribe etc. 229; restrain etc. 751; fold etc. 258.

pare, reduce, attenuate, rub down, scrape, file, grind, chip, shave, shear.

Adj. contracting etc. *v.*; astringent; shrunk, contracted etc. *v.*; strangulated, tabid, wizened, stunted, tabescent; marasmic; waning etc. *v.*; neap; compact; shriveled, preshrunk.

unexpanded etc. (expand etc. 194); inswept; contractile; compressible; smaller etc. small etc. 193).

196. Distance.—N. distance; space etc. 180; remoteness, farness; far- cry to; longinquity, elongation; offing, background; removedness; parallax; reach, span, stride; drift.

out-post, -skirt; horizon, sky-line; aphelion; foreign parts, *ultima Thule, ne plus ultra,* antipodes; long range, giant's stride.

dispersion etc. 73.

V. be -distant etc. *adj.*; extend −, stretch −, reach −, spread −, go −, get −, stretch away- to; range, outrange, outreach.

remain at a distance; keep −, stand- -away, − off, − aloof, − clear of.

Adj. distant; far -off, away; remote, telescopic, distal, wide of; stretching to etc. *v.*; yon, -der; ulterior; trans-marine, -pontine, -atlantic, -pacific, -continental, -polar, -equatorial, -alpine; tramontane; ultra-montane, -mundane; hyperborean, antihodean; inaccessible, out of the way; unapproached, -able; incontiguous.

Adv. far -off, − away; afar, -off; off; away; a -long, − great, − good- way off; wide away, aloof; wide −, clear- of; out of -the way, − reach; abroad, 'yonder, farther, further,' beyond; *outre mer,* over the border, far and wide, over the hills and far away; from pole to pole etc. (*over great space*) 180; to the -uttermost parts, − ends- of the earth; out of -hearing, − range, nobody knows where, *à perte de vue,* out of the sphere of, wide of the mark; a far cry to.

apart, asunder; wide -apart, − asunder; *longo intervallo;* at arm's length.

197. Nearness.—N. nearness etc. *adj.*; proximity, propinquity; vicinity, -age; neighborhood, adjacency; contiguity etc. 199.

short -distance, − step, − cut; earshot, close quarters, brief span; stone's throw; bow −, gun −, pistol- shot; hair's breadth, span; close-up.

purlieus, neighborhood, vicinage, *environs, alentours,* suburbs, confines, *banlieue,* borderland; whereabouts.

bystander; neighbor, borderer.

approach etc. 286; convergence etc. 290; perihelion.

V. be -near etc. *adj.*; adjoin, hang about, trench on; border-, verge upon; stand by, approximate, tread on the heels of, cling to, clasp, hug; cuddle, huddle; hang about the skirts of, hover over; burn; abut.

bring −, draw- -near etc. 286; converge etc. 290; crowd etc. 72; place -side by side etc. *adv.*

Adj. near, nigh; close-, near- at hand; close, neighboring, propinquent, bordering upon; adjacent, adjoining, limitrophe; proxim-ate, ~al; at hand, handy; near the mark, near run; home, intimate.

Adv. near,' nigh; hard −, 'fast- by; close -to, upon, − up; at the point of; next door to; within -reach, − call, − hearing, − earshot, − range; within an ace of; but a step, not far from, at no great distance; on the -verge, − brink, − skirts- of; in the -environs etc. *n.*; at one's -door, − feet, − elbow, − finger's end, − side; on the tip of one's tongue; under one's nose; within a -stone's throw etc. *n.*; in -sight, − presence- of; at close quarters; cheek by -jole, − jowl; beside, alongside, side by side, *tête-à-tête;* in juxtaposition etc. (*touching*) 199; yard-arm to yard-arm; at the heels of; on the confines of, at the threshold, bordering upon, verging to; in the way.

about; here-, there-abouts; roughly, in round

numbers; approxim- -ately, — atively; as good
as, well nigh.

198. Interval.—N. interval, interspace;
separation etc. 44; break gap, opening; hole etc.
260; chasm, *hiatus*, caesura; inter-ruption,-
regnum; interstice, *lacuna*, cleft, mesh, crevice,
chink, rime, creek, cranny, crack, chap, slit, slot,
fissure, scissure, rift, flaw, breach, fracture, rent,
gash, cut, leak, dike, ha-ha.

gorge, defile, ravine, canon, *crevasse*, abyss,
abysm; gulf; inlet, frith, strait, gully, gulch, nullah;
pass; notch; furrow etc. 259; yawning gulf; *hiatus -
maxime, — valde- deflendus*; parenthesis etc. (*interjacence*) 228; void etc. (*absence*) 187; incompleteness etc. 530.

V. gape etc. (*open*) 260; part, remove.

Adj. with an interval, far between; separated,
spaced, split.

Adv. at intervals etc. (*discontinuously*) 70;
longo intervallo.

199. Contiguity.—N. contiguity, contact,
proximity, apposition, juxtaposition, touching etc.
v.; abutment, osculation; meeting, appulse, ap-
pulsion, *rencontre*, rencounter, syzygy, coincidence, conjunction, coexistence; adhesion etc.
46.

border-land; frontier etc. (*limit*) 233; tangent.

V. be -contiguous etc. *adj.*; join, adjoin, abut
on, march with, border; tick, graze, touch, meet,
osculate, kiss, come in contact; coincide; coexist;
adhere etc. 46.

Adj. contiguous; touching etc. *v.*; in -contact
etc. *n.*, conterminous, end to end, osculatory; pertingent; tangential.

hand to hand; close to etc. (*near*) 197; with no -
interval etc. 198.

200. Length.—N. length, longitude, span, extent, mileage.

line, bar, rule, stripe, streak, spoke, radius.

lengthening etc. *v.*; pro-longation, -duction, -
traction; ten-sion, -sure; extension.

[Measures of length] line, nail, inch, hand,
palm, foot, cubit, yard, ell, fathom, rod, pole,
perch, furlong, mile, league; chain, meter, kilo-,
centi-, milli- etc meter.

pedometer, perambulator, odometer, odograph,
speedometer, cyclometer, log, telemeter, range finder; scale etc. (*measurement*) 466.

V. be -long etc. *adj.*; stretch out, sprawl; extend — , reach — , stretch -to; make a long
arm, 'drag its slow length along.'

render -long etc. *adj.*; lengthen, extend,
elongate; stretch; pro-long, -duce, -tract; let
— , pay — , draw — , spin- out; drawl.

enfilade, look along, view in perspective.

Adj. long, -some; lengthy, lank, wiredrawn, out-
stretched; stretched, drawn out, lengthened etc. *v.*;
sesquipedalian etc. (*words*) 577; interminable, no
end of.

line-ar, -al; longitudinal, oblong.

as long as -my arm, —to-day and to-morrow; un-
shortened etc. (shorten etc. 201).

Adv. lengthwise, at length, longitudinally, endlong, along; *tandem*; in a line etc. (*continuously*)
69; in perspective.

from -end to end; —stem to stern, —head to foot,
—the crown of the head to the sole of the foot, —
top to toe, —head to heels; fore and aft.

201. Shortness.—N. shortness etc. *adj.*; brevity;
littleness etc. 193; a span.

shortening etc. *v.*; abbrevia-tion, -ture;
abridgment, concision, retrenchment, curtailment,
decurtation; reduction etc. (*contraction*) 195;
epitome etc. (*compendium*) 596.

abridger, abstractor, epitomiser.

elision, ellipsis; conciseness etc. (*in style*) 572.

V. be -short etc. *adj.*; render -short etc. *adj.*;
shorten, curtail, abridge, abbreviate, take in,
reduce; compress etc. (*contract*) 195; epitomize
etc. 596.

retrench, cut short, obtruncate; scrimp, cut, chop
up, hack, hew; cut — , pare- down; clip, snip, dock,
lop, prune; shear, shave, mow, reap, crop; snub;
truncate, pollard, stunt, nip, nip in the bud, check
the growth of; [in drawing] foreshorten.

Adj. short, brief, curt; compendious, compact;
stubby, scrimp; shorn, stubbed; stumpy, thickset,
podgy, stocky, pug; squab, -by; squat, dumpy; little
etc. 193; curtailed of its fair proportions; short by;
oblate; concise etc. 572; summary.

Adv. shortly etc. *adj.*; in short etc. (*concisely*)
572.

202. Breadth. Thickness.—N. breadth, width,
latitude, amplitude; diameter, bore, calibre, radius;
superficial extent etc. (*space*) 180.

thickness, crassitude; corpulence etc. (*size*) 192;
dilatation etc. (*expansion*) 194.

V. be -broad etc. *adj.*; become — , render- -
broad etc. *adj.*; expand etc. 194; thicken, widen.

Adj. broad, wide, ample, extended; discous; fan-
like; out-spread, -stretched; wide as a church-door.

thick, dumpy, squab, squat, thickset, tubby; thick
as a rope, stubby etc. 201.

203. Narrowness. Thinness.—N. narrowness
etc. *adj.*; closeness, exility; exiguity etc. (*little*)
193.

line; hair's — , finger's -breadth; strip, streak,
vein.

thinness etc. *adj.*; tenuity; emaciation, slen-
derness, macilency, *marcor*.

shaving, slip etc. (*filament*) 205; threadpaper,
skeleton, shadow, scrag, anatomy, spindle-shanks,
barebones, lantern jaws, mere skin and bone.

middle construction, stricture, neck, waist, isthmus, wasp, hour-glass; ridge, *ghaut*, pass; ravine
etc. 198.

narrowing, coarctation, angustation, tapering;
contraction etc. 195.

V. be-narrow etc. *adj.*; narrow, taper, diminish,
contract etc. 195; render -narrow etc. *adj.*

Adj. narrow, close; slender, thin, fine; *svelte*;
thread-like etc. (*filament*) 205; finespun, taper,
slim, gracile, slight, slight-made; scant, -y; spare,
delicate, incapacious; contracted etc. 195; unexpanded etc. (expand etc. 194); slender as a thread,
capillary.

emaciated, lean, meager, gaunt, macilent; lank, -y; weedy, skinny, scrawny, scraggy; starv-ed, -eling; attenuated, shrivelled; wizened, pinched, peaky, skeletal, spindling, spindle- -legged, -shanked; extenuated, tabid, marcid, bare-bone, raw-boned; herring-gutted; worn to a shadow, lean as a rake; thin as a -lath,—whipping post,—wafer; hatchet-faced; lantern-jawed.

204. Layer.—**N.** layer, stratum, course, bed, zone, *substratum,*floor, flag, stage, story, tier, slab, escarpment, table, tablet, panel, plaque; board, plank; trencher, platter.

plate; lam-ina, -ella; sheet, flake, foil, wafer, scale, coat, peel, pellicle, ply, thickness, membrane, film, leaf, slice, shive, cut, rasher, shaving, integument etc. (*covering*) 223.

V. slice, shave, pare, peel; plate, coat, veneer; cover etc. 223.

Adj.lamell-ar, -ated, -iform; laminated, -iferous; micaceous; schist-ose, -ous; scaly; filmy, membranous, flaky, squamous; folia-ted, -ceous; stratified, -form; tabular, discoid, spathic.

205. Filament.—**N.** filament, line; fiber, fibril; funicle, vein, hair, capillament, *cilium*, tendril, gossamer; hair-stroke; harl.

wire, string, thread, packthread, cotton, sewing-silk, twine, twist, whip-cord, cord, rope, cable, yarn, hemp, oakum, jute, wool, worsted.

strip, shred, slip, spill, list, band, fillet, *fascia*, ribbon, riband, tape, roll, lath, slat, strake, splinter, shiver, shaving.

beard etc. (*roughness*) 256; ramification; strand.

Adj. fil-amentous, -aceous, -iform; fibr-ous, -illous; thread-like, wiry, stringy, ropy; capill-ary, -iform; funicular, wire-drawn; anguilliform; flagelliform; hairy etc. (*rough*) 256; ligulate.

206. Height.—**N.** height, altitude, elevation, ceiling; eminence, pitch; loftiness etc. *adj.*; sublimity.

tallness etc. *adj.*; stature, procerity; prominence etc. 250.

colossus etc. (*size*) 192; giant, grenadier, giraffe.

mount, -ain; hill, butte, monticle, fell, knap; cape; head-, fore-land; promontory; ridge, hog's back, dune; rising -. vantage- ground; down; moor, -land; Alp; up-, table-, high-lands; heights etc. (*summit*) 210; knoll, hummock, hillock, barrow, mound, mole, *kopje*; steeps, bluff, cliff, craig, tor, peak, pike, clough; escarpment, edge, ledge, brae; dizzy height.

tower, pillar, column, pylon, obelisk, monument, steeple, spire, minaret, *campanile*, belfry, turret, roof, dome, cupola, pagoda, pyramid; sky scraper; Eiffel tower.

pole, pikestaff, maypole, flagstaff; mast, top-, topgallant- mast.

ceiling etc. (*covering*) 223.

high water; high-, flood-, spring-tide.

altimetry etc. (*angle*) 244; altimeter, height-finder, hypsometer, barograph.

V. be -high etc. *adj.*; tower, soar, command;

hover; cap, culminate; overhang, hang over, impend, beetle; bestride, ride, mount; perch, surmount; cover etc. 233; overtop etc. (*be superior*) 33; stand on tiptoe.

become -high etc. *adj.*; grow, - higher, - taller; upgrow; rise etc. (*ascend*) 305.

render -high etc. *adj.*; heighten etc. (*elevate*) 307.

Adj. high, elevated, eminent, exalted, lofty, supernal; tall; gigantic etc. (*big*) 192; Patagonian; towering, beetling, soaring, hanging [gardens]; elevated etc. 307; upper; highest etc. (*topmost*) 210; monticulous, perching, hill-dwelling.

up-, moor-land; hilly, mountainous, alpine, subalpine, heaven-kissing; cloud-topt, -capt, -touching; aerial.

overhanging etc. *v.*; incumbent, overlying; super-incumbent, -natant, -imposed; prominent etc. 250.

tall as a -maypole, —poplar,—steeple; lanky etc. (*thin*) 203.

Adv. on high, high up, aloft, up, above, aloof, overhead; up—, above- stairs; in the clouds; on -tiptoe, —stilts,—the shoulders of; over head and ears; breast high.

over, upwards; from top to bottom etc. (*completely*) 52.

207. Lowness.—**N.** lowness etc. *adj.*; debasement, depression; prostration etc. (*horizontal*) 213; depression etc. (*concave*) 252.

molehill; lowlands; bottomlands; basement-ground-floor; *rez de chaussee* etc. 211; hold; feet, heels.

low water; low—, ebb—, neap—, spring- tide.

V. be -low etc. *adj.*; lie -low, —flat; underlie; crouch, slouch, wallow, grovel; lower etc. (*depress*) 308.

Adj. low, neap, debased; nether, -most; flat, level with the ground; lying low etc. *v.*; crouched, subjacent, squat, prostrate etc. (*horizontal*) 213.

Adv. under; be-, under-neath; below; down, -wards; adown, at the foot of; under-foot, -ground; down—, below-stairs; at a low ebb; below par.

208. Depth.—**N.** depth; deepness etc. *adj.*; profundity, depression etc. (*concavity*) 252.

hollow, pit, shaft, well, crater, abyss; gulf etc. 198; bowels of the earth, bottomless pit, hell.

soundings, sonar, depth of water, water, draught; submersion; plummet, sound, probe; sounding -rod, - line, - machine; lead; submarine, diving bell, bathysphere; diver.

V. be -deep etc. *adj.*; render -deep etc. *adj.*; deepen.

plunge etc. 310; sound, heave the lead, take soundings; dig etc. (*excavate*) 252.

Adj. deep, -seated; profound, sunk, buried; submerged etc. 310; sub-aqueous, -marine, -terranean, -terrene; underground.

bottom-, sound-, fathom-less; unfathom-ed, - able; abysmal; deep as a well, deep-sea.

knee-, ankle-deep.

Adv. beyond—, out of- one's depth; over head and ears, over one's head.

209. Shallowness.—**N.** shallowness etc. *adj.*; shoals; mere scratch; veneer, gloss, pinprick.

Adj. shallow. superficial; skin—, ankle—, knee-deep; just enough to wet one's feet; shoal, -y.

V. shallow, shoal, skim— over, —the surface, touch on.

210. Summit.—N. summit, -y; top, vertex, apex, zenith, pinnacle, acme, acropolis, culmination, meridian, utmost height, *ne plus ultra*, height, pitch, maximum, climax, apogee; culminating —, crowning —, turning- point; turn of the tide, fountain head; water-shed, -parting; sky, pole.

tip, -top; crest, crow's nest, cap, truck, peak, nib; end etc. 67; crown, brow; head, nob, noddle, pate, skull, cranium.

high places, heights.

top-, top-gallant mast, sky scraper; quarter —, hurricane- deck.

architrave, frieze, cornice, coping, coping-stone, zoophorus, capital, headpiece, capstone, epistyle, sconce, pediment, entablature; tympanum; ceiling etc. (*covering*) 223.

attic, loft, garret, house-top, upper story, roof.

topping, icing, frosting.

V. culminate, cap, crown, top; overtop etc. (*be superior to*) 33.

Adj. highest etc. (high etc. 206); top; top-, upper-most; tip-top; culminating etc. *v.*; meridi-an, -onal; capital, head, polar, supreme, supernal, top-gallant.

Adv. a-top, at the top of — the tree, — the heap.

211. Base.—N. base, -ment; plinth, dado, wainscot, baseboard; foundation etc. (*support*) 215; substructure, *sub stratum*, sump, ground, earth, pavement, floor, paving, flag, carpet, ground-floor, deck; footing, groundwork, basis; hold, bilge, orlop deck.

bottom, nadir, foot, sole, toe, hoof, keel, kelson, root.

Adj. bottom; under-, nether-most; fundamental; founded —, based —, grounded —, built- on.

212. Verticality.—N. verticality; erectness etc. *adj.*; perpendicularity; right angle, normal; azimuth circle.

wall, palisade, precipice, cliff, steep, bluff.

elevation, erection; square, plumb-line, plummet.

V. be -vertical etc. *adj.*; stand -up, — on end, — erect, — upright; stick —, cock-up.

render -vertical etc. *adj.*; set —, stick —, raise —, cock- up; erect, rear, raise, pitch, raise on its legs.

Adj. vertical, upright, erect, perpendicular, normal, plumb, straight, bolt upright; rampant; straight —, standing- up etc. *v.*; rectangular, orthogonal.

Adv. vertically etc. *adj.*; up, on end; up —, right- on end; *à plomb*, endwise; on one's legs; at right angles.

213. Horizontality.—N. horizontality; flatness; level, plane; stratum etc. 204; dead -level, — flat; level plane.

recumbency; lying down etc. *v.*; reclination, decumbence; de-, discumbency; proneness etc. *adj.*; accubation, supination, resupination, prostration; azimuth.

plain, floor, platform, bowling-green; cricket--ground; court; gridiron; base-ball diamond; hockey rink; tennis-, croquet-ground, — lawn; billiard table; terrace, estrade, esplanade, *parterre*, table-land, *plateau*, ledge.

spirit-, level; T-square.

V. be -horizontal etc. *adj.*; lie, recline, couch; lie -down, — flat, — prostrate; sprawl, loll; sit down.

render -horizontal etc. *adj.*; lay, — down, — out; level, flatten, even, raze, equalize, smooth, align; prostrate, knock down, floor, fell, ground.

Adj. horizontal, level, even, plane; flat etc. 251; flat as a -billiard table, — bowling green; alluvial; calm, — as a mill-pond; smooth, —as glass.

re-, de-, pro-, ac-cumbent; lying etc. *v.*; prone, supine, couchant, jacent, prostrate.

Adv. horizontally etc. *adj.*; on -one's back. —all fours, — its beam ends.

214. Pendency.—N. pend-, dependency; suspension, hanging etc. *v.*

pendant, drop, tippet, tassel, lobe, tail, train, flap, lappet, skirt, pig-tail, queue, pendulum, hanger, suspender, supporter.

peg, knob, button, hook, nail, stud, ring, staple, tenterhook; davit; fastening etc. 45; spar, horse, chande-, gase-, electro-lier.

V. be -pendent etc. *adj.*; hang, depend, swing, dangle, droop, sag; swag; daggle, flap, trail, flow.

suspend, hang, sling, hook up, hitch, fasten to, append.

Adj. pend-ent, -ulous; pensile; hanging etc. *v.*; dependent; suspended etc. *v.*; lowering, overhanging, beetling, decumbent; loose, flowing.

having a -peduncle etc. *n.*; pedunculate, tailed, caudate.

215. Support.—N. support, backing, ground, foundation, base, basis; *terra firma*; bearing, fulcrum, *point d'appui*, caudex, purchase, footing, hold, -locus standi; landing, — stage, — place; stage, platform; block; rest, resting-place; ground-work, *substratum*, sustentation, subvention; floor etc. (*basement*) 211.

supporter; aid etc. 707; prop, stand, anvil, fulciment; hod, stay, shore, skid, rib, sprag, truss, bandage; sleeper; stirrup, stilts, shoe, sole, heel, splint, lap; bar, rod, boom, sprit, outrigger.

staff, stick, crutch, alpenstock, bourdon, *bâton*, maulstick, colstaff, cowlstaff, staddle; stalk, pedicel, -icle, — uncle.

post, pillar, shaft, column, pilaster; pediment, pedestal; plinth, shank, leg, socle, zocle; buttress, jamb, mullion, abutment; pile, baluster, banister, stanchion, king post; balustrade.

frame, -work, body, *chassis, fuselage*; scaffold, skeleton, beam, rafter, girder, lintel, joist, cantilever, travis, trave, corner-stone, summer, transom; rung, round, step, sill.

columella, back-bone; key-stone; axle, -tree; axis; arch, ogive, mainstay.

trunnion, pivot, rowlock; peg etc. (*pendency*)

214; tie-beam etc. (*fastening*) 45; thole pin.

board, ledge, shelf, hob, bracket, trevet, trivet, arbor, rack, hatrack; mantel, -piece, -shelf; slab, console; counter, dresser; flange, corbel; table, trestle, teapoy; shoulder; perch; horse; easel, desk; retable, predella.

seat, throne, dais; divan, musnud; chair, bench, form, stool, camp-stool, sofa, settee, davenport, stall, miserere, arm –, easy –, elbow –, rocking-chair; couch, day bed, *fauteuil*, woolsack, ottoman, settle, squab, bench, box, dicky; saddle, pannel, pillion; side –, pack- saddle; pommel.

bed, berth, pallet, tester, crib, cot, bassinet, hammock, shakedown, camp bed, bunk, truckle-bed, cradle, litter, stretcher, bedstead; four-poster, French bed; bedding, mattress, *paillasse;* pillow, bolster; mat, rug, cushion.

stool, footstool, hassock, faldstool, *prie-dieu;* tabouret; tripod.

Atlas, Persides, Atlantes, Caryatides, Hercules.

V. be -supported etc.; lie –, sit –, recline –, lean –, loll –, rest –, stand –, step –, repose – , abut –, beat –, be based etc.- on; have at one's back; be-stride, -straddle.

support, bear, carry, hold, sustain, -shoulder; hold –, back –, bolster –, shore- up; up-hold, -bear; prop; under-prop,-pin, -set; bandage, etc. 43; brace, truss; cradle, pillow.

give –, furnish –, afford –, supply –, lend- -support, – foundations; bottom, found, base, ground, embed.

maintain, keep on foot; aid etc. 707.

Adj. support-ing, -ed, etc.*v.;* atlantean, columellar; sustentative, fundamental, basal.

Adv. astride on, astraddle; pick-a-back.

216. Parallelism.—N. parallelism; coextension, concentricity, collimation.

V. be –, lie- parallel to; collimate; equate, match.

Adj. parallel; coextensive, collateral, concentric, concurrent, abreast, aligned.

Adv. alongside, abreast etc. (*laterally*) 236.

217. Obliquity.—N. obliquity, inclination, skew, slope, slant; crookedness etc. *adj.*; slopeness; leaning etc. *v.*; bevel, bezel, ramp, tilt; bias, list, twist, warp, swag, cant, lurch; distortion etc. 243; bend etc. (*curve*) 245; tower of Pisa.

acclivity, rise, ascent, grade, gradient, *glacis*, rising ground, hill, bank, declivity, downhill, dip, fall, devexity; gentle –, rapid- slope; easy -ascent, – descent; shelving beach; *talus; montagne Russe; facilis descensus Averni.*

steepness etc. *adj.*; cliff, precipice etc. (*vertical*) 212; escarpment, scarp.

[Measure of inclination]clinometer, theodolite, level, sextant, quadrant, protractor; angle, sine, cosine, tangent etc. hypothenuse.

diagonal; zigzag, chevron.

V. be -oblique etc. *adj.*; slope, slant, lean, in-cline, shelve, stoop, decline, descent, bend, heel, careen, sag, swag, seel, slouch, cant, sidle.

render -oblique etc. *adj.*; sway, bias; slope, slant; incline, bend, crook; cant ,tilt; distort etc. 243.

Adj. oblique, inclined; sloping etc. *v.*; tilted etc.

v.; recumbent, clinal, skew, askew, slant, aslant, bias, plagiedral, indirect, wry, awry, ajee, crooked; knock-kneed etc. (*distorted*) 243; bevel, out of the perpendicular.

uphill, rising, ascending, acclivous; downhill, falling, descending; declining, declivous, devex, anticlinal; steep, abrupt, precipitous, breakneck.

diagonal; trans-verse, -versal; athwart, antiparallel; curved etc. 245.

Adv. obliquely etc. *adj.*; on –, all on- one side; askew, askant, askance, aslope, asquint, edgewise, at an angle; side-long, -ways; slope-, slant-wise; by a side wind.

218. Inversion.—N. in-, e-, sub-, re-, retro-, intro-version; contraposition etc. 237; contrariety etc. 14; reversal; turn of the tide.

overturn; upset, capsize; somer-sault, -set; summerset; *culbute*; revulsion; *pirouette*.

transposition, transposal, anastrophy, *metastasis, hyperbaton, anastrophe, hysteron--proteron,* hypallage, *synchysis, tmesis,* parenthesis; *metathesis;* palindrome; Spoonerism.

pronation and supination.

V. be -inverted etc.; turn –, go –, wheel-round, – about, – to the right about; turn –, go –, tilt –, topple-over; capsize, turn turtle.

in-, sub-, retro-, intro-vert; reverse; up-, over-turn, -set; turn -topsy turvy etc. *adj.; culbuter;* transpose, put the cart before the horse, turn the tables.

Adj. inverted etc. *v.*; wrong side -out, – up; inside out, upside down; bottom –, keel- upwards; supine, on one's head, topsy turvy, *sens dessus sens dessous.*

inverse; reverse etc. (*contrary*) 14; opposite etc. 237.

topheavy, unstable.

Adv. inversely etc.*adj.*; hirdie-girdie; heels over head, head over heels.

219. Crossing.—N. crossing etc. *v.*; inter-section, – lacement, – twinement, -digitation; decussation, transversion; convolution etc. 248.

reticulation, meshwork, network; inosculation, anastomosis, inter-texture, mortise.

net, *plexus*, web, mesh, twill, skein, sleeve, felt, lace; wicker; mat, -ting; plait, trellis, wattle, lattice, grating, *grille,* gridiron, tracery, fretwork, filigree, reticle; tissue, netting, mokes.

cross, crucifix, rood, crisscross, crux; chain, wreath, braid, cat's cradle,knot; entanglement etc. (*disorder*) 59.

[woven fabrics] cloth, linen, muslin, cambric, drill, homespun, tweed, broadcloth etc.

V. cross, decussate; inter-sect, -lace, -twine, - twist, -weave, -digitate, -link.

twine, entwine, weave, inweave, twist, wreathe; anastomose, inosculate, dovetail, splice, link.

mat, plait, plat, braid, felt, twill; tangle, entangle, ravel; net, knot; dishevel, raddle.

Adj. crossing etc.*v.*; crossed, matted etc. *v.*; transverse.

cross, cruciform, crucial; reti-form, -cular, -culated; arcolar, cancellated, mullioned, latticed, grated, barred, streaked; textile, secant, plexal; interfretted.

Adv. across, thwart, athwart, transversely, crosswise.

220. Exteriority.—N. exteriority; outside, exterior; surface, superficies; skin etc. (*covering*) 223; *superstratum*; disk, disc; face, facet, external, the open.

excentricity; circumjacence etc. 227.

V. be -exterior etc. *adj.*; lie around etc. 227.

place -exteriorly, — outwardly, — outside; put —, turn- out.

Adj. exter-ior, -nal; extraneous, outer, -most; out-ward, -lying, -side, -door; round about etc. 227; extramural.

superficial, skin-deep; frontal, discoid.

extraregarding; eccentric; outstanding; extrinsic etc. 6.

Adv. externally etc. *adj.*; out, without, over, outwards, *ab extra*, out of doors; *extra muros*.

in the open air; *sub -Jovè, — dio; à la belle étoile, al fresco.*

221. Interiority.—N. interiority; inside, -land, interior, endocrine; interspace, subsoil, *substratum.*

contents etc. 190; substance, pith, marrow; backbone etc. (*center*) 222; heart, bosom, breast, abdomen; vitals, viscera, entrails, bowels, belly, intestines, guts, chitterlings, womb, lap; gland, cell; internal organs, *penetralia*, recesses, innermost recesses; cave etc. (*concavity*) 252.

inhabitant etc. 188.

V. be -inside etc. *adj.*, — within etc. *adv.*

place —, keep- within; enclose etc. (*circumscribe*) 229; intern; embed etc. (*insert*) 300.

Adj. inter-ior, -nal; inner, inside, intimate, inward, intraregarding; in-, inner-most; deep-seated; visceral, intestine, -tinal; inland; subcutaneous; interstitial etc. (*interjacent*) 228; inwrought etc. (*intrinsic*) 5; enclosed etc. *v.*

home, domestic, indoor, intramural, vernacular; endemic.

Adv. internally etc. *adj.*; inwards, within, in, inly; here-, there-, where-in; *ab intra*, withinside; in —, within- doors; at home, in the bosom of one's family.

222. Centrality.—N. centrality, centricalness, center; middle etc. 68; focus etc. 74.

core, kernel; nucleus, nucleolus; heart, pole, axis, pivot, fulcrum, bull's eye; hub, nave, navel; *umbilicus*, spine, backbone, marrow, pith; hot-bed; concentration etc. (*convergence*) 290; centralization; symmetry.

center of -gravity, — pressure, — percussion, — oscillation, — buoyancy etc. metacenter.

V. be -central etc. *adj.*; converge etc. 290.

render central, centralize, concentrate; bring to a focus.

Adj. centr-al, -ical; middle etc. 68; axial, pivotal, focal, umbilical, concentric; middlemost, nuclear, centric, centraidal; spinal, vertebral.

Adv. middle; midst; centrally etc. *adj.*

223. Covering.—N. covering, cover; canopy, tilt, awning, baldachin, tent, marquee, *tente d'abri*, umbrella, parasol, sunshade; veil (*shade*) 424; shield etc. (*defense*) 717; hall.

roof, dome, cupola, mansard roof; ceiling; thatch, tile; pan-, pen-tile; tiling, shingles, slates, slating, leads; shed etc. (*abode*) 189.

top, lid, covercle, door, *operculum*, eyelid, blind, curtain.

bandage, plaster, lint, wrapping, dossil, finger stall.

coverlet, counterpane, sheet, quilt, comforter, eiderdown; tarpaulin, blanket, rug, drugget, linoleum, oilcloth; housing.

in-, tegument; skin, pellicle, fleece, fell, fur, ermine, miniver, sable, sealskin etc.; fabrikoid; leather, morocco, calf, pigskin, elk, kid, cowhide etc.; shagreen, hide; pelt, -ry; cuticle, *dermis*, scarf-skin, *epidermis.*

clothing etc. 225; mask etc. (*concealment*) 530.

peel, crust, bark, rind, *cortex*, husk, shell, coat. capsule; ferrule; sheath, -ing; pod, cod; casing, case, theca; *elytron; involucrum;* wrapp-ing, -er; cellophane; envelope, vesicle; dermatology, conchology.

armor, -plate, armoring; veneer, facing; pavement; scale etc. (*layer*) 204; coating, paint, stain; varnish etc. (*resin*) 356a; anointing etc. *v.*; inunction; incrustation; superposition, obduction, ground, enamel, whitewash, plaster, stucco, rough cast, pebble dash, compo; rendering; cerement; ointment etc. (*grease*) 356.

V. cover; super-pose, -impose; over-lay, -spread; wrap etc. 225; incase; face, case, veneer, pave, paper; tip, cap, bind, revet.

coat, paint, varnish, pay, incrust, stucco, cement, dab, plaster, tar; wash; be-, smear; be-, daub; anoint, do over; gild, plate, electroplate, japan, laquer, lacker, enamel, whitewash; lay it on thick.

over-lie, -arch; conceal etc. 528.

Adj. covering etc. *v.*; cutaneous, dermal, cortical, cuticular, tegumentary, skinny, scaly, squamous; covered etc. *v.*; imbricated, loricated, armor-plated, iron-clad; under cover, hooded, cloaked, cowled.

224. Lining.—N. lining, inner coating; coating etc. (*covering*) 223; stalactite, -agmite. filling, stuffing, wadding, padding, bushing. wainscot, *parietes,* wall brattice.

V. line, stuff, incrust, wad, pad, fill.

Adj. lined etc. *v.*

225. Investment.—N. investment; covering etc. 223; dress, clothing, raiment, drapery, costume, attire, guise, toilet, *toilette,* trim; habiliment; vesture, -ment; garment, garb, palliament, apparel, wardrobe, wearing apparel, clothes, things.

array; tailoring, millinery; best bib and tucker; finery etc. (*ornament*) 847; full dress etc. (*show*) 882; garniture; theatrical properties.

outfit, equipment, *trousseau;* uniform, khaki, regimentals; academicals, canonicals etc. 999; livery, gear, harness, turn out, accoutrement, caparison, suit, rigging, trappings, traps, slops, togs, toggery; masquerade.

dishabille, morning dress, lounge suit, tea-gown, *kimono*, *néglige*, dressing-gown, *peignoir*, wrapper, undress; shooting-coat; smoking jacket, mufti; rags, tatters, old clothes; mourning, weeds; duds; slippers.

robe, tunic, dolman, *paletot*, habit, gown, coat, coatee, frock, blouse, *pelisse*, middy, sagum, *toga*, smock-frock; frock-, dress-, morning-, tail- coat; dress-suit, — clothes, swallow-tail coat, dinner-, Eton-jacket.

cloak, pall; mantle, mantlet, mantua, shawl, *pelisse*, veil, yashmak; cape, tippet, kirtle, plaid, muffler, comforter, Balaclava helmet, haik, huke, chlamys, mantilla, tabard, housing, horse-cloth, burnous, *roquelaure, houppelande*; sur-, top-, over-, great-coat; *surtout*, spencer, cardigan, sweater, blazer; mackintosh, waterproof, slicker, raincoat, oilskin, trench coat, ulster, monkey-, pea-, pilot-jacket, redingote; wraprascal, poncho, cardinal, pelerine, talma.

jacket, jumper, vest, jerkin, waistcoat, doublet, *camisole*, gabardine; stays, *corsage*, corset, corselet, bodice; stomacher; skirt, petticoat, slip, farthingale, kilt, jupe, crinoline, bustle, hobble skirt, *panier*, apron, pinafore; loin cloth.

trousers; breeches, trews, pantaloons, unmentionables, inexpressibles, overalls, pajamas, smalls, small-clothes; tights, pants, shorts, drawers; knickerbockers, knickers, plus fours, bloomers, divided skirt; phil-, fill-ibeg.

head-dress, -gear; cap, *béret*, tam o' shanter, glengarry, topee, sombrero; hat; cocked —, high —, tall —, top —, silk —, opera —, crush - hat, *gibus*, beaver, castor, bonnet, tile, wideawake, billy-cock; bowler; soft felt —, straw —, leghorn- hat, panama; toque; wimple; night-, mob-, skull-cap, biretta; hood, cowl, coif; capote, calash; scull-cap; kerchief, snood; head, *coiffure*; crown etc. (*circle*) 247; *chignon*, pelt, wig, front, peruke; periwig; caftan, turban, fez, *tarboosh*, taj, shako, csako, busby; *képi*, forage cap, bearskin; helmet etc. 717; mask, domino.

body clothes; linen; shirt, sark, smock, shift, *chemise, lingerie*; night-gown, -shirt; bed-gown, *sac de nuit*; jersey, guernsey; underclothing, -waistcoat.

neck-erchief, -cloth; tie, ruff, collar, cravat, stock, handkerchief, bandana, scarf; bib, tucker; dicky; boa; girdle etc. (*circle*) 247; cummerbund.

shoe, pump, brogue, boot, slipper, sandal, galoche, galoshes, arctics, rubber boots, overshoes, patten, clog, sabot; high-low; Blucher —, Wellington —, Hessian —, jack —, top- boot; Balmoral; legging, puttee, buskin, greave, galligaskin, moccasin, *gamache*, gambado, gaiter, spatter-dash, spat, antigropeles; stocking, hose, gaskins, trunk-hose, sock, hosiery.

glove, gauntlet, mitten, cuff, muffettee, wristband, sleeve.

swaddling cloth, baby-linen, *layette*; pocket-handkerchief.

shroud, etc. 363.

clothier, tailor, milliner, *costumier*, sempstress, seamstress, snip; dress-, habit-, breeches-, shoemaker; cordwainer, cobbler, Crispin, hosier, hatter; draper, linendraper, haberdasher, mercer.

V.invest; cover etc. 223; envelop, lap, involve; in-, en-wrap; wrap; fold —, wrap —, lap —, muffle-up; overlap; sheathe, swathe, swaddle, roll up in, shroud, circumvest.

vest, clothe, array, dress, dight, drape, robe, enrobe, attire, tire, garb, habilitate, apparel, accouter, rig, fit out; bedizen, deck etc. (*ornament*) 847; perk; equip, harness, caparison; dress up.

wear; don; put —, huddle —, slip- on; mantle.
Adj. invested etc. *v.*; habited; dight, -ed; clad, *costumé*, shod, *chaussé*; *en grande tenue* etc. (*show*) 882.
sartorial.

226. Divestment.—N. divestment; taking off, stripping, removal etc. *v.*

nudity; bareness etc. *adj.*; undress; dishabille etc. 225, altogether; nu-, denu-dation; decortication, depilation, excoriation, desquamation; molting; exfoliation.

baldness, alopecia, acomia.

V. divest; uncover etc. (*cover* etc. 223); denude, bare, strip; undress, unclothe, disrobe etc. (dress, enrobe, etc. 225); uncoif; dismantle; uncase; put —, take —, cast- off; shed, doff; husk, peel, pare, decorticate, desquamate; excoriate, skin, scalp, flay, bark, expose, lay open; exfoliate, molt, mew; cast the skin.

Adj. divested etc. *v.*; bare, naked, nude; undressed, -draped, -clad, -clothed, -appareled; exposed; in dishabille; *décolleté*; bald, threadbare, ragged, callow, roofless.

in -a state of nature, — nature's garb, — buff, — native buff, — birthday suit; *in puris naturalibus*; with nothing on, stark naked; bald as a coot, bare as the back of one's hand; out at elbows; barefoot; bareback; leaf-, nap-, hairless, shaved, clean shaven, tonsured, beardless, bald-headed, acomous.

227. Circumjacence.—N. circumjacence, ambience; environment, encompassment; atmosphere, medium; surroundings, *entourage*.

outpost; border etc. (*edge*) 231; girdle etc. (*circumference*) 230; outskirts, *boulevards*, suburbs, purlieus, precincts, *faubourgs, environs, banlieue*; neighborhood, vicinity.

V.lie -around etc. *adv.*; surround, beset, compass, encompass, environ, inclose, enclose, encircle, circle, embrace, circumvent, lap, gird; begird, girdle, engird; skirt, twine round; hem in etc. (*circumscribe*) 229; besiege, invest, blockade.

Adj. circum-jacent, -ambient, -fluent; ambient; surrounding etc. *v.*; circumferential, suburban.

Adv. around, about; without; on -every side, — all sides; right and left, all round, round about; in the neighborhood.

228. Interjacence.—N. inter-jacence, -currence, -venience, -location, -digitation, -penetration; permeation.

inter-jection, -polation, -lineation, -spersion, -calation; embolism.

inter-vention, -ference, -position; in-, ob-trusion; insinuation; insertion etc. 300; dovetailing; infiltration; intromission.

intermedi-um, -ary; go-between, agent, middleman, medium, bodkin, intruder, interloper; parenthesis, episode; fly-leaf.

partition, *septum*, diaphragm, mid-riff; party-wall, panel, vail, bulkhead, brattice, *cloison*; half-way house.

V.lie —, come —, get- between; intervene, slide in, interpenetrate, permeate.

put between, introduce, intromit, import; throw –, wedge –, edge –, jam –, worm –, foist –, run –, plough –, work- in; interpose, -ject, -calate. -polate, -line, -leave, -sperse, -weave, -lard, -digitate; let in, dovetail, splice, mortise; insinuate, smuggle; infiltrate, ingrain.

interfere, put in an oar, thrust one's nose in; intrude, obtrude; have a finger in the pie; introduce the thin end of the wedge; thrust in etc. (*insert*) 300.

Adj. inter-jacent, -current, -venient, -vening etc. *v.*, -mediate, -mediary, -calary, -sitital, -costal, -mural, -planetary, -stellar; embolismal.

parenthetical, episodic: mediterranean; intrusive; embosomed; merged, mean, middle, medium, median.

Adv. between, betwixt; 'twixt; among, -st; amid, st; 'mid, -st; in the thick of; betwixt and between; sandwich-wise; parenthetically, *obiter dictum*.

229. Circumscription.—N. circumscription, limitation, inclosure; confinement etc. (*restraint*) 751; circumvallation, encincture; envelope etc. 232.

V. circumscribe, limit, bound, confine, restrict, enclose; surround etc. 227; compass about; imprision etc. (*restrain*) 751; hedge –, wall –, rail-in; fence –, hedge- round; embar; picket, corral.

enfold, bury, incase, pack up, enshrine, inclasp; wrap up etc. (*invest*) 225; embosom.

Adj. circumscribed etc. *v.*; begirt, lapt; circumambient; buried –, immersed- in; embosomed, in the bosom of, imbedded, encysted, mewed up; imprisoned etc. 751; land-locked, in a ring fence.

230. Outline.—N. outline, circumference; perimeter, -phery; ambit, circuit, lines, *tournure*, *contour*, profile, *silhouette*, lineaments; bounds, coastline.

zone, belt, girth, band, baldric, zodiac, girdle, tire, cingle, clasp, girt; *cordon* etc. (*inclosure*) 232; circlet etc. 247.

V. outline, delineate, *silhouette*, circumscribe etc. 229; profile, block out.

Adj. outlined etc. *v.*; circumferential, perimetric, peripheral.

231. Edge.—N. edge, verge, brink, brow, brim, margin, border, confines, skirt, rim, felloe, felly, flange, side, mouth; jaws, chops, chaps, *fauces*; lip, muzzle.

threshold, door, porch; portal etc. (*opening*) 260; coast, shore, strand, beach, bank, wharf, quay, dock.

frame, fringe, flounce, frill, list, trimming, edging, skirting, hem, selvedge, welt; furbelow, valance, exergue.

Adj. border, marginal, skirting; labial; labiated, marginated.

232. Inclosure.—N. inclosure, enclosure, envelope; package, box, crate, case etc. (*receptacle*) 191; wrapper; girdle etc. 230.

pen, fold, croft, sty; pen-, in-, sheep--fold; paddock, pound, corral, kraal; yard, compound; net, seine net.

wall; hedge, -row; *espalier*; fence etc. (*defence*) 717; pale, paling, balustrade, rail, railing, gunwale; quickset hedge, park paling, circumvallation, *enciente*, ring fence.

barrier, barricade; gate; -way; door, hatch, *cordon*; prison etc. 752.

dike, dyke, ditch, fosse, moat, trench.

V. inclose; circumscribe etc. 229.

233. Limit.—N. limit, boundary, bounds, confine, *enclave*, term, bourn, verge, kerb-stone, curb-stone, but, pale; termin-ation, -us; stint, frontier, precinct, marches.

boundary line, landmark; line of demarcation, – circumvallation; pillars of Hercules; Rubicon, turning-point; *ne plus ultra*; sluice, flood-gate.

V. limit, bound, confine, define, circumscribe, demarcate, delimit, encompass.

Adj. definite; contermin-ate, -able, terminable, limitable; terminal, frontier, border, bordering, boundary.

Adv. thus far, – and no further.

234. Front.—N. front; fore, – part; foreground; forefront, face, disk, disc, frontage, *façade*, *proscenium*, facia, frontispiece; priority, anteriority; obverse [of a medal].

fore, – front- rank, first line; van, -guard; advanced guard; outpost, scout.

brow, forehead, visage, physiognomy, phiz, features, countenance, map, mug; rostrum, beak, bow, stem, prow, prore, jib, bowsprit; forecastle, pioneer etc.(*precursor*) 64; metoposcopy.

V. be –, stand- in front etc. *adj.*; front, face, confront, breast, brave; bend forwards; come to the -front, – fore.

Adj. fore, forward, anterior, front, frontal, head-on, leading, first, primary.

Adv. before; in -front, – the van, – advance; ahead, right ahead; fore-, head-most; in the foreground; before one's -face, – eyes; face to face, *vis-à-vis*.

235. Rear.—N. rear, back, posterior-ity; rear - rank, – guard; background, *hinterland*.

occiput, nape, scruff, chine; heels; tail, rump, croup, buttock, posteriors, bottom, seat, backside, scut, breech, *dorsum*, loin; dorsal –, lumbar-region; hind quarters.

stern poop, after-part, counter; postern, heel-, tail-piece, crupper.

wake; train etc. (*sequence*) 281.

reverse; other side of the shield.

V. be -behind etc. *adv.*; fall astern; bend backwards; bring up the rear; follow etc. 622; tail, shadow.

Adj. back, rear; hind, -er, -most, -ermost; postern, -erior; dorsal, after; caudal, lumbar; mizzen.

Adv. behind; in the -rear, – ruck, – back-

ground; behind one's back; at the -heels, — tail, — back- of; back to back.

after, -most, aft, abaft, astern, stern- most, aback, rear-, hind-, back-ward.

236. Laterality.—N. laterality; side, flank, beam, quarter, lee; hand; cheek, jowl, jole, wing; profile; temple, *parietes*, loin, haunch, hip.

gable, -end; broadside; lee side.

points of the compass; East, Orient, Levant; West, occident; orientation.

V. be -on one side etc. *adv.*; flank, outflank; sidle; skirt, border.

Adj. lateral, sidelong; collateral; parietal, flanking, skirting; flanked; sideling.

many-sided; multi-, bi-, tri-, quadri- lateral.

East-ern, -ward, -erly; orient, -al, auroral, Levantine; West-ern, -ward, -erly; occidental, Hesperian; equatorial.

Adv. side-ways. -long; broadside on; on one side, abreast, abeam, alongside, beside, aside; by, — the side of; side by side; cheek by jowl etc. (*near*) 197; to -windward, — leeward; laterally etc. *adj.*; right and left; on her beam ends.

237. Contraposition.—N. contraposition, opposition; polarity; inversion etc. 218; opposite side; antithesis; reverse, inverse; counterpart; antipodes; opposite poles, North and South.

V. be -opposite etc. *adj.*; subtend.

Adj. opposite; reverse, inverse; antipodal, subcontrary; fronting, facing, diametrically opposite.

Northern, Septentrional, Boreal, arctic; Southern, Austral, antarctic, polar.

Adv. over, — the way, — against; against; face to face, vis-à-vis; as poles asunder.

238. Dextrality.—N. dextrality; right, — hand; dexter, offside, starboard.

Adj. dextral, right-handed; ambidextral; dexterous, dextrorsal etc.

239. Sinistrality.—N. sinistrality; left, — hand; *sinister*, nearside, larboard, port.

Adj. sinistral, sinister, sinistrorsal etc., left-handed, sinistromanual, sinistrous.

240. Form.—N. form, figure, shape, physique; con-formation, -figuration; make, formation, frame, construction, design, cut, set, build, trim, cut of one's jib; stamp, type, cast, mold; fashion; contour etc. (*outline*) 230; structure etc. 329.

feature, lineament, outline, turn; phase etc. (*aspect*) 448; posture, attitude, *pose*.

[Science of form] morphology.

[Similarity of form] isomorphism.

forming etc. *v.*; form-, figur-, efform- ation; sculpture.

V. form, shape, figure, fashion, efform, carve, cut, chisel, hew, cast; rough-hew, -cast; sketch; block —, hammer- out; trim; lick —, put- into

shape; model, knead, work up into, set, mold, sculpture; cast, stamp; built etc. (*construct*) 161.

Adj. formed etc. *v.*

[Receiving form] plastic, fictile, full- fashioned etc.

[Giving form] plasmic, etc.

[Similar in form] isomorphous etc.

241. Amorphism. [Absence of form.] —N. amorphism, informity, uncouthness; unlicked cub, rough diamond; *rudis indigestaque moles*; disorder etc. 59; deformity etc. 243.

disfigure-, deface-ment, deformation; mutilation.

V. [Destroy form] deface, disfigure, deform, mutilate, truncate; derange etc. 61.

Adj. shapeless, amorphous, malformed, formless; un-formed, -hewn, -fashioned, -shapen; rough, rude, Gothic, barbarous, rugged, in the rough; misshapen etc. 243.

242. Symmetry. [Regularity of form.]—N. symmetry, shapeliness, finish; beauty etc. 845; proportion, eurythmy, eurythmic, uniformity, parallelism; bi-, tri-, multi-lateral symmetry; centrality etc. 222.

arborescence, branching, ramification.

Adj. symmetrical, shapely, well set, finished; beautiful etc. 845; classic, chaste, severe.

regular, uniform, balanced; equal etc. 27; parallel, coextensive.

arbor-escent, -iform; dendr-iform, -oid; branching; ramous, ramose.

243. Distortion. [Irregularity of form.]—N. dis-, de-, con-tortion; knot, mop, warp, buckle, screw, twist; crookedness etc. (*obliquity*) 217; grimace; deformity; mal-, malcon-formation; monstrosity, misproportion, want of symmetry, *anamorphosis*; ugliness etc. 846; teratology.

V. distort, contort, twist, warp etc. *n.*; wrest, writhe, make faces, deform, misshape.

Adj. distorted etc. *v.*; out of shape, irregular, unsymmetric, awry, wry, askew, crooked, sinuous; anamorphous; not -true, — straight; on one side, crump, deformed; mis-shapen, -begotten; mis-, ill-proportioned; ill-made; grotesque, crooked as a ram's horn; hump-, hunch-, bunch-, crook-backed; bandy, bandy-, bow-legged; bow-, knock-kneed; splay-, club-footed; taliped; round-shouldered; snub-nosed; curtailed of one's fair proportions; scalene, stumpy etc. (*short*) 201; gaunt etc. (*thin*) 203; bloated etc. 194.

Adv. all manner of ways.

244. Angularity.—N. angular-ity, -ness; aduncity; angle, cusp, bend; fold etc. 258; notch etc. 257; fork, bifurcation.

elbow, knee, knuckle, ankle, groin, crotch, crane, fluke, scythe, sickle, zigzag, kimbo.

corner, nook, recess, niche, oriel.

right angle etc. (*perpendicular*) 212; obliquity etc. 217; angle of 45 degrees, miter; acute —, obtuse —, salient —, re-entrant —, spherical —, solid —, dihedral- angle.

angular -measurement, – elevation, – distance, – velocity; trigon-, goni-ometry; altimetry; clin-, graph-, goni-ometer; theodolite; transit circle; sextant, quadrant; dichotomy.

triangle, trigon, wedge; rectangle, square, lozenge, diamond; rhomb, -us; quadr-angle, -ilateral; parallelogram; quadrature; poly-, penta-, hexa-, hepta-, octa-, deca-gon.

Platonic bodies; cube, rhomboid; tetra-, penta-, hexa-, octa-, dodeca-, icosa-hedron; prism, pyramid; parallelopiped.

V. bend, fork, bifurcate, crinkle, divaricate, branch, ramify.

Adj. angular, bent, crooked, aduncous, uncinated, aquiline, jagged, serrated; falc-iform, -ated; furcular, furcated, forked, bifurcate, crotched; zigzag; dovetailed; knock-kneed, crinkled, akimbo, kimbo, geniculated; oblique etc. 217.

fusiform, wedge-shaped, cuneiform; tri-angular, -gonal, -lateral; quadr-angular, -ilateral; rectangular, square, foursquare, multilateral; polygonal etc. *n.*; cubical, rhomboidal, pyramidal.

245. Curvature.—**N.** curv-ature, -ity, -ation; incurv-ity, -ation; bend; flex- ure, -ion; conflexure; crook, hook, bought, bending; de-, inflexion; arcuation, devexity, turn; deviation, *détour*, sweep; curl, -ing; bough; recurv-ity, -ation; sinuosity etc. 248; aduncity.

curve, arc, arch, arcade, vault, dome, bow, crescent, *meniscus*, half-moon, lunule, horse-shoe, loop, crane-neck; para-, hyper-bola; catenary, festoon; conch-, cardi-oid; caustic, instep; tracery.

V. be -curved etc. *adj.*; sweep, swag, sag; deviate etc. 279; turn; re-enter.

render -curved etc. *adj.*; bend, curve, incurvate; de-, in-flect; crook; turn, round, arch, arcuate, arch over, loop the loop, concamerate; bow, coil, curl, recurve, frizzle.

Adj. curved etc. *v.*; curvi-form, -lineal, -linear, devex, devious; recurv-ed, -ous; *retroussé*; crump; bowed etc. *v.*; vaulted; hooked; falc-iform, -ated; semicircular, crescentic; lun-iform, -ular; semilunar, meniscal; conchoidal; cord-iform, -ated; cardioid; heart-, bell-, pear-, fig-shaped; reniform; lenti-form, -cular; bow-legged etc. (*distorted*) 243; oblique etc. 217; circular etc. 247.

246. Straightness.—**N.** straightness, rectilinearity, directness; inflexibility etc. (*stiffness*) 323; straight –, right –, direct-, bee- line; short cut.

V. be -straight etc. *adj*; have no turning; not -incline, – bend, – turn, – deviate- to either side; go straight; steer for etc. (*direction*) 278.

render straight, straighten, rectify; set –, put-straight; un-bend, -fold, -curl etc. 248, -ravel etc. 219, -wrap.

Adj. straight; rectiline-ar, -al; direct, even, right, true, in a line; unbent etc. *v.*; un-deviating, -turned, -distorted, -swerving; straight as an arrow etc. (*direct*) 278; inflexible etc. 323.

247. Circularity. [Simple circularity.]—**N.** circularity, roundness; rotundity etc. 249.

circle, circlet, ring, washer, areola, hoop, round-let, *annulus*, annulet, bracelet, armlet, armilla; ringlet; eye, loop, wheel; cycle, orb, orbit, rundle, zone, belt, *cordon*, band; sash, girdle, cestus, cincture, baldric, fillet, *fascia*, wreath, garland; crown, corona, coronet, chaplet, snood, necklace, collar; noose, lasso, lariat.

ellipse, oval, ovule; ellipsoid, cycloid; epicycloid, -cycle; semi-circle; quadrant, sextant, sector.

V. make -round etc. *adj.*; round.

go round; encircle etc. 227; describe -a circle etc. 311.

Adj. round, rounded, circular, annular, orbicular; oval, ovate; elliptic, -al; ovoid, egg-shaped; pear-shaped etc. 245; cycloidal etc. *n.*; spherical etc. 249.

248. Convolution. [Complex circularity.]—**N.** winding etc. *v.*; con-, in-, circum-volution; wave, undulation, tortuosity, anfractuosity; sinu-osity, -ation, sinuousness; meandering, circuit, circumbendibus, twist, twirl, windings and turnings, *ambages*; torsion; inosculation; reticulation etc. (*crossing*) 219.

coil, roll, curl, buckle, spire, spiral, helix, corkscrew, worm, volute, whorl, rundle; tendril; scollop, scallop, escalop; kink.

serpent, snake, eel, maze, labyrinth.

V. be -convoluted etc. *adj.*; wind, twine, turn and twist, twirl; wave, undulate, meander; inosculate; entwine, intwine; twist, coil, roll; wrinkle, curl, crisp, twill; frizz, -le; crimp, crape, indent, scollop, scallop; wring, intort; contort; wreathe etc. (*cross*) 219.

Adj. convoluted; winding, twisted etc. *v.*; tortile, tortive; wavy; und-ated, -ulatory; circling, snaky, snake-like, serpentine; serpent-, anguill-, vermiform; vermicular; mazy, tortuous, anfractuous, sinuous, flexuous, wavy, sigmoidal.

involved, intricate, complicated, perplexed; labyrinth-ic, -ian, -ine; circuitous; peristaltic; daedalian, curly.

wreathy, frizzly, *crêpé*, buckled; ravelled etc. (*in disorder*) 59.

spiral, coiled, helical, turbinated.

Adv. in and out, round and round.

249. Rotundity.—**N.** rotundity; roundness etc. *adj.*; cylindricity; spher-icity, -oidity; globosity.

cylin-der, -droid; barrel, drum; roll, -er; *rouleau*, column, rolling-pin, rundle; chimney-pot, drain-pipe.

cone, conoid; pear-, egg-, bell-shape.

sphere, globe, orb, orbit, ball, boulder, bowlder; spher-, ellips-, ge-, glob-oid, oblong –, oblate-spheroid; drop, spherule, globule, vesicle, bulb, bullet, pellet, *pelote*, clew, pill, marble, pea, knob, pommel, knot.

V. render -spherical etc. *adj.*; form into a sphere, sphere, roll into a ball; give -rotundity etc. *n.*; round.

Adj. rotund; round etc. (*circular*) 247; cylindric, -ical, -oid; columnar, lumbriciform; conic, -al; spher-ical, -oidal; glob-ular, -ated, -ous, -ose; egg-, bell-, pear-shaped; ov-oid, -iform; gibbous; campaniform, -ulate, -iliform; fungiform, bead-like,

moniliform, pyriform, bulbous; *teres atque rotundus*; round as -an orange, − an apple, − a ball, − a billiard ball, − a cannon ball.

250. Convexity.—N. convexity, prominence, projection, swelling, gibbosity, bilge, bulge, protuberance, protrusion; excrescency, camber.

intumescence; tumor; tubercle, -osity; excrescence; hump, hunch, bunch, gnarl.

tooth, knob, elbow, process, *apophysis*, condyle, bulb, node, nodule, nodosity, tongue, *dorsum*, boss, embossment, bump, clump; sugar-loaf etc. (*sharpness*) 253; bow; mamelon.

pimple, wen, wheal, *papula*, postule, pock, proud flesh, growth, goiter, *sarcoma*, caruncle, corn, bunion, wart, furnuncle, polypus, adenoid, fungus, fungosity, *exostosis*, bleb, blister, blain; boil etc. (*disease*) 655; bubble, blob.

papilla, nipple, teat, pap, breast, dug, mammilla; proboscis, .ose, neb, beak, snout, nozzle, snozzle; Adam's apple; belly, paunch, corporation; withers, back, shoulder, lip, flange.

peg, button, stud, ridge, rib, jutty, trunnion, snag.

cupola, dome, bee-hive; arch, balcony, eaves; pilaster.

relief, relievo, *cameo*; *basso-*, *mezzo-*, *alto-rilievo*; low-, bas-, high-relief.

hill etc. (*height*) 206; cape, promontory, mull; fore-, head-land; point of land, naze, ness, mole, jetty, hummock, ledge, spur.

V. be -prominent etc. *adj.*; project, bulge, protrude, bag, belly, pout, bouge, bunch; jut −, stand −, stick −, poke- out; stick −, bristle −, start −, cock −, shoot- up; swell −, hang −, bend-over; beetle.

render -prominent etc. *adj.*; raise 307; emboss, chase.

Adj. convex, prominent, protuberant, underhung, undershot; projecting etc. *v.*; bossed, bossy, nodular, bunchy; clav-ate, -ated; hummocky, *moutonné*, mammiform; papul-ous, -ose; hemispheric, bulbous; bowed, arched; bold; bellied; tuber-ous, -culous; tumorous; cornute, knobby, odontoid; lenti-form, -cular; gibbous.

salient, in relief, raised, *repoussé*; bloated etc. (*expanded*) 194.

251. Flatness.—N. flatness etc. *adj.*; smoothness etc. 255.

plane; level etc. 213; plate, platter, table, tablet, slab.

V. render flat, flatten, squash; level etc. 213.

Adj. flat, plane, even, flush, scutiform, discoid; level etc. (*horizontal*) 213; smooth; flat as -a pancake, − a fluke, − a flounder, − a board, − my hand.

252. Concavity.—N. concavity, depression, dip; hollow, -ness; indentation, *intaglio*, cavity, antrum, dent, dint, dimple, follicle, pit, *sinus*, *alveolus*, *lacuna*; excavation, trench, shaft, sap, mine, tunnel, burrow; trough etc. (*furrow*) 259; honeycomb.

cup, basin, crater, punch-bowl; cell etc. (*receptacle*) 191; socket, faucet.

valley, vale, dale, dell, gap, dingle, combe, bottom, slade, strath, glade, grove, glen, cave, cavern, cove; grot, -to; alcove, *cul-de-sac*, blind alley; gully etc. 198; arch etc. (*curve*) 245; bay etc. (*of the sea*) 343.

excavator, sapper, miner.

V. be -concave etc. *adj.*; retire, cave in.

render -concave etc. *adj.*; depress, hollow; scoop, − out; gouge, dig, delve, excavate, dent, dint, mine, sap, undermine, burrow, tunnel, stave in.

Adj. depressed etc. *v.*; concave, hollow, stove in; dished; spoon-like; retiring; retreating; cavernous; porous etc. (*with holes*) 260; cellular, spongy, spongious; honeycombed, alveolar; infundibul-ar, -iform; funnel-, bell-shaped; campaniform, capsular; vaulted, arched.

253. Sharpness.—N. sharpness etc. *adj.*; acuity, acumination; spinosity.

point, spike, spine, *spiculum*, tine; needle, pin; tack, nail; prick, -le; spur, rowel, barb; spit, cusp; horn, antler; snag; tag; thorn, bristle.

nib, tooth, incisor, tusk; spoke, cog, ratchet.

crag, crest *arête*, cone, peak, sugar-loaf, pike, *aiguille*; spire, pyramid, steeple.

beard, *chevaux de frise*, porcupine, hedgehog, brier, bramble, thistle; comb, awn, bur.

wedge; knife-, cutting- edge; blade, edge-tool, cutlery, knife, penknife, whittle, razor; scalpel, bistoury, lancet; chisel; ploughshare, coulter; hatchet, axe, pick-axe, mattock, pick, adze, bill; bill-hook, cleaver, cutter; skiver; scythe, sickle, scissors, shears; sword etc. (*arms*) 727; bodkin etc. (*perforator*) 262.

sharpener, hone, strop; grind-, whet-stone; steel, emery.

V. be -sharp etc. *adj.*; taper to a point; bristle with.

render -sharp etc. *adj.*; sharpen, point, aculeate, acuminate, whet, barb, spiculate, set, strop, grind.

cut etc. (*sunder*) 44.

Adj. sharp, keen; acute; aci-cular, -form; aculeated, -minated; pointed; tapering; conical, pyramidal; mucron-ate, -ated; spindle-, needle-shaped; spiked, spiky, ensiform, peaked, salient, cusp-ed; -idate, -idated; corn-ute, -uted, -iculate; prickly; spiny, spinous; thorny, bristling, muricated, pectinated, studded, thistly, briery; craggy etc. (*rough*) 256; snaggy; digitated, two-edged, fusiform; denti-form, -culated; toothed; odontoid; star-like; stell-ated, -iform; arrow-headed; arrowy, barbed, spurred, sagittal; spear-shaped, hastate; horned; conical.

cutting; sharp-, knife-edged; sharp −, keen-as a razor; sharp as a needle; sharpened etc. *v.*; set.

254. Bluntness.—N. bluntness etc. *adj.*; abruptness, dullness.

V. be −, render- blunt etc. *adj.*; obtund, dull; take off the -point, − edge; turn.

Adj. blunt, obtuse, dull, bluff.

255. Smoothness.—N. smoothness etc. *adj.*; polish, gloss; lubric-ity, -ation.

down, velvet, silk, satin; slide; bowling green etc. (*level*) 213; glass, ice; asphalt, pavement, flags.

roller, steam-roller; iron, flat-iron, tailor's goose; sand-, emery-paper; burnisher, turpentine and bees-wax.

V. smooth, -en; plane; file; mow, shave; level, roll; macadamize; polish, burnish, planish, levigate, calender, glaze; iron, hot-press, mangle; lubricate etc. (*oil*) 332.

Adj. smooth; polished etc. *v.*; even; level etc. 213; plane etc. (*flat*) 251; sleek, glossy; silken, silky; lanate, downy, velvety; glabrous, slippery, glassy, lubricous, oily, soft; unwrinkled; smooth as -glass, − ice, − velvet, − oil; slippery as an eel; wooly etc. (*feathery*) 256.

256. Roughness.—N. roughness etc. *adj.*; tooth, grain, texture, ripple; asperity, rugosity, salebrosity, corrugation, nodosity; arborescence etc. 242.

brush, hair, beard, shag, mane, whisker, mutton-chops, *moustache*, *mustachio*, imperial, Van Dyke, tress, lock, curl, ringlet, *fimbriae*, *cilia*, *villi*; eye-lashes, eye-brows, love-lock.

plum-age, -osity; plume, *panache*, crest; feather, tuft, tussock, fringe, toupee.

wool, velvet, plush, nap, pile, floss, fluff, fur, down; byssus, moss, bur.

V. be -rough etc. *adj.*; go against the grain.

render -rough etc. *adj.*; roughen, rough cast, knurl; ruffle, crisp, crumple, crinkle, corrugate, engrail; set on edge, stroke −, rub- the wrong way, rumple.

Adj. rough, uneven; scabrous, knotted; nodular; rug-ged, -ose, -ous; asperous, crisp, salebrous, gnarled, unpolished, unsmooth, rough-hewn; knurled, cross-grained, crag-gy, -ged; crankling, scraggy, jagged, unkempt, prickly etc. (*sharp*) 253; arborescent etc. 242; leafy, well-wooded; feathery; plum-ose, -igerous; tufted, fimbriated, hairy, bristly, ciliated, filamentous, hirsute; crin-ose, -ite; bushy, hispid, villous, pappous, bearded, pilous, shaggy, shagged; fringed, befringed; set-ous, -ose, - aceous; 'like quills upon the fretful porcupine;' rough as a -nutmeg grater, − bear.

downy, velvety, flocculent, wolly; lan-ate, -ated; lanugin-ous, ose; tomentous.

Adv. against the grain, in the rough, on edge.

257. Notch.—N. notch, dent, nick, cut; indent, -ation; serration; dimple.

embrasure, battlement, machicolation; saw, tooth, crenelle, scallop, scollop, vandyke.

V. notch, nick, cut, pink, mill, score, dent, in-dent, jag, scarify, scotch, crimp, scollop, crenulate, vandyke.

Adj. notched etc. *v.*; crenate, -d; dentate, -d; denticulate, -d; toothed, palmated, serrated.

258. Fold.—N. fold, plicature, pleat, plait, ply, crease; tuck, gather; flexion, flexure, joint, elbow, doubling, duplicature, wrinkle, rimple, crinkle, crankle, crumple, rumple, rivel, ruck, ruffle, dog's ear, corrugation, frounce, flounce, lapel; pucker, crow's feet.

V. fold, double, plicate, pleat, plait, crease, wrinkle, crinkle, crankle, curl, smock, cockle up, crocker, rimple, rumple, frizzle, frounce, rivel, twill, corrugate, ruffle, crimple, crumple, pucker; turn −, double- -down, − under; tuck, ruck, hem, gather.

Adj. folded etc. *v.*

259. Furrow.—N. furrow, groove, rut, *sulcus*, scratch, streak, *striae*, crack, score, incision, slit; chamfer, fluting.

channel, gutter, trench, ditch, dike, dyke, moat, fosse, trough, kennel; ravine etc. (*interval*) 198.

V. furrow etc. *n.*; flute, groove, carve, corrugate, plough; incise, chase, enchase, grave, engrave, etch, bite in, cross-hatch.

Adj. furrowed etc. *v.*; ribbed, straited, sulcated, fluted, canaliculated; bisculc-ous, -ate; trisulcate; corduroy.

260. Opening.—N. hole, foramen; puncture, blow-out, perforation; pin-, key-, loop-, port-, peep-, mouse-, pigeon-hole; eye, − of a needle; eyelet; slot.

opening; apert-ure, -ness; hiation, yawning, oscitancy, dehiscence, patefaction, pandiculation; gap, chasm etc. (*interval*) 198.

embrasure, window, casement, light; sky-, fan-light; lattice; bay-, bow-window; oriel; dormer, lantern.

out-, in-let; vent, vomitory; *embouchure*; orifice, mouth, sucker, muzzle, throat, gullet, placket; weasand, wizen, nozzle, *esophagus*.

portal, porch, gate, ostiary, postern, wicket, trap-door, hatch, door; arcade; gate-, door-, hatch-, gang-way; lych-gate.

way, path etc. 627; thoroughfare; channel, passage, tube, pipe; waterpipe etc. 350; air-pipe etc. 351; vessel, tubule, canal, gut, fistula; adjutage, ajutage; chimney, smoke stack, flue, tap, funnel, gully, tunnel, main; mine, pit, adit, shaft; gallery.

alley, aisle, glade, lane, vista.

bore, caliber; pore; blind orifice.

por-ousness, -osity; sieve, cullender, colander; grater, shredder; cribble, riddle, screen; honeycomb.

apertion, perforation; piercing etc. *v.*; terebration, empalement, pertusion, puncture, acupuncture, penetration.

opener, corkscrew, can opener, key, master-key, *passe-partout*.

V. open, ope, gape, dehisce, yawn, bilge; fly open.

perforate, pierce, empierce, tap, bore, drill; mine etc. (*scoop out*) 252; tunnel; trans-pierce, -fix; en-filade, impale, spike, spear, gore, spit, stab, pink, puncture, lance, trepan, trephine, stick, prick, rid-dle, punch; stave in.

cut a passage through; make -way, − room- for. un-cover, -close, -rip; lay −, cut −, rip −, throw-open.

Adj. open; perforated etc. *v.*; perforate; wide open, agape, ajar; un-closed, -stopped; oscitant, gaping, yawning; patent.

tubular, cannular, fistulous; per-vious, -meable; foraminous; vesi-, vas-cular; porous, follicular,

cribriform, honeycombed, infundibular, riddled; tubul-ous, -ated, piped.

opening etc. *v.*; aperient.

Int. *open sesame!*

261. Closure.—N. closure, occlusion, blockade; shutting up etc. *v.*; obstruction etc. (*hindrance*) 706; gag; embolism; contraction etc. 195; infarction; con-, ob-stipation; blind -alley, — corner; *cul-de-sac, caecum*; imperforation, -viousness etc. *adj.*; -meability; stopper etc. 263; *operculum*.

V. close, occlude, plug; block —, stop —, fill —, bung —, cork —, button —, stuff —, shut —, dam-up, obturate; blockade; obstruct etc. (*hinder*) 706; bar, bolt, stop, seal, plumb; choke, throttle; ram down, tamp, dam, cram; trap, clinch; put to —, shut- the door; batten down the hatches.

Adj. closed etc. *v.*; shut, operculated; unopened.

unpierced, imporous, caecal; imperforate, -vious, -meable; impenetrable; un-, im-passable; invious; path-, way-less; untrodden.

unventilated; air-, water-tight; hermetically sealed; tight, snug.

262. Perforator.—N. perforator, piercer, borer, auger, gimlet, stylet, drill, wimble, awl, bradawl, scoop, terrier, corkscrew, dibble, trocar, trepan, trephine, probe, bodkin, needle, stiletto, broach, reamer, rimer, warder, lancet; punch, -eon; spikebit, gouge; spear etc. (*weapon*) 727.

263. Stopper.—N. stopper, stopple; plug, cork, bung, spike, spill, stop-cock, tap; rammer; ram, -rod; piston; stopgap; wadding, stuffing, padding, stopping, dossil, pledget, tompion, tourniquet, obturator; wad.

cover etc. 223; valve, slide valve; vent-peg, spigot.

janitor, door —, gate- keeper, porter, commissionaire, *concierge*, warder, beadle, Cerberus, usher, guard, sentry, sentinel; ostiary.

264. Motion. [Successive change of place.*]—**N.** motion, movement, move; motivity, motility, going etc. *v.*; unrest.

stream, current, flow, flux, run, course, stir; conduction, evolution; kinematics.

step, rate, pace, tread, stride, gait, clip, port, footfall, cadence, carriage, velocity, angular velocity; progress, locomotion; journey etc. 266; voyage etc. 267; transit etc. 270.

restlessness etc. (*changeableness*) 149; mobility; movableness, motive power; laws of motion; mobilization.

V. be -in motion etc. *adj.*; move, go, hie, gang, budge, stir, pass, flit; hover -round, — about; shift, slide, slither, glide; roll, — on; flow, stream, run, drift, sweep along; wander etc. (*deviate*) 279; walk etc. 266; change —, shift- one's -place, — quarters; dodge; keep -going, — moving.

put —, set- in motion; move; impel etc. 276; propel etc. 284; render movable, mobilize.

Adj. moving etc. *v.*; in motion; motile, transitional; motory, motive; shifting, movable, mobile, mercurial, unquiet; restless etc. (*changeable*) 149; nomadic etc. 266; erratic etc. 279.

Adv. under way; on the -move, — wing, — tramp, — march.

*A thing cannot be said to *move* from one place to another, unless it passes in succession through every intermediate place; hence motion is only such a change of place as is *successive*. 'Rapid, swift, etc., as thought' are therefore incorrect expressions.

265. Quiescence.—N. rest; stillness etc. *adj.*; quiescence; stag-nation, -nancy; fixity, immobility, catalepsy; indisturbance; quietism.

quiet, tranquillity, calm; repose etc. 687; peace; dead calm, anticyclone; statue-like repose; silence etc. 403; not a -breath of air, — mouse stirring; sleep etc. (*inactivity*) 683.

pause, lull etc. (*cessation*) 142; stand, — still; standing still etc. *v.*; lock; dead -lock, — stop, — stand; full stop; fix; embargo.

resting-place; bivouac; home etc. (*abode*) 189; pillow etc. (*support*) 215; haven etc. (*refuge*) 666; goal etc. (*arrival*) 292.

V. be -quiescent etc. *adj.*; stand —, lie- still; keep quiet, repose, hold the breath.

remain, stay; stand, lie to, ride at anchor, remain *in situ*, mark time, tarry; bring —, heave —, lay- to; pull —, draw- up; hold, halt; stop, — short; rest, pause, anchor; cast —, come to an- anchor; rest on one's oars; repose on one's laurels, take breath; stop etc. (*discontinue*) 142.

stagnate, vegetate; *quieta non movere*; let -alone, — well alone; abide, rest and be thankful; keep within doors, stay at home, go to bed.

dwell etc. (*be present*) 186; settle etc. (*be located*) 184; alight etc. (*arrive*) 292.

stick, — fast; stand, — like a post; not stir a -peg, — step; be at a -stand etc. *n.*

quell, becalm, hush, stay; lull to sleep, lay an embargo on; put the brake on.

Adj. quiescent, still; motion-, move-less; fixed; stationary; at -rest, — a stand, — a stand-still, — anchor; stock-still; immotile; standing still etc. *v.*; sedentary, untravelled, stay-at-home; becalmed; stagnant, quiet; un-moved, -disturbed, -ruffled; calm, restful; cataleptic; immovable etc. (*stable*) 150; sleeping etc. (*inactive*) 683; silent etc. 403; still as -a statue; — a mouse, — a post, — a mouse, — death.

Adv. at a stand etc. *adj.*; *tout court*; at the halt.

Int. stop! stay! avast! halt! hold, — hard! whoa!

Phr. *requiescat in pace*.

266. Journey. [Locomotion by land.]—**N.** travel; traveling etc. *v.*; wayfaring, campaigning.

journey, excursion, expedition, tour, trip, grand tour, circuit, peregrination, discursion, ramble, pilgrimage, *trek*, course, ambulation, march, walk, hike, promenade, constitutional, stroll, saunter, tramp, jog-trot, turn, stalk, perambulation; noctambulation; somnambulism, sleep walking; outing, ride, drive, airing, jaunt.

equitation, horsemanship, riding, *manège*, ride and tie.

roving, vagrancy, pererration; marching and countermarching; nomadism; vagabond-ism, -age; gadding; flit, -ting; migration; e-, im-, de-, inter-migration.

plan, itinerary, guide; hand-, road- book; Baedeker, Murray, Bradshaw, time table.

procession, parade, cavalcade, caravan, file, *cortège*, column.

[Organs and instruments of locomotion] vehicle etc. 272; locomotive etc. 271; legs, feet, pegs, pins, trotters.

traveler etc. 268.

V. travel, journey, course; tour; take –, go- a journey, take –, go out for- -a walk etc. *n.*; have a run; take the air.

flit, take wing; migrate, emigrate, *trek*; rove, prowl, roam, range, patrol, pace up and down, traverse; scour –, traverse- the country; peragrate; per-, circum-ambulate; nomadize, wander, ramble, stroll, saunter, hover, go one's rounds, straggle; gad; – about; expatiate.

walk, march, step, tread, pace, plod, wend; promenade; trudge, tramp; stalk, stride, straddle, strut, foot it, stump, bundle, bowl along, toddle; paddle; tread –, follow –, pursue- a path.

take horse, ride, drive, trot, amble, canter, prance, fisk, frisk, *caracoler*; gallop etc. (*move quickly*) 274; motor, cycle, taxi; go by -car, – train, – tram, – bus, – plane.

peg –, jog –, wag –, shuffle- on; stir one's stumps; bend one's -steps, – course; make –, find –, wend –, pick –, thread –, plough-one's way; coast, slide, glide, skim, skate, ski; march in procession, file off, defile.

go –, repair –, resort –, hie –, betake oneself-to.

Adj. traveling etc. *v.*; ambulatory, itinerant, peripatetic, perambulatory, roving, rambling, gadding, discursive, vagrant, migratory, nomadic; circumforane-an, -ous; somnambular, nocti-, mundi-vagant; locomotive, automotive, self-moving.

way-faring, -worn; travel-stained.

Adv. on -foot, – horseback, – Shanks's mare; by the Marrowbone stage; *in transitu* etc. 270; *en route* etc. 282.

Int. come along!

267. Navigation. [Locomotion by water, or air.]—**N.** navigation; aquatics; boating, cruising, yachting; ship etc. 273; oar, scull, sweep, punt pole, paddle, – wheel, screw, propeller, stern wheel, sail, canvas.

natation, swimming; fin, flipper, fish's tail.

aeronautics, aviation, flying, winging, cruising, gliding, ballooning; blind –, instrument – flying; avigation, take-off.

flight, trip, run; solo –, nolo (pilotless) –, super-sonic –, test – flight; air -lift, -drop; shuttle, recon-naisence, mission, dry run (coll.); search mission, combat flight, sortie, air raid, bombing mission; air – support, – cover, – umbrella; formation flying, maneuvers, aerobatics, stunt flying (coll.), diving, rolling, barrel roll, spin, tail spin, loop, buzzing.

landing, instrument –, crash – landing.

angle, center, axis, stability, load, pressure, tor-sion, torque, thrust, propulsion, jet propulsion, pitch, lift, dray, yaw, resistance, drift, flow, wash.

course, heading, altitude; air -route, -lane.

voyage, sail, cruise, passage, circumnavigation, *periplus*; head-, stern-, lee-way.

astro-, cosmo- nautics; space –, in-terplanetary – travel; space – exploration, – flight.

mariner, aeronaut etc. 269.

V. sail; put to sea etc. (*depart*) 293; take ship, get under way; spread -sail, – canvas; gather way, have way on; make –, carry- sail; plough the -waves, – deep, – main, – ocean; walk the waters.

navigate, warp, luff, scud, boom, kedge; drift, course, cruise, coast; hug the -shore, – land; cir-cumnavigate.

ply the oar, row, paddle, pull, scull, punt, steam.

swim, float; buffet the waves, ride the storm, skim, *effleurer*, dive, wade.

fly, pilot, copilot, astronavigate, solo, take off, taxi, ascend, climb, stunt, spin, loop, roll, dive, buzz, land, descend, level off, bail out, parachute.

Adj. sailing etc. *v.*; seafaring, nautical, maritime, naval; sea-going, coasting; afloat; navigable, aquatic, natatory.

volitant, volant, aerostatic, aerial, aeronautic; alar, alate, pennate.

Adv. under -way, – sail, – canvas, – steam; on the wing.

268. Traveler.—N. traveler, wayfarer, voyager, itinerant, passenger.

tourist, excursionist, globe-trotter; explorer, ad-venturer, mountaineer, Alpine Club; peregrinator, wanderer, rover, straggler, rambler; bird of passage; gad-about, -ling; vagrant, scatterling, land-loper; waifs and estrays, wastrel, stray; loafer; tramp, -er, hobo, beachcomber, vagabond, nomad, Bohemian, gipsy, Arab, Wandering Jew, Hadji, pilgrim, palmer; peripatetic; somnambulist; sleep walker, noctambulist; emigrant, fugitive, refugee, *émigré*.

runner, courier, King's messenger; Mercury, Iris, Ariel, comet.

pedestrian, walker, foot-passenger; cyclist; wheelman.

rider, horseman, equestrian, cavalier, jockey, rough rider, trainer, breaker, huntsman.

driver, coachman, whip, Jehu, charioteer, postilion, post-boy, carter, wagoner, drayman, truckman; cab-man, -driver; *voiturier*, *vetturino*, *condottiere*; engine-driver; stoker, fireman, guard, brakeman, conductor; chauffeur, automobilist, motorist, motor –, truck –, taxi- driver.

269. Mariner.—N. sailor, mariner, navigator, argonaut; sea-man, -farer, -faring man; yachtsman; tar, jack tar, salt, gob, sea-dog, shellback, able seaman, A.B.; man-of-war's man, bluejacket, marine, jolly; midshipman, middy, reefer; captain, commander, master mariner, skipper, mate; ship-, boat-, ferry-, water-, lighter-, barge-, longshore-man, hoveller; bargee, gondolier; oar-, -sman; rower; boat-, cock-swain; coxswain; steersman, helmsman, pilot; crew; lascar.

aerial navigator, navigator; aero-, astro-, cosmo-naut; balloonist, Icarus, aviator, pilot, flyer, copilot, spaceman; fighter –, bomber – pilot; bombardier, gunner; meteorologist; stewardess, aviatrix, aviatress; ground crew, aeromechanic, aeronautical engineer; parachutist, paratrooper.

270. Transference.—N. transfer, -ence; trans-, e-location; displacement; *meta-stasis*, *-thesis*; removal; re-, a-motion; relegation; de-, asportation; extradition, conveyance, draft; carrying, carriage; convection, -duction, -tagion, infection; transfusion; transfer etc. (*of property*) 783.

transit, transition; passage, ferry, gestation; portage, porterage, carting, cartage; shoveling etc. *v.*; vect-ion, -ure, -itation; shipment, freight, wafture; trans-mission, -port, -portation, -umption, - plantation, -lation; shift-, dodg-ing; dispersion etc. 73; transposition etc. (*interchange*) 148; traction etc. 285.

[Thing transferred] drift, alluvium, detritus, *moraine*; gift, legacy, bequest, lease; freight, mails, cargo, luggage, baggage, goods.

V. trans-fer, -mit, -port, -place, -plant; convey, assign, carry, bear; fetch and carry; carry —, ferry-over; hand, pass, forward; shift; conduct, convoy, bring, fetch, reach.

send, delegate, consign, mail post, relegate, turn over to, pass the buck, deliver; ship, embark; waft; switch, shunt; transpose etc. (*interchange*) 148; displace etc. 185; throw etc. 284; drag etc. 285.

shovel, lade, dip, ladle, bale, decant, draft off, transfuse.

Adj. transferred etc. *v.*; drifted; movable, portable, -ative; conductive; contagious, infectious.

transferable, assignable, conveyable, devisable, negotiable, transmissible.

Adv. from -hand to hand, — pillar to post.

on —, by- the way; on the -road, — wing; as one goes; *in transitu, en route, chemin faisant, en passant*, in mid-progress.

271. Carrier.—N. carrier, porter, red cap, bearer, messenger, postman, tranter, conveyer; stevedore; coolie; conductor, locomotive, tractor, caterpillar tractor, motor.

beast of burden, cattle, horse steed, nag, palfrey, Arab, blood horse, thorough-bred, galloway, charger, courser, racer, hunter, jument, pony, filly, colt, foal, barb, roan, jade, hack, *bidet*, pad, cob, tit, punch, roadster, goer; race-, pack-, draft-, cart-, dray-, post-horse, mount; Shetland pony, sheltie; garran; jennet, genet, bayard, mare, stallion, gelding; stud.

Pegasus, Bucephalus, Rozinante.

ass, donkey, jackass, mule, hinny; sumpter -horse, — mule; reindeer; camel, dromedary, mehari, llama, elephant; carrier pigeon.

carriage etc. (*vehicle*) 272; ship etc. 273.

Adj. equine, asinine.

272. Vehicle.—N. vehicle, conveyance, carriage, car, caravan, van, furniture van, pantechnicon; wagon, wain, dray, cart, lorry.

carriole; sledge, sled, sleigh, bob-sleigh, toboggan, *luge*, truck, tram; limber, tumbrel, pontoon; barrow; wheel-, hand- -barrow, — cart, trolley; perambulator; Bath —, wheel —, sedan-chair, jinriksha, rickshaw; ekka; chaise; palan-keen, -quin; litter, horse-litter, brancard, crate, hurdle, stretcher, ambulance; velocipede, hobby-horse, coaster, scooter, go-cart; cycle; bi-, tri-, quadri-cycle; tandem, safety, skate, roller —, ice — skate; sled, sleigh; ski, snow-shoe.

equipage, turn-out; coach, chariot; *quadriga*, chaise, phaëton, break, brake, mail-phaëton, wagonette, drag, curricle, tilbury, whisky, landau, *barouche*, victoria, brougham, clarence, calash, *calèche*, britzska, *araba*, kibitka; berlin; sulky, *désobligeant*, sociable, *vis-à-vis, dormeuse*; jaunting —, outside- car; *tarantass*; runabout; shay.

post-chaise; diligence; stage; stage —, mail —, hackney —, glass- coach; stage-wagon; car, omnibus, bus, fly, *cabriolet*, cab, hansom, shofle, fourwheeler, growler, *droshki*, drosky.

dog-cart, trap, gig, whitechapel, buggy, four-in-hand, unicorn, random, tandem; shandredhan, *char-à-banc*.

automobile, motor-, auto-, touring-, racing-, cycle-, side-, steam-, electric- car; motor — cycle, — bike; motorized vehicle; bus, mini-bus; buggy, crate, tub, flivver, jalopy, wreck, clunker, jog, heap (all- slang); coupe, coup, sedan, convertible, hard-top; camper, trailer, mobile home; limosine, landaulette, cabriolet, *coupé, voiturette*, runabout, electromobile, taxi, -cab.

train; passenger —, express —, freight —, subway —, special —, corridor —, parliamentary —, luggage —, goods- train, *train de luxe*; 1st-, 2nd-, 3rd- class- -train, — carriage, — compartment; Pullman —, sleeping-, club-, observation-, dining-, restaurant-car; mail-, luggage-, brake-van, coach, car, carriage; rolling stock; horse-box, cattle- truck.

273. Ship.—N. ship, vessel, sail; craft, bottom. navy, marine, fleet, flotilla, squadron; shipping.

man of war etc. (*combatant*) 726; transport, tender, store-ship; merchant ship, merchantman; packet, liner; whaler, slaver, collier, coaster, tanker, freighter, freight steamer, cargo boat, lighter; fishing-, pilot- boat; trawler, drifter; cable ship; hulk; yacht; floating palace, ocean greyhound.

ship, bark, barque, brig, snow, hermaphrodite brig; brigantine, barquentine; schooner; topsail —, fore and aft —, three masted- schooner; *chasse-marée*; sloop, cutter, corvette, clipper, foist, yawl, dandy, ketch, smack, lugger, barge, hoy, cat-, -boat, buss; sail-er, -ing vessel, wind jammer; steamer, -boat, -ship; mail—, paddle —, screw —, sternwheel- steamer; tug; train-ferry; line of steamers etc.

boat, pinnace, launch, motor-boat, picket-boat; hydroplane; life-, long-, jolly-, bum-, fly-, cock-, ferry-, canal- boat, dory, dugout, galliot; shallop, gig, funny, skiff, dingy, scow, cockleshell, wherry, coble, punt, cog, lerret; eight-, four-, pair- oar; randan; out- rigger; float, raft, pontoon; prame, ice-yacht.

state barge, bucentaur.

catamaran, coracle, gondola, carvel, caravel; felucca, caique, canoe; trireme; galley, — foist; bilander, dogger, hooker, howker; argosy, carack; galliass, galleon; galliot, polacca, polacre, corsair, tartane, junk, lorcha, praam, proa, prahu, saick, sampan, xebec, dhow; dahabeah; nuggar, cayak, piroque; trireme.

submarine, submersible.

aircraft (*combatant*) etc. 726; flying machine, air mail, aero-, air-, mono-, bi-, tri-, hydro aero-

plane, plane, cabin —, transport —, propeller —
plane; *avion*, flying boat, glider; helicopter,
rotor —, gyro-plane, whirlybird, autogyro,
gyrodine; sea-, hydro-plane; amphibian; jet.
— plane; turbo-, ram-, pulse-, subsonic —, super-
sonic —, strato- jet; rocket — plane, — ship,; space
ship; war-, combat — plane; kamikaze, fleet, armada; trainer, fliight simulator; aerostat, dirigible,
blimp (coll.), zeppelin; parachute, chute
(coll.); kite.

    rocket, flying —, ballistic —, guided — missile;
projectile; rocket —, robot —, buzz-bomb;
multistage —, step —, test — rocket; booster;
satellite; flying saucer, unidentified flying object.
(UFO).

    nacelle, car, gondola, aileron; hangar, airport,
landing field, airdrome; catwalk, controls, rudder,
tail.

    Adj. marine, maritime, naval, nautical,
seafaring, sea-, ocean-going, sea-worthy.

    aerial, aeronautical, air-worthy, flying etc. *n.*

    Adv. afloat, aboard; on-board, — ship board, —
board ship.

274. Velocity.—N. velocity, speed, celerity;
swiftness etc. *adj.*; rapidity, eagle speed; expedition
etc. (*activity*) 682; pernicity; acceleration; haste
etc. 684.

    spurt, rush, dash, race, steeplechase; smart —,
lively —, swift etc. *adj.* —, rattling —, spanking —,
strapping- -rate, — pace; round pace; flying, flight.

    gallop, canter, trot, round trot, run, scamper;
hand —, full- gallop; swoop.

    lightning, light, electricity, wind; cannon-ball,
rocket, arrow, dart, quicksilver; telegraph, express
train; torrent; swallow flight.

    eagle, antelope, courser, race-horse, gazelle,
greyhound, hare, doe, squirrel.

    Mercury, Ariel, Camilla, Harlequin.

    [Measurement of velocity.] speedometer, log, -
line, tachometer.

    air speed, speed of sound, sonic —, subsonic —,
supersonic —, ultrasonic —, hypersonic —, tran-
sonic — speed.

    V. move quickly, trip, fisk; speed, hie, hasten,
sprint, spurt, post, spank, scuttle; scud, -dle, scurry;
scour, — the plain; scamper, sprint, dash, run, —
like mad; fly, race, run a race, cut away, cut and
run, shoot, tear, whisk, whiz, sweep, skim, brush;
cut —, bowl- along; rush etc. (*be violent*) 173;
dash -on, — off, — forward; bolt; trot, gallop,
bound, flit, spring, dart, boom; march in -quick, —
double-time; ride hard; et over the ground, scorch.

    hurry etc. (*hasten*) 684; accelerate, put on;
quicken, quicken —; mend- one's pace; clap spurs
to one's horse; make-haste, — rapid strides, — forced marches, — the best of one's way; put one's
best leg foremost, stir one's stumps, wing one's
way, set off at a score; carry —, crowd- sail; go off
like a shot, go ahead, gain ground; outstrip the
wind, fly on the wings of the wind.

    keep -up, — pace- with; outstrip etc. 303.

    Adj. fast, speedy, swift, rapid, quick, fleet; nim-
ble, agile, expeditious; express; active etc. 682;
flying, galloping etc. *v.*; light- nimble-footed;
winged; eagle-winged; mercurial, electric
telegraphic; light-legged; light of heel; swift as -an
arrow etc. *n.*; quick as -lightning etc. *n.*,
— thought.*

    Adv. swiftly etc. *adj.*; with -speed etc. *n.*; apace;
at -a great rate, — full speed, — railway speed; full -
drive, — gallop; post-haste, in full sail, tantivy; trippingly; instantaneously etc. 113; like a shot.

    under press of -sale, — canvas, — sail and steam;
velis et remis, on eagle's wing, in double quick
time; with -rapid, — giant- strides; *à pas de géant*;
in seven league boots; whip and spur; *ventre à
terre*; as fast as one's -legs, — heels- will carry one;
as fast on one can lay feet to the ground, at the top
of one's speed; by leaps and bounds; with haste etc.
684; in- high — gear, — speed.

    Phr. *vires acquirit eundo.*

    *See note on 274.

275. Slowness.—N. slowness etc. *adj.*; languor
etc. (*inactivity*) 683; drawl; creeping etc. *v.*, len-
tor.

    retardation; slackening etc. *v.*; delay etc.
(*lateness*) 133; claudication.

    jog-, dog-trot, walk; mincing steps; slow -march,
— time.

    slow -goer, — coach, — back; lingerer, loiterer,
sluggard, tortoise, snail; dawdle etc. (*inactive*) 683.

    V. move -slowly, etc. *adv.*; creep, crawl, lag,
slug, walk, drawl, linger, loiter, saunter; plod,
trudge, stump along, lumber; trail; drag; dawdle
etc. (*be inactive*) 683; grovel, worm one's way,
steal along; jog -, rub —, bundle- on; toddle,
waddle, wabble, slug; traipse, slouch, shuffle, halt,
hobble, limp, claudicate, shamble; flag, falter, totter, stagger; mince, step short; march in -slow time,
— funeral procession; take one's time; hang fire
etc. (*be late*) 133.

    retard, relax; slacken, check, moderate, rein in,
curb; reef; strike —, shorten —, take in- sail; put
on the drag, apply the brake; clip the wings; reduce
the speed, decelerate; slacken -speed, — one's
pace, lose ground; back -water, — pedal, put the
engines astern, throttle down.

    Adj. slow, slack; tardy, dilatory etc. (*inactive*)
683; gentle, easy; leisurely; deliberate, gradual; insensible, imperceptible; languid, sluggish,
apathetic, phlegmatic, slow-paced, tardigrade,
snail-like; creeping etc. *v.*

    Adv. slowly etc. *adj.*; leisurely; *piano, adagio*;
largo, larghetto; at half speed, under easy sail; at a
-foot's, — snail's, — funeral- pace; slower than
molasses in January; in slow time; with -mincing
steps, — clipped wings; *haud passibus aequis*; in-
low —, gear, — speed.

    gradually etc. *adj.*; *gradatim*; by -degrees, —
slow degrees, — inches, — little and little; step by
step; inch by inch, bit by bit, little by little,
seriatim; consecutively.

276. Impulse.—N. impulse, impulsion, impetus; momentum; push, pulsion, thrust, shove, jog,
jolt, brunt, booming, boost, throw; explosion etc.
(*violence*) 173; propulsion etc. 284; jet
propulsion; firing, launching, projection, trajection.

    percussion, concussion, collision, occursion,
clash, encounter, cannon, *carambole*, appulse,
shock, crash, bump; impact; *élan*; charge etc. (*attack*) 716; beating etc. (*punishment*) 972.

    blow, dint, stroke, knock, tap, rap, slap, smack,
pat, dab; fillip; slam, bang; hit, whack, thwack,

clout; cuff etc. 972; squash, dowse, whap, swap, punch, thump, swipe, jab, pelt, kick, punce, calcitration; *ruade*; arietation; cut, thrust, lunge, yerk.

hammer, sledge-hammer, mall, maul, mallet, flail; ram, -mer; battering-ram, monkey, pile-driver, punch, bat, tamper, tamping iron; cudgel etc. (*weapon*) 727; axe etc. (*sharp*) 253.

[Science of mechanical forces] mechanics, dynamics etc.

V. give an -impetus etc. *n.*; impel, push; start, give a start to, set going; drive, urge, boom; thrust, prod, foin; cant; elbow, shoulder, jostle, justle, hustle, hurtle, shove, jog, jolt, bean, encounter; run —, bump —, butt- against; knock —, run- one's head against; impinge.

fire, launch, project, traject, propel, 284.

strike, knock, hit, bash, tap, rap, bat, slap, flap, dab, pat, thump, beat, bang, slam, dash; punch, thwack, whack; hit — -, strike- hard; swap, batter, dowse, baste; pelt, patter, skelter, buffet, belabor, tamp; fetch one a blow, swat; poke at, pink, lunge, yerk; kick, calcitrate; butt; strike at etc. (*attack*) 716; whip etc. (*punish*) 972; propel etc. 284.

come —, enter- into collision; collide; foul; fall —, run- foul of.

throw etc.

Adj. impelling etc. *v.*; im-pulsive, -pellent; booming; dynamic, -al; impelled etc. *v.*

277. Recoil.—N. recoil; re-, retro-action; revulsion; rebound, *ricochet*; re-percussion, -calcitration; kick, *contre-coup*; springing back etc. *v.*; elasticity etc. 325; reflexion, reflex, reflux; reverberation etc. (*resonance*) 408; rebuff, repulse; return.

ducks and drakes; boomerang; spring; reactionist, reactionary.

V. recoil, resile, react; spring —, fly —, bound-back; rebound, reverberate, repercuss, recalcitrate, echo, *ricochet*.

Adj. recoiling etc. *v.*; re-fluent, -percussive, -calcitrant, -actionary; retroactive.

Adv. on the -recoil etc. *n.*

278. Direction.—N. direction, bearing, course, set, drift, tenor; tendency etc. 176; incidence; bending, trending etc. *v.*; dip, tack, aim, collimation; steer-ing, -age.

point of the compass, cardinal —, half —, quarter- points; North, East, South, West; N by E, ENE, NE by N, NE etc; rhumb, azimuth, line of collimation.

line, path, road, range, quarter, line of march; alignment; straight shot, bee-line.

course, bearing, heading, altitude, air -route, -lane, angle, center, axis, torsion, torque, pitch, lift, drift, flow, wash.

V. tend —, bend —, point- towards; conduct —, go- to; point -to, — at; bend, trend, verge, incline, dip, determine.

steer —, make- -for, — towards; aim —, level- at; take aim; keep —, hold- a course; be bound for; bend one's steps towards; direct —, steer —, bend —, shape- one's course; align —, align- one's march; go straight, — to the point; march -on, — on a point.

ascertain one's -direction etc. *n.*; *s'orienter*, see which way the wind blows; box the compass.

Adj. directed etc. *v.*, — towards; pointing towards etc. *v.*; bound for; aligned —, with; direct, straight; un-deviating, -swerving; straightforward; North, -ern, -erly, etc. *n.*

directable etc. *v.*

Adv. towards; on the -road, — high road- to; versus, to; hither, thither, whither; directly; straight, — forwards, — as an arrow; point blank; in a -direct, — straight- line -to, — for, — with; in a line with; full tilt at, as the crow flies.

before —, near —, close to —, against-, the wind; windwards, in the wind's eye.

through, *via*, by way of; in all -directions, — manner of ways; *quaqua-versum*, from the four winds.

279. Deviation.—N. deviation; swerving etc. *v.*; obliquation, warp, refraction; flection, flexion; sweep; de-flection, -flexure; declination.

diversion, digression, departure from, aberration, drift, sheer; divergence etc. 291; zigzag; *détour* etc. (*circuit*) 629.

[Desultory motion] wandering etc. *v.*; vagrancy, evagation; by-paths and crooked ways.

[Motion sideways, oblique motion] sidling etc. *v.*; *échelon*, leeway; knight's move (at chess).

V. alter one's course, deviate, depart from, turn, trend; bend, curve, etc. 245; swerve, heel, bear off.

intervert; deflect; divert, — from its course; put on a new scent, shift, shunt, switch, wear, draw aside, crook, warp, short circuit.

stray, straggle; sidle, edge; diverge etc. 291; tralineate, digress, divagate, wander; wind, twist, meander, meander around Robin Hood's barn; veer, tack, sheer; turn -aside, — a corner, — away from; wheel, steer clear of; ramble, rove, drift; go -astray, — adrift; yaw, dodge; step aside, ease off, make way for, shy.

fly off at a tangent; glance off; turn, wheel —, face- about; turn —, face- to the right about; wabble etc. (*oscillate*) 314; go out of one's way etc. (*perform a circuit*) 629; lose one's way.

Adj. deviating etc. *v.*; aberrant, errant; ex-, dis-cursive; devious, desultory, loose; rambling; stray, erratic, vagrant, undirected; circuitous, indirect, zigzag; crab-like.

Adv. astray from, round about, wide of the mark; to the right about; all manner of ways; circuitously etc. 629.

obliquely, sideling, like the move of the knight on a chessboard.

280. Precession. [Going before.]—N. precession, leading, heading; precedence etc. 62; priority etc. 116; the lead, *le pas*; van etc. (*front*) 234; precursor etc. 64.

V. go -before, — ahead, — in the van, — in advance; precede, forerun; usher in, introduce, herald, head, take the lead; lead, — the way, — the dance; get —, have- the start; steal a march; get -before, — ahead, — in front of; outstrip etc. 303; take precedence etc. (*first in order*) 62.

Adj. foremost, first, leading etc. *v.*

Adv. in advance, before, ahead, in the van; fore-head-most; in front.

Phr. *seniores priores.*

281. Sequence. [Going after.]—**N.** sequence, run; coming after etc. (*order*) 63; (*time*) 117; following; pursuit etc. 622.

follower, attendant, satellite, shadow, dangler, train.

V. follow; pursue etc. 622; go –, fly- after.

attend, beset, dance attendance on, dog, be-dog; tread -in the steps of, – close upon; be –, go –, follow- in the -wake, – trail, – rear- of; trail, follow as a shadow, hang on the skirts of; tread –, follow- on the heels of, tag after.

lag, get behind.

Adj. following etc. *v.*

Adv. behind; in the -rear etc. 235, – train of, wake of; after etc. (*order*) 63, (*time*) 117.

282. Progression. [Motion forwards; progressive motion.]—**N.** progress, -ion -iveness; advancing etc. *v.*; advance, -ment; ongoing; flood-tide, headway; march etc. 266; rise; improvement etc. 658.

V. advance; proceed, progress; get -on, – along, – over the ground; gain ground; jog –, rub –, wag- on; go with the stream; keep –, hold on-one's course; go –, move –, come –, get –, pass –, push –, press- -on, – forward, – forwards, – ahead; press onwards, step forward; make –, work –, carve –, push –, force –; edge –, elbow-one's way; make -progress, – head, – way, – headway; – advances, – strides, – rapid strides etc. (*velocity*) 274; go –, shoot- ahead; distance; make up leeway.

Adj. advancing etc. *v.*; pro-gressive, -fluent; advanced.

Adv. forward, onward; forth, on ahead, under way, *en route* for, on -one's way, – the way, – the road, – the high road- to; in -progress, – mid progress; *in transitu* etc. 270.

Phr. *vestigia nulla retrorsum.*

283. Regression. [Motion backwards.]—**N.** regress, -ion; retro-cession, -gression, -gradation, -action; *reculade*; retreat, withdrawal, retirement, remigration; recession etc. (*motion from*) 287; recess; crab-like motion.

re-fluence, -flux; backwater, regurgitation, ebb, return; resilience; reflexion (*recoil*) 277; *volte-face.*

counter -motion, – movement, – march; veering, tergiversation, recidivation, backsliding, fall, relapse; deterioration etc. 659.

turning point etc. (*reversion*) 145.

V. re-cede, -grade, -turn, -vert, -treat, -tire; retro-grade, -cede; back, – down, – out, crawl; withdraw; rebound etc. 277; go –, come –, turn –, hark –, draw –, fall –, get –, put –, run-back; lose ground; fall –, drop- astern; back water, put about; veer, – round; double, wheel, counter-march; ebb, regurgitate; *jib*, shrink, shy.

turn -tail, – round, – upon one's heel, – one's back upon; retrace one's steps, dance the back step; sound –, beat- a retreat; go home.

Adj. receding etc. *v.*; retro-grade, -gressive; re-gressive, -fluent, -flex, -cidivous, -silient; crab-like; reactionary etc. 277; counter-clockwise.

Adv. back, -wards; reflexively, to the right about; *à reculons*, *à rebours.*

Phr. *revenons à nos moutons*, as you were.

284. Propulsion. [Motion given to an object situated in front.]—**N.** pro-pulsion, -jection; *vis a tergo*; push etc. (*impulse*) 276; e-, jaculation; ejection etc. 297; throw, fling, toss, shot, discharge, shy.

[Science of propulsion] steam –, gas –, diesel –, jet –, rocket – propulsion, gunnery, ballistics, archery.

missile, projectile, ball, *discus*, javelin, hammer, quoit, brickbat, shot, bullet; arrow, shaft, gun etc. (*arms*) 727.

shooter, shot; gunner, gun-layer; archer, toxophilite; bow-, rifle-, marks- man; good –, crack- shot; sharpshooter etc. (*combatant*) 726.

V. propel, project, throw, fling, cast, pitch, chuck, toss, jerk, heave, shy, hurl; flirt, fillip.

dart, lance, tilt; e-, jaculate; fulminate, bolt, drive, sling, pitchfork.

send; send –, let –, fire- off; discharge, shoot; launch, send forth, let fly; dash.

put –, set- in motion; set agoing, start; give -a start, – an impulse- to; push, impel etc. 276; trun-dle etc. (*set in rotation*) 312; expel etc. 297.

carry one off one's legs; put to flight.

Adj. propelled etc. *v.*; propelling etc. *v.*; pro-pulsive, -jectile.

285. Traction. [Motion given to an object situated behind.]—**N.** traction; drawing etc. *v.*; draft, pull, tug, haul; rake; 'a long pull, a strong pull and a pull all together;' towage, haulage.

V. draw, pull, haul, lug, rake, drag, draggle, tug, tow, trail, trawl, train; take in tow.

wrench, jerk, twitch.

Adj. drawing etc. *v.*; tractive, tractile; ductile; pulling, hauling, tugging, towing.

286. Approach. Motion towards.]—**N.** ap-proach, approximation, appropinquation; access; appulse; afflux, -ion; advent etc. (*approach of time*) 121; pursuit etc. 622; convergence etc. 290.

V. approach, approximate; near; get –, go –, draw- near; come, – near, – to close quarters; move –, set in- towards; drift; make up to; gain upon; pursue etc. 622; tread on the heels of; bear up; make the land; hug the -shore, – land.

Adj. approaching etc. *v.*; approximative; con-vergent; affluent; impending, imminent etc. (*destined*) 152.

Adv. on the road.

Int. come hither! approach! here! come! come near!

287. Recession. [Motion from.]—**N.** recession, retirement, withdrawal; retreat; retrocession etc. 283; departure etc. 293; recoil etc. 277; flight etc. (*avoidance*) 623.

V. recede, go, move from, retire, ebb, withdraw, shrink; come –, move –, go –, get –, drift-away; depart etc. 293; retreat etc. 283; move –, stand –, sheer- off; swerve from; fall back, stand aside; run away etc. (*avoid*) 623.

remove, shunt, side track, switch off.

Adj. receding etc. *v.*

288. Attraction. [Motion towards, ac-tively.]—**N.** attract-ion, -iveness; pull; drawing to,

pulling towards, adduction, magnetism, gravity, attraction of gravitation; lure, bait, decoy.

lode-stone, -star; magnet, siderite, magnetite.

V. attract; draw –, pull –, drag- towards; adduce.

lure, bait, decoy.

Adj. attracting etc. *v.*; attrahent, attractive, adducent, adductive, alluring.

289. Repulsion. [Motion from, actively.]—**N.** repulsion; driving from etc. *v.*; repulse; abduction.

V. repel; push –, drive – etc. 276; from; chase, dispel; retrude; abduce, abduct; send away, repulse, dismiss.

keep at arm's length, turn one's back upon, give the cold shoulder; send packing; send -off, – away- with a flea in one's ear, – about one's business.

Adj. repelling etc. *v.*; repellant, repulsive; abducent, abductive.

290. Convergence. [Motion nearer to.]—**N.** con-vergence, -fluence, -course, -flux, -gress, -currence, -centration; appulse, meeting; corradiation.

assemblage etc. 72; resort etc. (*focus*) 74; asymptote.

V. converge, concur; come together, unite, meet, fall in with; close -with, – in upon; center round, – in; enter in; pour in.

gather together, unite, concentrate, bring into a focus.

Adj. converging etc. *v.*; con-vergent, -fluent, -current; centripetal; asymptotical.

291. Divergence. [Motion further off.]—**N.** diverg-ence, -ency; divarication, ramification, radiation; separation etc. (*disjunction*) 44; dispersion etc. 73; deviation etc. 279; aberration, declination.

V. diverge, divaricate, radiate; ramify; branch –, glance –, file- off; fly off, – at a tangent; spread, scatter, disperse etc. 73; deviate etc. 279; part etc. (*separate*) 44; splay apart.

Adj. diverging etc. *v.*; divergent, radiant, centrifugal; aberrant.

292. Arrival. [Terminal motion at.]—**N.** arrival, advent; landing; de-, disem-barkation; reception, welcome, *vin d'honneur.*

home, goal, bourn; landing-place, -stage; resting –, stopping -place; destination, harbor, haven, port; terminal, terminus, railway station, depot, airport; halt, halting -place, – ground; anchorage etc. (*refuge*) 666.

return, recursion, remigration; meeting; ren-, en-counter.

completion etc. 729.

V. arrive; get to, come to; come; reach, attain; come up, – with, – to; overtake; make, fetch; complete etc. 729; join, rejoin.

light, alight, dismount; land, go ashore; debark, disembark; put -in, – into; visit, cast anchor, pitch

one's tent; sit down etc. (*be located*) 184; get to one's journey's end; make the land; be in at the death; come –, get- -back, – home; return; come in etc. (*ingress*) 294; make one's appearance etc. (*appear*) 446; drop in; detrain; outspan.

come to hand; come -at, – across; hit; come –, light –, pop –, bounce –, plump –, burst –, pitch- upon; meet; en- ren-counter; come in contact.

Adj. arriving etc. *v.*; homewardbound; terminal.

Adv. here, hither.

Int. welcome! hail! all hail! good- day, – morrow; greetings! hullo! well!

293. Departure. [Initial motion from.]—**N.** departure, decession, decampment; embarkation; take-off; outset, start; removal; exit etc. (*egress*) 295; exodus, Hejira, flight.

leave-taking, *congé*, valediction, valedictory, adieu, farewell, good-bye, stirrup-cup.

starting -point, – post; point –, place- of -departure, – embarkation; port of embarkation.

V. depart; go, – away; take one's departure, set out; set –, march –, put –, start –, be –, move –, get –, whip –, pack –, go –, take oneself-off; start, issue, march out, debouch; go –, sally-forth; sally, set forward; be gone.

leave a place, quit, vacate, evacuate, abandon; go off the stage, make ones' exit; retire, withdraw, remove; go -one's way, – along, – from home; take -flight, – wing; spring, fly, flit, wing one's flight; fly –, whip- away; take off, hop off; embark; go -on board, – aboard; set sail; put –, go-to sea; sail, take ship; hoist blue Peter; get under way, weigh anchor; strike tents, break camp, decamp; walk one's chalks, make tracks, cut one's stick; cut and run; take leave; say –, bid- -good-bye etc. *n.*; disappear etc. 449; abscond etc. (*avoid*) 623; entrain, embus, emplane; saddle –, harness –, hitch- up; inspan.

Adj. departing etc. *v.*; valedictory; outward bound.

Adv. whence, hence, thence; with a foot in the stirrup; on the -wing, – move.

Int. begone! etc. (*ejection*) 297; to horse! all aboard! farewell! adieu! good-bye, – day! *au revoir! auf wiedersehen!* fare you well! so long! God -bless you, – speed! *bon voyage!*

294. Ingress. [Motion into.]—**N.** ingress; entrance, entry; introgression; influx; intrusion, inroad, incursion, invasion, irruption; pene-, interpene- tration; illapse, import, importation, infiltration; immigration; admission etc. (*reception*) 296; insinuation etc. (*interjacence*) 228; insertion etc. 300.

inlet; way in; mouth, door etc. (*opening*) 260; path etc. (*way*) 627; conduit etc. 350; immigrant, visitor, incomer, newcomer, colonist.

V. have the *entrée*; enter; go –, come –, pour –, flow –, creep –, slip –, pop –, break –, burst- -into, – in; set foot on; burst –, break-in upon; invade, intrude, butt in, horn in, crash; insinuate itself; inter-, penetrate; infiltrate; find one's way –, wriggle –, worm oneself- into.

give entrance to etc. (*receive*) 296; insert etc. 300.

Adj. incoming, ingressive etc. *n.*; inward bound.

Adv. inward.

295. Egress. [Motion out of.]—**N.** egress, exit, issue; emer-sion, -gence; disemboguement; out-break, -burst; e-, pro-ruption; emanation; evacuation; ex, trans-udation; extravasation, per-spiration, sweating, leakage, percolation, distillation, oozing; gush etc. (*water in motion*) 348; outpour, -ing; effluence, effusion; efflux, -ion; drain; dribbling etc. *v.*; defluxion; drainage; out-come, -put; discharge etc. (*excretion*) 299.

export; expatriation; e-, re-migration; *débouche*; exodus etc. (*departure*) 293; emigrant, migrant, *émigré*, colonist.

outlet, vent, spout, tap, sluice, floodgate; pore; vomitory, out-gate, sally-port; way out; mouth, door etc. (*opening*) 260; path etc. (*way*) 627; con-duit etc. 350; air-pipe etc. 351.

V. emerge, emanate, issue; go –, come –, move –, pass –, pour –, flow- out of; pass off, evacuate; migrate.

ex-, trans-ude; leak; run, – out, – through; per-, trans-colate; seep; strain, distil; perspire, sweat, drain, ooze; filter, filtrate; dribble, gush, spout, flow out; well, – out; pour, trickle etc. (*water in motion*) 348; effuse, extravasate, disem-bogue, discharge itself, debouch; come –, break-forth; burst- out, – through; find vent, escape etc. 671.

Adj. effused etc. *v.*; outgoing, outward bound.

Adv. outward.

296. Reception. [Motion into, actively.]—**N.** reception; admission, admittance, *entrée*, im-portation; initiation; intro-duction, -mission, ception; immission, ingestion, imbibition, ab-sorption, ingurgitation, inhalation; suction, sucking; eating, drinking etc. (*food*) 298; insertion etc. 300; interjection etc. 228.

V. give -entrance to, – admittance to, – the *entrée*; intro-duce, -mit; usher, admit, receive, im-port, initiate, bring in, open the door to, throw open, ingest, absorb, imbibe, inhale, infiltrate; let –, take –, suck- in; re-admit, -sorb, -absorb; snuff up; swallow, ingurgitate; enfulf, engorge; gulp; eat, drink etc. (*food*) 298.

Adj. admit-ting etc. *v.*, -ted etc *v.*; admissible; absorbent; introductory, introceptive, intromittent, initiatory.

297. Ejection. [Motion out of, actively.]—**N.** ejection, emission, effusion, rejection, expulsion, eviction, extrusion, trajection; discharge.

egestion, evacuation, vomition, disgorgement, voidance, eruption, eruptiveness; ruc-, eruc-tation; blood-letting, venesection, phlebotomy, paracen-tesis; tapping, drainage; clear-ance, -age, voidance; vomiting, excretion etc. 299.

deportation; banishment etc. (*punishment*) 972; rogue's march; relegation, extradition; dislodgment.

V. give -exit, – vent- to; let –, give –, pour –, send- out; des-, dis-patch; exhale, excern, ex-crete, disembogue, secrete, secern; extravasate,

shed, void, evacuate, egest, emit; open the -sluices, – floodgates; turn on the tap; extrude, detrude; ef-fuse, spend, expend; pour forth; squirt, spirt, spill, slop; perspire etc. (*exude*) 295; breathe, blow etc. (*wind*) 349.

tap, draw off; bale –, lade- out; let blood, broach.

eject, reject; expel, discard; cut, send to Coven-try, boycott, ostracize; *chasser*; banish etc. (*punish*) 972; throw etc. 284 -out, – up, – off, – away, – aside; push etc. 276 -out, – off, – away, – aside; shovel –, sweep- -out, – away; brush –, whisk –, turn –, send- -off, – away; discharge; send –, turn –, cast- adrift; turn –, bundle- out; throw overboard; give the sack to; send -packing, – about one's business, – to the right about; strike off the roll etc. (*abrogate*) 756; turn out-neck and heels, – head and shoulders, – neck and crop; pack off; send away with a flea in the ear; send to Jericho; bow out, show the door to, dismiss, fire, sack.

turn out of -doors, – house and home; evict, oust; exorcise, un-house, -kennel; dislodge; un-, dis-people; depopulate; relegate, deport.

empty; drain, – to the dregs; sweep off; clear, – off, – out, – away; such, draw off, extract; clean out, make a clean sweep of, clear decks, purge.

em-, dis-, disem-bowel; eviscerate, gut; unearth, root -out, – up; averruncate; weed –, get out; eliminate, get rid of, do away with, shake off; exen-terate.

vomit, spew, puke, keck, retch; belch, – out, eruct, eructate; cast –, bring- up; disgorge; ex-pectorate, salivate, clear the throat, hawk, spit, sputter, splutter, slobber, drool, drivel, slaver, slab-ber.

unpack, unlade, unload, unship; break bulk.

be let out; ooze etc. (*emerge*) 295.

Adj. emitt-ing, -ed etc. *v.*

begone! get you gone! get –, go- away, – along, – along with you! go your way! away, – with! off with you! go, – about your business! be off! avaunt! aroynt! get out!

298. Food. [Eating.]—**N.** eating etc. *v.*; deglutition, gulp, epulation, mastication, man-ducation, rumination, gastronomy, gastrology; panto-, hippo-, ichthyo-phagy etc.; gluttony etc. 957; carnivorousness, vegetarianism.

mouth, jaws, mandible, mazard, chops.

drinking etc. *v.*; potation, draught, libation; carousal etc. (*amusement*) 840; drunkenness etc. 959.

food, *pabulum*; aliment, nourishment, nutriment; susten-ance, -tation; nurture, sub-sistence, provender, feed, fodder, provision, ration, keep, commons, board; commissariat etc. (*provision*) 637; prey, forage, pasture, pasturage; fare, cheer; diet, -ary; regimen; belly timber, staff of life; bread, -and cheese; proteins, carbohydrates, vitamines.

comestibles, eatables, victuals, edibles, *ingesta*; grub, prog, tack, hard tack, meat; bread, -stuffs; cereals; viands, cates, delicacy, dainty, creature comforts, contents of the larder, flesh-pots; festal board; ambrosia; good -cheer, – living.

hors-d'oeuvre; soup, pottage, *potage*, broth,

bouillon, consommé, purée, borsch, stock, skilly, gumbo; fish, − cakes, − pie; joint, *rôti, pièce de résistance, relevé,* hash, *réchauffé,* stew, *ragoût,* fricassee, mince, *salim, goulash, bouillabaisse,* remove, *entrée, croquette, rissole,* sausage, curry, bubble and squeak; haggis, collops, giblets; poultry, game etc.; biscuit, bun, scone, rusk, pancake, pie, pastry, pasty, patty, *patisseria,* tart, turnover, *vol-au-vent, soufflé,* dumpling, pudding, duff, *compote,* fritters, cake, napoleon, *blancmange,* custard, jelly, jam, sweets etc. 396; *entremet;* oatmeal, porridge, hasty pudding, gruel; eggs, omelet, cheese, matzoon, savory; vegetable, salad, *mayonnaise,* fruit; sauce, condiment etc. 393; kickshaws.

table, *cuisine,* bill of fare, *menu, table d'hôte,* ordinary, *à la carte;* cover.

meal, repast, feed, spread; mess; dish, plate, course, side dish; regale; refresh-, entertain-ment; refection, collation, picnic, feast, banquet, junket; breakfast; lunch, -eon, *déjeuner,* bever, tiffin, tea, dinner, supper, snack, whet, bait, dessert; pot-luck, *table d'hôte, déjeuner à la fourchette;* hearty −, square −, substantial −, full- - meal; blow out; light refreshment; pemmican.

mouthful, bolus, gobbet, tit-bit, morsel, sop, sippet.

drink, beverage, liquor, broth, soup; potion, dram, draft, drench, swill; nip, peg, sip, sup, gulp.

wine, champagne, spirits, *liqueur* beer, porter, stout, ale, malt liquor, julep, Sir John Barleycorn, stingo, heavy wet, bitter, lager- beer, cider; grog, toddy, flip, purl, punch, negus, cup, bishop, posset, wassail; bitters, *apéritif,* high-ball, cocktail; whisky, rum, absinthe; gin etc. (*intoxicating liquor*) 959; coffee, chocolate, cocoa, tea, *maté,* the cup that cheers but not inebriates.

eating-house etc. 189.

V. eat, feed, fare, devour, swallow, take; gulp, bolt, snap; fall to; despatch, dispatch; discuss; take −, get −, gulp-down; lay −, tuck- in; lick, pick, peck; gormandize etc. 957; bite, champ, munch, cranch, craunch, crunch, chew, masticate, nibble, gnaw, mumble.

live on; feed −, batten −; fatten −, feast- upon; browse, graze, crop, regale; carouse etc. (*make merry*) 840; eat heartily, do justice to, play a good knife and fork, banquet.

break -bread, − one's fast; breakfast; lunch, dine, take tea, sup.

drink, − in, − up, − one's fill; quaff, sip, sup; suck, − up; lap; swig; swill; tipple etc. (*be drunken*) 959; empty one's glass, drain the cup; toss -off, − one's glass; wash down, crack a bottle, wet one's whistle.

cater, purvey etc. 637.

Adj. eatable, edible, esculent, comestible, alimentary; cereal, cibarious, dietetic; culinary; nutri-tive, -tious; succulent; drinkable, pot-able, - ulent; bibulous.

omn-, carn-, herb-, frug-, gramin-, phyt-ivorous; ichthyophagous.

prandial.

299. Excretion.—N. excretion, discharge, emanation; ejection etc. 297; exhalation, exudation, extrusion, secretion, effusion, extravasation, *ecchymosis,* evacuation, cacation, defecation, dysentery, dejection, *feces,* excrement;

perspiration, sweat; sub-, exud-ation; *diaphoresis;* sewage.

saliva, spittle, rheum; ptyalism, salivation, catarrh, distemper; diarrhea; *ejecta, egesta, sputum, sputa; excreta;* lava; *exuviae* etc. (*uncleanness*) 653.

hemorrhage, bleeding; catamenia, menses; outpouring etc. (*egress*) 295; leucorrhea.

V. excrete etc. (*eject*) 297; emanate etc. (*come out*) 295.

Adj. excretory, fecal, secretory; ejective, eliminant.

300. Insertion. [Forcible ingress.]—**N.** insertion, implantation, intercalation, embolism, introduction; interpolation, insinuation etc. (*intervention*) 228; planting etc. *v.*; injection, inoculation, importation, infusion; forcible -ingress etc. 294; immersion; submersion, -gence; dip, plunge; bath etc. (*water*) 337; interment etc. 363.

V. insert; intro-duce, -mit; put −, run- into; import; inject; interject etc. 228; infuse, instil, inoculate, impregnate, imbue, imbrue.

graft, ingraft, bud, plant, implant; dovetail.

obtrude; thrust −, stick −, ram −, stuff −, tuck −, press −, drive −, pop −, whip −, drop −, put- in; impact; empierce etc. (*make a hole*) 260.

embed; immerse, immerge, merge; bathe, soak etc. (*water*) 337; dip, plunge etc. 310.

bury etc. (*inter*) 363.

insert etc. -itself; plunge *in medias res.*

Adj. inserted etc. *v.*

301. Extraction. [Forcible egress.]—**N.** extraction; extracting etc. *v.*; removal, elimination, extrication, eradication, evolution.

evulsion, avulsion; wrench; expression, squeezing; extirpation, extermination; ejection etc. 297; export etc. (*egress*) 295; distillation.

extractor, corkscrew, forceps, pliers.

V. extract, draw, pit; take −, draw −, pull −, tear −, pluck −, pick −, get- out; wring from, wrench; extort; root −, weed −, grub −, rake-up, − out; eradicate; pull −, pluck- up by the roots; averruncate; unroot; uproot, pull up, extirpate, dredge.

remove; educe, elicit; evolve, extricate; eliminate etc. (*eject*) 297; eviscerate etc. 297.

express, squeeze −, press- out; distil.

Adj. extracted etc. *v.*

302. Passage. [Motion through.]—**N.** passage, transmission; permeation; pene-, interpene-tration; transudation, infiltration; *osmosis,* osmose, endos-, exos-mose; intercurrence; ingress etc. 294; egress etc. 295; path etc. 627; conduit etc. 350; opening etc. 260; journey etc. 266; voyage etc. 267.

V. pass, − through; perforate etc. (*hole*) 260; penetrate, permeate, thread, thrid, enfilade; go - through, − across; go −, pass- over; cut across; ford, cross; pass and repass, work; make −, thread −, worm −, force- one's way; make −, force- a passage; cut one's way through; find its -way, −

vent; transmit, make way, clear the course; traverse, go over the ground.

Adj. passing etc. *v.*; intercurrent; osmotic etc. *n.*

Adv. *en passant* etc. (*transit*) 270.

303. Overstep. [Motion beyond.]—**N.** transcursion, -ilience, -gression; infraction, intrusion; trespass; encroach-, infringe-ment; extravagation, transcendence; redundance etc. 641; ingress etc. 294.

V. transgress, surpass, pass; go-beyond, — by; show in —, come to the-front; shoot ahead of; steal a march —, gain-upon.

over-step, -pass, -reach, -go, -ride-leap, -jump, -skip, -lap, -shoot the mark; out-strip, -leap, -jump, -go, -step, -run, -ride, -rival, -do; beat, — hollow; distance; leave in the -lurch, — rear; go one better, throw into the shade; exceed, transcend, surmount; soar etc. (*rise*) 305.

encroach, intrude, trespass, infringe, invade, trench upon, intrench on; strain; stretch —, strain-a point; pass the Rubicon.

Adj. surpassing etc. *v.*

Adv. beyond the mark, ahead.

304. Shortcoming. [Motion short of.]—**N.** shortcoming, failure; delinquency; falling short etc. *v.*; de-fault, -falcation; leeway; labor in vain, no go.

incompleteness etc. 53; imperfection etc. 651; insufficiency etc. 640; noncompletion etc. 730; failure etc. 732.

V. come —, fall —, stop- -short, — short of; not reach; want; keep within -bounds, — the mark, — compass.

break down, stick in the mud, collapse, come to nothing; fall -through, — to the ground, — down; cave in, end in smoke, fizzle out, miss the mark, fail; lose ground; miss stays, slump.

Adj. unreached; deficient; short, — of; *minus*; out of depth; perfunctory etc. (*neglect*) 460.

Adv. within -the mark, — compass, — bounds; behindhand; *re infectâ*; to no purpose; far from it.

Phr. the bubble burst.

305. Ascent. [Motion upwards.]—**N.** ascent, ascension; rising etc. *v.*; rise, upgrowth; leap etc. 309; acclivity, hill etc. 217; stair, stairs, stair-case, -way, flight of -steps, — stairs; ladder, companion, — way; lift, elevator etc. 307.

rocket, lark; sky-rocket, -lark; Alpine Club.

V. ascend, rise, mount, arise, uprise; go —, get —, work one's way —, start —, spring —, shoot-up; zoom; aspire.

climb, clamber, ramp, scramble, swarm, *escalade*, surmount; scale, — the heights.

tower, soar, hover, spire, plane, swim, float, surge; leap etc. 309.

Adj. rising etc. *v.*; scandent, buoyant; supernatant, -fluitant; excelsior.

Adv. uphill.

306. Descent. [Motion downwards.]—**N.** descent, descension, declension, declination; fall;

falling etc. *v.*; drop, cadence; subsidence, lapse; come-down, downfall, tumble, slip, tilt, trip, lurch; cropper, *culbute*; titubation, stumble; fate of Icarus; dive, nose-dive, *volpané*.

avalanche, *débâcle*, landslip, slide.

V. descend; go —, drop —, come-down; fall, gravitate, drop, slip, slide, glissade, dive, plunge, settle; decline, slump, set, sink, droop, come down a peg.

dismount, alight, light, get down; swoop; stoop etc. 308; fall prostrate, precipitate oneself; let fall etc. 308.

tumble, trip, stumble, titubate, lurch, pitch, swag, topple; topple —, tumble- -down, — over; tilt, sprawl, plump down, come a cropper.

Adj. descending etc. *v.*; descendent, declivitous; downcast; decur-rent, sive; labent, deciduous; nodding to its fall.

Adv. down, -hill, -wards.

307. Elevation.—**N.** elevation; raising etc. *v.*; erection, lift; sublevation, upheaval; sublimation, exaltation; prominence etc. (*convexity*) 250.

lever etc. 633; crane, derrick, windlass, capstan, winch, dredger, lift, elevator, escalator, dumb waiter.

V. heighten, elevate, raise, lift, erect; set —, stick —, perch —, perk —, tilt- up; rear, hoist, heave; up-lift, -raise, -rear, -bear, -cast, -hoist, -heave; buoy, weigh, mount, give a lift; exalt, sublimate; place —, set- on a pedestal.

take —, drag —, fish- up; dredge.

stand —, rise —, get —, jump- up; spring to one's feet; hold -oneself, — one's head- up; draw oneself up to his full height.

Adj. elevated etc. *v.*; standing up; stilted, attollent, rampant.

Adv. on -stilts, — the shoulders of, — one's legs, — one's hind legs.

308. Depression.—**N.** lowering etc. *v.*; depression; dip etc. (*concavity*) 252; abasement; detrusion; reduction.

over-throw, -set, -turn; upset; prostration, subversion, precipitation.

bow; courtesy, curtsy; genuflexion, *kowtow*, obeisance, *salaam*.

V. depress, lower; let —, take- -down, — down a peg; cast; let -drop, — fall; sink, debase, bring low, abase, slash, reduce, detrude, pitch, precipitate.

over-throw, -turn, -set; upset, subvert, prostrate, level, fell; cast —, take —, throw —, fling —, dash —, pull —, cut —, knock —, hew- down; raze—, to the ground; humiliate, trample in the dust, pull about one's ears.

sit, — down; couch, squat, crouch, stoop, bend, bow, courtsey, curtsy; bob, duck, dip, genuflect, kneel; *kowtow, salaam*, make obeisance, prostrate oneself; bend, bow- the -head, — knee; incline the head; bow down; cower; recline etc. (*be horizontal*) 213.

Adj. depressed etc. *v.*; at a low ebb; prostrate etc. (*horizontal*) 213; detrusive.

309. Leap.—**N.** leap, jump, hop, spring, bound, vault, saltation.

dance, caper, gambol; curvet, caracole; *gambade, -bado*; capriole, demivolt; buck, – jump; hop, skip and jump.

kangaroo, jerboa, chamois, goat, frog, grasshopper, flea.

V. leap; jump -up, – over the moon; hop, spring, bound, vault, ramp, cut capers, gambol, trip, skip, dance, caper, curvet, *caracole*; foot it, bob, bounce, flounce, start, frisk etc. (*amusement*) 840; jump about etc. (*agitation*) 315; trip it on the light fantastic toe, dance oneself off one's legs.

Adj. leaping etc. *v.*; saltatory, frisky.

Adv. on the light fantastic toe.

310. Plunge.—**N.** plunge, dip, dive, header; ducking etc. *v.*; submergence, immersion, diver.

V. plunge, dip, souse, duck; dive, plump; take a -plunge, – header, make a plunge; bathe etc. (*water*) 337.

sub-merge, -merse; immerse, douse, sink, engulf, send to -the bottom, – Davy Jones' locker.

get out of one's depth; go -to the bottom, –down like a stone; founder, welter, wallow.

311. Circuition. [Curvilinear motion.]—**N.** circuition, circulation; turn, curvet; excursion; circum-vention, -navigation, -ambulation; north-west passage; ambit, gyre, lap, circuit etc. 629.

turning etc. *v.*; wrench; evolution; coil, helix, spiral; corkscrew.

V. turn, bend, wheel; go –, put- about; heel; go –, turn -round, – to the right about; turn on one's heel; make – , describe- a -circle, – complete circle; encircle; go –, pass- through -180°, – 360°.

circum-navigate, -aviate, -ambulate, -vent; put a girdle round the earth, go the round, make the round of.

turn –, round- a corner; double a point.

wind, circulate, meander; whisk, twirl; twist etc. (*convolution*) 248; make a *détour* etc. (*circuit*) 629.

Adj. turning etc. *v.*; circuitous; circumforaneous, -fluent; devious, roundabout, circumambient, -flex, -navigable.

Adv. round about.

312. Rotation. [Motion in a continued circle.]—**N.** rotation, revolution, gyration, circulation, roll; circum-rotation, -volution, -gyration; volutation, circination, turbination, *pirouette*, convolution.

verticity; whir, whirl, swirl, eddy, vortex, whirlpool, gurge; cyclone, tornado; surge; *vertigo*, dizzy round; Maelstrom, Charybdis; Ixion; wheel of Fortune.

wheel, screw, propeller, whirligig, rolling stone, windmill; top, teetotum, merry-go-round; roller; cog-, fly-wheel; spit; jack; caster.

axis, axle, spindle, spool, pivot, pin, hinge, pole, swivel, gimbals, arbor, bobbin, mandrel, shaft.

[Science of rotatory motion] trochilics, gyrostatics.

V. rotate; roll, – along; revolve, spin; turn, – round; circumvolve- circulate; gyre, gyrate, wheel,

whirl, swirl, twirl, trundle, troll, bowl; slew round.

roll up, furl; wallow, welter; box the compass; spin like a -top, – teetotum.

Adj. rotating etc. *v.*; rota-tory, -ry; circumrotatory, trochilic, vertiginous, gyratory; vortic-al, -ose.

Adv. head over heels, round and round, like a horse in a mill.

313. Evolution. [Motion in a reverse circle.]—**N.** evolution, unfolding, development; eversion etc. (*inversion*) 218.

V. evolve; un-fold, -roll, -wind, -coil, -twist, -furl, -twine, -ravel; disentangle; develop.

Adj. evolving etc. *v.*; evolved etc. *v.*

314. Oscillation. [Reciprocating motion, motion to and fro.]—**N.** oscillation; vibration, libration; motion of a pendulum; nutation; undulation; pulsation; pulse; throb; seismic disturbance.

alternation; coming and going etc. *v.*; ebb and flow, flux and reflux, ups and downs; wave, vibratiuncle, swing, beat, shake, wag, see-saw, dance, lurch, dodge; fluctuation, vacillation etc. (*irresolution*) 605.

seismometer, vibroscope, seismograph.

V. oscillate; vi-, li-brate; alternate, undulate, wave; sway, rock, swing; pulsate, beat, wag, -gle; nod, bob, courtesy, curtsy; tick; play; chatter, wamble, wabble; teeter, dangle, swag.

fluctuate, dance, curvet, reel, quake; quiver, quaver, shake, flicker; wriggle; roll, toss, pitch; flounder, stagger, totter, waddle; move –, bob- up and down etc. *adv.*; pass and repass, ebb and flow, come and go, shuttle; vacillate etc. 605.

brandish, shake, flourish.

Adj. oscillating etc. *v.*; oscill-, undul-, puls-, libr-atory; vibrat-ory, -ile; pendulous, shutterwise, seismic.

Adv. to and fro, up and down, backwards and forwards, see-saw, zigzag, wibble-wabble, in and out, from side to side, like buckets in a well.

315. Agitation. [Irregular motion.]—**N.** agitation, stir, tremor, shake, ripple, jog, jolt, jerk, shock, succession, trepidation, quiver, quaver, dance; jactit-ation, -ance; shuffling etc. *v.*; twitter, flicker, flutter.

disquiet, perturbation, commotion, turmoil, turbulence; tumult, -uation; hubbub, rout, bustle, fuss, racket, *subsultus*, staggers, megrims, epilepsy, fits, twitching, vellication, St. Vitus' dance.

spasm, throe, throb, palpitation, convulsion, paroxysm; tetanus.

disturbance etc. (*disorder*) 59; restlessness etc. (*changeableness*) 149.

ferment, -ation; ebullition, effervescence, hurly burly, *cahotage*; tempest, storm, ground swell, heavy sea, whirlpool, vortex etc. 312; whirlwind etc. (*wind*) 349.

V. be -agitated etc.; shake; tremble, – like an aspen leaf; quiver, quaver, quake, shiver, twitter, twire, dither, dodder; twitch, writhe, toss, shuffle, tumble, stagger, bob, reel, sway; wag –, -gle, wiggle; wriggle, – like an eel; squirm; dance, stumble,

shamble, flounder, totter, flounce, flop, curvet, prance.

throb, pulsate, beat, palpitate, go pit-a-pat; flutter, flitter, flicker, bicker; bustle.

ferment, effervesce, foam; boil, – over; bubble, – up; simmer.

toss –, jump- about; jump like a parched pea; shake like an aspen leaf; shake to its -center, – foundations; be the sport of the winds and waves; reel to and fro like a drunken man; move –, drive- from post to pillar and from pillar to post; keep between hawk and buzzard.

agitate, shake, convulse, toss, tumble, bandy, wield, brandish, flap, flourish, whisk, jerk, hitch, jolt; jog, -gle; hostle, buffet, hustle, disturb, stir, shake up, churn, jounce, wallop, whip, vellicate.

Adj. shaking etc. v.; agitated, tremulous; de-, sub-sultory; shambling; giddy-paced, saltatory, convulsive, jerky, unquiet, restless, all of a twitter.

Adv. by fits and starts; subsultorily etc. adj.; per saltum; hop, skip and jump; in -convulsions, – fits, pit-a-pat.

316. Materiality.—N. material-ity, -ness; materialization; corpor-eity, -ality; substantiality, material existence, incarnation, flesh and blood, plenum; physical condition.

matter, body, substance, brute matter, stuff, element, principle, protoplasm, plasma, parenchyma, material, substratum, hyle, corpus, pabulum; frame.

object, article, thing, something; still life; stocks and stones; materials etc. 635.

[Science of matter] physics; somatology, -ics; natural –, experimental- philosophy; physical science, philosophie positive, materialism, hylism; applied –, micro-, molecular -, nuclear – physics.

atomics, atomic science, nucleonics, quantum mechanics, radiology.

atom, radical, tracer, isotope, pleiad; atomic – nucleus, – cluster; nuclear particle, neutron, protron, shell, valence electron.

materialist, physicist, atomic scientist, radiologist.

V. materialize, incorporate, incarnate, substantiate, embody.

atomize, split –, smash – the atom; radio- activate.

Adj. material, bodily; corpor-eal, -al; physical; somat-ic, -oscopic; sensible, tangible, ponderable, palpable, substantial; fleshly, incarnate.

physical, bio-, electro-, geo-physical; atomic, nuclear, thermonuclear, radio-active.

objective, impersonal, neuter, unspiritual, materialistic.

317. Immateriality.—N. immaterial-ity, -ness; incorporeity, dematerialization, unsubstantiality, spirituality; inextension; astral plane.

personality; I, myself, me; ego, spirit etc. (soul) 450; astral body; immaterialism; spiritual-ism, - ist; subliminal –, subconscious- self.

V. disembody, spiritualize, dematerialize.

Adj. immateri-al, -ate; incorpor-eal, -al; asomatous, unextended; un-, dis-embodied; extramundane, supersensible, unearthly; pneumatoscopic; spiritual etc. (psychical) 450; aery.

personal, subjective.

318. World.—N. world, creation, nature, universe; earth, globe, wide world; cosmos; terraqueous globe, sphere; macro-, mega-cosm; music of the spheres; strato-, tropo-sphere.

heavens, sky, welkin, empyrean; starry -heaven, – host; firmament; vault –, canopy- of heaven; celestial spaces.

heavenly bodies, stars, luminaries, nebulae; galaxy, milky way, galactic circle, via lactea.

sun, orb of day, Apollo, Phoebus; photo-, chromo-sphere; solar system; planet, -oid, asteroid; comet; satellite; moon, orb of night, Diana, Luna; aerolite, meteor; falling –, shooting- star; meteorite.

constellation, zodiac, signs of the zodiac, Charles's wain, Great Bear, Southern Cross, Orion's belt, Cassiopeia's chair, Pleiades etc.

colures, equator, ecliptic, orbit.

[Science of heavenly bodies] astronomy; uranography, -logy; cosmo-logy, -graphy, -gony; eidouranion, orrery; geography; geodesy etc. (measurement) 466; star-gazing, -gazer; astronomer; cosmogonist, geodesist, geographer; observatory.

Adj. cosmic, cosmical, mundane; terr-estrial, - estrious, -aqueous, -ene, -eous; telluric, earthly, geotic, geodetic, cosmogonal, under the sun; sublunary, -astral.

solar, heliacal; lunar; celestial, heavenly, empyreal, sphery; starry, stellar; sider-eal, -al; astral; nebular.

Adv. in all creation, on the face of the globe, here below, under the sun.

319. Gravity.—N. gravi-ty, -tation; weight; heaviness etc. adj.; specific gravity; ponderosity, pressure, load; bur-den, -then; ballast, counterpoise; lump –, mass –, weight- of.

lead, millstone, mountain, Ossa on Pelion.

weighing, ponderation, trutination; weights; avoirdupois –, troy –, apothecaries'- weight; grain, scruple, drachm, ounce, pound, lb., load, stone, hundredweight, cwt., ton, quintal, carat, pennyweight, tod, gram, kilogram etc.

[Weighing instrument] balance, scales, steelyard, beam, weighbridge, spring balance, weighing machine.

[Science of gravity] statics.

V. be -heavy etc. adj.; gravitate, weigh, press, cumber, load.

[Measure the weight of] weigh, poise.

Adj. weighty; weighing etc. v.; heavy, – as lead; ponder-ous, -able; lump-ish, -y; cumber- burden-some; cumbrous, unwieldy, massive.

in-, superin-cumbent.

320. Levity.—N. levity; lightness etc. adj.; imponderability, imponderables, buoyancy, volatility.

feather, dust, mote, down, thistledown, flue, cobweb, gossamer, straw, cork, bubble; float, bouy; ether, air.

leaven, ferment, barm, yeast, enzyme.

V. be -light etc. *adj.*; float, swim, be buoyed up.
render -light etc. *adj.*; lighten, levitate; leaven.

Adj. light, subtile, subtle, airy; imponder-ous, -able; astatic, weightless, ethereal, sublimated; uncompressed, volatile; buoyant, floating etc. *v.*; barmy, frothy; portable.

light as -a feather, − thistle down, − air.
fermenting etc. *n.*

321. Density.—N. density, solidity; solidness etc. *adj.*; impenetra-, impermea-bility; incompressibility; imporosity; cohesion etc. 46; constipation, consistence, spissitude.

specific gravity; hydro-, areo-meter.

condensation; solid-ation, -ification; consolidation; concretion, caseation, coagulation; petrifaction etc. (*hardening*) 323; crystallization, precipitation; deposit, precipitate, silt; inspissation; thickening etc. *v.*

indivisibility, indiscerptibility, indissolvableness.

solid body, mass, block, knot, lump; con-cretion, -crete, -glomerate; cake, clot, stone, curd, coagulum, grume; bone, gristle, cartilage.

V. be -dense etc. *adj.*; become − . render- solid etc. *adj.*; solid-ify, -ate; concrete, set, take a set, consolidate, congeal, coagulate; curd, -le; fix, clot, cake, candy, precipitate, deposit, cohere, crystallize; petrify etc. (*harden*) 323.

condense, thicken, inspissate, incrassate; compress, squeeze, ram down, constipate.

Adj. dense, solid, solidified etc. *v.*; cohe-rent, -sive etc. 46; compact, close, serried, thickset; substantial, massive, lumpish; impenetrable, impermeable, imporous; incompressible; constipated; concrete etc. (*hard*) 323; knot-ted, -ty; gnarled; crystal-line, -lizable; thick, grumous, stuffy.

un-dissolved, -melted, -liquified, -thawed.
in-divisible, -discerptible, -frangible, -dissolvable, -dissoluble, -soluble, -fusible.

322. Rarity.—N. rarity; tenuity; absence of -solidity etc. 321; subtility; sponginess, compressibility.

rarefaction, expansion, dilatation, inflation, subtilization.

ether etc. (*gas*) 334.

V. rarefy, expand, dilate, subtilize, attenuate, thin.

Adj. rare, subtile, thin, fine, tenuous, compressible, flimsy, slight; light etc. 320; cavernous, spongy etc. (*hollow*) 252.

rarefied etc. *v.*; unsubstantial; uncom-pact, -pressed.

323. Hardness.—N. hardness etc. *adj.*; rigidity, renitence, inflexibility, temper, callosity, durity.

induration, petrifaction; lapid-ification, -escence; vitri-, ossi-, corni-fication; crystallization.

stone, pebble, flint, marble, rock, fossil, crag, crystal, quartz, granite, adamant; bone, cartilage; heart of oak, block, board, deal board; iron, steel; cast −, wrought- iron; nail; brick, concrete; cement.

V. render -hard etc. *adj.*; harden, stiffen, indurate, petrify, temper, ossify, vitrify.

Adj. hard, rigid, stubborn, stiff, firm; starch, -ed; stark, unbending, unlimber, unyielding; inflexible, tense; indurate, -d; gritty, proof.

adamant-ine, -ean; concrete, stony, rocky, lithic, granitic, vitreous; crystalline; horny, corneous; bony; oss-eous, -ific; cartilaginous; hard as a -stone etc. *n.*; stiff as -buckram, − a poker.

324. Softness.—N. softness, pliableness etc. *adj.*; flexibility; pli-ancy, -ability; sequacity, malleability; flabbiness; duct-, tract-ility; extend-, extensibility; plasticity; inelasticity; flaccidity, laxity.

clay, wax, butter, dough, pudding; cushion, pillow, feather-bed, pad, down, padding, wadding.

mollification; softening etc. *v.*

V. render -soft etc. *adj.*; soften, mollify, mellow, relax, temper; mash, knead, squash, *massage*.

bend, yield, relent, relax, give.

Adj. soft, tender, supple; pli-ant, -able; flex-ible, -ile; lithe, -some; lissom, limber, plastic; duc-tile; tract-ile, -able; malleable, extensile, sequacious, inelastic, mollient.

yielding etc. *v.*; flabby, limp, flimsy.

flaccid, flocculent, downy; spongy, edematous, medullary, doughy, argillaceous, mellow.

soft as -butter, − down, − silk; yielding as wax; tender as a chicken.

325. Elasticity.—N. elasticity, springiness, spring, resilience, renitency, buoyancy.

india-rubber, caoutchouc, gutta-percha, whalebone, gum elastic.

V. be -elastic etc. *adj.*; spring back etc. (*recoil*) 227.

Adj. elastic, tensile, springy, ductile, resilient, renitent, buoyant.

326. Inelasticity.—N. want of −, absence of- elasticity etc. 325; inelasticity etc. (*softness*) 324.

Adj. inelastic etc. (*soft*) 324.

327. Tenacity.—N. tenacity, toughness, strength; cohesion etc. 46; sequacity; stubbornness etc. (*obstinacy*) 606; viscidity etc. 352.

leather; gristle, cartilage.

V. be -tenacious etc. *adj.*; resist fracture.

Adj. tenacious, tough, cohesive, adhesive, strong, resisting, sequacious, stringy, gristly, cartilaginous, leathery, coriaceous, tough as whit-leather; stub-born etc. (*obstinate*) 606.

328. Brittleness.—N. brittleness etc. *adj.*; frag-, friab-, frangib-, fiss-ility; frailty; house of -cards, − glass.

V. be -brittle etc. *adj.*; live in a glass house.

break, crack, snap, split, shiver, splinter, crumble, break short, burst, fly, give way; fall to pieces; crumble -to, − into- dust.

Adj. breakable, brittle, frangible, fragile, frail, friable, delicate, gimcrack, shivery, fissile; splitting etc. *v.*; lacerable, splintery, crisp, crimp, short, brittle as glass.

329. Texture. [Structure.]—**N.** structure, organization, anatomy, frame, mold, fabric, construction; frame-work, carcass, architecture; stratification, cleavage.

substance, stuff, *compages*, *parenchyma*; constitution, staple, organism.

[Science of structures]organ-, oste-, my- splanchn-, neur-, angi-, aden-ology; angi-, aden-ography.

texture; inter-, con-texture; tissue, grain, web, surface; warp and -woof, – weft; tooth, nap etc. (*roughness*) 256; fineness –, coarseness- of grain.

[Science of textures] histology.

Adj. structural, organic; anatomic, -al.

text-ural, -ile; fine-, coarse-grained; fine, delicate, subtile, gossamery, filmy; coarse; homespun; linsey-woolsey.

330. Pulverulence. [State of powder.]—**N.** pulverulence; sandiness etc. *adj.*; efflorescence; friability.

powder, dust, sand, shingle; sawdust; grit; attrition; meal, bran, flour, *farina*, spore, sporule; crumb, seed, grain; particle etc. (*smallness*) 32; thermion; limature, filings, *débris*, *detritus*, scobs, magistery, fine powder; *flocculi*.

smoke; cloud of -dust, – sand, – smoke; puff –, volume -of smoke; sand –, dust- storm.

[Reduction to powder] pulverization, comminution, attenuation, granulation, disintegration, subaction, contusion, trituration, levigation, abrasion, detrition, multure; limation; filing etc. *v.*

[Instruments for pulverization] mill, millstone, grater, rasp, file, pestle and mortar, nutmeg grater, teeth, molar, grinder, chopper, grindstone, kern, quern, muller.

V. come to dust; be -disintegrated, – reduced to powder etc.

reduce –, grind- to powder; pulverize, comminute, granulate, triturate, levigate; scrape, file, abrade, rub down, grind, grate, rasp, pound, bray, bruise; con-tuse, -tund; beat, crush, cranch, craunch, crunch, muller, scranch, crumble, disintegrate; attenuate etc. 195.

Adj. powdery, pulverulent, granular, mealy, floury, farinaceous, branny, furfuraceous, flocculent, dusty, sandy, sabulous; aren-ose, -arious, -aceous; gritty; efflorescent, impalpable.

pulverizable; friable, crumbly, shivery; pulverized etc. *v.*; attrite; in pieces.

331. Friction.—**N.** friction, attrition; rubbing etc. *v.*; erasure; con-frication, -trition; affriction, abrasion, arrosion, limature, frication, rub; elbow-grease; rosin; *massage*.

V. rub, scratch, abrade, scrape, scrub, fray, rasp, graze, curry, scour, polish, rub out, erase, gnaw; file, grind etc. (*reduce to powder*) 330; *massage*.

set one's teeth on edge; rosin.

Adj. anatriptic, abrasive.

332. Lubrication. [Absence of friction. Prevention of friction.]—**N.** smoothness etc. 255; unctuousness etc. 355.

lubri-cation, -fication; anointment; oiling etc. *v.*

synovia; lubricant, graphite, glycerine, oil etc. 356; saliva; lather.

V. lubri-cate, -citate; oil, grease, lather, soap; wax.

Adj. lubricated etc. *v.*

333. Fluidity.—**N.** fluidity, liquidity; liquidness etc. *adj.*; gaseity etc. 334; liquefaction etc. 334.

fluid, inelastic fluid; liquid, liquor; lymph, humor, juice, sap, serum, blood, serosity, gravy, rheum, ichor, sanies.

solu-bility, -bleness.

[Science of liquids] hydro-logy, -statics, -dynamics, hydraulics. etc.

V. be -fluid etc. *adj.*; flow etc. (*water in motion*) 348; liquefy etc. 335.

Adj. liquid, fluid, serous, juicy, succulent, sappy; fluent etc. (*flowing*) 348.

liquefied etc. 335; uncongealed; soluble, hydrostatic etc. *n.*

334. Gaseity.—**N.** gaseity, gaseousness, vapourousness etc. *adj.*; flatulence, -lency; volatility, aeration, gasification.

elastic fluid, gas, air, vapor, ether, steam, fume, reek, *effluvium*, *flatus*; cloud etc. 353.

[Science of elastic fluids] pneumat-ics, -ostatics; aero-statics, -dynamics etc.

gas-, gaso-meter.

V. gassify, aerate, aerify; emit vapor etc. 336.

Adj. gaseous, aeriform, ethereal, aerial, airy, vaporous, volatile, evaporable; flatulent; aerostatic etc. *n.*

335. Liquefaction.—**N.** liquefaction; liquescen-ce, -cy, deliquescence; melting etc. (*heat*) 384; colliqu-ation, -efaction; thaw; de-, liquation; lixiviation, dissolution.

solution, apozem, lixivium, infusion, decoction, flux.

solvent, diluent, menstruum, alkahest, *aqua fortis*.

V. render -liquid etc 333; liquefy, run, deliquesce; melt etc. (*heat*) 384; solve; dissolve, resolve; liquate; hold in solution; leach, lixiviate.

Adj. lique-fied etc. *v.*, -scent, -fiable; deliquescent, soluble, colliquative; solvent.

336. Vaporization.—**N.** vapor-, volatilization; gasification; e-, vaporation; distillation, cohobation, sublimation, exhalation; volatility.

vaporizer, still, retort, spray, atomizer; fumigation, steaming.

V. render -gaseous etc. 334; vaporize, volatilize; distil, sublime; evaporate, exhale, smoke, transpire, emit vapor, fume, reek, steam, fumigate.

Adj. volatilized etc. *v.*; reeking etc. *v.*; volatile; evaporable, vaporizable.

337. Water.—N. water; serum, serosity; lymph; rheum; diluent.

dilution, maceration, lotion; washing etc. *v.*; immersion; humectation, infiltration, spargefaction; affusion, irrigation, *douche*, balneation, bath.

deluge etc. (*water in motion*) 348; high water, flood-, spring-tide.

V. be -watery etc. *adj.*; reek.

add water, water, wet; moisten etc. 339; dilute, dip, immerse; merge; im-, sub-merge; plunge, souse, duck, drown; soak, steep, macerate, pickle, wash, sprinkle, sparge, lave, bathe, affuse, splash, swash, douse, slosh, drench; dabble, slop, slobber, irrigate, inundate, deluge; syringe, inject, gargle; infiltrate, percolate.

Adj. watery, aqueous, aquatic, lymphatic; balneal, diluent; drenching etc. *v.*; diluted etc. *v.*; weak; wet etc. (*moist*) 339.

Phr. the waters are out.

338. Air.—N. air etc. (*gas*) 334; common −, atmospheric- air; atmosphere, stratosphere, isothermal layer, troposphere, Heaviside layer.

open; − air; sky, welkin; blue, − sky; cloud etc. 353.

weather, climate, rise and fall of the barometer, isobar.

[Science of air] pneumatics, aero-logy, -scopy, - graphy; meteorology, climatology; eudio-, baro-, aero-meter; aneroid, baro-graph, -scope; weather-gauge, -glass, -cock.

exposure to the -air, − weather; ventilation; aero-station; -nautics; -naut etc. 265 and 269.

V. air, ventilate; fan etc. (*wind*) 349.

Adj. containing air, flatulent, effervescent; windy etc. 349.

atmospheric, airy; aeri-al, -form; pneumatic; meteorological; weather-wise.

Adv. in the open air, out of doors, *à la belle étoile, al fresco; sub -Jove, − dio.*

339. Moisture.—N. moisture; moistness etc. *adj.*; hum-idity, -ectation; madefaction, dew; *serein*; marsh etc. 345; Hygromet-ry, -er.

V. moisten, wet; humect, -ate; sponge, damp, dampen, bedew; imbue, imbrue, infiltrate, saturate; seethe, sop; soak, drench etc. (*water*) 337.

be -moist etc. *adj.*; not have a dry thread; perspire etc. (*exude*) 295.

Adj. moist, damp; watery etc. 337; undried, humid, wet, dank, muggy, dewy; roric; roscid; juicy.

wringing wet; wet -through, − to the skin; saturated etc. *v.*

swashy, soggy, dabbled; reeking, seething, dripping, soaking, soft, sodden, sloppy, muddy; swampy etc. (*marshy*) 345; irriguous.

340. Dryness.—N. dryness etc. *adj.*; siccity, aridity, drought, ebb-, neap-tide, low water.

drying, ex-, de-siccation; evaporation; dehydration; arefaction, dephlegmation, drainage. drier, desiccator.

V. be -dry etc. *adj.*; render -dry etc. *adj.*; dry;

dry −, soak- up; sponge, swab, wipe; ex-, desiccate, dehydrate, anhydrate; drain, parch.

be fine, hold up.

Adj. dry, anhydrous, arid, waterless; dried etc. *v.*; undamped; juice-, sap- less; sear; husky; rainless, without rain, fine; dry as -a bone, − dust, − a stick, − a mummy, − a biscuit; disiccated; dehydrated; water-proof, -tight.

341. Ocean.—N. sea, ocean, main, deep, brine, salt water, waters, waves, billows, high seas, offing, great waters, watery waste, 'vasty deep,' briny ocean, herring pond, steamer track, the seven seas; wave, tide etc. (*water in motion*) 348.

hydrograph-y, -er, oceanography; Neptune, Thetis, Triton, Naiad, Nereid; sea-nymph, Siren, mer-maid, -man; trident, dolphin.

Adj. oceanic; mar-ine, -itime; pleagic, -ian; sea-going, -worthy; hydrographic.

Adv. at −, on- sea; afloat, on the high seas.

342. Land.—N. land, earth, ground, dry land, *terra firma.*

continent, mainland, peninsula, delta; tongue −, neck- of land; isthmus; oasis; promontory etc. (*projection*) 250; highland etc. (*height*) 206.

coast, shore, scar, strand, beach; bank, lea; sea-board, -side, -shore, -bank, -coast, -beach; rock-, iron- bound coast; loom of the land; derelict; innings; *alluvium*, alluvion.

soil, glebe, clay, loam, marl, clodge, chalk, gravel, mold, subsoil, clod, clot; rock, crag, cliff.

acres; real estate etc. (*property*) 780; landsman, land-lubber, farmer.

geography etc. 318; agriculture etc. 371.

V. land, come to land; set foot on -the soil, − dry land; come −, go- ashore.

Adj. earthy; continental, midland; littoral, riparian, ripuarian; alluvial; terrene etc. (*world*) 318; landed, predial, territorial.

Adv. ashore; on -shore, − land.

343. Gulf. Lake.—N. land covered with water, gulf, gulph, bay, inlet, bight, estuary, arm of the sea, fiord, armlet; frith, firth, ostiary, mouth; lagune, lagoon; indraught; cove, creek; natural harbor; roads; strait, narrows; Euripus; sound, belt, gut, kyles.

lake, loch, lough, mere, tarn, plash, broad, pond, pool, lin, puddle, well, artesian well, tank, sump; standing −, dead −; sheet of- water; fish −, mill-pond; race; ditch, dike, dyke, dam; reservoir etc. (*store*) 636.

Adj. lacustrine; land locked.

344. Plain.—N. plain, table land, mesa, face of the country; open −, champaign-country; basin, downs, waste, weary waste, desert, tundra, wild, steppe, pampas, savanna, prairie, champaign, heath, common, wold, veld; moor, -land, uplands, fell; bush; *plateau* etc. (*level*) 213; *campagna.*

meadow, mead, haugh, pasturage, park, field,

lawn, green, plat, plot, grass-plat, greensward,
sward, grass, turf, sod, heather; lea, ley, lay;
grounds.
Adj. campestrian, champaign, alluvial.

345. Marsh.—N. marsh, swamp, morass,
marish, moss, fen, bog, quagmire, slough, sump,
wash; mud, squash, slush.
Adj. marsh, -y; swampy, boggy, plashy, poachy,
quaggy, soft; muddy, sloppy, squashy, spongy;
paludal; moor-ish, -y; fenny.

346. Island.—N. island, isle, islet, eyot, ait,
holm, reef, atoll, breaker; archipelago; islander.
Adj. insular, sea-girt.

347. Stream. [Fluid in motion.]—**N.** stream
etc. (*of water*) 348, (*of air*) 349.
V. flow etc. 348; blow etc. 349.

348. River. [Water in motion.]—**N.** running
water.
jet, spirt, squirt, spout, splash, swash, rush, gush,
jet d'eau; sluice, chute.
water-spout, -fall; fall, cascade, force, foss; lin, -
n, ghyll, Niagara; cata-ract, -dupe, -clysm; *débâcle*,
inundation, deluge.
rain, -fall; *serein*; shower, scud; downpour,
cloud burst; driving –, pouring –, drenching-
rain; hyeto-logy, -graphy; rainy season, monsoon;
predominance of Aquarius, reign of St. Swithin;
mizzle, drizzle, *stilliciduim*, plash; dropping etc. *v.*
stream, course, flux, flow, profluence; effluence
etc. (*egress*) 295; defluxion; flowing etc. *v.*;
current, tide, race.
spring; fount, -ain; rill, rivulet, gill, gullet, rillet;
stream-, brook-let; runnel, sike, burn, beck, brook,
stream, river; reach; tributary.
body of water, torrent, rapids, flush, flood,
swash, spate; spring –, high –, full-tide; bore;
eagre, *hugre*; fresh, -et; undertow, indraught,
reflux, undercurrent, eddy, vortex, gurge,
whirlpool, Maelstrom, regurgitation, overflow;
confluence, corrivation.
wave, billow, surge, swell, ripple; roller, ground
swell, surf, breaker, white horses; comber, beachcomber; rough –, heavy –, cross –, long –,
short –, chopping –, choppy- sea, choppiness;
tidal wave.
[Science of fluids in motion] Hydrodynamics;
Hydraul-ics etc.; raingauge etc.
water-bearer, – carrier, Aquarius.
irrigation etc. (*water*) 337; pump; watering-pot,
– cart; hydrant, standpipe, hose, sprinkler,
drencher; fire engine, squirt, syringe.
V. flow, run; meander; gush, pour, spout, roll,
jet, well, issue; drop, drip, dribble, plash, squirt,
spurt, spirtle, trill, trickle, distil, percolate; stream,
overflow, inundate, deluge, flow over, splash,
swash, guggle, murmur, babble, bubble, purl,
gurgle, sputter, regurgitate; ooze, flow out etc.
(*egress*) 295.

rain, – hard, – in torrents, – cats and dogs, –
pitchforks; come down in sheets; pour with rain,
drizzle, mizzle, spit, sprinkle, set in.
flow –, fall –, open –, drain- into; discharge
itself, desembogue.
[Cause a flow] pour; pour out etc. (*discharge*)
297; shower down; irrigate, drench etc. (*wet*) 337;
spill, splash.
[Stop a flow] stanch; dam, -up etc. (*close*) 261;
obstruct etc. 706.
Adj. fluent; dif-, pro-, af-fluent; tidal; flowing
etc. *v.*; meand-ering, -ry, -rous; fluvi-al, -atile;
streamy, showery, rainy, drizzly, drizzling, pluvial,
pluviose, stillicidous.

349. Wind. [Air in motion.]—**N.** wind,
draught, *flatus*, *afflatus*, air; breath, – of air; puff,
whiff, zephyr; blow, drift; *aura*; stream, current;
under-current.
gust, blast, breeze, squall, gale, half a gale,
storm, tempest, hurricane, whirlwind, tornado,
samiel, cyclone, typhoon; simoon; harmattan,
monsoon, trade wind, sirocco, *mistral*, *bise*, *föhn*,
tramontane, levanter; capful of wind; fresh –,
stiff- breeze; keen blast; blizzard.
windiness etc. *adj.*; ventosity; rough –, dirty –,
ugly –, stress of- weather; dirty-, windy-,
mackerel- sky; mare's tail; thick –, black –,
white- squall.
anemography, aerodynamics; windgauge,
anemometer, weather-cock, vane.
suf-, insuf-, per-, in-, af-flation; blowing, fanning
etc. *v.*; ventilation.
sneezing etc. *v.*; sternutation; hic-cup, -cough;
catching of the breath; breathing etc.
Eolus, Eurus, Boreas, Zephyr, cave of Eolus.
air-pump, lungs, bellows, blow-pipe, fan,
blower; pulmotor, ventilator, punkah, aspirator,
exhauster, ejector.
V. blow, waft; blow -hard, – great guns, – a
hurricane etc. *n.*; whistle, roar, howl, ring in the
shrouds; stream, issue.
respire, breathe, in-, ex-hale, puff; whif, -fle;
gasp, wheeze; snuff, -le; sniff, -le; sneeze, cough,
belch.
fan, ventilate; in-, per-flate; blow –, pump- up.
Adj. blowing etc. *v.*; windy, airy, aeolian,
flatulent; breezy, gusty, squally; stormy, tempestuous, blustering; boisterous etc. (*violent*) 173.
pulmon-ic, -ary.

350. Conduit. [Channel for the passage of
water.]—**N.** conduit, channel, duct, watercourse,
race; head –, tail- race; adit, aqueduct, canal,
trough, flume, gutter, pantile; dike, canyon, ravine,
gorge, hollow, main, gully, moat, ditch, drain,
sewer, culvert, *cloaca*, sough, kennel, siphon,
piscina; pipe etc. (*tube*) 260; funnel; tunnel etc.
(*passage*) 627; water –, waste- pipe; emunctory,
gully-hole, artery, aorta, vein, blood vessel; lymphatic; throat, alimentary canal, intestine; pore,
spout, scupper; ad-, a-jutage; hose; gar-, gurgoyle; penstock, weir; flood-, water-gate; sluice,
lock, valve; rose; waterworks.
Adj. vascular etc. (*with holes*) 260.

351. Air-pipe. [Channel for the passage of
air.]—**N.** air-pipe, – shaft, – way, – passage, –

tube; shaft, flue, chimney, funnel, vent, blow-hole, nostril, nozzle, throat, weasand, *trachea*; *bronchus*, *-ia*; larynx, tonsils, wind-pipe, spiracle; ventiduct, -lator; louvre, Venetian blinds; blow-pipe etc. (*wind*) 349; pipe etc. (*tube*) 260.

352. Semiliquidity.—N. semiliquidity; stickiness etc. *adj.*; visc-idity, -osity; gumm-, glutin-, muc-osity; spiss-, crass-itude; lentor; adhesiveness etc. (*cohesion*) 46.

inspiss-, incrass-ation; thickening, coagulation.

jelly, aspic, mucilage, gelatin, isinglass; colloid, mucus, phlegm; pituite, lava; glair, starch, gluten, albumen, milk, cream, protein; syrup, treacle; gum, size, glue, paste; wax, bee's-wax; emulsoid, emulsion, soup; squash, mud, slush, slime, ooze; moisture etc. 339; marsh etc. 345.

V. inspiss-, incrass-ate; coagulate, gelatinize, gelatinify, gel, jell, emulsify, thicken; mash, squash, churn, beat up.

Adj. semi-fluid, -liquid; half-melted, -frozen; milky, muddy etc. *n.*; lact-eal, -ean, -eous, -escent, -iferous; emulsive, curdled, thick, succulent, uliginous.

gelat-, album-, mucilag-, glut-inous; gelatine, mastic, amylaceous, ropy, clammy, clotted; vis-cid, -cous; sticky, tacky; slab, -by; lentous, pituitous, mu-cid, -culent, -cous.

353. Bubble. [Mixture of air and water.] [Cloud.]**—N.** bubble; foam, froth, head, fume, spume, lather, suds, spray, surf, yeast, barm, spindrift.

cloud, vapor, fog, mist, haze, steam; scud, rack, *nimbus*; *cumulus*, woolpack, *cirrus*, *stratus*; cirro-, *cumulo-stratus*; *cirro-cumulus*; mackerel sky, mare's tail, dirty sky.

[Science of clouds] nephelognosy, nephology.

effervescence, fermentation; bubbling etc. *v.*

nebula; cloudiness etc. (*opacity*) 426; nebulosity etc. (*dimness*) 422.

V. bubble, boil, foam, froth, spume, mantle, sparkle, guggle, gurgle; effervesce, ferment, fizzle; aerate; cloud, overcast, befog.

Adj. bubbling etc. *v.*; frothy, nappy, effervescent, sparkling, *mousseux*, up, fizzy, with a head on.

cloudy etc. *n.*; vaporous, nebulous, overcast; nubiferous, nephological; foggy, brumous.

354. Pulpiness.—N. pulpiness etc. *adj.*; pulp, paste, dough, sponge, curd, pap, rob, jam, pudding, mush, fool, poultice, grume.

Adj. pulpy etc. *n.*; pultaceous, grumous.

V. pulp, pulpify, mash.

355. Unctuousness.—N. unctuousness etc. *adj.*; unctuosity, lubricity; ointment etc. (*oil*) 356; anointment; lubrication etc. 332.

V. oil etc. (*lubricate*) 332.

Adj. unctuous, oily, oleaginous, adipose, sebaceous; fat, -ty; greasy, waxy, butyraceous, soapy, saponaceous, pinguid, lardaceous; slippery.

356. Oil.—N. oil, fat, butter, cream, grease, tallow, suet, lard, dripping, margarine, oleomargarine, exunge, blubber; glycerine, stearine, elaine, oleagine; soap; soft soap, wax, cerement; paraffin, spermaceti, adipocere; petroleum, mineral −, rock −, crystal- oil, kerosene, vegetable −, colza −, olive −, linseed −, cotton seed −, rape −, nut −, fusel- oil; animal −, neat's foot −, signal −, train- oil; ointment, unguent, liniment, salve, pomade, pomatum, brilliantine, spike −, nard.

356a. Resin.—N. resin, rosin, colophony; gum; lac, shellac, sealing-wax; amber, -gris; bitumen, pitch, tar, asphalt, -e, -um; varnish, copal, mastic, magilp, lacquer, japan.

V. varnish etc. (*overlay*) 223.

Adj. resinous, bituminous, pitchy, tarry.

357. Organization.—N. organized -world, − nature; living −, animated- nature; living beings; organic remains, organism; fossils; animal and vegetable kingdom, *fauna* and *flora*, biota.

prot-oplasm, -ein; albumen; structure etc. 329; organ-ization, -ism.

[Science of living beings] biology; natural history,* organic −, bio-chemistry, anatomy, physiology, embryology, morphology, evolution, Darwinism, Lamarkism, zoology etc. 368; botany etc. 369; naturalist, biologist etc.

Adj. organ-ic, -ized.

*The term *Natural History* is also used as relating to all the objects in Nature whether organic or inorganic, and including therefore *Mineralogy, Geology, Meteorology*, etc.

358. Inorganization.—N. mineral -world, − kingdom; unorganized −, inorganic −, brute −, inanimate- matter.

[Science of the mineral kingdom] mineralogy; geo-logy, -gnosy, -scopy; metall-urgy, -ography; lithology; orycto-logy, -graphy.

V. turn to dust, pulverize.

Adj. in-organic, -animate; unorganized; azoic; mineral.

359. Life.—N. life; vi-tality, -ability; animation; vital -spark, − flame, − force.

respiration, wind; breath -of life, − of one's nostrils; life-blood; Archeus; existence etc. 1.

vivification, vitalization; revivification etc. 163; Prometheus; life to come etc. (*destiny*) 152.

[Science of life] physiology, etiology, embryology, biology; animal economy.

nourishment, staff of life etc. (*food*) 298.

V. be -alive etc. *adj.*; live, breathe, respire; subsist etc. (*exist*) 1; walk the earth; strut and fret one's hour upon a stage; be spared.

see the light, be born, come into the world; fetch −, draw- -breath, − the breath of life; quicken; revive; come to, − life.

give birth to etc. (*produce*) 161; bring to life, put into life, vitalize; vivi-fy, -ficate; reanimate etc. (*restore*) 660; keep -alive, − body and soul together, − the wolf from the door; support life.

have nine lives like a cat.

Adj. living, alive; in -life, — the flesh, — the land of the living; on this side of the grave, above ground, breathing, quick, animated, viable; lively etc. (*active*) 682; alive and kicking; tenacious of life.

vital; vivi-fying; -fied etc. *v.*; Promethean.

Adv. vivendi causâ.

360. Death.—N. death, dying etc. *v.*; de-cease, -mise; dissolution, departure, *obit*, release, rest, *quietus*, fall; loss, bereavement.

end etc. 67 — . cessation etc. 142 — , loss — , extinction — , ebb- of -life etc. 359.

death-warrant, -watch, -rattle, -bed; stroke — , agonies — , shades — , valley of the shadow — , jaws — , hand- of death; last -breath, — gasp, — agonies; dying -day, — breath, — agonies; swan song, *chant du cygne*; *rigor mortis*; Stygian shore; crossing the bar, the great adventure.

King -of terrors, — Death; Death, Angel of Death; mortality; doom etc. (*necessity*) 601.

euthanasia; happy release; break up of the system; natural -death, — decay; sudden — , violent- death; untimely end, watery grave; suffocation, *asphyxia*; heart failure; fatal disease etc. (*disease*) 655; death-blow etc. (*killing*) 361.

necrology, bills of mortality, obituary; death-song etc. (*lamentation*) 839.

V. die, expire, perish; meet one's -death, — end; pass away, be taken; yield — , resign- one's breath; resign one's -being, — life; end one's -days, — life, — earthly career; breathe one's last; cease to -live, — breathe; depart this life; be -no more etc. *adj.*; go — , drop — , pop -off; lose — , lay down — , relinquish — , surrender- one's life; drop — , sink- into the grave; close one's eyes; fall — , drop- dead, — down dead; break one's neck; give — , yield- up the ghost; be all over with one.

pay the debt to nature, shuffle off this mortal coil, take one's last sleep; go the way of all flesh; join the -greater number, — majority, — choir invisible, to life immortal awake; come — , turn- to dust; cross the Stygian ferry; go to -one's long account, — one's last home, — Davy Jones's locker, — the wall; receive one's death warrant, make one's will, die a natural death, go out like the snuff of a candle; come to an untimely end; catch one's death; go off the hooks, kick the bucket, pet out; go West; hop the twig, turn up one's toes; die a violent death etc. (*be killed*) 361; make the supreme sacrifice.

Adj. dead, lifeless; deceased, demised, departed, defunct; late, gone, no more; ex-, in-animate; out of the world, taken off, released; departed this life etc. *v.*; dead and gone; bereft of life, stone dead, dead as -a door nail, — a door post, — mutton, — a herring, — nits; launched into eternity, gathered to one's fathers, numbered with the dead, gone to a better land, behind the veil, beyond the grave, — mortal ken.

dying etc. *v.*; mori-bund, -ent, Acherontic; hippocratic; in -articulo, — extremis; in the -jaws, — agony- of death; going, — off; *aux abois*; on one's -last legs, — death bed; at -the point of death, — death's door, — the last gasp; near one's end, given over, booked, fey; with one foot in — , tottering on the brink of- the grave.

still-born; mortuary; deadly etc. (*killing*) 361.

Adv. post -obit, — mortem.

Phr. life -ebbs, — fails, — hangs by a thread; one's -days are numbered, — hour is come, — race is run, — doom is sealed; Death -knocks at the door, — stares one in the face; the breath is out of the body; the grave closes over one; *sic itur ad astra*.

361. Killing. [Destruction of life; violent death.]—N. killing etc. *v.*; homicide, man-slaughter, murder, assassination, trucidation, occision; lynching, effusion of blood; blood, -shed; gore, slaughter, carnage, butchery; *battue*, gladiatorial combat.

massacre; *fussillade*, *noyade*, *pogrom*; thuggism; racketeering.

death blow, finishing stroke, *coup de grâce*, *quietus*; execution etc. (*capital punishment*) 972; judicial murder; martyrdom.

butcher, slayer, murderer, Cain, assassin, cut-throat, garrotter, *bravo*, thug, racketeer, gunman, mobster, gangster, Moloch, *matador*, *sabreur*; *guet-à-pens*; gallows, executioner etc. (*punishment*) 975; man-eater.

regicide, parricide, fratricide, infanticide, aborticide etc.

suicide, *felo de se*, *suttee*, *hara kiri*, Juggernaut; immolation, holocaust.

suffocation, strangulation, *garrotte*; hanging etc. *v.*

deadly weapon etc. (*arms*) 727; Aceldama; the potter's field, the field of blood.

fatal accident, violent death, casualty.

[Destruction of animals] slaughtering; phthiozoics;* sport, -ting; the chase, venery; hunting, coursing, shooting, fishing; pig-sticking; sports-, hunts-, fisher-man; hunter, Nimrod; slaughterer, knacker, slaughter-house, shambles, *abattoir*.

V. kill, put to death, slay, shed blood; murder, assassinate, butcher, slaughter; victimize, im-molate; massacre; take away — , deprive of- life; make away with, put an end to; despatch, dispatch; burke settle, do, — to death, — for.

strangle, garrotte, hang, lynch, throttle, choke, stifle, suffocate, stop the breath, smother, asphyxiate, drown.

saber; cut -down, — to pieces, — the throat; jugulate; stab, run through the body, bayonet; put to the -sword, — edge of the sword.

shoot, — dead; blow one's brains out; brain, knock on the head; stone, lapidate; give — , deal- a death blow; give a -quietus, — coup de grâce.

behead, bowstring etc. (*execute*) 972.

hunt, shoot etc. *n.*

cut off, nip in the bud, launch into eternity, send to one's last account, bump off, rub out, sign one's death warrant, strike the death knell of.

give no quarter, pour out blood like water; decimate; run amuck, wade knee-deep — , imbrue one's hands- in blood.

die a violent death, welter in one's blood; dash — , blow- out one's brains; commit suicide; kill — -make away with — , put an end to- oneself.

Adj. killing etc. *v.*; murd-, slaught-erous; sanguin-ary, -olent; blood-stained, -thirsty;

homicidal, red-handed; bloody, -minded; ensanguined, gory, sanguineous.

mortal fatal, lethal; dead-, death-ly; mort-, lethiferous; unhealthy etc. 657; internecine; suicidal.

sporting; piscator-ial, -y.

Adv. in at the death.

*Bentham, 'Chrestomathia.'

362. Corpse.—N. corpse, corse, carcass, bones,
skeleton, dry-bones; defunct, relics, *relinquiae*,
remains, mortal remains, dust, ashes, earth, clay;
mummy; carrion; food for- worms, – fishes;
tenement of clay, this mortal coil.

shade, ghost, *manes*, apparition, etc. 980.

organic remains, fossils.

Adj. cadaverous, corpse-like; unburied etc. 363.

363. Interment.—N. interment, burial,
inhumation, sepulture, entombment; in-, humation;
obs-, ex-equies; funeral, wake, pyre, funeral pile;
cremation.

funeral -rite, – solemnity; knell, passing bell,
tolling; dirge etc. (*lamentation*) 839; cypress; *obit*,
dead march, muffled drum; coroner, mortician,
undertaker, mute, mourner, professional mourner,
pallbearer; elegy; funeral -oration, – sermon;
epitaph.

grave clothes, shroud; winding-sheet, cere-cloth;
cerement.

coffin, shell, sarcophagus, urn, pall, bier, hearse,
catafalque, cinerary urn.

grave, pit, sepulcher, tomb, vault, crypt,
catacomb, mausoleum, *Golgotha*, house of death,
narrow house, long home; cemetery, necropolis,
boneyard; burial-place, -ground; grave-, churchyard; God's acre; mortuary, tope, cromlech,
dolmen, menhir, barrow, tumulus, cairn; ossuary;
bone-, charnel-, dead-house; *Morgue*; lich-gate;
crematorium.

sexton, grave-digger.

monument, memorial, cenotaph, shrine; grave-,
head-, tomb-stone; *memento mori*; hatchment,
stone, cross.

exhumation, disinterment; necropsy, autopsy,
post mortem examination.

V. inter, bury, lay in – , consign to- the -grave,
– tomb; en-, in-tomb; inhume; lay out, prepare for
burial, embalm, mummify; conduct a funeral, hold
services; toll the knell; put to bed with a shovel.

exhume, disinter, unearth.

Adj. buried etc. *v.*; burial; fune-real, -brial; mortuary, sepulchral, cinerary; elegiac; necroscopic.

Adv. *in memoriam*; post-obit, -mortem;
beneath – , under- the sod.

Phr. hic jacet, ci-git, requiescat in pace.

364. Animality.—N. animal life; anima-tion, -
lity, -lization; breath.

flesh, – and blood; corporeal nature; *physique*;
strength etc. 159.

V. animalize, incorporate.

Adj. fleshly, incarnate, carnal, corporeal,
human.

365. Vegetability.—N. vegetable life; vegetation, -bility; herbage.

V. vegetate, germinate, sprout, shoot; cultivate.

Adj. vegetable etc. 367; rank, lush.

366. Animal.*—N. animal, – kingdom;
fauna; brute creation.

beast, brute, creature, created being; creeping
– , living- thing; dumb -animal, – creature.

flocks and herds, live stock; domestic – , wild-
animals; game, *ferae naturae*; beasts of the fields,
fowls of the air, denizens of the day.

vertebrate, bi-, quadru-ped, mammal, marsupial,
bird, reptile, batrachian, amphibian, fish, crustacean, shell fish, articulate, mollusc, worm, insect,
zoophyte; protozoon, animalcule etc. 193.

horse etc. (*beast of burden*) 271; cattle, kine, ox;
bull, -ock; steer, stot; cow, milch-cow, calf, heifer,
shorthorn; sheep; lamb, -kin; ewe – , pet-lamb;
ewe, ram, tup; pig, swine, boar, hog, shoat, sow;
tag, teg, wether.

dog, bitch, hound; pup, -py; whelp, cur, mutt,
mongrel; house-, watch-, sheep-, shepherd's, sport-
ing-, fancy-, lap-, toy-, bull-, badger-dog; mastiff;
blood-, grey-, stag-, deer-, fox-, otter-, hound;
harrier, beagle, spaniel, pointer, setter, retriever;
Newfoundland; water -dog, – spaniel; pug,
poodle; dachshund; Pinscher; turnspit; terrier; fox
– , Skye- terrier; Dandie Dinmont; colley.

cat; puss,-y; kitten; grimalkin; gib-, tom-cat;
mouser; fox, Reynard, vixen, stag, deer, hart, buck,
doe, roe, antelope.

bird; poultry, fowl, cock, hen, chicken, chan-
ticleer, partlet, rooster, dunghill cock, barn-door
fowl; feathered -tribes, – songster; singing – ,
dicky- bird; canary; finch; auk, dodo, moa, roc,
phoenix.

snake, serpent, viper, adder; newt, eft; asp, vermin.

Adj. animal, zoological.

equine, bovine, vaccine, canine, feline; fishy;
piscator-y, -ial; molluscous, vermicular.

*Extended lists of names of specific varieties of animals,
vegetables, etc., are beyond the scope of this work.

367. Vegetable.*—N. vegetable, – kingdom;
flora, verdure.

plant; tree, shrub, bush; creeper; vine; herb, -age;
grass.

annual; per-, bi-, tri-ennial; exotic.

timber; primeval – , virgin- forest; wood, -lands;
hurst; frith, holt, weald, park, chase, greenwood,
brake, grove, copse, coppice, *bocage*, tope, clump
of trees, thicket, spinet, spinney; under-, brushwood; boscage, scrub; the oak and the ash and the
bonny ivy tree.

bush, jungle, prairie; heath, -er; fern, bracken,
furze, gorse, whin, broom; grass, turf, grassland,
greensward, green, lawn, meadow; pas-ture, -
turage; turbary; sedge, rush, weed; fungus,
mushroom, toadstool; lichen, moss, conferva,
mold; seaweed etc.; growth, crop.

foliage, leafage, branch, bough, ramage; spray
etc. 51; leaf, frond, flag, petal, shoot, tendril.

flower, blossom, bud, bloom, bine; flowering
plant; tree, sapling, pollard; timber-, fruit-tree;
palm-, gum-tree; pulse, legume.

Adj. veget-able, -ous; herb-aceous, -al; botanic;
sylvan, silvan; arbor- ary, -eous, -escent, -ical; den-

dritic, dendriform; woody, grassy; ver-dant, -durous; floral, mossy; lign-ous, -eous; wooden, leguminous; end-, ex-ogenous.

*Extended lists of names of specific varieties of animals, vegetables, etc., are beyond the scope of this work.

368. Zoology. [The science of animals.]—N. zoo-logy, -nomy, -graphy, -tomy; anatomy; comparative anatomy; animal – , comparative-physiology; morphology.

anthrop-, ornith-, ichthy-, herpet-, ophi-, malac-, helminth-, entom-, oryct-, paleont-ology; ichthyetc. -otomy; taxidermy.

zo- etc. -ologist.

Adj. zoological etc. *n.*

369. Botany. [The science of plants.]—N. botany; phyto-graphy, -logy, -tomy; vegetable physiology, herborization, dendr-, myc-, fung-, alg-ology; flora, pomona; botanist etc.; botanic garden etc. (*garden*) 371; *hortus siccus, herbarium,* herbal.

herb-ist, -arist, -alist, -orist, -arian etc.

V. botanize, herborize.

Adj. botanical etc. *n.*

370. Cicuration. [The economy or management of animals.]—N. taming etc. *v.*; cicuration, zoohygiantics; domestication, -ity; *manège*; veterinary art; breeding, pisciculture, apiculture etc.

menagery, vivarium, zoological garden, zoo; bear-pit; aviary, apiary, hive; aquarium, fishery, fish hatchery; duck-, fish-pond; stud-farm; stock farm, dairy.

[Destruction of animals] phthisozoics etc. (*killing*) 361.

neat-, cow-, shep-herd, shepherdess; grazier; drover, cowboy, cowkeeper; trainer, breeder, groom, ostler etc. 746; veterinary surgeon, vet, horse doctor; farrier; keeper; game keeper.

cage etc. (*prison*) 752; hen-coop, bird-cage, cauf; sheep-fold etc. (*inclosure*) 232.

V. tame, domesticate, acclimatize, breed, tend, break in, train, corral, round up; cage, bridle etc. (*restrain*) 751; ride etc. 266.

drive, yoke, harness, hitch; groom, curry-comb; milk; shear; hatch; incubate.

Adj. pastoral, bucolic; tame, domestic, domesticated, broken in, gentle, docile.

371. Agriculture. [The economy or management of plants.]—N. agriculture, cultivation, husbandry, farming; georgics, geoponics; tillage, tilth, agronomy, gardening, spade husbandry, vintage; hort-, arbor-, silv-, citr-, vit-, flor-iculture; intensive culture; landscape gardening; forestry, afforestation.

husbandman, horticulturist, citriculturist, gardener, florist; agricult-or, -urist; yeoman, farmer, cultivator, tiller of the soil, ploughman, sower, reaper; woodcutter, backwoodsman, forester; vine grower, vintager; Boer; Triptolemus.

field, meadow, garden; botanic – , winter – , ornamental – , flower – , kitchen – , truck – , market – , hop- garden; nursery; green-, hot-, glass-house; conservatory, cucumber frame, *cloche,* bed, border, seed-plot; grass-plat, lawn; park etc. (*pleasure ground*) 840; *partere,* shrubbery, plantation, avenue, *arboretum,* pinery, *pinetum,* orchard, vineyard, vinery; orangery; farm etc. (*abode*) 189.

V. cultivate; till, – the soil; farm, garden; sow, plant; reap, mow, cut; manure, dress the ground, dig, delve, dibble, hoe, plough, plow, harrow, rake, weed, lop and top, force, transplant, thin out, bed out, prune, graft.

Adj. agr-icultural, -airan, -estic.

arable; predial, rural, rustic, country, bucolic, Boeotian; horticultural.

372. Mankind.—N. man, -kind; human -race, – species, – nature; humanity, mortality, flesh, generation.

[Science of man] anthropo-logy, -graphy, -sophy; ethno-logy, -graphy; humanitarianism.

human being; person, age; individual, creature, fellow creature, mortal, body, somebody, one; such a – , someone; soul, living soul; earthling; party, head, hand; *dramatis personae.*

people, persons, folk, public, society, world; community, – at large; general public; nation, -ality; state, realm; common-weal, -wealth; republic, body politic; million etc. (*commonalty*) 876; population etc. (*inhabitant*) 188.

cosmopolite; lords of the creation; ourselves.

Adj. human, mortal, personal, individual, national, civic, public, cosmopolitan; anthropoid.

373. Man.—N. man, male, he; manhood etc. (*adolescence*) 131; gentleman, sir, master; yeoman, wight, swain, fellow, guy, blade, *beau,* chap, gaffer, good man; husband etc. (*married man*) 903; Mr., mister, *monsieur, sahib, Herr, señor, signor;* boy etc. (*youth*) 129; Adonis.

[Male animal] cock, drake, gander, dog, boar, stag, hart, buck, horse, entire horse, stallion; gib-, tom-cat; he-, Billy-goat; ram, tup; bull, -ock; capon, ox, gelding; steer, stot.

Adj. male, he, masculine; manly, virile; un-womanly, -feminine.

374. Woman.—N. woman, she, female, petticoat, skirt, moll, broad.

feminality, feminity, muliebrity; womanhood etc. (*adolescence*) 131; feminism; gynecology, gyniatrics, gynics.

womankind; the -sex, – fair; fair – , softer- sex; weaker vessel; the distaff side.

dame, madam, *madame,* mistress, Mrs., lady, *mem-sahib, Frau, señora, signora, donna, belle,* matron, dowager, goody, gammer; good -woman, – wife; squaw; wife etc. (*marriage*) 903; matron-age, -hood.

Venus, nymph, wench, *grisette;* little bit of fluff; girl etc. (*youth*) 129.

inamorata (*love*) etc. 897; courtesan etc. 962.

spinster, old maid, virgin, bachelor girl, new woman, amazon.

[Female animal] hen, slut, bitch, sow, doe, roe, mare; she-, Nanny-goat; ewe, cow; lioness, tigress; vixen.

gynecaeum, harem, seraglio, zenana, purdah.

Adj. female, she; feminine, womanly, ladylike, matronly, maidenly; womanish, effeminate, unmanly, gynecic.

375. Physical Sensibility.—N. sensibility; sensitiveness etc. adj.; physical sensibility, feeling, perceptivity, anaphylaxis, susceptibility, esthetics; moral sensibility etc. 882.

sensation, impression, effect; consciousness etc. (knowledge) 490.

external senses.

V. be -sensible etc. adj. -of; feel, perceive.

render, -sensible etc. adj.; excite, stir, sharpen, cultivate, tutor.

cause sensation, impress; excite — , produce- an impression.

Adj. sens-ible, -itive, -uous; esthetic, perceptive, sentient; conscious etc. (aware) 490; impressionable, responsive, alive to.

acute, sharp, keen, vivid, lively, impressive, thinskinned.

Adv. to the quick.

376. Physical Insensibility.—N. insensibility, physical insensibility; obtuseness etc. adj.; palsy, paralysis, anesthesia, analgesia, narcosis, hypnosis, twilight sleep, stupor, coma, trance, catalepsy; sleep etc. (inactivity) 683; moral insensibility etc. 823; numbness etc. 381.

anesthetic agent, general — , local- anesthetic, opium, ether, chloroform, cocaine, novocaine, chloral; nitrous oxide, laughing gas; refrigeration.

V. be -insensible etc. adj.; have a -thick skin, — rhinoceros hide.

render -insensible etc. adj.; blunt, pall, obtund, benumb, deaden, paralyze; anesthetize, drug, dope; put under the influence of -chloroform etc. n.; hypnotize; stupefy, stun, narcotize.

Adj. insensible, unfeeling, senseless, comatose, dazed, impercipient, callous, thick-skinned, pachydermatous; hard, -ened; case-hardened; proof; obtuse, dull; anesthetic; paralytic, palsied, numb, dead.

377. Physical Pleasure.—N. pleasure; physical — , sensual — , sensuous- pleasure; bodily enjoyment, animal gratification, sensuality; hedonism, luxuriousness etc. adj.; dissipation, round of pleasure; titillation, gusto, creature comforts, comfort, ease; pillow etc. (support) 215; luxury, lap of luxury; purple and fine linen; bed of -down, — roses; velvet, clover; cup of Circe etc. (intemperance) 954.

treat; diversion, divertisement, entertainment; refreshment, regale; feast; délice; dainty etc. 394; bonne bouche.

source of pleasure etc. 829; happiness etc. (mental enjoyment) 827.

V. feel — , experience — , receive- pleasure; enjoy, relish; luxuriate — , revel — , riot — , bask — ,

swim — , wallow- in; feast on; gloat -over, — on; smack the lips.

live -on the fat of the land, — in comfort etc. adv.; bask in the sunshine, faire ses choux gras.

give pleasure etc. 829.

Adj. enjoying etc. v.; luxurious, voluptuous, sensual, hedonistic, comfortable, cosy, snug, in comfort, at ease.

agreeable etc. 829; grateful, refreshing, comforting, cordial, genial; sensuous; palatable etc. 394; sweet etc. (sugar) 396; fragrant etc. 400; melodious etc. 413; lovely etc. (beautiful) 845.

Adv. in -comfort etc. n.; on -a bed of roses etc. n.; at one's ease.

378. Physical Pain.—N. pain; suffering, -ance; bodily — physical -pain, — suffering; mental suffering etc. 828; dolor, ache; aching etc. v.; smart; shoot, -ing; twinge, twitch, gripe, head-, ear-, toothache; migraine, neuralgia, neuritis, lumbago, gout, sciatica; hurt, cut; sore, -ness; discomfort, malaise; tic douloureux.

spasm, cramp; nightmare, ephialtes; crick, stitch, kink; thrill, convulsion, throe; throb etc. (agitation) 315; pang.

sharp — , piercing — , throbbing — , shooting — , gnawing — , burning- pain; anguish, agony.

torment, torture; rack; cruci-ation, -fixion; martyrdom; martyr, toad under a harrow, vivisection.

V. feel — , experience — , suffer — , undergo- pain etc. n.; suffer, ache, smart, bleed; tingle, shoot; twinge, twitch, lancinate; writhe, wince, make a wry face; sit on -thorns, — pins and needles.

give — , inflict- pain; pain, hurt, chafe, sting, bite, gnaw, gripe, stab, grind; pinch, tweak; grate, gall, fret, prick, pierce, wring, convulse; torment, torture; rack, agonize; crucify; excruciate; break on the wheel, put to the rack; flag etc. (punish) 972; grate on the ear etc. (harsh sound) 410.

Adj. in -pain etc. n.; — a state of pain; pained etc. v.

painful; aching etc. v.; biting, poignant; sore, raw, tender, with exposed nerve.

379. Touch. [Sensation of pressure.] **—N.** touch; tact, -ion, -ility; feeling; palp-ation, -ability; manipulation; brush, tick, graze, contact etc. 199.

[Organ of touch] hand, finger, fore-finger, thumb, paw, teeler, antenna.

V. touch, feel, handle, finger, thumb, paw, fumble, grope, grabble; twiddle, tweedle; pass — , run-the fingers over, massage, rub, knead; palpate, stroke, manipulate, wield; throw out a feeler.

Adj. tact-ual, -ile; tangible, palpable; lambent.

380. Sensations of Touch.—N. itching etc. v.; titillation, formication, aura.

V. itch, tingle, creep, thrill, sting; prick, -le; tickle, titillate.

Adj. itching etc. v.

381. Numbness. [Insensibility to touch.] **—N.**

numbness etc. (*physical insensibility*) 376; pins
and needles.
local anesthetic,cocaine novocaine etc.; morphia.
V. benumb etc. 376; freeze, dull, deaden.
Adj. numb; benumbed etc. *v.*; intangible, impalpable.

382. Heat.—N. heat, caloric; temperature,
warmth, fervor, calidity; incal-, incand-, recal-,
decal-escence; glow, flush, blush; fever, hectic.
phlogiston; fire, spark, scintillation, flash, flame,
blaze; arc; bonfire; firework, pyrotechny; wild-fire;
sheet of fire, lambent flame; devouring element;
conflagration.
summer, dog-days, canicule; baking etc. 384 —,
white —, tropical —, Afric —, Bengal —, summer
—, blood- heat; heat wave, sirocco, simoon;
broiling sun; isolation; warming etc. 384.
sun etc. (*luminary*) 423; fire worshipper etc.
991; furnace etc. 386.
geyser, hot spring, volcano.
: Science of heat. pyrology; thermology, -otics;
thermometer etc. 389.
V. be -hot etc. *adj.*; glow, incandesce, flush,
sweat, swelter, bask, smoke, reek, stew, simmer,
seethe, boil, burn, singe, scorch, scald, grill, broil,
blaze, flame; smoulder; parch, fume, pant.
heat etc. (*make hot*) 384; thaw, fuse, melt, give.
Adj. hot, heated, warm, mild, genial, tepid,
lukewarm, unfrozen; therm-al, -ic; calorific; fervent, -id; ardent; aglow.
sunny, torrid, tropical, estival, canicular; close,
sultry, stifling, stuffy, suffocating, oppressive;
reeking etc. *v.*; baking etc. 384.
red —, white —, smoking —, bruning etc. *v.* —,
piping- hot; like -a furnace, — an oven; hot as -fire,
— pepper; hot enough to roast an ox.
fiery; incand-, incal-escent; candent, ebullient,
glowing, smoking; on fire; blazing etc. *v.*; in -
flames, — a blaze; alight, afire, ablaze; un-
quenched, -extinguished; smouldering; in a -heat,
— glow, — fever, — perspiration, — sweat;
sudorific; swelter-ing, -ed; blood-hot, -warm; warm
as -a toast, — wool; recalescent, thermogenic,
pyrotechnic, feverish, febrile, inflamed.
volcanic, plutonic, igneous; isother-mal, -mic, -
al.
Phr. Not a breath of air.

383. Cold.—N. cold, -ness etc. *adj.*; frigidity,
gelidity, algidity, inclemency, *fresco.*.
winter; depth of —, hard- winter; Siberia, Nova
Zembla; Ant-, arctic, North —, South- Pole.
ice; snow, — flake, — crystal – drift; sleet; hail,
-stone; rime, frost; hoar —, white —, hard —,
sharp- frost; icicle, thick-ribbed ice; fall of snow,
snow storm, heavy fall, *avalanche*; ice-berg, -floe;
floe, berg; *glacier*; *nevée*, *serac.*
[Sensation of cold] chilliness etc. *adj.*; chill
shivering etc. *v.*; goose- skin, -flesh; *rigor*,
horripilation, chattering of teeth; frostbite,
chilblain.
V. be -cold etc. *adj.*; shiver, starve, quake,
shake, tremble, shudder, didder, quiver; perish with
cold; chill etc. (*render cold*) 385.
Adj. cold, cool; chill, -y; gelid, frigid, algid;
fresh, keen, bleak, raw, inclement, bitter, biting,

niveous, cutting, nipping, piercing, pinching; clay-
cold; starved etc. (*made cold*) 385; shivering etc.
v.; aguish, *transi de froid*; frost- bitten, -bound, -
nipped.
cold as -a stone, — marble, — lead, — iron, —
a frog, — charity, — Christmas; cool as -a cucumber, — custard.
icy, glacial, frosty, freezing, wintry, brumal,
hibernal, boreal, arctic, antarctic, polar, Siberian,
hyemal; hyperbore-an, -al; ice-bound; frozen out.
un-warmed, -thawed, -heated; isocheimal, -
chimenal.
Adv. coldly, bitterly etc. *adj.*; *à pierre fendre.*

384. Calefaction.—N. increase of temperature;
heating etc. *v.*; cale-, tepe-, torre-faction; melting,
fusion; liquefaction etc. 335; burning etc. *v.*; kindling, combustion; in-, ac-cension; con-,
cremation; scorification; cauter-y, -ization;
ustulation, calcination; in-, cineration; cupellation;
carbonization.
ignition, inflammation, adustion, flagration; de-,
con-flagration; empyrosis, incendiarism; arson;
auto da fé; suttee.
boiling etc. *v.*; coction, ebullition, estuation,
elixation, decoction.
furnace etc. 386; blanket, flannel, fur, muffler,
wrap; wadding etc. (*lining*) 224; clothing etc. 225.
match etc. (*fuel*) 388; incendiary, pryomaniac;
pétroleur, *pétroleuse*; cauterant, caustic, lunar
caustic, apozem, moxa.
sunstroke, *coup de soleil*; insolation, sunburn.
pottery, ceramics, crockery, porcelain, china;
earthen-, stone-ware; pot, mug, *terra-cotta*, brick,
clinker; cinder, ash, *scoriae*; embers, dress, slag,
products of combustion, coke, carbon, charcoal.
inflamma-, combusti-bility.
[Transmission of heat] diathermancy, trans-
calency, diathermy.
V. heat, warm, chafe, stive, foment; make -hot
etc. 382; sun oneself, bask in the sun.
fire; set -fire to, — on fire; kindle, enkindle,
light, ignite, strike a light; apply the -match, —
torch- to; re-kindle, -lume; fan —, add fuel to- the
flame; poke —, stir —, blow- the fire; make a bonfire of; burn at the stake.
melt, thaw, fuse; liquefy etc. 335.
burn, inflame, roast, toast, fry, grill, singe,
parch, bake, torrefy, scorch; brand, cauterize, sear,
burn in; corrode, char, carbonize, calcine, incinerate; smelt, cupel, scorify; reduce to ashes; burn
to a cinder; commit —, consign- to the flames.
boil, digest, stew, cook, seethe, scald, parboil,
simmer; do to rags.
take —, catch- fire; blaze etc. (*flame*) 382.
Adj. heated etc. *v.*; molten, sodden; réchauffe;
heating etc. *v.*
inflammable, burnable, inflammatory, combustible; diatherm-al, -anous; burnt etc. *v.*;
volcanic.

386. Refrigeration.—N. refrigeration, in-
frigidation, reduction of temperature; cooling etc.
v.; con-gelation, -glaciation; ice etc. 383;
solidification etc. (*density*) 321; refrigerator etc.
387.

extincteur; fire, – engine, – extinguisher, – annihilator, – brigade, – man; sprinkler, hose, hydrant, standpipe.

incombusti-bility, -bleness etc. *adj.*

V. cool, fan, refrigerate, refresh, ice; congeal, freeze, glaciate; benumb, starve, pinch, chill, petrify, chill to the marrow, nip, cut, pierce, bite, make one's teeth chatter; damp, slack; quench; put –, stamp- out; extinguish.

go –, burn- out.

Adj. cooled etc. *v.*; frozen out; cooling etc. *v.*; .frigorific.

incombustible; un-, unin-flammable; fire-proof.

386. Furnace.—N. furnace, blast furnace, fire-box, stove, incinerator, destructor, crematorium, crematory, kiln, oven, oast-house; hot-, bake-, wash-house; laundry; conservatory; hearth, focus; athanor, hypocaust, reverberatory; volcano; forge, fiery furnace; *tuyère*, brasier, salamander, heater, warming-pan, foot-warmer, hot-water bottle; radiator; boiler, geyser, caldron, seething caldron, pot; urn, kettle; chafing-dish; retort, crucible, alembic, still; saggar.

fire-place, -dog, -irons; hearth, ingle, grate, range, kitchener; kitchen range; oil-, gas-, electric, -cooker, -stove; fireless cooker; fire; galley; ca-, cam-boose; poker, tongs, shovel, hob, trivet; and-, grid-iron; frying-, stew-pan etc.

hot –, Turkish –, Russian –, vapor –, shower –, warm- bath; *calidarium*, *tepidárium*, *sudatorium*, sudatory; *hammam*.

387. Refrigerator.—N. refrigerator, -y; *frigidarium*; cold storage; refrigerating-plant, – machine; ice-house, -pail, -bag, -chest, -pack; cooler, damper; wine-cooler, freezing mixture.

388. Fuel.—N. fuel, firing, combustible, coal, wallsend, anthracite, bituminous coal, slack, culm, cannel coal, lignite, briquette, coke, carbon, char-coal; turf, peat, fire-wood, bobbing, faggot, log, yule log, ember, cinder etc. (*products of combustion*) 384; kindling wood, tinder, touch-wood; fumigator, sulphur, brimstone; incense; port-fire; fire-barrel, -ball, -brand.

fuel oil, gas, gasoline, electricity.

brand, torch, fuse; wick; spill, match, safety match, light, lucifer, congreve, vesuvian, vesta, fusee, locofoco; linstock; illuminant.

candle etc. (*luminary*) 423; oil etc. (*grease*) 356; petrol, gasoline, methylated –, spirit; gas, acetylene.

Adj. carbonaceous; combustible, inflammable.

V. stoke, fire, feed, add fuel to the flames.

389. Thermometer.—N. thermo-meter, -scope, -stat, -pile, differential thermometer; pyro-, calori-meter; radio micrometer etc.

390. Taste.—N. taste, flavor, gust, *gusto*, relish, savor; sapor, sapidity; twang, smack, smatch; after-taste, tang.

tasting; de-, gustation.

palate, tongue, tooth, stomach.

V. taste, savor, smatch, smack, flavor, twang; tickle the palate etc. (*savory*) 394; smack the lips.

Adj. sapid, saporific; gusta-ble, -tory; strong; flavored, spiced, savory; palatable etc. 394.

391. Insipidity.—N. insipidity; tastlessness etc. *adj.*

V. be -tasteless etc. *adj.*

Adj. void of -taste etc. 390; insipid; jejune; taste-, gust-, savor-less; ingustible, mawkish, milk and water, weak, stale, flat, vapid, *fade*, wishy-washy, mild; untasted.

392. Pungency.—N. pungency, piquancy, poignancy, *haut-goût*, strong taste, twang, race, tang.

sharpness etc. *adj.*; acrimony, acridity; roughness etc. (*sour*) 397; unsavoriness etc. 395.

niter, saltpeter; mustard, cayenne, caviar; seasoning etc. (*condiment*) 393; brine.

dram, cordial, nip, pick-me-up, bracer, potion. nicotine, tobacco, snuff, quid; segar; cigar, -ette, gasper, fag; cheroot; weed; fragrant –, Indian-weed; pipe, clay pipe, churchwarden, brier, meer-schaum, hookah, hubble-bubble.

V. be -pungent etc. *adj.*; bite the tongue.

render -pungent etc. *adj.*; season, spice, salt, pepper, pickle, brine, devil, curry.

smoke, chew, take snuff.

Adj. pungent, strong; high-, full-flavored; high-tasted, -seasoned; gamy; sharp, stinging, rough, *piquant*, racy, biting, mordant; spicy; seasoned etc. *v.*; hot, – as pepper; peppery, vellicating, escharotic, meracious; acrid, acrimonious, bitter; rough etc. (*sour*) 397; unsavory etc. 395.

salt, saline, brackish, briny; salt as -brine, – a herring, – Lot's wife.

393. Condiment.—N. condiment, flavoring, salt, mustard, pepper, cayenne, curry, seasoning, sauce, spice, cinnamon, chillies, relish, *sauce piquante*, caviare, pot-herbs, onion, garlic, pickle, chutney, nutmeg etc.

V. season etc. (*render pungent*) 392.

394. Savoriness.—N. savoriness etc. *adj.*; relish, zest.

tit-bit, dainty, delicacy, ambrosia, nectar, *bonne bouche*; game, turtle, venison.

V. taste good, be -savory etc. *adj.*; tickle the - palate, – appetite; flatter the palate.

render -palatable etc. *adj.*

relish, like, smack the lips.

Adj. savory, well-tasted, to one's taste, tasty, good, palatable, nice, dainty, delectable; tooth-ful, -some; gustful, appetizing, lickerish, delicate, delicious, exquisite, rich, luscious, ambrosial.

Adv. *per amusare la bocca*.

Phr. *cela se laisse manger*.

395. Unsavoriness.—N. unsavoriness etc. *adj.*; amaritude; acri-mony, -tude; roughness etc. (*sour*) 397; acerbity, austerity; gall and worm-wood, rue, quassia, aloes; sickener.

V. be -unpalatable etc. *adj.*; sicken, disgust, nauseate, pall, turn the stomach.

Adj. un-savory, -palatable, -sweet; ill-flavored, un-appetizing, -eatable, inedible; bitter, − as gall; acrid, acrimonious; rough.

offensive, repulsive, nasty; sickening etc. *v.*; nauseous; loath-, ful-some; unpleasant etc. 830.

396. Sweetness.—N. sweetness, dulcitude, sac-charinity.

sugar, cane-, beet-sugar; saccharine, glucose, syrup, treacle, molasses, honey, manna; confection, -ary; sweets, grocery, conserve, preserve, *confiture*, jam, marmalade, julep; sugar-candy, -plum; licorice, liquorice, plum, lollipop, *bon bon*, *jujube*, comfit, sweetmeat, caramel, toffee, butterscotch.

nectar; hydromel, mead, metheglin, honeysuckle, *liqueur*, sweet wine.

pastry, pie, tart, puff, pudding, cake.

dulc-ification, -oration.

V. be sweet etc. *adj.*

render -sweet etc. *adj.*; sugar, saccharize, sweeten; edulcorate; dulc-orate, -ify; candy; mull.

Adj. sweet, sugary; sacchar-ine, -iferous; dulcet, honied, candied, luscious, nectarious, melliferous; sweetened etc. *v.*

sweet as -a nut, − sugar, − honey.

397. Sourness.—N. sourness etc. *adj.*; acid, -ity; acetous fermentation; acerbity.

vinegar, verjuice, crab, alum.

V. be −, turn- -sour etc. *adj.*; set the teeth on edge.

render -sour etc. *adj.*; acid-ify, -ulate.

Adj. sour; acid, -ulous, -ulated; acerb; tart, crab-bed; acet-ous, -ose; sour as vinegar, sourish, acescent, sub-acid; styptic, hard, rough; unripe, green.

398. Odor.—N. odor, smell, odorament, scent, effluvium; eman-, exhal-ation; fume, essence, trail, nidor, redolence.

sense of smell; scent; act of -smelling etc. *v.*

V. have an -odor etc. *n.*; smell, − of, − strong of; exhale; give out a -smell etc. *n.*; scent.

smell, scent, snuff, − up; sniff, nose, inhale.

Adj. odor-ous, -iferous; smelling, strong-scented; redolent, graveolent, nidorous, pungent.

[Relating to the sense of smell] olfactory, quick-scented..

399. Inodorousness.—N. inodorousness; absence −, want- of smell.

V. be -inodorous etc. *adj.*; not smell.

deodorize.

Adj. inodor-ous, -ate; scentless; without −, want-ing- smell etc. 398.

deodoriz-ed, -ing.

400. Fragrance.—N. fragrance, aroma, redolence, perfume, *bouquet*; sweet smell, aromatic perfume.

perfumery; incense; musk, frankincense; pastil, -le; myrrh, perfumes of Arabia, chypre; otto, ottar, attar; bergamot, balm, civet, *pot-pourri*, pulvil; nosegay, *boutonnière*; scent, -bag; *sachet*, scent-bottle, smelling bottle, *vinaigrette*; toilet water, *eau de Cologne*; thurible, censer, thurification.

perfumer; incense bearer.

V. be -fragrant etc. *adj.*; have a -perfume etc. *n.*; smell sweet, scent, perfume, thurify, embalm.

Adj. fragrant, aromatic, redolent, spicy, balmy, scented; sweet-smelling, -scented; perfum-ed, -atory; thuriferous; fragrant as a rose, muscadine, ambrosial.

401. Fetor.—N. fetor, fetidness; bad odor etc. *adj.*; -smell, − odor; stench, stink; mephitis, foul −, mal- odor; *empyreuma*; mustiness etc. *adj.*; ran-cidity; foulness etc. (*uncleanness*) 653.

stoat, polecat, skunk; asafetida; fungus, garlic; stink-pot, -bomb.

V. have a -bad smell etc. *n.*; smell; stink, − in the nostrils, − like a polecat; smell -strong etc. *adj.*; − offensively.

Adj. fetid; strong-smelling; high, bad, strong, fulsome, offensive, noisome, rank, rancid, reasty, tainted, musty, fusty, frouzy; olid, -ous; nidorous; smelling, stinking; putrid etc. 653; suffocating, mephitic; empyreumatic.

402. Sound.—N. sound, noise, strain; accent, twang, intonation, tone, tune; cadence; sonority, sonorousness etc. *adj.*; audibility; resonance etc. 408; voice etc. 580.

[Science of sound] acou-, acu-stics; catacoustics; cataphonics; phon-ics, -etics, -ology, -ography; diacoustics, -phonics.

telephone, phonograph etc. 418.

V. produce sound; sound, make a noise; give out −, emit- sound; phonetize, phonate; resound etc. 408.

Adj. sounding; soniferous; sonorific; resonant, audible, acoustic, auditory, distinct, stertorous; phonic, sonant; phonetic.

403. Silence.—N. silence; stillness etc. (*quiet*) 265; peace, hush, lull, rest; muteness etc. 581; solemn −, awful −, dead −, deathlike-silence.

V. be -silent etc. *adj.*; hold one's tongue etc. (*not speak*) 585.

render -silent etc. *adj.*; silence, still, hush; stifle, muffle, gag, stop; muzzle; put to silence etc. (*ren-der mute*) 581.

Adj. silent; still, -y; calm, quiet; noise-, sound-, speech-less; hushed etc. *v.*; mute etc. 581; aphonic.

soft, solemn, awful, deathlike, silent as the grave; inaudible etc. (*faint*) 405.

Adv. silently etc. *adj.*; *sub silentio*; in perfect silence.

Int. hush! 'sh! silence! soft! whist! tush! chut! tut! *pax!* mum's the word! hold your tongue! shut up! be

silent! be quiet! stop that noise! hold your row! dry
up! peace, be still!

Phr. one might hear a -feather, – pin- drop.

404. Loudness.—N. loudness, power; loud
noise, din; clang, -or; clatter, noise, bombilation,
roar, uproar, racket, static, grinders, hubbub,
fracas, charivari, trumpet blast, blare, flourish of
trumpets, fanfare, *tintamarre*, peal, swell, blast,
alarum, boom; resonance etc. 408.

vociferation; pandemonium, hullaballoo etc.
411; lungs; Stentor; megaphone; siren.

artillery, cannon, gunfire, shellburst, bomb;
thunder.

V. be -loud etc. *adj.*; peal, swell, clang, boom,
thunder, fulminate, roar; resound etc. 408; speak
up, shout etc. (*vociferate*) 411; bellow etc. (*cry as
an animal*) 412; give tongue.

rend the -air, – skies; fill the air; din –, ring
–, thunder- in the ear; pierce –, split –, rend-
the-ears, – head; deafen, stun; *faire le diable a
quatre*; make one's windows shake; awaken –,
startle- the echoes; make the welkin ring.

Adj. loud, sonorous; high-, big- sounding;
blatant; deep, full, powerful, noisy, clangorous,
multisonous, *fortisimo*; thundering, deafening etc.
v.; trumpet-tongued; ear-splitting, -rending, -
deafening; piercing; obstreperous, rackety,
uproarious; enough to wake the -dead, – seven
sleepers.

shrill etc. 410; clamorous etc. (*vociferous*) 411;
stentor-ian, -ophonic.

Adv. loudly etc. *adj.*; aloud; at the top of one's
voice, lustily, in full cry.

Phr. the air rings with.

405. Faintness.—N. faintness etc. *adj.*; faint
sound, whisper, breath; under-tone, -breath; murmur, hum, rustle, buzz, purr; plash; sough, moan,
sigh, susurration; tinkle; 'still small voice.'

hoarseness etc. *adj.*; raucity.

silencer, soft pedal, damper, mute, *sourdine*.

V. whisper, breathe, murmur, purl, hum, gurgle,
ripple, babble, flow; tinkle; mutter etc. (*speak imperfectly*) 583.

steal on the ear; melt in –, float on- the air.
muffle, mute, deaden, damp, stifle.

Adj. inaudible; scarcely –, just- audible; low,
dull; stifled, muffled; hoarse, husky; gentle, soft,
faint; floating; purling, flowing etc. *v.*; whispered
etc. *v.*; liquid; soothing; dulcet etc. (*melodious*)
413.

Adv. in a whisper, with bated breath, *sotto voce*,
between the teeth, aside; *pian-o, -issimo; a la sourdine; con sourdine*; out of earshot, inaudibly etc.
adj.

406. Snap. [Sudden and violent sounds.]—**N.**
snap etc. *v.*; rapping etc. *v.*; de-, crepitation;
smack, clap, report; thud; burst, explosion,
discharge, detonation, blow-out, back-fire, firing,
salvo, volley, pistol-shot.

squib, cracker, gun, rifle, pop-gun.

V. rap, snap, tap, knock; click; clash; crack, -

le; crash; pop; slam, bang, clap, thump, plump;
toot; back-fire, explode, burst on the ear.

Adj. rapping etc. *v.*

Int. crash! bang!

407. Roll. [Repeated and protracted
sounds.]—**N.** roll etc. *v.*; drumming etc. *v.*; tattoo; ding-dong; tantara; rataplan; whirr; rat-a-
tat; rub-a-dub; pit-a-pat; quaver, clutter,
charivari, racket; cuckoo; repetition etc. 104; peal
of bells, devil's tattoo; reverberation etc. 408.

drumfire, barrage.

machine gun.

V. roll, drum, rumble, rattle, clatter, rustle,
roar, drone, patter, clack.

hum, trill, shake; chime, peal, toll; tick, beat.

drum –, din- in the ear.

Adj. rolling etc. *v.*; monotonous etc. (*repeated*),
104; like a bee in a bottle.

408. Resonance.—N. resonance; ring etc. *v.*;
ringing etc. *v.*; tintinnabulation; reflection, reverberation, clangor.

low –, base –, bass –, flat –, grave –, deep
–, pedal- note; bass; *basso, – profondo*; bari-,
bary-tone; *contralto*.

V. re-sound. -verberate. -echo; ring. ding.
sing. jingle. gingle. chink. clink; tink. -le; chime;
gurgle etc. 405; plash. guggle. echo. ring in the ear.

Adj. resounding etc. *v.*; resonant, tinnient; tintinnabulary; deep-toned, -sounding, -mouthed;
hollow, sepulchral; gruff etc. (*harsh*) 410.

408a. Non-resonance.—N. thud, thump, dead
sound; non-resonance; muffled drums, cracked
bell; silencer, damper; mute, *sourdine*.

V. sound dead; stop –, damp- the -sound, –
reverberations; deaden, muffle.

Adj. non-resonant, dead, muted, muffled.

409. Sibilation. [Hissing sounds.]—**N.**
sibilation; hiss etc. *v.*; sternutation; high note etc.
410.

goose, serpent, snake.

V. hiss, buzz, whiz, rustle; fizz, -le, sizzle,
swish; wheeze, whistle, snuffle; squash; sneeze.

Adj. sibilant; hissing etc. *v.*; wheezy.

410. Stridor. [Harsh sounds.]—**N.** creak etc.
v.; creaking etc. *v.*; discord etc. 414; stridor; harshness, roughness, sharpness etc. *adj.*; cacophony.

acute –, high- note; *soprano*, treble, tenor, *alto*,
falsetto, *voce di testa*; shriek, cry etc. 411.

piccolo, fife, penny -whistle, – trumpet.

V. creak, grate, jar, burr, pipe, twang, jangle,
clank, clink; scream etc. (*cry*) 411; yelp etc. etc.
(*animal sound*) 412; buzz etc. (*hiss*) 409.

set the teeth on edge, écorcher les oreilles; pierce
–, split- the -ears, – head; offend –, grate upon
–, jar upon- the ear.

Adj. creaking etc. *v.*; strident, stridulous, harsh,

coarse, hoarse, horrisonous, raucous, metallic, rough, gruff, grum, sepulchral.

sharp, high, acute, shrill, high-pitched; trumpet-toned; piercing, ear-piercing; cracked; discordant etc. 414; cacophonous.

411. Cry.—N. cry etc. *v.*; voice etc. (*human*) 580; bark etc. (*animal*) 412.

vociferation, outcry, hullaballoo, chorus, clamor, hue and cry, plaint; lungs; stentor.

V. cry, roar, shout, bawl, brawl, halloo, halloa, hail, hoop, whoop, yell, bellow, howl, scream, screech, screak, shriek, shrill, squeak, squeal, squall, whine, whinny, pule, pipe, yaup.

cheer, hurrah; hoot; grumble, maon, groan.

snore, snort; grunt etc. (*animal sounds*) 412.

vociferate; raise –, lift up- the voice; call –, sing –, cry- out; exclaim; rend the air; thunder –, shout- at the -top of one's voice; – pitch of one's breath; *s'égosiller*; strain the -throat, – voice, – lungs; give a -cry etc.

Adj. crying etc. *v.*; clam-ant, -orous; vociferous; stentorian etc. (*loud*) 404; open-mouthed.

412. Ululation. [Animal sounds.]**—N.** cry etc. *v.*; crying etc. *v.*; ululation, latration, belling; reboation; call, note; bark, howl, yelp; twittering, woodnote; insect cry, fritinancy, drone; screech; cuckoo.

V. cry, ululate, howl, roar, bellow, blare, rebellow, bark, yelp; bay, – the moon; yap, growl; yarr, yawl, snarl, howl; grunt, -le; snort, squeak; neigh, bray; mew, mewl; purr, caterwaul, pule; bleat, low, moo; troat, croak, crow, screech, caw, coo, gobble, quack, cackle, gaggle, guggle; chuck, -le; cluck; clack; cheep, chirp, chirrup, twitter, sing, cuckoo; pout, wail, hum, buzz; hiss, blatter; hoot.

Adj. crying etc. *v.*; blatant, latrant; re-, mugient; deep-, full-mouthed.

Adv. in full cry.

413. Melody. Concord.—N. melody, rhythym, measure; rhyme etc. (*poetry*) 597.

pitch, *timbre*, intonation, tone, overtone.

scale, gamut; diapason; diatonic –, chromatic –, enharmonic- scale; key, clef, chords.

modulation, temperament, syncope, syncopation, preparation, suspension, resolution.

staff, stave, line, space, brace; bar, rest; *appogiato*, *-tura*; *acciaccatura*, shake, *arpeggio*.

note, musical note, notes of a sclae; sharp, flat, natural; high note etc. (*shrillness*) 410; low note etc. 408; interval; semitone; second, third, fourth etc.; diatessaron.

breve, semibreve, minim, crotchet, quaver; semi-, demisemi- quaver; sustained note, drone, burden.

tonic; key-, leading-, fundamental-, note; super-tonic, mediant, dominant; sub-mediant, -dominant, organ-, pedal-point; octave, tetrachord; major –, minor- -mode, – scale, – key; Doric mode, passage, phrase.

concord, harmony; unison, -ance; chime, homophony; euphon-y, -ism; tonality; consonance; concent; part.

orchestration; harmonization, – phrasing.

[Science of harmony] harmon-y, -ics; thorough-, fundamental- bass; counterpoint; faburden.

piece of music etc. 415; composer, harmonist, contrapuntist.

V. be -harmonious etc. *adj.*; harmonize, chime, symphonize, transpose; put in tune, tune, accord, string; score, arrange, orchestrate.

Adj. harmoni-ous, -cal; in -concord etc. *n.*, – tune, – concert; unisonant, concentual, symphonizing, isotonic, homophonous, assonant, consonant.

measured, rhythmical, diatonic, chromatic, enharmonic.

melodious, musical; tuneful, tunable; sweet, dulcet, canorous; mell-ow, -ifluous; soft; clear, – as a bell; silvery; euphon-ious, -ic, -ical; symphonious; enchanting etc. (*pleasure-giving*) 829; fine-, full-, silver-toned.

Adv. harmoniously etc. *adj.*

414. Discord.—N. discord, -ance; dissonance, cacaphony, caterwauling; harshness etc. 410; consecutive fifths.

[Confused sounds] Babel, pandemonium; Dutch –, cat's- concert; marrow-bones and cleavers.

V. be -discordant etc. *adj.* ; jar etc. (*sound harshly*) 410.

Adj. discordant; dis-, ab-sonant; out of tune, tuneless; un-musical, -tunable; un-, im-melodious; un-, in-harmonious; sing-song; cacophonous; jarring, harsh etc. 410.

415. Music.—N. music, classical –, modern –, descriptive- music; concert, recital; strain, tune, air, *motif*; melody etc. 413; *aria*, *arietta*; piece of music, *sonata*; *rond-o*, *-eau*; *pastorale*, *cavatina*, roulade, *fantasia*, *toccata*, *concerto*, overture, symphony, symphonic poem, tone poem, prelude, voluntary, *intermezzo*, variations, *cadenza*; cadence; fugue, canon, serenade, *nocturne*, *notturno*, rhapsody, romance, *aubade*, dithyramb; opera, operetta; oratorio; composition, movement, stave.

instrumental music; full-, orchestral- score; minstrelsy, tweedledum and tweedledee, band, orchestra etc. 416; concerted piece, potpourri, medley, *capriccio*, incidental music; improvisation; peal.

vocal music, vocalism; chaunt, chant; psalm, -ody; hymn; song etc. (*poem*) 597; canticle, canzonet, *cantata, bravura, coloratura*; lay, ballad, ditty, carol, barcarolle, pastoral, recitative, *recitativo, solfeggio*, tonic sol-fa.

Lydian measures; slow -music, – movement; *adagio* etc. *adv.*; minuet; siren strains, soft music, lullaby; *berceuse*, cradle song, dump; dirge etc. (*lament*) 839; pibroch; martial music, march, funeral-, dead- march; dance music; waltz etc. (*dance*) 840; rag-time, syncopation, jazz.

solo, duet, *duo, trio*; quartet; quintet, sextet, septet; part song, descant, glee, madrigal, catch, round, chorus, *chorale*; antiphon, -y; accompaniment, second –, alto –, tenor –, bass-part; score, thorough bass; counterpoint.

composer etc. 413; musician etc. 416.

V. compose, perform etc. 416; attune.

Adj. musical; instrumental, orchestral, vocal, choral, lyric, operatic; harmonious etc. 413.

Adv. *adagio; largo, larghetto, andan-te, -tino; alla capella; maestoso, moderato; allegr-o, -etto; spiritoso, vivace, veloce; prest-o, -issimo; pian-o, -issimo, fort-e, -issimo, sforzando; con brio; capriccioso; scherz-o, -ando; legato, sostenuto, staccato, crescendo,* diminuendo, *rallentando, af-fettuoso, arioso; parlante, cantabile; obbligato; pizzacato, tremolo, vibrato.*

416. Musician. [Performance of Music.]—**N.** musician, *artiste, virtuoso,* performer, player, minstrel; bard etc. (*poet*) 597; instrumental-, organ-, accompan-, pian-, violin-, flaut-, harp-ist; harper, fiddler, fifer, trumpeter, piper, drummer; catgut scraper.

band, orchestra, waits.

vocal-, melod-ist; singer, warbler; songst-, chaunt-er, -ress; *diva, cantatrice,* coloratura, soprano, mezzo-soprano, alto, contralto, tenor, baritone, bass, *basso, -profundo.*

choir, quire, chorister; chorus, − singer; choral society, festival, *eisteddfod.*

nightingale, philomel, thrush; siren; Orpheus, Apollo, the Muses, Erato, Euterpe, Terpsichore; tuneful -nine, − quire.

composer etc. 413.

performance, virtuosity, execution, touch, expression, solmization.

V. play, pipe, strike −, tune-up, sweep the chords, tickle −, paw- the ivories, vamp, tweedle; fiddle; strike the lyre, beat the drum; blow −, sound −, wind- the horn; grind the organ; touch the -guitar etc. (*instruments*) 417; thrum, strum, twang, drum, beat −, keep- time, conduct.

execute, perform; accompany; sing −, play- a second; compose, write music, set to music, arrange, harmonize, orchestrate.

sing, chaunt, chant, hum, warble, carol, chirp, chirrup, lilt, purl, quaver, trill, shake, twitter, whistle; sol-fa; intone.

have -an ear for music, − a musical ear, − a correct ear, − absolute pitch.

Adj. playing etc. *v.*; musical, lyric.

Adv. *adagio, andante* etc. (*music*) 415.

417. Musical Instruments.—N. musical instruments; band; string-, brass-, drum and fife-, military-, bugle-, German-, dance-, jazz-band; orchestra, string quartet; orchestration, orchestrelle.

[Stringed instruments] mono-, poly-chord; harp, lyre, lute, archlute, thearbo; mandol-a, -in, -ine; guitar; *ukulele;* psaltery, zither; bandore, cither, -n; gittern, rebeck, *bandurria,* banjo, zither banjo, *balalaika, samisen;* plectrum.

viol, -in, Cremona, Stradivarius; fiddle; kit; *vielle, viola, − d'amore, − di gamba;* tenor, *violoncello,* cello; bass, bass-, bass-viol; double-bass, *contrabasso, violone.* hurdy-gurdy; strings, catgut; bow, fiddlestick.

piano, -forte; grand −, concert grand −, baby −, upright −, cottage- piano; pianino, pianette; harpsi-, clavi-, clari-, mani-chord; *clavier,* spinet, virginals; dulcimer, *cymbalo;* Eolian harp; piano-organ, -player, electric piano, player-piano, pianola.

[Wind instruments] organ, church −, pipe −, American- organ; harmoni-um, -phon; accordion, seraphina, concertina; melodeon; barrel- organ; humming top.

flute, fife, piccolo, flageolet, penny-whistle, reed instrument; clari-net, -onet; bass clarionet; saxophone; basset horn, *corno di bassetto;* musette, shawm, oboe, hautboy, *cor Anglais, corno Inglese,* bassoon, double bassoon, *con-trafagotto;* bag-, union-pipes; ocarina, Pandean pipes; calliope; sirene, pipe, pitch-pipe; sourdet; whistle, catcall.

horn, bugle, key bugle, cornet, *cornet-à-pistons,* cornopean, clarion, trumpet, trombone, ophicleide, serpent; English-, French-, bugle-, sax-, flugel-, alt-, helicon-, post-horn; sackbut, euphonium, bombardon, tuba, bass tuba.

[Vibrating surfaces] cymbal, bell, gong, peal of bells, *carillon;* tambour, -ine; drum, tom-tom, tabor, -ret, -ourine, -orin; *sistrum, grand caisse,* bass-, big-, side-, kettle-drum; *tympani;* war drums; tymbal, timbrel, castanet, bones; musical-glasses, -stones; harmonica, sounding− board, rattle; gramophone, phonograph.

[Vibrating bars] reed, tuning-fork, triangle, Jew's harp, musical box, harmonicon, xylophone, marimba, *celeste.*

sord-ine, -et; *sourd-ine, -et;* mute.

418. Hearing. [Sense of sound.]—**N.** hearing etc. *v.*; audition, auscultation; eavesdropping; audibility; acoustics etc. 402.

acute −, nice −, delicate −, quick −, sharp −, correct −, musical -ear; ear for music.

ear, auricle, lug, acoustic organs, auditory apparatus, ear-drum, tympanum; ear-, speaking-trumpet, megaphone; telephone, radiophone, stethoscope, phonograph, gramophone, microphone.

hearer, auditor, listener, eavesdropper; audi-tory, -ence.

V. hear, overhear; hark, -en; list, -en; give −, lend −, bend- an ear; give attention; catch a sound, prick up one's ears; give -a hearing, − audience -to.

hang upon the lips of, be all ear, listen with both ears, monitor.

become audible; meet −, fall upon −, catch −, reach- the ear; be heard; ring in the ear etc. (*resound*) 408.

Adj. hearing etc. *v.*; auditory, auricular, aural, auditive, acoustic.

Adv. *arrectis auribis.*

Int. hark, − ye! hear! list, -en! *Oyez!* attention! lend me your ears!

419. Deafness.—N. deafness, hardness of hearing, surdity; inaudibility.

V. be -deaf etc. *adj.*; have no ear; shut −, stop −, close- one's ears; turn a deaf ear to.

render deaf, stun, deafen.

Adj. deaf, earless, surd; hard −, dull- of hearing; deaf-mute, stunned, deafened; stone deaf; deaf as -a post, − an adder, − a beetle, − a trunk-maker.

inaudible etc. 405; out of hearing.

420. Light.—N. light, ray, beam, stream, gleam, streak, pencil; sun-, moon-beam; dawn, aurora.

day; sunshine; light of -day, – heaven; sun etc. (*luminary*) 432, day-, broad day-, noontide- light; noon-tide, -day; glare.

glow etc. *v.*; afterglow, sunset; glimmering etc. *v.*; glint; play –, flood- of light; phosphorescence, flush, halo, glory, nimbus, aureole, *aureola*.

spark, *scintilla*; *facula*; sparkling etc. *v.*; emication, scintillation, flash, blaze, coruscation, fulguration; flame etc. (*fire*) 382; lightning, *ignis fatuus*, etc. (*luminary*) 423, radio-activity.

luster, sheen, shimmer, reflection; gloss, tinsel, spangle, brightness, brilliancy, splendor; ef-, refulgence; ful-gor, -gidity; dazzlement, resplendence, transplendency; . luminousness etc. *adj.*; luminosity; lucidity; renitency; radi-ance, -ation; irradiation, illumination, phosphorescence, luminescence.

. radiation, radiant heat, infra-red rays, visible radiation, ultra-violet –, actinic- rays, actinism; X –, Roentgen- rays; phot-, heli-ography; optical instruments etc. 445.

[Science of light] optics; photo-logy, -metry; di-, cat-optrics.

[Distribution of light] *chiaroscuro, clair-obscur*, clear obscure, breadth, light and shade, black and white, tonality, half-tone, mezzotint.

reflection, refraction, dispersion, double refraction, polarization, diffraction, interference.

illuminant etc. 423.

V. shine, glow, glitter, phosphoresce; glis-ter, -ten; twinkle, gleam; flare, – up; glare, beam, shimmer, glimmer, flicker, sparkle, scintillate, coruscate, flash, fulgurate, blaze; be -bright etc. *adj.*; reflect light, daze, dazzle, bedazzle, raidate, shoot out beams.

clear up, brighten.

lighten, enlighten; light, – up; irradiate, shine upon; give –, hang out- a light; cast –, throw –, shed- -luster, – light- upon; illum-e, -ine, -inate; relume, strike a light; kindle etc. (*set fire to*) 384.

Adj. shining etc. *v.*; lumin-ous, -iferous; luc-id, -ent, -ulent, -ific, -iferous; illuminating, light, -some; bright, vivid, splendent, nitid, lustrous, shiny, brilliant, beamy, scintillant, radiant, lambent; sheen, -y; glossy, burnished, glassy, sunny, orient, meridian; noon-day, -tide; cloudless, clear; unclouded, -obscured.

garish; re-, tran-splendent; re-, effulgent; ful-gid, -gent; relucent, splendid, blazing, in a blaze, ablaze, rutilant, meteoric, phosphorescent; aglow.

bright as silver; light –', bright- as -day, – noonday, – the sun at noonday.

optical, actinic; photo-genic, -graphic; heliographic, radioactive.

421. Darkness.—N. darkness etc. *adj.*; blackness etc. (*dark color*) 431; obscurity, gloom, murk; dusk etc. (*dimness*) 422;. tenebrosity, umbrageousness.

Cimmerian –, Stygian –, Egyptian- darkness; night; midnight; dead of –, witching time of-night; blind man's holiday; darkness -visible; – that can be felt; palpable, obscure; Erebus.

shade, shadow, umbra, penumbra, sciagraphy; *silhouette*; radiograph, skiagraph.

obscuration; ad-, ob-umbration; obtenebration, offuscation, caligation; extinction; eclipse, total eclipse; gathering of the clouds.

shading; distribution of shade; *chiaroscuro* etc. (*light*) 420.

noctivagation, noctograph, noctuary.

obscurantist.

V. be -dark etc. *adj.*

darken, obscure, shade; dim; tone down, lower; over-cast, -shadow; cloud, eclipse; ob-, of-fuscate; ob-, ad-umbrate, cast into the shade; be-cloud, -dim, -darken; cast –, throw –, spread- a -shade, – shadow, – gloom.

extinguish; put –, blow –, snuff- out; doubt.

Adj. dark, -some, -ling; obscure, tenebrous, tenebrious, sombrous, pitch dark, pitchy, caliginous; black etc. (*in color*) 431.

sunless, lightless etc. (*see* . sun, light etc. 423); somber, dusky; unilluminated etc. (*see* illuminate etc. 420); nocturnal; dingy, lurid, gloomy; murk-y, -some; shady, umbrageous; overcast etc. (*dim*) 422; cloudy etc. (*opaque*) 426; darkened etc. *v.*

dark as -pitch, – a pit, – Erebus.

benighted; noctivag-ant, -ous.

Adv. in the -dark, – shade; at night.

422. Dimness.—N. dimness etc. *adj.*; darkness etc. 421; paleness etc. (*light color*) 429.

half-light, *demi-jour*; partial -shadow, – eclipse; shadow of a shade; glimmer, -ing; nebulosity; cloud etc. 353; eclipse.

aurora, dusk, twilight, gloaming, blind man's holiday, shades of evening, crepuscule, cockshut time; break of day, daybreak, dawn.

moon-light, -beam, -shine; star- owl's-, candle-, rush-, fire-light; farthing candle.

V. be -, grow- -dim etc. *adj.*; flicker, twinkle, glimmer; loom, lower; fade; darken; pale, – its ineffectual fire.

render -dim etc. *adj.*; dim, bedim, obscure.

Adj. dim, dull, lack-luster, dingy, darkish, shorn of its beams; dark 421.

faint, shadowed forth; glassy; bleary; cloudy; misty etc. (*opaque*) 426; muggy, fuliginous; nebulous, -ar; obnubilated, overcast, crepuscular. twilight, muddy, lurid, leaden, dun, dirty; looming etc. *v.*

pale etc. (*colorless*) 429; confused etc. (*invisible*) 447.

423. Luminary. [Source of light.]**—N.** luminary; light etc. 420; flame etc. (*fire*) 382.

spark, *scintilla*; phosphorescence.

sun, orb of day, day star, Phoebus, Apollo, Helios, Phaethon, Hyperion, Ra, Aurora; star, orb, meteor; falling –, shooting- star; blazing –, dog-star; Sirius, canicula, Aldebaran; morning star, Lucifer, Phosphor, evening star; Hesperus, Venus, planet, moon etc. 318; constellation, galaxy; northern light, *aurora -borealis*, – *australis*, zodiacal light; mock sun, parhelion.

lightning, fork –, sheet –, summer- lightning, St. Elmo's fire; phosphorus; *ignis fatuus*; Jack o' – Friar's- lantern; Will o' the wisp, fire-drake, *Fata Morgana*.

glow-worm, fire-fly.

radium, luminous paint.

[Artificial light] gas; gas −, lime −, electric −, head −, search −, spot −, flash −, flood −, footlight; lamp, oil −, gas −, arc −, incandescent-lamp; flare; lant-ern, -horn; dark lantern, bull's eye, projector; candle, *bougie*, tallow −, wax- candle; dip, farthing dip; taper, rush-light; oil etc. (*grease*) 356; wick, burner; Argand, moderator, duplex; torch, *flambeau*, link, brand; cresset; gase-, chande-, electro-lier; candelabrum, *girandole*, sconce, luster, candle-stick.

firework, fizgig; pyrotechnics; Roman candle, Very light, star shell, parachute light; rocket, lighthouse etc. (*signal*) 550.

V. illuminate etc. (*light*) 420.

Adj. self-luminous, incandescent; phosphor-ic, -escent; luminescent, fluorescent, radiant etc. (*light*) 420.

424. Shade.—N. shade; awning etc. (*cover*) 223; parasol, sunshade, umbrella; screen, curtain, shutter, blind, gauze, veil, mantle, mask; cloud, mist, gathering of clouds; smoke screen; smoked glasses, colored spectacles; blinkers, blinders.

umbrage, glade; shadow etc. 421.

V. draw a curtain; put up −, close- a shutter; veil etc. *v.*; cast a shadow etc. (*darken*) 421; screen, obstruct the view.

Adj. shady, umbrageous, bowery.

425. Transparency.—N. transparen-ce, -cy; translucen-ce, -cy; diaphaneity; luc-, pelluc-, limpidity.

transparent medium, glass, crystal, mica; lymph, water.

v. be -transparent etc. *adj.*; transmit light.

Adj. transparent, pellucid, lucid, diaphanous; trans-, tra-lucent; limpid, clear, serene, crystalline, clear as crystal, vitreous, transpicuous, glassy, hyaline.

426. Opacity.—N. opacity; opaqueness etc. *adj.*

film; cloud etc. 353.

V. be -opaque etc. *adj.*; obstruct the passage of light; ob-, of-fuscate.

Adj. opaque, impervious to light.

dim etc. 422; turbid, thick, muddy, opacous, obfuscated, fuliginous, cloudy, hazy, foggy, vaporous, nubiferous, muggy.

smoky, fumid, murky, dirty.

427. Semitransparency.—N. semitransparency, opalescence, milkiness, pearliness; gauze, muslin; film; mist etc. (*cloud*) 353; frosted glass.

Adj. semi-transparent, -pellucid, -diaphanous, -opacous, -opaque; opal-escent, -ine; pearly, milky, frosted, mat; misty.

428. Color.—N. color, hue, tint, tinge, dye, complexion, shade, tincture, cast, livery, coloration, chromatism, glow, flush; tone, key.

pure −, positive −, primary −, primitive −, complementary- color; three primaries; spectrum, chromatic dispersion; broken −, secondary −, tertiary- color.

local color, coloring, keeping, tone, value, aerial perspective.

[Science of color] chromatics, spectrum analysis; prism, spectroscope.

pigment, coloring matter, paint, dye, wash, distemper, stain; medium; mordant; oil-paint etc. (*painting*) 556.

V. color, dye, tinge, stain, tint, tinct, tone, paint, wash, ingrain, grain, illuminate, emblazon, imbue; paint etc. (*fine art*) 556; daub.

Adj. colored etc. *v.*; colorific, tingent, tinctorial; chormatic, prismatic; full-, high-, deep-colored; doubly-dyed; polychromatic.

bright, vivid, intense, deep; fresh, unfaded; rich, gorgeous; highly colored; gay; variegated etc. 440.

gaudy, florid; garish; showy, flaunting, flashy; raw, crude; glaring, flaring; discordant, inharmonious.

mellow, harmonious, pearly, sweet, delicate, tender, refined.

429. Achromatism. [Absence of color.]**—N.** achromatism; de-, dis-coloration; pall-or, -idity; paleness etc. *adj.*; etoilation; neutral tint, monochrome, black-and-white.

V. lose -color etc. 428; fade, fly, go; become -colorless etc. *adj.*; turn pale, pale, whiten.

deprive of color, decolorize, bleach, tarnish, achromatize, blanch, etiolate, wash out, tone down.

Adj. uncolored, etc. (*see* color etc. 428); colorless, achromatic, hueless, pale, pallid; pale-, tallow-faced; faint, dull, cold, muddy, leaden, dun, wan, sallow, dead, dingy, ashy, ashen, ghastly, cadaverous, glassy, lack-luster; discolored etc. *v.*

light-colored, fair, *blond*; white etc. 430.

pale as -death, − ashes, − a witch, − a ghost, − a corpse.

430. Whiteness.—N. whiteness etc. *adj.*; argent.

albification, albescence, albinism, etiolation.

snow, paper, chalk, milk, lily, ivory, silver, alabaster; white lead, chinese −, flake −, ivory −, zinc- white, white-wash, -ning, whiting.

V. be -white etc. *adj.*

render -white etc. *adj.*; whiten- bleach, blanch, etiolate, whitewash, silver, frost.

Adj. white; milky, milk-, snow-white; snowy, niveous, candid, chalky; hoar, -y; frosted, silvery; argent, -ine; canescent.

whitish, creamy, pearly, ivory, fair, *blond*, ashblond, platinum blond; blanched etc. *v.*; high in tone, light.

white as -a sheet, − driven snow, − a lily, − silver; like -ivory etc. *n.*

431. Blackness.—N. blackness etc. *adj.*; darkness etc. (*want of light*) 421; swarthness, lividity, dark color, tone, color; *chiaroscuro* etc. 420.

nigrification, infuscation, denigration.

jet, ink, ebony, coal, pitch, soot, smudge, charcoal, sloe, raven, crow; black.

[Pigments] lamp –, ivory –, blue-black; writing –, printing –, printer's –, Indian- ink.

V. be -black etc. *adj.*

render -black etc. *adj.*; blacken, infuscate, denigrate; blot, -ch; smutch; smirch; darken etc. 421.

Adj. black, sable, swarthy, somber, dark, inky, ebon, atramentous, jetty; coal-, jet-black; fuliginous, pitchy, sooty, swart, dusky, dingy, murky, low-toned, low in tone; of the deepest dye.

black as -jet etc. *n.*, – my hat, – a shoe, – a tinker's pot, – November, – thunder, – midnight; nocturnal etc. (*dark*) 421; nigrescent; gray etc. 432; obscure etc. 421.

Adv. in mourning.

432. Gray.—N. gray etc. *adj.*; neutral tint, silver, pepper and salt, *chiaroscuro*, *grisaille*, grayness.

[Pigments] Payne's gray; black etc. 431.

Adj. gray, grey; steel –, iron- gray, dun, drab, dingy, leaden, livid, somber, sad, pearly; silver, -y, -ed; ash-en, -y; ciner-eous, -itious; grizzl-y, -ed; dove-, slate-, stone-, mouse-, ash-colored; mole; cool.

433. Brown.—N. brown etc. *adj.*

[Pigments] bister, ocher, sepia, Vandyke brown.

Adj. brown, adust, bay, dapple, auburn, chestnut, nutbrown, cinnamon, hazel, fawn, puce, *écru*, russet, tawny, fuscous, chocolate, maroon, foxy, tan, brunette, whitey-brown; snuff-, liver-colored; brown as -a berry, – mahogany; reddish brown; copper-, rust- colored; henna, bronze, khaki; russet, roan, sorrel.

sub-burnt; tanned etc. *v.*

V. render -brown etc. *adj.*; tan, embrown, bronze.

434. Redness.—N. red, scarlet, vermilion, cardinal, Post Office, red, carmine, crimson, pink, lake, *cerise*, cherry red, maroon, carnation, *couleur de rose*. *rose du Barry*; magenta, damask; flesh -color, – tint; color; fresh –, high- color; warmth; gules.

ruby, garnet, carbuncle; rose; rust, iron-mold.

[Dyes and pigments] cinnabar, cochineal; fuchsine; ruddle, madder, redlead; light –, Venetian- red; red ink, annotto.

redness etc. *adj.*; rub-escence, -icundity, -ification; erubescence, blush.

V. be –, become- -red etc. *adj.*; blush, flush, color up, mantle, redden.

render- red etc. *adj.*; redden, rouge; rub-ify, -ricate; incarnadine; ruddle.

Adj. red etc. *n.*; -dish; rufous, ruddy, florid, incarnadine, sanguine, bloody, gory; ros-y, -eate; blowz-y, -ed; brunt; rubi-cund, -form; lurid, stammel, blood-red; russet, murrey, carroty, sorrel, lateritious.

rose-, ruby-, cherry-, claret-, wine-, plum-,

flame-, flesh-, peach-, salmon-, brick-, brickdust-colored, reddish brown etc. 433.

red as -fire, – blood, – scarlet, – a turkeycock, – a lobster; warm, hot; foxy.

435. Greenness.—N. green etc. *adj.*; blue and yellow; vert.

emerald, verd antique, verdigris, malachite, beryl, aquamarine, reseda.

[Pigments] *terre verte*, verditer, bice, chlorophyl.

greenness, verdure, verdancy; viridity, -escence.

Adj. green, verdant; glaucous, olive; porraceous; green as grass.

emerald –, pea –, grass –, apple –, sea – olive –, bottle –, leaf- green.

greenish; vir-ent, -escent.

436. Yellowness.—N. yellow etc. *adj.*; or.

[Pigments] gamboge; cadmium –, chrome –, Indian –, lemon- yellow; orpiment, yellow ocher, Claude tint, aureolin.

crocus, saffron, topaz, gold.

jaundice; London fog; yellowness etc. *adj.*

Adj. yellow, aureate, gold, golden, gilt, gilded, flavous, citrine, fallow; fulv-ous, -id; sallow, luteous, fawny, creamy, sandy; xanth-ic, -ous; jaundiced.

gold-, citron-, saffron-, lemon-, sulphur-, amber- straw-, primrose-, cream-colored; flazen, yellowish, buff.

yellow as a -quince, – guinea, – crow's foot.

437. Purple.—N. purple etc. *adj.*; blue and red, bishop's purple; aniline dyes, gridelin, amethyst; purpure.

livid-ness, -ity.

V. empurple.

Adj. purple, violet, plum-colored, lavender, lilac, puce, *mauve*; livid.

438. Blueness.—N. blue etc. *adj.*; garter-blue; watchet.

[Pigments] ultramarine, smalt, cobalt, cyanogen; Prussian –, syenite- blue; bice, indigo, woad.

lapis lazuli, sapphire, turquoise.

blue-, bluish-ness; bloom

Adj. blue, azure, cerulean; sky-blue, -colored, -dyed; navy-blue, aquamarine, electric blue, royal blue, cyanic; bluish; atmospheric, retiring; cold.

439. Orange.—N. orange, red and yellow; gold; or; flame etc. color, *adj.*

[Pigments] ochre, Mars orange, cadmium.

V. gild, warm.

Adj. orange; ocherous; orange-, gold-, flame-, copper-, brass-, apricot-colored; warm, hot, glowing.

440. Variegation.—N. variegation; di-, trichromism; iridescence, irisation, play of colors, polychrome, maculation, spottiness, striae.

spectrum, rainbow, iris, tulip, peacock, chameleon, butterfly, tortoiseshell; mackerel, – sky; zebra, leopard, mother-of-pearl, nacre, opal, marble, batik.

check, plaid, tartan, patchwork; mar-, parquetry; mosaic, *tesserae*, tesselation, chess-board, checkers, chequers; harlequin; Joseph's coat; tricolor; patches, bands, stripes, spots etc of color.

V. be -variegated etc. *adj.*; variegate, stripe, streak, checker, chequer; be-, speckle, fleck; be-, sprinkle; stipple, maculate, dot, bespot; tattoo, inlay, tesselate, damascene; embroider, braid, quilt.

Adj. variegated etc. *v.*; many-colored, -hued; divers-, parti-colored; di-, poly-chromatic; bi-, tri-, versi-color; of all -the colors of the rainbow, – manner of colors; kaleidoscopic.

iridescent; opal-ine, -escent; prismatic, nacreous, pearly, shot, *gorge de pigeon*, *chatoyant*, irisated.

pied, piebald, skewbald; motley; mottled, marbled; pepper and salt, paned, dappled, clouded, cymophanous.

mosaic, tesselated, chequered, plaid; tortoiseshell etc. *n.*

spott-ed, -y; punctuated, powdered; speckled etc. *v.*; freckled, fleabitten, studded; fleck-ed, -ered; striated, barred, veined; brind-ed, -led; tabby; watered; grizzled; listed; embroidered etc. *v.*; daedal.

441. Vision.—N. vision, sight, optics, eye-sight.

view, look, espial, glance, ken, *coup d'oeil*; glimpse, peep, glint; gaze, stare, leer; perlustration; contemplation; conspect-ion, -uity; regard; survey; in-, intro-spection; *reconnaissance*, speculation, watch, espionage, *espionnage*, autopsy; ocular - inspection, – demonstration; sight-seeing.

macrography, micrography.

point of view; view-, stand- point; gazebo, loop-hole, *belvedere*, watchtower.

field of view; theater, amphitheater, arena, vista, horizon; commanding –, bird's eye –, panoramic- view; periscope.

visual organ, organ of vision; eye; naked –, unassisted- eye; eye-ball, retina, pupil, iris, cornea, white; optics, orbs; saucer –, goggle –, gooseberry-eyes.

short sight etc. 443; clear –, sharp –, quick –, eagle –, piercing-, –, penetrating- sight, – glance, – eye; perspicacity, discernment; catopsis.

eagle, hawk; cat, lynx; Argus.

evil eye; basilisk, cockatrice.

spectacles, telescope etc. 445.

V. see, behold, discern, perceive, have in sight, descry, sight, make out, discover, distinguish, recognize, spy, espy, ken; get –, have –, catch- a -sight, – glimpse- of; command of view of; witness, contemplate, speculate; cast –, set- the eyes on; be a -spectator etc. 444- of; look on etc. (*be present*) 186; see sights etc. (*curiosity*) 445; see at a glance etc. (*intelligence*) 498.

look, view, eye; lift up the eyes, open one's eye; look -at, – on, – upon, – over, – about one, – round; survey, scan, inspect; run the eye -over, – through; reconnoiter, glance -round, – on, – over; turn –, bend- one's looks upon; direct the eyes to, turn the eyes on, cast a glance, make eyes at.

observe etc. (*attend to*) 457; watch etc. (*care*) 459; see with one's own eyes; watch for etc. (*expect*) 507; peek, peep, peer, pry, take a peep; play at bo-peep.

look -full in the face, – hard at, – intently; strain one's eyes; fix –, rivet- the eyes upon; stare, gaze; pore over, gloat -over, – on; leer, ogle, glare; goggle; cock the eye, squint, gloat, look askance; give the glad eye.

Adj. seeing etc. *v.*; visual, ocular, -al; ophthalmic.

far-, clear-sighted etc. *n.*; eagle-, hawk-, lynx-, keen-, Argus-eyed.

visible etc. 446.

Adv. visibly etc. 446; in sight of, with one's eyes open.

at -sight, – first sight, – a glance, – the first blush; *primâ facie*.

Int. look! etc. (*attention*) 457.

Phr. the scales falling from one's eyes.

442. Blindness.—N. blindness, anopsia, cecity, excecation, *amaurosis*, cataract, ablepsy, prestriction; dim-sightedness etc. 443.

V. be -blind etc. *adj.*; not see; lose sight of; have the eyes bandaged; grope in the dark.

not look; close –, shut –, turn away – avert- the eyes; look another way; wink etc. (*limited vision*) 443; shut the eyes –, be blind- to; wink –, blink- at.

render -blind etc. *adj.*; blind, -fold; hoodwink, dazzle; put one's eyes out; throw dust into one's eyes; *jeter de la poudre aux yeux*; screen from sight etc. (*hide*) 528.

Adj. blind; eye-, sight-, vision-less; dark; stone-, sand-, stark-blind; undiscerning; dim-sighted etc. 443.

blind as -a bat, – a buzzard, – a beetle, – a mole, – an owl; wall-eyed.

blinded etc. *v.*

Adv. blind-ly, -fold; darkly.

443. Dim-sightedness. [Imperfect vision.] [Fallacies of vision.]—N. dim –, dull –, half –, short –, near –, long –, double –, astigmatic–, failing- sight; dim etc -sightedness; snow blindness; purblindness, lippitude; my-, presby-opia; confusion of vision; astigmatism; nystagmus; color-blindness, dichromism, chromato-pseudo-blepsis, Daltonism; nyctalopy; *strabismus*, strabism, squint, cast in the eye, swivel eye, goggle eyes; obliquity of vision.

winking etc. *v.*; nictitation; blinkard, albino.

dizziness, swimming, scotomy; cataract; ophthalmia.

[Limitation of vision] eye shade, blinker, blinder; screen etc. (*hider*) 530.

[Fallacies of vision] *deceptio visûs*; refraction, distortion, illusion, false light, *anamorphosis*, virtual image, *spectrum*, *mirage*, looming, phasma; phant-asm, -asma, -om; vision; specter, apparition, ghost; *ignis fatuus* etc. (*luminary*) 423; specter of the Brocken; magic mirror; magic lantern etc. (*show*) 448; mirror, lens etc. (*instrument*) 445.

V. be -dim-sighted etc. *n.*; see double; have a - mote in the eye, – mist before the eyes, – film over the eyes; see through a -prism, – glass darkly; wink, blink, nictitate; squint; look ask-ant, -ance; screw up the eyes, glare, glower.

dazzle, glare, blur, swim, loom.

Adj. dim-sighted etc. *n.*; my-, presby-opic; astigmatic; moon-, mope-, blear-, goggle-, gooseberry-, one-eyed; blind of one eye, monoculous; half-, pur-, color-blind; dichromatic.

blind as a bat etc. (*blind*) 442; winking etc. *v.*

444. Spectator.—N. spectator, beholder, observer, inspector, viewer, looker-on, onlooker, witness, eye-witness, bystander, passer by; sight-seer.

spy, scout; sentinel etc. (*warning*) 668.

v. witness, behold etc. (*see*) 441; look on etc. (*be present*) 186.

445. Optical Instruments.—N. optical instruments; lens, meniscus, magnifier, reading –, burning- glass; micro-, mega-, teino-scope; spectacles, glasses, barnacles, goggles, giglamps, eyeglass, *pince-nez*, monocle; periscopic lens; telescope, glass, lorgnette, binocular; spy-, opera-, field-glass, periscope, range finder.

mirror, reflector, speculum; looking-, pier-, cheval-, hand-glass.

prism; camera, *camera-lucida, -obscura*; projector, stereopticon, magic lantern etc. (*show*) 448; chro-, thau-matrope; stereo-, pseudo-, poly-, kaleido-scope.

photo-, opto-, erio-, actino-, luci-, radio-, spectro-meter; polari-, polemo-, spectro-scope, diffraction grating.

optics, optician, optometry, optometrist; microscop-y, -ist; photometry, photography; photographer.

446. Visibility.—N. visibility, perceptibility; conspicuousness, distinctness etc. *adj.*; conspicuity; appearance etc. 448; exposure; manifestation etc. 525; ocular -proof, – evidence, – demonstration; field of view etc. (*vision*) 441.

V. be –, become- -visible etc. *adj.*; appear, emerge, open to the view; meet –, catch- the eye; present –, show –, manifest –, produce –, discover –, reveal –, expose –, betray- itself; stand -forth, – out; show; arise; peep –, peer –, crop- out; start –, spring –, show –, turn –, crop- up; glimmer, glitter, glow, loom; glare; burst forth, scintillate; burst upon the -view, – sight; heave in sight; come -in sight, – into view, – out, – forth, – forward; see the light of day; break through the clouds; make its appearance, show its face, materialize, appear to one's eyes, come upon the stage, enter; float before the eyes, speak for itself. etc. (*manifest*) 525; attract the attention etc. 457; reappear; live in a glass house.

expose to view etc. 525.

Adj. visible, perceptible, perceivable, discernible, apparent; in -view, – full view, – sight; exposed to view, *en évidence*; unclouded.

obvious etc. (*manifest*) 525; plain, clear,

distinct, definite; well-defined, -marked; in focus; recognizable, palpable, autoptical; glaring, staring, conspicuous; stereoscopic; in -bold, – strong, – high- relief.

periscopic, panoramic.

before –, under- one's eyes; before one, *à vue d'oeil*, in one's eye, *oculis subjecta fidelibus*.

Adv. visibly etc. *adj.*; in sight of; before one's eyes etc. *adj.*; *veluti in speculum*.

447. Invisibility.—N. invisibility, nonappearance, imperceptibility; indistinctness etc. *adj.*; mystery, delitescence.

concealment etc. 528; latency etc. 526.

V. be -invisible etc. *adj.*; be hidden etc. (*hide*) 528; lurk etc. (*lie hidden*) 526; escape notice.

render -invisible etc. *adj.*; conceal etc. 528; put out of sight.

not see etc. (*be blind*) 442; lose sight of.

Adj. invisible, imperceptible; un-, in-discernible; un-, non-apparent; out of –; not in- sight; *à perte de vue*; behind the -scenes, – curtain; view-, sightless; in-, un-conspicuous; unseen etc. (*see* see etc. 441); covert etc. (*latent*) 526; eclipsed, under an eclipse.

dim etc. (*faint*) 422; mysterious, dark, obscure, confused; indistin-ct, -guishable; shadowy, indefinite, unde*f*ined; ill-defined, -marked; blurred, fuzzy, out of focus; misty etc. (*opaque*) 426; veiled etc. (*concealed*) 528; delitescent.

448. Appearance.—N. appearance, phenomenon, sight, spectacle, show, premonstration, scene, species, view, *coup d'oeil*; look-out, out-look, prospect, vista, perspective, bird's-eye view, scenery, landscape, picture, *tableau*; display, exposure, *mise en scène*; scenery, *décor*; rising of the curtain.

phant-asm, -om etc. (*fallacy of vision*) 443.

pageant, *spectacle*; peep-, raree-, gallanty-show; *ombres chinoises*; projector, optical –, magic-lantern, phantasmagoria, dissolving views; cinema, -tograph; bio-scope, -graph; moving pictures, movies, film, screen etc.; pan-, di-, cosm-, georama; *coup* –, *jeu- de théâtre*; pageantry etc. (*ostentation*) 882; insignia etc. (*indication*) 550.

aspect, phase, *phasis*, seeming; shape etc. (*form*) 240; guise, look, complexion, color, image, mien, air, cast, carriage, port, demeanor; presence, expression, first blush, face of the thing; point of view, light.

lineament, feature, trait, lines; out-line, -side; contour, *silhouette*, face, countenance, physiognomy, visage, phiz, mug, cast of countenance, profile, *tournure*, cut of one's jib, metoposcopy; outside etc. 220.

V. appear; be –, become- visible etc. 446; seem, look, show; present –, wear –, carry –, have –, bear –, exhibit –, take –, take on –, assume the -appearance, – semblance- of; look like; cut a figure, figure; present to the view; show etc. (*make manifest*) 525.

Adj. apparent, seeming, ostensible; on view.

Adv. apparently; to all -seeming, – appearance; ostensibly, seemingly, as it seems, on the face of it, *primâ facie*; at the first blush, at first sight; in the eyes of; to the eye.

449. Disappearance.—**N.** disappearance, evanescence, eclipse, occultation.

departure etc. 293; exit, vanishing point; dissolving views.

V. disappear, vanish, dissolve, fade, melt away, pass, go, avaunt; be -gone etc. *adj.*; leave -no trace, – 'not a rack behind;' go off the stage etc. (*depart*) 293; suffer –, undergo- an eclipse; be lost to –, retire from- -sight, – view.

lose sight of.

efface etc. 552.

Adj. disappearing etc. *v.*; evanescent; missing, lost; lost to -sight, – view; gone; *spurlos versenki.*

Int. vanish! disappear! avaunt! etc. (*ejection*) 297.

450. Intellect.—**N.** intellect, mind, understanding, reason, thinking principle; rationality; cogitative –, cognitive –, intellectual- faculties; faculties, senses, consciousness, observation, percipience, apperception, mentality, intelligence, intellection, intuition, association of ideas, instinct, flair, conception, judgment, wits, parts, capacity, intellectuality, reasoning power, brains, genius; wit etc. 498; ability etc. (*skill*) 698; wisdom etc. 498.

soul, spirit, ghost, inner man, heart, breast, bosom, *penetralia mentis, divina particula aurae*, heart's core; ego, psyche, pneuma, subconsciousness, subconscious, subliminal self; dual personality.

organ –, seat- of thought; *sensorium*, sensory, brain, gray matter; head, -piece; pate, noddle, skull, scull, *pericranium, cerebrum, cranium*, brain-pan, -box; sconce, upper story.

[Science of mind] metaphysics; psychics, psycho-logy, -metry, -genesis, -analysis, -physics, psychi-atry, -cal research, thought reading etc. 992; ideology; mental –, moral- philosophy; philosophy of the mind; pneumat-, phren-ology; no –, cranio-logy, -scopy.

ideal-ity, -ism; transcendental-, spiritual-ism; im-materiality etc. 317.

metaphysician, psychologist etc.

V. note, notice, mark; take -notice, – cognizance- of; be -aware, – conscious- of; realize; appreciate; ruminate etc. (*think*) 451; fancy etc. (*imagine*) 515; conceive, reason, understand.

Adj. [Relating to intellect] intellectual, mental, rational, subjective, metaphysical, nooscopic, spiritual; ghostly; psych-ical, -ological; cerebral. immaterial etc. 317; endowed with reason.

Adv. *in petto.*

450a. Absence or want **of Intellect.**—**N.** absence –, want- of -intellect etc. 450; imbecility etc. 499; brutality; brute -instinct, – force.

Adj. unendowed with reason.

451. Thought.—**N.** thought; exercitation –, exercise- of the intellect; reflection, cogitation, consideration, meditation, study, lucubration, speculation, deliberation, pondering; head-, brainwork; cerebration; mentation, deep reflection, close study, application etc. (*attention*) 457.

abstract thought, abstraction, contemplation, musing; brown study etc. (*inattention*) 458; reverie, Platonism; depth of thought, workings of the mind, thoughts, inmost thoughts; self-counsel, communing, -consultation.

association –, succession –, flow –, train –, current- of -thought, – ideas.

after –, mature- thought; reconsideration, second thoughts; retrospection etc. (*memory*) 505; excogitation; examination etc. (*inquiry*) 461; invention etc. (*imagination*) 515.

thoughtfulness etc. *adj.*

V. think, reflect, reason, cogitate, excogitate, consider, deliberate; bestow -thought, – consideration- upon; speculate, contemplate, meditate, ponder, muse, dream, ruminate; brood –, conover; animadvert, study; bend–, apply- the mind etc. (*attend*) 457; digest, discuss, hammer at, weigh, perpend; realize, appreciate; fancy etc. (*imagine*) 515; trow.

take into consideration; take counsel etc. (*be advised*) 695; commune with –, bethink- oneself; collect one's thoughts; revolve –, turn over –, run over- in the mind; chew the cud –, sleep- upon; take counsel of –, advise with- one's pillow.

rack –, ransack –, crack –, beat –, cudgel- one's brains; set one's -brain, – wits- to work.

harbor –, entertain –, cherish –, nurture- an idea etc. 453; take into one's head; bear in mind; reconsider.

occur; present –, suggest- itself; come –, get- into one's head; strike one, flit across the view, come uppermost, run in one's head; enter –, pass in –, cross –, flash on –, flash across –, float in –, fasten itself on –, be uppermost in –, occupy- the mind; have in one's mind.

make an impression; sink –, penetrate- into the mind; engross the thoughts.

Adj. thinking etc. *v.*; thoughtful, pensive, meditative, reflective, cogitative, museful, wistful, contemplative, speculative, deliberative, studious, sedate, introspective, Platonic, philosophical.

lost –, engrossed –, rapt –, absorbed- in thought etc. (*inattentive*) 458; deep musing etc. (*intent*) 457.

in the mind, under consideration, in contemplation.

Adv. all things considered; taking everything into account.

Phr. the mind being on the stretch; the -mind, – head- -turning, – running- upon.

452. Incogitancy. [Absence or want of thought.]—**N.** incogitancy, vacancy, inunderstanding; inanity, fatuity etc. 499; thoughtlessness etc. (*inattention*) 458.

V. not -think etc. 451; not think of; dismiss from the -mind, – thoughts etc. 451.

indulge in reverie etc. (*be inattentive*) 458.

put away thought; unbend –, relax –, divert- the mind.

Adj. vacant, unintellectual, unideal, unoccupied, unthinking, inconsiderate, thoughtless; absent etc. (*inattentive*) 458; diverted; irrational etc. 499; narrow-minded etc. 481.

un-thought of, -dreamt of, -considered; off one's mind; incogitable, not to be thought of, inconceivable.

453. Idea. [Object of thought.]—**N.** idea, notion, conception, thought, apprehension, impression, perception, image, sentiment, reflection, observation, consideration; abstract idea, principle; archetype.

view etc. (*opinion*) 484; theory etc. 514; conceit, fancy; phantasy etc. (*imagination*) 515.

point of view etc. (*aspect*) 448; field of view.

454. Topic. [Subject of thought.]—**N.** subject of –, material for- thought; food for the mind, mental *pabulum*.

subject, -matter; matter, theme, topic, what it is about, *thesis*, text, business, affair, matter in hand, argument; motion, resolution; head, chapter; case, point; proposition, theorem; field of inquiry; moot point, problem, etc. (*question*) 461.

V. float –, pass- in the mind etc. 451.

Adj. thought of; uppermost in the mind; *in petto*.

Adv. under -discussion, – consideration, – advisement; in -question, – the mind; on -foot, – the carpet, – the *tapis*; before the house, relative to etc. 9.

455. Curiosity. [The desire of knowledge.]—**N.** interest, thirst for knowledge; curi-osity, -ousness; inquiring mind; inquisitiveness.

sight-seer, quidnunc, newsmonger, Paul Pry, peeping Tom, eavesdropper; gossip etc. (*news*) 532; questioner, *enfant terrible*.

V. be -curious etc. *adj.*; take an interest in, stare, gape; prick up the ears, see sights, lionize; pry, speer; dig up.

Adj. curious, inquisitive, burning with curiosity, overcurious, nosey; inquiring etc. 461; prying; inquisitorial; agape etc. (*expectant*) 507; attentive etc. 457.

Phr. what's the matter? what next?

456. Incuriosity. [Absence of curiosity.]—**N.** incuriosity; incuriousness etc. *adj.*; *insouciance* etc. 866; indifference, apathy.

V. be -incurious etc. *adj.*; have no -curiosity etc. 455; take no interest in etc. 823; mind one's own business.

Adj. incurious, uninquisitive, uninterested, indifferent, bored; impassive etc. 823.

457. Attention.—**N.** attention; mindfulness etc. *adj.*; intent-ness, -iveness; thought etc. 451; adverten-ce, -cy; observ-ance, -ation; consideration, reflection, perpension; heed; particularity; notice, regard etc. *v.*; circumspection etc. (*care*) 459; study, scrutiny, once-over; in-, intro-spection; revision, -al.

active –, diligent –, exclusive –, minute –, close –, intense –, deep –, profound –, abstract –, labored, deliberate- -thought, – attention, – application, – study.

minuteness, attention to detail etc. 459.

absorption of mind etc. (*abstraction*) 458.

indication, calling attention to etc. *v.*

V. be -attentive etc. *adj.*; attend, advert to, observe, look, see, view, remark, notice, regard, take notice, mark; give –, pay- -attention, – heedto; listen in, incline –, lend- an ear to; trouble one's head about; give a thought –, animadvert- to; occupy oneself with; contemplate etc (*think of*) 451; look -at, – to, – after, – into, – over; see to; turn –, bend –, apply –, direct –, give- the -mind, – eye, – attention- to; have -an eye to, – in one's eye; bear in mind; take into -account, – consideration; keep in -sight, – view; have regard to, heed, mind, take cognizance of, be engaged in, entertain, recognize; make –, take- note of; note.

examine cursorily; glance -at, – upon, – over; cast –, pass- the eyes over; run over, turn over the leaves, dip into, perstringe; skim etc. (*neglect*) 460; take a cursory view of.

examine, – closely, – intently; scan, scrutinize, consider; give –, bend- one's mind to; overhaul, revise, pore over; inspect, review, pass under review; take stock of; fix –, rivet –, focus –, devote- the - eye, – mind, – thoughts, – attention- on or to; hear –, think- out; mind one's business.

revert –, hark back- to; watch etc. (*expect*) 507, (*take care of*) 459; hearken –, listen- to; prick up the ears; have –, keep- the eyes open; come to the point.

meet with attention; fall under one's -notice, – observation; be -under consideration etc. (*topic*) 454.

catch –, strike- the eye; attract notice; catch –, awaken –, wake –, invite –, solicit –, attract –, claim –, excite –, engage –, occupy –, strike –, arrest –, fix –, engross –, absorb –, rivet-theattention, – mind, – thoughts; be -present to, – uppermost in- the mind.

bring under one's notice; point -out, – to, – at, – the finger at; lay the finger on, indigitate, indicate; direct –, call- attention to; show; put a -mark etc. (*sign*) 550- upon; call soldiers to 'attention;' bring forward etc. (*make manifest*) 525.

Adj. attentive, mindful, heedful, observant, regardful; alive –, awake- to, alert; observing etc. *v.*; taken up –, occupied- with; engaged –, engrossed –, interested –, wrapped- in; absorbed, rapt; breathless; pre-occupied etc. (*inattentive*) 458; watchful etc. (*careful*) 459; intent on, openeyed, breathless, undistracted, upon the stretch; on the watch etc. (*expectant*) 507.

steadfast.

Int. see! look, – here, – out, – alive, – you, – to it! mark! lo! behold! soho! hark, – ye! mind! halloo! observe! lo and behold! attention! *nota bene*; N.B.; *, †; I'd have you to know; notice! take notice! O yes! *Oyez!*

Phr. this is –, these are- to give notice.

458. Inattention.—**N.** in-attention, -consideration; inconsiderateness etc. *adj.*; oversight; inadverten-ce, -cy; non-observance, disregard.

supineness etc. (*inactivity*) 683; *étourderie*; want of thought; heedlessness etc. (*neglect*) 460; *insouciance* etc. (*indifference*) 866.

abstraction; absence —, absorption- of mind; preoccupation, distraction, reverie, brown study, deep musing, fit of abstraction, woolgathering.

V. be -inattentive etc. *adj.*; overlook, disregard; pass by etc. (*neglect*) 460; not -observe etc. 457; think little of.

close —, shut- one's eyes to; wink at; pay no attention to; dismiss —, discard —, discharge- from one's -thoughts, — mind; drop the subject, think no more of; set —, turn —, put- aside; turn -away from, — one's attention from, — a deaf ear to, — one's back upon.

abstract oneself, dream, indulge in reverie.

escape -notice, — attention; come in at one ear and go out at the other; forget etc. (*have no remembrance*) 506.

call off —, draw off —, call away —, divert —, distract- the -attention, — thoughts, — mind; put out of one's head; dis-concert, -compose; put out, confuse, perplex, bewilder, fluster, muddle, dazzle; throw a sop to Cerberus.

Adj. inattentive; un-observant, -mindful, -heeding, -discerning; inadvertent; mind-, regard-, respect-less; listless etc. (*indifferent*) 866; blind, deaf; flighty, hand over head; cur-, percur-sory; giddy-, scatter-, hare-brained; unreflecting, *écervelé*, inconsiderate; off-hand, thoughtless, dizzy, muzzy, brainsick; giddy, — as a goose; wild, harum-scarum, ranipole, high-flying; heed-, careless etc. (*neglectful*) 460.

absent, absent-minded, abstracted, *distrait*; lost; lost —, wrapped- in thought, woolgathering; rapt, in the clouds, bemused; dreaming —, musing- on other things; pre-occupied, engrossed etc. (*attentive*) 457; in a -reverie etc. *n.*; off one's guard etc. (*inexpectant*) 508; napping; dreamy.

disconcerted, put out etc. *v.*; rattled.

Adv. inattentively, inadvertently etc. *adj.*; *per incuriam*, *sub silentio*.

Int. stand -at ease, — easy!

Phr. the attention wanders; one's wits gone a -woolgathering, — bird's nesting; it never entered into one's head; the mind running on other things; one's thoughts being elsewhere; had it been a bear it would have bitten you.

459. Care. [Vigilance.]—**N.** care, solicitude, heed; heedfulness etc. *adj.*; scruple etc. (*conscientiousness*) 939.

watchfulness etc. *adj.*; vigilance, *surveillance*, eyes of Argus, watch, vigil, look out, watch and ward, *l'oeil du maître*.

alertness etc. (*activity*) 682; attention etc. 457; prudence etc., circumspection etc. (*caution*) 864; forethought etc. 510; precaution etc. (*preparation*) 673; tidiness etc. (*order*) 58, (*cleanliness*) 652; accuracy etc. (*exactness*) 494; minuteness, attention to detail; meticulousness, nicety, circumstantiality.

V. be -careful etc. *adj.*; reck; take care etc. (*be cautious*) 864; pay attention to etc. 457; take care of; look —, see- -to, — after; keep -an eye, — a sharp eye- upon; keep -watch, — watch and ward; mount guard, set watch, watch; keep in -sight, — view; chaperon, play gooseberry; mind, — one's business.

look -sharp, — about one; look with one's own eyes; keep a -good, — sharp- look-out; have all one's -wits, — eyes- about one; watch for etc. (*ex-pect*) 507; stand to; keep one's eyes —, have the eyes —, sleep with one eye- open.

take precautions etc. 673; protect etc. (*render safe*) 664.

do one's best etc. 682; mind one's Ps and Qs, speak by the card, pick one's steps.

Adj. care-, regard-, heed-ful; taking care etc. *v.*; particular; prudent etc. (*cautious*) 864; considerate; thoughtful etc. (*deliberative*) 451; provident etc. (*prepared*) 673; alert etc. (*active*) 682; sure-footed.

guarded, on one's guard; on the -*qui vive*, — alert, — watch, — look-out; awake, broad awake, vigilant; watch-, wake-, wist-ful; Argus-, lynx-eyed; wide awake etc. (*intelligent*) 498; on the watch for etc. (*expectant*) 507.

tidy etc. (*orderly*) 58, (*clean*) 652; accurate etc. (*exact*) 494; scrupulous etc. (*conscientious*) 939; *cavendo tutus* etc. (*safe*) 664.

Adv. carefully etc. *adj.*; with care, gingerly.

Phr. *quis custodiet ipsos custodes?*

460. Neglect.—**N.** neglect; carelessness etc. *adj.*; trifling etc. *v.*; negligence; omission, laches, default; remissness, slackness, procrastination; supineness etc. (*inactivity*) 683; inattention etc. 458; *nonchalance* etc. (*insensibility*) 823; imprudence, recklessness etc. 863; slovenliness etc. (*disorder*) 59; (*dirt*) 653; improvidence etc. 674; non-completion etc. 730; inexactness etc. (*error*) 495.

paraleipsis [in rhetoric].

trifler, slacker, waster, waiter on Providence; Micawber.

V. be -negligent etc. *adj.*; take no care of etc. (take care of 459); neglect; let -slip, — go; lay —, set —, cast —, put- aside; keep —, leave- out of sight; lose sight of.

overlook, disregard; pass -over, — by; let pass; blink; wink —, connive- at; gloss over; take no -note, — notice, — thought, — account- of; pay no regard to; *laisser aller*; allow to lie on the table.

scamp, trifle, fribble; do by halves; skimp; cut; slight etc. (*despise*) 930; play —, trifle- with; slur; skim, — the surface; *effleurer*; take a cursory view of etc. 457.

slur —, slip —, skip —, jump- over; pertermit, miss, skip, jump, omit, give the go-by to, push aside, throw into the background, shelve, sink; ignore, shut one's eyes to, refuse to hear, turn a deaf ear to; leave out of one's calculation; not -attend to etc. 457, — mind; not trouble -oneself, — one's head- -with, — about; forget etc. 506; be caught napping etc. (*not expect*) 508; leave a loose thread; let the grass grow under one's feet.

render -neglectful etc. *adj.*; put —, throw- off one's guard.

Adj. neglecting etc. *v.*; unmindful, negligent, neglectful; heedless, careless, thoughtless; perfunctory, remiss, slack.

inconsiderate; un-, in-circumspect; off one's guard; un-wary, -watchful, -guarded; offhand.

supine etc. (*inactive*) 683; inattentive etc 458; *insouciant* etc. (*indifferent*) 823; imprudent, reckless etc. 863; slovenly etc. (*disorderly*) 59, (*dirty*) 653; inexact etc. (*erroneous*) 495; improvident etc. 674.

neglected etc. *v.*; un-heeded, -cared for, -

perceived, -seen, -observed, -noticed, -noted, -marked, -attended to, -thought of, -regarded, -remarked, -missed; shunted, shelved.

un-examined, -studied, -searched, -scanned, -weighed, -sifted, -explored.

Adv. negligently etc. *adj.*; hand over head, anyhow; in an unguarded moment etc. (*unexpectedly*) 508; *per incuriam*.

Int. never mind, no matter, let it pass; it will be all the same a hundred years hence.

461. Inquiry. [Subject of Inquiry. Question.]—**N.** inquiry; request etc. 765; search, research, quest; pursuit etc. 622.

examination, review, scrutiny, investigation, indagation; per-quisition, -scrutation, -vestigation; inqu-est, -isition; exploration; *exploitation*, ventilation.

sifting; calculation, analysis, dissection, resolution, induction; Baconian method.

strict —, close —, searching —, exhaustive-inquiry; narrow —, strict- search; study etc. (*consideration*) 451.

scire facias, ad referendum; trial.

questioning etc. *v.*; interroga-tion, -tory; third degree; interpellation; challenge, examination, cross-examination, catechism; feeler, Socratic method, zetetic philosophy; leading question; discussion etc. (*reasoning*) 476; questionnaire, questionary.

reconnoitering, *reconnaissance*; prying etc. *v.*; espionage, *espionnage*; domiciliary visit, peep behind the curtain; lantern of Diogenes.

question, query, problem, *desideratum*, point to be solved, porism; subject —, field- of -inquiry, — controversy; point —, matter- in dispute; moot-point; issue, question at issue; bone of contention etc. (*discord*) 713; plain —, fair —, open- question; enigma etc. (*secret*) 533; knotty point etc. (*difficulty*) 704; *quod-libet*; threshold of an inquiry.

inquirer, investigator, experimenter, inquisitor, inspector, querist, examiner, catechist; scrut-ator, -ineer; analyst; quidnunc etc. (*curiosity*) 455.

V. make -inquiry etc. *n.*; inquire, seek, search, frisk, speer, look -for, — about for, — out for; scan, reconnoiter, explore, sound, rummage, ransack, pry, peer, look round; look —, go- -over, — through; spy, over-haul.

scratch the head, slap the forehead.

look —, peer —, pry- into every hole and corner; look behind the scenes; trace up; hunt —, fish —, dig —, ferret- out; unearth; leave no stone unturned.

seek a -clue, — clew; hunt, track, trail, shadow, mouse, dodge, trace; follow the -trail, — scent; pursue etc. 622; beat up one's quarters; fish for; feel for etc. (*experiment*) 463.

investigate; take up —, institute —, pursue —, follow up —, conduct —, carry on —, prosecute- -an inquiry etc. *n.*; look -at, — into; pre-examine; discuss, canvass, agitate.

examine, study, consider, calculate; dip —, dive —, delve —, go deep- into; make sure of, probe, sound, fathom; probe to the -bottom, — quick; scrutinize, analyze, anatomize, dissect, parse, resolve, sift, winnow; view —, try- in all its phases; thresh out.

bring in question, subject to examination; put to

the proof etc. (*experiment*) 463; audit, tax, pass in review; take into consideration etc. (*think over*) 451; take counsel etc. 695.

ask, question, demand; put —, pop —, propose —, propound —, moot —, start —, raise —, stir —, suggsst —, put forth —, ventilate —, grapple with —, go into- a question.

put to the question, interrogate, catechize, pump, grill; cross-question, -examine; dodge; require an answer; pick —, suck- the brains of; feel the pulse.

be -in question etc. *adj.*; undergo examination.

Adj. inquiry etc. *v.*; inquisitive etc. (*curious*) 455; requisit-ive, -ory; catechetical, inquisitorial, analytic; in -search, — quest- of; on the look-out for, interrogative, zetetic; all-searching.

un-determined, -tried, -decided; in -question, — dispute, — issue, — course of inquiry; under -discussion, — consideration, — investigation etc. *n.*, *sub judice*, moot, proposed; doubtful etc. (*uncertain*) 475.

Adv. what? why? wherefore? whence? whither? where? *quaere?* how -comes, — happens, — is- it? what is the reason? what's -the matter, — up, in the wind? what on earth? when? who?

462. Answer.—N. answer, response, reply, replication, *riposte*, rejoinder, surrejoinder, rebutter, surrebutter, counter-evidence etc. 468, counter-charge, defence, plea; retort, repartee; contradiction etc. 536; rescript, -ion; antiphon, -y; acknowledgment; password; echo.

discovery etc. 480a; solution etc. (*explanation*) 522; rationale etc. (*cause*) 153; clue etc. (*indication*) 550.

Oedipus; oracle, etc. 513; return etc. (*record*) 551.

V. answer, respond, reply, rebut, retort, rejoin; give —, return for- answer; acknowledge, echo.

explain etc. (*interpret*) 522; solve etc. (*unriddle*) 522; discover etc. 480a; fathom, hunt out etc. (*inquire*) 461; satisfy, set at rest, determine.

Adj. answering etc. *v.*; respon-sive, -dent; oracular; antiphonal; conclusive.

Adv. because etc. (*cause*) 153; on the -scent, — right scent.

Int. *eureka!*

463. Experiment.—N. experiment; essay etc. (*attempt*) 675; research etc. (*investigation*) 461; trial, tentative method, *tâtonnement*.

verification, probation, *experimentum crucis*, proof, criterion, diagnostic test, tryout, crucial test, acid test.

crucible, reagent, check, touchstone, pix; assay, ordeal; ring.

empiricism, rule of thumb.

feeler; pilot —, messenger- balloon, *ballon d'essai*; pilot engine; scout; straw to show the wind.

speculation, random shot, leap in the dark.

analy-zer, -st; adventurer, explorer, sourdough, prospector; experiment-er, -ist, -alist; assayer.

V. experiment; essay etc. (*endeavor*) 675; try, assay, sample; make -an experiment, — trial of; give a trial to; put upon —, subject to- trial; experiment upon; rehearse; put —, bring —, submit-

to the -test, — proof; prove, verify, test, touch, practise upon, try one's strength.

grope; feel —, grope- -for, — one's way; fumble; *tâtonner, aller à tâtons*; put —, throw- out a feeler; send up a pilot balloon; see how the -land lies, — wind blows; consult the barometer; feel the pulse; fish —, bob- for; cast —, beat- about for; angle, trawl, cast one's net, beat the bushes.

venture, try one's fortune etc. (*adventure*) 675; explore etc. (*inquire*) 461.

Adj. experimental; probat-ive, ory, -ionary; analytic, docimastic; tentative; empirical; speculative, tentive.

under probation, on one's trial, on trial, on approval.

464. Comparison.—N. comparison, collation, contrast; identification.

sim-ile, -ilitude; allegory etc. (*metaphor*) 521.

V. compare -to, — with; collate, confront; place side by side etc. (*near*) 197; set —, pit- against one another; contrast balance.

identify, draw a parallel, parallel.

compare notes; institute a comparison; *parva componere magnis*.

Adj. comparative, relative; metaphorical etc. 521.

compared with etc. *v.*; comparable.

Adv. relatively etc. (*relation*) 9; as compared with etc. *v.*

465. Discrimination.—N. discrimination, distinction, differentiation, diagnosis, diorism; nice perception; perception —, appreciation- of difference; acuteness; estimation etc. 466; nicety, refinement; taste etc. 850; *critique*, judgement, tact; insight, discernment etc. (*intelligence*) 498; *nuances*.

V. discriminate, distinguish, differentiate, severalize; separate; draw the line, sift; separate —, winnow- the chaff from the wheat; split hairs.

estimate etc. (*measure*) 466; know -which is which, — one's stuff, — one's way about, — what is what, — 'a hawk from a handsaw.'

take into -account, — consideration; give —, allow- due weight to; weigh carefully.

Adj. discriminating etc. *v.*; dioristic, discriminative, critical, distinctive; nice.

Phr. *il y a fagots et fagots; rem acu tetigisti.*

465a. Indiscrimination.—N. indiscrimination; promiscuity; indistinctness, -ion; uncertainty etc. (*doubt*) 475; obtuseness.

V. not -indiscriminate etc? 465; overlook etc.' (*neglect*) 460- a distinction; con-found, -fuse, jumble; swallow whole.

Adj. indiscriminate, undiscriminating, promiscuous; undistinguish-ed, -able, -ing; unmeasured.

466. Measurement.—N. measurement, ad-measurement, mensuration, survey, valuation, ap-

praisment, assessment, assize; estim-ate, -ation; dead reckoning; reckoning etc. (*numeration*) 85; gauging etc. *v.*

metrology, weights and measures, compound arithmetic.

measure, yard measure, standard, rule, foot-rule, chain, tape, staff, compass, callipers; dividers; gage, gauge, planimeter; meter, line, rod, check.

volt, kilowatt, ampere, candle power; horse power; axle load; foot pound.

flood —, high water- mark; Plimsoll mark; index etc. 550.

scale; gradu-ation, -ated scale; nonius; vernier etc. (*minuteness*) 193; pedo (*length*)- 200, sounding line etc. (*depth*) 208, thermo (*heat* etc. 398)-, baro (*air* etc. 338)-, dynamo (*power*)- 276, anemo (*wind* 349)-, gonio (*angle* 244)- meter; landmark etc. (*limit*) 233; balance etc. (*weight*) 310; optical instruments etc. 445.

co-ordinates, ordinate and abscissa, polar co-ordinates, latitude and longitude, declination and right ascension, altitude and azimuth.

geo-, stereo-, hypso-metry; metage; surveying, land surveying; geo-desy, -detics, -desia; ortho-, alti-metry; *cadastre.*

astrolabe, armillary sphere.

land, -surveyor; geometer, topographer, cartographer, hydrographer.

V. measure, meter, mete; value, assess, rate, appraise, estimate, form as estimate, set a value on; appreciate; standardize.

span, pace, step; apply the -compass etc. *n.*; gauge, plumb, probe, calliper, sound, fathom etc. 208; heave the -log, — lead; weigh etc. 319; survey.

take an average etc. 29; graduate.

Adj. measuring etc. *v.*; metric, -al; measurable; geodetical, cadastral, topographical.

467. Evidence. [on one side]—**N.** evidence; facts, premises, *data, praecognita*, grounds.

indication etc. 550; criterion etc. (*test*) 463.

testi-mony, -fication; attestation; deposition etc. (*affirmation*) 535; examination.

admission etc. (*assent*) 488; authority, warrant, credential, diploma, voucher, certificate, docket; record etc. 551; document, muniments; *pièce justificative*; deed, warranty etc. (*security*) 771; signature, seal etc. (*identification*) 550; exhibit, citation, reference.

witness, indicator; eye-, ear-witness; deponent; sponsor.

oral —, documentary —, hearsay —, external —, extrinsic —, internal —, intrinsic —, circumstantial —, cumulative —, *ex parte* —, presumptive —, collateral —, constructive- evidence; proof etc. (*demonstration*) 478; evidence in chief; finger prints, dactylogram.

secondary evidence; confirmation, corroboration, adminicle, support; ratification etc. (*assent*) 488; authentication, verification; compurgation, wager of law, comprobation.

citation, reference.

V. be -evidence etc. *n.*; evince, show, betoken, tell of; indicate etc. (*denote*) 550; imply, involve, argue, bespeak, breathe.

have —, carry- weight; tell, speak volumes; speak for itself etc. (*manifest*) 525.

rest –, depend- upon; repose on.

bear -witness etc. *n.*; give -evidence etc. *n.*;
testify, depose, witness, vouch for; sign, seal, un-
dersign, set one's hand and seal, sign and seal,
deliver as one's act and deed, certify, attest;
acknowledge etc. (*assent*) 488.

make absolute, confirm, ratify, corroborate, endorse, countersign, support, bear out, vindicate,
uphold, warrant.

adduce, attest, cite, quote; refer –, appeal- to;
call, – to witness; bring -forward, – into court;
allege, plead; produce –, confront- witnesses;
collect –, bring together –, rake up- evidence.

have –, make out- a case; establish, circumstantiate, authenticate, substantiate, verify,
make good, quote chapter and verse; bring -home
to, – to book.

Adj. showing etc. *v.*; evidential, indica-tive, -
tory; deducible etc. 478; grounded –, founded –,
based- on; first hand, authentic, verifiable;
corroborative, confirmatory; significant, conclusive.

Adv. by inference; according to, witness, *a fortiori*; still -more, – less; *raison de plus*; in
corroboration etc. *n.* of; *valeat quantum*; under -
seal, – one's hand and seal.

468. Counter-evidence. [Evidence on the
other side, on the other hand.]—**N.** counter-
evidence; evidence on the other -side, – hand;
disproof; refutation etc. 479; negation etc. 536;
conflicting evidence.

plea etc. 617; vindication etc. 937; counter-
protest; *tu quoque* argument; other side –, reverse-
of the shield.

V. countervail, oppose; run counter; rebut etc.
(*refute*) 479; subvert etc. (*destroy*) 162; check,
weaken; contravene; contradict etc. (*deny*) 536;
tell another story, turn the -tables, – scale; alter
the case; cut both ways; prove a negative.

audire alteram partem.

Adj. countervailing etc. *v.*; contradictory, in
rebuttal.

un-attested, -authenticated, -supported by
evidence; suppositious, trumped up.

Adv. *per contra*, conversely, on the other hand.

469. Qualification.—**N.** qualification,
limitation, modification, coloring.

allowance, grains of allowance, consideration,
extenuating circumstances.

condition, proviso, exception; exemption; salvo,
saving clause; discount etc. 813.

V. qualify, limit, modify, affect, temper, leaven,
give a color to, introduce new conditions.

allow –, make allowance- for; admit exceptions,
take into account. –

take exception, object.

Adj. qualifying etc. *v.*; conditional; extenuatory;
exceptional etc. (*unconformable*) 83.

hypothetical etc. (*supposed*) 514; contingent etc.
(*uncertain*) 475.

Adv. provided, – always; if, unless, but, yet; according as; conditionally, admitting, supposing; on
the supposition of etc. (*theoretically*) 514; with the
understanding, even, although, though, for all that,
after all, at all events.

with grains of allowance, *cum grano salis*; *ex-
ceptis excipiendis*; wind and weather permitting; if
possible etc. 470.

subject to; with this -proviso etc. *n.*

470. Possibility.—**N.** possibility, potentiality;
what -may be, – is possible etc. *adj.*; compatibility
etc. (*agreement*) 23.

practicability, feasibility; practicableness etc.
adj.

contingency, chance etc. 156.

V. be -possible etc. *adj.*; stand a chance, have a
leg to stand on; admit of, bear.

render -possible etc. *adj.*; put in the way of.

Adj. possible; on the -cards, – dice; *in posse*,
within the bounds of possibility, conceivable,
credible, imaginable; compatible etc. 23.

practicable, feasible, workable, performable,
achievable; within -reach, – measurable distance;
accessible, superable, surmountable; at-, ob-
tainable; contingent etc. (*doubtful*) 475.

Adv. possibly, by possibility; perhaps, -chance, -
adventure; may be, haply, mayhap.

if possible, wind and weather permitting, God
willing, *Deo volente*, D.V.

471. Impossibility.—**N.** impossibility etc. *adj.*;
what -cannot, – can never- be; sour grapes; in-
feasibility, impracticability; hopelessness etc. 859.

V. be -impossible etc. *adj.*; have no chance
whatever.

attempt impossibilities; square the circle;
discover the -philosopher's stone – elixir of life, –
secret of perpetual motion; wash a blackamoor
white; skin a flint; make -a silk purse out of a sow's
ear, – bricks without straw; have nothing to go
upon; weave a rope of sand, build castles in the air,
prendre la lune avec les dents, extract sunbeams
from cucumbers, set the Thames on fire, milk a he-
goat into a sieve, catch a weasel asleep, *rompre
l'anguille au genou*, be in two places at once.

Adj. impossible; not -possible etc. 470; absurd,
contrary to reason; unlikely, at variance with facts;
unreasonable etc. 477; incredible etc. 485; beyond
the bounds of -reason, – possibility; from which
reason recoils; visionary; inconceivable etc. (*improbable*) 473; prodigious etc. (*wonderful*) 870;
un-, in-imaginable, unthinkable, not a Chinaman's
chance.

impracticable, unachievable; un-, in-feasible; insuperable; un-, in-surmountable; unat-, unob-
tainable; out of -reach, – the question; not to be -
had, – thought of; beyond control; desperate etc.
(*hopeless*) 859; incompatible etc. 24; inaccessible,
uncomeatable, impassable, impervious, in-
navigable, inextricable.

out of –, beyond- one's -power, – depth, –
reach, – grasp; too much for; *ultra crepidam*.

Phr. the grapes are sour; *non possumus*; *non
nostrum tantas componere lites.*

472. Probability.—**N.** probability, likelihood;
likeliness etc. *adj.*

vraisemblance, verisimilitude, plausibility;

color, semblance, show of; presumption; presumptive −, circumstantial- evidence; credibility.

reasonable −, fair −, good −, favorable- -chance, − prospect; prospect, well-grounded hope; chance etc. 156.

V. be -probable etc. *adj.*; give −, lend- color to; point to; imply etc. (*evidence*) 467; bid fair etc. (*promise*) 511; stand fair for; stand −, run- a good chance.

presume, infer, suppose, take for granted.

think likely, dare say, flatter oneself; expect etc. 507; count upon etc. (*believe*) 484.

Adj. probable, likely, hopeful, to be expected, in a fair way.

plausible, specious, ostensible, colorable, *ben trovato*, well-founded, reasonable, credible, easy of belief, presumable, presumptive, apparent.

Adv. probably etc. *adj.*; belike; in all -probability, − likelihood; very −, most- likely; as likely as not; like enough; ten etc. to one; apparently, seemingly, according to every reasonable expectation; *primâ facie*; to all appearance etc. (*to the eye*) 448.

Phr. the -chances. − odds- are; appearances −, chances- are in favor of; there is reason to -believe, − think, − expect; I dare say; all Lombard Street to a China orange.

---

473. Improbability.—N. improbability, unlikelihood; unfavorable −, bad −, little −, small −, poor −, scarcely any −, no −, not a ghost of a- chance; bare possibility; long odds; incredibility etc. 485.

V. be -improbable etc. *adj.*; have a -small chance etc. *n.*

Adj. improbable, unlikely, contrary to all reasonable expectation, implausible.

rare etc. (*infrequent*) 137; unheard of, inconceivable; un-, in-imaginable; incredible etc. 485; more than doubtful.

Int. not likely! no fear!

Phr. the chances are against.

---

474. Certainty.—N. certainty; necessity etc. 601; certitude, certainness, surety, assurance, sureness; dead −, moral- certainty; infallibleness etc. *adj.*; infallibility, reliability.

gospel, scripture, church, pope, court of final appeal; *res judicata, ultimatum*.

positiveness; dogmat-ism, -ist, -izer; *doctrinaire*, know-all, bigot, -ry; opinionist, Sir Oracle; *ipse dixit*; zealot.

fact; positive −, matter of- fact; *fait accompli*.

V. be -certain etc. *adj.*; stand to reason.

render -certain etc. *adj.*; in-, en-, as-sure; clinch, make sure; determine, decide, set at rest, 'make assurance double sure;' know etc. (*believe*) 484; dismiss all doubt.

dogmatize, lay down the law.

Adj. certain, sure, assured etc. *v.*; solid, well-founded.

unqualified, absolute, positive, determinate, definite, clear, unequivocal, categorical, unmistakable, decisive, decided, ascertained.

inevitable, unavoidable, ineluctable, avoidless.

unerring, infallible; unchangeable etc. 150; to be depended on, trustworthy, reliable, bound.

un-impeachable, -deniable, -questionable; indisputable, -contestable, -controvertible, -defeasible, -dubitable; irrefutable etc. (*proven*) 478; conclusive, without power of appeal, final.

indubious; without −, beyond a −, without a shade or shadow or- -doubt − question; past dispute; beyond all -question, − dispute; undoubted, -contested, -questioned, -disputed; question-, dount-less.

bigoted, fanatical, dogmatic, opinionat-ed, -ive, *doctrinaire*.

authoritative, authentic; official.

sure as -fate, − death and taxes, − a gun.

evident, self-evident, axiomatic; clear, − as day, − as the sun at noonday; obvious.

Adv. certainly etc. *adj.*; for certain, certes, sure, no doubt, doubtless, and no mistake, *flagrante delicto*, sure enough, to be sure, of course, as a matter of course, *à coup sur*, to a certainty, undoubtedly; in truth etc. (*truly*) 494; at -any rate, − all events; without fail; *coûte que coûte*; whatever may happen, if the worst come to the worst; come −, happen- what -may, − will; sink or swim; rain or shine.

Phr. *cela va sans dire*; there is -no question, − not a, shadow of doubt; the die is cast etc. (*necessity*) 601.

---

475. Uncertainty.—N. uncertainty, incertitude, doubt; doubtfulness etc. *adj.*; dubi-ety, -tation, -tancy, -ousness.

hesitation, suspense; perplexity, embarrassment, dilemma, quandary, Morton's fork, bewilderment; timidity etc. (*fear*) 860; indecision, vacillation etc. 605; *diaporesis*, indetermination.

vagueness etc. *adj.*; haze, fog; obscurity etc. (*darkness*) 421; ambiguity etc. (*double meaning*) 520; contingency, double contingency, possibility upon a possibility; conjecture; open question etc. (*question*) 461; *onus probandi*; blind bargain, pig in a poke, leap in the dark, something or other; needle in a bottle of hay; roving commission.

fallibility, unreliability, untrustworthiness, precariousness.

V. be -uncertain etc. *adj.*; wonder whether.

lose the -clue, − clew, − scent; miss one's way.

not know -what to make of etc. (*unintelligibility*) 519, − which way to turn, − whether one stands on one's head or one's heels; float in a sea of doubt, hesitate, flounder; lose -oneself, − one's head, − one's way, wander aimlessly; muddle one's brains.

render -uncertain etc. *adj.*; put out, pose, puzzle, perplex, embarrass; confuse, -found; bewilder, mystify, bother, nonplus, addle the wits, throw off the scent; *ambiguas in vulgus spargere voces*; keep in suspense.

doubt etc. (*disbelieve*) 485; hang −, tremble- in the balance; depend.

Adj. uncertain; casual; random etc. (*aimless*) 621; changeable etc. 149.

doubtful, dubious; indecisive; unsettled, -decided, -determined; in suspense, open to discussion; controvertible; in question etc. (*inquiry*) 461; insecure, unstable.

vague; in-determinate, -definite; ambiguous, equivocal; undefin-ed, -able; confused etc. (*in-distinct*) 447; mystic, mysterious, veiled, obscure, cryptic, oracular.

perplexing etc. *v.*; enigmatic, paradoxical; apocryphal, problematical, hypothetical; ex-perimental etc. 463.

fallible, questionable, precarious, slippery, ticklish, debatable, disputable; un-reliable, -trustworthy.

contingent, — on, dependent on; subject to; dependent on circumstances; occasional; provisional.

unauth-entic, -enticated, -oritative; un-ascertained, -confirmed; undemonstrated; un-told, -counted.

in a -state of uncertainty, — cloud, — maze; ignorant etc. 491; on the horns of a dilemma; afraid to say; out of one's reckoning, astray, adrift; as -sea, — fault, — a loss, — one's wit's end, — a *nonplus*; puzzled etc. *v.*; lost abroad, *désorienté*; dis-tracted, -traught.

Adv. *pendente lite*; *sub spe rati*.

Phr. Heaven knows; who can tell? who shall decide when doctors disagree?

476. Reasoning.—N. reasoning; ratio-cination, -nalism; dialectics, induction, generalization.

discussion, comment; ventilation; inquiry etc. 461.

argumentation, controversy, debate; polemics, wrangling; contention etc. 720; logomachy; dis-putation, -ceptation; paper war.

art of reasoning, logic.

process —, train —, chain- of reasoning; de-, in-duction; systhesis, analysis.

argument; case, plea, *plaidoyer*, opening; *lemma*, proposition, terms, premises, postulate, *data*, starting point, principle; inference etc. (*judgment*) 480.

pro-, syllogism; enthymeme, sorites, dilemma, *perilepsis, a priori* reasoning, *reductio ad ab-surdum*, horns of a dilemma, *argumentum ad hominem*, comprehensive argument.

reasoner, logician, dialectician; disputant; con-trover-sialist, -tist; wrangler, arguer, debater, polemic, casuist, rationalist; scientist.

logical sequence; good case; correct —, just —, sound —, valid —, cogent —, logical —, forcible —, persuasive —, persuasory —, consectary —, con-clusive etc. 478 —, subtle- reasoning; force of argument; strong -point, — argument.

arguments, reasons, pros and cons.

V. reason, argue, discuss, debate, dispute, wrangle; bandy -words, — arguments; chop logic; hold —, carry on- an argument; controvert etc. (*deny*) 536; canvass; comment —, moralize-upon; consider etc. (*examine*) 461.

open a -discussion, — case; join —, be at- issue; moot; come to the point; stir —, agitate —, ventilate —, torture- a question; try conclusions; take up a -side, — case.

contend, take one's stand upon, insist, lay stress on; infer etc. 480.

follow from etc. (*demonstration*) 478.

Adj. rational; reasoning etc. *v.*; rationalistic; argumentative, controversial, dialectic, polemical; discurs-ory, -ive; disputations.

debatable, controvertible.

logical; in-, de-ductive; synthetic, analytic; relevant etc. 23.

Adv. for, because, hence, whence, seeing that, since, sith, then, thence, so; for -that, — this, — which- reason; for-, inasmuch as; whereas, *ex con-cesso*, considering, in consideration of; there-, where-fore; consequently, *ergo*, thus, accordingly; *a fortiori*.

in -conclusion, — fine; finally, after all, *au bout du compte*, on the whole, taking one thing with another.

rationally etc. *adj.*

477. Sophistry. [The absence of reasoning.] **Intuition.** [False or vicious reasoning; show of reason.]—**N.** intuition, instinct, association; presen-timent; rule of thumb.

sophistry, paralogy, perversion, casuistry, jesuitry, equivocation, evasion, mental reservation; chicane, -ry; quiddit, quiddity; mystification; special pleading; speciousness etc. *adj.*; nonsense etc. 497; word-, tongue-fence.

false —, vicious- reasoning; *petitio principii, ignoratio elenchi*; *post hoc ergo propter hoc*; *non sequitur, ignotum per ignotius*.

misjudgment etc. 481; false teaching etc. 538.

sophism, solecism, paralogism; quibble, quirk, *elenchus*, elench, fallacy, *quodlibet*, subterfuge, subtlety, quillet; inconsistency, antilogy; 'a mockery, a delusion and a snare;' claptrap, mere words; 'lame and impotent conclusion.'

meshes —, cobwebs- of sophistry; flaw in an argument; weak point, bad case.

over-refinement; hair-splitting etc. *v.*

sophist, casuist, paralogist.

V. judge -intuitively, — by intuition; hazard a proposition, talk at random.

reason -ill, — falsely etc. *adj.*; paralogize; misjudge etc. 481.

pervert, quibble; equivocate, mystify, evade, elude; gloss over, varnish; misteach etc. 538; mislead etc. (*error*) 495; cavil, refine, subtilize, split hairs; misrepresent etc. (*lie*) 544.

beg the question, reason in a circle, cut blocks with a razor, beat about the bush, play fast and loose, blow hot and cold, prove that black is white and white black, travel out of the record, *parler à tort et à travers*, put oneself out of court, not have a leg to stand on.

Adj. intuitive, instinctive, impulsive; in-dependent of —, anterior to- reason; gratuitous; hazarded; unconnected.

unreasonable, illogical, false, unsound, invalid; unwarranted, not following; inconsequent, -ial; in-consistent, incongruous; abson-ous, -ant; un-scientific; untenable, inconclusive, incorrect; fall-acious, -ible; groundless, unproved.

deceptive, sophistical, sophisticated, casuistical, jesuitical; illus-ive, -ory; specious, hollow, plausible, *ad captandum*, evasive; irrelevant etc. 10.

weak, feeble, poor, flimsy, loose, vague, irrational; nonsensical etc. (*absurd*) 497; foolish etc. (*imbecile*) 499; frivolous, pettifogging, quib-bling; finespun, over-refined.

at the end of one's tether, *au bout de son latin*.

Adv. intuitively etc. *adj.*; by intuition; illogically etc. *adj.*

Phr. *non constat*; that goes for nothing.

478. Demonstration.—N. demonstration, proof; conclusiveness etc. *adj.*; *apodixis*, probation, comprobation.

logic of facts etc. (*evidence*) 467; *experimentum curcis* etc. (*test*) 463; argument etc. 476; irrefragability.

V. demonstrate, prove, establish, make good; show; evince etc. (*be evidence of*) 467; verify etc. 467; settle the question, reduce to demonstration, set the question at rest.

make out, — a case; prove one's point, have the best of the argument; draw a conclusion etc. (*judge*) 480.

follow, — of course; stand to reason; hold -good, — water.

Adj. demonstra-ting etc. *v.*, -tive, -ble; probative, unanswerable, conclusive; apodictic, -al; irre-sistible, -futable, -fragable, undeniable.

categorical, decisive, crucial.

demonstrated etc. *v.*; proven; unconfuted, -answered, -refuted; evident etc. 474.

deducible, consequential, consectary, inferential, following.

Adv. of course, in consequence, consequently, as a matter of course.

Phr. *probatum est*; there is nothing more to be said, Q.E.D., it must follow.

479. Confutation.—N. con-, re-futation; answer, complete answer; disproof, conviction, redargution, invalidation; expos-ure, -ition; clincher; retort; *reductio ad absurdum*; knock down —, *tu quoque-* argument.

V. con-, re-fute; parry, negative, disprove, redargue, expose, show the fallacy of, rebut, defeat; demolish etc. (*destroy*) 162; over-throw, -turn; scatter to the winds, explode, invalidate; silence; put —, reduce- to silence; clinch -an argument, — a question; give one a set down, stop the mouth, shut up; have, — on the hip; get the better of; confound, convince.

not leave a leg to stand on, cut the ground from under one's feet.

be confuted etc.; fail; expose —, show- one's weak point.

Adj. confut-ing, -ed etc. *v.*; capable of refutation; re-, con-futable.

condemned -on one's own showing, — out of one's own mouth.

Phr. the argument falls to the ground, *cadit quaestio*, it does not hold water, `suo sibi gladio hunc jugulo.`

480. Judgment. [Conclusion.]—**N.** result, conclusion, upshot; deduction, inference, ergotism, illation; corollary, porism; moral.

estimation, valuation, appreciation, judication; di-, ad-judication; arbitr- ament, -ement, -ation; assessment, ponderation.

award, estimate; review, criticism, *critique*, notice, report.

decision, determination, judgment, finding, verdict, sentence, decree, — nisi, — absolute, — interlocutory; dictum; *res judicata*.

plébiscite, referendum, voice, casting vote; vote etc. (*choice*) 609; opinion etc. (*belief*) 484; good judgment etc. (*wisdom*) 498.

judge, jurist, umpire; arbi-ter, -trator; assessor, referee; censor, reviewer, critic; *connoisseur*; commentator etc. 524; inspector, inspecting officer.

V. judge, conclude; come to —, draw —, arrive at- a conclusion; ascertain, determine, make up one's mind.

deduce, derive, gather, collect, draw an inference, make a deduction, weet, ween.

form an estimate, estimate, size up, appreciate, value, count, assess, rate, rank, account; regard, consider, think of; look upon etc. (*believe*) 484.

settle; pass —, give- an opinion; decide, try, pronounce, rule; pass -judgment; — sentence; sentence, doom; find; give —, deliver- judgment; adjud-ge, -icate; arbitrate, award, report; bring in a verdict; make absolute, set a question ar rest; confirm etc. (*assent*) 488.

comment, criticize; review, pass under review etc (*examine*) 457; investigate etc. (*inquire*) 461.

hold the scales, sit in judgment; try —, hear- a cause.

Adj. judging etc. *v.*; judicious etc. (*wise*) 498; determinate, conclusive, censorious, critical etc. 932.

Adv. on the whole, all things considered.

480a. Discovery. [Result of search or inquiry.]—**N.** discovery, invention, detection, disenchantment, disclosure, find, ascertainment, revelation.

trover etc. 775.

V. discover, find, determine, evolve; fix upon; find —, trace —, make —, hunt —, fish —, worm —, ferret —, root-out; fathom; bring —, draw-out; educe, elicit, bring to light, invent; dig —, grub —, fish- up; unearth, disinter.

solve, resolve; un-riddle, -ravel, -lock; pick —, open- the lock; find a -clue, — clew- to; interpret etc. 522; disclose etc. 529.

trace, get at; hit it, have it; lay one's -finger, — hands- upon; spot; get —, arrive- at the -turth etc. 494; put the saddle on the right horse, hit the right nail on the head.

be near the truth, burn; smoke, scent, sniff, smell a rat.

open the eyes to; see -through, — daylight, — in its true colors, — the cloven foot; detect; catch, — tripping.

pitch —, fall —, light —, hit —, stumble —, pop- upon; come across; meet —, fall in- with.

recognize, realize, verify, make certain of, identify.

Int. *eureka!*

481. Misjudgment.—N. misjudgment, obliquity of —, warped- judgment; mis-calculation, -computation, -conception etc. (*error*) 495; hasty conclusion.

prejud-gment, -ication, -ice; foregone conclusion; pre-notion, -vention, -conception, -
dilection, -possession, -apprehension, -sumption, -
sentiment; fixed –, preconceived- idea; *idée fixe*;
mentis gratissimus error; fool's paradise.

esprit de corps, party spirit, race –, class-
prejudice, partisanship, clannishness, *prestige*.

bias, warp, twist; hobby, fad, whim, craze, quirk,
crotchet, partiality, infatuation, blind side, mote in
the eye.

one-sided –, partial –, narrow –, confined –,
superficial- views, – ideas,– conceptions, –
notions; narrow mind; bigotry etc. (*obstinacy*)
606; *odium theologicum*; pedantry; hypercriticism.

doctrinaire etc. (*positive*) 474.

V. mis-judge, -estimate, -think, -conjecture, -
conceive etc. (*error*) 495; fly in the face of facts;
mis-calculate, -reckon, -compute.

overestimate etc. 482; underestimate etc. 483.

pre-, fore-judge; pre-suppose, -sume, -judicate;
dogmatize; have a -bias etc. *n.*; have only one idea;
jurare in verba magistri, run away with the notion;
jump –, rush- to a conclusion; look only at one
side of the shield; view –with jaundiced eye, –
through distorting spectacles; not see beyond one's
nose; *dare pondus fumo*; get the wrong sow by the
ear etc. (*blunder*) 699.

give a -bias, – twist; bias, warp, twist; prejudice, -possess.

Adj. misjudging etc. *v.*; ill-judging, wrong-
headed; prejudiced, prejudicial, etc. *v.*; jaundiced;
short-sighted, pur-blind; partial, one-sided, superficial.

narrow-minded; confined, insular, provincial,
parochial, illiberal, intolerant, narrow, besotted,
infatuated, fanatical, cracked, warped, *entêté*,
positive, dogmatic, dictatorial; conceited; opin-,
opini-ative; opinion-ed, -ate, -ative, -ated; self-
opinioned, wedded to an opinion, *opinâtre*;
bigoted etc. (*obstinate*) 606; crotchety, fussy, impracticable; unreason-able, -ing; stupid etc. 499;
credulous etc. 486.

misjudged etc. *v.*

Adv. *ex parte.*

Phr. nothing like leather; the wish the father to
the thought.

482. Overestimation.—N. overestimation etc.
v.; exaggeration etc. 549; vanity etc. 880; optim-,
pessim-ism, -ist; megalomania.

much -cry and little wool, – ado about nothing;
storm in a teacup; fine talking, rodomontade, gush,
hot air, gas, bombast.

egotism etc. 880; boasting etc. 884.

V. over-estimate, -rate, -value, -prize, -weigh, -
reckon, -strain, -praise; estimate too highly, attach
too much importance to, make mountains of
molehills, catch at straws; strain, magnify;
exaggerate etc. 549; set too high a value upon;
think –, make- -much, – too much- of;
outreckon.

extol, – to the skies; make the -most, – best, –
worst- of; eulogize, panegyrize, gush, puff, boost;
make two bites of a cherry.

have too high an opinion of oneself etc. (*vanity*)
880.

Adj. overestimated etc. *v.*; oversensitive etc.

(*sensibility*) 822; inflated, puffed up, exaggerated
etc. 549.

Phr. all his geese are swans; *parturiunt montes.*

483. Underestimation.—N. underestimation;
depreciation etc. (*detraction*) 934; pessim-ism, -ist;
undervaluing etc. *v.*; modesty etc. 881.

V. under-rate, -estimate, -value, -reckon;
depreciate; disparage etc. (*detract*) 934; not do
justice to; mis-, dis-prize; ridicule etc. 856; slight
etc. (*despise*) 930; neglect etc. 460; slur over, un-
der-state.

make -light, – little, – nothing, – no account-
of; minimize, belittle, run down, think nothing of;
set -no store by, – at naught; shake off as
dewdrops from the lion's mane.

Adj. depreciat-ing, -ed, -ive, -ory, etc. *v.*; un-
appreciated, -valued, -prized; pejorative.

484. Belief.—N. belief; credence; credit;
assurance; faith, trust, troth, confidence, presumption, sanguine expectation etc. (*hope*) 858; depen-
dence on, reliance on.

persuasion, conviction, convincement,
plerophory, self-conviction; certainty etc. 474;
opinion, mind, view; conception, thinking; impression etc. (*idea*) 453; surmise etc. 514; conclusion etc. (*judgment*) 480.

tenet, dogma, principle, way of thinking;
popular belief etc. (*assent*) 488.

firm –, implicit –, settled –, fixed –, rooted
–, deep-rooted –, staunch –, unshaken –,
steadfast –, inveterate –, calm –, sober –,
dispassionate –, impartial –, well-founded- -
belief, – opinion etc.; *uberrima fides.*

system of opinions, school, doctrine, articles,
canons; declaration –, profession- of faith; tenets,
credenda, creed; thirty-nine articles etc. (*orthodoxy*) 983*a*; catechism; assent etc. 488;
propaganda etc. (*teaching*) 537.

credibility etc. (*probability*) 472.

V. believe, credit; give -faith, – credit, –
credence- to; see, realize; assume, receive; set down
–, take- for; have –, take- it; consider, esteem,
presume.

count –, depend –, calculate –, pin one's faith
–, reckon –, lean –, build –, rely –, rest-
upon; lay one's account for; make sure of.

make oneself easy -about, – on that score; take
on -trust, – credit; take for -granted, – gospel;
allow –, attach- some weight to.

know, – for certain; have –, make- no doubt;
doubt not; be – rest- -assured etc. *adj.*; persuade
–, assure –, satisfy- oneself; make up one's mind.

give one credit for; confide –, believe –, put
one's trust- in; place –, repose- implicit confidence
in; take -one's word for, – at one's word; place
reliance on, rely upon, swear by, regard to.

think, hold; take, – it; opine, be of opinion,
conceive, trow, ween, fancy, apprehend; have –,
hold –, possess –, entertain –, adopt –, imbibe
–, embrace –, get hold of –, hazard –, foster
–, nurture –, cherish- -a belief, – an opinion etc.
n.

view –, consider –, take –, hold –, conceive
–, regard –, esteem –, deem –, look upon –,
account –, set down- as; surmise etc. 514.

get −, take- it into one's head; come round to an opinion; swallow etc. (*credulity*) 486.

cause to -be believed etc. *v.*; satisfy, persuade, have the ear of, gain the confidence of, assure; convince, -vict, -vert; put across, sell; wean, bring round; bring −, put −, win- over; indoctrinate etc. (*teach*) 537; cram down the throat; produce −, carry- conviction; bring −, drive- home to.

go down, find credence, pass current; be -received etc. *v.*, − current etc. *adj.*; possess −, take hold of −, take possession of- the mind.

Adj. believing etc. *v.*; certain, sure, assured, positive, cocksure, satisfied, confident, unhesitating, convinced, secure.

under the impression; impressed −, imbued −, penetrated- with.

confiding, trustful, suspectless; unsusp-ecting, -icious; void of suspicion; credulous etc. 486; wedded to.

believed etc. *v.*; accredited, putative; unsuspected.

worthy of −, deserving of −, commanding- -belief, − confidence; credible, reliable, trusted, trustworthy, to be - depended on, undoubted; satisfactory; probable etc. 472; fiduci-al, -ary; persuasive, impressive.

relating to belief, doctrinal.

Adv. in the -opinion, − eyes- of; *me judice*; me-seems, -thinks; to the best of one's belief; I -dare say, − doubt not, − have no doubt, − am sure; in my opinion; sure enough etc. (*certainty*) 474; depend −, rely- upon it; be −, rest- assured; I'll warrant you etc. (*affirmation*) 535.

485. Unbelief. Doubt.—N. un-, dis-, misbelief; discredit, miscreance; infidelity etc. (*irreligion*) 989; dissent etc. 489; change of -opinion etc. 484; retraction etc. 607.

doubt etc. (*uncertainty*) 475; skepticism, misgiving, demur; dis-, mis-trust; misdoubt, suspicion, jealousy, scruple, qualm; *onus probandi*. incredib-ility, -leness; incredulity; unbeliever etc. 487.

V. dis-believe, -credit; not -believe etc. 484; misbelieve; refuse to admit etc. (*dissent*) 489; refuse to believe etc. (*incredulity*) 487.

doubt; be -doubtful etc. (*uncertain*) 475; doubt the truth of; be -skeptical as to etc. *adj.*; diffide; dis-, mis-trust; suspect, smoke, scent, smell a rat; have −, harbor −, entertain- -doubts, − suspicions; have one's doubts.

demur, stick at, pause, hesitate, scruple, waver, stop and consider.

hang in -suspense, − doubt.

throw doubt upon, raise a question; bring −, call- in question; question, challenge, query; dispute; deny etc. 536; cavil; cause −, raise −, start −, suggest −, awake- a -doubt, − suspicion; ergotize.

startle, stagger; shake −, stagger- one's faith, − belief.

Adj. unbelieving; incredulous −, skeptical- as to; distrustful −, shy −, suspicious- of; doubting etc. *v.*

doubtful etc. (*uncertain*) 475; disputable; unworthy −, undeserving- of -belief etc. 484; questionable; sus-pect, -picious; open to -suspicion,

− doubt; staggering, hard to believe, incredible, not to be believed, inconceivable.

fallible etc. (*uncertain*) 475; undemonstrable; controvertible etc. (*untrue*) 495.

Adv. *cum grano salis.*

Phr. *fronti nulla fides; nimium ne crede colori; 'timeo Danaos et dona ferentes;' credat Judaeus Apella;* let those believe who may.

486. Credulity.—N.. credul-ity, -ousness etc. *adj.*; gull-, cull-ibility; gross credulity, infatuation; self-delusion, -deception; blind reasoning; superstition; one's blind side; bigotry etc. (*obstinacy*) 606; hyper-orthodoxy etc. 984; misjudgment etc. 481.

credulous person etc. (*dupe*) 547.

V. be -credulous etc. *adj.*; *jurare in verba magistri;* follow implicitly; swallow, − whole, gulp down; take on trust; take for -granted, − gospel; run away with -a notion, − an idea; jump −, rush- to a conclusion; think the moon is made of green cheese; take −, grasp- the shadow for the substance; catch at straws.

impose upon etc. (*deceive*) 545.

Adj. credulous, gullible; easily -deceived etc. 545; simple, green, soft, childish, silly, stupid; over-credulous, -confident; infatuated, superstitious; confiding etc. (*believing*) 484.

Phr. the wish the father to the thought; *credo quia impossibile.*

487. Incredulity.—N. incredul-ous-ness, -ity; skepticism, pyrrhonism; want of faith etc. (*irreligion*) 989.

suspiciousness etc. *adj.*; scrupulosity; suspicion etc. (*unbelief*) 485; dissent etc. 489.

unbeliever, skeptic, aporetic; atheist, agnostic, infidel, disbeliever, misbeliever, pyrrhonist etc. 989; heretic etc. (*heterodox*) 984.

v. be -incredulous etc. *adj.*; distrust etc. (*disbelieve*) 485; refuse to believe; shut one's -eyes, − ears- to; turn a deaf ear to; hold aloof; ignore; *nullis jurare in verba magistri.*

Adj. incredulous, skeptical, unbelieving, inconvincible; hard −, shy- of belief; suspicious, scrupulous, distrustful, heterodox etc. 984.

488. Assent.—N. assent, -ment; acquiescence, admission; nod; ac-, con-cord, -cordance; agreement etc. 23; affirm-ance, -ation; recognition, acknowledgment, avowal; confession, − of faith.

unanimity, common consent, *consensus*, acclamation, chorus, *vox populi*; popular −, current- -belief, − opinion; public opinion; concurrence etc. (*of causes*) 178; co-operation etc. (*voluntary*) 709.

ratification, confirmation, corroboration, approval, acceptance, *visa*; indorsement etc. (*record*) 551.

consent etc. (*compliance*) 762.

affirmant, consenter, covenantor, subscriber, endorser, upholder.

V. assent; give −, yield −, not- assent; acquiesce; agree etc. 23; receive, accept, accede,

accord, concur, lend oneself to, consent, coincide, reciprocate, go with; be -at one with etc. *adj.*; go along –, chime in –, strike in –, close- with; echo, enter into one's views, agree in opinion; vote –, give one's voice- for; recognize; subscribe –, conform –, defer- to; say -yes–, ditto, – amen; – aye- to.

acknowledge, own, admit, allow, avow, confess; concede etc. (*yield*) 762; come round to; abide by; permit etc. 760.

come to –, arrive at- -an understanding, – terms, – an agreement.

con-, af-firm; ratify, approve, endorse, countersign; visa; corroborate etc. 467.

go –, swim- with the stream, float with the current; be in the fashion, join in the chorus; be in every mouth.

Adj. assenting etc. *v.*; of one -accord, – mind; of the same mind, at one with, agreed, acquiescent, content; willing etc. 602.

un-contradicted, -challenged, -questioned, -controverted.

carried –, agreed- *-nem. con.* etc. *adv.*; unanimous; agreed on all hands, carried by acclamation.

affirmative etc. 535.

Adv. yes, yea, ay, aye, true; good; well; very well, – true; well and good; granted; *placet*; even –, just- so; to be sure, surely, 'thou hast said;' truly, exactly, precisely, that's just it, indeed, certainly, certes, *ex concesso*; of course, unquestionably, assuredly, no doubt, doubtless, undoubtedly.

be it so; so -be it, – let it be, so mote it be; amen; with all my heart; willingly etc. 602.

with one -consent, – voice, – accord; unanimously, *unâ voce*, by common consent, in chorus, to a man, *nem. con.*; *nemine -contradicente, – dissentiente*; without a dissentient voice; as one man, one and all, on all hands.

489. Dissent.—N. dissent; discordance etc. (*disagreement*) 24; difference –, diversity- of opinion.

non-conformity etc. (*heterodoxy*) 984; protestantism, recusancy, schism; disaffection; secession etc. 624; recantation etc. 607.

dissension etc. (*discord*) 713; discontent etc. 832; cavilling.

protest; contradiction etc. (*denial*) 536; non-compliance etc. (*rejection*) 764; disapprobation etc. 932; hartal.

dissent-ient, -er; non-juror, -content; recusant, sectary, schismatic, protestant, non-conformist, separatist, non-co-operator, conscientious objector, passive resister.

V. dissent, demur; call in question etc. (*doubt*) 485; differ in opinion, disagree; say -no etc. 536; refuse -assent, – to admit; cavil, protest, raise one's voice against, make bold to differ; repudiate; contradict etc. (*deny*) 536; agree to differ.

have no notion of, differ *toto caelo*; revolt -at, – from the idea.

shake the head, shrug the shoulders; look -askance, – askant.

secede; recant etc. 607.

Adj. dissenting etc. *v.*; negative etc. 536; dissident, -entient; unconsenting etc. (*refusing*) 764;

non-content, -juring; protestant, recusant; unconvinced, -verted.

unavowed, unacknowledged; out of the question. discontented etc. 832; unwilling etc. 603; extorted.

sectarian, denominational, schismatic, heterodox, intolerant.

Adv. no etc. 536; at -variance, – issue- with; under protest; *non placet*.

Int. God forbid! not for the world; not on your life; I beg to differ; I'll be hanged if; never tell me; your humble servant, pardon me; tell that to the marines.

Phr. many men many minds; *quot homines tot sententiae; tant s'en faut; il s'en faut bien.*

490. Knowledge.—N. knowledge; cogn-izance, -ition, -oscence; acquaintance, experience, ken, privity, insight, familiarity; com-, ap-prehension; recognition; appreciation etc. (*judgment*) 480; intuition; consci-ence, -ousness; preception, precognition; acroamatics.

light, enlightenment; glimpse, inkling; side light; glimmer, -ing; dawn; scent, suspicion; impression etc. (*idea*) 453; discovery etc. 480a.

system –, body- of knowledge; science, philosophy, pansophy; theory, Etiology; circle of the sciences; pandect, doctrine, body of doctrine; cy-, ency-clopedia; school etc. (*system of opinions*) 484.

tree of knowledge; republic of letters etc. (*language*) 560.

erudition, learning, lore, scholarship, reading, letters; literature; booklearning, bookishness; biblio-mania, -latry; information, general information; store of -knowledge etc.; education etc. (*teaching*) 537; culture, attainments; acquirements, -sitions; accomplishments, proficiency; practical knowledge etc. (*skill*) 698; higher education, liberal education; dilettantism; rudiments etc. (*beginning*) 66.

deep –, profound –, solid –, accurate –, acroatic –, acroamatic –, vast –, extensive –, encyclopedical- -knowledge, – learning; omniscience, pantology.

march of intellect; progress –, advance- of -science, – learning; schoolmaster abroad.

V. know, ken, scan, wot; wot –, be aware etc. *adj.*- of; ween, weet, trow, have, possess.

conceive; ap-, com-prehend; take; realize, understand, appreciate; fathom, make out; recognize, discern, perceive, see, get a sight of, experience.

know full well; have –, possess- some knowledge of; be *-au courant* etc. *adj.*; have -in one's head, – at one's fingers' ends; know by -heart, – rote; be master of; *connaître le dessous des cartes*, know what's what etc. 698.

see one's way; learn, discover etc. 480a.

come to one's knowledge etc. (*information*) 527.

Adj. knowing etc. *v.*; cognitive; acroamatic.

aware –, cognizant –, conscious- of; acquainted –, made acquainted- with; privy –, no stranger- to; *au -fait, – courant*; in the secret; up –, alive- to; sensible of; behind the -scenes, – curtain; let into; apprized –, informed- of; undeceived.

proficient –, versed –, read –, forward –,

strong —, at home- in; conversant —, familiar-with.

erudite, instructed, learned, lettered, educated; high-brow; well-conned, -informed, -read, -grounded, -educated; enlightened, shrewd, insightful, *savant*, blue, bookish, scholastic, solid, profound, deep-read, book-learned; accomplished etc. (*skilful*) 698; omniscient; self-taught, -educated.

known etc. *v.*; ascertained, well-known, recognized, received, notorious, noted; proverbial; familiar, — as household words, to every schoolboy; hackneyed, trite, commonplace.

knowable, cogn-oscible, -izable.

Adv. to —, to the best of- one's knowledge.

Phr. one's eyes being opened etc. (*disclosure*) 529.

491. Ignorance.—N. ignorance, nescience, *tabula rasa*, crass ignorance, *ignorance crasse*; unacquaintance; unconsciousness etc. *adj.*; dark-, blind-ness; incomprehension, inexperience, simplicity.

unknown quantities, *x*, *y*, *z*.

sealed book, *terra incognita*, virgin soil, unexplored ground; dark ages.

[Imperfect knowledge] smattering, superficiality, half-learning, sciolism, glimmering; bewilderment etc. (*uncertainty*) 475; incapacity.

[Affectation of knowledge] pedantry; charlatan-ry, -ism.

V. be -ignorant etc. *adj.*; not -know etc. 490; know -not, — not what, — nothing of; have no -idea, — notion, — conception; not have the remotest idea; not know chalk from cheese.

ignore, be blind to; keep in ignorance etc. (*conceal*) 528.

see through a glass darkly; have a -film over the eyes, — glimmering etc. *n.*; wonder whether; not know what to make of etc. (*unintelligibility*) 519; not pretend —, not take upon oneself- to say.

Adj. ignorant, nescient; un-knowing, -aware, -acquainted, -apprized, -witting, -weeting, -conscious; wit-, weet-less; a stranger to; unconversant.

un-informed, -cultivated, -versed, -instructed, -taught, -initiated, -tutored, -schooled, -guided, -enlightened; Philistine; behind the age.

shallow, superficial, green, rude, empty, half-learned, illiterate; un-read, -informed, -educated, -learned, -lettered, -bookish; empty-headed; lowbrow; pedantic.

in the dark; be-nighted, -lated; blind-ed, -fold; hoodwinked; misinformed; *au bout de son latin*, at the end of his tether; at fault; at sea etc. (*uncertain*) 475; caught tripping.

un-known, -apprehended, -explained, -ascertained, -investigated, -explored, -heard of, -perceived; concealed etc. 528; novel.

Adv. ignorantly etc. *adj.*; unawares; for -anything, — aught- one knows; not that one knows.

Int. God —, Heaven —, the Lord —, nobody-knows.

Phr. a little learning is a dangerous thing.

492. Scholar.—N. scholar, *connoisseur*, *savant*, pundit, schoolman, professor, graduate,

wrangler, moonshee; academ-ician, -ist; fellow, don, post graduate, advanced student; master —, bachelor- of arts; doctor, licentiate, gownsman; philo-sopher, -math: scientist, clerk; soph, -ist, -ister; linguist, classicist; glosso-, etymo-, philologist; philologer; lexico-, glosso-grapher; scholiast, commentator, annotator, grammarian; *littérateur*, *literati*, *dilettanti*, *illuminati*; Mezzofanti, admirable Crichton, Maecenas.

book-worm, *helluo librorum*, biblio-phile, -maniac; blue-stocking, *bas-bleu*; big-wig, learned Theban.

learned —, literary- man; *homo multarum literarum*; man of -learning, — letters, — education; high-brow, intelligentsia.

antiquar-ian, -y; archeologist; sage etc. (*wise man*) 500.

pendant, *doctrinaire*; pedagogue, Dr. Pangloss; pantologist.

teacher etc. 540; schoolboy etc. (*learner*) 541.

Adj. learned etc. 490; brought up at the feet of Gamaliel.

493. Ignoramus.—N. ignoramus, illiterate, moron, dunce, numskull; wooden spoon; no scholar.

sciolist, smatterer, dabbler, half-scholar; *charlatan*; wiseacre.

novice, griffin; greenhorn etc. (*dupe*) 547; tyro etc. (*learner*) 541.

lubber etc. (*bungler*) 701; fool etc. 501; pedant etc. 492.

Adj. bookless, shallow, simple, dense, dumb, thick, dull, ignorant etc. 491.

494. Truth. [Object of knowledge.]**—N.** fact, reality etc. (*existence*) 1; plain matter of fact; nature etc. (*principle*) 5; truth, verity; gospel; orthodoxy etc. 983a; authenticity; veracity etc. 543.

accuracy, exactitude; exact-, precise-ness etc. *adj.*; precision, delicacy; rigor, mathematical precision, punctuality; clockwork precision etc. (*regularity*) 80.

orthology; *ipsissima verba*; letter of the law, realism.

plain —, honest —, sober —, naked —, unalloyed —, unqualified —, stern —, exact —, intrinsic- truth; *nuda veritas*; the very thing; not an illusion etc. 495; real Simon Pure; unvarnished tale; the truth, the whole truth and nothing but the truth; just the thing.

V. be -true etc. *adj.*, — the case; stand the test; have the true ring; hold -good, — true, — water; conform to rule.

render —, prove- -true etc. *adj.*; substantiate etc. (*evidence*) 467.

get at the truth etc. (*discover*) 480a.

Adj. real, actual etc. (*existing*) 1; veritable, true; certain etc. 474; substantially —, categorically-true etc; true -to the letter; — to life, — to scale, — the facts, — as gospel; unimpeachable; veracious etc. 543; unre-, uncon-futed; un-ideal -imagined; realistic.

exact, accurate, definite, precise, well defined, just, right, correct, strict, severe; close etc. (*similar*) 17; literal; rigid, rigorous; scrupulous etc. (*con-*

scientious) 939; religiously exact, punctual, mathematical, scientific; faithful, constant, unerring; curious, particular, punctilious, meticulous, nice, delicate, fine.

genuine, authentic, legitimate, pukka; orthodox etc. 983*a*; official, *ex officio*.

pure, natural, sound, sterling; un-sophisticated, -adulterated, -varnished, -colored; in its true colors.

well-grounded, -founded; solid, substantial, tangible, valid; undis-torted, -guised; un-affected, -exaggerated, -romantic, -flattering.

Adv. truly etc.*adj*.; verily, indeed, in reality; as a matter of fact; beyond -doubt, – question; with truth etc. (*veracity*) 543; certainly etc. (*certain*) 474; actually etc. (*existence*) 1; in effect etc. (*intrinsically*) 5.

exactly etc. *adj*. ; *ad amussim*; *verbatim, – et literatim*; word for word, literally, *literatim*, *totidem verbis*, *sic*, to the letter, chapter and verse, *ipsissimis verbis*; *ad unguem*; to an inch; to a -nicety, – hair, – tittle, – turn, – T; *au pied de la lettre*; neither more nor less; in -every respect, – all respects; *sous tous les rapports*; at -any rate, – all events; strictly speaking.

Phr. the -truth, – fact- is; *rem acu tetigisti*.

495. Error.—N. error, fallacy; misconception, -apprehension, -understanding; inexactness etc. *adj*.; laxity; misconstruction etc. (*misinterpretation*) 523; miscomputation etc. (*misjudgment*) 481; *non-sequitur* etc. 477; misstatement, -report; anachronism; malapropism.

mistake, miss, fault, blunder, boner, bloomer, howler, *quid pro quo*, cross purposes, oversight, misprint, *erratum*, *corrigendum*, slip, blot, flaw, loose thread; trip, stumble etc. (*failure*) 732; botchery etc. (*want of skill*) 699; slip of the -tongue, – pen; *lapsus -linguae*, – *calami*, clerical error; bull etc. (*absurdity*) 497.

il-, de-lusion; false -impression, – idea; bubble; self-deceit, -deception; warped notion; mists- of error; superstition, exploded notion.

heresy etc. (*heterodoxy*) 984; hallucination etc. (*insanity*) 503; false light etc. (*fallacy of vision*) 443; dream etc. (*fancy*) 515; fable etc. (*untruth*) 546; bias etc. (*misjudgment*) 481; misleading etc. *v*.

V. be -erroneous etc. *adj*.

cause error; mis-lead, -guide; lead -astray, – into error; beguile, misinform etc. (*misteach*) 538; delude; give a false -impression, – idea; falsify, garble, misstate; deceive etc. 545; lie etc. 544.

err; be -in error etc. *adj*.; – mistaken etc. *v*.; be deceived etc. (*duped*) 547; mistake, receive a false impression, deceive oneself; fall into –, lie under –, labor under- -an error etc. *n*.; be in the wrong, blunder; mis-apprehend, -conceive, -understand, -reckon, -count, -calculate etc. (*misjudge*) 481.

play –, be- at cross purposes etc. (*misinterpret*) 523.

trip, stumble; lose oneself etc. (*uncertainty*) 475; go astray; fail etc. 732; take the wrong sow by the ear etc. (*mismanage*) 699; put the saddle on the wrong horse; reckon without one's host; take the shadow for the substance etc. (*credulity*) 486; dream etc. (*imagine*) 515.

Adj. erroneous, untrue, false, devoid of truth, fallacious, faulty, apocryphal, unreal, ungrounded,

groundless; unsubstantial etc. 4; heretical etc. (*heterodox*) 984; unsound; illogical etc. 477; wrong.

in-, un-exact; in-accurate, -correct; indefinite etc. (*uncertain*) 475.

illus-ive, -ory; delusive; mock; ideal etc. (*imaginary*) 515; spurious etc. 545; deceitful etc. 544; perverted.

controvertible, unsustain-able, -ed; unauthenticated, untrustworthy.

exploded, refuted, discarded.

in –, under an- error etc. *n*.; mistaken etc. *v*.; tripping etc. *v*.; out, – in one's reckoning; aberrant; beside –, wide of the- -mark, – truth; astray etc. (*at fault*) 475; on -a false, – the wrong-scent; in the wrong box; at cross purposes, all in the wrong, all abroad, at sea.

Adv. more or less.

496. Maxim.—N. maxim, aphorism; apo-, apoph-thegm; *dictum*, saying, gnome, adage, saw, proverb, epigram; sentence, *mot*, motto, word, by-word, precept, moral, phylactery, *protasis*, brocard.

axiom, postulate, theorem, *scholium*, truism.

reflection etc. (*idea*) 453; conclusion etc. (*judgment*) 480; golden rule etc. (*precept*) 697; principle, *principia*; profession of faith etc. (*belief*) 484; formula.

wise –, sage –, received –, admitted –, recognized- maxim etc.; true –, common –, hackneyed –, trite –, commonplace- saying etc.

Adj. aphoristic, proverbial, phylacteric; axiomatic, gnomic.

Adv. as -the saying is, – they say.

497. Absurdity.—N. absurd-ity, -ness etc. *adj*.; imbecility etc. 499; alogy, nonsense, paradox, inconsistency; stultiloqu-y, -ence, futility.

blunder, muddle, bull; Irish-, Hibernic-ism; slip-slop; anti climax; bathos; sophism etc. 477.

farce, burlesque, *galimatias*, *amphigouri*, rhapsody; farrago etc. (*disorder*) 59; extravagance, romance; sciomachy.

joke, catch, sell, pun, verbal quibble, macaronic; jargon, fustian, twaddle etc. (*no meaning*) 517; exaggeration etc. 549; moonshine, stuff; mare's nest.

vagary, tomfoolery, mummery, monkey trick, practical joke, *boutade*, *escapade*.

V. play the fool etc. 499; stultify, blunder, muddle; joke; talk nonsense, *parler à tort et à travers*; *battre la campagne*; be -absurd etc. *adj*.

Adj. absurd, nonsensical, preposterous, egregious, senseless, farcical, inconsistent, ridiculous, extravagant, quibbling, futile; macaronic, punning, paradoxical.

foolish etc. 499; sophistical etc. 477; unmeaning etc. 517; without rhyme or reason; fantastic.

Int. fiddle-de-dee! pish! pish and tush! pho! stuff and nonsense! rubbish! !rot! bosh! in the name of the Prophet—figs!

Phr. *credat Judaeus Apella*; tell it to the marines.

498. Intelligence. Wisdom.—N. intelligence, capacity, comprehension, understanding, intellect

etc. 450; nous, parts, sagacity, mother wit, wit, *esprit*, gumption, quick parts, grasp of intellect; acuteness etc. *adj.*; acumen, subtlety, penetration; perspica-cy, -city; discernment; long-headedness, due sense of, good judgment; discrimination etc. 465; craftiness, cunning etc. 702; refinement etc. (*taste*) 850.

head, brains, gray matter, headpiece, upper story, long head; eagle -eye, — glance; eye of a - lynx, — hawk.

wisdom, sapience, sense; good —, common —, plain —, horse- sense; clear thinking; rationality, reason; reasonableness etc. *adj.*; judgment; solidity, depth, profundity, caliber; enlarged views; reach —, compass- of thought; enlargement of mind.

genius, inspiration, *geist*, fire of genius, heaven-born genius, soul; talent etc. (*aptitude*) 698.

[Wisdom in action] prudence etc. 864; vigilance etc. 459; tact etc. 698; foresight etc. 510; sobriety, self-possession, *aplomb*, ballast, mental - poise, — balance.

a bright thought, inspiration, brainwave, not a bad idea.

V. be -intelligent etc. *adj.*; have all one's wits about one; understand etc. (*intelligible*) 518; catch —, take in- an idea; take a -joke, — hint.

see -through, — at a glance, — with half an eye, — far into, — through a millstone; penetrate; discern etc. (*descry*) 441; foresee etc. 510.

discriminate etc. 465; know what's what etc. 698; listen to reason.

Adj. [Applied to persons] intelligent, quick of apprehension, keen, acute, alive, brainy, awake, bright, quick, sharp; quick-, keen-, clear-, sharp- -eyed, -sighted -witted; wide awake; canny, shrewd, astute; clear-headed; far-sighted etc. 510; discerning, perspicacious, penetrating, piercing; argute nimble-, needle-witted; sharp as a needle; alive to etc. (*cognizant*) 490; clever etc. (*apt*) 698; arch etc. (*cunning*) 702; *pas si bête*; acute etc. 682.

wise, sage, sapient, sagacious, reasonable, rational, sound, in one's right mind, sensible, *abnormis sapiens*, judicious, strong-minded.

un-prejudiced, -biassed, -bigoted, -prepossessed; un-dazzled, -perplexed; of unwarped judgment, impartial, equitable, fair, broad-minded.

cool; cool-, long-, hard-, strong-headed; long-sighted, calculating, thoughtful, reflecting; solid, deep, profound.

oracular; heaven-directed, -born.

prudent etc. (*cautious*) 864; sober, staid, solid; considerate, politic, wise in one's generation; watchful etc. 459; provident etc. (*prepared*) 673; in advance of one's age; wise as -a serpent, — Solomon, — Solon.

[Applied to actions] wise, sensible, reasonable, judicious; well-judged, -advised; prudent, politic; expedient etc. 646.

499. Imbecility. Folly.—N. want of - intelligence etc. 498, — intellect etc. 450; shallow-, silli-, foolish-ness etc. *adj.*; imbecility, incapacity, vacancy of mind, poverty of intellect, clouded perception, poor head, apartments to let; stup-, stolidity; hebetude, dull understanding, meanest capacity; short-sightedness; incompetence etc. (*unskilfulness*) 699.

one's weak side; bias etc. 481; infatuation etc. (*insanity*) 503.

simplicity, puerility, babyhood; dotage, anility, second childishness, senile dementia, fatuity; idiocy, -tism; driveling.

folly, frivolity, desipience, irrationality, trifling, ineptitude, nugacity, inconsistency, lip-wisdom, conceit; sophistry etc. 477; giddiness etc. (*inattention*) 458; eccentricity etc. 503; extravagance etc. (*absurdity*) 497; rashness etc. 863.

act of folly etc. 699.

V. be -imbecile etc. *adj.*; have no -brains, — sense etc. 498.

trifle, drivel, *radoter*, dote; ramble etc. (*madness*) 503; play the -fool, — monkey, — goat, take leave of one's senses; not see an inch beyond one's nose; stultify oneself etc. 699; talk nonsense etc. 497.

Adj. [Applied to persons] un-intelligent, - intellectual, -reasoning; mind-, wit-, reason-, brainless; having no -head etc. 498; not -bright etc. 498; inapprehensible.

weak-, addle-, puzzle-, blunder-, muddle-, muddy-, pig-, beetle-, maggotty-, gross-headed; beef-, fat- -witted, -headed.

weak, feeble-minded; dull-, shallow-, rattle-, lack-brained; half-, nit-, short-, dull-, blunt-witted; shallow-, clod-, addle-pated; dim-, short-sighted; thick-skulled; weak in the upper story.

shallow, *borné*, weak, wanting, soft, nutty, sappy, spoony; dull, — as a beetle; stupid, heavy, insulse, obtuse, blunt, stolid, doltish, asinine; inapt etc. 699; prosaic etc. 843.

child-ish, -like; infant-ine, -ile; baby-, bab-ish; puerile; anile; simple etc. (*credulous*) 486.

fatuous, idiotic, imbecile, moronic, driveling; blatant, babbling; vacant; sottish; bewildered etc. 475.

blockish, unteachable; Boeot-ian, -ic; bovine; un-gifted, -discerning, -enlightened, -wise, -philosophical; apish.

foolish, silly, senseless, irrational, insensate, non-sensical, inept; maudlin.

narrow-minded etc. 481; bigoted etc. (*obstinate*) 606; giddy etc. (*thoughtless*) 458; rash etc. 863; eccentric etc. (*crazed*) 503.

[Applied to actions] foolish, unwise, indiscreet, injudicious, improper, unreasonable, without reason, ridiculous, silly, stupid, asinine; ill-imagined, -advised, -judged, -devised; inconsistent, irrational, unphilosophical; extravagant etc. (*nonsensical*) 497; sleeveless, idle; useless etc. 645; inexpedient etc. 647; frivolous etc. (*trivial*) 643; absurd etc. 497.

Phr. *Davis sum non Oedipus.*

500. Sage.—N. sage, wise man; pundit; master - mind, — spirit of the age; longhead, thinker, philosopher.

authority, oracle, mentor, luminary, shining light, *esprit fort*, *magnus Apollo*, Solon, Solomon, Nestor, Magi, 'second Daniel.'

man of learning etc. 492; expert etc. 700; wizard etc. 994.

[Ironically] wiseacre, bigwig.

Adj. wise, learned; authoritative, oracular; erudite etc. 490; venerable, reverenced, revered, *emeritus*.

501. Fool.—N. fool, idiot, tomfool, wiseacre, simpleton, Simple Simon, nit-wit, witling, dizzard, donkey, ass; ninny, -hammer; moron, dolt, booby, Tom Noddy, looby, hoddy-doddy, noddy, nonny, noodle, nizy, owl; goose, -cap; *imbécile*; gaby, *radoteur*, nincompoop, *badaud*, zany; trifler, babbler; pretty fellow; natural, *niais*.

child, baby, infant, innocent, milksop, sop.

oaf, lout, loon, lown, dullard, doodle, calf, colt, buzzard, block, put, stick, stock, numps, tony.

bull-, dunder-, addle-, block-, dull-, logger-, jolt-, jolter-, beetle-, gross-, thick-, giddy-head; num-, thick- skull; lack-, shallow-brain; half-, lack-wit; dunder-pate; fat-head, poor stick.

sawney, gowk; clod, -hopper; clod-, clot-poll, -pate; bull-calf; men of Boeotia, wise men of Gotham.

un sot à triple étage, sot; jobbernowl, changeling, mooncalf, *gobemouche*.

dotard, driveller; old -fogey, − woman; crone, grandmother.

greenhorn etc. (*dupe*) 547; dunce etc. (*ignoramus*) 493; lubber etc. (*bungler*) 701; madman etc. 504.

one who -will not set the Thames on fire, − did not invent gunpowder; *qui n'a pas inventé la poudre*; no conjuror.

502. Sanity.—N. sanity; soundness etc. *adj.*; rationality, normality, sobriety, lucidity, lucid interval; senses, sober senses, sound mind, *mens sana*.

V. be -sane etc. *adj.*; retain one's senses, − reason.

become -sane etc. *adj.*; come to one's senses, sober down.

render -sane etc. *adj.*; bring to one's senses, sober.

Adj. sane, rational, reasonable, *compos mentis*, of sound mind; sound, -minded.

self-possessed; sober, -minded.

in one's -sober senses, − right mind; in possession of one's faculties.

Adv. sanely etc. *adj.*

503. Insanity.—N. disordered -reason, − intellect; diseased −, unsound −, abnormal- mind; derangement, unsoundness.

insanity, lunacy; madness etc. *adj.*; mania, *rabies*, *furor*, mental aliénation, paranoia, aberration; *amentia*, dementation, -tia, -cy; *dementia praecox*; *morosis*, idiocy, phrenitis, frenzy, raving, incoherence, wandering, delirium, calenture of the brain, delusion, hallucination; lycanthropy, brain storm, *delirium tremens*, D.T.'s.

vertigo, dizziness, swimming; sunstroke, *coup de soleil*, siriasis.

fanatisism, infatuation, craze; oddity, eccentricity, twist, monomania; klepto-, dipso-mania; hypochondriasis etc. (*low spirits*) 837; *melancholia*, hysteria.

screw −, tile −, slate- loose; bee in one's bonnet, rats in the upper story.

dotage etc. (*imbecility*) 499.

V. be −, become- -insane etc. *adj.*; lose one's senses, − reason, − faculties, − wits; go −, run-

mad, run amuck; rave, dote, ramble, wander; drivel etc. (*be imbecile*) 499; have a -screw loose etc. *n.*, − devil; *avoir le diable au corps*; lose one's head etc. (*be uncertain*) 475.

derange, render −, drive- -mad etc. *adj.*; madden, dementate, addle the wits, derange the head, infatuate, befool; turn -the brain, − one's head.

Adj. insane, mad, lunatic; crazy, crazed, *aliéné*, *non compos mentis*; not right, cracked, touched; bereft of reason; unhinged, deranged, unsettled in one's mind; insensate, reasonless, beside oneself, demented, daft; phren-, fren-zied, -etic; possessed, − with a devil; far gone, maddened; moonstruck; shatterpated; barmy; mad-, scatter-, shatter-, crack-brained, off one's head; bug-house, *loco*.

maniacal; manic, manic-depressive; delirious, light-headed, incoherent, rambling, doting, wandering; frantic, raving, stark staring mad, amok, amuck.

corybantic, dithyrambic; rabid, giddy, vertiginous, dizzy, wild, haggard, mazed; flighty; distracted, -aught; bewildered etc. (*uncertain*) 475.

mad as a -March hare, − hatter; of -unsound mind etc. *n.* touched −, wrong −, not right- in one's -head, − mind, − wits, − upper story; out of one's -mind, − senses, − wits; not in one's right mind.

fanatical, infatuated, odd, eccentric; hypp-ed, -ish.

imbecile, silly etc. 499.

Adv. like one possessed.

Phr. the mind having lost its balance; the reason under a cloud; *tête -exaltée, -montée*.

504. Madman—N. madman, lunatic, maniac, bedlamite, candidate for Bedlam, raver, madcap; energumen; paranoiac; auto-, mono-, pyro-, megalo-, dipso-, klepto-maniac; hypochondriac etc. (*low spirit*) 837.

dreamer etc. 515; rhapsodist, seer, high-flier, enthusiast, crank, eccentric, nut, fanatic, *fanatico*; *exalté*; knight errant, Don Quixote.

idiot etc. 501.

505. Memory.—N. memory, remembrance; reten-tion, -tiveness; tenacity; *veteris vestigia flammae*; tablets of the memory; readiness.

reminiscence, recognition, recurrence, recollection, rememoration; retrospect, -ion; after-thought.

suggestion etc. (*information*) 527; prompting etc. *v.*; hint, reminder, token of remembrance, *memento*, *souvenir*, keepsake, relic, *memorandum*; remembrancer, flapper; memorial etc. (*record*) 551; commemoration etc. (*celebration*) 883.

things to be remembered, *memorabilia*.

art of −, artificial- memory; *memoria technica*; mnemo-nics, -technics; phrenotypics; Mnemosyne; memorandum-, note-, engagement-, prompt-book.

retentive −, tenacious −, green −, trustworthy −, capacious −, faithful −, correct −, exact −, ready −, prompt- memory.

V. remember, mind; retain the -memory, − remembrance- of; keep in view.

have −, hold −, bear −, carry −, keep −, retain- in *or* in the -thoughts, − mind, − memory, − remembrance; be in −, live in −, remain in −,

dwell in –, haunt –, impress- one's -memory, – thoughts, – mind.

sink in the mind; run in the head; not be able to get it out of one's head; be deeply impressed with; rankle etc. (*revenge*) 919.

recur to the mind; flash -on the mind, – across the memory.

recognize, recollect, bethink oneself, recall, call up, conjure up, retrace; look –, trace- -back, – backwards; think –, look back- upon; review; call –, recall –, bring- to mind; remembrance; carry one's thoughts back; rake up the past.

suggest etc. (*inform*) 527; prompt; put –, keep- in mind; remind; fan the embers; call –, summon –, rip- up; renew; *infandum renovare dolorem*; task –, tax –, jog –, flap –, refresh –, rub up –, awaken- the memory; pull by the sleeve; bring back the memory, put in remembrance, memorialize.

get –, have –, learn –, know –, say –, repeat- by -heart, – rote; drive –, get- into -one's head; say one's lesson; repeat, – as a parrot; have at one's finger's ends.

commit to memory; memorize; con, – over; fix –, rivet –, imprint –, impress –, stamp –, grave –, engrave –, store –, treasure up –, bot- tle up –, embalm –, enshrine- in the memory; load –, store –, stuff –, burden- the memory with.

redeem from oblivion; keep the memory -alive, – green; *tangere ulcus*; keep up the memory of; commemorate etc. (*celebrate*) 883.

make a note of etc. (*record*) 551.

Adj. remember-ing, -ed etc. *v.*; mindful, reminiscential; retained in the memory etc. *v.*; pent up in one's memory; fresh; green, – in remem- brance, still vivid; unforgotten, present to the mind; within one's -memory etc. *n.*; indelible; not to be forgotten, unforgettable, enduring; uppermost in one's thoughts; memorable etc. (*important*) 642.

Adv. by -heart, – rote; without book, *memoriter*.

in memory of; *in memoriam*; suggestive.

Phr. *manet altâ mente repostum; forsan et haec olim meminisse juvabit.*

506. Oblivion.—**N.** oblivion; forgetfulness etc. *adj.*; obliteration etc. 552, of –, insensibility etc. 823 to- the past.

short –, treacherous –, loose –, slippery –, failing- memory; decay –, failure –, lapse- of memory; memory like a sieve; waters of -Lethe, – oblivion, *amnesia*.

pardon, acquittal, amnesty, oblivion; absolution.

V. forget; be -forgetful etc. *adj.*; fall –, sink- into oblivion; have -a short memory etc. *n.* – no head.

forget one's own name, have on the tip of one's tongue, come in at one ear and go out at the other.

slip –, escape –, fade from –, die away from- the memory; lose, – sight of.

unlearn; efface etc. 552 –, discharge- from the memory; consign to -oblivion, – the tomb of the Capulets; think no more of etc. (*turn the attention from*) 458; cast behind one's back, wean one's thoughts from; let bygones be bygones etc. (*forgive*) 918.

Adj. forgotten etc. *v.*; unremembered, past recollection, bygone, out of mind; buried –, sunk-

in oblivion; clean forgotten; gone out of one's - head, – recollection.

forgetful, oblivious, mindless, heedless, Lethean; insensible etc. 823- to the past.

Phr. *non mi ricordo*; the memory -failing, – deserting one, – being at (*or* in) fault.

507. Expectation.—**N.** expect-ation, -ance, - ancy; anticipation, reckoning, calculation; con- tingency; foresight etc. 510.

contemplation, prospection, look out; prospect, perspective, horizon, vista; destiny etc. 152.

suspense, waiting, abeyance; curiosity etc. 455; anxious –, ardent –, eager –, breathless –, sanguine- expectation; torment of Tantalus.

presumption, hope etc. 858; trust etc. (*belief*) 484; prognostication, auspices etc. (*prediction*) 511.

V. expect; look -for, – out for, – forward to; hope for, anticipate; have in -prospect, – con- templation; keep in view; contemplate, promise oneself; not -wonder etc. 870 -at, – if.

wait, – tarry –, lie in wait, – watch –, bargain- for; keep a -good, – sharp- look-out for; await; stand at 'attention,' abide, bide one's –, mark- time; watch.

foresee etc. 510; prepare for etc. 673; forestall etc. (*be early*) 132; count upon etc. (*believe in*) 484; think likely etc. (*probability*) 472; make one's mouth water.

lead one to expect etc. (*predict*) 511; have in store for etc. (*destiny*) 152.

prick up one's ears, hold one's breath.

Adj. expectant; expecting etc. *v.*; in -expectation etc. *n.*; on the watch etc. (*vigilant*) 459; open- eyed, -mouthed; agape, gaping, all agog; on - tenterhooks, – tiptoe, – the tiptoe of expectation; *aux aguets*; ready; curious etc. 455; looking for- ward to; prepared for; on the rack.

expected etc. *v.*; long expected, foreseen; in prospect etc. *n.*; prospective; in -one's eye, – view, – the horizon; impending etc. (*destiny*) 152.

Adv. expectantly; in the event of; on the watch etc. *adj.*; with -breathless expectation etc. *n.*; – bated breath, – eyes, – ears strained; *arrectis auribus*; on edge.

Phr. we shall see; *nous verrons.*

508. Inexpectation.—**N.** in-, non-expectation; false expectation etc. (*disappointment*) 509; miscalculation etc. 481; unforeseen contingency, the unforeseen, the unexpected.

surprise, sudden burst, thunderclap, blow, shock; bolt out of the blue; eye-opener; wonder etc. 870.

V. not -expect etc. 507; be taken by surprise; start; miscalculate etc. 481; not bargain for; come –, fall- upon.

be -unexpected etc. *adj.*; come -unawares etc. *adv.*; turn up, pop, drop from the clouds; come –, burst –, flash –, bounce –, steal –, creep- upon one; come –, burst- like a thunder-clap; -bolt; take –, catch- -by surprise, – unawares, – napping. pounce –, spring a mine- upon.

surprise, startle, take aback, electrify, stun, stagger, take away one's breath, throw off one's guard; astonish etc. (*strike with wonder*) 870.

Adj. non-expectant; surprised etc. *v.*; un-warned, -aware; off one's guard; inattentive etc. 458.

un-expected, -anticipated, -prepared for, -looked for, -foreseen, -hoped for; dropped from the clouds; beyond –, contrary to –, against- expectation; out of one's reckoning; unheard of etc. (*exceptional*) 83; startling; sudden etc. (*instantaneous*) 113.

Adv. abruptly, unexpectedly, plump, pop, *à l'improviste*, unawares; without -notice, – warn-ing, – saying 'by your leave;' like a -thief in the night, – thunderbolt; in an unguarded moment; suddenly etc. (*instantaneously*) 113.

Int. heyday! etc. (*wonder*) 870.

Phr. little did one -think, – expect; nobody would ever -suppose, – think, – expect; who would have thought?'

509. Disappointment. [Failure of ex-pectation.]—**N.** disappointment, disillusionment; blighted hope, balk; blow; slip 'twixt cup and lip; non-fulfilment of one's hopes; sad –, bitter- disap-pointment; trick of fortune; afterclap; false –, vain- expectation; miscalculation etc. 481; fool's paradise; much cry and little wool.

V. be disappointed; look -blank, – blue; look –, stand- -aghast etc. (*wonder*) 870; find to one's cost; laugh on the wrong side of one's mouth; find one a false prophet.

disappoint; crush –, dash –, balk –, disap-point –, blight –, falsify –, defeat –, not realize- one's -hope, – expectation; balk, jilt, bilk; play one -false, – a trick; dash the cup from the lips; tantalize; dumb-found, -founder; disillusion, -ize; dissatisfy, disgruntle.

Adj. disappointed etc. *v.*; disconcerted, aghast; out of one's reckoning; disgruntled.

Phr. the mountain brought forth a mouse; *nascitur ridiculus mus*; *parturiunt montes*; *diis aliter visum*, the bubble burst; one's countenance falling.

510. Foresight.—**N.** foresight, prospicience, prevision, longsightedness; anticipation; providence etc. (*preparation*) 673.

fore-thought, -cast; pre-deliberation, -surmise; foregone conclusion etc. (*prejudgment*) 481; prudence etc. (*caution*) 864.

foreknowledge; *prognosis*; pre-cognition, -science, -notion, -sentiment; second sight; sagacity etc. (*intelligence*) 498.

prospect etc. (*expectation*) 507; foretaste; prospectus etc. (*plan*) 626.

V. foresee; look -forwards to, – ahead, – beyond; scent from afar; feel in one's bones; look –, pry –, peep into the future.

see one's way; see how the -land lies, – wind blows, – cat jumps.

anticipate; expect etc. 507; be beforehand etc. (*early*) 132; predict etc. 511; fore-know, -judge, -cast; surmise; have an eye to the -future, – main chance; *respicere finem*; keep a sharp look-out etc. (*vigilance*) 459; forewarn etc. 668.

Adj. foreseeing etc. *v.*; prescient; anticipatory; far-seeing, -sighted; sagacious etc. (*intelligent*) 498; weather-wise; provident etc. (*prepared*) 673; prospective etc. 507.

Adv. against the time when.

511. Prediction.—**N.** prediction, an-nouncement; program, programme etc. (*plan*) 626; premonition etc. (*warning*) 668; *prognosis*, prophecy, vaticination, Mantology, prognostication, premonstration, augur-y, -ation; a-, ha-riolation; fore-, a-boding; bode-, abode-ment; omin-ation, -ousness; auspices, forecast; sign, presage, prognostic; omen etc. 512; horoscope, nativity; sooth, -saying; fortune-telling; divination; crystal gazing, necromancy etc. 992; prophet etc. 512.

[Divination by the stars] astrology, horoscopy, astromancy, judicial astrology.*

[Place of prediction] *adytum*.

prefigur-ation, -ement; prototype, type.

V. predict, prognosticate, prophesy, vaticinate, divine, foretell, soothsay, augurate, tell fortunes; cast a -horoscope, – nativity; advise; forewarn etc. 668.

presage, augur, bode; a-, fore-bode, -cast; fore-, be-token; pre-figure, -show; portend; fore-show, -shadow, shadow forth, typify, ominate, signify, point to, precurse.

usher in, herald, premise, announce; lower.

hold out –, raise –, excite- -expectation, – hope; bid fair, promise, lead one to expect; be the -precursor etc. 64.

Adj. predicting etc. *v.*; predictive, prophetic, fatidical, vaticinal, oracular, Sibylline, haruspical, weatherwise.

ominous, presageful, portentous; augur-ous, -al, -ial; auspici-al, -ous; prescious, monitory, ex-tispicious, premonitory, precusory, significant of, pregnant with, big with the fate of.

Phr. 'coming events cast their shadows before.'

*The following terms, expressive of different forms of divination, have been collected from various sources, and are here given as a curious illustration of bygone super-stitions:

Divination *by oracles*, Theomancy; *by the Bible*, Bibliomancy; *by ghosts*, Psychomancy; *by spirits seen in a magic lens*, Cristallomantia; *by shadows or manes*, Sciomancy; *by appearances in the air*, Aeromancy, Chaomancy, *by the stars at birth*, Genethliacs; *by meteors*, Meteoromancy; *by winds*, Austromancy; *by sacrificial ap-pearances*, Aruspicy (or Haruspicy), Hieromancy, Hieroscopy; *by the entrails of animals sacrificed*, Hieromancy; *by the entrails of a human sacrifice*, An-thropomancy; *by the entrails of fishes*, Ichthyomancy; *by sacrificial fire*, Pyromancy; *by red-hot iron*, Sideromancy; *by smoke from the alter*, Capnomancy; *by mice*, Myomancy; *by birds*, Orniscopy, Ornithomancy; *by a cock picking up grains*, Alectryomancy (or Alectoromancy); *by fishes*, Ophiomancy; *by herbs*, Botanomancy; *by water*, Hydromancy; *by fountains*, Pegomancy; *by a wand*, Rhab-domancy; *by dough of cakes*, Crithomancy; *by meal*, Aleuromancy, Alphitomancy; *by salt*, Halomancy; *by dice*, Cleromancy; *by arrows*, Belomancy; *by a balanced hatchet*, Axinomancy; *by a balanced sieve*, Coscinomancy; *by a suspended ring*, Dactyliomancy; *by dots made at random on paper*, Geomancy; *by precious stones*, Lithomancy; *by pebbles*, Pessomancy; *by pebbles drawn from a heap*, Psephomancy; *by mirrors*, Catoptromancy; *by writings in ashes*, Tephramancy; *by dreams*, Oneiromancy; *by the hand*, Palmistry, Chiromancy; *by nails reflecting the sun's rays*, Onychomancy; *by finger rings*, Dactylomancy; *by numbers*, Arithmancy; *by drawing lots*, Sortilege; *by passages in books*, Stichomancy; *by the letters forming the name of the person*, Onomancy, Nomancy; *by the*

features. Anthroposcopy; *by the mode of laughing.* Geloscopy; *by ventriloquism,* Gastromancy; *by walking in a circle.* Gyromancy; *by dropping melted wax into water.* Ceromancy; *by currents.* Bletonism.

512. Omen.—N. omen, portent, presage, prognostic, augury, auspice; sigh etc. (*indication*) 550; herald, forerunner, harbinger etc. (*precursor*) 64.

bird of ill omen, signs of the times; gathering clouds; warning etc. 668.

prefigurement etc. 511.

513. Oracle.—N. oracle; prophet, -ess; seer, soothsayer, augur, fortune-teller, palmist, medium, clairvoyant, crystal gazer, witch, geomancer, *aruspex*; a-, ha-ruspice; Sibyl; Python, -ess; Pythia; Pythian –, Delphian- oracle; Monitor, Sphinx, Tiresias, Cassandra, Sibylline leaves; Zadkiel, Old Moore; sorcerer etc. 994; interpreter etc. 524.

514. Supposition.—N. supposition, assumption, postulation, condition, pre-supposition, hypothesis, postulate, *postulatum*, theory, *data*; pro-, position; *thesis*, theorem; proposal etc. (*plan*) 626.

bare –, vague –, loose- -supposition; – suggestion; conceit; conjecture; guess, – work; rough guess, shot; conjecturality; surmise, suspicion, inkling, suggestion, suggestiveness, association of ideas, hint; presumption etc. (*belief*) 484; divination, speculation.

theorist, speculator, doctrinarian, hypothesist.

V. suppose, conjecture, surmise, suspect, guess; divine; theorize; pre-sume, -surmise, -suppose; assume, fancy, wis, take it; give a guess, speculate, believe, dare say, take it into one's head, take for granted.

put forth; pro-pound, -pose; moot; hypothesize; start, put a case, submit, move, make a motion; hazard –, throw out –, put forward- a -suggestion, – conjecture.

allude to, suggest, hint, put it into one's head.

suggest itself etc. (*thought*) 451; run in the head etc. (*memory*) 505; marvel –, wonder- -if, – whether.

Adj. supposing etc. *v.*; given, mooted, postulatory; assumed etc. *v.*; supposit-ive, -itious; gratuitous, speculative, conjectural, hypothetical, suppositional, theoretical, academic, supposable; presumptive, putative.

suggestive, allusive, stimulating.

Adv. if, – so be; an; on the -supposition etc. *n.*; *ex hypothesi*; in -case, – the event of; *quasi*, as if, provided; perhaps etc. (*by possibility*) 470; for aught one knows.

515. Imagination.—N. imagination; originality; invention; fancy; inspiration; *verve*; empathy.

warm –, heated –, excited –, sanguine –, ardent –, fiery –, boiling –, wild –, bold –,

daring –, playful –, lively –, fertile- -imagination, – fancy.

'mind's eye;' 'such stuff as dreams are made of.'

ideal-ity, -ism; romanticism, utopianism, castle-building; dreaming; frenzy; ecs-, ex-tasy; calenture etc. (*delirium*) 503; reverie, brown study, trance; somnambulism.

conception, *vorstellung*, ercogitation, 'a fine frenzy,' poetic frenzy, divine afflatus; cloud-, dream-land; flight –, fumes- of fancy; 'thick-coming fancies;' creation –, coinage- of the brain; imagery, word painting.

conceit, maggot, figment, myth, dream, vision, shadow, chimera; phan-tasm, -tasy; fantasy, fancy; whim, -sey; vagary, rhapsody, romance, *extravaganza*; air-drawn dagger, bugbear, nightmare; flying Dutchman, great sea-serpent, man in the moon, castle in the air, *château en Espagne*; Utopia, Atlantis, happy valley, millennium, fairy land; land of Prester John, kingdom of Micomicon; work of fiction etc. (*novel*) 594; poetry etc. 597; drama etc. 599; Arabian nights; *le pot au lait*; dream of Alnaschar etc. (*hope*) 858; day –, golden- dream

illusion etc. (*error*) 495; phantom etc. (*fallacy of vision*) 443; *Fata Morgana* etc. (*ignis fatuus*) 423; vapor etc. (*cloud*) 353; stretch of the imagination etc. (*exaggeration*) 549.

idealist, romanticist, visionary; mopus; romancer, dreamer; somnambulist; rhapsodist etc. (*fanatic*) 504.

V. imagine, fancy, conceive; ideal-, real-ize; dream, – of; 'give to airy nothing a local habitation and a name.'

create, originate, devise, coin, fabricate; improvise, strike out something new.

set one's wits to work; strain –, crack- one's invention; rack –, ransack –, cudgel- one's brains; excogitate.

give -play, – the reins, – a loose- to the -imagination, – fancy; empathize; indulge in reverie.

conjure up a vision; fancy –, represent –, picture –, figure- to oneself; envisage.

float in the mind; suggest itself etc. (*thought*) 451.

Adj. imagined etc. *v.*; *ben trovato*; air-drawn, -built.

imagin-ing etc. *v.*, -ative; original, inventive, creative, fertile, productive; ingenious.

romantic, high-flown, flighty, extravagant, fanatic, enthusiastic, Utopian, Quixotic; preposterous, rhapsodical.

ideal, unreal; in the clouds, *in nubibus*; unsubstantial etc. 4; illusory etc. (*fallacious*) 495; fictitious, theoretical, hypothetical.

fabulous, legendary; myth-ic, -ological; chimerical; imagin-, vision-ary; notional; fan-cy, -ciful, -tastic, -tastical; whimsical; fairy, -like.

dreamy, entranced, vaporous.

516. Meaning. [Idea to be conveyed.] [Thing signified.]—**N.** meaning; signific-ation, -ance; sense, expression; im-, pur-port; drift, tenor, implication, connotation, essence, force, spirit, bearing, coloring; scope.

matter; subject, -matter; argument, text, sum and substance; gist etc. 5.

general –, broad –, substantial – colloquial –, literal –, plain –, simple –, accepted –, natural –, unstrained –, true etc. (*exact*) 494 –, honest etc. 543 –, *primâ facie* etc. (*manifest*) 525- meaning.

literality; literal interpretation; after acceptation; allusion etc. (*latency*) 526; suggestion etc. (*information*) 527; synonym; figure of speech etc. 521; acceptation etc. (*interpretation*) 522.

V. mean, signify, express, connote, denote; im-, pur-port; convey, imply, breathe, indicate, bespeak, bear a sense; tell –, speak- of; touch on; point –, allude- to; drive at; involve etc. (*latency*) 526; delcare etc. (*affirm*) 535.

understand by etc. (*interpret*) 522.

Adj. meaning etc. *v.*; expressive, suggestive, meaningful, allusive; signific-ant, -ative, -atory; pithy; full of –, pregnant with- meaning.

declaratory etc. 535; intelligible etc. 518; literal, metaphrastic; synonymous; tantamount etc. (*equivalent*) 27; implied etc. (*latent*) 526; explicit etc. 525; literal etc. 562.

Adv. to that effect; that is to say etc. (*being interpreted*) 522.

literally; evidently, from the context.

517. Unmeaningness. [Absence of meaning.]—**N.** unmeaningness etc. *adj.*; scrabble, scribble, scrawl, daub, (*painting*), strumming (*music*).

empty sound, dead letter, *vox et praeterea nihil*; 'a tale told by an idiot, full of sound and fury, signifying nothing;' 'sounding brass and a tinkling cymbal.'

nonsense, jargon, gibberish, jabber, mere words, hocus-pocus, fustian, rant, bombast, balderdash, palaver, patter, flummery, *verbiage*, babble, *bavardage*, *baragouin*, platitude, *niaiserie*; inanity, rigmarole, rodomontade; truism; *nugae canorae*; twaddle, twattle, fudge, trash; stuff, – and nonsense; bosh, rubbish, rot, drivel, moonshine, wishwash, fiddle-faddle, flapdoodle; absurdity etc. 497; vagueness etc. (*unintelligibility*) 519.

V. mean nothing; be -unmeaning etc. *adj.*; twaddle, quibble, rant, gabble, scrabble etc. *n.*

Adj. unmeaning; meaning-, sense-less; nonsensical; -void of -sense etc. 516.

in-, un-expressive; vacant, fatuous; not significant; insignificant,.

trashy, washy, inane, vague, trumpery, trivial, fiddle-faddle, twaddling, quibbling.

unmeant, not expressed; tacit etc. (*latent*) 526. inexpressible, undefinable, incommunicable.

Int. rubbish! etc. 497.

518. Intelligibility.—**N.** intelligibility, clearness, clarity, explicitness etc. *adj.*; lucidity, perspicuity; legibility, plain speaking etc. (*manifestation*) 525; precision etc. 494; a word to the wise.

V. be -intelligible etc. *adj.*; speak -for itself, – volumes; tell its own tale, lie on the surface.

render -intelligible etc. *adj.*; popularize, simplify, clear up; elucidate etc. (*explain*) 522.

understand, comprehend; take, – in; catch, grasp, recognize, follow, collect, master, make out;

see -with half an eye, – daylight, – one's way; enter into the ideas of; come to an understanding.

Adj. intelligible; clear, – as -day, – crystal, – noonday; lucid; per-, tran-spicuous; luminous, transparent; comprehensible.

easily understood, easy to understand, for the million, intelligible to the meanest capacity, popularized.

plain, distinct, explicit, clear-cut; positive; definite etc. (*precise*) 494.

graphic, vivid, telling; expressive etc. (*meaning*) 516; illustrative etc. (*explanatory*) 522.

un-ambiguous, -equivocal, -mistakable etc. (*manifest*) 525, -confused; legible, recognizable; obvious etc. 525.

Adv. in plain -terms, – words, – English.

Phr. he that runs may read etc. (*manifest*) 525.

519. Unintelligibility.—**N.** unintelligibility, incomprehensibility, imperspicuity; inconceivableness, vagueness etc. *adj.*; obscurity; ambiguity etc. 520; doubtful meaning; uncertainty etc. 475; perplexity etc. (*confusion*) 59; spinosity; *obscurum per obscurius*; mystification etc. (*concealment*) 528; latency etc. 526; transcendentalism.

paradox; enigma, riddle etc. (*secret*) 533; *dignus vindice nodus*; sealed book; steganography, freemasonry.

pons asinorum, asses' bridge; double –, high-Dutch, Greek, Hebrew; jargon etc. (*unmeaning*). 517.

obscurantist.

V. be -unintelligible etc. *adj.*; require -explanation etc. 522; have a doubtful meaning, pass comprehension.

render -unintelligible etc. *adj.*; conceal etc. 528; darken etc. 421; confuse etc. (*derange*) 61; perplex etc. (*bewilder*) 475.

not -understand etc. 518; lose, -- the clue; miss; not know what to make of, be able to make nothing of, give it up; not be able to -account for, – make either head or tail of; be at sea etc. (*uncertain*) 475; wonder etc. 870; see through a glass darkly etc. (*ignorance*) 491.

not understand one another; play at cross purposes etc. (*misinterpret*) 523.

Adj. un-intelligible, -accountable, -decipherable, -discoverable, -knowable, -fathomable; incognizable, -explicable, -scrutable; inap-, incomprehensible; insol-vable, -uble; impenetrable.

illegible, indecipherable, as Greek to one, unexplained, paradoxical; enigmatic, -al; puzzling, baffling.

obscure, dark, muddy, clear as mud, seen through a mist, dim, nebulous, shrouded in mystery; undiscernible etc. (*invisible*) 447; misty etc. (*opaque*) 426; hidden etc. 528; latent etc. 526.

indefinite etc. (*indistinct*) 447; perplexed etc. (*confused*) 59; undetermined, vague, loose, ambiguous; mysterious; mystic, -al; transcendental; occult, recondite, esoteric, abstruse, crabbed.

incon-ceivable, -ceptible; searchless; above –, beyond –, past- comprehension; beyond one's depth; unconceived.

inexpressible, undefinable, incommunicable, unutterable, ineffable, unpronounceable.

520. Equivocalness. [Having a double sense.]—**N.** equivocalness etc. *adj.*; double - meaning etc. 516; ambiguity, *double entendre*, pun, paragram, *calembour*, quibble, *équivoque*, anagram; conundrum etc. (*riddle*) 533; word-play etc. (*wit*) 842; homonym, -y; amphibo-ly, -logy; ambiloquy.

Sphinx, Delphic oracle.

equivocation etc. (*duplicity*) 544; white lie, mental reservation etc. (*concealment*) 528.

V. be -equivocal etc. *adj.*; have two -meanings etc. 516; equivocate etc. (*palter*) 544.

Adj. equivocal, ambiguous, amphibolous, homonymous; double-tongued etc. (*lying*) 544.

521. Metaphor.—**N.** figure of speech; *façon de parler*, way of speaking, colloquialism.

phrase etc. 566; figure, trope, metaphor, tralatition, metonymy, enallage, *catachresis*, *synecdoche*, *autonomasia*, irony, satire, figurativeness etc. *adj.*; image, -ry; *metalepsis*, type, anagoge, simile, personification, *prosopopaeia*, allegory, apologue, parable, fable; allusion, adumbration; application; euphemism; euphuism.

V. employ -metaphor etc. *n.*; personify, allegorize, adumbrate, shadow forth, apply, allude -, refer- to.

Adj. metaphorical etc. *n.*; figurative, catachrestical, typical, tralatitious, parabolic, allegorical, allusive, anagogical; ironical; colloquial.

Adv. so to -speak, - say, - express oneself; as it were.

Phr. *mutato nomine de te fabula nattatur.*

522. Interpretation.—**N.** interpretation, definition; explan-, explic-ation; solution, answer; rationale; plain -, simple -, strict- interpretation; meaning etc. 516.

translation; rend-ering, -ition; reddition; literal -, free- translation; key, crib; secret; clew etc. (*indication*) 550; Rosetta stone.

exegesis; ex-pounding, -position; Hermeneutics; comment, -ary; inference etc. (*deduction*) 480; illustration, exemplification; gloss, annotation, *scholium*, note; e-, di-lucidation, enucleation; *éclaircissement, mot de l'énigme.*

symptomat-, semei-ology; metoposcopy, physiognomy; diagnosis, prognosis; paleography etc. (*philology*) 560.

accept-ion, -ation, -ance; light, reading, lection, construction, version.

equivalent, - meaning etc. 516; synonym; para-, meta-phrase; convertible terms, apposition; dictionary etc. 562; polyglot.

V. interpret, explain, define, construe, translate, render; do - , turn- into; transfuse the sense of.

find out etc. 480*a*- -the meaning etc. 516- of; read; spell - , figure - , make- out; decipher, decode, unravel, disentangle, puzzle out; find the key of, enucleate, resolve, solve; read between the lines.

account for; find - , tell- the cause etc. 153- of; throw - , shed- light, - new light, - a fresh light- upon; clear up, elucidate.

illustrate, exemplify; unfold, expound, comment upon, annotate; popularize etc. (*render intelligible*) 518.

take - , understand - , receive - , accept- in a particular sense; understand by, put a construction on, be given to understand.

Adj. explanatory, expository; explica-tive, -tory; exegetical; hermeneutic, interpretive, illustrative, elucidative, annotative, scholiastic.

polyglot; literal; para-, meta-phrastic; cosignificative, synonymous; equivalent etc. 27.

Adv. in -explanation etc. *n.*; that is to say, *id est, videlicet*, to wit, namely, in other words.

literally, strictly speaking; in -plain, - plainer- - terms, - words, - English; more simply.

523. Misinterpretation.—**N.** misinterpretation, -apprehension, -understanding, -acceptation, -construction, -application; *catachresis*; cross -reading, - purposes; mistake etc. 495.

misrepresentation, perversion, exaggeration etc. 549; false -coloring, - construction; abuse of terms; parody, travesty; falsification etc. (*lying*) 544.

V. mis-interpret, -apprehend, -understand, -conceive, -judge, -doubt, -spell, -translate, -construe, -apply; mistake etc. 495.

misrepresent, pervert; garble etc. (*falsify*) 544; distort; detort; travesty, play upon words; stretch -, strain -, wrest- the -sense, - meaning; explain away; put a -bad, - false- construction on; give a false coloring, look through -rose colored -, - dark - spectacles.

be - , play- at cross purposes.

Adj. misinterpreted etc. *v.*; untranslat-ed, -able.

Adv. at cross purposes.

524. Interpreter.—**N.** interpreter, translator, ex-positor, -pounder, -ponent, -plainer; demonstrator.

scholiast, commentator, annotator; meta-, paraphrast.

spokesman, speaker, mouthpiece, prolocutor; diplomat etc. 758.

guide, courier, dragoman, *valet de place*, *cicerone*, showman; oneirocritic; Oedipus; oracle etc. 513.

525. Manifestation.—**N.** manifestation; unfolding; plainness etc. *adj.*; plain speaking; expression; showing etc. *v.*; exposition, demonstration, *séance*; exhibition, production; display, showing off etc. 882; premonstration. [Thing shown] exhibit, show.

indication etc. (*calling attention to*) 457; publicity etc. 531; disclosure etc. 529; openness etc. (*honesty*) 543, (*artlessness*) 703; *épachement*, prominence.

V. make - , render- -manifest etc. *adj.*; bring forth, - forward, - to the front, - into view; give notice, express; represent, set forth, exhibit; show,

– up; expose; produce; hold up –, expose- to view; set –, place –, lay- before -one, – one's eyes; tell to one's face; trot out, put through one's paces, unfold, show off, show forth, unveil, bring to light, display, demonstrate, unroll; lay open; draw –, bring- out; bring out in strong relief; call –, bring- into notice; hold up the mirror; wear one's heart upon his sleeve; show one's -face, – colors; manifest oneself; speak out; make no -mystery, – secret- of; unfurl the flag; proclaim etc. (*publish*) 531.

indicate etc. (*direct attention to*) 457; disclose etc. 529; elicit etc. 480a; interpret etc. 522.

be -manifest etc. *adj.*; appear etc. (*be visible*) 446; transpire etc. (*be disclosed*) 529; speak for itself, stand to reason; stare one in the face; loom large, appear on the horizon, rear its head; give - token, – sign, – indication of; tell its own tale etc. (*intelligible*) 518; go without saying.

Adj. manifest, apparent; salient, striking, demonstrative, prominent, in the foreground, notable, pronounced.

flagrant; notorious etc. (*public*) 531; arrant; stark staring; unshaded, glaring.

defin-ed, -ite; distinct, conspicuous etc. (*visible*) 446; obvious, evident, incontestable, unmistakable, not to be mistaken, plain, clear, palpable, self-evident, autoptical; intelligible etc. 518; clear as -day, – daylight, – noonday; plain as -a pikestaff, – the sun at noonday, – the nose on one's face, – the way to the parish church.

ostensible; open, – as day; overt, patent, express, explicit; naked, bare, literal, downright, undisguised, exoteric.

unreserved; frank, plain spoken etc. (*artless*) 703; barefaced, brazen, bold; shameless, daring, flaunting, loud.

manifested etc. *v.*; disclosed etc. 529; expressible, capable of being shown, producible; in-, un-concealable.

Adv. manifestly, openly etc. *adj.*; before one's eyes, under one's nose, to one's face, face to face, above board, *cartes sur table*, on the stage, in plain sight, in open court, in the open, – streets; at the cross roads; in market overt; in the face of -day, – heaven; in -broad –, open- daylight; without reserve; at first blush, *primâ facie*, on the face of; in set terms.

Phr. *cela saute aux yeux*; he that runs may read; you can see it with half an eye; it needs no ghost to tell us; the meaning lies on the surface; *cela va sans dire*; *res ipsa loquitur*.

526. Latency.—N. latency, inexpression; hidden –, occult- meaning; occultness, occultism, mysticism, mystery, cabala, symbolism, anagoge; silence etc. (*taciturnity*) 585; concealment etc. 528; more than meets the -eye, – ear; Delphic oracle; *les dessous des cartes*, undercurrent.

allusion, insinuation, implication; innuendo etc. 527; adumbration; 'something rotten in the state of Denmark.'

snake in the grass etc. (*pitfall*) 667; secret etc. 533.

darkness, invisibility, imperceptibility.

latent influence, power behind the throne; friend at court, wire puller.

V. be -latent etc. *adj.*; lurk, smoulder, underlie,

make no sign; escape -observation, – detection, – recognition; lie hid etc. 528.

laugh in one's sleeve; keep back etc. (*conceal*) 528.

involve, imply, implicate, connote, import, understand, allude to, infer, leave an inference; symbolize; whisper etc. (*conceal*) 528.

Adj. latent; lurking etc. *v.*; secret etc. 528; occult, symbolic, mystic; implied etc. *v.*; dormant.

un-apparent, -known, -seen etc. 441; in the background; invisible etc. 447; indiscoverable, dark; impenetrable etc. (*unintelligible*) 519; un-spied, -suspected.

un-said, -written, -published, -breathed, -talked of, -told etc. 527, -sung, -exposed, -proclaimed, -disclosed etc. 529, -pronounced, -mentioned, -expressed; not expressed, tacit.

un-developed, -solved, -explained, -traced, -discovered etc. 480a, -tracked, -explored, -invented.

indirect, crooked, inferential; by -inference, – implication; implicit, constructive; allusive, covert, muffled; steganographic; under-stood, -hand, -ground; concealed etc. 528; delitescent.

Adv. by a side wind; *sub silentio*; in the background; behind -the scenes, – one's back, – the veil; below the surface; on the tip of one's tongue; secretly etc. 528; between the lines; by a mutual understanding.

Phr. 'thereby hangs a tale.' 'that is another story.'

527. Information.—N. information, enlightenment, acquaintance, knowledge etc. 490; publicity etc. 531.

communication, intimation; not-ice, -ification; e-an-nunciation; announcement; representation, round robin, presentment.

case, estimate, specification, report, advice, monition; news etc. 532; return etc. (*record*) 551; account etc. (*description*) 594; statement etc. (*affirmation*) 535.

mention; acquainting etc. *v.*; instruction etc. (*teaching*) 537; outpouring; intercommunication, communicativeness.

informant, authority, teller, announcer, annunciator, harbinger, herald, intelligencer, commentator, columnist, reporter, exponent, mouthpiece; informer, keek, eavesdropper, delator, detective, sleuth; *mouchard*, spy, stool pigeon, newsmonger; messenger etc. 534; *amicus curiae*.

valet de place, cicerone, pilot, guide; guide-, hand-book; *vade mecum*; manual; map, plan, chart, gazetteer; itinerary etc. (*journey*) 266.

hint, suggestion, wrinkle, innuendo, inkling, whisper, passing word, word in the ear, subaudition, cue, by-play; gesture etc. (*indication*) 550; gentle – broad- hint; *verbum sapienti*; word to the wise; insinuation etc. (*latency*) 526.

V. tell; inform, – of; acquaint, – with; impart, – to; make acquainted with, bring to the ears of, apprise, advise, enlighten, awaken.

let fall, mention, express, intimate, represent, communicate, make known; publish etc 531; notify, signify, specify, convey the knowledge of.

let one –, have one to- know; serve notice, give one to understand; give notice; set –, lay –, put-

before; point out, put into one's head; put one in possession of; instruct etc. (*teach*) 537; direct the attention to etc. 457.

an-nounce, -nunciate; report, – progress; bring –, send –, leave –, write- word; tele-graph, -phone; ring –, call- up; wire; retail, render an account; give an account etc. (*describe*) 594; state etc. (*affirm*) 535.

disclose etc. 529; show cause; explain etc. (*interpret*) 522.

hint; give an inkling of; give –, drop –, throw out- a hint; insinuate; allude –, make allusion- to; glance at; tip off, tip the wink etc. (*indicate*) 550; suggest, prompt, give the cue, breathe; whisper, – in the ear.

give a bit of one's mind; tell one plainly, – once for all; speak volumes.

un-deceive, -beguile; set right, correct, open the eyes of, disabuse.

be -informed of etc.; know etc. 490; learn etc. 539; get scent of, gather from; awaken –, open one's eyes- to; become -alive, – awake- to; keep posted; hear, overhear, understand.

come to one's -ears, – knowledge; reach one's ears.

Adj. informed etc. *v.*; *communiqué*; reported etc. *v.*; published etc. 531; advisory.

expressive etc. 516; explicit etc. (*open*) 525, (*clear*) 518; plain-spoken etc. (*artless*) 703.

declara-, nuncupa-, exposi-tory; declarative, enunciative, communicat-ive, -ory; oral.

Adv. from information received; according to -rumor, – report; in the air; from what one can gather.

Phr. a little bird told me.

528. Concealment.—N. concealment; hiding etc. *v.*; occultation, mystification.

seal of secrecy; screen etc. 530; disguise etc. 530; masquerade; masked battery; hiding place etc. 530; cipher, code, crypt-, stegan-ography; invisible –, sympathetic- ink; palimpsest; freemasonry.

stealth, -iness; obreption; slyness etc. (*cunning*) 702.

latit-ancy, -ation; seclusion etc. 893; privacy, secrecy, secretness; *incognita*.

reticence; reserve; mental –, reservation, aside; *arrière pensée*, suppression, evasion, white lie, misprision; silence etc. (*taciturnity*) 585; suppression of truth etc. 544; underhand dealing; close-, secretive-ness etc. *adj.*; mystery.

latency etc. 526; snake in the grass; secret etc. 533.

V. conceal, hide, secrete, stow away, put out of sight; lock –, seal –, bottle- up.

cover, screen, cloak, veil, shroud; screen from -sight, – observation; draw the veil; draw –, close- the curtain; curtain, shade, eclipse, throw a veil over; be-cloud, -fog, -mask; mask, disguise; ensconce, muffle, smother; whisper.

keep -from, – back, – to oneself; keep -snug, – close, – secret, – dark; bury; sink, suppress; keep -from, – out of- -view, – sight; keep in –, throw into- the -shade, – background; cover up one's tracks; stifle, hush up, withhold, reserve; fence with a question; ignore etc. 460.

code, codify, use a cipher.

keep -a secret, – one's own counsel; hold one's tongue etc. (*silence*) 585; make no sign, not let it go further; not breathe a -word, – syllable- about; not let the right hand know what the left is doing; hide one's light under a bushel, bury one's talent in a napkin.

keep –, leave- in -the dark, – ignorance; blind, – the eyes; blindfold, hoodwink, mystify; puzzle etc. (*render uncertain*) 475; bamboozle etc. (*deceive*) 545.

be -concealed etc. *v.*; suffer an eclipse; retire from sight, couch; hide oneself; lie -hid, – in ambush, – low, – perdu, – snug, – close; seclude oneself etc. 893; lurk, sneak, skulk, slink, pussyfoot, prowl; steal -into, – out of, – by, – along; play at -bopeep, – hind and seek; hide in holes and corners.

Adj. concealed etc. *v.*; hidden; veiled, secret, recondite, mystic, cabalistic, occult, dark; cryptic, -al, private, privy, *in petto*, auricular, clandestine, close, inviolate.

behind a -screen etc. 530; under -cover, – an eclipse; in -ambush, – hiding, – disguise; in a -cloud, – fog, – mist, – haze, – dark corner; in the -shade, – dark; clouded, wrapt in clouds; invisible etc. 447; buried, underground, *perdu*; incommunicado; secluded etc. 893.

un-disclosed etc. 529; -told etc. 527; covert etc. (*latent*) 526; mysterious etc. (*unintelligible*) 519.

irrevealable, inviolable; confidential; esoteric; not ot be spoken of.

obreptitious, furtive, stealthy, feline; skulking etc. *v.*; surreptitious, underhand, hole and corner; sly etc. (*cunning*) 702; secretive, evasive, non-committal, reserved, reticent, uncommunicative, buttoned up; close, – as wax; taciturn etc. 585.

Adv. secretly etc. *adj.*; in -secret, – private, – one's sleeve, – holes and corners; in the dark etc. *adj.*

januis clausis, with closed doors, *à huis clos*; hugger-mugger, *à la dérobée*; under the -cloak of, – rose, – table; *sub rosâ, en tapinois*, in the background, aside, on the sly, with bated breath, *sotto voce*, in a whisper, without beat of drum, *à la sourdine*.

in –, strict- confidence; confidentially etc. *adj.*; between -ourselves, – you and me; *entre nous, inter nos*, under the seal of secrecy; in -code, – cipher.

underhand, by stealth, like a thief in the night; stealthily etc. *adj.*; behind -the scenes, – the curtain, – one's back, – a screen etc. 530; *incognito; in camerâ*.

Phr. it -must, – will- go no further; 'tell it not in Gath,' nobody the wiser.

529. Disclosure.—N. disclosure; retection; un-veiling etc. *v.*; deterration, revealment, revelation; divulgence, expos-ition, -ure; *exposé*; whole truth; tell-tale etc. (*news*) 532.

acknowledgment, avowal; confession, -al; shrift. bursting of a bubble; *dénouement*.

V. dis-close, -cover, -mask; draw –, draw aside –, lift –, raise –, lift up –, remove –, tear- the -veil, – curtain; un-mask, -veil, -fold, -cover, -seal, -kennel; take off –, break- the seal; lay -open, – bare; expose; open, – up; bare, bring to light; evidence; make -clear, – evident, – manifest; evince.

divulge, reveal, break; let into the secret; reveal the secrets of the prison-house; tell etc. (*inform*) 527; breathe, utter, blab, peach; let -out, − fall, − drop, − the cat out of the bag; betray; tell tales, − out of school; come out with; give -vent, − utterance- to; open the lips, blurt out, vent, whisper about; speak out etc. (*make manifest*) 525; make public etc. 531; unriddle etc. (*find out*) 480a; split; blow the gaff; break the news.

acknowledge, allow, concede, grant, admit, own, confess, avow, throw off all disguise, turn inside out, make a clean breast; show one's -hand, − cards; unburden −, disburden- one's -mind, − conscience, − heart; open −, lay bare −, tell a piece of- one's mind; unbosom oneself, own to the soft impeachment; say −, speak- the truth; turn -King's, − Queen's, − States's- evidence.

raise −, drop −, lift −, remove −, throw off-the mask; expose; debunk; lay open; un-deceive, -beguile; disabuse, set right, correct, open the eyes of; *désillusionner*.

be -disclosed etc.; transpire, come to light; come in sight etc. (*be visible*) 446; become known, escape the lips; come −, ooze −, creep −, leak −, peep −, crop- out; show its -face, − colors; discover etc. itself; break through the clouds, flash on the mind.

Adj. disclosed etc. *v.*

Int. out with it!

Phr. the murder is out; a light breaks in upon one; the scales fall from one's eyes; the eyes are opened.

530. Ambush. [Means of concealment.]—**N.** hiding-place; secret -place,   drawer; recess, hole, funk hole, holes and corners; closet, crypt, *adytum*, abditory, *oubliette*, safe, − deposit.

am-bush, -buscade; stalking horse; lurking-hole, -place; secret path, backstairs; retreat etc. (*refuge*) 666.

screen, cover, shade, blinder; veil, curtain, blind, *purdah*, cloak, cloud.

mask, vizor, visor, disguise, masquerade dress, domino; *camouflage*.

pitfall etc. (*source of danger*) 667; trap etc. (*snare*) 545.

v. ambush, ambuscade, lie in ambush etc. (*hide oneself*) 528; lie in wait for; set a trap for etc. (*deceive*) 545.

Adv. *aux aguets*.

531. Publication.—N. publication; public -announcement etc. 527; promulgation, propagation, proclamation, pronouncement, encyclical, *pronunciamento*; circulation, indiction, edition, imprint, impression, printing; hue and cry.

publicity, notoriety, currency, flagrancy, cry, *bruit*; *vox populi*; report etc. (*news*) 532.

the Press, fourth estate, public press, newspaper, periodical, journal, gazette; house organ, trade publication, tabloid, daily, weekly, monthly, quarterly, annual, magazine, monograph, book; review; news sheet, special edition, supplement, feature, rotogravure, comic strips; leaflet, pamphlet; telegraphy; publisher etc. *v.*

circular, − letter; manifesto, advertisement,

puff, placard, bill, *affiche*, broadside, poster; notice etc. 527; program.

V. publish; make -public, − known etc. (*information*) 527; speak −, talk- of; broach, utter; put forward; circulate, propagate, promulgate; spread −, abroad; rumor, diffuse, disseminate, evulgate; put −, give −, send- forth; emit, edit, get out; issue; cover, report; bring −, lay −, drag-before the public; give -out, − to the world; put −, bandy −, hawk −, buzz −, whisper −, bruit −, blaze- about; drag into the -open day, − limelight; voice.

proclaim, herald, blazon; blaze −, noise-abroad; sound a trumpet; trumpet −, thunder-forth; give tongue; announce with -beat of drum, − flourish of trumpets; proclaim -from the housetops, − at Charing Cross, at the cross roads; declare, declaim.

advertise, placard; post, − up; *afficher*, publish in the Gazette, send round the crier.

raise a -cry, − hue and cry, − report; set news afloat.

telegraph, cable, wireless, broadcast.

be -published etc; be −, become- public etc. *adj.*; come out; go −, fly −, buzz −, blow- about; get -about, − abroad, − afloat, − wind; find vent; see the light; go forth, take air, acquire currency, pass current; go -the rounds, − the round of the newspapers, − through the length and breadth of the land; *virum volitare per ora*; pass from mouth to mouth; spread; run −, spread- like wildfire.

Adj. published etc. *v.*; current etc. (*news*) 532; in circulation, public; notorious; flagrant, arrant; open etc. 525; trumpet-tongued; encyclical, promulgatory; exoteric.

Adv. publicly etc. *adj.*; in open court, with open doors; in the limelight.

Int. *Oyez!* O yes! notice!

Phr. notice is hereby given; this is −, these are- to give notice.

532. News.—N. news; information etc. 527; piece −, budget- of -news, − information; report, story, yarn, copy, filler, intelligence, tidings; stop press news.

word, advice, *aviso*, message; dis-, des-patch; telegram, cable, wireless telegram, radio-gram, marconi-gram, communication, errand, embassy; *bulletin*.

microphone; public address system, P.A.; walkie talkie, radio -telephone, -phone.

radio, wireless (Eng.), high fidelity, hi fi, radio set, transistor, receiver; speaker, loudspeaker, amplifier, tweeter, woofer; transmitter, broadcaster; AM −, FM −, short wave − transmitter; radio station, studio, control room, network, hookup, circuit; frequency, kilocycles, megacycles; band, channel, modulation, amplification; broadcast, program, newscast, network show, commerical announcement, serial, sound effects; signature, station − identification, − break; radio listener, audiophile.

television, TV, video, color television; television −, live − broadcast, telecast, TV show; televising, telecasting, transmission, television channel, video, audio, beam, reception, image, test pattern; rain, snow, ghost; television −, TV − station, mobile unit, TVmobile, transmitter, televisor, boost, camera; set, monitor, tube, screen.

rumor, hearsay, *on dit*, flying rumor, news stirring, cry, buzz, *bruit*, fame; talk, *ouï-dire*, scandal, eavesdropping; town —, table- talk; tittle-tattle; *canard*, topic of the day, idea afloat.

fresh —, stirring —, old — stale- news; glad tidings; old —, stale- story.

narrator etc. (*describe*) 594; news-, scandal-monger; tale-bearer; tell-tale, gossip, tattler, busybody, chatterer; informer.

broad-, news-, sports-caster; commentator, announcer, master of ceremonies, M.C., programmer, sound man, radioman, ham, radiooperator.

television technician, TV man, cameraman, soundman.

V. transpire etc. (*be disclosed*) 529; rumor etc. (*publish*) 531.

broadcast, radio, transmit, send, release, beam; sign — on, — off; go on —, go off — the air, monitor; listen —, tune — in.

tele-vise, -cast; color cast.

Adj. many-tongued; rumored; publicly —, currently- -rumored, — reported; rife, current, floating, afloat, going about, in circulation, in everyone's mouth, all over the town.

Adv. as the story -goes, — runs; as they say, it is said.

---

533. Secret.—N. secret; dead —, profound-secret; *arcanum*, mystery; latency etc. 526; Asian mystery; sealed book, secrets of the prison-house; *le dessous des cartes*.

enigma, riddle, puzzle, nut to crack, conundrum, charade, rebus, logogriph; mono-, ana-gram; acrostic, cross-word puzzle; Sphinx; *crux criticorum*.

maze, labyrinth, Hyrcynian wood.

problem etc. (*question*) 461; paradox etc. (*difficulty*) 704; unintelligibility etc. 519; *terra incognita* etc. (*ignorance*) 491.

Adj. secret etc. (*concealed*) 528.

---

534. Messenger.—N. messenger, envoy, emissary, legate; nuncio, internuncio; intermediary; ambassador etc. (*diplomatist*) 758.

marshal, flag-bearer, herald, crier, trumpeter, bellman, pursuivant, *parlementaire*, *apparitor*.

courier, runner, dawk, *estafette*; Hermes, Mercury, Iris, Ariel.

postman, letter carrier, telegraph boy, messenger boy, district messenger; despatch rider, commissionaire, erand-boy.

mail; post, -office; letter-bag; mail -boat, — train, — coach, — van, aerial mail; tele-graph, -phone; cable, wire; carrier-pigeon; wireless telegraph, -phone; radiotele-graph, -phone.

journalist, newspaperman, reporter; gentleman —, representative- of the press; sob sister; penny-a-liner; special —, war —, own- correspondent; spy, scout; informer etc. 527.

---

535. Affirmation.—N. affirm-ance, -ation; statement, allegation, assertion, predication, declaration, word, averment.

asseveration, adjuration, swearing, oath, affidavit; deposition etc. (*record*) 551; avouchment, assurance; protest, -ation; profession; acknowledgment etc. (*assent*) 488; pledge.

vote, voice, suffrage, ballot.

remark, observation; position etc. (*proposition*) 514; saying, *dictum*, sentence, *ipse dixit*.

emphasis, positiveness, peremptoriness; dogmatism etc. (*certainty*) 474; dogmatist etc. 887.

V. assert; make -an assertion etc. *n.*; have one's say; say, affirm, predicate, declare, state, represent; protest, profess.

put -forth, — forward; advance, allege, propose, propound, enunciate, enounce, broach, set forth, hold out, maintain, contend, pronounce, pretend.

depose, depone, aver, avow, avouch, asseverate, swear; make —, take one's- oath; make —, swear —, put in- an affidavit; take one's Bible oath, kiss the book, vow, *vitam impendere vero*; swear till -one is black in the face, — all's blue; be sworn, call Heaven to witness; vouch, warrant, certify, assure, swear by bell, book and candle.

swear by etc. (*believe*) 484; insist —, take one's stand- upon; emphasize, lay stress on; assert -roundly, — positively; lay down, — the law; raise one's voice, dogmatize, have the last word; rap out; repeat; re-assert, -affirm.

announce etc. (*information*) 527; acknowledge etc. (*assent*) 488; attest etc. (*evidence*) 467; adjure etc. (*put to one's oath*) 768.

Adj. asserting etc. *v.*; declaratory, predicatory, pronunciative, affirmative, *soi-disant*; positive; certain etc. 474; express, explicit etc. (*patent*) 525; absolute, emphatic, flat, broad, round, pointed, marked, distinct, decided, confident, assertive, insistent, trenchant, dogmatic, definitive, formal, solemn, categorical, peremptory; unretracted; predicable, affirmable.

Adv. affirmatively etc. *adj.*; in the affirmative. with emphasis, *ex cathedrâ*, without fear of contradiction.

I must say, indeed, i' faith, let me tell you, why, give me leave to say, marry, you may be sure, I'd have you to know; upon my -word, — honor; by my troth, egad, I assure you; by -jingo, — Jove, — George, — etc.; troth, seriously, sadly; in —, in sober- -sadness, — truth, — earnest; of a truth, truly, pardi, perdy; in all conscience, upon oath; be assured etc. (*belief*) 484; yes etc. (*assent*) 488; I'll -warrant, — warrant you, — engage, — answer for it, — be bound, — venture to say, — take my oath; in fact, as a matter of fact, forsooth, joking apart; so help me God; not to mince the matter.

Phr. quoth he; *dixi*.

---

536. Negation.—N. ne-, abne-gation; denial; dis-avowal, -claimer; abjuration; contra-diction, -vention; recusation, protest; rebuttal; recusancy etc. (*dissent*) 489; flat —, emphatic- -contradiction, — denial; *démenti*.

qualification etc. 469; repudiation etc. 610; retraction etc. 607; confutation etc. 479; refusal etc. 764; prohibition etc. 761.

V. deny; contra-dict, -vene; controvert, give denial to, gainsay, negative, shake the head.

dis-own, -affirm, -claim, -avow; recant etc. 607; revoke etc. (*abrogate*) 756.

dispute, impugn, traverse, rebut, join issue upon; bring −, call- in question etc. (*doubt*) 485.

deny -flatly, − peremptorily, − emphatically, − absolutely, − wholly, − entirely; give the lie to, belie.

repudiate etc. 610; set aside, ignore etc. 460; rebut etc. (*confute*) 479; qualify etc. 469; refuse etc. 764.

Adj. denying etc. *v.*; denied etc. *v.*; contradictory; negat-ive, -ory; revocatory; recusant etc. (*dissenting*) 489; at issue upon.

Adv. no, nay, not, nowise; not a -bit, − whit, − jot; not -at all, −, in the least, − so; no such thing; nothing of the -kind, − sort; quite the contrary, *tout au contraire*, far from it; *tant s'en faut*; on no account, in no respect; by -no, − no manner of-means; negatively.

phr. there never was a greater mistake; I know better; *non haec in foedera*.

537. Teaching.—N. teaching etc. *v.*; instruction; edification; education; pedagogy; tuition; tutor-, tutel-age; direction, guidance.

qualification, preparation; train-, school-ing etc. *v.*; discipline; exer-cise, -citation; drill, practice.

persuasion, proselytism, propagandism, *propaganda*; in-doctrination, -culcation, oculation.

explanation etc. (*interpretation*) 522; lesson, lecture, sermon, homily; apologue, parable; discourse, prelection, preachment, disquisition.

exercise, task; *curriculum*; course, − of study; grammar, three R's, initiation, A.B.C. etc. (*beginning*) 66.

elementary −, primary −, secondary −, grammar school −, high school −, college −, university −, technical −, liberal −, classical −, religious −, denominational −, moral −, secular-education; technical −, vocational- training; university extension lectures; propaedeutics, moral tuition; evening classes, correspondence course.

physical education, gymnastics, calisthenics, eurythmics; *sloyd*.

V. teach, instruct, edify, school, tutor; cram, prime, coach; enlighten etc. (*inform*) 527.

in-culcate, -doctrinate, -oculate, -fuse, -stil, -fix, -graft, -filtrate; im-bue, -pregnate, -plant; graft, sow the seeds of, disseminate, propagandize.

give an idea of; put -up to, − in the way of; set right.

sharpen the wits, enlarge the mind; give new ideas, open the eyes, bring forward, 'teach the young idea how to shoot;' improve etc. 658.

expound etc. (*interpret*) 522; lecture; prelect; read −, give- a -lesson, − lecture, − sermon, − discourse; hold forth, preach; sermon-, moral-ize; point a moral.

train, discipline; bring up, − to; educate, form, ground, prepare, qualify, drill, exercise, practice, habituate, familiarize with, nurture, dry-nurse, breed, rear, take in hand; break, − in; tame; pre-instruct; initiate; inure etc. (*habituate*) 613.

put to nurse, send to school.

direct, guide; direct attention to etc. (*attention*) 457; impress upon the -mind, − memory; beat into, − the head; convince etc. (*belief*) 484.

Adj. teaching etc. *v.*; taught etc. *v.*; educational;

scholastic, academic, doctrinal; disciplinal; instructive, didactic, hortative, pedagogic, tutorial.

Phr. the schoolmaster abroad.

538. Misteaching—N. mis-teaching, -information, -intelligence, -guidance, -direction, -persuasion, -instruction, -leading etc. *v.*; per-version, false teaching; sophistry etc. 477; college of Laputa; the blind leading the blind.

V. mis-inform, -teach, -direct, -guide, -instruct, -correct; pervert; put on a false −, throw off the-scent; deceive etc. 545; mislead etc. (*error*) 495; misrepresent; lie etc. 544; *ambiguas in vulgum spargere voces*, preach to the wise, teach one's grandmother to suck eggs.

render unintelligible etc. 519; bewilder etc. (*uncertainty*) 475; mystify etc. (*conceal*) 528; un-teach.

Adj. misteaching etc. *v.*; unedifying.

Phr. *piscem natare doces.*

539. Learning.—N. learning; acquisition of -knowledge etc. 490, − skill etc. 698; acquirement, attainment; edification; scholarship, erudition; lore; information; self-instruction; study, reading, perusal; inquiry etc. 461.

ap-, prenticeship; pupil-age, -arity; tutelage, novitiate, matriculation.

docility etc. (*willingness*) 602; aptitude etc. 698.

V. learn; acquire −, gain −, receive −, take in −, drink in −, imbibe −, pick up −, gather −, get −, obtain −, collect −, glean- -knowledge, − information, − learning.

acquaint oneself with, master; make oneself -master of, − acquainted with; grind, cram; get −, coach- up; learn by -heart, − rote.

read, spell, peruse; con −, pore −, thumb- over; wade through; dip into; run the eye -over, − through; turn over the leaves.

study; be -studious etc. *adj.*; consume the mid-night oil, mind one's book.

go to -school, − college, − the university; serve -an (*or* one's) apprenticeship, − one's time; learn one's trade; be -informed etc. 527; be -taught etc. 537.

Adj. studious; schol-astic, -arly; teachable; docile etc. (*willing*) 602; apt etc. 698; industrious etc. 682; learned erudite.

Adv. at one's books; *in statu pupillari* etc. (*learner*) 541.

540. Teacher.—N. teacher, trainer, instructor, institutor, master, tutor, don, director, Corypheus, dry nurse, coach, grinder, crammer; governor, bear-leader; governess, duenna; disciplinarian.

professor, lecturer, reader, prelector, prolocutor, preacher; Boanerges; pastor etc. (*clergy*) 996; schoolmaster, dominie, usher, pedagogue, abecedarian; schoolmistress, dame, monitor, proctor, pupil-teacher.

expositor etc. 524; preceptor; guide; mentor etc. (*adviser*) 695; pioneer, apostle, missionary, propagandist, moonshee; example etc. (*model for imitation*) 22.

professorship etc. (*school*) 542.

tutelage etc. (*teaching*) 537.

Adj. professorial, tutorial etc. 537.

541. Learner.—N. learner, scholar, student, *alumnus, élève,* pupil; ap-, prentice; articled clerk; school-boy, -girl, beginner, tyro, abecedarian, alphabetarian.

recruit, novice, neophyte, tenderfoot, inceptor, *débutant,* catechumen, probationer; undergraduate; freshman, frosh; sophomore, junior, senior; junior –, senior- soph; sophister, questionist, fellow-, commoner, pensioner, exhibitioner, sizar, scholar, fellow, advanced –, post graduate –, research- student.

class, form, grade, standard, remove; pupilage etc. (*learning*) 539.

disciple, follower, apostle, proselyte; fellow student, school-mate, -fellow, class mate, condisciple.

Adj. *in statu pupillari,* in leading strings, sophomoric.

542. School.—N. school, academy, university, *alma mater,* college, seminary, Lyceum; instit-ute, -ution, *conservatoire; palaestra, gymnasium.*

day –, boarding –, public –, preparatory –, elementary –, primary –, nursery –, dame's –, grammar –, Board –, County –, Council –, parochial –, denominational –, Sunday –, religious –, collegiate –, secondary –, continuation –, night –, correspondence –, secretarial –, military –; law –, medical –, business –, technical- school; technical –, training- college; Polytechnic; training ship; *Kindergarten,* nursery, *crèche,* reformatory.

pulpit, desk, reading desk, ambo, class-, lecture-room, theater, amphitheater, forum, stage, rostrum, platform, hustings, tribune.

school –, horn –, text-book; grammar, primer, abecedary, rudiments, manual, *vade mecum,* Lindley, Murray, Cocker.

professor-, lecture-, reader-ship; chair; schoolmaster etc. 540.

School Board, Council of Education; *propaganda.*

Adj. scholastic, academic, collegiate; educational.

Adv. *ex cathedrâ.*

543. Veracity.—N. veracity; truthfulness, frankness etc. *adj.;* truth, sooth, sincerity, candor, honesty, fidelity; plain dealing, *bona fides;* love of truth; probity etc. 939; ingenuousness etc. (*artlessness*) 703.

the truth the whole truth and nothing but the truth; honest –, sober- truth etc. (*fact*) 494; unvarnished tale; light of truth.

V. speak –, tell- the truth; speak by the card; paint in its –, show oneself in ones -true colors; make a clean breast etc. (*disclose*) 529; speak one's mind etc. (*be blunt*) 703; not -lie etc. 544, – deceive etc. 545.

Adj. truthful, true; ver-acious, -edical; scrupulous etc. (*honorable*) 939; sincere, candid, frank, open, straightforward, unreserved; open-, true-, simple- hearted; honest, trustworthy; undissembling (dissemble etc. 544); guileless, pure; unperjured, ture blue, as good as one's word;

unaffected, unfeigned, *bonâ fide;* outspoken, ingenuous etc. (*artless*) 703; undisguised etc. (*real*) 494.

Adv. truly etc. (*really*) 494; on oath; in plain words etc. 703; in –, with –, of a –, in good –, very- truth; as the -dial to the sun, – needle to the pole; honor bright; troth; in good -sooth, – earnest; unfeignedly, with no nonsense, in sooth, sooth to say, *bonâ fide, in foro conscientiae;* without equivocation; *cartes sur table,* from the bottom of one's heart; by my troth etc. (*affirmation*) 535.

544. Falsehood.—N. false-hood, -ness; fals-ity, -ification; misrepresentation; deception etc. 545; untruth etc. 546; guile; bad faith; lying etc. *v.;* misrepresentation; mendacity, perjury, false swearing; forgery, invention, fabrication; subreption; covin.

perversion –, suppression- of truth; *suppressio veri;* perversion, distortion, false coloring; exaggeration etc. 549; prevarication, equivocation, shuffling, fencing, evasion, fraud; *suggestio falsi* etc. (*lie*) 546; mystification etc. (*concealment*) 528; simulation etc. (*imitation*) 19; dis-simulation, -sembling; deceit.

sham; pretence, pretending, malingering.

lip-homage, – service; mouth honor; hollowness; mere -show, – outside, eye-wash, window dressing; duplicity, double dealing, insincerity, hypocrisy, cant, humbug, casuistry; jesuit-ism, -ry; pharisaism; Machiavelism, 'organized hypocrisy;' crocodile tears, mealy-mouthedness, quackery; charlatan-ism, -ry; gammon; bun-kum, -come; flam, ban, flim-flam, cajolery, flattery; Judas kiss; perfidy etc. (*bad faith*) 940; *il volto sciolto i pensieri stretti.*

unfairness etc. (*dishonesty*) 940; artfulness etc. (*cunning*) 702; misstatement etc. (*error*) 495.

V. be -false etc. *adj.,* – a liar etc. 548; speak -falsely etc. *adv.;* tell a -lie etc. 546; lie, fib; lie like a trooper; swear falsely, forswear, perjure oneself, bear false witness.

mis-state, -quote, -cite, -report, -represent; belie, falsify, pervert, distort; put a false construction upon etc. (*misinterpret*) 523.

prevaricate, equivocate, quibble; palter, – to the understanding; *répondre en Normand;* trim, shuffle, fence, mince the truth, beat about the bush, blow hot and cold, play fast and loose.

garble, gloss over, disguise, give a color to; give –, put- a -gloss, – false coloring- upon; color, varnish, cook, dress up, embroider; varnish right and puzzle wrong, exaggerate etc. 549.

invent, fabricate; trump –, get- up; forge, hatch, concoct; romance etc. (*imagine*) 515; cry 'wolf!'

dis-semble, -simulate; feign, assume, put on, pretend, make believe; play -false, – a double game; coquet; act –, play- a part; affect etc. 855; simulate, pass off for; counterfeit, fake, sham, make a show of; malinger; swing the lead; say the grapes are sour.

cant, play the hypocrite, sham Abraham, *faire pattes de velours,* put on the mask, clean the outside of the platter, lie like a conjuror; hang out –, hold out –, sail under- false colors; 'commend the poisoned chalice to the lips;' *ambiguas in vulgus spargere voces;* deceive etc. 545.

Adj. false, deceitful, mendacious, unveracious,

fraudulent, untruthful, dishonest; faith-, truth-, troth-less; un-fair, -candid; evasive; un-, dis-ingenuous; hollow, insincere, *Parthis mendacior*; forsworn.

canting; hypocrit-, jesuit-, pharisa-ical; tartuffish; Machiavelian; double-tongued, -faced, -handed, -minded, -hearted, -dealing; two-faced, bare-faced; Janus-faced; smooth-faced, -spoken, -tongued; plausible; mealy-mouthed; affected etc. 855.

collus-ive, -ory; artful etc. (*cunning*) 702; perfidious etc. 940, spurious etc. (*deceptive*) 545; untrue etc. 546; falsified etc. *v.*; covinous.

Adv. falsely etc. *adj.*; *à la Tartufe*, with a double tongue; out of whole cloth; slily etc. (*cunning*) 702.

545. Deception.—N. deception; falseness etc. 544; untruth etc. 546; impos-ition, -ture; fraud, deceit, guile; fraudulen-ce, -cy; covin; knavery etc. (*cunning*) 702; misrepresentation etc. (*falsehood*) 544.

delusion, gullery, bluff, spoof, *blague*; juggl-ing, -ery; sleight of hand, legerdemain; presti-giation, -digitation; magic etc. 992; conjur-ing, -ation; hocus pocus, jockeyship; trickery, coggery, hanky-panky, chicanery, pettifogging, sharp practice; *super-cherie*, cozenage, circumvention, ingannation, collusion; treachery etc. 940; practical joke.

trick, cheat, wile, ruse, blind, feint, plant, bubble fetch, catch, chicane, juggle, reach, hocus, bite; thimble-rig, card-sharping, artful dodge, machination, swindle, hoax; tricks upon travellers; confidence trick; strategem etc. (*artifice*) 702; theft etc. 791.

snare, trap, pitfall, decoy, gin; sprin-ge, -gle; noose, hook; bait, decoy-duck, tub to the whale, baited trap, *guet-à-pens*; cobweb, net, meshes, toils, mouse-trap, bird-lime; ambush etc. 530; trap-door, sliding panel, false bottom; spring-net, -gun; mask, -ed battery; mine; booby trap.

Cornish hug; wolf in sheep's clothing etc. (*deceiver*) 548; disguise, -ment; false colors, masquerade, mummery, borrowed plumes; *pattes de velours*.

mockery etc. (*imitation*) 19; copy etc. 21; counterfeit, sham, brummagem, make-believe, forgery, fraud, fake; lie etc. 546; 'a mockery, a delusion, and a snare,' hollow mockery.

whited –, painted- sepulcher; tinsel, paste, false jewelry, scagliola, ormolu, German silver, Britannia metal, paint; jerry building; man of straw.

illusion etc. (*error*) 495; *ignis fatuus* etc. 423; *mirage* etc. 443.

V. deceive, take in; defraud, cheat, jockey, do, cozen, diddle, nab, gyp, chouse, double cross, play one false, bilk, cully, jilt, bite, pluck, swindle, victimize; abuse; mystify; blind one's eyes; blindfold, hoodwink, spoof, bluff; throw dust into the eyes, 'keep the word of promise to the ear and break it to the hope,' 'draw a herring across the trail.'

impose –, practice –, play –, put –, palm –, foist- upon; snatch a verdict.

circumvent, overreach, out-reach, -wit, maneuvre; steal a march upon, give the go-by to, leave in the lurch.

set –, lay- a -trap, – snare- for; bait the hook, forlay, spread the toils, lime; decoy, waylay, lure,

beguile, delude, inveigle; tra-, tre-pan; kidnap; let-, hook-in; trick; en-, in-trap, -snare, entoil, benet; nick, springe; catch, – in a trap; sniggle, entangle, illaqueate, hocus, practice on one's credulity, dupe, gull, hoax, fool, befool, bamboozle; hum, -bug; gammon, stuff up, dope, sell; play a -trick, – practical joke- upon one; balk, trip up, throw a tub to a whale; fool to the top of one's bent, send on -a wild goose chase, – a fool's errand; make -game, – a fool, – an April fool, – an ass- of; trifle with, cajole, flatter; come over etc. (*influence*) 615; gild the pill, make things pleasant, divert, put a good face upon; dissemble etc. 544.

cog, – the dice, play with marked cards; live by one's wits, play at hide and seek; obtain money under false pretences etc. (*steal*) 791; conjure, juggle, practice chicanery; gerrymander.

play –, palm –, foist –, fob- off.

lie etc. 544; misinform etc. 538; mislead etc. (*error*) 495; betray etc. 940; be -deceived etc. 547.

Adj. deceived etc. *v.*; deceiving etc. *v.*; cunning etc. 702; prestigi-ous, -atory; decept-ive, -ious; deceitful, covinous; delus-ive, -ory; illus-ive, -ory; elusive, insidious, *ad captandum vulgus*.

untrue etc. 546; mock, sham, make-believe, counterfeit, faked, pseudo, spurious, so-called, pretended, feigned, trumped up, bogus, scamped, fraudulent, tricky, factitious, artificial, bastard; surreptitious, illegitimate, contraband, adulterated, sophisticated; unsound, rotten at the core; colorable; disguised; meretricious; tinsel, pinchbeck, plated; catch-penny; Brummagem; simulated etc. 544.

Adv. under -false colors, – the garb of, – cover of; over the left.

Phr. *fronti nulla fides.*

546. Untruth.—N. untruth, falsehood, lie, story, thing that is not, fib, bounce, crammer, taradiddle, whopper.

forgery, fabrication, invention; mis-statement, -representation; perversion, falsification, gloss, *suggestio falsi*; exaggeration etc. 549.

fiction; fable, nursery tale; romance etc. (*imagination*) 515; untrue –, false –, trumped up- -story, – statement; thing devised by the enemy; *canard*; shave, sell, hum, yarn, traveler's tale, Canterbury tale, cock and bull story, fairy tale, clap-trap.

myth, moonshine, bosh, all my eye, -and Betty Martin, mare's nest, farce.

irony; half truth, white lie, pious fraud; mental reservation etc. (*concealment*) 528.

pretence, pretext; false -plea etc. 617; subterfuge, evasion, shift, shuffle, make-believe; sham etc. (*deception*) 545.

profession, empty words; Judas kiss etc. (*hypocrisy*) 544; disguise etc. (*mask*) 530.

V. have a false meaning; not ring true.

pretend, sham, feign, counterfeit, make believe.

Adj. untrue, false, trumped up; void of –, without- foundation; far from the truth, false as dicer's oaths; unfounded, *ben trovato*, invented, fabulous, fabricated, forged; fict-, fact-, supposit-, surrept-itious; e-, il-lusory; ironical; satirical; evasive; *soi-disant* etc. (*misnamed*) 565.

Phr. *se non e vero e ben trovato.*

547. Dupe.—N. dupe, gull, gudgeon, *gobemouche*, cull, cully, victim, sucker, pigeon, April fool; laughing stock etc. 857; Cyclops, simple Simon, flat, mug, greenhorn; fool etc. 501; puppet, cat's paw.

V. be -deceived etc. 545, – the dupe of; fall into a trap; swallow –, nibble at- the bait; bite; catch a Tartar.

Adj. credulous etc. 486; mistaken etc. (*error*) 495.

548. Deceiver.—N. deceiver etc. (deceive etc. 545); dissembler, hypocrite; sophist, Pharisee, Jesuit, Mawworm, Pecksniff, Joseph Surface, Tartufe, Janus; serpent, snake in the grass, cockatrice, Judas, wolf in sheep's clothing; Molly Maguire; jilt; shuffler.

liar etc. (lie etc. 544; story-teller, perjurer, false-witness, *menteur à triple étage*, Scapin.

imposter, pretender, capper, decoy, fraud, *soi-disant*, humbug; adventurer; Cagliostro, Fernam Mendez Pinto; ass in lion's skin etc. (*bungler*) 701; actor etc. (*stage player*) 599.

quack, *charlatan*, mountebank, saltimbanco, *saltimbanque*, empiric, quacksalver, medicaster.

conjuror, juggler, magician, necromancer, trickster, prestidigitator, medium, jockey; crimp; decoy-duck, stool pigeon; rogue, knave, cheat; swindler etc. (*thief*) 792; jobber.

549. Exaggeration.—N. exaggeration; expansion etc. 194; hyperbole, stretch, strain, coloring; high coloring, caricature, *caricatura*; extravagance etc. (*nonsense*) 497; Baron Munchausen; men in buckram, yarn, fringe, embroidery, traveler's tale; Pelion upon Ossa.

storm in a teacup; much ado about nothing etc. (*over-estimation*) 482; puffery etc. (*boasting*) 884; rant etc. (*turgescence*) 577.

figure of speech, *façon de parler*; stretch of- fancy, – the imagination; flight of fancy etc. (*imagination*) 515.

false coloring etc. (*falsehood*) 544; aggravation etc. 835.

V. exaggerate, magnify, pile up, aggravate; amplify etc. (*expand*) 194; overestimate etc. 482; hyperbolize; over-charge, -state, -draw, -lay, -shoot the mark, -praise; make -much, – the most- of; strain, – a point; stretch, – a point; go great lengths; spin a long yarn; draw –, shoot with- a long-bow; deal in the marvelous.

out -Herod Herod, run riot, talk at random.

heighten, overcolor; color -highly, – too highly; embroider, *broder*; flourish; color etc. (*misrepresent*) 544; puff etc. (*boast*) 884.

Adj. exaggerated etc. *v.*; overwrought; bombastic etc. (*magniloquent*) 577; hyperbolical, on stilts; fabulous, extravagant, preposterous, egregious, *outré*, high-flying.

Adv. hyperbolically etc. *adj.*

550. Indication.—N. indication; symbol-ism, -ization; semeio-logy, -tics; sign of the times.

lineament, feature, *trait*, characteristic, trick, diagnostic; divining-rod; cloven hoof; footfall; means of recognition; earmark.

sign, symbol; ind-ex, -ice, -icator; point, -er; marker; exponent, note, token, symptom.

type, figure, emblem, cipher, device; representation etc. 554; epigraph, motto, posy.

gest-ure, -iculation; pantomime; wink, glance, leer; nod, shrug, beck; touch, nudge; grip; dactylology, -nomy; freemasonry, telegraphy, chirology, by-play, dumb-show; cue; hint etc. 527; clue, clew, key, scent, tract etc. 551.

signal, -post; rocket, blue light; watch-fire, -tower; telegraph, semaphore, flag-staff; cresset, fiery cross; calumet; heliograph, signal-, flash-lamp; radar, radar signal, pulse –, microwave –, radar; tracing, blips, pips.

mark, line, stroke, dash, score, stripe, streak, scratch, tick, dot, point, notch, nick, blaze; asterisk, red letter, Italics, heavy type, inverted commas, quotation marks, sublineation, underlining, jotting; print; impr-int, -ess, ession; note, annotation, mark of exclamation.

[For identification] badge, criterion; counter-check, -mark, -sign, -foil, duplicate, tally; label, tab, ticket, stub, billet, letter, counter, *tessera*, card, bill, check; witness, voucher; stamp; *cachet*; trade –, Hall- mark; broad arrow; signature; address –, visiting- card; *carte de visite*; credentials etc. (*evidence*) 467; passport, identity book; attestation; hand, – writing, sign-manual; cipher; monogram, – mark, seal, sigil, signet; autograph, -y, paraph, brand; superscription; in-, en-dorsement; title, heading, rubric, docket; *mot -de passe*, – *du guet*; *passe-parole*; shibboleth; watch-, catch-, pass-word; open *sesame*.

insignia, banner, -et, -ol; bandrol; flag, colors, streamer, standard, eagle, labarum, oriflamb, *oriflamme*; figure-head; ensign; pen-non, -nant, -dant; burgee, blue Peter, jack, ancient, gonfalon, union-jack; tricolor, stars and stripes, bunting.

hearldry, crest; coat of –, arms; armorial bearings, hatchment; e-, scutcheon; shield, supporters; livery, uniform; cockade, *epaulette*, brassard, chevron; garland, chaplet, love-knot, fillet, favor.

[Of locality] beacon, cairn, post, staff, flagstaff, hand, pointer, vane, cock, weathercock; guide-, hand-, finger-, directing-, sign-post; pillars of Hercules, pharos, signal fire; land-, sea-mark; lighthouse, balize; pole-, load-, lode-star; cynosure, guide; address, direction, name; sign, -board.

[Of the future] warning etc. 668; omen etc. 512; prefigurement etc. 511. [Of the past] trace record etc. 551. [Of danger] warning etc. 668; alarm etc. 669. [Of authority] scepter etc. 747. [Of triumph] trophy etc. 733. [Of quantity] gauge etc. 466. [Of distance] mile-stone, -post. [Of disgrace] brand, fool's cap, stigma, mark of Cain. [For detection] check, tell-tale; test etc. (*experiment*) 463.

notification etc. (*information*) 527; advertisement etc. (*publication*) 531.

word of command, call; bugle-, trumpet-call; reveille, taps; bell, alarum, cry; battle –, rallying-cry.

church, bell, angelus, sacring bell; muezzin.

exposition etc. (*explanation*) 522; proof etc. (*evidence*) 463; pattern etc. (*prototype*) 22.

V. indicate; be the -sign etc. *n.*- of; denote,

betoken; argue, testify etc. (*evidence*) 467; bear the
-impress etc. *n.*- of; con-note, -notate.

represent, stand for; typify etc. (*prefigure*) 511;
symbolize.

put -an indication, – a mark, – etc. *n.*; note,
mark, tick, blaze, stamp, earmark; set one's seal
upon; label, ticket, docket; dot, spot, score, dash,
trace, chalk; print; im-print, -press, surprint;
engrave, stereotype, electrotype.

signal, transmit, send, radiate, beam, deflect,
echo, bounce back, return.

make a -sign etc. *n.*; signalize; give –, hang out-
a signal; beck, -on; gesture; not; wink, glance, leer,
nudge, shrug, tip the wink; gesticulate; raise –,
hold up- the-finger, – hand; saw the air, suit the
action to the word.

wave –, unfurl –, hoist –, hang out- a banner
etc. *n.*; wave -the hand, – a kerchief; give the cue
etc. (*inform*) 527; show one's colors; give –,
sound- an alarm; beat the drum, sound the trumpets, raise a cry.

sign, seal, attest etc. (*evidence*) 467; underline
etc. (*give importance to*) 642; call attention to etc.
(*attention*) 457; give notice etc. (*inform*) 527.

Adj. indicat-ing etc. *v.*; -ive, -ory; de-, con-
notative; diacritical, representative, typical, symbolic, pantomimic, pathognomonic, symptomatic,
ominous, characteristic, demonstrative, diagnostic,
exponential, emblematic, armorial; individual etc.
(*special*) 79.

known –, recognizable- by; indicated etc. *v.*;
pointed, marked.

[Capable of being denoted] denotable; indelible.

Adv. in token of; symbolically etc. *adj.*; in
dumb show.

Phr. *ecce signum*; *ex ungue leonem*, *ex pede
Herculem.*

551. Record.—N. trace, vestige, relic, remains;
scar, *cicatrix*; foot-step, -mark, -print; track, mark,
wake, trail, spoor, scent, *piste*.

monument, hatchment, escutcheon, slab, tablet,
trophy, achievement; obelisk, pillar, column,
monolith, cromlech, dolmen; memorial; *memento*
etc. (*memory*) 505; testimonial, medal, ribbon, order; commemoration etc. (*celebration*) 883.

record, note, minute; *dossier*; register, -try; census, roll etc. (*list*) 86; cartulary, diptych,
Domesday book; entry, memorandum, indorsement, inscription, copy, duplicate, docket;
notch etc. (*mark*) 550; muniment, deed etc.
(*security*) 771; document, deposition, *procès-
verbal*; affidavit; certificate etc. (*evidence*) 467.

note-, memorandum-, pocket-, commonplace-
book; portfolio; scoring-board, -sheet; bulletin
board; card index, file; pigeon-holes, *excerpta, adversaria*, jottings, dottings.

gazette, -er; newspaper, magazine etc. 531;
alman-ac, -ack; calendar, ephemeris, noctuary,
diary, log, journal, account-, cash-, day-book,
ledger.

archive, scroll, state-paper, Congressional
Record, return, blue-book; statistics etc. 86;
compte rendu; Acts –, Transactions –,
Proceedings- of; Hansard's Debates; chronicle, annals; legend; history, biography etc. 594.

registration; en-, in-rolment; tabulation; entry,

booking; signature etc. (*identification*) 550; recorder etc. 553; journalism.

drawing, photograph etc. 554; phonograph –,
gramophone- record; music roll.

V. record; put –, place- upon record; go on
record; chronicle, calendar, hand down to
posterity; keep up the memory of etc. (*remember*)
505; commemorate etc. (*celebrate*) 883; report
etc. (*inform*) 527; commit to –, reduce to-
writing; put –, set down- -in writing, – in black
and white; put –, jot –, take –, write –, note
–, set-down; note, minute, put on paper; take –,
make- a -note, – minute, – memorandum; make
a return.

mark etc. (*indicate*) 550; sign etc. (*attest*) 467.

enter, book; post, – up; insert, make an entry
of; mark –, tick- off; register, list, docket, enroll,
inscroll; file etc. (*store*) 636.

Adv. on record.

552. Obliteration. [Suppression of sign.]—**N.**
obliteration; erasure, rasure; effacement; interference; cancel, -lation; cassation; cir-
cumduction; deletion, blot; *tabula rasa.*

V. efface, obliterate, erase, rase, expunge, cancel; blot –, take –, rub –, scratch –, strike –,
wipe –, wash –, sponge- out; wipe –, rub- off;
wipe away; deface, render illegible; draw the pen
through, apply the sponge.

interfere, jam, black-, block-out; clutter, screen.

be -effaced etc.; leave no -trace etc. 449; 'leave
not a rack behind.'

Adj. obliterated etc. *v.*; out of print; printless;
leaving no trace; intestate; un-recorded, -registered,
-written.

Int. *dele*; out with it!

553. Recorder.—N. recorder, notary, clerk;
regis-trar, -trary, -ter; prothonotary; amanuensis,
secretary, scribe, stenographer, remembrancer,
book-keeper, *custos rotulorum*, Master of the
Rolls.

annalist; histori-an, -ographer; chronicler, journalist, reporter, columnist; biographer etc.
(*narrator*) 594; antiquary etc. (*antiquity*) 122;
memorialist.

draughtsman etc. 559; engraver 558;
photographer, cinematographer, camera man.

Recording instrument, recorder, camera,
phonograph, gramophone, dictaphone,
telegraphone, telautograph, printing telegraph, tape
recorder, ticker, time recorder, cash register, turn-
stile, speedometer, voting machine, seismograph,
radar, oscilloscope, teletypewriter, pari-mutuel,
photostat.

554. Representation.—N. represent-ation, -
ment; imitation etc. 19; illustration, delineation,
depictment, portrayal; imagery, portraiture,
iconography; design, -ing; art, fine arts; painting
etc. 556; sculpture etc. 557; engraving etc. 558;
photography, radiography, skiagraphy.

person-ation, -ification; impersonation; drama
etc. 599.

picture, drawing, sketch, draught, draft; tracing; copy etc. 21; photo-, helio-graph; daguerreo-, talbo-, calo-, helio-type; cabinet, *carte-de-visite*, snapshot; X-ray photograph; radio-gram, -graph, skia-graph, -gram.

image, likeness, icon, portrait; striking −, speaking- likeness; very image; effigy, fac-simile.

figure, − head; puppet, doll, *figurine*, aglet, manikin, lay-figure, model, *marionnette*, *fantoccini*, bust; waxwork, statue, -tte, automaton, Robot.

hieroglyphic, anaglyph; dia-, mono-gram, graph.

map, plan, chart; ground plan, projection, elevation; ichno-, carto-graphy; atlas; outline, scheme; view etc. (*painting*) 556.

artist, draughtsman etc. 559.

V. represent, delineate; depict, -ure; portray; picture; take − , catch- a likeness etc. *n.*; hit off, photograph, daguerreotype; figure; shadow -forth, − out; adumbrate; body forth; describe etc. 594; trace, copy; mold.

dress up; illustrate, symbolize.

paint etc. 556; carve etc. 557; engrave etc. 558.

person-ate, -ify; impersonate; assume a character; pose as; act; play etc. (*drama*) 599; mimic etc. (*imitate*) 19; hold the mirror up to nature.

Adj. represent-ing etc. *v.*, -ative; illustrative; represented etc. *v.*; imitative, figurative.

like etc. 17; graphic etc. (*descriptive*) 594.

555. Misrepresentation.—N. misrepresentation, distortion, exaggeration; daubing etc. *v.*; bad likeness, daub, sign-painting; scratch, caricature; *anamorphosis*.

V. misrepresent, distort, overdraw, travesty, parody, burlesque, exaggerate, caricature, daub.

Adj. misrepresented etc. *v.*

556. Painting.—N. painting; depicting; drawing etc. *v.*; design; perspective, skiagraphy; *chiaroscuro* etc. (*light*) 420; composition; treatment, values, atmosphere, tone, technique.

historical −, portrait −, miniature −, landscape −, marine −, flower −, scene- painting; scenography.

school, style; the grand style, high art, *genre*, portraiture; ornamental art etc. 847.

mono-, poly-chrome; *grisaille*.

pallet, palette; easel; brush, pencil, stump; blacklead, charcoal, crayons, chalk, pastel; paint etc. (*coloring matter*) 428; water-, body-, oil-color; oils, oil-paint; varnish etc. 356*a*; *gouache*, tempera, distemper, fresco, water-glass; enamel; encaustic painting; *graffito*, *gesso*; mosiac; tapestry.

picture, painting, piece, *tableau*, canvas; oil etc.- painting; fresco, cartoon; easel − , cabinet- picture; drawing, draught, draft; pencil etc. − , watercolor- drawing; sketch; outline; study.

portrait etc. (*representation*) 554; whole − , full − , half- length; kitcat, head; miniature; shade, *silhouette*; profile.

landscape, sea-piece, -scape; view, scene, prospect; interior; bird's- eye view; pan-, di-orama; still life.

picture − , art- gallery; *studio*, *atelier*.

V. paint, design, limn, draw, sketch, pencil, scratch, shade, stipple, hatch, dash off, chalk out, square up; color, dead-color, wash, varnish; draw in -pencil etc. *n.*; paint in -oils etc. *n.*; stencil; depict etc. (*represent*) 554.

Adj. painted etc. *v.*; pictorial, graphic, picturesque, decorative; classical, romantic, pre-Raphaelite, modern, cubist, futurist, vorticist.

pencil, oil etc. *n.*

Adv. in -pencil etc. *n.*

Phr. *fecit, delineavit.*

557. Sculpture.—N. sculpture, insculpture; carving etc. *v.*; statuary, ceramics, plastic arts.

high − , low − , bas- relief; relievo; *basso-*, *alto-*, *mezzo-relievo*; *intaglio*, anaglyph; medal, -lion; *cameo.*

marble, bronze, *terra cotta*; ceramic ware, pottery, porcelain, china, earthenware, faïence, enamel, *cloisonné.*

statue etc. (*image*) 554; cast etc. (*copy*) 21; glyptotheca.

V. sculpture, carve, cut, chisel, model, mold, cast.

Adj. sculptured etc. *v.*; in relief, anaglyptic, ceroplastic, ceramic; parian; marble etc. *n.*

558. Engraving.—N. engraving, chalcography; line − , mezzotint − , stipple − , chalk- engraving; dry-point, bur; etching, aquatinta; plate − , copper-plate − , steel − , wood-, process-, photo-engraving; xylo-, ligno-, glypto-, cero-, litho-, chromolitho-, photolitho-, zinco-, glypho- -graphy, -graph.

impression, print, engraving, plate; steel-, copper-plate; etching; mezzo-, aqua-, litho-tint; cut; woodcut, block; stereo-, grapho-, auto-, helio-type; half-tone; *photogravure, rotogravure.*

graver, *burin*, etching-point, style; plate, stone, wood-block, negative; die, punch, stamp.

printing; plate − , copper-plate − , intaglio − , anastatic − , lithographic − , color − , three color-printing; type-printing etc. 591.

illustr-, illumin-ation; *vignette*, initial letter, *cul de lampe*, tail-piece.

V. engrave, grave, stipple, scrape, etch; bite, − in; lithograph etc. *n.*; print.

Adj. insculptured; engraved etc. *v.*

Phr. *sculpsit, imprimit.*

559. Artist.—N. artist; painter, limner, drawer, sketcher, delineator; cartoon-, caricatur-ist, designer, engraver; draughtsman; copyist; enameller, -list.

historical − , landscape − , genre − , marine − , flower − , portrait − , miniature − , scene − , sign-painter; engraver; Apelles; sculptor, carver, chaser, modeller, lapidary, *figuriste*, statuary; Phidias, Praxiteles; Royal Academician.

photographer, retoucher.

560. Language.—N. language; phraseology etc.
569; speech etc. 582; tongue, lingo, vernacular,
slang; mother −, vulgar −, native- tongue;
household words; King's or Queen's English;
idiom; dialect etc. 563.

volapuk, esperanto, ido, occidental, Ro.

confusion of tongues, Babel, *pasigraphie*; pantomime etc. (*signs*) 550; *onomatopaeia*.

phil-, gloss-, glott-ology; linguistics,
chrestomathy; paleo-logy; -graphy; comparative
grammar.

literature, letters, polite literature, *belles lettres*,
muses, humanities, *literae humaniores*, republic of
letters, dead languages, classics; genius of a
language; scholarship etc. (*knowledge*) 490.

linguist etc. (*scholar*) 492.

V. speak, say, express by words etc. 566.

Adj. lingu-al, -istic; dialectic; vernacular,
current, colloquial, slangy; bilingual, polyglot;
literary.

561. Letter.—N. letter; character; hieroglyphic
etc. (*writing*) 590; type etc. (*printing*) 591;
capitals; majus-, minus-cule; alphabet, ABC,
abecedary, christcross row, chrisscross row.

consonant, vowel, diphthong; mute, surd;
sonant, liquid, labial, dental, palatal, gutteral.

syllable; mono-, dis-, poly-syllable; affix, prefix,
suffix.

spelling, orthography; phon-ography, -etic
spelling; ana-, meta-grammatism.

cipher, monogram, anagram; double − acrostic.

V. spell.

Adj. literal; alphabetical, abecedarian; syllabic;
uncial etc. (*writing*) 590; phonetic, voiced, mute
etc. *n.*

562. Word.—N. word, term, vocable; name
etc. 564; phrase etc. 566; root, etymon; derivative;
part of speech etc. (*grammar*) 567.

dictionary, vocabulary, word book, lexicon, index, glossary, thesaurus, *gradus, delectus*, concordance.

etymology, lexicology, derivation; phonology,
orthoepy; gloss-, termin-, orism-ology; paleology
etc. (*philology*) 560; comparative philology.

lexicograph-er, -y; glossographer etc. (*scholar*)
492; etymologist; logolept.

verbosity, verbiage, loquacity etc. 584.

Adj. verbal, literal; titular, nominal. [Similarly
derived] conjugate, paronymous; derivative.

Adv. verbally etc. *adj.*; *verbatim* etc. (*exactly*)
494.

563. Neology.—N. neolo-gy; -gism; new-
fangled expression; barbarism; caconym; archaism,
black letter, monkish Latin; corruption; missaying,
antiphrasis.

paronomasia, play upon words; wordplay etc.
(*wit*) 842; *double-entente* etc. (*ambiguity*) 520;
palindrome, paragram, clinch; abuse of -language,
− terms.

dialect, brogue, *patois*, provincialism, broken
English, *lingua franca*; Brit-, Gall-, Scott-, Hibern-
icism; American-ism; Gipsy lingo, Romany, pidgin
English.

dog Latin, macaronics, gibberish, confusion of
tongues, Babel; jargon.

colloquialism etc. (*figure of speech*) 521; by-
word; technicality, lingo, slang, cant, *argot*, St.
Giles's Greek, thieves' Latin, peddler's French,
flash tongue, Billingsgate, Wall Street slang.

pseudonym etc. (*misnomer*) 565; Mr. So-and-so;
what d'ye call 'em, what's his name; thingum-my, -
bob; *je ne sais quoi.*

neologist, coiner of words.

V. coin words.

Adj. neologic, -al; rare; archaic; obsolete etc.
(*old*) 124; colloquial, dialectic, slang, cant.

564. Nomenclature.—N. nomenclature;
naming etc. *v.*; nuncupation, nomination, baptism;
orismology; *onomatopaeia*; antonomasia.

name; appella-tion, -tive; designation; title;
head, -ing, caption; denomination; by-name,
epithet.

style, proper name; prae-, ag-, cog-nomen;
patronymic, surname; cognomination; compellation, description; empty -title, − name; handle to one's name; namesake, eponym.

synonym, antonym.

term, expression, noun; by-word; convertible
terms etc. 522; technical term; cant etc. 563.

V. name, call, term, denominate, designate,
style, entitle, intitule, clepe, dub, christen, baptize,
nickname, characterize, specify, define, distinguish
by the name of; label etc. (*mark*) 550.

be -called etc. *v.*; take −, bear −, go (*or* be
known) by −, go (*or* pass) under −, rejoice in- the
name of.

Adj. named etc. *v.*; hight, yclept, known as;
what one may -well, − fairly, − properly, − fitly-
call.

nuncupa-tory, -tive; cognominal, titular,
nominal; orismological.

565. Misnomer.—N. misnomer; *lucus a non
lucendo*; Mrs. Malaprop; what d'ye call 'em etc.
(*neologism*) 563.

nickname, *sobriquet*, by-name, handle,
moniker; assumed -name, − title; *alias*; *nom de -
guerre*, − *plume*, − *theâtre*; pseudonym, pen
name, stage name.

V. mis-name, -call, - term; nickname; assume -a
name, − an alias.

Adj. misnamed etc. *v.*; pseudonymous; *soi-
disant*; self-called, -styled, -christened; so-called.
nameless, anonymous; without a −, having no-
name; innominate, unnamed.

Adv. in no sense.

566. Phrase.—N. phrase, expression, set
phrase; sentence, paragraph; figure of speech etc.
521; idi-om, -otism; turn of expression.

paraphrase etc. (*synonym*) 522; periphrase etc. (*circumlocution*) 573; motto etc. (*proverb*) 496. phraseology etc. 569.

V. express, phrase; word, – it; give -words, – expression- to; voice; arrange in –, clothe in –, put into –, express by- words; couch in terms; find words to express; speak by the card.

Adj. expressed etc. *v.*; idiomatic.

Adv. in -round, – set, – good, set- terms; in set phrases.

567. Grammar.—**N.** grammar, accidence, syntax, *praxis*, analysis, paradigm, punctuation; parts of speech, inflexion, case, declension, conjugation; *jus et norma loquendi*; Lindley Murray etc. (*school-book*) 542; correct style; philology etc. (*language*) 560.

V. parse, analyze; decline, conjugate; punctuate.

Adj. grammatical; syntactic; inflexional.

568. Solecism.—**N.** solecism; bad –, false –, faulty- grammar; slip, error; slip of the -pen, – tongue; *lapsus calami-*, – *linguae*; *faux pas*; slipslop; bull.

V. use -bad, – faulty- grammar; solecize, commit a solecism; murder the -King's, – Queen's-English; break Priscian's head.

Adj. ungrammatical; in-correct, -accurate; faulty, improper, incongruous, abnormal.

569. Style.—**N.** style, diction, phraseology, wording; manner, strain; composition; mode of expression, choice of words, literary power, ready pen, pen of a ready writer; command of language etc. (*eloquence*) 582; authorship; *la morgue littéraire*.

V. express by words etc. 566; write.

570. Perspicuity.—**N.** perspicuity etc. (*intelligibility*) 518; plain speaking etc. (*manifestation*) 525; defin-iteness, -ition; exactness etc. 494; perspicuousness, logical acuteness.

Adj. lucid etc. (*intelligible*) 518; explicit etc. (*manifest*) 525; exact etc. 494.

571. Obscurity.—**N.** obscurity etc. (*unintelligibility*) 519; involution; hard words; ambiguity etc. 520; vagueness etc. 475, inexactness etc. 495; what d'ye call 'em etc. (*neologism*) 563; cloudiness, confusion.

Adj. obscure etc. *n.*; crabbed, involved, confused.

572. Conciseness.—**N.** conciseness etc. *adj.*; brevity, 'the soul of wit,' laconism; Tacitus; ellipsis; syncope; abridgment etc. (*shortening*) 201; compression etc. 195; epitome etc. 596; monostitch; portmanteau word, telescope word, protogram.

V. be -concise etc. *adj.*; condense etc. 195; abridge etc. 201; abstract etc. 596; come to the point.

Adj. concise, brief, short, terse, close; to the point, exact; neat, compact, condensed, pointed; laconic, curt, pithy, trenchant, summary; pregnant; compendious etc. (*compendium*) 596; succinct; elliptical, epigrammatic, crisp, sententious.

Adv. concisely etc. *adj.*; briefly, summarily; in-brief, – short, – a word, – few words, – a nutshell; for shortness sake; to -come to the point, – make a long story short, – cut the matter short, – be brief; it comes to this, the long and short of it is.

573. Diffuseness.—**N.** diffuseness etc. *adj.*; amplification etc. *v.*; dilating etc. *v.*; verbiage, wordiness, cloud of words, *copia verborum*; flow of words etc. (*loquacity*) 584.

poly-, tauto-, batto-, perisso-logy; pleonasm, exuberance, redundance; thrice-told tale; prolixity; circumlocution, *ambages*; periphra-se, -sis; roundabout phrases; episode; expletive; penny-a-lining; padding, drivel, twaddle, rigmarole; richness etc. 577.

V. be -diffuse etc. *adj.*; run out on, descant, expatiate, enlarge, dilate, amplify, expand, inflate, pad; launch –, branch- out; rant.

maunder, prose; harp upon etc. (*repeat*) 104; dwell on, insist upon.

digress, ramble, *battre la campagne*, beat about the bush, perorate, spin a long yarn, protract; spin –, swell –, draw- out; drivel.

Adj. dif-, pro-fuse; wordy, verbose, largiloquent, copious, exuberant, effusive, pleonastic, lengthy; long, -some, -winded, -spun, -drawn out; diffusive, spun out, protracted, prolix, prosing, maundering; circumlocutory, periphrastic, ambagious, roundabout; digressive; dis-, ex-cursive; rambling, episodic; flatulent, frothy.

Adv. diffusely etc. *adj.*; at large, *in extenso*; about it and about it.

574. Vigor.—**N.** vigor, power, force; boldness, raciness etc. *adj.*; spirit, point, antithesis, piquancy; *verve*, glow, fire, warmth, ardor, enthusiasm; 'thoughts that breathe and words that burn;' strong language; punch; gravity, sententiousness; elevation, loftiness, sublimity.

eloquence; command of -words, – language.

Adj. vigorous, nervous, powerful, forcible, trenchant, mordant, biting, incisive, impressive; sensational.

spirited, lively, glowing, sparkling, racy, bold, slashing; pungent, *piquant*, full of point, pointed, pithy, antithetical; sententious.

lofty, elevated, sublime, grand, weighty, ponderous; eloquent; vehement, petulant, impassioned; poetic.

Adv. in -glowing, – good set, – no measured-terms.

575. Feebleness.—**N.** feebleness etc. *adj.*;

Adj. feeble, bald, tame, meager, insipid, nerve-

les, jejune, vapid, trashy, cold, frigid, poor, dull, dry, languid; pros-ing, -y, -aic; unvaried, monotonous, weak, frail, washy, wishy-washy, sloppy; sketchy, slight; careless, slovenly, loose, lax; slip-shod, -slop; inexact; dis-jointed, -connected; puerile, childish; flatulent; rambling etc. (*diffuse*) 573.

576. Plainness.—N. plainness etc. *adj.*; simplicity, severity; plain -terms, – English; Saxon English; household words.

V. speak plainly; call a spade 'a spade;' plunge *in medias res*; come to the point.

Adj. plain, simple; un-ornamented, -adorned, -varnished; home-ly, -spun; neat; severe, chaste, pure, Saxon; commonplace, matter of fact, natural, prosaic, sober, unimaginative.

dry, unvaried, monotonous etc. 575.

Adv. in plain -terms, – words, – English, – common parlance; point blank.

577. Ornament.—N. ornament; floridness etc. *adj.*; turg-idity, -escence; altiloquence etc. *adj.*; orotundity; declamation, teratology; well-rounded periods; elegance etc. 578.

inversion, antithesis, alliteration, *paronomasia*; figurativeness etc. (*metaphor*) 521.

flourish; flowers of -speech, – rhetoric; euphuism, -emism.

big-, high-sounding words; macrology, *sesquipedalia verba*, sesquipedalianism; Alexandrine; inflation, pretension; rant, bombast, fustian; bunkum, balderdash, prose run mad; fine writing; Minerva press.

phrasemonger; euph-uist, -emist.

V. ornament, overlay with ornament, overcharge; smell of the lamp.

Adj. ornamented etc. *v.*; beautified etc. 847; ornate, florid, rich, flowery; euph-uistic, -emistic; sonorous; high-, big-sounding; inflated, swelling, tumid; turg-id, -escent; pedantic, pompous, stilted; high-flown, -flowing; sententious, rhetorical, declamatory; grandiose; grand-, magn-, altiloquent; sesquipedal, -ian; Johnsonian, mouthy; bombastic; fustian; frothy, flashy, flaming, flamboyant.

antithetical, alliterative; figurative etc. 521; artificial etc. (*inelegant*) 579.

Adv. *ore rotundo*; with rounded phrase.

578. Elegance.—N. elegance, purity, grace, ease, felicity, distinction, gracefulness, refinement, readiness etc. *adj.*; concinnity, euphony, numerosity, balance, rythm, symmetry, proportion; restraint; good taste, propriety.

well rounded –, well turned –, flowing-periods; the right word in the right place; antithesis etc. 577.

purist, stylist.

V. point an antithesis, round a period.

Adj. elegant, polished, classical, Attic, correct, Ciceronian, artistic; chaste, pure, Saxon, academical.

graceful, easy, readable, fluent, flowing, tripping; unaffected, natural, unlabored; mellifluous; euph-onious, -emistic; rhythmical, balanced, symmetrical.

felicitous, happy, neat; well –, neatly- -put, – expressed.

579. Inelegance.—N. inelegance; vulgarity, bad taste; stiffness etc. *adj.*; unlettered Muse; barbarism; slang etc. 563; solecism etc. 568; mannerism etc. (*affectation*) 855; euphuism; fustian etc. 577; cacophony; want of balance; words that -break the teeth, – dislocate the jaw.

V. be -inelegant etc. *adj.*

Adj. inelegant, graceless, ungraceful, unpolished; harsh, abrupt; dry, stiff, cramped, formal, *guindé*; forced, labored, awkward; artificial, mannered, ponderous; turgid etc. 577; affected, euphuistic; barbarous, uncouth, grotesque, rude, crude, halting; vulgar, offensive to ears polite.

580. Voice.—N. voice; vocality; organ, lungs, bellows; good –, fine –, powerful etc. (*loud*) 404 –, musical etc. 413- voice; intonation; tone etc. (*sound*) 402- of voice.

vocalization; cry etc. 411; strain, utterance, prolation; exclam-, ejacul-, vocifer-ation; enunci-, articul-ation; articulate sound; distinctness; clearness, – of articulation; stage whisper; delivery; attack.

accent, -uation; emphasis, stress; broad –, strong –, pure –, native –, foreign- accent; pronunciation.

[Word similarly pronounced] homonym.

orthoepy; euphony etc. (*melody*) 413.

gastri-, ventri-loquism; ventriloquist; polyphonism, -ist.

[Science of voice] phonology etc. (*sound*) 402.

V. sing, speak, utter, breathe, voice; give -utterance, – tongue; cry etc. (*shout*) 411; ejaculate, rap out; vocalize, prolate, articulate, enunciate, enounce, pronounce, accentuate, aspirate, deliver, mouth; emit, murmur, whisper, – in the ear, croon, yodel.

Adj. vocal, phonetic, oral; ejaculatory, articulate, distinct, stertorous; enunciative; accentuated, aspirated; euphonious etc. (*melodious*) 413.

581. Aphony—N. aphony, *aphonia*; dumbness etc. *adj.*; obmutescence; absence –, want- of voice; dysphony; silence etc. (*taciturnity*) 585; raucity; harsh etc. 410 –, unmusical etc. 414- voice; *falsetto*, 'childish treble;' mute, dummy, deaf mute.

V. keep silence etc. 585; speak -low, – softly; whisper etc. (*faintness*) 405.

silence; render -mute, – silent etc. 403; muzzle, muffle, suppress, smother, gag, strike dumb, dumbfound, -founder; drown the voice, put to silence, stop one's mouth, cut one short.

stick in the throat.

Adj. aphon-ous, -ic, dumb, mute; deaf-mute, –

and dumb; mum; tongue-tied; breath-, tongue-, voice-, speech-, word-less; mute as a -fish, — stock-fish, — mackerel; silent etc. (*taciturn*) 585; muzzled; in-articulate, -audible.

croaking, raucous, hoarse, husky, dry, hollow, sepulchral, hoarse as a raven.

Adv. with -bated breath, — the finger on the lips; *sotto voce*; in a -low tone, — cracked voice, — broken voice; in an aside.

Phr. *vox faucibus haesit.*

582. Speech.—**N.** speech, faculty of speech; locution, talk, parlance, verbal intercourse, prolation, oral communication, word of mouth, *parole*, palaver, prattle; effusion.

oration, recitation, delivery, say, address, speech, lecture, harangue, sermon, *tirade*, screed, formal speech, salutatory, peroration; prelection; speechifying; soliloquy etc. 589; allocution etc. 586; interlocution etc. 588.

oratory; elo-cution, -quence; rhetoric, declamation; grandi-, multi-loquence; burst of eloquence; facundity; talkativeness; flow —, command- of -words, — language; *copia verborum*; power of speech, gift of the gab; *usus loquendi.*

speaker etc. *v.*; spokesman, pro-, inter-locutor; mouthpiece, Hermes; ora-tor, -trix, -tress; Demosthenes, Cicero; rhetorician; stump —, platform- orator, tub-thumper; elocutionist; speech-maker, patterer, *improvisatore.*

V. speak, — of; say, utter, pronounce, deliver, give utterance to; utter —, pour- forth; breathe, let fall, come out with; rap —, blurt- out; have on one's lips; have at the -end, — tip- of one's tongue.

break silence; open one's -lips, — mouth; lift —, raise- one's voice; give —, wag the- tongue; talk, outspeak; put in a word or two.

hold forth; make —, deliver- -a speech etc. *n.*; speechify, harangue, declaim, stump, flourish, spout, rant, recite, lecture, preach, sermonize, discourse, be on one's legs; have —, say- one's say; expatiate etc. (*speak at length*) 573; speak one's mind.

soliloquize etc. 589; tell etc. (*inform*) 527; speak to etc. 586; talk together etc. 588.

be -eloquent etc. *adj.*; have -a tongue in one's head, — the gift of the gab etc. *n.*

pass —, escape- one's lips; fall from the -lips, — mouth.

Adj. speaking etc., spoken etc. *v.*; oral, lingual, phonetic, not written, unwritten, outspoken; eloquent, -cutionary; orat-, rhetorical; declamatory; grandiloquent etc. 577; talkative etc. 584.

Adv. orally etc. *adj.*; by word of mouth, *vivâ voce*, from the lips of.

Phr. quoth —, said- he etc.

583. Stammering. [Imperfect Speech.]—**N.** inarticulateness; stammering etc. *v.*; hesitation etc. *v.*; impediment in one's speech; aphasia, titubancy, traulism; whisper etc. (*faint sound*) 405; lisp, drawl, tardiloquence; nasal -tone, — accent; twang; *falsetto* etc. (*want of voice*) 581; broken -voice, — accents, — sentences.

brogue etc. 563; slip of the tongue, *lapsus linguae.*

V. stammer, stutter, hesitate, falter, hammer; balbu-tiate, -cinate; haw, hum and haw, be unable to put two words together.

mumble, mutter; maund, -er; whisper etc. 405; mince, lisp; jabber, gabble, gibber; sp-, spl-utter; muffle, mump; drawl, mouth; croak; speak -thick, — through the nose; snuffle, clip one's words; murder the -language, — King's (*or* Queen's) English; mis-pronounce, -say.

Adj. stammering etc. *v.*; inarticulate, guttural, nasal; tremulous.

Adv. *sotto voce* etc. (*faintly*) 405.

584. Loquacity.—**N.** loquac-ity, -iousness; talkativeness etc. *adj.*; garrulity; multiloquence, much speaking, effusion, wordiness.

jaw; gab, -ble; jabber, chatter; prate, prattle, cackle, clack; twaddle, trattle, rattle; *caquet, -terie*; blabber, *bavardage*, bibble-babble, gibble-gabble; small talk etc. (*converse*) 588.

fluency, flippancy, volubility, flowing tongue; flow, — of words; *flux de -bouche, — mots, — paroles*; *copia verborum, cacoëthes loquendi*; verbosity etc. (*diffuseness*) 573; gift of the gab etc. (*eloquence*) 582.

talker; chatter-er, -box; babbler etc. *v.*; rattle; ranter; sermonizer, proser, driveller; wind bag; gossip etc. (*converse*) 588; magpie, jay, parrot, poll, Babel; *moulin à paroles.*

V. be -loquacious etc. *adj.*; talk glibly, pour forth, patter; prate, palaver, prose, chatter, prattle, clack, jabber, jaw; rattle, — on; twaddle, twattle; babble, gabble; out-talk; talk oneself -out of breath, — hoarse; maunder, gush, blatter; talk a donkey's hind leg off; expatiate etc. (*speak at length*) 573; gossip etc. (*converse*) 588; din in the ears etc. (*repeat*) 104; talk -at random, — nonsense etc. 497; be hoarse with talking.

Adj. loquacious, talkative, conversational, garrulous, linguacious, multiloquous; chattering etc. *v.*; chatty etc. (*sociable*) 892; declamatory etc. 582; open-mouthed.

fluent, voluble, glib, flippant; long-tongued, -winded etc. (*diffuse*) 573.

Adv. trippingly on the tongue; glibly etc. *adj.*

Phr. the tongue running -fast, — loose, — on wheels.

585. Taciturnity.—**N.** silence, muteness, ob-mutescence; taciturnity, pauciloquy, costiveness, curtness; reserve, reticence etc. (*concealment*) 528; *aposiopesis.*

man of few words.

V. be -silent etc. *adj.*; keep silence; hold one's -tongue, — peace, — jaw; not speak etc. 582; say nothing; seal —, close —, put a padlock on- the -lips, — mouth; put a bridle on one's tongue; keep one's tongue between one's teeth; make no sign, not let a word escape one; keep a secret etc. 528; not have a word to say; lay —, place- the finger on the lips; render mute etc. 581.

stick in one's throat.

Adj. silent, mute, mum; silent as -a post, — a stone, — the grave etc. (*still*) 403; dumb etc. 581.

taciturn, sparing of words; close, — mouthed, —

tongued; laconic, costive, inconversable, curt; reserved; reticent etc. (*concealing*) 528.

Int. tush! silence! mum! hush! *chut!* hist! tut! etc. 403.

586. Allocution.—N. allocution, alloquy, address; speech etc. 582; apostrophe, interpellation, appeal, invocation, salutation; word in the ear.
[Feigned dialogue] dialogism.
platform etc. 542; audience etc. (*interview*) 588.
V. speak to, address, accost, make up to, apostrophize, appeal to, invoke; hail, salute; call to, halloo.
take -aside, − by the button, button-hole; talk to in private.
lecture etc. (*make a speech*) 582.
Int. soho! halloo! hey! hist! hi!

587. Response etc.; *see* Answer 462.

588. Interlocution.—N. interlocution; collocution, colloquy, converse, conversation, confabulation, talk, discourse, verbal intercourse; communion, oral communication, commerce; dia-, duo-, tria-logue.
causerie, chat, chit-chat; small −, table −, teatable −, town −, village −, idle- talk; tattle, gossip, tittle-tattle; babble, -ment; *tripotage*, cackle, prittle-prattle, *on dit*; talk of the -town, − village.
conference, parley, interview, audience, *pourparler*; *tête-à-tête*; reception, *conversazione*; congress etc. (*council*) 696; pow-wow.
hall of audience, *durbar*, coliseum, assembly hall, auditorium.
palaver, debate, logomachy, war of words, controversy.
talker, gossip, tattler; Paul Pry; tabby; chatterer etc. (*loquacity*) 584; interlocutor etc. (*spokesman*) 582; conversation-ist, -alist; dialogist.
'the feast of reason and the flow of soul;' *mollia tempora fandi*.
V. talk together, converse, confabulate; hold −, carry on −, join in −, engage in- a conversation; put in a word; shine in conversation; bandy words; parley; palaver; chat, gossip, tattle; prate etc. (*loquacity*) 584.
discourse −, confer −, commune −, commerce- with; hold -converse, − conference, − intercourse; talk it over; be closeted with; talk with one -in private, − *tête-à-tête*.
Adj. conversing etc. *v.*; interlocutory; conversational, -able; discursive, -coursive; chatty etc. (*sociable*) 892; colloquial, *tête-à-tête*, confabulatory.

589. Soliloquy.—N. soliloquy, monologue, apostrophe.
solilo-quist, -quizer, monologist.

V. soliloquize; say −, talk- to oneself; say aside, think aloud, apostrophize.
Adj. soliloquizing etc. *v.*
Adv. aside.

590. Writing.—N. writing etc. *v.*; chiro-, stelo-, cero-graphy, graphology; stylography; pen-craft, -script, -manship; quill-driving; typewriting.
writing, manuscript, MS., *literae scriptae*; these presents.
stroke −, dash- of the pen; *coup de plume*; line; pen and ink.
letter etc. 561; uncial writing, cuneiform character, arrow-head, Ogham, Runes, futhorc; hieroglyphic, hieratic, demotic; script; contraction.
short-hand; steno-, brachy-, tachy-graphy; secret writing, writing in cipher; crypt-, stegan-ography; phono-, pasi-, poly-, logo-graphy.
copy; tran-, re-script; draft, rough −, fair- copy; handwriting; signature, sign-manual; auto-, mono-, holo-graph; hand, fist; mark.
calligraphy; good −, running −, flowing −, cursive −, legible −, copperplate −, round −, bold-hand.
cacography; *griffonage*, *barbouillage*; bad −, cramped −, crabbed −, illegible- hand; scribble etc. *v.*; *pattes de mouche*; ill-formed letters; pothooks and hangers.
stationery; pen, quill, goose-quill, reed; stylographic-, fountain-pen; pencil, style, stylus; paper, foolscap, parchment, vellum, papyrus, pad, tablet, block, note book, slate, marble, pillar, table, black board.
ink-bottle, -pot, -stand, -well, -horn; typewriter.
transcription etc. (*copy*) 21; inscription etc. (*record*) 551; superscription etc. (*indication*) 550.
composition, authorship; *cacoethes scribendi*.
writer, scribe, amanuensis, scrivener, secretary, clerk, penman, copyist, transcriber, quill-driver; writer for the press etc. (*author*) 593.
shorthand writer, stenographer; typewriter, typist.
V. write, pen; copy, engross; write out, − fair; transcribe; scribble, scrawl, scrabble, scratch; interline; stain paper; write down etc. (*record*) 551; sign etc. (*attest*) 467; take down, − in shorthand; typewrite, type.
compose, indite, draw up, redact, draft, formulate; dictate; inscribe, throw on paper, dash off; concoct.
take -up the pen, − pen in hand; shed −, spill −, dip one's pen in- ink.
Adj. writing etc. *v.*; written etc. *v.*; in -writing, − black and white; under one's hand.
uncial, Runic, cuneiform, hieroglyphical etc. *n.*
Adv. *currente calamo*; pen in hand.

591. Printing.—N. printing; block −, type-printing, lino-, mono-type; plate printing etc. (*engraving*) 558; the press etc. (*publication*) 531; composition.
print, letterpress, text, matter, standing type; context, note, page, column; over-running; head-, foot-line, title.
typography; stereo-, electro-, apro-type; type,

black letter, heavy type, font, fount; pi, pie; capitals etc. (*letters*) 561; diamond, pearl, nonpareil, minion, brevier, bourgeois, long primer, small pica, pica, english, great primer.

folio etc. (*book*) 593; copy, impression, pull, proof, galley –, author's –, page- proof, revise.

printer, compositor, reader; printer's devil.

V. print; compose; put –, go- to press; pass –, see- through the press; publish etc. 531; bring out; appear in –, rush into- print.

Adj. printed etc. *v.*; in type; typographical etc. *n.*

592. Correspondence.—N. correspondence, letter, epistle, note, *billet*, post-, letter-card, missive, circular, form letter; favor, *billet-doux*; des-, dis-patch; *bulletin*, communication etc. 532; these presents; rescript, -ion; post etc. (*messenger*) 534; letter writer, correspondent.

V. correspond, – with; write –, send a letter-to; keep up a correspondence; drop a line to; despatch; communicate with; circularize.

Adj. epistolary.

593. Book.—N. book, -let; writing, work, volume, tome, opuscule; tract, -ate; *livret*; *brochure*, *libretto*, handbook, treatise, text-book, codex, manual, pamphlet, monograph, enchiridion, circular, publication; book of poems; novel; chap-book.

part, issue, number, *livraison*; album, portfolio; periodical, serial, magazine, *ephemeris*, annual, journal.

paper, bill, sheet, broadsheet, screed; leaf, -let; fly-leaf, page; quire, ream.

chapter, section, head, article, paragraph, passage, clause, supplement, appendix; *feuilleton*. folio, quarto, octavo; duo-, sexto-, octo-decimo.

en-, cyclopedia, dictionary, lexicon, thesaurus, concordance, anthology, bibliography; compilation, compendium, catalogue etc. 86; library, bibliotheca; the press etc. (*publication*) 531.

writer, author, *littérateur*, essayist, journalist, publicist; scribe, penman, war –, special –, correspondent; pen, scribbler, the scribbling race; ghost, hack, literary hack, Grub-street writer; writer for –, gentlemen of –, representative of- the press; reporter, penny-a-liner; editor, sub-editor; playwright etc. 599; poet etc. 597.

bookseller, publisher; biblio-pole, -polist, - grapher; librarian; book -collector, – worm.

book -shop, – club, circulating –, lending –, public- library; publishing house.

knowledge of books, bibliography; book-learning etc. (*knowledge*) 490.

594. Description.—N. description, account, statement, report; *exposé* etc. (*disclosure*) 529; specification, particulars, scenario, plot; state –, summary- of facts; brief etc. (*abstract*) 596; return etc. (*record*) 551; *catalogue raisonné* etc. (*list*) 86; guide-book etc. (*information*) 527.

delineation etc. (*representation*) 554; sketch, vignette; monograph; minute –, detailed –, particular –, circumstantial –, graphic- account; narration, recital, rehearsal, relation.

histori-, chron-ography; historic Muse, Clio; history; bi-, autobi-ography; necrology, obituary.

narrative, history; memoir, memorials; annals etc. (*chronicle*) 551; tradition, legend, saga, epic, epos, story, tale, historiette; personal narrative, journal, letters, life, adventures, fortunes, experiences, confessions; anecdote, ana, *trait*.

work of fiction, short story, novelette, novel, romance, penny dreadful, shilling, shocker, Minerva press; fairy –, nursery- tale; fable, allegory, parable, apologue.

relator etc. *v.*; *raconteur*; historian etc. (*recorder*) 553; biographer, fabulist, novelist, story teller, romancer, teller of tales, spinner of yarns, anecdotist.

V. describe; set forth etc. (*state*) 535; draw a picture, picture; portray etc. (*represent*) 554; characterize, particularize; narrate, relate, recite, recount, sum up, run over, recapitulate, rehearse, fight one's battles over again.

unfold etc. (*disclose*) 529- a tale; tell; give –, render- an account of; report, make a report, draw up a statement.

detail; enter into –, descend to- -particulars, - details.

Adj. descriptive, graphic, narrative, epic, suggestive, well-drawn; historic; auto-, biographical, realistic, expository, tradition-al, -ary; legendary; fabulous, mythical; anecdotic, storied; described etc. *v.*

595. Dissertation.—N. dissertation, treatise, essay; *thesis*, theme; tract, -ate, -ation, excursus; discourse, memoir, disquisition, lecture, sermon, homily, pandect.

commentary-, review, *critique*, criticism, article; lead-er, -ing article, editorial; argument, running commentary.

investigation etc. (*inquiry*) 461; study etc. (*consideration*) 451; discussion etc. (*reasoning*) 476; exposition etc. (*explanation*) 522.

commentator, critic, essayist, pamphleteer; publicist, reviewer, leader writer, editor, annotator.

V. dissert –, descant –, write –, touch- upon a subject; dissertate; treat of –, take up –, ventilate –, discuss –, deal with –, go into –, canvass –, handle –, do justice to- a subject; comment, criticize, interpret etc. 522.

Adj. dis-cursive, -coursive; disquisitional, disquisitionary; expository, critical.

596. Compendium.—N. compend, -ium; abstract, *précis*, epitome, *multum in parvo*, analysis, pandect, digest, sum and substance, brief, abridgment, summary, *aperçu*, draft, minute, note; synopsis, textbook, *conspectus*, outlines, syllabus, contents, heads, prospectus.

album; scrap –, note –, memorandum –, commonplace- book; extracts, *excerpta*, cuttings; fugitive -pieces, – writings; *spicilegium*, flowers,

anthology, miscellany, *collectanea, analecta*; compilation.

recapitulation, *résumé*, review.

abbrevia-tion, -ture; contraction; shortening etc. 201; compression etc. 195.

V. abridge, abstract, epitomize, summarize; make – , prepare – , draw – , compile- an abstract etc. *n.*

recapitulate, review, skim, run over, sum up.

abbreviate etc. (*shorten*) 201; condense etc. (*compress*) 195; compile etc. (*collect*) 72; edit, blue pencil.

Adj. compendious, synoptic, analectic, analytical; abridged etc. *v.*

Adv. in -short, – epitome, – substance, – few words.

Phr. it lies in a nutshell.

597. Poetry.—N. poetry, poetics, poesy, Muse, Calliope, tuneful Nine, Parnassus, Helicon, Pierides, Pierian spring, afflatus, inspiration.

versification, rhyming, making verses; prosody, scansion, orthometry.

poem; epic, – poem; epopee, *epopaea*, ode, epode, idyl, lyric, eclogue, pastoral, bucolic, georgic, dithyramb, anacreontic, sonnet, roundelay, *rondel, rondoletto, rondeau, rondo*, triolet; madrigal, canzonet, *cento*, monody, elegy, palinode; rhapsody.

dramatic – , lyric- poetry; opera; posy, anthology.

song, ballad, lay; love – , drinking – , war – , folk – , sea- song; lullaby; music etc. 415; nursery rhymes.

[Bad poetry] doggerel, Hudibrastic verse, prose run mad; macaronics; macaronic – , leonineverse; runes.

canto, stanza, distich, verse, line, couplet, triplet, quatrain, sestet; *strophe, antistrophe*, refrain, chorus, burden.

verse, rhyme, assonance, crambo, meter, measure, foot, numbers, strain, rhythm; accentuation etc. (*voice*) 580; iambus, dactyl, spondee, trochee, anapaest etc.; hex-, pent-ameter; Alexandrine; blank verse, alliteration.

elegiacs etc. *adj.*; elegiac etc. *adj.* -verse, – meter, – poetry.

poet, – laureate; laureate; minor poet, bard, lyrist, scald, troubadour, *trouvère*; mistrel; minne-, meister-singer; *improvisatore*; versifier, sonneteer; ballad monger; rhym-er, -ist, -ester; poetaster.

V. poetize, sing, versify, make verses, rhyme, scan.

Adj. poetic, -al; lyric, -al; tuneful; epic; dithyrambic etc. *n.*; metrical; a-, catalectic; elegiac, iambic, trochaic, spondaic, anapest; Ionic, Sapphic, Alcaic, Pindaric.

598. Prose.—N. prose, – writer, pros-aism, -aist, -er.

V. prose, write prose.

write -prose, – in prose.

Adj. pros-y, -aic; unpoetical.

rhymeless, unrhymed, in prose, not in verse.

599. Drama.—N. drama, the -drama, – stage,

– theater, – play; theatricals, dramaturgy, histrionic art, buskin, sock, *cothurnus*, Melpomene and Thalia, Thespis.

play, stage-play, piece, five-act play, tragedy, comedy, opera, comic opera, *vaudeville, comedietta, lever de rideau*, curtain raiser, interlude, afterpiece, exode, farce, *divertissement, extravaganza*, burletta, harlequinade, pantomime, mimodrama, burlesque, *opéra bouffe*, musical comedy, review, revue, intimate revue, variety, cabaret entertainment, *ballet, spectacle*, masque, *drame, comédie drame*; melo-drama, -drame; *comédie larmoyante*, emotional drama, sensation drama, tragi-, farcical-comedy; mono-drame, - logue; duologue; trilogy; charade, *proverbe*; mystery, miracle – , morality- play.

act, scene, *tableau*; in-, intro-duction; pro-, epilogue, curtain; *libretto*, book, script.

performance, representation, show, *mise en scène*, stagery, *jeu de théâtre*, stage-craft; acting; gesture etc. 550; impersonation etc. 554; stage business, gag, patter, buffoonery.

theater; play-, opera-house; house; music hall; *cabaret*; amphitheater, circus, hippodrome; puppet-show, *fantoccini*; *marionnettes*, Punch and Judy.

cinema, -tograph-, picture – , theater, the pictures, the movies, the talkies.

auditory, *auditorium*, front of the house, stalls, boxes, balcony, dress – , upper- -circle, – boxes, amphitheater, pit, gallery; *foyer*; greenroom; dressing rooms, *coulisses.*

flat; drop, – scene; wing, screen, side-scene; transformation scene, curtain, act-drop, safety –, fire- curtain; *proscenium*, forestage.

stage, revolving stage, scene, the boards; star –, grave – , trap, mezzanine floor; flies; gridiron, floats, battens, footlights; lime – , spot – , flood – , bunch-lights; scenery, set, *décor*; orchestra.

theatrical -costume, – properties, props.

part, *rôle*, character, cast, *dramatis personae*; *répertoire.*

actor, player; stage – , strolling- player; old –, stager, performer; mime, -r; *artiste*; com-, tragedian, straight man; *tragédienne*, Thespian, Roscius, star.

pantomimist, clown, harlequin, *buffo*, buffoon, *farceur, grimacier*, pantaloon, columbine; *Pierrot, Pierrette*; punch, -inello; *pulcinell-o, -a*; mute, *figurante*, general utility; super, -numerary, extra.

mummer, guiser, guisard, gysart, masque.

mountebank, Jack Pudding; tumbler, posturemaster, acrobat, equilibrist, juggler, contortionist; *danseuse, ballerina*, ballet -dancer, – girl, *coryphée; bayadère, geisha*; chorus -singer, – girl.

company; first tragedian, *prima donna*, lead, leading lady, protagonist; *jeune premier*; juvenile lead, *débutant, -e*; light – , genteel – , low- comedy, – comedian; *soubrette*, walking gentleman, *amoroso*, heavy, heavy father, *ingénue, jeune veuve, commère, compère.*

property man, *costumier*, machinist, stage hand, electrician, prompter, call-boy; director, manager; stage – , acting – , business- manager; *entrepreneur, impresario*, producer, press agent.

dramatic -author, – writer; play-writer, -wright; dramatist, mimographer; dramatic critic.

V. act, play, perform; stage, produce, put on the stage; personate etc. 554; mimic etc. (*imitate*) 19; enact; play – , act – , go through – , perform- a

part; rehearse, spout, gag, rant; 'strut and fret one's hour upon a stage;' tread the -stage, − boards; come out;, star.

Adj. dramatic; theatric, -al; scenic, histrionic, anctorial, comic, tragic, buskined, farcical, tragicomic, melodramatic, operatic; stagey spectacular; stagestruck.

Adv. on the -stage, − boards; before -the floats, − an audience; in the limelight, behind the footlights; behind the scenes.

600. Will.—N. will, volition, conation, velleity; will and pleasure, free-will; freedom etc. 748; discretion; choice, inclination, intent, purpose, option etc. (*choice*) 609; voluntariness; spontane-ity, -ousness; originality.

pleasure, wish, desire, mind; frame of mind etc. (*inclination*) 602; intention etc. 620; predetermination etc. 611; self-control etc. determination etc. (*resolution*) 604; will-power.

V. will, list; see −, think- -fit; determine etc. (*resolve*) 604; settle etc. (*choose*) 609; volunteer.

have a will of one's own; do what one chooses etc. (*freedom*) 748; have it all one's own way; have one's -will, − own way.

use − , exercise- one's discretion; take -upon oneself, − one's own course, − the law into one's own hands; do -of one's own accord, − upon one's own -responsibility, − authority; take the bit between one's teeth; take responsibility; originate etc. (*cause*) 153.

Adj. voluntary, volitive, volitional, wilful; free etc. 748; optional; discretion-al, -ary; volitient; dictatorial.

minded etc. (*willing*) 602; prepense etc. (*predetermined*) 611; intended etc. 620; autocratic; unbidden etc. (bid etc. 741); spontaneous; original etc. (*causal*) 153.

Adv. voluntarily etc. *adj.*; at -will, − pleasure; *à -volonté, − discrétion; al piacere; ad -libitum, − arbitrium*; as -one thinks proper, − it seems good to.

of one's own -accord, − free will; *proprio −, suo −, ex mero- motu*; out of one's own head; by choice etc. 609; purposely etc. (*intentionally*) 620; deliberately etc. 611.

Phr. *stet pro ratione voluntas; sic volo sic jubeo.*

601. Necessity.—N. involuntariness; instinct, blind −, natural- impulse; inborn −, innate-proclivity; the force of circumstances.

necessi-ty, -tation, necessarianism; obligation; compulsion etc. 744; subjection etc. 749; stern −, hard −, dire −, imperious −, inexorable −, iron −, adverse- -necessity, − fate; what must be.

desti-ny, -nation; fatality, fate, *kismet*, doom, foredoom, election, predestination; pre-, foreordination; lot, fortune; fatalism, determinism; inevitableness etc. *adj.*; spell etc. 993.

star, -s; planet, -s; astral influence; sky, Fates, Norns, *Parcae*, Sisters three, Clotho, Lachesis, Atropos; book of fate; God's will, will of Heaven; wheel of Fortune, Ides of March, Hobson's choice.

last -shift, − resort; *dernier ressort; pis aller*

etc. (*substitute*) 147; necessaries etc. (*requirement*) 630.

necess-arian, -itarian; fatalist, determinist; automaton.

V. lie under a necessity; be -fated, − doomed, − destined etc., − in for, − under the necessity of; have no -choice, − alternative; be- obliged −, forced −, driven −, one's -fate etc. *n.*- to; be -pushed to the wall, − driven into a corner, − unable to help, − drawn irresistibly.

destine, doom, foredoom, devote; pre-destine, - ordain; cast a spell etc. 992; necessitate; compel etc. 744.

Adj. necessary; needful etc. (*requisite*) 630.

fated; destined etc. *v.*; fateful; elect; spell-bound.

compulsory etc. (*compel*) 744; uncontrollable, inevitable, unavoidable, irrestible, irrevocable, inexorable, binding; avoid-, resist-less; written in the book of fate.

involuntary, instinctive, automatic, blind, mechanical; un-conscious, -witting, -thinking; unintentional etc. (*undesigned*) 621; impulsive etc. 612.

Adv. necessarily etc. *adv.*; of -necessity, − course; *ex necessitate rei*; needs must; perforce etc. 744; *nolens volens*; will he nil he, willy nilly, *bon gré mal gré*, willing or unwilling, *coûte que coûte*, forcefully.

faute de mieux; by stress of; if need be.

Phr. it cannot be helped; there is no- help for, − helping- it; it -will, − must, − must needs- be, − be so, − have its way; the die is cast; *jacta est alea; che sarà sarà*; 'it is written;' one's- days are numbered, − fate is sealed; *Fata obstant; diis aliter visum.*

602. Willingness.—N. willingness, voluntariness etc. *adj.*; willing mind, heart.

disposition, inclination, leaning, *animus*; frame of mind, humor, mood, vein; bent etc. (*turn of mind*) 820; *penchant* etc. (*desire*) 865; aptitude etc. 698.

doc-ility, -ibleness, tractability; persuasi-bleness, -bility; pliability etc. (*softness*) 324.

geniality, cordiality; goodwill; alacrity, readiness, earnestness, forwardness, enthusiasm; zeal, eagerness etc. (*desire*) 865.

assent etc. 488; compliance etc. 762; pleasure etc. (*will*) 600.

labor of love, self-appointed task; volunteer, - ing, gratuitous service; unpaid worker, amateur.

V. be -willing etc. *adj.*; incline, lean to, mind, propend; had as lief; lend −, give −, turn- a willing ear; have -a, − half a, − a great- mind to; hold −, cling- to; desire etc. 865.

see −, think- -good, − fit, − proper; acquiescence etc. (*assent*) 488; comply with etc. 762.

swallow −, nibble at- the bait; gorge the hook; swallow hook, line and sinker; have −, make- no scruple of; make no bones of; jump −, catch- at; meet half way; volunteer, offer oneself etc. 763.

Adj. willing, minded, fain, disposed, inclined, favorable, favorably- minded, -inclined, -disposed; nothing loth; in the -vein, − mood, − humor, − mind.

ready, forward, enthusiastic, earnest, eager; bent upon etc. (*desirous*) 865; predisposed, propense.

docile; persua-dable, -sible; suasible, easily persuaded, facile, easy-going; amenable; tractable etc.
(*pliant*) 324; genial, gracious, cordial, hearty; content etc. (*assenting*) 488.

voluntary, gratuitous, spontaneous; unasked etc.
(ask etc. 765); unforced etc. (*free*) 748.

Adv. willing etc. *adj.*; fain, freely, as lief, heart
and soul; with -pleasure, – all one's heart, – open
arms; with -good, – right good- will; *de bonne
volonté, ex animo; con amore*, heart in hand,
nothing loth, without reluctance, of one's own accord, graciously, with a good grace, without demur.

à la bonne heure; by all -means, – manner of
means; to one's heart's content; yes etc. (*assent*)
488.

Int. sure, -ly! of course!

603. Unwillingness.—N. unwillingness etc.
adj.; indispos-ition, -edness; disinclination, aver-
sation, aversion; nolleity, nolition; renitence; reluctance; indifference etc. 866; backwardness etc.
adj.; slowness etc. 275; want of -alacrity, –
readiness; indocility etc. (*obstinacy*) 606.

scrupul-ousness, -osity; qualms of conscience,
delicacy, demur, scruple, qualm, shrinking, recoil;
hesitation etc. (*irresolution*) 605; fastidiousness
etc. 868.

averseness etc. (*dislike*) 867; dissent etc. 489;
refusal etc. 764.

slacker, scrimshanker, *embusqué*, unwilling
worker, forced labor.

V. be -unwilling etc. *adj.*; nill; dislike etc. 867;
grudge, begrudge; not be able to find it in one's
heart to, not have the stomach to.

demur, stick at, scruple, stickle; hang fire, run
rusty, slack, shirk, scamp, give up, fight shy of, not
pull fair; recoil, shrink, swerve; hesitate etc. 605;
avoid etc. 623.

oppose etc. 708; dissent etc. 489; refuse etc.
764.

Adj. unwilling; not in the vein, loth, shy of,
disinclined, indisposed, averse, reluctant, not content; adverse etc. (*opposed*) 708; laggard, back-
ward, remiss, slack, slow to; renitent; indifferent
etc. 866; scrupulous; squeamish etc. (*fastidious*)
868; repugnant etc. (*dislike*) 867; rest-iff, -ive;
demurring etc. *v.*; unconsenting etc. (*refusing*)
764; involuntary etc. 601; grudging, irreconcilable.

Adv. unwilling etc. *adj.*; grudgingly, with a
heavy heart; with -a bad, – an ill- grace; against
–, sore against- -one's wishes, – one's will, – the
grain; *invitâ Minervâ; à contre coeur; malgré soi*;
in spite of -one's teeth, – oneself; *nolens volens*
etc. (*necessity*) 601; perforce etc. 744; under
protest; no etc. 536; not for the world, far be it
from me; not if I can help it; if I must I must.

604. Resolution.—N. determination, will; iron
–, unconquerable- will; will of one's own,
decision, resolution, backbone, grit; strength of -
mind, – will; resolve etc. (*intent*) 620; *intransigeance*; firmness etc. (*stability*) 150; energy,
manliness, vigor, game, pluck; resoluteness etc.
(*courage*) 861; zeal etc. 682; *aplomb*; desperation;
devot-ion, -edness.

mastery over self; self-control, -command, -

mastery, -possession, -reliance, -government, -
restraint, -conquest, -denial; moral -courage, –
strength, – fiber; perseverance etc. 604a; tenacity;
obstinacy etc. 606; bull-dog; British lion.

V. have -determination etc. *n.*; know one's own
mind; be -resolved etc. *adj.*; make up one's mind,
will resolve, determine; decide etc. (*judgment*)
480; form –, come to- a -determination, –
resolution, – resolve; conclude, fix, seal, determine once for all, bring to a crisis, drive matters to
an extremity; take a decisive step etc. (*choice*) 609;
take upon oneself etc. (*undertake*) 676.

devote oneself –, give oneself up- to; throw
away the scabbard, kick down the ladder, nail
one's colors to the mast, set one's back against the
wall, set one's teeth, put one's foot down, burn
one's bridges, take one's stand; stand firm etc.
(*stability*) 150; steel oneself; stand no nonsense,
not listen to the voice of the charmer.

buckle to; put –, lay –, set- one's shoulder to
the wheel; put one's heart into; run the gantlet,
make a dash at, take the bull by the horns; beard
the lion in his den; rush –, plunge- *in medias res*;
go in for; insist upon, make a point of; set one's
heart, – mind- upon.

stick at nothing; make short work of etc. (*activity*) 682; not stick at trifles; go -all lengths, –
the whole hog; persist etc. (*persevere*) 604a; go
down with colors flying, die game; go through fire
and water, ride in the whirlwind and direct the
storm.

Adj. resolved etc. *v.*determined; strong-willed, -
minded; resolute etc. (*brave*) 861; self-possessed,
plucky, tenacious; decided, definitive, peremptory;
un-hesitating, -flinching, -shrinking; firm, cast iron,
indomitable, game to the backbone; inexorable,
relentless, not to be -shaken, – put down; *tenax
propositi*; inflexible etc. (*hard*) 323; obstinate etc.
606; steady etc. (*persevering*) 604a; unbending,
unyielding, irrevocable; firm as a rock; grim.

earnest, serious; set –, bent –, intent- upon.
steeled –, proof- against; *in utrumque paratus*.

Adv. resolutely etc. *adj.*; in –, in good- earnest;
seriously, joking apart, earnestly, heart and soul; on
one's metal; manfully, like a man, with a high
hand; with a strong hand etc. (*exertion*) 686.

at any -rate, – risk, – hazard, – price, –
cost, – sacrifice; at all -hazards, – risks, –
events; cost what it may; *coûte que coûte; à tort et
à travers*; once for all; neck or nothing; rain or
shine; with colors nailed to the mast.

Phr. *spes sibi quisque*.

604a. Perseverance. —N. perseverance; continuance etc. (*inaction*) 143; permanence etc. (*absence of change*) 141; firmness etc. (*stability*) 150.

constancy, steadiness; singleness –, tenacity- of
purpose; persistence, plodding, patience; sedulity
etc. (*industry*) 682; pertina-cy, -city, -ciousness;
iteration etc. 104.

bottom, game, pluck, stamina, backbone, grit;
indefatiga-bility, -bleness; bulldog courage.

V. persevere, persist; hold -on, – out; die in the
last ditch, be in at the death; stick –, cling –,
adhere- to ; stick to one's text, keep on; keep to –,
maintain- one's -course, – ground; bear –, keep
–, hold-up; plod; stick to work etc. (*work*) 686;

continue etc. 143; follow up; die -in harness, – at one's post.

Adj. persevering, constant; stead-y, -fast; undeviating, -wavering, -faltering, -swerving, -flinching, -sleeping, -flagging, -drooping; steady as time; uninter-, un-remitting; plodding; industrious etc. 682; strenuous etc. 686; pertinacious; persisting, -ent.

solid, sturdy, staunch, stanch, ture to oneself; unchangeable etc. 150; unconquerable etc. (*strong*) 159; indomitable, game to the last, indefatigable, untiring, unwearied, never tiring.

Adv. through -evil report and good report, – thick and thin, – fire and water; *per fas et nefas*; without let, sink or swim, at any price, *vogue la galère*; in sickness and in health.

Phr. never say die; *vestigia nulla retrorsum*.

605. Irresolution.—N. irresolution, infirmity of purpose, indecision; in-, un-determination, loss of will power; unsettlement; uncertainty etc. 475; demur, suspense; hesi-tating etc. *v.*, -tation, -tancy; vacillation; ambivalence; changeableness etc. 149; fluctuation; alternation etc. (*oscillation*) 314; caprice etc. 608; lukewarmness.

fickleness, levity, *légèreté*; pliancy etc. (*softness*) 324; weakness; timidity etc. 860; cowardice etc. 862; half measures.

waverer, ass between two bundles of hay; shuttlecock, butterfly; timeserver, opportunist, turn coat.

V. be -irresolute etc. *adj.*; hang –, keep- in suspense; heave '*ad referendum*;' think twice about, pause; dawdle etc. (*inactivity*) 683; remain neuter; dilly dally. hesitate, boggle, hover, wobble, shilly-shally, hum and haw, demur, not know one's own mind; debate, balance; dally –, coquet- with; will and will not, *chasser-balancer*; go half-way, compromise, make a compromise; be thrown off one's balance, stagger like a drunken man; be afraid etc. 860; let 'I dare not' wait upon 'I would;' falter, waver.

vacillate etc. 149; change etc. 140; retract etc. 607; fluctuate; alternate etc. (*oscillate*) 314; keep off and on, play fast and loose; blow hot and cold etc. (*caprice*) 608.

shuffle, palter, blink; trim.

Adj. irresolute, infirm of purpose, double-minded, half-hearted; un-decided, -resolved, -determined; drifting; shilly-shally; fidgety, tremulous; wobbly; hesitating etc. *v.*; off one's balance; at a loss etc. (*uncertain*) 475.

vacillating etc. *v.*; unsteady etc. (*changeable*) 149; unsteadfast, fickle, unreliable, irresponsible, unstable, without ballast; capricious etc. 608; volatile, frothy; light, -some, -minded; giddy; fast and loose.

weak, feeble-minded, frail; timid etc. 860; cowardly etc. 862; facile; pliant etc. (*soft*) 324; unable to say 'no,' easy-going.

revocable, reversible.

Adv. irresolutely etc. *adj.*; irresolvedly; in faltering accents; off and on; from pillar to post; see-saw etc. 314.

Int. 'how happy could I be with either!'

606. Obstinacy.—N. obstinateness etc. *adj.*; obstinacy, tenacity; perseverance etc. 604*a*; im-

movability; old school; inflexibility etc. (*hardness*) 323; obdur-acy, -ation; dogged resolution; resolution etc. 604; ruling passion; blind side.

self-will, contumacy, perversity; pervica-cy, -city; indocility.

bigotry, intolerance, dogmatism; opinia-try, -tiveness; fixed idea etc.; intractibility, incorrigibility; (*prejudgment*) 481; fanaticism, zealotry, infatuation, monomania, opinionativeness.

mule; opin-ionist, -ionatist, -iator, -ator; stickler, dogmatist, die-hard, bitter-ender; bigot; zealot, enthusiast, fanatic.

V. be -obstinate etc. *adj.*; stickle, take no denial, fly in the face of facts; opinionate, be wedded to an opinion, hug a belief; have one's own way etc. (*will*) 600; persist etc. (*persevere*) 604*a*; have –, insist on having- the last word.

die -hard, – fighting, fight -against destiny, – to the last ditch; not yield an inch, stand out.

Adj. obstinate, tenacious, stubborn, obdurate, case-hardened; inflexible etc. (*hard*) 323; immovable, not to be moved; inert etc. 172; unchangeable etc. 150; inexorable etc. (*determined*) 604; mulish, obstinate as a mule, pig-headed.

dogged; sullen, sulky; un-moved, -influenced, -affected.

wilful, self-willed, perverse; res-ty, -tive, -tiff; pervicacious, wayward, refractory, unruly; head-y, -strong; *entete*; contumacious; cross-grained.

arbitrary, dogmatic, opinionated, positive, bigoted; prejudiced etc. 481; prepossessed, infatuated; stiff-backed, -necked, -hearted; hard-mouthed, hidebound; unyielding; im-pervious, -practicable, -persuasible; unpersuadable; in-, un-tractable; incorrigible, deaf to advice, impervious to reason; crotchety etc. 608.

Adv. obstinately etc. *adj.*

Phr. *non possumus*; no surrender.

607. Tergiversation.—N. change of -mind, – intention, – purpose; afterthought.

tergiversation, recantation; palinode, -ody; renunciation; abjur-ation, -ement; defection etc. (*relinquishment*) 624; going over etc. *v.*; apostasy; retract-ion, -ation; withdrawal, disavowal etc. (*negation*) 536; revo-cation, -kement; reversal; repentance etc. 950; *redintegratio amoris*.

coquetry, flirtation; vacillation etc. 605; backsliding, recidivation.

turn-coat, | -tippet; rat, apostate, renegade, mugwump; con-, per-vert; proselyte, deserter; backslider, recidivist; black leg.

time-server, -pleaser; timist, Vicar of Bray, trimmer, ambidexter; weathercock etc. (*changeable*) 149; Janus.

V. change one's -mind, – intention, – purpose, – note; abjure, renounce; withdraw from etc. (*relinquish*) 624; wheel –, turn –, veer- round; turn a *pirouette*; go over –, pass –, change –, skip- from one side to another; go to the right about; box the compass, shift one's ground, go upon another tack; back down, crawl, crawfish.

apostatize, change sides, go over, rat; recant, retract; revoke; rescind etc. (*abrogate*) 756; recall, forswear, abjure, unsay; come -over, – round- to an opinion.

draw in one's horns, eat one's words; eat –,

swallow- the leek; swerve, flinch, back out of, retrace one's steps, think better of it; come back −, return- to one's first love; turn over a new leaf etc. (*repent*) 950.

trim, shuffle, play fast and loose, blow hot and cold, coquet, flirt, hold with the hare but run with the hounds; straddle; *nager entre deux eaux*; wait to see how the -cat jumps, − wind blows.

Adj. changeful etc. 149; irresolute etc. 605; ductile, slippery as an eel, trimming, ambidextrous, timeserving; coquetting etc. *v.*

revocatory, reactionary.

Phr. 'a change came o'er the spirit of my dream.'

608. Caprice.—N. caprice, fancy, humor; whim, -sey, -wham; crotchet, *capriccio*, quirk, freak, maggot, fad, vagary, prank, fit, flim-flam, *escapade*, *boutade*, wild-goose chase; capriciousness etc. *adj.*; kink.

V. be -capricious etc. *adj.*; have a maggot in the brain; take it into one's head, strain at a gnat and swallow a camel; blow hot and cold; play -fast and loose, − fantastic tricks.

Adj. capricious; erratic, eccentric, fitful, hysterical; full of -whims etc. *n.*; maggoty; inconsistent, fanciful, fantastic, whimsical, crotchety, particular, humorsome, freakish, skittish, wanton, wayward; contrary; captious; arbitrary; unrestrained, undisciplined; not amenable to reason; uncomfortable etc. 83; penny wise and pound foolish; fickle etc. (*irresolute*) 605; frivolous, sleeveless, giddy, volatile.

Adv. by fits and starts, without rhyme or reason, at one's own sweet will.

Phr. *nil fuit unquam six impar sibi*; the deuce is in him.

609. Choice.—N. choice, option; discretion etc. (*volition*) 600; preoption; alternative; dilemma; *ambarras de choix*; adoption, co-optation; novation; decision etc. (*judgment*) 480.

election, poll, ballot, vote, voice, suffrage, plumper, cumulative vote; *plebiscitum, plébiscite, vox populi; referendum*, electioneering; voting etc. *v.*; franchise; ballot box; slate, ticket.

selection, excerption, gleaning, eclecticism; *excerpta*, gleanings, cuttings, scissors and paste; pick etc. (*best*) 650.

preference, prelation; predilection etc. (*desire*) 865.

V. offer for one's choice, set before; hold out −, present −, offer- the alternative; put to the vote.

use −, exercise −, one's- -discretion, − option; adopt −, take up, embrace, espouse; choose, elect, co-opt; take −, make- one's choice; make choice of, fix upon.

vote, poll, hold up one's hand; divide.

settle; decide etc. (*adjudge*) 480; list etc. (*will*) 600; make up one's mind etc. (*resolve*) 604.

select; pick, − and choose; pick −, single- out, excerpt; cull, glean, winnow; sift −, separate −, winnow- the chaff from the wheat; pick up, pitch upon; pick one's way; indulge one's fancy.

set apart, reserve, mark out for; mark etc. 550.

prefer; have -rather, − as lief; fancy etc. (*desire*) 865; be persuaded etc. 615.

take a -decided, − decisive- step; commit oneself to a course; pass −, cross- the Rubicon; cast in one's lot with; take for better or for worse.

Adj. optional; co-optative; discretional etc. (*voluntary*) 600; on approval.

eclectic; choosing etc. *v.*; preferential; chosen etc. *v.*; choice etc. (*good*) 648.

Adv. optionally etc. *adj.*; at pleasure etc. (*will*) 600; either, − the one or the other; at the option of; whether or not; once for all; for one's money.

by -choice, − preference; in preference; rather, before.

609a. Absence of Choice.—N. no −, Hobson's- choice; first come, first served; necessity etc. 601; not a pin to choose etc. (*equality*) 27; any, the first that comes.

neutrality, indifference; indecision etc. (*irresolution*) 605.

V. be -neutral etc. *adj.*; have no choice; waive, not vote; abstain −, refrain- from voting; leave undecided; make a virtue of necessity.

Adj. neu-tral, -ter; indifferent; undecided etc. (*irresolute*) 605.

Adv. either etc. (*choice*) 609.*

610. Rejection.—N. rejection, repudiation, exclusion; declination; refusal etc. 764.

V. reject; set −, lay- aside; give up; decline etc. (*refuse*) 764; exclude, except, eliminate; pluck, spin; cast.

repudiate, scout, set at naught; fling −, cast −, thrown −, toss- -to the winds, − to the dogs, − overboard, − away; send to the right about; disclaim etc. (*deny*) 536; discard etc. (*eject*) 297, (*have done with*) 678.

Adj. rejected etc. *v.*; reject-aneous, -itious; not chosen etc. 609, − to be thought of; out of the question.

Adv. neither, − the one nor the other; no etc. 536.

Phr. *non haec in foedera.*

611. Predetermination.—N. premeditation, -deliberation, -determination, -destination; foreordination; foregone conclusion; *parti pris*; resolve, propendency; intention etc. 620; project etc. 626.

V. pre-determine, -destine, -meditate, -resolve, -concert; foreordain; resolve beforehand.

Adj. pre-pense, -meditated etc. *v.*, -designed; advised, studied, designed, calculated; aforethought; intended etc. 620; foregone.

well-laid, -devised, -weighed; maturely considered; cut and dried; cunning.

Adv. advisedly etc. *adj.*; with premeditation, deliberately, all things considered, with eyes open, in cold blood; intentionally etc. 620.

612. Impulse.—N. impulse, sudden thought; *impromptu*, improvisation; inspiration, hunch, flash, spurt.

improvisatore, *improvisatrice,* improviser, extemporizer; creature of impulse.

V. flash on the mind.

say what comes uppermost; improvise, extemporize; rise to the occasion; spurt.

Adj. extemporaneous, impulsive, indeliberate; improvis-ed, -ate, -atory; un-, unpre-meditated; *improvisé*; unprompted, -guided; natural, unguarded; spontaneous etc. (*voluntary*) 600; instinctive etc. 601.

Adv. extem-pore, -poraneously; offhand, *impromptu, à l'improviste*; improviso; on the spur of the -moment, — occasion.

613. Habit.—N. habit, -ude; assuetude, - faction; wont; run, way.

common —, general —, natural —, ordinary —, habitual- -course, — run, — state- of things; matter of course; beaten -path, — track, — ground.

prescription, custom, use, usage, immemorial usage, practice; tradition; prevalence, observance; conventionalism, -ity; mode, fashion, vogue; *etiquette* etc. (*gentility*) 852; order of the day, cry; conformity etc. 82.

habitué, addict.

one's old way, old school, consuetude, *veteris vestigia flammae; laudator temporis acti.*

rule, standing order, precedent, routine; redtape, -tapism; pipe-clay; rut, groove.

cacoëthes; bad —, confirmed —, inveterate —, intrinsic etc. 5- habit; addiction, trick.

training etc. (*education*) 537; seasoning, hardening, inurement; radication; second nature, acclimatization; knack etc. (*skill*) 698.

V. be -wont etc. *adj.*

fall into a custom etc. (*conform to*) 82; tread —, follow- the beaten -track, — path; *stare super antiquas vias;* move in a rut, run on in a groove, go round like a horse in a mill, go on in the old jobtrot way.

habituate, inure, harden, season, caseharden; accustom, familiarize; naturalize, acclimatize; keep one's hand in; train etc. (*educate*) 537.

get into the -way, — knack- of; learn etc. 539; cling —, adhere- to; repeat etc. 104; acquire —, contract —, fall into- a -habit, — trick; addict oneself —, take- to; accustom oneself to.

be -habitual etc. *adj.*; prevail; come into use, become a habit, take root; gain —, grow- upon one.

Adj. habitual; ac-, customary; prescriptive; accustomed etc. *v.*; traditional; of -daily, — everyday- occurrence; wonted, usual, general, ordinary, common, frequent, every-day, household, jog-trot; well-trodden, -known; familiar, vernacular, trite, commonplace, banal, bromidic, conventional, regular, set, stock, officinal, established, stereotyped; pre-vailing, -valent; current, received, acknowledged, recognized, accredited; of course, admitted, understood.

conformable etc. 82; according to -use, — custom, — routine; in -vogue, — fashion; fashionable etc. (*genteel*) 852.

wont; used — given — addicted —, attuned —, habituated etc. *v.*- to; in the habit of; *habitué;* at home in etc. (*skilful*) 698; seasoned; permeated —, imbued- with; devoted —, wedded- to; never free from.

hackneyed, fixed, rooted, deep-rooted, ingrafted, permanent, inveterate, besetting; naturalized; ingrained etc. (*intrinsic*) 5.

Adv. habitually etc. *adj.*; always etc. (*uniformly*) 16.

as -usual, — is one's wont, — things go, — the world goes, — the sparks fly upwards; *more -suo, — solito.*

as a rule, for the most part; generally etc. *adj.*; most often, — frequently.

Phr. *cela s'entend.*

614. Desuetude.—N. desuetude, disusage; disuse etc. 678; want of -habit, — practice; inusitation; newness to; new brooms.

infraction of usage etc. (*unconformity*) 83; non-prevalence; 'a custom more honored in the breach than the observance.'

V. be -unaccustomed etc. *adj.*; leave off —, cast off —, break off —, wean oneself of —, violate —, break through —, infringe- -a habit, — a custom, — a usage; break one's fetters; disuse etc. 678; wear off.

Adj. un-accustomed, -used, -wonted, -seasoned, -inured, -habituated, -trained; new; green etc. (*unskilled*) 699; fresh, original, unhackneyed.

unusual etc. (*unconformable*) 83; unconventional, non-observant; disused etc. 678.

Adv. just for once.

615. Motive.—N. motive, springs of action.

reason, ground, call, principle; mainspring, *primum mobile,* key-stone; the why and the wherefore; *pro* and *con,* reason why; secret —, ulterior- motive, *arrière-pensée;* intention etc. 620.

inducement, consideration; attraction etc. 288; loadstone; magnet, -ism, -ic force; allect-ation, -ive; temptation, enticement, *agacerie,* allurement, witchery; bewitch-ment, -ery; charm; spell etc. 993; fascination, blandishment, cajolery; seduc-tion, - ement; honeyed words, voice of the tempter, son of the Sirens; forbidden fruit, golden apple.

persuasi-bility, -bleness; attractability; impress-, suscept-ibility; softness; persuas-, attract-iveness; tantalization.

influence, prompting, dictate, instance; impuls-e, -ion; incit-ement, -ation; press, instigation; provocation etc. (*excitation of feeling*) 824; inspiration; per-, suasion; encouragement, advocacy; exhortation, advice etc. 695; solicitation etc. (*request*) 765; lobbying.

incentive, stimulus, spur, fillip, whip, goad, rowel, provocative, whet, dram.

bribe, lure, decoy, — duck; bait, trail of a red herring; bribery and corruption; sop, — for Cerberus.

prompter, tempter; seduc-er, -tor; suggester, coaxer, wheedler; instigator, firebrand, incendiary; Siren, Circe; *agent provocateur;* lobbyist.

V. induce, move; draw, — on; bring in its train, give an -impulse etc. *n.*- to; inspire; put up to, prompt, call up; attract, beckon.

stimulate etc. (*excite*) 824; spirit up, inspirit; a-, rouse; ecphorize; animate, incite, provoke, instigate, set on, actuate; act —, work —, operate-

upon; encourage; pat –, clap- on the -back, – shoulder.

influence, weigh with, bias, sway, incline, dispose, predispose, turn the scale, inoculate; lead, – by the nose; have –, exercise- influence- -with, – over, – upon; go –, come- round one; turn the head, magnetize.

persuade; prevail -with, – upon; overcome, carry; bring -round, – to one's senses; draw –, win –, gain –, come –, talk- over; procure, enlist, engage; invite, court.

tempt, seduce, overpersuade, entice, allure, captivate, fascinate, intrigue, bewitch, carry away, charm, conciliate, wheedle, coax, lure, suggest; inveigle; tantalize; cajole etc. (deceive) 545.

tamper with, bribe, suborn, grease the palm, bait with a silver hook, gild the pill, make things pleasant, put a sop into the pan, throw a sop to, bait the hook.

enforce, force; impel etc. (push) 276; propel etc. 284; whip, lash, goad, spur, prick, urge; egg –, hound –, hurry- on; drag etc. 285; exhort; advise etc. 695; call upon etc.; press etc. (request) 765; advocate.

set -an example, – the fashion; keep in countenance; back up.

be -persuaded etc.; yield to temptation, come round; concede etc. (consent) 762; obey a call; follow -advice, – the bent, – the dictates of; act on principle.

Adj. impulsive, motive; suas-, persuas-, hortative, -ory; protreptical; inviting, tempting etc. v.; seductive, attractive, irresistible; fascinating etc. (pleasing) 829; provocative etc. (exciting) 824.

induced etc. v.; disposed; persuadable etc. (docile) 602; spellbound; instinct –, smitten- with; inspired etc. v.- by.

Adv. because, therefore etc. (cause) 155; from -this, – that- motive; for -this, – that- reason; for; by reason –, for the sake –, on the score –, on account- of; out of, from, as, forasmuch as.

for all the world; on principle.

615a. Absence of Motive.—N. absence of motive; caprice etc. 608; chance etc. (absence of design) 621.

V. have no motive; scruple etc. (be unwilling) 603.

Adj. without rhyme or reason; aimless etc. (chance) 621.

Adv. capriciously; out of mere caprice.

616. Dissuasion.—N. dissuasion, dehortation, expostulation, remonstrance; deprecation etc. 766.

discouragement, damper, wet blanket; warning.

cohibition etc. (restraint) 751; curb etc. (means of restraint) 752; check etc. (hindrance) 706.

reluctance etc. (unwillingness) 603; contraindication.

V. dissuade, dehort, cry out against, remonstrate, expostulate, warn, contraindicate.

disincline, indispose, shake, stagger; dispirit; discourage, -hearten, -enchant; deter; hold –, keep-back etc. (restrain) 751; render -averse etc. 603;

repel; turn aside etc. (deviation) 279; wean from; act as a drag etc. (hinder) 706; throw cold water on, damp, cool, chill, blunt, calm, quiet, quench; deprecate etc. 766.

Adj. dissuading etc. v.; dissuasive; dehortatory, expostulatory; monit-ive, -ory.

dissuaded etc. v.; uninduced etc. (induce etc. 615); unpersuadable etc. (obstinate) 606; averse etc. (unwilling) 603; repugnant etc. (dislike) 867.

617. Plea. [Ostensible motive, ground, or reason assigned.]—N. plea, pretext; allegation, advocation; ostensible -motive, – ground, – reason; excuse etc. (vindication) 937; color; gloss, guise.

loop-, starting-hole; how to creep out of, salvo, come off.

handle, peg to hang on room, locus standi; stalking horse, cheval de bataille, cue.

pretence etc. (untruth) 546; put off, subterfuge, dust thrown in the eyes; blind; moonshine; mere –, shallow- pretext; lame -excuse, – apology, tub to a whale; flase plea, sour grapes; makeshift, shift, white lie; special pleading etc. (sophistry) 477; soft sawder etc. (flattery) 933.

V. plead, allege; shelter oneself under the plea of; excuse etc. (vindicate) 937; gloss over; lend a color to; furnish a -handle etc. n.; make a -pretext, –handle- of; use as a plea etc. n.; take one's stand upon, make capital out of; pretend etc. (lie) 544.

Adj. ostensible etc. (manifest) 525; excusing; alleged, apologetic; pretended etc. 545.

Adv. ostensibly; under -color, – the plea, – the pretence- of.

618. Good.—N. good, benefit, advantage; improvement etc. 658; interest, service, behoof, behalf; weal; main chance, summum bonum, common weal; 'consummation devoutly to be wished;' gain, boot; profit, harvest.

boon etc. (gift) 784; good turn; blessing, benison; world of good; piece of good -luck, – fortune; nuts, prize, windfall, godsend, waif, treasure trove.

good fortune etc. (prosperity) 734; happiness etc. 827.

[Source of good] goodness etc. 648; utility etc. 644; remedy etc. 662; pleasure-giving etc. 829.

Adj. commendable etc. 931; useful etc. 644; good etc., beneficial etc. 648.

V. benefit, profit, advantage, serve, help, avail; do good to, gain, prosper, flourish.

Adv. well, aright, satisfactorily, favorably, not amiss; all for the best; to one's -advantage etc. n.; in one's -favor, – interest etc. n.

Phr. so far so good.

619. Evil.—N. evil, ill, harm, hurt, mischief, nuisance; machinations of the devil, Pandora's box, ills that flesh is heir to.

blow, buffet, stroke, scratch, bruise, wound, gash, mutilation; mortal -blow, – wound; im-

medicabile vulnus; damage, loss etc. (*deterioration*) 659.

disadvantage, prejudice, drawback.

disaster, accident, casualty; mishap etc. (*misfortune*) 735; bad job, devil to pay; calamity, bale, woe, catastrophe, tragedy; ruin etc. (*destruction*) 162; adversity etc. 735.

mental suffering etc. 828. [Evil spirit] demon etc. 980. [Cause of evil] bane etc. 663. [Production of evil] badness etc. 649; painfulness etc. 830; evil doer etc. 913.

outrage, wrong, injury, foul play; bad –, ill-turn; disservice; spoliation etc. 791; grievance, crying evil.

V. be in trouble etc. (*adversity*) 735; harm, injure, hurt, do disservice to.

Adj. disastrous, bad etc. 649; awry, out of joint; disadvantageous, injurious, harmful.

Adv. amiss, wrong, ill, to one's cost.

620. Intention.—N. intent, -ion, -ionality; purpose; *quo animo*; project etc. 626; undertaking etc. 676; predetermination etc. 611; design, ambition.

contemplation, mind, *animus*, view, purview, proposal; study; look out.

final cause; *raison d'être*; *cui bono*; object, aim, end; 'the be all and the end all;' drift etc. (*meaning*) 516; tendency etc. 176; destination, mark, point, butt, goal, target, bull's-eye, quintain; prey, quarry, game.

decision, determination, resolve; set –, settled-purpose; *ultimatum*; resolution etc. 604; wish etc. 865; *arrière-pensée*; motive etc. 615.

[Study of final causes] teleology.

V. intend, purpose, design, mean; have to; propose to oneself; harbor a design; have in -view, – contemplation, – one's eye, – *petto*; have an eye to.

bid –, labor- for; be –, aspire –, endeavour- after; be –, aim –, drive –, point –, level- at; take aim; set before oneself; study to.

take upon oneself etc. (*undertake*) 676; take into one's head; meditate, contemplate; think –, dream –, talk- of; premeditate etc. 611; compass, calculate; dest-ine, -inate, propose.

project etc. (*plan*) 626; have a mind to etc. (*be willing*) 602; desire etc. 865; pursue etc. 622.

Adj. intended etc. *v.*; intentional, advised, express, determinate; prepense etc. 611; bound for; intending etc. *v.*; minded, disposed, inclined; bent upon etc. (*earnest*) 604; at stake, on the -anvil, – *tapis*; in -view; – prospect, – the breast of; *in petto*; teleological.

Adv. intentionally etc. *adj.*; advisedly, wittingly, knowingly, designedly, purposely, on purpose, by design, studiously, pointedly; with -intent etc. *n.*; deliberately etc. (*with premeditation*) 611; with one's eyes open, in cold blood.

for; with -a view, – an eye- to; in order -to, – that; to the end –, with the intent- that; for the purpose –, with the view –, in contemplation -, on account- of.

in pursuance of, pursuant to; *quo animo*; to all intents and purposes.

621. Chance.†[Absence of purpose in the succession of events.]—**N.** chance etc. 156; lot, fate etc. (*necessity*) 601; luck; good luck etc. (*good*) 618; bad luck etc. 735; wheel of fortune; mascot; swastika.

speculation, venture, stake, flutter, flier, gamble, game of chance; mere –, random- shot; blind bargain, leap in the dark; pig in a poke etc. (*uncertainty*) 475; fluke, pot-luck.

drawing lots; sorti-legy, -tion; *sortes*, – *Virgilianae*; *rouge et noir*, hazard, *roulette*, pitch and toss, chuck-farthing, cup-tossing, heads or tails, cross and pile, wager; bet, -ting; risk, stake, plunge; gambling; the turf.

stock exchange, bourse, board of trade, curb exchange.

gaming-, gambling-, betting-house; hell; betting ring, totalizator; dice, – box; dicer; gam-bler, -ester, plunger, stock operator, manipulator, punter; man of the turf; adventurer, speculator; bookmaker, layer, backer.

V. chance etc. (*hap*) 156; stand a chance etc. (*be possible*) 470.

toss up; cast –, draw- lots; leave –, trust- -to chance, – to the chapter of accidents; tempt fortune; chance it, take one's chance; run –, incur –, encounter- the -risk, – chance; stand the hazard of the die.

speculate, try one's luck, set on a cast, raffle, put into a lottery, buy a pig in a poke, shuffle the cards.

risk, venture, hazard, stake; lay, – a wager; make a bet, wager, bet, gamble, game, play for; play at chuck-farthing.

Adj. fortuitous etc. 156; unintentional, -ded; accidental; not meant; un-designed, -purposed; unpremeditated etc. 612; never thought of.

indiscriminate, promiscuous; undirected, random; aim-, drift-, design-, purpose-, cause-less; without purpose.

possible etc. 470.

Adv. casually etc. 156; unintentionally etc. *adj.*; unwittingly.

en passant, by the way, incidentally; as it may happen; at -random, – a venture, – haphazard; as luck would have it, by -chance, – good fortune; un-, -luckily.

† See note on 156.

622. Pursuit. [Purpose in action.]—**N.** pursuit; pursuing etc. *v.*; prosecution; pursuance; enterprise etc. (*undertaking*) 676; business etc. 625; adventure etc. (*essay*) 675; quest etc. (*search*) 461; scramble, hue and cry, game; hobby.

chase, hunt, *battue*, race, steeplechase, hunting, coursing; ven-ation, -ery; fox-chase; sport, -ing; shooting, angling, fishing, hawking.

pursuer; hunt-er, -sman; sportsman, Nimrod, the field; hound etc. 366.

V. pursue, prosecute, follow; run –, make –, be –, hunt – prowl- after; shadow; carry on etc. (*do*) 680; engage in etc. (*undertake*) 676; set about etc. (*begin*) 66; endeavor etc. 675; court etc. (*request*) 765; seek etc. (*search*) 461; aim at etc. (*intention*) 620; follow the trail etc. (*trace*) 461; fish for etc. (*experiment*) 463; press on etc. (*haste*) 684; run a race etc. (*velocity*) 274.

chase, give chase, course, dog, hunt, hound, stalk; tread –, follow- on the heels of etc. (*sequence*) 281.

rush upon; rush headlong etc. (*violence*) 173;

ride −, run- full tilt at; make a leap −, jump −, snatch- at; run down; start game.

tread a path; take −, hold- a course; shape −, direct −, bend- one's -steps, − course; play a game; fight −, elbow- one's way; follow up; take -to, − up; go in for; ride one's hobby.

Adj. pursuing etc. *v.*; in quest of etc. (*inquiry*) 461; in -pursuit, − full cry, − hot pursuit; on the scent.

Adv. in pursuance of etc. (*intention*) 620; after.

Int. tally-ho! yoicks! so-ho!

623. Avoidance. [Absence of pursuit.]—N. abst-ention, -inence; forbearance; refraining etc. *v.*; inaction etc. 681; neutrality.

avoidance, evasion, elusion; seclusion etc. 893.

avolation, flight; escape etc. 671; retreat etc. 287; recoil etc. 277; departure etc. 293; rejection etc. 610.

shirker etc. *v.*; slacker; truant; fugitive, refugee; runa-way, -gate; renegade; deserter.

V. abstain, refrain, spare, not attempt; not do etc. 681; maintain the even tenor of one's way.

eschew, keep from, let alone, have nothing to do with; keep −, stand −, hold- -aloof, − off; take no part in, have no hand in.

avoid, shun; steer −, keep- clear of; fight shy of; keep -one's, − at a respectful- distance; keep −, get- out of the way; evade, elude, turn away from; set one's face against etc. (*oppose*) 708; deny oneself.

shrink; hang −, hold −, draw- back; recoil etc. 277; retire etc. (*recede*) 287; flinch, blink, blench, shy, shirk, dodge, parry, make way for, give place to.

beat a retreat; turn -tail, − one's back; take to one's heels; run, -away, − for one's life; cut and run; be off, − like a shot; fly, flee; fly −, flee −, run away- from; take −, take to- flight; desert, elope; make −, scamper −, sneak −, shuffle −, sheer- off; break −, burst −, tear oneself −, slip −, slink −, steal- -away, − away from; slip cable, part company, turn on one's heel; sneak out of, play truant, give one the go by, give leg bail, take French leave, slope, decamp, flit, bolt, abscond, levant, skedaddle, absquatulate, cut one's stick, walk one's chalks, show a light pair of heels, make oneself scarce; escape etc. 671; go away etc. (*depart*) 293; abandon etc. 624; reject etc. 610.

lead one a -dance, − a merry chase, − pretty dance; throw off the scent, play at hide and seek.

Adj. unsought, unattempted; avoiding etc. *v.*; neutral; shy of etc. (*unwilling*) 603; elusive, evasive, distant; fugitive, runaway; shy, wild.

Adj. lest, in order to avoid.

Int. forbear! keep −, hands- off! *sauve qui peut!* devil take the hindmost.

624. Relinquishment.—N. relinquish-, abandon-ment; desertion, defection, secession, withdrawal; cave of Adullam; *nolle prosequi.*

discontinuance etc. (*cessation*) 142; renunciation etc. (*recantation*) 607; abrogation etc. 756; resignation etc. (*retirement*) 757; desuetude etc. 614; cession etc. (*of property*) 782.

V. relinquish, give up, abandon, desert, forsake, leave in the lurch; depart −, secede −, withdraw- from; back − out of, − down from, leave, go back on one's word, quit, take leave of, bid a long farewell; vacate etc. (*resign*) 757.

renounce etc. (*abjure*) 607; forego, have done with, drop; write off; disuse etc. 678; discard etc. 782; wash one's hands of; drop all idea of; *nolle-pros.*; lose interest in.

break −, leave- off; desist; stop etc. (*cease*) 142; hold −, stay- one's hand; quit one's hold; give over, shut up shop.

throw up the -game, − cards; give up the -point, − argument; pass to the order of the day, move the previous question, table the motion.

Adj. unpursued; relinquished etc. *v.*; relinquishing etc. *v.*

Int. avast etc.! (*stop*) 142.

625. Business.—N. business, occupation, employment; pursuit etc. 622; what one is doing-, − about; affair, concern, matter, case, undertaking.

matter in hand, irons in the fire; thing to do, *agendum*, task, work, job, chore, errand, transaction, commission, mission, charge, care; duty etc. 926.

part, *rôle*, cue; province, function, look-out, department, capacity, sphere, orb, field, line; walk, − of life; beat, round, routine; race, career.

office, place, post, incumbency, living situation, appointment, billet, berth, employ; service etc. (*servitude*) 749; engagement; undertaking etc. 676.

vocation, calling, profession, *métier*, cloth, faculty; industry, art; industrial arts; craft, mystery, handicraft; trade etc. (*commerce*) 794.

exercise; work etc. (*action*) 680; avocation; press of business etc. (*activity*) 682.

V. pass −, employ −, spend- one's time in; employ oneself -in, − upon; occupy −, concern-oneself with; make it one's -business etc. *n.*; undertake etc. 676; enter a profession; betake oneself to, turn one's hand to; have to do with etc. (*do*) 680.

drive a trade; carry on −, do −, transact- -business, − a trade etc. *n.*; keep a shop; ply one's task, − trade; labor in one's vocation; pursue the even tenor of one's way; attend to -business, − one's work.

officiate, serve, act; act −, play- one's part; do duty; serve −, discharge −, perform- the -office, − duties, − functions- of; hold −, fill- -an office, − a place, − a situation; hold a portfolio.

be -about, − doing, − engaged in, − employed in, − occupied with, − at work on; have one's hands in, have in hand; have one's -hands, − shoulders; bear the burden; have one's hands full etc. (*activity*) 682.

be -in the hands of, − on the stocks, − on the anvil; pass through one's hands.

Adj. business-like; work-a-day; professional; official, functional; busy etc. (*actively employed*) 682; on −, in- -hand, − one's hands; afoot; on -foot, − the anvil; going on; acting.

Adv. in the course of business, all in a day's work; professionally etc. *adj.*

626. Plan.—N. plan, scheme, design, project; propos-al, -ition; suggestion; resolution, motion;

precaution etc. (*provision*) 673; deep-laid etc.
(*premeditated*) 611- plan etc.; racket.

system etc. (*order*) 58; organization etc.
(*arrangement*) 60; germ etc. (*cause*) 153; Five
Year Plan.

sketch, skeleton, outline, draught, draft,
ébauche, brouillon; rough-cast, − draft, −
draught, − copy; proof, revise.

forecast, *programme*, prospectus, scenario; *carte
du pays*; card; bill, protocol; order of the day, list
of agenda, *memorandum*; bill of fare etc. (*food*)
298; base of operations; platform, plank.

rôle; policy etc. (*line of conduct*) 692.

contrivance, invention, expedient, receipt,
nostrum, artifice, device, gadget; stratagem etc.
(*cunning*) 702; trick etc. (*deception*) 545; alternative, loophole, shift etc. (*substitute*) 147; last
shift etc. (*necessity*) 601.

measure, step; stroke, − of policy; master
stroke; trump-, court-card; *chaval de bataille*,
great gun; *coup*, − *d'état*; clever −, bold −,
good- -move, − hit, − stroke; bright -thought, −
idea, great idea.

intrigue, cabal, plot, frame-up, conspiracy, complot, machination; under-, counter-plot.

schem-ist, -atist; stragetist, machinator, schemer;
projector, author, builder, artist, promoter,
designer etc. *v.*; conspirator; *intrigant* etc. (*cunning*) 702.

V. plan, scheme, design, frame, contrive,
project, forecast, sketch; conceive, devise, invent
etc. (*imagine*) 515; set one's wits to work etc. 515;
spring a project; fall −, hit- upon; strike −, chalk
−, cut −, lay −, map-out; lay down a plan; shape
−, mark- out a course; predetermine etc. 611; concert, preconcert, preestablish; prepare etc. 673;
hatch, − a plot; concoct; take -steps, − measures.

cast, recast, systematize, organize; arrange etc.
60; digest, mature.

plot; counter-plot, -mine; dig a mine; lay a train;
intrigue etc. (*cunning*) 702.

Adj. planned etc. *v.*; strategic, -al; planning etc.
v.; in course of preparation etc. 673; under consideration; on the *-tapis*, − carpet, − table.

627. Method. [Path.]—**N.** method, way, manner, wise, gait, form, mole, fashion, tone, guise;
modus operandi; procedure etc. (*line of conduct*)
692.

path, road, route, course; line of -way, − road;
trajectory, orbit, track, beat, tack.

steps; stair, -case; flight of stairs, ladder, stile.

bridge, viaduct, gauntry, pontoon, stepping
stone, plank, gangway, catwalk, drawbridge; pass,
ford, ferry, tunnel, subway, elevated; pipe etc. 260.

door; gateway etc. (*opening*) 260; channel,
passage, avenue, means of access, approach,
perron, adit, entrance; artery, lane, alley, aisle,
lobby, corridor, cloister; back- door, -stairs; secret
passage; covert-way.

road-, path-, stair-way; thoroughfare; highway,
pike, turnpike, trail, parkway, *boulevard*; turnpike
−, royal −, coach- road; broad −, King's −,
Queen's- highway; beaten -track, − path; horse −,
bridle- road, − track, − path; pathway; walk,
trottoir, foot-path, pavement, flags, side-walk; by
−, cross- -road, − path, − way; cut; short -cut

etc. (*mid-course*) 628; *carrefour*; private −, oc-
cupation- road; highways and byways; rail-, tram-
road, -way; funicular, ropeway, causeway; defile,
cutting; canal etc. (*conduit*) 350; street etc.
(*abode*) 189.

Adv. how; in what -way, − manner; by what
mode; so, in this way, after this fashion, on these
lines.

one way or another, anyhow; somehow or other
etc. (*instrumentality*) 631; by way of; *viâ*; *in transitu* etc. 270; on the high road to.

Phr. *hae tibi erunt artes*.

628. Mid-course.—**N.** middle-, mid-course;
moderation, mean etc. 29; middle etc. 68; *juste
milieu*, *mezzo termine*, golden mean, *aurea
mediocritas*.

straight etc. (*direct*) 278 -course, − path; short
−, cross- cut; short- circuit; great circle sailing.

neutrality; half −, half and half- measures; compromise.

V. keep in −, steer −, preserve- -a middle, −
an even- course; go straight etc. (*direct*) 278.

go half way, compromise, make a compromise.

Adj. neutral, average, even, impartial,
moderate, straight etc. (*direct*) 278.

629. Circuit.—**N.** circuit, round-about way,
digression, divagation, *détour*, circum-ambience, -
ambulation, bendibus, *ambages*, loop; winding etc.
(*circuition*) 311; zigzag etc. (*deviation*) 279.

V. perform −, make- a circuit; go -round about,
− out of one's way; make a *détour*; meander etc.
(*deviate*) 27; circumambulate.

lead a pretty dance; beat about, − the bush;
make two bites of a cherry.

adj. circuitous, indirect, round-about; zig-zag
etc. (*deviating*) 279; circum-ambient, -ambulatory.

Adv. by -a side wind, − an indirect course; in a
roundabout way; from pillar to post.

630. Requirement.—**N.** requirement, need,
wants, necessities; necessaries, − of life; stress,
exigency, pinch, *sine quâ non*, matter of necessity;
case of -need, − life or death.

needfulness, essentiality, necessity, in-
dispensability, urgency, prerequisite.

requisition etc. (*request*) 765, (*exaction*) 741;
run upon; demand −, call- for.

desideratum etc. (*desire*) 865; want etc.
(*deficiency*) 640.

charge, claim, command, injunction, requisition,
mandate, order, *ultimatum*.

V. require, need, want, have occasion for, entail;
not be able to -do without, − dispense with;
prerequire.

render necessary, necessitate, create a necessity
for, call for, put in requisition; make a requisition
etc. (*ask for*) 765, (*demand*) 741,

stand in need of; lack etc. 640; desiderate; desire
etc. 865; be -necessary etc. *adj*.

Adj. required etc. *v.*; requisite, needful,

necessary, imperative, essential, indispensable, prerequisite; called for; in -demand, – request.

urgent, exigent, pressing, instant, crying, absorbing.

in want of; destitute of etc. 640.

Adv. *ex necessitate rei* etc. (*necessarily*) 601; of –, out of stern- necessity; at a pinch.

Phr. there is no time to lose; it cannot be - spared, – dispensed with.

631. Instrumentality.—N. instrumentality; aid etc. 707; subservien-ce, -cy; mediation, intervention, -mediacy, medium, inter-medium, -mediary, vehicle, hand; agency etc. 170.

minister, handmaid, servant, slave, maid, valet; midwife, *accoucheur*, obstetrician; go-between; cat's paw; stepping-stone.

key; master –, pass –, latch- key; 'open seseme;' passport, *passe partout*, safe-conduct; influence.

instrument etc. 633; expedient etc. (*plan*) 626; means etc. 632.

V. subserve, minister, tend, mediate, intervene; come –, go- between, interpose; pull the strings; be -instrumental etc. *adj.*; pander to.

Adj. instrumental; useful etc. 644; ministerial, subservient, mediatorial; inter-mediate, -vening; conducive.

Adv. through, by, *per*; where-, there-, here-by; by the -agency etc. 170- of; by dint of; by –, invirtue of; through the -medium etc. *n.*- of; along with; on the shoulders of; by means of etc. 632; by –, with- -the aid etc. (*assistance*) 707- of.

per fas et nefas, by fair means or foul; somehow, – or other; by hook or by crook.

632. Means.—N. means, resources, revenue, wherewithal, ways and means, income; capital etc. (*money*) 800; stock in trade etc. 636; provision etc. 637; a shot in the locker; appliances etc. (*machinery*) 633; means and appliances; conveniences; cards to play; expendients etc. (*measures*) 626; two strings to one's bow; sheet anchor etc. (*safety*) 666; aid etc. 707; medium etc. 631.

V. find –, have –, possess- means etc. *n.*; provide the wherewithal.

Adj. instrumental etc. 631; mechanical etc. 633.

Adv. by means of, with; by -what, – all, – any, – some- means; where-, here-, there-with; wherewithal.

how etc. (*in what manner*) 627; through etc. (*by the instrumentality of*) 631; with – –, by- the aid etc. (*assistance*) 707- of; by the -agency etc. 170- of.

633. Instrument.—N. machinery, mechanism, engineering.

instrument, organ, tool, implement, utensil, contrivance, machine, motor, engine, lathe, gin, mill, pump.

gear; tack-le, -ling, trice, rigging, gear, apparatus, appliances; plant, *matériel*; harness, trap-pings, fittings, accouterments; equip-ment, -age; appointments, furniture, upholstery; chattels; paraphernalia etc. (*belongings*) 780; *impedimenta*.

mechanical powers; lever, -age; mechanical advantage; crow, -bar; handspike, gavelock, jemmy, arm, limb, wing; oar, paddle; pulley, sheave; parbuckle; wheel and axle; wheel-, clock-work; wheels within wheels; piñion, gear wheel, spur –, bevel-gearing, chains, belting, crank, winch, capstan, windlass, crane, derrick, hoist, lift etc. 307; cam; pedal; wheel etc. (*rotation*) 312; inclined plane; wedge; screw; jack; spring, mainspring.

handle, hilt, haft, shaft, heft, shank, blade, trigger, tiller, helm, treadle, key; turnscrew, screwdriver, spanner, wrench.

hammer etc. (*impulse*) 276; edge tool etc. (*cut*) 253; borer etc. 262; vice, teeth etc. (*hold*) 781; nail, rope etc. (*join*) 45; peg etc. (*hang*) 214; support etc. 215; spoon etc. (*vehicle*) 272; arms etc. 727; oar etc. (*navigation*) 267.

Adj. instrumental etc. 631; mechanical, machinal, automatic, self-acting; brachial.

634. Substitute.—N. substitute etc. 147; deputy etc. 759; proxy, alternative, understudy.

635. Materials.—N. material, raw material, stuff, stock, staple; building materials, bricks and mortar; metal; stone; clay, brick; crockery etc. 384; compo, -sition; reinforced –, ferro-, concrete; cement; wood, ore, timber; gravel, cobbles, macadam, asphalt, tarmac.

materials; supplies, munition, fuel, grist, household stuff; *pabulum* etc. (*food*) 298; ammunition etc. (*arms*) 727; contingents; relay, reinforcement; baggage etc. (*personal property*) 780; means etc. 632.

Adj. raw etc. (*unprepared*) 674; wooden etc. *n.*

636. Store.—N. stock, fund, mine, vein, lode, quarry; spring; fount, -ain; well, -spring; milch-cow.

stock in trade, supply; heap etc. (*collection*) 72; treasure; reserve, *corps de réserve*, reserve fund, nest-egg, savings, *bonne bouche*.

crop, harvest, mow, vintage; yield, product, gleanings.

store, accumulation, hoard, rick, stack; lumber; relay etc. (*provision*) 637.

store-house, -room, -closet; depository, *dépôt*, *cache*, safe deposit, vault, pantechnicon, repository, -servatory, -pertory; *repertorium*; promptuary, warehouse, *entrepôt*, magazine, dump, buttery, larder, pantry, panary, lanary, still-room, spence; crib, garner, granary, silo, barn; bunker; thesaurus; bank etc. (*treasury*) 802; armoury; arsenal; dock; gallery, museum, library, conservatory, hot-house; manag-ery, -erie, aquarium, zoological gardens.

reservoir, cistern, tank, sump, pond, mill-pond; gasometer.

budget, quiver, bandolier, portfolio; coffer etc. (*receptacle*) 191.

conservation; storing etc. v.; storage.

dictionary etc. 562; list etc. 86.

V. store; put –, lay –, set- by; stow away; set –, lay- apart; store –, hoard –, treasure –, lay –, heap –, put –, garner –, save- up; *cache*; accumulate, amass, hoard, fund, garner, save, bank.

conserve, reserve; keep –, hold- back; husband, – one's resources.

deposit; stow, stack, load, dump; harvest; heap, collect etc. 72; lay -in, – down, – by, store etc. *adj.*; keep, file [papers] lay in etc. (*provide*) 637; preserve etc. 670; put by for a rainy day.

Adj. stored etc. v.; in -store, – reserve, – ordinary; spare, supernumerary.

637. Provision.—N. provision, supply; grist, – to the mill; subvention etc. (*aid*) 707; resources etc. (*means*) 632.

provising etc. v.; purveyance; reinforcement; commissary, commissariat.

rations; iron –, emergency- rations; provender etc. (*food*) 298; *viaticum*; ensilage.

caterer, purveyor, commissary, quartermaster, steward, housekeeper, maniple, feeder, batman; victualler, storekeeper, grocer, provision merchant, green-, grocer, *comprador*, *restaurateur*; sutler etc. (*merchant*) 797; innkeeper, publican, confectioner, baker, butcher, wine merchant, vintner.

V. provide; make -provision, – due provision for; lay in, – a stock, – a store.

sup-ply, -peditate; furnish; find, – one in; arm.

cater, victual, provision, purvey, forage; beat up for; stock, – with; make good, replenish; fill, – up; recruit, feed, ration.

have in -store, – reserve; keep, – by one, – on foot; have to fall back upon; store etc. 636; provide against a rainy day etc. (*economy*) 817.

638. Waste.—N. consumption, expenditure, exhaustion; dispersion etc. 73; ebb; leakage etc. (*exudation*) 295; loss etc. 776; wear and tear; waste; prodigality etc. 818; misuse etc. 679; wasting etc. v.; rubbish etc. (*useless*) 645.

mountain in labor.

v. spend, expend, use, consume, swallow up, exhaust, deplete; impoverish; spill, drain, empty; disperse etc. 73.

cast –, throw –, fling –, fritter- away; burn the candle at both ends, waste; squander etc. 818.

'waste its sweetness on the desert air;' cast -one's bread upon the waters, – pearls before swine; employ a steam engine to crack a nut, waste powder and shot, break a butterfly on a wheel; labor in vain etc. (*useless*) 645; cut a whetstone with a razor, pour water into a sieve; tilt at windmills.

leak etc. (*run out*) 295; run to waste; ebb; melt away, run dry, dry up.

Adj. wasted etc. v.; at a low ebb.

wasteful etc. (*prodigal*) 818; penny wise and pound foolish.

Phr. *magno conatu magnas nugas; le jeu n'en vaut pas la chandelle.*

639. Sufficiency.—N. sufficiency, adequacy, enough, withal, *quantum sufficit*, satisfaction, competence; no less.

mediocrity etc. (*average*) 29.

fill; fullness etc (*completeness*) 52; plen-itude, -ty; abundance; copiousness etc. *adj.*; amplitude, galore, lots, profusion; full measure; 'good measure pressed down, shaken together and running over.'

luxuriance etc. (*fertility*) 168; affluence etc. (*wealth*) 803; fat of the land; 'a land flowing with milk and honey;' cornucopia; horn of -plenty, – Amalthaea; mine etc. (*stock*) 636.

outpouring; flood etc. (*great quantity*) 31; tide etc. (*river*) 348; repletion etc. (*redundance*) 641; satiety etc. 869; rich man etc. 803.

V. be -sufficient etc. *adj.*; suffice, do, just do, satisfy, pass muster; have -enough etc. *n.*; eat –, drink –, have- one's fill; roll –, swim- in; wallow in etc. (*superabundance*) 641.

abound, exuberate, teem, flow, stream, rain, shower down; pour, – in; swarm; bristle with.

render -sufficient etc. *adj.*; replenish etc. (*fill*) 52.

Adj. sufficient, enough, adequate, up to the mark, commensurate, competent, satisfactory, valid, tangible.

measured; moderate etc. (*temperate*) 953.

full etc. (*complete*) 52; ample; plen-ty, -tiful, -teous; plenty as blackberries; copious, abundant; abounding etc. v.; replete, enough and to spare, flush; choke-full; well-stocked, -provided; liberal; unstint-ed, -ing; stintless; without stint; un-sparing, -measured; lavish etc. 641; wholesale.

rich, luxuriant etc. (*fertile*) 168; affluent etc. (*wealthy*) 803; wantless; big with etc. (*pregnant*) 161.

un-exhausted, -wasted; exhaustless, inexhaustible.

Adv. sufficiently, amply etc. *adj.*; full; in -abundance etc. *n.*; with no sparing hand; to one's heart's content, *ad libitum*, without stint.

Phr. cut and come again.

640. Insufficiency.—N. insufficiency; inadequa-cy, -teness; incompetence etc. (*impotence*) 158; deficiency etc. (*incompleteness*) 53; imperfection etc. 651; shortcoming etc. 304; paucity; stint; scantiness etc. (*smallness*) 32; none to spare; bare subsistence.

scarcity, dearth; want, need, lack, poverty, exigency; inanition, starvation, famine, drought.

dole, pittance, mite; short -allowance, – commons; half-rations; banyan –, fast- day, Lent.

emptiness, poorness etc. *adj.*; depletion, vacancy, flaccidity; ebb-tide; low water; 'a beggarly account of empty boxes;' indigence etc. (*poverty*) 804; insolvency etc. (*non-payment*) 808; poor man etc. 804; bankrupt etc. 808.

V. be -insufficient etc. *adj.*; not -suffice etc. 639; come short of etc. 304; run dry.

want, lack, need, require; *caret*; be in want etc. (*poor*) 804; live from hand to mouth.

render- insufficient etc. *adj.*; drain of resources; impoverish etc. (*waste*) 638; stint etc. (*begrudge*) 819; put on short -commons, – allowance.

do -insufficiently etc. *adv.*; scotch the snake.

Adj. insufficient, inadequate; too -little etc. 32; not -enough etc. 639; unequal to; incompetent etc. (*impotent*) 158; 'weighed in the balance and found wanting;' perfunctory etc. (*neglect*) 460; deficient

etc. (*incomplete*) 53; wanting etc. *v.*; imperfect etc. 651; ill-furnished, -provided, -stored, -off.

slack, at a low ebb; empty, vacant, bare; short –, out –, destitute –, devoid –, bereft etc. 789 –, denuded- of; dry, drained.

un -provided, -supplied, -furnished; un-replenished, -fed; un-stored, -treasured; empty-handed.

meager, poor, thin, scrimp, sparing, spare, stinted, stunted; skimpy; starv-ed, -eling; half-starved, emaciated, famine-stricken, famished, underfed, undernourished; jejune.

scant etc. (*small*) 32; scarce; not to be had, – for love or money, – at any price; scurvy; stingy etc. 819; at the end of one's tether; without - resources etc. 632; in want etc. (*poor*) 804; in debt etc. 806.

Adv. insufficiently etc. *adj.*; in default –, for want- of; failing.

641. Redundance.—N. redundance; too - much, – many; superabundance, -fluity, -fluence, -saturation; nimiety, transcendency, exuberance, profuseness; profusion etc. (*plenty*) 639; repletion, enough in all conscience, *satis superque*, lion's share; more than -enough etc. 639; plethora, engorgement, congestion, load, surfeit, sickener; turgescence etc. (*expansion*) 194; over-dose, - measure, -supply, -flow; inundation etc. (*water*) 348; *avalanche*.

accumulation etc. (*store*) 636; heap etc. 72; drug, – in the market; glut; crowd; burden.

excess; sur-, over-plus, epact; margin; remainder etc. 40; duplicate; surplusage; expletive; work of –, supererogation; *bonus, bonanza*.

luxury; intemperance etc. 954; extravagance etc. (*prodigality*) 818; exorbitance, lavishment.

pleonasm etc. (*diffuseness*) 573; too many irons in the fire; embarrassment of riches; money to burn.

V. super-, over-abound; know no bounds, swarm; meet one at every turn; creep –, bristle-with; overflow; run –, flow –, well –, brim-over; run riot; over-run, -stock, -lay, -charge, -dose, - feed, -burden, -load, -do, -whelm, -shoot the mark etc. (*go beyond*) 303; surcharge, supersaturate, gorge, glut, load, drench, whelm, inundate, deluge, flood; drug, – the market.

choke, cloy, accloy, suffocate; pile up, lay it on, – with a trowel, lay on thick; impregnate with; lavish etc. (*squander*) 818.

send –, carry- coals to Newcastle, – owls to Athens; teach one's grandmother to suck eggs; *pisces natare docere*; kill the slain, 'gild refined gold,' 'paint the lily;' butter one's bread on both sides, put butter upon bacon; employ a steam-engine to crack a nut etc. (*waste*) 638.

exaggerate etc. 549; wallow in; roll in etc. (*plenty*) 639; remain on one's hands, hang heavy on hand, go a begging.

Adj. redundant; too -much, – many; exuberant, inordinate, superabundant, excessive, overmuch, replete, profuse, lavish; prodigal etc. 818; exorbitant; overweening; extravagant; overcharged etc. *v.*; supersaturated, drenched, overflowing; running -over, – to waste, – down.

crammed –, filled- to overflowing; gorged, stuffed, ready to burst; dropsical, turgid, plethoric, full-blooded; obese etc. 194; voluminous.

superfluous, unnecessary, needless, super-vacaneous, uncalled for, to spare, in excess; over and above etc. (*remainder*) 40; *de trop*; adscititious etc. (*additional*) 37; supernumerary etc. (*reserve*) 636; on one's hands, spare, duplicate, supererogatory, expletive; *un peu fort*.

Adj. over, too, over and above; over –, too-much; too far; without –, beyond – out of-measure; with ... to spare; over head and ears; up to one's eyes, – ears; *extra*; beyond the mark etc. (*transcursion*) 303; over one's head.

Phr. It never rains but it pours.

642. Importance.—N. importance, consequence, moment, prominence, consideration, mark, materialness.

import, significance, concern; emphasis, interest.

greatness etc. 31; superiority etc. 33; notability etc. (*repute*) 873; weight etc. (*influence*) 175; value etc. (*goodness*) 648; usefulness etc. 644.

gravity, seriousness, solemnity; no -joke, – laughing matter; pressure, urgency, stress; matter of life and death.

memorabilia, notabilia, great doings; red-letter day.

great -thing, – point; main chance, 'the be all and end all,' cardinal point, outstanding feature; substance, gist etc. (*essence*) 5; sum and substance, *gravamen*, head and front; important –, principal –, prominent –, essential- part; half the battle; *sine quâ non*; breath of one's nostrils etc. (*life*) 359; cream, salt, core, kernel, heart, nucleus; key, -note, -stone, corner stone; trumpcard etc. (*device*) 626; salient points.

top-sawyer, first fiddle, *prima donna*, chief, big-wig; triton among the minnows.

V. be -important etc. *adj.*, – somebody, – something; import, signify, matter, be an object; carry weight etc. (*influence*) 175; make a figure etc. (*repute*) 873; be in the ascendant, come to the front, lead the way, take the lead, play first fiddle, throw all else into the shade; lie at the root of; deserve –, merit –, be worthy- of notice, – regard, – consideration.

attach –, ascribe –, give- importance etc. *n.*- to; value, care for; set store -upon, – by; mark etc. 550; mark with a white stone, underline; write –, put –, print- in -italics, – capitals, – large letters, – large type, – letters of gold; accentuate, emphasize, lay stress on.

make -a fuss, – a stir, – a piece of work, – much ado- about; make -of, – much of.

Adj. important; of -importance etc. *n.*; momentous, material; to the point; not to be -overlooked, – despised, – sneezed at; egregious; weighty etc. (*influential*) 175; of note etc. (*repute*) 873; notable, prominent, salient, signal, memorable, remarkable; worthy of -remark, – notice; never to be forgotten; stirring, eventful.

grave, serious, earnest, noble, grand, solemn, impressive, commanding, imposing.

urgent, pressing, critical, instant.

paramount, essential, vital, all-absorbing, radical, cardinal, chief, main, prime, primary, principal, leading, capital, foremost, overruling; of vital etc. importance.

in the front rank, first-rate, A1; superior etc. 33; considerable etc. (*great*) 31; marked etc. *v.*; rare etc. 137.

significant, telling, trenchant, emphatic, pregnant; *tanti.*

Adv. materially etc. *adj.*; in the main; above all, *par excellence*, to crown all.

643. Unimportance.—N. unimportance, insignificance, nothingness, immateriality.

triviality, trivia, fribble, levity, frivolity; paltriness etc. *adj.*; poverty; smallness etc. 32; vanity etc. (*uselessness*) 645; matter of - indifference. 866; no object; side issue.

nothing, − to signify, − worth speaking of, − particular, − to boast of, − to speak of; small −, no great −, trifling etc. *adj.*-matter; mere -joke, − nothing; hardly −, scarcely- anything; nonentity, cipher, figurehead; no great shakes, *peu de chose*; child's play; small beer.

toy, plaything, popgun, paper pellet, gimcrack, geegaw, bauble, trinket, *bagatelle*, kickshaw, knicknack, whim-wham, trifle, 'trifles light as air.'

trumpery, trash, rubbish, stuff, *fatras*, frippery; 'leather or prunello;' chaff, drug, froth, bubble, smoke, cobweb; weed; refuse etc. (*inutility*) 645; scum etc. (*dirt*) 653.

joke, jest, snap of the fingers; fudge etc. (*unmeaning*) 517; fiddlestick, − end; pack of nonsense, mere farce.

straw, pin, fig, continental, button, rush; bulrush, feather, halfpenny, farthing, brass farthing, doit, peppercorn, jot, rap, pinch of snuff, old song.

minutiae, details, minor details, small fry; dust in the balance, feather in the scale, drop in the ocean, flea-bite, molehill; fingle-fangle.

nine days' wonder, *ridiculus mus*; flash in the pan etc. (*impotence*) 158; much ado about nothing etc. (*overestimation*) 482; storm in a teacup.

V. be -unimportant etc. *adj.*; not -matter etc. 642; go for −, matter −, signify -little, − nothing, − little or nothing; not matter a -straw etc. *n.*

make light of etc. (*underestimate*) 483; catch at straws etc. (*overestimate*) 482.

Adj. unimportant; of -little, − small, − no- account, − importance etc. 642; immaterial; un-, non-essential; not vital; irrelevant, incidental, indifferent.

subordinate etc. (*inferior*) 34; *médiocre* etc. (*average*) 29; passable, fair, respectable, tolerable, commonplace; uneventful, mere, common; ordinary etc. (*habitual*) 613; inconsiderable, so-so, insignificant, inappreciable, nugatory.

trifling, trivial; slight, slender, light, flimsy, frothy, idle; puerile etc. (*foolish*) 499; airy, shallow; weak etc. 160; powerless etc. 158; frivolous, petty, niggling; pid-, ped-dling; fribble, inane, ridiculous, farcical; fini-cal, -kin; fiddle-faddle, namby-pamby, wishy-washy, milk and water.

poor, paltry, pitiful; contemptible etc. (*contempt*) 930; sorry, mean, meager, shabby, miserable, wretched, vile, scrubby, scrannel, weedy, niggardly, scurvy, putid, beggarly, worthless, twopenny-half penny, cheap, trashy, catchpenny, gimcrack, trumpery, one-horse; toy.

not worth -the pains, − while, − mentioning, − speaking of, − a thought, − a curse, − a straw, − rap etc. *n.*; beneath −, unworthy of- -notice, −

regard, − consideration, − contempt; *de lanâ caprinâ*; vain etc. (*useless*) 645.

Adv. slightly etc. *adj.*; rather, somewhat, pretty well, fairly well, tolerably.

for aught one cares.

Int. no matter! pish! tush! tut! pshaw! pugh! pooh, -pooh! fudge! bosh! humbug! fiddle-stick, − end! fiddlededee! never mind! *n'importe!* what - signifies, − matter, − boots it, − of that, − 's the odds! a fig for! stuff ! nonsense! stuff and nonsense!

Phr. *magno conatu magnas nugas*; *le jeu n'en vaut pas la chandelle*; it -matters not, − does not signify; it is of no -consequence, − importance.

644. Utility.—N. utility; usefulness etc. *adj.*; efficacy, efficiency, adequacy; service, use, stead, avail; help etc. (*aid*) 707; applicability etc. *adj.*; subservience etc. (*instrumentality*) 631; function etc. (*business*) 625; value; worth etc. (*goodness*) 648; money's worth; productiveness etc. 168; *cui bono* etc. (*intention*) 620; utilization etc. (*use*) 677; step in the right direction.

common weal, public good; utilitarianism etc. (*philanthropy*) 910.

V. be -useful etc. *adj.*; avail, serve; subserve etc. (*be instrumental to*) 631; conduce etc. (*tend*) 176; answer −, serve- -one's turn, − a purpose.

act a part etc. (*action*) 680; perform −, discharge- -a function etc. 625; do −, render- -a service, − good service, − yeoman's service; bestead, stand one in good stead; be the making of; help etc. 707.

bear fruit etc. (*produce*) 161; bring grist to the mill; profit, remunerate; benefit etc. (*do good*) 648.

find one's -account, − advantage- in; reap the benefit of etc. (*be better for*) 658.

render useful etc. (*use*) 677.

Adj. useful; of -use etc. *n.*; serviceable, usable, proficuous, good for; subservient etc. (*instrumental*) 631; conducive etc. (*tending*) 176; subsidiary etc. (*helping*) 707.

advantageous etc. (*beneficial*) 648; profitable, gainful, remunerative, worth one's salt; in-, valuable; prolific etc. (*productive*) 168.

adequate; ef-ficient, -ficacious; effect-ive, -ual; practicable, expedient etc. 646.

applicable, available, ready, handy, at hand, tangible; commodious, adaptable; of all work.

Adv. usefully etc. *adj.*; *pro bono publico.*

645. Inutility.—N. inutility; uselessness etc. *adj.*; inefficacy, futility; inep-, inap-titude; un-subservience; inadequacy etc. (*insufficiency*) 640; inefficiency etc. (*incompetence*) 158; unskilfulness etc. 699; disservice; unfruitfulness etc. (*unproductiveness*) 169; labor -in vain, − lost, − of Sisyphus; lost -trouble, − labor; work of Penelope; sleeveless errand, wild goose chase, mere farce.

tautology etc. (*repetition*) 104; supererogation etc. (*redundance*) 641.

vanitas vanitatum, vanity, inanity, worthlessness, nugacity; triviality etc. (*unimportance*) 643.

caput mortuum, waste paper, dead letter; blunt tool.

litter, rubbish, lumber, odds and ends, cast-off clothes; button-top; shoddy; rags, orts, trash, refuse, sweepings, scourings, off-scourings, dross, slag, waste, rubble, dottle, drast, *débris*; stubble, leavings; broken meat; dregs etc. (*dirt*) 653; weeds, tares; rubbish heap, dust hole; *rudera*, deads.

fruges consumere natus etc. (*drone*) 683.

V. be -useless etc. *adj.*; go a begging etc. (*redundant*) 641; fail etc. 732.

seek –, strive- after impossibilities; use vain efforts, labor in vain, roll the stone of Sisyphus, beat the air, lash the waves; *battre l'eau avec un bâton, donner un coup d'épée dans l'eau,* fish in the air, milk the ram, drop a bucket into an empty well, sow the sand; bay the moon; preach –, speak- to the winds; whistle jigs to a milestone; kick against the pricks, *se battre contre des moulins*; lock the stable door when the steed is stolen etc. (*too late*) 135; hold a farthing candle to the sun; cast pearls before swine etc. (*waste*) 638; carry coals to Newcastle etc. (*redundance*) 641; wash a blackamoor white etc. (*impossible*) 471.

render -useless etc. *adj.*; dis-mantle, -mast, -mount, -qualify, -able; unrig; cripple, lame etc. (*injure*) 659; spike guns, clip the wings; put out of gear.

Adj. useless, inutile, inefficacious, futile, unavailing, bootless; inoperative etc. 158; inadequate etc. (*insufficient*) 640; in-, un- subservient: inept, inefficient etc. (*impotent*) 158; of no -avail etc. (*use*) 644; ineffectual etc. (*failure*) 732; incompetent etc. (*unskilful*) 699; 'stale, flat and unprofitable;' superfluous etc. (*redundant*) 641; dispensable; thrown away etc. (*wasted*) 638; abortive etc. (*immature*) 674.

worth-, value-less; unsaleable; not worth a straw etc. (*trifling*) 643; dear at any price.

vain, empty, inane; gain-, profit-, fruit-less; unserviceable, -profitable; ill-spent; unproductive etc. 169; *hors de combat*; barren, sterile, impotent, unproductive; effete, past work etc. (*impaired*) 659; obsolete etc. (*old*) 124; fit for the -dust-hole, – wastepaper basket; good for nothing; of no earthly use; not worth -having, – powder and shot; leading to no end, uncalled for; un-necessary, -needed, superfluous.

Adv. uselessly etc. *adj.*; to -little, – no, – little or no- purpose.

Int. *cui bono?* what's the good!

646. Expedience. [Specific subservience.]—**N.** expedien-ce, -cy; desirableness, -bility etc. *adj.*; fitness etc. (*agreement*) 23; utility etc. 644; propriety; advantage; opportunism, pragmatism.

high time etc. (*occasion*) 134.

V. be -expedient etc. *adj.*; suit etc. (*agree*) 23; befit; suit – befit- the -time, – season, – occasion.

conform etc. 82.

Adj. expedient; desir-, advis-, accept-able; convenient; worth while, meet; fit, -ting; due, proper, eligible, seemly, becoming; befitting etc. *v.*; opportune etc. (*in season*) 134; *in loco*; suitable etc. (*accordant*) 23; applicable etc. (*useful*) 644; practical, effective, pragmatical; suitable, handy.

Adv. in the right place; conveniently etc. *adj.*; in the nick of time.

Phr. *operae pretium est.*

647. Inexpedience.—**N.** enexpedien-ce, -cy; undesira-bleness, -bility etc. *adj.*; discommodity, impropriety; unfitness etc. (*disagreement*) 24; inutility etc. 645; inconvenience, inadvisability; disadvantage.

V. be -inexpedient etc. *adj.*; come amiss etc. (*disagree*) 24; embarrass etc. (*hinder*) 706; put to inconvenience; pay too dear for one's whistle.

Adj. inexpedient, undesirable; un-, in-advisable; objectionable; troublesome, in-apt, -eligible, -admissable, -convenient; in-, dis-commodious; disadvantageous; inappropriate, unsuitable, unfit etc. (*inconsonant*) 24.

ill-contrived, -advised; unsatsifactory; unprofitable etc., unsubservient etc. (*useless*) 645; inopportune etc. (*unseasonable*) 135; out of –, in the wrong- place; improper, unseemly.

clumsy, awkward; cum-brous, -bersome; lumbering, unwieldy, hulky; unmanageable etc. (*impracticable*) 704; impedient (*in the way*) 706.

unnecessary etc. (*redundant*) 641.

Phr. it will never do.

648. Goodness. [Capability of producing good. Good qualities.]—**N.** goodness etc. *adj.*; excellence, merit; virtue etc. 944; value, worth, price.

super-excellence, -eminence; superiority etc. 33; perfection etc. 650; *coup de maître*; master-piece, *chef d'oeuvre*, prime, flower, cream, *élite*, pick, A1, none such, *nonpareil, crême de la crême,* flower of the flock, cock of the roost, salt of the earth; champion.

tid-bit; gem, – of the first water; *bijou*, precious stone, jewel, pearl, diamond, ruby, brilliant, treasure; good thing; *rara avis*, one in a thousand.

beneficence etc. 906; good man etc. 948.

V. be -beneficial etc. *adj.*; produce –, do- good etc. 618; profit etc. (*be of use*) 644; benefit; confer a -benefit etc. 618.

be the making of, do a world of good, make a man of.

produce a good effect; do a good turn, confer an obligation; improve etc. 658.

do no harm, break no bones.

be -good etc. *adj.*; excel, transcend etc. (*be superior*) 33; bear away the bell.

stand the -proof, – test; pass -muster, – an examination.

challenge comparison, vie, emulate, rival.

Adj. harm-, hurt-less; unobnoxious; in-nocuous, -nocent, -offensive.

beneficial, valuable, of value; serviceable etc. (*useful*) 644; advantageous, profitable, edifying; salutary etc. (*healthful*) 656.

favorable; propitious etc. (*hopegiving*) 858; fair.

good, – as gold; excellent; better; superior etc. 33; above par; nice, fine; genuine etc. (*true*) 494.

best, choice, select, picked, elect, eximious, *recherché*, rare, priceless; unpara-goned, -lleled etc. (*supreme*) 33; superlatively etc. 33- good; super-fine, -excellent; bonzer; of the first water; first-rate, -class; high-wrought; exquisite, very best, crack, prime, tip-top, gilt-edged, capital, cardinal; standard etc. (*perfect*) 650; inimitable.

admirable, estimable; praiseworthy etc. (*approve*) 931; pleasing etc. 829; *couleur de rose*, precious, of great price; costly etc. (*dear*) 814; worth -its weight in gold, – a Jew's eye, – a king's

ransom; matchless, peerless, invaluable, inestimable, precious as the apple of the eye.

tolerable etc. (*not very good*) 651; up to the mark, un-exceptionable, -objectionable; satisfactory, tidy.

in -good, − fair- condition; fresh; unspoiled; sound etc. (*perfect*) 650.

Adv. beneficially etc. *adj.*; well etc. 618.

649. Badness. [Capability of producing evil. Bad qualities.]—**N.** hurtfulness etc. *adj.*; virulence.

evil doer etc. 913; bane etc. 663; plague-spot etc. (*insalubrity*) 657; evil star, ill wind; snake in the grass, skeleton in the closet; *amari aliquid*, thorn in the side; Jonah, jinx, hoodoo.

malignity; malevolence etc. 907; tender mercies [ironically].

ill-treatment, annoyance, molestation, abuse, oppression, persecution, outrage; misusage etc. 679; injury etc. (*damage*) 659.

badness etc. *adj.*; peccancy, abomination; painfulness etc. 830; pestilence etc. (*disease*) 655; guilt etc. 947; depravity etc. 945.

V. be -hurtful etc. *adj.*; cause −, produce −, inflict −, work −, do- evil etc. 619; damnify, endamage, hurt, harm, scathe; injure etc. (*damage*) 659; pain etc. 830.

wrong, aggrieve, oppress, persecute; trample −, tread −, bear hard −, put-upon; overburden; weigh -down, − heavy on; victimize; run down; molest etc. 830.

maltreat, abuse; ill-use, -treat; thwart, buffet, bruise, scratch, maul; smite etc. (*scourge*) 972; do -violence, − harm, − a mischief; stab, pierce, outrage.

do −, make- mischief; bring −, get- into trouble.

destroy etc. 162.

Adj. hurt-, harm-, scath-, bane-, bale-ful; injurious, deleterious, detrimental, noxious, pernicious, mischievous, full of mischief, mischiefmaking, malefic, malignant, nocuous, noisome; prejudicial; dis-serviceable, advantageous; widewasting.

unlucky, sinister; obnoxious, untoward, disastrous.

oppressive, burdensome, onerous; malign etc. (*malevolent*) 907.

corrupting etc. (corrupt etc. 659) virulent, venomous, envenomed, corrosive; poisonous etc. (*morbific*) 657; deadly etc. (*killing*) 361; destructive etc. (*destroying*) 162; inauspicious etc. 859.

bad, ill, arrant, as bad bad can be, dreadful; horrid, -rible; dire; rank, peccant, foul, fulsome; rotten, − at the core.

vile, base, villainous; mean etc. (*paltry*) 643; injured etc., deteriorated etc. 659; unsatisfactory, exception, -able, indifferent; below par etc. (*imperfect*) 651; ill-contrived, -conditioned; wretched, sad, grievous, deplorable, lamentable; piti-ful, -able, woeful etc. (*painful*) 830.

evil, wrong; depraved etc. 945; shocking; reprehensible etc. (*disapprove*) 932.

hateful, − as a toad; abominable, detestable, execrable, cursed, accursed, confounded; damn-ed, -able; infernal; diabolic etc. (*malevolent*) 907.

inadvisable etc. (*inexpedient*) 647; unprofitable etc. (*useless*) 645; incompetent etc. (*unskilful*) 699; irremediable etc. (*hopeless*) 859.

Adv. badly etc. *adj.*; wrong, ill; to one's cost; where the shoe pinches.

Phr. bad is the best; the worst come to the worst.

650. Perfection.—**N.** perfection; perfectness etc. *adj.*; indefectibility; inpecc-ancy, -ability.

pink, *beau idéal*, phoenix, paragon; pink −, acme- of perfection; *ne plus ultra*; summit etc. 210.

cygne noir; philosopher's stone; chrysolite, Koh-i-noor, black tulip.

model, standard, pattern, mirror, admirable Chrichton; trump; very prince of.

master-piece, -stroke, super-excellence etc. (*goodness*) 648; transcendence etc. (*superiority*) 33.

V. be -perfect etc. *adj.*; transcend etc. (*be supreme*) 33.

bring to perfection, perfect, ripen, mature; consummate, complete etc. 729; put in trim etc. (*prepare*) 673; put the finishing touch to.

Adj. perfect, faultless, ideal; indefective, -ficient, -fectible; immaculate, spotless, impeccable; free from -imperfection etc. 651; un-blemished, -injured etc. 659; sound, − as a roach; in perfect condition; scathless, intact, harmless; seaworthy etc. (*safe*) 644; right as a trivet; *in seipso totus teres atque rotundus*; consummate etc. (*complete*) 52; finished etc. 729; complete in itself.

best etc. (*good*) 648; model, standard; inimitable, unparagoned, unparalleled etc. (*supreme*) 33; superhuman, divine; beyond all praise etc. (*approbation*) 931; *sans peur et sans reproche*.

Adv. to perfection, to the limit; perfectly etc. *adj.*; *ad unguem*; clean, − as a whistle.

651. Imperfection.—**N.** imperfection; imperfectness etc. *adj.*; deficiency; inadequacy etc. (*insufficiency*) 640; peccancy etc. (*badness*) 649; immaturity etc. 674.

fault, defect, weak point; screw loose; rift within the lute; fly in the ointment; flaw etc. (*break*) 70; gap etc. 198; twist etc. 243; taint, attainder; bar sinister, hole in one's coat; blemish etc. 848; weakness etc. 160; half-blood, touch of the tar brush; shortcoming etc. 304; drawback; seamy side.

mediocrity; no great -shakes, − catch; not much to boast of.

V. be -imperfect etc. *adj.*; have a -defect etc. *n.*; lie under a disadvantage; spring a leak.

not −, barely- pass muster; fall short etc. 304.

Adj. imperfect; not -perfect etc. 650; de-ficient, -fective; faulty, unsound, mutilated, tainted; out of -order, − tune; cracked, leaky; sprung; warped etc. (*distort*) 243; lame; injured etc. (*deteriorated*) 659; peccant etc. (*bad*) 649; frail etc. (*weak*) 160; inadequate etc. (*insufficient*) 640; crude etc. (*unprepared*) 674; incomplete etc. 53; found wanting; below par; shorthanded; below −, under- its full -strength, − complement.

indifferent, middling, ordinary, mediocre; average etc. 29; so-so; *cosi-cosi*, milk and water; tolerable, fair, passable; pretty -well, – good; rather –, moderately- good; good –, well-enough; decent; not -bad, – amiss; inobjectionable, admissable, bearable, only better than nothing.

secondary, inferior; second-rate, -best, one-horse.

Adv. almost etc.; to a limited extent, rather etc. 32; pretty, moderately; only; considering, all things considered, enough.

Phr. *surgit amari aliquid.*

652. Cleanness.—N. cleanness etc. *adj.*; purity; cleaning etc. *v.*; purification, defecation etc. *v.*; purgation, lustration; de-, abs-tersion; epuration, mundation, lustration, ablution, lavation, colature; disinfection etc. *v.*; drain-, sewerage.

lavatory, bath, -room; swimming pool, natatorium; public baths; hot –, cold –, Turkish –, Swedish –, Russian – vapor- bath; *hammam*, laundry, washhouse; washerwoman, laundress, laundryman; scavenger, cleaner, sweeper, goodie; crossing sweeper, white wings, dustman, sweep.

brush; broom, besom, carpet-sweeper, vacuum-cleaner, mop, squilgee, rake, shovel, sieve, riddle, screen, filter; scraper, strigil.

napkin, *serviette*, cloth, table-, carving-cloth, table-linen, napery, maukin, handkerchief, towel, sudary; doyley, doily, duster, sponge, mop, swab.

cover, drugget, mat, doormat.

soap, wash, -lotion, detergent, cathartic, purgative; purifier etc. *v.*; dentifrice, tooth-powder, -paste; mouth wash; disinfectant.

V. be –, render- clean etc. *adj.*

clean, -se; mundify, rinse, wring, flush, full, wipe, mop, sponge, scour, swab, scrub, holystone, brush up.

wash, shampoo, lave, launder, buck; abs-, de-terge; clear, purify; de-purate, -spumate, -fecate; purge, expurgate; Bowdlerize; elutriate, lixiviate, edulcorate, clarify, refine, rack; fil-ter, -trate; drain, strain.

disinfect, sterilize, pasteurize, fumigate, ventilate, deodorize; whitewash.

sift, winnow, screen, riddle, pick, weed, comb, rake, brush, sweep.

rout –, clear –, sweep etc.- out; make a clean sweep of.

Adj. clean, -ly; pure; immaculate; spot-, stain-, taint-less; without a stain, un-stained, -spotted, -soiled, -sullied, -tainted, -infected, -adulterated; aseptic; sweet, – as a nut.

neat, spruce, tidy, trim, gimp, clean as a new penny, like a cat in pattens; cleaned etc. *v.*; kempt.

Adv. neatly etc. *adj.*; clean as a whistle.

653. Uncleanness.—N. uncleanness etc. *adj.*; impurity; immundi-ty, -city; impurity etc. [of mind] 961.

defilement, contamination etc. *v.*; defedation; soil-ure, -iness; abomination; leaven; taint, -ure; fetor etc. 401.

decay; putre-scence, -faction; corruption; mold, must, mildew, dry-rot, *mucor*, rubigo, caries.

slovenry; slovenliness etc. *adj.*; squalor.

dowdy, drab, slut, malkin, slattern, sloven, slam-merkin, scrub, draggletail, mudlark, dustman, sweep; beast.

dirt, filth, soil, slop; dust, cobweb, flue; smoke, soot, smudge, smut, grime, raff.

sordes, dregs, grounds, lees; sedi-, settle-ment; heel-tap; dross, -iness; mother, precipitate, *scoria*, ashes, cinders, recrement, slag; scum, froth.

hog-wash, swill, ditch-, dish-, bilge-water; rins-ings, cheese-parings; sweepings etc. (*useless refuse*) 645; off-, out-scourings; off-scum; *caput mortuum, residuum*, sprue, feculence, clinker, draff; scurf, -iness; *exuviae*, morphew; fur, -fur; dandruff; tartar.

riffraff; vermin, louse, cootie, flea, bug.

mud, mire, quagmire, *alluvium*, silt, sludge, slime, slush, slosh.

spawn, offal, garbage, carrion; *excreta* etc. 299; -slough, peccant humor, pus, matter, suppuration, *lienteria*; *feces*, excrement, ordure, dung; sew-, sewer-age; muck, coprolite; guano, manure, compost.

dunghill, *coluvies*, mixen, midden, bog, laystall, sink, w.c., water-, earth-closet, latrine, privy, jakes, John's, cess, -pool; sump, sough, *cloaca*, drain, sewer, common sewer; Cloacina; dust-hole.

sty, pig-sty, lair, den, Augean stable, sink of corruption; slum, rookery.

V. be –, become- unclean etc. *adj.*; rot, putrefy, fester, rankle, reek; stink etc. 401; mold, -er; go bad etc. *adj.*

render -unclean etc. *adj.*; dirt, -y; soil, smoke, tarnish, slaver, spot, smear, daub, blot, blur, smudge, smutch, smirch; d-, dr-abble, -aggle; spat-ter, slubber; be-smear etc.; -mire, -slime, -grime, -foul; splash, stain, distain, maculate, sully, pollute, defile, debase, contaminate, taint, leaven; corrupt etc. (*injure*) 659; cover with -dust etc. *n.*; drabble in the mud.

wallow in the mire; slob-, slab-ber.

Adj. unclean, dirty, filthy, grimy; soiled etc. *v.*; not to be handled with kid gloves; dusty, snuffy, smutty, sooty, smoky; thick, turbid, dreggy; slimy.

uncleanly, slovenly, untidy, sluttish, dowdy, slat-ternly, draggletailed; un-combed, -kempt, -scoured, -swept, -wiped, -washed, -strained, -purified; squalid.

nasty, coarse, foul, impure, offensive, abominable, beastly, reeky, reechy; fetid etc. 401.

moldy, lentiginous, musty, mildewed, rusty, moth-eaten, mucid, rancid, bad, gone bad, touched, fusty, reasty, rotten, corrupt, tainted, high, fly-blown, maggoty; putr-id, -escent, -efied; purulent, carious, peccant, fec-al, -ulent; ster-coraceous, excrementitious; scurfy, impetiginous; gory, bloody; rotting etc. *v.*; rotten as -a pear, -cheese.

crapulous etc. (*intemperate*) 954; gross etc. (*impure in mind*) 961.

654. Health.—N. health, sanity; soundness etc. *adj.*; vigor; good –, perfect –, excellent –, rude –, robust- health; bloom, *mens sana in corpore sano*; Hygeia; incorrupti-on, -bility; good state –, clean bill- of health, eupepsia.

V. be in health etc. *adj.*; bloom, flourish.

keep -body and soul together, – on one's legs; enjoy -good, – a good state of - health; have a clean bill of health.

return to health; recover etc. 660; get better etc. (*improve*) 658; take a -new, − fresh- lease of life; convalesce, be convalescent, recruit; restore to health; cure etc. (*restore*) 660.

Adj. health-y, -ful; in -health etc. *n.*; well, sound, strong, fit, hearty, hale, fresh, blooming, green, whole; florid, flush, hardy, stanch, staunch, brave, robust, vigorous, weather-proof; convalescent.

un-scathed, -injured, -maimed, -marred, -tainted; sound of wind and limb, safe and sound; without a scratch.

on one's legs; sound as a -roach, − bell; fresh as -a daisy, − a rose, − April; picture of health; bursting with health; fit as a fiddle; hearty as a buck; in -fine, − high- feather; in -good case, − full bloom; in fine fettle; pretty bobbish, tolerably well, as well as can be expected.

sanitary etc. (*health-giving*) 656; sanatory etc. (*remedial*) 662.

655. Disease.*—N. disease, illness, sickness etc. *adj.*; ailing etc. *v.*; 'the ills that flesh is heir to;' morb-idity, -osity; infirmity, ailment, indisposition; complaint, disorder, malady; distemper, -ature.

visitation, attack, seizure, stroke, fit, epilepsy, apoplexy, shock, shell-shock.

delicacy, loss of health, valetudinarianism, in-validism, cachexy; *cachexia*, atrophy, *marasmus*; indigestion, *dyspepsia*; decay etc. (*deterioration*) 659; malnutrition, decline, consumption, palsy, paralysis, prostration; occupational diseases.

taint, pollution, infection, contagion, septicity, septicaemia, blood poisoning, pyaemia, epi-, endemic; murrain, plague, pestilence, virus, pox.

sore, ulcer, abscess, fester, boil; pimple etc. (*swelling*) 250; carbuncle, gathering, whitlow, imposthume, peccant humor, issue; rot, canker, cancer, *carcinoma*, *caries*, mortification, corruption, gangrene, *sphacelus*, leprosy, eruption, rash, breaking out, venereal disease.

fever, calenture; inflammation.

fatal etc. (*hopeless*) 859- -disease etc.; dangerous illness, galloping consumption, churchyard cough; general breaking up, break up of the system.

[Disease of the mind] neurasthenia; idiocy etc. 499; insanity etc. 503.

martyr to disease; cripple; 'the halt, the lame and the blind;' valetudinar-y, -ian; invalid, patient, case; sick-room, -chamber, hospital etc. 662.

[Science of disease] path-, eti-, nos-ology, therapeutics, diagnosis, prognosis.

V. be -ill etc. *adj.*; ail, suffer, labor under, be affected with, complain of; droop, flag, languish, halt; sicken, peak, pine, waste away, fail, lose strength; gasp.

keep one's bed; feign sickness etc. (*falsehood*) 544; malinger.

lay -by, − up; take −, catch- -a disease etc. *n.*, − an infection; be stricken by; break out.

Adj. diseased; ailing etc. *v.*; ill, − of; taken ill, seized with; indisposed, unwell, sick, squeamish, poorly, seedy; affected −, afflicted- with illness; laid up, confined, bed-ridden, invalided, in hospital, on the sick list; out of -health, − sorts; valetudinary.

un-sound, -healthy; sickly, morbose, healthless,

infirm, chlorotic, unbraced, drooping, flagging, lame, halt, crippled, halting.

morbid, tainted, vitiated, peccant, contaminated, poisoned, septic, tabid, mangy, leprous, cankered; rotten, − to, − at- the core; withered, palsied, paralytic, tuberculous; dyspeptic.

touched in the wind, broken-winded, spavined, gasping; *hors de combat* etc. (*useless*) 645.

weak-ly, -ened etc. (*weak*) 160; decrepit; decayed etc. (*deteriorated*) 659; incurable etc. (*hopeless*) 859; in declining health; cranky; in a bad way, in danger, prostrate; moribund etc. (*death*) 360.

morbific, epidemic etc. 657.

*Extended lists of different diseases are beyond the scope of this work.

656. Salubrity.—N. salubrity, salubriousness; healthiness etc. *adj.*

fine -air, − climate; eudiometer.

[Preservation of health] *hygiène*; valetudinarian, -ism, preventorium, sanitarian; *sanitarium*, *sanitorium*, immunity.

V. be -salubrious etc. *adj.*; agree with, be good for; assimilate etc. 23.

Adj. salu-brious, -tary, -tiferous, wholesome; health-y, -ful; sanitary, prophylactic, benign, bracing, tonic, invigorating, good for, nutritious, hyg-eian, -ienic.

in-noxious, -nocuous, -nocent; harmless, uninjurious, uninfectious; immune.

sanative etc. (*remedial*) 662; restorative etc. (*reinstate*) 660; useful etc. 644.

657. Insalubrity.—N. insalubrity, unhealthiness etc. *adj.*; non-naturals; plague spot; malaria etc. (*poison*) 663; death in the pot, contagion.

Adj. insalubrious; un-healthy, -wholesome; noxious, noisome, foul; morbi-fic, -ferous; mephitic, septic, azotic, deleterious; pesti-lent, -ferous, -lential; virulent, venomous, envenomed, poisonous, toxic, narcotic.

contagious, infectious, catching, taking, communicable, epidemic, zymotic, sporadic, endemic, pandemic, epizoötic.

innutritious, indigestible, ungenial; uncongenial etc. (*disagreeing*) 24.

deadly etc. (*killing*) 361.

658. Improvement.—N. improvement; a-, melioration; betterment; mend, amendment, emendation; mending etc. *v.*; advancement; advance etc. (*progress*) 282; ascent etc. 305; promotion, preferment; elevation etc. 307; increase etc. 35.

cultiv-, civiliz-ation; menticulture, culture, march of intellect; eugenics, euthenics, meliorism, telesis.

reform, -ation; revision, radical reform; second thoughts, correction, *limae labor*, refinement, elaboration; purification etc. 652; repair etc. (*restoration*) 660; recovery etc. 660.

revise; revised −, new- edition.

reformer, radical, progressive.

V. improve; be –, become –, get- better; mend, amend.

advance etc. (*progress*) 282; ascend etc. 305; increase etc. 35; fructify, ripen, mature; pick up, come about, rally, take a favorable turn; turn -over a new leaf, – the corner; raise one's head, sow one's wild oats; recover etc. 660.

be -better etc. *adj.*, – improved by; turn to - right, – good, – best- account; profit by, reap the benefit of; make -good use of, – capital out of; place to good account; take advantage of.

render better, improve, emend, make over, better; a-, meliorate; correct.

improve –, refine- upon; rectify; enrich, mellow, elaborate, fatten.

promote, cultivate, advance, forward, enhance; bring -forward, – on; foster etc. 707; invigorate etc. (*strengthen*) 159.

touch –, rub –, brush –, furbish –, bolster –, vamp –, brighten –, warm- up; polish, cook, make the most of, set off to advantage; prune; repair etc. (*restore*) 660; put in order etc. (*arrange*) 60.

review, revise, edit, redact; make -corrections, – improvements etc. *n.*; doctor etc. (*remedy*) 662; purify etc. 652.

relieve, refresh, revive, infuse new blood into, recruit, re-invigorate, renew, revivify, freshen, build -afresh, – anew; uplift, inspire.

re-form, -model, -organize; new model, civilize.

view in a new light, think better of, appeal from Philip drunk to Philip sober.

palliate, mitigate; lessen etc. 36- an evil.

Adj. improving etc. *v.*; progressive, improved etc. *v.*; better, – off, – for; all the better for; better advised.

reform-, emend-atory; reparatory etc. (*restorative*) 660; remedial etc. 662.

corrigible, improvable, curable, accultural.

Adv. on -consideration, – reconsideration, – second thoughts, – better advice; *ad melius inquirendum*; on the -mend,' – up grade.

659. Deterioration.—N. deterioration, debasement; want, ebb; recession etc. 287; retrogradation etc. 283; decrease etc. 36.

degenera-cy, -tion, -teness; degradation; depravation, -ement; depravity etc. 945; demoralization, retrogression.

impairment, inquination, injury, damage, loss, detriment, delaceration, outrage, havoc, inroad, ravage, scath; perversion, prostitution, vitiation, discoloration, oxidation, pollution, defedation, poisoning, venenation, leaven, contamination, canker, corruption, adulteration, alloy.

decl-ine, -ension, -ination; decadence, -cy; falling off etc. *v.*; caducity, decrepitude, senility.

decay, dilapidation, ravages of time, wear and tear; cor-, e-rosion; mouldi-, rotten-ness; moth and rust, dry-rot, blight, marasmus, atrophy, collapse; disorganization; *délabrement* etc. (*destruction*) 162.

wreck, mere wreck, honeycomb, *magni nominis umbra*.

V. be –, become- -worse, – deteriorated etc. *adj.*; have seen better days, deteriorate, degenerate,

fall off; wane etc. (*decrease*) 36; ebb; retrograde etc. 283; decline, droop; go down etc. (*sink*) 306; go -downhill, – on from bad to worse, – farther and fare worse; jump out of the frying pan into the fire.

run to -seed, – waste; swale, sweal; lapse, be the worse for; break, – down; spring a leak, crack, start; shrivel etc. (*contract*) 195; fade, go off, wither, molder, rot, rankle, decay, go bad; go to - fall into- decay; 'fall into the sear and yellow leaf,' rust, crumble, shake; totter, – to its fall; perish etc. 162; die etc. 360.

[*Render less good*] deteriorate; weaken etc. 160; put back; taint, infect, contaminate, poison, empoison, envenom, canker, corrupt, exulcerate, pollute, vitiate, inquinate; de-, em-base; denaturalize, leaven; de-flower, -bauch, -file, - prave, -grade; stain etc. (*dirt*) 653; discolor; alloy, adulterate, sophisticate, tamper with, prejudice.

pervert, prostitute, demoralize, brutalize; render vicious etc. 945; compromise.

embitter, ex-, acerbate, aggravate.

injure, impair, labefy, damage, harm, hurt, shend, scathe, spoil, mar, despoil, dilapidate, waste; overrun; ravage; pillage etc. 791.

wound, stab, pierce, maim, lame, surbate, cripple, hough, hamstring, hit between the wind and water, scotch, mangle, mutilate, disfigure, blemish, deface, warp.

blight, rot; cor-, e-rode, eat away; wear -away, – out; gnaw, – at the root of; sap, mine, undermine, shake, sap the foundations of, break up; dis-organize, -mantle, -mast; destroy etc. 162.

damnify etc. (*aggrieve*) 649; do one's worst; knock down; deal a blow to; play -havoc, – sad havoc, – the mischief, – the deuce, – the very devil- -with, – among; decimate.

Adj. unimproved etc. (improve etc. 658); deteriorated etc. *v.*; altered, – for the worse; injured etc. *v.*; sprung; withering, spoiling, etc. *v.*; on the -wane; – decline; tabid; degenerate; worse; the –, all the- worse for; out of -repair, – tune; imperfect etc. 651; the worse for wear; battered; weather-ed, -beaten; stale, *passé*, shaken, dilapidated, frayed, faded, wilted, shabby, second-hand, second-rate, threadbare; worn, – to- -a thread, – a shadow, – the stump, rags; reduced, – to a skeleton, skeletonized; far gone.

decayed etc. *v.*; moth-, worn-eaten; mildewed, rusty, moldy, spotted, seedy, time-worn, moss-grown; discolored; effete, wasted, crumbling, moldering, rotten, cankered, blighted, tainted; depraved etc. (*vicious*) 945; decrep-id, -it; broken down; done, – for, – up; worn out, used up; fit for the -dust-hole, – wastepaper basket; past work etc. (*useless*) 645.

at a low ebb, in a bad way, on one's last legs, washed -up; – out; undermined, deciduous; nodding to its fall etc. (*destruction*) 162; tottering etc. (*dangerous*) 665; past cure etc. (*hopeless*) 859; fatigued etc. 688; backward, retrograde etc. (*retrogressive*) 283; deleterious etc. 649; behind the times.

Adv. on the down grade; beyond hope.

Phr. out of the frying pan into the fire; *aegrescit medendo*.

660. Restoration.—N. restor-ation, -al; re-instatement, -placement, -habilitation, -

establishment, -construction; reproduction etc. 163; re-novation, -newal; reviv-al, -escence; refreshment etc. 689; re-suscitation, -animation, -vivification, -viction; Phoenix; reorganization.

renaissance, renascence, rebirth, second youth, rejuvenation, rejuvenescence, new birth; regeneration, -cy, -teness; palingenesis, reconversion, resurgence, resurrection.

redress, retrieval, reclamation, recovery; convalescence; resumption, *résumption*.

recurrence etc. (*repetition*) 104; *réchauffé*, *rifacimento*.

cure, recure, sanation; healing etc. *v*.; redintegration; rectification, instauration.

repair, reparation, mending; recruiting etc. *v*.; cicatrization; disinfection; tinkering.

reaction; redemption etc. (*deliverance*) 672; restitution etc. 790; relief etc. 834.

mender, repairer, renewer; tinker, cobbler; doctor etc. 662; *vis medicatrix* etc. (*remedy*) 662. curableness.

V. return to the original state; recover, rally, revive; come -to, – round, – to oneself; pull through, weather the storm, be oneself again; get well, – round, – the better of, – over, – about; rise from -one's ashes, – the grave; resurge, resurrect; survive etc. (*outlive*) 110; resume, reappear; come to, – life again; live –, rise- again; relive.

heal, skin over, cicatrize; right itself.

restore, put back, place *in statu quo*; re-instate, -place, -seat, -habilitate, -establish, -estate, -install.

re-construct, -build, -organize, -constitute; reconvert; re-new, -novate; recondition; regenerate; rejuvenate.

re-deem, -claim, -cover, -trieve; rescue etc. (*deliver*) 672.

redress, recure; cure, heal, remedy, doctor, physic, medicate; break of; bring round, set on one's legs.

re-suscitate, -vive, -animate, -vivify, -call to life; reproduce etc. 163; warm up; reinvigorate, refresh etc. 689.

redintegrate, make whole; recoup etc. 790; make -good, – all square; rectify; put –, set- -right, – to rights, – straight; set up, correct; put in order etc. (*arrange*) 60; refit, recruit; fill up, – the ranks; reinforce.

repair, mend; put in -repair, – thorough repair, – complete repair; retouch, botch, vamp, tinker, doctor, cobble; do –, patch –, plaster –, vamp-up; darn, fine-draw, heel-piece; stop a gap, stanch, staunch, caulk, calk, careen, splice, bind up wounds.

Adj. restored etc. *v*.; *redivivus*, convalescent; in a fair way; none the worse; rejuvenated, renascent.

restoring etc. *v*.; restorative, recuperative; sana-, repara-tive, -tory; curative, remedial.

restor-, recover-, san-, remedi-, retriev-, cur-able.

Adv. *in statu qho*; as you were.

Phr. *revenons à nos moutons.*

661. Relapse.—N. relapse, lapse; falling back etc. *v*.; retrogradation etc. (*retrogression*) 283; deterioration etc. 659.

[Return to, or recurrence of a bad state] backsliding, recidivation, recrudescence.

V. relapse, lapse; fall –, slide –, sink- back;

have a relapse; return; retrograde etc. 283; recidivate; fall off etc. 659- again.

662. Remedy.—N. remedy, help, redress; antidote, anti-toxin, -biotic; anti-, counter-poison, prophylactic, antiseptic, germicide, bactericide, corrective, restorative, stimulant, pick-me-up, tonic; sedative etc. 174; palliative; febrifuge; alterant, -ative; specific; emetic, carminative; narcotic etc. *adj*.; Nepenthe, Mithridate.

cure; radical –, perfect –, certain- cure; sovereign remedy.

physic, medicine, patent medicine, Galenicals, simples, drug, wonder –, miracle – drugs; potion, draught, dose, pill, bolus, lozenge, tablet, tabloid, capsule; electuary; linct-us, -ure; medicament.

nostrum, receipt, recipe, prescription; catholicon, panacea, elixir, *elixir vitae*, philosopher's stone; balm, balsam, cordial, theriac, ptisan.

salve, ointment, cerate, oil, lenitive, lotion, cosmetic; plaster; epithem, embrocation, liniment, cataplasm, sinapism, arquebusade, traumatic, vulnerary, pepastic, poultice, collyrium, depilatory. compress, pledget; bandage etc. (*support*) 215.

treatment, medical treatment, regimen; diet-ary, -etics; *vis medicatrix*, – *naturae*; *médicine expectante*; seton, blood-letting, bleeding, venesection, phlebotomy, cupping, leeches; operation, surgical operation; tonsillectomy, appendectomy; injection, electrolysis, massage.

pharma-cy, -cology, -ceutics; acology; materia medica, pharmacopoeia, therapeutics, therapy, posology, pathology etc. 655; home-, hetero-, all-, hydr-opathy; cold water –, open air- cure; dietetics; sur-, chirur-gery, osteopathy; healing art, leechcraft, practice of medicine; ortho-paedy, -praxy; dentistry, midwifery, obstetrics, gynecology.

faith -cure, – healing, Christian science; psychotherapy, -analysis, psychiatry.

hospital, infirmary, clinic; pest-, lazar-house; lazaretto, lazaret; lock hospital; *maison de santé*; *ambulance*; dispensary; *sanatorium, sanitarium*, spa, baths, pump-room, well; *hospice*; Red Cross; nursing home; asylum.

doctor, physician, surgeon; medical –, general-practitioner, consultant, specialist; medical attendant; medical student, medico; chemist, apothecary, pharmacopolist, druggist; leech; Aesculapius, Hippocrates, Galen; *accoucheur*, gynecologist, midwife, oculist, aurist, dentist; operator; osteopath, bonesetter; nurse, monthly nurse, sister; dresser; *masseur, masseuse.*

V. apply a -remedy etc. *n*.; doctor, dose, physic, nurse, minister to, attend; dress the wounds, plaster, bandage, poultice; heal, cure, work a cure, kill or cure, remedy, stay (disease), snatch from the jaws of death; prevent etc. 706; relieve etc. 834; palliate etc. 658; restore etc. 660; drench with physic; consult, operate, extract, deliver; bleed, cup, let blood, transfuse; electrolyse; psychoanalyse.

Adj. remedial; restorative etc. 660; corrective, palliative, healing; sana-tory, -tive; prophylactic; salutiferous etc. (*salutary*) 656; medic-al, -inal; therapeutic, surgical, chirurgical, orthopedic, epulotic, paregoric, tonic, corroborant, analeptic, balsamic, anodyne, hypnotic, neurotic, narcotic,

sedative, lenitive, demulcent, emollient;
depuratory; deter-sive, -gent; abstersive, disinfectant, febrifugal, alternative; traumatic,
vulnerary.

dietetic, alimentary; nutrit-ious, -ive; peptic;
alexi-pharmic, -teric; remedi-, cur-able.

663. Bane. —N. bane, curse, thorn in the -side,
-flesh, bugbear, *bête noire*; evil etc. 619; hurtfulness etc. (*badness*) 649; painfulness etc. (*cause
of pain*) 830; scourge etc. (*punishment*) 975; *dam-
nosa hereditas*; white elephant.

sting, fang, thorn, tang, bramble, briar, nettle.

poison, leaven, virus, venom; intoxicant; arsenic,
Prussic acid, antimony, tartar emetic, strychnine,
nicotine, cyanide of potassium, corrosive sublimate;
curare; hyoscine etc.; poison-, mustard-, tear-gas;
carbon di-, mon-oxide; ptomaine poisoning,
botulism; miasm, mephitis, malaria, azote, sewer
gas; pest, stench etc. 401.

rust, worm, moth, moth and rust, fungus,
mildew; dry-rot; canker, -worm; cancer; torpedo;
viper etc. (*evil-doer*) 913; demon etc. 980.

hemlock, hellebore, nightshade, *belladonna*,
henbane, aconite; Upas tree.

drugs, dope, opium, morphia, morphine,
cocaine, heroin, hashish, bhang.

[*Science of poisons*] Toxicology.

Adj. baneful etc. (*bad*) 649; poisonous etc. (*unwholesome*) 657.

664. Safety.—N. safety, security, im-
pregnability; invulnera-bility, -bleness etc. *adj.*;
danger -past, — over; storm blown over; coast
clear; escape etc. 671; means of escape, safety-
valve; safeguard, palladium, sheet anchor, rock,
tower of strength.

guardian-, ward-, warden-ship; tutelage, custody,
safe keeping; preservation etc. 670; protection,
auspices.

safe-conduct, escort, convoy; guard, sheild etc.
(*defense*) 717; guardian angel, tutelary -god, —
deity, — saint; *genius loci*.

protector, guardian; ward-en, -er; preserver,
custodian, *duenna chaperon*, third person.

watch-, ban-dog; Cerberus; watch-, patrol-,
police-man, constable, peeler, bobby, copper, cop,
bull, flat-foot, detective, armed guard; sentinel,
sentry, scout etc. (*warning*) 668; garrison; guard-
ship.

[*Means of safety*] refuge etc., anchor etc. 666;
precaution etc. (*preparation*) 673; quarantine, *cordon sanitaire*. [Sense of security] confidence etc.
858.

V. be -safe etc. *adj.*; keep one's head above
water, tide over, save one's bacon; ride out —,
weather- the storm; light upon one's feet; bear a
charmed life; escape etc.· 671; possess nine lives.

make —, render- -safe etc. *adj.*; protect, watch
over; take care of etc. (*care*) 459; preserve etc.
670; cover, screen, shelter, shroud, flank, ward;
guard etc. (*defend*) 717; secure etc. (*restrain*) 751;
intrench, fence round etc. (*circumscribe*) 229;
house, nestle, ensconce; take charge of.

escort, convoy; garrison; watch, mount guard,
patrol, scout, spy.

make assurance double sure etc. (*caution*) 864;
take up a loose thread; take precautions etc.
(*prepare for*) 673; take in a reef; double reef topsails.

seek safety; take —, find- shelter etc. 666; run
into port.

Adj. safe, secure, sure; in -safety, — security;
have an anchor to windward; on the safe side; under the -shield of, — shade of, — wing of, —
shadow of one's wing; under -cover, — lock and
key; out of -danger, — the meshes, — harm's way;
in -harbor, — port; on sure ground, at anchor, high
and dry, above water, on *terra firma*; un-
threatened, -molested; protected etc. *v.*; cavendo
tutus; panoplied etc. (*defended*) 717.

snug, sea-, air-worthy; weather-, water-, fire-,
bomb-proof.

defensible, tenable, proof against, invulnerable;
un-assailable, -attackable; im-pregnable, -perdible;
founded on a rock; inexpugnable.

safe and sound etc. (*preserved*) 670; harmless;
scathless etc. (*perfect*) 650; unhazarded; not -
dangerous etc. 665.

protecting etc. *v.*; guardian, tutelary; per-
servative etc. 670; trustworthy etc. 939.

Adv. *ex abundanti cautelâ*; with impunity.

Phr. all's well; all clear; *salva res est*; *suave
mari magno*; safety first.

665. Danger.—N. danger, peril, insecurity,
jeopardy, risk, hazard, venture, precariousness,
slipperiness; instability etc. 149; defenselessness
etc. *adj.*

exposure etc. (*liability*) 177; vulnerability;
vulnerable point, heel of Achilles; forlorn hope etc.
(*hopelessness*) 859.

[Dangerous course] leap in the dark etc.
(*rashness*) 863; road to ruin, *facilis descensus
Averni*, hair-breadth escape.

cause for alarm; source of danger etc. 667.
[Approach of danger] rock —, breakers- ahead;
storm brewing; clouds -in the horizon, —
gathering; warning etc. 668; alarm etc. 669. [Sense
of danger] apprehension etc. 860.

V. be -in danger etc. *adj.*; be exposed to —, run
into —, incur —, encounter- -danger etc. *n.*; run a
risk; lay oneself open to etc. (*liability*) 177; lean
on —, trust to- a broken reed; feel the ground
sliding from under one, have to run for it; have the
-chances, — odds- against one.

hang by a thread, totter; tremble on the -verge,
— brink; sleep — stand -on a volcano; sit on a
barrel of gunpowder, live in a glass house.

bring —, place —, put- in -danger etc. *n.*; endanger, expose to danger, imperil; jeopard, -ize,
compromise; sail too near the wind etc. (*rash*) 863;
put one's head in the lion's mouth.

adventure, risk, hazard, venture, stake, set at
hazard; run the gauntlet etc. (*dare*) 861; engage in
a forlorn hope.

threaten etc. 909- danger; run one hard; lay a
trap for etc. (*deceive*) 545.

Adj. in -danger etc. *n.*; endangered etc. *v.*;
fraught with danger; danger-, hazard-, peril-, parl-;
pericul-ous; unsafe, unprotected etc. (*safe, protect
etc.* 664); insecure, untrustworthy, unreliable; built
upon sand, on a sandy basis.

defence-, fence-, guard-, harbor-less; unshielded;
vulnerable, expugnable, unsheltered, exposed;
open to etc. (liable) 177.

aux abois, at bay; on -the wrong side of the wall,
– a lee shore, – the rocks.

at stake, in question; precarious, aleatory,
critical, ticklish; slip-pery, -py; hanging by a thread
etc. *v.*; with a halter round one's neck; between –
the hammer and the anvil, – Scylla and Charybdis, – two fires; on the -edge, – brink, – verge of
a- -precipice, – volcano; in the lion's den, on slippery ground, under fire; not out of the wood.

un-warned, -admonished, -advised; unprepared
etc. 674; off one's guard etc. (inexpectant) 508.

tottering; un-stable, -steady; shaky, top-heavy,
tumble-down, ramshackle, crumbling,
waterlogged; help-, guide-less; in a bad way;
reduced to – , at- the last extremity; trembling in
the balance; nodding to its fall etc. (destruction)
162.

threatening etc. 909; ominous, ill-omened; alarming etc. (fear) 860; explosive; poisonous etc. 657.

adventurous etc. (rash) 863, (bold) 861.

Int. stop! look out! beware! take care!

Phr. incidit in Scyllam qui vult vitare Charybdim; nam tua res agitur paries dum proximus ardet.

666. Refuge. [Means of safety.]—N. refuge,
sanctuary, retreat, fastness; stronghold, keep, last
resort; ward; prison etc. 752; asylum, ark, home,
almshouse, refuge for the destitute; hiding-place
etc. (ambush) 530; *sanctum sanctorum* etc.
(privacy) 893.

roadstead, anchorage; breakwater, mole, port,
haven; harbor, – of refuge; sea-port; pier, jetty,
embankment, quay.

covert, shelter, abri, screen, lee-wall, wing,
shield, umbrella; splash-, dash-board, mudguard.

wall etc. (inclosure) 232; fort etc. (defence)
717.

anchor, kedge; grap-nel, -pling iron; sheet-,
mushroom-anchor, main-stay; support etc. 215;
check etc. 706; ballast.

jury-mast; vent-peg; safety -valve, – lamp;
lightning conductor.

means of escape etc. (escape) 671; life-boat,
swimming belt, cork jacket; life preserver, breeches
buoy; parachute, plank, stepping-stone.

safeguard etc. (protection) 664.

V. seek – , take – , find- refuge etc. *n.*; seek – ,
find- safety etc. 664; throw oneself into the arms
of; claim sanctuary; take to the -hills, – woods;
make port, reach shelter, bar – , bolt – , lock -the
door, – gete; let the portcullis down; raise the
drawbridge.

667. Pitfall. [Source of danger.]—N. rocks,
reefs, coral reef, sunken rocks, snags; sands,
quicksands, Goodwin sands, sandy foundation;
slippery ground; breakers, shoals, shallows, bank,
shelf, flat, lee shore, iron-bound coast; rock – ,
breakers- ahead; derelict.

precipice; abyss, chasm, pit, crevasse; maelstrom,
whirlpool, eddy, vortex, rapids, current, bore, tidal
wave; storm, squall, hurricane, whirlwind; volcano;

ambush etc. 530; pitfall, trap-door; trap etc.
(snare) 545.

sword of Damocles; wolf at the door, snake in
the grass, viper in one's bosom, death in the pot;
latency etc. 526.

ugly customer, dangerous person, *le chat qui
dort*; firebrand, hornet's nest.

Phr. *latet anguis in herbâ*; *proximus ardet
Ucalegon*.

668. Warning.—N. warning, caution, *caveat*;
notice etc. (information) 527; premoni-tion, -
shment; prediction etc. 511; contraindication;
symptom; lesson, dehortation; admonition,
monition; alarm etc. 669.

handwriting on the wall, *tekel upharsin*, yellow
flag; fog-signal, -horn; siren; monitor, warning
voice, Cassandra, signs of the times, Mother
Carey's chickens, stormy petrel, bird of ill omen,
gathering clouds, clouds in the horizon, cloud no
bigger than a man's hand, death-watch.

watch-tower, beacon, signal-post; light-house etc.
(indication of locality) 550.

sent-inel, -ry, watch, -man; watch and ward;
watch-, ban-, house-dog; patrol, vedette, picket,
bivouac, scout, spy, spial; advanced – , rear-guard,
lookout, flagman.

cautiousness etc. 864.

V. warn, caution; fore-, pre-warn; ad-, premonish; give -notice, – warning; menace etc.
(threaten) 909; put on one's guard; sound the
alarm etc. 669; croak.

beware, ware; take -warning, – heed at one's
peril; watch out for; keep watch and ward etc.
(care) 459.

Adj. warning etc. *v.*; premonitory, monitory,
cautionary; admonitory, -tive; ominous,
threatening, lowering, minatory, symptomatic.

warned etc. *v.*; on one's guard etc. (careful) 459;
(cautious) 864.

Adv. in terrorem etc. (threat) 909.

Int. beware! ware! take care! mind – , take care-
what you are about; mind! look out!

Phr. ne reveillez pas le chat qui dort; foenum
habet in cornu.

669. Alarm. [Indication of danger.]—N.
alarm; alarum, larum, alarm bell, tocsin, *alerte*,
beat of drum, sound of trumpet, note of alarm, hue
and cry, signal of distress, S.O.S.; blue-lights; war-
cry, -whoop; warning etc. 668; fog-signal, -horn;
siren; yellow flag; danger signal; red -light, – flag;
fire -bell, – alarm; burglar alarm, police whistle,
watchman's rattle.

false alarm, cry of wolf; bug-bear, -aboo.

V. give – , raise – , sound – , beat- the *or* an -
alarm etc. *n.*; alarm; warn etc. 668; ring the tocsin;
battre la générale; cry wolf.

Adj. alarming etc. *v.*

Int. sauve qui peut! qui vive? who goes there?

670. Preservation.—N. preservation; safe
keeping; conservation etc. (storage) 636; maintenance, upkeep, support, sustentation, con-

servatism; *vis conservatrix*; salvation etc. (*deliverance*) 672; drying etc. *v.*

[Means of preservation] prophylaxis; preserv-er, -ative; canned goods; cold pack; hygi-astics, -antics; cover, durgget; *cordon sanitaire*.

[Superstitious remedies] charm etc. 993.

V. preserve, maintain, keep, sustain, support; keep -up, – alive; not willingly let die; shore –, bank- up; nurse; save, rescue; be –, make- safe etc. 664; take care of etc. (*care*) 459; guard etc. (*defend*) 717.

stare super antiquas vias; hold one's own; hold –, stand- -one's ground etc. (*resist*) 719.

embalm, dry, cure, smoke, salt, pickle, season, kyanize, bottle, pot, tin, can; husband etc. (*store*) 636.

Adj. preserving etc. *v.*; conservative; prophylatic; preserva-tory, -tive; hygienic.

preserved etc. *v.*; un-impaired, -broken, -injured, -hurt, -singed, -marred; safe, – and sound; intact, with a whole skin, without a scratch.

Phr. *nolumus leges Angliae mutari*.

671. Escape.—N. escape, scape; avolation, elopment, flight, get-away; evasion etc. (*avoidance*) 623; retreat; narrow –, hairbreadth- escape; close –, near- shave; come off, impunity.

[Means of escape] loophole etc. (*opening*) 260; path etc. 627; secret -door, – passage; refuge etc. 666; vent, – peg; safety-valve; drawbridge, fire-escape.

reprieve etc. (*deliverance*) 672; liberation etc. 750.

refugee etc. (*fugitive*) 623.

V. escape, scape; make –, effect –, make good- one's escape, make a get-away; get -off, – clear off, – well out of; *échapper belle*, save one's bacon; weather the storm etc. (*safe*) 664; escape scot-free.

elude etc., make off etc. (*avoid*) 623; march off etc. (*go away*) 293; give one the slip; slip through the -hands, – fingers; slip the collar, wriggle out of; break -loose, – from prison; break –, slip –, get- away; find -vent, – a hole to creep out of.

Adj. escap-ing, -ed etc. *v.*; stolen away, fled.

Phr. the bird has flown.

672. Deliverance.—N. deliverance, extrication, rescue; repriev-e, -al; respite; ransom; liberation etc. 750; truce, armistice; redemption, salvation; riddance; gaol delivery; exemption, day of grace; redeemableness.

V. deliver, extricate, rescue, save, redeem, ransom, free, liberate, release, set free, redeem, emancipate; bring -off, – through; *tirer d'affaire*, get the wheel out of the rut; snatch from the jaws of death, come to the rescue; rid; retrieve etc. (*restore*) 660; be –, get- rid of.

Adj. saved etc. *v.*; extric-, redeem-, rescu-able.

Phr. to the rescue!

673. Preparation.—N. preparation; providing etc. *v.*; provi-sion, -dence; anticipation etc. (*foresight*) 510; precaution, -concertation,

disposition; forecast etc. (*plan*) 626; rehearsal, not of preparation.

[Putting in order] arrangement etc. 60; clearance; adjustment etc. 23; tuning; equipment, outfit, accoutrement, armament, array.

ripening etc. *v.*; maturation, evolution; elaboration, concoction, digestion; gestation, hatching, incubation, sitting.

groundwork, datum, first stone, cradle, stepping-stone; foundation, scaffold etc. (*support*) 215; scaffolding, *échafaudage*.

[Preparation -of men] training etc. (*education*) 537; inurement etc. (*habit*) 613; novitiate; [– of food] cook-ing, -ery; brewing, culinary art; [– of the soil] till-, plough-, sow-ing; semination, cultivation.

[State of being prepared] prepared-, readi-, ripe-, mellow-ness; maturity; *un impromptu fait à loisir.*

[Preparer] preparer, teacher, coach, trainer, pioneer; *avant-courrier*, *-coureur*; sappers and miners, paver, navvy; packer, stevedore; warmingpan; precursor etc. 64.

V. prepare; get –, make- ready; make preparations, settle preliminaries, get up, sound the note of preparation; address oneself to.

set –, put- in order etc. (*arrange*) 60; forecast etc. (*plan*) 626; prepare –, plough –, dress- the ground; till –, cultivate- the soil; predispose, sow the seed, lay a train, dig a mine; lay –, fix- the -foundations, – basis, -groundwork; dig the foundations, erect the scaffolding; lay the first stone etc. (*begin*) 66.

rough-hew; cut out work; block –, hammer-out; lick into shape etc. (*form*) 240.

elaborate, mature, ripen, mellow, season, bring to maturity; nurture etc.

(*aid*) 707; hatch, cook, brew; temper; anneal, smelt; dry, cure etc. 670.

equip, arm, man; fit-out, -up; furnish, rig, dress, garnish, betrim, accouter, array, fettle, fledge; dress –, furbish –, brush –, vamp- up; refurbish; sharpen one's tools, trim one's foils, set, prime, attune; whet the -knife, – sword; wind –, screw- up; adjust etc. (*fit*) 27; put in- trim, – train, – gear, – working order, – tune, – a groove for, – harness; pack, stow away, store.

train etc. (*teach*) 537; inure etc. (*habituate*) 613; breed; prepare etc.- for; rehearse; make provision for; take -steps, – measures, – precautions; provide, – against; beat up for recruits; open the door to etc. (*facilitate*) 705.

set one's house in order, make all snug; clear - decks, – for action; close one's ranks; shuffle the cards.

prepare oneself; serve an apprenticeship etc. (*learn*) 539; lay oneself out for, get into harness, gird up one's loins, buckle on one's armor, *reculer pour mieux sauter*, prime and load, shoulder arms, get the steam up, put the horses to.

guard –, make sure- against; forearm, make sure, prepare for the evil day, have a rod in pickle, provide against a rainy day, feather one's nest; lay in provisions etc. 637; make investments; keep on foot.

be -prepared, – ready etc. *adj.*; hold oneself in readiness, watch and pray, keep one's powder dry; lie in wait for etc. (*expect*) 507; anticipate etc. (*foresee*) 510; *principiis obstare*; *veniente occurrere morbo*.

Adj. preparing etc. *v.*; in -preparation, – course

of preparation, − agitation, − embryo, − hand, − train; afoot, afloat; on -foot, − the stocks, − the anvil; under consideration etc. (*plan*) 626; brewing, hatching, forthcoming, brooding; in -store for, − reserve.

precautionary, provident; prepara-tive, -tory; provisional, inchoate, under revision; preliminary etc. (*precedent*) 62.

prepared etc. *v.*; in readiness; ready, − to one's hand, − made, cut and dried; ready for use, reach me down; made to one's hand, handy, on the table, made to order; in gear; in working -order, − gear; snug; in practice.

ripe, mature, mellow; practiced etc. (*skillet*) 698; labored, elaborate, highly-wrought, smelling of the lamp, worked up.

in -full feather, − best bib and tucker; in −, at-harness; in − the saddle, − arms, − battle array, − war paint; up in arms; armed -at all points, − to the teeth, − *cap-à-pie*; sword in hand; booted and spurred.

in utrumque −, *semper- paratus*; on the alert etc. (*vigilant*) 459; at one's post.

Adv. in -preparation, − anticipation of; afoot, astir, abroad; abroach.

674. Non-preparation.—N. non-, absence of −, want of- preparation; unpreparedness; in-culture, inconcoction, improvidence.

immaturity, crudity; rawness etc. *adj.*; abortion; disqualification.

[Absence of art] nature, state of nature; virgin soil, unweeded garden; rough diamond, neglect etc. 460.

rough copy etc. (*plan*) 626; germ etc. 153; raw material etc. 635.

improvisation etc. (*impulse*) 612.

V. be -unprepared etc. *adj.*; want −, lack-preparation; lie fallow; *s'embarquer sans biscuits*; live from hand to mouth.

[Render unprepared] dismantle etc. (*render useless*) 645; undress etc. 226.

extemporize, improvise.

surprise, pay a surprise visit, take by surprise, drop in upon, take unawares; take pot-luck.

Adv. un-prepared etc. prepare etc. 673] without -preparation etc. 673; incomplete etc. 53; rudimen-tal, embryonic, abortive; immature, unripe, raw, green, crude; coarse; rough, -cast, -hewn; in the rough; un-hewn, -formed, -fashioned, -wrought, - labored, -blown, -cooked, -boiled, -concocted, - cút, -polished.

callow, un-hatched, -fledged, -nurtured, -licked, -taught, -educated, -cultivated, -trained, -tutored, - drilled, -exercised; precocious, premature; un-, in-digested; un-mellowed, -seasoned, -leavened.

fallow; un-sown, -tilled; natural, in a state of na-ture; undressed; in dishabille, *en déshabille, en négligé.*

un-, dis-qualified; unfitted; ill-digested; un-begun, -ready, -arranged, -organized, -furnished, - provided, -equipped, -trimmed; out of -gear, − or-der; dismantled etc. *v.*

shiftless, improvident, unthrifty, thoughtless, unguarded; happy-go-lucky; caught napping etc. (*inexpectant*) 508; unpremeditated etc. 612.

Adv. extempore etc. 612.

675. Essay.—N. essay, trial, endeavor, aim, at-tempt; venture, adventure, speculation, *coup d'essai, début*; probation etc. (*experiment*) 463.

V. try, essay; experiment etc. 463; endeavor, strive; tempt, tackle, take on, attempt, make an at-tempt; venture, adventure, speculate, take one's chance, tempt fortune; try one's -fortune, − luck, −, hand; use one's endeavor; feel −, grope −, pick- one's way.

try hard, push, make a bold push, use one's best endeavor; do one's best etc. (*exertion*) 686.

Adj. essaying etc. *v.*; experimental etc. 463; tentative, empirical, probationary.

Adv. experimentally etc. *adj.*; on trial, at a ven-ture; by rule of thumb.

if one may be so bold.

676. Undertaking.—N. undertaking, compact etc. 769; engagement etc. (*promise*) 768; enter-em-prise; venture etc. 675; pilgrimage; matter in hand etc. (*business*) 625; move; first move etc. (*beginning*) 66.

V. undertake; engage −, embark- in; launch −, plunge- into; volunteer; apprentice oneself to; engage etc. (*promise*) 768; contract etc. 769; take upon -oneself, − one's shoulders; devote oneself to etc. (*determination*) 604.

take -up, − in hand; tackle; set −, go- about; set −, fall- -to, − to work; launch forth; set up shop; put in -hand, − execution; set forward; break the neck of a business, be in for; put one's hand to; betake oneself to, turn one's hand to, go to do; begin etc. 66; broach, institute, etc. (*originate*) 153; put −, lay- one's -hand to the plough, − shoulder to the wheel.

have in hand etc. (*business*) 625; have many irons in the fire etc. (*activity*) 682.

Adj. undertaking etc. *v.*; on the anvil etc. 625; adventurous, venturesome.

Int. here goes!

677. Use.—N. use; employ, -ment; exer-cise, - citation; appli-cation, -ance; adhibition, disposal; consumption; agency etc. (*physical*) 170; usufruct; usefulness etc. 644; recourse, resort, avail; pragmatism.

[Conversion to use] utilization, service, wear. [Way of using] usage.

V. use, make use of, employ, put to use; apply, put in -action, − operation, − practice; set -in motion, − to work.

ply, work, wield, handle, manipulate; play, − off; exert, exercise, practice, avail oneself of, profit by; resort −, have recourse −, recur −, take −, betake oneself- to; take -up with, − advantage of; lay one's hands on, try.

render useful etc. 644; mold; turn to -account, − use; convert to use, utilize, administer; work up; call −, bring- into play; put into requisition; call −, draw- forth; press −, enlist- into the service; bring to bear upon, devote, dedicate, consecrate, apply, adhibit, dispose of; make a -handle, − cat's paw- of.

fall beak upon, make a shift with; make the -most, − best- of.

use −, swallow- up; consume, absorb, expend; tax, task, wear, put to task.

Adj. in use; used etc. *v.*; well-worn, -trodden. useful etc. 644; subservient etc. (*instrumental*) 631; utilitarian; pragmatical.

678. Disuse.—N. forbearance, abstinence; disuse; relinquishment etc. 782; desuetude etc. (*want of habit*) 614.

V. not use; do without, dispense with, let alone, not touch, forbear, abstain, spare, waive, neglect; keep back, reserve.

lay -up, – by, – on the shelf, – up in a napkin; shelve; set –, put –, lay- aside; disuse, leave off, have done with; supersede; discard etc. (*eject*) 297; dismiss, give warning.

throw aside etc. (*relinquish*) 782; make away with etc. (*destroy*) 162; cast –, heave –, throw-overboard; cast to the -dogs, – winds; dismantle etc. (*render useless*) 645.

lie –, remain- unemployed etc. *adj.*

Adj. not used etc. *v.*; un-employed, -applied, -disposed of, -spent, -exercised, -touched, -trodden, -essayed, -gathered, -culled; uncalled for, not required.

disused etc. *v.*; done with; run down, used up, cast off.

679. Misuse.—N. mis-use, -usage, - employment, -application, -appropriation.

abuse, profanation, prostitution, desecration; waste etc. 638.

V. mis-use, -employ, -apply, -appropriate.

desecrate, abuse, profane, prostitute; waste etc. 638; over-task, -tax, -work; squander etc. 818.

cut a whetstone with a razor, employ a steam-engine to crack a nut; catch at a straw.

Adj. misused etc. *v.*

680. Action.—N. action, performance; doing etc. *v.*; perpetration; exercise, -citation; movement, operation, evolution, work; labor etc. (*exertion*) 686; *praxis*, execution; procedure etc. (*conduct*) 692; handicraft; business etc. 625; agency etc. (*power at work*) 170.

deed, act, overt act, stitch, touch, gest; trans-action, job, doings, dealings, proceeding, measure, step, maneuver, bout, passage, move, stroke, blow; *coup*, – *de main*, – *d'état*; *tour de force* etc. (*display*) 882; feat, exploit, stunt; achievement etc. (*completion*) 729; handiwork, workmanship, crafts-manship; manufacture; stroke of policy etc. (*plan*) 626.

actor etc. (*doer*) 690.

V. do, perform, execute; achieve etc. (*complete*) 729; transact, enact; commit, perpetrate, inflict; exercise, prosecute, carry on, work, practice, play.

employ oneself, ply one's task; officiate, have in hand etc. (*business*) 625; labor etc. 686; be at work; pursue a course; shape one's course etc. (*conduct*) 692.

act, operate; take -action, – steps; strike a blow, lift a finger, stretch forth one's hand; take in hand etc. (*undertake*) 676; put oneself in motion; put in practice; carry into execution etc. (*complete*) 729; act upon.

be -an actor etc. 690; take –, act –, play –, perform- a part in; participate in; have a -hand in, – finger in the pie; have to do with; be a -party to, – participator in; bear –, lend- a hand; pull an oar, run in a race; mix oneself up with etc. (*meddle*) 682.

be in action; come into operation etc. (*power at work*) 170.

Adj. doing etc. *v.*; acting; in action; in harness; on duty; at work; in operation etc. 170; up to one's ears in work, in the midst of things.

Adv. in the -act, – midst of, – thick of; red-handed, *in flagrante delicto*; while one's hand is in.

681. Inaction.—N. inaction, passiveness, ab-stinence from action; non-interference; Fabian –, conservative- policy; neglect etc. 460; stagnation, vegetation; loafing.

inactivity etc. 683; rest etc. (*repose*) 687; quiescence etc. 265; want of –, in- occupation; unemployment; idle hours, time hanging on one's hands, *dolce far niente*; sinecure.

V. not -do, – act, – attempt; be -inactive etc. 683; abstain from doing, do nothing, hold, spare; not -stir, – move, – lift- a -finger, – foot, – peg; fold one's -arms, – hands; leave –, let- alone; let -be, – pass, – things take their course, – it have its way, – well alone; *quieta non movere*; *stare super antiquas vias*; rest and be thankful, live and let live; lie –, rest- upon one's oars; *laisser -aller,* – *faire*; stand aloof; refrain etc. (*avoid*) 623; keep oneself from doing; remit –, relax- one's efforts; desist etc. (*relinquish*) 624; stop etc. (*cease*) 142; pause etc. (*be quiet*) 265.

wait, lie in wait, bide one's time, take time, tide it over.

cool –, kick- one's heels; loaf, while away the -time, – tedious hours; pass –, fill –, beguile- the time; talk against time; waste time etc. (*inactive*) 683.

lie -by, – on the shelf, – in ordinary, – idle, – to, – fallow; keep quiet, slug; have nothing to do, whistle for want of thought; twiddle one's thumbs.

undo, do away with; take -down, – to pieces; destroy etc. 162.

Adj. not doing etc. *v.*; not done etc. *v.*; undone; passive; un-occupied, -employed; out of -employ, – work, – a job; fallow; *désœuvré*.

Adv. *re infectâ*, at a stand, *les bras croisés*, with folded arms; with the hands -in the pockets, – behind one's back; *pour passer le temps*.

Int. so let it be! stop! etc. 142; hands off!

Phr. nothing doing; *cunctando restituit rem.*

682. Activity.—N. activity; briskness, liveliness etc. *adj.*; animation, life, vivacity, spirit, verve, dash, energy, go.

nimbleness, agility; smartness, quickness etc. *adj.*; velocity etc. 274; alacrity, promptitude; des-, dis-patch; expedition; haste etc. 684; punctuality etc. (*early*) 132.

eagerness, zeal, ardor, *perfervidum ingenium*, *empressement*, earnestness, intentness; *abandon*; vigor etc. (*physical energy*) 171; devotion etc. (*resolution*) 604; exertion etc. 686.

industry, assiduity; assiduousness etc. *adj.*; sedulity; laboriousness; drudgery etc. (*labor*) 686; painstaking, diligence; perseverance etc. 604*a*; indefatigable; habits of business.

vigilance etc. 459; wakefulness; sleep-, restlessness; *pervigilium, insomnia*; racketing.

movement, bustle, hustle, stir, fuss, ado, bother, pottering; fidget, -iness; flurry etc. (*haste*) 684.

officiousness; dabbling, meddling; inter-ference, -position, -meddling, butting in, intrusiveness; tampering with, intrigue.

press of business, no sinecure, plenty to do, many irons in the fire, great doings, busy hum of men, battle of life, thick of -things, — the action; the madding corwd.

housewife, busy bee; new brooms; sharp fellow, blade; hustler, devotee, enthusiast, fan, zealot, fanatic; meddler, intermeddler, intriguer, busybody, kibitzer, pickthank.

V. be -active etc. *adj.*; busy oneself in; stir, -about, — one's stumps; bestir —, rouse- oneself; speed, hasten, peg away, lay about one, bustle, fuss; raise —, kick up- a dust; push; make a -push, — fuss, — stir; go ahead, push forward; flight —, elbow- one's way; make progress etc. 282; toil etc. (*labor*) 686; drudge, plod, persist etc. (*persevere*) 604*a*; keep -up the ball, — the pot boiling.

look sharp; have all one's eyes about one etc. (*vigilance*) 459; rise, arouse oneself, get up early, hustle, push; be about, keep moving, steal a march, kill two birds with one stone; seize the opportunity etc. 134; lose no time, not lose a moment, make the most of one's time, not suffer the grass to grow under one's feet, improve the shining hour, make short work of; dash off; make haste etc. 684; do one's best, take pains etc. (*exert oneself*) 686; do —, work- wonders.

have -many irons in the fire, — one's hands full, — much on one's hands; have other -things to do, — fish to fry; be busy; not have a moment -to spare, — that one can call one's own.

have one's fling, run the round of; go all lengths, stick at nothing, run riot.

outdo; over-do, -act, -lay, -shoot the mark; make a toil of a pleasure.

have a hand in etc. (*act in*) 680; take an active part, put in one's oar, have a finger in the pie, mix oneself up with, trouble one's head about, intrigue; agitate.

tamper with, meddle, moil; inter-meddle, -fere, -pose; obtrude; poke —, thrust- one's nose in, butt in.

Adj. active; brisk, — as a lark, — as a bee; lively, animated, vivacious; alive, — and kicking; frisky, spirited, stirring.

nimble, — as a squirrel; agile; light-, nimble-footed; featly, tripping.

quick, prompt, yare, instant, ready, alert, spry, sharp, smart, slick, go-ahead; fast etc. (*swift*) 274; quick as a lamplighter, expeditious; awake, broad awake; wide awake etc. (*intelligent*) 498.

forward, eager, ardent, strenuous, zealous, enterprising, pushing, in earnest; resolute etc. 604.

industrious, assiduous, diligent, sedulous, notable, painstaking; intent etc. (*attention*) 457; indefatigable etc. (*persevering*) 604*a*; unwearied; unsleeping, sleepless, never tired; plodding, hard-working etc. 686; business-like, workaday.

bustling; restless, — as a hyena; fussy, fidgety, pottering; busy, — as a hen with one chicken.

working, laboring, at work, on duty, in harness; up in arms; on one's legs, at call; up and -doing, — stirring.

busy, occupied; hard at -work, — it; up to one's ears in, full of business, busy as a bee.

meddling etc. *v.*; meddlesome, pushing, officious, overofficious, *intrigant*.

astir, stirring; a-going, -foot; on foot; in full swing; eventful; on the alert etc. (*vigilant*) 459.

Adv. actively etc. *adj.*; with -life and spirit, — might and main etc. 686, — haste etc. 684, — wings; full tilt, *in mediis rebus*.

Int. be —, look- -alive, — sharp! move —, push-on! keep moving! go ahead! stir your stumps! *age quod agis!*

Phr. *carpe diem* etc. (*opportunity*) 134; *nulla dies sine lineâ*; *nec mora nec requies*; no sooner said than done etc. (*early*) 132; catch a weasel asleep.

---

683. Inactivity.—N. inactivity; inaction etc. 681; inertness etc. 172; obstinacy etc. 606.

lull etc. (*cessation*) 142; quiescence etc. 265; rust, -iness.

idle-, remiss-ness etc. *adj.*; sloth, indolence, indiligence; otiosity, dawdling etc. *v.*

dullness etc. *adj.*; languor; segni-ty, -tude; len-tor; sluggishness etc. (*slowness*) 275; procrastination etc. (*delay*) 133; torp-or, -idity, -escence; stupor etc. (*insensibility*) 823; somnolence; drowsiness etc. *adj.*; nodding etc. *v.*; oscitation, -ancy; pandiculation, hypnotism, lethargy; heaviness, heavy eye-lids, sand in the eyes.

sleep, slumber; sound —, heavy —, balmy-sleep; Morpheus, dreamland; coma, trance, catalepsy, hypnosis, *ecstasis*, dream, hibernation, nap, doze, snooze, *siesta*, wink of sleep, forty winks, snore; Hypnology.

dull work; pottering; relaxation etc. (*loosening*) 47; Castle of Indolence.

[Cause of inactivity] lullaby, *berceuse*; anesthetic, sedative etc. 174; torpedo.

idler, drone, droil, dawdle, mopus; do-little, *fainéant*, dummy, sleeping partner; afternoon farmer; truant etc. (*runaway*) 623; lounger, *lazzarone*, floater, loafer, tramp, beggar, cadger; lubber, -bard; slow-coach etc. (*slow*) 275; opium —, lotus- eater; slug; lag-, slug-gard, lie-abed; slumberer, dormouse, marmot; waiter on Providence, *fruges consumere natus*.

V. be -inactive etc. *adj.*; do nothing etc. 681; move slowly etc. 275; let the grass grow under one's feet; take one's time, dawdle, poke, drawl, droil, lag, hang back, slouch; loll, -op; lounge, loaf, loiter; go to sleep over; sleep at one's post; *ne battre que d'une aile*.

take -it easy, — things as they come; lead an easy life, vegetate, swim with the stream, eat the bread of idleness; loll in the lap of -luxury, — indolence; waste —, consume —, kill —, lose time; burn daylight, waste the precious hours.

idle —, trifle —, fritter —, fool- away time; spend —, take- time in; ped-, pid-dle; potter, put-ter, dabble, faddle, fribble, fiddle-faddle; dally, dilly-dally.

sleep, slumber, be asleep; hibernate; oversleep; sleep like a -top, — log, — dormouse; sleep -soundly, — heavily; doze, drowze, snooze, nap; take a -nap etc. *n.*; dream; snore; settle —, go —,

go off- to sleep; drop off; fall −, drop- asleep; close −, seal up- -the -eyes, − eyelids; weigh down the eyelids; get sleepy, nod, yawn; go to bed, turn in.

languish, expend itself, flag, hang fire; relax.

render -idle etc. adj.; sluggardize; mitigate etc. 174.

Adj. inactive; motionless etc. 265; unoccupied etc. (doing nothing) 681.

indolent, lazy, slothful, idle, otiose, lusk, remiss, slack, inert, torpid, sluggish, languid, supine, heavy, dull, leaden, lumpish; exanimate, soulless; listless; dron-y, -ish; lazy as Ludlam's dog.

dilatory, laggard; lagging etc. v.; slow etc. 275; rusty, flagging; lackadaisical, maudlin, fiddle-faddle; pottering etc. v.; shilly-shally etc. (irresolute) 605.

sleeping etc. v.; alseep; fast −, dead −, sound-alseep; in a sound sleep; sound as a top, dormant, comatose; in the -arms, − lap- of Morpheus.

sleep-y, -ful; dozy, drowsy, somnolent, torpescent; lethargic, -al; heavy, − with sleep; napping; somni-fic, -ferous; sopor-ous, -ific, -iferous; hypnotic; balmy, dreamy; un-, una-wakened.

sedative etc. 174.

Adv. inactively etc. adj.; at leisure etc. 685.

Phr. the eyes begin to draw straws.

684. Haste.—**N.** haste, urgency; des-, dis-patch; acceleration, spurt, spirt, forced march, rush, dash; velocity etc. 274; precipit-ancy, -ation, -ousness etc. adj.; impetuosity; brusquerie; hurry, scurry, scuttle, drive, scramble, push, hustle, bustle, fuss, fidget, flurry, flutter, splutter.

V. haste, hasten; make -haste, − a dash etc. n.; hurry −, dash −, whip −, push −, press- -on, −-forward; hurry, skurry, scuttle along, bundle on, dart to and fro, bustle, flutter, scramble; plunge, − headlong; run, race, speed; dash off; rush etc. (violence) 173.

bestir oneself etc. (be active) 682; lose -no time, −. not a moment, − not an instant; make short work of; make the best of one's -time, − way.

be -precipitate etc. adj.; jump at; be in -haste, − a hurry etc. n.; have -no time, − not a moment- -to lose, − to spare; work -under pressure, − against time.

quicken etc. 274; accelerate, expedite, put on, precipitate, urge, whip, spur, flog, goad.

Adj. hasty, hurried, brusque; scrambling, cursory, precipitate, headlong, furious, boisterous, impetuous, hot-headed; feverish, fussy; pushing.

in -haste, − a hurry etc. n.; in -hot, − all- haste; breathless, pressed for time, hard pressed, urgent.

Adv. with -haste, − all haste, − breathless speed; in haste etc. adj.; apace etc. (swiftly) 274; amain; all at once etc. (instantaneously) 113; at short notice etc., immediately etc. (early) 132; posthaste; by -express, − telegraph, − wire, − wireless, − air mail.

hastily, precipitately etc. adj.; helter-skelter, hurry-skurry, holusbolus; slap-dash, -bang; full-tilt, -drive; heels over head, head and shoulders, headlong, à corps perdu.

by -fits and starts, − spurts; hop, skip and jump.

Phr. sauve qui peut, devil take the hindmost, no time to be lost; no sooner said than done etc. (early) 132; a word and a blow.

Int. hurry up! look alive! get a move on! buck up! double march! rush! urgent!

685. Leisure.—**N.** leisure; spare -time, − hours, − moments; vacant hour; time, − to spare, − on one's hands; holiday etc. (rest) 687; otium cum dignitate, ease.

V. have -leisure etc. n.; take one's -time, − leisure, − ease; repose etc. 687; move slowly etc. 275; while away the time etc. (inaction) 681; be -master of one's time, − an idle man; desipere in loco.

Adj. leisurely; slow etc. 275; deliberate, quiet, calm, undisturbed; at -leisure, − one's ease, − a loose end.

Phr. time hanging heavy on one's hands.

686. Exertion.—**N.** exertion, effort, strain, tug, pull, stress, force, pressure, throw, stretch, struggle, spell, spurt, spirt; stroke −, stitch- of work.

'a stong pull, a long pull and a pull all together;' dead lift; heft; gymnastics, sports; exer-cise, -citation; wear and tear; ado; toil and trouble; uphill −, hard −, warm- work; harvest time.

labor, work, toil, travail, manual labor, sweat of one's brow, swink, operoseness, drudgery, slavery, fagging, hammering; limae labor.

trouble, pains, duty; resolution etc. 604; energy etc. (physical) 171.

V. exert oneself; exert −, tax- one's energies; use exertion.

labor, work, toil, moil, sweat, fag, drudge, slave, drag a lengthened chain, wade through, strive, strain; make −, stretch- a long arm; pull, tug, ply; ply −, tug at- the oar; do the work; take the laboring oar.

bestir oneself (be active) 682; take trouble, trouble oneself.

work hard; rough it; put forth -one's strength, − a strong arm; fall to work, bend the bow; buckle to, set one's shoulder to the wheel etc. (resolution) 604; work like a -Briton, − horse, − carthorse, − galley-slave, − coalheaver; labor −, work-day and night; redouble one's efforts; do double duty; work double -hours, − tides; sit up, burn the -midnight oil, − candle at both ends; stick to etc. (persevere) 604a; work −, fight- one's way; lay about one, hammer at.

take pains; do one's -best, − level best, − utmost; do -the best one can, − all one can, − all in one's power, − as much as in one lies, − what lies in one's power; use one's -best, − utmost- endeavor; try one's -best, − utmost; play one's best card; put one's -best, − right- leg foremost; have one's whole soul in one's work, put all one's strength into, strain every nerve; spare no -efforts, − pains; go all lengths; go through fire and water etc. (resolution) 604; move heaven and earth, leave no stone unturned.

Adj. laboring etc. v.

laborious, operose, elaborate, strained; toil-, trouble-, burden-, weari-some; uphill; herculean, gymnastic, athletic, palestric.

hardworking, painstaking, strenuous, energetic.

hard at work, on the stretch.

Adv. laboriously etc. adj.; lustily; with -might and main, − all one's might, − a strong hand, − sledge-hammer; − much ado; to the best of one's abilities, totis viribus, vi et armis, manibus pedibusque, tooth and nail, unguibus et rostro,

hammer and tongs, heart and soul; through thick and thin etc. (*perseverance*) 604a.

by the sweat of one's brow, *suo Marte*.

come to oneself etc. (*revive*) 660; feel like a giant refreshed.

Adj. refreshing etc. *v.*; recuperative etc. 660. refreshed etc. *v.*; un-tired, -wearied.

687. Repose.—N. repose, rest, silken repose; sleep etc. 683.

relaxation, breathing time; halt, pause etc. (*cessation*) 142; respite.

day of rest, *dies non*, Sabbath, Lord's day, holiday, red-letter day, vacation, recess.

V. repose; rest, – and be thankful; take -rest, – one's ease.

relax, unbend, slacken; take breath etc. (*refresh*) 689; rest upon one's oars; pause etc. (*cease*) 142; stay one's hand.

lie down; recline, – on a bed of down, – on an easy chair; go to -rest, – bed, – sleep etc. 683.

take a holiday, shut up shop; lie fallow etc. (*inaction*) 681.

Adj. reposing etc. *v.*; unstrained.

Adv. at rest.

688. Fatigue.—N. fatigue; weariness etc. 841; yawning, drowsiness etc. 683; lassitude, tiredness, fatigation, exhaustion; sweat.

anhelation, shortness of breath, panting; faintness; collapse, prostration, swoon, fainting, *deliquium*, syncope, lipothymy.

V. be -fatigued etc. *adj.*; yawn etc. (*get sleepy*) 683; droop, sink, flag; lose -breath, – wind; gasp, pant, puff, blow, drop, swoon, faint, succumb.

fatigue, tire, weary, bore, irk, fag, jade, harass, exhaust, knock up, wear out, prostrate.

tax, task, strain; over-task, -work, -burden, -tax, -strain.

Adj. fatigued etc. *v.*; weary etc. 841; drowsy etc. 683; drooping etc. *v.*; haggard; toil-, way-worn; footsore, surbated, weatherbeaten; faint; done –, used –, knock- up; exhausted, prostrate, spent; over-tired,--spent, -fatigued; forspent; unre-freshed, -stored.

worn, – out; battered, shattered, pulled down, seedy, altered.

breath-, wind-less; short of – –, out of -breath, – wind; blown, puffing and blowing; short-breathed; anhelous; broken-, short-winded.

ready to drop, more dead than alive, dog -tired, – weary, walked off one's legs, tired to death, on one's last legs, played out, *hors de combat*.

fatiguing etc. *v.*; tire-, irk-, weari-some; weary; trying.

689. Refreshment.—N. bracing etc. *v.*; recovery of -strength etc. 159; restoration, revival etc. 660; repair, refection, refocillation, refreshment, regalement, bait; relief etc. 834.

V. brace etc. (*strengthen*) 159; reinvigorate; air, freshen up, refresh, recruit; repair etc. (*restore*) 660; fan, revocillate.

breathe, respire; draw –, take –, gather –, take a long –, regain –, recover- breath; get better, raise one's head; recover –, regain –, renew one's strength etc. 159; perk up.

690. Agent.—N. doer, actor, agent, performer, perpetrator, operator; execu-tor, -trix; practitioner, worker, stager.

bee, ant, working bee, laboring oar, shaft horse, servant –, maid- of all work, general servant, factotum.

workman, artisan; crafts-, handicrafts-man; mechanic, operative; working –, laboring- man; hewers of wood and drawers of water, laborer, navvy; hand, man, day laborer, journeyman, hack; mere -tool etc. 633; porter, docker, stevedore, beast of burden, drudge, fag.

maker, artificer, artist, wright, manufacturer, architect, contractor, builder, mason, bricklayer, smith, forger, Vulcan; black-, tin-smith; carpenter; ganger, platelayer.

machinist, mechanician, engineer, electrician, plumber, gasfitter etc.

semp-, sem-, seam-stress; needle-, char-, work-woman; tailor, cordwainer.

minister etc. (*instrument*) 631; servant etc. 746; representative etc. (*commissioner*) 758; (*deputy*) 759.

co-worker, fellow-worker, party to, participator in, co-operator, colleague, associate, collaborator, *particeps criminis, dramatis personae; personnel.*

Phrs. '*quorum pars magna fui.*'

691. Workshop.—N. work-shop, -house; laboratory; manufactory, mill, factory, armory, arsenal, mint, forge, loom; cabinet, *studio, bureau, atelier;* hive, – of industry; nursery; hot-house, -bed; kitchen, kitchenette; dock, -yard; slip, yard, wharf; found-ry, -ery; furnace; vineyard, orchard, farm, kitchen garden.

melting pot, crucible, alembic, caldron, mortar, *matrix.*

692. Conduct.—N. dealing, transaction etc. (*action*) 680; business etc. 625.

tactics, game, policy, polity; general-, statesman-, seaman-ship; strate-gy, -gics; plan etc. 626.

husbandry; house-keeping, -wifery; stewardship; *ménage;* regimen, *régime;* econom-y, -ics; political economy; management; government etc. (*direction*) 693.

execution, manipulation, treatment, campaign, career, life, course, walk, race.

conduct; behavior; de-, com-portment; carriage, *maintien,* demeanor, guise, bearing, manner, mien, air, observance.

course –, line- of -conduct, – action, – proceeding; *rôle;* process, ways, practice, procedure, *modus operandi;* method etc., path etc. 627.

V. transact, execute; des-, dis-patch; proceed with, discharge; carry -on, – through, – out, – into effect; work out; go –, get- through; enact; put into practice; officiate etc. 625.

behave –, comport –, demean –, carry –, bear –, conduct –, acquit- oneself.

run a race, lead a life, play a game; take –, adopt- a course; steer –, shape- one's course; play one's- part, – cards; shift for oneself; paddle one's own canoe.

conduct; manage etc. (*direct*) 693.

deal –, have to do- with; treat, handle a case; take -steps, – measures.

Adj. conducting etc. *v.*; strategical, business-like, practical, economic, executive.

693. Direction.—**N.** direction; manage-ment, -ry; government, gubernation, conduct, legislation, regulation, guidance; steer-, pilot-age; reins, – of government; helm, rudder, controls, joy stick, needle, compass, binnacle; guiding –, load –, lode –, pole- star; cynosure.

super-vision, -intendence; *surveillance*, oversight; eye of the master; control, charge, auspices; board of control etc. (*council*) 696; command etc. (*authority*) 737.

premier-, senator-ship; director etc. 694; chair, seat, portfolio.

statesmanship; state-, king-craft.

minis-try, -tration; administration; steward-, proctor-ship; agency.

V. direct, manage, govern, conduct; order, prescribe, cut out work for; head, lead; lead –, show- the way; take the lead, lead on; regulate, guide, steer, pilot; take –, be at- the helm; have –, handle –, hold –, take- the reins, handle the ribbons; drive, tool; tackle.

super-intend, -vise; overlook, control, keep in order, look after, see to, oversee, legislate for; ad-minister, ministrate; patronize; have the -care, – charge- of; have –, take- the direction; pull the -strings, – wires; rule etc. (*command*) 737; have –, hold- -office, – the portfolio; preside, – at the board; take –, occupy –, be in- the chair; pull the stroke oar.

Adj. directing etc. *v.*; executive, supervisory, hegemonic.

Adv. at the -helm, – head of, in charge of; under the auspices of.

694. Director.—**N.** director, manager, gover-nor, rector, comptroller; super-intendent, -visor; intendant; over-seer, -looker; foreman, boss, straw boss; supercargo, husband, inspector, visitor, ranger, surveyor, aedile, moderator, monitor, task-master; master etc. 745; leader, ringleader, demagogue, corypheus, conductor, fugleman, precentor, bellwether, agitator.

guiding star etc. (*guidance*) 693; adviser etc. 695; guide etc. (*information*) 527; pilot; helms-man; steers-man, -mate; man at the wheel; wire-puller.

driver, whip, Jehu, charioteer; coach-, car-, cab-man, jarvey; postilion, *vetturino*, muleteer, team-ster; whipper in; engineer, engine driver, motor-man, *chauffeur*.

head, – man; principal, president, speaker; chair, -man; captain etc. (*master*) 745; superior; dean; mayor etc. (*civil authority*) 745; vice-

president, prime minister, premier, vizier, grand vizier; dictator.

officer, functionary, minister, official, red-tapist, bureaucrat; man –, Jack- in office; office-bearer; person in authority etc. 745.

statesman, strategist, legislator, lawgiver, politi-cian, administrator, statist, statesmonger; Minos, Draco; arbiter etc. (*judge*) 967; king maker, power behind the throne.

board etc. (*council*) 696.

secretary, – of state; Reis Effendi; vicar etc. (*deputy*) 759; steward, factor; agent etc. 758; bailiff, middleman; ganger, clerk of works; land-reeve; factotum, major-domo, seneschal, house-keeper, shepherd, *croupier*; proctor, procurator, curator, librarian.

Adv. *ex officio.*

695. Advice.—**N.** advice, counsel, adhortation; word to the wise; suggestion, submonition, recom-mendation, advocacy, consultation.

exhortation etc. (*persuasion*) 615; expostulation etc. (*dissuasion*) 616; admonition etc. (*warning*) 668; guidance etc. (*direction*) 693.

instruction, charge, injunction.

adviser, prompter; counsel, -lor; monitor, men-tor, Nestor, *magnus Apollo*, senator; teacher etc. 540.

guide, manual, chart etc. (*information*) 527.

physician, leech, archiater; arbiter etc. (*judge*) 967.

refer-ence, -ment; consultation, conference, parley, *pourparler* etc. 696.

V. advise, counsel; give -advice, – counsel, – a piece of advice; suggest, prompt, submonish, recommend, prescribe, advocate; exhort etc. (*per-suade*) 615.

enjoin, enforce, charge, instruct, call; call upon etc. (*request*) 765; dictate.

expostulate etc. (*dissuade*) 616; admonish etc. (*warn*) 668.

advise with; lay heads –, consult- together; compare notes; hold a council, deliberate, be closeted with.

confer, consult, refer to, call in; take –, follow-advice; follow implicitly; be advised by, have at one's elbow, take one's cue from.

Adj. recommendatory; hortative etc. (*per-suasive*) 615; dehortatory etc. (*dissuasive*) 616; ad-monitory etc. (*warning*) 668; consultative.

Int. go to!

696. Council.—**N.** council, committee, sub-committee, *comitia*, court, chamber, cabinet, board, bench, staff; consultation.

senate, *senatus*, parliament, house, – of Lords, – Peers, – Commons, legislature, legislative assembly, federal council, chamber of deputies, directory, *reichsrath, rigsdag, cortes,* storthing, witenagemote, *junta*, divan, *musnud, sanhedrim,* Amphictyonic council; *duma, zemstvo, soviet, cheka, ogpu; Dail Eireann*; caput, consistory, chapter, syndicate; court of appeal etc. (*tribunal*) 966; board of -control, – works; vestry; county –, borough –, district –, parish –, town- council, local board.

cabinet –, privy- council, royal commission; cockpit, convocation, synod, congress, congregation, convention, diet, states-general, aulic council.

League of Nations, assembly, *caucus*, conclave, *clique*, conventicle; meeting, sitting, *séance*, conference, session, hearing, palaver, *pourparler*, *durbar*, pow-wow, house; *quorum*.

senator; member, – of parliament; councilor, M.P., representative of the people.

Adj. senatorial, curule, parliamentary.

697. Precept.—N. precept, direction, instruction, charge; prescript, -ion; *recipe*, receipt; golden rule; maxim etc. 496.

commandment, rule, ruling, canon, law, code, *corpus juris*, *lex scripta*, common –, unwritten –, canon- law; the Ten Commandments; act, statute, convention, rubric, stage direction, regulation; form, -ula, -ulary; technicality; nice point.

order etc. (*command*) 741.

698. Skill.—N. skill, skilfulness, address; dexter-ity, -ousness; adroitness, expertness etc. *adj* ; proficiency, competence, craft, callidity, facility, knack, trick, sleight; master-y, -ship; excellence, panurgy; ambidext-erity, -rousness; sleight of hand etc. (*deception*) 545.

sea-, air-, marks-, horse-manship; tight-, ropedancing.

accomplish-, acquire-, attain-ment; art, science; techn-icality, -ology, -ique; practical –, technicalknowledge; technocracy; finish, technic.

knowledge of the world, world wisdom, *savoirfaire*; tact; mother wit etc. (*sagacity*) 498; discretion etc. (*caution*) 864; *finesse*; craftiness etc. (*cunning*) 702; management etc. (*conduct*) 692; *ars celare artem*; self-help.

cleverness, talent, ability, ingenuity, capacity, parts, talents, faculty, endowment, *forte*, turn, gift, genius, flair, feeling; intelligence etc. 498; sharpness, readiness etc. (*activity*) 682; invention etc. 515; apt-ness, -itude; turn –, capacity –, geniusfor; felicity, capability, *curiosa felicitas*, qualification, habilitation.

proficient etc. 700.

masterpiece, *coup de maître*, *chef- d'oeuvre*, *tour de force*; good stroke etc. (*plan*) 626.

V. be -skilful etc. *adj* ; excel in, be master of; have -a turn for etc. *n*.

know -what's what, – a hawk from a handsaw, – what one is about, – on which side one's bread is buttered, – what's o'clock, – a thing or two; have cut one's -eye, – wisdom- teeth.

see -one's way, – where the wind lies, – which way the wind blows; have -all one's wits about one, – one's hand in; *savoir vivre*; *scire quid valeant humeri quid ferre recusent*

look after the main chance; cut one's coat according to one's cloth; live by one's wits; exercise one's discretion, feather the oar, sail near the wind; stoop to conquer etc. (*cunning*) 702; play one's -cards well, – best card; hit the right nail on the head, put the saddle on the right horse.

take advantage of, make the most of; profit by etc. (*use*) 677; make a hit etc. (*succeed*) 731; make a virtue of necessity; make hay while the sun shines etc. (*occasion*) 134.

Adj. skilful, dexterous, adroit, expert, apt, slick, handy, quick, deft, ready, resourceful, gain; smart etc. (*active*) 682; proficient, good at, up to, at home in, master of, a good hand at, *au fait*, thoroughbred, masterly, crack, accomplished; conversant etc. (*knowing*) 490.

experienced, practiced, skilled; up –, well upin; in -practice, – proper cue; competent, efficient, qualified, capable, fitted, fit for, up to the mark, trained, initiated, prepared, primed, finished.

clever, able, ingenious, felicitous, gifted, talented, endowed, cute, inventive etc. 515; shrewd, sharp etc. (*intelligent*) 498; cunning etc. 702; alive to, up to snuff, not to be caught with chaff; discreet.

neat-handed, fine-fingered, ambidextrous, surefooted; cut out –, fitted- for.

technical, artistic, scientific, daedalian, shipshape; workman-, business-, statesman-like.

Adv. skilfully etc. *adj* ; well etc. 618; artistically; with -skill, – consummate skill; *secundum artem*, *suo Marte*; to the best of one's abilities etc. (*exertion*) 686; like a machine.

699. Unskillfulness.—N. unskillfulness etc. *adj* ; want of -skill etc. 698; incompeten-ce, -cy; inability, -felicity, -dexterity, -experience; clumsiness; disqualification, unproficiency; quackery.

folly, stupidity etc. 499; indiscretion etc. (*rashness*) 863; thoughtlessness etc. (*inattention*) 458, (*neglect*) 460.

mis-management, -conduct; impolicy; maladministration; mis-rule, -government, -application, -direction, -feasance.

absence of rule, rule of thumb; bungling etc. ν ; failure etc. 732; screw loose; too many cooks.

blunder etc. (*mistake*) 495; *étourderie*, *gaucherie*, act of folly, *balourdise*; botch, -ery; bad job, sad work.

sprat sent out to catch a whale, much ado about nothing, wildgoose chase.

bungler etc. 701; fool etc. 501.

layman, amateur.

V. be -unskillful etc. *adj*; not see an inch beyond one's nose; blunder, bungle, boggle, fumble, muff, botch, bitch, flounder, loppet, stumble, trip; hobble etc. 275; put one's foot in it; make a -mess, – hash, – sad work- of; overshoot the mark.

play -tricks with, – Puck; mismanage, -conduct, -direct, -apply, -send.

stultify –, make a fool of –, commit- oneself; act foolishly; play the fool; put oneself out of court; lose one's -head, – cunning.

begin at the wrong end; do things by halves etc. (*not complete*) 730; make two bites of a cherry; play at cross purposes; strain at a gnat and swallow a camel etc. (*caprice*) 608; put the cart before the horse; lock the stable door when the horse is stolen etc. (*too late*) 135.

not know -what one is about, – one's own interest, – on which side one's bread is buttered; stand in one's own light, quarrel with one's bread and butter, throw a stone in one's own garden, kill the goose which lays the golden eggs, pay dear for

one's whistle, cut one's own throat, burn one's fingers; knock —, run- one's head against a stone wall; fall into a trap, catch a Tartar, bring the house about one's ears; have too many -eggs in one basket (*imprudent*) 863, — irons in the fire.

mistake etc. 495; take the shadow for the substance etc. (*credulity*) 486; be in the wrong box, aim at a pigeon and kill a crow; take — , get- the wrong sow by the ear, — the dirty end of the stick; put -the saddle on the wrong horse, — a square peg into a round hole, — new wine into old bottles.

cut a whetstone with a razor; hold a farthing candle to the sun etc. (*useless*) 645; fight with —, grasp at- a shadow; catch at straws, lean on a broken reed, reckon without one's host, pursue a wildgoose chase; go on a fool's —, sleeveless-errand; go further and fare worse; loose —, miss-one's way; fail etc. 732.

Adj. un-skillful etc. 698; unskilled, inexpert; bungling etc. *v.* ; awkward, clumsy, unhandy, lubberly, *gauche*, *maladroit*; left-, heavy-handed; slovenly, slatternly; gawky.

adrift, at fault.

in-, un-apt; inhabile; un-tractable, -teachable; giddy etc. (*inattentive*) 458; inconsiderate etc. (*neglectful*) 460; stupid etc. 499; inactive etc. 683; incompetent; un-, dis-, ill-qualified; unfit; quackish; raw, green, inexperienced, rusty, out of practice.

un-accustomed, -used, -trained etc. 537; - initiated, -conversant etc. (*ignorant*) 491; shiftless; unbusinesslike, unpractical; unstatesmanlike.

un-, ill-, mis-advised; ill-devised, -imagined, - judged, -contrived, -conducted; un-, mis-guided; misconducted, foolish, wild; infelicitous; penny wise and pound foolish etc. (*inconsistent*) 608.

Phr. one's fingers being all thumbs; the right hand forgets its cunning.

il se noyerait dans une goutte d'eau.

incidit in Scyllam qui vult vitare Charybdim; *out of the frying pan into the fire.*

700. Proficient.—**N.** proficient, expert, adept, dab; *connoisseur* etc. (*scholar*) 492; master, hand; top-sawyer, *prima donna*, first fiddle, *chef de cuisine*; protagonist; past master; profess-or, -ional, specialist.

picked man; medalist, prizeman.

veteran; old -stager, — campaigner, — soldier, — file, — hand; man of -business, — the world.

nice —, good —, clean- hand; practised —, experienced- -eye, — hand; marksman; good —, dead —, crack- shot; rope-dancer, funambulist, acrobat, contortionist; cunning man; conjuror etc. (*deceiver*) 548; wizard etc. 994.

genius; master-mind, — head, — spirit.

cunning —, sharp -blade, — fellow; jobber; cracksman etc. (*thief*) 792; politician, tactician, diplomat, -ist, strategist.

pantologist, admirable Crichton, Jack of all trades; prodigy of learning; walking encyclopedia; mine of information.

701. Bungler.—**N.** bungler; blunderer, -head; marplot, fumbler, lubber, lout, oaf, duffer, stick, clown; bad —, poor- -hand, — shot; butter-fingers.

no conjuror, flat, muff, slow coach, looby, lub-

ber, swab; clod, yokel, hick, awkward squad, novice, greenhorn, jaywalker, *blanc-bec*.

land lubber; fresh water —, fair weather- sailor; horse-marine; fish out of water, ass in lion's skin, jackdaw in peacock's feathers; quack etc. (*deceiver*) 548; Lord of Misrule.

sloven, slattern, trapes.

Phr. *il n'a pas inventé la poudre*; he will never set the Thames on fire.

702. Cunning.—**N.** cunning, craft; cunningness, craftiness etc. *adj.*; subtlety, artificiality; maneuvring etc. *v.*; temporization; circumvention.

chicane, -ry; sharp practice, knavery, jugglery; concealment etc. 528; nigger in the woodpile; guile, duplicity etc. (*falsehood*) 544; foul play.

diplomacy, politics; Machiavellism; jobbery, back-stairs influence, gerrymandering.

art, -ifice; device, machination; plot etc. (*plan*) 626; maneuver, stratagem, dodge, artful dodge, wile; trick, -ery etc. (*deception*) 545; *ruse*, — *de guerre*; finesse, side-blow, thin end of the wedge, shift, go by, subterfuge, evasion; white lie etc. (*untruth*) 546; juggle, *tour de force*; tricks -of the trade, — upon travelers; imposture, deception; *expiè-glerie*, net, trap etc. 545.

Ulysses, Machiavel, sly boots, fox, reynard; Scotch-, Yorkshire-man; Jew, Yankee; intriguer, *intrigant*, schemer, trickster.

V. be -cunning etc. *adj.*; have cut one's eye-teeth; contrive etc. (*plan*) 626; live by one's wits; maneuver; intrigue, gerrymander, finesse, double, temporize, stoop to conquer, *reculer pour mieux sauter*, circumvent, steal a march upon; overreach etc. 545; throw off one's guard; surprise etc. 508; outdo, get the better of, snatch from under one's nose; snatch a verdict; waylay, undermine, introduce the thin end of the wedge; play -a deep game, — tricks with; have an axe to grind; *ambiguas in vulgum spargere voces*; flatter, make things pleasant.

Adj. cunning, crafty, artful; skilful etc. 698; subtle, feline, vulpine; cunning as a -fox, — serpent; deep, — laid; profound; designing, contriving; intriguing etc. *v.*; strategic, diplomatic, politic, Machiavellian, time-serving, artificial; trick-y, -sy; wily, sly, slim, insidious, stealthy, foxy; underhand etc. (*hidden*) 528; subdolous, deceitful etc. 545; double-tongued, -faced; shifty; crooked; arch, pawky, shrewd, acute; sharp, — as a needle; canny, astute, leery, knowing, up to snuff, too clever by half, not to be caught with chaff.

Adv. cunningly etc. *adj.*; slily, on the sly, by a side wind.

Phr. diamond cut diamond.

703. Artlessness.—**N.** artlessness etc. *adj.*; nature, simplicity; innocence etc. 946; *bonhomie*, *naiveté*, *abandon*, candor, sincerity; singleness of - purpose, — heart; honesty etc. 939; plain speaking; *épanchement*.

rough diamond, matter of fact man; *le palais de vérité*; *enfant terrible*.

V. be -artless etc. *adj.*; look one in the face; wear one's heart upon his sleeves for daws to peck

at; think aloud; speak -out, — one's mind; be free with one, call a spade a spade.

Adj. artless, natural, pure, native, simple, plain, inartificial, untutored, unsophisticated, *ingénu*, unaffected, *naïve*; sincere, frank; open, — as day; candid, ingenuous, guileless, unsuspicious, childlike; honest etc. 939; innocent etc. 946; Arcadian; undesigning, straightforward; unreserved, unvarnished, above-board; simple-, single-minded; frank-, open-, single-, simple-hearted; open and above-board.

free-, plain-, out-spoken; blunt, downright, direct, matter of fact, unpoetical; unflattering.

Adv. in plain -words, — English; without mincing the matter; not to mince the matter etc. (*affirmation*) 535.

Phr. *Davus sum non Oedipus; liberavi animam meam.*

704. Difficulty.—N. difficulty; hardness etc. *adj.*; impracticability etc. (*impossibility*) 471; tough —, hard —, uphill- work; hard —, Herculean —, Augean- task; task of Sisyphus, Sisyphean labor, tough job, teaser, rasper, dead lift.

dilemma, embarrassment; perplexity etc. (*uncertainty*) 475; involvement; intricacy; entanglement etc. 59; cross fire; awkwardness, delicacy, ticklish card to play, deadlock, knot, Gordian knot, *dignus vindice nodus*, net, meshes, maze; coil etc. (*convolution*) 248; crooked path.

nice —, delicate —, subtle —, knotty-point; vexed question, *vexata quaestio*, poser; puzzle etc. (*riddle*) 533; paradox; hard —, nut to crack; bone to pick, *crux, pons asinorum*, where the shoe pinches.

nonplus, quandary, strait, pass, pinch, pretty pass, stress, brunt; critical situation, crisis; trial, rub, emergency, exigency, scramble.

scrape, hobble, slough, quagmire, hot water, hornet's nest; sea —, peck- of troubles; pretty kettle of fish; pickle, stew, *imbroglio*, mess, muddle, botch, fuss, bustle, ado; false position; set fast, stand; dead -lock, — set; fix, horns of a dilemma, *cul de sac*; hitch; stumbling block etc. (*hindrance*) 706.

V. be -difficult etc. *adj.*; run one hard, go against the grain, try one's patience, put one out; put to one's -shifts, — wit's end; go hard with —, try- one; pose, perplex etc. (*uncertainty*) 475; bother, nonplus, gravel, bring to a dead lock; be -impossible etc. 471; be in the way of etc. (*hinder*) 706.

meet with —, labor under —, get into —, plunge into —, struggle with —, contend with —, grapple with- difficulties; labor under a disadvantage; be -in difficulty etc. *adj.*

fish in troubled waters, buffet the waves, swim against the stream, scud under bare poles.

have -much ado with, — a hard time of it; come to the -push, — pinch; bear the brunt.

grope in the dark, lose one's way, weave a tangled web, walk among eggs.

get into a -scrape etc. *n.*; bring a hornet's nest about one's ears; be put to one's shifts; flounder, boggle, struggle; not know which way to turn etc. (*uncertainty*) 475; get -tangled up, — wound up; *perdre son latin*; stick - at, — in the mud, — fast; come to a -stand, — dead lock; hold the wolf by the ears.

render -difficult etc. *adj.*; encumber, embarrass, ravel, entangle; put a spoke in the wheel etc. (*hinder*) 706; lead a pretty dance.

Adj. difficult, not easy, hard, tough; trouble-, toil-, irk-some; operose, laborious, onerous, arduous, Herculean, formidable; sooner —, more easily- said than done; difficult —, hard- to deal with; ill-conditioned, crabbed; not -to be handled with kid gloves, — made with rosewater.

awkward, unwieldy, unmanageable; intractable, stubborn etc. (*obstinate*) 606; perverse, refractory, plaguy, trying, thorny, rugged; knot-ted, -ty; invious; path-, track-less; labyrinthine etc. (*convoluted*) 248; intricate, complicated etc. (*tangled*) 59; impracticable etc. (*impossible*) 471; not -feasible etc. 470; desperate etc. (*hopeless*) 859.

embarrassing, perplexing etc. (*uncertain*) 475; delicate, ticklish, critical; beset with -, full of -, surrounded by -, entangled by -, encompassed with- difficulties.

under a difficulty; in -difficulty, — hot water, — the suds, — a cleft stick, — a fix, — the wrong box, — a scrape etc. *n.*; — deep water, — a fine pickle; *in extremis*; between -two stools, — Scylla and Charybdis; surrounded by -shoals, — breakers, — quicksands; at cross purposes; not out of the wood.

reduced to straits; hard —, sorely- pressed; run hard; pinched, put to it, straitened; hard -up, — put to it, — set; put to one's shifts; puzzled, at a loss etc. (*uncertain*) 475; at -the end of one's tether, — one's wit's end, — a nonplus, — a standstill; graveled, nonplussed, stranded, aground; stuck —, set- fast; up a tree, at bay, *aux abois*, driven -into a corner, — from post to pillar, — to extremity, — to one's wit's end, — to the wall; *au bout de son latin*; out of one's -depth, — reckoning; put —, thrown -out.

accomplished with difficulty; hard-fought, -earned.

Adv. with -difficulty, — much ado; hardly etc. *adj.*; uphill; against the -stream, — grain; *à rebours*; *invitâ Minervâ*; in the teeth of; at —, upon- a pinch; at long odds.

Phr. ay there's the rub; *hic labor hoc opus*; things are come to a pretty pass.

705. Facility.—N. facility, ease; easiness etc. *adj.*; capability; feasibility etc. (*practicability*) 470; flexibility, pliancy etc. 324; smoothness etc. 255; convenience.

plain —, smooth —, straight- sailing; mere child's play, holiday task.

smooth water, fair wind; smooth — royal- road; clear -coast, — stage; *tabula rasa*; *full play* etc. (*freedom*) 748.

disen-cumbrance, -tanglement; deoppilation; permission etc. 760.

V. be -easy etc. *adj.*; go on —, run- smoothly; have -full play etc. *n.*; go —, run- on all fours; obey the helm, work well.

flow —, swim —, drift —, go- with the- -stream, — tide; see one's way; have -it all one's own way, — the game in one's own hands; walk over the course, win -at a canter, — hands down; make -light of, — nothing of; be at home in etc. (*skilful*) 698.

render -easy etc. *adj.*; facilitate, smooth, ease; popularize; lighten, – the labor; free, clear; dis-encumber, -embarrass, -entangle, -engage; deob-struct, unclog, extricate, unravel; untie –, cut- the knot; disburden, unload, exonerate, emancipate, free from, deoppilate; humor etc. (*aid*) 707; lubricate etc. 332; relieve etc. 834.

leave -a hole to creep out of, – a loophole, – the matter open; give -the reins to, – full play, – full swing; make way for; open the -door to, – way; prepare –, smooth –, clear- the -ground, – way, – path, – road; pave the way, bridge over; permit etc. 760.

Adj. easy, facile; feasible etc. (*practicable*) 470; easily -managed, – accomplished; within reach, accessible, easy of access, for the million, open to.

manageable, wieldy; towardly, tractable; sub-missive; yielding, ductile; pliant etc. (*soft*) 324; glib, slippery; smooth etc. 255; on -friction wheels, – velvet; convenient.

un-, dis-burdened, -encumbered, -embarrassed; exonerated; un-loaded, -obstructed, -trammeled, -impeded, -restrained etc. (*free*) 748; at ease, light.

at – , quite at- home; in -one's element, – smooth water.

Adv. easily etc. *adj.*; readily, smoothly, swim-mingly, *ad lib.*, on easy terms, single-handed.

Phr. touch and go.

Int. all clear!

706. Hindrance.—N. prevention, preclusion, obstruction, stoppage; prohibition; inter-ruption, -ception, -clusion; hindrance, impedition; retard-ment, -ation; constriction; embarrassment, op-pilation; coarctation, stricture, restriction; anchor etc. 666; restraint etc. 751 & 752; inhibition etc. 761; blockade etc. (*closure*) 261; picketing.

inter-ference, -position; obtrusion; dis-couragement, -countenance, -approval, -approbation; opposition etc. 708.

impedimen', let, obstacle, obstruction, knot, knag; check, hitch, *contretemps, impasse*, screw loose, grit in the oil.

bar, stile, barrier; turn-stile, -pike; gate, port-cullis; bulwark, parapet, barricade etc. (*defence*) 717; wall, dead wall, breakwater, groyne; bulkhead, block, buffer; stopper etc. 263; boom, dam, weir, burrock.

drawback, objection; stumbling-block, -stone; lion in the path; snag; snags and sawyers.

en-, in-cumbrance; clog, skid, shoe, spoke; brake, drag, – chain, – weight; stay, stop; preven-tive, prophylactic; contraception; load, burden, far-del, *onus*, millstone round one's neck, *im-pedimenta*; dead weight; lumber, pack; nightmare, Ephialtes, incubus, old man of the sea; remora.

difficulty etc. 704; insuperable etc. 471- ob-stacle; estoppel; ill wind; head wind etc. (*op-position*) 708; trammel, tether etc. (*means of restraint*) 752; hold back, counterpoise; damper, wet blanket, hinderer, marplot, kill-joy, dog in the manger, interloper; trail of a red herring; opponent etc. 710.

V. hinder, impede, impedite, embarrass.

keep – , stave – , ward- off; picket; obviate; a-, ante-vert; turn aside, draw off, prevent, forefend, nip in the bud; retard, slacken, check, let; counter-act, -check; preclude, debar, foreclose, estop;

inhibit etc. 761; shackle etc. (*restrain*) 751; restrict, restrain, cohibit.

obstruct, filibuster, stop, stay, bar, bolt, lock; block, – up; belay, barricade; block –, stop- the way; dam up etc. (*close*) 261; put on the -brake etc. *n.*; scotch –, lock –, put a spoke in- the wheel; put a stop to etc. 142; traverse, contravene; inter-rupt, -cept; oppose etc. 708; hedge -in, – round; cut off; interclude.

inter-pose, -fere, -meddle etc. 682.

cramp, hamper; clog, – the wheels; cumber; en-, in-cumber; handicap; choke; saddle – , load-with; overload, lay; lumber, trammel, tie one's hands, put to inconvenience; in-, discommode; discompose; hustle, drive into a corner; choke off.

run – , fall- foul of; cross the path of, break in upon.

thwart, frustrate, disconcert, balk, foil, baffle, snub, override, circumvent; defeat etc. 731; spike guns etc. (*render useless*) 645; spoil, mar, clip the wings of; cripple etc. (*injure*) 659; put an ex-tinguisher on; damp; dishearten etc. (*dissuade*) 616; discountenance, throw cold water on, spoil sport; lay –, throw- a wet blanket on; cut the ground from under one, take the wind out of one's sails, undermine; be – , stand- in the way of; act as a drag; hang like a millstone round one's neck.

Adj. hindering etc. *v.*; obstr-uctive, -uent; im-pedi-tive, -ent; intercipient; prophylactic etc. (*remedial*) 662.

in the way of, unfavorable; onerous, bur-densome; cumb-rous, -ersome; obtrusive.

hindered etc. *v.*; wind-bound, water-logged, heavy laden; hard pressed.

unassisted etc. (*see* assist etc. 707); single-handed, alone; deserted etc. 624.

707. Aid.—N. aid, -ance; assistance, help, opitulation, succor, support, lift, advance, fur-therance, promotion; coadjuvancy etc. (*co-operation*) 709.

patronage, championship, countenance, favor, interest, advocacy, auspices.

sustentation, subvention, subsidy, bounty, alimentation, nutrition, nourishment, maintenance; manna in the wilderness; food etc. 298; means etc. 632.

ministr-y, -ation; subministration; accomodation.

relief, rescue; help at a dead lift; supernatural aid; *deus ex machinâ*.

supplies, reinforcements, succors, contingents, recruits; support etc. (*physical*) 215; adjunct, ally etc. (*helper*) 711.

V. aid, assist, help, succor, lend one's aid; come to the aid etc. *n*- of; contribute, subscribe to; bring –, give –, furnish –, afford –, supply- -aid etc. *n.*; render assistance; give –, stretch –, lend –, bear –, hold out- a -hand, – helping hand; give one a -lift, – cast, – turn; take -by the hand, – in tow; help a lame dog over a stile, lend wings to.

relieve, rescue; set -up, – agoing, – on one's legs; bear –, pull- through; give new life to, be the making of; reinforce, recruit; set –, put –, push-forward; give -a lift, – a shove, – an impulse- to; promote, further, forward, advance; speed, ex-pedite, quicken, hasten.

support, sustain, uphold, prop, hold up, bolster.

cradle, nourish; nurture, nurse, dry nurse, suckle, put out to nurse; manure, cultivate, force; foster; cherish, foment; feed −, fan- the flame.

serve; do service to, tender to, pander to; ad-, sub-, minister to; tend, attend, wait on; take care of etc. 459; entertain; smooth the bed of death.

oblige, accomodate, consult the wishes of; humor, cheer, encourage.

second, stand by; back, − up; pay the piper, abet; work −, make interest −, stick up −, take up the cudgels- for; take up −, espouse −, adopt- the cause of; advocate, beat up for recruits, press into the service; squire, give moral support to, keep in countenance, countenance, patronize; lend - oneself, − one's countenance- to; smile −, shine- upon; favor, befriend, take up, take in hand, enlist under the banners of; side with etc. (co-operate) 709.

be of use to; subserve etc. (instrument) 631; benefit etc. 648; render a service etc. (utility) 644; conduce etc. (tend) 176.

Adj. aiding etc. v.; auxiliary, adjuvant, helpful; coadjuvant etc. 709; subservient, ministrant, ancillary, accessory, subsidiary.

at one's beck; friendly, amicable, favorable, propitious, well-disposed; neighborly; obliging etc. (benevolent) 906.

Adv. with −, by- -the aid etc. n.- of; on −, in- behalf of; in -aid, − the service, − the name, − favor, − furtherance- of; on account of; for the sake of, on the part of; non obstante.

Int. help! save us! to the rescue! S.O.S.!

708. Opposition.—**N.** opposition, antagonism, oppug-nancy, -nation; impugnation; contravention; counteraction etc. 179; counterplot.

cross-fire, under-current; head-wind.

clashing, collision, conflict, lack of harmony, contest.

competition, two of a trade, rivalry, emulation; race; war to the knife.

absence of -aid etc. 707; resistance etc. 719; restraint etc. 751; hindrance etc. 706.

V. oppose, contract, run counter to; withstand etc. (resist) 719; control etc. (restrain) 751; hinder etc. 706; antagonize, oppugn, fly in the face of, go dead against, kick against, fall foul of; set −, pit- against; face, confront, cope with; make a -stand, − dead set- against; set -oneself, one's face- against; protest −, vote −, raise one's voice- against; disfavor, turn one's back upon; set at naught, slap the face, slam the door in one's face.

be −, play- at cross purposes; counter-work, - mine; thwart, overthwart.

stem, breast, encounter; stem −, breast- the tide, − current, − flood; buffet the waves; beat up −, make head- against; grapple with; kick against the pricks etc. (resist) 719; contend etc. 720 −, do battle etc. (warfare) 722- -with, − against.

contra-dict, -vene; belie; go −, run −, beat −, militate- against; come in conflict with.

emulate etc. (compete) 720; rival, spoil one's trade.

Adj. oppos-ing, -ed etc. v.; adverse, antagonistic; ambivalent; contrary etc. 14; at variance etc. 24; at issue, at war with; in opposition; 'agin the Government.'

un-favorable, -friendly; hostile, inimical, cross, unpropitious.

in hostile array, front to front, with crossed bayonets, at daggers drawn; up in arms; resistant etc. 791.

competitive, emulous.

Adv. against, versus, counter to, in conflict with, at cross purposes.

against the -grain, − current, − stream, − wind, − tide; with a headwind; with the wind - ahead, − in one's teeth.

in spite of, in despite, in defiance; in the -way, − teeth, − face- of; across; a-, over-thwart; where the shoe pinches.

though etc. 30; even; quand même; per contra.

Phr. nitor in adversum.

709. Co-operation.—**N.** co-operation; coadju-vancy, -tancy; coagency, coefficiency; concert, con-currence, complicity, participation; union etc. 43; amalgamation, combination etc. 48; collusion.

association, alliance, colleagueship, jointstock, copartnership, trust, cartel, pool, ring, combine; in-terlocking directorate; confederation etc. (party) 712; federation, coalition, fusion; a long pull, a strong pull and a pull all together; log-rolling, freemasonry.

unanimity etc. (assent) 488; esprit de corps, party spirit; clan-, partisan-ship; reciprocity, con-cord etc. 714.

V. co-operate, co-adjute, concur; conduce etc. 178; combine, cartelize, unite one's efforts; keep −, draw −, pull −, club −, hang −, hold −, league −, band −, be banded- together; stand −, put- shoulder to shoulder; act in concert, join forc-es, fraternize, cling to one another, conspire, con-cert, lay one's heads together; confederate, be in league with; collude, understand one another, play into the hands of, hunt in couples.

side −, take side −, go along −, go hand in hand −, join hands −, make common cause −, strike in −, unite −, join −, mix oneself up −, take part −, play along −, cast in one's lot- with; join −, enter into- partnership with; rally round, follow the lead of; come to, pass over to, come into the views of; be −, row −, sail- in the same boat; sail on the same tack.

be a party to, lend oneself to; participate; have a -hand in, − finger in the pie; take −, bear- part in; second etc. (aid) 707; take the part of, play the game of; espouse a -cause, − quarrel.

Adj. co-operating etc. v.; in -co-operation etc. n., − league etc. (party) 712; coadju-vant, -tant; hand and glove with.

favorable etc. 707- to; un-opposed etc. 708.

Adj. as one man etc. (unanimously) 488; shoulder to shoulder; in co-operation with.

710. Opponent.—**N.** opponent, antagonist, ad-versary; adverse party, opposition; enemy etc. 891; assailant.

oppositionist, obstructive; obscurantist; brawler, wrangler, brangler, disputant, extremist, irrecon-cilable, diehard, bitter-ender.

malcontent; Jacobin, Fenian etc. 742;
demagogue, reactionist.

passive resister, conscientious objector.

rival, competitor, contestant.

711. Auxiliary.—N.
auxiliary; recruit;
assistant; adju-vant, -tant; adjunct; help, er, -mate,
-ing hand; midwife; colleague, partner, mate, confrère, co-operator; coadju-tor, -trix; collaborator.

ally; friend etc. 890; confidant, fidus Achates,
pal, chum, buddy, alter ego.

confederate; ac-, complice; accessory, – after
the fact; particeps criminis.

aide-de-camp, secretary, clerk, associate, marshal; right-hand; candle-, bottle-holder; hand-maid;
servant etc. 746; puppet, cat's-paw; stooge, dependent, creature, jackal; tool, âme damnée; satellite,
adherent, parasite.

votary, disciple; secta-rian, -ry; seconder, backer,
upholder, supporter, abettor, advocate, partisan,
champion, patron, friend at court, mediator.

friend in need, Jack at a pinch, deus ex
machinâ, guardian angel, fairy godmother; special
providence, tutelary genius.

712. Party.—N.
party, faction, side,
denomination, class, communion, set, crowd, crew,
band, horde, posse, phalanx; regiment etc. 726;
family, clan etc. 166.

Tories, Conservatives, Unionists, Whigs,
Liberals, Radicals, Labour party, Socialists, Com-
munists etc.; Republicans, Democrats, Farmer-
Labor; Fascisti, Revolutionaries etc. 742.

community, body, fellowship, sodality,
solidarity; con-, fraternity, sorority; brother-, sisterhood.

Freemasons, Knights Templars, Odd Fellows,
Ku Klux Klan etx.

knot, gang, clique, ring, circle; coterie, club,
casino.

corporation, corporate body, guild; establishment, company, copartnership, firm, house, joint
concern, joint-stock company, trust, investment
trust, combine etc. 709.

society, association; instit-ute, -ution; union;
trade-union; league, syndicate, alliance, Verein,
Bund, Zollverein, combination; league –,
alliance- offensive and defensive; coalition;
federation; confedera -tion, -cy; junto, cabal,
camarilla, camorra, brigue; freemasonry; party
spirit etc. (co-operation) 709.

staff; cast, dramatis personae.

V. unite, join; club together etc. (co-operate)
709; cement –, form- a party etc. n.; associate etc.
(assemble) 72.

Adj. in -league, – partnership, – alliance etc.
n.

bonded –, banded –, linked etc. (joined) 43-
together; embattled; confederated, federative, joint,
corporate, leagued, fraternal, masonic, cliquish.

Adv. hand in hand, side by side, shoulder to
shoulder, en masse, in the same boat.

713. Discord.—N.
disagreement etc. 24; dis-
cord, -accord, -sidence, -sonance; jar, clash, shock;
jarring, jostling etc. ɤ ; screw loose.

variance, difference, dissension, misunderstanding, cross purposes, odds, brouillerie;
division, split, rupture, disruption, division in the
camp, house divided against itself, rift within the
lute; disunion, breach; schism etc. (dissent) 489;
feud, faction.

quarrel, dispute, rippet, spat, tiff, tracasserie,
squabble, altercation, words, high words; wrangling
etc. ɤ ; jangle, brabble cross questions and crooked
answers, snip-snap; family jars.

polemics; litigation; strife etc. (contention) 720;
warfare etc. 722; outbreak, open rupture; breaking
off of negotiations, recall of ambassadors;
declaration of war.

broil, brawl, row, racket, hubbub, rixation; embroilment, embranglement, imbroglio, fracas,
breach of the peace, piece of work, scrimmage,
rumpus; breeze, squall; riot, disturbance etc.
(disorder) 59; commotion etc. (agitation) 315;
bear garden, Donnybrook Fair.

subject of dispute, ground of quarrel, battle
ground, disputed point; bone -of contention, – to
pick; apple of discord, casus belli; question at issue
etc. (subject of inquiry) 461; vexed question,
vexata quaestio, brand of discord.

troublous times; cat-and-dog life; contentiousness etc. adj ; enmity etc. 889; hate etc.
898; Kilkenny cats; disputant etc. 710; strange
bedfellows.

V. be -discordant etc. adj ; disagree, come amiss
etc. 24; clash, jar, jostle, pull different ways, conflict, have no measures with, misunderstand one
another; live like cat and dog; differ; dissent etc.
489; have a -bone to pick, – crow to pluck- with.

fall out, quarrel, dispute, litigate; controvert etc.
(deny) 536; squabble, wrangle, jangle, brangle,
bicker, nag; spar etc. (contend) 720; have -words
etc. n. with; fall foul of.

split; break –, break squares –, part company-
with; declare war, try conclusions; join –, part in-
issue; pick a quarrel, fasten a quarrel on; sow –,
stir up- -dissension etc. n.; embroil, estrange, entangle, disunite, widen the breach; set -at odds, -
together by the ears; set –, pit- against; rub up the
wrong way.

get into hot water, fish in troubled waters, brawl;
kick up a -row, – dust; turn the house out of window.

Adj. discordant; disagreeing etc. ɤ ; out of tune,
dissonant, inharmonious, harsh, grating, jangling,
ajar, on bad terms; dissentient etc. 489; inconsistent, contradictory, incongruous, discrepant;
un- reconciled, -pacified.

quarrelsome, unpacific; gladiatorial, controversial, polemic, disputatious; factious; liti-gious,
-gant; pettifogging.

at odds, at loggerheads, at daggers drawn, at
variance, at issue, at cross purposes, at sixes and
sevens, at feud, at high words; up in arms, together
by the ears, in hot water, embroiled.

torn, disunited.

Phr. quot homines tot sententiae; no love lost
between them, non nostrum tantas componere
lites.

714. Concord.—N.
concord, accord, harmony,
symphony, homology; aggreement etc. 23; sympathy etc. (love) 897; response; union, unison,

unity; bonds of harmony; peace etc. 721; unanimity etc. (*assent*) 488; league etc. 712; happy family.

rapprochement; *réunion*; amity etc. (*friendship*) 888; reciprocity; alliance, *entente cordiale*, good understanding, conciliation, arbitration, peacemaker etc. 724.

V. agree etc. 23; accord, harmonize with; fraternize; be -concordant etc. *adj.* ; go hand in hand; blend −, tone in- with; run parallel etc. (*concur*) 178; understand one another; pull together etc. (*co-operate*) 709; put up one's horses together, sing in chorus.

side −, sympathize −, go −, chime in −, fall in- with; come round; be pacified etc. 723; assent etc. 488; enter into the -ideas, − feelings- of; reciprocate.

hurler avec les loups; go −, swim- with the stream.

pour oil on troubled waters, keep in good humor, render accordant, put in tune; come to an understanding, meet half-way; keep the −, remain at- peace.

Adj. concordant, congenial; agreeing etc. *v.*; in-accord etc. *n.*; harmonious, united, cemented; banded together etc. 712; allied; friendly etc. 888; fraternal; conciliatory; at one with; of one mind etc. (*assent*) 488.

at peace, in still water; tranquil etc. (*pacific*) 721.

Adv. with one voice etc. (*assent*) 488; in concert with, hand in hand; on one's side, unanimously.

715. Defiance.—N. defiance; daring etc. *v.*; dare, challenge, *cartel*; threat etc. 909; war-cry, -whoop.

V. defy, dare, beard; brave etc. (*courage*) 861; bid defiance to; set at -defiance, − naught; hurl defiance at; dance the war dance; snap the fingers at, laugh to scorn; disobey etc. 742.

show -fight, − one's teeth, − a bold front; bluster, look big, stand akimbo; double −, shake-the fist; threaten etc 909.

challenge, call out; throw −, fling- down the - gauntlet, − gage, − glove.

Adj. defiant; defying etc. *v.* ; with arms akimbo, rebellious, insolent; reckless, greatly daring.

Adv. in -defiance, − the teeth- of; under one's very nose.

Int. do your worst! come if you dare! come on! marry come up! hoity toity!

Phr. *noli me tangere*; *nemo me impune lacessit*.

716. Attack.—N. attack; assault, − and battery; onset, onslaught, charge.

aggression, drive, offence; incursion, inroad; invasion; irruption; outbreak; *estrapade*, *ruade*; *coup de main*, sally, *sortie*, *camisade*, raid, foray; run - at, − against; dead set at.

storm, -ing; boarding, *escalade*; siege, investment, obsession, bombardment, cannonade; air raid.

fire, volley; platoon −, file −, rapid-fire; *fusillade*; sharp-shooting, sniping; broadside; raking −, cross −, machine gun- fire; − volley of grapeshot, *feu d'enfer*; salvo.

cut, thrust, lunge, pass, *passado*, *carte* and tierce, home thrust, *coup de pied*; kick, punch, etc. (*impulse*) 276.

battue, *razzia*, *Jacquerie*, *dragonnade*; devastation etc. 162.

assailant, aggressor, invader.

base of operations, point of attack.

V. attack, assault, assail; set −, fall- upon; charge, impugn, break a lance with, enter the lists.

assume −, take- the offensive; be −, become-the aggressor; strike the first blow, fire the first shot, throw the first stone at; lift a hand −, draw the sword- against; take up the cudgels; advance −, march- against; march upon, invade, harry; come on, show fight.

strike at, poke at, thrust at; aim −, deal- a blow at; give −, fetch- one a -blow, − kick; have a -cut, − shot, − fling, − shy- at; be down −, pounce-upon; fall foul of, pitch into, launch out against; bait, slap on the face; make a -thrust, − pass, − set, − dead set- at; dunt; bear down upon.

close with, come to close quarters, bring to bay.

ride full tilt against; let fly at, dash at, run a tilt at, rush at, tilt at, run at, fly at, hawk at, have at, let out at; make a -dash, − rush at; attack tooth and nail; strike home; drive −, press- one hard; be hard upon, run down, strike at the root of.

lay about one, run amuck.

fire -upon, − at, − a shot at; shoot at, pop at, level at, let off a gun at; open fire, pepper, bombard, shell, pour a broadside into; fire -a volley, − red-hot shot; spring a mine.

throw -a stone, − stones- at; stone, lapidate, pelt; hurl -at, − against, − at the head of.

beset, besiege, beleaguer; lay siege to, invest, open the trenches, plant a battery, sap, mine; storm, board, scale the walls.

cut and thrust, bayonet, butt; kick, strike etc. (*impulse*) 276; whip etc. (*punish*) 972.

Adj. attacking etc. *v.*; aggressive, offensive, obsidional.

up in arms; on the warpath; over the top.

Adv. on the offensive.

Int. 'up and at them!'

717. Defense.—N. defense, protection, guard, ward; shielding etc. *v.*; propugnation; preservation etc. 670; guardianship.

self-defense, -preservation; resistance etc. 719.

safeguard etc. (*safety*) 664; screen etc. (*shelter*) 666, (*concealment*) 530; barrage; fortification; muni-tion, -ment; bulwark, fosse, moat, ditch, in-trenchment, trench, dugout, gas mask; dike, dyke; parapet, parados, sunk fence, embankment, mound, mole, bank; earth- field-work, gabions; fence, wall, dead wall, contravallation; paling etc. (*inclosure*) 232; palisade, haha, stockade, *stoccado*, *laager*, *sangar*; barri-er, -cade; boom; port-cullis, *chevaux de frise*; aba-, abat-, abba-tis; *vallum*, circumvallation, battlement, rampart, scarp; e-, counter-scarp; glacis, casemate.

mine, countermine.

buttress, abutment; shore etc. (*support*) 215.

breastwork, *banquette*, curtain, mantlet, bastion, demilune, redan, ravelin; advanced −, horn −, out- work, lunette; barb-acan, -ican; redoubt; fort-elage, -alice; lines; coast defense.

loop-hole, machicolation; sally-port, postern gate.

hold, stronghold, fastness; asylum etc. (*refuge*)
666; keep, donjon, fortress, citadel; capitol, castle;
tower, − of strength; fort, barracoon, pah, sconce,
martello tower, peel-house, block-house, rath;
wooden walls; turret, barbette.

buffer, corner-stone, fender, apron, mask, gauntlet, thimble, carapace, armor, shield, buckler;
target, targe, aegis, breastplate, cuirass, plastron,
habergeon, mail, coat of mail, brigandine, hauberk,
lorication, helmet, helm, basinet, sallet, salade,
heaume, morion, murrion, armet, cabaset, vizor,
casquetel, siege-cap, head-piece, casque, steel
helmet, tin hat; *pickelhaube*, csako; shako etc.
(*dress*) 225; bearskin; panoply; truncheon etc.
(*weapon*) 727.

garrison, picket, piquet; defender, protector;
guardian etc. (*safety*) 664; trabant, body guard,
champion; knight-errant, Paladin; propugner.

V. defend, forfend, fend; shield, screen, shroud;
fence round etc. (*circumscribe*) 229; fence, intrench; guard etc. (*keep safe*) 664; guard against;
take care of etc. (*vigilance*) 459; bear harmless;
keep −, ward −, beat- off; hinder etc. 706.

parry, repel, propugn, put to flight; give a warm
reception to [*ironical*] ; hold −, keep- at -bay, −
arm's length.

stand −, act- on the defensive; show fight; maintain −, stand- one's ground; stand by; hold one's
own; bear −, stand- the brunt; fall back upon,
hold, stand in the gap.

Adj. defending etc. *v.*; defensive; mural; armed,
− at all points, − cap-à-pie, − to the teeth;
panoplied; accoutred, harnessed; iron-plated, -clad;
loop-holed, castellated, machicolated; casemated;
defended etc. *v.*; proof against, bomb-, bullet-
proof; protective.

Adv. defensively; on the -defense, − defensive;
in defense; at bay, *pro aris et focis*.

Int. no surrender! *il ne passeront pas!*

Phr. defense not defiance.

718. Retaliation.—N. retaliation, reprisal,
retort; counter-stroke, -blast, -plot, -project;
retribution, *lex talionis*; reciprocation etc.
(*reciprocity*) 12.

requital, desert, tit for tat, give and take, blow
for blow, *quid pro quo*, a Roland for an Oliver,
measure for measure, an eye for an eye, diamond
cut diamond, the biter bit, a game at which two can
play; boomerang.

recrimination etc. (*accusation*) 938; revenge etc.
919; compensation etc. 30; reaction etc. (*recoil*)
277.

V. retaliate, retort, turn upon; pay -off, − back;
pay in -one's own, − the same- coin; cap;
reciprocate etc. 148; turn the tables upon, return
the compliment; give -a *quid pro quo* etc. *n.*, − as
much as one takes; give and take, exchange -blows,
− fisticuffs; be -quits, − even- with; pay off old
scores.

serve one right, be hoist on one's own petard,
throw a stone in one's own garden, cathch a Tartar.

Adj. retaliating etc. *v.*; retalia-tory, -tive;
retributive, recriminatory, reciprocal.

Adv.. in retaliation; *en revanche*.

Phr. *mutato nomine de te fabula narratur; par
pari refero; tu quoque*; you're another; *suo sibi
gladio hunc jugulo*.

719. Resistance.—N. resistance, stand, front,
oppugnation; opposition etc. 708; renitence, reluc-
tation, recalcitration, recalcitrance; repugnance;
kicking etc. *v.*

repulse, rebuff.

insurrection etc. (*disobedience*) 742; strike; turn
−, lock −, barring- out; *levée en masse,
Jacquerie*; riot etc. (*disorder*) 59.

V. resist; not -submit etc. 725; repugn, reluctate,
withstand; stand up −, strive −, bear up −, be
proof −, make head- against; stand, − firm, −
one's ground, − the brunt of, − out; hold -one's
ground, − one's own, − out.

breast the -wave, − current; stem the -tide, −
torrent; face, confront, grapple with; show a bold
front etc. (*courage*) 861; present a front; make a
−, take one's- stand.

kick, − against; recalcitrate, kick against the
pricks; oppose etc. 708; fly in the face of; lift the
hand against etc. (*attack*) 716; rise up in arms etc.
(*war*) 722; strike, turn out; draw up a round robin
etc. (*remonstrate*) 932; revolt etc. (*disobey*) 742;
make a riot.

prendre le mors aux dents; take the bit between
the teeth; sell one's life dearly, die hard, keep at
bay; repel, repulse.

Adj. resisting etc. *v.*; resist-ive, -ant; refractory
etc. (*disobedient*) 742; recalcitrant, re-nitent, -
pulsive, -pellant; up in arms.

proof against; unconquerable etc. (*strong*) 159;
stubborn, unconquered; indomitable etc. (*persevering*) 604a; unyielding etc. (*obstinate*) 606.

Int. hands off! keep off!

720. Contention.—N. contention, strife; contest, -ation; struggle; belligerency; opposition etc.
708.

controversy, polemics; debate etc. (*discussion*)
476; war of words, logomachy, litigation; paper
war, ink slinging; high words etc. (*quarrel*) 713;
sparring etc. *v.*

competition, rivalry, corrival-ry, -ship; agonism,
concours, match, race, horse-racing, heat, steeple
chase, point-to-point race, handicap; boat race,
regatta; field-day; sham fight, Derby day; turf,
sporting, bull-fight, tauromachy, *gymkhana*, rodeo,
Olympiad.

wrestling, *ju-jitsu*, pugilism, boxing, fisticuffs,
spar, mill, set-to, scrap, round, bout, event; prize-
fighting; quarter-staff, single stick; gladiatorship,
gymnastics; athletic-s, − sports; games of skill etc.
840.

shindy; *fracas* etc. (*discord*) 713; clash of arms;
tussle, scuffle, broil, fray; affray, -ment; velitation;
col-, luctation; brabble, *brique*, scramble, *mêlée*,
scrimmage, stramash, bush-fighting.

free −, stand up −, hand to hand −, running-
fight.

conflict, skirmish; ren-, en-counter; *rencontre*,
collision, affair, brush, fight; battle, − royal; combat, action, engagement, joust, tournament; tilt, -
ing; tourney, list; pitched battle, guerilla warfare.

death-struggle, struggle for life or death, Armageddon; hard knocks, sharp contest, tug of war.

naval -engagement, − battle; *naumachia*, sea-
fight.

duel, -lo; single combat, monomachy, satisfac-

tion, *passage d'armes*, passage of arms, affair of honor; triangular duel; hostile meeting, digladiation; appeal to arms etc. (*warfare*) 722.

deeds —, feats- of arms; pugnacity; combativeness etc. *adj.*; bone of contention etc. 713.

V. contend; contest, strive, struggle, scramble, wrestle; spar, square; exchange -blows, — fisticuffs; scrap, mix with, fib, justle, tussle, tilt, box, stave, fence; skirmish; fight etc. (*war*) 722; wrangle etc. (*quarrel*) 713.

contend etc. —, grapple —, engage —, close —, buckle —, bandy —, try conclusions —, have a brush etc. *n.* —, tilt- with; encounter, fall foul of, pitch into, clapperclaw, run a tilt at; oppose etc. 708; reluct.

join issue, come to blows, be at loggerheads, set-to, come to the scratch, exchange shots, measure swords, meet hand to hand; take up the -cudgels, — glove, — gauntlet; enter the lists; couch one's lance; give satisfaction; appeal to arms etc. (*warfare*) 722.

lay about one; break the peace.

compete —, cope —, vie —, race- with; outvie, emulate, rival; run a race; contend etc. —, stipulate —, stickle- for; insist upon, make a point of.

Adj. contending etc. *v.*; together by the ears, at loggerheads, at war, at issue.

competitive, rival; belligerent; contentious, combative, bellicose, unpeaceful; warlike etc. 722; quarrelsome etc. 901; pugnacious; pugilistic, gladiatorial; palestric, -al.

Phr. *a verbis ad verbera*; a word and a blow.

721. Peace.—N. peace; amity etc. (*friendship*) 888; harmony etc. (*concord*) 714; tranquility etc. (*quiescence*) 265; truce etc. (*pacification*) 723; pacificism; pipe —, calumet- of peace.

piping time of peace, quiet life; neutrality.

V. be at peace; keep the peace etc. (*concord*) 714; make peace etc. 723.

Adj. pacific; peace-able, -ful; calm, tranquil, untroubled, halcyon; bloodless; neutral.

Phr. the storm blown over; the lion lies down with the lamb.

722. Warfare.—N. warfare; fighting etc. *v.*; hostilities; war, arms, the sword; Mars, Bellona, grim visaged war, *horrida bella*, Armageddon.

appeal to -arms, — the sword; ordeal —, wager- of battle; *ultima ratio regum*, arbitrament of the sword.

battle array, campaign, crusade, expedition; mobilization; state of siege; battle-field etc. (*arena*) 728; warpath.

art of war, tactics, strategy, castrametation; general-, soldier-ship; aerial —, submarine —, naval —, chemical-, atomic-, guerilla- warfare; military evolutions, ballistics, gunnery; chivalry; poison gas; gun-powder, shot, — and shell.

battle, tug of war etc. (*contention*) 720; service, campaigning, active service, tented field; fiery cross, trumpet, clarion, bugle, pibroch, slogan; war-cry, -whoop; battle cry, beat of drum, rappel, tom-tom; word of command; pass-, watch-word.

war to the -death, — knife; *guerre à -mort*, - outrance*; open —, internecine —, civil- war.

V. arm; raise —, mobilize- troops; raise up in arms; take up the cudgels etc. 720; take up —, fly to —, appeal to- -arms, — the sword; draw —, unsheathe- the sword; dig up the hatchet; go to —, declare —, wage —, let slip the dogs of- war; cry havoc; kindle —, light- the torch of war; raise one's banner, send round the fiery cross; hoist the black flag; throw —, fling- away the scabbard; enrol, enlist, join up; take the field; take the law into one's own hands; do —, give —, join —, engage in —, go to- battle; flesh one's sword; set to, fall to, engage, measure swords with, draw the trigger, cross swords; come to -blows, — close quarters; fight; combat; contend etc. 720; battle —, break a lance- with.

serve; see —, be on- -service, — active service; campaign; wield the sword, shoulder a musket, smell powder, be under the fire; spill —, imbrue the hands in- blood; be on the warpath.

carry on -war, — hostilities; keep the field; fight the good fight; go over the top; cut one's way through; fight -it out, — like devils, — one's way, — hand to hand; sell one's life dearly.

Adj. conten-ding, -tious etc. 720; armed, — to the teeth, — cap-à-pie; sword in hand; in —, under —, up in- arms; at war with; bristling with arms; in -battle array, — open arms, — the field; embattled.

unpacific, unpeaceful; belligerent, combative, armigerous, bellicose, martial, warlike; mili-tary, -tant; soldier-like, -ly; chivalrous; strategical, internecine.

Adv. *flagrante bello*, in the -thick of the fray, — cannon's mouth; at the -swords's point, — point of the bayonet.

Int. *vae victis!* to arms! to your tents O Israel!

Phr. the battle rages.

723. Pacification.—N. pacification, conciliation; reconcil-iation, -ement; shaking of hands, accomodation, arrangement, adjustment; terms, compromise; amnesty, deed of release.

peace-offering; olive-branch; overtures; pipe —, calumet —, preliminaries- of peace.

truce, armistice; suspension of -arms, — hostilities; breathing-time; convention; *modus vivendi*; flag of truce, white flag, *parlementaire*, cartel.

hollow truce, *pax in bello*; drawn battle.

V. pacify, tranquilize, compose; allay etc. (*moderate*) 174; reconcile, propitiate, placate, conciliate, meet half-way, hold out the olive-branch, heal the breach, make peace, restore harmony, bring to terms.

settle —, arrange —, accommodate- -matters, — differences; set straight; make up a quarrel, *tantas componere lites*; come to -an understanding, — terms; bridge over, hush up; make -it, — matters- up; shake hands.

raise a siege; put up —, sheathe- the sword; bury the hatchet, lay down one's arms, turn swords into ploughshares; smoke the calumet of peace, close the temple of Janus; keep the peace etc. (*concord*) 714; be -pacified etc.; come round.

Adj. conciliatory, pacificatory; composing etc *v.*; pacified etc. *v.*

Phr. *requiescat in pace*.

724. Mediation.—N. media-tion, -torship, -tization; inter-vention, -position, -ference, - meddling, -cession; parley, negotiation, arbitration; flag of truce etc. 723; good offices, peace -offering; diploma-tics, -cy; compromise etc. 774.

mediator, intercessor, peacemaker, make-peace, negotiator, go-between; diplomatist etc. (con-signee) 758; moderator, propitiator, umpire, ar-bitrator.

V. media-te, -tize; inter-cede, -pose, -fere, -vene; step in, negotiate; meet half-way; arbitrate; *magnas componere lites.*

Adj. mediatory, propitiatory, diplomatic.

725. Submission.—N. submission, yielding, acquiescence, compliance; non-resistance; obedience etc. 743; submissiveness, deference.

surrender, cession, capitulation, resignation.

obeisance, homage, kneeling, genuflexion, cour-tesy, curtsy, *salaam, kowtow,* prostration.

V. succumb, submit, yield, bend, resign, defer to, accede.

lay down −, deliver up- one's arms;,hand over one's sword; lower −, haul down −, strike- one's flag, − colors; deliver the keys of the city.

surrender, − at discretion; cede, capitulate, come to terms, retreat, beat a retreat; draw in one's horns etc. (*humility*) 879; give -way, − ground, − in, − up; cave in; suffer judgment by default; bend, − to one's yoke, − before the storm; reel back; bend −, knuckle- -down, − to, − under; knock under.

humble oneself; eat -dirt, − the leek, − humble pie; bite −, lick- the dust; be −, fall- at one's feet; craven; crouch before, throw oneself at the feet of; swallow the -leek, − pill; kiss the rod; turn the other cheek; *avaler des couleuvres,* gulp down.

obey etc. 743; kneel to, bow to, pay homage to, cringe to, truckle to; bend the -neck, − knee; kneel, fall on one's knees, bow submission, cour-tesy, curtsy, *kowtow;* make obeisance.

pocket the affront; make -the best of, − a virtue of necessity; grin and abide, shrug the shoulders, resign oneself; submit with a good grace etc. (*bear with*) 826.

Adj. surrendering etc. *v.*; submissive, resigned, crouching; down-trodden; down on one's marrow bones; on one's bended knee; weak-kneed, un-, non-resisting; pliant etc. (*soft*) 324; undefended.

untenable, indefensible; humble etc. 879.

Phr. have it your own way; it can't be helped; amen etc. (*assent*) 488.

726. Combatant.—N. combatant; disputant, controversialist, polemic, litigant, belligerent; com-petitor, rival, corrival; fighter, assailant, aggressor; champion, Paladin; moss-trooper, swashbuckler, fire-eater, duellist, bully, bludgeon-man, rough, fighter, fighting-man, prize-fighter, pugilist, pug, boxer, bruiser, the fancy, gladiator, athlete, wrestler; fighting-, game-cock; swordsman, *sabreur.*

warrior, soldier, Amazon, man-at-arms, ar-migerent; campaigner, veteran; red-coat, military man, *rajpoot,* brave.

armed force, troops, soldiery, military, forces, sabaoth, the army, standing army, regulars, the line, troops of the line, militia, territorials, yeomanry, volunteers, trainband, fencible; auxiliary −, reserve- forces; reserves, *posse comitatus,* national guard, *gendarme,* beefeater; guards, -man; yeoman of the guard, life guards, household troops.

janissary; myrmidon; Mama-, Mame-luke; spahee, *spahi,* Cossack, Croat, Pandour; irregular, free lance, *franc-tireur, bashi-bazouk,* guerilla, *condottiere;* mercenary.

levy, draught, commando; *Land-wehr, -sturm;* conscript, recruit, rookie, cadet, raw levies.

private, − soldier; Tommy Atkins, rank and file, peon, trooper, doughboy, sepoy, *askari, legionnaire,* legionary, food for powder, cannon fodder; officer etc. (*commander*) 745; subaltern, ensign, shave-tail, standard bearer, non-com; spear-pike-man; halberdier, lancer; musketeer, carabineer, rifleman, sharpshooter, yager, skir-misher; grenadier, fusileer; archer, bowman.

horse and foot; horse −, foot- soldier; cavalry, horse, artillery, horse −, field −, heavy −, moun-tain- artillery, infantry, light horse, *voltigeur, Uhlan,* mounted rifles, dragoon, hussar, trooper; light −, heavy- dragoon; heavy; *cuirassier;* gunner, cannoneer, bombardier, artillery-man, matross; sapper, − and miner; engineer; light infantry, rifles, *chasseur, zouave;* military train, supply and transport, coolie.

army, − corps, *corps d'armée,* host, division, column, wing, detachment, *escadrille,* garrison, flying column, brigade, regiment, *corps,* battalion, squadron, company, platoon, battery, subdivision, section, squad; piquet, picket, guard, rank, file; legion, phalanx, cohort; cloud of skirmishers; impi.

war-horse, charger, *destrier.*

armored -train, − car; tank.

marine, man of war's. man etc. (*sailor*) 269; navy, first line of defense, wooden walls; naval forces, fleet, flotilla, armada, squadron.

man-of-war, warship; H.M.S., U.S.S.; capital ship; line-of-battle ship, battle ship; super-, dread-nought, battle −, armored −, protected − light-cruiser; scout, flotilla leader; destroyer, torpedo boat; submarine, submersible, U-boat; submarine chaser, eagle boat, mystery ship, Q-boat; mine-layer, -sweeper; ship of the line, iron-clad, turret-ship, ram, Monitor, floating battery; first-rate, frigate, sloop of war, corvette, gunboat, bomb-vessel, fire-boat; flag ship, guard ship, cruiser; air-plane carrier; privateer; tender; depôt −, parent-ship; store −, troop- ship; transport, catamaran.

aircraft etc. 273; air force, scout, fighter, bomb-er, troop carrier, aerial patrol, seaplane, flying boat, torpedo plane; airship, Zeppelin, rigid −, semi-rigid −, non-rigid- airship; dirigible −, free −, captive −, kite −, observation- balloon.

anti-aircraft guns, searchlights, sound locators; catapult.

727. Arms.—N. arm, -s; weapon, deadly weapon; arma-ment, -ture; panoply, stand of arms; armor etc. (*defense*) 717; armory etc. (*store*) 636.

ammunition; powder, − and shot; explosive; propellant; gun-powder, -cotton; dynam-, melin-, cord-, lydd-ite; trinitrotoluene, T.N.T., ammonal; cartridge; ball cartridge, *cartouche,* fire-ball; dud,

black Marie; 'villainous saltpeter;' poison –, mustard –, lachrymatory –, tear- gas.

sword, saber, broadsword, cutlass, falchion, scimitar, cimeter, brand, whinyard, bilbo, glaive, glave, rapier, skean, Toledo, Ferrara, tuck, claymore, creese, kris, *kukri*, dagger, dirk, hanger, poniard, stiletto, stylet, dudgeon, bayonet; sword-bayonet, -stick; side arms, foil, blade, steel; axe, bill; pole-, battle-axe; gisarm, halberd, partisan, tomahawk, bowie-knife; at-, att-, yat-aghan; yatachan; good –, trusty –, naked- sword; cold –, naked-steel.

club, mace, truncheon, staff, bludgeon, cudgel, life-preserver, shillelagh, sprig; hand-, quarter-staff; bat, cane, stick, knuckle-duster, sand bag.

gun, piece; fire-arms; artillery, ordnance; siege –, battering-train; park, battery; cannon, gun of position, heavy –, siege –, field –, mountain –, anti-aircraft –, breech loading –, quick firing-gun; field piece, mortar, trench mortar; mine –, flame- -thrower, napalm; howitzer, carronade, culverin, basilisk; falconet jingal, swivel, *pederero, bouche à feu*; smooth bore, rifled cannon; Armstrong –, Lancaster –, Paixhan –, Whitworth –, Parrott –, Krupp –, Gatling –, Maxim –, Vickers –, Hotchkiss –, Lewis –, machine- gun; tommy gun, Thompson's submachine gun; *mitrailleu-r, -se*; pompom; blow pipe.

small arms; musket, -ry, firelock, flintlock, fowling-piece, shot gun, rifle, *fusil*, caliver, carbine, blunderbuss, musketoon, Brown Bess, matchlock, harquebuss, *arquebuse*, haguebut; petronel; smallbore; breech-, muzzle-loader; Minié –, Enfield –, Westly Richards –, Snider –, Springfield –, Martini-Henry –, Lee-Metford –, Lee-Enfield –, Mauser –, Männlicher –, magazine –, repeating- rifle; needle-gun, *chassepot*; pis-tol, -et; revolver, automatic pistol, automatic; wind-, air-gun; flame –, gas- projector.

bow, cross-bow, arbalest, balister, catapult, sling; battering-ram etc. (*impulse*) 276; gunnery; ballistics etc. (*propulsion*) 284.

missile, bolt, projectile, shot, pellet, ball; grape; grape –, canister –, bar –, cannon –, langrel –, langrage –, round –, chain- shot; explosive; incendiary –, expanding –, soft-nosed –, dum-dum- bullet; slug, stone, brickbat; hand –, rifle-grenade; high explosive –, incendiary –, stink-, A-, H-, atomic –, hydrogen – bomb; petard, torpedo, carcass, rocket; congreve, – rocket; shrapnel, *mitraille*; thunderbolt; mine, land mine, infernal machine.

pike, lance, spear, spontoon, javelin, assagai, throwing stick, dart, djerrid, arrow, reed, shaft, bolt, boomerang, harpoon, gaff.

728. Arena.—N. arena, field, platform; scene of action, theater; walk, course; hustings; stage, boards etc. (*playhouse*) 599; amphitheater; Coli-, Colos-eum; Flavian amphitheater, hippodrome, circus, race-course, track, *stadium*, *corso*, turf, cockpit, bear-garden, play-ground, playing fields, *gymnasium*, *palaestra*, ring, lists; tilt-yard, -ing ground; *Campus Martius, Champ de Mars*; aerodrome, airport, air base, flying field.

theater –, seat- of war; battle-field, -ground; field of -battle, – slaughter; no man's land; Aceldama, camp; the enemy's camp; trysting- place etc. (*place of meeting*) 74.

729. Completion.—N. completion; ac-complish-, achieve-, fulfil-ment; performance, execution; des-, dis-patch; consummation, culmination, climax; finish, conclusion, ef-fectuation; close etc. (*end*) 67; terminus etc. (*arrival*) 292; winding up; *finale, dénouement,* catastrophe, issue, upshot, result; final –, last –, crowning –, finishing- -touch, – stroke; last finish, *coup de grâce*; crowning of the edifice; coping-, keystone; missing link etc. 53; super-structure, *ne plus ultra*, work done, *fait accompli.*

elaboration; finality; completeness etc. 52.

V. effect, -uate; accomplish, achieve, compass, consummate, hammer out; bring to -maturity, – perfection; perfect, complete; elaborate.

do, execute, make; go –, get- through; work out, enact; bring -about, – to bear, – to pass, – through, – to a head.

des-, dis-patch; knock –, finish –, polish- off; make short work of; dispose of, set at rest; perform, discharge, fulfil, realize; put in -practice, – force; carry -out, – into effect, – into execution; make good; be as good as one's word.

. do thoroughly, not do by halves, go the whole hog; drive home; be in at the death etc. (*persevere*) 604a; carry through, play out, exhaust, deliver the goods, fill the bill.

finish, bring to a close etc. (*end*) 67; wind up, stamp, clinch, seal, set the seal on, put the seal to; give the -final touch etc. *n.* to; put the -last, – finishing- hand to; crown, – all; cap.

ripen- culminate; come to a -head, – crisis; come to its end; die -a natural death, – of old age; run -its course, – one's race; touch –, reach –, attain- the goal; reach etc. (*arrive*) 292; get in the harvest.

Adj. completing, final; conclu-ding, -sive; crowning etc.. *v.*; exhaustive, complete, mature, perfect, consummate.

done, completed etc. *v.*; done for, sped, wrought out; highly wrought etc. (*preparation*) 673; thorough etc. 52; ripe etc. (*ready*) 673.

Adv. completely etc. (*thoroughly*) 52; to crown all, out of hand.

Phr. the race is run; *actum est*; *finis coronat opus; consummatum est; c'en est fait*; it is all over; the game is played out, the bubble has burst.

730. Non-Completion.—N. non-completion, -fulfilment; shortcoming etc. 304; incompleteness etc. 53; drawn -battle, – game; work of Penelope, task of Sisyphus.

non-performance, inexecution; neglect etc. 460.

V. not -complete etc. 729; leave -unfinished etc. *adj.*, – undone; neglect etc. 460; let -alone, – slip; lose sight of.

fall short of etc. 304; do things by halves; scotch the snake, not kill it; hang fire; be slow; collapse etc. 304.

Adj. not completed etc. *v.*; incomplete etc. 53; uncompleted, unfinished; unaccomplished; un-performed, unexecuted; sketchy, addle.

in progress, in hand; going on, proceeding; on one's hands; on the fire; on the stocks; in preparation; lacking the finishing touch.

Adv. *re infectâ.*

731. Success.—N. success, -fulness; speed; advance etc. (*progress*) 282.

trump card; hit, stroke; lucky –, fortunate –, good- -hit, – stroke; bold –, master- stroke; *coup de maître,* checkmate; half the battle, prize; profit etc. (*acquisition*) 775; best seller.

continued success; good fortune etc. (*prosperity*) 734; time well spent.

advantage over; edge; upper-, whiphand; ascendancy, mastery; expugnation, conquest, victory, subdual; subjugation etc. (*subjection*) 749.

triumph etc. (*exultation*) 884; proficiency etc. (*skill*) 698; conqueror, victor, winner, champion; master of the -situation, – position.

V. succeed; be -successful etc. *adj.*; gain one's- end, – ends; crown with success.

gain –, attain –, carry –, secure –, win- -a point, – an object; put over; make a go of; manage to, contrive to; accomplish etc. (*effect, complete*) 729; do –, work- wonders.

come off -well, – successfully, – with flying colors; make short work of; take –, carry- by storm; bear away the bell; win -one's spurs, – the battle; win –, carry –, gain- the -day, – prize, – palm; climb on the bandwagon; have -the best of it, – it all one's own way, – the game in one's own hands, – the ball at one's feet, – one on the hip; walk over the course; carry all before one, remain in possession of-the field; score a success, win hands down.

speed; make progress etc. (*advance*) 282; win –, make –, work –, find- one's way; strive to some purpose; prosper etc. 734; drive a roaring trade; make profit etc. (*acquire*) 775; reap –, gather the -fruits, – benefit of, – harvest; make one's fortune, get in the harvest, turn to good account; turn to account etc. (*use*) 677.

triumph, be triumphant; gain –, obtain- -a victory, – an advantage; chain victory to one's car.

surmount –, overcome –, get over- -a difficulty, – an obstacle etc. 706; *se tirer d'affaire;* make head against; stem the -torrent, – tide, – current; weather the storm, – a point; turn a corner, keep one's head above water, tide over; master; get –, have –, gain- the -better of, – best of, – upper hand, – ascendancy, – whip hand, – start of; distance; surpass etc. (*superiority*) 33.

defeat, conquer, vanquish, discomfit; over-come, throw, -power, -master, -match, -set, -ride, -reach; out-wit, -do, -flank, -maneuver, -general, -vote; take the wind out of one's adversary's sails; beat, – hollow; rout, lick, drub, floor, worst; put -down, – to flight, – to the rout, – *hors de combat;* – out of court.

silence, quell, nonsuit, checkmate, upset, confound, nonplus, trump; baffle etc. (*hinder*) 706; circumvent, elude; trip up – the heels of; drive -into a corner, – to the wall; run hard, put one's nose out of joint.*

settle, do for; break the -neck of, – back of; capsize, sink, shipwreck, drown, swamp; subdue; subjugate etc. (*subject*) 749; reduce; make the enemy bite the dust; victimize, roll in the dust, trample under foot, put an extinguisher upon.

answer, – the purpose; avail, prevail, take effect, do, turn out well, work well, take, tell, bear fruit; hit -it, – the mark, – the right nail on the head; nick it; turn up trumps, make a hit; find one's account in.

Adj. succeeding etc. *v.*; successful; prosperous

etc. 734; triumphant; flushed –, crowned- with success; victorious; set up; in the ascendant; unbeaten etc. (*see* beat etc. *v.*); well-spent; felicitous, effective, in full swing.

Adv. successfully etc. *adj.*; with flying colors, in triumph, swimmingly; *à merveille,* beyond all hope; to some –, good- purpose; to one's heart's content.

Phr. *veni vidi vici,* the day being one's own, one's star in the ascendant; *omne tulit punctum.*

732. Failure.—N. failure; non-success, -fulfilment; dead failure, successlessness; abortion, miscarriage; *brutum fulmen* etc. 158; labor in vain etc. (*inutility*) 645; no go; inefficacy; inefficaciousness etc. *adj.*; vain –, ineffectual –, abortive- -attempt, – efforts; flash in the pan, 'lame and impotent conclusion;' frustration; slip 'twixt cup and lip etc. (*disappointment*) 509.

blunder etc. (*mistake*) 495; fault, omission, miss, oversight, slip, trip, stumble, claudication, footfall; false –, wrong- step; *faux pas,* titubation, *bévue, faute,* lurch; botchery etc. (*want of skill*) 699; scrape, jam, mess, muddle, foozle, *fiasco,* breakdown.

mishap etc. (*misfortune*) 735; split, collapse, smash, blow, explosion.

repulse, rebuff, defeat, rout, overthrow, discomfiture; beating, drubbing; *quietus,* nonsuit, subjugation; check-, fool's-mate.

fall, downfall, ruin, perdition; wreck etc. (*destruction*) 162; death-blow; bankruptcy etc. (*non-payment*) 808.

losing game, *affaire flambée.*

victim, prey; bankrupt.

V. fail, be -unsuccessful etc. *adj.*; not -succeed etc. 731; make -vain efforts etc. *n.*; do –, labor –, toil- in vain; lose one's labor, take nothing by one's motion; bring to naught, make nothing of; wash a blackamoor white etc. (*impossible*) 471; roll the stone of Sisyphus etc. (*useless*) 645; do by halves etc. (*not complete*) 730; lose ground etc. (*recede*) 283; flunk; fall short of etc. 304.

miss, – one's aim, – the mark, – one's footing, – stays; slip, trip, stumble; make a -slip etc. *n.*, – blunder etc. 495, – mess of, – botch of; bitch it, miscarry, abort, go up like a rocket and come down like the stick, reckon without one's host; get the wrong sow by the ear etc. (*blunder, mismanage*) 699.

limp, halt, hobble, titubate; fall, tumble; lose one's balance; fall -to the ground, – between two stools; flounder, falter, stick in the mud, run aground, split upon a rock; run –, knock –, dash- one's head against a stone wall; break one's back; break down, sink, drown, founder, have the ground cut from under one; get into -trouble, – a mess, – a scrape; come to grief etc. (*adversity*) 735; go to -the wall, – the dogs, – pot; lick –, bite- the dust; be -defeated etc. 731; have the worst of it, lose the day, come off second best, lose; fall a prey to; succumb etc. (*submit*) 725; not have a leg to stand on.

come to nothing, end in smoke; fall -to the ground, – through, – dead, – still-born, – flat; slip through one's fingers; hang –, miss- fire; flash in the pan, collapse; topple down etc. (*descent*) 305; go to wrack and ruin etc. (*destruction*) 162.

go amiss, go wrong, go cross, go hard with, go on a wrong tack; go on –, come off –, turn out

−, work- ill; take -a wrong, − an ugly- turn; gang
agley.

be all -over with, − up with; explode; dash one's
hopes etc. (*disappoint*) 509; defeat the purpose;
upset the apple cart; sow the wind and reap the
whirlwind, jump out of the frying pan into the fire.

Adj. unsuccessful, successless; failing, tripping
etc. *v.*; at fault; unfortunate etc. 735.

abortive, addle, still-born; fruitless, sterile,
bootless; ineffect-ual, -ive; inefficient etc. (*impotent*) 158; inefficacious; lame, hobbling,
décousu; insufficient etc. '640; unavailing etc.
(*useless*) 645; of no effect.

aground, grounded, swamped, stranded, cast
away, wrecked, foundered, capsized, shipwrecked,
non-suited; foiled; defeated etc. 731; struck −,
borne −, broken- down; down-trodden; over-
borne, -whelmed; all up with; beaten to a frazzle.

lost, undone, ruined, broken; bankrupt etc. (*not
paying*) 808; played out; done -up,· − for; dead
beat, ruined root and branch, *flambé*, knocked on
the head; destroyed etc. 162.

frustrated, thwarted, crossed, unhinged, disconcerted, dashed; thrown -off one's balance, − on
one's back, − on one's beam ends; unhorsed, in a
sorry plight; hard hit.

stultified, befooled, dished, hoist on one's own
petard, victimized, sacrificed.

wide of the mark etc. (*error*) 495; out of one's
reckoning etc. (*inexpectation*) 508; left in the
lurch; thrown away etc. (*wasted*) 638; unattained;
uncompleted etc. 730.

Adv. unsuccessfully etc. *adj.*; to little or no purpose, in vain, *re infectâ*.

Phr. the bubble has burst, the game is up, all is
lost; the devil to pay; *parturiunt montes* etc:
(*disappointment*) 509.

733. Trophy.—N. trophy; medal, prize, palm;
ribbon, blue ribbon, *cordon bleu*; citation; cup,
laurel, -s; bays, crown, chaplet, wreath, civic
crown; Victoria Cross, V.C., *Croix de Guerre*,
Iron Cross; Distinguished Service Cross, Medal of
Honor, Congressional Medal; insignia etc. 550;
feather in one's cap etc. (*honor*) 873; decoration
etc. 877; garland, triumphal arch.

triumph etc. (*celebration*) 883; flying colors etc.
(*show*) 882.

monumentum aere perennius.

734. Prosperity.—N. prosperity, welfare, well-
being; affluence etc. (*wealth*) 803; success etc. 731;
thrift, roaring trade; chicken in every pot, the full
dinner paid; good −, smiles of- fortune; blessings,
godsend.

luck; good −, run of- luck; sunshine; fair -
weather, − wind; palmy −, bright −, halcyon-
days; piping times, tide, flood, high tide.

Saturnia regna, Saturnian age; golden -time, −
age; bed of roses; fat of the land, milk and honey,
loaves and fishes, fleshpots of Egypt.

made man, lucky dog, *enfant fâte,* spoiled child
of fortune.

upstart, *parvenu, nouveau riche*, profiteer, skipjack, mushroom.

V. prosper, thrive, flourish; be -prosperous etc.
adj.; drive a roaring trade; go on -well, −
smoothly, − swimmingly; sail before the wind,
swim with the tide; run -smooth, − smoothly, −
on all fours.

rise −, get on- in the world; work −, make-
one's way; look up; lift −, raise- one's head, make
one's -fortune, − pile, feather one's nest.

flower, blow, blossom, bloom, fructify, bear
fruit, fatten, batten.

keep oneself afloat; keep −, hold- one's head
above water; light −, fall- on one's -legs, − feet;
drop into a good thing; bear a charmed life; bask in
the sunshine; have a -good, − fine- time of it; have
a run, − of luck; have the -good fortune etc. *n.* to;
take a favorable turn; live -on the fat of the land,
− in clover.

Adj. prosperous; thriving etc. *v.*; in a fair way,
buoyant; well -off, − to do, − to do in´the world;
set up, at one's ease; rich etc. 803; in good case; in
-full, − high- feather; fortunate, lucky, in luck;
born -with a silver spoon in one's mouth, − under
a lucky star; on the sunny side of the hedge.

auspicious, propitious, providential.

palmy, halcyon; agreeable etc. 829; *couleur de
rose*.

Adv. prosperously etc. *adj.*; swimmingly; as
good luck would have it; beyond all -expectation,
− hope, − one's wildest dreams.

Phr. one's star in the ascendant, all for the best,
one's course runs smooth.

735. Adversity.—N. adversity, evil etc. 619;
failure etc. 732; bad −, ill −, evil −, adverse −,
hard- -fortune, − hap, − luck, − lot; frowns of
fortune; evil -dispensation, − star, − genius; ups
and downs of life, broken fortunes; hard -case, −
lines, − life; sea −, peck- of troubles; hell upon
earth; slough of despond; jinx.

trouble, humiliation, hardship, curse, blight,
blast, load, pressure.

pressure of the times, iron age, evil day, time out
of joint; hard −, bad −, sad- times; rainy day,
cloud, dark cloud, gathering clouds, ill wind;
visitation, infliction; affliction etc. (*painfulness*)
830; bitter -pill, − cup; care, trial; the sport of fortune.

mis-hap, -chance, -adventure, -fortune; disaster,
calamity, catastrophe; accident, casualty, cross,
reverse, check, *contretemps*, rub, pinch, setback.

losing game; falling etc. *v.*; fall, down-fall,
come-down; ruin-ation, -ousness; undoing;
extremity; ruin etc. (*destruction*) 162.

V. be -ill off etc. *adj.*; go hard with; fall on evil,
− days; go on ill; not -prosper etc. 734.

go -downhill, − to rack and ruin etc. (*destruction*) 162, − to the dogs; fall, − from one's high
estate; decay, sink, decline, go down in the world;
have seen better days; bring down one's grey hairs
with sorrow to the grave; come to grief; be all -
over, − up- with; bring a -wasp's, − hornet's- nest
about one's ears.

Adj. unfortunate, unblest, unhappy, unlucky;
im-, un-prosperous; luck-, hap-less; out of luck; in
trouble, in a bad way, in an evil plight; under a
cloud; clouded; ill −, badly- off; in adverse circumstances; poor etc. 804; behindhand, down in
the world, decayed, undone; on the road to ruin,

on its last legs, on the wane; in one's utmost need.

planet-struck, devoted; born -under an evil star, – with a wooden ladle in one's mouth; ill-fated, -starred, -omened; inconspicuous, ominous, doomed, unpropitious.

adverse, untoward; disastrous, calamitous, ruinous, dire, deplorable.

Adv. if the worst come to the worst, as ill luck would have it, from bad to worse, out of the frying pan into the fire.

Phr. one's star is on the wane; one's luck -turns, – fails; the game is up, one's doom is sealed, the ground crumbles under one's feet, *sic transit gloria mundi, tant va la cruche à l'eau qu'à la fin elle se casse.*

736. Mediocrity.—N. moderate –, average-circumstances; respectability; middle classes, *bourgeoisie*; mediocrity; golden mean etc. (*mid-course*) 628, (*moderation*) 174.

V. jog on; go –, get on- -fairly, – quietly, – peaceably, – tolerably, – respectably; steer a middle course etc. 628.

Adj. middling, so-so, fair, medium, moderate, mediocre, second-, third- etc. -rate.

737. Authority.—N. authority; influence, patronage, power, preponderance, credit, *prestige*, prerogative, jurisdiction; right etc. (*title*) 924.

divine right, dynastic rights, authoritativeness; absolut-eness, -ism; despotism, tyranny; *jus nocendi.*

command, empire, sway, rule; domin-ion, -ation; sovereignty, supremacy, suzerainty; lord-, head-ship; chiefdom; seignior-y, -ity, hegemony, patriarchate, patriarchy; master-y, -ship, -dom; government etc. (*direction*) 693; dictation, control.

hold, grasp; grip, -e; reach; iron sway etc. (*severity*) 739; fangs, clutches, talons; rod of empire etc. (*scepter*) 747.

reign, regnancy, *régime*, dynasty; director-, dictator-ship; protector-ate, -ship; caliphate, pashalic, electorate; presiden-cy, -tship; administration; pro-, consulship; prefecture; seneschalship; magistra-ture, -cy; raj.

empire; monarchy; king-hood, -ship; royalty, regality, autocracy, monocracy, arist-archy, -ocracy; oligarchy, democracy, demogogy; republic, -anism; federalism; socialism, collectivism; communism, bolshevism, syndicalism; mob law, mobocracy, ochlocracy, ergatocracy; *vox populi, imperium in imperio*; bureaucracy; beadle-, bumble-dom; stratocracy; martial law, military -power, – government; feodality, feudal system, feudalism.

Thearchy, diarchy; du-, tri-, heter-archy; du-, triumvirate; auto-cracy, -nomy; limited monarchy; constitutional -government, – monarchy; home rule, autonomy; self-government, -determination; representative government; Soviet government.

gyn-archy, -ocracy, -aeocracy; petticoat government, matriarchate, matriarchy.

[Vicarious authority] commission etc. 755; deputy etc. 759; permission etc. 760.

country, state, realm, commonwealth, canton,

constituency, toparchy, municipality, polity, body politic, *posse comitatus.*

person in authority etc. (*master*) 745; judicature etc. 965; cabinet etc. (*council*) 696; usurper; seat of -government, – authority; head-quarters.

[Acquisition of authority] accession; installation etc. 755; usurpation.

V. authorize etc. (*permit*) 760; warrant etc. (*right*) 924; dictate etc. (*order*) 741; have –, hold –, possess –, exercise –, exert –, wield- -authority etc. *n.*

be -at the head of etc. *adj.*; hold –, be in –, fill an- office; hold –, occupy- a post; be -master etc. 745.

rule, sway, command, control, administer; govern etc. (*direct*) 693; lead, preside over, reign; possess –, be seated on –, occupy- the throne; sway –, wield- the scepter; wear the crown.

have –, get- the -upper, – whip- hand; gain a hold upon, preponderate, dominate, boss, rule the roost; over-ride, -rule, -awe; lord it over, hold in hand, keep under, make a puppet of, lead by the nose, hold in the hollow of one's hand, turn round one's little finger, bend to one's will, hold one's own, wear the breeches; have -the ball at one's feet, – it all one's own way, – the game in one's own hand, – on the hip, – under one's thumb; be master of the situation; take the lead, play first fiddle, set the fashion; give the law to; carry with a high hand; lay down the law; 'ride in the whirlwind and direct the storm;' rule with a rod of iron etc. (*severity*) 739.

ascend –, mount- the throne, take the reins, – into one's hand; assume -authority etc. *n.*, – the reins of government; take –, assume the- command.

be -governed by, – in the power of; be under -the rule of, – the domination of.

Adj. ruling etc. *v.*; regnant, at the head, dominant, paramount, supreme, predominant, preponderant, in the ascendant, influential; gubernatorial; imperious; authoritative, executive, administrative, clothed with authority, official, *ex officio,* ministerial, bureaucratic, departmental, imperative, peremptory, overruling, absolute; hegemonic, -al; arbitrary; compulsory etc. 744; stringent.

regal, sovereign; royal, -ist; monarchical, kingly; imperial, -istic; princely; feudal; aristo-, auto-cratic; oligarchic etc. *n.*; democratic, republican, dynastic.

at one's command; in one's -power, – grasp; under control; authorized etc. (*due*) 924.

Adv. in the name of, by the authority of, *de par le Roi,* in virtue of; under the auspices of, in the hands of.

at one's pleasure; by a -dash, – stroke- of the pen; *ex mero motu; ex cathedrâ.*

Phr. the grey mare the better horse; 'every inch a king.'

738. Laxity. [Absence of authority.]—**N.** laxity; lax-, loose-, slack-ness; toleration etc. (*lenity*) 740; freedom etc. 748.

anarchy, interregnum; relaxation; loosening etc. *v.*; remission; dead letter, *brutum fulmen,* misrule; license, licentiousness; insubordination etc. (*disobedience*) 742; lynch law etc. (*illegality*) 964; nihilism.

[Deprivation of power.] dethronement, deposition, usurpation, abdication.

V. be -lax etc. *adj.*; *laisser -faire*, – *aller*; hold a loose rein; give -the reins to, – rope enough, – a loose to; tolerate; relax; misrule.

go beyond the length of one's tether; have one's - swing, – fling; act without -instructions, – authority; act on one's own responsibility, usurp authority.

dethrone, depose; abdicate.

Adj. lax, loose; slack; remiss etc. (*careless*) 460; weak.

relaxed; licensed; reinless, unbridled; anarchical; unauthorized etc. (*unwarranted*) 925.

---

739. Severity.—N. severity; strictness, formalism, harshness etc. *adj.*; rigor, stringency, austerity; inclemency etc. (*pitilessness*) 914*a*; arrogance etc. 885.

arbitrary power; absolut-, despot-ism; dictatorship, autocracy, tyranny, domineering, oppression; assumption, usurpation; inquisition, reign of terror, martial law; iron -heel, – rule, – hand, – sway; tight grasp; brute -force, – strength; coercion etc. 744; strong –, tight- hand.

hard -lines, – measure; tender mercies [ironical.]; sharp practice; bureaucracy, red tape; pipe-clay, officialism.

tyrant, disciplinarian, martinet, stickler, formalist, bashaw, despot, hard master, Draco, oppressor, inquisitor, extortioner, harpy, vulture, bird of prey.

V. be -severe etc. *adj.*

assume, usurp, arrogate, take liberties; domineer, bully etc. 885; tyrannize, inflict, wreak, stretch a point, put on the screw; be hard upon; bear –, lay- a heavy hand on; be –, come- down upon; ill-treat; deal-hardly with, – hard measure to; rule with a rod of iron, chastise with scorpions; dye with blood; oppress, override; trample –, tread- -down, – upon, – under foot; crush under an iron heel, ride roughshod over; rivet the yoke; hold –, keep- a tight hand; force down the throat; coerce etc. 744; give no quarter etc. (*pitiless*) 914*a*.

Adj. severe; strict, hard, harsh, dour, rigid, stiff, stern, rigorous, uncompromising, exacting, exigent, *exigeant*, inexorable, inflexible, obdurate, austere, relentless, Spartan, Draconian, stringent, strait-laced, puritanical, prudish, searching, unsparing, ironhanded, hard-headed, peremptory, absolute, positive, arbitrary, imperative; coercive etc. 744; tyrannical, despotic, masterful, extortionate, grinding, withering, oppressive, inquisitorial; inclement etc. (*ruthless*) 914*a*; cruel etc. (*malevolent*) 907; haughty, arrogant etc. 885.

Adv. severely etc. *adj.*; with a -high, – strong, – tight, – heavy-hand.

at the point of the -sword, – bayonet.

Phr. *Delirant reges plectuntur Achivi.*

---

740. Leniency.—N. leni-ency, -ence, -ty; moderation etc. 174; toler-ance, -ation; mildness, gentleness; favor; indulgen-ce, -cy; clemency, mercy, forbearance, quarter; compassion etc. 914.

V. be -lenient etc. *adj.*; tolerate, bear with; *parcere subjectis*, give quarter.

indulge, allow one to have his own way, spoil.

Adj. lenient; mild, – as milk; gentle, soft; tolerant, indulgent, easy-going; clement etc. (*compassionate*) 914; forbearing; complaisant, long-suffering.

---

741. Command.—N. command, order, ordinance, act, *fiat*, bidding, *dictum*, hest, behest, call, beck, nod.

des-, dis-patch; message, direction, injunction, charge, instructions; appointment, fixture.

demand, exaction, imposition, requisition, claim, reclamation, revendication; *ultimatum* etc. (*terms*) 770; request etc. 765; requirement.

dictation; dict-ate, mand-ate; *caveat*, decree, decree -nisi, – absolute, *senatus consultum*; precept; pre-re-script; writ, ordination, bull, edict, decretal, dispensation, prescription, brevet, placet, ukase, *firman*, hatti-sheriff, warrant, passport, *mittimus*, *mandamus*, summons, subpoena, *nisi prius*, interpellation, citation; word, – of command; *mot d'ordre*; bugle –, trumpet- call; beat of drum, tattoo; order of the day; enactment etc. (*law*) 963; *plébiscite* etc. (*choice*) 609.

V. command, order, decree, enact, ordain, dictate, direct, give orders.

prescribe, set, appoint, mark out; set –, prescribe –, impose- a task; set to work, put in requisition etc. 926.

bid, enjoin, charge, call upon, instruct; require, – at the hands of; exact, impose, tax, task; demand; insist on etc. (*compel*) 744.

claim, lay claim to, revendicate, reclaim.

cite, summon; call –, send- for; subpoena; beckon.

issue a command; make –, issue –, promulgate- -a requisition, – a decree, – an order etc. *n.*; give the -word of command, – word, – signal; call to order; give –, lay down- the law; assume the command etc. (*authority*) 737; remand.

be -ordered etc.; receive an order etc. *n.*

Adj. commanding etc. *v.*; authoritative etc. 737; decret-ory, -ive, -al; imperative, jussive, decisive, final.

Adv. in a commanding tone; by a -stroke, – dash- of the pen; by order, at beat of drum, on the first summons; at the word of command.

Phr. the decree is gone forth; *sic volo sic jubeo*; *le Roi le veut.*

---

742. Disobedience.—N. disobedience, insubordination, contumacy; infraction, -fringement; violation, non-compliance; non-observance etc. 773.

revolt, rebellion, mutiny, outbreak, rising, uprising, putsch, insurrection, *émeute*; riot, tumult etc. (*disorder*) 59; strike etc. (*resistance*) 719; barring out; defiance etc. 715.

mutinousness etc. *adj.*; mutineering; sedition, treason; high –, petty –, misprison of- treason; *premunire*, *lèse- majesté*; violation of law etc. 964; defection, secession, revolution, *sabotage*, bolshevism, *Sinn Fein*.

insurgent, mutineer, rebel, revolter, rioter, traitor, *carbonaro, sansculottes*, red republican, communist, Fenian, chartist, *frondeur*; seceder, runagate, brawler, anarchist, demagogue; suffragette; Spartacus, Masaniello, Wat Tyler, Jack Cade; bolshevist, bolshevik, maximalist, ringleader.

V. disobey, violate, infringe; shirk; set at defiance etc. (*defy*) 715; set authority at naught, run riot, fly in the face of, bolt, take the law into one's own hands; kick over the traces.

turn −, run- restive; champ the bit; strike etc. (*resist*) 719; rise, − in arms; secede; mutiny, rebel.

Adj. disobedient; uncompl-ying, -iant; unsubmissive; unruly, ungovernable; insubordinate, impatient of control; rest-iff, -ive; refractory, contumacious; recusant etc. (*refuse*) 764; recalcitrant; resisting etc. 719; lawless, mutinous, seditious, insurgent, riotous, revolutionary.

disobeyed, unobeyed; unbidden.

743. Obedience.—N. obedience; observance etc. 772; compliance; submission etc. 725; subjection etc. 749; non-resistance; passiveness, passivity, resignation.

allegiance, loyalty, fealty, homage, deference, devotion, fidelity, constancy.

submiss-ness, -iveness; ductility etc. (*softness*) 324; obsequiousness etc. (*servility*) 886.

V. be -obedient etc. *adj.*; obey, bear obedience to; submit etc. 725; comply, answer the helm, come at one's call; do -one's bidding, − what one is told, − suit and service; attend to orders, serve - devotedly, −, loyally, − faithfully.

follow, − the lead of, − to the world's end; serve etc. 746; play second fiddle.

Adj. obedient; compl-ying, -iant; law-abiding, loyal, faithful, leal, devoted; at one's -call, − command, − orders, − beck and call; under - beck and call; − control.

restrainable; resigned, passive; submissive etc. 725; henpecked; pliant etc. (*soft*) 324.

unrestrain-ed, -ing.

Adv. obediently etc. *adj.*; in compliance with, in obedience to.

Phr. to hear is to obey; as −, if- you please; at your service.

744. Compulsion.—N. compulsion, coercion, coaction, constraint, eminent domain, duress, enforcement, press, conscription.

force; brute −, main −, physical- force; the sword, *ultima ratio*; club −, mob −, lynch- law; *argumentum baculinum, le droit du plus fort*, martial law.

restraint etc. 751; necessity etc. 601; *force majeure*; Hobson's choice; the spur of necessity.

V. compel, force, make, drive, coerce, constrain, enforce, necessitate, oblige.

force upon, press; cram −, thrust −, force- down the throat; say it must be done, make a point of, insist upon, take no denial; put down, dragoon.

extort, wring from; put −, turn- on the screw; drag into; bind, − over; pin −, tie- down; require, tax, put in force; commandeer; restrain etc. 751.

Adj. compelling etc. *v.*; coercive, coactive; inexorable etc. 739; compuls-ory, -atory; obligatory, stringent, peremptory, binding.

forcible, not to be trifled with; irresistible etc. 601; compelled etc. *v.*; fain to.

Adv. by -force etc. *n.*, − force of arms; on compulsion, perforce; *vi et armis*, under the lash; at the point of the -sword, − bayonet; forcibly; by a strong arm.

under protest, in spite of one's teeth; against one's will etc. 603; *nolens volens* etc. (*of necessity*) 601; by stress of -circumstances, − weather; under press of; *de rigueur*.

745. Master.—N. master, *padrone*; lord, − paramount; command-er, -ant; captain; chief, -tain; *sahib*, sirdar, sachem, sheik, head, senior, governor, *duce*, ruler, dictator; leader etc. (*director*) 694.

lord of the ascendant; cock of the -walk, − roost; grey mare; mistress.

potentate; liege, − lord; suzerain, sovereign, monarch, autocrat, despot, tyrant, oligarch, overlord.

crowned head, emperor, king, anointed king, majesty, *imperator*, protector, president, stadtholder, judge.

caesar, kaiser, czar, sultan, grand Turk, caliph, imaum, shah, padishah, sophi, mogul, great mogul, khan, cham; lama, tycoon, mikado, inca, cazique; domn; vaivode; wai-, way-wode; landamman; seyyid, cacique.

prince, duke etc. (*nobility*) 875; arch-duke, doge, elector; seignior; mar-, land-grave; rajah, emir, nizam, nawab, negus.

empress, queen, sultana, czarina, princess, infanta, duchess, margravine, begum, maharani.

regent, viceroy, exarch, palatine, khedive, hospodar, beglerbeg, three-tailed bashaw, pasha, pashaw, bashaw, bey, beg, dey, scherif, tetrarch, satrap, mandarin, subhadar, nabob, maharajah; burgrave; laird etc. (*proprietor*) 779; High Commissioner.

the -authorities, − powers that be, − government; staff, *état major*, aga, official, man in office, person in authority.

[Naval authorities] admiral, -ty, − of the fleet; rear-, vice-, port-admiral; senior-, naval officer, S.N.O., commodore, captain, commander, lieutenant-commander, lieutenant, sub-lieutenant, midshipman, warrant −, petty- officer, leading seaman; skipper, mate, master.

[Military authorities] marshal, field-marshal, *maréchal*; general, -issimo; commander-in-chief, *seraskier, hetman*; lieutenant-, major-general; commandant; colonel, lieutenant-colonel, major, captain, centurion, skipper, lieutenant, second-lieutenant, officer, staff-officer, *aide de camp*, brigadier, brigade-major, adjutant, *jemidar*, ensign, cornet, cadet, subaltern, warrant officer, quartermaster, noncommissioned officer, N.C.O.; sergeant, -major; top-sergeant, color sergeant; corporal, -major; lance-, acting-corporal; drum major; shavetail.

[Air authorities] air -marshal, − commodore; group captain, squadron leader, wing commander, flight lieutenant, flying −, pilot- officer.

[Civil authorities] judge etc. 967; mayor, -alty; prefect, chancellor, archon, provost, magistrate, syndic; alcalde, alcaid; burgomaster, *corregidor*, seneschal, alderman, warden, constable, portreeve; lord mayor, sheriff; officer etc. (*executive*) 965.

746. Servant.—N. subject, liegeman; servant, retainer, follower, henchman, servitor, domestic, menial, help, lady help, *employé*, *attaché*; official.

retinue, suite, *cortège*, staff, court.

attendant, squire, usher, page, buttons, donzel, footboy; dog robber; train-, cup-bearer; waiter, busboy, tapster, butler, livery servant, lackey, footman, flunkey, valet, *valet de chambre*; boots; scout, gyp; equerry, groom; jockey, hostler, ostler, tiger, orderly, messenger, cad, gillie, caddie; *wallah*; journeyman, herdsman, swineherd.

bailiff, castellan, seneschal, chamberlain, *major-domo*, groom of the chambers.

secretary; under −, assistant- secretary; clerk; clerical staff, stenographer, subsidiary; agent etc. 758; subaltern; under-ling, -strapper; man.

maid, -servant, waitress; handmaid; *confidente*, lady's maid, abigail, *soubrette*; nurse, *bonne*, *ayah*; nurse-, nursery-, house-, parlor-, waiting-, chamber-, kitchen-, scullery-, between −, laundry −, dairy-maid; *femme* −, *fille- de chambre*; *camarista*; *chef de cuisine*, *cordon bleu*, cook, scullion, Cinderella; maid −, servant- of all work, tweeny, general servant, girl, slavey; laundress, bed-maker, goodie, char-woman etc. (*worker*) 690.

serf, vassal, slave, negro, helot; bondsman, -woman; bondslave; *âme damnée*, *odalisque*, ryot, *adscriptus glebae*; vill-ain, -ein; bead-, bede-sman; sizar; pension-er, -ary; client; dependant, -ent; hanger on, stooge, satellite; parasite etc. (*servility*) 886; led captain; *protégé*, ward, hireling, mercenary, puppet, creature.

badge of slavery; bonds etc. 752.

V. serve; minister to, wait −, attend −, dance attendance −, pin oneself- upon; squire, tend, hang on the sleeve of, char, do for; fag; valet.

Adj. in the train of; in one's -pay, − employ; at one's call etc. (*obedient*) 743; in bonds.

747. Scepter. [Insignia of authority.]—N. scepter, regalia, rod of empire, sword of state, mace, *fasces*, wand; staff, − of office; *bâton*, truncheon; flag etc. (*insignia*) 550; ensign −, emblem −, badge −, insignia- of authority, rank marks, brassard, badge, sash; cocked −, brass- hat.

epaulette, aiguilette, crown, star, eagle, bar, double bar, pip, stripe, chevron, curl, ring, anchor, shoulder-strap, tab.

throne, chair, musnud, divan, dais, woolsack.

toga, pall, mantle, robes of state, ermine, purple.

crown, coronet, diadem, tiara, triple crown, miter, crozier, cardinal's hat etc.; cap of maintenance; decoration; title etc. 877; portfolio.

key, signet, seals, talisman; helm; reins etc. (*means of restraint*) 752.

748. Freedom.—N. freedom, liberty, independence; license etc. (*permission*) 760; facility etc. 705.

scope, range, latitude, play; free −, full- -play, − scope; free stage and no favor; swing, full swing, elbow-room, margin, rope, wide berth; Liberty Hall.

franchise, denization; free −, freed-, livery-man; denizen.

autonomy, self-government, homerule, self-determination, liberalism, free trade; non-interference etc. 706.

immunity, exemption; emancipation etc. (*liberation*) 750; en-, af-franchisement; rights, privileges.

free land, freehold; allodium; frankalmoigne, mortmain.

independent, free-lance, -thinker, -trader.

V. be -free etc. *adj.*; have -scope etc. *n.*, − the run of, − one's own way, − a will of one's own, − one's fling; do what one -likes, − wishes, − pleases, − chooses; go at large, feel at home, paddle one's own canoe; stand on one's -legs, − rights; shift for oneself.

take a liberty; make -free with, − oneself quite at home; use a freedom; take -leave, − French leave.

set free etc. (*liberate*) 750; give the reins to etc. (*permit*) 760; allow −, give- scope etc. *n.* to; give a horse his head.

make free of; give the -freedom of, − franchise; en-, af-franchise.

laisser -faire, − *aller*; live and let live; leave to oneself; leave −, let- alone; mind one's own business.

Adj. free, − as air; out of harness, independent, at large, loose, scot free; left -alone, − to oneself.

in full swing; uncaught, unconstrained, unbuttoned, unconfined, unrestrained, unchecked, unprevented, unhindered, unobstructed, unbound, uncontrolled, untrammeled.

unsubject, ungoverned, unenslaved, unenthralled, unchained, unshackled, unfettered, unreined, unbridled, uncurbed, unmuzzled, unimpeded.

unrestricted, unlimited, unconditional; absolute; discretionary etc. (*optional*) 600.

unassailed, unforced, uncompelled.

unbiassed, unprejudiced, uninfluenced, spontaneous.

free and easy; at −, at one's- ease; *dégagé*, quite at home; wanton, rampant, irrepressible, unvanquished.

exempt; freed etc. 750; freeborn; autonomous, freehold, allodial; *gratis* etc. 815.

unclaimed, going a begging.

Adv. freely etc. *adj.*; *ad libitum* etc. (*at will*) 600.

749. Subjection.—N. subjection; depend-ence, -ance, -ency; subordination; thrall, thraldom, enthralment, subjugation, bondage, serfdom; feudal- -ism, -ity; vassalage, villenage; slavery, enslavement, involuntary servitude.

service; servi-tude, -torship; tendence, employ, tutelage, clientship; liability etc. 177; constraint etc. 751; oppression etc. (*severity*) 739; yoke etc. (*means of restraint*) submission etc. 725; obedience etc. 743.

V. be -subject etc. *adj.*; be −, lie- at the mercy of; depend −, lean −, hang- upon; fall -a prey to, − under; play second fiddle.

be a -mere machine, − puppet, − football; not dare to say one's soul is his own; drag a chain.

serve etc. 746; obey etc. 743; submit etc. 725.

break in, tame; subject, subjugate; master etc. 731; tread -down, − under foot; weigh down; drag at one's chariot wheels; reduce to -subjection, −

slavery; en-, in-, be-thral; enslave, lead captive; take into custody etc. (*restrain*) 751; rule etc. 737; drive into a corner, hold at the sword's point; keep under; hold in -bondage, - leading strings, - swaddling clothes.

Adj. subject, dependent, subordinate; feud-al, -atory; in subjection to, under control; in -leading strings, - harness; subjected, enslaved etc. *v.*; con-strained etc. 751; subservient, servile, fawning, slavish, obsequious, cringing; down-trodden; over-borne, -whelmed; under the lash, on the hip, led by the nose, henpecked; the -puppet, - sport, - plaything- of; under one's -orders, - command, - thumb; like dirt under one's feet; a slave to; at the mercy of; in the -power, - hands, - clutches- of; at the feet of; at one's beck and call etc. (*obedient*) 743; liable etc. 177; parasitical; stipendiary.

Adv. under.

750. Liberation.—N. liberation, disengagement, release, disenthrallment, enlargement, emancipation; af-, en-franchisement; manumission; discharge, dismissal.

deliverance etc. 672; redemption, extrication, acquittance, absolution; acquittal etc. 970; escape etc. 671.

V. liberate, free; set -free, - clear, - at liberty; render free, emancipate, release; en-, af-franchise; manumit; enlarge; dis-band, -charge, -miss, -enthral; let -go, - loose, - out, - slip; cast -, turn- adrift; deliver etc. 672; absolve etc. (*acquit*) 970; reprieve.

unfetter etc. 751; untie etc. 44; loose etc. (*disjoin*) 44; loosen, relax; un-bolt, -bar, -close, -cork, -clog, -hand, -bind, -latch, -chain, -harness; dis-engage, -entangle; clear, extricate, unloose.

gain -, obtain -, acquire- one's -liberty etc. 748; get -rid, - clear- of; deliver oneself from; shake off the yoke, slip the collar; break -loose, - prison; tear asunder one's bonds, cast off trammels; escape etc. 671.

Adj. at -liberty, - large, free, liberated etc. *v.*; out of harness etc. 748; adrift.

Int. unhand me! let me go!

751. Restraint.—N. restraint; hindrance etc. 706; coercion etc. (*compulsion*) 744; cohibition, constraint, repression; discipline, control, self-restraint etc. 604.

confinement; durance, duress; im-, prisonment; incarceration, coarctation, entombment, man-cipation, durance vile, thrall, -dom, limbo, cap-tivity; blockade; quarantine; detention.

arrest, -ation; custody, keep, care, charge, ward, restringency.

curb etc. (*means of restraint*) 752; *lettres de cachet*.

limitation, restriction, protection, monopoly; prohibition etc. 761; economic pressure.

prisoner etc. 754.

V. restrain, check; put -, lay- under restraint; en-, in-, be-thral; restrict; debar etc. (*hinder*) 706; constrain; coerce etc. (*compel*) 744; curb, control; hold -, keep- -back, - from, - in, - in check, - within bounds; hold in -leash, - leading strings; withhold.

keep under; repress, suppress; smother; pull in, rein in; hold, - fast; keep a tight hand on; prohibit etc. 761; in-, co-hibit.

enchain; fasten etc. (*join*) 43; fetter, shackle; en-trammel; bridle, muzzle, gag, pinion, manacle, handcuff, tie one's hands, hobble, bind hand and foot; swathe, swaddle; pin -, peg- down; tether, picket; tie, - up, - down; secure; forge fetters.

confine; shut -, clap -, lock -, box -, mew -, bottle -, cork -, seal -, button- up; shut -, hem -, bolt -, wall -, rail- in; impound, pen, coop; enclose etc. (*circumscribe*) 229; cage; in-, en-cage; close the door upon; cloister; imprison, immure; incarcerate, entomb; clap -, lay- under hatches; put in -irons, - a strait waistcoat; throw -, cast- into prison; put into bilboes.

arrest; take -up, - charge of, - into custody; take -, make- -prisoner, - captive; captivate; lead -captive, - into captivity; send -, commit- to prison; commit; give in -charge, - custody; subjugate etc. 749.

Adj. re-, con-strained; imprisoned etc. *v.*; pent up; jammed in, wedged in; under -restraint, - lock and key, - hatches; serving -, doing- time; in swaddling clothes; on *parole*; in custody etc. (*prisoner*) 754; cohibitive; coactive etc. (*compulsory*) 744.

stiff, restringent, straitlaced, hide-bound.

ice-, wind-, weather-bound; 'cabined, cribbed, confined;' in Lob's pound, laid by the heels.

Adv. in captivity, under arrest, behind the bars, in -prison, - jail, - durance vile.

752. Prison. [Means of restraint.]**—N.** prison, -house; jail, gaol, cage, coop, den, death house, condemned -, cell; stronghold, fortress, keep, donjon, dungeon, *Bastille, oubliette*; bridewell, house of correction, hulks, tool-booth, panopticon, penitentiary, guard-room, clink, can, stir, tronk, jug, lock-up, hold; round -, watch -, station -, sponging-house; station; house of detention, black hole, pen, fold, pound; enclosure etc. 232; penal settlement; chain gang; debtors' prison; reform-atory; federal penitentiary, state prison; criminal lunatic asylum; bilboes, stocks, limbo, quod.

Dartmoor, Newgate, Fleet, Marshalsea; King's (*or* Queen's) Bench; Sing Sing, Dannemora.

bond; strap, bandage, splint, tourniquet; irons, pinion, gyve, fetter, shackle, trammel, manacle, handcuff, bracelets, darbies, strait waistcoat, strait-jacket.

yoke, collar, halter, harness; muzzle, gag, bit, brake, curb, snaffle, bridle; rein, -s; ribbons, lines, bearing-rein; martingale, leading string; tether, picket, band, guy, chain; cord etc. (*fastening*) 45.

bolt, bar, lock, padlock, rail, wall; paling, palisade; fence; barrier, barricade.

brake, drag etc. (*hindrance*) 706.

753. Keeper.—N. keeper, custodian, *custos*, ranger, warder, jailer, gaoler, turnkey, castellan, guard; watch, -dog, -man; Charley; sen-try, -tinel; watch and ward; *concierge*, coast-guard, *guarda costa*, gamekeeper.

escort, body guard, convoy.

protector, governor, duenna; guardian; gover-ness etc. (*teacher*) 540; nurse, *bonne, ayah, amah.*

754. Prisoner.—N. prisoner, captive, *détenu*, close prisoner.

jail-bird, ticket-of-leave man.

V. stand committed; be -imprisoned etc. 751.

Adj. imprisoned etc. 751; in -prison, — quod, — durance vile, — limbo, — custody, — charge, — chains; under -lock and key, — hatches; on *parole*; detained at his Majesty's pleasure.

755. Commission. [Vicarious authority.]—**N.** commission, delegation; con-, as-signment; procuration; deputation, legation, mission, embassy; agency, agentship; power of attorney, proxy; clerkship.

errand, charge, *brevet*, diploma, *exequatur*, permit etc. (*permission*) 760.

appointment, nomination, return; charter; ordination; installation, inauguration, investiture; accession, coronation, enthronement.

vicegerency; regency, regentship.

viceroy etc. 745; consignee etc. 758; deputy etc. 759.

V. commission, delegate, depute; consign, assign; charge; in-, en-trust; turn over to; commit, — to the hands of; authorize etc. (*permit*) 760.

put in commission, accredit, engage, hire, bespeak, appoint, name, nominate, return, ordain; install, induct, inaugurate, invest, crown; en-roll, -list.

employ, empower; give power of attorney to; set —, place- over; send out.

be commissioned, be accredited; represent, stand for; stand in the -stead, — place, — shoes- of.

Adj. commissioned etc. *v.*

Adv. *per procuratione.*

756. Abrogation.—N. abrogation, annulment, nullification; cancelling etc. *v.*; cancel; revo-cation, -kement; repeal, rescission, defeasance.

dismissal, *congé*, demission; depos-al, -ition; sack, dethronement; disestablish-, disendow-ment; deconsecration.

aboli-tion, -shment; dissolution.

counter-order, -mand; repudiation, retractation; recantation etc. (*tergiversation*) 607.

V. abrogate, annul, cancel; destroy etc. 162; abolish; revoke, repeal, rescind, reverse, retract, recall; over-rule, -ride; set aside; disannul, dissolve, quash, nullify, declare null and void; dis-establish, -endow; deconsecrate.

disclaim etc. (*deny*) 536; ignore, repudiate; recant etc. 607; divest oneself, break off.

counter-mand, -order; do away with; sweep —, brush- away; throw -overboard, — to the dogs; scatter to the winds, cast behind.

dismiss, discard; cast —, turn- -off, — out, — adrift, — out of doors, — aside, — away; send -off, — away, — about one's business; discharge, get rid of, fire out, fire etc. (*eject*) 297; jilt.

cashier; break; oust; set down, unseat, -saddle; un-, de-, disen-throne; depose, uncrown; unfrock, strike off the roll; dis-bar, -bench.

be -abrogated etc.; receive its quietus.

Adj. abrogated etc. *v.*; *functus officio.*

Int. get along with you! begone! go about your business! away with!

757. Resignation.—N. resignation, retirement, abdication, renunciation, abjuration, disclaimer, abandonment, relinquishment.

V. resign; give —, throw- up; lay down, throw up the cards, wash one's hands of, abjure, renounce, forego, disclaim, abandon, relinquish, retract, demit; deny etc. 536.

abrogate etc. 756; desert etc. (*relinquish*) 624; get rid of etc. 782.

abdicate; vacate, — one's seat; accept the stewardship of the Chiltern Hundreds; retire; tender —, send in —, hand in- one's resignation.

Adj. abdicant, renunciatory etc. *v.*

Phr. 'Othello's occupation's gone.'

758. Consignee.—N. consignee, trustee, nominee, committee.

delegate; commiss-ary, -ioner; emissary, envoy, commissionaire; messenger etc. 534.

diplomatist, diplomat, *corps diplomatique*, embassy; am-, em-bassador; representative, resident, consul, legate, nuncio, internuncio, *chargé d' affaires, attaché.*

vicegerent etc. (*deputy*) 759; plenipotentiary.

functionary, placeman, curator; treasurer etc. 801; agent, factor, bailiff, steward, clerk, secretary, attorney, solicitor, proctor, broker, underwriter, commission agent, auctioneer, one's man of business; factotum etc. (*director*) 694; caretaker.

negotiator, go between; middleman; under agent, *employé*; servant etc. 746.

salesman; commercial, — traveler; bagman, *commis-voyageur*, touter.

newspaper —, own —, war —, special-correspondent; reporter.

759. Deputy.—N. deputy, substitute, vice, proxy, *locum tenens*, delegate, representative, next friend, surrogate, secondary.

regent, vicegerent, vizier, minister, vicar; premier etc. (*director*) 694; chancellor, prefect, provost, warden, lieutenant, archon, consul, proconsul; viceroy etc. (*governor*) 745; commissioner etc. 758; plenipotentiary, *alter ego.*

team, eight, eleven; champion.

V. be -deputy etc. *n.*; stand —, appear —, hold a brief —, answer- for; represent; stand —, walk- in the shoes of; stand in the stead of.

substitute, ablegate, accredit; commission, empower, delegate etc. 755.

Adj. acting; vice, -regal; accredited to.

Adv. in behalf of, by proxy.

760. Permission.—N. permission, leave; allow-, suffer-ance; toler-ance, -ation; liberty, law, license, concession, grace; indulgence etc. (*lenity*) 740; favor, dispensation, exemption, release; connivance; vouchsafement.

authorization, warranty, accordance, admission.

permit, warrant, *brevet*, precept, sanction, authority, *firman*; pass, -port; furlough, license, *carte blanche*, ticket of leave; grant, charter, patent.

V. permit; give -permission etc. *n.*, — power;

let, allow, admit; suffer, bear with, tolerate, recognize; concede etc. 762; accord, vouchsafe, favor, humor, gratify, indulge, stretch a point; wink at, connive at; shut one's eyes to.

grant, empower, charter, enfranchise, privilege, confer a privilege, license, authorize, warrant; sanction; entrust etc. (*commission*) 755.

give -*carte blanche*, – the reins to, – scope to etc. (*freedom*) 748; leave -alone, – it to one, – the door open; open the -door to, – floodgates; give a loose to.

let off; absolve etc. (*acquit*) 970; release, exonerate, dispense with.

ask –, beg –, request- -leave, – permission.

Adj. permitting etc. *v.*; permissive, indulgent; permitted etc. *v.*; patent, chartered, permissible, allowable, lawful, legitimate, legal; legalized etc. (*law*) 963; licit; unforbid, -den; unconditional.

Adv. permissibly; by –, with –, on- -leave etc. *n.*; *speciali gratiâ*; under favor of; *pace*; *ad libitum* etc. (*freely*) 748, (*at will*) 600; by all means etc. (*willingly*) 602; yes etc. (*assent*) 488.

761. Prohibition.—N. pro-, in-hibition; *veto*, disallowance; interdict, -ion; injunction; embargo, ban, *verboten*, taboo, proscription; *index expurgatorius*; restriction etc. (*restraint*) 751; hindrance etc. 706; forbidden fruit.

V. pro-, in-hibit; forbid, put one's *veto* upon, disallow; bar; debar etc. (*hinder*) 706, forefend.

keep -in, – within bounds; restrain etc. 751; cohibit, withhold, limit, circumscribe, clip the wings of, restrict, narrow; interdict, taboo; put –, place- under -an interdiction, – the ban; proscribe, censor; exclude, shut out; shut –, bolt –, show- the door; warn off; dash the cup from one's lips; forbid the banns.

Adj. prohibit-ive, -ory; interdictive; proscriptive; restrictive, exclusive; forbidding etc. *v.*

prohibited etc. *v.*; not -permitted etc. 760; unlicensed, contraband, under the ban of; illegal etc. 964; unauthorized, not to be thought of.

Adv. on no account etc. (*no*) 536.

Int. forbid it heaven! etc. (*deprecation*) 766. hands –, keep- off! hold! stop! avast!

Phr. that will never do.

762. Consent.—N. consent; assent etc. 488; acquiescence; approval etc. 931; compliance, agreement, concession; yield-ance, -ingness; accession, acknowledgment, acceptance, agnition.

settlement, ratification, confirmation, adjustment.

permit etc. (*permission*) 760; promise etc. 768.

V. consent; assent etc. 488; yield assent, admit, allow, concede, grant, yield; come -over, – round; give in to, acknowledge, agnize, give consent, comply with, acquiesce, agree to, fall in with, accede, accept, embrace an offer, close with, take at one's word, have no objection.

satisfy, meet one's wishes, settle, come to terms etc. 488; not -refuse etc. 764; turn a willing ear etc. (*willingness*) 602; jump at; deign, vouchsafe; promise etc. 768.

Adj. consenting etc. *v.*; agreeable, compliant; agreed etc. (*assent*) 488; unconditional.

Adv. yes etc. (*assent*) 488; by all means etc. (*willingly*) 602; if –, as- you please; be it so, so be it, well and good, of course.

763. Offer.—N. offer, proffer, presentation, tender, bid, overture; propos-al, -ition; motion, invitation; candidature; offering etc. (*gift*) 784.

V. offer, proffer, present, tender; bid; propose, move; make -a motion, – advances; start; invite, hold out, place- at one's disposal, – in one's way, put forward.

hawk about; offer for sale etc. 796; press etc. (*request*) 765; lay at one's feet.

offer –, present- oneself; volunteer, come forward, be a candidate; stand –, bid- for; seek; be at one's service; go a begging; bribe etc. (*give*) 784.

Adj. offer-ing, -ed etc. *v.*; in the market, for sale, to let, disengaged, on hire.

764. Refusal.—N. refusal, rejection; non-, incompliance; denial; declining etc. *v.*; declension; peremptory –, flat –, point blank- refusal; repulse, rebuff; discountenance.

recusancy, renunciation, abnegation, negation, protest, disclaimer; dissent etc. 489; revocation etc. 756.

V. refuse, reject, deny, decline; nill, negative; refuse –, withhold- one's assent; shake the head; close the -hand, – purse; grudge, begrudge, be slow to, hang fire.

be deaf to; turn -a deaf ear to, – one's back upon; set one's face against, discountenance, not hear of, have nothing to do with, wash one's hands of, stand aloof, forswear, set aside, cast behind one; not yield an inch etc. (*obstinacy*) 606.

resist, cross; not -grant etc. 762; repel, repulse; shut –, slam- the door in one's face; rebuff; send -back, – to the right about, – away with a flea in the ear; deny oneself, not be at home to; discard etc. (*repudiate*) 610; rescind etc. (*revoke*) 756; disclaim, protest; dissent etc. 489.

Adj. refusing etc. *v.*; rest-ive, -iff; recusant; uncomplying, noncompliant, unconsenting, uncomplaisant, protestant; not willing to hear of, deaf to.

refused etc. *v.*; ungranted, out of the question, not to be thought of, impossible.

Adv. no etc. 536; on no account, not for the world; no thank you.

Phr. *non possumus*; [ironically] your humble servant; *bien obligé.*

765. Request.—N. requ-est, -isition; claim etc. (*demand*) 741; petition, suit, prayer; begging letter, round-robin.

motion, overture, application, canvass, address, appeal, apostrophe; imprecation; rogation; proposal, proposition.

orison etc. (*worship*) 990; incantation etc. (*spell*) 993.

mendicancy; asking, panhandling, begging etc. *v.*; postulation, solicitation, invitation, entreaty, importunity, supplication, instance, impetration; imploration, obsecration, obtestation, invocation, interpellation.

V. request, ask; beg, crave, sue, pray, petition, solicit, invite, pop the question, make bold to ask; beg -leave, – a boon; apply to, call to, put to; call -upon, – for; make –, address –, prefer –, put up- a -request, – prayer, – petition; make - application, – a requisition; ask –, trouble- one for; claim etc. (*demand*) 741; offer up prayers etc. (*worship*) 990; whistle for.

beg hard, entreat, beseech, plead, supplicate, implore, apostrophize; conjure, adjure; obtest; cry to, kneel to, appeal to; invoke, evoke; impetrate, imprecate, ply, press, urge, beset, importune, dun, tax, clamor for; cry -aloud, – for help; fall on one's knees; throw oneself at the feet of; come down on one's marrow-bones.

beg from door to door, send the hat round, go a begging; mendicate, mump, cadge, panhandle, beg one's bread.

dance attendance on, besiege, knock at the door.

bespeak, canvass, tout, make interest, court; seek, bid for etc. (*offer*) 763; publish the banns.

Adj. requesting etc. *v.*; precatory; suppli-ant, -cant, -catory; invoc-, imprec-, rog-atory; postulant, mendicant.

importunate, clamorous, urgent; solicitous; cap in hand; on one's -knees, – bended knees, – marrow-bones.

Adv. prithee, do, please, pray; be so good as, be good enough; have the goodness, vouchsafe, will you, I pray thee, if you please.

Int. for -God's, – heaven's, – goodness', – mercy's- sake.

766. Deprecation. [Negative request.]—**N.** deprecation, expostulation; remonstrance; intercession, mediation.

V. deprecate, protest, expostulate, enter a protest, intercede for.

Adj. deprecatory, expostulatory, intercessory, mediatorial.

deprecated, protested.

un-, unbe-sought; unasked etc. (*see* ask etc. 765).

Int. cry you mercy! God forbid! forbid it Heaven! Heaven -forefend, – forbid! far be it from! hands off! etc. (*prohibition*) 761.

767. Petitioner.—**N.** petitioner, solicitor, applicant; suppli-ant, -cant; suitor, candidate, claimant, postulant, aspirant, competitor, bidder; place –, pot- hunter; prizer.

beggar, mendicant, mumper, sturdy beggar, cadger, panhandler.

canvasser, barker, touter etc. 768.

sycophant, parasite etc. 886.

768. Promise.—**N.** promise, undertaking, word, troth, plight, pledge, *parole*, word of honor, vow; oath etc. (*affirmation*) 535; profession, assurance, warranty, guarantee, insurance, obligation; contract etc. 769.

engagement, pre-engagement; affiance; betroth, -al, -ment; marriage -compact, – vow.

V. promise; give a -promise etc. *n.*; undertake, engage; make –, form- an engagement; enter - into, – on- an engagement; bind –, tie –, pledge –, commit –, take upon- oneself; vow; swear etc. (*affirm*) 535; give –, pass –, pledge –, plight- one's -word, – honor, – credit, – troth; betroth, plight faith; take the vows.

assure, warrant, guarantee, vouch for, avouch, covenant, bind; attest etc. (*bear witness*) 467.

hold out an expectation; contract an obligation; become -bound to, – sponsor for; answer –, be answerable- for; secure; give security etc. 771; underwrite.

adjure, administer an oath, put to one's oath, swear a witness.

Adj. promising etc. *v.*; promissory; votive; under hand and seal; upon -oath, – affirmation.

promised etc. *v.*; affianced, pledged, bound; committed, compromised; in for it.

Adv. as one's head shall answer for; upon my honor.

Phr. in for a penny, in for a pound.

768a. Release from engagement.—**N.** release etc. (*liberation*) 750.

Adj. absolute; unconditional etc. (*free*) 748.

769. Compact.—**N.** compact, contract, agreement, bargain, deal, transaction; affidation; pact, -ion; bond, covenant, indenture.

stipulation, settlement, convention; compromise, *cartel*.

protocol, treaty, *concordat*, *Zollverein*, *Sonderbund*, charter, *Magna Charta*, Pragmatic Sanction.

negotiation etc. (*bargaining*) 794; diplomacy etc. (*mediation*) 724; negotiator etc. (*agent*) 758.

ratification, completion, signature, seal, sigil, signet.

V. contract, covenant, agree for, engage etc. (*promise*) 768.

treat, negotiate, stipulate, make terms; bargain etc. (*barter*) 794.

make –, strike- a bargain; come to -terms, – an understanding; compromise etc. 774; set at rest; close, – with; conclude, complete, settle; confirm, ratify, clench, subscribe, underwrite; en-, in-dorse; put the seal to; sign, seal etc. (*attest*) 467; indent.

take one at one's word, bargain by inch of candle.

Adj. contractual, agreed etc. *v.*; conventional; under hand and seal; signed, sealed and delivered.

Phr. *caveat emptor*.

770. Conditions.—**N.** conditions, terms; articles, – of agreement.

clauses, provisions; proviso etc. (*qualification*) 469; covenant, stipulation, obligation, *ultimatum*, *sine quâ non*; *casus foederis*.

V. make –, come to- -terms etc. (*contract*) 769; make it a condition, stipulate, insist upon, make a point of; bind, tie up.

Adj. conditional, provisional, guarded, fenced, hedged in.

Adv. conditionally etc. (*with qualification*) 469; provisionally, *pro re natà*; on condition; with a reservation.

771. Security.—N. security; guaran-ty, -tee; gage, waranty, bond, tie, pledge, plight, mortgage, debenture, hypothecation, bill of sale, lien, pignus, pawn, pignoration; real security; bottomry; collateral, vadium.

stake, deposit, earnest, handsel, caution.

promissory note; bill, – of exchange; I.O.U.: personal security, covenant, specialty; *parole* etc. (*promise*) 768.

acceptance, indorsement, signature, execution, stamp, seal.

spon-sor, -sion, -sorship; surety, bail; main-pernor, hostage.

recognizance; deed –, covenant- of indemnity.

authentication, verfication, warrant, certificate, voucher, docket, doquet; record etc. 551; probate, attested copy.

receipt; ac-, quittance; discharge, release.

muniment, title-deed, instrument; deed, – poll; assurance, insurance, indenture; charter etc. (*compact*) 769; charter-poll; paper, parchment, settlement, will, testament, last will and testament, codicil.

V. give -security, – bail, – substantial bail; go bail; pawn, impawn, hock, spout, mortgage, hypothecate, impignorate.

guarantee, warrant, assure; accept, indorse, underwrite, insure.

execute, stamp; sign, seal etc. (*evidence*) 467.

let, set; grant –, take –, hold- a lease; hold in pledge; lend on security etc. 787.

Adj. secure, -ed; pledged etc. *v.*; in pawn, on deposit.

772. Observance.—N. observance, performance, compliance; obedience, etc. 743; fulfilment, satisfaction, discharge; acquit-tance, -tal.

adhesion, acknowledgment; fidelity etc. (*probity*) 939; exact etc. 494- observance.

V. observe, comply with, respect, acknowledge, abide by; cling to, adhere to, be faithful to, act up to; meet, fulfil; carry -out, – into execution; execute, perform, keep, satisfy, discharge; do one's office.

perform –, fulfill –, discharge –, acquit oneself of- an obligation; make good; make good –, keep- one's -word, – promise; redeem one's pledge; keep faith with, stand to one's engagement.

Adj. observant, faithful, true, loyal; honorable etc. 939; true as the -dial to the sun, – needle to the pole; punct-ual, -ilious; meticulous; literal etc. (*exact*) 494; as good as one's word.

Adv. faithfully etc. *adj.*

773. Non-observance.—N. non-observance etc. 772; evasion, inobservance, failure, omission, neglect, laches, laxity, informality.

infringement; infraction; violation, transgression.

retractation, repudiation, nullification; protest; forfeiture.

lawlessness; disobedience etc. 742; bad faith etc. 940.

V. fail, neglect, omit, elude, evade, give the go by to, cut, set aside, ignore; shut –, close- one's eyes to, avoid.

infringe, transgress, pirate, violate, break, trample under foot, do violence to, drive a coach and six through.

discard, protest, repudiate, fling to the winds, set at naught, nullify, declare null and void; cancel etc. (*wipe off*) 552.

retract, go back from, be off, forfeit, go from one's word, palter; stretch –, strain- a point.

Adj. violating etc. *v.*; lawless, transgressive; elusive, evasive; lax, casual; non-observant.

unfulfilled etc. (*see* fulfil etc. 772).

774. Compromise.—N. com-promise, -mutation, -position; middle term, *mezzo termine*; compensation etc. 30; adjustment, mutual concession.

V. com-promise, -mute, -pound; take the mean; split the difference, meet one half way, give and take; come to terms etc. (*contract*) 769; submit to –, abide by- arbitration; patch up, bridge over, fix up, arrange; adjust, – differences; agree; make -the best of, – a virtue of necessity; take the will for the deed.

775. Acquisition.—N. acquisition; gaining etc. *v.*; obtainment; procur-ation, -ement; purchase, descent, inheritance; gift etc. 784.

recovery, retrieval, revendication, replevin; redemption, salvage, trover; find, *trouvaille*, foundling.

gain, thrift; money-making, -grubbing; lucre, filthy lucre, loaves and fishes, the main chance, pelf; emolument etc. 973; wealth etc. 803.

profit, earnings, winnings, innings, clean-up, pickings, perquisite, net profit; income etc. (*receipt*) 810; pro-ceeds, -duce, -duct; out-come, -put; return, fruit, crop, harvest, tilth; second crop, aftermath; benefit etc. (*good*) 618.

sweepstakes, trick, prize, pool.

[Fraudulent acquisition] subreption; theft, stealing etc. 791.

V. acquire, get, gain, win, earn, obtain, procure, gather, annex; collect etc. 72; pick, – up; glean, take etc. 789.

find; come –, pitch –, light- upon; scrape -up, – together; get in, reap and carry, net, bag, stack, bring home, secure, come across, derive, draw, get in the harvest.

profit; make –, draw- profit; turn to -profit, – account; make -capital out of, – money by; obtain a return, reap the fruits of; reap –, gain- an advantage; turn -a penny, – an honest penny; make the pot boil, bring grist to the mill; make –, coin –, raise- money; raise -funds, – the wind; fill one's pocket etc. (*wealth*) 803.

treasure up etc. (*store*) 636; realize, clear; produce etc. 161; take etc. 789.

get back, recover, regain, retrieve, revendicate, replevy, redeem, come by one's own.

come -by, – in for; receive etc. 785; inherit; step into, – a fortune, – the shoes of; succeed to.

get -hold of, – between one's finger and thumb, – into one's hand, – at; take – , come into – , enter into- possession.

be -profitable etc. *adj.*; pay, answer.

accrue etc. (*be received*) 785.

Adj. acquir-ing, -ed etc. *v.*; acquisitive; productive, profitable, advantageous, gainful, remunerative, paying, lucrative.

776. Loss.—N. loss; de-, perdition; forfeiture, lapse.

privation, bereavement; deprivation etc. (*dispossession*) 789; riddance.

V. lose; incur – , experience – , meet with- a loss; miss; mislay, let slip, allow to slip through the fingers, squander; be without etc. (*exempt*) 777a; forfeit.

get rid of etc. 782; waste etc. 638.

be lost, lapse.

Adj. losing etc. *v.*; not having etc. 777a.

shorn of, deprived of; denuded, bereaved, bereft, *minus*, cut off; dispossessed etc. 789; rid of, quit of; out of pocket.

lost etc. *v.*; long lost; irretrievable etc. (*hopeless*) 859; irredentist; off one's hands.

Int. farewell to! adieu to! good riddance!

777. Possession.—N. possession, seisin; ownership etc. 780; occupancy; hold, -ing; tenure, tenancy, feodality, dependency; villenage; socage, chivalry, knight service.

exclusive possession, impropriation, monopoly, corner; retention etc. 781; pre-possession, -occupancy; nine points of the law.

future possession, heritage, inheritance, heirship, reversion, fee, seigniority, feud, fief.

bird in hand, *uti possidetis*, *chose* in possession.

V. possess, have, hold, occupy, enjoy; be -possessed of etc. *adj.*; have -in hand etc. *adj.*; own etc. 780; command.

inherit; come -to, – in for.

engross, monopolize, forestall, regrate, impropriate, have all to oneself, corner; have a firm hold of etc. (*retain*) 781; get into one's hand etc. (*acquire*) 775.

belong to, appertain to, pertain to; be -in one's possession etc. *adj.*; vest in.

Adj. possessing etc. *v.*; worth; possessed of, seized of, master of, in possession of; endowed – , blest – , instinct – , fraught – , laden – , charged – , instilled – , with.

possessed etc. *v.*; on hand, by one; in hand, in store, in stock; in one's -hands, – grasp, – possession; at one's -command, – disposal; one's own etc. (*property*) 780.

unsold, unshared.

777a. Exemption.—N. exemption; exception, immunity, privilege, release etc. 927a; absence etc. 187.

V. not -have etc. 777; be -without etc. *adj.*

Adj. exempt from, devoid of, without, un-possessed of, unblest with, immune from.

not -having etc. 777; unpossessed; untenanted etc. (*vacant*) 187; without an owner.

unobtained, unacquired.

778. Participation. [Joint possession.]—N. participation; co-, joint-tenancy; possession – , tenancy- in common; joint – , common- stock; co-, partnership; communion; community of - possessions, – goods; communalism, communism, socialism, collectivism; co-operation etc. 709; profit sharing.

snacks, co-portion, picnic, hotchpotch; co-heirship, -parceny, -parcenary; gavelkind.

participator, sharer; co-, partner; shareholder; co-, joint-tenant; tenants in common; co-heir, - parcener.

communist, socialist.

V. par-ticipate, -take; share, – in; come in for a share; go -shares, – snacks, – halves; share and share alike.

have – , possess – , be seized- -in common, – as joint tenants etc. *n.*

join in; have a hand in etc. (*co-operate*) 709.

Adj. partaking etc. *v.*; communistic, socialistic, co-operative, profit sharing.

Adv. share and share alike.

779. Possessor.—N. possessor, holder; occupant, -ier; tenant; person – , man- -in possession etc. 777; renter, lodger, lessee, under-lessee; zemindar, ryot; tenant -on sufferance, – at will, – from year to year, – for years, – for life.

owner; propriet-or, -ress, -ary; impropriator, master, mistress, lord.

land-holder, -owner, -lord, -lady; lord -of the manor, – paramount; heritor, laird, vavasor, landed gentry, mesne lord.

cestui-que-trust, beneficiary, mortgagor.

grantee, feoffee, relessee, devisee; legat-ee, -ary. trustee; holder etc.- of the legal estate; mort-gagee.

right – , rightful- owner.

[Future possessor] heir, – apparent; – presumptive; heiress; inherit-or, -ress, -rix; reversioner, remainder-man.

780. Property.—N. property, possession, *suum cuique, meum et tuum*.

owner-, proprietor, lord-ship; seignority; empire etc. (*dominion*) 737.

interest, stake, estate, right, title, claim, demand, holding; tenure etc. (*possession*) 777; vested – , contingent – , beneficial – , equitable- interest; use, trust, benefit; legal – , equitable- estate; seisin.

absolute interest, paramount estate, freehold; fee, – simple, – tail; estate -in fee, – in tail, – tail; estate in tail -male, – female, – general.

limitation, term, lease, settlement, strict settlement, particular estate; estate -for life, – for years, – *pur autre vie*; remainder, reversion, expectancy, possibility.

dower, dowry, *dot*, jointure, marriage portion, appanage, inheritance, heritage, patrimony, alimony; legacy etc. (*gift*) 784.

assets, belongings, means, resources, circumstances; wealth etc. 803; money etc. 800; what one -is worth, – will cut up for; estate and effects.

landed –, real- -estate, – property; realty; land, -s; subdivision; plot, site; tenements; hereditaments; corporeal –, incorporeal- hereditaments; acres; ground etc. (*earth*) 342; acquest; messuage.

territory, state, kingdom, principality, realm, empire, protectorate, margravate, dependancy, colony, sphere of influence, mandate.

manor, honor, domain, demesne; farm, ranch, plantation, *hacienda*; allodium etc. (*free*) 748; fieff, feoff, feud, zemindary, dependency.

free-, copy-, lease-holds; chattels real; fixtures, plant, heirloom easement; folkland; right of - common, – user.

personal -property, – estate, – effects; personalty, chattels, goods, effects, movables; stock, – in trade; things, traps, rattle-traps, paraphernalia; equipage etc. 633.

parcels, appurtenances.

impedimenta; lug-, bag-gage; bag and baggage; pelf; cargo, lading.

rent-roll; income etc. (*receipts*) 810.

patent, copyright; *chose* in action; credit etc. 805; debt etc. 806.

V. possess etc. 777; be the -possessor etc. 779- of own; have for one's own, – very own; come in for, inherit; enfeoff.

savor of the realty.

be one's own -property etc. *n*.; belong to; appertain to.

Adj. one's own; landed, predial, manorial, allodial, seignorial; free-, copy-, lease-hold; feu-, feo-dal; hereditary, entailed, personal.

Adv. to one's -credit, – account; to the good.

to one and -his heirs for ever, – the heirs of his body, – his heirs and assigns, – his executors, administrators and assigns.

781. Retention.—N. retention; retaining etc. *v*.; keep, detention, custody; tenacity, firm hold, grasp, gripe, grip, iron grip.

fangs, teeth, claws, talons, nail, hook, tentacle, *tenaculum*; bond etc. (*vinculum*) 45.

clutches, tongs, forceps, pincers, nippers, pliers, tweezers, vise.

paw, hand, finger, wrist, fist, neaf, neif.

bird in hand; captive etc. 754.

V. retain, keep; hold –, fast, – tight, – one's own, – one's ground; clinch, clench, clutch, grasp, gripe, hug, have a firm hold of.

secure, withold, detain; hold –, keepback; keep close; husband etc. (*store*) 636; reserve; have –, keep- in stock etc. (*possess*) 777; enfail, tie up, settle.

Adj. retaining etc. *v*.; retentive, tenacious.

unforfeited, undeprived, undisposed, uncommunicated.

incommunicable, inalienable; in mortmain; in strict settlement.

Phr. *uti possidetis*.

782. Relinquishment.—N. relinquishment, abandonment etc. (*of a course*) 624; renunciation,

expropriation, dereliction; cession, surrender, dispensation; resignation etc. 757; riddance.

derelict etc. *adj.*; jetsam; waif, foundling, orphan.

v. relinquish, give up, surrender, yield, cede; let -go, – slip; spare, drop, resign, forego, renounce, abjure, abandon, expropriate, give away, dispose of, part with; lay -aside, – apart, – down, – on the shelf etc. (*disuse*) 678; set –, put- aside; make away with, cast behind; discard, cast off, dismiss; maroon.

give -notice to quit, – warning; supersede; be –, get- -rid of, – quit of; eject etc. 297.

rid –, disburden –, divest –, djspossess- oneself of; wash one's hands of; divorce, desert; disinherit, cut off.

cast –, throw –, pitch –, fling- -away, – aside, – overboard, – to the dogs; cast –, throw –, sweep- to the winds; put –, turn –, sweep- away; jettison.

quit one's hold.

Adj. relinquished etc. *v*.; cast off, derelict; unowned, unappropriated, unculled; left etc. (*residuary*) 40; divorced; disinherited.

Int. away with!

783. Transfer.—N. transfer, conveyance, assignment, alienation, abalienation; demise, limitation; conveyancing; transmission etc. (*transference*) 270; enfeoffment, bargain and sale, lease and release; exchange etc. (*interchange*) 148; barter etc. 794; substitution etc. 147.

succession, reversion; shifting -use, – trust; devolution.

V. transfer, convey, alien, -ate; assign; grant etc. (*confer*) 784; consign; make –, hand- over; pass, hand, transmit, negotiate; hand down; exchange etc. (*interchange*) 148.

change -hands, – from one to another; devolve, succeed; come into possession etc. (*acquire*) 775; take over.

abalienate; disinherit; dispossess etc. 789; substitute etc. 147.

Adj. alienable, negotiable, transferable, reversional.

Phr. estate coming into possession.

784. Giving.—N. giving etc. *v*.; bestowal, donation; present-ation, -ment; accordance; con-, cession; delivery, consignment, dispensation, communication, endowment; invest-ment, -iture; award.

almsgiving, charity, liberality, generosity; philanthropy etc. 910.

[Thing given] gift, donation, present, *cadeau*; fairing; free gift, boon, favor, benefaction, grant, offering, oblation, sacrifice, immolation.

grace, act of grace, *bonus, bonanza*.

allowance, contribution, subscription, subsidy, tribute, subvention.

bequest, legacy, devise, will, dotation, appanage; dowry; voluntary -settlement, – conveyance etc. 783; amortization.

alms, largess, bounty, dole, sportule, donative, help, oblation, offertory, Peter's pence, *honorarium*, gratuity, Maundy money, Christmas

box, Easter offering, vail, tip, *douceur*, drink money, *pourboire, trinkgeld, backsheesh*; fee etc. (*recompense*) 973; consideration.

bribe, bait, ground-bait; peace-offering, handsel.

giver, grantor etc. *v.*; donor, feoffer, settlor; almoner; testator; investor, subscriber, contributor; fairy godmother; Santa Claus, benefactor etc. 816.

V. deliver, hand, pass, put into the hands of; hand −, make −, deliver −, pass −, turn- over.

present, give away, dispense, dispose of; give −, deal −, dole −, mete −, fork −, shell −, squeeze- out.

pay etc. 807; render, impart, communicate.

concede, cede, yield, part with, shed cast; spend etc. 809.

give, bestow, confer, grant, accord, award, assign.

entrust, consign, vest in.

make a present; allow, contribute, subscribe, donate, furnish its quota.

invest, endow, settle upon; bequeath, leave, devise.

furnish, supply, help; ad-, minister to; afford, spare; accommodate −, indulge −, favor- with; shower down upon; lavish, pour on, thrust upon; tip, bribe; tickle −, grease- the palm; offer etc. 763; sacrifice, immolate.

Adj. giving etc. *v.*; given etc. *v.*; allow-ed, -able; concessional; communicable; charitable, eleemosynary, sportulary, tributary; *gratis* etc. 815.

785. Receiving.—N. receiving etc. *v.*; acquisition etc. 775; reception etc. (*introduction*) 296; suscipiency, acceptance, admission.

re-, ac-cipient; assignee, devisee; lega-tee, -tary; grantee, feoffee, donee, relessee, lessee.

sportulary, stipendiary; beneficiary; pension-er, -ary; almsman.

income etc. (*receipt*) 810.

v. receive; take etc. 789; acquire etc. 775; admit.

take in, catch, touch; pocket; put into one's - pocket, − purse; accept; take off one's hands.

be received; come -in, − to hand; pass −, fall- into one's hand; go into one's pocket; fall to one's - lot, − share; come −, fall- to one; accrue; have - given etc. 784 to one.

Adj. receiving etc. *v.*; re-, suscipient.

received etc. *v.*; given etc. 784; second-hand.

not given, unbestowed etc. (*see* give, bestow etc. 784).

786. Apportionment.—N. apportion-, allot-, consign-, assign-, appoint-ment; appropriation; dispensation, -tribution; allocation, division, deal; repartition; administration.

dividend, portion, contingent, share, allotment, lot, cut, split, measure, dose; dole, meed, pittance; *quantum*, ration; ratio, proportion, quota, *modicum*, mess, allowance.

V. apportion, divide; cut, split, divvy; distribute, administer, dispense; billet, allot, detail, cast, share, mete; portion −, parcel −, dole- out; deal, carve.

partition, assign, appropriate, appoint.

come in for one's share etc. (*participate*) 778.

Adj. apportioning etc. *v.*; respective.

Adv. respectively, each to each.

787. Lending.—N. lending etc. *v.*; loan, advance, accommodation, feneration; mortgage etc. (*security*) 771; investment.

mont de piété, pawnshop, hock shop, spout, my uncle's.

lender, pawnbroker, money lender, usurer, Jew, Shylock.

V. lend, advance, loan, accommodate with; lend on security; pawn etc. (*security*) 771.

intrust, invest; place −, put- out to interest; sink, risk.

let, demise, lease, set, under-, sub-let.

Adj. lending etc. *v.*; lent etc. *v.*; unborrowed etc. (*see* borrowed etc. 788).

Adv. in advance; on -loan, − security.

788. Borrowing.—N. borrowing, pledging, pawning.

borrowed plumes; plagiarism etc. (*thieving*) 791. replevin.

V. borrow, desume; pawn.

hire, rent, farm; take a -lease, − demise; take −, hire- by the -hour, − mile, − year etc.

raise −, take up- money; float bonds; raise the wind; fly a kite, borrow of Peter to pay Paul; run into debt etc. (*debt*) 806.

make use of, plagiarize, pirate.

replevy.

789. Taking.—N. taking etc. *v.*; reception etc. (*taking in*) 296; deglutition etc. (*taking food*) 298; appropriation, prehension, prensation; capture, caption; ap-, de-prehension; abreption, seizure; abduction, -lation; subtraction etc. (*subduction*) 38; abstraction, ademption.

dispossession; depriv-ation, -ement; bereavement; divestment; disherison; distraint, distress; sequestration, confiscation, attachment, execution; eviction etc. 297.

rapacity, extortion, vampirism, predacity, bloodsucking; theft etc. 791.

resumption; repris-e, -al; recovery etc. 775.

clutch, swoop, wrench; grip etc. (*retention*) 781; haul, take, catch; scramble.

taker, captor, capturer; vampire; extortioner.

V. take, catch, hook, nab, bag, sack, pocket, put into one's pocket, scrounge; receive; accept.

reap, crop, cull, pluck; gather etc. (*get*) 775; draw.

ap-, im-propriate; assume, possess oneself of; take possession of; commandeer; lay −, clap- one's hands on; help oneself to; make free with, dip one's hands into, lay under contribution; intercept; scramble for; deprive of.

take −, carry −, bear- -away, − off; abstract; hurry off −, run away- with; abduct; steal etc. 791; ravish; seize; pounce −, spring- upon; swoop -to, − down upon; take by -storm, − assault; snatch, reave.

snap up, nip up, whip up, catch up; kidnap, crimp, capture, lay violent hands on.

get −, lay −, take −, catch −, lay fast −, take firm- hold of; lay by the heels, take prisoner; fasten upon, grip, grapple, embrace, gripe, clasp, grab, clutch, collar, throttle, take by the throat, claw, clinch, clench, make sure of.

catch at, jump at, make a grab at, snap at, snatch at; reach, make a long arm, stretch forth one's hand.

take -from, − away from; deduct etc. 38; retrench etc. (*curtail*) 201; dispossess, ease one of, snatch from one's grasp; tear −, tear away −, wrench −, wrest −, wring- from; extort; deprive of, bereave; disinherit, cut off with a shilling.

oust etc. (*eject*) 297; divest; levy, distrain, confiscate; sequest-er, -rate, accroach; usurp; despoil, strip, fleece, shear, displume, impoverish, eat out of house and home; drain, − to the dregs; gut, dry, exhaust, swallow up; absorb etc. (*suck in*) 296; draw off; suck, − like a leech, − the blood of.

retake, resume; recover etc. 775.

Adj. taking etc. *v.*; privative, prehensile; pred-aceous, -al, -atory, -atorial; rap-acious, -torial; ravenous; parasitic; all-devouring, -engulfing.

bereft etc. 776.

Adv. at one fell swoop.

Phr. give an inch and take an ell.

790. Restitution.—**N.** restitution, return; ren-, red-dition; reinstatement, restoration; reinvestment, recuperation; repatriation; rehabilitation etc. (*reconstruction*) 660; reparation, atonement, indemnity, compensation, recompense.

release, replevin, redemption; recovery etc. (*getting back*) 775; remitter, reversion.

V. return, restore; recondition; give −, carry −, bring- back; render, − up; give up; let go, un-clutch; dis-, re-gorge; regurgitate; recoup, reimburse, repay, indemnify, reinvest, remit, rehabilitate; repair etc. (*make good*) 660.

redeem, recover etc. (*get back*) 775; take back again; revest, revert.

Adj. restoring etc. *v.*; recuperative etc. 660; in full restitution, to compensate for.

Phr. *suum cuique.*

791. Stealing.—**N.** stealing etc. *v.*; theft, thievery, robbery, latrociny, direption; abstraction, appropriation; plagiar-y, -ism; rape, kidnapping, depredation; raid, hold up.

spoliation, plunder, pillage; sack, -age; rapine, *brigandage*; highway robbery, foray, *razzia*; black-mail; piracy, privateering, buccaneering; filibuster-ing, -ism; burglary; house-breaking; cattle-stealing, -rustling, -lifting.

peculation, embezzlement; fraud etc. 545; lar-ceny, petty larceny, pilfering, shop-lifting.

thievishness, rapacity, kleptomania, Alsatia; den of -Cacus, − thieves.

license to plunder, letters of marque.

V. steal, thieve, rob, purloin, pilfer, filch, lift, prig, bag, nim, crib, cabbage, palm; abstract; appropriate, plagiarize.

convey away, carry off, abduct, kidnap, shanghai, impress, crimp; make −, walk −, run-off with; run away with; spirit away; seize etc. (*lay violent hands on*) 789.

plunder, pillage, rifle, sack, loot, ransack, spoil, spoliate, despoil, strip, sweep, gut, forage, levy black-mail, pirate, pickeer, maraud, lift cattle, rustle, poach, smuggle, run.

stick −, hold- up.

swindle, peculate, embezzle; sponge, mulct, rook, bilk, pluck, pigeon, skin, fleece, diddle; defraud etc. 545; obtain under false pretences; live by one's wits

rob −, borrow of- Peter to Paul; set a thief to catch a thief.

disregard the distinction between *meum* and *tuum*.

Adj. thieving etc. *v.*; thievish, light-fingered; fur-acious, -tive; piratical; pred-aceous, -al, -atory, -atorial; raptorial etc. (*rapacious*) 789.

stolen etc. *v.*

Phr. *sic vos non vobis.*

792. Thief.—**N.** thief, robber, *homo trium literarum*, pilferer, rifler, filcher, plagiarist.

spoiler, depredator, pillager, marauder; harpy, shark, land-shark, falcon, moss-trooper, bushranger, Bedouin, brigand, freebooter, bandit, thug, dacoit, pirate, corsair, viking, Paul Jones; buccan-eer, -ier; piqu-, pick-eerer; rover, ranger, privateer, filibuster; rapparee, wrecker, picaroon; smuggler, poacher, plunderer; racketeer.

highwayman, Dick Turpin, Claude Duval, Macheath, knight of the road, footpad, sturdy beggar; abductor, kidnapper.

cut-, pick-purse; pick-pocket, light-fingered gen-try; sharper; card-, skittle-sharper; crook; thimble-rigger; rook, Greek, blackleg, leg, welsher, defaulter; Autolycus, Cacus, Barabbas, Jeremy Diddler, Robert Macaire, artful dodger, trickster; swell mob, *chevalier d'industrie*; shop-lifter.

swindler, peculator; forger, coiner, counterfeiter, shoful; fence, receiver of stolen goods, duffer; smasher.

burglar, housebreaker; cracks-, mags-man; Bill Sikes, Jack Sheppard, Jonathan Wild, Raffles, cat burglar.

793. Booty.—**N.** booty, spoil, plunder, price, loot, graft, swag, pickings, boodle; *spolia opima*, prey; blackmail; stolen goods.

Adj. looting etc. *n.*; manubial, spoliative.

794. Barter.—**N.** barter, exchange, scorse, truck system; interchange etc. 148.

a Roland for an Oliver; *quid pro quo*; commutation, -position.

trade, commerce, mercature, buying and selling, bargain and sale; traffic, business, nundination, custom, shopping; commercial enterprise, speculation, jobbing, stock-jobbing, *agiotage*, brokery, arbitrage.

dealing, transaction, negotiation, bargain.

free trade.

V. barter, exchange, truck, scorse, swop; interchange etc. 148; commutate etc. (*substitute*) 147; compound for.

trade, traffic, buy and sell, give and take, nun-dinate; carry on −, ply −, drive- a trade; be in -

business, — the city; keep a shop, deal in, employ one's capital in.

trade — , deal — , have dealings- with; transact — , do- business with; open — , keep- an account with.

bargain; drive — , make- a bargain; negotiate, bid for; dicker, haggle, higgle; chaffer, huckster, cheapen, beat down; stickle, — for; out-, under-bid; ask, charge; strike a bargain etc. (*contract*) 769.

speculate, give a sprat to catch a herring; buy in the cheapest and sell in the dearest market; rig the market.

Adj. commercial, mercantile, trading; interchangeable, marketable, staple, in the market, for sale.

wholesale, retail.

Adv. across the counter; on 'change.

795. Purchase.—N.
purchase, emption; buying, purchasing, shopping; pre-emption, refusal.

coemption, bribery; slave trade.

buyer, purchaser, *emptor*, vendee; patron, employer, client, customer, *clientèle*.

V. buy, purchase, invest in, procure; rent etc. (*hire*) 788; repurchase, buy in.

keep in one's pay, bribe, suborn; pay etc. 807; spend etc. 809.

make — , complete- a purchase; buy over the counter; pay cash for.

shop, market, go a shopping.

Adj. purchased etc. *v.*

Phr. *caveat emptor.*

796. Sale.—N.
sale, vent, disposal; auction, roup, Dutch auction; custom etc. (*traffic*) 794.

vendi-bility, -bleness.

seller, salesman; peddler, smous; vender, vendor, consignor; merchant etc. 797; auctioneer.

V. sell, vend, dispose of, effect a sale; sell -over the counter; — by auction etc. *n.*; dispense, retail; deal in etc. 794; sell -off, — out; turn into money; realize; bring -to, — under- the hammer; put up to auction; auction, offer — , put up- for sale; hawk, peddle, bring to market; offer etc. 763; undersell; dump, unload.

let; mortgage etc. (*security*) 771.

Adj. under the hammer, in the market, for sale.

saleable, marketable, vendible, in demand, having a ready sale; unsaleable etc., unpurchased, unbought; on one's hands.

797. Merchant.—N.
merchant, trader, dealer, monger, chandler, salesman; changer; regrater; shop-keeper, -man; trades-man, -people, -folk.

retailer; chapman, hawker, huckster, higgler; peddler, smous, pedlar, *colporteur*, cadger, Autolycus; sutler, *vivandière*; coster-man, -monger; market woman; cheap jack; caterer etc. 637; tallyman.

money-broker, -changer, -lender; stock-broker, -jobber; cambist, usurer, moneyer, banker.

jobber; broker etc. (*agent*) 758; buyer etc. 795; seller etc. 796.

concern; firm etc. (*partnership*) 712.

798. Merchandise.—N.
merchandise, ware, commodity, effects, goods, article, stock, produce, staple commodity; stock in trade etc. (*store*) 636; cargo etc. (*contents*) 190.

799. Mart.—N.
mart; market, -place, *forum*; fair, bazaar, staple; stock — , exchange; 'change, bourse, Wall Street, Rialto, hall, guildhall; toll-booth, custom-house; Tattersalls.

shop, stall, booth; wharf; office, chambers, counting-house, *bureau*; coun-, comp-ter.

ware-house, -room; *dépôt*, interposit, *entrepôt*, *emporium*, establishment; store etc. 636.

open market, market-overt.

800. Money.—N.
money -matters, — market; finance; accounts etc. 811; funds, treasure; capital, stock; assets etc. (*property*) 780; wealth etc. 803; supplies, ways and means, wherewithal, sinews of war, almighty dollar, needful, cash.

sum, amount; balance, -sheet; sum total; proceeds etc. (*receipts*) 810.

currency, circulating medium, specie; coin, — of the realm; piece, hard cash, dollar, sterling coin; pounds, shillings and pence; L s. d., guineas; pocket, breeches pocket, purse; money in hand; the best, ready, — money; filthy lucre, shekels, roll, jack, rhino, blunt, dust, bawbees, brass, dibs, dough, mopus, tin, salt, chink, oof, spondulics, pile, wads.

precious metals, gold, silver, copper, nickel; bullion, bar, ingot, nugget.

petty cash; pocket-, pin-money; small — , change; small coin, loose cash; doit, stiver, rap, mite, farthing, *sou*, penny, shilling, bob, tanner, tester, groat, guinea, ducat; *rouleau*; *wampum*; good — , round — , lump- sum; power — , mint — , tons- of money; plum, lac of rupees, millions, money-bags, miser's hoard, stocking, mine of wealth etc. 803.

[Science of coins] numismatics, chrysology.

paper-money; money — , postal — , Post Office-order; note, — of hand; bank — , treasury- note; Bradbury; promissory note; I.O.U., bond; bill, — of exchange; draft, check, order, warrant, *coupon*, debenture, exchequer bill, *assignat*, greenback, gold — , silver- certificate.

copper; nickel, dime, quarter, two bits, half a dollar, dollar, buck, simoleon, fiver, tenner, a twenty, a sawbuck, a century, a grand; eagle, double eagle.

gold standard, bimetallism, fiat money; rate of — , exchange; in-, de-flation.

remittance etc. (*payment*) 807; credit etc. 805; liability etc. 806; solvency etc. 803.

draw-er, -ee; oblig-or, -ee; moneyer, coiner, counterfeiter, forger.

false — , bad- money; base — , counterfeit- coin, flash note, slip, kite; Bank of Elegance.

argumentum ad crumenam.

V. amount to, come to, mount up to; touch the pocket; draw, — upon; endorse etc. (*security*) 771; issue, utter, circulate; discount etc. 813.

forge, counterfeit, coin, circulate — , pass- bad money.

Adj. monetary, pecuniary, crumenal, fiscal, financial, sumptuary, numismatical; sterling; solvent etc. 803.

801. Treasurer.—N. treasurer; bursar, -y; purser, purse-bearer; cash-keeper, banker; depositary; questor, receiver, steward, trustee, chartered —, accountant; Accountant-General, almoner, liquidator, paymaster, cashier, teller; cambist; money-changer etc. (*merchant*) 797.

financier, Chancellor of the Exchequer, minister of finance; Secretary of the Treasury, Director of the Budget, Controller of Currency.

802. Treasury.—N. treasury, bank, exchequer, almonry, fisc, hanaper, bursary; safe; strong-box, -hold, -room; coffer; chest etc. (*receptacle*) 191; depository etc. 636; till, -er; cash-box, -register, purse, pocketbook, wallet; money-bag, -belt, -box, *porte-monnaie*.

purse-strings; pocket, breeches pocket.

sinking fund; stocks; government —, public —, parliamentary- -stocks, — funds, — securities, bonds; gild-edged securities; Consols, Liberty bonds, government bonds, *crédit mobilier*.

803. Wealth.—N. wealth, riches, fortune, handsome fortune, opulence, affluence; good —, easy- circumstances; independence; competence etc. (*sufficiency*) 639; solvency, soundness, solidity.

provision, livelihood, maintenance; alimony, dowry; means, resources, substance; property etc. 780; command of money.

income etc. 810; capital, money; round sum etc. (*treasure*) 800; mint of money, mine of wealth, El Dorado, Pactolus, Golconda, Potosi, *bonanza*; philosopher's stone.

long —, full —, well lined —, heavy- purse; purse of Fortunatus.

pelf, Mammon, lucre, filthy lucre; loaves and fishes; fleshpots of Egypt.

rich —, moneyed —, warm- man; man of substance; capitalist, millionaire, Nabob, Croesus, Midas, Plutus, Dives, Timon of Athens; Timo-, Pluto-cracy; Danaë.

V. be -rich etc. *adj.*; roll —, wallow- in -wealth, — riches; have money to burn.

afford, well afford; command -money, — a sum; make both ends meet, hold one's head above water.

become -rich etc. *adj.*; fill one's -pocket etc. (*treasury*) 802; feather one's nest, clean up —. make- a fortune; make money etc. (*acquire*) 775. enrich, imburse.

worship -Mammon, — the golden calf.

Adj. wealthy, rich, affluent, opulent, moneyed, monied, worth -a great deal, — much; well -to do, — off; warm; well —, provided for.

made of money; rich as Croesus; rolling in -riches, — wealth.

flush, — of -cash, — money, — tin; in -funds, — cash, — full feather; solvent, solid, sound, pecunious, out of debt, all straight; able to pay 20s in the L.

Phr. one's ship coming in.

804. Poverty.—N. poverty, indigence, penury, pauperism, destitution, want; need, -iness; lack, necessity, privation, distress, difficulties, wolf at the door.

bad —, poor —, needy —, embarrassed —, reduced —, straitened- circumstances; slender —, narrow- means; straits; hand to mouth existence, *res angusta domi*, low water, impecuniosity.

beggary; mendi-cancy, -city; broken —, loss of-fortune; insolvency etc. (*non-payment*) 808.

empty -purse, — pocket; light purse; beggarly account of empty boxes.

poor man, pauper, mendicant, mumper, beggar, starveling; *pauvre diable*.

V. be -poor etc. *adj.*; want, lack, starve, live from hand to mouth, have seen better days, go down in the world, be on one's uppers, come upon the parish; go to -the dogs, — wrack and ruin; not have a -penny etc. (*money*) 800, — shot in one's locker; beg one's bread; *tirer le diable par la queue*; run into debt etc. (*debt*) 806.

render -poor etc. *adj.*; impoverish; reduce, — to poverty; pauperize, fleece, ruin, bring to the parish.

Adj. poor, indigent; poverty-striken; badly —, poorly —, ill- off; poor as -a rat, — a church mouse, — Job's turkey, — Job; fortune-, dower-, money-, penni-less; unportioned, unmoneyed; impecunious; broke, flat; out —, short- of -money, — cash; without —, not worth- a rap etc. (*money*) 800; *qui n'a pas le sou*, out of pocket, hard up; out at -elbows, — heels; seedy, bare-footed; beggar-ly, -ed; destitute; fleeced, strapped, stripped; bereft, bereaved; reduced.

in -want etc. *n.*; needy, necessitous, distressed, pinched, straitened; put to one's -shifts, — last shifts; unable to -keep the wolf from the door, — make both ends meet; embarrassed, under hatches; involved etc. (*in debt*) 806; insolvent etc. (*not paying*) 808.

Adv. in formâ pauperis.
Phr. zonam perdidit.

805. Credit.—N. credit, trust, tick, score, tally, account.

letter of credit, circular note; duplicate; mortgage, lien, debenture, paper credit, floating capital; draft; securities.

creditor, lender, lessor, mortgagee; dun; usurer.

V. keep —, run up- an account with; entrust, credit, accredit.

place to one's -credit, — account; give —, take-credit; fly a kite.

Adj. credit-ing, -ed; accredited.

Adv. on -credit etc. *n.*; to the -account, — credit- of.

806. Debt.—N. debt, obligation, liability, indebtment, debit, score.

arrears, deferred payment, deficit, default; insolvency etc. (*non-payment*) 808; bad debt.

interest; usance, usury; premium; floating -debt, — capital.

debtor, debitor; mortgagor; defaulter etc. 808; borrower.

V. be -in debt etc. *adj.*; owe; incur —, contract- a debt etc. *n.*; run up -a bill, — a score, — an account; go on tick, put on the cuff; borrow etc. 788; run —, get- into debt; outrun the constable.

answer —, go bail- for; back- one's note.

Adj. indebted; liable, chargeable, answerable for.

in -debt, – embarrassed circumstances, – difficulties; incumbered, involved; involved –, plunged –, deep –, over head and ears- in debt; deeply involved; fast tied up; insolvent etc. (*not paying*) 808; *minus*, out of pocket.

unpaid; unrequieted, unrewarded; owing, due, in arrear, outstanding.

807. Payment.—N. pay-, defray-ment;' discharge; ac-, quittance; settlement, clearance, liquidation, satisfaction, reckoning, arrangement.

acknowledgment, release; receipt, – in full, – in full of all demands; voucher.

repayment, reimbursement, retribution; pay etc. (*reward*) 973; money paid etc. (*expenditure*) 809.

ready money etc. (*cash*) 800; stake, remittance, instalment.

payer, liquidator etc. 801.

V. pay, defray, make payment; pay -down, – on the nail, – ready money, – at sight, – in advance; cash, honor a bill, acknowledge; redeem; pay in kind.

pay one's -way, – shot, – footing; pay -the piper, – sauce for all, – costs; do the needful; come across; shell –, fork- out; come down with, – the dust; tickle –, grease- the palm; expend etc. 809; put –, lay- down.

discharge, settle, quit, acquit oneself of; account –, reckon –, settle –, be even –, be quits- with; strike a balance; settle –, balance –, square- accounts with; quit scores; foot the bill; wipe –, clear- off old scores; satisfy; pay in full; satisfy –, pay in full of- all demands; clear, liquidate; pay -up, – old debts.

disgorge, make repayment; repay, refund, reimburse, retribute; make compensation etc. 30.

Adj. paying etc., paid etc. '*v.*; owing nothing, out of debt, all straight, clear of -debt, – encumbrance; unowed, never indebted.

Adv. to the tune of; on the nail; money –, cash-down; cash on delivery.

808. Non-payment.—N. non-payment; default, defalcation; protest, repudiation; application of the sponge; whitewashing.

insolvency, bankruptcy, failure; overdraft, overdrawn account; insufficiency etc. 640; run upon a bank.

waste paper bonds; dishonored –, protested-bills; bogus cheque.

bankrupt, insolvent debtor, lame duck, man of straw, welsher, stag, defaulter, absconder, levanter.

V. non -pay etc. 807; fail, break, stop payment; become -insolvent, – bankrupt; be gazetted.

protest, dishonor, repudiate, nullify.

pay under protest; button up one's pockets, draw the purse strings; apply the sponge; pay over the left shoulder, get whitewashed; swindle etc. 791; run up bills, fly kites.

Adj. not paying; in debt etc. 806; behindhand, in arrear; beggared etc. (*poor*) 804; unable to make both ends meet; *minus*; worse than nothing.

insolvent, bankrupt, in the gazette, gazetted, ruined.

unpaid etc. (*outstanding*) 806; gratis etc. 815; unremunerated.

809. Expenditure.—N. expenditure, money going out; out-goings, -lay; expenses, disbursement; prime cost etc. (*price*) 812; circulation; run upon a bank.

[Money paid] payment etc. 807; pay etc. (*remuneration*) 973; bribe etc. 973; fee, footing, garnish; subsidy; tribute, Peter's pence; contingent, quota; donation etc. 784.

pay in advance, earnest, handsel, deposit, instalment.

investment; purchase etc. 795.

V. expend, spend; run –, get- through; pay, disburse; open –, loose –, untie- the purse strings; lay –, shell –, fork- out; bleed; make up a sum, invest, sink money.

fee etc. (*reward*) 973; pay one's way etc. (*pay*) 807; subscribe etc. (*give*) 784; subsidize, bribe.

Adj. expend-ing, -ed etc. *v.*; sumptuary, liberal etc. 816; openhanded, lavish etc. 818; extensive etc. 814.

810. Receipt—N. receipt, accountable –, conditional –, binding –, return- receipt; value received, money coming in; income, incomings, innings, revenue, return, proceeds; gross receipts, net profit; earnings etc. (*gain*) 775.

rent, – roll; rent-al, -age; rack-rent.

premium, *bonus*; sweepstakes, tontine, prize, drawing.

pension, annuity; jointure etc. (*property*) 780; alimony, pittance; emolument etc. (*remuneration*) 973.

V. receive etc. 785; take money; draw –, derive- from; get, be in receipt of, acquire etc. 775; take etc. 789.

bring in, yield, afford, pay, return; accrue etc. (*be received from*) 785.

Adj. receiv-ing, -ed etc. *v.*; profitable etc. (*gainful*) 775.

811. Accounts.—N. accounts, accompts; commercial –, monetary- arithmetic; statistics etc. (*numeration*) 85; money matters, finance, budget, bill, score, reckoning, account.

books, account book, ledger; day –, cash –, pass- book; journal; debtor and creditor –, cash –, petty cash –, running- account; account-current; balance, – sheet; *compte rendu*, account settled.

book-keeping, audit; double –, single- entry; reckoning etc. 85.

chartered –, certified public –, accountant; auditor, actuary, bookkeeper; financier etc. 801; accounting party.

V. keep accounts, enter, post, book, credit, debit, carry over; take stock; balance –, make up –, square –, settle –, wind up –, cast up –, add up –, tot up- accounts; make accounts square.

bring to book, audit, tax, surcharge and falsify.

falsify –, garble –, cook –, doctor- an account.

Adj. monetary etc. 800; account-able, -ing; statistical.

812. Price.—N. price, amount, cost, expense, prime cost, charge, figure, demand, damage, fare, hire; wages etc. (*remuneration*) 973.

dues, duty, toll, tax, impost, cess, sess, tallage, levy, capitation-, poll-, income-, sur-, sales-, super-tax; gabel, *gabelle*; gavel, *octroi*, custom, tariff, excise, assessment, taxation, benevolence, tithe, tenths, exactment, ransom, salvage; broker-, wharf-, lighter-, ton-, freight-age.

worth, rate, value, valuation, appraisement, money's worth, par value; penny etc. -worth; price current, market price, quotation; what it will -fetch etc. *v.*

bill etc. *(account)* 811; shot.

V. bear –, set –, fix- a price; appraise, assess, price, charge, demand, ask, require, exact, run up; distrain; run up a bill etc. *(debt)* 806; have one's price; liquidate.

amount to, come to, mount up to; stand one in. fetch, sell for, cost, bring in, yield, afford.

Adj. priced etc. *v.*; to the tune of, *ad valorem*; mercenary, venal.

Phr. no penny, no paternoster; *point d'argent, point de Suisse*, no longer pipe, no longer dance, no song, no supper.

one may have it for.

813. Discount.—N. discount, abatement, concession, reduction, depreciation, allowance, qualification, set off, drawback, poundage, *agio*, percentage; rebate, -ment; backwardation, contango; salvage; tare and tret.

V. discount, bate; a-, re-bate; deduct, reduce, mark down, take off, allow, give, make allowance; tax, depreciate.

Adj. discounting etc. *v.*

Adv. at a discount, below par.

814. Dearness.—N. dearness etc. *adj.*; high –, famine –, fancy- price; overcharge; extravagance; exorbitance, extortion; heavy pull upon the purse; Pyrrhic victory.

V. be -dear etc. *adj.*; cost -much, – a pretty penny; rise in price, look up.

overcharge, bleed, fleece, skin, extort.

pay -too much, – through the nose, –, too dear for one's whistle.

Adj. dear; high, -priced; of great price, expensive, costly, precious, worth a Jew's eye, dear bought; unreasonable, extravagant, exorbitant, extortionate.

at a premium; not to be had, – for love or money; beyond –, above- price; priceless, of priceless value.

Adv. dear, -ly; at great –, heavy- cost; *à grands frais*.

Phr. prices looking up; *le jeu ne vaut pas la chandelle*.

815. Cheapness.—N. cheapness, low price; depreciation; bargain; good penny etc.- worth, *bon marché*.

[Absence of charge] gratuity; free -quarters, – seats, – admission,] warren; pass, Annie Oakley; run of one's teeth; nominal price, peppercorn rent; labor of love.

drug in the market.

V. be -cheap etc. *adj.*; cost little; come down –, fall- in price.

buy for -a mere nothing, – an old song; have one's money's worth; cheapen, beat down.

Adj. cheap; low, – priced; moderate, reasonable; in-, un-expensive; well –, worth the money; *magnifique et pas cher*; good –, cheap- at the price; dirt –, dog- cheap; cheap, -as dirt, – and nasty; catchpenny.

reduced, marked down, half-price, depreciated, unsaleable.

gratuitous, *gratis*, free, for love, – nothing; cost-, expense-less; without charge, not charged, un-taxed; scot –, shot –, rent- free; free of -cost, – expense; honorary, unbought, unpaid, complimentary.

Adv. for a mere song; at -cost price, – prime cost, – a reduction, – a bargain; on the cheap.

816. Liberality.—N. liberality, generosity, munificence; bount-y, -eousness, -ifulness; hospitality; charity etc. *(beneficence)* 906.

benefactor, free giver, Lady Bountiful.

V. be -liberal etc. *adj.*; spend –, bleed- freely; shower down upon; open one's purse strings etc. *(disburse)* 809; spare no expense, give -with both hands, – *carte blanche*.

Adj. liberal, free, generous; charitable etc. *(beneficent)* 906; hospitable; bount-iful, -eous; handsome; unsparing, ungrudging; open-, free-, full-handed; open-, large-, free-hearted; munificent, princely, unstinting.

overpaid.

Adv. liberally, ungrudgingly, with open hand.

817. Economy.—N. economy, frugality; thrift, -iness; prudence, care, husbandry, good housewifery, savingness, retrenchment.

savings; prevention of waste, save-all; cheese parings and candle ends; parsimony etc. 819.

V. be -economical etc. *adj.*; economize, save; retrench; cut- down expenses, – one's coat according to one's cloth, make both ends meet, keep within compass, meet one's expenses, pay one's way; keep one's head above water; husband etc. *(lay by)* 636; save –, invest- money; put out to interest; provide –, save- for, – against- a rainy day; feather one's nest; look after the main chance.

Adj. economical, frugal, careful, thrifty, saving, chary, spare, sparing; parsimonious etc. 819.

underpaid.

Adv. sparingly etc. *adj.*; *ne quid nimis*.

818. Prodigality.—N. prodi-gality, -gence; un-thriftiness, waste, -fulness; profus-ion, -eness; extravagance; squandering etc. *v.*; lavishness; malversation.

prodigal; spend-, waste-thrift; losel, play-boy, spender, squanderer, locust.

V. be -prodigal etc. *adj.*; squander, lavish, sow broadcast; pour forth like water; pay through the nose etc. *(dear)* 814; spill, waste, dissipate, exhaust, drain, eat out of house and home, overdraw, outrun the constable; run -out, – through; misspend; throw -good money after bad, – the helve after the hatchet; burn the candle at both ends; make ducks and drakes of one's money;

squander one's substance, spend money like water; fool –, potter –, muddle –, fritter –, throw-away one's money; pour water into a sieve, kill the goose that lays the golden eggs; *manger son blé en herbe.*

Adj. prodigal, profuse, thriftless, unthrifty, improvident, wasteful, losel, extravagant, lavish, dissipated, over liberal; full-handed etc. (*liberal*) 816.

penny wise and pound foolish.

Adv. with an unsparing hand; money burning one's pocket; recklessly profuse.

Int. hang the expense!

819. Parsimony.—N. parsimony, parcity; parsimoniousness, stinginess etc. *adj.*; stint; illiberality, avarice, tenacity, avidity, rapacity, extortion, venality, cupidity; selfishness etc. 943; *auri sacra fames.*

miser, niggard, churl, screw, tightwad, skinflint, crib, codger, muckworm, money-grubber, pinch-fist, scrimp, lickpenny, hunks, curmudgeon, *Harpagon*, Silas Marner, harpy, extortioner, Jew, usurer.

V. be -parsimonious etc. *adj.*; grudge, begrudge, stint, skimp, pinch, gripe, screw, dole out, hold back, withhold, starve, famish, live upon nothing, skin a flint.

drive a -bargain, – hard bargain; cheapen, beat down; stop one hole in a sieve; have an itching palm, grasp, grab.

Adj. parsimonious, penurious, stingy, miserly, mean, shabby, peddling, scrubby, pennywise, near, niggardly, frugal to excess; close; fast-, close-, strait-handed; close-, hard-, tight-fisted; tight, sparing, chary; grudging, griping etc. *v.*; illiberal, ungenerous, churlish, hidebound, sordid, mercenary, venal, covetous, usurious, avaricious, greedy, extortionate, rapacious.

Adv. with a sparing hand.

820. Affections.—N. affections, character, qualities, disposition, nature, spirit, tone; temper, -ament; *diathesis*, idiosyncrasy; cast –, habit –, frame- of -mind, – soul; predilection, turn; natural –, turn of mind; bent, bias, predisposition, proneness, proclivity; propen-sity, -sedness, -sion, -dency; vein, humor, mood, grain, mettle; sympathy etc. (*love*) 897.

soul, heart, breast, bosom, inner man; heart's -core, – strings, – blood; heart of hearts, *penetralia mentis*; secret and inmost recesses of the –, cockles of one's- heart; inmost -heart, – soul; back-bone.

passion, pervading spirit; ruling –, master-passion; *furore*; fulness of the heart, heyday of the blood, flesh and blood, flow of soul, force of character.

V. have –, possess- -affections etc. *n.*; be of a -character etc. *n.*; be -affected etc. *adj.*; breathe.

Adj. affected, characterized, formed, molded, cast; at-, tempered; framed; pre-, disposed; prone, inclined; having a -bias etc. *n.*; tinctured –, imbued –, penetrated –, eaten up- with.

inborn, inbred, ingrained, in the grain, congenital, inherent, bred in the bone; deep-rooted, ineffaceable, inveterate; pathoscopic.

Adv. in one's -heart etc. *n.*; at heart; heart and soul etc. 821; in the -vein, – mood.

821. Feeling.—N. feeling; suffering etc. *v.*; endurance, tolerance, sufferance, supportance, experience, response; sympathy etc. (*love*) 897; impression, inspiration, affection, sensation, emotion, pathos, deep sense.

fire, warmth, glow, unction, *gusto*, vehemence; ferv-or, -ency; heartiness, cordiality; earnestness, eagerness; *empressement*, ardor, zeal, passion, enthusiasm; *verve, furore*, fanaticism; excitation of feeling etc. 824; fulness of the heart etc. (*disposition*) 820; passion etc. (*state of excitability*) 825; ecstasy etc. (*pleasure*) 827.

blush, suffusion, flush; hectic; tingling, thrill, kick, tun-, shock; agitation etc. (*irregular motion*) 315; quiver, heaving, flutter, flurry, fluster, twitter, tremor; throb, -bing; pulsation, palpitation, painting; trepid-, perturb-ation; ruffle, hurry of spirits, pother, stew, ferment.

V. feel; receive an -impression etc. *n.*; be -impressed with etc. *adj.*; entertain –, harbor –, cherish- -feeling etc. *n.*

respond; catch the -flame, – infection; enter the spirit of.

bear, suffer, support, sustain, endure, brook, thole, aby; abide etc. (*be composed*) 826; experience etc. (*meet with*) 151; taste, prove; labor –, smart- under; bear the brunt of, brave, stand.

swell, glow, warm, flush, blush, change color, mantle; turn -color, – pale, – red, – black in the face; blench, crimson, whiten, pale, tingle, thrill, heave, pant, throb, palpitate, go pit-a-pat, tremble, quiver, flutter, twitter; stagger, reel; shake etc. 315; be -agitated, – excited etc. 824; look -blue, – black; wince, draw a deep breath.

impress etc. (*excite the feelings*) 824.

Adj. feeling etc. *v.*; sentient; sensuous; sensorial, -y; emo-tive, -tional; of –, with- feeling etc. *n.*

warm, quick, lively, smart, strong, sharp, acute, cutting, piercing, incisive; keen, – as a'razor; trenchant, pungent, racy, *piquant*, poignant, caustic.

impressive, deep, profound, indelible; deep-, home-, heart-felt; swelling, soul-stirring, deep-mouthed, heart-expanding, electric, thrilling, rapturous, ecstatic.

earnest, wistful, eager, breathless; fer-vent, -vid; gushing, passionate, warmhearted, hearty, cordial, sincere, zealous, enthusiastic, glowing, ardent, burning, red-hot, fiery, flaming; boiling, – over.

pervading, penetrating, absorbing; rabid, raving feverish, fanatical, hysterical; impetuous etc. (*excitable*) 825; overmastering.

impressed –, moved –, touched –, affected –, penetrated –, seized –, imbued etc. 820-with; devoured by; wrought up etc. (*excited*) 824; struck all of a heap; rapt; in a -quiver etc. *n.*; enraptured etc. 829.

Adv. heart and soul, from the bottom of one's heart, *ab imo pectore, de profundis*, at heart, *con amore*, heartily, devoutly, over head and ears.

Phr. the heart -big, – full, – swelling, – beating, – pulsating, – throbbing, – thumping, – beating high, – melting, – overflowing, – bursting, – breaking.

822. Sensibility.—N. sensi-bility, -bleness, -tiveness; moral sensibility; impress-, affect-ibility; suscepti-bleness, -bility, -vity; mobility; viva-city, -ciousness; tender-, soft-ness; sentimental-ity, -ism.

excitability etc. 825; fastidiousness etc. 868; physical sensibility etc. 375.

sore -point, − place; where the shoe pinches.

V. be -sensible etc. *adj.*; have a -tender, − warm, − sensitive- heart.

take to −, treasure up in the- heart; shrink.

'die of a rose in aromatic pain;' touch to the quick.

Adj. sensi-ble, -tive; impressi-ble, -onable; suscepti-ve, -ble; alive to, impassion-able, -ed; gushing; warm-, tender-, soft-hearted; tender −, as a chicken; soft, sentimental, romantic; enthusiastic, highflying, spirited, mettlesome, vivacious, lively, expressive, mobile, tremblingly alive; excitable etc. 825;• over-sensitive, without skin, thin-skinned; fastidious etc. 868.

Adv. sensibly etc. *adj.*; to the -quick, − inmost core.

---

823. Insensibility.—N. insensi-bility, -bleness; moral insensibility; inertness, *inertia, vis inertiae*; impassi-bility, -bleness; inappetency, apathy, phlegm, dulness, hebetude, supineness, lukewarmness, insusceptibility, unimpressibility.

cold -fit, − blood, − heart; cold-, cool-ness; frigidity, *sang-froid*; stoicism, imperturbation etc. (*inexcitability*) 826; *nonchalance*, unconcern, dry eyes; *insouciance* etc. (*indifference*) 866; recklessness etc. 863; callousness; heart of stone, stock and stone, marble, deadness.

torp-or, -idity; obstupefaction, lethargy, coma, trance; sleep etc. 683; suspended animation; stup-or, -efaction; paralysis, palsy; numbness etc. (*physical insensibility*) 376.

neutrality; quietism, vegetation.

V. be -insensible etc. *adj.*; have a rhinoceros hide; show -insensibility etc. *n.*; not -mind, − care, − be affected by; have no desire for etc. 866; leave −, feel −, take- no interest in; *nil admirari*; not care a -straw etc. (*unimportance*) 643 for; disregard etc. (*neglect*) 460; set at naught etc. (*make light of*) 483; turn a deaf ear to etc. (*inattention*) 458; vegetate.

render -insensible, − callous; blunt, obtund, numb, benumb, paralyze, chloroform, deaden, hebetate, stun, stupefy; brut-ify, -alize.

inure; harden, − the heart; steel, case-harden, sear.

Adj. insensible, unconscious; impassi-ve, -ble; blind to, deaf to, dead to; un-, in-susceptible; unimpress-ionable, -ible; passion-, spirit-, heart-, soul-less; unfeeling, unmoral.

apathetic; leuco-, phlegmatic; dull, frigid; cold, -blooded, -hearted; unemotional; cold as charity; flat, obtuse, inert, supine, sluggish, torpid; sleepy etc. (*inactive*) 683; languid, half-hearted, tame; numb, -ed; comatose; anesthetic etc. 376; stupefied, chloroformed, palsy-stricken.

indifferent, lukewarm; Laodicean; careless, mindless, regardless; inattentive etc. 458; neglectful etc. 460; disregarding.

unconcerned, *nonchalant, pococurante, insouciant, sans souci*; unambitious etc. 866.

un-affected, -ruffled, -impressed, -inspired, -excited, -moved, -stirred, -touched, -shocked, -struck; unblushing etc. (*shameless*) 885; unanimated; vegetative.

callous, thick-skinned, pachydermatous, impervious; hard, -ened; inured, case-hardened; steeled −, proof- against; imperturbable etc. (*inexcitable*) 826; unfelt.

Adv. insensibly etc. *adj.*; *aequo animo*; without being -moved, − touched, − impressed; in cold blood; with -dry eyes, − withers unwrung.

Phr. never mind; it is of no consequence etc. (*unimportant*) 643; it cannot be helped; nothing coming amiss; it is all -the same, − one- to.

---

824. Excitation.—N. excitation of feeling; mental −, excitement; suscitation, galvanism, stimulation, piquancy, provocation inspiration, calling forth, infection; interest, animation, agitation, perturbation; subjugation, fascination, intoxication; en-, ravishment; entrancement, high pressure.

unction, impressiveness etc. *adj.*; emotional appeal; melodrama; psychological moment, crisis; sensationalism.

trail of temper, *casus belli*; irritation etc. (*anger*) 900; passion etc. (*state of excitability*) 825; thrill etc. (*feeling*) 821; repression of feeling etc. 826.

V. excite, affect, touch, move, impress, strike, interest, intrigue, animate, inspire, impassion, smite, infect; stir −, fire −, warm- the blood; set astir; a-, wake; a-, waken; call forth; e-, pro-voke; raise up, summon up, call up, wake up, blow up, get up, light up; raise; get up steam, rouse, arouse, stir, fire, kindle, enkindle, apply the torch, set on fire, inflame, illuminate.

stimulate; ex-, suscitate; inspirit; spirit up, stir up, work up; infuse life into, five new life to; bring −, introduce- new blood; quicken, sharpen, whet; work upon etc. (*incite*) 615; hurry on, give a fillip, put on one's mettle.

fan the -fire, − flame; blow the coals, stir the embers; fan, − into a flame; foster, heat, warm, foment, raise to a fever heat; keep -up, − the pot boiling; revive, rekindle; rake up, rip up.

stir −, play on −, come home to- the feelings; touch -a string, − a chord, − the soul, − the heart; go to one's heart, penetrate, pierce, go through one, touch to the quick, open the wound; possess −, pervade −, penetrate −, imbrue −, absorb −, affect −, disturb- the soul.

absorb, rivet the attention; sink into the -mind, − heart; prey on the mind; intoxicate; over-whelm, -power; *bouleverser*, upset, turn one's head.

fascinate; enrapture etc. (*give pleasure*) 829.

agitate, perturb, ruffle, fluster, flutter, shake, disturb, faze, startle, shock, stagger; give one a -shock, − turn; strike -dumb, − all of a heap; stun, astound, electrify, galvanize, petrify.

irritate, sting; cut, − to the -heart, − quick; try one's temper; fool to the top of one's bent, pique; infuriate, madden, make one's blood boil; lash into fury etc. (*wrath*) 900:

be -excited etc. *adj.*; flash up, flare up; catch the infection; thrill etc. (*feel*) 821; mantle; work oneself up; seethe, boil, simmer, foam, fume, flame, rage, rave; run mad etc. (*passion*) 825.

Adj. excited etc. *v.*; wrought up, on the *qui vive*, astir, sparkling; in a -quiver etc. 821, − fever, − ferment, − blaze, − state of excitement; in hysterics; black in the face, over-wrought; hot, red-hot, flushed, feverish; all -of a twitter, − of a flutter, − of a dither, − in a pucker; with -quivering lips, − tears in one's eyes.

flaming; boiling, − over; ebullient, seething; foaming, − at the mouth; fuming, raging, carried away by passion, wild, raving, frantic, mad, dis-

tracted, distraught, beside oneself, out of one's wits, amuck, ready to burst, *bouleversé*, demoniacal.

lost, *eperdu*, tempest-tossed; haggard; ready to sink.

stung to the quick, up, on one's high ropes.

exciting etc. *v.*; impressive, warm, glowing, fervid, swelling, imposing, spirit-stirring, thrilling; high-wrought; soul-stirring, -subduing; heart-swelling, -thrilling; agonizing etc. (*painful*) 830; telling, sensational, melodramatic, hysterical; overpowering, -whelming; more than flesh and blood can bear.

piquant etc. (*pungent*) 392; spicy, appetizing, provocative, *provaquant*, tantalizing.

Adv. till one is black in the face.

Phr. the heart -beating high, — going pit-a-pat, — leaping into one's mouth; the blood -being up, — boiling in one's veins; the eye -glistening, — 'in a fine frenzy rolling;' the head turned.

825. Excitability. [Excess of sensitiveness.]—**N.** excitability, impetuosity, vehemence; boisterousness etc. *adj.*; turbulence; impatience, intolerance, non-endurance; irritability etc. (*irascibility*) 901; itching etc. (*desire*) 865; wincing; disquiet, -ude; restlessness; fidge-ts, -tiness; agitation etc. (*irregular motion*) 315.

trepidation, perturbation, ruffle, hurry, -skurry, fuss, flurry; fluster, flutter; pother, stew, ferment; whirl; thrill etc. (*feeling*) 821; state —, fever- of excitement; transport.

passion, excitement, flush, heat; fever, -heat; fire, flame, fume, blood boiling; tumult; effervescence, ebullition; boiling, — over; whiff, gust, storm, tempest; scene, breaking out, burst, fit, paroxysm, explosion; out-break, -burst; agony.

violence etc. 173; fierceness etc. *adj.*; rage, fury, *furor*, *furore*, desperation, madness, distraction, raving, delirium, brain storm; frenzy, hysterics; intoxication; tearing —, raging- passion, towering rage; anger etc. 900.

fascination, infatuation, fanaticism; Quixot-ism, -ry; *tête montée*.

V. be -impatient etc. *adj.*; not be able to -bear etc. 826; bear ill, wince, chafe, champ the bit; be in a -stew etc. *n.*; be out of all patience, fidget, fuss, not have a wink of sleep; toss, — on one's pillow.

lose one's temper etc. 900; break —, burst —, fly- out; go —, fly- -off, — off the handle, — off at a tangent; explode; flare up, flame up, fire up, burst into a flame, take fire, fire, burn; boil, — over; foam, fume, rage, rave, rant, tear; go —, run- -wild, — mad; go into hysterics; run -riot, — amuck; *battre la campagne, faire le diable à quatre*, play the deuce; raise -Cain, — the devil.

Adj. excitable, easily excited, in an excitable state; high strung; irritable etc. (*irascible*) 901; impatient, intolerant.

feverish, febrile, hysterical; delirious, mad, moody, maggoty-headed.

unquiet, mercurial, electric, galvanic, hasty, hurried, restless, fidgety, fussy; chafing etc. *v.*

startlish, mettlesome, high mettled, skittish.

vehement, demonstrative, violent, wild, furious, fierce, fiery, hot-headed, mad-cap.

over-zealous, enthusiastic, impassioned, fanatical; rabid etc. (*eager*) 865.

rampant, clamorous, uproarious, turbulent, tempestuous, tumultuary, boisterous.

impulsive, impetuous, passionate; uncontroll-ed, -able; ungovernable, irrepressible, stanchless, inextinguishable, burning, simmering, volcanic, ready to burst forth.

excit-ed, -ing etc. 824.

Int. pish! pshaw!

Phr. *noli me tangere.*

826. Inexcitability. [Absence of excitability, or of excitement.]—**N.** inexcit-, imperturb-, inirritability; even temper, tranquil mind, dispassion; tolerance, toleration, patience.

passiveness etc. (*physical inertness*) 172; hebetude, -ation; impassibility etc. (*insensibility*) 823; stupefaction.

coolness, calmness etc. *adj.*; composure, placidity, indisturbance, imperturbation, *sangfroid*, tranquility, serenity, quiet, -ude; peace of mind, mental calmness.

staidness etc. *adj.*; gravity, sobriety, Quakerism; philosophy, equanimity, stoicism, command of temper; self-possession, -control, -command, -restraint; presence of mind.

submission etc. 725; resignation; suffer-, support-, endur-, long-suffer-, forbear-ance; longanimity; fortitude; patience -of Job, — 'on a monument,' — 'sovereign o'er transmuted ill;' moderation; repression —, subjugation- of feeling; restraint etc. 751.

tranquilization etc. (*moderation*) 174.

V. be -composed etc. *adj.*

laisser -faire, — aller; take things -easily, — as they come; take it easy, run on, live and let live; take -easily, — cooly, — in good part; *aequam serva e mentem.*

bear, — well, — the brunt; go through, support, endure, brave, disregard.

tolerate, suffer, stand, bide; abide, aby; bear —, put up —, abide- with; acquiesce; submit etc. (*yield*) 725; submit with a good grace; resign —, reconcile- oneself to; brook, digest, eat, swallow, pocket, stomach; make -light of, — the best of, — a virtue of necessity; put a good face on, keep one's countenance; carry -on, — through; check etc. 751- oneself.

compose, appease etc. (*moderate*) 174; propitiate; repress etc. (*restrain*) 751; render insensible etc. 823; overcome —, allay —, repress- one's -excitability etc. 825; master one's feelings.

make -oneself, — one's mind- easy; set one's mind at -ease, — rest.

calm —, cool- down; thaw, grow cool.

be -borne; — endured; go down.

Adj. in-, un-excitable; imperturbable; un-susceptible etc. (*insensible*) 823; un-, dis-passionate; cold-blooded, inirritable; enduring etc. *v.*; stoical, Platonic, philosophic, staid, stayed; sober, — minded; grave; sober —, grave- as a judge; sedate, demure, cool-, level-headed; steady.

easy-going, peaceful, placid, calm; quiet, — as a mouse; tranquil, serene; cool, — as -a cucumber, — custard; undemonstrative.

temperate etc. (*moderate*) 174; composed, collected; un-excited, -stirred, -ruffled, -disturbed, -perturbed, -impassioned; unoffended; unresisting.

meek, tolerant; patient, — as Job; submissive etc. 725; tame; content, resigned, chastened, subdued, lamblike; gentle, — as a lamb; *suaviter in modo*; mild, — as mother's milk; soft as pep-

permint; armed with patience, bearing with, clement, forbearant, long-suffering.

Adv. 'like patience on a monument smiling at grief;' *aequo animo*, in cold blood etc. 823; more in sorrow than in anger.

Int. patience! and shuffle the cards.

827. Pleasure.—**N.** pleasure, gratification, enjoyment, fruition; ob-, de-lectation; relish, zest; *gusto* etc. (*physical pleasure*) 377; satisfaction etc. (*content*) 831; complacency.

well-being; good etc. 618; snugness, comfort, ease; cushion etc. 215; *sans souci*, mind at ease.

joy, gladness, delight, glee, cheer, sunshine; cheerfulness etc. 836.

treat, refreshment; frolic, fun, lark, gambol, merry-making; amusement etc. 840; luxury etc. 377; hedonism.

mens sana in corpore sano.

happiness, felicity, bliss; beati-tude, -fication; enchantment, transport, rapture, ravishment, ecstasy; *summum bonum*; paradise, elysium etc. (*heaven*) 981; third −, seventh- heaven; unalloyed - happiness etc.

honeymoon; palmy −, halcyon- days; golden- age, − time; *Saturnia regna*, Eden, Arcadia, happy valley, Agapemone; Cockaigne.

V. be pleased etc. 829; feel −, experience- pleasure etc. *n.*; joy; enjoy −, hug- oneself; be in - clover etc. 377, − elysium etc. 981; tread on enchanted ground; fall −, go- into raptures.

feel at home, breathe freely, bask in the sunshine.

be -pleased etc. 829- with; receive −, derive- pleasure etc. *n.*- from; take -pleasure etc. *n.*- in; delight in, rejoice in, indulge in, luxuriate in; gloat over etc. (*physical pleasure*) 377; enjoy, relish, like; love etc. 897; take -to, − a fancy to; have a liking for; enter into the spirit of.

take in good part.

treat oneself to, solace oneself with.

Adj. pleased etc. 829; not sorry; glad, -some; pleased as Punch.

happy, blest, blessed, blissful, beatified; happy as -a king, − the day is long; thrice happy, *ter quaterque beatus*; enjoying etc. *v.*; joyful etc. (*in spirits*) 836; hedonic.

in -a blissful state, − paradise etc. 981; − raptures, − ecstasies, − a transport of delight.

comfortable etc. (*physical pleasure*) 377; at ease; content etc. 831; *sans souci*, in clover.

overjoyed, entranced, enchanted; enraptured; en-, ravished; transported; fascinated, captivated.

with -a joyful face, − sparkling eyes.

pleasing etc. 829; ecstatic, beat-ic, -ific; painless, unalloyed, without alloy, cloudless.

Adv. happily etc. *adj.*; with pleasure etc. (*willingly*) 60; with -glee etc. *n.*

phr. one's heart leaping with joy.

828. Pain.—**N.** mental suffering, pain, dolor; suffer-ing, -ance, ache, smart etc. (*physical pain*) 378; passion.

displeasure, dissatisfaction, discomfort, discomposure, disquiet; *malaise*; inquietude, uneasiness, vexation of spirit; taking; discontent etc. 832.

dejection etc. 837; weariness etc. 841.

annoyance, irritation, worry, infliction, visitation; plague, bore; bother, -ation; stew, vexation, mortification, chagrin, *esclandre*; *mauvais quart d'heure*.

care, anxiety, solicitude, trouble, trial, ordeal, fiery ordeal, shock, blow, cark, dole, fret, burden, load.

concern, grief, sorrow, distress, affliction, woe, bitterness, gloom, heartache; heavy −, aching −, bleeding −, broken- heart; heavy affliction, gnawing grief; unhappiness, infelicity, misery, tribulation, wretchedness, desolation; despair etc. 859; extremity, prostration, depth of misery.

nightmare, *ephialtes*, incubus.

anguish, agony; throe, tor-ture, -ment; crucifixion, martyrdom; pang, twinge, stab; the rack, the stake; purgatory etc. (*hell*) 982.

hell upon earth; iron age, reign of terror; slough of despond etc. (*adversity*) 735; peck −, sea- of troubles; ills that flesh is heir to etc. (*evil*) 619; miseries of human life; unkindest cut of all.

sufferer, victim, prey, martyr; object of compassion, wretch, shorn lamb.

V. feel −, suffer −, experience −, undergo −, bear −, endure- pain etc. *n.*; smart, ache etc. (*physical pain*) 378; suffer, bleed, ail; be the victim of; bear − take up- the cross.

labor under afflictions; quaff the bitter cup, have a bad time of it; fall on evil days etc. (*adversity*) 735; go hard with, come to grief, fall a sacrifice to, drain the cup of misery to the dregs, sup full of horrors.

sit on thorns, be on pins and needles, wince, fret, chafe, worry oneself, be in a taking, fret and fume, take -on, − to heart.

grieve; mourn etc. (*lament*) 839; yearn, repine, pine, droop, languish, sink; give way; despair etc. 859; break one's heart; weigh upon the heart etc. (*inflict pain*) 830.

Adj. in −, in a state of −, full of- pain etc. *n.*; suffering etc. *v.*; pained, afflicted, worried, displeased etc. 830; aching, griped, sore etc. (*physical pain*) 378; on the rack; in limbo; between hawk and buzzard.

un-comfortable, -easy; ill at ease; in a -taking, − way; disturbed; discontented etc. 832; out of humor etc. 901a; weary etc. 841.

heavy laden, stricken, crushed, a prey to, victimized, ill-used.

unfortunate etc. (*hapless*) 735; to be pitied; doomed, devoted, accursed, undone, lost, stranded.

unhappy, infelicitous, poor, wretched, miserable, woe-begone; cheerless etc. (*dejected*) 837; careworn.

concerned, sorry; sorrow-ing, -ful; cut up, chagrined, horrified, horror-stricken; in −, plunged in −, a prey to- grief etc. *n.*; in tears etc. (*lamenting*) 839; steeped to the lips in misery; heart-stricken, -broken, -scalded; broken-hearted; in despair etc. 859.

Phr. 'the iron entered into our soul;' *haeret lateri lethalis arundo;* one's heart bleeding.

829. Pleasurableness. [Capability of giving pleasure; cause or source of pleasure.]—**N.** pleasurable-, pleasant-, agreeable-ness etc. *adj.*; pleasure giving, jocundity, delectability; amusement etc. 840.

attraction etc. (*motive*) 615; attractiveness, -

ability; invitingness etc. *adj.*; charm, fascination, captivation, enchantment, witchery, seduction, winsomeness, winning ways, amenity, amiability, sweetness.

loveliness etc. (*beauty*) 845; sunny –, brightside; sweets etc. (*sugar*) 396; goodness etc. 648; manna in the wilderness, land flowing with milk and honey.

treat; regale etc. (*physical pleasure*) 377; dainty; tit-, tid-bit; nuts, *sauce piquante*.

V. cause –, produce –, create –, give –, afford –, procure –, offer –, present –, yieldpleasure etc. 827.

please, charm, delight; gladden etc. (*make cheerful*) 836; take, captivate, fascinate; enchant, entrance, enrapture, transport, bewitch; en–, ravish.

bless, beatify; satisfy; gratify –, desire etc. 865; slake, satiate, quench; indulge, humor, flatter, tickle; tickle the palate etc. (*savory*) 394; regale, refresh; enliven; treat; amuse etc. 840; take –, tickle –, hit- one's fancy; meet one's wishes; win –, gladden –, rejoice –, warm the cockles of- the heart; do one's heart good.

attract, allure etc. (*move*) 615; stimulate etc. (*excite*) 824; interest, intrigue.

make things pleasant, popularize, gild the pill, sweeten.

Adj. causing pleasure etc. *v.*; pleasure-giving; pleas-ing, -ant, -urable; agreeable, cushy; grat-eful, -ifying; leef, lief, acceptable; welcome, – as the roses in May; welcomed; favorite; to one's -taste, – mind, – liking, – heart's content; satisfactory etc. (*good*) 648.

refreshing; comfortable; cordial; genial; glad, -some; sweet, delectable, nice, dainty; delic-ate, -ious; dulcet; luscious etc. 396; palatable etc. 394; luxurious, voluptuous; sensual etc. 377.

attractive etc. 615; inviting, prepossessing, engaging; win-ning, -some; taking, fascinating, captivating, killing; seduc-ing, -tive; alluring, enticing; appetizing etc. (*exciting*) 824; cheering etc. 836; bewitching; interesting, absorbing, enchanting, entrancing, enravishing.

charming; delightful, felicitous, exquisite; lovely etc. (*beautiful*) 845; ravishing, rapturous; heartfelt, thrilling, ecstatic; beat-ic, -ific; seraphic; empyrean; elysian etc. (*heavenly*) 981.

palmy, halcyon, Saturnian.

Phr. *decies repetita placebit*.

830. Painfulness. [Capability of giving pain; cause or source of pain.]—**N.** painfulness etc. *adj.*; trouble, care etc. (*pain*) 828; trial; af–, in-fliction; cross, blow, stroke, burden, load, curse; bitter -pill, – draught, – cup; waters of bitterness.

annoyance, grievance, nuisance, vexation, mortification, sickener; bore, bother, pother, hot water, sea of troubles, hornet's nest, plague, pest.

cancer, ulcer, sting, thorn; canker etc. (*bane*) 663; scorpion etc. (*evil-doer*) 913; dagger etc. (*arms*) 727; scourge etc. (*instrument of punishment*) 975; carking –, canker worm of- care.

mishap, misfortune etc. (*adversity*) 735; *désagrément, esclandre*; rub.

source of -irritation, – annoyance; wound, sore subject, skeleton in the closet; thorn in -the flesh, – one's side; where the shoe pinches, gall and wormwood.

sorry sight, heavy news, provocation; affront etc. 929; head and front of one's offending.

infestation, molestation; malignity etc. (*malevolence*) 907.

V. cause –, occasion –, give –, bring –, induce –, produce –, create –, inflict- pain etc. 828; pain, hurt, wound.

pinch, prick, gripe etc. (*physical pain*) 378; pierce, lancinate, cut.

hurt –, wound –, grate upon –, jar upon- the feelings; wring –, pierce –, lacerate –, break –, rend- the heart; make the heart bleed; tear –, rend- the heart-strings; draw tears from the eyes.

sadden; make -unhappy etc. 828; plunge into sorrow, grieve, fash, afflict, distress; cut -up, – to the heart.

displease, annoy, incommode, discommode, discompose, trouble, disquiet, disturb, thwart, cross, perplex, molest, tease, rag, tire, irk, vex, mortify, wherret, worry, plague, bother, pester, bore, pother, harass, harry, badger, heckle, bait, beset, infest, persecute, importune, be troublesome.

wring, harrow, torment, torture; put to the -rack, – question; break on the wheel, rack, scarify; cruci-ate, -fy; convulse, agonize; barb the dart; plant a -dagger in the breast, – thron in one's side.

irritate, provoke, sting, nettle, try the patience, pique, fret, rile, tweak the nose, chafe, gall; sting –, wound –, cut- to the quick; aggrieve, affront, enchafe, enrage, ruffle, sour the temper; give offence etc. (*resentment*) 900.

maltreat, bite, snap at, assail, bully; smite etc. (*punish*) 972.

sicken, disgust, revolt, nauseate, disenchant, repel, offend, shock, stink in the nostrils; go against –, turn- the stomach; make one sick, set the teeth on edge, go against the grain, grate on the ear; stick in one's -throat, – gizzard; rankle, gnaw, corrode, horrify, appal, freeze the blood; chill the spine; make the -flesh creep, – hair stand on end; make the blood -curdle, – run cold; make one shudder.

haunt, – the memory; weigh –, prey- on the -heart, – mind, – spirits; bring one's grey hairs with sorrow to the grave; add a nail to one's coffin.

Adj. causing pain, hurting etc. *v.*; hurtful etc. (*bad*) 649; painful; dolor-ific, -ous; unpleasant; un–, dis-pleasing; disagreeable, unpalatable, bitter, distasteful; uninviting; unwelcome; undesir-able, -ed; obnoxious; unacceptable, unpopular, thankless.

unsatisfactory, untoward, unlucky, uncomfortable.

distressing; afflict-ing, -ive; joy-, cheer-, comfortless; dismal, disheartening; depress-ing, -ive; dreary, melancholy, grievous, piteous; woeful, rueful, mournful, deplorable, pitiable, lamentable; sad, affecting, touching, pathetic.

irritating, provoking, stinging, annoying, aggravating, mortifying, galling; unaccommodating, invidious, vexatious; trouble-, tire-, irk-, weari-some; plagu-ing, -y; awkward.

importunate; teas-, pester-, bother-, harass-, worry-, torment-, cark-ing.

in-toler-, -suffer-, -support-able; un-bear-, -endur-able; past bearing; not to be -borne, – endured; more than flesh and blood can bear; enough to -drive one mad, – provoke a saint, – make a parson swear, – try the patience of Job.

shocking, terrific, grim, appalling, crushing; dreadful, fearful, frightful; thrilling, tremendous,

dire; heart-breaking, -rending, -wounding, -corroding, -sickening; harrowing, rending.

odious, hateful, execrable, repulsive, repellent, abhorrent; horri-d, -ble, -fic, -fying; offensive; nause-ous, -ating; disgust-, sicken-, revolt-ing; nasty; loath-some, -ful; fulsome; vile etc. (bad) 649; hideous etc. 846.

sharp, acute, sore, severe, grave, hard, harsh, cruel, biting, acrimonious, caustic; cutting, corroding, consuming, racking, excruciating, searching, searing, grinding, grating, agonizing; envenomed.

ruinous, disastrous, calamitous, tragical; desolating, withering; burdensome, onerous, oppressive; cumb-rous, -ersome.

Adv. painfully etc. adj.; with -pain etc. 828; deuced.

Int. hinc illae lachrymae! woe is me!

Phr. surgit amari aliquid; the place being too hot to hold one; the iron entering into the soul.

831. Content.—N. content, -ment, -edness; complacency, satisfaction, entire satisfaction, ease, heart's ease, peace of mind; serenity etc. 826; cheerfulness etc. 836; ray of comfort; comfort etc. (well-being) 827.

re-, conciliation; resignation etc. (patience) 826. waiter on Providence.

V. be -content etc. adj.; rest -satisfied, – and be thankful; take the good the gods provide, let well alone, feel oneself at home, hug oneself, lay the flattering unction to one's soul.

take -up with, – in good part; assent etc. 488; be reconciled to, make one's peace with; get over it; take -heart, – comfort; put up with etc. (bear) 826.

render -content etc. adj.; set at ease, comfort; set one's -heart, – mind- at -ease, – rest; speak peace; conciliate, reconcile, win over, propitiate, disarm, beguile; content, satisfy; gratify etc. 829.

be -tolerated etc. 826; go down, – with; do.

Adj. content, -ed; satisfied etc. v.; at -ease, – one's ease, – home; with the mind at ease, sans souci, sine curâ, easy-going, not particular; conciliatory; unrepining, of good comfort; resigned etc. (patient) 826; cheerful etc. 836.

un-afflicted, -vexed, -molested, -plagued; serene etc. 826; at rest; snug, comfortable; in one's element.

satisfactory, satisfying, ample, sufficient, adequate, tolerable.

Adv. to one's heart's content; à la bonne heure; all for the best.

Int. amen etc. (assent) 488; very well, so much the better, well and good; it –, that- will do; it cannot be helped.

Phr. nothing comes amiss.

832. Discontent.—N. discontent, -ment; dissatisfaction; dissent etc. 489; labor unrest.

disappointment, mortification; cold comfort; regret etc. 833; repining, taking on etc. v.; inquietude, vexation of spirit, soreness; heartburning, -grief; querulousness etc. (lamentation) 839; hypercriticism.

malcontent, grumbler, growler, croaker, laudator temporis acti; censurer, complainer, faultfinder, murmurer, Adullamite, Diehard, Bitterender.

the Opposition, cave of Adullam, indignation meeting, 'winter of our discontent.'

V. be -discontented etc. adj.; quarrel with one's bread and butter; repine; regret etc. 833; wish one at the bottom of the Red Sea; take -on, – to heart; shrug the shoulders; make a wry –, pull a long-face; knit one's brows; look -blue, – black, – black as thunder, – blank, – glum.

take -in bad part, – ill; fret, chafe, make a piece of work; grumble, croak, grouse; lament etc. 839.

cause -discontent etc. n.; dissatisfy, disappoint, mortify, put out, disconcert; cut up; dishearten.

Adj. discontented; dissatisfied etc. v.; unsatisfied, ungratified; dissident; dissentient etc. 489; malcontent, exigent, exacting, hypercritical.

repining etc. v.; regretful etc. 833; down in the mouth etc. (dejected) 837.

in -high dudgeon, – a fume, – the sulks, – the dumps, – bad humor; glum, sulky; sour, – as a crab; soured, sore; out of -humor, – temper.

disappointing etc. v.; unsatisfactory.

Int. so much the worse!

Phr. that –, it- will never do.

833. Regret.—N. regret, repining; home sickness, nostalgia; mal –, maladie- du pays; lamentation etc. 839; contrition, compunction, penitence etc. 950.

bitterness, heart-burning.

laudator temporis acti etc. (discontent) 832.

V. regret, deplore; bewail etc. (lament) 839; repine, cast a longing lingering look behind; rue, – the day; repent etc. 950; infandum renovare dolorem.

prey –, weigh –, have a weight- on the mind; leave an aching void.

Adj. regretting etc. v.; regretful; home-sick.

regretted etc. v.; much to be regretted, regrettable; lamentable etc. (bad) 649.

Int. what a pity! hang it!

Phr. 'tis -pity, – too true.

834. Relief.—N. relief; deliverance; refreshment etc. 689; easement, softening, alleviation, mitigation, palliation etc. 174; soothing, lullaby; cradle song, berceuse.

solace, consolation, comfort, encouragement.

lenitive, restorative etc. (remedy) 662; poultice etc. v.; cushion etc. 215; crumb of comfort, balm in Gilead; aspirin.

V. relieve, ease, alleviate, mitigate, palliate, soothe, adulce; salve; soften, – down; foment, stupe, poultice; assuage, allay.

cheer, comfort, console; encourage, bear up, pat on the back, give comfort, set at ease; enliven, gladden –, cheer- the heart.

remedy; cure etc. (restore) 660; refresh; pour -balm into, – oil on.

smoothe the ruffled brow of care, temper the wind to the shorn lamb, lay the flattering unction to one's soul.

disburden etc. (free) 705; take off a load of care.

be relieved; breathe more freely, draw a long breath; take comfort; dry –, wipe- the -tears, – eyes.

Adj. relieving etc. *v.*; consolatory, soothing; assua-ging, -sive; bal-my, -samic; lenitive, palliative; anodyne etc. (*remedial*) 662; curative etc. 660.

835. Aggravation.—N. aggravation, heightening; exacerbation; exasperation; overestimation etc. 482; exaggeration etc. 549.

V. aggravate, render worse, heighten, embitter, sour; ex-, acerbate; exasperate, envenom; tease, provoke, enrage.

add fuel to the -fire, – flame; fan the flame etc. (*excite*) 824; go from bad to worse etc. (*deteriorate*) 659.

Adj. aggravated etc. *v.*; worse, unrelieved; aggravable; aggravating etc. *v.*

Adv. out of the frying pan into the fire, from bad to worse, worse and worse.

Int. so much the worse!

836. Cheerfulness.—N. cheerfulness etc. *adj.*; geniality, gaiety, *l'allegro*, cheer, good humor, spirits; high –, animal –, flow of- spirits; glee, high glee, light heart; sunshine of the -mind, – breast; *gaieté de coeur*, *bon naturel*.

liveliness etc. *adj.*; life, alacrity, vivacity, animation, *allégresse*; jocundity, joviality, jollity; levity; jocularity etc. (*wit*) 842.

mirth, merriment, hilarity, exhilaration; laughter etc. 838; merry-making etc. (*amusement*) 840; heyday, rejoicing etc. 838; marriage bells.

nepenthe, Euphrosyne.

optimism etc. (*hopefulness*) 858; self-complacency.

V. be -cheerful etc. *adj.*; have the mind at ease, smile, put a good face upon, keep up one's spirits; view -the bright side of the picture, – things *en couleur de rose*; *ridentem dicere verum*, cheer up, brighten up, light up, bear up; chirp, take heart, cast away care, drive dull care away, perk up.

rejoice etc. 838; carol, chirrup, lilt; frisk, rollick, give a loose to mirth.

cheer, enliven, elate, exhilarate, gladden, in-spirit, animate, raise the spirits, inspire; put in good humor; cheer –, rejoice- the heart; delight etc. (*give pleasure*) 829.

Adj. cheerful; happy etc. 827; cheer-y, -ly; of good cheer, smiling; blithe; in –, in good- spirits; in high -spirits, – feather; happy as -the day is long, – a king; gay; – as a lark; *allegro*; light, -some, -hearted; buoyant, *débonnaire*, bright, free and easy, airy; janty, jaunty, canty; spright-ly, -ful; spry; spirit-ed, -ful; lively, animated, breezy, vivacious; brisk, – as a bee; sparkling, sportive; full of -play, – spirit; all alive.

sunny, palmy; hopeful etc. 858.

merry, – as -a -cricket, – grig, – marriage bell; joyful, joyous, jocund, jovial; jolly, – as a thrush, – as a sandboy; blithesome; glee-ful, -some; hilarious, rattling.

play-ful, -some; *folâtre*, playful as a kitten, tricksy, frisky, frolicsome; gamesome; jocose, jocular, waggish; mirth-, laughter-loving; mirthful, rollicking.

elate, -d; exulting, jubilant, flushed; rejoicing etc. 838; cock-a-hoop.

cheering, inspiriting, exhilarating; cardiac, -al; pleasing etc. 829; flourishing, halcyon.

Adv. cheerfully etc. *adj.*

Int. never say die! come! cheer up! hurrah! etc. 838; 'hence loathed melancholy!' begone dull care! away with melancholy!

837. Dejection.—N. dejection; dejectedness etc. *adj.*; depression, prostration; lowness –, depression- of spirits; weight –, oppression –, damp- on the spirits; low –, bad –, drooping –, depressed- spirits; heart sinking; heaviness –, failure- of heart.

heaviness etc. *adj.*; infestivity, gloom; weariness etc. 841; *taedium vitae*, disgust of life; *mal du pays* etc. (*regret*) 833.

melancholy; sadness etc. *adj.*; *il penseroso*, *melancholia*, dismals, mumps, mopes, lachrymals, dumps, blues, blue devils, doldrums, vapors, megrims, spleen, horrors, hypochondriasis, pessimism; despondency, slough of Despond; disconsolateness etc. *adj.*; hope deferred, blank despondency.

prostration, – of soul; broken heart; despair etc. 859; cave of -despair, – Trophonius.

demureness etc. *adj.*; gravity, solemnity; long –, grave- face.

hypochondriac, seek-sorrow, self-tormentor, *heautontimorumenos*, *malade imaginaire*, *médecin tant pis*; croaker, pessimist; mope, mopus.

[Cause of dejection] affliction etc. 830; sorry sight; *memento mori*; damper, wet blanket, Job's comforter; death's head, skeleton at the feast.

V. be -dejected etc. *adj.*; grieve; mourn etc. (*lament*) 839; take on, give way, lose heart, despond, droop, sink.

lower, look downcast, frown, pout; hang down the head; pull –, make- a long face; laugh on the wrong side of the mouth; grin a ghastly smile; look -blue, – like a drowned man; lay –, take- to heart.

mope, brood over; fret; sulk; pine, – away; yearn; repine etc. (*regret*) 833; despair etc. 859.

refrain from laughter, keep one's countenance; be –, look- grave etc. *adj.*; repress a smile, keep a straight face.

depress; dis-courage, -hearten; dis-pirit; damp, dull, deject, lower, sink, dash, knock down, un-man, prostrate, break one's heart; frown upon; cast a -gloom, – shade- on; sadden; damp –, dash –, wither- one's hopes; weigh –, lie heavy –, prey- on the -mind, – spirits; damp –, depress- the spirits.

Adj. cheer-, joy-, spirit-less; uncheer-ful, -y; unlively; unhappy etc. 828; melancholy, dismal, somber, dark, gloomy, adust, *triste*, clouded, murky, lowering, frowning, lugubrious, Acherontic, funereal, mournful, lamentable, dreadful.

dreary, flat; dull, – as -a beetle, – ditchwater; depressing etc. *v.*

'melancholy as a gib cat;' oppressed with –; a prey to- melancholy; down-cast, -hearted; down -in the mouth, – on one's luck; heavy-hearted; in the -dumps, – suds, – sulks, – doldrums; in doleful dumps, in bad humor; sullen; mumpish, dumpish; mopish, moping; moody, glum; sulky etc. (*discontented*) 832; out of -sorts, – humor, – heart, – spirits; ill at ease, low-spirited, in low spirits, a cup

too low; weary etc. 841; dis-couraged, -heartened; desponding; *chop-, jaw-, crest-fallen.

sad, pensive, *penseroso*, tristful; dole-some, -ful; woebegone, lachrymose, in tears, melancholic, hypped, hypochondriacal, bilious, jaundiced, atrabilious, saturnine, splenetic; lackadaisical.

serious, sedate, staid, stayed; grave, – as -a judge, – an undertaker, – a mustard pot; sober, solemn, demure; grim; grim-faced, -visaged; rueful, wan, long-faced.

disconsolate; un-, in-consolable; forlorn, comfortless, desolate, *désolé*, sick at heart; soul-, heart-sick; *au désepoir*; in despair etc. 859; lost.

overcome; broken-, borne-, bowed-down; heart-stricken etc. (*mental suffering*) 828; cut up, dashed, sunk, unnerved, unmanned; down-fallen, -trodden; broken-hearted; care-worn.

Adv. with -a long face, – tears in one's eyes; sadly etc. *adj.*

Phr. the countenance falling; the heart -failing, – sinking within- one.

838. Rejoicing. [Expression of pleasure.]—**N.** rejoicing, exultation, triumph, jubilation, heyday, flush, revelling; merry-making etc. (*amusement*) 840; jubilee etc. (*celebration*) 883; *paean*, *Te Deum* etc. (*thanksgiving*) 990; congratulation etc. 896; applause etc. 971.

smile, simper, smirk, grin; broad –, sardonic-grin.

laughter, giggle, titter, crow, cheer, chuckle, snicker, snigger, shout; Homeric laughter, horse –, hearty- laugh; guffaw; burst –, fit –, shout –, roar –, peal- of laughter; cachinnation.

risibility; derision etc. 856.

Momus; Democritus the Abderite; rollicker; Laughter holding both his sides.

V. rejoice; thank –, bless- one's stars; congratulate –, hug- oneself; rub –, clap- one's hands; smack the lips, fling up one's cap; dance, skip, caleer; sing, carol, chirrup, chirp; hurrah; cry for –, leap with- joy; exult etc. (*boast*) 884; triumph; hold jubilee etc. (*celebrate*) 883; make merry etc. (*sport*) 840; sing a paean of joy.

smile, simper, smirk; grin, – like a Cheshire cat; mock, laugh in one's sleeve; laugh, – outright; giggle, titter, snigger, crow, smicker, chuckle, snicker, cackle; burst -out, – into a fit of laughter; shout, split, roar.

shake –, split –, hold both- one's sides; roar –, die- with laughter.

raise laughter etc. (*amuse*) 840.

Adj. rejoicing etc. *v.*; jubilant, exultant, triumphant; flushed, elated; laughing etc. *v.*; risible; ready to -burst –, split –, die with laughter; convulsed with laughter.

laughable etc. (*ludicrous*) 853.

Int. hip, hip, -hurrah! huzza! aha! hail! tolderolloll! tra-la la! Heaven be praised! *io triumphe! tant mieux!* so much the better.

Phr. the heart leaping with joy.

839. Lamentation. [Expression of pain.]—**N.** lament, -ation; wail, complaint, plaint, murmur, mutter, grumble, groan, moan, whine, whimper, sob, sigh, suspiration, heaving, deep sigh.

cry etc. (*vociferation*) 411; scream, howl; out-cry, wail of woe, frown, scowl.

tear; weeping etc. *v.*; flood of tears, fit of crying, lachrymation, melting mood, weeping and gnashing of teeth.

plaintiveness etc. *adj.*; languishment; condolence etc. 915.

mourning, weeds, willow, cypress, crêpe, crape, deep mourning; sackcloth and ashes; knell etc. 363; dump, deathsong, dirge, coronach, keen, *nenia*, requiem, elegy, *epicedium*; threne; mon-, thren-ody; jeremiad; ululation.

mourner, professional mourner, keener; grumbler etc. (*discontent*) 832; Niobe; Heraclitus.

V. lament, mourn, deplore, grieve, weep over; be-wail, -moan; keen; condole with etc. 915; fret etc. (*suffer*) 828; wear –, go into –, put on-mourning; wear the willow, – sackcloth and ashes; *infandum renovare dolorem* etc. (*regret*) 833; give sorrow words.

sigh; give –, heave –, fetch- a sigh; 'waft a sigh from Indus to the pole;' sigh 'like furnace;' wail.

cry, weep, sob, greet, blubber, pipe, snivel, bib-ber, whimper, pule; pipe one's eye; drop –, shed- -tears, – a tear; melt –, burst- into tears; *fondre en larmes*; cry -oneself blind, – one's eyes out.

scream etc. (*cry out*) 411; mew etc. (*animal sounds*) 412; groan, moan, whine, yammer; roar; roar –, bellow- like a bull; cry out lustily, rend the air, yell.

frown, scowl, make a wry face, grimace, gnash one's teeth, wring one's hands, tear one's hair, beat one's breast, roll on the ground, burst with grief.

complain, murmur, mutter, grumble, growl, clamor, make a fuss about, croak, grunt, maunder; deprecate etc. (*disapprove*) 932.

cry out before one is hurt, complain without cause.

Adj. lamenting etc. *v.*; in mourning, in sackcloth and ashes; crying, sorrowing, -ful etc. (*unhappy*) 828; mourn-, tear-ful; lachrymose; plaint-ive, -ful, quer-ulous, -imonious; in the melting mood.

in tears, with tears in one's eyes; with -moistened, – watery- eyes; bathed –, dissolved-in tears; 'like Niobe all tears.'

elagiac, epicedial, threnetic.

Adv. *de profundis*; *les larmes aux yeux*.

Int. heigh-ho! alas! alack! O dear! ah –, woe is-me! lackadaisy! well –, lack –, alack- a day! well-a-way! alas the day! *O tempora! O mores!* what a pity! *miserabile dictu!* O lud lud! too true!

Phr. tears -standing in, – starting from- the eyes; eyes, -suffused, – swimming, – brimming –, over- flowing- with tears.

840. Amusement.—**N.** amuse-, entertain-ment; diver-sion, -tissement; reaction, relaxation, solace; pastime, *passetemps*, sport; labor of love; pleasure etc. 827.

fun, frolic, merriment, whoopee, jollity; jovial-ity, -ness; heyday; laughter etc. 838; jocos-ity, -eness; droll-, buffoon-, tomfool-ery; mummery, masquing, pleasantry; wit etc. 842; quip, quirk.

play; game, – at romps; gambol, romp, prank, antic, rig, lark, spree, skylarking, vagary, trick, monkey trick, *gambade*, *fredaine*, *escapade*, *échappée*, bout, *espièglerie*; practical joke etc. (*ridicule*) 856.

dance; round –, square –, solo –, step –, tap –, clog –, skirt –, sand –, folk –, morris-

dance, *pas seul*, step, turn, *chassé*, cut, shuffle, double shuffle; hop, reel, rigadoon, saraband, hornpipe, bolero, fandango, pavan, tarantella, minuet, waltz, polka; galop, -ade; Schottische, *pas de quatre*, Boston, one-, two-step, rumba, tango, maxixe, fox-, turkey-trot, shimmy, ragtime, cakewalk, jazz, blues, Charleston; jig, breakdown, fling, strathspey; *allemande*; gavot, -te; mazurka, morisco; quadrille, lancers, country dance, *cotillon*, polonaise, Sir Roger de Coverley, Swedish dance; *ballet* etc. (*drama*) 599; ball; *bal, — masqué, — costumé*; masquerade, fancy dress ball; *thé dansant*; Terpsichore, choreography, Russian ballet, classical dancing; eurythmics; nautch dance, *danse du ventre*, cancan.

festivity, merry-making; party etc. (*social gathering*) 892; *fête*, festival, gala, *ridotto*; revel-s, -ry, -ling; carnival, brawl, saturnalia, high jinks; feast, banquet etc. (*food*) 298; regale, *symposium*, wassail; carous-e, -al; jollification, junket, wake, pic-nic, *fête champêtre*, garden party, gymkhana, regatta, track meet, field day, jamboree, treat.

round of pleasures, dissipation, a short life and a merry one, racketing, holiday making, high jinks.

rejoicing etc. 838; jubilee etc. (*celebration*) 883.

bonfire, fireworks, *feu-de-joie*, rocket, catherine wheel, roman candle etc.

holiday; gala —, red letter —, play- day; high days and holidays; high —, Bank- holiday; May —, Derby- day; Saint —, Easter —, Whit- Monday; King's birthday, Empire Day; *mi-carême*; *Bairam*; wayzgoose, bean feast, beano.

place of amusement, theater etc. 599; concert-, ball-, assembly-room; music-hall, cinema, movies, talkies, vaudeville; hippodrome, circus, rodeo; *casino*, *kursaal*; winter garden; park, pleasance, arbor; garden etc. 371; pleasure-, play-, cricket-, football-, polo-, croquet-, archery-, hunting-ground; golf links, race course, stadium, gridiron, bowl, speedway, racing track, ring; gymnasium, swimming pool; shooting gallery; tennis-, racket-court; bowling-green, -alley; croquet-lawn, rink, skating rink; roller-coaster, roundabout, carousel, merry-go-round; swing; *montagne russe*; switch-back, scenic railway etc.

game, — of -chance, — skill; athletic sports, gymnastics; fencing; archery, rifle-shooting; tournament, pugilism etc. (*contention*) 720; sporting etc. 622; horse-racing, the turf; aquatics etc. 267; skating, roller skating; ski-running, -joring, -jumping, bobsleighing, luging, tobogganing, winter sports; sliding; cricket, tennis, lawn —, table —, deck-tennis, rackets, fives, squash, ping pong, trap bat and ball, battledore and shuttlecock, badminton, *la grâce*; pall mall, tip-cat, croquet, golf, curling, hockey, basketball, soccer, football, Rugby, Association, *pallone*, polo; tent-pegging, tilting at the ring, quintain, greasy pole; quoits, *discus*; throwing the hammer, putting the -weight, — shot, tossing the caber; knurr and spell; leap-frog; hop, skip and jump; French and English, tug of war; blind man's buff, hunt the slipper, hide-and-seek, kiss in the ring; snapdragon; cross questions and crooked answers; jig-saw puzzle; rounders, base-ball, *la crosse* etc.; angling; swimming, diving, water-polo.

billiards, pool, pyramids, snooker, bagatelle; bowls, skittles, ninepins, kail, American bowls.

cards; bridge, auction, contract, whist, rubber; round game, coon-can, loo, cribbage, *bésique*, pinocle, euchre, drole, *écarté*, skat, picquet, all-fours, quadrille, ombre, reverse, Pope Joan, commit; bo-, boa-ston; *vingt-et-un*; *quinze*, thirty-one, put-and-take, speculation, connections, brag, cassino, lottery, commerce, snip-snap-snorem, lift smoke, blind hookey, Polish bank, poker, banker; faro; Earl of Coventry, Napoleon, nap, patience; pairs; old maid, fright, beggar-my-neighbor; *baccarat, chemin de fer, monté, roulette*.

chess, draughts, backgammon, dominoes, checkers, mah jong, merelles, nine men's morris, go-bang, solitaire; game of —, fox and-goose; lotto; etc.

morra; gambling etc. (*chance*) 621.

toy, plaything, bauble; doll etc. (*puppet*) 554; teetotum; knick-knack etc. (*trifle*) 643; magic lantern etc. (*show*) 448; peep-, puppet-, raree-, gallanty-show; marionettes, Punch and Judy; toy-shop; 'quips and cranks and wanton wiles, nods and becks and wreathed smiles.'

sportsman, gamester, gambler etc. 621; reveler, master of the -ceremonies, — revels; *arbiter elegantiarum*.

V. amuse, entertain, divert, eliven; tickle, — the fancy; titillate, raise a smile, put in good humor; cause —, create —, occasion —, raise —, excite —, produce —, convulse with- laughter; set the table in a roar, be the death of one.

recreate, solace, cheer, rejoice; please etc. 829; interest; treat, regale.

amuse oneself; game; play, — a game, — pranks, — tricks; sport, disport, toy, wanton, revel, junket, feast, carouse, banquet, make merry; drown care; drive dull care away; frolic, gambol, frisk, romp; caper; dance etc. (*leap*) 309; keep up the ball; run a rig, sow one's wild oats, have one's fling, paint the town red, take one's pleasure; see life; *desipere in loco*, play the fool.

make —, keep- holiday; go a Maying.

while away —, beguile- the time; kill time, dally.

Adj. amusing, entertaining, diverting etc. *v.*; recreative, lusory; pleasant etc. (*pleasing*) 829; laughable etc. (*ludicrous*) 853; witty etc. 842; festive, -al; jovial, jolly, jocund, roguish, rompish; sporting; playful — as a kitten; sportive, ludibrious.

amused etc. *v.*; 'pleased with a feather, tickled with a straw.'

Adv. 'on the light fantastic toe,' at play, in sport.

Int. *vive la bagatelle! vogue la galère!*

Phr. *Deus nobis haec otia fecit; dum vivimus vivamus.*

841. Weariness.—N. weariness, defatigation, boredom, *ennui*; lassitude etc. (*fatigue*) 688; drowsiness etc. 683.

disgust, nausea, loathing, sickness; satiety etc. 869; *taedium vitae* etc. (*dejection*) 837.

wearisome-, tedious-ness etc. *adj.*; dull work, tedium, monotony, twice told tale.

bore, button-hole, proser, wet blanket; heavy hours, 'the enemy' [time].

V. weary; tire etc. (*fatigue*) 688; bore; bore —, weary —, tire- -to death, — out of one's life, — out of all patience; set —, send- to sleep.

pall, sicken, nauseate, disgust.

harp on the same string; drag its -slow, — weary-length along.

never hear the last of; be -tired etc. *adj.* -of, – with; yawn; died with *ennui*.

Adj. wearying etc. *v.*; wearing; weari-, tire-, irksome; uninteresting, stupid, bald, devoid of interest, dry, monotonous, dull, arid, tedious, humdrum, mortal, flat; pros-y, -ing; slow; soporific, somniferous, dormitive.

disgusting etc. *v.*; unenjoyed.

weary; tired etc. *v.*; drowsy etc. (*sleepy*) 683; uninterested, flagging, used up, worn out, *blasé*, life-weary, weary of life; sick of.

Adv. wearily etc. *adj.*; *usque ad nauseam*.

Phr. time hanging heavily on one's hands; *toujours perdrix*; *crambe repetita*.

842. Wit.—N. wit, -tiness; attic -wit, – salt; atticism; salt, *esprit*, point, fancy, whim, humor, drollery, pleasantry.

farce, buffoonery, fooling, tomfoolery; harlequinade etc. 599; broad -farce, – humor; fun, *espièglerie*; *vis comica*.

jocularity; jocos-ity, -eness; facetiousness; waggery, -ishness; whimsicality; comicality etc. 853.

smartness, ready wit, banter, *badinage*, *persiflage*, retort, repartee, *quid pro quo*; ridicule etc. 856.

facetiae, quips and cranks; jest, joke, capital joke; standing -jest, – joke; conceit, quip, quirk, crank, quiddity, *concetto*, *plaisanterie*, brilliant idea; merry –, bright –, happy- thought; sally; flash, – of wit, – of merriment; scintillation; *mot*, – pour rire; witticism, smart saying, *bon mot*, *jeu d'esprit*, epigram; jest book; dry joke, *quodlibet*, cream of the jest.

word-play, *jeu de mots*; play -of, – upon-words; pun, -ning; *double entente* etc. (*ambiguity*) 520; quibble, verbal quibble; conundrum etc. (*riddle*) 533; anagram, acrostic, double acrostic, *nugae canorae*, trifling, idle conceit, *turlupinade*.

old joke, Joe Miller, chestnut, hoary-headed jest.

V. joke, jest, cut jokes; crack a joke; perpetrate a -joke, – pun; make -fun of, – merry with; set the table in a roar etc. (*amuse*) 840; scintillate.

retort, flash back; banter etc. (*ridicule*) 856; *ridentem dicere verum*; joke at one's expense.

Adj. witty, attic, salty; quick-, nimble-witted; keen, clever, smart, brilliant, pungent, jocular, jocose, funny, waggish, facetious, whimsical, humorous, gilbertian; playful etc. 840; merry and wise; pleasant, sprightly, *spirituel*, sparkling, epigrammatic, full of point, *ben trovato*; comic etc. 853.

Adv. in joke, in jest, in sport, in play.

843. Dullness.—N. dullness, heaviness, flatness; infestivity etc. 837; stupidity etc. 499; want of originality, dearth of ideas.

prose, matter of fact; heavy book, *conte à dormir debout*; platitude.

V. be -dull etc. *adj.*; prose, platitudinize, take *au sérieux*, be caught napping.

render -dull etc. *adj.*; damp, depress, throw cold water on, lay a wet blanket on; fall flat upon the ear; hang fire.

Adj. dull, – as ditch water; dry, insipid, jejune; unentertaining, uninteresting, unlively,

unimaginative; heavisome, heavy-gaited; insulse; dry as dust; pros-y, -ing, -aic; matter of fact, commonplace, banal, pointless; 'weary, flat, stale and unprofitable.'

stupid, slow, flat, sluggish, ponderous, humdrum, monotonous; melancholic etc. 837; stolid etc. 499; plodding.

Phr. *Davus sum non Oedipus*.

844. Humorist.—N. humorist, wag, wit, reparteeist, epigrammatist, gag man, punster; *bel esprit*, life of the party; wit-snapper, -cracker, -worm; joker, jester, jokesmith, Joe Miller, *drôle de corps*, *gaillard*, spark, *persiffleur*, banterer.

buffoon, *farceur*, merry-andrew, mime, tumbler, acrobat, mountebank, charlatan, posturemaster, harlequin, punch, *pulcinella*, scaramouch, clown; wearer of the -cap and bells, – motley; motley fool; pantaloon, gipsy; jack -pudding, – in the green, – a dandy; zany; mad-cap, pickle-herring, witling, caricaturist, *grimacier*.

845. Beauty.—N. beauty, the beautiful, *le beau idéal*, loveliness.

[Science of the perception of beauty] Callaesthetics.

form, elegance, grace, beauty unadorned; symmetry etc. 242; comeliness, fairness etc. *adj.*; pulchritude, polish, gloss; good -effect, – looks; *belle tournure*; bloom, brilliancy, radiance, splendor, gorgeousness, magnificence; sublimi-ty, -fication.

concinnity, delicacy, refinement; charm, *je ne sais quoi*, style, *chic*, swank.

Venus, – of Milo; Aphrodite, Hebe, the Graces, Peri, Houri, Cupid, Apollo, Hyperion, Adonis, Antinous, Narcissus; Helen of Troy.

peacock, butterfly; flower, flow'ret gay, rose, lily, asphodel; garden; flower of, pink of; *bijou*; jewel etc. (*ornament*) 847; work of art.

pleasurableness etc. 829.

beautifying; landscape gardening; decoration etc. 847; calisthenics.

V. be -beautiful etc. *adj.*; shine, beam, bloom; become one etc. (*accord*) 23; set off, grace, flatter one.

render -beautiful etc. *adj.*; beautify; polish, burnish; gild etc. (*decorate*) 847; set out.

'snatch a grace beyond the reach of art.'

Adj. beaut-iful, -eous; handsome; pretty; lovely, graceful, elegant; delicate, dainty, refined, exquisite; fair, personable, comely, seemly; bonny; good-looking; well-favored, -made, -formed, -proportioned; proper, shapely; symmetrical etc. (*regular*) 242; harmonious etc. (*color*) 428; sightly.

fit to be seen, passable, not amiss.

goodly, dapper, tight, jimp; gimp; janty, jaunty; natty, quaint, trim, tidy, neat, spruce, smart, tricksy.

bright, -eyed; rosy-, cherry-cheeked; rosy, ruddy; blooming, in full bloom.

brilliant, shining; beam-y, -ing; sparkling, swanky, splendid, resplendent, dazzling, glowing; glossy, sleek.

showy, specious; rich, gorgeous, superb; magnificent, grand, fine, sublime, imposing; majestic 873.

artistic, -al; aesthetic; pict-uresque, -orial; *fait à piendre*, paintable; well-composed, -grouped, - varied; curious.

enchanting etc. (*pleasure-giving*) 829; attractive etc. (*inviting*) 615; becoming etc. (*accordant*) 23; ornamental etc. 847.

undeformed, undefaced, unspotted; spotless etc. (*perfect*) 650.

846. Ugliness.—N. ugliness etc. *adj.*; deformity, inelegance; disfigurement etc. (*blemish*) 848; want of symmetry, inconcinnity; distortion etc. 243; squalor etc. (*uncleanness*) 653.

forbidding countenance, vinegar aspect, hanging look, wry face, '*spretae injuria formae.*'

eyesore, object, figure, sight, fright, specter, scarecrow, hag, harridan, satyr, witch, toad, baboon, monster, Caliban, Aesop, '*monstrum horrendum informe ingens cui lumen ademptum.*'

V. be -ugly etc. *adj.*; look ill, grin horribly a ghastly smile, make faces.

render -ugly etc. *adj.*; deface; dis-, de-figure; deform, spoil, distort etc. 243; blemish etc. (*injure*) 659; soil etc. (*render unclean*) 653.

Adj. ugly, – as -sin, – a toad, – a scarecrow, – a dead monkey; plain, bald etc. 226; homely etc. (*unadorned*) 849; ordinary, unornamental, inartistic; unsightly, unseemly, uncomely, unshapely, unlovely; sightless, seemless; not fit to be seen; unbeaut-eous, -iful; beautiless; shapeless etc. (*amorphous*) 241; course; garish, over-decorated etc. 882.

mis-shapen, -proportioned; monstrous; gaunt etc. (*thin*) 203; dumpy etc. (*short*) 201; curtailed of its fair proportions; ill-made, -shaped, -proportioned; crooked etc. (*distorted*) 243; hard-featured, - visaged; ill-, hard-, evil-favored; ill-looking; unprepossessing.

graceless, inelegant; ungraceful, ungainly, uncouth; stiff; rugged, rough, gross, rude, awkward, clumsy, slouching, rickety; gawky; lump-ing, -ish; lumbering; hulk-y, -ing; unwieldy.

squalid, haggard; grim, -faced, -visaged; grisly, ghastly; ghost-, death-like; cadaverous, gruesome.

frightful, hideous, odious, uncanny, forbidding, repellant, repulsive; horri-d, -ble; shocking etc. (*painful*) 830.

foul etc. (*dirty*) 653; dingy etc. (*colorless*) 429; gaudy etc. (*color*) 428; disfigured etc. *v.*; discolored (*blemished*) etc. 848.

847. Ornament.—N. ornament, -ation, -al art; ornat-ture, -eness; adorn-ment, decoration, embellishment; architecture.

garnish, polish, varnish, French polish, gilding, japanning, lacquer, ormolu, enamel.

cosmetics, rouge, powder, lipstick, lip salve, mascara; manicure, nail polish; permanent – . Marcel – , finger-wave.

pattern, diaper, powdering, panelling, graining, pargeting, inlay, detail; texture etc. 329; richness; tracery, molding, beading, reeding, fillet, listel, strapwork, *coquillage*, flourish, *fleur-de-lis*; arabesque, fret, *anthemion*; egg and -tongue, – dart; *astragal*, zigzag, *acanthus*, *cartouche*; pilaster etc. (*projection*) 250; cyma, ogee.

em-, broidery, needlework; knitting, crochet, tatting, brocade, *brocatelle*, beads, bugles; galloon, lace, gimp, *guipure*, fringe, trapping, border, edging, insertion, *motif*, trimming; *passementerie*; drapery, hanging, tapestry, arras; millinery, ermine.

wreath, festoon, garland, lei, chaplet, flower, nosegay, *bouquet*, posy, 'daisies pied and violets blue.'

tassle, knot; shoulder-knot, *épaulette*, epaulet, aigulet, *aiguilette*, frog; star, rosette, bow; feather, plume, *panache, aigrette*.

jewel, -ry, -lery; bijoutry; *bijou, -terie*; diadem, tiara; pendant, trinket, locket, necklace, armilla, bracelet, bangle, armlet, anklet, ear-, nose- ring, carcanet, chain, *châtelaine*, albert, brooch, torque.

gem, precious stone; diamond, brilliant, beryl, aquamarine, alexandrite, cat's eye, emerald, calcedony, chrysoprase, cornelian, jasper, bloodstone, agate, heliotrope; girasol, -e; onyx, plasma; sard, -onyx; garnet, lapis-lazuli, opal, peridot, chrysolite, sapphire, ruby; spinel, -le; balais; oriental – , topaz; turquois, -e; zircon, jacinth, hyacinth, carbuncle, amethyst; moonstone; pearl, coral.

finery, frippery, gewgaw, gimcrack, knick-knack, tinsel, spangle, sequin, *clinquant*, pinch-beck, paste; excess of ornament etc. (*vulgarity*) 851; gaud, pride, ostentation; frills and furbelows.

illustration, illumination, *vignette*; *fleuron*; head-, tail-piece; *cul-de-lampe*; flowers of rhetoric etc. 577; work of art, article of vertu, *bric-à-brac*, curio, *bibelot*.

V. ornament, embellish, enrich, decorate, adorn, beautify, adonize.

· smarten, furbish, polish, gild, varnish, whitewash, enamel, japan, lacquer, paint, grain.

garnish, trim, dizen, bedizen, prink, prank; trick – , fig- out; deck, bedeck, dight, bedight, array; dress, – up, preen, spruce up, titivate; spangle, bespangle, powder; embroider, work; chase, tool, emboss, fret; emblazon, blazon, illuminate; illustrate.

become etc. (*accord with*) 23.

Adj. ornamented, beautified etc. *v.*; ornate, rich, gilt, begilt, tesselated, enamelled, inlaid; festooned; topiary.

smart, gay, tricksy, flowery, glittering; new-gilt, - spangled; fine, – as -a Mayday queen, – fivepence, – a carrot fresh scraped; pranked out, bedight, well-groomed.

in full dress etc. (*fashion*) 852; *en grande - tenue*, – *toilette*; in best bib and tucker, in Sunday best, *endimanché*; dressed to advantage.

showy, flashy; gaudy etc. (*vulgar*) 851; garish; gorgeous.

ornamental, decorative; becoming etc. (*accordant*) 23.

848. Blemish.—N. blemish, disfigurement, deformity; defect etc. (*imperfection*) 651; flaw; injury etc. (*deterioration*) 659; spots on the sun; eyesore.

stain, blot, slur; spot, -tiness; speck, -le; blur, freckle, mole, *macula*, patch, blotch, birthmark, blain, maculation, tarnish, smudge, smear; dirt etc. 653; bruise, black eye, scar, wem; pustule; excrescence, pimple etc. (*protuberance*) 250.

V. disfigure etc. (*injure*) 659; speckle; render ugly etc. 846.

Adj. pitted, freckled, discolored, bloodshot, bruised, disfigured; stained etc. *n.*; imperfect etc. 651; injured etc. (*deteriorated*) 659.

849. Simplicity.—N. simplicity; plain-, homeli-ness; undress, nudity, nakedness, beauty unadorned, chastity, chasteness.

V. be -simple etc. *adj.*

render -simple etc. *adj.*; simplify, chasten, strip of ornament.

Adj. simple, plain; home-ly, -spun; ordinary, household.

natural, unaffected; free from -affectation, − ornament; *simplex munditiis*; *sans façon, en déshabillé*, nude, naked.

chaste, inornate, severe.

un-adorned, -ornamented, -decked, -garnished, -arranged, -trimmed, -varnished.

bald, flat, dull, blank.

850. Taste. [Good taste.]**—N.** taste; good −, refined −, cultivated- taste; delicacy, refinement, fine feeling, gust, *gusto*, tact, *finesse*; nicety etc. (*discrimination*) 465; polish, elegance, grace.

virtu; dilettanteism, virtuosity; fine art; cul-ture, -ivation.

[Science of taste] esthetics.

man of -taste etc.; *connoisseur*, judge, critic, *conoscente, virtuoso, amateur, dilettante*, Aristarchus, Corinthian, *arbiter elegantarum*, stagirite, euphemist.

'caviar to the general.'

V. appreciate, judge, criticize, discriminate etc. 465.

Adj. in good taste; tasteful, tasty; unaffected, pure, chaste, classical, attic; cultivated, refined; dainty; esthetic, artistic; elegant etc. 578; euphemistic.

to one's -taste, − mind; after one's fancy; *comme il faut*; *tiré à quatre épingles*.

Adv. elegantly etc. *adj.*

Phr. *nihil tetigit quod non ornavit.*

851. Vulgarity. [Bad taste.]**—N.** vulgar-ity, -ism; barbar-, Vandal-, Gothic-ism; *mauvais goût*, bad taste; Babbittry; *gaucherie*, awkwardness, want of tact; ill-breeding etc. (*discourtesy*) 895; ungentlemanly behavior.

coarseness etc. *adj.*; indecorum, misbehavior.

low-, homeli-ness; low life, *mauvais ton*, rusticity; boorishness etc. *adj.*; brutality; rowdy-, ruffian-, blackguard-ism; ribaldry; slang etc. (*neology*) 563.

bad joke, *mauvaise plaisanterie*.

[Excell of ornament] gaudi-, tawdri-ness; false ornament; finery, frippery, trickery, tinsel, gewgaw, *clinquant*.

rough diamond, tomboy, hoyden, cub, unlicked cub; clown etc. (*commonalty*) 876; Hun, Goth, Vandal, Boeotian; vulgarian; snob, cad, bounder, gent; *parvenu* etc. 876; frump, dowdy; slattern etc. 653.

V. be -vulgar etc. *adj.*; misbehave; talk −, smell of the- shop.

Adj. in bad taste, vulgar, unrefined, gutter.

coarse, indecorus, ribald, gross; unseemly, unbeseeming, unpresentable; *contra bonos mores*; ungraceful etc. (*ugly*) 846.

dowdy, slovenly etc. (*dirty*) 653; ungenteel, shabby genteel; low etc. (*plebeian*) 876;uncourtly; uncivil etc. (*discourteous*) 895; ill-bred, -mannered; underbred; ungentleman-ly, -like; unladylike, unfeminine; wild, − as an unbacked colt.

unkempt, uncombed, untamed, unlicked, unpolished, uncouth, plebeian; incondite; heavy, rude, awkward; home-ly, -spun, -bred; provincial, hick, countrified, rustic, uncultivated, freshwater; boorish, clownish; savage, brutish, blackguard, rowdy, snobbish; barbar-ous, -ic; Gothic, unclassical, doggerel, heathenish, tramontane, outlandish; Bohemian.

obsolete etc. (*antiquated*) 124; unfashionable, old-fashioned, out of date; new-fangled etc. (*unfamiliar*) 83; fantastic, odd etc. (*ridiculous*) 853.

particular; affected etc. 855; meretricious; extravagant, monstrous, horrid; shocking etc. (*painful*) 830.

gaudy, tawdry, bedizened, tricked out, gingerbread; obtrusive, flaunting, loud, flashy, garish, showy.

852. Fashion.—N. fashion, style, *ton, bon ton*, society; good −, polite- society; drawing room, civilized life, civilization, town, *beau monde*, high life, court; world; fashionable −, gay- world; Vanity Fair; show etc. (*ostentation*) 822.

manners, breeding etc. (*politeness*) 894; air, demeanor etc. (*appearance*) 448; *savoir faire*; gentlemanliness, gentility, decorum, pròpriety, *bienséance*; conventions −, dictates- of society; Mrs. Grundy; convention, -ality; punctilio; form, -ality; etiquette, point of etiquette; custom etc. 613; mode, vogue, style, go; rage etc. (*desire*) 865; prevailing taste, *dernier cri*, dress etc. 225.

man −, woman- of -fashion, − the world; height −, pink −, star −, glass −, leader- of fashion; *arbiter elegantiarum* etc. (*taste*) 850; upper ten thousand etc. (*nobility*) 875; *élite* etc. (*distinction*) 873.

V. be -fashionable etc. *adj.*, − the rage etc. *n.*; have a run, pass current.

follow −, conform to −, fall in with- the fashion etc. *n.*; go with the stream etc. (*conform*) 82; *savoir -vivre, − faire*; keep up appearances, behave oneself.

set the −, bring into- fashion; give a tone to −, cut a figure in- society, rub shoulders with nobility, keep one's carriage.

Adj. fashionable; in -fashion etc. *n.*; *à la mode, comme il faut*; admitted −, admissible- in -society etc. *n.*; presentable, decorous, punctilious, conventional etc. (*customary*) 613; genteel; well-bred, -mannered, -behaved, -spoken; gentleman-like, -ly; ladylike; civil, polite etc. (*courteous*) 894.

polished, refined, thoroughbred, courtly; *distingué*, aristocratic, unembarrassed, poised, *dégagé*; ja-, jau-nty; dashing, fast, showy, high toned, toney.

modish, stylish, in the latest style, *recherché*; new-fangled etc. (*unfamiliàr*) 83.

'in -court, − full, − evening- dress; *en grande tenue* etc. (*ornament*) 847.

Adv. fashionably etc. *adj.*; for fashion's sake.

853. Ridiculousness.—N. ridiculousness etc. *adj.*; comical-, odd-ity etc. *adj.*; extravagance, drollery.

farce, comedy; burlesque etc. (*ridicule*) 856; buffoonery etc. (*fun*) 840; frippery; doggerel verses; Irish bull, Hibernianism, Hibernicism; Spoonerism; absurdity etc. 497; bombast etc. (*unmeaning*) 517; anticlimax, bathos; monstrosity etc. (*unconformity*) 83; laughing stock etc. 857.

V. be -ridiculous etc. *adj.*; pass from the sublime to the ridiculous; make one laugh; play the fool, make a fool of oneself, commit an absurdity.

play a joke on, make a -fool of, − sucker of, − monkey of.

Adj. ridiculous, ludicrous; comic, -al; droll, funny, laughable, *pour rire*, grotesque, farcical, odd; whimsical, − as a dancing bear; fanciful, fantastic, queer, rum, quizzical, waggish, quaint, *bizarre*; eccentric etc. (*unconformable*) 83; strange, outlandish, out of the way, *baroque*, *rocaille*, rococo; awkward etc. (*ugly*) 846.

absurd, extravagant, *outré*, monstrous, preposterous, bombastic, inflated, stilted, burlesque, mock heroic.

drollish; serio-, tragic-comic; gimcrack, contemptible etc. (*unimportant*) 643; doggerel; ironical etc. (*derisive*) 856; risible.

Phr. *'risum teneatis amici?' rideret Heraclitus.*

854. Fop.—N. fop, fine gentleman; swell; dand-y, -iprat; exquisite, coxcomb, toff, beau, macaroni, blade, blood, buck, man about town, fast man; fribble, jemmy, spark, popinjay, puppy, prig, *petit maître*; jacka-napes, -dandy; man milliner; Jemmy Jessamy, carpet-knight, masher, Dundreary, Johnnie, dude.

belle, fine lady, *coquette*, flirt.

855. Affectation.—N. affectation; affectedness etc. *adj.*; acting a part etc. *v.*; pretence etc. (*falsehood*) 544; (*ostentation*) 882; boasting etc. 884.

charlatanism, quakery, shallow profundity, humbug, pretension, airs, pedantry, purism, precisianism, euphuism, prunes and prisms; teratology etc. (*altiloquence*) 577.

mannerism, *simagrée*, grimace.

conceit, foppery, dandyism, man millinery, coxcombry, puppyism.

stiffness, formality, buckram; prudery, demureness, coquetry, mock modesty, *minauderie*, sentimentalism; *mauvaise honte*, false shame.

affector, performer, actor; pedant, pedagogue, *doctrinaire*, purist, euphuist, mannerist; shoneen; *grimacier*; lump of affectation, *précieuse ridicule*, *bas bleu*, blue stocking, poetaster; prig, hypocrite; charlatan etc. (*deceiver*) 548; *petit maître* etc. (*fop*) 854; flatterer etc. 935; *coquette*, prude, puritan; precisian, formalist.

V. affect, act a part, put on; give oneself airs etc. (*arrogance*) 885; boast etc. 884; coquet; simper, mince, attitudinize, strike a pose, pose; flirt a fan; over-act, -play, -do.

Adj. affected, full of affectation, pretentious, pedantic, stilted, stagey, theatrical, big-sounding, *ad captandum*, canting, insincere.

not natural, unnatural; self-conscious; *maniéré*; artificial; over-wrought, -done, -acted; euphuistic etc. 577.

stiff, starch, formal, prim, smug, demure, *tiré à*. quatre *épingles*, quakerish, puritanical, prudish, pragmatical, priggish, conceited, coxcomical, foppish, dandified; fini-cal, -kin, -cky, mincing, simpering, namby-pamby, sentimental, languishing.

856. Ridicule.—N. ridicule, derision; sardonic -smile, − grin; irrision; snigger; scoffing etc. (*disrespect*) 929; mockery, quiz, banter, irony, *persiflage*, raillery, chaff, *badinage*; quizzing etc. *v.*

squib, satire, skit, quip, quib, grin.

parody, burlesque, travesty; farce etc. (*drama*) 599; caricature, take-off.

buffoonery etc. (*fun*) 840; practical joke, horse-play.

V. ridicule, deride; laugh at, grin at, smile at; snigger; laugh in one's sleeve; banter, rally, chaff, joke, twit, quiz, poke fun at, jolly, roast, rag; fleer; play −, play tricks- upon; fool, − to the top of one's bent; show up.

satirize, parody, caricature, burlesque, travesty.

turn into ridicule; make merry with; make -fun, − game, − a fool, − an April fool- of; rally; scoff etc. (*disrespect*) 929.

raise a laugh etc. (*amuse*) 840; play the fool, make a fool of oneself.

be ridiculous etc. 853.

Adj. deris-ory, -ive; mock; sarcastic, ironical, quizzical, burlesque, Hudibrastic; scurrilous etc. (*disrespectful*) 929.

Adv. in -ridicule etc. *n.*

857. Laughing-stock. [Object and cause of ridicule.]**—N.** laughing-, jesting-, gazing-stock; butt, game, fair game; April fool etc. (*dupe*) 547.

original, oddity; queer −, odd- fish; quiz, square toes; old −, fogey or fogy..

monkey; buffoon etc. (*jester*) 844; pantomimist etc. (*actor*) 599.

jest etc. (*wit*) 842.

858. Hope.—N. hope, -s; desire etc. 865; fervent hope, sanguine expectation, trust, confidence, reliance; faith etc. (*belief*) 484; affiance, assurance; secur-eness, -ity; reassurance.

good -omen, − auspices; promise; well-grounded hopes; good −, bright- prospect; clear sky.

as-, pre-sumption; anticipation etc. (*expectation*) 507.

hopefulness, buoyancy, optimism, enthusiasm, heart of grace, aspiration; optimist, utop-ian, -ist; Pollyanna.

castles in the air, *châteaux en Espagne*, hope chest, *le pot au lait*, Utopia, millennium; day −, golden- dream; dream of Alnaschar; airy hopes, fool's paradise; *mirage* etc. (*fallacies of vision*) 443; fond hope.

beam −, ray −, gleam −, glimmer −, dawn −, flash −, star- of hope; cheer; bit of blue sky,

silver lining of the cloud, bottom of Pandora's box, balm in Gilead.

anchor, sheet-anchor, main-stay; staff etc. (*support*) 215; heaven etc. 981.

V. hope, trust, confide, rely on, put one's trust in, lean upon; pin one's -hope, — faith- upon etc. (*believe*) 484.

feel —, entertain —, harbor —, indulge —, cherish —, feed —, foster —, nourish —, encourage —, cling to —, live in- hope etc. *n.*; see land; feel —, rest- -assured, — confident etc. *adj.*

presume; promise oneself; expect etc. (*look forward to*) 507.

hope for etc. (*desire*) 865; anticipate.

be -hopeful etc. *adj.*; look on the bright side of, view on the sunny side, make the best of it, hope for the best; put -a good, — a bold, — the best-face upon; keep one's spirits up; take heart, — of grace; be of good -heart, — cheer; flatter oneself, lay the flattering unction to one's soul.

catch at a straw, hope against hope, count one's chickens before they are hatched.

give —, inspire —, raise —, hold out- hope etc. *n.*; raise expectations; encourage, hearten, cheer, assure, reassure, buoy up, embolden; promise, bid fair, augur well, be in a fair way, look up, flatter, tell a flattering tale.

Adj. hoping etc. *v.*; in -hopes etc. *n.*; hopeful, confident; secure etc. (*certain*) 484; sanguine, in good heart, buoyed up, buoyant, elated, flushed, exultant, enthusiastic; utopian.

unsus-pecting, -picious; fearless, free —, exempt from- -fear, — suspicion, — distrust, — despair; undespairing, self-reliant.

probable, on the high road to; within sight of -shore, — land; promising, propitious; of —, full of-promise; of good omen; auspicious, *de bon augure*; reassuring; encouraging, cheering, inspiriting, looking up, bright, roseate, *couleur de rose*, rose-colored.

Adv. hopefully etc. *adj.*

Phr. *nil desperandum*; never say die, *dum spiro spero, latet scintillula forsan*, all is for the best, *spero meliora*; the wish being father to the thought; 'hope told a flattering tale;' *rusticus expectat dum defluat amnis.*

859. Hopelessness. [Absence, want, or loss of hope.]—**N.** hopelessness etc. *adj.*; despair, desperation; despondency etc. (*dejection*) 837; pessimism.

hope deferred, dashed hopes; vain expectation etc. (*disappointment*) 509.

airy hopes etc. 858; forlorn hope; bad -job, — business; *enfant perdu*; gloomy —, black spots in the- horizon; slough of Despond, cave of Despair. Job's comforter; bird of -bad, — ill-omen.

V. despair; lose —, give up —, abandon —, relinquish- -all hope, — the hope of; give -up, — over; yield to despair; falter; despond etc. (*be dejected*) 837; *jeter le manche après la cognée.*

inspire —, drive to- despair etc. *n.*; disconcert; dash —, crush —, shatter —, destroy- one's hopes; hope against hope.

Adj. hopeless, desperate, despairing, in despair, *au désespoir*, forlorn; inconsolable etc. (*dejected*) 837; broken-hearted.

out of the question, not to be thought of; im-practicable etc. 471; past -hope, — cure, — mending, — recall; at one's last gasp etc. (*death*) 360; given -up, — over.

incurable, cureless, immedicable, remediless, beyond remedy; incorrigible; irre-parable, -mediable, -coverable, -versible, -trievable, -claimable, -deemable, -vocable; ruined, undone; immitigable.

unpromising, unpropitious; inauspicious, ill-omened, threatening, clouded over, lowering, ominous.

Phr. *'lasciate ogni speranza voi ch' entrate;'* its days are numbered; the worst come to the worst.

860. Fear.—N. fear, timidity, diffidence, want of confidence; apprehensive-, fearful-ness etc. *adj.*; solicitude, anxiety, care, apprehension, misgiving; mistrust etc. (*doubt*) 485; suspicion, qualm; hesitation etc. (*irresolution*) 605.

nervous-, restless-ness etc. *adj.*; in-, dis-quietude; flutter, trepidation, fear and trembling, perturbation, tremor, quivering, shaking, trembling, throbbing heart, palpitation, ague fit, cold sweat; abject fear etc. (*cowardice*) 862; mortal funk, heart-sinking, despondency; despair etc. 859.

fright; affright, -ment; alarm, pavor, dread, awe, terror, horror, dismay, consternation, panic, scare, stampede [of horses].

intimidation, terrorism, reign of terror.

[Object of fear] bug-bear, -aboo; scarecrow; hobgoblin etc. (*demon*) 980; daymare, nightmare, Gorgon, Medusa, mormo, ogre, Hurlothrumbo, raw head and bloody bones, fee faw fum, *bête noire, enfant terrible.*

alarmist etc. (*coward*) 862.

V. fear, stand in awe of; be -afraid etc. *adj.*; have -qualms etc. *n.*; apprehend, sit upon thorns, eye askance; distrust etc. (*disbelieve*) 485.

hesitate etc. (*be irresolute*) 605; falter, funk, cower, crouch; skulk etc. (*cowardice*) 862; let 'I dare not' wait upon 'I would;' take -fright, — alarm; start, wince, flinch, shy, shrink; fly etc. (*avoid*) 623.

tremble, shake; shiver, — in one's shoes; shudder, flutter; shake —, tremble- -like an aspen leaf, — all over; quake, quaver, quiver, quail; get the wind up.

grow —, turn- pale; blench, stand aghast; not dare to say one's soul is one's own.

inspire —, excite- -fear, — awe; raise apprehensions; give —, raise —, sound- an alarm; alarm, startle, scare, cry 'wolf,' disquiet, dismay; fright, -en; affright, terrify; astound; frighten from one's propriety; frighten out of one's -wits, — senses, — seven senses; awe; strike -all of a heap, — an awe into, — terror; harrow up the soul, appal, unman, petrify, horrify.

make one's -flesh creep, — hair stand on end, -- blood run cold, — teeth chatter; chill one's spine; take away —, stop- one's breath; make one -tremble etc.

haunt, obsess, beset; prey —, weigh- on the mind.

put in -fear, — bodily fear; terrorize, intimidate, cow, daunt, over-awe, abash, deter, discourage; browbeat, bully; threaten etc. 909.

Adj. fearing etc. *v.*; frightened etc. *v.*; in -fear, — a fright etc. *n.*; haunted with the -fear etc. *n.*- of.

afraid, fearful; tim-id, -orous; nervous, diffident, coy, faint-hearted, tremulous, shaky, afraid of one's shadow, apprehensive, restless, fidgety; more frightened than hurt.

aghast; awe-, horror-, terror-, panic- -struck, -stricken; frightened to death, white as a sheet; pale, — as -death, — ashes, — a ghost; breathless, in hysterics.

inspiring fear etc. *v.*; alarming; formidable, redoubtable; perilous etc. (*danger*) 665; portentous; fear-ful, -some; dread, -ful; fell; dire, -ful; shocking; terri-ble, -fic; tremendous; horri-d, -ble, -fic; ghastly; awful, awe-inspiring, eerie, weird; revolting etc. (*painful*) 830.

Adv. *in terrorem.*

Int. 'angels and ministers of grace defend us!'

Phr. *ante tubam trepidat; horresco referens,* one's heart failing one, *obstupui steteruntque comae et vox faucibus haesit.*

861. Courage. [Absence of fear.]—**N.** courage, bravery, valor; resolute-, bold-ness etc. *adj.*; spirit, daring, gallantry, intrepidity; contempt —, defiance- of danger; derring-do; audacity; rashness etc. 863; dash; defiance etc. 715; confidence, self-reliance.

man-liness, -hood; nerve, pluck, mettle, game; heart, — of grace; spunk, gameness, grit, face, virtue, hardihood, fortitude; firmness etc. (*stability*) 150; heart of oak; bottom, backbone etc. (*perseverance*) 604*a.*

resolution etc. (*determination*) 604; tenacity, bull-dog courage.

prowess, heroism, chivalry.

exploit, feat, achievement; heroic -deed, — act; bold stroke.

man, — of mettle; hero, demigod, paladin, heroine, Amazon, Hector, Joan of Arc; lion, tiger, panther, bulldog; game-, fighting-cock; bully, fire-eater etc. 863; dare-devil.

V. be -courageous etc. *adj.*; dare, venture, make bold; face —, front —, affront —, confront —, brave —, defy —, despise —, mock- danger; look in the face; look -full, — boldly, — danger- in the face; face; meet, — in front; brave, beard; defy etc. 715.

take —, muster —, summon up —, pluck up-courage; nerve oneself, take heart; take —, pluck up- heart of grace; hold up one's head, screw one's courage to the sticking place; come -to, — up to- the scratch; stand, — to one's guns, — fire, — against; bear up — against; hold out etc. (*persevere*) 604*a.*

put a bold face upon; show —, present- a bold front, face the music; show fight.

bell the cat, take the bull by the horns, beard the lion in his den, march up to the cannon's mouth, go through fire and water, run the gauntlet, go over the top.

give —, infuse —, inspire- courage; reassure, encourage, embolden, inspirit, cheer, hearten, nerve, put upon one's mettle, rally, raise a rallying cry; pat on the back, make a man of, keep in countenance.

Adj. courageous, brave, val-iant, -orous; gallant, intrepid; spirit-ed, -ful; high-spirited, -mettled; mettlesome, game, plucky; man-ly, -ful; resolute; stout, -hearted; iron-, lion-hearted; heart of oak; Penthesilean.

bold, — spirited; daring, audacious; fear-, daunt-, dread-, awe-less; un-daunted, -appalled, -dismayed, -awed, -blenched, -abashed, -alarmed, -flinching, -shrinking, -blenching; apprehensive; confident, self-reliant; bold as -a lion, — brass.

enterprising, adventurous; ventur-ous, -esome; dashing, chivalrous; soldierly etc. (*warlike*) 722; heroic.

fierce, savage; pugnacious etc. (*bellicose*) 720.

strong-minded, hardy, doughty; firm etc. (*stable*) 150; determined etc. (*resolved*) 604; dogged, indomitable etc. (*persevering*) 604*a.*

up to, — the scratch; upon one's mettle; reassured etc. *v.*; unfeared, undreaded.

Phr. one's blood being up.

862. Cowardice. [Excess of fear.]—**N.** cowardice, pusillanimity; cowardliness etc. *adj.*; timidity, effeminacy.

poltroonery, baseness; dastard-ness, -y; abject fear, funk; Dutch courage; fear etc. 860; white feather, faint heart.

coward, poltroon, dastard, sneak, recreant; shy —, dunghill- cock; coistril, milksop, white-liver, nidget, cur, craven, one that cannot say 'Boo' to a goose; Bob Acres, Jerry Sneak.

alarm-, terror-, pessim-ist; runagate etc. (*fugitive*) 623; shirker.

V. quail etc. (*fear*) 860; be -cowardly etc. *adj.*, — a coward etc. *n.*; funk; cower, skulk, sneak; flinch, shy, fight shy, slink, turn tail; run away etc. (*avoid*) 623; show the white feather, have cold feet, show a yellow streak.

Adj. coward, -ly; fearful, shy; tim-id, -orous; skittish; poor-spirited, spirit-less, soft, effeminate.

weak-minded; infirm of purpose etc. 605; weak-, faint-, chicken-, lily-, pigeon-hearted; yellow; white-, lily-, milk-livered; milksop, smock-faced; unable to say 'Boo' to a goose.

dastard, -ly; base, craven, sneaking, dunghill, recreant; unwar-, unsoldier-like.

'in face a lion but in heart a deer.'

unmanned; frightened etc. 860.

Int. *sauve qui peut!* devil take the hindmost!

Adv. in fear and trembling, in fear of one's life, in a blue funk.

Phr. *ante tubam trepidat,* one's courage oozing out.

863. Rashness.—**N.** rashness etc. *adj.*; temerity, want of caution, imprudence, indiscretion; over-confidence, presumption, audacity.

precipit-ancy, -ation; impetuosity; levity; foolhardi-hood, -ness; heed-, thought-lessness etc. (*inattention*) 458; carelessness etc. (*neglect*) 460; desperation; Quixotism, knight-errantry; fire-eating.

gam-ing, -bling; blind bargain, leap in the dark, fool's paradise; too many eggs in one basket.

desperado, rashling, mad-cap, dare-devil, Hotspur, fire-eater, bully, *bravo,* Hector, scapegrace, *enfant perdu;* Don Quixote, knight-errant, Icarus; adventurer; gam-bler, -ester; dynamitard.

V. be -rash etc. *adj.*; stick at nothing, play a desperate game; run into danger etc. 665; play with -fire, — edge tools.

carry too much sail, sail too near the wind, ride at single anchor, go out of one's depth.

take a leap in the dark, buy a pig in a poke.

donner tête baissée; knock one's head against a wall etc. (*be unskilful*) 699; rush on destruction; kick against the pricks, tempt Providence, go on a forlorn hope.

count one's chickens before they are hatched; reckon without one's host; catch at straws; trust to –, lean on- a broken reed.

Adj. rash, incautious, indiscreet, injudicious; imprudent, improvident, temerarious; uncalculating; heedless; careless etc. (*neglectful*) 460; without ballast, heels over head; giddy etc. (*inattentive*) 458; wanton, reckless, wild, madcap; desperate, devil-may-care.

hot-blooded, -headed, -brained; head-long, - strong; break-neck; fool-hardy; harebrained; precipitate, impulsive.

over-confident, -weening; ventur-esome, -ous; adventurous, Quixotic; fire-eating, cavalier; free-and-easy.

off one's guard etc. (*inexpectant*) 508.

Adv. post haste, *à corps perdu*, hand over head, *tête baissée*, head- foremost; happen what may.

Phr. neck or nothing, the devil being in one.

864. Caution.—N. caution; cautiousness etc. *adj.*; discretion, prudence, cautel, heed, circumspection, calculation, deliberation; safety first.

foresight etc. 510; vigilance etc. 459; warning etc. 668.

coolness etc. *adj.*; self-possession, -command; presence of mind, *sang froid*; well-regulated mind; worldly wisdom, Fabian policy.

V. be -cautious etc. *adj.*; take -care, – heed, – good care; have a care; mind, – what one is about; be on one's guard etc. (*keep watch*) 459; make assurance double sure; ca' canny.

bespeak etc. (*be early*) 132.

think twice, look before one leaps, keep one's weather eye open, count the cost, look to the main chance, cut one's coat according to one's cloth; feel one's -ground, – way; see how the land lies etc. (*foresight*) 510; wait to see how the cat jumps; bridle one's tongue; *reculer pour mieux sauter* etc. (*prepare*) 673; let well alone, let sleeping dogs lie, *ne pas réveiller le chat qui dort.*

keep out of -harm's way, – troubled waters; keep at a respectful distance, stand aloof; keep –, be- on the safe side.

husband one's resources etc. 636.

caution etc. (*warn*) 668.

Adj. cautious, wary, guarded; on one's guard etc. (*watchful*) 459; *cavendo tutus*; *in medio tutissimus.*

care-, heed-ful; cautelous, stealthy, chary, shy of, circumspect, prudent, canny, safe, non-committal, discreet, politic; sure-footed etc. (*skilful*) 698.

unenterprising, unadventurous, cool, steady, self-possessed; over-cautious.

suspicious, leery, vigilant.

Adv. cautiously, gingerly etc. *adj.*

Int. have a care! look out! *cave canem!*

Phr. *timeo Danaos*; *festina lente.*

865. Desire.—N. desire, wish, fancy, fantasy; want, need, exigency.

mind, inclination, leaning, bent, *animus*, partiality, *penchant*, predilection; propensity etc. 820; willingness etc. 602; liking, love, fondness, relish.

longing, hankering; solicitude, anxiety; yearning, coveting; aspiration, ambition, vaulting ambition; eagerness, zeal, ardor, *empressement*, breathless impatience, over-anxiety; solicitude, impetuosity etc. 825.

appet-ite, -ition, -ence, -ency; sharp appetite, keenness, hunger, stomach, twist; thirst, -iness; drouth, mouth-watering; itch, -ing; prurience, *cacoëthes*, cupidity, lust, concupiscence.

edge of -appetite, – hunger; torment of Tantalus; sweet –, lickerish- tooth; itching palm; longing –, wistful –, sheep's-eye.

avidity; greed, -iness; covetous-, ravenous-ness etc. *adj.*; grasping, craving, canine appetite, rapacity; voracity etc. (*gluttony*) 957.

passion, rage, *furore*, mania, *manie*; inextinguishable desire; dips-, klept-, mon-omania.

[Person desiring] desirer, lover, *amateur*, votary, devotee, aspirant, solicitant, candidate; cormorant etc. 957; sycophant.

[Object of desire] *desideratum*; want etc. (*requirement*) 630; 'consumation devoutly to be wished;' attraction, magnet, allurement, fancy, temptation, seduction, lure, fascination, *prestige*, height of one's ambition, idol; whim, -sey; maggot; hobby, -horse.

Fortunatus' cap, wishing cap, love potion.

V. desire; wish, – for; be -desirous etc. *adj.*; have a -longing etc. *n.*; hope etc. 858.

care for, affect, like, list; take to, cling to, take a fancy to; fancy; prefer etc. (*choose*) 609.

have -an eye, – a mind- to; find it in one's heart etc. (*be willing*) 602; have a fancy for, set one's eyes upon; cast a sheep's eye –, look sweet- upon; take into one's head, have a heart, be bent upon; set one's -cap at, – heart upon, – mind upon; covet.

want, miss, need, lack, desiderate, feel the want of; would fain -have, – do; would be glad of.

be -hungry etc. *adj.*; have a good appetite, play a good knife and fork; hunger –, thirst –, crave –, lust –, itch –, hanker –, run mad- after; raven –, itch- for; burn to.

desiderate; sigh –, cry –, gape –, gasp –, pine –, pant –, languish –, yearn –, long –, be on thorns –, hope- for; aspire after; catch at, grasp at, jump at.

woo, court, solicit; fish –, spell –, whistle –, put up- for; ogle.

cause –, create –, raise –, excite –, provoke- desire; whet the appetite; appetize, titillate, allure, attract, take one's fancy, tempt; hold out - temptation, – allurement; tantalize, make one's mouth water, *faire venir l'eau à la bouche.*

gratify desire etc. (*give pleasure*) 829.

Adj. desirous; desiring etc. *v.*; orectic, appetitive; inclined etc. (*willing*) 602; partial to; fain, wishful, optative; anxious, wistful, curious; at a loss for, sedulous, solicitous.

craving, hungry, sharp-set, peckish, ravening, with an empty stomach, esurient, lickerish, thirsty, athirst, parched with thirst, pinched with hunger, famished, dry, drouthy; hungry as a -hunter, – hawk, – horse, – church mouse.

greedy, – as a hog; over-eager, voracious; ravenous, – as a wolf; open-mouthed, covetous, rapacious, grasping, extortionate, exacting, sordid,

alieni appetens; insati-able, -ate; unquenchable, quenchless; omnivorous.

unsatisfied, unsated, unslaked.

eager, avid, keen; burning, fervent, ardent; agog; all agog; breathless; impatient etc. (*impetuous*) 825; bent −, intent −, set- -on, − upon; mad after, *enragé*, rabid, dying for, devoured by desire.

aspiring, ambitious, vaulting, sky-aspiring.

desirable; popular; desired etc. *v.*; in demand; pleasing etc. (*giving pleasure*) 829; appeti-zing, -ble; tantalizing.

Adv. wistfully etc. *adj.*; fain.

Int. would -that, − it were! O for! *esto perpetua!* if only!

Phr. the wish being the father to the thought; *sua cuique voluptas*; *hoc erat in votis*, the mouth watering, the fingers itching; *aut Caesar aut nullus*.

866. Indifference.—**N.** indifference, neutrality; coldness etc. *adj.*; unconcern, *insouciance, nonchalance*; want of -interest, − earnestness; anorexy, inappetency; apathy etc. (*insensibility*) 823; supineness etc. (*inactivity*) 683; disdain etc. 930; recklessness etc. 863; inattention etc. 458.

V. be -indifferent etc. *adj.*; stand neuter; take no interest in etc. (*insensibility*) 823; have no -desire etc. 865, − taste, − relish- for; not care for; care nothing -for, − about; not care a -straw etc. (*unimportance*) 643 -about, − for; not mind.

set at naught etc. (*make light of*) 483; spurn etc. (*disdain*) 930.

Adj. indifferent, cold, frigid, lukewarm; cool, − as a cucumber; unconcerned, *insouciant*, phlegmatic, *pococurante*, easy-going, devil-may-care, careless, listless, lackadaisical, feckless; half-hearted; un-ambitious, -aspiring, -desirous, -solicitous, -attracted.

un-attractive, -alluring, -desired, -desirable, - cared for, -wished, -valued, all one to.

insipid etc. 391; vain.

Adv. for aught one cares.

Int. never mind.

867. Dislike.—**N.** dis-like, -taste, -relish, - inclination, -placency.

reluctance; backwardness etc. (*unwillingness*) 603.

repugnance, disgust, queasiness, turn, nausea, loathing; avers-eness, -ation, -ion; abomination, antipathy, abhorrence, horror; mortal −, rooted-antipathy, − horror; hatred, detestation; hate etc. 898; animosity etc. 900; hydrophobia.

sickener; gall and wormwood etc. (*unsavory*) 395; shuddering, cold sweat.

V. dis-, mis-like, -relish; mind, object to; have rather not, not care for; have −, conceive −, entertain −, take- -a dislike, − an aversion- to; have no -taste, − stomach- for.

shun, avoid etc. 623; eschew; withdraw −, shrink −, recoil- from; not be able to -bear, − abide, − endure; shrug the shoulders at, shudder at, turn up the nose at, look askance at; make a - mouth, − wry face, − grimace; make faces.

loathe, nauseate, abominate, detest, abhor; hate etc. 898; take amiss etc. 900; have enough of etc. (*be satiated*) 869.

cause −, excite- dislike; disincline, repel, sicken; make −, render- sick; turn one's stomach, nauseate, wamble, disgust, shock, stink in the nostrils; go against the -grain, − stomach; stick in the throat; make one's blood run cold etc. (*give pain*) 830; pall.

Adj. disliking etc. *v.*; averse to, loth, adverse; shy of, sick of, out of conceit with; disinclined; heart-, dog-sick; queasy.

disliked etc. *v.*; uncared for, unpopular; out of favor; repulsive, repugnant, repellent; abhorrent, insufferable, fulsome, nauseous; loath-some, -ful; offensive; disgusting etc. *v.*; disagreeable etc. (*painful*) 830; unsavory etc. 395.

Adv. *usque ad nauseam.*

Int. faugh! foh! ugh!

868. Fastidiousness.—**N.** fastidiousness etc. *adj.*; nicety, meticulosity, hypercriticism, difficulty in being pleased, *friandise*, epicurism, *omnia suspendens naso*.

discrimination, discernment, good taste, perspicacity.

epicure, gourmet.

[Excess of delicacy] prudery, prudishness, primness.

V. be -fastidious etc. *adj.*; split hairs, discriminate, have a sweet tooth.

mince the matter; turn up one's nose at etc. (*disdain*) 930; look a gift horse in the mouth, see spots on the sun.

Adj. fastidious, meticulous, exacting, nice, delicate, *délicat*, finical, finicky, difficult, dainty, lickerish, squeamish, thin-skinned; s-, queasy; hard −, difficult- to please; querulous, particular, over-particular, straitlaced, prudish, prim, scrupulous; censorious etc. 932; hypercritical, discriminating, discerning, perspicacious.

Phr. *noli me tangere.*

869. Satiety.—**N.** satiety, satisfaction, saturation, repletion, glut, surfeit; weariness etc. 841.

spoiled child; *enfant gâté*; too much of a good thing, *toujours perdrix*; *crambe repetita*.

V. sate, satiate, satisfy, saturate, cloy, quench, slake, pall, glut, gorge, surfeit; bore etc. (*weary*) 841; tire etc. (*fatigue*) 688; spoil.

have -enough of, − quite enough of, − one's fill, − too much of; be -satiated etc. *adj.*

Adj. satiated etc. *v.*; overgorged; *blasé*, used up, sick of, heart-sick.

Int. enough! hold! *eheu jam satis!*

870. Wonder.—**N.** wonder, marvel; astonish-, amaze-, wonder-, bewilder-ment; amazedness etc. *adj.*; admiration, awe; stup-or, -efaction; stound, fascination, sensation; surprise etc. (*inexpectation*) 508; cynosure.

note of admiration; thaumaturgy etc. (*sorcery*) 992.

V. wonder, marvel, admire; be -surprised etc. *adj.*; start; stare; open −, rub −, turn up- one's eyes; gloar; gape, open one's mouth, hold one's breath; look −, stand- -aghast, − agog; look blank

etc. (*disappointment*) 509; *tomber des nues*; not believe one's -eyes, – ears, – senses.

not be able to account for etc. (*unintelligible*) 519; not know whether one stands on one's head or one's heels.

surprise, astonish, amaze, astound; dumbfound, -er; startle, dazzle; strike, – with -wonder, – awe; electrify; stun, stupefy, petrify, confound, bewilder, flabbergast; stagger, throw on one's beam ends, fascinate, turn the head, take away one's breath, strike dumb; make one's -hair stand on end, – tongue cleave to the roof of one's mouth; make one stare.

take by surprise etc. (*be unexpected*) 508.

be -wonderful etc. *adj.*; beggar –, baffle-description; stagger belief.

Adj. surprised etc. *v.*; aghast, all agog, breathless, agape; open-mouthed; awe-, thunder-, moon-, planet-struck; spell-bound; lost in -amazement, – wonder, – astonishment; struck all of a heap, unable to believe one's senses, like a duck in thunder.

wonderful, wondrous; surprising etc. *v.*; unexpected etc. 508; unheard of; mysterious etc. (*inexplicable*) 519; miraculous; *foudroyant*.

in-describable, -expressible, -effable; un-utterable, -speakable.

monstrous, prodigious, stupendous, marvelous; in-conceivable, -credible; in-, un-imaginable; strange etc. (*uncommon*) 83; passing strange.

striking etc. *v.*; over-whelming; wonder-working.

Adv. wonderfully etc. *adj.*; fearfully; for a –, in the name of- wonder; strange to say; *mirabile -dictu*, – visu; to one's great surprise.

with -wonder etc. *n.*, – gaping mouth, – open eyes, – upturned eyes; eyes starting out of one's head.

Int. lo, – and behold! O! hey-day! halloo! what! indeed! really! surely! humph! hem! good -lack, – heavens, – gracious! – lord! by jove! gad so! well a day! dear me! only think! lack-a-daisy! my -stars, – goodness! gracious goodness! goodness gracious! mercy on us! heavens and earth! God bless me! bless -us, – my heart! odzookens! *O gemini!* adzooks! hoity-toity! strong! Heaven save –, bless-the mark! can such things be! zounds! 'sdeath! what -on earth, – in the world! who would have thought it! etc. (*inexpectation*) 508; fancy! did you ever? you don't say so! what do you say to that! how now! where am I? well I'm blowed! etc.

Phr. *vox faucibus haesit*; one's hair standing on end.

871. Expectance. [Absence of wonder.]—**N.** expectan-ce, -cy etc. (*expectation*) 507; calmness, composure, tranquillity, serenity, coolness, imperturbability etc. 826.

nine days' wonder.

V. expect etc. 507; not -be surprised, – wonder etc. 870; *nil admirari*, make nothing of.

Adj. expecting etc. *v.*; unamazed, astonished at nothing; *blasé* etc. (*weary*) 841; unimaginative, calm, serene, imperturbable etc. 826; expected etc. *v.*; foreseen.

common, ordinary etc. (*habitual*) 613.

Int. no wonder; of course; why not?

872. Prodigy.—**N.** prodigy, phenomenon; wonder, -ment; genius, marvel, miracle; freak, monster etc. (*unconformity*) 83; curiosity, lion, infant prodigy, sight, spectacle; *jeu* –, *coup- de théâtre*; gazing-stock; sign; portent etc. 512.

bursting of a -shell, – bomb; volcanic eruption, peal of thunder; thunder-clap, -bolt.

what no words can paint; wonders of the world; *annus mirabilis*; *dignus vindice nodus*.

873. Repute.—**N.** distinction, mark, name, figure; repute, reputation, character; good –, high-repute; note, notability, notoriety, *éclat*, 'the bubble reputation,' vogue, celebrity; fame, famousness; renown; populairty, *aura popularis*; esteem, approval, approbation etc. 931; credit, *succès d'estime*, prestige, talk of the town; name to conjure with.

glory, honor; luster etc. (*light*) 420; illustriouness etc. *adj.*

account, regard, respect; reputableness etc. *adj.*; respectability etc. (*probity*) 939; good -name, – report; fair name.

dignity; stateliness etc. *adj.*; solemnity, grandeur, splendor, nobility, majesty, sublimity.

rank, standing, brevet rank, precedence, *pas*, station, place, *status*; position, – in society; order, degree, *locus standi*, caste, condition.

greatness etc. *adj.*; eminence; height etc. 206; importance etc. 642; pre-, super-eminence; high mightiness, primacy; top of the -ladder, – tree.

elevation; ascent etc. 305; super-, ex-altation; dignification, aggrandizement.

dedication, consecration, enthronement, canonization, apotheosis, deification, celebration, enshrinement, glorification.

hero, man of mark, great card, celebrity, worthy, lion, *rara avis*, notability, somebody; man of rank etc. (*nobleman*) 875; pillar of the -state, – society, – church.

chief etc. (*master*) 745; first fiddle etc. (*proficient*) 700; scholar etc. 492; cynosure, mirror; flower, pink, pearl; paragon etc. (*perfection*) 650; choice and master spirits of the age; *élite*; star, sun, constellation, galaxy.

ornament, honor, feather in one's cap, halo, aureole, nimbus; halo –, blaze- of glory; blushing honors; laurels etc. (*trophy*) 733.

memory, posthumous fame, niche in the temple of fame; immor-tality, -tal name; *magni nominis umbra*.

V. be conscious of glory; be proud of etc. (*pride*) 878; exult etc. (*boast*) 884; be vain of etc. (*vanity*) 880.

be -distinguished etc. *adj.*; shine etc. (*light*) 420; shine forth, figure; make –, cut- a -figure, – dash, – splash.

rival, surpass; out-shine, -rival, -vie, -jump; emulate, vie with, eclipse; throw –, cast- into the shade; overshadow.

live, flourish, glitter, scintillate, flaunt; gain –, acquire- honor etc. *n.*; play first fiddle etc. (*be of importance*) 642; bear the -palm, – bell; lead the way; take -precedence, – the wall of; gain –, win--laurels, – spurs, – golden opinions etc. (*approbation*) 931; graduate, take one's degree, pass one's examination, win a -scholarship, – fellowship.

make -a, – some- -noise, – noise in the world; leave one's mark, exalt one's horn, star, have a run, be run after; enjoy popularity, come -into vogue, – to the front; raise one's head.

enthrone, signalize, immortalize, deify, exalt to the skies; hand one's name down to posterity.

consecrate; dedicate to, devote to; enshrine, inscribe, blazon, lionize, blow the trumpet, crown with laurel.

confer −, reflect- honor etc. *n.* on; shed a luster on; redound to one's honor, ennoble.

give −, do −, pay −, render- honor to; honor, accredit, pay regard to, dignify, glorify; sing praises to etc. (*approve*) 931; look up to; exalt, aggrandize, elevate, nobilitate.

Adj. distinguished, *distingué*, noted; of -note etc. *n.*; honored etc. *v.*; popular; fashionable etc. 852.

in good odor; in −, in high- favor; reput-, respect-, credit-able.

remarkable etc. (*important*) 642; notable, notorious; celebrated, renowned; in every one's mouth, talked of; fam-ous, -ed; far-famed; conspicuous, to the front; foremost; in the -front rank, − ascendant.

imperishable, deathless, immortal, never fading, *aere perennius*; time-honored.

illustrious, glorious, splendid, brilliant, radiant; bright etc. 420; full-blown; honorific.

eminent, prominent; high etc. 206; in the zenith; at the -head of, − top of the tree; peerless, of the first water; superior etc. 33; super-, pre-eminent.

great, dignified, proud, noble, honorable, worshipful, lordly, grand, stately, august, princely, imposing, solemn, transcendent, majestic, sacred, sublime, heaven-born, heroic, *sans peur et sans reproche*; sacrosanct.

Int. hail! all hail! *ave! viva! vive!* long life to! glory −, honor- be to!

Phr. one's name -being in every mouth, − living for ever; *sic itur ad astra, fama volat, aut Caesar aut nullus*; not to know him argues oneself unknown; none but himself could be his parallel, *palmam qui meruit ferat.*

874. Disrepute.—**N.** disrepute, discredit; ill-, bad- -repute, -name, -odor, -favor; disapprobation etc. 932; in-gloriousness, derogation; a-, debasement; abjectness etc. *adj.*; degradation, dedecoration; 'a long farewell to all one's greatness;' odium, obloquy, opprobrium, ignominy.

dishonor, disgrace, shame, humiliation; scandal, baseness, vileness; perfidy, turpitude etc. (*improbity*) 940; infamy.

tarnish, taint, defilement, pollution.

stain, blot, spot, blur, stigma, brand, reproach, imputation, slur.

crying −, burning- shame; *scandalum magnatum*, badge of infamy, blot in one's escutcheon; bend −, bar- sinister; champain, point champain; by- word of reproach; Ichabod.

argumentum ad verecundiam; sense of shame etc. 879.

V. be -inglorious etc. *adj.*; incur -disgrace etc. *n.*; have −, earn- a bad name; put −, wear- a halter round one's neck; disgrace −, expose-oneself.

play second fiddle; lose caste; pale one's ineffectual fire; recede into the shade; fall from one's high estate; keep in the background etc. (*modesty*) 881; be conscious of disgrace etc. (*humility*) 879; look -blue, − foolish, − like a fool; cut a -poor,

− sorry- figure; laugh on the wrong side of the mouth; make a sorry face, go away with a flea in one's ear, slink away.

cause -shame etc. *n.*; shame, disgrace, put to shame, dishonor; throw −, cast −, fling −, reflect- dishonor etc. *n.* upon; be a -reproach etc. *n.* to; derogate from.

tarnish, stain, blot, sully, taint; discredit, degrade, debase, defile; beggar; expel etc. (*punish*) 972.

impute shame to, brand, post, stigmatize, vilify, defame, slur, cast a slur upon, hold up to shame, send to Coventry; tread −,' trample- under foot; show up, drag through the mire, heap dirt upon; reprehend etc. 932.

bring low, put down, snub; take down a peg, − lower, − or two.

obscure, eclipse, outshine, take the shine out of; throw −, cast- into the shade; overshadow; leave −, put- in the background; push into a corner, put one's nose out of joint; put out, − of countenance.

upset, throw off one's center; discompose, disconcert; put to the blush etc. (*humble*) 879.

Adj. disgraced etc. *v.*; blown upon; shorn of -its beams, − one' glory; overcome, down-trodden; loaded with -shame etc. *n.*; in -bad repute etc. *n.*; out of -repute, − favor, − fashion, − countenance; at a discount; under -a cloud, − an eclipse; unable to show one's face; in the -shade, − background; out at elbows, down in the world, down and out.

inglorious; nameless, renownless, obscure, unknown to fame; un-noticed, -noted, -honored, -glorified.

shameful; dis-graceful, -creditable, -reputable; despicable; questionable; unbecoming, unworthy; derogatory; degrading, humiliating, *infra dignitatem*, dedecorous; scandalous, infamous, too bad, unmentionable; ribald, opprobrious; arrant, shocking, outrageous, notorious, shady.

ignominious, scrubby, dirty, abject, vile, beggarly, pitiful, low, mean, shabby; base etc. (*dishonorable*) 940.

Adv. to one's shame be it spoken.

Int. fie! shame! for shame! *proh pudor! O tempora! O mores!* ough! *sic transit gloria mundi!*

875. Nobility.—**N.** nobility, rank, condition, distinction, optimacy, blood, *pur sang*, birth, high descent, order; quality, gentility; blue blood of Castile; *ancien régime*.

high life, *haut monde*; upper -classes, − ten thousand; *élite*, aristocracy, great folks; fashionable world etc. (*fashion*) 852; salariat.

peer, -age; house of -lords, − peers; lords, − temporal and spiritual; *noblesse*; baronage, knightage; noble, -man; lord, -ling; grandee, *magnifico, hidalgo*; don, -ship; aristocrat, swell, three-tailed bashaw; gentleman, squire, squireen, patrician, laureate.

gentry, gentlefolk; squirarchy, better sort; *magnates, primates, optimates.*

king etc. (*master*) 745; prince, crown prince, *Dauphin*; duke; marquis, -ate; earl, viscount, baron, thane, banneret; baronet, -cy; knight, -hood; count, armiger, laird; sig-, seig-nior; esquire, boyar, margrave, vavasor, sheik, emir, ameer, scherif, *pasha*, effendi, sahib.

queen etc. 745; princess, begum, duchess, mar-chioness; countess etc.; lady, dame.

personage —, man- of -distinction, — mark, — rank; nota-bles, -bilities; celebrity, big-wig, magnate, great man, star; *magni nominis umbra*; 'every inch a king;' grand Panjandrum

V. be -noble etc. *adj.*

Adj. noble, exalted; of -rank etc. *n.*; princely, titled, patrician, aristocratic; high-, well-born; of gentle blood; genteel, *comme il faut*, gen-tlemanlike, courtly etc. (*fashionable*) 852; highly respectable.

Adv. in high quarters.

876. Commonalty.—N. commonalty,
democracy; obscurity; low -condition, — life, — society, — company; *bourgeoisie*; mass of -the people, — society; Brown, Jones, and Robinson; Tom, Dick, and Harry; lower —, humbler- -classes, — orders; vulgar —, common- herd; rank and file, *hoc genus omne*; the -many, — general, — crowd, — people, — populace, — multitude, — million, — masses, — mobility, — peasantry; king Mob; proletariat, *fruges consumere nati*, great unwashed; man in the street

mob; rabble, — rout; chaff, rout, horde, *canaille*; scum —, *residuum* —, dregs- of -the people, — society; swinish multitude, *faex populi*; *profanum* —, *ignobile- vulgus*; vermin; riff-raff, tag-rag and bobtail; small fry.

commoner, one of the people, democrat, plebeian, republican, proletary, *prolétaire*, *roturier*, Mr. Snooks, *bourgeois*, *épicier*, Philistine, cockney; *grisette, demi-monde*.

peasant, countryman, boor, carle, churl; vill-ain, -ein; serf, kern, tyke, tike, chuff, ryot, fellah; long-shoreman; swain, clown, hind; clod, -hopper; hob-nail, yokel, hick, rube, cider squeezer, bog-trotter, bumpkin; ploughman, -boy; rustic, chawbacon, tiller of the soil; hewers of wood and drawers of water, groundling; gaffer, loon, put, cub, Tony Lumpkin, looby, lout, under-ling; *gamin*, gut-tersnipe, street arab, mudlark; rough, rowdy, ruf-fian, roughneck; pot-walloper, slubberdegullion; vulgar —, low- fellow; cad, curmudgeon.

upstart, *parvenu*, *nouveau-riche*, skipjack; nobody, — one knows; *hesterni quirites*, *pessoribus orti*; *bourgeois gentilhomme*, *novus homo*, snob, gent, mushroom, no one knows who, adventurer; man of straw.

beggar, panhandler, gaberlunzie, muckworm, mudlark, *sans-culotte*, raff, tatterdemalion, caitiff, ragamuffin, Pariah, outcast of society, tramp, weary Willie, bum, vagabond, *chiffonaier*, rag-picker, Cinderella, cinderwench, scrub, jade; boots, gossoon.

Goth, Vandal, Hottentot, savage, barbarian, Yahoo; unlicked cub, rough diamond.

barbar-ousness, -ism; Boeotia.

V. be -ignoble etc. *adj.*, — nobody etc. *n.*

Adj. ignoble, common, mean, low, base, vile, sorry, scrubby, beggarly, below par; no great shakes etc. (*unimportant*) 643; home-ly, -spun; vulgar, low-minded; snobbish, *parvenu*.

plebeian, proletarian; of -low, — mean- -parentage, — origin, extraction; low-, base-, earth-born, low bred; mushroom, dunghill, risen from the ranks; unknown to fame, obscure, untitled.

rustic, uncivilized; lout-, boor-, clown-, churl-, brut-, raff-ish; rude, unlicked, unpolished.

barbar-ous, -ian, -ic, -esque; cockney, born within sound of Bow bells.

underling, menial, servile, subaltern.

Adv. below the salt.

877. Title.—N. title, honor; knighthood etc.
(*nobility*) 875.

royal —, serene- highness, excellency, grace; lordship, worship, Rt. Hon., rever-ence, -end; esquire, sir; madam, *madame*; master, mistress, Mr., Mrs., *signor*, *señor*, *Mein Herr*, *mynheer*; your —, his- honor; handle to one's name.

decoration, laurel, palm, wreath, garland, bays, medal, ribbon, riband, blue ribbon, *cordon*, cross, crown, coronet, star, garter; feather, — in one's cap; chevron, epaulet, *épaulette*, colors, cockade; livery; order, arms, armorial bearings, shield, scutcheon, crest, reward etc. 973.

878. Pride.—N. dignity, self-respect, *mens sibi conscia recti*.

pride; haughtiness etc. *adj.*; high notions, *hauteur*; vainglory, crest; arrogance etc. (*assumption*) 885; pomposity etc. 882.

proud man, highflier; fine -gentleman, — lady; *grande dame*.

V. be -proud etc. *adj.*; put a good face on; look one in the face; stalk abroad, perk oneself up; presume, swagger, strut; rear —, lift up —, hold up- one's head; hold one's head high, look big, take the wall, 'bear like the Turk no rival near the throne,' carry with a high hand; ride the —, mount on one's- high horse; set one's back up, bridle, toss the head; give oneself airs etc. (*assume*) 885; boast etc. 884.

pride oneself on; glory in, take pride in; pique —, plume —, hug- oneself; stand upon, be proud of; put a good face on; not -hide one's light under a bushel, — put one's talent in a napkin; not think small beer of oneself etc. (*vanity*) 880.

Adj. dignified; stately; proud, -crested; lordly, baronial; lofty-minded; high-souled, -minded, -mettled, -handed, -plumed, -flown, -toned.

haughty, paughty, insolent, lofty, high, mighty, swollen, puffed up, flushed, blown; vain-glorious; purse-proud, fine; proud as -a peacock, Lucifer; bloated with pride.

supercilious, disdainful, bumptious, magisterial, imperious; high-handed, — and mighty; over-weening, consequential; arrogant etc. 885; un-blushing etc. 880.

stiff, -necked; starch; perked —, stuck- up; in buckram, straitlaced; prim etc. (*affected*) 855.

on one's -high horses, — tight ropes, — high ropes; on stilts; *en grand seigneur*.

Adv. with head erect, with one's nose in the air.

Phr. *odi profanum vulgus et arceo*.

879. Humility.—N. hum-ility, -bleness; meek-, low-ness; lowli-ness, -hood; abasement, self-abasement, -effacement; submission etc. 725; resignation.

condescension; affability etc. (*courtesy*) 894.

modesty etc. 881; verecundity, blush, suffusion, confusion; sense of -shame, — disgrace; humiliation, mortification; let —, set- down.

V. be -humble etc. *adj.*; deign, vouchsafe, condescend; humble —, demean- oneself; stoop, — to conquer; carry coals; submit etc. 725; submit with a good grace etc. (*brook*) 826; yield the palm.

lower one's -tone, — note; sing small, draw in one's horns, sober down; hide one's -face, — diminished head; not dare to show one's face, take shame to oneself, not have a word to say for oneself; feel —, be conscious of- -shame, — disgrace; drink the cup of humiliation to the dregs; eat -humble pie, — one's words, — dirt; be humiliated, receive a snub.

blush -for, — up to the eyes; redden, change color; color up; hang one's head, look foolish, feel small.

render humble; humble, humiliate; let —, set —, take —, tread —, frown- down; snub, abash, abase, make one sing small, strike dumb; teach one -his distance, — his place; take down a peg, — lower; throw —, cast- into the shade etc. 874; stare —, put- out of countenance; put to the blush; confuse, ashame, mortify, disgrace, crush; send away with a flea in one's ear.

get a set down.

Adj. humble, lowly, meek; modest etc. 881; humble-, sober-minded; unoffended; submissive etc. 725; servile etc. 886.

condescending; affable etc. (*courteous*) 894.

humbled etc. *v.*; bowed down, resigned; abashed, ashamed, dashed; out of countenance; down in the mouth; down on one's -knees, — marrow-bones; humbled in the dust, brow-beaten; chap-, crest-fallen; dumbfoundered, flabbergasted, struck all of a heap.

shorn of one's glory etc. (*disrepute*) 874.

Adv. with -downcast eyes, — bated breath, — bended knee; on all fours, on one's feet.

under correction, with due deference.

Phr. I am your -obedient, — very humble- servant; my service to you.

880. Vanity.—**N.** vanity; conceit, -edness; self-conceit, -complacency, -confidence, -sufficiency, — esteem, -love, -approbation, -praise, -glorification, — laudation, -gratulation, -applause, -admiration; *amour-propre*; selfishness etc. 943.

airs, pretensions, mannerism; egotism; prigg-ism, -ishness; coxcombery, gaudery, vainglory, elation; pride etc. 878; ostentation etc. 882; assurance etc. 885.

vox et praeterea nihil; *cheval de bataille*.

ego-ist, -tist; peacock, coxcomb etc. 854; Sir Oracle etc. 887.

V. be -vain etc. *adj.*, — vain of; pique oneself etc. (*pride*) 878; lay the flattering unction to one's soul.

have -too high, — an overweening- opinion of -oneself, — one's talents; blind oneself as to one's own merit; not think -small beer, — *vin ordinaire*- of oneself; put oneself forward; fish for compliments; give oneself airs etc. (*assume*) 885; boast etc. 884.

render -vain etc. *adj.*; inspire with -vanity etc. *n.*; inflate, puff up, turn up, turn one's head.

Adj. vain, — as a peacock; conceited, assured, overweening, pert, forward, perky; vain-glorious, high-flown; ostentatious etc. 882; puffed up, inflated, flushed.

self-satisfied, -confident, -sufficient, -flattering, — admiring, -applauding, -glorious, -opinionated; *entêté* etc. (*wrong-headed*) 481; wise in one's own conceit, pragmatical, overwise, pretentious, priggish, egotistic, -al; *soi-disant* etc. (*boastful*) 884; arrogant etc. 885.

un-abashed, -blushing; un-constrained, — ceremonious; free and easy.

Adv. vainly etc. *adj.*

Phr. how we apples swim!

881. Modesty.—**N.** modesty; humility etc. 879; diffidence, timidity; retiring disposition, unobtrusiveness, bashfulness etc. *adj.*; *mauvaise honte*; blush, -ing; verecundity; self-knowledge.

reserve, constraint; demureness etc. *adj.*; blushing honors.

V. be -modest etc. *adj.*; retire, reserve oneself; give way to; draw in one's horns etc. 879; hide one's face.

keep -private, — in the background, — one's distance; pursue the noiseless tenor of one's way, 'do good by stealth and blush to find it fame,' hide one's light under a bushel, cast a sheep's eye.

Adj. modest, diffident; humble etc. 879; timid, timorous, bashful; shy, nervous, skittish, coy, sheepish, shamefaced, blushing, over-modest.

unpreten-ding, -tious; un-obtrusive, -assuming, — ostentatious, -boastful, -aspiring; poor in spirit.

out of countenance etc. (*humbled*) 879.

reserved, constrained, demure.

Adv. humbly etc. *adj.*; quietly, privately; without -ceremony, — beat of the drum; *sans façon*.

882. Ostentation.—**N.** ostentation, display, show, flourish, parade, *étalage*, pomp, array, state, solemnity; dash, splash, glitter, strut, swank, side, swagger, pomposity; preten-se, -sions; showing off; fuss.

magnificence, splendor; *coup d'oeil*; grand doings.

coup de théâter; stage -effect, — trick; clap-trap; *mise en scène*; *tour de force*; chic.

demonstration, flying colors; tomfoolery; flourish of trumpets etc. (*celebration*) 883; pageant, -ry; spectacle, exhibition, procession; turn —, set- out; grand function; *fête*, gala, field-day, review, march past, promenade, insubstantial pageant.

dress; court —, full —, evening — ball —, fancy- dress; tailoring, millinery, man-millinery, frippery; foppery, equipage.

ceremon-y, -ial; ritual; form, -ality; etiquette; punct-o, -ilio, -ilious-ness; starched-, stateli-ness.

mummery, solemn mockery, mouth honor.

attitudinarian; fop etc. 854.

V. be -ostentatious etc. *adj.*; come —, put oneself- forward; attract attention, star it.

make —, cut-a -figure, — dash — splash; strut, blow one's own trumpet; figure, — away; make a show, — display; glitter.

show -off, — one's paces; parade, march past;

display, exhibit, put forward, hold up; trot –, hang- out; sport, brandish, blazon forth; dangle, – before the eyes.

cry up etc. (*praise*) 931; prôner, flaunt, emblazon, prink, set off, mount, have framed and glazed.

put a good, – smiling- face upon; clean the outside of the platter etc. (*disguise*) 544.

Adj. ostentatious, showy, dashing, pretentious, ja-, jau-nty; grand, pompous, palatial; high-sounding; turgid etc. (*big-sounding*) 577; garish, gorgeous, gaudy, – as a -peacock, – butterfly, – tulip; flaunting, flashing, flaming, glittering; gay etc. (*ornate*) 847; colorful.

splendid, magnificent, sumptuous.

theatrical, dramatic, spectacular, scenic, ceremonial, ritual, -istic.

solemn, stately, majestic, formal, stiff, ceremonious, punctilious, starch-ed, -y.

en grande tenue, in best bib and tucker, in Sunday best, endimanché.

Adv. with -flourish of trumpet, – beat of drum, – flying colors, – a brass band.

ad captandum vulgus.

883. Celebration.—**N.** celebration, solemnization, jubilee, diamond jubilee, commemoration, ovation, paean, triumph, jubilation.

triumphal arch, bonfire, salute; salvo, – of artillery; *feu de joie*, flourish of trumpets, *fanfare*, colors flying, illuminations, fireworks.

inauguration, installation, presentation; début, coming out, birthday anniversary, bi-, ter-, centenary; silver –, golden –, diamond- wedding, - day; coronation; Lord Mayor's show; harvest home, red letter day, festival; trophy etc. 733; Te Deum etc. (*thanksgiving*) 990; fête etc. 882; holiday etc. 840.

V. celebrate, keep, signalize, do honor to, commemorate, solemnize, hallow, mark with a red letter, hold high festival, maffick.

pledge, drink to, toast, hob and nob.

inaugurate, install, instate, induct, chair.

rejoice etc. 838; kill the fatted calf, hold jubilee, roast an ox, fire a salute.

Adj. celebrating etc. v.; commemorative, celebrated, immortal.

Adv. in -honor, – commemoration, – celebration of.

Int. hail! all hail! *io -paean, – triumphe!* 'see the conquering hero comes!'

884. Boasting.—**N.** boasting etc. v.; boast, vaunt, crake, preten-ce, -sions; puff, -ery; flourish, fanfaronnade; gasconade; bluff, swank, brag, - gardism; bravado, bunkum, Buncombe; high-falutin; jact-itation, -ancy; bounce, rant, bluster; venditation, vaporing, rodomontade, bombast, fine talking, tall talk, magniloquence, teratology, heroics; jingoism, Chauvinism; exaggeration etc. 549; gas, hot air.

vanity etc. 880; *vox et praeterea nihil*; much cry and little wool, *brutum fulmen.*

exultation; glorification; flourish of trumpets; triumph etc. 883.

boaster; bragg-art, -adocio; hot air merchant;

Gascon, *fanfaron*, pretender, fourflusher, soi-disant; windbag, blowhard, bluffer; chauvinist; blusterer etc. 887; charlatan, jack-pudding, trumpeter; puppy etc. (*fop*) 854.

V. boast, make a boast of, brag, vaunt, puff, show off, flourish, crake, crack, trumpet, strut, swagger, vapor, bluff; draw the long bow.

exult, crow over, neigh, chuckle, triumph; glory, gloat, jubilate; throw up one's cap; talk big, *se faire valoir, faire claquer son fouet*, take merit to oneself, make a merit of, sing *Io triumphe*, holloa before one is out of the wood.

Adj. boasting etc. v.; magniloquent, flaming, Thrasonic, stilted, gasconading, braggart, boastful, pretentious, *soi-disant*; vain-glorious etc. (*conceited*) 880.

elate, -d; jubilant, triumphant, exultant; in high feather; flushed, – with victory; cock-a-hoop; on stilts.

vaunted etc. v.

Adv. vauntingly etc. adj.; with a brass band.

Phr. 'let the galled jade wince.'

885. Insolence. [Undue assumption of superiority.]—**N.** insolence; haughtiness etc. adj.; arrogance, airs; overbearance, brashness, bumptiousness, contumely, disdain; domineering etc. v.; tyranny etc. 739.

impertinence; cheek, nerve, sauce; sauciness etc. adj.; flippancy, dicacity, petulance, procacity, bluster; swagger, -ing etc. v.; bounce; terrorism; jingoism, chauvinism.

as-, pre-sumption; beggar on horseback; usurpation.

impudence, assurance, audacity, self-assertion, hardihood, front, face, brass; shamelessness etc. adj.; effrontery, hardened front, face of brass.

assumption of infallibility.

malapert, saucebox etc. (*blusterer*) 887.

V. be -insolent etc. adj.; bluster, vapor, swagger, swell, give oneself airs; snap one's fingers, kick up a dust; swear etc. (*affirm*) 535; rap out oaths; roister.

arrogate; as-, pre-sume; make -bold, – free; take a liberty, give an inch and take an ell.

domineer, bully, dictate, hector; lord it over, bulldoze; *traiter de haut, regarder de haut en bas*; exact; snub, huff, beard, fly in the face of; put to the blush; bear –, beat- down; browbeat, intimidate; trample –, tread- down, – under foot; dragoon, ride roughshod over, terrorize.

out-face, -look, -stare, -brazen, -brave; stare out of countenance; brazen out; lay down the law; teach one's grandmother to suck eggs; assume a lofty bearing; talk –, look- big; put on big looks, act the *grand seigneur*; mount –, ride- the high horse; toss the head, carry with a high hand.

tempt Providence, want snuffing.

Adj. insolent, haughty, arrogant, imperious, magisterial, dictatorial, arbitrary; high-handed, high and mighty; contumelious, supercilious, overbearing, intolerant, domineering; overweening, high-flown.

flippant, pert, cavalier, saucy, forward, impertinent, fresh, malapert.

precocious, assuming, would-be, bumptious.

bluff; brazen-, browed-faced, shameless, aweless, unblushing, unabashed; bold-, bare-faced; dead –, lost- to shame.

impudent, audacious, presumptuous, free and easy, devil-may-care, rollicking; janty, jaunty; roistering, blustering, hectoring, swaggering, vaporing; thrasonic, fire-eating, 'full of sound and fury.'

Adv. insolently, with a high hand; *ex cathedrâ*.

Phr. one's bark being worse than his bite.

886. Servility.—N. servility; slavery etc. (*subjection*) 749; obsequiousness etc. *adj.*; subserviency; abasement; pros-tration, -ternation; genuflexion etc. (*worship*) 990; fawning etc. *v.*; tuft-hunting, time-serving, flunkeyism; sycophancy etc. (*flattery*) 933; humility etc. 879.

sycophant, parasite, yes-man; toad, -y, -eater; tuft-hunter; snob, flunkey, lap-dog, spaniel, lickspittle, smell-feast, *Graeculus esuriens*, hanger on, stooge, *cavaliere servente*, led captain, carpet knight; time-server, fortune-hunter, Vicar of Bray, Sir Pertinax Mac Sycophant, flatterer etc. 935; doer of dirty work; *âme damnée*, tool; reptile; slave etc. (*servant*) 746; courtier; sponge, jackal; truckler.

V. cringe, bow, stoop, kneel, bend the knee; fall on one's knees, prostrate oneself; worship etc. 990.

sneak, crawl, crouch, cower, truckle to, grovel, fawn, toady, lick the feet of, kiss the hem of one's garment.

pay court to; feed —, fatten —, batten- on; dance attendance on, pin oneself upon, hang on the sleeve of, *avaler des couleuvres*, keep time to, fetch and carry, do the dirty work of.

go with the stream, follow the crowd, worship the rising sun, hold with the hare and run with the hounds.

Adj. servile, obsequious; supple, — as a glove; soapy, oily, pliant, cringing, fawning, slavish, groveling, sniveling, mealy-mouthed; beggarly, sycophantic, parasitical; abject, prostrate, down on one's marrow-bones; base, mean, sneaking; crouching etc. *v.*

Adv. hat —, cap- in hand.

887. Blusterer.—N. bluster-, swagger-, vapor-, roister-, brawl-er; brazen-face; *fanfaron*; braggart etc. (*boaster*) 884; bully, terrorist, rough, rough-neck; hooligan, hoodlum, larrikin, ruffian; Mohock, -hawk; drawcansir, swashbuckler, Captain Boabdil, Sir Lucius O'Trigger, Thraso, Pistol, Parolles, Bombastes Furioso, Hector, Chrononhotonthologos; jingo; desperado, dare-devil, fire-eater; fury etc. (*violent person*) 173; rowdy.

puppy etc. (*fop*) 854; prig; Sir Oracle, dogmatist, *doctrinaire*, stump orator, jack-in-office; saucebox, malapert, jackanapes, minx; bantam-cock.

888. Friendship.—N. friendship, amity; friendliness etc. *adj.*; brotherhood, fraternity, sodality, confraternity, sorosis, sisterhood; harmony etc. (*concord*) 714; peace etc. 721.

firm —, staunch —, intimate —, familiar —, bosom —, cordial —, tried —, devoted —, lasting —, fast —, sincere —, warm —, ardent- friendship.

cordiality, fraternization, *entente cordiale*, good

understanding, *rapprochement*, sympathy, fellow-feeling, response, welcomeness; *camaraderie*.

affection etc. (*love*) 897; favoritism; goodwill etc. (*benovolence*) 906; partiality.

acquaintance, familiarity, intimacy, intercourse, fellowship, knowledge of; introduction.

V. be -friendly etc. *adj.*, — friends etc. 890; — acquainted with etc. *adj.*; know; have the ear of; keep- company with etc. (*sociality*) 892; hold communication —, have dealings —, sympathize- with; have a leaning to; bear good will etc. (*benevolence*) 906; love etc. 897; make much of; befriend etc. (*aid*) 707; introduce to.

set one's horses together; hold out —, extend the right hand of -friendship; — fellowship; become -friendly etc. *adj.*; make -friends etc. 890 with; break the ice, be introduced to; make —, pick —, scrape- acquaintance with; get into favor, gain the friendship of.

shake hands with, fraternize, embrace; receive with open arms, throw oneself into the arms of; meet half way, take in good part.

Adj. friendly, amic-able, -al; well affected, unhostile, neighborly, brotherly, fraternal, sisterly, sympathetic, harmonious, hearty, cordial, warm-hearted, devoted.

friends —, well —, at home —, hand in hand-with; on -good, — friendly, — amicable, — cordial, — familiar, — intimate- terms, — footing; on -speaking, — visiting- terms; in one's good -graces, — books.

acquainted, familiar, intimate, thick, hand and glove, hail fellow well met, free and easy; welcome.

Adv. amicably etc. *adj.*; with open arms; *sans cérémonie*; arm in arm.

889. Enmity.—N. enmity, hostility; unfriendliness etc. *adj.*; discord etc. 713.

alienation, estrangement; dislike etc. 867; hate etc. 898; antagonism.

heartburning; animosity etc. 900; malevolence etc. 907.

V. be -inimical etc. *adj.*; keep —, hold- at arm's length; be at loggerheads; bear malice etc. 907; fall out; take umbrage etc. 900; harden the heart, alienate, estrange.

Adj. inimical, unfriendly, hostile; at -enmity, — variance, — swords points, — daggers drawn, — open war with; up in arms against; in bad odor with.

on bad —, not on speaking- terms; cool; cold, -hearted; estranged, alienated, disaffected, irreconcilable.

890. Friend.—N. friend, — of one's bosom, intimate acquaintance, neighbor, well-wisher; *alter ego*; best —, bosom —, fast- friend; *amicus usque ad aras*; *fidus Achates*; *persona grata*.

favorer, *fautor*, patron, backer, Maecenas; tutelary saint, good genius, advocate, partisan, sympathizer; ally; friend in need etc. (*auxiliary*) 711.

associate, compeer, comrade, mate, companion, *confrère, camarade, confidante*, colleague; old —, crony; side-kick; chum, buddy, bunkie, roommate, pal; play-fellow, -mate; classmate, schoolfellow; bed-fellow, -mate; maid of honor.

compatriot; fellow –, countryman, – townsman.

shop-, ship-, mess-mate; fellow –, boon –, potcompanion; co-partner.

Arcades ambo, Pylades and Orestes, Castor and Pollux, Nisus and Euryalus, Damon and Pythias, *par nobile fratrum*.

host, Amphitryon, Boniface; guest, visitor, frequenter, *habitué*; *protégé*.

891. Enemy.—N. enemy; antagonist, foeman; open –, bitter- enemy; opponent etc. 710; back friend.

public enemy, enemy to society, traitor, anarchist etc. 743.

Phr. every hand being against one.

892. Sociality.—N. soci-ality, -ability, -ableness etc. *adj.*; social intercourse; consociation; intercourse, -community; consort-, companion-, fellow-, comrade-ship; clubbism; *esprit de corps.*

conviviality; good -fellowship, – company, *camaraderie*; joviality, jollity, *savoir -vivre*, festivity, festive board, merry-making; loving cup; hospitality, heartiness; cheer.

welcome, -ness; greeting; hearty –, warm –, welcome- reception; urbanity etc. (*courtesy*) 894; intimacy, familiarity.

good –, jolly- fellow, good mixer, Rotarian; *bon enfant.*

social –, family- circle; circle of acquaintance, *coterie*, society, company.

social -gathering, – *réunion*; assembly etc. (*assemblage*) 72; party, entertainment, reception, *levée*, at home, *conversazione*, *soirée*, *matinée*, evening –, morning –, afternoon –, garden –, dinner –, tea –, cocktail- party; symposium, singsong; kettle-, drum; *partie carrée*, dish of tea, *ridotto*, rout, housewarming; ball, prom, hop, dance, *thé dansant*; festival etc. (*amusement*) 840; wedding breakfast; 'the feast of reason and the flow of soul.'

visit, -ing; round- of visits; call, morning call; interview etc. (*interlocution*) 588; assignation; tryst, -ing place; appointment.

club etc. (*association*) 712.

V. be -sociable etc. *adj.*; know; be -acquainted etc. *adj.*; associate –, sort –, keep company –, walk hand in hand -with; eat off the same trencher, club together, consort, bear one company, join; make acquaintance with etc. (*friendship*) 888; make advances, fraternize, embrace; intercommunicate.

be –, feel –, make oneself- at home with; make free with; crack a bottle with; take pot luck with, receive hospitality, live at free quarters.

visit, pay a visit; interchange -visits, – cards; call -at, – upon; leave a card; drop-in, look in; look one up, beat up one's quarters.

entertain; give a -party etc. *n.*; be at home, see one's friends, hang out, keep open house, do the honors; receive, – with open arms; welcome; give a warm reception etc. *n.* to; kill the fatted calf.

Adj. sociable, companionable, clubbable, clubby, conversable, cosy, cosey, chatty, conversational; homiletical.

convivial; fest-ive, -al; jovial, jolly, hospitable.

welcome, – as the roses in May; *fêté*, entertained.

free and easy, hail fellow well met, familiar, on visiting terms, acquainted.

social, neighborly; international, cosmopolitan, gregarious.

Adv. *en famille*, in the family circle; *sans - façon*, – *cérémonie*, arm in arm.

893. Seclusion. Exclusion.—N. seclusion, privacy; retirement; concealment; reclusion, recess; snugness etc. *adj.*; delitescence; rustication, *rus in urbe*; solitude; solitariness etc. (*singleness*) 87; isolation; loneliness etc. *adj.*; estrangement from the world, anchoritism, voluntary exile; aloofness.

cell, hermitage; convent etc. 1000; *sanctum sanctorum*; study, library, den; hide-out.

depopulation, desertion, desolation; wilderness etc. (*unproductive*) 169; howling wilderness; rotten borough, Old Sarum.

exclusion, excommunication, banishment, exile, ostracism, proscription; cut, – direct; dead cut.

inhospit-ality, -ableness etc. *adj.*; un-, dissociability; domesticity, Darby and Joan.

recluse, hermit, eremite, cenobite; anchor-et, - ite; Simon Stylites; Troglodyte, Timon of Athens, Santon, *solitaire*, ruralist, disciple of Zimmermann, closet cynic, Diogenes; outcast, Pariah, castaway, outsider, pilgarlic; wastrel, foundling, orphan.

V. be –, live- secluded etc. *adj.*; keep –, stand –, hold oneself- -aloof, – in the background; keep snug; shut oneself up; deny –, secludeoneself; creep into a corner, rusticate, *aller planter ses choux*; retire, – from the world; hermetize, take the veil; abandon etc. 624.

cut, – dead; refuse to -associate with, – acknowledge; look cool –, turn one's back –, shut the door- upon; repel, blackball, excommunicate, exclude, exile, expatriate; banish, outlaw, maroon, ostracize, proscribe, cut off from, send to Coventry, keep at arm's length, draw a cordon round; boycott, blockade, lay an embargo on, isolate.

depopulate; dis-, un-people.

Adj. secluded, sequestered, retired, delitescent, private, bye; out of the -world, -way; in a backwater; 'the world forgetting by the world forgot.' snug, domestic, stay-at-home.

unsociable; un-, dis-social; inhospitable, cynical, inconversable, unclubbable, *sauvage*, eremetic.

solitary; lone-ly, -some; isolated, single.

excluded, estranged; unfrequented; uninhabitable, -ed; tenantless; un-tenanted, -occupied; abandoned; deserted, – in one's utmost need; unfriended; kith-, friend-, home-less; lorn, forlorn, desolate.

un-visited, -introduced, -invited, -welcome; under a cloud, left to shift for oneself, derelict, outcast, outside the gates.

banished etc. *v.*; under an embargo.

Phr. *noli me tangere.*

894. Courtesy.—N. courtesy; respect etc. 928; good -manners, – behavior, – breeding; manners; politeness etc. *adj.*; *bienséance*, urbanity, comity, gentility; gentle –, breeding; polish, presence,

cultivation, culture; civili-ty, -zation; amenity, suavity; good -temper, − humor; amiability, easy temper, complacency, soft tongue, mansuetude; condescension etc. (*humility*) 879; affability, complaisance, *prévenance*, amiability, gallantry, chivalry; pink of -politeness, − courtesy.

compliment; fair −, soft −, sweet- words; honeyed phrases, flattering remarks, ceremonial; salutation, reception, presentation, introduction, *accueil*, greeting, recognition; welcome, *abord*, respects, *devoir*, regards, remembrances; kind -regards, − remembrances; love, best love, duty; deference.

obeisance etc. (*reverence*) 928; bow, courtesy, curtsy, scrape, *salaam*, *kow-tow*, bowing and scraping; kneeling; genuflexion etc. (*worship*) 990; obsequiousness etc. 886; capping, shaking hands etc. *v.*; grip of the hand, embrace, hug, squeeze, *accolade*, loving cup, *vin d'honneur*, pledge; love token etc. (*endearment*) 902; kiss, buss, salute.

mark of recognition, not; 'nods and becks and wreathed smiles;' valediction etc. 293; condolence etc. 915.

V. be -courteous etc. *adj.*; show -courtesy etc. *n.*

mind one's P's and Q's, behave oneself, be all things to all men, conciliate, speak one fair, take in good part; make −, do- the amiable; look as if butter would not melt in one's mouth; mend one's manners.

receive, do the honors, usher, greet, hail, bid welcome; welcome, − with open arms; shake hands; hold out − , press − , squeeze the hand; bid God speed; speed the parting guest; cheer, serenade.

salute; embrace etc. (*endearment*) 902; kiss, − hands; drink to, pledge, hob and nob; move to, nod to; smile upon.

uncover, cap; touch −, take off- the hat; doff the cap; pull the forelock; present arms; make way for; bow; make one's bow; scrape, curtsy, courtesy; bob a -curtsy, − courtesy; kneel; bow − , bend- the knee; salaam, *kowtow*.

visit, wait upon, present oneself, pay one's respects, pay a visit etc. (*sociability*) 892; dance attendance on etc. (*servility*) 886; pay attentions to; do homage to etc. (*respect*) 928.

prostrate oneself etc. (*worship*) 990.

give −, send- one's duty etc. *n.* to.

render -polite etc. *adj.*; polish, civilize, humanize.

Adj. courteous, polite, civil, mannerly, urbane; well-behaved, -mannered, -bred, -brought up, gently bred, of gentle -breeding, − manners, good-mannered, polished, civilized, cultivated; refined etc. (*taste*) 850; gentlemanlike etc. (*fashion*) 852; gallant, chivalrous, on one's good behavior.

fine −, fair −, soft- spoken; honey-mouthed, -tongued; oily, unctuous, bland, suave; obliging, conciliatory, complaisant, complacent; obsequious etc. 886.

ingratiating, winning; gentle, mild; good-humored, cordial, gracious, amiable, tactful, addressful, affable, genial, friendly, familiar; neighborly.

Adv. courteously etc. *adj.*; with a good grace; with -open, − outstretched- arms; *à bras ouverts*; *suaviter in modo*, in good humor.

Int. hail! welcome! well met! *ave!* all hail! good -day, − morning etc., − morrow! God speed! *pax vobiscum!* may your shadow never be less! *chin-chin!*

895. Discourtesy.—N. discourtesy; ill-breeding; ill −, bad −, ungainly- manners; insuavity; grouchiness; un-courteous etc. *adj.*, tactlessness; rusticity, inurbanity; illiberality, incivility, displacency.

disrespect etc. 929; procacity, impudence; barbar-ism, -ity; misbehavior, brutality, blackguard--ism, conduct unbecoming a gentleman, *grossièreté*, *brusquerie*; vulgarity etc. 851.

churlishness etc. *adj.*; spinosity, perversity; moroseness etc. (*sullenness*) 901*a*.

bad-, ill-temper; sternness etc. *adj.*; austerity, moodishness, captiousness etc. 901; cynicism; tartness etc. *adj.*; acrimony, acerbity, virulence, asperity.

scowl, black looks, frown; short answer, rebuff; hard words, contumely; unparliamentary language, personality.

bear, bruin, brute, grouch, blackguard, beast; unlicked cub; frump, cross-patch; saucebox etc. 887.

V. be -rude etc. *adj.*; insult etc. 929; treat with discourtesy; take a name in vain; make -bold, − free- with; take a liberty; stare out of countenance, ogle, point at, put to the blush.

cut; turn -one's back upon, − on one's heel; give the cold shoulder; keep at -a distance, − arm's length; look -cool, − coldly, − black- upon; show the door to, send away with a flea in the ear.

lose one's temper etc. (*resentment*) 900; sulk etc. 901*a*; frown, scowl, glower, pout; snap, snarl, growl.

render -rude etc. *adj.*; brut-alize, -ify.

Adj. dis-, un-courteous; uncourtly; ill-bred, -mannered, -behaved, -conditioned; unbred; un-manner-ly, -ed; im-, un-polite; un-polished, -civilized, -genteel; ungentleman-like, -ly; unladylike; blackguard; vulgar etc. 851; dedecorous; foul-mouthed, -spoken; abusive.

un-civil, -gracious, -ceremonious; cool; pert, forward, obtrusive, impudent, rude, saucy, precocious; insolent etc. 885.

repulsive; un-complaisant, -accommodating, -neighborly, -gallant; inaffable; un-gentle, -gainly; rough, rugged, bluff, blunt, gruff; churl-, boor-, bear-ish; brutal, *brusque*; stern, harsh, austere; cavalier.

tart, sour, crabbed, sharp, short, trenchant, sarcastic, crusty, biting, caustic, virulent, bitter, acrimonious, venomous, contumelious; snarling etc., *v.*; surly, − as a bear; perverse; grim, sullen etc. 901*a*; peevish etc. (*irascible*) 901.

Adv. discourteously etc. *adj.*; with -discourtesy etc. *n.*, − a bad grace.

896. Congratulations.—N. con-, gratulation; felicitation; salute etc. 894; condolence etc. 915; compliments of the season; good −, best- wishes.

V. con-, gratulate; felicitate, compliment; give −, wish one- joy; tender −, offer- one's congratulations; wish -many happy returns of the day, − a merry Christmas and a happy new year.

congratulate oneself etc. (*rejoice*) 838.

Adj. con-, gratulatory.

897. Love.—N. love; fondness etc. *adj.*; liking; inclination etc. (*desire*) 865; regard, dilection, admiration, fancy.

affection, sympathy, fellow-felling; tenderness etc. *adj.*; heart, brotherly love; benevolence etc. 906; attachment.

yearning, tender passion, *affaire de coeur*, *amour*, gallantry, passion, flame, devotion, fervor, enthusiasm, transport of love, rapture, enchantment, infatuation, adoration, idolatry.

narcissism, Oedipus complex, Electra complex.

Cupid, Venus, Eros; myrtle; true lover's knot; love -token, – suit, – affair, – tale, – story; the old story, plighted love; courtship etc. 902; *amourette*.

maternal love.

attractiveness, charm; popularity; favorite etc. 899.

lover, suitor, follower, admirer, adorer, wooer, amoret, beau, sweetheart, inamorato, swain, young man, flame, love, truelove; leman, Lothario, gallant, paramor, *amoroso*, *cavaliere servente*, captive, *cicisbeo*; *caro sposo*, Don Juan, sheik, ladies' man, squire of dames, Knave of Hearts.

inamorata, lady-love, idol, darling, duck, Dulcinea, angel, goddess, *cara sposa*; mistress.

betrothed, affianced, *fiancée*.

flirt, *coquette*; amorette; pair of turtle doves; abode of love, *agapemone*.

V. love, like, affect, fancy, care for, take an interest in, be partial to, sympathize with; be -in love etc. *adj.*- with; have –, entertain –, harbor –, cherish- a -love etc. *n.* for; regard, revere; take to, bear love to, be wedded to; set one's affections on; make much of, feast one's eyes on; hold dear, prize, treasure; hug, cling to, cherish, pet, caress etc. 902.

burn; adore, idolize, love to distraction, *aimer eperdument*; dote -on, – upon.

take a fancy to, fall for, be stuck on, look sweet upon; become -enamored etc. *adj.*; fall in love with, lose one's heart; desire etc. 865.

excite love; win –, gain –, secure –, engage- the -love, – affections, – heart; take the fancy of; have a place in –, wind round- the heart; attract, attach, endear, charm, fascinate, captivate, bewitch, seduce, enamor, enrapture, turn the head.

get into favor; ingratiate –, insinuate –, worm- oneself; propitiate, curry favor with, pay one's court to, make a date with, *faire l'aimable*, set one's cap at, flirt, coquet.

Adv. loving etc. *v.*; fond of; taken –, struck- with; smitten, bitten; attached to, wedded to; enamored; charmed etc. *v.*; in love; lovesick; over head and ears in love.

affectionate, tender, sweet upon, sympathetic, loving, fond, amorous, amatory; erotic, uxurious, ardent, passionate, rapturous, devoted, motherly.

loved etc. *v.*; beloved; well –, dearly- beloved; dear, precious, darling, pet, little; favorite, popular.

congenial; to –, after- one's -mind, – taste, – fancy, – own heart.

in one's good -graces etc. (*friendly*) 888; dear as the apple of one's eye, nearest to one's heart.

lovable, adorable; lovely, sweet; attractive, seductive, winning; charming, engaging, interesting, enchanting, captivating, fascinating, intriguing, bewitching; amiable, like an angel, angelic, seraphic.

898. Hate.—N. hate, hatred, vials of hate; Hymn of Hate.

dis-affection, -favor; alienation, estrangement, coolness; enmity etc. 889; animosity etc. 900.

umbrage, pique, grudge; dudgeon, spleen; bitterness, – of feeling; ill –, bad- blood; acrimony; malice etc. 907; implacability etc. (*revenge*) 919.

repugnance etc. (*dislike*) 867; odium, unpopularity; loathing, detestation, antipathy; object of -hatred, – execration; abomination, aversion, *bête noire*; enemy etc. 891; bitter pill; source of annoyance etc. 830.

V. hate, detest, abominate, abhor, loathe; recoil –, shudder- at; shrink from, view with horror, hold in abomination, revolt against, execrate; scowl etc. 895; disrelish etc. (*dislike*) 867.

owe a grudge; bear -spleen, – a grudge, – malice etc. (*malevolence*) 907; conceive an aversion to.

excite –, provoke- hatred etc. *n.*; be -hateful etc. *adj.*; stink in the nostrils; estrange, alienate, repel, set against, sow dissension, set by the ears, envenom, incense, irritate, rile, ruffle, vex; horrify etc. 830.

Adj. hating etc. *v.*; abhorrent; averse from etc. (*disliking*) 867; set against.

bitter etc. (*acrimonious*) 895; implacable etc. (*revengeful*) 919.

un-loved, -beloved, -lamented, -deplored, -mourned, -cared for, -endured, -valued; disliked etc. 867.

crossed in love, forsaken, rejected, love-lorn, jilted.

obnoxious, hateful, odious, abominable, repulsive, offensive, shocking; disgusting etc. (*disagreeable*) 830.

invidious, spiteful; malicious etc. 907.

insulting, irritating, provoking.

[Mutual hate] at -daggers drawn, – swords points; not on speaking terms etc. (*enmity*) 889.

Phr. no love lost between.

899. Favorite.—N. favorite, pet, cosset, minion, idol, jewel, spoiled child, *enfant gâté*; led captain; crony; fondling; apple of one's eye, man after one's own heart; *persona grata*.

love, dear, darling, duck, honey, jewel; mopsey, moppet; sweetheart etc. (*love*) 897.

general –, universal- favorite; idol of the people; matinée idol, movie –, radio- star.

900. Resentment.—N. resentment, displeasure, animosity, anger, wrath, indignation; vexation, exasperation, bitter resentment, wrathful indignation.

pique, umbrage, huff, miff, soreness, dudgeon, acerbity, virulence, bitterness, acrimony, asperity, spleen, gall; heart-burning, -swelling; rankling.

ill –, bad- -humor, – temper; irascibility etc. 901; ill blood etc. (*hate*) 898; revenge etc. 919.

excitement, irritation; warmth, bile, choler, ire, fume, pucker, dander, ferment, ebullition; towering -passion, – rage, *acharnement*, angry mood; taking, pet, tiff, passion, fit, tantrums.

burst, explosion, paroxysm, storm, rage, fury, desperation; violence etc. 173; fire and fury; vials of wrath; gnashing of teeth, hot blood, high words.

scowl etc. 895; sulks etc. 901a.

[Cause of umbrage] affront, provocation, offence; indignity etc. (*insult*) 929; grudge, crow to pluck, sore subject; red rag to a bull; *casus belli*.

Furies, Erinys, Eumenides, Alecto, Megaera, Tisiphone.

buffet, slap in the face, box on the ear, rap on the knuckles.

V. resent; take -amiss, − ill, − to heart, − offence, − umbrage, − huff, − exception; take in - ill part, − bad part, − dudgeon; *ne pas entendre raillerie*; breathe revenge, cut up rough.

fly −, fall −, get- into a -rage, − passion; bridle −, bristle −, froth −, fire −, flare- up; open −, pour out- the vials of one's wrath.

pout, knit the brow, frown, scowl, lower, snarl, growl, gnarl, gnash, snap; redden, color; look - black, − black as thunder, − daggers; bite one's thumb; show −, grind- one's teeth; champ the bit.

chafe, mantle, fume, kindle, fly out, take fire; boil, − over; boil with -indignation, − rage; rage, storm, foam; vent one's -rage, − spleen; lose one's temper, stand on one's hind legs, stamp the foot, kick up a row, fly off the handle, cut up rough; stamp −, quiver −, swell −, foam- with rage; burst with anger; raise Cain, breathe fire and fury.

have a fling at; bear malice etc. (*revenge*) 919.

cause −, raise- anger; affront, offend; give - offence, − umbrage; anger; hurt the feelings; insult, discompose, fret, ruffle, nettle, heckle, huff, pique; excite etc. 824; irritate, stir the blood, stir up bile; sting, − to the quick; rile, provoke, chafe, wound, incense, inflame, enrage, aggravate, add fuel to the flame, fan into a flame, widen the breach, envenom, embitter, exasperate, infuriate, kindle wrath; stick in one's gizzard; rankle etc. 919.

put out of humor; put one's -monkey, − backup; set −, get- one's back up; raise one's -gorge, − dander, − choler; work up into a passion; make - one's blood boil, − the ears tingle; throw into a ferment, madden, drive one mad; lash into -fury, − madness; fool to the top of one's bent; set by the ears.

bring a hornet's nest about one's ears.

Adj. angry, wrath, irate; ire-, wrath-ful; cross etc. (*irascible*) 901; sulky etc. 901a; bitter, virulent; acrimonious etc. (*discourteous*) etc. 895; violent etc. 173.

warm, burning; boiling, − over; fuming, raging; foaming, − at the mouth; convulsed with rage.

offended etc. *v.*; waxy, *acharné*; wrought, worked up; indignant, hurt, sore, peeved; set against.

fierce, wild, rageful, furious, mad with rage, fiery, infuriate, rabid, savage; relentless etc. 919.

flushed with -anger, − rage; in a -huff, − stew, − fume, − pucker, − passion, − rage, − fury; on one's high ropes, up in arms; in high dudgeon.

Adv. angrily etc. *adj.*; in the height of passion; in the heat of -passion, − the moment.

Phr. one's -blood, − back, − monkey- being up; *fervens difficili bile jecur*; the gorge rising, eyes flashing fire; the blood -rising, − boiling; *haeret lateri lethalis arundo*.

901. Irascibility.—N. irascibility, temper; crossness etc. *adj.*; susceptibility, procacity,

petulance, irritability, tartness, acerbity, protervity; pugnacity etc. (*contentiousness*) 720.

excitability etc. 825; bad −, fiery −, crooked −, irritable etc. *adj.*- temper; *genus irritabile*, hot blood.

ill humor etc. (*sullenness*) 901a; asperity etc., churlishness etc. (*discourtesy*) 895.

huff etc. (resentment) 900; a word and a blow.

Sir Fretful Plagiary; brabbler, Tartar; shrew, vixen, virago; termagant, dragon, scold, Xanthippe; porcupine; spit-fire; fire-eater etc. (*blusterer*) 887; fury etc. (*violent person*) 173.

V. be -irascible etc. *adj.*; have a -temper etc. *n.*, − devil in one; fire up etc. (be angry) 900.

Adj. irascible; bad-, ill-tempered; irritable, susceptible; excitable etc. 825; thin-skinned etc. (*sensitive*) 822; fretful, fidgety; on the fret.

hasty, over-hasty, quick, warm, hot, testy, touchy, techy, tetchy; like -touchwood, − tinder; huffy; pet-tish, -ulant; waspish, snapp-y, -ish, peppery, fiery, passionate, choleric, shrewish, 'sudden and quick in quarrel.'

querulous, captious, mood-y, -ish; quarrelsome, contentious, disputatious; pugnacious etc. (*bellicose*) 720; cantankerous, exceptious, restive etc. (*perverse*) 901a; churlish etc. (*discourteous*) 895.

cross, − as -crabs, − two sticks, − a cat, − a dog, − the tongs; like a bear with a sore head; fractious, peevish, *acariâtre*.

in a bad temper; sulky etc. 901a; angry etc. 900.

resent-ful, -ive; vindictive etc. 919.

Int. pish!

901a. Sullenness.—N. sullenness etc. *adj.*; morosity, spleen; churlishness etc. (*discourtesy*) 895; irascibility etc. 901.

moodiness etc. *adj.*; perversity; obstinacy etc. 606; torvity, spinosity; crabbedness etc. *adj.*

ill −, bad- -temper, − humor; sulks, dudgeon, mumps, doleful dumps, doldrums, fit of the sulks, *bouderie*, black looks, scowl; huff etc. (*resentment*) 900.

V. be -sullen etc. *adj.*; sulk; frown, scowl, lower, glower, grouse, grouch, crab, gloam, pout, have a hang-dog look, glout.

Adj. sullen, sulky; ill-tempered, -humored, - affected, -disposed; in -an ill, − a bad, − a shocking- -temper, − humor; out of -temper, − humor; knaggy, torvous, crusty, crabbed; sore as a boil; surly etc. (*discourteous*) 895.

moody; spleen-ish, -ly; splenetic, cankered.

cross, -grained; perverse, wayward, humorsome; restive; cantankerous, refractory, intractable, exceptious, sinistrous, deaf to reason, unaccommodating, rusty, crust, froward.

dogged etc. (*stubborn*) 606.

grumpy, glum, grim, grum, morose, frumpish; in the -sulks etc. *n.*; out of sorts; scowl-, glower-, growl-ing.

peevish etc. (*irascible*) 901.

902. Endearment. [Expression of affection or love.]—**N.** endearment, caress; blandish-, blandiment; *épanchement*, fondling, billing and cooing, dalliance.

embrace, salute, kiss, buss, smack, osculation,

deosculation; amorous glances; ogle, side glance, sheep's eyes.

courtship, wooing, suit, addresses, the soft impeachment; love-making; an affair; serenading; caterwauling.

flirting etc. v.; flirtation, gallantry; coquetry, spooning.

ture lover's knot, plighted love, engagement, bethrothal; love -tale, − token, − letter; *billet-doux*, valentine.

honeymoon; Strephon and Chloe, 'Arry and 'Arriet.

V. caress, fondle, pet, dandle, nurse; pat, − on the -head, − cheek; chuck under the chin, smile upon, coax, wheedle, cosset, coddle, cocker; make -of, − much of, pamper; cherish, foster, kill with kindness.

clasp, hug, cuddle; fold −, strain- in one's arms; nestle, nuzzle, neck, embrace, kiss, buss, smack, blow a kiss; salute etc. (*courtesy*) 894.

bill and coo, spoon, toy, dally, flirt, coquet; galli-, gala-vant; philander; make love; pay one's - court; − addresses, − attentions- to; serenade; court, woo; set one's cap at; be −, look- sweet upon; ogle, cast sheep's eyes upon; *faire les yeux doux*.

fall in love with, win the affections etc. (*love*) 897; die for.

propose; make −, have- an offer; pop the question; plight one's -troth, − faith; become - engaged, − betrothed.

Adj. caressing etc. v.; 'sighing like furnace;' love-sick, spoony.

carressed etc. v.

903. Marriage.—N. marriage, matrimony, wedlock, union, intermarriage, *vinculum matrimonii*, nuptial tie, knot.

married state, coverture, bed, cohabitation.

match; betrothment etc. (*promise*) 768; wedding, nuptials, Hymen, bridal; e-, spousals; leading to the altar etc. v.; nuptial benediction, *epithalamium*,

torch −, temple- of Hymen; hymeneal altar; honeymoon.

bride, bridegroom; brides-maid; -man.

best −, grooms-man, page, usher.

married -man, − woman, − couple; neogamist, Benedick, partner, spouse, mate, yokemate; husband, man, consort, baron; old −, good- man; wife of one's bosom; help-meet, -mate, rib, better half, grey mare, old woman, good wife; feme, − coverte; squaw, lady; matron, -age, -hood; man and wife; wedded pair, Darby and Joan.

affinity, soul-mate.

mono-, bi-, di-, deutero-, tri-, poly-gamy; mormonism; poly-andry; Turk, Bluebeard.

unlawful −, left-handed −, companionate −, morganatic −, ill-assorted- marriage; *mésalliance*; *mariage de convenance*; an affair.

match-maker, marriage broker, matrimonial agent.

V. marry, wive, take to oneself a wife; be - married, − spliced; go −, pair- off; wed, espouse, lead to the hymeneal altar, take 'for better, for worse,' give one's hand to, bestow one's hand upon; remarry; intermarry.

marry, join, handfast; couple etc. (*unite*) 43; tie

the nuptial knot; give -away, − in marriage; affy, affiance; betroth etc. (*promise*) 768; publish −, bid- the banns; be asked in church.

Adj. married etc. v.; one, − bone and one flesh. marriageable, nubile.

engaged, betrothed, affianced.

matrimonial, marital, conjugal, connubial, wedded; nuptial, hymeneal, spousal, bridal.

Phr. the gray mare the better horse.

904. Celibacy.—N. celibacy, singleness, single blessedness; bachelor-hood, -ship; miso-gamy, - gyny.

virginity, *pueelage*; maiden-hood, -head.

unmarried man, bachelor, agamist, old bachelor; miso-gamist, -gynist; celibate.

unmarried woman, spinster; maid, -en; virgin, *feme sole*, old maid; bachelor girl; nun etc.

V. live single; keep bachelor hall.

Adj. un-married, -wedded; wife-, spouse-less; single, virgin, celibate.

905. Divorce.—N. divorce, -ment; separation; judicial separation, separate maintenance; *separatio a -mensâ et thoro*, − vinculo matrimonii.

widowhood, viduage, viduity, weeds.

widow, -er; relict; dowager; *divorcée*; cuckold.

V. live -separately, − apart; separate, divorce, disespouse, put away; wear the horns.

906. Benevolence.—N. benevolence, Christian charity; God's -love, − grace; good-will; philanthropy etc. 910; unselfishness etc. 942.

good -nature, − feeling, − wishes; kind-, kindliness etc. *adj.*; lovingkindness, benignity, brotherly love, charity, humanity, fellow-feeling, sympathy; goodness −, warmth- of heart; *bon-homie*; kind-heartedness; amiability, milk of human kindness, tenderness; love etc. 897; friendship etc. 888.

toleration, consideration, generosity; mercy etc. (*pity*) 914.

charitableness etc. *adj.*; bounty, alms-giving; good works, beneficence, the luxury of doing good.

acts of kindness, a good turn; good −, kind- - offices, − treatment.

good Samaritan, sympathizer, well-wisher, philanthropist, *bon enfant*; altruist.

V. be -benevolent etc. *adj.*; have one's heart in the right place, bear good will; wish -well, − God speed; view −, regard- with an eye of favor; take in good part; take −, feel- an interest in; be −, feel-interested- in; sympathize with, feel for; fraternize etc. (*be friendly*) 888.

enter into the feelings of others, do as you would be done by, meet halfway.

treat well; give comfort, smooth the bed of death; do -good, − a good turn; benefit etc. (*goodness*) 648; render a service, be of use; aid etc. 707.

Adj. benevolent; kind, -ly; wellmeaning; amiable; obliging, accommodating, indulgent, considerate, gracious, complacent, good-humored.

warm-, soft-, kind-, tender-, large-, broad-hearted; merciful etc. 914; philanthropic etc. 910; charitable, beneficent, humane, benign, benignant; bount-eous, -iful etc. 816.

good-, well-natured; spleenless; sympath-izing, -etic; complaisant etc. (*courteous*) 894; kindly, well-meant, -intentioned.

fatherly, motherly, brotherly, sisterly; pat-, mat-, frat-ernal; friendly etc. 888.

Adv. with -a good intention, – the best intentions.

Int. God speed! much good may it do!

907. Malevolence.—N. malevolence; bad intent, -ion; un-, dis-kindness; ill -nature, – will, – blood; bad blood; enmity etc. 889; hate etc. 898; malignity; malice, – aforethought, – prepense; maliciousness etc. *adj.*; spite, despite; resentment etc. 900.

uncharitableness etc. *adj.*; incompassionateness etc. 914*a*; gall, venom, rancor, rankling, virulence, mordacity, acerbity; churlishness etc. (*discourtesy*) 895.

hardness of heart, heart of stone, obduracy; cruelty; cruelness etc. *adj.*; brutality, savagery; ferity, -ocity; barbarity, inhumanity, immanity, truculence, ruffianism; evil eye, cloven -foot, – hoof; Inquisition; torture.

ill –, bad- turn; affront etc. (*disrespect*) 929; outrage, atrocity; ill usage; intolerance, bigotry, persecution; tender mercies [ironical]; 'unkindest cut of all.'

V. be -malevolent etc. *adj.*; bear –, harbor- spleen, – a grudge, – malice; betray –, show- the cloven foot.

hurt etc. (*physical pain*) 378; annoy etc. 830; injure, harm, wrong; do -harm, – an ill office- to; outrage; disoblige, malign, plant a thorn in the breast.

molest, worry, harass, haunt, harry, bait, tease, throw stones at; play the devil with; hunt down, dragoon, hound; persecute, oppress, grind; maltreat; ill-treat, -use.

wreak one's malice on, do one's worst, break a butterfly on the wheel; dip –, imbrue- one's hands in blood; have no mercy etc. 914*a*.

Adj. male-, unbene-volent; unbenign; ill-disposed, -intentioned, -natured, -conditioned, - contrived; evil-minded, -disposed.

malicious; malign, -ant; rancorous; de-, spiteful; mordacious, caustic, bitter, envenomed, acrimonious, virulent; un-amiable, -charitable; maleficent, venomous, grinding, galling.

harsh, disobliging; un-kind, -friendly, -gracious; treacherous; inofficious; invidious; uncandid; churlish etc. (*uncourteous*) 895; surly, sullen etc. 901*a*.

cold, -blooded, -hearted; hard-, flint-, marble-, stony-hearted; hard of heart, unnatural; ruthless etc. (*unmerciful*) 914*a*; relentless etc. (*revengeful*) 919.

cruel; brut-al, -ish; savage, – as a -bear, – tiger; ferine, feral, ferocious; inhuman; barbarous, fell, untamed, tameless, truculent, incendiary; bloodthirsty etc. (*murderous*) 361; atrocious.

fiend-ish, -like; demoniacal; diabolic, -al; devilish, infernal, hellish, Satanic.

Adv. malevolently etc. *adj.*; with -bad intent etc. *n.*

908. Malediction.—N. malediction, malison, curse, imprecation, denunciation, execration,

anathema, ban, proscription, excommunication, commination, thunders of the Vatican, fulmination, *maranatha*, aspersion, vilification, vituperation, scurrility.

abuse; foul –, bad –, strong –, un-parliamentary- language, Limehouse; Billingsgate, sauce, evil speaking; cursing etc. *v.*; profane swearing, oath.

threat etc. 909; more bark than bite; invective etc. (*disapprobation*) 932.

V. curse, accurse, imprecate, damn, swear at; slang; curse with bell, book and candle; invoke –, call down- curses on the head of; devote to destruction.

execrate, beshrew, scold; anathematize etc. (*censure*) 932; hold up to execration, denounce, proscribe, excommunicate, fulminate, thunder against; threaten etc. 909; curse up hill and down dale.

curse and swear; swear, – like a trooper; fall a cursing, rap out an oath, damn, cuss.

Adj. curs-ing, -ed etc. *v.*; maledictory.

Int. woe to! beshrew! *ruat coelum!* ill –, woe- betide! confusion seize! damn! confound! blast! curse! devil take! hang! out with! a plague –, out- upon! aroynt! *honi soit!*

Phr. *delenda est Carthago.*

909. Threat.—N. threat, menace; defiance etc. 715; abuse, minacity, intimidation; fulmination; commination etc. (*curse*) 908; gathering clouds etc. (*warning*) 668.

V. threat, -en; menace; snarl, growl, gnarl, mutter, bark, bully.

defy etc. 715; intimidate etc. 860; keep –, hold up –, hold out- *in terrorem*; shake –, double –, clinch- the fist at; thunder, talk big, fulminate, use big words, bluster, look daggers.

Adj. threatening, menacing; mina-tory, -cious; comminatory, abusive; *in terrorem*; ominous etc. (*predicting*) 511; defiant etc. 715; under the ban.

Int. *vae victis!* at your peril! do your worst!

910. Philanthropy.—N. philanthropy; altruism, humanit-y, -arianism; universal benevolence; *deliciae humani generis;* cosmopolitanism, utilitarianism, the greatest happiness of the greatest number, social science, sociology.

common weal, public welfare, socialism, communism.

patriotism, civism, nationality, love of country, *amor patriae*, public spirit.

chivalry, knight errantry; generosity etc. 942.

philanthropist, altruist etc. 906; utilitarian, Benthamite, socialist, communist, cosmopolite, citizen of the world, *amicus humani generis*; knight errant; patriot.

Adj. philanthropic, altruistic, humanitarian, utilitarian, cosmopolitan; public-spirited, patriotic; humane, large-hearted etc. (*benevolent*) 906; chival-ric, -rous, generous etc. 942.

Adv. pro -bono publico, – aris et focis.

Phr. 'humani nihil .a me alienum puto.'

911. Misanthropy.—N. misanthropy, incivism; egotism etc. (*selfishness*)· 943; moroseness etc. 901*a*; cynicism; defeatism.

misanthrope, misanthropist, egotist, cynic, man-
hater, Timon, Diogenes.

woman-hater, misogynist.

Adj. misanthropic, antisocial, unpatriotic;
egotistical etc. (*selfish*) 943; morose etc. 901*a*.

912. Benefactor.—N. benefactor, savior, good
genius, tutelary saint, patron, guardian angel, fairy
godmother, good Samaritan; *pater patriae*; salt of
the earth etc. (*good man*) 948; auxiliary etc. 711.

913. Evil-doer. [*Maleficent being.*]—N. evil-
-doer, – worker; wrong doer etc. 949; mischief
maker, marplot; oppressor, tyrant; firebrand, incendiary, pyromaniac, anarchist, destroyer, Hun,
Boche, Vandal, iconoclast; communist; terrorist,
apache, gunman, gangster, racketeer.

savage, brute, ruffian, barbarian, semi-barbarian,
caitiff, desperado; Mo-hock, -hawk; bludgeon man,
bully, rough, hooligan, larrikin, dangerous classes,
ugly customer; thief etc. 792.

cockatrice, scorpion, hornet; viper, adder; snake,
– in the grass; serpent, cobra, asp, rattlesnake,
anaconda; canker-, wire-worm; locust, Colorado
beetle; torpedo; bane etc. 663.

cannibal; Anthropophag-us, -ist; bloodsucker,
vampire, ogre, ghoul, gorilla; vulture; gyr-, ger-
falcon.

wild beast, tiger, hyaena, butcher, hangman; cut-
throat etc. (*killer*) 361; blood-, sleuth-, hell-hound.

hag, hellhag, beldam, Jezebel.

monster; fiend etc. (*demon*) 980; homicidal
maniac, devil incarnate, demon in human shape;
Frankenstein's monster.

harpy, siren, vampire; Furies, Eumenides etc.
900.

Attila, scourge of the human race.

Phr. *foenum habet in cornu.*

914. Pity.—N. pity, compassion, com-
miseration; bowels, – of compassion; condolence
etc. 915; sympathy, fellow-feeling, tenderness,
yearning, forbearance, humanity, mercy, clemency,
exorability; leniency etc. (*lenity*) 740; charity, ruth,
long-suffering.

melting mood; *argumentum ad misericordiam*;
quarter, grace, *locus poenitentiae.*

sympathizer, champion, partisan.

V. pity; have –, show –, take- pity etc. *n.*;
commiserate, compassionate; condole etc. 915;
sympathize; feel –, be sorry –, yearn- for; weep,
melt, thaw, enter into the feelings of.

forbear, relent, relax, give quarter, wipe the
tears, *parcere subjectis*, give a *coup de grâce*, put
out of one's misery; be cruel to be kind.

raise –, excite- pity etc. *n.*; touch, soften; melt,
– the heart; appeal to one's better feelings;
propitiate, disarm.

ask for -mercy etc. *n.*; supplicate etc. (*request*)
765; cry for quarter, beg one's life, kneel;
deprecate.

Adj. pitying etc. *v.*; pitiful, compassionate, sympathetic, touched.

merciful, clement, ruthful; humane;
humanitarian etc. (*philanthropic*) 910; tender, –

hearted, – as a chicken; soft, – hearted; unhardened; lenient etc. 740; exorable, forbearing;
melting etc. *v.*; weak.

Int. for pity's sake! mercy! have –, cry you-
mercy! God help you! poor -thing, – dear, –
fellow! woe betide! *quis talia fando temperet a
lachrymis!*

Phr. one's heart bleeding for; *haud ignara mali
miseris succurrere disco.*

914a. Pitilessness.—N. pitilessness etc. *adj.*;
inclemency; inexorability, hardness of heart; inflexibility; severity etc. 739; malevolence etc. 907.

V. have no – , shut the gates of- mercy etc. 914;
give no quarter.

Adj. piti-, merci-, ruth-, bowel-less; unpitying,
unmerciful, inclement; in-, un-compassionate;
inexorable, inflexible; harsh etc. 739; cruel etc.
907; unrelenting etc. 919.

915. Condolence.—N. condolence; lamen-
tation etc. 839; sympathy, consolation.

V. condole with, console, sympathize etc. 914;
share one's misery; feel for; express –, testify- pity;
afford –, supply- consolation; lament etc. 839-
with; send one's condolences.

916. Gratitude.—N. gratitude, thankfulness,
gratefulness, feeling of obligation.

acknowledgement, recognition, thanksgiving,
giving thanks.

thanks, praise, benediction; paean; *Te Deum*
etc. (*worship*) 990; grace, – before, – after-
meat; thank-offering.

requital.

V. be -grateful etc. *adj.*; thank; give –, render
–, return –, offer –, tender- thanks etc. *n.*;
acknowledge, requite.

feel –, be –, lie- under an obligation; *savoir
gré*; not look a gift horse in the mouth; never
forget, overflow with gratitude; thank –, bless-
one's stars; fall on one's knees.

Adj. grateful, thankful, obliged, beholden, indebted to, under obligation.

Int. thanks! many thanks! gramercy! much
obliged! thank you! thank Heaven! Heaven be
praised!

917. Ingratitude.—N. ingratitude,
thanklessness, oblivion of benefits; unthankfulness.

'benefits forgot;' thankless -task, – office.

V. be -ungrateful etc. *adj.*; forget benefits; look
a gift horse in the mouth.

Adj. un-grateful, -mindful, -thankful; thankless,
ingrate, wanting in gratitude, insensible of benefits.

forgotten; un-acknowledged, -thanked, -
requited, -rewarded; ill-requited.

Int. thank you for nothing! *'et tu Brute!'*

918. Forgiveness.—N. forgiveness, pardon,
condonation, grace, remission, absolution, amnesty, oblivion; indulgence; reprieve.

conciliation; reconciliation etc. (*pacification*) 723; propitiation.

excuse, exoneration, quittance, release, indemnity; bill −, act −, covenant −, deed- of indemnity; exculpation etc. (*acquittal*) 970.

longanimity, placability, forbearance; *amantium irae*; *locus poenitentiae*.

V. forgive, − and forget; pardon, condone, think no more of, let bygones be bygones, shake hands; forget an injury, bury the hatchet; clean the slate.

excuse, pass over, overlook; wink at etc. (*neglect*) 460; bear with; allow −, make allowances- for; let one down easily, not be too hard upon, pocket the affront; blot out one's transgression.

let off, remit, absolve, give absolution, reprieve; acquit etc. 970.

beg −, ask −, implore- pardon etc. *n.*; conciliate, propitiate, placate; make up a quarrel etc. (*pacify*) 723; let the wound heal.

Adj. forgiving, placable, conciliatory.

forgiven etc. *v.*; un-resented, -avenged, revenged.

Adv. cry you mercy.

Phr. *veniam petimusque damusque vicissim*; more in sorrow than in anger.

919. Revenge.—N. revenge, -ment; vengeance; avenge-ment, -ance; sweet revenge, *vendetta*, death-feud, eye for an eye, blood for blood, a Roland for an Oliver; retaliation etc. 718; day of reckoning.

rancor, vindictiveness, implacability; malevolence etc. 907; ruthlessness etc. 914a.

avenger, vindicator, Nemesis, Eumenides.

V. re-, a-venge; take −, have one's- revenge; breathe -revenge, − vengeance; wreak one's -vengeance, − anger; give no quarter.

have -accounts to settle, − a crow to pluck, − a rod in pickle; pay off old scores.

keep the wound green; harbor -revenge, − vindictive feeling; bear malice; rankle, − in the breast; have at one's mercy.

Adj. revenge-, venge-ful; vindictive, rancorous; pitiless etc. 914a; ruthless, rigorous, avenging, retaliative.

unforgiving, unrelenting; inexorable, stony-hearted, implacable; relent-, remorse-less.

aeternum servans sub pectore vulnus; rankling, immitigable.

Phr. *manet -cicatrix,− altâ mente repostum*. revenge is sweet.

920. Jealousy.—N. jealous-y, -ness; jaundiced eye, heartburning; green-eyed monster; yellows; Juno.

V. be -jealous etc. *adj.*; view with -jealousy, − a jealous eye.

Adj. jealous, − as a Barbary pigeon; jaundiced, yellow-eyed, horn-mad.

921. Envy.—N. envy; enviousness etc. *adj.*; rivalry; *jalousie de métier*.

V. envy, covet, lust after, crave, burst with envy, regard with envious eyes.

Adj. envious, invidious, covetous; *alieni appetens*.

922. Right.—N. right; what -ought to, − should- be; fitness etc. *adj.*; *summum jus*.

justice, equity; equitableness etc. *adj.*; propriety; fair play, impartiality, measure for measure, give and take, *lex talionis*, square deal.

Astraea, Nemesis, Themis.

scales of justice, even-handed justice, retributive justice, *suum cuique*; clear stage −, fair field- and no favor; Queensberry rules.

morals etc. (*duty*) 926; law etc. 963; honor etc. (*probity*) 939; virtue etc. 944.

V. be -right etc. *adj.*; stand to reason.

see -justice done, − one righted, − fair play; do justice to; recompense etc. (*reward*) 973; hold the scales even, give and take; serve one right, put the saddle on the right horse; give -every one, − the devil- his due; *audire alteram partem*.

deserve etc. (*be entitled to*) 924.

Adj. right, good; just, reasonable; fit etc. 924; equ-al, -able, -itable; evenhanded, fair, − and square.

legitimate, justifiable, rightful; as it -should, − ought to- be; lawful etc. (*permitted*) 760, (*legal*) 963.

deserved etc. 924.

Adv. rightly etc. *adj.*; in -justice, − equity, − reason.

without -distinction of, − regard to, − respect to- persons; upon even terms.

Int. all right!

923. Wrong.—N. wrong; what -ought not to, − should not- be; *malum in se*; unreasonableness, grievance; shame.

injustice; unfairness etc. *adj.*; iniquity, foul play, partiality, leaning; favor, -itism; nepotism, party spirit, partisanship; undueness etc. 925; unlawfulness etc. 964.

robbing Peter to pay Paul etc. *v.*; the wolf and the lamb; vice etc. 945.

a custom more honored in the breach than the observance.

V. be -wrong etc. *adj.*; cry to heaven for vengeance.

do -wrong etc. *n.*; be -inequitable etc. *adj.*; favor, lean towards; encroach; impose upon; reap where one has not sown; give an inch and take an ell; rob Peter to pay Paul.

Adj. wrong, -ful; bad, too bad; unjust, -fair; in-, un-equitable; unequal, partial, one-sided.

objectionable; un-reasonable, -allowable, -warrantable, -justifiable; not cricket, not playing the game; improper, unfit; unjustified etc. 925; illegal etc. 964; iniquitous, criminal; immoral etc. 945; injurious etc. 649.

in the wrong, − box.

Adv. wrongly etc. *adj.*

Phr. it will not do; this is too bad.

924. Dueness.—N. due, -ness; right, privilege, prerogative, prescription, title, claim, pretension, demand, birthright.

immunity, license, liberty, franchise; vested - interest, – right; licitness.

sanction, authority, warranty, charter; warrant etc. (*permission*) 760; constitution etc. (*law*) 963; tenure; bond etc. (*security*) 771.

deserts, merits, dues.

claimant, appellant; plaintiff etc. 938.

V. be -due etc. *adj.* to, – the due etc. *n.* of; have -right, – title, – claim- to; be entitled to; have a claim upon; belong to etc. (*property*) 780.

deserve, merit, be worthy of, richly deserve.

demand, claim; call upon –, come upon –, appeal to- for; re-vendicate, -claim; exact; insist -on, – upon; challenge; take one's stand, make a point of, require, lay claim to, assert, assume, arrogate, make good; substantiate; vindicate a -claim, – right; make out a case.

give –, confer- a right; sanction, entitle; authorize etc. 760; sanctify, legalize, ordain, prescribe, allot.

give every one his due etc. 922; pay one's dues; have one's -due, – rights; stand upon one's rights.

use a right, assert, enforce, put in force, lay under contribution.

Adj. having a right to etc. *v.*; entitled to; claiming; deserving, meriting, worthy of.

privileged, allowed, sanctioned, warranted, authorized; ordained, prescribed, constitutional, chartered, enfranchised.

prescriptive, presumptive; absolute, indefeasible; un-, in-alienable.

imprescriptible, inviolable, unimpeachable, unchallenged; sacrosanct.

due to, merited, deserved, condign, richly deserved, *emeritus*.

allowable etc. (*permitted*) 760; lawful, licit, legitimate, legal; legalized etc. (*law*) 963.

square, unexceptionable, right; equitable etc. 922; due, *en règle*; fit, -ting; correct, proper, meet, befitting, becoming, seemly; decorous, creditable, up to the mark, right as a trivet; just –, quite- the thing; *selon les règles*.

Adv. duly, *ex officio, de jure*; by -right, – divine right; as is -fitting, – proper, – fitting and proper; *jure divino, Dei gratiâ*, in the name of.

Phr. *civis Romanus sum.*

925. Undueness. [Absence of right.] —**N.** undueness etc. *adj.*; *malum prohibitum*; impropriety; illegality etc. 964.

falseness etc. *adj.*; emptiness –, invalidity- of title; illegitimacy.

loss of right, disfranchisement, forfeiture.

usurpation, assumption, tort, violation, breach, encroachment, presumption, seizure, stretch, exaction, imposition, lion's share.

usurper, pretender, Carlist; imposter.

V. be -undue etc. *adj.*; not be -due etc. 924.

infringe, encroach, trench on, exact; arrogate, – to oneself; give an inch and take an ell; stretch –, strain- a point; usurp, violate, do violence to; sail under false colors.

dis-franchise, -entitle, -qualify; invalidate.

relax etc. (*be lax*) 738; misbehave etc. (*vice*) 945; misbecome.

Adj. undue; unlawful etc. (*illegal*) 964; unconstitutional, *ultra vires*; illicit; un-authorized, - warranted, -allowed, -sanctioned, -justified; un-, dis-entitled, -qualified; un-privileged, -chartered.

illegitimate, bastard, spurious, false; usurped, tortious.

un-deserved, -merited, -earned; unfulfilled.

forfeited, disfranchised.

improper; un-meet, -fit, -befitting, -seemly; un-, mis-becoming; seemless; *contra bonos mores*; not the thing, out of the question, not to be thought of; preposterous, pretentious, would- be.

926. Duty. —**N.** duty, what ought to be done, moral obligation, accountableness, liability, *onus*, responsibility; bounden –, imperative- duty; call, – of duty.

allegiance, fealty, tie; engagement etc. (*promise*) 768; part; function, calling etc. (*business*) 625.

morality, morals, decalogue; case of conscience; conscientiousness etc. (*probity*) 939; conscience, inward monitor, still small voice within, sense of duty, tender conscience.

dueness etc. 924; propriety, fitness, seemliness, amenableness, decorum; the -thing, – proper thing; the -right, – proper- thing to do.

[Science of morals] eth-ics, -ology; deon-, aretology; moral –, ethical-philosophy; casuistry, polity.

observance, fulfilment, discharge, performance, acquittal, satisfaction, redemption; good behavior.

V. be -the duty of, – incumbent etc. *adj.* on, – responsible etc. *adj.*; behoove, become, befit, beseem; belong –, pertain- to; fall to one's lot; devolve on; lie -upon, – on one's head, – at one's door; rest -with, – on the shoulders of.

take upon oneself etc. (*promise*) 768.

be –, become- -bound to, – sponsor for; be responsible for; incur a -responsibility etc. *n.*; be –, stand –, lie- under an obligation; have to answer for, owe it to oneself.

impose a -duty etc. *n.*; enjoin, require, exact; bind, – over; saddle with, prescribe, assign, call upon, look to, oblige.

enter upon –, perform –, observe –, fulfil –, discharge –, adhere to –, acquit oneself of –, satisfy- -a duty, – an obligation; act one's part, redeem one's pledge, do justice to, be at one's post; do duty; do one's duty etc. (*be virtuous*) 944.

be on one's good behavior, mind one's P's and Q's.

Adj. obligatory, binding; imperative, peremptory; stringent etc. (*severe*) 739; behooving etc. *v.*; incumbent –, chargeable- on; under obligation; obliged –, bound –, tied- by; saddled with.

due –, beholden –, bound –, indebted- to; tied down; compromised etc. (*promised*) 768; in duty bound.

amenable, liable, accountable, responsible, answerable.

right, meet etc. (*due*) 924; moral, ethical, casuistical, conscientious, ethological.

Adv. with a safe conscience, as in duty bound, on one's own responsibility, at one's own risk, *suo periculo*; *in foro conscientiae*; *quamdiu se bene gesserit*; at one's post, on duty.

Phr. *dura lex sed lex.*

927. Dereliction of Duty. —**N.** dere; liction of duty; fault etc. (*guilt*) 947- sin etc. (*vice*) 945; non-observance, -performance, -co-operation; neglect, carelessness, laziness, incompetence, eye-service,

relaxation, infraction, violation, transgression, failure, evasion, indolence; dead letter.

slacker, loafer, striker, non-co-operator.

V. violate; break, – through; infringe; set - aside, – at naught; trample -on, – under foot; slight, neglect, evade, renounce, forswear, repudiate; wash one's hands of; escape, transgress, fail.

call to account etc. (*disapprobation*) 932.

927a. Exemption.—N. exemption, freedom, irresponsibility, immunity, liberty, license, release, exoneration, excuse, dispensation, absolution, franchise, renunciation, discharge; exculpation etc. 970; *aegrotat*.

V. be -exempt etc. *adj.*

exempt, release, acquit, discharge, quit-claim, remise, remit; free, set at liberty, let off, pass over, spare, excuse, dispense with, give dispensation, license; stretch a point; absolve etc. (*forgive*) 918; exonerate etc. (*exculpate*) 970; save the necessity.

Adj. exempt, free, immune, at liberty, scot free; released etc. *v.*; unbound, unencumbered; irresponsible, unaccountable, not answerable; excusable.

928. Respect.—N. respect, regard, consideration; courtesy etc. 894; attention, deference, reverence, honor, esteem, estimation, veneration, admiration; approbation etc. 931.

homage, fealty, obeisance, genuflexion, kneeling, prostration; obsequiousness etc. 886; salaam, *kowtow*, bow, presenting arms, salute.

respects, regards, duty, *devoirs*, *égards*.

devotion etc. (*piety*) 987.

V. respect, regard, revere, -nce; hold in reverence, honor, venerate, hallow; esteem etc. (*approve of*) 931; think much of; entertain –, bear- respect for; have a high opinion of; look up to, defer to; pay -attention, – respect etc. *n*.- to; do –, render- honor to; do the honors, hail; show courtesy etc. 894; salute, present arms; do –, pay-homage to; pay tribute to; kneel to, bow to, bend the knee to; fall down before, prostrate oneself, kiss the hem of one's garment; worship etc. 990.

keep one's distance, make room, observe due decorum, stand upon ceremony.

command –, inspire- respect; awe, impose, overawe, dazzle.

Adj. respecting etc. *v.*; respectful, deferential, decorous, reverential, obsequious, ceremonious, bare-headed, cap in hand, on one's knees; prostrate etc. (*servile*) 886.

respected etc. *v.*; in high -esteem, – estimation; time-honored, venerable, *emeritus*.

Adv. in deference to; with -all, – due, – the highest- respect; with submission.

saving your -grace, – presence; *salva sit reverentia*; *pace tanti nominis*.

Int. hail! all hail! *esto perpetua!* may your shadow never be less!

929. Disrespect.—N. dis-respect, -esteem, -estimation, -favor, -repute; low estimation; disparagement etc. (*dispraise*) 932; (*detraction*) 934.

irreverence; slight, neglect; *spretae injuria formae*; superciliousness etc. (*contempt*) 930.

vilipendency, contumely, affront, dishonor, insult, indignity, outrage, discourtesy etc. 895; practical joking; scurrility, scoffing, sibilation; ir-, derision; mockery; irony etc. (*ridicule*) 856; sarcasm.

hiss, hoot, gibe, flout, jeer, scoff, gleek, taunt, sneer, quip, fling, wipe, slap in the face.

V. hold in disrespect etc. (*despise*) 930; misprize, disregard, slight, undervalue, depreciate, trifle with, set at naught, pass by, push aside, overlook, turn one's back upon, laugh in one's sleeve; be -disrespectful etc. *adj.*, – discourteous etc. 895; treat with -disrespect etc. *n.*; set down, browbeat.

dishonor, desecrate; insult, affront, outrage.

speak slightingly of; disparage etc. (*dispraise*) 932; vilipend, call names; throw –, fling- dirt; drag through the mud, point at, indulge in personalities; make -mouths, – faces; bite the thumb; take –, pluck- by the beard; toss in a blanket, tar and feather.

have –, hold- in derision; deride, scoff, sneer, laugh at, snigger, ridicule, gibe, mock, jeer, taunt, twit, niggle, gleek, gird, flout, fleer; roast, turn into ridicule; guy, burlesque etc. 856; laugh to scorn etc. (*contempt*) 930; smoke; fool; make -game, – a fool, – an April fool- of; play a practical joke; rag; lead one a dance, run the rig upon, have a fling at, scout, hiss, hoot, mob.

Adj. disrespectful; aweless, irreverent; disparaging etc. 934; insulting etc. *v.*; supercilious etc. (*scornful*) 930; rude, derisive, contemptuous, sarcastic; scurri-le, -lous; contumelious.

un-respected, -worshipped, -envied, -saluted; un-dis-regarded.

Adv. disrespectfully etc. *adj.*

930. Contempt.—N. contempt, disdain, scorn, sovereign contempt; despi-sal, -ciency; vilipendency, contumely; slight, sneer, spurn, by-word.

contemptuousness etc. *adj.*; scornful eye; smile of contempt; derision etc. (*disrespect*) 929.

[State of being despised] despisedness.

V. despise, contemn, scorn, disdain, feel contempt for, view with a scornful eye, disregard, slight, not mind; pass by etc. (*neglect*) 460.

look down upon; hold -cheap, – in contempt, – in disrespect; think -nothing, – small beer- of; make light of; underestimate etc. 483; esteem -slightly, – of small or no account; take no account of, care nothing for; set no store by; not care a -straw etc. (*unimportance*) 643; set at naught,-laugh in one's sleeve, snap one's fingers at, shrug one's shoulders, turn up one's nose at, pooh-pooh, damn with faint praise; sneeze –, whistle –, sneer- at; curl up one's lip, toss the head, *traiter de haut*; laugh at etc. (*be disrespectful*) 929.

point the finger of –, hold up to –, laugh to-scorn; scout, hoot, flout, hiss, scoff at.

turn -one's back, – a cold shoulder- upon; tread –, trample- -upon, – under foot; spurn, kick; fling to the winds etc. (*repudiate*) 610; send away with a flea in the ear.

Adj. contemptuous; disdain-, scorn-ful; withering, contumelious, supercilious, cynical, haughty, bumptious, cavalier; derisive.

contemptible, despicable; pitiable; pitiful etc.
(*unimportant*) 643; despised etc. *v.*; down-
trodden; unenvied.

Adv. contemptuously etc. *adj.*

Int. a fig for etc. (*unimportant*) 643; bah! never
mind! away with! hang it! fiddle-de-dee!

931. Approbation.—N. approbation; approv-
al, -ement; sanction, advocacy; nod of approbation;
esteem, estimation, good opinion, golden opinions,
admiration; love etc. 897; appreciation, regard, account, popularity, *kudos*, credit; repute etc. 873.

commendation, praise; laud, -ation; good word;
meed —, tribute- of praise; encomium; eulog-y, -
ium; *éloge*, panegyric; homage, hero worship;
benediction, blessing, benison.

applause, plaudit, clap; clapping, — of hands;
accl-aim, -amation; cheer; paean, hosannah; shout
—, peal —, chorus —, thunders- of -applause etc.
Kentish fire; Prytaneum; blurb.

V. approve; think -good, — much of, — well of,
— highly of; esteem, value, prize; set great store -
by, — on.

do justice to, appreciate; honor, hold in esteem,
look up to, admire; like etc. 897; be in favor of,
wish God speed; hail, — with satisfaction.

stand —, stick- up for; uphold, hold up, countenance, sanction; clap —, pat- on the back; keep
in countenance, endorse, give credit, recommend;
mark with a white -mark, — stone.

commend, praise; be-, laud; compliment, pay a
tribute, bepraise; clap, the hands; applaud,
cheer, acclaim, acclamate, encore; panegyrize,
eulogize, cry up, *prôner*, puff; extol, — to the
skies; magnify, glorify, exalt, boost, swell, make
much of; flatter etc. 933; bless, give a blessing to;
have —, say- a good word for; speak -well, —
highly, — in high terms- of; sing —, sound —,
chaunt —, resound- the praises of; sing praises to;
cheer —, applaud- to the -echo, — very echo.

redound to the -honor, — praise, — credit- of;
do credit to; deserve -praise etc. *n.*; recommend itself; pass muster.

be -praised etc.; receive honorable mention; be
in -favor, — high favor- with; ring with the praises
of, win golden opinions, gain credit, find favor
with, stand well in the opinion of; *laudari a
laudato viro*.

Adj. approving etc. *v.*; in favor of; lost in admiration.

commendatory, complimentary, benedictory,
laudatory, panegyrical, eulogistic, encomiastic, ac-
clamatory, lavish of praise; uncritical.

approved, praised etc. *v.*; un-censured, -
impeached; popular, in good odor; in high esteem
etc. (*respected*) 928; in —, in high- favor.

deserving —, worthy of- praise etc. *n.*;
praiseworthy, commendable, of estimation; good
etc. 648; meritorious, estimable, creditable,
plausible, unimpeachable; beyond all praise.

Adv. commendably, with credit, to admiration;
well etc. 681; with three times three.

Int. hear, hear! well done! *brav-o! -a! -i!
bravissimo! euge! macte virtute!* so far so good,
that's right, quite right; *optime!* one cheer more;
may your shadow never be less! *esto perpetua!*
long life to! *viva! enviva!* God speed! *valete et
plaudite! encore! bis!*

Phr. *probatum est.*

932. Disapprobation.—N. disappro-bation, -
val; improbation; dis-esteem, | -valuation, -
placency; odium; dislike etc. 867; dissent etc. 489.

dis-praise, -commendation; blame, censure,
obloquy; detraction etc. 934; disparagement,
depreciation; denunciation; condemnation etc.
971; ostracism; boycott; black-list, -ball; *index -
expurgatorius*, — *librorum prohibitorum*.

animadversion, reflection, stricture, objection,
exception, criticism; sardonic -grin, — laugh; sarcasm, insinuation, innuendo; bad —, poor —, left-
handed- compliment.

satire; sneer etc. (*contempt*) 930; taunt etc.
(*disrespect*) 929; cavil, carping, censoriousness;
hypercriticism etc. (*fastidiousness*) 868.

reprehension, remonstrance, expostulation,
reproof, reprobation, admonition, increpation,
reproach; rebuke, reprimand, castigation, jobation,
lecture, curtain lecture, blow up, wigging, dressing,
— down; rating, scolding, trimming; correction, set
down, rap on the knuckles, *coup de bec*, rebuff;
slap, — on the face; home thrust; hit, frown, scowl,
black look.

diatribe; jeremiad; *tirade*, philippic.

clamor, outcry, hue and cry; hiss, -ing; sibilation,
cat-call; execration etc. 908.

chiding, upbraiding etc. *v.*; exprobration, abuse,
vituperation, invective, objurgation, contumely,
personal remarks; hard —, cutting —, bitter-
words.

evil-speaking; bad language etc. 908; personality.

V. disapprove; dislike etc. 867; lament etc. 839;
object to, take exception to; be scandalized at,
think ill of; view with -disfavor, — dark eyes, —
jaundiced eyes; *nil admirari*, disvalue, improbate.

frown upon, look grave; bend —, knit- the
brows; shake the head at, shrug the shoulders; turn
up the nose etc. (*contempt*) 930; look -askance, —
black upon; look with an evil eye; make a wry -
face, — mouth- at; set one's face against.

dis-praise, -commend, -parage; deprecate, speak
ill of, not speak well of; slate, condemn etc. (*find
guilty*) 971.

blame; lay —, cast- blame upon; censure, *fron-
der*, reproach, pass censure on, reprobate, impugn.

remonstrate, expostulate, recriminate.

reprehend, chide, admonish; bring —, call- -to
account, — over the coals, — to order; take to
task, reprove, lecture, bring to book; read a -lesson,
— lecture- to; rebuke, correct.

reprimand, chastise, castigate, lash, blow up,
trounce, trim, *laver la tête*, overhaul; give it one,
— finely; gibbet.

accuse etc. 938; impeach, denounce; hold up to -
reprobation, — execration; expose, brand, gibbet,
stigmatize; show —, pull —, take- up; cry 'shame'
upon; be outspoken; raise a hue and cry against.

execrate etc. 908; exprobrate, speak daggers,
vituperate; abuse, —, like a pickpocket; scold, rate,
objurage, upbraid, fall foul of; jaw; rail, — at, — in
good set terms; bark at; anathematize, call names;
call by -hard, — ugly- names; a-, re-vile; vili-fy, -
pend; bespatter; backbite; clapperclaw; rave —,
thunder —, fulminate- against; load with
reproaches; lash with the tongue.

exclaim —, protest —, inveigh —, declaim —,
cry out —, raise one's voice- against.

decry; cry —, run —, frown- down; clamor, hiss,

hoot, mob, ostracize; draw up –, sing- a round robin; black-ball, -list.

animadvert –, reflect- upon; glance at; cast - reflection, – reproach, – a slur- upon; insinuate, damn with faint praise; 'hint a fault and hesitate dislike;' not to be able to say much for.

scoff at, point at; twit, taunt etc. (*disrespect*) 929; sneer at etc. (*despise*) 230; satirize, lampoon; defame etc. (*detract*) 934; depreciate, find fault with, criticize, cut up; pull –, pick- to pieces; take exception; cavil; peck –, nibble –, carp- at; be - censorious etc. *adj.*; pick -holes, – a hole, – a hole in one's coat; make a fuss about.

take –, set- down; snub, snap one up, give a rap on the knuckles; throw a stone -at, – in one's gar- den; have a -fling, – snap- at; have words with, pluck a crow with; give one a -wipe, – lick with the rough side of the tongue.

incur blame, excite disapprobation, scandalize, shock, revolt; get a bad name, forfeit one's good opinion, be under a cloud, come under the ferule, bring a hornet's nest about one's ears.

take blame, stand corrected; have to answer for.

Adj. disapproving etc. *v.*; scandalized.

disparaging, condemnatory, damnatory, denun- ciatory, reproachful, abusive, objurgatory, clamorous, vituperative; defamatory etc. 934.

satirical, sarcastic, sardonic, cynical, dry, sharp, cutting, biting, severe, virulent, withering, trench- ant, hard upon; censorious, critical, captious, carping, hypercritical; fastidious etc. 868; sparing of –, grudging- praise.

disapproved, chid etc. *v.*; in bad odor, blown upon, unapproved; unblest; at a discount, ex- ploded; weighed in the balance and found wanting.

blameworthy, reprehensible etc. (*guilt*) 947; to –, worthy of- blame, answerable, un- commendable, exceptionable, not to be thought of, bad etc. 649; vicious etc. 945.

un-lamented, -bewailed, -pitied.

Adv. with a wry face; reproachfully etc. *adj.*

Int. it is too bad! it -won't, – will never- do! marry come up! Oh! come! 'sdeath!

forbid it Heaven! God –, Heaven- forbid! out –, fie- upon it! away with! tut! *O tempora! O mores!* shame! fie, – for shame! out on you! tell it not in Gath!

933. Flattery.—N. flattery, adulation, gloze; bland-ishment, -iloquence; cajolery; fawning, wheedling etc. *v.*; captation, coquetry, sycophancy, obsequiousness, flunkeyism, toad-eating, tuft- hunting; snobbishness.

incense, honeyed words, flummery; bun-kum, - combe; blarney, *placebo*, butter; soft -soap, – sawder; rose water.

voice of the charmer, mouth honor; lip-homage; euphemism; unctuousness etc. *adj.*

V. flatter, praise to the skies, puff; wheedle, cajole, glaver, coax; fawn, –, upon; humor, gloze, soothe, pet, coquet, slaver, butter; be-spatter, - slubber, -plaster, -slaver; lay it on thick, overpraise; earwig, cog, collogue; truckle –, pander *or* pandar –, pay court- to; court; creep into the good graces of; curry favor with, hang on the sleeve of; fool to the top of one's bent; lick the dust.

lay the flattering unction to one's soul, gild the pill, make things pleasant.

overestimate etc. 482; exaggerate etc. 549.

Adj. flattering etc. *v.*; adulatory; mealy-, honey- mouthed; honeyed; smooth, – tongued; soapy, oily, unctuous, blandiloquent, specious; fine-, fair- spoken; plausible, servile, sycophantic, fulsome; courtier-ly, -like.

Adv. *ad captandum.*

934. Detraction.—N. detraction, disparagement, depreciation, vilification, obloquy, scurrility, scandal, defamation, aspersion, traducement, slander, calumny, obtrectation, evil- speaking, backbiting, *scandalum magnatum.*

personality, libel, squib, lampoon, skit, pasquinade; *chronique scandaleuse.*

sarcasm, cynicism; criticism (*disapprobation*) 932; invective etc. 932; envenomed tongue; *spretae injuria formae.*

detractor etc. 936.

V. detract, derogate, decry, depreciate, disparage; run –, cry- down; minimize, make light of; belittle, sneer at etc. (*contemn*) 930; criticize, pull to pieces, pick a hole in one's coat, asperse, cast aspersions, blow upon, bespatter, blacken; vili- fy, -pend; avile; give a dog a bad name, brand, malign, backbite, libel, lampoon, traduce, slander, defame, calumniate, bear false witness against; speak ill of behind one's back.

'damn with faint praise, assent with civil leer; and without sneering, others teach to sneer.'

fling dirt etc. (*disrespect*) 929; anathematize etc. 932; dip the pen in gall, view in a bad light.

Adj. detracting etc. *v.*; defamatory, detractory, derogatory; disparaging, libellous; scurril-e, -ous; abusive; foul-spoken, -tongued, -mouthed; slan- derous; calumni-ous, -atory; sar-castic, -donic; satirical, cynical.

935. Flatterer.—N. flatterer, adulator; eu- logist, -phemist; optimist, encomiast, *laudator*, whitewasher, booster.

toad-y, -eater; sycophant, courtier, pickthank, Sir Pertinax MacSycophant; *flâneur, prôneur*; puffer, touter, *claqueur*; claw-back, ear-wig, doer of dirty work; parasite, hanger on etc. (*servility*) 886.

936. Detractor.—N. detractor, reprover; cens- or, -urer; cynic, critic, caviller, carper, word- catcher.

defamer, backbiter, slanderer, knocker, Sir Ben- jamin Backbite, lampooner, satirist, traducer, libeller, calumniator, dearest foe, dawplucker, Thersites; Zoilus; good-natured –, candid- friend [satirically] ; reviler, vituperator, castigator; shrew etc. 901.

disapprover, *laudator temporis acti.*

937. Vindication.—N. vindication, justification, warrant; exoneration, exculpation; acquittal etc. 970; whitewashing.

extenuation; pallia-tion, -tive; softening, mitigation.

reply, defense; recrimination etc. 938.

apology, gloss, varnish; plea etc. 617; salvo; ex-

cuse, extenuating circumstances; allowance, − to be made; *locus poenitentiae.*

apologist, vindicator, justifier; defendant etc. 938.

justifiable charge, true bill.

V. justify, warrant; be an -excuse etc. *n.*- for; lend a color, furnish a handle; vindicate; ex-, disculpate; acquit etc. 970; clear, set right, exonerate, whitewash.

extenuate, palliate, excuse, soften, apologize, varnish, slur, gloze; put a -gloss, − good face- upon; mince; gloss over, bolster up, help a lame dog over a stile.

advocate, defend, plead one's cause; stand −, stick −, speak- up for; contend −, speak- for; bear out, keep in countenance, support; plead etc. 617; say in defense; plead ignorance; confess and avoid, propugn, put in a good word for.

take the will for the deed, make allowance for, do justice to; give -one, − the Devil- his due.

make good; prove -the truth of, − one's case; be justified by the event.

Adj. vindicat-ed, -ing etc. *v.*; vindicat-ive, -ory; palliative; exculpatory; apologetic.

excusable, defensible, pardonable; veni-al, -able; specious, plausible, justifiable.

Phr. *'honi soit qui mal y pense.'*

938. Accusation.—N. accusation, charge, im- putation, slur, inculpation, exprobration, delation; crimination; in-, ac-, re-crimination; *tu quoque* argument; invective etc. 932.

de-nunciation, -nouncement; libel, challenge, citation, arraignment; im-, ap-peachment; in- dictment, bill of indictment, true bill; lawsuit etc. 969; condemnation etc. 971.

gravamen of a charge, head and front of one's offending, *argumentum ad hominem*; scandal etc. (*detraction*) 934; *scandalum magnatum.*

accuser, prosecutor, plaintiff, complainant, petitioner; relator, informer; appellant.

accused, defendant, prisoner, panel, co-, respon- dent; litigant.

V. accuse, charge, tax, impute, twit, taunt with, reproach.

brand with reproach; stigmatize, slur; cast a - stone at, − slur on; incriminate; inculpate, im- plicate; call to account etc. (*censure*) 932; take to- blame, − task; put in the black book.

inform against, indict, denounce, arraign; im-, ap-peach; have up, show up, pull up, challenge, cite, lodge a complaint; prosecute, bring an action against etc. 969.

charge −, saddle- with; lay to one's -door, − charge; lay the blame on, bring home to; cast −, throw- in one's teeth; cast the first stone at.

have −, keep- a rod in pickle for; have a crow to pluck with.

trump up a charge.

Adj. accusing etc. *v.*; accusat-ory, -ive; im- putative, denunciatory; re-, criminatory.

accused etc. *v.*; suspected; under -suspicion, − a cloud, − *surveillance*; in -custody, − detention; in the -lock up, − watch house, − house of deten- tion.

accusable, imputable; in-defensible, -excusable; un-pardonable, -justifiable; vicious etc. 945.

Int. look at home; *tu quoque* etc. (*retaliation*) 718.

939. Probity.—N. probity, integrity, rectitude; uprightness etc. *adj.*; honesty, faith; honor; good faith, *bona fides*; purity, clean hands.

fairness etc. *adj.*; fair play, justice, equity, im- partiality, principle; grace.

constancy; faithfulness etc. *adj.*; fidelity, loyalty; incorrupt-ion, -ibility.

trustworthiness etc. *adj.*; truth, candor, singleness of heart; veracity etc. 543; tender con- science etc. (*sense of duty*) 926.

punctil-iousness, -io; delicacy, nicety; scrupul- osity, -ousness etc. *adj.*; scruple; point, − of honor; punctuality.

dignity etc. (*repute*) 873; respectability, -bleness etc. *adj.*; gentleman; man of -honor, − his word; *fidus Achates, preux chevalier; galantuomo*; truepenny, trump, brick; true Briton, white man, sportsman.

court of honor, a fair field and no favor; *argumentum ad verecundiam.*

V. be -honorable etc. *adj.*; deal -honorably, − squarely, − impartially, − fairly; speak the truth etc. (*veracity*) 543; tell the truth and shame the devil, *vitam impendere vero*; show a proper spirit, make a point of; do one's duty etc. 944; play the game.

redeem one's pledge etc. 926; keep −, be as good as- one's -promise, − word; keep faith with, not fail.

give and take, *audire alteram partem*, give the devil his due, put the saddle on the right horse.

redound to one's honor.

Adj. upright; honest, − as daylight; veracious etc. 543; virtuous etc. 944; honorable; fair, right, just, equitable, impartial, even-handed, square; fair −, open- and aboveboard.

constant, − as the northern star; faithful, loyal, staunch; true, − blue, − to one's colors, − to the core, − as the needle to the pole; true-hearted, trust-y, -worthy; as good as one's word, to be depended on, incorruptible.

manly, straightforward etc. (*ingenuous*) 703; frank, candid, open-hearted.

conscientious, tender-conscienced, right-minded; high-principled, -minded; scrupulous, religious, strict; nice, punctilious, correct, punctual; respect-, reput-able; gentlemanlike.

inviol-able, -ate; un-violated, -broken, -betrayed; un-bought, -bribed.

innocent etc. 946; pure; stainless; un-stained, - tarnished, -sullied, -tainted, -perjured; uncorrupt, - ed; unde-filed, -praved, -bauched; *integer vitae scelerisque purus; justus et tenax propositi.*

chivalrous, jealous of honor, *sans peur et sans reproche*; high-spirited.

supra-mundane, unworldly, overscrupulous.

Adv. honorably etc. *adj.*; *bona fide*; on the square, in good faith, honor bright, *foro con- scientiae*, with clean hands; by fair means.

940. Improbity.—N. improbity; dishon-esty, -our; deviation from rectitude; disgrace etc. (*disrepute*) 874; fraud etc. (*deception*) 545; lying etc. 544; bad −, Punic- faith; *mala −, Punica, fides*; infidelity; faithlessness etc. *adj.*; Judas kiss, betrayal; scrap of paper.

breach of -promise, − trust, − faith; prodition, disloyalty, divided allegiance, treason, high

treason; apostacy etc. (*tergiversation*) 607; non-observance etc. 773.

shabbiness etc. *adj.*; villainy; baseness etc. *adj.*; abjection, debasement, turpitude, moral turpitude, laxity, trimming, shuffling.

perfidy; perfidiousness etc. *adj.*; treachery, double-dealing; unfairness etc. *adj.*; knavery, roguery, rascality, foul-play; jobb-ing, -ery; Tammany, graft; venality, nepotism; corruption, job, shuffle, fishy transaction, barratry; sharp practice, heads I win, tails you lose; mouth-honor etc. (*flattery*) 933.

V. be -dishonest etc. *adj.*; play false; break one's -word, – faith, – promise; jilt, betray, forswear; shuffle etc. (*lie*) 544; live by one's wits, sail near the wind; play with marked cards.

disgrace –, dishonor –, demean –, degrade-oneself; derogate, stoop, grovel, sneak, lose caste; sell oneself, go over to the enemy; seal one's infamy.

Adj. dishon-est, -orable; un-conscientious, -scrupulous; fraudulent etc. 545; knavish; disgraceful etc. (*disreputable*) 874; wicked etc. 945.

false-hearted, disingenuous; unfair, one-sided; double, -tongued, -faced; time-serving, crooked, tortuous, insidious Machiavellian, dark, slippery; questionable; fishy; perfidious, treacherous, perjured.

infamous, arrant, foul, base, vile, low, ignominious, blackguard;

contemptible, abject, mean, shabby, little, paltry, dirty, scurvy, scabby, sneaking, groveling, scrubby, rascally, pettifogging; beneath one; not cricket.

low-minded, -thoughted; base-minded.

undignified, indign; unbe-coming, -seeming, fitting; de-rogatory, -grading; *infra dignitatem*; ungentleman-ly, -like; un-knightly, -chivalric, -manly, -handsome; recreant, inglorious.

corrupt, venal; debased, mongrel.

faithless, of bad faith, false, unfaithful, disloyal; untrustworthy; trust-less; troth-less; lost to shame, dead to honor.

Adv. dishonestly etc. *adj.*; *malâ fide*, like a thief in the night, by crooked paths; by foul means.

Int. *O tempora! O mores!*

941. Knave.—**N.** knave, rogue, villain; Seapin, rascal; Lazarillo de Tormes; bad man etc. 949; blackguard etc. 949.

traitor, betrayer, arch-traitor, conspirator, stool pigeon, Judas, Catiline; reptile, serpent, snake in the grass, wolf in sheep's clothing, sneak, Jerry Sneak, tell-tale, squealer, mischief-maker, trimmer; renegade etc. (*tergiversation*) 607; truant, recreant; sycophant etc. (*servility*) 886.

942. Disinterestedness.—**N.** disinterestedness etc. *adj.*; generosity; liberal-ity, -ism; altruism; benevolence etc. 906; elevation, loftiness of purpose, exaltation, magnanimity; chival-ry, -rous spirit; heroism, sublimity.

self-denial, -abnegation, -effacement, -sacrifice; -immolation, -control etc. (*resolution*) 604; stoicism, devotion, martyrdom, *suttee*.

labor of love.

V. be -disinterested etc. *adj.*; make a sacrifice, lay one's head on the block; put oneself in the place of others, do as one would be done by, do unto others as we should men should do unto us.

Adj. disinterested; unselfish; self-denying, -sacrificing, -devoted; generous.

handsome, liberal, noble; noble-, high-minded; princely, great, high, elevated, lofty, exalted, spirited, stoical, magnanimous; great-, large-hearted, chivalrous, heroic, sublime.

un-bought, -bribed; uncorrupted etc. (*upright*) 939.

943. Selfishness.—**N.** selfishness etc. *adj.*; self-love, -indulgence, -worship, -interest; ego-tism, -ism; egocentrism, narcissism; *amour propre* etc. (*vanity*) 880; nepotism.

worldliness etc. *adj.*; world wisdom.

illiberality; meanness etc. *adj.*

time-server; tuft-, fortune-hunter; self-seeker; jobber, worldling; egotist, egoist, monopolist, nepotist, profiteer; temporizer, trimmer; dog in the manger, charity that begins at home.

V. be -selfish etc. *adj.*; please –, indulge –, coddle- oneself; consult one's own -wishes, – pleasure; look after one's own interest; feather one's nest; take care of number one, have an eye to the main chance, know on which side one's bread is buttered; give an inch and take an ell; wangle.

Adj. selfish; self-seeking, -indulgent, -interested; wrapt up –, centered- in self; egotistic, -al; egoistical; egocentric.

illiberal, mean, ungenerous, narrowminded; mercenary, venal; covetous etc. 819.

unspiritual; earthly, -minded; mundane; worldly, -minded, -wise; time-serving.

interested; *alieni appetens sui profusus*.

Adv. ungenerously etc. *adj.*; to gain some private ends; from selfish –, interested- motives.

Phr. *après nous le déluge.*

944. Virtue.—**N.** virtue; virtuousness etc. *adj.*; morality; moral rectitude; integrity etc. (*probity*) 939; nobleness etc. 873.

morals; ethics etc. (*duty*) 926; cardinal virtues.

merit, worth, desert, excellence, credit; self-control etc. (*resolution*) 604; self-denial etc. (*temperance*) 953.

well-doing; good -actions, – behavior; discharge –, fulfilment –, performance- of duty; well spent life; innocence etc. 946.

V. be -virtuous etc. *adj.*; practice -virtue etc. *n.*; do –, fulfil –, perform –, discharge- one's duty; redeem one's pledge etc. 926; act well, – one's part; fight the good fight; acquit oneself well; command –, master- one's passions; keep -straight, – in the right path.

set -an, – a good- example; be on one's -good, – best- behavior.

Adj. virtuous, good; innocent etc. 946; meritorious, deserving, worthy, desertful, correct; dut-iful, -eous; moral; right, -eous, -minded; well-intentioned, creditable, laudable, commendable, praiseworthy; above –, beyond- all praise; excellent, admirable; sterling, pure, noble.

exemplary; match-, peer-less; saint-ly, -like; heaven-born, angelic, seraphic, godlike.

Adv. virtuously etc. *adj.*; *e merito.*

945. Vice.—N. vice; evil-doing, – courses; wrong doing; wickedness, viciousness etc. *adj.*; iniquity, peccability, demerit; sin, Adam; old – offending- Adam.

immorality, impropriety, indecorum, scandal, laxity, looseness of morals; want of -principle, – ballast; obliquity, backsliding, infamy, demoralization, pravity, depravity, pollution; hardness of heart; brutality etc. (*malevolence*) 907; corruption etc. (*debasement*) 659; knavery etc. (*improbity*) 940; profligacy; lust etc. 961; flagrancy, atrocity; cannibalism.

infirmity; weakness etc. *adj.*; weakness of the flesh, frailty, imperfection; error; weak side; foible; fail-ing, -ure; crying –, besetting- sin; defect, deficiency, shortcoming; cloven foot.

lowest dregs of vice, sink of iniquity, Alsatian den; *gusto picaresco.*

fault, crime; criminality etc. (*guilt*) 947.

sinner etc. 949.

V. be -vicious etc. *adj.*; sin, commit sin, do amiss, err, transgress; misdemean –, forget –, misconduct- oneself; mis-do, -behave; fall, lapse, slip, trip, offend, trespass; deviate from the -line of duty, – path of virtue etc. 944; take a wrong course, go astray; hug a -sin, – fault; sow one's wild oats.

render -vicious etc. *adj.*; demoralize, brutalize; corrupt etc. (*degrade*) 659.

Adj.* vicious; sinful; sinning etc. *v.*; wicked, iniquitous, bad, immoral, unrighteous, wrong, criminal; naughty, incorrect; undut-eous, -iful.

unprincipled, lawless, disorderly, *contra bonos mores*, indecorous, unseemly, improper; dissolute, profligate, scampish; unworthy; worth-, desert-less; disgraceful, recreant; reprehensible, blameworthy, uncommendable; dis-creditable, -reputable.

base, sinister, scurvy, foul, gross, vile, black, grave, facinorous, felonious, nefarious, shameful, scandalous, infamous, villainous, of a deep dye, heinous; flag-rant, -itious; atrocious, incarnate, accursed.

Mephistophelian, satanic, diabolic, hellish, infernal, stygian, fiend-ish, -like, hell-born, demoniacal, devilish.

mis-created, -begotten; demoralized, corrupt, depraved.

evil-minded, -disposed; ill-conditioned; malevolent etc. 907; heart-, grace-, shame-, virtue-less; abandoned, lost to virtue; unconscionable; sunk –, lost –, deep –, steeped- in iniquity.

incorrigible, irreclaimable, obdurate, reprobate, past praying for; culpable, reprehensible etc. (*guilty*) 947.

unjustifiable; in-defensible, -excusable; inexpiable, unpardonable, irremissible.

weak, frail, lax, infirm, imperfect, indiscreet; demoralizing, degrading.

Adv. wrong; sinfully etc. *adj.*; without excuse.

Int. *O tempora! O mores!*

*Most of these adjectives are applicable both to the act and to the agent.

946. Innocence.—N. innocence; guiltlessness etc. *adj.*; incorruption, impeccability.

clean hands, clear conscience, *mens sibi conscia recti.*

innocent, new born babe, lamb, dove.

V. be -innocent etc. *adj.*; *nil conscire sibi nullâ pallescere culpâ.*

acquit etc. 970; exculpate etc. (*vindicate*) 937.

Adj. innocent, not guilty, unguilty; guilt-, fault-, sin-, stain-, blood-, spot-less; clear, immaculate; *rectus in curiâ*; un-spotted, -blemished, -erring; undefiled etc. 939; unhardened, Saturnian; Arcadian etc. (*artless*) 703.

in-, un-culpable; unblam-ed, -able; blameless, inerrable, above suspicion; irrepr-oachable, -ovable, -ehensible; un-exceptionable, -objectionable, -impeachable; salvable, venial etc. 937.

harmless; in-offensive, -noxious, -nocuous; dove-, lamb-like; pure, harmless as doves; innocent as -a lamb, – the babe unborn; more sinned against than sinning.

virtuous etc. 944; un-reproved, -impeached, -reproached.

Adv. innocently etc. *adj.*; with clean hands; with a -clear, – safe- conscience.

947. Guilt.—N. guilt, -iness; culpability; crimin-ality, -ousness; deviation from rectitude etc. (*improbity*) 940; sinfulness etc. (*vice*) 945; peccability.

mis-conduct, -behavior, -doing, -deed; malpractice, fault, sin, error, transgression; dereliction, delinquency; indiscretion, lapse, slip, trip, *faux pas*, *peccadillo*; flaw, blot, omission; fail-ing, -ure.

offence, trespass; mis-demeanor, -feasance, -prision, tort; mal-efaction, -feasance, -versation; crime, felony.

enormity, atrocity, outrage; deadly –, mortal –, unpardonable- sin; died without a name.

corpus delicti.

Adj. guilty, to blame, culpable, peccable, in fault, censurable, reprehensible, blameworthy, uncommendable, illaudable; weighed in the balance and found wanting; exceptionable, objectionable.

Adv. *in flagrante delicto*; red-handed, in the very act.

948. Good Man.—N. good man, worthy.

good woman, goddess, *madonna*, virgin.

model, paragon etc. (*perfection*) 650; good example; hero, demigod, seraph, angel; innocent etc. 946; saint etc. (*piety*) 987; benefactor etc. 912; philanthropist etc. 910; Aristides.

brick, trump, rough diamond, ugly duckling.

salt of the earth; one in ten thousand; one of the best.

Phr. *si sic omnes!*

949. Bad Man.—N. bad man, wrongdoer, worker of iniquity; evil-doer etc. 913; sinner; the -wicked etc. 945; bad example.

rascal, scoundrel, villain, miscreant, caitiff; wretch, reptile, viper, serpent, cockatrice, basilisk, urchin; tiger, monster; devil etc. (*demon*) 980; devil incarnate; demon in human shape, Nana Sahib; hell-hound, -cat; rake-hell.

bad woman, jade, Jezebel, adultress, etc. 962.

scamp, scapegrace, rip, runagate, ne'er-do-well, reprobate, *roué*, rake; limb; one who has sold him-

self to the devil, fallen angel, *âme damnée*, *vaurien*, *mauvais sujet*, loose fish, sad, dog; lost —, black-sheep; castaway, recreant, defaulter; prodigal etc. 818; libertine etc. 962.

rough, rowdy, ugly customer, ruffian, hoodlum, bully; Jonathan Wild; hangman; incendiary; thief etc. 792; murderer etc. 361.

culprit, delinquent, criminal, melefactor, misdemeanant; felon; convict, jail-bird, ticket-of-leave man; outlaw.

blackguard, *polisson*, loafer, sneak; raps-, rascallion; cullion, mean wretch, varlet, kern, *âme-de-boue*, *drôle*; cur, dog, hound, whelp, mongrel; lown, loon, runnion, outcast, vagabond; rogue etc. (*knave*) 941; scum of the earth, riff-raff; *Arcades ambo*.

Int. sirrah!

950. Penitence.—N. penitence, contrition, compunction, repentance, remorse; regret etc. 833.

self-reproach, -reproof, -accusation, -condemnation, -humiliation; stings —, pangs —, qualms —, prickings —, twinge —, twitch —, touch —, voice- of conscience; compunctious visitings of nature.

acknowledgment, confession etc. (*disclosure*) 529; apology etc. 952; recantation etc. 607; penance etc. 952; resipiscence.

awakened conscience, deathbed repentance, *locus poenitentiae*, stool of repentance, cutty stool.

penitent, Magdalen, prodigal son, returned prodigal, a sadder and wiser man.

V. repent, be sorry for; be -penitent etc. *adj.*; rue; regret etc. 833; think better of; recant etc. 607; knock under etc. (*submit*) 725; plead guilty; sing -*miserere*, - *de profundis*; cry *peccavi*; own oneself in the wrong; acknowledge, confess etc. (*disclose*) 529; humble oneself; beg pardon etc. (*apologize*) 952; turn over a new leaf, put on the new man, turn from sin; reclaim; repent in sackcloth and ashes etc. (*do penance*) 952; learn by experience.

Adj. penitent; repenting etc. *v.*; repentant, contrite; conscience-smitten, -stricken; self-accusing, -convicted.

penitenti-al, -ary; chastened, reclaimed; not hardened; un-hardened.

Adv. *meâ culpâ*.

Phr. *peccavi*; *erubuit*; *salva res est*; *vous l'avez voulu*, *Georges Dandin*.

951. Impenitence.—N. impenitence, irrepentance, recusance.

hardness of heart, seared conscience, induration, obduracy.

V. be -impenitent etc. *adj.*; steel —, harden- the heart; die -game, — and make no sign.

Adj. impenitent uncontrite, obdurate; hard, -ened; seared, recusant; unrepentant; relent-, remorse-, grace-, shrift-less.

lost, incorrigible, irreclaimable.

unre-claimed, -formed; unrepented, unatoned.

952. Atonement.—N. atonement, reparation; compromise, composition; compensation etc. 30; quittance, quits; indemni-ty, -fication; expiation,

redemption, reclamation, conciliation, propitiation.

amends, apology, *amende honorable*, satisfaction; peace —, sin —, burnt- offering; scapegoat, sacrifice.

penance, fasting, maceration, sackcloth and ashes, white sheet, shrift, flagellation, lustration; purga-tion, -tory.

V. atone, — for; expiate; propitiate; make -amends, — good; reclaim, redeem, repair, ransom, absolve, purge, shrive, do penance, stand in a white sheet, repent in sackcloth and ashes.

set one's house in order, wipe off old scores, make matters up; pay the -forfeit, — penalty.

apologize, beg pardon, express regret, *faire amende honorable*, give satisfaction; come —, fall-down on one's -knees, — marrow bones.

Adj. propitiatory, expiatory; sacrific, -ial, -atory; piacul-ar, -ous.

953. Temperance.—N. temperance, moderation, sobriety, soberness.

forbearance, abnegation; self-denial, -restraint, -control etc. (*resolution*) 604.

frugality; vegetarianism, teetotalism, total abstinence, prohibition, abst-inence, -emiousness, asceticism etc. 955; system of -Pythagoras, — Cornaro; Pythagorism, Stoicism.

vegetarian; Pythagorean, gymnosophist; teetotaler etc. 958; abstainer.

V. be -temperate etc. *adj.*; abstain, forbear, refrain, deny oneself, spare; know when one has had enough; take the pledge; look not upon the wine when it is red.

Adj. temperate, moderate, sober, frugal, sparing; abst-emious, -inent; within compass; measured etc. (*sufficient*) 639.

Pythagorean; vegetarian; teetotal, pussy-foot.

954. Intemperance.—N. intemperance; sensuality, animalism, carnality; pleasure; effeminacy, silkiness; luxur-y, -iousness; lap of -pleasure, — luxury.

indulgence; high-, free- living, in-abstinence, self-indulgence; voluptuousness etc. *adj.*; epicurism, -eanism; sybaritism.

dissipation; licentiousness etc. *adj.*; debauchery; crapulence.

revel-s, -ry; debauch, carousal, jollification, drinking bout, wassail, Saturnalia, orgies; excess, too much; intoxication etc. 959.

Circean cup; drug habit etc. 663.

V. be -intemperate etc. *adj.*; indulge, exceed; live -well, — high, — on the fat of the land; give a loose to -indulgence etc. *n.*; dine not wisely but too well; wallow in -voluptuousness etc. *n.*; plunge into dissipation.

revel, rake, live hard, run riot, sow one's wild oats; slake one's -appetite, — thirst; swill; pamper.

Adj. intemperate, inabstinent, intoxicated etc. 958; sensual, self-indulgent; voluptuous, luxurious, licentious, wild, dissolute, rakish, fast, debauched.

brutish, crapulous, swinish, piggish, hoggish, bestial.

Paphian, Epicurean, Sybaritical; bred —, nursed- in the lap of luxury; indulged, pampered, full-fed.

954a. Sensualist.—N. Sybarite, voluptuary, Sardanapalus, man of pleasure, carpet knight; epicure, -an; *gourm-et, -and;* gormandizer, gutling, glutton, pig, hog; votary −, swine- of Epicurus; sensualist; Heliogabalus; free −, hard- liver; libertine etc. 962; hedonist.

955. Asceticism.—N. asceticism, puritanism, sabbatarianism; cynicism, austerity; total abstinence.

mortification, maceration, sackcloth and ashes, flagellation; penance etc. 952; fasting etc. 956; martyrdom.

ascetic; anchor-et, -ite; martyr; *Heautontimorumenos;* hermit etc. (*recluse*) 893; puritan, sabbatarian, cynic.

Adj. ascetic, austere, puritanical; cynical; over-religious.

956. Fasting.—N. fasting; exrophagy; famishment, starvation; banting.

fast, *jour maigre;* fast −, banyan-day; Lent, quadragesima; Rama-dan, -zan; spare −, meager-diet; lenten -diet, − entertainment; *soupe maigre,* short -rations, − commons; Barmecide feast; hunger strike.

V. fast, starve, clem, famish, perish with hunger; dine with Duke Humphrey; make two bites of a cherry.

Adj. lenten, quadragesimal; unfed; starved etc. *v.;* half-starved; fasting etc. *v.;* hungry etc. 865.

957. Gluttony.—N. gluttony; greed; greediness etc. *adj.;* voracity.

epicurism; good −, high- living; edacity, gulosity, crapulence; gutt-, guzz-ling; over-indulgence.

good cheer, blow out; feast etc. (*food*) 298; gastronomy.

epicure, *bon vivant, gourmand;* glutton, cormorant, hog, belly-god, Apicius, gastronome, gormandizer.

V. gormandize, gorge; over-gorge, -eat- oneself; engorge, eat one's fill, cram, stuff, stodge, glut, satiate; gutt-le, guzz-le; bolt, devour, gobble up; gulp etc. (*swallow food*) 298; raven, eat out of house and home.

have the stomach of an ostrich; play a good knife and fork etc. (*appetite*) 865.

Adj. gluttonous, greedy; gormandizing etc. *v.;* edacious, omnivorous, crapulent, swinish, voracious, devouring.

pampered; over-fed, -gorged.

958. Sobriety.—N. sobriety; teetotalism, temperance etc. 953.

water-drinker; teetotal-er, -ist; abstáiner, Good Templar, Rechabite, band of hope; prohibitionist, pussyfoot.

V. take the pledge.

Adj. sober, − as a judge; dry, on the water wagon.

959. Drunkenness.—N. drunkenness etc. *adj.;* intemperance; drinking etc. *v.;* inebri-ety, -ation; ebri-ety, -osity; befuddlement; insobriety; intoxication; temulency, bibacity, wine-bibbing; com-, potation; deep potations, bacchanals, *bacchanalia,* libations.

oino-, dipso-mania; *delirium tremens,* d.t., alcohol, -ism.

drink; alcoholic drinks, alcohol, booze; gin, blue ruin, grog, brandy, port wine; punch, -bowl; cup, rosy wine, flowing bowl; drop, − too much; dram; beer, wine, spirits etc. (*beverage*) 298; cocktail, nip, peg; stirrup cup.

drunkard, sot, toper, tippler, bibber, wine-bibber; hard −, gin −, dram- drinker; soak, soaker, sponge, tun; love-, toss-pot; thirsty soul, reveller, carouser; Bacchanal, -ian; Bacch-al, -ante; devotee to Bacchus, dipsomaniac.

V. get −, be- drunk etc. *adj.;* see double; take a -drop, − glass- too much; drink, tipple, tope, booze, bouse, guzzle, swill, soak, sot, lush, bib, swig, carouse; sacrifice at the shrine of Bacchus; take to drinking; drink -hard, − deep, − like a fish; have one's swill, drain the cup, splice the main brace, take a hair of the dog that bit you.

liquor, − up; wet one's whistle, take a whet; lift one's elbow; crack a −, pass the- bottle; toss of etc. (*drink up*) 298; go to the -ale, − public house.

make one-drunk etc. *adj.;* inebriate, fuddle, fuzzle, get into one's head.

Adj. drunk, tipsy; intoxicated; inebri-ous, -ate, -ated; in one's cups; in a state of -intoxication etc. *n.;* temulent, -ive; fuddled, mellow, cut, boosy, fou, fresh, merry, elevated, squiffy; plastered, befuddled, sozzlęd; flush, -ed; flustered, disguised, groggy, beery, topheavy; potvaliant, glorious; potulent; over-come, -taken; whittled, screwed, tight, primed, oiled, corned, raddled, sewed up, lushy, nappy, muddled, muzzy, bosky, obfuscated; maudlin; crapulous, dead −, blind- drunk.

inter pocula; in −, the worse for- liquor, having had a drop too much, half seas over, three sheets in the wind; under the table, blind to the world, one over the eight.

drunk as -a piper, − a fiddler, − a lord, − Chloe, − an owl, − David's sow, − a wheelbarrow.

drunken, bibacious, bibulous, sottish; given −, addicted- to -drink, − the bottle; toping etc. *v.;* wet.

Phr. *nunc est bibendum.*

960. Purity.—N. purity; decency, decorum, delicacy; continence, chastity, honesty, virtue, modesty, shame; pudicity, *pucelage,* virginity.

vestal, virgin, Joseph, Hippolytus; Lucretia, Diana; prude.

Adj. pure, undefiled, modest, delicate, decent, decorous; *virginibus puerisque;* chaste, continent, virtuous, honest, Platonic.

961. Impurity.—N. impurity; uncleanness etc. (*filth*) 653; immodesty; grossness etc. *adj.;* indelicacy, indecency; impudicity; obscenity, ribaldry, smut, bawdry, *double entendre, équivoque;* Aretinism; pornography.

concupiscence, lust, carnality, flesh, salacity; pruriency, lechery, lasciviency, lubricity, lewdness.

incontinence, intrigue, *faux pas*; *amour, -ette*; gallantry; dabauchery, libertinism, *libertinage*, fornication; *liaison*; wenching, venery, dissipation.

seduction; defloration, defilement, abuse, violation, rape; incest.

social evil, harlotry, stupration, whoredom, concubinage, cuckoldom, adultery, advoutry, *crim. con.*; free love.

seraglio, harem, zenana; brothel, bagnio, stew, bawdy-house, *lupanar*, house of ill fame, *bordel*, kip.

V. be -impure etc. *adj.*; intrigue; debauch, defile, assault, attack, seduce; prostitute; abuse, violate, deflower; commit -adultery etc. *n.*

Adj. impure; unclean etc. (*dirty*) 653; not to be mentioned to ears polite; immodest, shameless; indecorous, -delicate, -decent; loose, suggestive; *risqué*, coarse, gross, broad, free, equivocal, smutty, fulsome, ribald, obscene, bawdy, pornographic.

concupiscent, prurient, lickerish, rampant, lustful; carnal, -minded; lewd, lascivious, lecherous, libidinous, erotic, ruttish, salacious; Paphian; voluptuous; incestuous.

· unchaste, -light, wanton, licentious, adulterous, debauched, dissolute; of -loose character; — easy virtue; frail, gay, riggish, incontinent, meretricious, rakish, gallant, dissipated; no better than she should be; on the -town, — streets, — *pavé*, — loose.

adulterous, incestuous, bestial.

962. Libertine.—**N.** libertine; voluptuary etc. 954*a*; rake, debauchee, loose fish, rip, rake-hell, fast man; *intrigant*, gallant, seducer, fornicator, lecher, satyr, goat, whoremonger, *paillard*, adulterer, gay deceiver, Lothario, Don Juan, Bluebeard.

adulteress, advoutress, courtesan, prostitute, strumpet, tart, hustler, chippy, broad, harlot, whore, punk, *fille de joie*; woman, — of the town; street-walker, Cyprian, miss, piece; frail sisterhood, fallen woman; demirep, wench, trollop, trull, baggage, hussy, drab, bitch, jade, skit, rig, quean, mopsy, slut, minx, harridan; woman -of easy virtue etc. (*unchaste*) 961; wanton, fornicatress; Jezebel, Messalina, Delilah, Thaïs, Phryne, Aspasia, Lais, *lorette, cocotte, petite dame, grisette; demi-monde*; white slave.

concubine, mistress, fancy woman, kept woman, doxy, *chère amie, bona roba.*

pimp; pand-er, -ar; bawd, *conciliatrix*, procuress, mackerel; wittol.

963. Legality.—**N.** legality; legitima-cy, -teness, legitimization.

legislature; law, code, *corpus juris*, constitution, pandect, charter, act, enactment, statute, rule; canon etc. (*precept*) 697; ordinance, institution, regulation; by-, bye-law, rescript; decree etc. (*order*) 741; *ordonnance*; standing order; *plébiscite* etc. (*choice*) 609.

legal process; form, -ula, -ality; rite; arm of the law; *habeas corpus.*

[Science of law] jurisprudence, nomology; legislation, codification.

equity, common law; *lex* —, *lex nonscripta*, unwritten law; law of nations, international law, *jus gentium; jus civile;* civil —, criminal —, canon —, statute —, ecclesiastical- law; *lex mercatoria.*

constitutional-ism, -ity; justice etc. 922.

V. legalize, legitimize; enact, ordain; decree etc. (*order*) 741; pass a law; legislate; codify, formulate; authorize.

Adj. legal, legitimate; according to law; vested, constitutional, chartered, legalized; lawful etc. (*permitted*) 760; statut-able, -ory; legislat-orial, -ive.

Adv. legally etc. *adj.*; in the eye of the law; *de jure.*

964. Illegality. [Absence or violation of law.]—**N.** lawlessness; breach —, violation- of law; disobedience etc. 742; unconformity etc. 83.

arbitrariness etc. *adj.*; antinomy, violence, brute force, despotism, outlawry.

mob —, lynch —, club —, Lydford —, martial —, drumhead- law; *coup d'état; le droit du plus fort; argumentum baculinum.*

illegality, informality, unlawfulness, illegitimacy, bar sinister.

trover and conversion; smuggling, boot-legging, rum-running, poaching; simony.

speakeasy, speakie, blind pig.

V. offend against —, violate- the law; set the law at defiance, ride rough-shod over, drive a coach and six through a statute; make the law a dead letter, take the law into one's own hands.

smuggle, run, poach.

Adj. illegal; prohibited etc. 761; not allowed, unlawful, illegitimate, illicit, contraband, actionable.

unchartered, unconstitutional; unwarrant-ed, -able; unauthorized; informal, unofficial; in-, extrajudicial.

lawless, arbitrary; despotic, -al; summary, irresponsible; un-answerable, -accountable.

null and void; a dead letter.

Adv. illegally etc. *adj.*; with a high hand, in violation of law.

965. Jurisdiction. [Executive.]—**N.** jurisdiction, judicature, administration of justice, soc; executive, commission of the peace; magistracy etc. (*authority*) 737.

judge etc. 967; tribunal etc. 966; municipality, corporation, bailiwick, shrievalty; lord lieutenant; lord —, mayor, city manager, alderman etc. 745; sheriff, bailie, shrieve, chief —, constable; police, — force; constabulary, bumbledom.

officer, proctor, high —, commissioner; bailiff, tipstaff, bum-bailiff, catchpoll, beadle; police-man, -constable, -sergeant; *sbirro, alguazil, gendarme,* kavass, *lictor,* macebearer, *huissier,* bedel.

press-gang; exciseman, gauger, custom-house officer, *douanier.*

coroner, edile, aedile, portreeve, paritor; *posse comitatus.*

V. judge, sit in judgment.

Adj. executive, administrative, municipal;

inquisitorial, causidical; judic-atory, -iary, -ial; juridical.

Adv. *coram judice.*

966. Tribunal.—N. tribunal, court, board, bench, judicatory, curia; court of -justice, − law, − arbitration; inquisition; guild.

justice −, judgment −, mercy- seat; woolsack; bar, − of justice; dock; forum, hustings, *bureau*, drum-head; jury-, witness-box.

senate-house, town-hall, theater; House of - Lords, − Commons.

assize, eyre; ward-, burgh-mote; superior courts of Westminister; court of -record, − oyer and ter-miner, − assize, − appeal − error; High court of -Judicature, − Appeal; Judicial Committee of the Privy Council; Star-Chamber; Court of -Chancery, − King's *or* Queen's Bench, − Exchequer, − Common Pleas, − Probate, − Arches, − Ad-miralty, − Criminal Appeal; Lords Justices' −, Rolls −, Vice Chancellor's −, Stannary −, Divorce −, Palatine −, ecclesiastical −, county −, police- court; sessions; quarter −, petty-sessions; court -leet, − baron, − of pie poudre, − of common council; board of green cloth.

court-martial; drum-head court-martial; *durbar*, divan; Areopagus; *rota.*

Adj. judicial etc. 965; appellate; curial.

967. Judge.—N. judge; justi-ce, -ciar, -ciary; chancellor; justice −, judge- of assize; recorder, common serjeant; puisne −, assistant −, county court- judge; conservator −, justice- of the peace, J.P.; court etc. (*tribunal*) 966; grand −, petty −, coroner's- jury; panel, juror, juryman; twelve men in a box; magistrate, police magistrate, stipendiary, the great unpaid, beak; his -worship, − honor, − lordship; deemster, moderator.

Lord -Chancellor, − Justice; Master of the Rolls, Vice-Chancellor; Lord Chief -Justice, − Baron; Mr. Justice; Baron, − of the Exchequer.

jurat, assessor; arbi-ter, -trator; umpire; refer-ee, -endary; revising barrister; domesman; censor etc. (*critic*) 480; official −, receiver.

archon, tribune, praetor, *ephor*, syndic, *podestà*, mullah, ulema, mufti, cadi, kadi; Rhadamanthus. litigant etc. (*accusation*) 938.

V. adjudge etc. (*determine*) 480; try a -case, − prisoner.

Adj. judicial etc. 965.

Phr. 'a Daniel come to judgment.'

968. Lawyer.—N. lawyer, jurist, legist, civilian, pundit, publicist, jurisconsult, legal adviser, ad-vocate; barrister, − at law; counsel, -lor; King's *or* Queen's counsel; K.C.; Q.C.; silk gown, leader; junior, − counsel; stuff gown, serjeant-at-law; bencher, tubman; judge etc. 967.

bar, legal profession, gentleman of the long robe; junior −, outer −, inner- bar; Inns of Court; equity draftsman, conveyancer, pleader, special pleader.

solicitor, attorney, proctor; notary, − public; scrivener, cursitor; writer, − to the signet; S.S.C.; limb of the law; pettifogger.

V. practice -at, − within- the bar; plead; call −, to called- -to, − within- the bar; take silk.

Adj. learned in the law; at the bar; forensic.

969. Lawsuit.—N. lawsuit, suit, action, cause, petition; litigation; dispute etc. 713.

citation, arraignment, prosecution, im-peachment; accusation etc. 938; presentment, true bill, indictment.

apprehension, arrest; committal; imprisonment etc. (*restraint*) 751.

writ, summons, subpoena, *latitat*, *nisi prius*; *habeas corpus.*

pleadings; declaration, bill, claim; *procès-verbal*, bill of right, information, *corpus delicti*; affidavit, state of facts; answer, replication, plea, demurrer, rebutter, rejoinder; surre-butter, - joinder.

suitor, party to a suit; litigant etc. 938; libellant.

hearing, trial; verdict etc. (*judgment*) 480; ap-peal, − motion; writ of error; *certiorari.*

case, decision, precedent, ruling; decided case, reports.

V. go to −, appeal to the- law; bring to -justice, − trial, − the bar; put on trial, pull up; accuse etc. 938; prefer −, file- a claim etc. *n.*; take the law of, inform against.

serve with a writ, cite, apprehend, arraign, sue, prosecute, bring an action against, indict, impeach, attach, distrain, commit; arrest; summon, -s; give in charge etc. (*restrain*) 751.

empanel a jury, implead, join issue; close the pleadings; set down for hearing.

try, hear a cause; sit in judgment; adjudicate etc. 480.

Adj. litigious etc. (*quarrelsome*) 713; *qui tam*; *coram* −, *sub- judice.*

Adv. *pendente lite.*

Phr. *adhuc sub judice lis est.*

970. Acquittal.—N. acquit-tal, -ment; clearance, exculpation, exoneration; discharge etc. (*release*) 750; *quietus*, absolution, compurgation, reprieve, respite; pardon etc. (*forgiveness*) 918. [Exemption from -punishment] impunity, im-munity.

V. acquit, exculpate, exonerate, clear; absolve, whitewash, assoil, discharge, release; liberate etc. 750.

reprieve, respite; pardon etc. (*forgive*) 918; let off, − scot free.

Adj. acquitted etc. *v.*; un-condemned, - punished, -chastised; recommended to mercy.

971. Condemnation.—N. condemnation, con-viction, proscription, damnation; death warrant; penalty etc. 974.

attain-der, -ture, -tment.

V. condemn, convict, cast, bring home to, find guilty, damn, doom, sign the death warrant, sen-tence, pass sentence on, attaint, confiscate, proscribe, sequestrate; non-suit.

disapprove etc. 932; accuse etc. 938.

stand condemned.

Adj. condem-, dam-natory; condemned etc. *v.*; non-suited etc. (*failure*) 732; self-convicted.

Phr. *mutato nomine de te fabula narratur.*

972. Punishment.—N. punishment, punition; chast-isement, -ening; correction, castigation.

discipline, infliction, trial; judgment; penalty etc. 974; retribution; thunderbolt, Nemesis; requital etc. (*reward*) 973; penology; retributive justice.

lash, scaffold etc. (*instrument of punishment*) 975; imprisonment etc. (*restraint*) 751; chain gang; transportation, banishment, expulsion, deportation, exile, involuntary exile, ostracism; penal servitude, hard labor; galleys etc. 975; beating etc. *v.*; flagellation, fustigation, gantlet, *strappado*, *estrapade*, *bastinado*, *argumentum baculinum*, stick law, rap on the knuckles, box on the ear; blow etc. (*impulse*) 276; stripe, cuff, kick, buffet, pummel; slap, – in the face; wipe, douse; *coup de grâce*; torture, rack; picket, -ing; *dragonnade*; capital punishment, extreme penalty; execution; hanging etc. *v.*; de-capitation, -collation; *garrot-te*, *-to*; electrocution, lethal chamber; crucifixion, impalement; martyrdom, *auto-da-fé*; *noyade*; *hara-kiri*, happy despatch.

V. punish; chast-ise, -en; castigate, correct, inflict punishment, administer correction, deal retributive justice.

visit upon, pay; pay –, serve- out; settle with, get even with, get one's own back; do for; make short work of, give a lesson to, strafe, serve one right, make an example of; have a rod in pickle for; give it one.

strike etc. 276; deal a blow to, administer the lash, smite; slap, – the face; smack, cuff, box the ears, spank, thwack, thump, beat, lay on, swinge, buffet; thresh, thrash, pummel, drub, leather, trounce, baste, belabor; lace, – one's jacket; dress, give a -dressing, – down; trim, warm, wipe, tund, cob, bang, strap, comb, lash, lick, larrup, whallop, whop, flog, scourge, whip, birch, cane, give the stick, switch, flagellate, horsewhip, *bastinado*, towel, rub down with an oaken towel, rib roast, dust one's jacket, fustigate, pitch into, lay about one, beat black and-blue; beat to a -mummy, – jelly; give a black eye; hit on the head; sandbag.

tar and feather; pelt, stone, lapidate; mast-head, keelhaul.

execute; bring to the -block, – gallows; behead; de-capitate, -collate; guillotine; hang, turn off, gibbet, bowstring, hang, draw and quarter; shoot; decimate; burn; electrocute; break on the wheel, crucify; em-, im-pale; flay; lynch; put to death.

torture; put -on, – to- the rack; picket.

banish, exile; trans-, de-port; expel, ostracize; rusticate; drum out; dismiss, -bar, -bench; strike off the roll, unfrock; post.

suffer, – for, – punishment; be -flogged, – hanged etc.; come to the gallows, dance upon nothing, die in one's shoes, be rightly served.

Adj. punishing etc. *v.*; penal; puni-tory, -tive; inflictive, castigatory; punished etc. *v.*

Int. *à la lanterne!*

973. Reward.—N. reward, recompense, remuneration, prize, meed, guerdon, reguerdon; indemni-ty, -fication, price; quittance; compensation; reparation, *ersatz*, assythment, redress; retribution, reckoning, acknowledgment, requital, amends, sop; atonement, consideration, return, *quid pro quo*; salvage, perquisite; vail etc. (*donation*) 784; *douceur*, bribe, bait, baksheesh,

tip; hush-, smart-money; black-mail; carcelage; *solatium*.

allowance, salary, stipend, wages; pay, -ment; emolument; tribute, batta, shot, scot; premium, fee, *honorarium*; hire.

crown etc. (*decoration of honor*) 877.

V. re-ward, -compense, -pay, -quite; re-, munerate; compensate; fee, tip, bribe; pay one's footing etc. (*pay*) 807; make amends, indemnify, atone; satisfy, acknowledge.

get for one's pains, reap the fruits of.

Adj. remunerat-ive, -ory; munerary, compensatory, retributive, reparatory.

974. Penalty.—N. penalty; retribution etc. (*punishment*) 972; pain, pains and penalties; *peine forte et dure*; penance etc. (*atonement*) 952; the devil to pay.

fine, mulct, amercement; forfeit, -ure; escheat, damages, deodand, sequestration, confiscation, premunire.

V. penalize, fine, mulct, amerce, sconce, confiscate; sequest-rate, -er; escheat; estreat, forfeit.

975. Scourge. [Instrument of punishment.]—N. scourge, rod, cane, stick; ra-, rat-tan; birch, – rod; rod in pickle; switch, ferule, cudgel, truncheon; rubber hose.

whip, lash, strap, thong, cowhide, knout; cat, – o'-nine-tails, *sjambok*, quirt; rope's end.

pillory, stocks, whipping-post; cuck-, duck-ing stool; brank; triangle, wooden horse, maiden, thumbscrew, boot, rack, wheel, iron heel; treadmill, crank, galleys.

scaffold; block, axe, *guillotine*; stake; cross; gallows, gibbet, Tyburn tree; drop, noose, rope, halter, bowstring; electric-chair, lethal chamber.

house of correction etc. (*prison*) 752.

gaol-, jail-er; executioner; hang-, heads-man; Jack Ketch; lyncher.

976. Deity.—N. Deity, Divinity; God-head, -ship; Omnipotence, Providence.

[Quality of being divine] divin-eness, -ity.

God, Lord, Jehovah, *Deus*; The -Almighty, – Supreme Being, – First Cause; *Ens Entium*; Author –, Creator- of all things; Author of our being; The -Infinite, – Eternal; The All-powerfull, -wise, -merciful, -holy; The Omni-potent, -scient.

[Attributes and perfections] infinite -power, – wisdom, – goodness, – justice, – truth, – love, – mercy; omni-potence, -science, -presence; unity, immutability, holiness, glory, majesty, sovereignty, infinity, eternity.

The -Trinity, – Holy Trinity, – Trinity in Unity, – Triune God; Three in One and One in Three.

God the Father; The -Maker, – Creator, – Preserver.

[Functions] creation, preservation, divine government; The-ocracy, -archy; providence; ways –, dealings –, dispensations –, visitations- of Providence.

God the Son, Jesus, Christ; The -Messiah, – Anointed, – Savior, – Redeemer, – Mediator,

— Intercessor, — Advocate, — Judge; The Son of -God, — Man, — David; The Only Begotten; The Lamb of God, The Word; Em-, Im-manuel; The -King of Kings and Lord of Lords, — King of Glory, — Prince of Peace, — Good Shepherd, — Way, — Truth, — Life, — Bread of Life, — Light of the World; The -Lord our, — Sun of-Righteousness.

The -Incarnation, — Hypostatic Union, — Word made Flesh.

[Functions] salvation, redemption, atonement, propitiation, mediation, intercession, judgment.

God the Holy Ghost, The Holy Spirit, Paraclete; The -Comforter, — Consoler, — Spirit of Truth, — Dove.

[Functions] inspiration, unction, regeneration, sanctification, consolation.

eon, aeon, special providence, *Deus ex machinâ*; *Avatar*.

V. create, uphold, preserve, govern etc.

atone, redeem, save, propitiate, mediate etc.

predestinate, elect, call, ordain, bless, justify, sanctify, glorify etc.

Adj. almighty, holy, hallowed, sacred, divine, heavenly, celestial; messianic; sacrosanct; all-powerful, -wise, -seeing, -knowing; omnipotent, omniscient; supreme.

super-human, -natural; ghostly, spiritual, hyperphysical, unearthly; the-istic, -ocratic, deistic; anointed.

Adv. *jure divino*, by divine right; *Deo volente*, D.V.

977. Angel. [Beneficent spirits.]—**N.** angel, archangel; heavenly host, choir invisible, host of heaven, sons of God; Michael, Gabriel etc.; seraph, -im; cherub, -im; ministering spirit, morning star; saint, *Madonna*; Our Lady, the Blessed Virgin, the Virgin Mary.

Adj. angelic, seraphic, cherubic.

978. Satan. [Maleficent spirits.]—**N.** Satan, the Devil, Lucifer, Ahrimanes, Belial; Sammael, Zamiel, Beelzebub, the Prince of the Devils; Mephistopheles, his satanic majesty.

the tempter; the evil -one, — spirit; the -author of evil, — wicked one, — old Serpent; the Prince of -darkness, — this world, — the power of the air; the -foul, — arch- fiend; the devil incarnate; the -common enemy, — angel of the bottomless pit; Abaddon, Apollyon, Mammon.

fallen agnels, unclean spirits, devils; the -rulers, — powers- of darkness; inhabitants of Pàndemonium; demon etc. 980.

diabolism; devil-ism, -ship, -dom, -ry, -worship; *diablerie*; satanism, manicheism; the cloven foot; black magic etc. 992.

Adj. satanic, diabolic, devilish, infernal, hellborn.

979. Jupiter.—**N.** god, -dess; heathen gods and goddesses; Pantheon; Jupiter, Jove, Zeus, Apollo, Mars, Mercury, Neptune, Vulcan, Bacchus, Pluto, Saturn, Cupid, Eros, Pan; Juno, Ceres, Proserpina, Dina, Minerva, Pallas, Athenae, Venus, Aphrodite, Vesta; The Fates etc. 601.

Allah, Brahma, Vishnu, Siva, Shiva, Krishna, Juggernaut, Buddha; Ra, Isis, Osiris; Belus, Bel, Baal, Asteroth etc.; Thor, Odin; Mumbo Jumbo; good —, tutelary- genius; demiurge, familiar, — spirit; Sibyl; fairy, fay; sylph, -id; Ariel, peri, nymph, nereid, dryad, oread, sea-maid, Banshee, Benshie, Ormuzd; Oberon, Titania, Mab, hamadryad, naiad, mermaid, kelpie, Ondine, nix, nixie, sprite; denizens of the air; pixy etc. (*bad spirit*) 980.

mythology; heathen —, fairy- mythology; Lemprière, folklore.

Adj. fairy-, sylph-like; sylphic.

980. Demon.—**N.** demon, -ry, -ism, -ology; evil genius, fiend, familiar, — spirit, devil; bad —, un-clean- spirit; cacodemon, incubus, Frankenstein's monster, succubus and succuba, Titan, Shedim, Mephistopheles, Asmodeus, Moloch, Belial, Ahriman, fury, The Furies etc. 900; harpy; Friar Rush.

vampire, ghoul; af-, ef-freet; afrite; ogre, -ss; gnome, gin, djinn, imp, deev, *lamia*; bo-gie, -gle; nis, kobold, flibbertigibbet, fairy, brownie, pixy, elf, dwarf, urchin, Puck, Robin Goodfellow; lepre-, cluri-chaune; troll, dwerger, sprite, oaf, changeling, bad fairy, nixe, pigwidgeon, Will-o'-the-wisp; Erl King.

[Supernatural appearance] ghost, specter, apparition, genie, spirit, shade, shadow, vision, phantom etc. 443; materialization (*spiritualism*) 992; hob-, goblin; wraith, spook, werwolf, boggart, banshee, *loup-garou, lemures*; evil eye.

nisse, necks; mer-man, -maid, -folk; siren, Lorelei; satyr, faun.

Adj. supernatural, weird, uncanny, unearthly, spectral; ghost-ly, -like; elf-in, -like; fiend-ish, -like; impish, demoniacal; haunted.

981. Heaven.—**N.** heaven; kingdom of -heaven, — God; heavenly kingdom; throne —, presence- of God; inheritance of the saints in light.

Paradise, Eden, abode of the blessed; Holy City, New Jerusalem; celestial bliss, glory.

[Mythological -heaven] Olympus; [— paradise] Elysium, Elysian fields, Arcadia, bowers of bliss, garden of the Hesperides, Islands of the Blessed; happy hunting-ground; third —, seventh-heaven; Valhalla (Scandinavian); Nirvana (Buddhist).

future state, eternity, eternal life, life after death, eternal home, resurrection, translation; resuscitation etc. 660; apotheosis, deification.

Adj. heavenly, celestial, supernal, unearthly, from on high, paradisiacal, beatific, elysian, Olympian, Arcadian.

982. Hell.—**N.** hell, bottomless pit, place of torment; habitation of fallen angels; Pandemonium, Abaddon, Domdaniel.

hell fire; everlasting -fire, — torment; lake of fire and brimstone; fire that is never quenched, worm that never dies.

purgatory, limbo, gehenna, abyss.

[Mythological hell] Tartarus, Hades, Avernus, Styx, Stygian creek, pit of Acheron, Cocytus,

Phlegethon, Lethe; infernal regions, *inferno*, shades below, realms of Pluto.

Pluto, Rhadamanthus, Erebus, Charon, Cerberus; Tophet.

Adj. hellish, infernal, stygian.

983. Theology. [Religious Knowledge.]—**N.** Theology (natural and revealed); Theo-gony, -sophy; Divinity; Hagio-logy, -graphy; Caucasian mystery; monotheism; religion; religious -persuasion, – sect, – denomination; cult; creed etc. (*belief*) 484; articles –, declaration –, profession –, confession- of faith.

theolog-ue, -ian; divine, schoolman, canonist, monotheist.

Adj. theological, religious; canonical; denominational; sectarian etc. 984.

983a. Orthodoxy.—**N.** orthodoxy; strictness, soundness, religious truth, true faith; truth etc. 494.

Christian-ity, -ism; Catholic-ism, -ity; 'the faith once delivered to the saints;' hyperorthodoxy etc. 984; iconoclasm.

the Holy –, the Orthodox- Church; Catholic –, Universal –, Apostolic –, Established- Church; temple of the Holy Ghost; Church –, body –, members –, disciples –, followers- of Christ; Christian, – community; true believer; canonist etc. (*theologian*) 983; Christendom, collective body of Christians, the Church Militant.

canons etc. (*belief*) 484; thirty-nine articles; Apostles' –, Nicene –, Athanasian- Creed; Church Catechism; textuary.

Adj. orthodox, sound, literal, strict, faithful, catholic, schismless, Christian, evangelical, scriptural, divine, monotheistic; true etc. 494.

984. Heterodoxy. [Sectarianism.]—**N.** heterodoxy; error etc. 495; false doctrine, heresy, schism; schismantic-ism, -alness; recusancy, backsliding, apostasy; atheism etc. (*irreligion*) 989.

bigotry etc. (*obstinacy*) 606; fanaticism, iconoclasm; hyperorthodoxy, precisianism, bibliolatry, hagiolatry, sabbatarianism, puritanism; idolatry etc. 991; superstition etc. (*credulity*) 486; dissent etc. 489.

sectar-ism, -ianism; nonconformity; secularism; syncretism, religious sects; the clash of creeds.

protestant-, advent-, Arian-, Erastian-, Calvin-, quaker-, method-, anabapt-, Pusey-, tractarian-, ritual-, Origen-, Sabellian-, Socinian-, De-, The-, mon-, material-, positiv-, latitudinairan-ism etc.

High –, Low –, Broad –, Free- Church; ultramontanism; monasticism; pap-ism, -istry; papacy; Anglican-, Catholic-, Roman-ism; popery, Scarlet Lady, Church of Rome, Greek Church; Christian Science, The Church of Christ Scientist.

pagan-, heathen-, ethic-ism; mythology; animism; poly-, di-, tri-, pan-theism; dualism; heathendom.

Juda-, Gentil-, Mahometan-, Islam-, Turc-, Brahmin-, Hindoo-, Buddh-, Lama-, Confucian-, Shinto-, Sabian-, Gnostic-, Soofee-, Hylothe-, Mormon-ism.

Theosophy; Spiritualism, Occultism.

heretic, antichrist; pagan, heathen; pai-, pay-nim; *giaour*; gentile; pan-, poly-theist; idolator; misbeliever, apostate, backslider.

bigot etc. (*obstinacy*) 606; fanatic, dervish, abdal, iconoclast.

latitudinarian, limitarian, Deist, Theist, Unitarian; positivist, materialist; agnostic, sceptic etc. 989.

schismatic; sectar-y, -ian, -ist; seceder, separatist, recusant, dissenter; non-conformist, -juror; Huguenot, Protestant; orthodox dissenter, Congregationalist, Independent; Episcopalian, Presbyterian; Lutheran, Calvinist, Quaker, Methodist, Weslayan; Ana-, Baptist; Dunker; Mormon, Latter-day Saint, Irvingite, Sandemanian, Glassite, Erastian; Sub-, Supra-lapsarian; Gentoo, Antinomian, Swedenborgian, Adventist, Plymouth Brother; Theosophist etc.

Catholic, Roman Catholic, Romanist, papist, ultramontane; Old Catholic, tractarian, Anglican, Puseyite, ritualist; Puritan.

Jew, Hebrew, Rabbist; Mahometan, Mohammedan, Mussulman, Moslem, Islamite, Osmanli; Brahm-in, -an; Parsee, Sofi, Soofee; Buddhist; Zoroastrian, Magi, Gymnosophist, fire-worshipper, Sabian, Gnostic, Sadducee, Rosicrucian etc.

Adj. heterodox, heretical; un-orthodox, -scriptural, -canonical; antiscriptural, apocryphal; un-, anti-christian; schismatic, recusant, iconoclastic; sectarian; dis-senting, -sident; secular etc. (*lay*) 997.

pagan; heathen, -ish; ethnic, -al; gentile, painim; pan-, poly-theistic; agnostic, sceptic.

Judaical, Mohammedan, Moslem, Brahminical, Buddhist etc. *n*.; Romish, Protestant etc. *n*.

bigoted etc. (*prejudiced*) 481; (*obstinate*) 606; superstitious etc. (*credulous*) 486; fanatical; idolatrous etc. 991; visionary etc. (*imaginative*) 515.

985. Revelation.—**N.** revelation, inspiration, *afflatus*.

Word, – of God; Scripture; the -Scriptures, – Bible, – Book of Books; Holy -Writ, – Scriptures; inspired writings, Gospel.

Old Testament, Septuagint, Vulgate, Pentateuch; Octateuch; the -Law, – Jewish Law, – Prophets; major –, minor- Prophets; Hagio-grapha, -logy; Hierographa; Apocrypha.

New Testament; Gospels, Evangelists, Acts, Epistles, Apocalypse, Revelations.

Talmud; Mishna, Masorah.

prophet etc. (*seer*) 513; evangelist, apostle, disciple, saint; the –, the Apostolical- fathers; Holy Men of old, inspired -writers, – penmen.

Adj. scriptural, biblical, sacred, prophetic; evangel-ical, -istic; apostolic, -al; inspired, theopneustic, apocalyptic, ecclesiastical, canonical, textuary.

986. Pseudo-Revelation.—**N.** the -Koran, -Alcoran; Ly-king, Shaster, Vedas, Zendavesta, Vedidad, Purana, Edda; Go-, Gau-tama; Book of Mormon.

[False prophets and religious founders] Buddha, Zoroaster, Zerdhusht, Confucius, Mahomet.

[Idols] golden calf etc. 991; Baal, Moloch, Dagon.

987. Piety.—N. piety, religion, theism, faith; religiousness, holiness etc. *adj.*; saintship; religionism; sanctimony etc. (*assumed piety*) 988; reverence etc. (*respect*) 928; humility, veneration, devotion; prostration etc. (*worship*) 990; grace, unction, edification; sancti-ty, -tude; consecration.

spiritual existence, odor of sanctity, beauty of holiness.

theopathy, beatification, adoption, regeneration, conversion, justification, sanctification, salvation, inspiration, bread of life; Body and Blood of Christ.

believer, convert, theist, Christian, devotee, pietist; the -good, — righteous, — just, — believing, — elect; Saint, *Madonna*.

the children of -God, — the kingdom, — light.

V. be -pious etc. *adj.*; have -faith etc. *n.*; believe, receive Christ; revere etc. 928; worship etc. 950; be -converted etc.

convert, edify, sanctify, hallow, keep holy, beatify, regenerate, inspire, consecrate, enshrine.

Adj. pious, religious, devout, devoted, reverent, godly, heavenly minded, humble; pure, — in heart; holy, spiritual, pietistic; saint-ly, -like; seraphic, sacred, solemn.

believing, faithful, Christian, Catholic.

elected, adopted, justified, sanctified, regenerated, inspired, consecrated, converted, unearthly, not of the earth.

988. Impiety.—N. impiety; sin etc. 945; irreverence; profan-eness etc. *adj.*, -ity, -ation; blasphemy, desecration, sacrilege; scoffing etc. *v.*

[Assumed piety] hypocrisy etc. (*falsehood*) 544; pietism, cant, pious fraud; lip-devotion, -service, -reverence; mis-devotion, formalism, austerity; sanctimon-y, -iousness etc. *adj.*; pharisaism, precisianism; sabbat-ism, -arianism; *odium theologicum*, sacerdotalism; bigotry etc. (*obstinacy*) 606, (*prejudice*) 481.

hardening, backsliding, declension, perversion, reprobation apostasy, recusancy.

sinner etc. 949; scoffer, blasphemer; sacrilegist; worldling; hypocrite etc. (*dissembler*) 548; Scribes and Pharisees; Tartufe, Maw-worm.

bigot; saint [ironically]; Pharisee, sabbatarian, formalist, methodist, puritan, pietist, precisian, religionist, devotee, ranter, fanatic, wowser.

the -wicked, — evil, — unjust, — reprobate; son of -men, — Belial, — the wicked one; children of darkness.

V. be -impious etc. *adj.*; profane, desecrate, blaspheme, revile, scoff; swear etc. (*malediction*) 908; commit sacrilege.

snuffle; turn up the whites of the eyes; idolize.

Adj. impious; irreligious etc. 989; desecrating etc. *v.*; profane, irreverent, sacrilegious, blasphemous.

un-hallowed, -sanctified, -regenerate; hardened, perverted, reprobate.

hypocritical etc. (*false*) 544; canting, pietistical, sanctimonious, unctuous, pharisaical, over-righteous, righteous over much.

bigoted, fanatical etc. 481 and 606; priest-ridden.

Adv. under the -mask, — cloak, — pretence, — form, — guise- of religion.

989. Irreligion.—N. irreligion, indevotion; ungodliness etc. *adj.*; laxity, quietism, apathy, in-difference, passivity.

scepticism, doubt; un-, dis-belief; incredul-ity, -ousness etc. *adj.*; want of -faith, — belief; pyrrhonism; doubt etc. 485; agnosticism.

atheism, deism; hylotheism; materialism; positivism; nihilism.

infidelity, freethinking, antichristianity, rationalism.

atheist, anti-christian, sceptic, unbeliever, deist, infidel, pyrrhonist; *giaour*, heathen, alien, gentile, Nazarene; *esprit fort*, freethinker, latitudinarian, rationalist; materialist, positivist, nihilist, agnostic.

V. be -irreligious etc. *adj.*; disbelieve, lack faith; doubt, question etc. 485.

dechristianize; serve Mammon, love darkness better than light.

Adj. irreligious; in-, un-devout; devout-, god-, grace-less; un-godly, -holy, -sanctified, -hallowed; atheistic, without God.

sceptical, free-thinking; un-believing, -converted; incredulous, faithless, lacking faith; deistical; un-, anti-christian.

worldly, mundane, earthly, carnal, unspiritual; worldly etc.- minded.

Adv. irreligiously etc. *adj.*

990. Worship.—N. worship, adoration, devotion, aspiration, latria, homage, service, humiliation; kneeling, genuflexion, prostration.

prayer, invocation, supplication, rogation, in-tercession, orison, holy breathing; petition etc. (*request*) 765; collect, litany, Lord's prayer, pater-noster, *Ave Maria*, rosary; bead-roll; latria, dulia, hyperdulia, vigils; revival; cult.

thanksgiving; giving —, returning- thanks; grace, praise, glorification, benediction, doxology, hosanna; h-, allelujah; *Te Deum*, *non nobis Domine*, *nunc dimittis*; paean.

psalm, -ody; hymn, plainsong, chant, chaunt, response, anthem, motet; antiphon, -y.

oblation, sacrifice, incense, libation; burnt —, votive —, thank-offering; offertory, collection.

discipline; self-discipline, -examination, -denial; fasting.

divine service, office, duty; morning prayer; mass, matins, evensong, vespers, compline; holy day etc. (*rites*) 998.

worshipper, congregation, communicant, celebrant.

V. worship, lift up the heart, aspire; revere etc. 928; adore, do service, pay homage; humble oneself, kneel; bow —, bend- the knee; fall -down, — on one's knees; prostrate oneself, bow down and worship, recite the rosary.

pray, invoke, supplicate; put —, offer- up -prayers, — petitions; beseech etc. (*ask*) 765; say one's prayers, tell one's beads.

return —, give- thanks; say grace, bless, praise, laud, glorify, magnify, sing praises; give benedic-tion, lead the choir, intone, chant, sing.

propitiate, offer sacrifice, fast, deny oneself; vow, offer vows, give alms.

work out one's salvation; go to church; attend -service, — mass; communicate etc. (*rite*) 998.

Adj. worshipping etc. *v.*; devout, devotional, reverent, pure, solemn; fervid etc. (*heartfelt*) 821.

Int. h-, allelujah! hosanna! glory be to God! O Lord! pray God that! God -grant, — bless, — save, — forbid! *sursum corda*.

991. Idolatry.—**N.** idol-atry, -ism; demon-ism, -olatry; idol —, demon —, devil —, fire- worship; zoolatry, fetishism, Mari-, Bibli-, ecclesi-, heli-olatry.

deification, apotheosis, canonization; hero worship.

sacrifices, hecatomb, holocaust; human sacrifices, immolation, mactation, infanticide, self-immolation, *suttee*.

idol, golden calf, graven image, fetish, *avatar*, Juggernaut, joss, *lares et penates*; Baal etc. 986. idolator etc. *n.*

V. worship -idols, — pictures, — relics; put on a pedestal, bow down to, prostrate oneself before, make sacrifice to; deify, canonize, idolize.

Adj. idolatrous.

992. Sorcery.—**N.** sorcery; superstition; occult -art, — sciences; black —, magic; the black art, necromancy, theurgy, thaumaturgy; demon-ology, -omy, -ship; *diablerie*, bedevilment; witch-craft, -ery; glamor; fetis-hism, -ism; ghost dance; hoodoo, voodoo; Shamanism [Esquimaux]', vampirism; conjuration; bewitchery, exorcism, enchantment, incantation, obsession, possession, mysticism, second sight, mesmerism, animal magnetism; od —, odylic- force; electro-biology, *clairvoyance*; spiritualism, spirit-rapping, table-turning; thought reading, telepathy, thought transference, automatic writing, *planchette*, ouija board; crystal gazing; spirit manifestation, materialization, astral body, ectoplasm etc.

divination etc. (*prediction*) 511; sortilege, ordeal, *sortes Virgiliance*; hocus-pocus etc. (*deception*) 545; oracle etc. 513.

V. practice -sorcery etc. *n.*; cast a -horoscope, — nativity; conjure, exorcise, charm, enchant; bewitch, -devil; overlook, look on with the evil eye; entrance, mesmerize, magnetize; fascinate etc. (*influence*) 615; taboo; wave a wand; rub the -ring, — lamp; cast a spell; call up spirits, — from the vasty deep; raise spirits from the dead; raise —, lay-ghosts; command genii.

Adj. magic, -al; mystic, weird, cabalistic, talismanic, phylacteric, incantatory; charmed etc. *v.*

993. Spell.—**N.** spell, charm, incantation, exorcism, weird, cabala, exsufflation, cantrap, runes, abracadabra, hocus-pocus, open *sesame*, counter-charm, Ephesian letters, bell, book and candle, Mumbo-jumbo, evil-eye, fee-faw-fum.

talisman, amulet, periapt, telesm, phylactery, philter, wish-bone, merry-thought, mascot, scarab, swastika; fetish; *agnus Dei*.

wand, caduceus, rod, divining rod, lamp of Aladdin, magic carpet, seven-league boots; magic ring; wishing —, Fortunatus's- cap.

994. Sorcerer.—**N.** sorcerer, magician; thaumat-, the-urgist; conjuror, necromancer, seer, wizard, witch; fairy etc. 980; *lamia*, hag, warlock, charmer, exorcist, voodoo, mage, diviner, dowser; cunning| —, medicine- | man, witch doctor; Shaman, figure-flinger, ecstatica, medium, *clairvoyant*, mesmerist, hypnotist; *deus ex machinâ*; astrologer; soothsayer etc. 513.

Katerfelto, Cagliostro, Merlin, Comus, Mesmer, Rosicrucian; Hecate, Circe, Lilith, siren, weird sisters; witch of Endor.

995. Churchdom.—**N.** church, -dom; ministry, apostleship, priesthood, prelacy, hierarchy, church government, christendom, pale of the church.

clerical-, sacerdotal-, episcopalian-, ultramontan-ism; Theocracy; ecclesiolog-y, -ist; priestcraft, *odium theologicum*.

monach-ism, -y; monasticism, monkhood.

[Ecclesiastical offices and dignities] pontificate, primacy, archbishopric, archiepiscopacy; prelacy; bishop-ric, -dom; episcop-ate, -acy; see, diocese; deanery, stall; canon-ry, -icate; prebend, -aryship; benefice, incumbency, glebe, advowson, living, cure, — of souls; rectorship; vicar-iate, -ship; pastor-ate, -ship; deacon-ry, -ship; -curacy; chaplain, -cy, -ship; cardinal-ate, -ship; abbacy, presbytery.

holy orders, ordination, institution, consecration, induction, reading in, preferment, translation, presentation.

popedom, papacy; the -Vatican, — apostolic see, — see of Rome; religious sects etc. 984.

council etc. 696; conclave, college of cardinals, convocation, synod, consistory, chapter, vestry, presbytery; sanhedrim, *congé d'élire*; ecclesiastical courts, consistorial court, court of Arches.

V. call, ordain, induct, prefer, translate, consecrate, present, elect, bestow.

take -orders, — the veil, — vows.

Adj. ecclesi-astical, -ological; clerical, sacer-dotal, priestly, prelatical, pastoral, ministerial, capitular, theocratic; hierarchical, archiepiscopal; episcopal, -ian; canonical; mon-astic, -achal; monkish; abbati-al, -cal; pontifical, papal, apostolic; untramontane, priest-ridden.

996. Clergy.—**N.** clergy, clericals, ministry, priesthood, presbytery, the cloth, the pulpit.

clergyman, divine, ecclesiastic, churchman, priest, presbyter, hierophant, pastor, shepherd, minister, clerk in holy orders; father, – in Christ; *padre*, *abbé*, *curé*; patriarch, reverend; black coat; confessor; sky pilot.

dignitaries of the church; ecclesi-, hier-arch; eminence, reverence, elder, primate, metropolitan, archimandrite, archbishop, bishop, prelate, diocesan, suffragan, dean, subdean, archdeacon, prebendary, canon, rural dean, rector, parson, vicar, perpetual curate, residentiary, beneficiary, incumbent, chaplain, curate, — in charge; deacon, -ess; preacher; lay reader, lecturer; capitular; missionary, propagandist, Jesuit, revivalist, field preacher.

churchwarden, sidesman; clerk, precentor, choir; almoner, *suisse*, verger, beadle, sexton, sacristan; acol-yth, -othyst, -yte; thurifer; chorister, choir boy.

[Roman Catholic priesthood] Pope, *Papa*, Holy

Father, pontiff, high priest, cardinal; ancient —, flamen; confessor, penitentiary; spiritual director.

cenobite, conventual, abbot, prior, monk, friar, lay brother, beadsman, mendicant, pilgrim, palmer; canon-regular, -secular; Jesuit, Franciscan, Friars minor, Minorites; Observant, Capuchin, Dominican, Carmelite; Augustinian; Gilbertine; Austin-, Black-, White-, Grey-, Crossed-, Crutched- Friars; Bonhomme, Carthusian, Benedictine, Cistercian, Trappist, Cluniac, Premonstratensian, Maturine; Templar, Hospitaller.

abb-, prior-, canon-ess; mother superior; *religieuse*, nun, sister, *beguine*, novice, postulant.

[Under the Jewish dispensation] prophet, priest, high priest, Levite; Rabbi, -n; scribe.

[Mohammedan etc.] mullah, ulema, imauam, sheik; so-fi, -phi; mufti, hadji, muezzin, dervish; fakir, -quir; brahmin, gooroo, druid, bonze, santon, abdal, Lama, talapoin, caloyer etc.

V. take orders etc. 995.

Adj. the —, the very —, the Right- Reverend; ordained, in orders, called to the ministry.

997. Laity.—N. laity, flock, fold, congregation, assembly, brethren, people.

temporality, secularization.

layman, civilian; parishioner, catechumen; secularist.

V. secularize.

Adj. secular, lay, laical, civil, temporal, profane.

998. Rite.—N. rite; ceremon-y, -ial; ordinance, observance, function, duty; form, -ulary; solemnity, sacrament; incantation etc. (*spell*) 993; service, psalmody etc. (*worship*) 990; liturgies.

ministration; preach-ing, -ment; predication, sermon, homily, exhortation, lecture, discourse, pastoral.

baptism, christening, chrism; immersion; baptismal regeneration; font; circumcision.

confirmation; imposition —, laying on- of hands; churching, purification, ordination etc. (*churchdom*) 995; excommunication.

Eucharist, Lord's supper, communion; the —, the holy- sacrament; celebration, high celebration; *missa cantata*; offertory; introit; consecration; con-, tran-substantiation; real presence; elements, bread and wine; mass; high —, low —, dry- mass.

matrimony etc. 903; burial etc. 363; visitation of the sick.

seven sacraments, impanation, extreme unction, last rites, *viaticum*, invocation of saints, canonization, transfiguration, auricular confession; fasting; maceration, flagellation, sackcloth and ashes; penance etc. (*atonement*) 952; absolution; telling of beads, reciting the rosary, processional; thurification, incense, holy water, aspersion.

relics, rosary, beads, reliquary, host, cross, rood, crucifix, pax, pix, pyx, *agnus Dei*, censer, thurible, patera, urceole; chalice, patten, Holy Grail, sangrail; seven-branch candle stick, monstrance, sacring bell.

ritual, rubric, canon, ordinal; liturgy, prayerbook, book of common prayer, pietas, euchology,

litany, lectionary; missal, breviary, mass-book, bead-roll.

psalter; psalm —, hymn- book; hymn-al, -ology; psalmody.

ritual-, ceremonial-ism; sabbat-ism, -arianism; ritualist, sabbatarian.

holyday, feast, fast; Sabbath, Passover, Pentecost; Advent, Christmas, Noel, Epiphany, Lent, Shrove Tuesday, Ash Wednesday, Maundy Thursday; Passion —, Holy- week; Good Friday, Easter, Ascension Day, Whitsuntide; Trinity Sunday, Corpus Christi; All-Saints' —, — Souls'- Day; Candle-, Lam-, Martin-, Michael-mas; hogmanay; Ramadan, -zan; Bairam etc. etc.

V. perform service, do duty, minister, officiate, baptize, dip, sprinkle; confirm, lay hands on; give —, administer —, take —, receive —, attend —, partake of- the -sacrament, — communion; communicate; celebrate mass; administer —, receive-extreme unction; anele, shrive, absolve, confess; do penance; genuflect; cross oneself, make the sign of the cross.

excommunicate, ban with bell, book and candle.

preach, sermonize, predicate, lecture.

Adj. ritual, -istic; ceremonial, liturgic; baptismal, eucharistical; paschal.

999. Canonicals.—N. canonicals, vestments; robe, gown, Geneva gown, frock, pallium, surplice, cassock, dalmatic, scapulary, cope, scarf, tunicle, chasuble, alb, *alba*, stole; fan-on, -nel; tonsure, cowl, hood; calo-te, -tte; bands; capouch, amice, orarium, ephod; apron, lawn sleeves, pontificals, pall; miter, tiara, triple crown; -shovel —, cardinal's- hat; biretta; crosier; pastoral staff; costume etc. 225.

1000. Temple.—N. place of worship; house of -God, — prayer.

temple, cathedral, minister, church, kirk, chapel, meeting-house, bethel, tabernacle, conventicle, *basilica*, fane, holy place, chantry, oratory.

synagogue; mosque; marabout; pantheon; pagoda; joss-house; dagobah, tope; kiosk.

parsonage, rectory, vicarage, manse, deanery, glebe, church house; Vatican; bishop's palace; Lambeth.

altar, shrine, sanctuary, Holy of Holies, *sanctum sanctorum*, sacrarium, -isty; communion —, holy —, Lord's- table; table of the Lord; pyx; baptistery, font; piscina, stoup; aumbry; sedile; reredos; roodloft, — screen; jube.

chancel, quire, choir, nave, aisle, transept, lady chapel, vestry, crypt, cloisters, porch; triforum, clerestory, churchyard, *golgotha*, calvary, Easter sepulcher; stall, pew, sitting; pulpit, ambo, lectern, reading-desk, confessional, prothesis, credence, baldachin, *baldacchino*; jesse, apse, belfry; chapter-house; presbytery.

monastery, priory, abbey, friary, convent, nunnery, cloister.

Adj. claustral, cloistered; monast-ic, -erial; conventual.

INDEX

The numbers refer to the headings under which the words or phrases occur. When the same word or phrase may be used in various senses, the several headings under which it, or its synonyms, will be found, according to those meanings, are indicated by the words printed in Italics. These words in Italics are not intended to explain the meaning of the word or phrase to which they are annexed, but only to assist in the required reference.

When the word given in the Index is itself the title or heading of a category, the number of reference is printed in blacker type, thus: **abode 189.**

put in – 677
suit the – to the word 550
thick of the – 682
activate 171
actionable 964
active physical 171
  voluntary 682
  – service 722
  – thought 457
activity 682
actor
  impostor 548
  player 599
  agent 690
  affectation 855
Acts record 551
  Apostolic 985
actual existing 1
  present 118
  real 494
actuary 85, 811
actuate 176, 615
actum est 729
acu tetigisti, rem 465, 494
acuity 253
aculeated 253
acumen 498
acuminated 253
acupuncture 260
acustics 402
acute energetic 171
  physically violent 173
  pointed 253
  physically sensible 375
  musical tone 410
  perspicacious 498
  cunning 702
  strong feeling 821
  morally painful 830
  – angle 244
  – ear 418
  – note 410
acutely 31
acuteness 465
ad
  – eundem 27
  – hominem 79
  – infinitum 105
  – instar 82
  – interim 106
  – lib 705
  – rem 23
A.D. 106
adage 496
adagio music 415
  slow 275
Adam sin 945
  – 's apple 250
adamant 159, 323
adapt 23, 27
  – oneself to 82
adaptable
  conformable 82
  useful 644
add increase 35
  join 37
  numerically 85
  – up 811
addendum 39
adder 913
addict habit 613
adding machine 85
additament 39

addition
  extrinsical 6
  increase 35
  adjunction 37
  thing added 39
  arithmetical 85
addle barren 169
  incomplete 730
  abortive 732
  – the wits, 475, 503
addlehead 501
addleheaded 499
address
  residence 189
  direction 550
  speech 582
  speak to 586
  skill 698
  request 765
  – oneself to 673
addresses
  courtship 902
addressful 894
adduce
  bring to 288
  evidence 467
adulce 834
ademption 789
adenoid 250
adenology 329
adept 700
adequate power 157
  sufficient 639
  for a purpose 644
adhere stick 46
  – to 604a, 613
  – to an obligation 772
  – to a duty 926
adherent
  follower 711
adhesive, 46, 327, 352
adhibit 677
adhortation 695
adieu departure 293
  loss 776
adipocere 356
adipose 355
adit orifice 260
  conduit 350
  passage 627
adjacent 197
adjection 37
adjective 39
adjoin 197, 199
adjourn 133
adjudge 480
adjudicate 480
adjunct
  thing added 39
  accompaniment 88
  aid 707
  auxiliary 711
adjuration 535, 536
adjure 765, 768
adjust adapt 23
  equalize 27
  order 58
  prepare 673
  settle 723, 762
  – differences 774
adjutage 260, 350
adjutant
  auxiliary 711
  military 745
adjuvant helping 707

auxiliary 711
admeasurement 466
adminicle 467
administer
  utilize 677
  conduct 693
  exercise authority 737
  distribute 786
  – correction 972
  – oath 768
  – sacrament 998
  – to aid 707
  give 784
administration of justice 965
administrative 737, 965
administrator 694
admirable 648, 744
admiral 745
Admiralty, court of – 966
admirari, nil – 871, 932
admiration
  wonder 870
  love 897
  respect 928
  approval 931
admired disorder 59
admirer 897
admissible
  relevant 23
  receivable 296
  tolerable 651
  – in society 852
admit
  composition 54
  include 76
  let in 296
  assent 488
  acknowledge 529
  permit 760
  concede 762
  accept 785
  – exceptions 469
  – of 470
admitted
  customary 613
  – maxim &c. 496
admixture 41
admonish
  warn 668
  advise 695
  reprove 932
ado activity 682
  exertion 686
  difficulty 704
  make much –
  about 542
  much – about nothing
  overestimate 482
  unimportant 643
  unskilful 699
adolescence 131
Adonis 845
adonize 847
adopt
  naturalize 184
  choose 609
  – a cause aid 707
  – a course 692
  – an opinion 484
adoption
  religious 987

adore 897, 990
adorn 847
adown 207
adrift unrelated 10
  disjoined 44
  dispersed 73
  uncertain 475
  unapt 699
  free 750
  go – deviate 279
  turn – disperse 73
  liberate 750
  dismiss 756
adroit 698
adscititious
  extrinsic 6
  added 37
  redundant 641
adscriptus glebae 746
adulation 933
adulator 935
adulterate mix 41
  deteriorate 659
adulterated 545
adulterer 962
adultery 961
adumbrate
  darkness 421
  allegorize 521
  represent 554
adumbration
  semblance 21
  allusion 526
aduncity 244, 245
adust
  color 433
  gloomy 837
adustion 384
advance increase 35
  course 109
  progress 282
  assert 535
  improve 658
  aid 707
  succeed 731
  lend 787
  in – precedence 62
  front 234
  precession 280
  in – of 33
  in – of one's age 498
  – against 716
  – of learning &c. 490
advanced 282
  – in life 128
  – guard 234
  – student 541
  – work 717
advances, make –
  offer 763
  social 892
advantage
  superiority 33
  influence 175
  good 618
  expedience 646
  mechanical – 633
  dressed to – 847
  find one's – in 644
  gain an – 775
  set off to – 658

take – of 677, 698
– over success 731
advantageous
  beneficial 648
  profitable 775
advene 37
advent
  futurity 121
  event 151
  approach 286
  arrival 292
Advent 998
adventism 984
adventitious 6, 156
adventive 156
adventure event 151
  chance 156
  pursuit 622
  danger 665
  trial 675
  the great – 360
adventurer
  traveler 268
  deceiver 548
  experimenter 463
  gambler 621
  rash 863
  ignoble 876
adventures 594
adventurous
  undertaking 676
  bold 861
  rash 863
adversaria 551
adversary 710
adverse
  contrary 14
  opposed 708
  unprosperous 735
  disliking 867
  – party 710
adversity 735
advert 457
advertise 531
advice notice 527
  news 532
  counsel 695
advisable 648
advise predict 511
  inform 527
  counsel 695
  – with one's pillow 451
advised predetermined 611
  intended 620
  better – 658
adviser 540, 695
advocacy 931
advocate
  prompt 615
  recommend 695
  aid 707
  auxiliary 711
  friend 890
  vindicate 937
  counsellor 968
Advocate, the – 976
advocation 617
advoutress 962
advoutry 961
advowson 995
adynamic 160
adytum room 191
  prediction 511
  secret place 530
adze 253
adzooks 870

aidless 160
aigrette 847
aiguille 253
aiguillette 747, 847
aigulet 847
ail 655, 828
aileron 267, 273
ailment 655
aim 278, 620, 675
– a blow at 716
aimable 894
faire l' – 897
aimer éperdument
897
aimless *without*
motive 615a
chance 621
air *unsubstantial* 4
broach 66
lightness 320
gas 334
atmospheric **338**
wind 349
tune 415
appearance 448
refresh 689
demeanor 692
fashionable 852
beat the – 645
fill the – 404
fine – *salubrity* 656
fish in the – 645
fowls of the – 366
in the – 527
rend the – 404
take – 531
air-balloon 273
air base 728
air-commodore 745
aircraft 273, 726
air-drawn 515
airdrome 273
air-force 726
air-gun 727
airing 266
air-mail 273
airman 269
airmanship 698
air-marshal 745
air-passage 351
air-pipe **351**
airport 273, 292,
728
air-pump 349
air-raid 716
airs *affectation* 855
pride 878
vanity 880
arrogance 885
air-shaft 351
air service 267
airship 273, 726
air-tight 261
airways 267
airworthy 273, 664
airy [*see* air]
windy 349
unimportant 643
gay 836
– hopes 858, 859
give to – nothing
a local habita-
tion &c. 515
aisle *passage* 260
way 627
in a church 1000
ait 346
ajar *open* 260

discordant 713
ajee 217
ajutage 260, 350
akimbo *angular* 244
stand – 715
akin *related* 9
*consanguineous*11
similar 17
al fresco 220
alabaster *white* 430
alack! 839
alacrity *willing* 602
active 682
cheerful 836
Aladdin's lamp 993
alar 267
alarm *warning* 668
notice of danger
669
fear 860
cause for – 665
give an – *indicate*
550
alarmist 862
alarum 114, 550, 669
alas! 839
alate 267
alb 999
albeit 30
albert
chain 847
albification 430
albinescence 430
albinism 430
albino 443
album 593, 596
albumen
semi-liquid 352
protein 357
Alcaic 597
alçaid 745
alcalde 745
alcazar 189
alchemy 144
alcohol 995
Alcoran 986
alcove 191, 252
Aldebaran 423
alderman 745
ale 298
alea, jacta est – 601
aleatory 665
Alecto 173
alectromancy 511
alehouse 189
go to the – 959
alembic
conversion 144
vessel 191
furnace 386
laboratory 691
alentours 197
alert *watchful* 457,
459
active 682
alerte 669
aleuromancy 511
Alexandrine
ornate style 577
verse 597
alexandrite 848
alexipharmic 662
alexiteric 662
algebra 85
algid 383
algology 369
algorithm 85
alguazil 965

alias
otherwise 18
pseudonym 565
alibi 187
alien *irrelevant* 10
foreign 57
transfer 783
gentile 989
alienable 783
alienate
transfer 783
estrange 44, 889
set against 898
alienation
mental – 503
alieni appetens
grasping 865
envious 921
selfish 943
alienism 54
align 278
alight *stop* 265
arrive 292
descend 306
on fire 382
alike 17
share and share –
778
aliment *food* 298
alimentary 662
– canal 350
alimentation
aid 707
alimony
property 780
provision 803
income 810
aliquot 51, 84
aliter visu: diis –
601
alive
living 359
intelligent 498
active 682
cheerful 836
be – with 102
keep – *continue*
143
keep the memory
– 505
look – 684
– to *attention* 457
cognizant 490
informed 527
able 698
sensible 822
alkahest 335
all *whole* 50
complete 52
generality 78
– absorbing 642
in – ages 112
– aboard 495
– agog 865
– in all 50
– along 106
– along of 154
– but 32
– colors 440
– considered 451,
480
– day long 110
– devouring 190
in – directions 278
– engrossing 190
at – events *com-
pensation* 30
qualification 469

true 494
resolve 604
– fours *easy* 705
cards 840
– in good time 152
– hail! *welcome* 292
honor to 873
celebration 883
courtesy 894
– hands *everybody*
78
on – hands 488
– of a dither 824
– of a heap 72
– knowing 976
– manner of *differ-
ence* 15
multiform 81
with – one's might
686
– at once 113
– one 27, 866
– out 52
– over *end* 67
universal 78
destruction 162
space 180
at – points 52
– in one's power
686
– powerful
mighty 159
God 976
in – quarters 180
with – respect 928
in – respects 52,
494
– right! 922
– Saints' day 998
– searching 461
– seeing 976
on – sides 227
– sorts *diverse* 16a
mixed 41
multiform 81
– talk 4
– things to all
men 894
– the time 106
at – times 136
– together 50
– ways 243, 279
– wise 976
– the world and
his wife 78
of – work
useful 644
maid – 746
Allah 979
allay
moderate 174
pacify 723
relieve 834
– excitability 826
allective 615
allege *evidence* 467
assert 535
plea 617
allegiance 743, 926
allegory 464, 521,
594
allegro *music* 415
cheerful 836
allelujah 990
allemande 840
all-embracing 76
alleviate 174, 834
alley *court* 189

passage 26
way 627
alliance *relation* 9
kindred 11
*physical co-opera-
tion* 178
*voluntary co-oper-
ation* 709
party 712
union 714
allied to *like* 17
alligation 43
align 278
alliteration
similarity 17
style in writing
577
poetry 597
allocation 60, 786
allocution **586**
allodium *free* 748
property 780
allopathy 662
alloquy 586
allot *arrange* 60
distribute 786
due 924
allow *assent* 488
admit 529
permit 760
consent 762
give 784
– to have one's
own way 740
allowable 760, 924
allowance
qualification 469
gift 784
allotment 786
discount 813
salary 973
with grains of –
485
make – for *forgive*
918
vindicate 937
alloy *mixture* 41
combination 48
debase 659
allude *hint* 514
mean 516
refer to 521
latent 526
inform 527
allure *move* 615
create desire 865
alluring 829
allusive
relative 9
alluvial *level* 213
land 342
plain 344
alluvium
deposit 40
land 342
soil 653
ally *combine* 48
auxiliary 711
friend 891
alma mater 542
almanac
list 86
chronometry 114
record 551
almighty 157
Almighty, the – 976
almoner
treasurer 801

science 357
  comparative – 368
anatriptic 331
ancestral
  bygone 122
  old 124
  aged 128
ancestry 166
anchor
  connection 45
  stop 265
  safeguard 666
  badge 747
  hope 858
  at – *fixed* 150
  stationed 184
  safe 664
  cast – *settle* 184
  arrive 292
  have an – to wind-
    ward 664
  sheet – *means* 632
anchorage
  location 184
  roadstead 189
  refuge 866
anchored 150
anchorite 893, 955
ancien régime 875
ancient *old* 124
  flag 550
  – *times* 122
ancientness 122
ancillary 707
and 37, 88
andante 415
andiron 386
androgynous 83
anecdote 594
anele 998
anemia 160
anemography 349
ἀνεμώλια βάζειν 497
anemometer
  wind 349
  measure 466
anent 9
aneroid 338
anesthesia 376,
  381, 683
anew *again* 104
  newly 123
anfractuosity 248
angel
  object of love 897
  good person 948
  supernatural
    being **977**
  fallen –
    bad man 949
    devil 978
  guardian –
    safety 664
    auxiliary 711
    benefactor 912
  – of Death 362
  – 's visits 137
angelic 944
angels and minis-
  ters of grace de-
  fend us! 860
angelus 550
anger 900
  more in sorrow
    than in – 826,
    918
angiology 329
angle 244

try 463
  at an – 217
Anglicanism 984
angling 622, 840
anguille au genou,
  rompre l' – 158,
  471
anguilliform 205,
  248
anguis in herbâ 667
anguish
  physical 378
  moral 828
angular 244
  – *velocity* 264
angularity **244**
angusta domi, res
  – 804
angustation 203
anhelation 688
anhydrate 340
anhydrous 340
aniline dyes 437
anility 128, 499
animadvert
  consider 451
  attend to 457
  reprehend 932
animal **366**
  female – 374
  – cries 412
  – economy 359
  – gratification 377
  – life 364
  – physiology 368
  – spirits 836
  – and vegetable
    kingdom 357
animalcule 193, 366
animalism
  sensuality 954
animality **364**
animate
  induce 615
  excite 824
  enliven 836
animation
  life 359
  animality 364
  activity 682
  vivacity 836
  suspended – 823
animism 984
animo, ex – 602
  quo – 620
animosity
  dislike 867
  enmity 889
  hatred 898
  anger 900
animus
  willingness 602
  intention 620
  desire 865
ankle 244
  – *deep* 208, 209
anklet 847
ankylosis 150
annalist 114, 553
annals
  chronology 114
  record 551
  account 594
anneal 673
annex
  addition 37
  adjunct 39
  junction 43

acquire 775
Annie Oakley 815
annihilate 2, 162
anniversary 138
anno 106
Anno Domini
  era 106
  old age 124
annotation 522, 550
annotator 524
  scholar 492
  interpreter 524
  editor 595
annotto 434
announce
  predict 511
  inform 527
  publish 531
  assert 535
announcer 527
annoy
  molest 649, 907
  disquiet 830
annoyance 828
  source of – 830
annual *periodic* 138
  plant 367
  book 593
annuity 810
annul 162, 750
annular 247
annunciate 527
annus magnus 108
anodyne
  lenitive 174
  remedial 662
  relief 834
anoint *coat* 223
  lubricate 332
  oil 355
anointed
  deity 976
  king 745
anomaly 59, 83
  disorder 59
  irregularity 83
anon 132
anonymous 565
anopsia 442
anorexy 866
another
  different 15
  repetition 104
  – *story* 468, 526
  go upon – tack.607
  – *time* 119
answer
  to an inquiry **462**
  confute 479
  solution 522
  succeed 731
  pecuniary profit
    775
  pleadings 969
  require an – 461
  – for *deputy* 759
  promise 768
  go bail 806
  I'll – for it 535
  – the helm 745
  – the purpose 731
  – to *correspond* 9
  – one's turn 644
answerable
  agreement 23
  liable 177
  bail 806
  duty 926

censurable 932
ant 690
Antaeus 159, 192
antagonism
  difference 14
  physical 179
  voluntary 708
  enmity 889
antagonist 710, 891
antagonistic 24
antarctic 237
antecedence 62, 116
antecedent 64
antechamber 191
ante Christum 106
antedate 115
antediluvian 124
antelope 274
antemundane 124
antenna 379
anteposition 62
anterior
  in order 62
  in time 116
  in place 234
  – to *reason* 477
anteroom 191
antevert 706
anthem 990
anthemion 847
anthology
  book 533
  collection 596
  poem 597
anthracite 388
anthropoid 372
anthropology
  zoology 368
  mankind 372
anthropomancy 511
anthropophagi 913
anthroposcopy 511
anthroposophy 372
antic 840
anti-aircraft gun
  564, 727
antichambre,
  faire – 133
antichristian 984,
  989
antichronism 115
anticipate
  anachronism 115
  priority 116
  future 121
  early 132
  expect 507
  foresee 510
  prepare 673
  hope 858
  in – 116
anticlimax
  decrease 36
  bathos 497, 853
anticlinal 217
anticyclone 265
antidote 662
antigropelos 225
antilogarithm 84
antilogy 477
antimony 663
Antinomian 984
antinomy 964
Antinous 845
antiparallel 217
antipathy 867, 898
antiphon *music* 415
  answer 462

worship 990
antiphrasis 563
antipodes
  difference 14
  distance 196
  contraposition
    237
antipoison 660
antiquary
  past times 122
  scholar 492
  historian 553
antiquas vias,
  stare super –
    613, 670
antiquated 128
antique 124
antiquity 122
antiscriptural 984
antiseptic 652, 662
antisocial 911
antistrophe 597
antithesis
  contrast 14
  difference 15
  opposite 237
  style 574, 577
antitoxin 662
antitype 22
antler 253
antonomasia
  metaphor 521
  nomenclature 564
antonym 14
antrum 252
anvil *support* 215
  on the –
  intended 620
  in hand 625
  preparing 673
anxiety *pain* 828
  fear 860
  desire 865
anxious expectation
  507
any *some* 25
  part 51
  no choice 609a
  at – *price* 604a
  at – *rate*
  certain 474
  true 494
  at all hazards 604
anybody 78
anyhow 460, 627
anything one
  knows, for – 491
aorist 109, 119
aorta 350
apace *early* 132
  swift 274
apache 913
apart 44, 87
  set – 636
  wide – 196
apartment 191
  –s 189
  – to let
  imbecile 499
apathetic 275
apathy
  indifference 465
  insensibility 823
  irreligion 989
ape *imitate* 19
Apelles 559
aperçu 596
aperture 260

apex 210
aphasia 583
aphelion 196
aphonic 403
aphony **581**
aphorism 496
aphrodite 845, 979
apiary 370
apiculture 370
Apicius 957
apiece 79
apish 19, 499
aplanatic 429
aplomb
  stability 150
  self-possession
  498
  resolution 604
Apocalypse 985
Apocrypha 985
apocryphal
  uncertain 475
  erroneous 495
  heterodox 984
apodictic 478
apodosis 67
apogee 210
apograph 21
Apollo *sun* 318
  music 416
  luminary 423
  beauty 845
  god 979
  magnus – 500, 695
Apollyon 978
apologue
  metaphor 521
  teaching 537
  description 594
apology *excuse* 617
  vindication 937
  penitence 950
  atonement 952
apophthegm 496
apophysis 250
apoplexy 158, 655
aporetic 487
aposiopesis 585
apostasy
  recantation 607
  dishonor 940
  heterodoxy 984
apostate
  convert 144
  turncoat 607
  impiety 988
apostle *teacher* 540
  disciple 541
  inspired 985
  –'s creed 983a
apostolic 985
  – church 983a
  – see 995
apostrophe
  address 586
  soliloquy 589
  appeal 765
apothecary 662
  –'s weight 319
apothegm 496
apotheosis
  resuscitation 163
  canonization 873
  heaven 981
  hero worship 991
apozem 335, 384
appal 830, 860
appanage

property 780
  gift 784
apparatus 633
apparel 225
apparent
  visible 446
  appearing 448
  probable 472
  manifest 525
  heir – 779
apparition
  fallacy of vision
  443
  spirit 980
apparitor 534
appeach 938
appeal 586, 765
  court of – 966
  – to arms 722
  – motion 969
  – from Philip
    drunk to Philip
    sober 658
  – to *call to witness*
  467
  – to for (*claim*) 924
appear 446, 525
  – for 759
  – in print 591
appearance **448**
  make one's – 292
  to all – 448
  probable 472
appearances
  keep up – 852
appease 174
appellant 924, 938
appellate 966
appellation 564
append *add* 37
  sequence 63
  hang 214
appendage 39
appendectomy 662
appendix
  adjunct 39
  sequel 65
  end 67
  book 593
appertain
  related to 9
  component 56
  belong 777
  property 780
appetite 865
  tickle the –
  savory 394
appetizing 865
  exciting 824
applaud 931
apple – of discord
  713
  golden –
    allurement 615
  – of one's eye *good*
  648
  love 897
  favorite 899
  – off another tree
  15
  how we –s swim!
  880
apple-green 435
apple-pie order 58
appliance *use* 677
  –s *means* 632
  machinery 633
applicable *relevant*

23
  useful 644
  expedient 646
applicability 9
applicant 767
application *study*
  457
  metaphor 521
  use 677
  request 765
apply, *use* 677
  – a match 384
  – the match to a
    train 66
  – the mind 457
  – a remedy 662
appoggiatura 413
appointment
  employment 625
  order 741
  charge 755
  assignment 786
  interview 892
appointments
  gear 633
apportion *arrange*
  60
  disperse 73
  allot 786
apportionment **786**
appositeness 9
apposition
  relation 9
  relevancy 23
  closeness 199
  paraphrase 522
appraise 466, 812
appreciate
  realize 450, 451
  measure 466
  judge 480
  know 490
  taste 850
  approve 931
apprehend
  believe 484
  know 490
  fear 860
  seize 789
apprehension
  idea 453
  taking 789
apprentice 541
  – oneself 676
apprenticeship 539,
  673
apprise 527
apprised of 490
approach
  of time 121
  impend 152
  nearness 197
  move **286**
  path 627
approaching 9
approbation **931**
appropinquation
  286
appropriate *fit* 23
  peculiar 79
  expedient 646
  assign 786
  take 789
  steal 791
approval 488, 931
  on – 609
approximate
  related to 9

resemble 17
  in mathematics 85
  nearness 197
  approach 286
appulse *meeting* 199
  collision 276
  approach 286
  convergence 290
appurtenance
  part 51
  component 56
  belongings 780
  accompaniment
  88
appurtenant 9
après nous le
  déluge 943
apricot *color* 439
April
  – fool 547, 857
  make an – fool of
  545
  – showers 149
apron *extension* 39
  clothing 225
  defence 717
  canonicals 999
àpropos [*see* à]
aprotype 591
apse 1000
apt *consonant* 23
  tendency 176, 177
  docile 539
  willing 602
  clever 698
aqua-fortis 335
aquamarine 435
aquarium 370
Aquarius 348, 636
aquatic *water* 337
aquatics 267
aquatinta 558
aqueduct 350
aqueous 337
aquiline 244
A.R. 106
Arab *wanderer* 268
  horse 271
  street – 876
araba 272
arabesque 847
Arabian
  – perfumes 400
  – nights 515
arable 371
arbalest 727
arbiter *critic* 480
  director 694
  adviser 695
  judge 967
  – *elegantiarum*
  revels 840
  taste 850
  fashion 852
arbitrage 794
arbitrament 480
  judgment 480
  – of the sword 722
arbitrary
  without relation
  10
  irregular 83
  wilful 606
  capricious 608
  authoritative 737
  severe 739
  insolent 885
  lawless 964

– power 739
arbitrate
  adjudicate 480
  mediate 724
arbitration
  court of – 966
  submit to – 774
arbitrium, ad – 600
arbor 215, 312
arbor *abode* 189
  summer-house
  191
  plaisance 840
arborescent
  ramifying 242
  rough 256
  trees 367
arboriculture 371
arc 245
  heat 382
arcade *street* 189
  curve 245
  gateway 260
Arcades ambo
  alike 17
  friends 890
  bad men 949
Arcadia 827, 981
Arcadian 703, 946
arcanum 533
arch *great* 31
  support 215
  curve 245
  convex 250
  concave 252
  clever 498
  cunning 702
  triumphal – 733,
  883
archaic *old* 124
archaism 122, 563
archangel 977
archbishop 996
archbishopric 995
archdeacon 996
archduchy 181
archduke 745
archegenesis 161
archeologist
  pastimes 122
  scholar 492
archeology 122
archer 726
archery 840
Arches, court of –
  966, 995
archetype 22
archetypal 20
Archeus 359
archfiend 978
archiater 695
archiepiscopal 995
archimandrite 996
archipelago 346
architect 164, 690
architectonic 161
architecture
  arrangement 60
  construction 161
  fabric 329
  ornament 847
architrave 210
archive 551
archlute 417
archon *ruler* 745
  deputy 759
  judge 967
archtraitor 941

arctic *northern* 237
  cold 383
arctics 225
arcuation 245
ardent *fiery* 382
  eager 682
  feeling 821
  loving 897
  – expectation 507
  – imagination 515
ardet, proximus –
  665, 667
ardor *vigor* 574
  activity 821
  feeling 821
  desire 865
arduous 704
area 181, 182
arefaction 340
arena *space* 180
  region 181
  field of view 441
  field of battle **728**
arenaceous 330
areola 247
areolar 219
areometer 321
Areopagus 966
arête 253
aretinism 961
aretology 926
Argand lamp 423
argent 430
argillaceous 324
argosy 273
argot 563
argonaut 269
argue *evidence* 467
  reason 476
  indicate 550
  dissectation 595
argument *disagreement* 24
  topic 454
  discussion 476
  meaning 516
  have the best of
    an – 478
argumentum
  – baculinum
    compel 744
    lawless 964
    punish 972
  – ad crumenam
    800
  – ad hominem
    reasoning 476
    accuse 938
  – ad verecundiam
    939
Argus-eyed 441, 459
argute 498
aria 415
arianism 984
arid 340
  unproductive 169
  uninteresting 841
Ariel *courier* 268
  swift 274
  messenger 534
  spirit 979
arietation 276
arietta 415
aright *well* 618
Ariman [see Ahri-
  manes]
ariolation 511
arioso 415

aris et focis, pro –
  defence 717
  philanthropy 910
arise *exist* 1
  begin 66
  happen 151
  mount 305
  appear 446
  – from 154
Aristarchus 850
Aristides
  good man 948
aristocracy
  power 737
  fashion 852
  nobility 875
ἄριστον μέτρον 628
Arithmetic 511
arithmetic 85
ark *abode* 189
  asylum 666
arm *part* 51
  power 157
  instrument 633
  provide 637
  prepare 673
  war 722
  weapon 727
  make a long – 200
  – chair 215
  – in arm
    together 88
    friends 888
    sociable 892
  – of the law 963
  – of the sea 343
armada 726
Armageddon 720,
  722
armament 673, 727
armed 717
  – at all points 673
  – force 726
  – itself 58
  – guard 664
armet 717
armful 25
armiger 875
armigerent 726
armigerous 722
armilla 247, 847
armillary sphere
  466
armipotent 157
armistice
  cessation 142
  respite 672
  pacification 723
armless 158
armlet *ring* 247
  gulf 343
  ornament 847
armor *cover* 223
  defence 717
  arms 727
  buckle on one's –
    673
  – plated 223
armored
  – car 726
  – cruiser 726
  – train 726
armorial bearings
  550, 877
armory *store* 636
  workshop 691
arm's length
  at – 196
  keep at –

repel 289
defence 717
enmity 889
seclusion 893
discourtesy 895
arms **727** [see arm]
  heraldry 550
  war 722
  honors 877
  clash of – 720
  deeds of – 720
  with folded – 681
  in – *infant* 129
  throw oneself into
    the – of 666, 880
  under – 722
  up in – *active* 682
    discord 713
    resistance 719
    resentment 900
    enmity 889
Armstrong gun 727
army *collection* 72
  multitude 102
  troops 726
aroma 400
around 227
  lie – 220
arouse *move* 615
  excite 824
  – oneself 682
aroynt *begone* 297
  malediction 908
arquebusade 662
arquebuse 727
arraign 938, 969
arrange
  set in order 60
  plan 626
  compromise 774
  – with creditors
    807
  – matters
    pacify 723
  – music 413, 416
  – in a series 69
  – under 76
arrangement 23, 60
  [see arrange]
  order 58
  temporary – 111
arrant *identical* 31
  manifest 525
  notorious 531
  bad 649
  disreputable 874
  base 940
arras 847
array *order* 58, 60
  series 69
  assemblage 72
  multitude 102
  dress 225
  prepare 673
  adorn 847
  ostentation 882
  battle – 722
arrear, in – 53, 808
arrears *debt* 806
arrectis auribus
  hear 418
  expect 507
arrest *stop* 142
  restrain 751
  in law 969
  – the attention 457
arrière-pensée

after-thought 65
mental reservation
  528
motive 615
set purpose 620
arrival **292**
arrive *happen* 151
  reach 292
  complete 729
  – at a conclusion
    480
  – at the truth 480a
arrogant *severe* 739
  proud 878
  insolent 885
arrogate 885, 924
  – to oneself
    undue 925
arrondissement 181
arrosion 331
arrow *swift* 274
  missile 284
  arms 727
  broad – 550
arrow-head
  form 253
  writing 590
'Arry and 'Arriet
  902
ars celare artem
  698
arsenal *store* 636
  workshop 661
arsenic 663
arson 384
art *representation*
  554
  business 625
  skill 698
  cunning 702
  fine – 850
  work of – 845, 847
  – gallery 556
artery 350, 627
artes, hae tibi
  erunt – 627
artesian well 343
artful 544, 702
  – dodge 545, 702
article *thing* 3
  part 51
  matter 316
  chapter 593
  review 595
  goods 798
articled clerk 541
articles
  thirty-nine – 983a
  – of agreement
    770
  – of faith 484, 983
articulate 366
articulation
  junction 43
  speech 580
articulo, in –
  transient 111
  dying 360
artifice 626, 702
artificer 690
artificial
  fictitious 545
  cunning 702
  affected 855
  – language 579
artillery
  explosion 404
  arms 727

artilleryman 726
artisan 690
artist *painter* &c.
  559
  contriver 626
  agent 690
artiste *music* 416
  drama 599
artistic *skilful* 698
  beautiful 845
  taste 850
  – language 578
artlessness **703**
aruspex 513
aruspicy 511
arundo, haeret
  lateri lethalis –
  828
as *motive* 615
  – broad as long 27
  – can be 52
  – good as 27
  – if *similar* 17
  suppose 514
  – little as may be
    32
  – it may be
    circumstance 8
    event 151
    chance 156
  – much again 90
  – soon as 120
  – they say 496, 532
  – things are 7
  – things go 151,
    613
  – to 9
  – usual 82
  – it were 17, 521
  – you were 141,
    283
  – well as 37
  – the world wags
    151
ascend *be great* 31
  increase 35
  rise 305
  improve 658
ascendancy
  power 157
  influence 175
  success 731
ascendant
  lord of the – 745
  in the –
    influence 175
    important 642
    success 731
    authority 737
    repute 873
  one's star in the –
    prosperity 734
ascension
  [see ascend]
  calefaction 384
  – Day 998
ascent
  [see ascend]
  gradient 217
  rise **305**
  glory 873
ascertain *fix* 150
  determine 480
ascertained 474,
  490
ascertainment 480a
asceticism **955**
ascititious

attract – 882
call to – 457
call – to 550
give – 418
pay –s to 894
pay one's –s to 902
attenuate
decrease 36
weaken 158
reduce 195
rarefy 322
attenuated 203
attest
bear testimony 467
affirm 535
adjure 768
attested copy 771
attic *simple* 42
garret 191
summit 210
style 578
wit 842
taste 850
Attila 913
attire 225
attitude
circumstance 8
situation 183
posture 240
attitudinarian 882
attitudinize 855
attollent 307
attorney
consignee 758
at law 968
power of – 755
attract
bring towards 288
induce 615
allure 865
excite love 897
– the attention 457
visible 446
attraction
[*see* attract]
natural power 157
bring towards 288
attractive
[*see* attract]
pleasing 829
beautiful 845
attrahent 288
attribute
speciality 79
accompaniment 88
power 157
–s of the Deity 976
– to 155
attribution 155
attrite 330
attrition 330, 331
attroupement 72
attune *music* 415
prepare 673
attuned to
habit 613
attunement 23
auburn 433
A.U.C. 106
auction 796, 840
auctioneer 758, 796
auctorial 599
audacity
courage 861

rashness 863
insolence 885
audible 402
become – 418
scarcely – 405
audience
hearing 418
conversation 588
before an – 599
audire alteram partem
counter-evidence 468
right 922
justice 939
audit
numeration 85
examination 461
accounts 811
auditive 418
auditor
hearer 418
accountant 811
auditorium 189, 588
auditory
sound 402
hearing 418
theater 599
– apparatus 418
au fait 698
au fond 5
auf wiedersehen 293
Augean
– stable 653
– task 704
auger 262
aught 51
for – one cares
unimportant 643
indifferent 866
for – one knows
ignorance 491
conjecture 514
augment
increase 35
thing added 39
expand 194
augur 513
– well 858
augurate 511
augury 512
august 873
Augustinian 996
auk 366
auld lang syne 122
aulic council 696
aumbry 1000
aunt 11
aura *wind* 349
sensation 380
aurea mediocritas 628
aureate 436
aureola 420
aureole 420, 873
aureolin 436
auribus, arrectis – 418
auricular *hearing* 418
clandestine 528
– confession 998
auri sacra fames 819
aurist 662
aurora
dawn 125

light 420, 423
twilight 422
– australes 423
– borealis 423
Auroral 236
ausculation 418
auspice *omen* 512
auspices
influence 175
prediction 511
protection 664
direction 693
aid 707
under the – of 693, 737
auspicious
opportune 134
prosperous 734
hopeful 858
austerity
harsh taste 395
severe 739
discourteous 895
ascetic 955
pietism 988
austral 237
austromancy 511
authentic 467
certain 474
true 494
authentication
evidence 467
security 771
author 164, 593
projector 626
dramatic – 599
– of our being 976
– of evil 978
– 's proof 591
authoritative 474, 741
authority
testimony 467
sage 500
informant 527
power 737
permission 760
right 924
ensign of – 747
person in – 745
do upon one's own – 600
authorized *due* 924
legalized 963
authorship
production 161
style 569
writing 590
autobiography 594
autocar 272
autochthonous 188
autocracy 737, 739
autocrat 745
autocratic 600, 737
auto-da-fe 384, 972
autograph 550, 590
Autolycus *thief* 792
pedlar 797
automaniac 504
automatic 601, 633
– pistol 727
– writing 992
automaton 554, 601
automobile 272
automobilist 268
automotive 266
autonomasia 521
autonomy 737, 748

autopsy
post-mortem 363
vision 441
autoptical 446, 535
autotype 558
autumn 126
auxiliary 711
additional 34
helpful 707
– forces 726
avail *benefit* 618
useful 644
succeed 731
of no – 645
– oneself of 677
avalanche *fall* 306
snow 383
redundance 641
avaler les couleu-vres 725, 886
avant-courier 64, 673
avant-propos 64
avarice 819
avast! *stop* 142, 265
desist 624
forbid 761
avatar *change* 140
deity 976
idol 991
avaunt! 297, 449
ave! *honor* 873
courtesy 894
Ave maria 990
avenge 919
avenue
plantation 371
way 627
aver 535
average *mean* 29, 628
mediocre 651
– circumstances 736
take an – 466
Averni, facilis de-scensus – 217, 665
Avernus 982
averruncate 297, 301
aversion *unwilling-ness* 603
dislike 867
hate 898
avert 706
– the eyes 442
aviary 370
aviation 267
aviator 269
avidity *avarice* 819
desire 865
airette 273
avile 932, 934
avion 273
aviso 532
avocation 625
avoidance 623
avoidless 474, 601
avoirdupois 319
avolation 623, 671
avouch 535, 768
avow *assent* 488
disclose 529
assert 535
avulsion 44, 301
avuncular 11
await *future* 121

be kept waiting 133
impend 152
expect 507
awake *attentive* 457
careful 459
intelligent 498
active 682
– to life immortal 360
awaken *inform* 527
excite 824
– the attention 457
– the memory 505
award *adjudge* 480
give 784
aware 490
away 187, 196
break – 623
fly – 293
move – 287
take – from 789
get &c. – 671
throw &c. –
eject 297
reject 610
waste 638
relinquish 782
– from *unrelated* 10
– with! 930, 932
do – with *undo* 681
abrogate 756
awe *fear* 860
wonder 870
respect 928
aweless *fearless* 861
insolent 885
disrespectful 329
awful 31, 860
– silence 403
awhile 111
awkward
inelegant 579
inexpedient 647
unskilful 699
difficult 704
painful 830
ugly 846
vulgar 851
ridiculous 853
– squad 701
awl 262
awn 253
awning 223, 424
awry *oblique* 217
distorted 243
evil 619
axe *edge tool* 253
impulse 276
weapon 727
for beheading 975
have an – to grind 702
Axinomancy 511
axiom 496
axiomatic 474
axis *support* 215
center 222
rotation 312
axle 312
wheel and – 633
axle load 466
axletree 215
ay 488
ayah 746, 753
aye *ever* 112
yes 488
azimuth

relief 834
Balmoral *boot* 225
balmy
  sleep 683
balneal 337
balourdise 699
balsam 662
balsamic
  salubrious 834
balustrade
  support 215
  inclosure 232
bam 544
bambino 129
bamboozle 545
ban *exclude* 55
  prohibit 761
  denounce 908
  under the — 909
  — with bell, book,
    and candle 998
banal 613, 843
band *ligature* 45
  assemblage 72
  filament 205
  belt 230
  ring 247
  music 415, 416,
    417
  party 712
  shackle 752
  — of hope 958
  — together 709
  — with 720
bandage 43, 45
  support 215
  cover 223
  remedy 662
  restraint 752
  the eyes -d 442
bandana 225
bandbox 191
banded together
  178, 712
bandit 792
bandog 664, 668
bandolier 636
bandore 417
bandrol 550
bands 999
bandurria 417
bandy
  exchange 148
  agitate 315
  — about 531
  — legged 243
  — words 476, 588
bane 619, **663**
baneful 649
bang *impel* 276
  sound 406
  beat 972
bangle 847
banish *eject* 297
  seclude 893
  punish 972
banister 215
banjo 417
bank *acclivity* 217
  side of lake 342
  store 636
  sand 667
  fence 717
  money 802
  sea — 342
  — of elegance 800
  — holiday 840
  — up 670

banker 797, 801
  game 840
bank-note 800
bankruptcy 732, 808
banlieue 197, 227
banner 550
  enlist under the -s
    of 707
  raise one's — 722
banneret 875
banns
  forbid the — 761
  publish the —
    ask 765
    marriage 903
banquet 298, 840
banquette 717
banshee 979, 980
bantam cock 887
banter 842, 856
banterer 844
banting 956
banyan *stint* 640
  fast 956
baptism *name* 564
  rite 998
Baptist 984
baptistery 1000
bar *except* 38
  exclude 55
  hotel 189
  line 200
  support 215
  inclosure 232
  close 261
  music 413
  hindrance 706
  insignia 747
  prison 752
  prohibit 761
  ingot 800
  tribunal 966
  legal profession
    968
  — sinister *flaw* 651
    disrepute 874
    illegal 964
  crossing the — 360
Barabbas 792
baragouin 517
barb *spike* 253
  nag 271
  — the dart *pain* 830
baronet 875
barbacan 717
barbarian
  uncivilized 876
  evil-doer 913
barbaric 851, 876
barbarism
  neology 563
  bad style 579
  vulgarity 851
  discourtesy 895
barbarous
  unformed 241
  plebeian 876
  maleficent 907
barbette 717
barbican 717
barbouillage 590
barcarolle 415
bard 416, 597
bare *mere* 32
  nude 226
  manifest 525
  disclose 529
  scanty 640

— back 226
— bone 203
— faced *deceitful*
  544, *insolent* 885
— foot 226, 804
— headed 928
  scud under - poles
    704
— possibility 473
— supposition 514
bargain
  compact 769
  barter 794
  cheap 815
  into the - 37
  — for 507
  — and sale *transfer
    of property* 783
barge 273
bargee 269
baritone 408
bark *rind* 223
  strip 226
  ship 273
  yelp 412
  — at *threaten* 909
  censure 932
  more - than bite
    908
  - worse than bite
    885
barker 767
barleycorn
  little 193
Barleycorn, Sir
  John - 298
barm *leaven* 320
  bubbles 353
Barmecide feast
  956
barmy 320, 503
barn 189
barnacles 445
barndoor fowl 366
barograph 206, 338
barometer *air* 338
  measure 466
  consult the — 463
baron *peer* 875
  husband 903
  court — 966
  — of the Exchequer
    967
baronet 875
baronial 878
baroque 853
baroscope 338
barouche 272
barque 273
barrack 189
barracoon 717
barrage 407, 717
barratry 940
barred 219, 440
barrel 191, 249
  — organ 417
barren 169, 645
barricade *fence* 232
  obstacle 706
  defence 717
  prison 752
barrier [*see* barri-
  cade]
barring *save* 38
  excluding 55
  except 83
  — out *resist* 719
  disobey 742

barrister 968
  revising — 967
barrow
  mound 206
  vehicle 272
  grave 363
barter
  reciprocate 12
  interchange 148
  commerce **794**
barytone 408
basal 215
bas-bleu
  scholar 492
  affectation 855
base
  site 183
  lowest part **211**
  support 215
  bad 649
  cowardly 862
  shameful 874
  servile 886
  dishonorable 940
  vicious 945
  — ball 840
  — born 876
  — coin 800
  — note 408
  — of operations
    plan 626
    attack 716
  — viol 417
baseball diamond
  213
baseboard 211
based on *ground of*
  belief 467
baseless 2, 4
basement *cellar* 191
  lowest part 207,
    211
bash 276
bashaw 739, 745
bashful 881
bashi bazouk 726
basilica 1000
basilisk *sight* 441
  cannon 737
  serpent 949
basin *dock* 189
  vessel 191
  hollow 252
  plain 344
basinet 717
basis
  lowest part 211
  support 215
  preparation 673
bask *physical enjoy-
  ment* 377
  warmth 382
  prosperity 734
  moral enjoyment
    827
basket 191
  — of 190
bas-relief 250, 557
bass *music* 415
  — note 408
  — viol 417
basset horn 417
bassinet 191, 215
bassoon 417
basso-profondo 408
basso-rilievo 250,
  557
bastard 545, 925

baste *beat* 276
  punish 972
Bastille 752
bastinado 972
bastion 717
bat 276, 727
batch 25, 72
bate *diminish* 36
  subtract 38
  reduce price 813
bated breath
  with — *faint sound*
    405
  expecting 507
  hiding 528
  whisper 581
  humble 879
bath 337, 652
  public -s 652
  warm — 386
  - room 191, 652
Bath chair 272
bathe *immerse* 300
  plunge 310
  water 337
bathos 497
bathysphere 208
batik 440
batman 637
bâton *support* 215
  scepter 747
batrachian 366
batta 973
battalion 726
batten
  feed 298
  stage lighting 599
  — down the
    hatches 261
  — on 886
batter *destroy* 162
  beat 276
battered 659, 688
battering-ram 276
battering-train 727
battery *electric* 153
  artillery 726
  guns 727
  floating — 726
  plant a — 716
battle 720, 722
  half the — 642
  win the — 731
  — array *order* 60
  prepare 673
  war 722
  — axe 727
  — cruiser 726
  — cry 550, 722
  — field *arena* 728
  — ground *discord*
    713
  — ship 726
  — with *oppose* 708
battledore and
  shuttlecock
  interchange 148
  game 840
battlement 257, 717
battre
  — la campagne
    nonsense 497
  diffuse style 573
  excitable 825
  — l'eau avec un
    bâton 645
  — le fer sur l'en-
    clume 134

ask 765
– one's bread 765
  poor 804
– leave 760
– one's life 914
– pardon 952
– the question 477
beget 161
begetter 164, 166
beggar *idler* 683
  petitioner 767
  poor 804
  degrade 874
  low person 876
  sturdy – 792
  – description 83, 870
  – my neighbor 840
  – on horseback 885
beggared
  bankrupt 808
beggarly *mean* 643
  vile 874
  vulgar 876
  servile 886
  – account of empty boxes 640, 804
begging
  go a –
    too much 641
    useless 645
    offered 763
    free 748
  – letter 765
begilt 847
begin 66
  – again 104
beginner 541
beginning 66
begird 227, 229
beglerbeg 745
begone
  depart 293
  ejection 297
  abrogate 756
  – dull care 836
Begotten, the only
  – 976
begrime 653
begrudge
  unwilling 603
  refuse 764
  stingy 819
beguile *mislead* 495
  deceive 545
  reconcile 831
  – the time
    inaction 681
    amusement 840
beguine 996
begum 745, 875
behalf 618, 707
  in – of 759
behave oneself
  conduct 692
  fashion 852
  courtesy 894
behavior 692
  on one's good –
    894, 944
behead 361, 972
behemoth 192
behest 741
behind
  in order 63
  in space 235

sequence 281
– the age 124, 491
– one's back 187
speak ill of – one's
  back 934
– the bars 751
– the scenes
  cause 153
  unseen 447
  cognizant 490
  latent 526
  hidden 528
  playhouse 599
  – time 133
behindhand
  late 133
  shortcoming 304
  adversity 735
  insolvent 808
behold 441, 457
beholden 916, 926
beholder 444
behoof 618
behoove 926
being 1, 3
  created – 366
  human – 372
  time – 106
Bel 979
belabor 276, 972
belated *late* 133
  ignorant 491
belaud 931
belay *join* 43
  restrain 706
belch 297
beldam 130, 913
beldame 173
beleaguer 716
bel esprit 844
belfry 206, 1000
Belial 978, 980
  sons of – 988
belie *deny* 536
  falsify 544
  contradict 708
belief 484, 983
  easy of – 472
  hug a – 606
believe
  [*see* belief]
  suppose 514
  reason to – 472
  – who may 485
  not – one's senses 870
believer
  religious 987
  true – 983a
belike 472
belittle
  decrease 36
  underestimate 482
  disparage 934
bell 417, 550
  alarm – 669
  bear away the –
    goodness 648
    success 731
    repute 873
  church – 350
  cracked – 408a
  passing – 363
  – book and candle
    swear 535
    curse 908
  spell 993
  rite 998

– the cat 861
– shape 249, 252
belladonna 663
belle 374, 854
  a la – étoile 220, 845
belles-lettres 560
belli, casus – 824
bellicose 720, 722
bellied 250
belligerent
  contentious 720
  warlike 722
  combatant 726
belling 412
bellman 354
bello, flagrante –
  722
Bellona 722
bellow *loud* 404
  cry 411
  animal cry 412
  wail 839
bellows 349, 580
bells, peal of – 407
bellwether 64, 694
belly *receptacle* 191
  inside 221
  convex 250
  –ful 52, 639
  – god 957
  – timber 298
belomancy 511
belong to *related* 9
  component 56
  included 76
  attribute 157
  property 777, 780
  duty 926
beloved 897
below 207
  here – 318
  – the mark 32
  – par 34, 207
  bad 649
  indifferent 651
  discount 813
  ignoble 876
  – its full strength 651
  – stairs 207
belt *outline* 230
  ring 247
  strait 343
  swimming – 666
belting 633
Belus 979
belvedere 441
bemask 528
bemingle 41
bemire 653
bemoan 839
bemused 458
bench *support* 215
  council 696
  tribunal 966
Bench, King's –
  752
bencher 968
bend *oblique* 217
  angle 244
  curve 245
  incline 278
  deviate 279
  depression 308
  circuit 311
  give 324
  submit 725

– backwards 235
– the bow 686
– the brows 932
– one's course 27
– the knee
  bow down 308
  submit 725
  humble 879
  servile 886
  courtesy 894
  respect 928
  worship 990
– one's looks upon 441
– the mind 457
– over 250
– to rules &c. 82
– sinister 874
– one's steps 622
– to tend 176
– towards 278
– to one's will 737
beneath 207
  – one 940
  – notice 643
Benedick 903
Benedictine 996
benediction
  gratitude 916
  approval 931
  worship 990
  nuptial – 903
benefaction 784
benefactor 816, 912
benefice 995
beneficent 906
beneficial 648
  – interest 780
beneficiary
  possessor 779
  receive 785
  clergy 996
benefit *good* 618
  use 644
  do good 648
  aid 707
  acquisition 775
  property 780
  benevolence 906
  reap the – of 131
benefits forgot 917
bene gesserit,
  quamdiu se –
  926
benet 545
benevolence
  tax 812
  love 897
  kindness 906
  universal – 910
Bengal heat 382
benighted
  dark 421
  ignorant 491
benign 656, 906
benignant 906
benison 618, 931
Benjamin's mess
  33, 50
Benshie 979
bent *tendency* 176
  angle 244
  turn of mind 820
  desire 865
  fool to the top of
    one's – 856
  – on *willing* 602
  resolved 604

intention 620
desirous 865
Benthamite 910
ben trovato
  likely 472
  imagination 515
  untruth 546
  wit 842
benumb
  insensible 376
  cold 385
  deaden affections 823
beplaster 933
bepraise 931
bequest 270
  gift 784
bereavement
  death 360
  loss 776
  take away 789
bereft *poor* 804
  – of life 360
  – of reason 503
béret 225
berg, ice – 383
bergamot 400
berlin 272
berth *lodging* 189
  bed 215
  office 625
beryl *green* 435
  jewel 847
beseech 765, 990
beseem 926
berserk 173, 503
beset *surround* 227
  follow 281
  attack 716
  entreat 765
  annoy 830
  haunt 860
  – with difficulties 704
besetting 78, 613
  – sin 945
beshrew 908
beside *except* 83
  near 197
  alongside 236
  – the mark 10, 495
  – oneself 503, 824
besides 37
besiege
  surround 227
  attack 716
  solicit 765
bésique 840
besmear 233, 653
besom 652
besotted 481
bespangle 847
bespatter *dirt* 653
  disapprove 932
  flatter 933
  detract 934
bespeak *early* 132
  evidence 467
  indicate 516
  engage 755
  ask for 765
bespeckle 440
bespot 470
besprinkle 41, 440
best 648, 650

all for the —
  good 618
  prosper 734
  content 831
  hope 858
bad is the — 649
do one's —
  care 459
  try 675
  activity 682
  exertion 686
have the — of it 731
make the — of it
  over-estimate 482
  use 677
  submit 725
  compromise 774
  take easily 826
  hope 858
the — 800
to the — of one's
  belief 484
— bib and tucker
  prepared 673
  ornament 847
  ostentation 882
— friends 890
— intentions 906
— man 903
— part 31, 50
— seller 731
make the — of
  one's time 684
bestead 644
bestial 954, 961
bestir oneself
  activity 682
  haste 684
  exertion 686
bestow 784
— one's hand 903
— thought 451
bestraddle 215
bestrew 73
bestride 206, 215
bet 621
betake oneself to
  journey 266
  business 625
  use 677
bête, pas si — 498
bête noire *bane* 663
  fear 860
  hate 898
bethel 1000
bethink 451, 505
bethral 749, 751
betide 151
betimes 132
betoken
  evidence 467
  predict 511
  indicate 550
betray *disclose* 529
  deceive 545
  dishonor 940
— itself *visible* 446
betrayer 941
betrim 673
betroth 768, 903
betrothed 897
better *good* 648
  improve 658
appeal to one's —
  feelings 914
get — *health* 654
  improve 658
  refreshment 689

restoration 660
get the — of, 479,
  702, 731
think — of 658, 950
seen — days
  deteriorate 659
  adversity 735
  poor 804
only — than noth-
  ing 651
— sort 875
for — for worse
  choice 609
  marriage 903
between 228
— cup and lip 111
far — 198
lie — 228
— the lines 526
vibrate — two ex-
  tremes 149
— ourselves 528
— two fires 665
— maid 746
betwixt 228
bevel 217
— gearing 653
bever 298
beverage 298
bévue 732
bevy 72, 102
bewail *regret* 833
  lament 839
beware 665, 668
bewilder
  put out 458
  uncertainty 475
  astonish 870
bewitch
  fascinate 615
  please 829
  excite love 897
  exorcise 992
bey 745
beyond *superior* 33
  distance 196
go — 303
— compare 31, 33
— control 471
— one's depth 208,
  519
— expression 31
— one's grasp 471
— hope 731, 534
— the mark 303,
  641
— measure 641
— possibility 471
— praise
  perfect 650
  approbation 931
  virtue 944
— price 814
— question 474, 494
— reason 471
— remedy 859
— seas 57
bezel 217
bhang 663
bias *influence* 175
  tendency 176
  slope 217
  prepossession 481
  disposition 820
bib *pinafore* 225
  drink 959
bibber *weep* 839

tope 959
bibble-babble 584
bibelot 847
bibendum, nunc
  est — 959
Bible 895
— oath 535
biblioclasm 162
bibliography 593
bibliolatry
  learning 490
  heterodoxy 984
  idolatry 991
bibliomancy 511
bibliomania 490
bibliomaniac 492
bibliophile 492
bibliopole 593
bibliotheca 593
bibulous 298, 959
bicameral 90
bicapital 90
bice 435, 438
bicentenary 98,
  138, 883
bicker *flutter* 315
  quarrel 713
bicolor 440
biconjugate 91
bicuspid 91
bicycle 272
bid *order* 741
  offer 763
— the banns 903
— defiance 715
— fair *tend* 176
  probable 472
  promise 511
  hope 858
— a long farewell
  624
— for *intend* 620
  offer 763
  request 765
  bargain 794
bidder 767
bide *wait* 133
  remain 141
  take coolly 806
— one's time 133
  watch 507
  inactive 681
bidet 271
biennial
  periodic 138
  plant 367
bienséance 852, 894
bier 363
bifacial 90
bifarious 90
bifid 91
bifold 90
biform 90
bifurcate 91, 244
big *in degree* 31
  in size 192
  wide 194
look — *defy* 715
  proud 878
  insolent 885
talk — 885, 909
— sounding
  loud 404
  words 577
  affected 855
— swollen 194
— with ₤.1
— with the fate of

511
bigamy 903
biggin 191
bight 343
bigot *positive* 474
  prejudice 481
  obstinate 606
  heterodox 984
  impious 988
bigotry 907
bigwig *scholar* 492
  sage 500
  nobility 875
bijou *goodness* 648
  beauty 845
  ornament 847
bilander 273
bilateral 90, 236
bilbao 727
bilboes 752
put into — 751
bile 900
bilge *base* 211
  convex 250
  yawn 260
— water 653
bilious 837
bilingual 560
bilk
  disappoint 509
  cheat 545
  steal 791
bill *list* 86
  hatchet 253
  placard 531
  ticket 550
  paper 593
  plan 626
  weapon 727
  money order 800
  money account
  811
  charge 812
  in law 969
true — 969
— and coo 902
— of exchange 771
— of fare *food* 298
  plan 626
— of indictment
  938
—s of mortality 360
— of sale 771
billet *locate* 184
  ticket 550
  apportion 786
billet *epistle* 592
— doux 902
billfold 191
billhook 253
billiard — ball 249
— room 191
— table *flat* 213
billiards 840
Billingsgate 563,
  908
billion 98
billow *sea* 348
  river 341
billy-cock 225
billy-goat 373
bimetallism 800
bin 191
binary 91
bind *connect* 43
  cover 223
  compel 744
  condition 770

obligation 926
— hand and foot
  751
— oneself 768
— over 744
— up wounds 660
binding 681, 744
bine 367
binnacle 693
binocular 445
binomial 89
biogenesis 161
biograph 448
biography 594
biology 357, 359
bioscope 448
biota 357
biparous 89
biplane 273
biplicity 89
biquadrate 96
birch *flog* 972
— rod 975
bird 366
kill two —s with
  one stone 682
—'s eye view 441,
  448
—s of a feather 17
the — has flown
  187, 671
— in hand 777, 781
— of ill omen
  omen 512
  warning 668
  hopeless 859
— of passage 268
— of prey 739
a little — told me
  527
birdcage 370
birdlime *glue* 45
  trap 545
biretta 999
birth *beginning* 66
  production 161
  paternity 166
  nobility 875
— place 153
— right 924
birthday 138, 883
— suit 226
birthmark 848
bis *repeat* 104
  approval 931
biscuits, s'embar-
  quer sans — 674
bise 349
bisection 68, **91**
bishop *punch* 298
  clergy 996
—'s palace 1000
—'s purple 437
bishopric 995
bisque 33
bissextile 138
bister 433
bistoury 253
bisulcate 259
bit
  small quantity 32
  part 51
  interval 106
  curb 752
just a — 26
— by bit
  by degrees 26

by instalments 51
in detail 79
slowly 275
- *between the teeth* 600, 719
bitch *animal* 366
  female 374
  clumsy 699
  fail 732
  impure 962
bite *eat* 298
  physical pain 378
  cold 385
  cheat 545
  dupe 547
  etch 558
  mental pain 830
- *the dust* 725
- *in* 259
- *the thumb* 900, 929
- *the tongue* 392
biter *bit* 718
biting *pain* 378
  cold 383
  pungent 392
  painful 830
  discourteous 895
  censorious 932
bitten 897
bitter *beer* 298
  cold 383
  taste 392, 395
  painful 830
  acrimonious 895
  hate 898
  angry 900
  malevolent 907
- *end* 67
- *ender* 606, 710, 832
- *pill* 735
- *words* 932
bitterly *greatly* 31
bitterness
  [see bitter]
  pain 828
  regret 833
bitumen 356a
bituminous coal 388
bivouac
  encamp 184
  camp 189
  repose 265
  watch 668
bi-weekly 138
bizarre 83, 853
blab 529
blabber 584
black *color* 431
  crime 945
  look — feeling 821
  discontent 832
  angry 900
- *art* 992
- *and blue*
  beat 972
- *board* 590
- *book* 938
- *eye* 848, 972
- *in the face*
  swear 535
  excitement 821, 824
- *flag* 722
- *hole crowd* 72
  prison 752

- *lead* 556
- *letter old* 124
  barbarism 563
  print 591
- *list* 932
- *looks*
  discourteous 895
  sullen 901a
  disapprove 932
  magic 998
- *mail theft* 791
  booty 793
  bribe 973
- *sheep* 949
- *spots in the horizon* 859
- *swan* 83
- *and white*
  chiaroscuro 420
  colorless 429
  record 551
  writing 590
  prove that — is white 477
blackamoor 431
  wash a — white 471
blackball 55, 893, 932
blackcoat 996
blacken [see black]
  defame 934
blackguard
  vulgar 851
  rude 895
  base 940
  vagabond 949
blackleg 792
black Maria 727
blackness 431
blacksmith 690
bladder 191
blade *edge tool* 253
  man 373
  instrument 633
  sharp fellow 682
  proficient 700
  sword 727
  fop 854
blague 545
blain 250, 848
blame 155, 932
  lay — on 938
  take — 932
blameless 946
blameworthy
  disapprove 932
  vice 945
  guilt 947
blanc-bec 701
blancmange 298
blanch 429, 430
bland 174, 894
blandiloquence 933
blandishment
  inducement 615
  endearment 902
  flattery 933
blank 2, 4
  empty 187
  simple 849
  look —
  disappointed 509
  discontent 832
  wonder 870
  point — 576
- *cartridge* 158
- *verse* 597
blanket 223, 384

wet — 174
  toss in a — 929
blare 404, 412
blarney 933
blasé 841, 869
blasphemy 988
blast
  destroy 162
  explosion 173
  wind 349
  sound 404
  adversity 735
  curse 908
- *furnace* 386
blatant *loud* 404
  cry 412
  silly 499
blather 584
blatter 412
blaze *heat* 382
  light 420
  mark 550
  excitement 824
- *abroad* 531
blazer 225
blazing
  luminary 423
- *the eyes hide* 528
blazon *publish* 531
  repute 873
  ornament 847
  ostentation 882
blé: manger son —
  on herbe 818
bleach 429, 430
bleak 383
blear-eyed 443
bleary 422
bloat 412
blob 250
bleed
  physical pain 378
  remedy 662
  spend money 809
  extort money 814
  moral pain 828
  make the heart — 830
- *freely liberal* 816
bleeding
  hemorrhage 299
  remedy 662
- *heart* 828
blemish
  imperfection 651
  injure 659
  ugly 846
  defect **848**
blench *avoid* 623
  whiten 821
  fear 860
blend 41, 48
- *with* 714
bless
  give pleasure 829
  approve 931
  divine function 976
  worship 990
- *my heart* 870
- *one's stars* 838, 916
blessed 827
  abode of the — 981
blessedness
  single — 904
blessing *good* 618
  approval 931
blessings 734

blest 827
- *with* 177
bletonism 511
blight
  deteriorate 659
  adversity 735
- *hope* 509
blighty 189
blimp 273
blind 223
  shade 424
  cecity 442
  inattentive 458
  ignorant 491
  conceal 528
  screen 530
  deception 545
  instinctive 601
  pretext 617
  insensible 823
  drunk 959
- *alley* 261
- *bargain*
  uncertain 475
  purposeless 62
  rash 863
- *the eyes hide* 528
  deceive 545
- *hookey* 840
- *lead the blind* 538
- *man's buff* 840
- *man's holiday*
  evening 126
  dark 421, 422
- *to one's own merit* 880
- *to the world* 959
- *of one eye* 443
- *reasoning* 486
- *side prejudice* 481
  credulity 486
  obstinacy 606
blinders 424, 443
blindness **442**
blind pig 964
blink *wink* 443
  neglect 460
  falter 605
  avoid 623
- *at blind to* 442, 458
blinkard 443
blinker 424, 530
bliss 827
  celestial 981
blister 250
blithe 836
blizzard 349
bloated
  expanded 194
  misshapen 243
  convex 250
- *with pride* 878
blob 250
block *mass* 192
  support 215
  dense 321
  hard 323
  fool 501
  engraving 558
  writing 590
  hinder 706
  execution 975
  bring to the — 972
  wood — 558
- *of buildings* 189

- *out* 230, 240, 973
- *printing* 591
- *up* 261, 706
blockade
  surround 227
  close 261
  restrain 751
  exclude 893
blockhead 501
blockhouse 717
blockish 499
blond 429, 430
blood
  consanguinity 11
  fluid 333
  kill 361
  fop 854
  nobility 875
  dye with —
  severe 739
  hands in — cruel 907
  in the — 5
  life — 359
  new — 658, 824
  spill — war 722
- *for blood* 919
- *boil excite* 824, 825
  anger 900
- *run cold* 830, 860
- *heat* 382
- *horse* 271
- *hound* 913
- *letting* 297, 662
- *poisoning* 655
- *red* 434
- *stained* 361
- *sucker* 789, 913
- *thirsty*
  murderous 361
  cruel 907
- *up excited* 824
  angry 900
bloodless 160
  peace 721
  virtue 946
bloody [see blood]
  red 434
  unclean 653
  cruel 907
bloom *youth* 127
  flower 367
  blue 438
  health 654
  prosperity 734
bloomer 495
bloomers 225
blooming 654, 845
blossom
  flower 154, 161, 367
  prosperity 734
blot *blacken* 431
  error 495
  obliterate 552
  dirty 653
  blemish 848
  disgrace 874
  guilt 947
- *out destroy* 162
  forgive 918
blotch 848
blouse 225
blow *expand* 194
  knock 276
  wind 349

unexpected 508
disappointment
509
evil 619
action 680
get wind 688
failure 732
prosper 734
pain 828, 830
come to –s 720, 722
deal a – at 716
deal a – to 972
death – 360, 361
– for blow 718
– one's brains out
361
– the coals 824
– down 162
– the fire 384
– the gaff 529
– hole 351
– the horn 416
– hot and cold
lie 544
irresolute 605
tergiversation 607
caprice 608
– a kiss 902
– off *disperse* 73
– out *food* 298
darken 421
gorge 957
– over *past* 122
– pipe 349, 727
– the trumpet 873
– one's own
trumpet 882
– up *destroy* 162
eruption 173
inflate 194
wind 349
excite 824
objurgate 932,
934
blower 349
blowhard 884
blown [*see* blow]
fatigued 688
proud 878
storm – over 664,
721
– upon 874, 932
blow-out 406
blowzy *swollen* 194
red 434
blubber *fat* 356
cry 839
Blucher boot 225
bludgeon 727
– man 726, 913
blue *sky* 338
color 438
learned 490
bit of – *hope* 858
look –
disappointed 509
feeling 821
discontent 832
disrepute 874
out of the – 508
swear till all's –
535
true – 543, 939
– book 86, 551
– blood 875
– devils 837
– jacket 269
– light 550, 669

– pencil 174, 596
– moon 110
– Peter 293, 550
– and red 437
– ribbon 733, 877
– ruin 959
– stocking
scholar 492
affectation 855
– and yellow 435
Bluebeard
marriage 903
libertine 962
blueness 438
blues 837, 840
bluff *violent* 173
high cliff 206
blunt 254
deceive 545
boasting 884
insolent 885
discourteous 895
blunder *error* 495
absurdity 497
awkward 699
failure 732
– *upon* 156
blunderbuss 727
blunderhead 701
blunderheaded 499
blunt *weaken* 160
inert 172
moderate v. 174
obtuse 254
benumb 376
damp v. 616
plain-spoken 703
cash 800
deaden 823
discourteous 895
– tool 645
– witted 499
bluntness 254
blur
imperfect vision
443
dirt 653
blemish 848
stigma 874
blurb 931
blurred
invisible 447
blurt out 529, 582
blush *flush* 382
redden 434
feel 821
humbled 879
modest 881
at first – *see* 441
appear 448
manifest 525
put to the –
humble 897
browbeat 885
discourtesy 895
blushing honors
873, 881
bluster *violent* 173
defiant 715
boasting 884
insolent 885
threaten 909
blusterer 887
blustering [*see*
bluster]
windy 349
Bo to a goose, not
say – 862.

boa 225
boanerges 540
boar 366, 373
board *layer* 204
support 215
food 298
hard 323
council 696
attack 716
tribunal 966
festive – 892
go by the – 158,
162
go on – 293
on – 186, 273
preside at the –
693
– of trade 621
– school 542
boarding-house 189
boarder 188
boards 599, 728
boast 884
not much to – of
651
boasting 884
boaston 840
boat 273
in the same – 88
– race 720
boating 267
boatman 269
boatswain 269
bob *depress* 308
leap 309
oscillate 314
agitate 315
money 800
– a curtsy 894
– for *fish* 463
Bobadil, Captain –
887
bobbed
hair 53
bobbin 312
bobbing *fuel* 388
bobbish 654
bobby *police* 664
bobsleigh 272
bobsleighing 840
bobtailed 53
bocage 367
**bocca, per amusare
la** – 394
Boche 913
boddice 225
bode 511
bodega 189
bodily
substantially 3
wholly 50
material 316
– enjoyment 377
– fear 860
– pain 378
bodkin
go between 228
perforator 262
body *substance* 3
whole 50
assemblage 72
frame 215
matter 316
party 712
in a – *together* 88
– and blood of
Christ 987
– clothes 225

– color 556
– of doctrine 490
– forth 554
– guard 717, 753
– of knowledge
490
– politic
mankind 372
authority 737
keep – and soul
together 654
– of water 438
Boeotian *rustic* 371
stupid 499
fool 501
vulgar 851
ignoble 876
Boer 371
bog 345, 653
– trotter 876
boggart 980
boggle *hesitate* 605
awkward 699
difficulty 704
bogie 980
truck 272
bogle 980
bogus 545
Bohemian
unconventional 83
nomad 268
ungenteel 851
boil *violence* 173
effervesce 315
bubble 353
heat 382, 384
ulceration 655
excitement 824,
825
anger 900
– down 195
boiler 386
boisterous
violent 173
hasty 684
excitable 825
bold *prominent* 250
unreserved 525
vigorous 574
brave 861
make – with 895
show a –front 715,
861
– faced 885
– push *essay* 675
– relief *visible* 446
– stroke *plan* 626
success 731
bole 50
bolero 840
bollard 45
bolshevik 144, 146
bolshevist 737, 742
bolster *support* 215
repair 658
aid 707
– up *vindicate* 937
bolt *sift* 42
fasten 43
fastening 45
close 261
move rapidly 274
propel 284
run away 623
escape 671
hindrance 706
shaft 727
disobey 742

shackle 752
thunder – 872
– the door 761
– food 298, 957
– in 751
– upright 212
bolthead 191
bolus *mouthful* 298
remedy 662
bomb 404, 727
– proof 664, 717
– vessel 726
bombard 716
bombardier 726
bombardon 417
bombast
unmeaning 517
magniloquence
577
ridiculous 853
boasting 884
exaggeration 549
Bombastes Furioso
887
bomber
aeroplane 726
bombilation 404
bon de – augure
858
– *enfant social* 892
kindly 906
– gré mal gré 601
– marché 815
– mot 842
– naturel 836
– ton 852
– vivant 957
– voyage 293
bona – fides
veracity 543
probity 939
– roba 962
bonanza 641, 784
wealth 803
bonbon 396
bond *relation* 9
tie 45
compact 769
security 771
money 800
right 924
– of union 9, 45
government – 802
Liberty – 802
bondage 749
bonded together
712
bonds [*see* bond]
fetters 752
funds 802
in – *service* 746
tear asunder one's
– 750
– of harmony 714
bondsman 746
bone *strength* 159
dense 321
hard 323
bred in the – 5
feel it in one's –
510
– of contention
713, 720
one – and one flesh
903
– to pick *difficulty*
704
discord 713

hold a – for 759
 – case 191
briefly anon 132
brier
  sharp 253
  pipe 390
  bane 663
brig 273
brigade 726
brigadier 745
brigand 792
brigandage 791
brigandine 717
brigantine 273
bright shine 420
  color 428
  intelligent 498
  cheery 836
  beauty 845
  glory 873
  – days 734
  – eyed 845
  – prospect 858
  – side 829
look at the – side
  836, 858
  – thought
  sharp 498
  good stroke 626
  wit 842
brighten up
  furbish 658
brigue 712, 720
brilliant
  shining 420
  good 648
  wit 842
  beautiful 845
  gem 847
  glorious 873
  – idea 842
brilliantine 356
brim 231
  – over 641
brimful 52
brimstone 388
brindled 440
brine 341, 392
bring 270
  – about 153, 729
  – back 790
  – back to the
    memory 505
  – to bear upon
    relation 9
  – action 170
  – into being 161
  – to a crisis 604
  – forth 161
  – forward
    evidence 467
    manifest 525
    teach 537
    improve 658
  – grey hairs to the
    grave 735, 830
  – grist to the mill
    644
  – home 775
  – home to 155
  – in receive 296
    income 810
    price 812
  – to life 359
  – to light 480a
  – low 874
  – to maturity 673,
    729

– to mind 505
 – under one's
    notice 457
 – off 672
 – out
  discover 480a
  manifest 525
  publish 591
 – over
  persuade 484
 – to perfection
  677
 – into play 677
 – to a point 74
 – in question 461
 – up the rear 235
 – round
  persuade 615
  restore 660
 – to terms 723
 – to convert 144
  halt 265
 – together 72
 – in its train 88
 – to trial 969
 – up develop 161
  vomit 297
  educate 537
 – in a verdict 480
 – word 527
brink 231
  on the –
  almost 32
  coming 121
  near 197
  – of the grave 360
briny 392
  – ocean 341
brio music 415
  active 682
brisk prompt 111
  energetic 171
  active 682
  cheery 836
bristle 253
  – up stick up 250
  angry 900
  – with 639, 641
  – with arms 722
bristly 256
Britannia metal
  545
Briticism 563
British 188
  – lion 604
Briton, true – 939
  work like a – 686
brittleness 328
britzska 272
broach begin 66
  found 153
  reamer 262
  tap 297
  publish 531
  assert 535
broad general 78
  space 202
  lake 343
  emphatic 535
  indelicate 961,
    962
  – accent 580
  – awake 459, 682
  – daylight 420,
    525
  – farce 842
  – grin 838
  – highway 627

 – hint 527
 – meaning 516
 – minded 498
broadcast
  disperse 73
  spread 78
  publish 531
  sow – 818
broadcloth 219
broadhearted 906
broadsheet 593
broad-shouldered
  159
broadside 236
  publication 531
  cannonade 716
broadsword 727
Brobdingnagian
  192
brocade 847
brochure 593
Brocken, specter of
  the 443
broder 549
brogue boot 225
  dialect 563
broidery 847
broil heat 382
  fry 384
  fray 713, 720
broke poor 804
broken
  discontinuous 70
  weak 160
  – color 428
  – down
  decrepit 659
  failing 732
  dejected 837
  – English 563
  – fortune 735, 804
  – heart 828, 837
  hopeless 859
  – reed 160, 665
  – meat 645
  – voice 581, 583
  – winded
  disease 655
  fatigue 688
broker 758, 797
brokerage pay 812
brokery 794
bromidic 613
bronchia 351
bronze alloy 41
  brown 433
  sculpture 557
brooch 847
brood 102, 167
  – over 451, 847
brooding
  preparing 673
brook stream 348
  bear 821, 826
broom 652
broth 298
brothel 961
brother kin 11
  similar 17
  equal 27
brotherhood 712
brotherly
  friendship 888
  love 897
  benevolence 906
brougham 272
brought to bed 161
brouillerie 713

brouillon 626
brow top 210
  edge 231
  front 234
browbeat
  intimidate 860
  swagger 885
  disrespect 929
  –en humbled 879
brown 433
  – Bess 727
  – study 451, 458
Brown, Jones and
  Robinson 876
brownie 980
browse 298
bruin 895
bruise powder 330
  hurt 619
  injure 649
  blemish 848
bruiser 726
bruit
  report 531, 532
brumal 126, 383
brumous 353
Brummagem 545
brunette 433
brunt beginning 66
  impulse 276
  bear the –
  difficulty 704
  defence 717
  endure 821, 826
brush rough 256
  rapid motion 274
  graze 379
  clean 652
  fight 720
  paint – 556
  – away reject 297
  abrogate 756
  – up clean 652
  furbish 658
  prepare 673
brushwood 367
brusque violent 173
  haste 684
  discourtesy 895
brutal vulgar 851
  rude 895
  savage 907
brutalize
  [see brutal]
  corrupt 659
  deaden 823
  vice 945
brute animal 366
  rude 895
  maleficent 913
  – force
  strength 159
  violence 173
  animal 450a
  severe 739
  compulsion 744
  lawless 964
  – matter 316, 358
Brute, et tu 917
brutish [see brute]
  vulgar 851
  ignoble 876
  intemperate 954
brutum fulmen
  impotent 158
  failure 732
  lax 738
  boast 884

bubble
  unsubstantial 4
  transient 111
  little 193
  convexity 250
  light 320
  water 348
  air 353
  error 495
  deceit 545
  trifle 643
  – burst
  fall short 304
  disappoint 509
  fail 732
  – reputation 873
  – and squeak 298
  – up agitation 315
buccaneer 791, 792
bucentaur 273
Bucephalus 271
buck stag 366
  male 373
  wash 652
  money 800
  fop 854
  – basket 191
  – jump 309
  – up 684
bucket 191
  kick the – 360
  drop – in empty
    well 645
  like –s in well 314
buckle tie 43
  fastening 45
  distort 243
  curl 248
  – on one's armor
    673
  – to 604, 686
  – with grapple 720
buckler 717
buckram 855, 878
  men in – 549
bucolic
  pastoral 370
  poem 597
bud 367
  beginning 66
  germ 153
  expand 194
  graft 300
  – from 154
Buddha 979, 986
Buddhism 984
budding young 127
buddy 711, 890
budge 264
budget heap 72
  bag 191
  store 636
  finance 811
  – of news 532
buff 436
  blind man's – 840
  native – 226
buffer
  hindrance 706
  defence 717
buffet 191
  strike 276
  agitate 315
  evil 619
  bad 649
  affront 900
  smite 972
  – the waves 704,

708
bar 189
buffo 599
buffoon *actor* 599
  humorist 844
  butt 857
buffoonery 840, 842
bug 653
bugaboo 669, 860
bugbear
  imaginary 155
  bane 663
  alarm 669
  fear 860
buggy 272
bugle
  instrument 417
  war-cry 722
  ornament 847
  — call 550, 741
build *construct* 161
  form 240
  — anew 658
  — upon a rock 150
  — up *compose* 54
  — upon *belief* 484
builder 626, 690
building material
  635
buildings 189
built on *basis* 211
bulb 249, 250
bulge 250
bulk 50, 192
  — large 31
bulkhead 228, 706
bull *animal* 366
  male 373
  error 495
  absurdity 497
  solecism 568
  police 664
  ordinance 741
  — in a china shop
  59
  like a — at a gate
  173
  take the — by the
  horns 604, 861
Bull, John — 188
bullcalf 501
bulldog *animal* 366
  pluck 604, 604a
  courage 861
bulldoze 885
bullet *ball* 249
  arms 727
  missile 284
bulletin 532, 592
  — board 551
bullfight 720
bullhead 501
bullion 800
bullseye *centre* 222
  lantern 423
  aim 620
bully *fighter* 726
  maltreat 830
  frighten 860
  courage 861
  rashness 863
  bluster 885
  blusterer 887
  threaten 909
  evil doer 913
  bad man 949
bulrush
  worthless 643

bulwark 706, 717
bum 876
bumbailiff 965
bumbledom 737,
  965
bumboat 273
bump 250, 276
  — off 361
bumper 52
bumpkin 876
bumptious
  proud 878
  insolent 885
  contemptuous 930
bun 298
bunch *collection* 72
  protuberance 250
  — light 599
bunchbacked 243
Buncombe
  [*see* bunkum]
Bund 712
bundle *packet* 72
  go 266
  — on 275, 684
  — out 297
bung 263
  — up 261
bungalow 189
bungle 59, 699
bungler 701
bunion 259
bunk 186, 215
bunker 181
bunkie 890
bunkum *lie* 544
  style 577
  boast 884
  flattery 933
bunting 550
buoy *raise* 307
  float 320
  hope 858
buoyant
  floating 305
  light 320
  elastic 325
  prosperous 734
  cheerful 836
  hopeful 858
bur *clinging* 46
  sharp 253
  rough 256
  in engraving 558
burden *lading* 190
  weight 319
  melody 413
  poetry 597
  too much 641
  clog 706
  oppress 828
  care 830
  — the memory 505
  — of a song
  repetition 104
burdensome
  [*see* burden]
  hurtful 649
  laboring 686
bureau *chest* 191
  office 691
  shop 799
  tribunal 960
bureaucracy 737
bureaucrat 694
burgee 550
burgeon
  [*see* bourgeon]

burgess 188
burgh 189
burgher 188
burghmote 966
burglar 792
  — alarm 669
burglary 791
burgomaster 745
burgrave 745
burial 363
buried *deep* 208
  imbedded 229
  hidden 528
  — in a napkin 460
  — in oblivion 506
burin 558
burke 361
burlesque
  imitation 19
  travesty 21
  absurdity 497
  misrepresent 555
  drama 599
  comic 853
  ridicule 856
burletta 599
burly 192
burn *near* 197
  rivulet 348
  hot 382
  consume 384
  near the truth
  480a
  excited 825
  love 897
  punish 972
  — the candle at
  both ends
  waste 638
  exertion 686
  prodigal 818
  — daylight 683
  — one's bridges 604
  — one's fingers 699
  — in 384
  — out 385
  — to 865
burner 423
burning [*see* burn]
  passion 821
  angry 900
  — glass 445
  — with curiosity
  455
  — pain 378
  — shame 874
burnish *polish* 255
  shine 420
  beautify 845
burnous 225
burnt [*see* burn]
  red 434
  — offering 952, 990
burr 410
burrock 706
burrow *lodge* 184
  excavate 252
bursar 801
bursary 802
burst *disjoin* 44
  instantaneous 113
  explosion 173
  brittle 328
  sound 406
  paroxysm 825
bubble —
  disclosure 529
  all over 729

ready to —
  replete 641
  excited 824
  — of anger 900
  — away 623
  — of eloquence 582
  — of envy 921
  — into a flame 825
  — forth *begin* 66
  expand 194
  be seen 446
  —ing with health
  654
  — with grief 839
  — in 294
  — of laughter 838
  — out 295
  — upon *arrive* 292
  unexpected 508
  — into tears 839
burthen
  [*see* burden]
bury *enclose* 229
  inter 363
  conceal 528
  — the hatchet 918
  — one's talent 528
busboy 746
busby 225
bush *branch* 51
  jungle 344
  shrub 367
  beat about the —
  629
bushel *much* 31
  multitude 102
  receptacle 191
  size 192
  hid under a — 460
  not hide light un-
  der a — 878
bush-fighting 720
bushing 224
bushranger 792
bushy 256
business *event* 151
  topic 454
  occupation **625**
  commerce 794
  full of — 682
  man of —
  proficient 700
  consignee 758
  mind one's —
  incurious 456
  attentive 457
  careful 459
  let alone 748
  send about one's —
  297
  stage — 599
business-like
  orderly 58
  business 625
  active 682
  practical 692
  skilful 698
buskin *dress* 225
  drama 599
buss *boat* 273
  courtesy 894
  endearment 902
bust 554
bustle *energy* 171
  dress 225
  agitation 315
  activity 682
  haste 684

difficulty 704
bustling
  [*see* bustle]
  eventful 151
busy 682
busybody 532, 682.
but
  on the other hand
  30
  except 83
  limit 233
  qualifying 469
  — now 118
butcher *kill* 361
  provisions 637
  evil-doer 913
butler 746
butt *cask* 191
  push 276
  aim 620
  attack 716
  laughing-stock
  857
  — in 294, 682
  — end 67
butte 206
butter 357
  flattery 933
  — bread on both
  sides 641
  — not melt in
  mouth 894
buttered *side*
  know — skill 698
  selfish 943
  not know — 699
butter-fingers 701
butterfly
  variegated 440
  fickle 605
  beauty 845
  gaudy 882
  break — on wheel
  waste 638
  spite 907
butter-scotch 396
buttery 636
buttock 235
button *fasten* 43
  fastening 45
  little 193
  hanging 214
  knob 250
  trifle 643
  take by the — 586
  — hole 586
  — up *close* 261
  restrain 751
  — up one's pockets
  808
buttoned-up
  reserved 528
buttonholder 841
buttons *page* 746
button-top
  useless 645
buttress
  strengthen 159
  support 215
  defence 717
butyraceous 355
buxom 836
buy 795
  — a pig in a poke
  621
  — and sell 794
buzz *hiss* 409
  insect cry 412

publish 531
news 532
buzzard *fool* 501
blind as a – 442
between hawk
and –
agitation 315
worry 315
by *alongside* 236
instrumental 631
go – *pass* 303
– air mail 684
– and by 121, 132
– the card 82
– the hour &c.
hire 788
– itself 87
– means of 632
– no means 32
have – one 637,
777
– my troth &c.c. 535
– the way
à propos 9
beside the purpose
10
parenthetical 134
– wire 684
– wireless 684
bye *departure* 293
sequestered 893
bygone 122, 506
let –s be bygones
918
by-law 963
by-name 565
by-path 279
by-play 527, 550
byre 189
byssus 256
bystander 197, 444
byway 627
by-word
maxim 496
cant term 563, 564
reproach 574
contempt 930

C

C 3 160
cab 272
cabal *plan* 626
confederacy 712
cabala 526, 993
cabalistic 528, 992
cabaret 599
cabasset 717
cabbage 791
caber, tossing the –
840
cabin 189, 191
cabined, cribbed,
confined 751
cabinet
photograph 554
receptacle 191
workshop 691
council 696
– *picture* 556
cabin plane 273
cable 45, 205
news 531, 532
slip – 623
telegraphic – 534
cabman 268, 694
caboose 386

cabriolet 272
cacation 299
cache 636
cachet 530
lettre de – 751
cachexy 160, 655
cachinnation 838
cacique 745
cackle *of geese* 412
chatter 584
talk 588
laugh 838
cacodemon 980
cacoëthes 613, 865
– *loquendi* 584
– *scribendi* 590
cacography 590
caconym 563
cacophony
stridor 410
discord 414
style 579
Cacus 792
den of – 791
cad *servant* 746
vulgar 851
plebeian 876
cadastre 86, 466
cadaverous
corpse 362
pale 429
hideous 846
caddie 746
caddy 191
cadeau 784
cadence *pace* 264
fall 306
sound 402
music 415
cadenza 415
cadet *junior* 129
soldier 726
officer 745
cadge 765
cadger *idler* 683
beggar 767
huckster 797
cadi 967
cadit quaestio 479
cadmium 439
cadre 726
caduceus 993
caducity
fugacity 111
age 128
impotence 158
decay 659
Caesar 745
aut – aut nullus
ambition 865
fame 873
caesura
disjunction 44
discontinuity 70
cessation 142
interval 198
caetera desunt 53
caeteris paribus 27
café 189
cafeteria 189
caftan 225
cage *receptacle* 191
restrain 751
prison 752
Cagliostro 548, 994
cahotage 59, 315
Cain 361
mark of – 550

raise – 825
caique 273
cairn 363, 550
caisse
grand – 417
caisson 191
caitiff *churl* 876
ruffian 913
villain 949
cajolery
imposition 544,
545
persuasion 615
flattery 933
cake *stick* 46
food 298
consolidate 321
sweet 396
– *walk* 840
calabash 191
calamity *evil* 619
adversity 735
suffering 830
calamo, currente –
590
calash *cap* 225
vehicle 272
calcedony 847
calcine 384
calcitrate 276
calculate
reckon 85
investigate 461
expect 507
intend 620
– *upon* 484
calculated
tending 176
premeditated 611
calculation
[*see calculate*]
caution 864
calculating [*ditto*]
prudent 498
– *machine* 85
calculus 85
caldron
convert 144
vessel 191
heat 386
laboratory 691
calèche 272
caleer 838
calefaction 384
calembour 520
calendar *list* 86
chronicle 114
record 551
calender 255
calenture 503, 655
calf *young* 129
give birth 161
leather 223
animals 366
fool 501
golden – 986, 991
Caliban 846
caliber *degree* 26
size 192
breadth 202
opening 260
intellectual
capacity 498
calibrate 26
calidarium 356
calidity 382
caliginous 421
caliph 745

caliphate 737
calisthenics
training 537
beauty 845
caliver 727
calk 660
call *cry* 412
signal 550
name 564
motive 615
visit 892
sanctify 976
ordain 995
at one's – 682, 743
within – 197
– to account 932
– attention to 457
– to the bar 968
– into being 161
– of duty 926
– for *require* 630
order 741
ask 765
– forth
resort to 677
excite 824
– in *advice* 695
– to mind 505
– to the ministry
996
– *names* 929, 932
– into notice 525
– off the attention
458
– to order 741
– out *cry* 411
challenge 715
– over *number* 85
– into play 677
– in question 485
– the roll 85
– up 527
– up spirits 992
– to 586
– up *recollect* 505
motive 615
excite 824
– *upon*
demand 741
request 765
visit 892
duty 924, 926
– to witness 467
callæsthetics 845
callant 129
call-boy
theatre 599
called, so – 545
callidity 698
calligraphy 590
calling
business 625
Calliope 417, 597
callipers 466
callosity 323
callous 376, 823
callow *young* 127
infant 129
bare 226
unprepared 674
calm *physical* 174
quiet 265
dissuade 616
leisure 685
peace 721
moral 826
unamazed 871
– *belief* &c. 484

– before a storm
145
calmative 174
caloric 382
calorimeter 389
calote 999
caloyer 996
calotype 556
calumet *token* 550
– of peace 721, 723
calumniator 936
calumny 934
calvary 1000
Calvinism 984
calyx 191
cam 633
camarade 890
camaraderie 888,
892
camarilla 712
camarista 746
camber 250
cambist 797, 801
camboose 386
camel 271
swallow a – 608,
694
cameo *convex* 250
sculpture 557
camera 445, 553
in – 528
– *lucida* 445
– *obscura* 445
camerated 191
camilla 274
camisade 716
camisole 225
camorra 712
camouflage 530
camp *locate* 184
abode 189
military 728
– bed 215
– stool 215
campagna 180, 344
campaign 692, 722
campaigner 726
campaigning 722
campaniform 249,
252
campanile 206
campestrian 344
Campus Martius
728
can *power* 157
mug 191
preserve 670
jail 752
best one – 686
– it be! 870
canaille 876
canal *opening* 260
conduit 350
way 627
– boat 273
canard 532, 546
canary 366
cancan
dance 840
cancel
compensate 30
neutralize 179
obliterate 552
abrogate 756
repudiate 773
cancellated 219
cancelli 191
cancer *disease* 655

bane 663
  painful 830
candelabrum 423
candent 382
candid *white* 430
  sincere 543
  ingenuous 703
  honorable 939
candidate 767, 865
candidature 763
candle 423
  bargain by inch of
    — 769
  burn — at both
    ends 686
  not fit to hold a —
    to 34
  — ends 40, 817
  — holder 711
  — light 126, 422
  — power 466
  — stick 423, 998
  hold — to sun 645
Candlemas 998
candor
  veracity 543
  artlessness 705
  honor 939
candy *dense* 321
  sweet 396
cane *weapon* 727
  punish 972
  scourge 975
canescent 430
Canicula 423
canicular 382
caniculated 259
canine 366
  — *appetite* 865
canister 191
canker *disease* 655
  deterioration 659
  bane 663
  pain 830
canned goods 670
cannel coal 388
cankered
  sullen 901a
cankerworm 663
  evil-doer 913
  care 830
cannibal 913
cannibalism 945
cannon
  collision 276
  loud 404
  arms 727
  — *fodder* 726
  —'s *mouth war* 722
  courage 861
cannonade 716
cannonball 249, 274
cannoneer 726
cannot 271
cannular 260
canny 498, 702
ca' — 864
canoe 273
  paddle one's own
    — 748
canon *rule* 80
  ravine 198
  music 415
  belief 484
  precept 697
  priest 996
  rite 998
  — *law* 697

canonical
  regular 82
  inspired 985
  ecclesiastical 995
canonicals 999
canonist 983
canonization
  repute 873
  deification 991
  rite 998
canonry 995
canopy 223
  — of heaven 318
canorous 413
cant *oblique* 217
  jerk 276
  hypocrisy 544
  neology 563
  impiety 988
cantabile 415
cantankerous 901,
    901a
cantata 415
  missa — 998
cantatrice 416
canteen 189, 191
canter 266, 274
  win at a — 705
canterbury
  receptacle 191
Canterbury tale
    546
cantharides 171
canticle 415
cantilever 215
canting 855
cantle 51
cantlet 32, 51
canto 597
canton 181, 737
cantonment 184,
    189
cantrap 993
canty 836
canvas *sail* 267
  picture 556
  under press of —
    274
canvass
  investigate 461
  discuss 476
  dissert 595
  solicit 765
canvasser 767
canyon 350
canzonet 415, 597
caoutchouc 325
cap *be superior* 33
  height 206
  summit 210
  cover 223
  hat 225
  retaliate 718
  complete 929
  salute 894
  fling up one's —
    838
  Fortunatus's — 993
  set one's — at 897,
    902
  — and bells 844
  — fits 23
  — in hand
  request 765
  servile 886
  respect 928
  — of maintenance
    747

capability
  endowment 5
  power 157
  skill 698
  facility 705
capacious *space* 180
  — *memory* 505
capacity
  endowment 5
  power 157
  space 180
  size 192
  intellect 450
  wisdom 498
  office 625
  talent 698
cap-à-pie
  armed —
  prepared 673
  defence 717
  war 722
caparison 225
cape *height* 206
  cloak 225
  projection 250
capella, alla — 415
caper *leap* 309
  dance 840
capful *quantity* 25
  small 32
  — of wind 349
capillament 205
capillary
  hairlike 205
  thin 203
capital *city* 189
  top 201
  letter 561
  important 642
  excellent 648
  money 800
  wealth 803
  make — out of
  pretext 617
  acquire 775
  print in —s 642
  — *messuage* 189
  — *punishment* 972
  ship 726
capitalist 803
capitation 85
  — *tax* 812
capitol 189, 717
capitular 995, 996
capitulate 725
capnomancy 511
capon 373
caponize 38, 158
capote 225
capouch 999
capper 548
capriccio *music* 415
  whim 608
caprice 608
  out of — 615a
capricious
  irregular 139
  changeable 149
  irresolute 605
  whimsical 608
capriole 309
capsize 218, 731
capsized 732
capstan 307, 633
capstone 210
capsular 252
capsule *vessel* 190

tunicle 223
  medicine 662
captain 269, 745
captandum, ad —
  sophistry 477
  deception 545
  affectation 855
  ostentation 882
  flattery 933
captation 933
captious
  capricious 608
  irascible 901
  censorious 932
caption
  taking 789
  beginning 66
  heading 564
captivate
  induce 615
  restrain 751
  please 829
captivated 827
captivating 829, 897
captive
  prisoner 754
  adorer 897
  lead — 749
  make — 751
  — *balloon* 273
captivity 751
capture 789
Capuchin 996
caput 696
  — *mortuum* 645,
    653
caquet 584
car 272
carabineer 726
carack 273
caracole 309
caracoler 266
carafe 191
caramel 396
carambole 276
carapace 717
cara sposa 897
carat 309
caravan 266, 272
caravansary 189
caravel 273
carbine 727
carbohydrates 298
carbon 388
  — dioxide 663
  — monoxide 663
carbonaro 742
carbonization 384
carboy 191
carbuncle *red* 434
  abscess 655
  jewel 847
carcanet 847
carcass
  structure 329
  corpse 362
  bomb 727
carcelage 973
carcinoma 655
card *unravel* 60
  ticket 550
  plan 626
  address — 550
  by the — 82
  great — 873
  house of —s 328,
  leave a — 892
  on the —s 152, 177,

470
  play one's — 692
  play one's best —
    686
  play one's —s well
    698
  playing —s 840
  shuffle the —s
    begin again 66
    change 140
    chance 621
    prepare 673
  speak by the —
    care 459
    veracity 543
  throw up the —s
    757
  ticklish — 704
  trump — 626
  — index 60, 86, 551
  —s to play 632
cardcase 191
cardiac 836
cardigan 225
cardinal *intrinsic* 5
  dress 225
  red 434
  important 642
  excellent 648
  priest 995, 996
  —'s hat 747
  — points 278
  — virtues 944
cardioid 245
card-sharper 792
card-sharping 545
care *attention* 459
  business 625
  adversity 735
  custody 751
  economy 817
  pain 828
  fear 860
  for aught one —s
    643, 866
  begone dull — 836
  drive — away 840
  have the — of 693
  take — 665, 864
  take — of 459
  — *for important*
    642
  desire 865
  love 897
careen *slope* 217
  repair 660
career 625, 692
careless
  inattentive 458
  neglectful 460,
    927
  feeble 575
  insensible 823
  indifferent 866
caress 897, 902
caret *incomplete* 53
  want 640
careworn 828, 837
cargo 270
  large quantity 31
  contents 190
  property 780
  goods 798
  — *boat* 273
caricature
  likeness 19
  copy 21

circumfluent
lie round 227
move round 311
circumforaneous
traveling 266
circuition 311
circumfuse 73
circumgyration 312
circumjacence **227**
circumlocution 573
circumnavigate
navigation 267
circuition 311
circumrotation 312
circumscribe
surround 229
limit 233, 761
circumspection **229**
circumspection
attention 457
care 459
caution 459
circumstance
phase 8
event 151
circumstances
property 780
bad – 804
depend on – 475
good – 803
under the – 8
circumstantial 8
– *account* 594
– *evidence* 467
probability 472
circumstantiality
459
circumstantiate 467
circumvallation
enclosure 229,
232
defence 717
line of – 233
circumvent
environ 227
move round 311
cheat 545
cunning 702
hinder 706
defeat 731
circumvest 225
circumvolution
winding 248
rotation 312
circus
buildings 189
drama 599
arena 728
amusement 840
cirrus 353
cistern
receptacle 191
store 636
Cistercian 996
cit 188
citadel 717
citation 467, 733
cite
quote as example
82
as evidence 467
summon 741
accuse 938
arraign 969
cithern 417
citizen 188
– of the world 910
citriculture 371

citrine 436
city 189
in the – 794
city manager 965
civet 400
civic 372
civil *courteous* 894
laity 997
– authorities 745
– crown 733
– law 963
– war 722
civilian *lawyer* 968
layman 997
civilization
improvement 658
fashion 852
courtesy 894
civilized life 852
civism 910
clack *clatter* 407
animal cry 412
talkative 584
clad 225
claim *requisition*
630
demand 741
property 780
right 924
lawsuit 969
– the attention
457
claimant
petitioner 767
right 924
clair-obscur 420
clairvoyance 992
clairvoyant 513, 994
clamant 411
clamber 305
clammy 352
clamor *cry* 411
wail 839
– against 932
– for 765
clamorous
[*see* clamor]
loud 404
excitable 825
clamp *fasten* 43
fastening 45
clan *race* 11
class 75
family 166
party 712
clandestine 528
clangor 404
clank 410
clannishness 481
clanship 709
clap *explosion* 406
applaud 931
thunder –
prodigy 872
– the hands
rejoice 838
– on 31
– on the shoulder
615
– together 43
– up *imprison* 751
clapperclaw
contention 720
censure 932
claptrap
pretence 546
display 882
claquer 935

faire – son fouet
884
clarence 272
claret color 434
clarify 652
clarinet 417
clarion *music* 417
war 722
clarity 518
clash *disagree* 24
cross 179
concussion 276
sound 406
oppose 708
discord 713
– of arms 720
clasp *fasten* 43
fastening 45
stick 46
come close 197
belt 230
embrace 902
class *arrange* 60
category **75**
learners 541
party 712
– prejudice 481
– room 542
classic *old* 124
symmetry 242
classical
elegant writing
578
taste 850
– art 556
– dancing 840
– education 537
– music 415
classicist 492
classics 560
classify 60
classmate 890
clatter 404, 407
claudication
slowness 275
failure 732
clause *part* 51
passage 593
condition 770
clausis, januis –
528
claustral 110
clavate 250
clavichord 417
clavier 417
claw *hook* 781
grasp 789
– back 935
clay *soft* 324
earth 342
corpse 362
material 635
– pipe 392
clay-cold 383
claymore 727
clean
entirely 52
perfect 650
unstained 652
– bill of health 654
– breast
disclose 529
– forgotten 506
– hand
proficient 700
with – hands
honesty 939
innocence 946

– out *empty* 297
– shaven 226
– sweep
revolution 146
destruction 162
clean-up 775
clear *simple* 42
sound 413
light 420
transparent 425
visible 446
certain 474
intelligible 518
manifest 525
easy 705
liberate 750
profit 775
vindicate 937
innocent 946
acquit 975
all – 664, 705
coast – 664
get – off 671
keep – of 623
make – 529
– for action
prepare 673
– articulation 580
– conscience 946
– the course 302
– cut 518
– the ground
facilitate 705
– of *distant* 196
– off *pay* 807
– out *empty* 297
clean 652
– sighted
vision 441
shrewd 498
– sky *hope* 858
– stage
occasion 134
easy 705
– right 922
– thinking 498
– the throat 297
– up *light* 420
intelligible 518
interpret 522
clearheaded 498
clear-obscure 420
cleat 45
cleavage
cutting 44
structure 329
cleave *sunder* 44
adhere 46
bisect 91
cleaver 253
cledge 342
clef 413
cleft *divided* 44
bisected 91
chink 198
in a – stick
difficulty 704
clem 956
clement
lenient 740
long-suffering
826
compassionate
914
clench *compact* 769
retain 781
take 789
clepe 564

clepsydra 114
clerestory 191, 1000
clergy 996
clerical 995, 996
– error 495
– staff 746
clerk *scholar* 492
recorder 553
writer 590
helper 711
servant 746
agent 758
clergy 996
articled – 541
– in holy orders
995
– of works 694
clerkship
commission 755
cleromancy 511
clever
intelligent 498
skilful 698
smart 842
too – by half 702
clew *ball* 249
interpretation 522
indication 550
seek a – 461
click 406
client
dependant 746
customer 795
clientship
subjection 749
cliff *height* 206
vertical 212
steep 217
land 342
climacteric 128
climate *region* 181
weather 338
fine – 656
climatology 338
climax
supremacy 33
summit 210
culmination 729
climb 305
– on the band-
wagon 731
clime 181
clinal 217
clinch *fasten* 43
close 261
certify 474
pun 563
complete 729
clutch 781
snatch 789
– an argument 47
– the fist at 909
clincher 479
cling *adhere* 46
– to *near* 197
willing 602
persevere 604a
habit 613
observe 772
desire 865
love 897
– to hope 858
– to one another
709
clinic 662
clink
resonance 408
stridor 410

co-operate 709
Coelebs 904
coemption 795
coequal 27
coerce *compel* 744
  restrain 751
coetaneous 120
coeternal
  perpetual 112
  synchronous 120
coeur, à contre –
  603
coeval 120
  – with birth 5
coexist *exist* 1
  accompany 88
  synchronism 120
  contiguity 199
coextension
  equality 27
  parallelism 216
  symmetry 242
coffee 298
coffee-house 189
coffee-pot 191
coffer *chest* 191
  store 636
  money chest 802
cofferdam 55
coffin 363
  add a nail to one's
  – 830
cog *tooth* 253
  boat 273
  deceive 545
  flatter 933
cogent
  powerful 157
  – *reasoning* 476
cogitate 451
cogitative faculties
  450
cognate
  consanguineous
  11
  related 9
  similar 16
cognition 490
cognitive faculties
  450
cognizance 490
  take – of
  intellect 490
  attention 457
cognomen 564
cognoscence 490
cog-wheel 312
cohabitation
  location 184
  marriage 903
coheir 778
coherence *unite* 46
  dense 321
cohesive 46
cohibit
  restrict 706
  restrain 751
  prohibit 761
cohobation 336
cohort 726
cohue 72
coif 225
coiffure 225
coign of vantage 33
coil *disorder* 59
  curve 245
  convolution 248
  circuition 311

shuffle off this
  mortal – 360
coin *fabricate* 161
  imagine 515
  money 800
  – *money* 775
  – *words* 563
coincidence
  identity 13
  in time 120
  chance 156
  concurrence 178
  in place 199
  in opinion 488
coiner *thief* 792
coistril 862
coition 42
coke 388
colander 260
colature 652
cold *frigid* **383**
  color 429, 438
  style 575
  insensible 823
  indifferent 866
  in – blood
  premeditated 611
  purposely 620
  unfeeling 823
  dispassionate 826
  – *comfort* 832
  – *shoulder*
  discourtesy 895
  contempt 930
  – *steel* 727
  – *storage* 387
  – *sweat fear* 860
  dislike 867
  – *water cure* 662
  throw – water on
  dissuade 616
  hinder 706
  dull 843
cold feet 862
coldhearted
  unfeeling 823
  hostile 889
  malevolent 907
cold pack 670
Coliseum 189, 588,
  728
collaboration 178
collaborator 690,
  711
collapse
  prostration 158
  contract 195
  shortcoming 304
  deteriorate 659
  fatigue 688
  failure 732
collar *dress* 225
  circlet 247
  shackle 752
  seize 789
  slip the – 750
collate 464
collateral
  relation 9, 11
  parallel 216
  lateral 236
  security 771
  – *evidence* 467
collation
  repast 298
  comparison 464
colleague
  accompany 88

co-worker 696
co-operation 709
  auxiliary 711
  friend 890
collect
  assemble 72
  opine 480
  understand 518
  acquire 775
  prayer 990
  – *evidence* 467
  – *knowledge* 539
  – one's thoughts
  451
collectanea
  assemblage 72
  compendium 596
collected *calm* 826
collection
  assemblage 72
  offertory 998
collectively
  whole 50
  generality 78
  together 88
collectivism 737,
  778
college 542
  go to – 539
  – of cardinals 996
  – education 537
colleen 129
colley 366
collide 276
collier 273
colligate 72
collimation 216,
  278
colliquate 335
collision *disagreement* 24
  clash 179
  percussion 276
  opposition 708
  encounter 720
collocate
  arrange 60
  assemble 72
  place 184
collocution 588
collogue 933
colloid 352
collop 51, 298
colloquial
  figure of speech
  521
  neology 563
  conversation 588
  – *meaning* 516
colluctation 720
collusion *deceit* 545
  conspiring 709
collusive 544
colluvies 653
collyrium 662
Cologne
  eau de – 398
colon 142
colonel 745
colonist 188
colonize 184, 294,
  295
colonnade
  series 69
  houses 189
colony 184, 188, 780
colophon 65
colophony 356a

Colorado beetle 913
color *hue* **428**
  tone 431
  appearance 448
  probability 472
  disguise 544
  paint 556
  plea 617
  be angry 900
  all –s 440
  change –
  shame 879
  give a – to
  change 140
  qualify 469
  probable 472
  falsehood 472
  lend a – to
  plea 617
  vindicate 937
  man of – 431
  show in true –s
  543
  – *blindness* 443
  – *printing* 558
  – *sergeant* 745
  –ed *spectacles* 424
  – *too highly* 549
  – up *redden* 434
  blush 879
colorable
  ostensible 472
  deceptive 545
coloration 428
coloratura 415, 416
colorful 882
coloring
  [see color]
  meaning 516
  false – 523
  – *matter* 428
colorless
  weak 160
  pale 429
colors
  ensign 550
  decoration 877
  with – *flying*
  resolution 604
  false – 544, 545
  flying –
  display 882
  celebration 883
  lower one's – 735
  nail one's – to the
  mast 604
  show one's –
  manifest 525
  disclose 529
  true to one's – 939
Colosseum 728
colossus 192, 206
colporteur 797
colstaff 215
colt *young* 129
  horse 271
  fool 501
columbine 599
columella 215
column *series* 69
  height 206
  support 215
  cylinder 249
  caravan 266
  monument 551
  printing 591
  troop 726
columnist 527, 553

colures 318
coma *inactive* 683
  insensible 376,
  823
comb *teeth* 253
  clean 652
  punish 972
combat 720, 722
combat, hors de –
  useless 645
  tired 688
combatant **726**
combe 252
comber 348
combination **48**
  arithmetical 84
  party 712
combine *unite* 48
  co-operate 709
combustible 388
combustion 384
come *happen* 151
  approach 286
  arrive 292
  cheer up! 836
  out upon! 932
  to – *future* 121
  destiny 152
  – about 658
  – across
  discover 480a
  acquire 775
  pay up 807
  – after
  sequence 63
  posterior 117
  – between 631
  cut and – again
  639
  – of age 131
  – amiss
  disagreeable 24
  ill-timed 135
  – back 283
  – before 116
  – by 775
  – at one's call 743
  – to a determination 604
  – down with 807
  – into existence
  be 1
  begin 66
  – first *superior* 33
  precede 62
  – forth
  egress 295
  appear 446
  – forward 763
  – from 154
  – to the front 303
  – and go 314
  – to hand 785
  – to a head
  climax 33
  complete 52
  – in *ingress* 294
  receipt 785
  – in for
  property 778, 780
  – to one's knowledge 527
  – to life 359
  – what may 474
  – near 286
  – to nothing
  unproductive 169
  fail 732

– of thought 498
compassion 914
  object of – 828
compatible
  consentaneous 23
  possible 470
compatriot
  inhabitant 188
  friend 890
compeer equal 27 _
  friend 890
compel 744
compellation 564
compendency 43
compendious 201
compendium **596**
  book 593
compensate
  make up for 30
  requite 973
compensation **30**
compère 599
competence
  power 157
  sufficiency 639
  skill 698
  wealth 803
competition
  opposition 708
  contention 720
competitor
  opponent 710
  combatant 726
  candidate 767
compilation
  collect 72
  book 593
  compendium 596
compile 54
complacent
  pleased 827
  content 831
  courteous 894
  kind 906
complain 839
complainant 938
complaint
  illness 655
  murmur 839
  lodge a – 938
  – without cause
  839
complaisant
  lenient 740
  courteous 894
  kind 906
complement
  adjunct 39
  remainder 40
  part 52
  arithmetic 84
complementary
  correlation 12
  colour 428
complete
  entire 52
  accomplish 729
  compact 769
  – answer 479
  – circle 311
  in a – degree 31
completeness 52
completion **729**
complex 59
complexion
  state 7
  color 428
  appearance 448

compliance
  conformity 82
  obedience 743
  consent 762
  observance 772
complicate
  derange 61
complicated
  disorder 59
  convolution 248
complice 711
complicity 709
compliment
  courtesy **894**, 896
  praise 931
  poor – 932
  –s of season 896
complimentary
  free 815
complot 626
comply [see compli-
  ance]
compo coating 223
  material 635
component **56**
componere lites
  723, 724
comport
  – oneself 692
  – with 23
compos mentis 502
compose
  make up 54, 56
  produce 161
  moderate 174
  music 416
  write 590
  printing 591
  pacify 723
  assuage 826
composed
  self-possessed 826
composer
  music 413
composite 41
composition **54**
  [see compose]
  combination 48
  piece of music 415
  picture 556
  style 569
  writing 590
  building material
  635
  compromise 774
  barter 794
  atonement 952
compositor
  printer 591
compost 653
composure 826, 871
compotation 959
compote 298
compound
  mix 41
  combination 48
  limited space 182
  enclosure 232
  compromise 774
  – arithmetic 466
  – for substitute 147
  barter 794
comprador 637
comprehend
  compose 54
  include 76
  know 490
  understand 518

comprehension [see
  comprehend]
  intelligence 498
comprehensive 76
  complete 50
  general 78
  wide 192
  – argument 476
compress
  contract 195
  curtail 201
  condense 321
  remedy 662
compressible 322
comprise 76
comprobation
  evidence 467
  demonstration 478
compromise
  dally with 605
  mid-course 628
  taint 659
  danger 665
  pacify 723
  compound **774**
  atone 952
compromised
  promised 768
compter 799
compte rendu
  record 551
  accounts 811
comptroller 694
compulsion **744**
compunction 833,
  950
compurgation
  evidence 467
  acquittal 970
compute 85
comrade 890
comradeship 892
con think 451
  get by heart 505
  learn 539
conation 600
conatu magnas
  nugas, magno –
  waste 638
  unimportance 643
conatus 176
concamerate 245
concatenation
  junction 43
  continuity 69
concavity **252**
conceal
  invisible 447
  hide 528
  cunning 702
concealment **528**,
  893
concede
  assent 488
  admit 529
  permit 760
  consent 762
  give 784
conceit idea 453
  folly 499
  supposition 514
  imagination 515
  wit 842
  affectation 855
  vanity 880
conceited
  dogmatic 481

conceivable 470
conceive begin 66
  beget 161
  teem 168
  believe 484
  understand 490
  imagine 515
  plan 626
concent 413
concentrate
  assemble 72
  centrality 222
  converge 290
concentric 216, 222
conception
  [see conceive]
  intellect 450
  idea 453
concern
  relation 9
  event 151
  business 625
  importance 642
  firm 797
  grief 828
  – oneself with 625
concert
  agreement 23
  synchronism 120
  music 415
  act in – 709
  in – musical 413
  concord 714
  – measures 626
concertina 417
concerto 415
concert-room 840
concession
  permission 760
  consent 762
  compromise 774
  giving 784
  discount 813
concesso, ex –
  reasoning 476
  assent 488
concetto 842
conchoid 245
conchology 223
concierge 163, 753
conciliate
  talk over 615
  pacify 723
  satisfy 831
  courtesy 894
  atonement 952
conciliatory [see
  conciliate]
  concord 714
  forgiving 918
conciliatrix 962
concinnity
  agreement 23
  style 578
  beauty 845
conciseness **572**
concision 201
conclave
  assembly 72
  council 696
  church 995
conclude
  end 67
  infer 480
  resolve 604
  complete 729
  compact 769
conclusion

[see conclude]
  sequel 65
  germination 161
  judgment 480
  try –s 476
  forgone – 611
  hasty – 481
conclusive
  [see conclude]
  answer 462
  evidence 467
  certain 474
  proof 478
  – reasoning 476
concoct lie 544
  write 590
  plan 626
  prepare 673
concomitant
  accompany 88
  same time 120
  concurrent 178
concord agree 23
  music **413**
  assent 488
  harmony **714**
concordance 562
  book 593
concordant 173
concordat 769
concordia discors
  24, 59
concours 720
concourse
  assemblage 72
  convergence 290
concremation 384
concrete existent 3
  mass 46
  definite 79
  density 321
  hardness 323
  materials 635
concubinage 961
concubine 926
concupiscence 865,
  961
concur
  co-exist 120
  causation 178
  converge 290
  assent 488
  concert 709
concurrence **178**,
  216
concussion 276
condemnation 932,
  971
condemned cell 752
condense
  compress 195
  dense 321
condensed
  concise 572
condescend 879
condign 924
condiment **393**
condisciple 541
condition state 7
  modification 469
  supposition 514
  term 770
  repute 873
  rank 875
  in – plump 192
  in good – 648
  on – 770
  in perfect – 650

physical – 316
conditional 8
conditions **770**
condolence 914, **915**
condone 918
condottiere
  traveller 268
  fighter 726
conduce
  contribute 153
  tend 176
  concur 178
  avail 644
conducive 631
conduct
  transfer 270
  music 416
  procedure **692**
  lead 693
safe –
  passport 631
  safety 664
– a funeral 363
– an inquiry 461
– to 278
conduction 264
conductor 269
  conveyer 271
  director 694
lightning – 666
conduit **350**
conduplicate 89
condyle 250
cone *round* 249
  pointed 253
confabulation 588
confection 396
  confectionary 396
confectioner 637
confederacy
  co-operation 709
  party 712
confederate 711
confer *advise* 695
  give 784
– benefit 648
– power 157
– privilege 760
– right 924
– with 588
conference [*see*
  confer]
  council 696
confess *assent* 488
  avow 529
  penitence 950,
  998
– and avoid 937
confession [*see*
  confess]
  auricular – 998
– of faith 983
confessional 1000
confessions
  biography 594
confessor 996
confidant 711
confidante
  servant 746
  friend 890
confidence
  trust 484
  hope 858
  courage 861
in – 528
– trick 545
confident 535
configuration 240

confine
  region 182
  circumscribe 229
  limit 231, 233
  imprison 751
confined
  narrow judgment
  481
  ill 655
confinement
  childbed 161
confines of
  on the – 197
confirm
  corroborate 467
  assent 488
  consent 762
  compact 769
  rite 998
confirmed 150
– habit 613
confiscate *take* 789
  condemn 971
  penalty 974
confiture 396
conflagration 382,
  384
conflexure 245
conflict
  opposition 708
  discord 713
  contention 720
conflicting
  contrary 14
  counteracting 179
– evidence 468
confluence
  junction 43
  convergence 290
  river 348
conflux
  assemblage 72
  convergence 290
conform *assent* 488
– to rule 494
conformable 23,
  178
conformation 54,
  240
conformity **82,** 178
confound
  disorder 61
  destroy 162
  not discriminate
  465a
  perplex 475
  defeat 731
  astonish 870
  curse 908
confounded
  great 31
  bad 649
confraternity
  party 712
  friendship 888
confrère
  colleague 711
  friend 890
confrication 331
confront *face* 234
  compare 464
  oppose 708
  resist 719
– danger 861
– witnesses 467
confucianism 984
Confucius 986
confuse *derange* 61

perplex 458
  obscure 519
  not discriminate
  465a
  abash 879
confused *disorder*
  59
  invisible 447
  uncertain 475
  style 571
confusion
  [*see* confuse]
– seize 908
– of tongues 560,
  563
– of vision 443
– worse-con-
  founded 59
confutation **479**
congé 293, 756
– d'élire 995
congeal *dense* 321
  cold 385
congeneric
  similar 17
  included 76
congenial
  related 9
  agreeing 23
  concord 714
  love 897
congenital 5, 820
congeries 72
congestion 641
conglaciation 385
conglobation 72
conglomerate
  cohere 46
  assemblage 72
  council 696
  dense 321
conglutinate 46
congratulate 896
– oneself 838
congratulation **896**
congregation
  assemblage 72
  worshippers 990
  laity 997
Congregationalist
  984
congress
  assembly 72
  convergence 290
  conference 588
  council 698
Congressional
  Medal 733
Congressional
  Record 551
congreve *fuel* 388
– rocket 727
congruous
  agreeing 23
  (*expedient* 646)
conical *round* 249
  pointed 253
conjecture 475, 514
conjoin 43
conjoint 48
conjointly 37
conjugal 903
conjugate
  words 562
  grammar 567
– in all its tenses
  &c. 104
conjugation

junction 43
  pair 89
  phase 144
  grammar 567
conjunction 43
in – with 37
conjuncture
  contingency **8**
  occasion 134
conjure *deceive* 545
  entreat 765
  sorcery 992
  name to – with
  873
– up *recall* 505
– up a vision 505
conjuror
  deceiver 548
  sorcerer 994
connaître les des-
  sous des cartes
  490
connate
  intrinsic 5
  kindred 11
  cause 153
connatural
  uniform 16
  similar 17
connect *relate* 9
  link 43
connection
  [*see* connect]
  kin 11
  in – with 9
connections
  cards 840
connective 45
conned, well – 490
connive
  overlook 460
  co-operate 709
  allow 760
connoisseur
  critic 480
  scholar 492
  taste 850
connotate 550
connote 516, 550
  imply 526
connubial 903
connuted 9
conoscente 850
conquer 731
conquered
  (*failure* 732)
conquering hero
  comes 883
conqueror 731
consanguinity **11**
consciarecti, mens-
  pride 878
  innocence 946
conscience
  knowledge 490
  moral sense 926
  in all – *great* 31
  affirmation 535
  awakened – 950
  qualms of – 603
  clear – 946
  stricken – 950
  tender – 926
  honor 939
conscientious 926
  scrupulous 939
– objector 489
conscious

intuitive 450
  knowledge 490
– of disgrace 874
– of glory 873
conscript 726
conscription 744
consecrate *use* 677
  dedicate 873
  sanctify 987
  holy orders 995
consecration
  rite 998
consectory 478
– reasoning 476
consecution 63
consecutive
  following 63
  continuous 69
– fifth 414
consecutively
  slowly 275
consensus 488
– of opinion 23
consent *assent* 488
  compliance **762**
  with one – 178
consentaneous
  agreeing 23
  (*expedient* 646)
consequence
  event 151
  effect 154
  importance 642
  in – 478
  of no – 643
  take the –s 154
consequent 63
consequential
  deducible 478
  arrogant 878
consequently
  reasoning 476
  effect 154
conservation
  permanence 141
  storage 636
  preservation 670
conservatism 141,
  670
conservative 141,
  712
– policy 681
conservatoire 542
conservator
  of the peace 967
conservatory
  receptacle 191
  floriculture 371
  furnace 386
  store 636
conserve 396, 636
consider *think* 451
  attend to 457
  examine 461
  adjudge 480
  believe 484
considerable
  in degree 31
  in size 192
  important 642
considerate
  careful 459
  judicious 498
  benevolent 906
consideration
  purchase money
  147
  thought 451

contrition
  abrasion 331
  regret 833
  penitence 950
contrivance 633
contrive
  produce 161
  plan 626
  – to succeed in 731
contriving
  cunning 702
control
  power 157
  influence 175
  regulate 693
  authority 737
  restrain 751
  board of – 696
  under –
  obedience 743
  subjection 749
controller of
  currency 801
controls 273, 693
controversial
  discussion 476
  discordant 713
controversialist
  476, 726
controversy
  disagreement 24
  discussion 476
  debate 588
  contention 720
controvert
  deny 536
controvertible
  uncertain 475
  debatable 476
  untrue 495
contumacy
  obstinacy 606
  disobedience 742
contumely
  arrogance 885
  rudeness 895
  disrespect 929
  scorn 930
  reproach 932
contund 330
contuse 330
conundrum pun
  520
  riddle 533
  wit 842
convalescence 654,
  660
convection 270
convenance
  mariage de – 903
convene 72
conveniences 632
convenient 646, 705
convent 1000
conventicle
  assembly 72
  council 696
  chapel 1000
convention
  agreement 23
  assembly 72
  rule 80
  council 696
  precept 697
  treaty of peace
  723
  compact 769

–s of society 852
conventional 82,
  613
conventual 996,
  1000
convergence 290
convergent 286
conversable
  talk 588
  sociable 892
conversant
  know 490
  skilful 698
conversation 588
conversational
  loquacious 584
  interlocution 588
  sociable 892
conversazione 588,
  892
converse
  reverse 14
  talk 588
conversely 468
conversion 144
  trover and – 964
convert
  change to 140, 144
  opinion 484
  tergiversation 607
  religion 987
  – to use 677
convertible 13, 27
  – terms 522
convexity 250
convey
  transfer 270
  mean 516
  assign 783
  – away 791
  – the knowledge
  of 527
conveyance
  [see convey]
  vehicle 272
conveyancer 968
conveyancing 783
convict
  convince 484
  condemned 949
  condemn 971
convicted, self –
  950
conviction
  confutation 479
  belief 484
  prove guilty 971
convince
  belief 484
  confute 479
  teach 537
convivial 892
convocate 72
convocation
  council 696
  church 995
convoke 72
convolution
  coil 248
  rotation 312
convoy
  accompany 88
  transfer 270
  guard 664
  escort 753
convulse
  derange 61

violent 173
  agitate 315
  bodily pain 378
  mental pain 830
convulsed with
  – laughter 838
  – rage 900
convulsion
  [see convulse]
  disorder 59
  revolution 146
in –s 325
coo 412
cook heat 384
  falsify 544
  improve 658
  prepare 673
  servant 746
too many –s 699
  – accounts 811
cool moderate 174
  cold 383
  refrigerate 385
  grey 432
  dissuade 616
  cautious 864
  indifferent 866
  unamazed 871
  unfriendly 889
  discourteous 895
look – upon
  unsocial 893
take –ly 826
  – down 826
  – one's heels
  kept waiting 133
  inaction 681
cooler 387
coolheaded
  judicious 498
  unexcitable 826
coolie
  bearer 271
  military 726
coolness
  insensibility 823
  estrangement 898
coon-can 840
coop abode 189
  restrain 751
  prison 752
co-operation
  physical 178
  voluntary 709
  participation 778
co-operator 690, 711
co-optation 609
co-ordinate
  equal 27
  arrange 60
  measure 466
cootie 653
cop 664
copal 356a
coparcener 778
copartner
  accompanying 88
  participator 778
  associate 890
copartnership
  co-operation 709
  party 712
cope equal 27
  oppose 708
  contend 720
  canonicals 999
copia verborum

diffuse 573
  loquacious 584
coping stone
  top 210
  completion 729
copious
  diffuse style 573
  abundant 639
coportion 778
copper money 800
  policeman 664
copper-colored
  433, 439
copper-plate
  engraving 558
  writing 590
coppice 367
coprolite 653
copse 367
copula 45
copulation 43
copy
  imitate 19
  facsimile 21
  prototype 22
  news 532
  record 551
  represent 554
  write 590
  for the press 591
  plan 626
  – book 22
copyhold 780
copyist
  imitator 19
  artist 559
  writer 590
copyright 780
coquet lie 544
  change the mind
  607
  affected 855
  endearment 902
  flattery 933
  – with
  irresolute 605
coquette
  affected 854, 855
  flirt 897
coquillage 847
coracle 273
coral 847
  – reef 667
coram judice
  jurisdiction 965
  lawsuit 969
cor Anglais 417
corbeille 191
corbel 215
cord tie 45
  filament 205
cordage 45
cordated 245
cordial
  pleasure 377
  dram 392
  willing 602
  remedy 662
  feeling 821
  grateful 829
  friendly 888
  courteous 894
cordiform 245
cordite 727
cordon
  inclosure 232
  circularity 247

decoration 877
  – bleu 733, 746
  – sanitaire
  safety 664
  preservation 670
corduroy 259
cordwainer
  shoemaker 225
  artificer 690
core gist 5
  source 153
  center 222
  gist 642
  true to the – 939
coriaceous 327
Corinthian 850
co-rival
  [see corrival]
cork plug 263
  lightness 320
  – jacket 666
  – up close 261
  restrain 751
corking pin 45
corkscrew
  spiral 248
  perforator 262
  circuition 311
cormorant
  desire 865
  gluttony 957
corn
  projection 250
Cornaro 953
cornea 441
corned 959
cornelian 847
corneous 323
corner place 182
  receptacle 191
  angle 244
  monopoly 777
  – creep into a –
  893
in a dark – 528
  drive into a – 706
  push into a – 874
  rub off –s 82
  – turn a – 311
  turn the – 658
  – stone
  support 215
  importance 642
  defence 717
cornet music 417
  officer 745
cornice 210
corniculate 253
cornification 323
Cornish hug 545
corno 417
cornopean 417
cornucopia 639
cornute
  – projecting 250
  sharp 253
corollary
  adjunct 39
  deduction 480
corona 247
coronach 839
coronation
  enthronement 755
  celebration 883
coroner 363, 965
  –'s jury 967
coronet hoop 247

insignia 747
title 877
corporal
  corporeal 316
  officer 745
corporate 43
  – *body* 712
corporation
  bulk 192
  convex 250
  association 712
  jurisdiction 965
corporeal 3, 316,
  364
  – *hereditaments*
    780
corporeity 316
corps *assemblage* 72
  troops 726
  à – perdu
  haste 684
  rash 863
  – de reserve 636
corpse 362
corpulence 192
corpus 316
  – Christi 998
  – delicti
  guilt 947
  lawsuit 969
  – juris
  precept 697
  law 963
corpuscle
  small 32
  little 193
corradiation
  focus 74
  convergence 290
corral 232, 370
correct
  orderly 58
  true 494
  inform 527
  disclose 529
  improve 658
  repair 660
  due 924
  censure 932
  honorable 939
  virtuous 944
  punish 972
  – *ear* 416, 418
  – *memory* 505
  – *reasoning* 476
  – *style*
  grammatical 567
  elegant 578
correction
  [*see* correct]
  house of – 752
  under – 879
corrective 662
corregidor 745
correlation
  relation 9
  reciprocity **12**
correspondence
  correlation 12
  similarity 17
  agreement 23
  writing **592**
  – *course* 537
correspondent
  messenger 534
  journalist 593
  consignee 758
corresponding

similar 17
agreeing 23
corridor *region* 181
  place 191
  passage 627
  – *train* 272
corrigendum 495
corrigible 658
corrival 726
corrivalry 720
corrivation 348
corroborant 662
corroboration
  evidence 467
  assent 488
corrode *burn* 384
  erode 659
  afflict 830
corrosive
  [*see* corrode]
  acrid 171
  destructive 649
  – *sublimate* 663
corrugate
  derange 61
  constrict 195
  roughen 256
  rumple 258
  furrow 259
corruption
  decomposition 49
  neology 563
  foulness 653
  disease 655
  deterioration 659
  improbity 940
  vice 945
corrupting
  noxious 649
corsage 225
corsair 273, 792
corse 362
corselet 225
corset 225
corso 728
cortège
  adjunct 39
  continuity 69
  accompaniment
    88
  journey 266
  suite 746
cortes 696
cortex
  cortical 223
coruscate 420
corvette 273, 726
corybantic 503
coryphée 599
Corypheus
  teacher 540
  director 694
coscinomancy 511
cosey 892
cosignificative 522
cosine 217
cosmetic
  remedy 662
  ornament 847
cosmic 318
cosmogony &c. 318
cosmopolitan
  abode 189
  mankind 372
  philanthropic 910
  sociality 892
cosmorama 448
cosmos 60, 318

Cossack 726
cosset
  darling 899
  caress 902
cost 812
  pay –s 807
  to one's –
  evil 619
  badness 649
  – what it may 604
  – *price* 815
costermonger 797
costless 815
costly 814
costive
  taciturn 585
costume 225
  theatrical – 599
costumé 225
  bal – 840
costumier 225
  theatrical 599
cosy *snug* 377
  sociable 892
cot *abode* 189
  bed 215
cote 189
cotenancy 778
coterie *class* 75
  junto 712
  society 892
coterminous 120
cothurnus 599
cotillon 840
cottage 189
  – *piano* 417
cottager 188
cotter 188
cotton 205
  – *seed oil* 356
couch *lie* 213
  bed 215
  stoop 308
  lurk 528
  – one's *lance* 720
  – in *terms* 566
couchant 213
couci-couci 651
cough 349
  churchyard – 655
couleur de rose
  good 648
  prosperity 734
  view en – 836
coulisses 599
coulter 253
council
  senate **696**
  church 995
  hold a – 695
  – of education 542
  – school 542
councillor 696
counsel
  advice 695
  lawyer 968
  keep one's own –
    528
  take – *think* 451
  inquire 461
  be *advised* 695
count *clause* 51
  item 79
  compute 85
  estimate 480
  lord 875
  – one's chickens
    before they are

hatched 858,
  863
  – the cost 864
  – upon
  believe 484
  expect 507
  to be –ed on one's
  fingers 103
countenance
  face 234
  appearance 448
  favor 707
  approve 931
  keep in –
  conform 82
  induce 615
  encourage 861
  vindicate 937
  keep one's –
  brook 826
  not *laugh* 837
  out of –
  abashed 879
  put out of – 874
  stare out of – 885
  – *falling*
  disappointment
    509
  dejection 837
counter *contrary* 14
  number 84
  table 215
  stern 235
  token 550
  shop-board 799
  over the –
  barter 794
  buy 795
  sell 796
  run – 179
  – to 708
counteract
  compensate 30
  physically 179
  hinder 706
  voluntarily 708
counteraction 14,
  179
counterbalance 30
counterblast
  counteract 179
  retaliate 718
countercharge 462
counterchange
  correlation 12
  interchange 148
countercharm 993
countercheck
  mark 550
  hindrance 706
counterclaim 30
counter-evidence
  468
counterfeit
  imitate 19
  copy 21
  simulate 544
  sham 545
  coinage 792
counterfoil 550
countermand 756
countermarch 266,
  283
countermark 550
countermine
  plan 626
  oppose 708
countermotion 283

counterorder 756
counterpane 223
counterpart
  match 17
  copy 21
  reverse 237
counterplot
  plan 626
  oppose 708
  retaliate 718
counterpoint 415
counterpoise
  compensate 30
  weight 319
  hinder 706
counter-poison 662
counterpole 14
counter-project 718
counter-protest 468
counter-revolution
  146
counterscarp 717
countersign
  evidence 467
  assent 488
  mark 550
counterstroke 718
countervail
  outweigh 28
  compensate 30
  evidence 468
counterwork 708
countess 875
counting-house 799
countless 105
countrified 189
  vulgar 851
country
  region 181
  abode 189
  rural 371
  authority 737
  love of – 910
country-dance 840
countryman
  commonalty 876
  friend 890
county 181
  – seat 189
  – town 189
  – school 542
  – council 696
  – court 966
coup
  instantaneous 113
  action 680
  – de bec
  attack 716
  censure 932
  – d'épée dans
    l'eau 645
  – d'essai 675
  – d'état
  revolution 146
  plan 626
  action 680
  lawless 964
  – de grâce
  end 67
  death-blow 361
  completion 729
  punishment 972
  – de main
  violence 173
  action 680
  attack 716
  – de maître
  excellent 648

642
best 648
- color
  white 430
  yellow 436
- of the jest 842
creamy 352
crease 258
create cause 153
  produce 161
  imagine 515
created being 366
creation
  [see create]
  effect 154
  world 318
Creator 976
creator 164
creature thing 3
  effect 154
  animal 366
  man 372
  parasite 711
  slave 746
- comforts
  food 298
  pleasure 377
crèche 542
credat Judaeus
  Apella
  unbelief 485
  absurdity 497
credence belief 484
  church 1000
credenda 484
credential 467
credible
  possible 470
  probable 472
  belief 484
credit belief 484
  influence 737
  pecuniary 805
  account 811
  repute 873
  approbation 931
  desert 944
  to one's -
  property 780
crédit mobilier 802
creditable right 924
creditor 805
credo quia
  impossibile 486
credulity 486
credulous person
  dupe 547
creed belief 484
  theology 983
  Apostles' - 983a
creek interval 198
  water 343
creel 191
creep crawl 275
  tingle 380
  (inactivity 683)
- in 294
- into a corner 893
- into the good
  graces of 933
- out 529
- upon one 508
- with
  multitude 102
  redundance 641
creeper 367
creeping
  sensation 380

- thing 366
creese 727
cremation
  of corpses 363
  burning 384
crematorium 363,
  386
crematory 386
crème de la crème
  648
Cremona 417
crenate 257
crenele 257
crenulate 257
creole 57
crêpé 248, 839
crepidam, ultra -
  471
crepitation 406
crepuscule
  dawn 125
  dusk 422
crescendo
  increase 35
  musical 415
crescent
  growing 35
  street 189
  curve 245
cresset 423, 550
crest supremacy 33
  summit 210
  pointed 253
  tuft 256
  sign 550
  armorial 877
  pride 878
  on the - 33
crest-fallen
  dejected 837
  humble 879
crevasse 198, 667
crevice 198
crew assemblage 72
  inhabitants 188
  mariners 269
  party 712
crib bed 215
  key 522
  granary 636
  steal 791
  parsimony 819
cribbage 840
cribbed, confined,
  cabined - 751
cribble 260
cribriform 260
Crichton,
  Admirable -
  scholar 492
  perfect 650
  proficient 700
crick pain 378
cricket game 840
  not - 940
- ground 213
crier 534
  send round the -
  531
crim. con. 961
crime 945, 947
criminal 923, 945
  culprit 949
- law 963
  court of - appeal
  966
criminality 947
criminate 938

crimp crinkle 248
  notch 257
  brittle 328
  deceiver 548
  take 789
  steal 791
crimple 258
crimson 434, 821
cringe submit 725
  subject 749
  servility 886
crinite 256
crinkle angle 244
  convolution 248
  roughen 256
  fold 258
crinoline 225
cripple disable 158
  weaken 160
  injure 659
crippled
  disease 655
crisis
  conjuncture 8
  present time 118
  opportunity 134
  event 151
  strait 704
  excitement 824
  bring to a - 604
  come to a - 729
crisp rumpled 248
  rough 256
  brittle 328
  style 572
Crispin 225
criss-cross 219
cristallomantia 511
criterion test 463
  evidence 467
  indication 550
crithomancy 511
critic judge 480
  taste 850
  detractor 936
critical
  contingent 8
  opportune 134
  discriminating
  465
  important 642
  dangerous 665
  difficult 704
  censorious 932
criticism
  judgment 480
  dissertation 595
  disapprobation
  932
  detraction 934
critique
  [see criticism]
croak cry 412
  hoarseness 581
  stammer 583
  warning 668
  discontent 832
  lament 839
croaker 832, 837
Croat 726
crochet 847
crock 191
crockery 384
crocodile tears 544
crocus yellow 436
Croesus 803
croft 189, 232
Croix de Guerre 733

cromlech 363, 551
crone veteran 130
  fool 501
crony friend 890
  favourite 899
crook curve 245
  deviation 279
  thief 792
crooked
  sloping 217
  distorted 243
  angular 244
  latent 526
  crafty 702
  ugly 846
  dishonorable 940
- path 704
- temper 901
- ways 279
croon 580
crop
  stomach 191
  harvest 154
  shorten 201
  eat 298
  vegetable 367
  store 636
  gather 775
  take 789
  second - 167, 775
- out visible 446
  disclose 529
- up begin 66
  take place 151
  reproduction 163
cropper fall 306
croquet game 840
- ground level 213
croquette 298
crosier 747, 999
cross mix 41
  across 219
  pass 302
  grave 363
  oppose 708
  failure 732
  disaster 735
  refuse 764
  pain 830
  decoration 877
  fretful 901
  punishment 975
  rites 998
  fiery - 722
  proclaim at the -
  roads 531
  red - 662
  -ed bayonets 708
- breed 63
- cut 628
- fire interchange
  148
  difficulty 704
  opposition 708
  attack 716
  -ed in love 898
- the mind 451
- the path of 706
- and pile 621
- purposes 14
  disorder 59
  error 495
  misinterpret 523
  unskilful 699
  difficulty 704
  opposition 708
  discord 713
- oneself 998

- questions
  inquiry 461
  discord 713
  game 840
- road 627
- the Rubicon 609
- sea 348
- swords 722
crossbow 727
cross-examine 461
cross-grained 256
  obstinate 606
  sulky 901a
crossing 219
- sweeper 652
crosspatch 895
crossroads 8
cross-word puzzle
  533
crotch 244
crotchet
  eccentric 83
  music 413
  misjudgment 481
  obstinacy 606
  caprice 608
crouch lower 207
  stoop 308
  fear 860
  servile 886
- before 725
croup 235
croupier 694
crow cry 412
  black 431
  rejoice 838
  boast 884
  pluck a - with 932
  as the - flies 278
  -'s foot (age) 128
  -'s nest 210
- to pluck
  discord 713
  anger 900
  accuse 938
crowbar 633
crowd 72
  multitude 102
  close 197
  redundance 641
  party 712
  vulgar 876
  in the - mixed 41
  madding - 682
crown top 210
  circle 247
  complete 729
  trophy 733
  scepter 747
  install 755
  decoration 877
  reward 973
  to - all 33, 642
  -ed head 745
- with laurel 873
- with success 731
crowning
  [see crown]
  superior 33
  end 67
- point 210
cruche à l'eau &c.
  tant va la - 735
crucial
  crossing 219
  proof 478
- test 463
cruciate

physical pain 378
mental pain 830
crucible
  dish 191
  conversion 144
  furnace 386
  experiment 463
  laboratory 691
  put into the – 163
crucifix 219, 998
crucifixion 828
cruciform 219
crucify
  physical torture
    378
  mental agony 830
  execution 972
crucis, experimen-
    tum – 463
crude *color* 428
  - *style* 579
  unprepared 674
cruel
  painful 830
  inhuman 907
  – to be kind 914
cruelly *much* 31
cruet 191
cruise
  vessel 191
  navigation 267
cruiser 726
cruising 267
crumb *small* 32
  powder 330
  – of comfort 834
crumble
  decrease 36
  weak 160
  destruction 162
  brittle 328
  pulverize 330
  spoil 659
  – into dust
  decompose 49
  – under one's feet
    735
crumbling
  [see crumble]
  dangerous 665
crumenal 800
crump
  distorted 243
  curved 245
crumple
  ruffle 256
  fold 258
  – up *destroy* 162
  crush 195
crunch
  shatter 44
  chew 298
  pulverize 330
crupper 235
crusade 722
crush *crowd* 72
  destroy 162
  compress 195
  pulverize 330
  humble 879
  – under an iron
    heel 739
  – one's hopes
  disappoint 509
  hopeless 859
crushed 828
crushing 830
crust 223

crustacean 366
crusty 895, 901*a*
crutch
  support 215
  angle 244
  –ed Friars 996
crux 219, 704
  – *criticorum* 533
cry *human* 411
  animal 412
  publish 531, 532
  call 550
  voice 580
  vogue 613
  weep 839
  far – to 196
  full – *loud* 404
  raise a – 550
  – aloud
  implore 765
  – out against
  dissuade 616
  censure 932
  – down 932, 934
  – for 865
  – before hurt 839
  – for joy 838
  – you mercy
  deprecate 766
  pity 914
  forgive 918
  – shame 932
  – to beseech 765
  – up 931
  – for vengeance
    923
  – wolf *false* 544
  alarm 669
  – and little wool
  overrate 482
  boast 884
  disappoint 509
crying [see cry]
  urgent 630
  weary 841
  – evil 619
  – shame 874
  – sin 945
crypt *cell* 191
  grave 363
  ambush 530
  altar 1000
cryptic 475, 528
cryptography
  hidden 528
  writing 590
crystal *hard* 323
  transparent 425
  snow – 383
  – *gazer* 513
  – *gazing* 511, 992
  – *oil* 356
  clear as – 519
crystalline
  dense 321
  hard 323
  transparent 425
crystallization 321,
    323
csako 225, 717
cub *young* 129
  vulgar 851
  clown 876
  unlocked – 241
cubby-hole 191
cube
  three dimensions
    92, 93

form 244
cubicle 191
cubist 556
cubit 200
cucking stool 975
cuckold 905
cuckoldom 961
cuckoo
  imitation 19
  repetition 104
  sound 407
  cry 412
cuddle 196, 902
cudgel *beat* 276
  weapon 727
  punish 975
  take up the –s
  aid 707
  attack 716
  contention 720
  – one's brains
  think 451
  imagine 515
cue *hint* 527
  watchword 550
  plea 617
  rôle 625
  take one's – from
    695
  in proper – 698
cuff *sleeve* 225
  blow 276
  punishment 972
cui bono 644, 645
cuique voluptas
  sui – 865
cuirass 717
cuirassier 726
cuisine 298
  batterie de – 957
culbute
  inversion 218
  fall 306
cul-de-lampe
  engraving 558
  ornament 847
cul-de-sac
  concave 252
  closed 261
  difficulty 704
culinary 298
  – *art* 673
cull *dupe* 547
  choose 609
  take 789
cullender 260
cullibility 486
cullion 949
cully *deceive* 545,
    547
culm 388
culminate
  maximum 33
  height 206
  top 210
  complete 729
culpability *vice* 945
  guilt 947
culprit 949
cult 983
cultivate *till* 365,
    371
  sharpen 375
  improve 658
  prepare 673
  aid 707
cultivated
  courteous 894

– *taste* 850
cultivator 371
culture
  knowledge 490
  improvement 658
  taste 850
  politeness 894
culverin 727
culvert 350
cum multis aliis 37,
    102
cumber *load* 319
  obstruct 706
cumbersome
  incommodious
    647
  disagreeable 830
cummerbund 225
cumulative 72
  increasing 35
  assembled 72
  – *evidence* 467
  – *vote* 609
cumulus 353
cunctando restituit
  rem 681
cunctation 133
cuneiform 244
  – *character* 590
cunning
  prepense 611
  sagacious 698
  artful 702
  – *fellow* 700
  – *man* 994
cup *vessel* 191
  hollow 252
  beverage 298
  remedy 662
  trophy 733
  tipple 959
  between – and lip
    111
  in one's –s 959
  – that cheers &c.
    298
  – of humiliation
    879
  dash the – from
    one's lips 509
  – too low 837
cupbearer 746
cupboard 191
cupellation 384
Cupid *beauty* 845
  love 897
  gods 979
cupidity
  avarice 819
  desire 865
cupola *height* 206
  roof 223
  dome 250
cup-tossing 621
cur *dog* 366
  coward 862
  sneak 949
curable 658, 660,
    662
curacy 995
curare 663
curate 996
curative 660
curator 694, 758
curb *moderate* 174
  slacken 275
  dissuade 616
  restrain 751

shackle 752
curb exchange 621
curbstone 233
curd *density* 321
  pulp 354
  (*cohere* 46)
curdle *condense* 321
  (*cohere* 46)
  make the blood –
    830
curdled 352
cure *reinstate* 660
  remedy 662
  preserve 670
  benefice 995
curé 996
cureless 859
curfew 126
curia 966
curio 847
curiosa felicitas 698
curiosity
  unconformity 83
  inquiring 455
  phenomenon 872
curious
  exceptional 83
  inquisitive 455
  true 494
  beautiful 845
  desirous 865
curiously *very* 31
curl *bend* 245
  convolution 248
  hair 256
  cockle up 258
  badge 747
  – up one's lip 930
curling *game* 840
curmudgeon
  miser 819
  plebeian 876
currency
  publicity 531
  money 800
current *existing* 1
  usual 78
  present 118
  happening 151
  flow 264
  of water 348
  of air 349
  rife 531, 532
  language 560
  habit 613
  danger 667
  account – 811
  against the – 708
  go with the – 82
  pass –
  believed 484
  fashion 852
  stem the – 708
  – *belief* 488
  – of events 151
  – of ideas 451
  – of time 109
currente calamo
    590
curricle 272
curriculum 537
curry *food* 298
  rub 331
  condiment 392,
    393
  – favour with
  love 897
  flatter 933

– to *insensible* 823
deafen *loud* 404
deafness 419
deal *much* 31
 arrange 60
 bargain 768
 allot 786
 – a blow
 injure 659
 attack 716
 punish 972
 – board 323
 – in 794
 – out *scatter* 73
 give 784
 – with
 treat of 595
 handle 692
 barter 794
dealer 797
dealings *action* 680
 have – with
 trade 794
 friendly 888
dean 128, 694, 996
deanery *office* 995
 house 1000
dear
 high-priced 814
 loved 897
 favorite 899
 Ó – ! *lament* 839
 – at any price 646
 – me *wonder* 870
 pay – for whistle
 647
dearest foe 936
dearness 814
dearth 640
 – of ideas 843
death 360
 house of – 363
 in at the –
 arrive 292
 kill 361
 persevere 604a
 pale as –
 colorless 429
 fear 860
 put to – 361, 972
 still as – 265
 violent – 361
 be the – of one
 amuse 480
 –'s head 837
 – in the pot
 unhealthy 657
 hidden danger
 667
**deathbed repent-
 ance** 950
death-blow
 end 67
 killing 361
 failure 732
death-house 752
deathless
 perpetual 112
 fame 873
deathlike
 silent 403
 hideous 846
death-song 839
death-struggle 720
death-warrant 971
death-watch 668
débâcle 145
 destruction 162

downfall 306
 torrent 348
debar *hinder* 706
 restrain 751
 prohibit 761
debark 292
debase *depress* 308
 foul 653
 deteriorate 659
 degrade 874
debased
 lowered 207
 dishonored 940
debate *reason* 476
 talk 588
 hesitate 605
 dispute 720
debatable 475
debauch
 spoil 659
 intemperance 954
 impurity 961
debauchee 962
debenture
 security 771
 money 800
 credit 805
debility 160
debit *debt* 806
 accounts 811
debitor 806
débonnaire 836
debouch 293, 295
débris
 fragments 51
 crumbled 330
 useless 645
debt 806
 out of – 803
 get out of – 807
 – of nature 360
debtor 806
 – and creditor 811
debunk 529
début *beginning* 66
 essay 675
 celebration 883
débutant
 learner 541
 drama 599
decade *ten* 98
 period 108
decadence 659
decagon 244
decalescence 382
decalogue 926
decamp
 go away 293
 run away 623
decant 270
decanter 191
decapitate *kill* 361
 punish 972
decay *decrease* 36
 decompose 49
 shrivel 195
 unclean 653
 disease 655
 spoil 659
 adversity 735
 natural – 360
 – of memory 506
decayed
 [see *decay*]
 old 124
 rotten 160
decease 360
deceit

falsehood 544
 deception 545
 cunning 702
deceived
 in error 495
 duped 547
deceiver 548
 gay – 962
decelerate 275
decennium 108
decent
 mediocre 651
 pure 960
decentralize 49
deceptio visûs 443
deception 545
**deceptive reason-
 ing** 477
decession 293
dechristianize 989
decide
 turn the scale 153
 judge 480
 choose 609
decided *great* 31
 ended 67
 certain 474
 resolved 604
 take a – step 609
deciduous
 transitory 111
 falling 306
 spoiled 659
decies repetita
 placebit 829
decimal 84, 98, 99
decimate
 subtract 38
 tenth 99
 few 103
 weaken 160
 kill 361
 play havoc 659
 punish 972
decipher 522
decision
 judgment 480
 resolution 604
 intention 620
 law case 969
decisive
 certain 474
 proof 478
 commanding 741
 take a – step 609
deck *floor* 211
 beautify 847
declaim 531, 582
 – against 932
declamatory
 style 577
 speech 582
declaration
 affirmation 535
 law pleadings 969
 – of faith
 belief 484
 theology 983
 – of war 713
declaratory
 meaning 516
 inform 527
declare
 publish 531
declension
 [see *decline*]
 grammar 567
 backsliding 988

declensions 5
declination
 [see *decline*]
 deviation 279
 measurement 466
 rejection 610
decline *decrease* 36
 old 124
 weaken 160
 descent 306
 grammar 567
 be unwilling 603
 reject 610
 disease 655
 become worse 659
 adversity 735
 refuse 764
 – of day 126
 – of life 128
declivity *slope* 217
 descent 306
decoction 335, 384
decode 522
decollate 972
décolleté 226
decoloration 429
decomposition 49
deconsecrate 756
decontrol 158
décor 448, 599
decoration
 insignia 747
 ornament 847
 title 877
decorative 556
decorous
 [see *decorum*]
 fashionable 862
 proper 924
 respectful 928
decorticate 226
decorum
 fashion 852
 duty 926
 purity 960
décousu
 discontinuous 70
 failure 732
decoy *attract* 288
 deceive 545
 deceiver 548
 entice 615
decrease 36, 195
decree
 judgment 480
 order 741
 law 963, 969
decrement
 decrease 36
 thing deducted 40a
 contraction 195
decrepit *old* 128
 weak 158, 160
 disease 655
 decayed 659
decrepitate 406
decrescendo 36
decretal 741
decry *underrate* 483
 censure 932
 detract 934
decumbent 213
decuple 98
decursive 306
decurtation 201
decussation 219
dedecorous
 disreputable 874

discourteous 895
dedicate *use* 677
 inscribe 873
deduce *deduct* 38
 infer 480
deducible
 evidence 467
 proof 478
deduct *retrench* 38
 deprive 789
 subtract 813
deduction
 [see *deduce*]
 decrement 40a
 reasoning 476
deed *evidence* 467
 record 551
 act 680
 security 771
 –s of arms 720
 – without a name
 947
deem 484
deemster 967
deep *great* 31
 profound 208
 sea 341
 sonorous 404
 cunning 702
 plough the – 267
 – color 428
 – in debt 806
 – game 702
 – knowledge 490
 – mourning 839
 – note 408
 – potations 959
 – reflection 451
 – sense 821
 – sigh 839
 – study 457
 in – water 704
deepen 35
deep-dyed
 intense 171
 black 431
 vicious 945
deep-felt 821
deep-laid *plan* 626
deep-mouthed
 resonant 408
 bark 412
 thrilling 821
deep-musing 458
deep-read 490
deep-rooted
 stable 150
 strong 159
 belief 484
 habit 613
 affections 820
deep-sea 208
deep-seated 208,
 221
deer 366
 in heart a – 862
deev 980
deface
 destroy form 241
 obliterate 552
 injure 659
 render ugly 846
defalcation
 incomplete 53
 contraction 195
 shortcoming 304
 non-payment 808
defame *shame* 874

censure 932
detract 934
defamer 936
defatigation 841
default
  incomplete 53
  shortcoming 304
  neglect 460
  insufficiency 640
  debt 806
  non-payment 808
  in − of 187
  judgment by − 725
defaulter *thief* 792
  non-payer 808
  rogue 949
defeasance 756
defeat
  confute 479
  succeed 731
  failure 732
  − one's hope 509
defeatism 911
defecate 652
defecation 299
defect
  decrement 40a
  incomplete 53
  imperfect 651
  failing 945
defection
  relinquishment 624
  disobedience 742
defective
  incomplete 53
  insufficient 640
  imperfect 651
defence
  plea 462
  resist 717
  vindication 937
  first line of − 726
defenceless
  impotent 158
  weak 160
  exposed 665
defendant 938
defensible *safe* 664
  excusable 937
defensive alliance 712
defer 133
  − to *assent* 488
  submit 725
  respect 928
deference
  obedience 743
  humility 879
  courtesy 894
  respect 928
defiance **715**, 909
  threat 909
  in − *opposition* 708
  set at − *disobey* 742
  − of danger 861
deficiency
  [see deficient]
  vice 945
deficient
  inferior 34
  incomplete 53
  shortcoming 304
  insufficient 640
  imperfect 651
deficit
  incompleteness 53
  debt 806

defigure 846
defile
  interval 198
  march 266
  dirt 653
  spoil 659
  shame 874
  impure 961
define
  specify 79
  limit 233
  explain 522
  name 564
definite
  [see define]
  visible 446
  certain 474
  exact 494
  intelligible 518
  manifest 525
  perspicuous 570
definition
  interpretation 521
definitive *final* 67
  affirmative 535
  decided 604
deflagration 384
deflate 195
deflation
  currency 800
deflect
  curve 245
  deviate 279
deflower
  spoil 659
  violate 961
defluxion
  egress 295
  flowing 348
defœdation 653, 659
deform 241
deformity
  distortion 243
  ugliness 846
  blemish 848
defraud *cheat* 545
  swindle 791
defray 807
deft *suitable* 23
  clever 698
defunct 360, 362
defy 715
  disobey 742
  threaten 909
  − danger 861
dégagé *free* 748
  fashion 852
degenerate 659
deglutition 298
degradation
  deterioration 659
  shame 874
  dishonor 940
degree **26**
  term 71
  honor 873
  by −s 26
  by slow −s 275
degustation 390
dehiscence 260
dehort
  dissuade 616
  advise 695
dehydrate 340
Dei gratiâ 976
deification 873, 981
deify

hono
  idolatry 991
deign
  condescend 762
  consent 879
Deism
  heterodoxy 984
  irreligion 989
Deity **976**
  tutelary − 664
dejection
  excretion 299
  melancholy **837**
déjeûner 298
délabrement 162
delaceration 659
delation 938
delator 527
delay 133
dele 552
delectable
  savory 394
  agreeable 829
delectation 827
delectus 562
delegate
  transfer 270
  commission 755
  consignee 758
  députy 759
delenda est Carthago
  destroy 162
  curse 908
delete 162
deleterious
  pernicious 649
  unwholesome 657
deletion 552
deletory
  destructive 162
deliberate
  slow 275
  think 451
  attentive 457
  leisure 685
  advise 695
  cautious 864
deliberately
  [see deliberate]
  late 133
  with *premeditation* 611
delicacy *weak* 160
  slender 203
  dainty 298
  brittleness 328
  texture 329
  savory 394
  color 428
  exact 494
  scruple 603
  ill health 655
  difficult 704
  pleasing 829
  beauty 845
  taste 850
  fastidious 868
  honor 939
  pure 960
delicate *ear* 418
délice 377
delicious *taste* 394
  pleasing 829
delicti, corpus −
  guilt 947
  lawsuit 969
delicto, in

flagrante − 947
delight
  pleasure 827
  pleasing 829
Delilah 962
delimit 233
delineate
  outline 230
  represent 554
  describe 594
delineator 559
delineavit 556
delinquency 304, 947
delinquent 949
deliquation 335
deliquesce 36
deliquescence 335
deliquium
  paralysis 158
  fatigue 688
delirant reges plectuntur Achivi 739
delirium
  raving 503
  passion 825
  − *tremens* 503, 959
delitescence
  invisible 447
  latency 526
  seclusion 893
deliver
  transfer 270
  utter 580, 582
  birth 662
  rescue 672
  liberate 750
  give 784
  relieve 834
  − as one's act and deed 467
  − the goods 729
  − judgment 480
  − a speech 582
deliverance **672**
delivery
  [see deliver]
  bring forth 161
  cash on − 807
dell 252
Delphic oracle
  prophetic 513
  equivocal 520
  latent 526
delta 342
delude *error* 495
  deceive 545
deluge *crowd* 72
  water 337
  flood 348
  redundance 641
delusion
  [see delude]
  insane 503
  self − *credulous* 486
delve *dig* 252
  till 371
  − into *inquire* 461
demagogue
  director 694
  malcontent 710
  rebel 742
demagogy 737
demand
  inquire 461

order 741
  ask 765
  price 812
  claim 924
  in − *require* 630
  desire 865
  saleable 796
demarcation 233
dematerialize 317
demean oneself
  conduct 692
  humble 879
  dishonor 940
demeanor
  aid 448
  conduct 692
  fashion 852
demency 503
dementia 503
demerit 945
demesne
  abode 189
  property 780
demi- 91
demigod *hero* 861
  angel 948
demigration 266
demijohn 191
demi-jour 422
demi-lune 717
demi-monde
  plebeian 876
  licentious 962
démenti 536
demirep 962
demise *death* 360
  transfer 783
  lease 787
demisemiquaver 413
demission 756
demit 757
demiurge
  deity 979
demivolt 309
demobilize 73
democracy *rule* 737
  commonalty 876
Democrats
  party 712
Democritus 838
demoiselle 129
demolish 479
demon *violent* 173
  bane 663
  devil **980**
  − in human shape 913, 949
  − *worship* 991
demoniacal
  malevolent 907
  furious 824
  wicked 945
demonology
  demons 980
  sorcery 992
demonstration
  number 85
  proof **478**
  manifest 525
  ostentation 882
  ocular − 441, 446
demonstrative
  manifest 525
  indicative 550
  vehement 825
demonstrator 524
demoralize

unnerve 158
spoil 659
vicious 945
Demosthenes 582
demotic 590
demulcent
  mild 174
  soothing 662
demur
  disbelieve 485
  dissent 489
  unwilling 603
  hesitate 605
  without – 602
demure
  grave 826
  sad 837
  affected 855
  modest 881
demurrage 132
demurrer 969
den *abode* 189
  study 191, 893
  sty 653
  prison 752
  – *of thieves* 791
denary 98
denaturalize
  corrupt 659
denaturalized
  abnormal 83
dendriform 242, 367
dendrology 369
denial
  negation 536
  refusal 764
  self– 953
denigrate 431
denization 748
denizen
  inhabitant 188
  freeman 748
  –s *of the air* 979
  –s *of the day* 366
**Denmark, rotten in
  the state of** –
  526
denomination
  class 75
  name 564
  sect 712
  religious – 983
denominational
  dissent 489
  theological 983
  – *education* 537
denominator 84
denote
  specify 79
  mean 516
  indicate 550
dénouement
  end 67
  result 154
  disclosure 529
  completion 729
denounce
  curse 908
  disapprove 932
  accuse 938
dense
  crowded 72
  ignorant 493
density 321
dent 252, 257
dental 561
denticulated 253,
  257

dentifrice 652
dentistry 662
denude 226
denuded *loss* 776
  – *of*
  insufficient 640
denunciation
  [see denounce]
deny *dissent* 489
  negative 556
  refuse 764
  – *oneself*
  avoid 623
  seclude 893
  temperate 953
  ascetic 990
Deo volente 470,
  976
deobstruct 705
deodand 974
deodorize 399
  clean 652
deontology 926
deoppilation 705
deorganization 61
deosculation 902
depart 293
  – *from*
  deviate 15, 279
  relinquish 624
  – *this life* 360
departed
  non-existent 2
department
  class 75
  region 181
  business 625
departure 293
  new – 66
  point of – 293
depend *hang* 214
  contingent 475
  – *upon*
  be the effect of 154
  evidence 467
  trust 484
  – *on circumstan-
  ces* 475
**depended on, to
  be** –
  certain 474
  reliable 484
  honorable 939
dependency 777,
  780
dependent
  effect 154
  liable 177
  hanging 214
  puppet 711
  servant 746
  subject 749
deperdition 776
dephlegmation 340
depict 554, 556
  describe 594
depilation 226
depilatory 662
depletion 638, 640
deplorable *bad* 649
  disastrous 735
  painful 830
deplore *regret* 833
  complain 839
  remorse 950
deploy 194
depone 535
deponent 467

depopulate
  eject 297
  desert 893
deportation
  removal 270
  emigration 297
  expulsion 972
deportment 692
depose
  evidence 467
  declare 535
  dethrone 738, 756
deposit *place* 184
  precipitate 321
  store 636
  security 771
  payment 809
depositary 801
deposition
  [see depose,
  deposit]
  record 551
depository 636
depôt *terminal* 292
  store 636
  shop 799
  – *ship* 726
deprave *spoil* 659
depraved *bad* 649
  vicious 945
deprecation 766
  pity 914
  disapprove 932
depreciation
  decrease 36
  underestimate 483
  discount 813
  cheap 815
  disrespect 929
  censure 932
  detraction 934
  accusation 938
depredation 791
depredator 792
deprehension 789
depression
  lowness 207
  depth 208
  concavity 252
  lowering 308
  dejection 837
  dulness 843
depressing
  painful 830
deprive *subduct* 38
  take 798
  – *of life* 361
  – *of power* 158
  – *of property* 789
  – *of strength* 160
deprived of 776
depth *physical* 208
  mental 498
  out of one's – 304
  310
  – *bomb* 727
  – *of misery* 828
  – *of thought* 451
  – *of winter* 383
depurate *clean* 652
  improve 658
depuratory 662
deputation 755
depute 755
**deputies, chamber
  of** – 696
deputy 759
dequantitate 36

derangement 61
  mental – 503
Derby-day 720
derelict *land* 342
  danger 667
  relinquish 782
  outcast 893
dereliction
  relinquishment
  624, 782
  guilt 947
  – *of duty* 927
deride
  ridicule 856
  disrespect 929
  contempt 930
derivation
  origin 153, 154,
  155
  verbal 562
derive
  attribute 155
  deduce 480
  acquire 775
  income 810
dermal 223
dermatology 223
dernier
  – *cri* 850
  – *ressort* 601
dérobée, à la – 528
derogate
  underrate 483
  disparage 934
  dishonor 940
  – *from* 874
derogatory
  shame 874
  dishonor 940
derrick 307, 633
derring-do 861
dervish 996
désagrément 830
descant *music* 415
  diffuseness 573
  loquacity 584
  dissert 595
descend *slope* 217
  go down 306
  – *to particulars*
  special 79
  describe 594
descendant 167
**descensus Averni,
  facilis** – 665
descent *lineage* 166
  fall 306
  inheritance 775
description
  kind 75
  name 564
  narration 594
descriptive music
  415
descry 441
desecrate
  misuse 679
  disrespect 929
  profane 988
desert
  unproductive 169
  empty 187
  plain 344
  run away 623
  relinquish 624,
  782
  merit 944
  waste sweetness

on – *air* 638
deserted
  outcast 893
deserter 144, 607,
  623
desertless 945
deserts 924
deserve
  be entitled to 924
  merit 944
  – *notice* 642
  – *belief* 484
désespoir, au –
  dejected 837
  hopeless 859
déshabillé, en –
  not dressed 226
  unprepared 674
  homely 849
desiccate 340
desiccator 340
desiderate *need* 630
  desire 865
desideratum
  inquiry 461
  requirement 630
  desire 865
design
  prototype 22
  form 240
  delineation 554
  painting 556
  intention 620
  plan 626
designate
  specify 79
  call 564
designation 75
designed
  aforethought 611
designer 164, 559
designing
  cunning 702
designless 621
désillusioner 529
desinence *end* 67
  discontinuance
  142
desipience 499
desipere in loco 840
desirable 646
desire 865
  will 600
  have no – *for* 866
desist
  discontinue 142
  relinquish 624
  inaction 681
desk *box* 191
  support 215
  school 542
  pulpit 1000
désobligeant 272
désoeuvré 681
desolate *alone* 87
  ravage 162
  afflicted 828
  dejected 837
  secluded 893
desolating
  painful 830
désorienté 475
despair *grief* 828,
  859
despatch *eject* 297
  kill 361
  news 532
  epistle 592

at a – 34
lie under a – 651
disadvantageous
647, 649
disaffection
dissent 489
enmity 889
hate 898
disaffirm 536
disagreeable 830,
867
disagreement
difference 15
incongruity **24**
dissent 489
discord 713
disallow 761
disannul 756
disappearance 449
disappointment
balk **509**
fail 732
discontent 832
disapprobation 706,
932
disapprover 936
disarm *disable* 158
weaken 160
reconcile 831
propitiate 914
disarrange 61
disarray
disorder 59
undress 226
disaster *evil* 619
failure 732
adversity 735
calamity 830
disastrous *bad* 649
disavow 536
disband
separate 44
disperse 73
liberate 750
disbar
abrogate 756
punish 972
disbarment 55
disbelief 485, 487
religious 989
disbench 756, 972
disbowel 297
disbranch 44
disburden
facilitate 705
– one's mind 529
– oneself of 782
disburse 809
disc 220, 234
discard *eject* 297
relinquish 624
disuse 678
abrogate 756
refuse 764
repudiate 773
surrender 782
– from one's
thoughts 458
discarded 495
disceptation 476
discern *see* 441
know 490
discernible 446
discernment 498,
868
discerption 44
discharge
violence 173

propel 284
emit 297
excrete 299
sound 406
acquit oneself 692
complete 729
liberate 750
abrogate 756
pay 807
exempt 927a
acquit 970
– a duty 926, 944
– a function
business 625
utility 644
– itself *egress* 295
river 348
– from the mem-
ory 506
– from the mind
458
– an obligation
772
discind 44
disciple *pupil* 541
votary 711
Christian 985
disciplinarian
master 540
martinet 739
discipline
order 58
teaching 537
training 673
restraint 751
punishment 972
religious 990
disclaim *deny* 536
repudiate 756
abjure 757
refuse 764
disclosure 480a, **529**
discoid *layer* 204
frontal 220
flat 251
discoloration 429
discolored
shabby 659
ugly 846
blemish 848
discomfit 731
discomfiture 732
discomfort
physical 378
mental 828
discommend 932
discommode
hinder 706
annoy 830
discommodious
645, 647
discompose
derange 61
put out 458
hinder 706
pain 830
disconcert 874
anger 900
discomposure 828
disconcert
derange 61
distract 458
disappoint 509
hinder 706
discontent 832
confuse 879
disconcerted
hopeless 859

disconformity 83
disconguity 24
disconnected
style 575
disconnection
irrelation 19
disjunction 44
discontinuity 70
disconsolate 837
discontent **832**
discontinuance
cessation 142
relinquishment
624
discontinuity 70
discord
difference 15
disagreement 24
of sound **414**
of color 428
dissension **713**
discount
decrease 36
decrement 40a
money **813**
at a –
disrepute 874
disapproved 932
discountenance
disfavor 706
refuse 764
discourage
dissuade 616
sadden 837
frighten 860
discourse
teach 537
speech 582
talk 588
dissert 595
sermon 998
discourtesy 895
discous 202
discover
perceive 441
solve 462
find 480a
disclose 529
– itself
be seen 446
discovery 480a
discredit
disbelief 485
dishonor 874
discreditable
vicious 945
discreet *careful* 459
cautious 864
discrepancy 15
discrepant 24, 713
discrete
separate 44, 70
single 87
discretion *will* 600
choice 609
skill 698
caution 864
surrender at – 725
use – 609
years of – 131
discrétion à – 600
discrimination
difference 15
nice perception
465
wisdom 498
taste 850
fastidiousness 868

disculpate 937
discumbency 213
discursion 266
discursive
moving 264
migratory 266
wandering 279
argumentative 476
diffuse style 573
conversable 588
disserting 595
discus 840
discuss *eat* 298
reflect 451
inquire 461
reason 476
dissert 595
discussion
[see *discuss*]
open to – 475
under – 461
disdain
indifference 866
fastidious 868
arrogance 885
pride 878
contempt 930
disease 655
occupational – 655
–d *mind* 503
disembark 292
disembarrass 705
disembody
decompose 49
disperse 73
spiritualize 317
disembogue
emit 295
eject 297
flow out 348
disembowel 297,
301
disembroil 60
disenable 158
disenchant
discover 480a
dissuade 616
displease 830
disencumber 705
disendow 756
disengage
detach 44
facilitate 705
liberate 750
disengaged
to let 763
disentangle
separate 44
arrange 60
unroll 313
decipher 522
facilitate 705
liberate 750
disenthral 750
disenthrone 756
disentitle 925
disespouse 905
disestablish
displace 185
abrogate 756
disesteem 929, 932
disfavor
oppose 708
hate 898
disrespect 929
view with – 932
disfigure
deface 241

injure 659
deform 846
blemish 848
disfranchise 925
disgorge *emit* 297
flow out 348
restore 790
pay 807
disgrace
shame 874
dishonor 940
sense of – 879
disgraceful
vice 945
disgruntle 509
disguise
unlikeness 18
conceal 528
mask 530
falsify 544
untruth 546
disguised in drink
959
disgust *taste* 395
offensive 830
weary 841
dislike 867
hatred 898
– of life 837
dish *destroy* 162
plate 191
food 298
– of tea 892
dishabille
undress 225
unprepared 674
dishearten
dissuade 616
pain 830
discontent 832
deject 837
dished 252, 732
disherison 789
dishevel
loose 47
untidy 59
disorder 61
disperse 73
intermix 219
dishonest *false* 544
base 940
dishonour
disrepute 874
disrespect 929
baseness 940
– bills 808
dish-water 653
disillusion 509
disincline
dissuade 616
dislike 867
disinclined 603
disinfect
purify 652
restore 660
disinfectant 662
disingenuous
false 544
dishonorable 940
disinherit
relinquish 782
transfer 783
deprive 789
disintegrate
separate 44
decompose 49
pulverize 330
disinter *exhume* 363

discover 480a
disinterested 942
disjecta membra
  separate 44
  disorder 59
  dispersed 73
  – poetae 597
disjoin 44
disjointed
  disorder 59
  powerless 158
  style 575
disjunction 44
disjunctive 70
diskindness 907
dislike 867
  reluctance 603
  hate 898
dislocate
  separate 44
  put out of joint 61
dislocated
  disorder 59
dislodge
  displace 185
  eject 297
disloyal 940
dismal
  depressing 830
  dejected 837
dismantle
  destroy 162
  divest 226
  render useless 645
  injure 659
  disuse 678
dismask 529
dismast
  render useless 645
  injure 659
  disuse 678
dismay 860
dismember
  separate 44
  disperse 73
dismiss
  send away 289
  discharge 297
  discard 678
  liberate 750
  abrogate 756
  relinquish 782
  punish 972
  – from the mind
    452, 458
dismount
  arrive 292
  descend 306
  render useless 645
disnest 185
disobedience 742
  non-observance
    773
disoblige 907
disorder
  confusion **59**
  derange 61
  turbulent 173
  disease 655
  –ed intellect 503
disorderly
  unprincipled 945
disorganize
  derange 61
  destroy 162
  spoil 659
disorganized 59
disown 536

dispair 44
disparage
  underrate 483
  disrespect 929
  dispraise 932
  detract 934
disparity
  different 15
  dissimilar 18
  disagreeing 24
  unequal 28
  isolated 44
dispart 44
dispassionate 826
  – *opinion* 484
dispatch
  [see despatch]
dispel *scatter* 73
  destroy 162
  displace 185
  repel 289
dispensable
  useless 645
dispensary 662
dispensation
  [see dispense]
  command 741
  licence 760
  relinquishment
    782
  exemption 927a
  –s of Providence
    976
dispense
  disperse 73
  give 784
  apportion 786
  retail 796
  – with
    disuse 678
  permit 760
  exempt 927a
  cannot be –d with
    630
dispeople
  eject 297
  expatriate 893
disperse
  separate 44
  scatter 73
  diverge 291
  waste 638
dispersion 73
  – of light 420
  chromatic – 428
dispirit
  discourage 616
  sadden 837
displacement
  derange 61
  remove **185**
  transfer 270
displacency
  dislike 867
  incivility 895
  disapprobation
    932
displant 185
display *appear* 448
  show 525
  parade 882
displease 830
displeasure 828
  anger 900
displosion 173
displume 789
disport 840
disposal

[see dispose]
  at one's – 763, 777
dispose
  arrange 60
  tend 176
  induce 615
  – of *use* 677
  complete 729
  relinquish 782
  give 784
  sell 796
disposed 620
disposition
  nature 5
  order 58
  arrangement 60
  inclination 602
  mind 820
dispossess
  transfer 783
  take away 789
  – *oneself of* 782
dispraise 932
dispread 73
disprize 483
disproof
  counter-evidence
    468
  confutation 479
disproportion
  irrelation 10
  disagreement 24
disprove 479
disputable 475, 485
disputant 710, 726
disputatious 901
dispute
  discuss 476
  doubt 485
  deny 536
  discord 713
  in – 461
disqualification
  incapacitate 158
  useless 645
  unprepared 674
  unskilful 699
  disentitle 925
disquiet
  changeable 149
  agitation 315
  excitement 825
  uneasiness 828
  give pain 830
disquietude
  apprehension 860
disquisition 539,
  595
disregard
  overlook 458
  neglect 460
  make light of 483
  insensible to 823,
    826
  disrespect **929**
  contempt 930
  – of time 115
disrelish 867, 898
disreputable 874
  vicious 945
disrepute 874, 929
disrespect 929
  despise 930
disrobe 226
disruption
  disjunction 44
  destruction 162
  discord 713

dissatisfaction
  disappointment
    509
  sorrow 828
  discontent 832
dissect
  anatomize 44, 49
  investigate 461
dissemblance 18
dissemble 544
dissembler 548
disseminate
  scatter 73
  pervade 186
  publish 531
  teach 537
dissension 713
  sow – 898
dissent
  disagree **489**
  refuse 764
  heterodoxy 984
dissentient 15
dissentious 24
dissertation 595
disservice
  disadvantage 619
  useless 645
disserviceable 649
dissever 44
dissidence
  disagreement 24
  dissent 489
  discord 713
  discontent 832
  heterodoxy 984
dissilience 173
dissimilarity 18
dissimulate 544
dissipate *scatter* 73
  destroy 162
  pleasure 377
  prodigality 818
  amusement 840
  intemperance 954
  dissolute 961
dissocial 893
dissociate 44
dissociation
  irrelation 10
  separation 44
dissolute 961
  profligate 945
  intemperate 954
dissolution
  [see dissolve]
  decomposition 49
  destruction 162
  death 360
dissolve *vanish* 2, 4
  liquefy 335
  disappear 449
  abrogate 756
dissolving views
  448, 449
dissonance
  disagreement 24
  unmusical 414
  discord 713
dissuasion 616
dissyllable 561
distaff
  – side 374
distain *dirty* 653
  ugly 846
distal 196
distance 196
  overtake 282

  go beyond 303
  defeat 731
  angular – 244
  keep at a –
    discourtesy 895
  keep one's –
    avoid 623
  modest 881
  respect 928
  teach one his – 879
  – of time
    long time 110
  past 122
distaste 867
distasteful 830
distemper 299, 428
  color 428
  painting 556
  disease 655
distend 194
distended 192
distich 89, 597
distil *come out* 295
  extract 301
  evaporate 336
  drop 348
distinct
  disjoined 44
  audible 402
  visible 446
  intelligible 518
  manifest 525
  express 535
  articulate 580
distinction
  difference 15
  discrimination
    465
  style 578
  fame 873
  rank 875
  – without a differ-
    ence 27
distinctive 15
  – feature 79
distinctness 15
distingué 852, 873
distinguish
  perceive 441
  discriminate 465
  – by the name of
    564
distinguishable 15
distinguished
  superior 33
  repute 873
Distinguished
  Service Cross
  733
distortion
  obliquity 217
  twist **243**
  of vision 443
  misinterpret 523
  falsehood 544
  misrepresent 555
  ugly 846
distract 458
distracted
  confused 475
  insane 503
  excited 824
distraction
  passion 825
  love to – 897
distrain *take* 789
  appraise 812
  attach 969

distrait 458

distraught 824

distress
 distraint 789
 poverty 804
 affliction 828
 cause pain 830
 signal of – 669

distressingly
 excessively 31

distribute
 arrange 60
 disperse 44, 73
 allot 786

district 181
 – council 696

distrust
 disbelief 485
 fear 860

distrustful 487

disturb
 derange 61
 change 140
 agitate 315
 excite 824
 distress 828, 830

disturbance 59

disunion
 discord 24
 separation 44
 disorder 59
 discord 713

disuse
 desuetude 614
 relinquish 624
 unemploy **678**

disused
 old 124

disvalue 932

ditch
 inclosure 232
 trench 259
 water 343
 conduit 350
 defence 717
 to the last – 606

ditch-water 653

ditheism 984

dither 315

dithyramb
 music 415
 poetry 597

dithyrambic 503

ditto 13, 104
 say – to 488

ditty 415
 – box 191

diurnal 138

diuturnity **110**

diva 416

divagate 279, 629

divan *sofa* 215
 council 696
 throne 747
 tribunal 966

divaricate *differ* 15
 bifurcate 91
 diverge 291

dive *swim* 267
 fly 267
 plunge 306, 310
 – into *inquire* 461

divellicate 44

diver 208

divergence
 difference 15
 variation 20a
 disagreement 24

deviation 279

separation **291**

divers *different* 15
 multiform 81
 many 102
 – *coloured* 440

diverse 15

diversify
 very 20a
 change 140

diversion
 change 140
 deviation 279
 pleasure 377
 amusement 840

diversity
 difference 15
 irregular 16a
 dissimilar 18
 multiform 81
 – of opinion 489

divert *turn* 279
 deceive 545
 amuse 840
 – the mind 452, 458

divertissement
 diversion 377
 drama 599
 amusement 840

Dives 803

divest *denude* 226
 take 789
 – oneself of
 abrogate 756
 relinquish 782

divestment **226**

divide *differ* 15
 separate 44
 part 51
 arrange 60
 arithmetic 85
 bisect 91
 vote 609
 apportion 786

dividend *part* 51
 number 84
 portion 786

divina particula
 aurae 450

divination
 prediction 511
 sorcery 992

divine *predict* 511
 guess 514
 perfect 650
 of God 976, 983, 983a
 clergyman 996

divine afflatus 515
 – right
 authority 737
 due 924
 – service 990

diving 840

diving-bell 208

divining-rod 550, 993

Divinity *God* 976
 theology 983

divisible
 number 84

division
 [see divide]
 part 51
 class 75
 arithmetic 85
 discord 713

military 726

divisor 84

divorce
 separation 44
 relinquish 782
 matrimonial **905**

Divorce Court 966

divulge 529

divulsion 44

divvy 786

dixi 535

dizen 847

dizzard 501

dizzy
 dimsighted 443
 confused 458
 vertigo 503
 – height 206
 – round 312

djerrid 727

djinn 980

do *fare* 7
 suit 23
 produce 161
 cheat 545
 act 680
 complete 729
 succeed 731
 I beg 765
 all one can – 686
 plenty to – 682
 thing to – 625
 – away with
 destroy 162
 eject 297
 abrogate 756
 – battle 722
 – one's bidding
  743
 – business 625
 – to death 361
 – as done by 906, 942
 – for *destroy* 162
 kill 361
 conquer 731
 serve 746
 punish 972
 – good 906
 – harm 907
 – honor 873
 – into
 translate 522
 – justice to 595
 – like 19
 – little 683
 – no harm 648
 – nothing 681
 – nothing but 136
 – one's office 772
 – as others do 82
 – over 223
 – as one pleases
  748
 – a service
 useful 644
 avl 707
 – up 660
 have to – with
  680, 692
 – without 678
 – the work 686
 – wrong 923

docere, pisces na-
 tare – 641

docile *domesticated*
 370
 learning 539

willing 602

docimastic 463

dock *diminish* 36
 cut off 38
 port 189
 shorten 201
 edge 231
 store 636
 tribunal 966

docked
 incomplete 53

docker 690

docket
 list 86
 evidence 467
 note 550
 record 551
 security 771

dockyard 691

doctor
 learned man 492
 restore 660
 remedy 662
 after death the –
  135
 – accounts 811
 when –s disagree
  475

doctrinaire
 positive 474
 pedant 492
 affectation 855
 blusterer 887

doctrinal 537

doctrinarian 514

doctrine *tenet* 484
 knowledge 490

document 551

documentary
 evidence 467

dodder 315

doddering 128

dodecahedron 244

dodge *change* 140
 shift 264
 deviate 279
 oscillate 314
 pursue 461
 avoid 623
 stratagem 702

dodger, artful – 792

dodo 366
 extinct as the –
  122

doe *swift* 274
 deer 366
 female 374

doer
 originator 164
 agent 690

doff 226
 – the cap 894

dog *follow* 281
 animal 366
 male 373
 pursue 622
 wretch 949
 cast to the –s
 destroy 162
 reject 610
 disuse 678
 abrogate 756
 relinquish 782
 fire – 386
 go to the –s
 destruction 162
 fail 732
 adversity 735

poverty 804

sea – 269

watch –
 safety 664
 warning 668
 keeper 753
 hair of – that bit
  you 959
 let sleeping –s lie
  141
 – in manger 706, 943
 –tired 686
 –s of war 722

dog-cart 272

dog-cheap 815

dog-days 382

doge 745

dogged
 obstinate 606
 valour 861
 sullen 901a

dogger 273

doggerel
 verse 597
 ridiculous 851, 853

dog-hole 189

dog-Latin 563

dogma *tenet* 484
 theology 983

dogmatic
 certain 474
 positive 481
 assertion 535
 obstinate 606

dogmatist 887

dog's ear 258

dog robber 746

dog-sick 867

dog-star 423

dog-trot 275

dog-weary 688

doily 852

doing
 up and – 682
 what one is – 625

doings
 events 151
 actions 680
 conduct 692

doit *trifle* 643
 coin 800

dolce far niente 681

doldrums
 dejection 837
 sulks 901a

dole
 small quantity 32
 scant 640
 give 784
 allot 786
 parsimony 819
 grief 828

doleful 837
 – dumps 901a

doll *small* 193
 image 554

dollar 800

dolman 225

dolmen 363, 551

dolor
 physical 378
 moral 828

dolorem, infandum
 renovare – 833

dolorous 830

dolphin 341

dolt 501
doltish 499
domain
  class 75
  region 181
  property 780
Domdaniel 982
dome *high* 206
  roof 223
  curvature 245
  convex 250
Domesday book
  list 86
  record 551
domesman 967
domestic
  inhabitant 188
  home 189
  interior 221
  servant 746
  secluded 893
  - *animals* 366
domesticate
  locate 184
  acclimatize 613
  - *animals* 370
domicile 189
domiciled 186
domiciliary 188
  - *visit* 461
dominant 175
  note in music 413
domination 737
dominical 998
domineer
  tyrannize 739
  insolence 885
Domini, anno - 106
Dominican 996
Dominie 540
dominion 181, 737
domino *dress* 225
  mask 530
  game 840
domn 745
don *put on* 225
  scholar 492
  teacher 540
  noble 875
Don Juan 897
donation 784
done *finished* 729
  work - 729
  - *for spoilt* 659
  failure 732
  - *up*
  impotent 158
  tired 688
  have - *with*
  cease 142
  relinquish 624
  disuse 678
donee 785
donjon 717, 752
donkey *ass* 271
  fool 501
  talk a -'*s hind leg*
  off 584
donna 374
Donnybrook Fair
  disorder 59
  discord 713
donor 784
donzel 746
doodle 501
doom *end* 67
  fate 152
  destruction 162

death 360
judgment 480
necessity 601
sentence 971
- sealed
death 360
adversity 735
doomed 735, 828
doomsday
  end 67
  future 121
till - 112
door *entrance* 66
  cover 223
  brink 231
  barrier 232
  opening 260
  passage 627
at one's - 197
beg from door to -
  765
bolt the - 666
close the - upon
  751
death's - 360
keep within -s 265
lie at one's - 926
lock the - 666
open a - to
  liable 177
open the - to
  receive 296
  facilitate 705
  permit 760
show the - to
  eject 297
  discourtesy 895
  - *mat* 652
doorkeeper 263
doorway 260
dope 376, 545, 663
doquet
  security 771
Dorado, El - 803
Doric mode 413
dormant
  inert 172
  latent 526
  asleep 683
dormer 260
dormeuse 272
dormir debout,
  conte à - 843
dormitive 841
dormitory 191
dormouse 683
dorp 189
dorsal 235
dorser 191
dorsum 235, 250
dory 273
dose *quantity* 25
  part 51
  medicine 662
  apportion 786
dosser 191
dossier *bundle* 72
  record 551
dossil 223, 263
dot *small* 32
  place 182
  little 193
  variegate 440
  mark 550
  dowry 780
on the - 113
dotage 128, 499
dotard 130, 501

dotation 784
dottle 40, 645
dote *drivel* 499, 503
  - *upon* 897
douanier 965
double
  similar 17
  increase 35
  duplex 90
  substitute 147
  fold 258
  turn 283
  finesse 702
march at the - 274
see -
  dim sight 443
  drunk 959
- acrostic
  letters 561
  wit 842
- dutch 518
- entry 811
- the fist 909
- march 684
- meaning 520
- a point 311
in - quick time
  274
- reef topsails 664
- sure 474
work - tides 686
- up
  render powerless
  158
double bar 747
double-bass 417
double-cross 545
double-dealing
  lie 544
  cunning 940
double-distilled 171
double-dyed 428
double-eagle 800
double-edged 90,
  171
double entendre
  ambiguity 520
  impure 961
double-faced
  lie 544
  cunning 702, 940
double-headed 90
double-minded 605
double-shotted 171
doublet 225
double-tongued
  lie 544
  cunning 702, 940
doubt
  uncertain 475
  disbelieve **485**
  sceptic 989
doubtful 475
  more than - 473
  - *meaning*
  unintelligible 519
doubtless
  certain 474
  belief 484
  assent 488
douceur 784, 973
douche 337
dough 324, 354, 800
doughty 861
dour 739
douse
  immerse 310
  splash 337

blow 972
Dove
  Holy Ghost 976
dove
  innocent 946
  roar like sucking -
  174
dovecote 189
dovetail
  agree 23
  join 43
  intersect 219
  intervene 228
  angle 244
  insert 300
dowager 374, 905
dowdy 653, 851
dower 780, 803, 810
dowerless 804
down
  below 207
  light 320
bear - upon 716
bed of -
  pleasure 377
  repose 687
come - 306
get - 306
go -
  sink 306
  calm 826
keep - 36
money - 807
take -
  lower 308
  rebuff 874
  humble 879
- on one's mar-
  row-bones 886
- in the mouth 837
- and out 874
- in price 815
go - like a stone
  310
be - upon
  attack 716
  severe 739
downcast 306, 837
  - *eyes* 879
downfall
  destruction 162
  fall 306
  failure 732
  misfortune 735
downhill 217, 306
go -
  adversity 735
downpour 348
downright
  absolute 31
  manifest 525
  sincere 703
dowis 206, 344
down-trodden
  submission 725
  vanquished 732
  subject 749
  dejected 837
  disrepute 874
  contempt 930
downwards 306
downy
  smooth 255
  plumose 256
  soft 324
dowry 780, 784
dowse 276
dowser 994

doxology 990
doxy 897
doyer 128
doyley 652
doze 683
dozen 98
drab *color* 432
  slut 653
  hussy 962
drabble 653
drachm 319
Draco 694, 739
draff 653
draft [see also
  draught]
  multitude 102
  drawing 554, 556
  write 590
  abstract 596
  plan 626
  cheque 800
  credit 805
  - *off displace* 185
  transfer 270
draft-horse 271
drag *carriage* 272
  crawl 275
  traction 285
  impediment 706
put on the - 275
  - a chain
  tedious 109, 110
  exertion 686
  subjection 749
  - into
  implicate 54
  compel 744
  - through mire
  disrepute 874
  disrespect 929
  - on *tedious* 110
  - into open day
  531
  - towards
  attract 288
  - slow length
  long 200
  weary 841
draggle 285, 653
  - *tail* 59
drag-net
  all sorts 78
dragoman 524
dragon *monster* 83
  violent 173
  animal 366
  irascible 901
dragonnade
  attack 716
  punish 972
dragoon
  soldier 726
  compel 744
  insolent 885
  worry 907
drain
  flow out 295
  empty 297
  dry 340
  conduit 350
  waste 638
  clean 652
  unclean 653
  exhaust 789
  dissipate 818
  - the cup
  drink 298
  drunken 959

dynamitard 863
dynamite 727
dynamo 153
dynasty 737
dysentery 299
dyspepsia 655
dysphony 581

E

each 79
– to each 786
– other 12
– in his turn 148
eager
willing 602
active 682
ardent 821
desirous 865
– expectation 507
eagle
standard 550
money 800
– boat 726
– eye *sight* 441
intelligence 498
– winged *swift* 274
insignia 747
eagre 348
ean 161
ear 418
corn 154
come to one's –s 527
din in the –
loud 404
drum 407
all – 418
have the – of
belief 484
friendship 888
lend an –
hear 418
attend 457
meet the – 418
nice – 418
no – 419
offend the – 410
pick up the –s
attention 457
expectation 507
put about one's –s 308
quick – 418
reach one's –s 527
ring in the – 408
set by the –s
discord 713
hate 898
resentment 900
split the –s 404
together by the –s
discord 713
contention 720
up to one's –s
redundance 641
active 680, 682
willing – 602
word in the – 586
– for music 416, 418
in at one – out at the other
inattention 458
forget 506
not for –s polite 961

make the –s tingle
anger 900
– ache 378
ear-drum 418
earl 875
earless 419
earliness **132**
early 132
get up – 682
earmark 550
earn 775
earnest *willing* 602
determined 604
emphatic 642
pledge 771
pay in advance 809
eager 821
in –
affirmation 535
veracious 543
strenuous 682
ear-piercing 410
ear-ring 847
ear-shot 197
'out of – 405
ear-splitting 404
earth *ground* 211
world 318
land 342
corpse 362
what on –
inquiry 461
wonder 870
– closet 653
earthenware
baked 384
sculpture 557
earthling 372
earthly 318
end of one's –
career 360
of no – use 645
earthly-minded 943, 989
earthquake 146, 173
earthwork 717
earwig *flatter* 933, 935
ear-witness 467
ease *bodily* 377
style 578
leisure 685
facility 705
mental 827
content 831
at one's –
prosperous 734
mind at –
cheerful 836
set at – *relief* 834
take one's – 687
– off *deviate* 297
– one of *take* 789
easel *support* 215
painting 556
– picture 556
easement
property 780
relief 834
easily
[*see* easy]
let one down – 918
– accomplished 705
– deceived 486
– persuaded 602

East 236, 278
Easter *period* 138
rite 998
– Monday *holiday* 840
– offering *gift* 784
– sepulcher 1000
easy *gentle* 275
style 578
facile 705
make oneself –
about 484
take it –
inactive 683
inexcitable 826
– ascent 217
– of belief 472
– chair *support* 215
repose 687
– circumstances 803
– going *willing* 602
irresolute 605
lenient 740
inexcitable 826
contented 831
indifferent 866
– sail *moderate* 174
slow 275
– temper 894
– terms 705
– to understand 518
– virtue 961
eat *food* 298
tolerate 826
– dirt 725, 879
– one's fill *enough* 639
gorge 957
– heartily 298
– one's words 879
– out of house and home *take* 789
prodigal 818
gluttony 957
– of the same trencher 892
– one's words 607
eatables 298
eaten up with 820
eau, battre l' – 645
faire venir l' – à la bouche 865
mettre de l' – dans son vin 174
eaves 250
eavesdropper 455, 527
eavesdropping 418, 532
ébauche 626
ebb *decrease* 36
contract 195
regress 283
recede 287
waste 638
spoil 659
low – 36
low 207
depression 308
insufficient 640
– and flow 314
– of life 360

ebb-tide *low* 207
dry 340
ebony 431
ebriety 959
ebullient
violent 173
hot 382
excited 824
ebullition
energy 171
violence 173
agitation 315
heating 384
excitation 825
anger 900
écarté 840
ecce
– iterum Crispinus 104
– signum 550
eccentric 220
irregular 83
foolish 499
crazed 503, 504
capricious 608
ecchymosis 299
ecclesiastic
church 995
clergy 996
ecclesiastical
canonical 985
– court 966
– law 963
ecclesiolatry 991
écervelé 458
échafaudage 673
échappée 840
échapper belle 671
échelon 279
echo *imitate* 19
copy 21
repeat 104
reflection 277
resonance 408
answer 462
assent 488
applaud to the – 931
awake –es 404
éclaircissement 522
éclat 873
eclectic 609
eclipse *surpass* 33
disappearance 449
hide 528
outshine 873, 874
partial – *dim* 422
total – *dark* 421
under an –
invisible 447
out of repute 874
ecliptic 318
eclogue 597
economic pressure 751
economy
order 58
conduct 692
frugality **817**
animal – 359
écorcher les oreilles 410
ecphorize 615
écru 433
ecstasis 683
ecstasy
frenzy 515

transport 821
rapture 827
ecstatic 829
ecstatica 994
ectoplasm 992
ectype 21
ecumenical 78
edacity 957
Edda 986
eddy
whirlpool 348
current 312
danger 667
edematous 194, 324
Eden 827
edge *energy* 171
height 206
brink **231**
sidle 279
advantage 731
cutting – 253
on – 256, 507
take the – off 174
– of hunger 865
– in 228
– one's way 282
edge-tools 253
play with – 863
edgewise 217
edging
obliquity 217
border 231
ornament 847
edible 298
edict 741
edification
building 161
teaching 537
learning 539
piety 987
edifice 161
edifying *good* 648
edile 965
edit
publication 531
condense 596
revise 658
edition, new – 658
editor 593
educate 537
educated 490
self – 490
education
teaching 537
knowledge 490
man of – 492
higher – 490
educational 537, 542
educe *extract* 301
discover 480a
educt 40
eduction 40a
edulcorate 396, 652
eel 248
wriggle like an – 315
eerie 860
efface
delete 162
disappear 449
obliterate 552
– from the memory 506
effect
consequence **154**
product 161
impression 375

complete 729
carry into – 692
with crushing –
  162
in – 5
take – 731
to that – 516
effective
  capable 157
  useful 644
effectuation 729
expedient 646
effects 780, 798
effectual 731
effectually 52
effectuate 729
effeminate
  weak 160
  womenlike 374
  timorous 862
  sensual 954
effeminize 158
effendi 875
effervesce
  energy 171
  violence 173
  agitate 315
  bubble 353
  excited 825
effervescent 338
effete *old* 128
  weak 160
  useless 645
  spoiled 659
efficacious
  [*see* efficient]
efficient
  power 157
  agency 170
  utility 644
  skill 698
effigy 21, 554
effleurer *skim* 267,
  460
efflorescence 330
effluxion of time
  109
effluence *egress* 295
  flow 348
effluvium 334, 398
efflux 295
efformation 240
effort 686
effreet 980
effrontery 885
effulgence 420
effuse
  pour out 295, 297
  excrete 299
  speech 582
  loquacity 584
effusion of blood
  361
effusive 573
eft 366
eftsoons 117
egad 535
égards 928
egesta 299
egestion 297
egg *beginning* 66
  cause 153
  food 298
walk among –s
  704
too many –s in
  one basket
  unskilful 699

(*imprudent* 863)
– and dart
  ornament 847
– on 615
egg-shaped 247,
  249
ego *intrinsic* 5
  speciality 79
  immaterial 317
  non – 6
egocentrism 943
egotism
  vanity 880
  cynicism 911
  selfishness 943
egregious
  exceptional 83
  absurd 497
  exaggerated 549
  important 642
egregiously 31, 33
egress **295**
Egyptian darkness
  421
eheu! *fugaces*
  labuntur anni
  111
eiderdown 223
eidouranion 318
Eiffel tower 206
eight *number* 98
  boat 273
  representative 759
eisteddfod 72, 416
eighty 98
either *choice* 609
  happy with – 605
ejaculate
  propel 284
  utter 580
ejection 185, **297**
ejecta 299
ejector 349
eke *also* 37
  – out *complete* 52
  spin out 110
ekka 272
El Dorado 803
elaborate
  improve 658
  prepare 673
  laborious 686
  work out 729
elaine 356
élan 276
elapse 109, 122
elastic fluid 334
elasticity
  power 157
  strength 159
  energy 171
  spring **325**
elate *cheer* 836
  rejoice 838
  hope 858
  vain 880
  boast 884
elbow *angle* 244
  projection 250
  push 276
  at one's –
  near 197
  advice 695
lift one's –
  drink 959
out at –s
  undress 226
  poor 804

disrepute 874
– one's way
  progress 282
  pursuit 622
  active 682
elbow-chair 215
elbow-grease 331
elbow-room 180,
  748
elder *older* 124
  aged 128
  veteran 130
  clergy 996
elect *choose* 609
  good 648
  predestinate 976
  pious 987
  clergy 996
election
  numerical 84
  necessity 601
electioneering 609
elector 745
electorate 737
Electra complex
  897
electric
  swift 274
  sensation 821
  excitable 825
  car 272
  – blue 438
  – chair 974
  – light 423
  – piano 417
electrician 599, 690
electricity 157, 388
electrify
  unexpected 508
  excite 824
  astonish 870
electro-biology 992
electrocution 972
electrolier 214, 423
electrolyze 49
electro-magnetism
  157
electromobile 272
electron 32
electronics 157
electroplate 223
electrotype 21, 591
electuary 662
eleemosynary 784
elegance
  in style 578
  beauty 845
  taste 859
  Bank of – 800
elegy *interment* 363
  poetry 597
  lament 839
element
  component 56
  beginning 66
  cause 153
  matter 316
  in one's –
  facility 705
  content 831
  devouring – 382
  out of its – 195
elementary 42
  – education 537
  – school 542
elements
  Eucharist 998
elench 477

elephant
  large 192
  carrier 271
  white – *bane* 663
elevated
  tipsy 959
elevation
  height 206
  vertical 212
  raising **307**
  plan 554
  – of style 574
  improvement 658
  glory 873
  – of mind 942
  angular – 244
élève 541
eleven 98
  representative 759
eleventh hour
  evening 126
  late 133
  opportune 134
elf *infant* 129
  little 193
  imp 980
elicit *cause* 153
  draw out 301
  discover 480a
  manifest 525
eligible 646
Elijah's mantle 63
eliminant 299
eliminate
  subduct 38
  simplify 42
  exclude 55
  weed 103
  extract 301
  reject 610
elision 44, 201
élite *best* 648
  distinguished 873
  aristocratic 875
elixation 384
elixir 662
  – of life 471
elk 223
ell 200
  take an –
  take 789
  insolence 885
  wrong 923
  undue 925
  selfish 943
ellipse 247
ellipsis *shorten* 201
  style 572
ellipsoid 247, 249
elocation 185, 270
elocution 582
éloge 931
elongation 196, 200
elopement 623, 671
eloquence 572, 582
else 37
elsewhere 187
elucidate 522
elude
  sophistry 477
  avoid 623
  escape 671
  succeed 731
  palter 773
elusive 545
elusory 546
elutriate 652
elysian 829, 981

Elysium 827, 981
elytron 223
Elzevir edition 193
emaciation 195,
  203, 640
emanate 151
  go out of 295
  excrete 299
  – from 544
emanation 398
emancipate
  facilitate 705
  free 748, 750
emasculate
  impotent 158
embalm
  interment 363
  perfume 400
  preserve 670
  – in the memory
  505
embankment
  esplanade 189
  refuge 666
  fence 717
embar 229
embargo
  stoppage 265
  prohibition 761
  exclusion 893
embark
  transfer 270
  depart 293
  – in *begin* 66
  engage in 676
embarquer sans
  biscuits, s' – 674
embarras de
  – *choix* 609
embarrass 641,
  704, 706
embarrassed 804,
  806
embarrassing 475
embase 659
embassy
  errand 532
  commission 755
  consignee 758
embattled
  arranged 60
  leagued 712
  war array 722
embed
  locate 184
  base 215
  enclose 221
  insert 300
embellish 847
embers 384
embezzle 791
embitter
  deteriorate 659
  aggravate 835
  acerbate 900
emblazon
  color 428
  ornament 847
  display 882
emblem 550, 747
embody
  join 43
  combine 48
  form a whole 50
  compose 54
embolden
  hope 858
  encourage 861

embolism 228, 261, 300
embonpoint 192
embosomed
  lodged 184
  interjacent 228
  circumscribed 229
emboss *convex* 250
  ornament 847
embouchure 260
embowel 297
embrace
  cohere 46
  compose 54
  include 76
  enclose 227
  choose 609
  take 789
  friendship 888
  sociality 892
  courtesy 894
  endearment 902
  – an offer 760
embrangle 61
embranglement 713
embrasure 257, 260
embrocation 662
embroider
  variegate 440
  lie 544
  ornament 847
embroidery
  adjunct 39
  exaggeration 549
embroil *derange* 61
  discord 713
embroilment 59
embrown 433
embryo
  beginning 66
  cause 153
  in – *destined* 152
  preparing 673
embryology 357
embryonic 193, 674
embus 293
embusqué 603
emendation 658
emerald *green* 435
  jewel 847
emerge 295, 446
emergency
  circumstance 8
  event 151
  difficulty 704
emeritus 500, 928
emersion 295, 446
emery
  sharpener 253
  – paper
  smooth 255
emetic *remedy* 662
émeute 742
emication 420
emigrant 57, 268
emigrate 266, 295
emigré 268, 295
eminence
  height 206
  fame 873
  church dignitary 996
eminent domain 744
eminently 33
emir 745, 875
emissary
  messenger 534

consignee 758
emission 297
emit *eject* 297
  publish 531
  voice 580
  – vapour 336
Emmanuel 976
emmet 193
emollient 662
emolument
  acquisition 775
  receipt 810
  remuneration 973
emotion 821
  –al appeal 824
  –al drama 599
empale 260, 972
empanel 86, 969
empathy 515
emperor 745
emphasis 580
emphatic 535, 642
emphatically 31
empierce
  perforate 260
  insert 300
empire 737, 789
  – day 840
empiric 548
empirical 463, 675
empiricism 463
emplane 293
employ
  business 625
  use 677
  servitude 749
  commission 755
  in one's – 746
  – one's capital in 794
  – oneself 680
  – one's time in 625
employé
  servant 746
  agent 758
employer 795
empoison 659
emporium 799
empower
  power 157
  commission 755
  accredit 759
  permit 760
empress 745
empressement
  activity 682
  emotion 821
  desire 865
emprise 676
emption 795
emptor 795
  caveat – 769
empty *clear* 185
  vacant 187
  deflate 195
  drain 297
  ignorant 491
  waste 638
  deficient 640
  useless 645
  beggarly account of – boxes
  poverty 804
  – one's glass 298
  – purse 804
  – sound 517
  – stomach 865

– *title name* 564
  undue 925
  – words 546
empty-handed 640
empty-headed·4, 491
empurple 437
empyrean *sky* 318
  blissful 829
empyreuma 41
empyrosis 384
emulate *imitate* 19
  goodness 648
  rival 708
  compete 720
  glory 873
emulsion 352
emunctory 350
en – bloc 50
  – masse 50
  – passant
  parenthetical 10
  transient 111
  à propos 134
  – rapport 9
  – règle *order* 58
  conformity 82
  – route
  journey 266
  progress 282
enable 157
enact *drama* 599
  action 680
  conduct 692
  complete 729
  order 741
  law 963
enallage 521
enamel *coating* 223
  painting 556
  ornament 847
enameller 559
enamor 897
encage 751
encamp 184, 189
encampment 184
encaustic 556
enceinte
  with child 161
  region 181
  inclosure 232
enchafe 830
enchain 751
enchant *please* 829
enchanted 827
enchanting 845, 897
enchantment
  sorcery 992
enchase 43, 259
enchiridion 593
enchorial 188
encincture 229
encircle 76, 227, 311
enclave *close* 181
  boundary 233
enclose 227, 229
enclosure
  region 181
  envelope 232
  fence 752
encomiast 935
encomium 931
encompass 227, 233
  –ed with difficulties 704
encore 104, 931

encounter
  undergo 151
  clash 276
  meet 292
  withstand 708
  contest 720
  – danger 665
  – risk 621
encourage
  animate 615
  aid 707
  comfort 834
  hope 858
  embolden 861
encroach
  transcursion 303
  do wrong 923
  infringe 925
encumber 704, 706
encumbrance
  clear of – 807
encyclical 531
encyclopedia 490, 593
  walking – 700
encyclopedical
  general 78
  – *knowledge* 490
encysted 229
end
  termination 67
  effect 154
  object 620
  at an – 142
  come to its – 729
  one's journey's – 292
  on – 212
  put an – to
  destroy 162
  kill 361
  begin at the wrong – 699
  – one's days 360
  –s of the earth 196
  – to end *space* 180
  touching 199
  – of life 360
  – in smoke 732
  – of one's tether
  sophistry 477
  ignorant 491
  insufficient 640
  difficult 704
endamage 649
endanger 665
endear 897
endearment 902
endeavor
  pursue 622
  attempt 675
  use one's best – 686
  – after 620
endemic
  special 79
  interior 221
  disease 657
endimanché 847, 882
endless
  multitudinous 102
  infinite 105
  perpetual 112
endlessly 16
endlong 200

endocrine 221
endogenous 367
endorse
  evidence 467
  assent 488
  compact 769
  - a bill 800
  approve 931
endorsement 550
endosmose 302
endow
  confer power 157
  endowed with
  possessed of 777
endowment
  intrinsic 5
  power 157
  talent 698
  gift 784
endrogynous 83
endue 157
endure *time* 106
  last 110
  persist 143
  continue 141
  undergo 151
  feel 821
  submit to 826
  unable to – 867
  – for ever 112
  – pain 828
enduring
  indelible 505
endwise 212
enemy *time* 841
  foe 891
  the common – 978
  thing devised by the – 546
  – to society 891
energumen 504
energy *power* 157
  strength 159
  physical 171
  resolution 604
  activity 682
enervate 158, 160
enfant, bon – 906
  – gâté
  prosperity 734
  satiety 869
  favorite 899
  – perdu
  hopeless 859
  reckless 863
  – terrible
  curiosity 455
  artless 703
  object of fear 860
enfeeble 160
enfeoff 780, 783
Enfield rifle 727
enfilade
  lengthwise 200
  pierce 260
  pass through 302
enfold 229
enforce *urge* 615
  advise 695
  compel 744
  require 924
enfranchise
  free 748
  liberate 750
  permit 760
enfranchised 924
engage
  bespeak 132

induce 615
undertake 676
do battle 722
commission 755
promise 768
compact 769
I'll –
  affirmation 535
  – the attention
  457
  – with 720
engaged
  marriage 903
  be – 135
  – in *attention* 457
engagement
  business 625
  battle 720
  betrothal 902
engaging
  pleasing 829
  amiable 897
engender 161
engine 153, 633
engine–driver 268
engineer 690, 694,
  726
engineering 633
engird 227
English 188
  broken – 563
  king's – 560
  murder the king's
  – 568
  plain –
    intelligible 518
    interpreted 522
    style 576
    – horn 417
engorge
  swallow 296
  gluttony 957
engorgement
  too much 641
engrail 256
engrave
  furrow 259
  mark 550
  – in the memory
  505
engraver 559
engraving 21, 22,
  558
engross *write* 590
  possess 777
  – the thoughts
    thought 451
    attention 457
engrossed in
  thought 451
engulf
  destroy 162
  plunge 310
  swallow up 296
enhance
  increase 35
  improve 658
enharmonic 413
enigma
  question 461
  secret 533
enigmatic
  uncertain 475
  unintelligible 517
  obscure 519
enigme, mot d' –
  522
enjoin *advise* 695

command 741
prescribe 926
enjoy
  physically 377
  possess 777
  morally 827
  – health 654
  – popularity 873
  – a state 7
enkindle *heat* 384
  excite 824
enlarge
  increase 35
  swell 194
  in writing 573
  liberate 750
  – the mind 537
enlarged views 498
enlighten
  illumine 420
  inform 527
  teach 537
enlightened
  knowledge 490
enlist *engage* 615
  war 722
  commission 755
  under the ban-
  ners of 707
  – into the service
  677
enliven
  delight 829
  cheer 836
  amuse 840
enmity **889**
ennoble 873
ennui 841
enormity
  crime 947
enormous *great* 31
  big 192
  – number 102
enough *much* 31
  no more! 142
  sufficient 639
  moderately 651
  satiety 869
  know when one
    has had – 953
  – in all conscience
  641
  – to drive one
    mad 830
  – and to spare 639
enounce 535, 580
enrage 830, 900
enragé 865
enrapture
  excite 824
  beatify 829
  love 897
enraptured 827
enravish 829
enravished 827
enravishment 824
enrich
  improve 658
  wealth 803
  ornament 847
enrobe 225
enroll *list* 86
  record 551
  – troops 722
  commission 755
ens *essence* 1
Ens Entium 976
ensample 22

ensanguined 361
ensconce
  conceal 528
  safety 664
ensconced
  located 184
ensemble 50
enshrine
  circumscribe 229
  repute 873
  sanctify 987
  – in the memory
  505
ensiform 253
ensign
  standard 550
  officer 726
  master 745
  – of authority 747
ensilage 637
enslave 749
ensnare 545
ensue *follow* 63, 117
  happen 151
ensure 474
entablature 210
entail *cause* 153
  tie up property
  781
entangle
  interlink 43
  derange 61
  ravel 219
  entrap 545
  embroil 713
entangled
  disorder 59
  – by difficulties
  704
entend, cela s' – 613
entente
  agreement 23
  alliance 714
  friendship 888
enter *go in* 294
  appear 446
  note 551
  accounts 811
  – into the compo-
    sition of 56
  – into details
    special 79
    describe 594
  – into an engage-
    ment 768
  – into the feelings
    of 914
  – into the ideas of
    understand 518
    concord 714
  – in *converge* 290
  – the lists
    attack 716
    contention 720
  – the mind 451
  – a profession 625
  – into the spirit of
    feel 821
    delight 827
  – upon 66
  – into one's views
    488
enterprise
  pursuit 622
  undertaking 676
  commercial – 794
enterprising
  active 171, 682

courageous 861
entertain
  bear in mind 457
  support 707
  amuse 840
  sociality 892
  – doubts 485
  – feeling 821
  – an idea 451
  – an opinion 484
entertainment 840
  pleasure 377
  repast 298
entêté 481, 606
enthral
  subjection 749
  restraint 751
enthrone 873
enthronement 755
enthusiasm
  language 574
  willingness 602
  feeling 821
  hope 858
  love 897
enthusiast
  madman 504
  obstinate 606
  active 682
enthusiastic
  imaginative 515
  sensitive 822
  excitable 825
  sanguine 858
enthymeme 476
entice 615
enticing 829
entire *whole* 50
  complete 52
  continuous 69
  – horse 373
entirely *much* 31
entitle *name* 564
  give a right 924
entity 1
entoil 545
entomb *inter* 363
  imprison 751
Entomology 368
entourage 88, 183,
  227
entozoon 193
entrails 221
entrammel 751
entrance
  beginning 66
  ingress 294
  way 627
  enrapture 827,
  829
  magic 992
  give – to 296
entranced 515
entrancement 824
entrap 545
entrain 293
entre nous 528
entreat 765
entrée
  reception 296
  dish 298
  give the – 296
  have the – 294
  – dish 191
entremet 298
entrepôt 636, 799
entrepreneur 599
entre-sol 191

entrust
  commission 755
  give 784
  credit 805
entry *beginning* 66
  ingress 294
  record 551
entwine *join* 43
  intersect 219
  convolve 248
enucleate 522
enumerate 85
  – among 76
enumeration 86
enunciate
  inform 527
  affirm 535
  voice 580
envelop 225
envelope 223, 232
envenom
  deprave 659
  exasperate 835
  hate 898
  anger 900
envenomed
  bad 649
  insalubrious 657
  painful 830
  malevolent 907
  – tongue 934
environ 227
environment 183
environs 197
  in such and such –
  183
envisage 515, 861
envoy
  messenger 534
  consignee 758
envy **921**
enwrap 225
enzyme 320
Eolian harp 417
Eolus 349
eon 976
épanchement
  manifest 525
  artless 703
  endearment 902
epact 641
épaulette
  badge 550, 747
  ornament 847
  decoration 877
éperdu 824
épergne 191
ephemeral 111
ephemeris
  calendar 114
  record 551
  book 593
Ephesian letters
  993
ephialtes
  physical pain 378
  hindrance 706
  mental pain 828
ephod 999
ephor 967
epic 594, 597
epicedium 839
epicene 81, 83
épicier 876
epicure
  fastidious 868
  sybarite 954a
  glutton 957

epicurean 954
Epicurus, system
of - 954
epicy-cle, -cloid
247
epidemic
general 78
disease 655
insalubrity 657
epidermis 223
epigenesis 161
epigram 496, 842
epigrammatic 572
epigrammatist 844
epigraph 550
epilepsy 315, 655
epilogue
sequel 65
end 67
drama 599
èpingles, tiré à
quatre - 855
Epiphany 998
episcopal 995
Episcopalian 984
episcopate 995
episode
adjunct 39
discontinuity 70
interjacence 228
episodic
irrelative 10
style 573
epistle 592
Epistles 985
epistrophe 104
epistyle 210
epitaph 363
epithalamium 903
epithem 662
epithet 564
epitome
miniature 193
short 201
concise 572
epizoötic 657
epoch *time* 106
instant 113
date 114
present time 118
epode 597
eponym 564
epopoea 597
epos 594
epulation 298
epulotic 662
epuration 652
equable 16, 922
equal *even* 27
equitable 922
- chance 156
- times 120
- to *power* 157
equality 13, **27**
equalize 213
equanimity 826
equate 27, 30
equations 85
equator 68, 318
equatorial 68, 236
equerry 746
equestrian 268
equibalanced 27
equidistant 68
equilibration 27
equilibrist 599
equilibrium 27
equine *carrier* 271

horse 366
equinox 125, 126
equip 225, 673
equipage
vehicle 272
instruments 633
display 882
equiparent 27
equipment 633
equipoise &c. 27, 30
equiponderate 30
equitable *wise* 498
just 922
due 924
honorable 939
- interest 780
equitation 266
equity *right* 922
honor 939
law 963
in - 922
- draftsman 968
equivalent
identical 13
equal 27
compensation 30
substitute 147
translation 522
equivocalness
dubious 475
double meaning
520
impure 961
equivocate
sophistry 477
palter 520
lie 544
equivocation
[*see* equivocate]
without - 543
équivoque
double meaning
520
impure 961
era *time* 106, 108
date 114
eradicate
destroy 162
extract 301
erase *destroy* 162
obliterate 331, 552
Erastian 984
erasure 552
Erato 416
ere 116
- long 132
- now 116
past 122
Erebus *dark* 421
hell 982
erect *build* 161
vertical 212
raise 307
with head - 878
- the scaffolding
673
erewhile 116, 122
ergatocracy 737
ergo 476
ergotism 480
ergotize 485
eriometer 445
Erinys 900
Erl King 980
ermine
badge of authority
747
ornament 847

erode 36, 659
Eros 897, 979
erosion 36
erotic 897, 961
err - *in opinion* 495
- *morally* 945
errand
message 532
business 625
commission 755
errand-boy 534
errant 279
erratic
irregular 139
changeable 149
wandering 279
capricious 608
erratum 495
erroneous 495
error *fallacy* **495**
vice 945
guilt 947
court of - 966
writ of - 969
ersatz 973
erst 122
erubescence 434
erubuit salva res
est 95
eruct 297
eructate 297
erudition 490, 539
eruption
upheaval 146
violence 173
egress 295, 297
disease 655
volcanic - 872
escadrille 726
escalade
mounting 305
attack 716
escalator 307
escalop 248
escapade
absurdity 497
freak 608
prank 840
escape
flight **671**
liberate 750
evade 927
means of - 664,
666
- the lips
disclosure 529
speech 582
- the memory 506
- notice &c.
invisible 447
inattention 458
latent 526
escarp 717
escarpment
stratum 204
height 206
oblique 217
escharotic
caustic 171
pungent 392
eschatology 67
escheat 144, 974
eschew
avoid 623
dislike 867
esclandre 828, 830
escort
accompany 88

safeguard 664
keeper 753
escritoire 191
esculent 298
escutcheon 550
esophagus 260
esoteric
private 79
concealed 528
Espagne, château
en - *fancy* 515
espalier 232
especial 79
especially 33
espial 441
espiéglerie
cunning 702
fun 840
wit 842
espionnage 441,
461
esplanade
houses 189
flat 213
espouse
choose 609
marriage 903
- a cause *aid* 707
co-operate 709
esprit
shrewdness 498
wit 842
bel - 844
- de corps
bias 481
co-operation 709
sociality 892
(*party* 712)
espy 441
esquire 875, 877
essay
experiment 463
dissertation 595
endeavor **675**
essayist 593, 595
esse 1
essence
nature 5
scent 398
essential
intrinsic 5
great 31
required 630
important 642
essentially
intrinsically 5
substantially 3
essential stuff 5
establish
settle 150
create 161
place 184
evidence 467
demonstrate 478
- equilibrium 27
established
permanent 141
habit 613
- church 983a
establishment
party 712
shop 799
estafete 534
estaminet 189

estate *condition* 7
property 780
come to man's -
131
esteem
believe 484
repute 873
approve 931
in high - 928
estimable 648
estimate
measure 466
adjudge 480
information 527
- too highly 482
estimation
[*see* esteem,
estimate]
estime
succès d' - 873
estival 382
esto perpetua!
perpetuity 112
permanence 141
desire 865
estop 706
estrade 213
estrange
alienate 44, 889
discord 713
hate 898
estranged
secluded 893
estrapade
attack 716
punishment 972
estreat 974
estuary 343
estuation 384
esurient 865
et - cetera
add 37
include 76
plural 100
- hoc genus omne
similar 17
include 76
multiform 81
étalage 882
état major 745
etch *furrow* 259
engraving 558
eternal 112
- home 981
Eternal, the - 976
eterne 112
eternify 112
eternity 112
an - 110
launch into - 360,
361
ether
lightness 320
rarity 322
vapor 334
anesthetic 376
ethereal 4
ethicism 984
ethics 926
Ethiopian 431
-'s skin 150
Ethiopian's skin
unchangeable 150
ethnology 372
ethnic 984
ethology 926
ethos 5
etiolate 429, 430

expose]
appearance 448
– to weather 338
expound
interpret 522
teach 537
expounder 524
express
rapid 274
squeeze out 301
mean 516
declare 525
inform 527
journal 531
intentional 620
by – *haste* 684
– *train* 272
– by words 566
expressed, well –
578
expressible 525
expression [*see*
express]
musical 416
aspect 448
nomenclature 564
phrase 566
mode of – 569
new fangled – 563
expressive
meaning 516
sensibility 822
exprobation 932,
938
expropriation 782
expugnable 665
expugnation 731
expulsion 55 [*see*
expel]
expunge 162, 552
expurgate 38, 652
expurgatorious,
index – 761
exquisite
savory 394
excellent 648
pleasurable 829
beautiful 845
fop 854
exquisitely 31
exsiccate 340
exsudation 299
exsufflation 993
exsuscitate 824
extant 1
extasy [*see* ecstasy]
extemporaneous
[*see* extempore]
transient 111
extempore
instant 113
early 132
occasion 134
off-hand 612
unprepared 674
extend
expand 194
prolong 200
– to 196
extended 202
extensibility 324
extensile 324
extension [*see*
extend] 35, 142,
180
– of time 110
extensive 31, 180
– knowledge 490

extenso, in –
whole 50
diffuse 573
extent 26, 180
extenuate
decrease 36
weaken 160
excuse 937
extenuated 203
extenuating cir-
cumstances
469, 937
extenuatory 469
exteriority 220
exterminate 162
extermination 301
external 57, 220
– evidence 467
– senses 375
extinct
inexistent 2
past 122
destroyed 162
darkness 421
become – 4
extincteur 385
extinction of life
360
extinguish
destroy 162
blow out 385
darken 421
extinguisher 165
put an – upon
hinder 706
defeat 731
extirpate 301
extispicious 511
extol
over-estimate 482
praise 931
extort *extract* 301
compel 744
despoil 789
extorted
dissent 489
extortion 814, 819
extortionate 739,
865
extra 37, 599, 641
ab – 220
extract
draw off 297
take out 301
quotation 596
remedy 662
extraction 301
paternity 166
– of roots 85
extractor 301
extradition 270, 297
extrajudicial 964
extramundane 317
extramural 220
extraneous
extrinsic 6
not related 10
foreign 57
outside 220
extraneousness 57
extraordinary
great 31
exceptional 83
extraregarding 220
extravagant
inordinate 31
violent 173
absurd 497

foolish 499
fanciful 515
exaggerated 549
excessive 641
high-priced 814
prodigal 818
vulgar 851
ridiculous 853
extravagation 303
extravaganza
fanciful 515
drama 599
extravasate 295,
297
extreme
inordinate 31
end 67
– unction 998
extremis, in –
dying 360
difficulty 704
extremist 710
extremity *end* 67
adversity 735
tribulation 828
drive matters to
an – 604
at the last – 665
extricate
take out 301
deliver 672
facilitate 705
liberate 750
extrinsicality 6
extrinsic evidence
467
extrusion 297, 299
exuberant
– *style* 573
redundant 639
exudation 295, 299
exulcerate 659
exult 838, 884
exultant 858
exulting 836
exunge 356
exuviae 653
eye *circle* 247
opening 260
organ of sight 441
all my – and
Betty Martin
546
appear to one's
– 446
before one's –s
front 234
visible 446
manifest 525
cast the –s on
see 441
cast the –s over
attend to 457
catch the – 457
close the –s
blind 442
death 360
sleep 683
dry –s 823
fix the –s on 457
have an – to
attention 457
intention 620
desire 865
in one's –
visible 446
expectant 507
in the –s of

appearance 448
belief 484
keep an – upon
459
look with one's
own –s 459
make –'s at 441
mind's – 515
with moistened –s
839
open the –s to
480a
with open –s 870
set one's –s upon
865
shut one's –s to
inattention 458
permit 760
to the –s 448
under the –s of
186
up to one's –s
641
have one's –s
about one 459
– askance 860
–s draw straws 683
an – for an – 718,
919
– glistening 824
in the – of the law
963
– of the master
693
– of a needle 260
–s open
attention 457
care 459
intention 620
–s opened
disclosure 529
– s out 442
eye-ball 441
eyebrows 256
eyeglass 445
eyelashes 256
eyeless 442
eyelet 260
eyelid 223
eye-shade 443
eye-sight 441
eyesore 846, 848
eye-teeth
have cut one's –
adolescence 131
skill 698
cunning 702
eye-wash 544
eye-witness
spectator 444
evidence 467
eyot 346
eyre 966
eyry 189

F

Fabian policy
delay 133
inaction 681
caution 864
fable *error* 495
metaphor 521
fiction 546
description 590
fabric *state* 7
effect 154

texture 329
fabricate
composition 54
make 161
invent 515
falsify 544
fabrication *lie* 546
fabula narratur, de
te – *retaliate* 718
condemn 971
fabulist 594
fabulous
enormous 31
imaginary 515
untrue 546
exaggerated 549
faburden 413
façade 234
face *exterior* 220
covering 223
front 234
aspect 448
oppose 708
resist 719
brave 861
impudence 885
change the – of
146
fly in the – of
disobey 742
put a good – upon
sham 545
calm 826
cheerful 836
hope 858
pride 878
display 882
vindicate 93
in the – of
presence 186
opposite 708
look in the –
see 441
proud 878
make –s
distort 243
ugly 846
disrespect 929
on the – of
manifest 525
show –
present 186
visible 446
not show –
disreputable 874
bashful 879
to one's – 525
wry – 378
– about 279
set one's – against
708
– of the country
344
on the – of the
earth
space 180
world 318
– to face *front* 234
contraposition
237
manifest 525
– of the thing
appearance 448
facet 220
facetiae 842
facetious 842
facia 234
facile *willing* 602

irresolute 605
easy 705
facile princeps 33
facilis descensus
  Averni
sloping 217
danger 665
facilitate 705
facility skill 698
easy 705
facing covering 223
facinorous 945
façon de parler 521,
  549
fac-simile 21, 554
fact existence 1
event 151
certainty 474
truth 494
in – 535
faction 712, 713
factious 24
factitious 545, 546
factor
numerical 84
director 694
consignee 758
factory 691
factotum
agent 690
manager 694
employé 758
facts evidence 467
summary of – 594
at variance with –
  471
facula 420
faculties 450
in possession of
  one's – 502
faculty
power 157
profession 625
skill 698
facundity 582
fad 481, 608
faddle 683
fade vanish 4
transient 111
become old 124
droop 160
grow dim 422
lose color 429
disappear 449
spoil 659
– from the
  memory 506
fade 391
fadge 23
fæx populi 876
fag cigarette 392
labor 686
fatigue 688
drudge 690, 746
– end
remainder 40
end 67
faggot 72, 388
fagots et fagots 15,
  465
faïence 557
fail droop 160
shortcoming 304
be confuted 479
illness 655
not succeed 732

not observe 773
not pay 808
dereliction 927
failing [see fail]
incomplete 53
insufficient 640
vice 945
guilt 947
– heart 837
– luck 735
– memory 506
– sight 443
– strength 160
failure 732
heart – 360
fain willing 602
compulsive 744
wish 865
fainéant 683
faint
small in degree 32
impotent 158
weak 160
sound 405
dim 422
color 429
swoon 688
– heart fear 860
cowardice 862
damn with –
  praise 930, 932,
  934
faintness 405
fair in degree 31
pale 429
white 430
wise 498
important 643
good 648
moderate 651
mart 799
beautiful 845
just 922
honorable 939
– chance 472
– copy copy 21
writing 590
– field
occasion 134
– game 857
by – means 631,
  940
– name 873
– play 922, 923
– question 461
– sex 374
in a – way
tending 176
probable 472
convalescent 658
prosperous 734
hopeful 858
– weather 734
– weather sailor
  701
– wind 705
– words 894
fairing 784
fairly
intrinsically 5
get on – 736
– well 643
fair-spoken
courtesy 894
flattery 933
fairy fanciful 515
fay 979

imp 980
– godmother 711,
  784, 912
– tale 545, 594
fairy-land 515
fait: au –
knowledge 490
skilful 698
– accompli
certain 474
complete 729
faith belief 484
hope 858
honor 939
piety 987
declaration of –
  983
bad – 544
i' – 535
keep – with
observe 772
plight –
promise 768
love 902
true –
orthodox 983a
want of –
incredulity 487
irreligious 989
– healing 662
faithful [see faith]
like 17
copy 21
exact 494
obedient 743
– memory 505
– to 772
faithless false 544
dishonorable 940
sceptical 989
fake 544, 545
fakir 996
falcate 244, 245
falchion 727
falciform
[see falcate]
falcon 792
falconet 727
faldstool 215
fall autumn 126
happen 151
perish 162
slope 217
regression 283
descend 306
die 360
fail 732
adversity 73
vice 945
let – lower 308
inform 527
water– 348
– asleep 683
– astern 235, 283
– away 105
– back return 283
recede 287
relapse 661
– back upon 677,
  717
have to – back
  upon 637
– a cursing 908
– of the curtain 67
– into a custom 82
– of day 125
– dead 360

– into decay 659
– down 990
– down before 928
– upon the ear 418
– flat on the ear
  843
– at one's feet 725
– foul of blow 276
hinder 706
oppose 708
discord 713
attack 716
contention 720
censure 932
– for 897
– to the ground
be confuted 479
fail 732
– into a habit 613
– from one's high
  estate
adversity 735
disrepute 874
– in order 58
continuity 69
event 151
– into
conversion 144
river 348
– in with agree 23
conform 82
converge 2
discover 480a
concord 714
consent 762
– on one's knees
submit 725
servile 886
gratitude 916
worship 990
– of the leaf 126
– from the lips 582
– in love with 897
– to one's lot
event 151
chance 156
receive 785
duty 926
– under one's
  notice 457
– into oblivion 506
– off decrease 36
deteriorate 659
– off again 661
– out happen 151
quarrel 713
enmity 889
– into a passion
  900
– to pieces
disjunction 44
destruction 162
brittle 328
– a prey to 732,
  749
– in price 815
– into raptures
  827
– short inferior 32
contract 195
shortcoming 304
– of snow 383
– through fail 734
– to eat 298
take in hand 676
do battle 722
– into a trap 547

– under
inclusion 76
subjection 749
– upon
discover 480a
unexpected 508
devise 626
attack 716
– in the way of 186
– to work 686
fallacy sophistry
  477
error 495
show the – of 497
fallen angel 949,
  978
fallible 475, 477
falling-out 24
falling star 318, 423
fallow
unproductive 169
yellow 436
unready 674
inactive 681
false imitation 10
sophistry 477
error 495
untrue 544, 546
spurious 925
dishonorable 940
– alarm 669
– coloring
misinterpretation
  523
falsehood 544
– construction
  523, 544
– doctrine 984
– expectation 509
– hearted 940
– impression 495
– light vision 443
– money 800
– ornament 851
– plea untruth 546
plea 617
– position 704
– pretences 791
– prophet
disappoint 509
pseudo-revelation
  986
– reasoning 477
– scent 495, 538
– shame 855
– statement 546
– step 732
– teaching 538
– witness
deceiver 548
detraction 934
falsehood 544, 546
falsetto squeak 410
want of voice 581
falsify error 495
falsehood 544,
  546
– accounts 811
– one's hope 509
falter slow 275
stammer 583
hesitate 605
slip 732
hopeless 859
fear 860
faltering accents
  605

fame *greatness* 31
 news 532
 renown 873
familiar
 known 490
 habitual 613
 sociable 892
 affable 894
 – *spirit* 979, 980
 on – *terms* 888
familiarize
 teach 537
 habit 613
famille, en – 892
family
 kin 11
 class 75
 ancestors 166
 posterity 167
 party 712
 in the bosom of
  one's – 221
 happy – 714
 – *circle* 892
 – *jars* 713
 – *likeness* 17
 – *tie* 11
 in the – *way* 161
famine 640
 – *price* 814
famine-stricken
 640
famish
 stingy 819
 fasting 956
famished
 insufficient 640
 hungry 865
famous 873
famously 31
fan *blow* 349
 cool 385
 refresh 689
 stimulate 824
 flirt a – 855
 – the embers 505
 – the flame
 violence 173
 heat 384
 aid 707
 excite 824
 – into a flame
 anger 900
 –shaped 194
fanatic
 madman 504
 imaginative 515
 zealot 682
 religious – 988
fanatical
 misjudging 481
 insane 503
 emotional 821
 excitable 825
 heterodox 984
 over-righteous 988
fanaticism 606
fanciful
 imaginative 515
 capricious 608
 ridiculous 853
fancy *think* 451
 idea 453
 believe 484
 suppose 514
 imagine 515
 caprice 608

choice 609
 pugilism 726
 wit 842
 desire 865
 wonder 870
 love 897
 after one's – 850
 indulge one's –
  609
 take a – to
  delight in 827
 desire 865
 take one's –
  please 829
 – *dog* 366
 – *dress* 840
 – *price* 814
 – *woman* 962
fandango 840
fandi, mollia tem-
  pora – 588
fane 1000
fanfare *loudness*
  404
 celebration 883
fanfaron 887
fanfaronnade 884
fangs *venom* 663
 rule 737
 retention 781
fan-light 260
fan-like 202
fannel 999
fanon 999
fantasia 415
fantastic *odd* 83
 absurd 497
 imaginative 515
 capricious 608
 unfashionable 851
 ridiculous 853
fantasy
 imagination 515
 desire 865
fantoccini 554, 599
faquir 996
far – *away* 196
 – be it from
 unwilling 603
 deprecation 766
 – between
 disjunction 44
 few 103
 interval 198
 – from it
 unlike 18
 shortcoming 304
 no 536
 – from the truth
  546
 – and near 180
 – off 196
 – and wide 31,
  180, 196
farce
 absurdity 497
 untruth 546
 drama 599
 wit 842
 ridiculous 853
 mere –
 unimportant 643
 useless 645
farceur
 actor 599
 humorist 844
fardel

bundle 72
 hindrance 706
fare *state* 7
 food 298
 price 812
bill of –
 list 86
farewell
 departure 293
 relinquishment
  624
 loss 776
 – to greatness 874
far-famed 873
far-fetched 10
far-flung 73
far-gone
 much 31
 insane 503
 spoiled 654
farinaceous 330
farm *till* 371
 property 780
 rent 788
farmer 188, 342,
  371
 afternoon – 683
farm-house 189
Farmer-Labor 712
faro 840
farrago 59
farrier 370
farrow
 produce 161
 litter 167
 multitude 102
far-sighted 442, 510
farther 196
 [*and see further*]
farthing
 quarter 97
 worthless 643
 coin 800
 – *candle* 422
farthingale 225
fasces 747
fascia 205, 247
fascicule 51
fasciculated 72
fascinate
 influence 615
 excite 824
 please 829
 astonish 870
 love 897
 conjure 992
fascinated
 pleased 827
fascination [*see*
  fascinate]
 infatuation 825
 desire 870
fascine 72
Fascisti 712
fas et nefas, per –
  604a, 631
fash 830
fashion
 state 7
 form 240
 custom 613
 method 627
 ton 852
 after a –
 middling 32
 after this – 617
 follow the – 82

be in the – 488
 man of – 852
 set the –
 influence 175
 authority 737
 for –'s sake 852
fast *joined* 43
 steadfast 150
 rapid 274
 fashionable 852
 intemperate 954
 not eat 956
 worship 990
 rite 998
 stick – 704
 – *asleep* 683
 – *by* 197
 – day 956
 – *friend* 890
 – and loose
 sophistry 477
 falsehood 544
 irresolute 605
 tergiversation 607
 caprice 608
 – man *fop* 854
 libertine 962
fasten *join* 43
 hang 214
 restrain 751
 – on the mind 451
 – on a quarrel upon
  713
 – *upon* 789
fastening 45
fast-handed 819
fastidious
 censorious 932
fastidiousness 868
fasting
 insufficiency 640
 worship 990
 penance 952
 abstinence 956
fastness
 asylum 666
 defence 717
fat *corpulent* 192
 expansion 194
 unctuous 355
 oleaginous 356
 kill the –ted calf
 celebration 883
 sociality 892
 – in the fire
 disorder 59
 violence 173
 – of the land
 pleasure 377
 enough 639
 prosperity 734
 intemperance 95
fata – Morgana
 occasion 134
 ignis fatuus 423
 – obstant 601
fatal 361
 – disease 655
fatalism 601
fatality 601
fate *end* 67
 necessity 601
 chance 621
 be one's – 156
 sure as – 474
Fates 601, 979
fat-head 501

father *eldest* 128
 paternity 166
 priest 996
 Apostolical –s 985
 gathered to one's
  –s 360
 heavy – 599
 – upon 155
Father, God the –
  976
fatherland 189
fatherless 158
fatherly 906
fathom
 length 200
 investigate 461
 solve 462
 measure 466
 discover 480a
 knowledge 490
fathomless 208
fatidical 511
fatigation 688
fatigue **688**
fatras 643
fatten
 expand 194
 improve 658
 prosperous 734
 – on *parasite* 886
 – upon
 feed 298
fatuity 4, 499
fatuous 517
fat-witted 499
faubourg 227
fauces 231
faucet 252
faugh! 867
fault
 break 70
 error 495
 imperfection 651
 failure 732
 vice 945
 guilt 947
 at –
 uncertain 475
 ignorant 491
 unskilful 699
 find – with 932
faultless 650, 946
faulty 495, 651
faun 980
fauna 366
faut: comme il –
 taste 850
 fashion 852
 il s'en – bien 489
 tant s'en – 536
faute 732
 – de mieux
 substitution 147
 necessity 601
fauteuil 215
fautor 890
faux pas
 error 568
 failure 732
 misconduct 947
 intrigue 961
favor
 resemble 16
 badge 550
 letter 592
 aid 707
 indulgence 740

permit 760
gift 784
partiality 923
appearances in –
of 472
get into –
friendship 888
love 897
in – repute 873
approbation 931
in – of
approve 931
under – of 760
view with – 906
– with 784
favorable
occasion 134
willing 602
good 648
aid 707
– prospect 472
– to 709
take a – turn
improve 658
prosperity 734
favorably
well 618
favorer 890
favorite
pleasing 829
beloved 897, **899**
favoritism
friendship 888
wrong 923
fawn color 433
cringe 749, 886
flatter 993
fay 979
fealty
obedience 743
duty 926
respect 928
fear **860**
fearful
painful 830
timid 862
fearfully 31, 870
fearless hope 858
courage 861
fearsome 860
feasible 470, 705
feast period 138
repast 298
pleasure 377
revel 840
rite 998
– one's eyes 897
feast of reason
conversation 588
– and flow of soul
sociality 892
feat action 680
courage 861
– of arms 720
– of strength 159
feather
class 75
tuft 256
light 320
trifle 643
ornament 847
decoration 877
in full –
prepared 673
prosperous 734
rich 803
hear a – drop 403

in high –
health 654
cheerful 884
pleased with a –
840
– in one's cap
honor 873
decoration 877
– one's nest
prepare 673
prosperity 734
wealth 803
economy 817
selfish 943
– the oar 698
– in the scale 643
feather-bed 324
feathered tribes
366
feathery 256
featly 682
feature
character 5
component 56
form 240
appearance 448
press 531
lineament 550
– in 56
features
face 234
febrifuge 662
febrile 382, 825
fecal 653
feces 299, 653
fecit 556
feckless 866
feculence 653
fecund 168
fecundate 161
federal council 696
– penitentiary 752
federalism 737
federation 48, 709,
712
fee possession 777
property 780
pay 809
reward 973
feeble weak 160
illogical 477
feeble-minded 497,
605
feebleness
style **575**
feed eat 298
supply 637
– the flame 707
fee-faw-fum
bugbear 860
spell 993
feel sense 375
touch 379
emotion 821
– for try 463
benevolence 906
pity 914
condole with 915
– the pulse 461
– the want of 865
– one's way
essay 675
caution 864
feeler 379
inquiry 461
experiment 463
feeling 698, **821**

feet low 207
walkers 266
at one's –
near 197
subjection 749
humility 879
fall at one's –
submit 725
fall on one's –
prosper 734
lick the – of
servile 886
light upon one's
safe 664
spring to one's –
307
throw oneself at
the – of
entreat 765
feign 544, 546
feigned 545
feint 545
felicitas, curiosa –
698
felicitate 896
felicitous
agreeing 23
- style 578
skilful 698
successful 731
pleasant 829
felicity 827
feline cat 366
stealthy 528
cunning 702
fell destroy 162
mountain 206
lay flat 21
skin 223
lay low 308
moor 344
dire 860
malevolent 907
fellah 876
felloe 231
fellow similar 17
equal 27
companion 88
dual 89
man 373
scholar 492, 541
fellow-commoner
541
fellow-companion
890
fellow-countryman
890
fellow-creature 372
fellow-feeling
friendship 888
love 897
benevolence 906
pity 914
fellowship
partnership 712
distinction 873
friendship 888
companionship
890
good – 892
fellow-student 541
fellow-worker 690
felly 231
felo-de-se 361
felon 949
felonious 945
felony 947

felt texture 219
heart– 821
felucca 273
female 374
feme coverte 903
feme sole 904
feminality
weakness 160
woman 374
feminine 374
feminism 374
femme de chambre
746
fen 345
fence enclose 232
evade 544
defence 717
fight 720
prison 752
thief 792
– round 229
– with a question
528
fenced 770
fenceless 665
fencible 726
fencing 840
feneration 787
fend 717
fender 717
Fenian 710, 742
fenum habet in
cornu 668, 913
feodal 780
feodality 737, 777
feoff property 780
feoffee 779, 785
feoffer 784
ferae naturae 366
feral 907
ferine 907
ferment
disorder 59
energy 171
violence 173
agitation 315
lightness 320
effervesce 353
emotion 821
excitement 824,
825
anger 900
fermentation,
acetous – 397
fern 367
ferocity 173, 907
Ferrara
sword 727
ferret out 461, 480a
ferro-concrete 635
ferrule 223
ferry 270, 627
ferry-boat 273
ferry-man 269
fertile 161, 168
– imagination 515
ferule 975
come under the –
932
fervent hot 382
desirous 865
– hope 858
fervid hot 382
heartfelt 821
excited 824
fervour heat 382
animation 821
love 897

festal eating 298
social 892
fester 653, 655
festina lente 864
festival
music 416
celebration 883
festivity 840, 892
festoon 245, 847
fetch bring 270
arrive 292
evasion 545
sell for 812
– one a blow
strike 276
attack 716
– and carry
servile 886
– a sigh 839
fête 840, 882
fêté 892
fetishism 992
fetid 401
fetish 991, 993
fetter 751, 752
fettle 673
state 5
prepare 673
in fine – 159, 654
fetus 129, 153
feu
– d'enfer 716
– de joie
amusement 840
celebration 883
feud discord 713
possess 777
property 780
death – 919
feudal 737, 780
feudatory 749
feuilleton 593
fever heat 382
disease 655
excitement 825
feverish hurry 684
animated 821
excited 824
few
a – 100
– and far between
70
– words
concise 572
taciturn 585
compendium 596
fewness **103**
fey 360
fez 225
fiancée 897
fiasco 732
fiat 481
– money 800
fib falsehood 544,
546
thump 720
fiber link 45
filament 205
moral – 60
fickle 149, 605
fictile 240
fiction untruth 546
work of – 594
fictitious 515, 546
fiddle 416, 417
fiddle-de-dee
absurd 497

unimportant 643
　contempt 930
fiddlefaddle
　unmeaning 517
　trifle 643
　dawdle 683
fiddler 416
fiddlestick 417
　– end 643
fidelity
　veracity 543
　obedience 743
　observance 772
　honor 939
fidget changes 149
　activity 682
　hurry 684
　excitability 825
fidgety
　irresolute 605
　fearful 860
　irascible 901
fiducial 156
fiduciary 484
fidus Achates
　auxiliary 711
　associate 743
　friend 890
fie disreputable 874
　– upon it
　censure 932
fief 777
field opportunity
　134
　scope 180
　region 181
　plain 344
　agriculture 371
　business 625
　arena 728
　property 780
　the – hunting 622
　beasts of the – 366
　playing –s 728
　the potter's – 361
　take the – 722
　– artillery 726
　the – of blood 361
　– of inquiry
　topic 454
　inquiry 461
　– of view
　vista 441
　idea 453
field-day
　contention 720
　amusement 840
　display 882
field-glass 445
field-marshal 745
field-piece 727
field-preacher 996
field-work 717
fiend 913, 980
fiend-like
　malevolent 907
　wicked 945
　fiend 980
fierce violent 173
　passion 825
　daring 861
　angry 900
fiery violent 173
　hot 382
　strong feeling 821
　excitable 825
　angry 900
　irascible 901

– cross 550, 722
– furnace 386
– imagination 515
– ordeal 828
fife 417
fifer 416
fifth 98, 99
fifty 98
fig
　unimportance 643
　in the name of the
　prophet –s! 497
　– out 847
fight
　contention 720
　warfare 722
　show –
　defence 717
　courage 861
　– one's battles
　again 594
　– against destiny
　606
　– the good fight
　944
　– it out 722
　– shy avoid 603,
　623
　coward 862
　– one's way
　pursue 622
　active 682
　exertion 686
fighter 726
fighting-cock 726,
　861
fighting-man 726
figment 515
figurante 599
figurate number 84
figuration 240
figurative
　metaphorical 521
　representing 554
　– style 577
figure
　number 84
　form 240
　appearance 448
　metaphor 521
　indicate 550
　represent 554
　price 812
　ugly 846
　cut a –
　repute 873
　display 882
　poor – 874
　– to oneself 515
　– of speech 521
　– out 522
　exaggeration 549
figure-flinger 994
figure-head 4, 550,
　554, 643
figurine 554
figuriste 559
filaceous 205
filament 205
filamentous 256
filch 791
filcher 762
file subduct 38
　arrange 60
　row 69
　assemblage 72
　list 86
　reduce 195

smooth 255
pulverize 330
record 551
store 636
soldiers 726
– a claim &c. 969
– off march 266
diverge 291
file-fire 716
filial 167
filiation
　consanguinity 11
　attribution 155
　posterity 167
filibuster 133, 706,
　792
filibustering 791
filiform 205
filigree 219
filings 330
fill complete 52
　occupy 186
　contents 190
　stuff 224
　provision 637
eat one's – 957
have one's –
　enough 639
　satiety 869
　– the bill 229
　– an office
　business 625
　government 737
　– out
　expand 194
　–ed to overflow-
　ing 641
　– one's pocket 803
　– time 106
　– up compensate
　30
　compose 54
　close 261
　restore 660
　– up the time
　inaction 681
fille
　– de chambre 746
　– de joie 962
filled
　– to overflowing
　641
filler 532
fillet band 45
　filament 205
　circle 247
　insignia 550
　ornament 847
fillibeg 225
filling 224
fillip
　impulse 276
　propulsion 284
　stimulus 615
　excite 824
filly 271
film layer 204
　opaque 426
　semitransparent
　427
　– over the eyes
　dim sight 443
　cinema 448
　ignorant 491
filmy texture 329
filter percolate 295
　clean 652
filth 653

–y lucre 800
filtrate 652
fimbriated 256
fin 267
final ending 67
　conclusive 474
　completing 729
　court of – appeal
　474
　– cause 620
　– stroke 729
　– touch 729
finale end 67
　completion 729
finality 67, 729
finally
　for good 141
　on the whole 476
finance 800, 811
　minister of – 801
financier 801
finch 366
find
　eventuality 151
　adjudge 480
　discover 480a
　acquire 775
　– one's account in
　644
　– the cause of 522
　– a clue to 480a
　– to one's cost 509
　– credence 484
　– it in one's heart
　602
　– in provide 637
　– the key of 522
　– the meaning 522
　– means 632
　– oneself be 1
　present 186
　– out 480a
　– vent 671
　– one's way 731
　– one's way into
　294
finding
　judgment 480
fine small 32
　large 192
　thin 203
　rare 322
　not raining 340
　exact 494
　good 648
　beautiful 845
　adorned 847
　proud 878
　mulct 974
　in – end 67
　after all 476
　– air 656
　– arts 554
　– feather 159, 654
　– feeling 850
　– frenzy 515
　– gentleman
　fop 854
　proud 878
　– grain 329
　– lady 854, 878
　one – morning 106
　some – morning
　119
　– powder 330
　– talking
　overrate 482

boast 884
– writing 577
– time of it 734
– voice 580
fine-draw 660
fine-fingered 698
fine-spoken 894,
　933
fine-spun thin 203
　sophistry 477
fine-toned 413
finem, respicere –
　510
finery 847, 851
finesse tact 698
　artifice 702
　taste 850
finger touch 379
　hold 781
　lay the – on
　point out 457
　discover 480a
　lift a – 680
　not lift a – 681
　point the – at 457
　turn round one's
　little – 737
　–'s breadth 203
　at one's –s' end
　near 197
　know 490
　remember 505
　– on the lips
　aphony 581
　taciturnity 585
　– in the pie
　cause 153
　interfere 228
　act 680
　active 682
　co-operate 709
fingerling 193
finger-post 550
finger-print 467
finger-stall 223
fingle-fangle 643
finical
　trifling 643
　affected 855
　fastidious 868
finicky 855, 868
finikin 643
finis 67
　– coronat opus
　729
finish lend 67
　symmetry 242
　complete 729
　skill 698
finished
　absolute 31
　perfect 650
　skilled 698
finishing
　– stroke 361
　– touch 729
finite 32
fiord 343
fire energy 171
　heat 382
　make hot 384
　stoke 388
　vigor 574
　discharge 756
　enthusiasm 821
　excite 824, 825
　catch – 384

foozle 732
fop 854
foppery 882
foppish 855
for *cause* 155
  tendency 176
  reason 476
  motive 615
  intention 620
  preparation 673
have –
  price **812**
– all that
  notwithstanding 30
  qualification 469
– all the world
  like 17
– aught one
  knows 156
– better for worse 78
– ever 112
– example 82
– form's sake 82
– good
  complete 52
  diuturnity 110
  permanence 141
– the most part
  great 31
  general 78
  special 79
– the nonce 118
– nothing 815
– a season 106
– a time 111
– the time being 106
forage
  food 298
  provision 637
  steal 791
forage-cap 225
foramen 260
foraminous 260
forasmuch as
  relating to 9
  cause 155
  reason 476
  motive 615
foray *attack* 716
  robbery 791
forbear
  avoid 623
  spare 678
  lenity 740
  sufferance 826
  pity 914
  abstain 953
  forbearance 918
forbid 761
  God –
  dissent 489
  deprecation 766
  censure 932
  prayer 990
forbidden fruit
  seduction 615
  prohibition 761
forbidding
  ugly 846
force *corps* 72
  power 157
  strength 159
  agency 170
  energy 171

violence 173
cultivate 371, 707
cascade 348
– *of style* 574
urge 615
exertion 686
compulsion 744
armed – 726
brute – 964
put in – 924
– of argument 476
– of arms 744
– of character 820
– down the throat
severe 739
compel 744
– *majeure* 744
– open 173
– one's way
  progression 282
  passage 302
forced *irrelative* 10
– *style* 579
be – to 601
– labor 603
– march 744
forcefully 601
forceps
  extraction 301
  grip 781
forces 726
forcible [see force]
ford 302, 627
fore 234
fore and aft
  complete 52
  lengthwise 200
– *schooner* 273
fore part 234
forearm 673
forebears 166
forebode 511
forecast
  foresight 510
  prediction 511
  plan 626
foreclose 706
foredoom 152, 601
forefathers 166
forefend
  prohibit 761
forefinger 379
forego
  relinquish 624
  renounce 757
  surrender 782
foregoing 62, 116
foregone
  past 122
– conclusion
  prejudged 481
  predetermined 611
foreground 234
  in the –
  manifest 525
forehead 234
foreign
  alien 10
  extraneous 57
– *accent* 580
– *parts* 196
foreigner 57
forejudge
  prejudge 481
  foresight 510
foreknow 510

foreland 206, 254
forelay 545
fore ock
  pull the – 894
  take time by the –
  early 132
  occasion 134
foreman 694
foremost
  superior 33
  beginning 66
  front 234
  in advance 280
  important 642
  reputed 873
forenoon 125
forensic 968
foreordain 152
foreordination 601, 611
forerun 62, 116, 280
forerunner 64, 512
foresee 507, 510
foreseen 871
foreshadow 152, 511
foreshorten 201
foreshow 511
foresight 116, **510**
  caution 864
forest 367
forestage 599
forestry 371
forestall
  prior 116
  early 132
  possession 777
foretaste 510
foretell 511
forethought 459, 510
foretoken 511
forewarn 511, 668
foreword 64
forfeit *fail* 773
  lose 776
  penalty 974
– one's good
  opinion 932
forfeiture
  disfranchisement 925
forfend 706, 717
forgather 72
forge *imitate* 19
  produce 161
  furnace 386
  trump up 544
  workshop 691
– *fetters* 751
forged
  false 546
forger
  maker 690
  thief 792
forgery
  deception 545
forget 506
  hand – cunning 699
– benefits 917
– injury 918
– oneself 945
forgive **918**
forgo
  relinquish 624
  renounce 757

  surrender 782
forgotten
  past 122
  ingratitude 917
  not to be – 505
– by the world 893
fork *bifid* 91
  pointed 244
– *lightning* 423
– out
  give 784
  pay 807
  expenditure 809
forlorn
  dejected 837
  hopeless 859
  deserted 893
– hope
  danger 665
  rashness 863
form *state* 7
  likeness 21
  make up 54
  order 58
  arrange 60
  convert 144
  produce 161
  bench 215
  shape **240**
  educate 537
  pupils 541
  manner 627
  beauty 845
  fashion 852
  etiquette 882
  law 963
  rite 998
– letter 592
– part of 56
– a party 712
– a resolution 604
formal [see form]
  regular 82
  definitive 535
– *style* 579
  affected 855
  stately 882
– *speech* 582
formalism 739, 988
formalist 82
formality [see formal]
  ceremony 852
  affectation 855
  law 963
formation
  composition 54
  production 161
  shape 240
formative 153
formed [see form]
  attempered 820
former
– *in order* 62
  prior in time 116
  past 122
formication 380
formidable 704, 860
formless 241
formula *rule* 80
  arithmetic 84
  maxim 496
  precept 697
  law 963
formulary 998
formulate 590

fornication 961
fornicator 962
foro conscientiæ
  veracity 543
  duty 926
  probity 939
forsake 624
forsaken 898
forsooth 535
forspent 688
forswear *lie* 544
  tergiversation 607
  refuse 764
  transgress 927
  improbity 940
fort 666, 717
fort
  le droit du plus –
  compulsion 744
  illegality 964
  un peu – 641
fortalice 717
forte 415, 698
fortelage 717
forth 282
  come –
  egress 295
  visible 446
  go – *depart* 293
  the decree has gone – 741
forthcoming 152, 673
forthwith 132
fortification 717
fortify 159
fortiori, a – 467, 476
fortissimo 404
fortiter in re 171
fortitude 826, 861
fortnightly 138
fortress 717, 752
fortuitous
  extrinsic 6
  chance 156
  undersigned 621
– concourse of atoms 59
fortunate
  opportune 134
  successful 731
  prosperous 734
Fortunatus's – cap
  wish 865
  spell 993
– purse 803
fortune *chance* 156
  fate 601
  wealth 803
  be one's – 151
  clean up a – 803
  evil – 621, 735
  good – 734
  make one's –
  succeed 731
  wealth 803
  tempt –
  hazard 621
  essay 675
  trick of – 509
  try one's – 675
  wheel of – 601, 621
fortune-hunter 886, 943
fortuneless 804
fortune-teller 513
fortune-telling 511

fortunes of
narrative 594
forty 98
– *winks* 683
forum 799
school 542
tribunal 966
forward *early* 132
transmit 270
advance 282
willing 602
improve 658
active 682
help 707
vain 880
insolent 885
uncourteous 895
bend – 234
come –
in sight 446
offer 763
display 882
look – *to* 507
move – 282
press – *haste* 684
put – *aid* 507
offer 763
put oneself – 880
set – 676
– *in knowledge* 490
foss 348
fosse
inclosure 232
ditch 259
defence 717
fossil
ancient 124
hard 323
organic 357
dry bones 362
foster *aid* 707
excite 824
caress 902
– *a belief* 484
fou 959
foudroyant 870
foul
collide 276
bad 649
dirty 653
unhealthy 657
ugly 846
base 940
vicious 945
fall – *of*
oppose 708
quarrel 713
attack 716
fight 720
censure 932
run – *of*
impede 706
– *fiend* 978
– *means* 940
– *language*
malediction 908
– *odor* 401
– *play evil* 619
cunning 702
wrong 923
improbity 940
foul-mouthed 934
foul-spoken 934
found 153, 215
foundation
beginning 66
stability 150

base 211
support 215
lay the –*s* 673
sandy – 667
shake to its –*s* 315
founded
well – 472
– *on base* 211
evidence 467
founder
originator 164
sink 310
fail 732
religious –*s* 986
foundery 691
founding 22
foundling
trover 775
derelict 782
outcast 893
fount *type* 591
fountain
source 153
river 348
store 636
– *head* 210
– *pen* 590
four 95
on all –*s* 13, 23
horizontal 213
easy 705
prosperous 734
humble 879
– *in hand* 272
– *score &c.* 98
– *square* 244
– *times* 96
from the – *winds* 278
fourflusher 884
fourfold 96
four-oar 273
four-poster 215
fourth 96, 97
musical 413
– *estate* 531
four-wheeler 272
fowl 366
fowling-piece 727
fox *animal* 366
– *cunning* 702
– *chase* 622
fox-trot 840
foxy *color* 433, 434
cunning 720
foyer 191, 599
fracas
disorder 59
noise 404
discord 713
contention 720
fraction *part* 51
numerical 84
less than one **100a**
fractious 901
fracture
disjunction 44
discontinuity 70
fissure 198
fragile 160, 328
fragment
small 32, 193
part 51, **100a**
fragrance 400
fragrant weed 392
frail *weak* 160
brittle 328

feeble 575
irresolute 605
imperfect 651
failing 945
impure 961
– *sisterhood* 962
frais, à grands – 481
frame
condition **7**
make 161
support 215
border 231
form 240
substance 316
structure 329
contrive 626
cucumber – 371
have –*d and glazed* 822
– *of mind*
inclination 602
disposition 820
frame-up 626
framework
support 215
structure 329
franchise
voting 609
freedom 748
right 924
exemption **927a**
Franciscan 996
franc-tireur 726
frangible 160, 328
frank *open* 525
sincere 543
artless 703
honorable 939
frankalmoigne 748
Frankenstein 913, 980
frankincense 400
frantic
violent 173
delirious 503
excited 824
fraternal
brother 11
concord 714
friendly 888
fraternity
[*see* fraternal]
party 712
fraternize
co-operate 48, 709
agree 714
sympathize 888
associate 892
fratricide 361
Frau 374
fraud
falsehood 544
deception 545
pretender 548
dishonor 940
pious – 988
fraught *full* 52
pregnant 161
possessing 777
– *with danger* 665
fray *rub* 331
battle 720
in the thick of the – 722
frayed 659
frazzle

beaten to a – 732
freak 608, 872
– *of Nature* 83
freckle 848
freckled 440
fredaine 840
free
detached 44, 47
unconditional 52
liberate 672
unobstructed 705
at liberty 748, 750
gratis 815
liberal 816
insolent 885
exempt **927a**
impure 961
– *balloon* 273
– *and easy*
cheerful 836
adventurous 863
vain 880
insolent 885
friendly 888
sociable 892
– *fight* 720
– *from*
simple 42
never – *from* 613
– *gift* 784
– *from imperfection* 650
– *lance* 726
– *land* 748
– *liver* **954a**
– *love* 961
make – *of* 748
– *play* 170, 748
– *quarters*
cheap 815
hospitality 892
– *space* 180
– *stage* 748
– *trade*
commerce 794
– *translation* 522
– *will* 600
make – *with*
frank 703
take 789
sociable 892
uncourteous 895
freebooter 792
freeborn 748
freedman 748
freedom **748**
free-handed 816
freehold 780
freely
willingly 602
freeman 748
freemasonry
unintelligible 519
secret 528
sign 550
co-operation 709
party 712
free-spoken 703
freethinker 989
freeze
benumb 381
cold 385
– *the blood* 830
freezing 38.5
– *mixture* 387
freight *lade* 184
cargo 190

transfer 270
freightage 812
freighter 273
freight train 272
French
peddler's – 563
– *and English* 840
– *horn* 417
– *leave avoid* 623
freedom 748
– *polish* 847
frenetic 503
frenzy
madness 503
imagination 515
excitement 825
frequency **136**
frequent
in number 104
in time 136
in space 186
habitual 613
visit 892
fresco *cold* 383
painting 556
al –
out of doors 220
in the air 338
fresh *additional* 37
new 123
flood 348
cold 383
color 428
remembered 505
unaccustomed 614
good 648
healthy 654
impertinent 885
tipsy 959
– *breeze* 349
– *color* 434
– *news* 532
freshen 658, 689
freshet 348
freshman 541
freshwater 851
freshwater sailor 701
fret *suffer* 378
grieve 828
gall 830
discontent 832
sad 837
ornament 847
irritate 900
– *and fume* 828
fretful 901
fret-work 219
friable 328, 330
friandise 868
friar 996
–*'s lantern* 423
– *Rush* 980
Black –*s* 996
friary 1000
fribble
slur over 460
trifle 643
dawdle 683
fop 854
fricassee 298
frication 331
friction *force* 157
obstacle 179
rubbing **331**
on – *wheels* 705
friend 711, **890**

delight 827
globated 249
globe
  sphere 249
  world 318
  on the face of the
   — 318
  — trotter 268
globule 32, 249
glomeration 72
gloom 421, 827, 837
gloomy horizon 859
glorification 884
glorify
  honor 873
  approve 931
  worship 990
glorious
  illustrious 873
  tipsy 959
glory
  light 420
  honor 873
  heaven 981
  King of — 976
  — in 878, 884
  — be to God 990
gloss *smooth* 255
  sheen 420
  interpretation 522
  falsehood 546
  plea 617
  beauty 845
  — of novelty 123
  — over
   neglect 460
   sophistry 477
   falsehood 544
   vindicate 937
glossary 86, 562
glossographer 492
glossologist 492
glossology 560, 562
glossy [see gloss]
glottology 560
glout 901a
glove 225
  take up the — 720
  throw down the —
   715
glow *warm* 382
  shine 420
  appear 446
  color 428
  style 574
  passion 821
glower
  glare 443
  discourteous 895
  sullen 901a
glowing
  [see glow]
  orange 439
  excited 824
  beautiful 845
  — terms 574
glow-worm 423
gloze 933, 937
glucose 396
glue *cement* 45
  cementing 46
  semiliquid 352
glum
  discontented 832
  dejected 837
  sulky 901a
glut

redundance 641
  satiety 869
gluttony 957
glutinous 352
glutton 954a, 957
gluttony 957
glycerine 332, 356
glyphography 558
glyptography 558
glyptotheca 557
gnarl *protuberance*
  250
  anger 900
  threat 909
gnarled 256, 321
gnash one's teeth
  839, 900
gnat *little* 193
  strain at a — &c.
  caprice 608
gnaw *eat* 298
  rub 331
  injure 659
gnawing
  — *grief* 828, 830
  — *pain* 378
gnome 496, 980
gnomic 496
gnomon 114
Gnostic 984
go
  cease to exist 2
  energy 171, 682
  move 264
  recede 287
  depart 293
  fade 429
  disappear 449
  fashion 852
  come and — 314
  as things — 613
  — about
   turn round 311
   published 531
   undertake 676
  — across 302
  — after
   in time 117
   in motion 281
  — ahead
   energetic 171
   precede 280
   advance 282
   active 682
  — against 708
  — astray 495
  — away 293
  — back 283, 624
  — bad 659
  — bail 771
  — before 280
  — between
   interjacent 228
   instrumental 631
   mediate 631, 724
  — beyond 303
  — by the board
   158
  — about your
   business
   ejection 297
   dismissal 756
  — by
   conform to 82
   elapse 109
   past 122
   outrun 303

subterfuge 702
give the — by to
  neglect 460
  deceive 545
  avoid 623
  not observe 773
  — by the name of
   564
  — deep into 461
  — down *sink* 306
   decline 659
  — down with
   believed 484
   tolerated 826
   content 831
  — farther and fare
   worse 659
  — forth *depart* 293
   publish 531
  — halves 91
  — hand in hand
   accompany 88
   same time 120
  — hard 704
  — on ill 735
  — in 294
  — in for
   resolution 604
   pursuit 622
  — into
   ingress 294
   inquire 461
   dissert 595
  — all lengths
   complete 52
   resolve 604
   exertion 686
  — mad 503
  — near 286
  — no further
   keep secret 528
  — for nothing
   sophistry 477
   unimportant 643
  — off *explode* 173
   depart 293
   die 360
   wither 360
   marry 903
  — on *time* 106
   continue 143
   advance 282
  — on for ever 112
  — one better 303
  — out
   cease 142
   egress 295
   extinct 385
  — out of one's
   head 506
  — over
   passage 302
   explore 461
   apostate 607
   faithless 940
  — to pieces 162
  — on record 551
  — round 311
  — shares 778
  — to sleep 683
  — through
   meet with 151
   pass 302
   explore 461
   perform 599
   conduct 692
   complete 729

endure 826
  — to extend 196
  travel 266
  direction 278
  remonstrance 695
  — up 305
  — to war 722
  — with
   assent 488
   concord 714
  — with the stream
   conform 82
   servile 886
  — from one's word
   773
goad 615
  hasten 684
goal *end* 67
  reach 292
  object 620
  reach the —
   complete 729
goat *substitute* 147
  jumper 309
  lecher 962
  he — *male* 373
  play the — 499
gob 269
gobang 840
gobbet
  small piece 32
  food 298
gobble *cry* 412
  gormandize 957
  eat 298
gobemouche 501,
  547
go-between 758
goblet 191
goblin 980
go-cart 272
GOD 976
  house of — 1000
  kingdom of — 981
  sons of — 977
  —'s acre 363
  — bless me! 870
  — bless you
   farewell 293
  — forbid 766
  —'s grace 906
  — grant 990
  — knows 491
  —'s love 906
  for —'s sake 765
  —'s will 601
  — willing 470
god 979
  household —s 189
  tutelary — 664
goddess *love* 897
  good woman 948
  heathen 979
Godhead 976
godlike 987
godly 944
godsend *good* 618
  prosperity 734
Godspeed
  farewell 293
  hope 858
  courtesy 894
  benevolence 906
  approbation 931
goer *horse* 271
goes [see go]
  as one — 270

here — 676
Gog and Magog 192
goggle 441
  — eyes 443
goggles 445
going [see go]
  general 78
  rumor 532
  — to happen 152
  — on
   incomplete 53,
   730
   current 151
   transacting 625
goiter 250
Golconda 803
gold *yellow* 436
  orange 439
  money 800
  write in letters
   of — 642
  worth its weight
   in — 648
gold certificate 800
golden [see gold]
  — age
   prosperity 734
   pleasure 827
  — apple 615
  — calf
   wealth 803
   idol 985
   idolatry 991
  — dream
   imagination 515
   hope 858
  — mean
   moderation 174
   mid-course 628
  — opinions 931
  — opportunity 134
  — rule
   precept 697
  — season of life
   127
  — wedding 883
golf 840
Golgotha 363, 1000
Goliath 159, 192
goloshes 225
gondola 273
gondolier 269
gone [see go]
  past 122
  absent 187
  dead 360
  — bad 653
  — by
   antiquated 124
  — out of one's rec-
   ollection 506
gonfalon 550
gong 417
goniometer 244,
  466
good
  complete 52
  palatable 394
  assent 488
  benefit 618
  beneficial 648
  right 922
  virtuous 944
  pious 987
  as — as 197
  be so — as 765
  do — 906

groove
furrow 259
habit 613
in a – 16
move in a – 82
put in a – for 673

grope
feel 379
experiment 463
try 675
in the dark 442,
704

gross
great 31
whole 50
number 98
ugly 846
vulgar 851
vicious 945
impure 961
– credulity 486
– receipts 810

grosshead 501
grossheaded 499
grossièreté 895
grot [*see* grotto]
grotesque
odd 83
distorted 243
– *style* 579
ridiculous 853

grotto
alcove 191
hollow 252

grouch 895, 901a
ground
cause 153
region 181
base 211
lay down 213
support 215
coating 223
land 342
plain 344
evidence 467
teach 537
motive 615
plea 617
above – 359
down to the – 52
dress the – 371
fall to the – 732
get over the – 274
go over the – 302
level with the –
162
maintain one's –
persevere 604a
play– 840
prepare the – 673
stand one's –
defend 717
resist 719
– bait 784
– cut from under
one 732
– floor
chamber 191
low 207
base 211
– on
attribute 155
– plan 554
– of quarrel 713
– sliding from
under one 665
– swell

agitation 315
waves 348
grounded
stranded 732
well– 490
– on *basis* 211
evidence 467
groundless
unsubstantial 4
illogical 477
erroneous 495
groundling 876
grounds
dregs 653
groundwork
precursor 64
cause 153
basis 211
support 215
preparation 673
group
marshal 60
cluster 72
– *captain* 745
grouping 60
grouse 852, 901a
grout 45
grove
street 189
glade 252
wood 367
grovel
below 207
move slowly 275
cringe 886
base 940
grow
increase 35
become 144
expand 194
– from
effect 154
– into 144
– less 195
– taller 206
– together 46
– up 194
– upon one 613
grower 164
growl *cry* 412
complain 839
discourtesy 895
anger 900
threat 909
growler *cab* 272
discontented 832
sulky 901a
grown up 131
growth [*see* grow]
development 161
– *in size* 194
tumor 250
vegetation 367
groyne 706
grub
small animal 193
food 298
– up
eradicate 301
discover 480a
Grub-street writer
593
grudge
unwilling 603
refuse 764
stingy 819
hate 898

anger 900
bear a – 907
owe a – 898
grudging 603
– *praise* 932
gruel 298
gruesome 846
gruff
harsh sound 410
discourteous 895
grum
harsh sound 410
morose 901a
grumble
cry 411
complain 832,
839
grume 321, 354
grumous 321, 354
grumpy 901a
Grundy, Mrs. 852
grunt 412
complain 839
guano 653
guarantee 768, 771
guard
traveling 268
safety 664
defence 717
soldier 726
sentry 753
advanced – 668
mount –
care 459
safety 664
off one's –
inexpectant 508
throw off one's –
cunning 702
on one's –
careful 459
cautious 864
rear – 668
– against
prepare 673
defence 717
– ship 664, 726
guarda costa 753
guarded
conditions 770
guardian
safety 664
defence 717
keeper 753
– angel
helper 711
benefactor 912
guardless 665
guard-room 752
gubernation 693
gubernatorial 737
gudgeon 547
guerdon 973
guernsey 225
guerre:
nom de – 565
– à outrance &c.
722
guerilla 726
– *warfare* 720
guess 514
guesswork 514
guest 890
paying – 188
guet:
mot de – 550
–à-pens 545

guffaw 838
guggle
gush 348
bubble 353
resound 408
cry 412
guide
pattern 22
courier 524
teach 537
teacher 540
indicate 550
direct 693
director 694
advise 695
guide-book 527
guided by, be – 82
guideless 665
guide-post 550
guiding star 693
guild 712, 966
guildhall 799
guile
deceit 544, 545
cunning 702
guileless 543, 703
guillotine 972, 975
guilt 947
guiltless 946
guilty:
find – 971
plead – 950
guindé 579
guinea 800
guipure 847
guisard 599
guise
state 7
dress 225
appearance 448
plea 617
mode 627
conduct 692
guiser 599
guitar 417
gulch 198
gules 434
gulf
interval 198
deep 208
lake 343
gull 545, 547
gullible 486
gullet *throat* 260
rivulet 348
gully *gorge* 198
hollow 252
opening 260
conduit 350
gulosity 957
gulp *swallow* 296
take food 298
– down
credulity 486
submit 725
gum *fastening* 45
fasten 46
resin 356a
– elastic 325
– tree 367
gumbo 298
gummy 352
gumption 498
gun *report* 406
weapon 727
great – 626
blow great –s 349

sure as a – 474
gunboat 726
gunfire 404
gunman 361
gunner 776
gunnery
warfare 722
cannon 727
gunlayer 284
gunpowder
warfare 722
ammunition 727
not invent – 665
sit on barrel of –
501
gunroom 193
gun-shot 197
gunwale 232
gurge 312, 348
gurgle
flow 348
bubble 353
faint sound 405
resonance 408
gurgoyle 350
gush
flow out 295
flood 348
exaggeration 482
talk 584
gushing
emotional 821
impressible 822
gusset 43
gust *wind* 349
physical taste 390
passion 825
moral taste 850
gustation 390
gustful 394
gustless 391
gusto [*see* gust]
physical pleasure
377
emotion 821
gut *destroy* 162
opening 260
strait 343
eviscerate 297
sack 789
steal 791
gutling 954a
guts *inside* 221
guttapercha 325
gutter *groove* 259
conduit 350
vulgarity 851
guttersnipe 876
guttle 957
guttural
letter 561
inarticulate 583
guy
fastening 45, 752
fellow 373
disrespect 929
grotesque 853
guzzle
gluttony 957
drunkenness 959
gybe [*see* jibe]
gymkhana 720, 840
gymnasium 191
school 542
arena 728, 840
gymnast 159
gymnastics

unprepared 674
poor 804
–s off! avoid 623
leave alone 681
prohibition 761
– over
transfer 783
give 784
win –s down 731
with the –s in the
pockets 681
hand-bag 191
hand-barrow 272
handbook
travel 266
information 527
book 593
handcuff 751, 752
handfast 903
handful
quantity 25
small 32
few 103
handicap
equalize 27
inferiority 34
encumber 706
race 720
handicraft 625, 680
handicraftsman 690
effect 154
doing 680
handkerchief
clothes 225
cleaner 652
handle
feel, touch 379
name 565
dissert 595
plea 617
instrument 633
use 677
manage 693
furnish a – 937
make a – of 677
– a case 693
– to one's name
name 564
honor 877
handmaid
instrumentality
631
auxiliary 711
servant 746
handpost 550
handsel
begin 66
security 771
gift 784
pay 809
handsome
liberal 816
beautiful 845
disinterested 942
– fortune 803
handspike 633
handstaff 727
handwriting
signature 550
autograph 590
– on the wall
warning 668
handy
near 197
useful 644, 646
ready 673
dexterous 698

hang
pendency 214
kill 361
curse 908
execute 972
– about 133, 197
– back 133, 623
– in the balance
133
– in doubt 485
– fire late 133
cease 142
unproductive 169
inert 172
slow 275
reluctance 603
inactive 683
not finish 730
fail 732
refuse 764
dullness 843
– on hand 641
– down the head
837
– over the head
152
– it! regret 833
contempt 930
– out a light 420
– upon the lips of
418
– on
accompany 88
– out
display 882
entertain 892
– over
destiny 152
height 206
project 250
– out a signal 550
– on the sleeve of
servant 746
servility 886
flattery 933
– in suspense 605
– by a thread 665
– together
joined 43
cohere 46
concur 178
co-operate 709
– upon
effect 154
dependency 749
hangar 191, 273
hang-dog look 901a
hanged if, I'll be –
489
hanger
weapon 727
suspender 45, 214
pothooks and –s
590
– on
accompaniment
88
servant 746
servile 886
hanging [see hang]
elevated 307
ornament 847
– look 846
hangman
evil-doer 913
bad man 949
executioner 97u̇

hank tie 45
hanker 865
hanky-panky 545
Hansard 551
hansom 272
hap 156
haphazard
chance 156, 621
hapless
unfortunate 735
(miserable 828)
(hopeless 859)
haply
possibly 470
(by chance 156)
happen 151
– as it may
chance 621
– what may
certain 474
reckless 863
happening 151
happiness
[see happy]
the greatest – of
the greatest
number 910
happy fit 23
opportune 134
style 578
glad 827
cheerful 836
– despatch 972
– go lucky 674
– hunting grounds
981
– returns of the
day 896
– thought 842
– valley
imagination 515
delight 827
harangue 582
hara-kiri 972
harass
fatigue 688
vex 830
worry 907
harbinger
precursor 64
omen 512
informant 527
harbor
abode 189
haven 292
refuge 666
cherish 821
natural – 343
– a design 620
in – 664
– an idea 451
harborless 665
hard strong 159
dense 323
physically insen-
sible 376
sour 397
difficult 704
severe 739
morally insen-
sible 823
grievous 830
impenitent 951
blow – 349
go –
difficult 704

failure 732
adversity 735
pain 828
hit – 276
look – at 441
not be too – upon
918
strike –
energy 171
impulse 276
try – 675
work – 686
– at it 682
– bargain 819
– of belief 487
– to believe 485
– by 197
– case 735
– cash 800
– earned 704
– and fast rule 80
– fought 704
– frost 383
– of hearing 419
– heart
malevolent 907
vicious 945
impenitent 951
– hit 732
– knocks 720
– life 735
– lines
adversity 735
severity 739
– liver 954a
– lot 735
– master 739
– measure 739
– names 932
– necessity 601
– nut to crack 704
– to please 868
– pressed
haste 684
difficulty 704
hindrance 706
– put to it 704
– set 704
– tack 298
– task 703
– time 704
– up 704, 804
– upon
attack 715
severe 739
censure 932
– winter 383
– words
obscure 571
rude 895
censure 932
– work 686
– at work 682
harden [see hard]
strengthen 159
accustom 613
– the heart
insensible 823
enmity 889
impenitence 951
hardened
impious 988
– front
insolent 885
hardening
habit 613
hard-featured 846

hard-fisted 819
hard-headed 498,
739
hardihood 861, 885
hardly
scarcely 32
deal – with 739
– any few 103
– anything
small 32
unimportant 643
– ever 137
hard-mouthed 606
hardness 323
– of heart 914a
hardship 735
hardy
strong 159
healthy 654
brave 861
hare 274
hold with the –
and run with
the hounds
fickle 607
servile 886
hare-brained 458,
863
harem 961
hariolation 511
hark 418, 457
– back 283
harl 205
harlequin
changeable 149
nimble 274
motley 440
pantomimic 599
humorist 844
harlequinade 599
harlot 962
harlotry 961
harm
evil 619
badness 649
malevolence 907
harmattan 349
harmless
impotent 158
good 648
perfect 650
salubrious 656
safe 664
innocent 946
bear – 717
harmonica 417
harmonics 413
harmonist 413
harmonize 178, 416
harmonium 417
harmony
agreement 23
order 58
music 413
color 428
concord 714
peace 721
friendship 888
harness
fasten 43
fastening 45
accouterment 225
yoke 370
instrument 633
restraint 752
in –
prepared 673

in action 680
active 682
subjection 749
– up 293
harp
　repeat 104
　musical instrument 417
　weary 841
Harpagon 819
harper 416
harpist 416
harpoon 727
harpsichord 417
harpy
　relentless 739
　thief 792
　miser 819
　evil-doer 913
　demon 980
harquebuss 727
harridan 846, 962
harrier 366
harrow
　agriculture 371
　– up the soul 860
harrowing 830
harry *pain* 830
　attack 716
　persecute 907
Harry, old – 978
harsh
　acrid 171
　sound 410
　style 579
　discordant 713
　severe 739
　disagreeable 830
　morose 895
　malevolent 907
　– *voice* 581
hart 366, 373
hartal 142, 489
harum-scarum 59, 458
haruspice 513
Haruspicy 511
harvest
　effect 154
　profit 618
　store 636
　acquisition 775
　get in the –
　complete 729
　succeed 731
　– home
　celebration 883
　– time
　autumn 126
　exertion 686
has been 122
hash *mix* 41
　cut 44
　confusion 59
　food 298
　make a – 699
hashish 863
hasp 43, 45
hassock 215
hastate 253
haste
　velocity 274
　activity 682
　hurry **684**
hasten
　promote 707
hasty

transient 113
　hurried 684
　impatient 825
　irritable 901
　– *pudding* 298
hat 225
　cardinal's – 999
　send round the –
　765
　shovel – 999
　– in hand 886
hatch
　produce 161
　gate 232
　opening 260
　chickens 370
　fabricate 544
　shading 556
　plan 626
　prepare 673
　– a plot 626
hatches, under –
　restraint 751
　prisoner 754
　poor 804
hatchet
　cutting 253
　bury the – 918
　dig up the – 722
　throw the helve
　after the – 818
hatchet-faced 203
hatchment
　funeral 363
　arms 550
　record 551
hatchway 260
hate 867, **898**
hateful 649, 830
hath been, the
　time – 122
hatrack 215
hatter 225
　mad as a – 503
hatti-sheriff 741
hatred [see hate]
　object of – 898
hauberk 717
haud passibus
　æquis 28, 275
haugh 344
haughty
　proud 878
　insolent 885
　contemptuous 930
haul *drag* 285
　catch of *fish* &c.
　789
　– down one's flag
　725
　– in 10
haunch 236
haunt *focus* 74
　presence 186
　abode 189
　alarm 860
　persecute 907
　– the memory
　remember 505
　trouble 830
haunted 980
haut
　traiter de –
　insolence 885
　contempt 930
hautboy 417
haut-goût 392

haut-monde 875
hauteur 878
have *confute* 479
　ken 49
　possess 777
　– the advantage
　28, 33
　– at 716
　– no choice 609a
　– done! 142
　– to do with 9
　– no end 112
　– other fish to fry
　135
　– it
　discover 480a
　believe 484
　– one to know 527
　– some knowledge
　of 490
　– nothing to do
　with 10
　– for one's own
　780
　– rather 609
　– one's rights 924
　– the start 116
　– in store 152, 637
　– to 620
　– up 638
　– it your own way
　submission 725
haven 292, 666
haversack 191
havoc
　destruction 162
　cry – *war* 722
　play – *spoil* 659
haw 583
hawk *spit* 297
　stammer 583
　eye of a – 498
　– about
　publish 531
　offer 763
　sell 796
　– at 716
　between – and
　buzzard 315,
　828
　know a – from a
　handsaw 465,
　698
hawker 796
hawk-eyed 441
hawking *chase* 622
hawser 45
hay while the sun
　shines, make –
　134
haycock 72
hazard
　chance 156, 621
　danger 665
　at all –s 604
　– a conjecture 514
　– a proposition
　477
haze *mist* 353
　uncertainty 475
　in a –
　hidden 528
hazel 433
hazy *opaque* 426
he 373
head *precedence* 62
　beginning 66

class 75
　summit 210
　coiffure 225
　lead 280
　froth 353
　person 372
　intellect 450
　topic 454
　wisdom 498
　picture 556
　nomenclature 564
　chapter 593
　direct 693
　director 694
　master 745
　at the – of
　direction 693
　authority 737
　repute 873
　bow the – 308
　bring to a – 729
　come into one's –
　451
　come to a – 729
　drive into one's –
　505
　gain – 175
　get into one's –
　thought 451
　learn 505
　belief 484
　intoxicate 959
　give a horse his –
　748
　hang one's – 879
　have in one's – 490
　from – to heels 52,
　200
　hit on the – 912
　knock on the –
　361
　knock one's –
　against
　impulse 276
　unskilful 699
　fail 732
　lie on one's – 926
　lift up one's – 878
　make – against
　oppose 708
　resistance 719
　success 731
　never entered
　into one's – 458
　have no – 506
　on one's – 218
　off one's – 503
　can't get out of
　one's – 505
　over – and ears
　deep 641
　debt 806
　love 897
　put into one's –
　supposition 514
　information 527
　put out of one's –
　458
　run in the – 505
　not know whether
　one stands on –
　or heels
　uncertain 475
　wonder 870
　take into one's –
　thought 451
　caprice 608

intention 620
　turn the – 824
　trouble one's –
　about 457
　as one's – shall
　answer for 768
　with – erect 878
　from – to foot 200
　– and front
　important 642
　– and front of
　one's offending
　provocation 830
　charge 938
　– over heels
　inversion 218
　rotation 312
　– *light* 423
　– *line* 591
　– and shoulders
　irrelevant 10
　complete 52
　haste 684
　make neither – nor
　tail of 519
　hold one's – up
　307
　– above water
　safe 664
　prosperous 743
　wealth 803
　with a – on 353
headache 378
head-dress 225
header 310
head-foremost
　violent 173
　rash 863
head-gear 225
heading *prefix* 64
　beginning 66
　indication 550
　title 564
headland
　height 206
　projection 250
headlong
　hurry 684
　rush 863
　rush –
　violence 173
headman 694
headmost
　front 234
　precession 280
head-piece
　summit 210
　intellect 450
　helmet 717
　ornament 847
head-quarters
　focus 74
　abode 189
　authority 737
head-race 350
head-stone 363
heads
　compendium 596
　– or tails 156, 621
　lay – together
　advice 695
　co-operate 709
　– I win tails you
　lose
　unfair 940
headship 737
headsman 975

high-brow 492
higher 33
highest 210
highfalutin 884
high-flavored 392
high-flier
  madman 504
  proud 878
high-flown
  imaginative 515
  style 577
  proud 878
  vain 880
  insolent 885
high-flying
  inattentive 458
  exaggerated 549
  ostentatious 822
highlands 206
high-low 225
high-mettled
  excitable 825
  brave 861
high-minded
  honorable 939
  magnanimous 942
highness *title* 877
high-pitched 410
high-seasoned 392
high-souled 878
high-sounding
  loud 404
  words 577
  display 882
high-spirited 861, 939
hight 564
high-toned 852
high-water
  completeness 52
  height 206
  crater 337
  – mark
  measure 466
highway 627
  –s and byways 627
  – robbery 791
highwayman 792
high-wrought
  good 648
  prepared 673
  excited 824
hike 266
hilarity 836
hill *height* 206
  convexity 250
  ascent 305
  descent 306
  take to the –s 666
  –dwelling 206
hillock 206
hilt 633
hinc illæ lachrymæ 155
hind *back* 235
  clown 876
  on one's – legs
  elevation 307
  anger 900
  – quarters 235
hinder 706
hindermost 67, 235
Hindooism 984
hindrance 706
hinge *fasten* 43

fastening 45
  cause 153
  depend upon 154
  rotate 312
hinny 271
hint *reminder* 505
  suppose 514
  inform 527
  take a – 498
  – a fault &c. 932
hinterland 235
hip 236
  have on the –
  confute 479
  success 731
  authority 737
  subjection 749
  – hip, hurrah! 838
hipped [*see* hypped]
hippocentaur 80
Hippocrates 662
hippocratic 360
hippodrome
  drama 599
  arena 728
  amusement 840
hippogriff 83
Hippolytus 960
hippophagy 298
hippopotamus 192
hirdie-girdie 218
hire
  commission 755
  borrowing 788
  price 812
  reward 973
  on – 763
hireling 746
hirsute 256
hispid 256
hiss *sound* 409
  animal cry 412
  disrespect 929
  contempt 930
  disapprobation 932
hist! 585, 586
histology 329
historian 553
historic 594
historiette 594
historical:
  – painter 559
  – painting 556
historiographer 553
historiography 594
history *past* 122
  record 551
  narrative 594
History, Natural – 357
histrionic 599
hit *chance* 156
  strike 276
  reach 292
  succeed 731
  censure 932
  (*punish* 972)
  good – 626
  make a – 731
  – one's fancy 829
  – the mark 731
  – off 545
  – upon
  discover 480a
  plan 626
hitch

fasten 43
  knot 45
  stoppage 142
  hang 214
  jerk 315
  harness 370
  difficulty 704
  hindrance 706
  – up 293
hither 278, 292
  come – 286
hitherto 122
hive
  multitude 102
  location 184
  abode 189
  bees 871
  workshop 691
H.M.S. 726
hoar *aged* 128
  white 430
  – frost 383
hoard 636
hoarse
  husky 405
  harsh 410
  voiceless 581
  talk oneself – 584
hoary [*see* hoar]
hoax 545
hob *support* 215
  stove 386
  – and nob
  celebration 883
  courtesy 894
hobble
  limp 275
  awkward 699
  difficulty 704
  fail 732
  shackle 751
  – skirt 225
hobbledehoy 129
hobby
  crotchet 481
  pursuit 622
  desire 865
hobby-horse 272
hobgoblin
  fearful 860
  demon 980
hobo 268
hobnail 876
Hobson's choice
  necessity 601
  no choice 609a
  compulsion 744
hoc genus omne 876
hock 771
hock shop 787
hockey 840
hockey rink 213
hocus 545
hocus-pocus
  interchange 148
  unmeaning 517
  cheat 545
  conjuration 992
  spell 993
hod
  receptacle 191
  support 215
  vehicle 272
hoddy-doddy 501
hodge-podge 41, 59
hoe 272, 371

hog *animal* 366
  sensualist 954a
  glutton 957
  (greedy as a – 865
  go the whole – 604
hog's back 206
hogmanay 998
hogshead 191
hog-wash 653
hoist 307
  – the black flag 722
  – a flag 550
  – on one's own petard
  retaliation 718
  failure 732
hoity-toity! 815, 870
hold *cohere* 46
  contain 54
  remain 141
  cease 142
  go on 143
  happen 151
  receptacle 191
  cellar 207
  base 211
  support 215
  halt 265
  believe 484
  be passive 681
  defend 717
  power 737
  restrain 751
  prison 752
  prohibit 761
  possess 777
  retain 781
  enough! 869
  have a firm – 781
  have a – upon 175
  gain a – upon 737
  get – of 789
  quit one's – 782
  take – 175
  – aloof
  stay away 187
  distrust 487
  avoid 623
  – an argument 476
  – authority 737
  – back *avoid* 623
  store 636
  hinder 706
  restrain 751
  retain 781
  miserly 819
  – one's breath
  wonder 870
  – converse 588
  – a council 695
  – fast 751, 781
  – forth *teach* 537
  speak 582
  – good 478, 494
  – one's ground 141
  – in hand 737
  – one's hand
  cease 142
  relinquish 624
  – hard 265
  – up one's head 861
  – a lease 771

  – a meeting 72
  – off 623
  – office 693
  – on
  continue 141, 143
  persevere 604a
  – out [*see below*]
  – one's own
  preserve 670
  defend 717
  resist 719
  – oneself in readiness 673
  – in remembrance 505
  – both one's sides 838
  – a situation 625
  – in solution 335
  – to 602
  – together 43, 709
  – one's tongue 403, 585
  – up [*see below*]
  – oneself up 307
hold out
  endure 106
  affirm 535
  persevere 604a
  resist 719
  offer 763
  brave 861
  – expectation
  predict 511
  promise 768
  – temptation 865
hold up
  continue 143
  support 215
  not rain 340
  aid 707
  rob 791
  display 882
  extol 931
  – one's hand
  sign 550
  threat 909
  – to execration
  cures 908
  censure 932
  – the mirror 525
  – to scorn 930
  – to shame 874
  – to view 525
holder 779
holdfast 45
holding
  tenancy 777
  property 780
hole *place* 182
  hovel 189
  receptacle 191
  opening 260
  ambush 530
  – in one's coat 651
  – and corner
  place 182
  peer into – 461
  hiding 528, 530
  – to creep out of
  plea 617
  escape 671
  facility 705
holiday *leisure* 685
  repose 687
  amusement 840
  – task *easy* 705

holiness *God* 976
 piety 987
holloa 411
 – before one is out
  of the wood 884
hollow
 unsubstantial 4
 completely 52
 incomplete 53
 depth 208
 concavity 252
 channel 350
 – *sound* 408
 specious 477
 false 544
 voiceless 581
 beat – 731
 – truce 723
holm 346
holocaust
 kill 361
 sacrifice 991
 (*destruction* 162)
holograph 590
holster 191
holt 367
holus bolus 684
Holy *of God* 976
 pious 987
 keep – 987
 – breathing 990
 – Church 983a
 – City 981
 – day 998
 – Ghost 976
 temple of the –
  Ghost 983a
 – men of old 985
 – orders 995
 – place 1000
 – Scriptures 985
 – Spirit 976
 – water 998
 – week 998
holystone 652
homage
 submission 725
 fealty 743
 reverence 928
 approbation 931
 worship 990
home *focus* 74
 habitation 189
 near 197
 interior 221
 arrival 292
 refuge 666
 at – *party* 72
 present 186
 within 221
 at ease 705
 social gathering
  892
 be at –
 – *to visitors* 892
 feel at –
 freedom 748
 pleasure 827
 content 831
 look at –
 accusation 938
 make oneself at –
 free 748
 sociable 892
 not be at – 764
 stay at – 265
 at – in

knowledge 490
 skill 698
 at – with
  friendship 888
 bring – to
  evidence 467
 belief 484
 accuse 938
 condemn 971
 come – 292
 eternal – 98
 from – 187
 get – 292
 go – 283
 go from – 293
 long – 363
 strike –
  energy 171
 attack 716
 – *stroke* 170
 – *thrust*
  attack 716
 censure 932
home-bred 851
home-felt 821, 824
home-rule 737, 748
homeless
 unhoused 185
 banished 893
homely
 language 576
 unadorned 849
 common 851, 876
homeopathic
 small 32
 little 193
Homeopathy 662
Homeric
 – laughter 838
home-sick 833
home-spun
 texture 329
home-stall 189
homestead 189
homeward bound
  292
homicidal maniac
  913
homicide 361
homiletical 892
homily
 teaching 537
 advice 595
 sermon 998
hominem, argu-
  mentum ad –
  938
homogeneity
 relation 9
 identity 13
 uniformity 16
 simplicity 42
homogenesis 161
homologous 23
homology
 relation 9
 uniformity 16
 equality 27
 concord 714
homonym
 equivocal 520
 vocal sound 580
homophony 413
homunculus 193
Hon. 817
hone 253
honest

veracious 543
 honorable 939
 pure 960
 – *meaning* 516
 turn an – penny
  775
 – *truth* 494
honey
 sweet 396
 favorite 899
 milk and – 734
honeycomb
 concave 252
 opening 260
 deterioration 659
honeyed
 – *phrases* 894
 – *words*
 allurement 615
 flattery 933
honeymoon
 pleasure 827
 endearment 902
 marriage 903
honey-mouthed
  894, 933
honeysuckle 396
honorarium 784, 973
honorary 815
honor
 demesne 780
 glory 873
 title 877
 respect 928
 approbation 931
 probity 939
 affair of – 720
 do – to 883
 do the –s
 sociality 892
 courtesy 894
 respect 928
 his – *judge* 967
 in – of 883
 man of – 939
 upon my – 535,
  768
 word of – 768
 – be to 873
 – a bill 807
 – in the breach
  923
 – bright
 veracity 543
 probity 939
honte, mauvaise –
  881
hood 225, 999
hooded 223
hoodlum 887
hoodoo 649
hoodwink
 ignore 491
 blind 442
 hide 528
 deceive 545
hoof 211
 cloven – 907
hook *fasten* 43
 fastening 45
 hang 214
 curve 245
 deceive 545
 retain 781
 take 789
 by – or by crook
  631

hookah 392
hooker *ship* 273
hookey, blind – 840
hooks, go off the
  360
hooligan 887, 913
hoop *circle* 247
 cry 411
hoot *cry* 411, 412
 deride 929
 contempt 930
 censure 932
hop *leap* 309
 dance 840, 892
 – off 293
 – skip and jump
  leap 309
 agitation 315
 haste 684
 game 840
 – the twig 360
hope 858
 band of – 958
 beyond – 658, 734
 dash one's –s 837
 excite – 511
 foster – 858
 well-grounded –
  472
 – against hope 859
 – for the best 858
 – deferred
 dejection 837
 lamentation 859
 – for *expect* 507
 desire 865
 hope chest 858
hopeful *infant* 129
 probable 472
 hope 858
hopelessness 471,
  859
Hop-o'-my-thumb
  193
hopper 191
horary 108
horde
 assemblage 72
 party 712
 commonalty 876
horizon
 distance 196
 view 441
 expectation 507
 appear on the –
  525
 gloomy – 859
horizontality 213
horn
 receptacle 191
 sharp 253
 music 417
 draw in one's –s
 recant 607
 submit 725
 humility 879
 exalt one's – 873
 wear the –s 905
 –s of a dilemma
 reasoning 476
 difficulty 704
 – in 294
 – mad 920
 – of plenty 639
hornbook 542
hornet
 evil-doer 913

–'s nest
 pitfall 667
 difficulty 704
 adversity 735
 painful 830
 resentment 900
 censure 932
hornpipe 840
hornwork 717
horny 323
Horny, old – 978
horology 114
horoscope 511, 992
horresco referens
  860
horrible *great* 31
 noxious 649
 dire 830
 ugly 846
 fearful 860
horrid [see horrible]
 vulgar 851
horrida bella 722
horrific [see
  horrible]
horrified 828, 860
horrify 830, 860
horripilation 383
horrisonous 410
horror 860, 867
 view with – 898
horrors 837
 sup full of – 828
horror-stricken 828
hors de combat
 impotent 158
 useless 645
 tired out 688
 put – 731
hors-d'oeuvre 298
horse *hang on* 214
 stand 215
 carrier 271
 animal 366
 male 373
 cavalry 726
 ride the high –
  885
 put the –s to 673
 put up one's –s at
  184
 put up one's –s
  together
 concord 714
 friendship 888
 take – 266
 to – 293
 war – 726
 work like a – 686
 – artillery 726
 – of another color
  15
 – doctor 370
 – and foot 726
 – laugh 838
 – marine 701
 like a – in a mill
  613
 – racing
 pastime 840
 contention 720
 – soldier 726
 – track 627
horseback 266
horse-cloth 225
horseman 268
horsemanship

riding 266
skill 698
horseplay 856
horse power 466
horse-shoe 245
horse-whip 972
hortation 615, 695
hortative 537
horticulture 371
hortus siccus 369
hosanna 931, 990
hose
  stockings 225
  pipe 348, 350
  extinguisher 385
hosier 225
hospice 189, 662
hospitable 816, 892
hospital 189, 662
  in – 655
hospitality
  [see hospitable]
hospodar 745
host collection 72
  multitude 102
  army 726
  friend 890
  rite 998
  reckon without
    one's –
    error 495
    unskilful 699
    rash 863
  – of heaven 977
  – in himself 175
hostage 771
hostel 189
hostelry 189
hostile
  disagreeing 24
  opposed 708
  enmity 889
  in – array 708
  – meeting 720
hostilities 722
hostility 889
hostler 746
hot violent 173
  warm 382
  pungent 392
  red 434
  orange 439
  excited 824
  irascible 901
  make – 384
  – air 482, 884
  – bath 386
  – blood rash 863
    angry 900
    irascible 901
  blow – and cold
    inconsistent 477
    falsehood 544
    tergiversation 607
    caprice 608
  in – haste 684
  in – pursuit 622
  – water
    difficulty 704
    quarrel 713
    painful 830
  – water bottle 386
hot air merchant
  884
hot-bed cause 153
  centre 222
  workshop 691

Hotchkiss gun 727
hotchpotch
  mixture 41
  confusion 59
  participation 778
hotel 189
hot-headed 684,
  825
hothouse
  conservatory 371,
    636
  furnace 386
  workshop 691
hot-press 255
Hotspur 863
Hottentot 876
hough 659
hound animal 366
  hunt 622
  persecute 907
  wretch 949
  hold with the hare
    but run with the
    –s 607
  – on 615
houppelande 225
hour period 108
  point of time 113
  present time 118
  improve the shin-
    ing – 682
  one's – is come
    occasion 134
    death 360
  – after hour 110
hour-glass
  chronometer 114
  contraction 195
  narrow 203
Houri 845
hourly time 106
  frequent 136
  periodical 138
house family 166
  locale 184
  abode 189
  theater 599
  make safe 664
  council 696
  firm 712
  before the – 454
  keep – 184
  eat out of – and
    home
    prodigal 818
    gluttony 957
  turn out of – and
    home 297
  – of cards 160
  – of correction
    prison 752
    punishment 975
  – of death 363
  – of detention 752
  – divided against
    itself 713
  bring the – about
    one's ears 699
  – of Commons
    696, 966
  – of God 1000
  – of Lords 696,
    875, 966
  set one's – in
    order 952
  – of peers 696, 875
  – of prayer 1000

  – built on sand
    160
  turn – out of win-
    dow 713
housebreaker 792
housebreaking 791
house-dog 366
household
  inhabitants 188
  abode 189
  – gods 189
  – stuff 635
  – troops 726
  – words
    known 490
    language 560
    plain 576, 849
householder 188
housekeeper 637,
  694
housekeeping 692
houseless 185
housemaid 746
house-organ 531
Houses of Parlia-
  ment 191, 696
house-top 210
  proclaim from –
    531
house-room 180
house-warming 892
housewife 682
housewifery 692,
  817
housing
  lodging 189
  covering 223
  horse-cloth 225
hovel 189
hoveller 269
hover high 206
  rove 266
  soar 267
  ascend 305
  irresolute 605
  – about
    move 264
  – over
    near 197
how way 627
  means 632
  – comes it?
    attribution 155
    inquiry 461
  – now 870
howbeit 30
however
  degree 26
  notwithstanding
    30
  except 83
howitzer 727
howker 273
howl
  wind 349
  human cry 411
  animal cry 412
  lamentation 839
howler 495
howling wilderness
  169, 893
hoy 273
hoyden girl 129
  rude 851
hub 222
hubble-bubble 392
hubbub stir 315

noise 404
  discord 713
huckster 794, 797
huddle
  disorder 59
  derange 61
  collect 72
  hug 197
  – on 225
Hudibrastic 856
  – verse 597
hue 428
  – and cry cry 411
    proclaim 531
    pursuit 622
    alarm 669
  raise a – and cry
    932
hueless 429
huff 885, 900
huffy 901
hug cohere 46
  border on 197
  retain 781
  courtesy 894
  love 897
  endearment 902
  – a belief 606
  – oneself
    pleasure 827
    content 831
    rejoicing 838
    pride 878
  – the shore
    navigation 267
    approach 286
    – a sin 945
huge 31, 192
hugger-mugger 528
Huguenot 984
huis clos, à – 528
huissier 965
huke 225
hulk body 50
  ship 273
hulks 752
hulky big 192
  unwieldy 647
  ugly 846
hull 50
hullabaloo 404, 411
hullo! 292
hum
  faint sound 405
  continued sound
    407
  animal sound 412
  sing 416
  deceive 545, 546
  – and haw
    stammer 583
    irresolute 605
  busy – of men 682
human 372
  – race 372
  – sacrifices 991
humane
  benevolent 906
  philanthropic 910
  merciful 914
humanitarian 372,
  910
humanities 560
humanize 894
humano capiti cer-
  vicem jungere
  equinam 24

humation 363
humble meek 879
  modest 881
  pious 987
  –r classes 876
  – oneself
    submit 725
    meek 879
    penitent 950
    worship 990
  eat – pie 725, 879
  your – servant
    dissent 489
    refusal 764
humbug
  falsehood 544
  deception 545
  deceiver 548
  trifle 643
  affectation 855
humdrum 841, 843
humectate 337, 339
humid 339
humiliate 308
humiliation
  adversity 735
  disrepute 874
  sense of shame
    879
  worship 990
  self – 950
humility 879, 987
humming-top 417
hummock 206, 250
humorist 844
humor essence 5
  tendency 176
  liquid 333
  disposition 602
  caprice 608
  aid 707
  indulge 760
  affections 820
  please 829
  wit 842
  flatter 933
  (fun 840)
  in the – 602
  out of – 901a
  peccant –
    unclean 853
    disease 655
humorous 842
humorsome
  capricious 608
  sulky 901a
hump 250
hump-backed 243
humph! 870
Humphrey, dine
  with Duke – 956
Humpty-dumpty
  193
Hun 165, 851, 913
hunch 250, 612
hunch-backed 243
hundred
  number 98
  many 102
  region 181
  the same a – years
    hence 460
hundredth 99
hundredweight 319
hunger 865
hunger-strike 956
hunks 819

ill-defined 447
ill-devised 499, 699
ill-digested 674
ill-disposed 901a,
907
illegality **964**
illegible 519
render — 552
— hand 590
illegitimate
deceitful 545
undue 925
illegal 964
ill-fated 735
ill-flavored 395
ill-furnished 640
illiberal
narrow-minded
481
stingy 819
uncourteous 895
selfish 943
illicit 925, 964
ill-imagined 499,
699
illimited 105
ill-intentioned 907
illiterate 491, 493
ill-judged 499, 699
ill-judging 481
ill-made 243, 846
ill-mannered 851,
895
ill-marked 447
ill-matched 24
ill-mated 24
ill-natured 907
illogical 477, 495
ill-omened 605, 859
ill-proportioned 243
ill-provided 640
ill-qualified 699
ill-requited 917
ill-spent 646
ill-tempered 901
ill-timed 135
ill-treat *bad* 649
severe 739
malevolent 907
illuminant 388
illuminate
enlighten 420
color 428
excite 824
ornament 847
illuminati 492
illumination
[*see* illuminate]
book-illustration
558
celebration 883
ill-use 907
ill-used 828
illusion
fallacy of vision
443
error 495
illusive, illusory
sophistical 477
erroneous 495
deceitful 545, 546
illustrate
exemplify 82
interpret 522
represent 554
engravings 558
ornament 847

illustrious 873
image
likeness **17**
copy 21
appearance 448
idea 453
metaphor 521
representation
554
graven — *idol* 991
imagery *fancy* 515
metaphor 521
representation
554
imaginable 470
imaginary
non-existing 2
fancied 515
— *quantity* 84
imagination **515**
imaum 745, 996
imbecile 158, 499
imbécile 501
imbecility **499**
imbed [*see* embed]
imbedded 229
imbibe 296
— *learning* 539
imbrangle 61
imbricated 223
imbroglio
disorder 59
difficulty 704
discord 713
imbrue
impregnate 300
moisten 339
— one's hands in
blood
killing 361
war 722
— the soul 824
imbue *mix* 41
impregnate 300
moisten 339
tinge 428
teach 537
imbued
affections 820
— with
belief 484
habit 613
feeling 821
imburse 803
imitation
copying **19**
copy 21
representation
554
immaculate
perfect 650
clean 652
innocent 946
immanent 5, 132
immanity 907
Immanuel 976
immaterial
unsubstantial 4
immateriality
spiritual **317**
trifling 643
immature 123, 674
immeasurable 31,
105
immediate
continuous 69
immediately 113,

132
immedicabile
vulnus 619
immedicable 859
immelodious 414
immemorial 124
from time — 122
— usage 613
immense *great* 31
infinite 105
- *size* 192
immerge)
immerse}
introduce 300
dip 337
immersed in 229
immethodical 59
immigrant
alien 57
entering 294
immigration 266,
294
imminent 152, 286
immiscible 47
immission 296
immitigable
hopeless 859
revenge 919
immix 41
immobility 150, 265
immoderately 31
immodest 961
immolation
killing 361
giving 784
sacrifice 991
immoral 923, 945
immortal
perpetual 112
glorious 873
celebrated 883
immotile 265
immovable
stable 150
quiescent 265
obstinate 606
immundicity 653
immunity
health 656
freedom 748
right 924
exemption 777a,
927a
immure 751
immutable
stable 150
deity 976
imo pectore, ab —
821
imp 980
impact *contact* 43
impulse 276
insertion 300
impair 659
impale *transfix* 260
execute 972
impalpable
small 193
powder 330
intangible 381
impanation 998
impar sibi 608
imparity 28
impart *inform* 527
give 784
impartial
judicious 498

neutral 628
just 922
honorable 939
— *opinion* 484
impassable
closed 261
impossible 471
impasse 706
impassible 823
impassion 824
impassionable 822
impassioned
- *language* 574
excited 825
impassive 823
impatient 825
— *of control* 742
impawn 771
impeach
censure 932
accuse 938
go to law 969
impeachment,
soft — 902
impeccability 650,
946
impecunious 804
impede 706
impediment 706
— *in speech* 583
impedimenta 633,
780
impel *push* 276
induce 615
impend
future 121
imminent 132
destiny 152
overhang 206
impenetrable
closed 261
solid 321
unintelligible 519
latent 526
impenitence **951**
imperative
require 630
command 737,
741
severe 739
duty 926
imperator 745
imperceptible
small 32
minute 193
slow 275
invisible 447
latent 526
impercipient 376
imperdible 664
imperfect
incomplete 53
failing 651
vicious 945
imperfection **651**
inferiority 34
vice 945
imperfectly 32
imperforate 261
imperial
trunk 191
beard 256
authority 737
imperil 665
imperious
command 737
proud 878

arrogant 885
— *necessity* 601
imperishable 112
stable 150
glorious 873
imperium in
imperio 737
impermanent 111
impermeable
closed 261
dense 321
impersonal
general 78
neuter 316
impersonate 19,
554
impersonator 19
imperspicuity 519
impersuasible 606
impertinent
irrelevant 10
insolent 885
imperturbable 823,
826
impervious
closed 261
impossible 471
insensible 823
— *to light* 426
— *to reason* 606
impetiginous 653
impetrate 765
impetuous
boisterous 173
hasty 684
excitable 825
rash 863
eager 865
impetus 276
impi 726
impiety **988**
impignorate 787
impinge 276
implacable 848, 919
implant *insert* 300
teach 537
implanted
adventitious 6
implausible 473
implead 969
implement 633
impletion 52
implex 41
implicate *involve* 54,
526
accuse 938
implicated *related* 9
component 56
implication
disorder 59
meaning 516
latency 526
implicit 526
— *belief* 484
implore 765
imply *evidence* 467
mean 516
involve 526
impolicy 699
impolite 895
imponderable 4,
320
imporous 261, 321
import
put between 228
ingress 294
take in 296

insert 300
mean 516
imply 526
be of consequence 642
importance **642**
greatness 30
attach – to 642
attach too much – to 482
of no – 643
importune 765, 830
impose *order* 741
awe 928
– upon
credulity 486
deceive 545
be unjust 923
imposing
important 642
exciting 824
glorious 873
imposition [*see* impose]
undue 925
– of hands 998
impossibile, credo quia – 486
impossibilities, seek after – 645
impossibility **471**
impossible 471
refusal 764
– quantity
algebra 84
impost 812
imposthume 655
impostor 548, 925
imposture 545
impotence **158**
impotent conclusion 732
impound 791
impoverish
weaken 160
waste 638
despoil 789
render poor 804
impracticable
impossible 471
misjudging 481
obstinate 606
difficult 704
imprecation
prayer 765
curse 908
impregnable 159, 664
impregnate *mix* 41
combine 48
fecundate 161, 168
insert 300
teach 537
– with 641
impresario 599
imprescriptible 924
impress *cause*
sensation 375
mark 550
compel 791
excite feeling 824
– upon the mind
memory 505
teach 537
impressed with
belief 484

feeling 821
impressible
motive 615
sensibility 822
impression
sensation 375
idea 453
belief 484
printing 531
mark 550
engraving 558
print 591
emotion 821
make an –
act 171
thought 451
impressionable 375, 822
impressive
language 574
important 642
feeling 821, 824
imprimis 66
imprimit 558
imprint
publisher 531
indication 550
– in the memory 505
imprison
circumscribe 229
restrain 751
punish 972
improbability **473**
improbate 932
improbity **940**
impromptu 612
– fait à loisir 673
improper
incongruous 24
foolish 499
solecism 568
inexpedient 647
wrong 923
unmeet 925
vicious 945
– time 135
impropriate 777, 789
impropriator 779
improve 658
– the occasion 134
– the shining hour 682
– upon 658
improvement **658**
improvident
careless 460
not preparing 674
prodigal 818
rash 863
improvisation
music 415
improvisatore
speech 582
poetry 597
impulse 612
improvise
imagination 515
impulse 612
unprepared 674
improvise, à l'– 508, 612
improvisatrice 612
imprudent 460, 863
impudent 885, 895

impudicity 961
impugn *deny* 536
attack 716
blame 932
impugnation 708
impuissance 158
impulse *push* **276**
sudden thought **612**
motive 615
blind – 601
creature of – 612
give an – to
propel 284
aid 707
impulsive [*see* impulse]
intuitive 477
excitable 825
rash 863
impunity *escape* 671
acquittal 970
with – *safely* 664
impurity 653, **961**
imputation
ascribe 155
slur 874
accuse 938
in 221
go – 294
– as much as
relation 9
degree 26
– the circumstances 8
– doors 221
– durancevile 751
– for
undertake 676
promise 768
– re 9
– and out 314
–s and outs 182
in : – articulo 111
– extenso *whole* 50
diffuse 573
– jail 751
– limine 66
– loco 23
– medias res 68
– prison 751
– propriâ personâ 79
– toto 52
– transitu
transient 111
transfer 270
– statu pupillari 127
– statu quo 141
– vogue 1
inability 158, 699
inabstinent 954
inaccessible 196, 471
inaccurate 495, 568
inaction 172, **683**
inactivity **683**, 172
inadequate
powerless 158
insufficient 640
useless 645
imperfect 651
inadmissible
incongruous 24
excluded 55

extraneous 57
inexpedient 647
inadvertence 458
inadvisable 647
inaffable 895
inalienable
retention 781
right 924
inamorata 897
inane *void* 4
unmeaning 517
unthinking 452
insufficient 640
trivial 643
useless 645
inanimate 360
– matter 358
inanition 158
inanity [*see* inane]
inappetency 823, 866
inapplicable 10, 24
inapposite 10, 24
inappreciable 33, 193
unimportant 643
inapprehensible
stolid 499
unintelligible 519
inappropriate 24, 647
inapt
incongruous 24
impotent 158
useless 645
inexpedient 647
unskilful 699
inarticulate 581, 583
inartificial 703
inartistic 846
inasmuch *whereas* 9
however 26
because 476
inattention **458**
inaudible
silence 403
faint sound 405
deaf 419
voiceless 581
inaugural
precursor 64
inaugurate
begin 66
cause 153
install 755
celebrate 883
inauspicious
untimely 135
untoward 649
hopeless 859
inbeing 5
inborn, inbred
intrinsic 5
affections 820
– proclivity 601
inca 745
incage 751
incalculable 31, 105
incalescence 382
incandescence 382
incandescent 423
incantation
invocation 765
sorcery 992
spell 993
incantatory 992

incapable 158
incapacious 203
incapacitate 158
incapacity
impotence 158
ignorance 491
stupidity 499
incarcerate 751
incarnadine 434
incarnate
intrinsic 5
bodily 316
fleshly 364
vicious 945
devil –
bad man 949
Satan 978
Incarnation 976
incase 223, 229
incautious 863
incendiary
destroy 162
burn 384
influence 615
malevolent 907
evil-doer 913
bad man 949
incense *fuel* 388
fragrant 400
hate 898
anger 900
flatter 933
worship 990
rite 998
incension
burning 384
incentive 615
inception 66
inceptive 153
inceptor 541
incertitude 475
incessant
repeated 104
ceaseless 112
frequent 136
incest 961
inch *small* 32
length 200
by –es 275
to an – 494
not yield an – 606
give an – and take an ell 789
– by inch
by degrees 26
in parts 51
slowly 275
not see an – beyond one's nose 699
inchoation 66, 673
incide 44
incidence 278
incident 151
incidental
extrinsic 6
circumstance 8
irrelative 10
occurring 151
casual 156
liable 177
chance 621
trivial 643
– music 415
incinerate 384
incipience 66
incircumspect 460

incision 44, 259
incisive *energy* 171
  vigor 574
  feeling 821
incisor 253
incite
  exasperate 173
  urge 615
incivility 895
incivism 911
inclasp 229
inclement
  violent 173
  cold 383
  severe 739
  pitiless 914a
inclination
  [*see* incline]
  will 600
  affection 820
  desire 865
  love 897
incline *tendency* 176
  slope 217
  direction 278
  willing 602
  induce 615
  – an ear to 457
  – the head 308
inclined
  disposed 620
  – plane 633
inclose
  surround 227
inclosure **232**
include
  composition 54
  – *in a class* 76
inclusion **76**
inclusive
  additive 37
  component 56
  class 76
incogitancy **452**
incognita, terra –
  491
incognito 528
incognizable 519
incoherence
  physical **47**
  mental 503
incombustible 385
income *means* 632
  profit 775
  property 780
  wealth 803
  receipt 810
  – tax 812
incoming
  ingress 294
  receipt 810
incommensurable
  10
  – *quantity* 84, 85
incommode 706
  hinder 706
incommunicable
  unmeaning 517
  unintelligible 519
  retention 781
incommunicado
  528
incommutable 150
incomparable 33
incompassionate
  914a
incompatible 24

incompatibility 15
incompetence
  inability 158
  incapacity 499
  unskilful 699
  dereliction 927
incompleteness **53**
  non-completion
  730
incompliance 764
incomprehensible
  infinite 105
  unintelligible 519
incomprehension
  491
incompressible 321
inconcealable 525
inconceivable
  unthinkable 452
  impossible 471
  improbable 473
  incredible 485
  unintelligible 519
  wonder 870
inconceptible 519
inconcinnity
  disagreement 24
  ugliness 846
inconclusive 477
inconcoction 674
incondite 851
incongruous
  differing 15
  disagreeing 24
  illogical 477
  ungrammatical
  568
  discordant 713
inconnection 10, 44
inconsequence
  irrelation 10
inconsequential 477
inconsiderable 32,
  643
inconsiderate
  thoughtless 452
  inattentive 458
  neglectful 460
  foolish 699
inconsistent
  contrary 14
  disagreeing 24
  illogical 477
  absurd 497
  foolish 499
  capricious 608
  discord 713
inconsolable 837
inconsonant
  disagreeing 24
  fitful 149
inconspicuous 447
inconstant 149
incontestable 159,
  474, 525
incontiguous 196
incontinent 961
incontinently 132
incontrollable 173
incontrovertible
  150, 474
inconvenience 647
  put to – 706
inconversable 585,
  893
inconvertible 143
inconvincible 487

incorporate 48
  combine 48
  include 76
  materialize 316
incorporation 761
incorporeal 317
  – *hereditaments*
  780
incorrect
  illogical 477
  erroneous 495
  solecism 568
  vicious 945
incorrigible
  obstinate 606
  hopeless 859
  vicious 945
  impenitent 951
incorruption
  probity 939
  innocence 946
incrassate
  increase 194
  density 321
  – *fluids* 352
increase
  – *in degree* **35**
  – *in number* 102
  – *in size* 194
incredible
  great 31
  impossible 471
  improbable 473
  doubtful 485
  wonderful 870
incredulity 487, 989
increment
  increase 35
  addition 37
  adjunct 39
  expansion 194
increpation 932
incriminate 938
incrust 223, 224
incubate 370
incubation 673
incubus
  hindrance 706
  pain 828
  demon 980
inculcate 6, 537
inculpable 946
inculpate 938
inculture 674
incumbency
  business 625
  churchdom 995
incumbent
  inhabitant 188
  high 206
  weight 319
  duty 926
  clergyman 996
incumber 706
incumbered 806
incunabula 66, 127
incur 177
  – *blame* 932
  – *danger* 665
  – *a debt* 806
  – *disgrace* 874
  – *a loss* 776
  – *the risk* 621
incurable
  ingrained 5
  disease 655
  hopeless 859

incuriam, per –
  458, 460
incuriosity **456**
incursion 294, 716
incurvation 245
indagation 461
indebted
  owing 806
  gratitude 916
  duty 926
indecent 961
indeciduous 150
indecipherable 519
indecision 475, 605
indecisive 475
indeclinable 150
indecorous
  vulgar 851
  vicious 945
  impure 961
indeed *existing* 1
  very 31
  assent 488
  truly 494
  assertion 535
  wonder 870
indefatigable
  persevering 604a
  active 682
indefeasible
  stable 150, 474
  due 924
indefectible 650
indefensible
  powerless 158
  submission 725
  accusable 938
  wrong 945
indeficient 650
indefinite
  great 31
  unspecified 78
  infinite 105
  misty 447
  uncertain 475
  inexact 495
  vague 519
indeliberate 612
indelible *stable* 150
  memory 505
  mark 550
  feeling 821
indelicate 961
indemnity
  compensation 30
  restitution 790
  forgiveness 918
  atonement 952
  reward 973
  deed of – 771
indenization 184
indent *scollop* 248
  list 86
indentation 252,
  257
indenture 769, 771
independence
  irrelation 10
  freedom 748
  wealth 803
Independent 984
indescribable 31,
  870
indesinent 112
indestructible 150
indeterminate
  indefinite 78

  chance 156
  uncertain 475
  irresolute 605
indevotion 989
index
  arrangement 60
  exponent 84
  list 86
  sign 550
  words 62
index expurga-
  torius 761, 932
indexterity 699
Indian:
  – file 69
  – rubber 325
  – summer 126
  – weed 392
indicate
  specify 79
  direct attention to
  457
  mean 516
  mark 550
indication **550**
indicative
  evidence 467
indict *accuse* 938
  arraign 969
indiction 108, 531
indifference
  incuriosity 456
  unwillingness 603
  no choice 609a
  insensibility 823
  unconcern **866**
  irreligion 989
  matter of – 643
indifferent
  [*see* indifference]
  unimportant 643
  bad 649
indigence
  insufficiency 640
  poverty 804
indigenous 5, 186
indigested 674
indigestible 657
indigestion 657
indigitate 457
indign 940
indignation 900
  – *meeting* 832
indignity 900, 929
indigo 438
indiligence 683
indirect
  oblique 217
  devious 279
  latent 526
  circuitous 629
indiscernible 447
indiscerptible
  whole 50
  unity 87
  dense 321
indiscoverable 526
indiscreet 499, 863,
  945
indiscretion
  guilt 947
indiscriminate
  mixed 41
  unarranged 59
  multiform 81
  casual 621
indiscrimination

inebriation 959
intra, ab – 221
intractable
  obstinate 606
  difficult 704
  sullen 901a
intramural 221
intransient 110
intransigeance 604
intransitive 110
intransmutable
  110, 150
intrap 545
intraregarding 221
intrench 717
  – on 303
intrepid 861
intricate
  confused 59
  convoluted 248
  difficult 704
intrigant
  meddlesome 682
  cunning 702
  libertine 962
intrigue fascinate
  615, 897
  plot 626
  activity 682
  cunning 702
  excite 824
  interest 829
  licentiousness 961
intrinsic 5
  – evidence 467
  – habit 613
  – truth 494
intrinsicality 5
introception 296
introduce lead 62
  interpose 228
  precede 280
  insert 300
  – new blood 140
  – new conditions
  469
  – to 888
introduction
  [see introduce]
  preface 64
  reception 296
  drama 599
  friendship 888
  courtesy 894
introductory
  precursor 64
  beginning 66
  priority 116
introgression 294
introit 998
intromission 228
intromit
  discontinue 142
  receive 296
introspection 441,
  457
introspective 451
introvert 218
intrude
  interfere 24
  inopportune 135
  intervene 228
  enter 294
  encroach 303
intruder 57
intrusiveness 682
intrust 755, 787

intuition mind 450
  unreasoning 477
  knowledge 490
intumescence 194,
  250
intwine 43, 243
inunction 223
inundate
  effusion 337
  flow 348
  redundance 641
inunderstanding
  452
inurbanity 895
inure 613, 673
inured
  insensible 823
inusitation 614
inutility 645
invade ingress 294
  encroach 303
  attack 716
invalid
  powerless 158
  illogical 477
  diseased 655
  undue 925
invalidate
  disable 158
  weaken 160
  confute 479
invaluable 648
invariable
  intrinsic 5
  uniform 16
  conformable 82
  stable 150
invasion
  ingress 294
  attack 716
invective 932
inveigh 932
inveigle 545, 615
invent
  discover 480a
  imagine 515
  lie 544
  devise 626
invented
  untrue 546
invention 480a
inventive
  skilful 698
inventor 164
inventory 86
inverse 14, 218
inversion
  derangement 61
  change 140
  of position 218
  contraposition
  237
  reversion 145
  language 577
invertebrate 158
invest
  empower 157
  clothe 225
  besiege 227, 716
  commission 755
  give 784
  lend 787
  expend 809
  – in locate 184
  purchase 795
  – money 817
  – with ascribe 155

investigate 461
investment 225
  – trust 712
  make –s 673
inveterate old 124
  established 150
  inborn 820
  – belief 484
  – habit 613
invidious
  painful 830
  hatred 898
  spite 907
  envy 921
invigorate
  strengthen 159
invigorating
  healthy 656
invincible 159
inviolable
  secret 528
  right 924
  honor 939
inviolate
  permanent 141
  secret 528
  honorable 939
invious closed 261
  pathless 704
invisibility 447
invisible small 193
  not to be seen 447
  concealed 526
  – ink 528
  become – 4
invitâ Minervâ 603,
  704
invite induce 615
  offer 763
  ask 765
  – the attention
  457
inviting
  [see invite]
  pleasing 829
invoice 86
invoke address 586
  implore 765
  pray 990
  – curses 908
  – saints 998
involucrum 223
involuntary
  necessary 601
  unwilling 603
  – servitude 749
involution [see
  involve]
  algebra 85
involve include 54
  derange 61
  wrap 225
  evince 467
  mean 516
  latency 526
involved
  disorder 59
  convoluted 248
  obscure style 571
  in debt 806
involvement 704
invulnerable 664
inward intrinsic 5
  inside 221
  – bound 294
  – monitor 926
inweave 219

inwrap 225
inwrought 5
io triumphe! 838,
  883
Ionic 597
iota 32
I. O. U. 771, 800
ipse dixit 474, 535
ipsissima verba 494
ipso facto 1
irae
  amantium — 918
  tantaene animis
  coelestibus — 900
irascibility 901
irate 900
ire 900
iridescent 440
Iris 268, 534
iris 440, 441
Irish Bull 353
Irishism 497
irk 688, 830
irksome
  tiresome 688
  difficult 704
  painful 830
  weary 841
iron strength 159
  smooth 255
  hard 323
  resolution 604
  rule with a rod of
  – 739
  – age adversity 735
  pain 828
  – cross 733
  – gray 432
  – grip 159
  – gripe 781
  – heel 739
  – necessity 601
  – rule 739
  – entering into the
  soul 828, 830
  – sway 739
  – will 604
iron-bound coast
  land 342
  danger 667
iron-clad
  covering 223
  defence 717
  man of war 726
iron-handed 739
iron-hearted 861
iron-mold 434
irons 752
  fire – 386
  put in – 751
  – in the fire
  business 625
  redundance 641
  active 682
  unskilful 699
irony
  figure of speech
  521
  untruth 546
  ridicule 856
irradiate 420
irrational
  number 84
  illogical 477
  silly 499
irreclaimable
  hopeless 859

vicious 945
  impenitent 951
irreconcilable
  unrelated 10
  discordant 24
  unwilling 603
  opponent 710
  enmity 889
irrecoverable
  past 122
  hopeless 859
irredeemable 859
irredentist 776
irreducible
  discordant 24
  out of order 59
  unchangeable 150
irrefragable 478
irrefutable 474, 478
irregular
  diverse 16a
  out of order 59
  multiform 81
  against rule 83
  – in recurrence
  139
  distorted 243
  combatant 726
irregularity 139
irrelation 10
irrelevant
  unrelated 10
  unaccordant 24
  sophistical 477
  unimportant 643
irreligion 989
irremediable
  bad 649
  hopeless 859
  (spoiled 659)
irremissible 945
irremovable 150
irreparable
  hopeless 859
irrepentance 951
irreprehensible 946
irrepressible
  violent 173
  free 748
  excitable 825
irreproachable 946
irreprovable 946
irresistible
  strong 159
  demonstration
  478
  necessary 601
irresoluble 150
irresolution 605
irresolvable 87
irresolvedly 605
irrespective 10
irresponsible
  irresolute 605
  exempt 927a
  arbitrary 964
irretrievable
  stable 150
  lost 776
  hopeless 859
irrevealable 528
irreverence 929,
  988
irreversible
  stable 150
  hopeless 859
irrevocable

stable 150
  necessary 601
  resolute 604
  hopeless 859
irrigate 337
irriguous 339
irrision 856, 929
irritabile, genus –
  901
irritable 825, 901
irritate *violent* 173
  excite 824
  pain 830
  provoke 898
  incense 900
irritation
  [*see* irritate]
  pain 828
  ·source of – 830
irritating
  [*see* irritate]
  stringent 171
irruption 294, 716
Irvingite 984
Ishmael 83
is: that – 118
  – to be 152
Isis 979
Islamism 984
island 181, **346**
  –s of the blessed
  981
islander 188
isle 346
isobar 338
isocheimal 383
isochronal 114
isochronous 27, 120
isolate 44, 893
isolated 10, 87
isomorphism 240
isoperimetrical 27
isothermal 382
  – layer 338
isotonic 413
issue *distribute* 73
  focus 74
  event 151
  effect 154
  posterity 167
  depart 293
  egress 295
  stream 348, 349
  inquiry 461
  publication 531
  book 593
  ulcer 655
  dénouement 729
  money 800
  at – *discussion* 476
  dissent 489
  negation 536
  opposition 708
  discord 713
  contention 720
  in – 461
  join – *lawsuit* 969
  – a command 741
issueless 169
isthmus
  connection 45
  narrow 203
  land 342
italics *mark* 550
  put in –
  importance 642
itch *titillation* 380

desire 865
itching palm 819
item
  addition 37, 39
  part 51
  speciality 79
  unit 87
iteration 104
itinerant 266, 268
itinerary 266, 527
itur ad astra, sic –
  360
ivory 430
Ixion 312

J

jab 276
jabber
  unmeaning 517
  stammer 583
  chatter 584
jacent 213
jacet, hic – 363
jacinth 847
jack
  rotation 312
  ensign 550
  instrument 633
  money 800
Jack – Cade 742
  – Ketch 975
  – o' lantern 423
  – in office
    director 694
    bully 887
  – at a pinch 711
  – Pudding
    actor 599
    humorist 844
    boaster 884
  before one can say
  ' – Robinson'
  132
  – tar 269
  – of all trades 700
jack-a-dandy 844,
  854
jackal
  auxiliary 711
  servility 886
jackanapes 854,
  887
Jackass 271
jack-boot 225
jackdaw in pea-
  cock's feathers
  701
jacket 225
  cork – 666
Jacobin 710
Jacquerie 716, 719
jacta est alea 601
jactitation
  tossing 315
  boasting 884
jaculation 284
jade *horse* 271
  fatigue 688
  low woman 876
  scamp 949
  drab 962
jag 257
jagged 244
jail 752

– bird
  prisoner 754
  bad man 949
jailer 753, 975
jakes 653
jalousie de métier
  921
jam *squeeze* 43
  crowd 72
  food 298
  pulp 354
  sweet 396
  scrape 732
  – in *interpose* 228
jamb 215
jamboree 840
jammed in 751
jangle
  harsh sound 410
  quarrel 713
janissary 726
janitor 263
janty *gay* 836
  pretty 845
  stylish 852
  showy 882
  insolent 885
January 138
januis clausis 528
Janus *deceiver* 607
  tergiversation 607
  close the temple
  of – 723
Janus-faced 544
japan *coat* 223
  resin 356a
  ornament 847
jar *clash* 24
  vessel 191
  agitation 315
  stridor 410
  discord 713
  – upon the feel-
  ings 830
jardinière 191
jargon
  absurdity 497
  no meaning 517
  unintelligible 519
  neology 563
jarvey 694
jasper 847
jaundiced
  yellow 436
  prejudiced 481
  dejected 837
  jealous 920
  view with – eyes
  disapprove 932
jaunt 266
jaunting car 272
jaunty [*see* janty]
javelin 727
jaw *chatter* 584
  scold 932
jaw-fallen 837
jaws *mouth* 231
  eating 298
  – of death 360
jay 584
jaywalker 701
jazz 415, 840
  – band 417
jealous of honor
  939
jealousy **920**
  suspicion 485

jecur, difficili bile –
  900
jeer 929
Jehovah 976
Jehu 268, 694
jejune *insipid* 391
  style 575
  scanty 640
  dull 843
jell 352
jelly 298, 352
  beat to a – 972
jemidar 745
jemmy *lever* 633
  dandy 854
je ne sais quoi
  exceptional 83
  what d'ye call 'em
  563
  beauty 845
jennet 271
jeopardy 665
jerboa 309
jeremiad
  lament 839
  invective 932
Jericho, send to –
  297
jerk *start* 146
  throw 284
  pull 285
  agitate 315
jerkin 225
jerks, by – 70
Jerry Sneak 862,
  941
jersey 225
Jerusalem
  the new – 981
Jessamy, Jemmy –
  854
jesse 1000
jest *trifle* 643
  wit 842
jest-book 842
jester 844
jesting-stock 857
Jesuit *deceiver* 548
  priest 996
jesuitical 477, 544
Jesus 976
jet *ship* 273
  stream 348
  – black 431
  – propulsion 267
jetsam 73, 782
jettison 782
jetty *protection* 250
  harbor 666
jeu
  le – n'en vaut pas
  la chandelle
  waste 638
  unimportant 643
  dear 814
  – d'esprit 842
  – de mots 842
  – de théâtre 599
jeune
  – premier 599
  – veuve 599
Jew *cunning* 702
  lender 787
  rich 803
  extortioner 819
  heretic 984
  worth a –'s eye

648, 814
  –'s harp 417
jewel *gem* 648
  ornament 847
  favorite 899
jewelery, false –
  545
Jezebel *wicked* 913
  wretch 949
  courtesan 962
jib *front* 234
  regression 283
  cut of one's –
  form 240
  appearance 448
jibe 140
jiffy 113
jig 840
jig-saw puzzle 840
jilt *disappoint* 509
  deceive 545
  deceiver 548
  cast off 756
  dishonor 940
jilted 898
jimp 845
jingal 727
jingle 408
jingo 887
jingoism 884
jinks, high – 840
jinriksha 272
jinx 649, 735
Joan of Arc 861
job *business* 625
  action 680
  unfair 940
  tough – 704
Job:
  patience of – 826,
  830
  poor as – 804
  –'s comforter
    dejection 837
    hopeless 859
jobation 932
jobber
  deceiver 548
  tactician 700
  merchant 797
  trickster 943
jobbernowl 501
jobbery 702, 940
jobbing *barter* 794
jockey *rider* 268
  deceive 545
  deceiver 548
  servant 746
jocose 836, 842
jocoseness *fun* 840
jocular 836, 842
jocund 836, 840
jocundity 829
Joe Miller 842, 844
jog *push* 276
  shake 315
  – the memory 505
  – on *continue* 143
  trudge 266
  slow 275
  advance 282
  mediocrity 736
joggle 315
jog-trot
  trudge 266
  slow 275
  habit 613

sad 837
– one's course 282
– an eye upon 459
– the field 722
– firm 150
– on foot
continuance 143
support 215
preparation 673
– from conceal 528
refrain 623
not do 681
restrain 751
– going
continue 143
move 264
– one's ground 141
– one's hand in 613
– one's head above
water 731, 817
– hold 150
– holy 987
– house 184
– in ignorance 528
– in restrain 751
prohibit 761
– on one's legs 654
– a good look out
for 507
– in mind 505
– moving 682
– off avoid 623
hinder 706
defend 717
resist 719
prohibition 761
– on do often 136
continue 143
persevere 604a
– to oneself 528
– in order 693
– out
- of the way 187
- of harm's way
864
– pace with 27,
120
– the peace 714
– posted 527
– the pot boiling
143
– one's promise
772
– quiet 265
– a secret 528
– a shop 625
– in sight 459
– silence 585
– straight 944
– in suspense
uncertainty 475
irresolution 605
– in the thoughts
505
– time
punctual 132
music 416
– to 604a
– together 709
– under
authority 737
subjection 749
restraint 751
– up [see below]
– in view
attend to 457
remember 505

expect 507
– waiting 133
– watch 459
– one's word 939
keep up
continue 143
preserve 670
stimulate 824
– appearances 852
– the ball 682, 840
– a correspond-
ence 592
– the memory of
505
– one's spirits 836
– with 274
keeper 370, 753
keeping
congruity 23
in – 82
safe – safety 664
preservation 670
keepsake 505
keg 191
kelpie 979
kelson 211
kempt 652
ken 441, 490
beyond mortal –
360
kennel
assemblage 72
hovel 189
ditch 259
conduit 350
Kentish fire 931
képi 225
kérb-stone 233
kerchief 225
wave a – 550
kern quern 330
low fellow 876
varlet 949
kernel heart 5
cause 153
central 222
important 642
kerosene 356
ketch
ship 273
Ketch, Jack – 975
kettle vessel 191
caldron 386
– drum music 417
tea-party 892
– of fish
disorder 59
difficulty 704
key cause 153
opener 260
music 413
color 428
interpretation 522
indication 550
instrument 631,
633
emblem of au-
thority 747
deliver the –s of
the city 725
key-hole 260
key-note model 22
rule 80
music 413
key-stone
support 215
motive 615

importance 642
completion 729
khaki 225, 433
khan inn 189
governor 745
khedive 745
kibitka 272
kibitzer 682
kick impulse 276
recoil 277
assault 716
thrill 821
spurn 930
punish 972
– against
oppose 708
resist 719
– against the
pricks
useless 645
rash 863
unequal 28
superior 33
– up a dust
active 682
discord 713
insolent 885
– a row 900
– one's heels
kept waiting 133
nothing to do 681
– off 62
– up a row
violent 173
discord 713
– over the traces
742
kicking, alive and –
359
kickshaw food 298
trifle 643
kid child 129
progeny 167
leather 223
not to be handled
with – gloves
dirty 653
difficult 704
kidnap
deceive 545
take 789
steal 791
kidney class 75
kilderkin 191
Kilkenny cats 713
kill 361
– or cure 662
– the fatted calf
883
– the goose with
golden eggs 699
– with kindness
902
– the slain 641
– time 106
inactivity 683
amusement 840
– two birds with
one stone 682
killing 361
delightful 829
kill-joy 706
kiln 386
kilowatt 466
kilt 225
kimbo 244
kimono 225

kin 75
kind class 75
benevolent 906
– regards 894
kinder-garten 542
kindle cause 153
produce 161
quicken 171
inflame 173
set fire to 384
excite 824
incense 900
kindling wood 388
kindred 9, 11
kine 366
kinematics 264
kinetic energy 157
king 745
every inch a –
authority 737
rank 875
–maker 694
King –'s Bench
752, 966
–'s birthday 268
–'s counsel 968
– Death 360
–'s English 560
–'s evidence 529
–'s highway 627
–'s ransom 648
– of Kings 976
kingcraft 693
kingdom
region 181
property 780
– of heaven 981
kingly 737
king-post 215
kink 248, 378, 608
kiosk 189, 1000
kip 961
kirk 1000
kirtle 225
kismet 601
kiss touch 199
courtesy 894
endearment 902
– the book 535
– the hem of one's
garment 928
– in the ring 840
– the rod 725
kit class 75
equipment 191
fiddle 417
–bag 191
kitcat 556
kitchen 191, 691
– maid 746
– range 386
kitchener 386
kitchenette 691
kite fly 273
bill 800
fly a – credit 805
insolvency 808
– balloon 273, 726
kith 11
kithless 87
kitten animal 366
young 129
bring forth 161
playful as a – 836,
840
kleptomania
insanity 502

stealing 791
desire 865
kleptomaniac 504
knack 698
get into the – 613
knacker 361
knag 706
knaggy 901a
knap 206
knapsack 191
knave 548, 941
– of hearts 897
knavery
deception 545
cunning 702
improbity 940
vice 945
knead mix 41
mold 240
soften 324
stroke 379
knee angle 244
bend the –
stoop 30
submission 725
down on one's –s
humble 879
on one's –s
beg 765
respect 928
atone 952
on the –s of the
gods 121, 152
knee-deep 208, 209
kneel stoop 308
submit 725
beg 765
servility 886
courtesy 894
ask mercy 914
respect 928
worship 990
knell 363
strike the death –
361
knickerbockers 225
knicknack 643, 847
knife 253
play a good – and
fork eat 298
appetite 865
war to the – 708
knight 875
– errant
madman 504
defender 717
rash 863
philanthropist
910
–'s move 279
– service 777
– of the road 792
– Templar 71
knit 43
well – 159
– the brow
discontent 832
anger 900
disapprobation
932
knitting 847
knob pendency 214
ball 249
protuberance 250
knock blow 276
sound 406
hard –s 720

landscape
  prospect 448
  —.gardening
  agriculture 71
  beauty 845
  — painting 556
  — painter 559
land-shark 792
land-slip 306
landsman 342
Landsturm 726
land-surveying 466
Landwehr 726
lane 189, 260, 627
langrel 727
lang-syne 122
language 560
  command of — 582
  strong —
    vigor 574
    malediction 908
languid weak 160
  inert 172
  slow 275
  - style 575
  inactive 683
  torpid 823
languish
  decrease 36
  ill 655
  inactive 683
  repine 828
  — for 865
languishing
  weak 160
  affected 855
languishment
  lament 839
languor
  [see languid]
lank 200
lanky 203, 206
lantern
  window 260
  lamp 423
  magic — 448
  — of Diogenes 461
  — jaws 203
lanterne, à la — 972
lanuginous 256
lanyard 45
Laodicean 822
lap abode 189
  support 215
  interior 221
  wrap 225
  encompass 227,
    229
  drink 298
  — of luxury
    pleasure 377
    inactivity 683
    voluptuousness
      954
lap-dog animal 366
  servile 886
lapel 39
lapidary 559
lapidate kill 361
  attack 716
  punish 972
lapidescence 323
lapis lazuli
  blue 438
  jewel 847
lappet 39, 214
lapse course 109

past 122
  conversion 144
  fall 306
  degeneracy 659
  relapse 661
  loss 776
  vice 945
  guilt 947
  — of memory 506
  — of time 109
lapsus calami 495
lapsus linguae
  mistake 495
  solecism 508
  stammering 583
Laputa, college of —
  538
larboard 239
larceny 791
lard 356
lardaceous 355
larder 636
  contents of the —
    298
lares et penates
  home 189
  idols 991
large
  quantity 31
  size 192
  at — diffuse 573
    free 748
  become — 194
  — number 102
  — type 642
large-hearted
  liberal 816
  benevolent 906
  disinterested 942
larger 194
largest 784
largest portion 192
larghetto 275, 415
largiloquent 573
largo 275, 415
lariat 45, 247
lark ascent 305
  pleasure 827
  sprec 840
  with the — 125
larmes:
  fondre en — 839
  — aux yeux 839
larmoyante,
  comédie — 599
larrikin 887, 913
larrup 972
larum 404, 669
larva 129
larynx 351
lascar 269
lasciate ogni spe-
  ranza 859
lascivious 961
lash tie together 43
  violence 173
  incite 615
  censure 932
  punish 972
  scourge 975
  under the — com-
    pelled 744
  subject 749
  — into fury 909
  — with the tongue
    931
  — the waves 645

lass girl 129
lassitude 680, 841
lasso 45, 247
last model 22
  - in order 67
  endure 106
  durable 110
  - in time 122
  continue 141
  at — 133
  breathe one's —
    360
  game to the —
    604a
  never hear the —
    of 104
  — but one &c. 67
  die in the — ditch
    604a
  — for ever 112
  at the — extremity
    665
  — finish 729
  — gasp 360
  go to one's — home
    360
  on — legs weak 160
  dying 360
  spoiled 659
  adversity 735
  — resort 666
  — rites 998
  — shift 601
  — sleep 360
  — stage 67
  — straw 153
  — stroke 729
  — touch 729
  — word
    affirmation 535
    obstinacy 606
  — year &c. 122
latch 43, 45
latchet 45
latch-key 631
late past 122
  new 123
  tardy 133
  dead 360
  too — 135
lately 122, 123
latency 526
lateness 133
latent 172, 526
  — organism 153
later 117
laterality 236
lateritious 434
latest 118
latet anguis in
  herbâ 66
lath 205
  thin as a — 203
lathe
  region 181
  machine 633
lather 332, 353
Latin
  au bout de son —
    704
  perdre son — 704
  thieves' — 563
latitancy 528
latitat 969
latitude extent 180
  region 181
  breadth 202

measurement 466
  freedom 748
  — and longitude
    situation 183
latitudinarian 984,
  989
latration 412
latria 990
latrines 653
latrociny 791
latter sequent 63
  past 122
Latter-day Saint
  984
latterly 123
lattice crossing 219
  opening 260
laud 931, 990
laudable 944
laudanum 174
laudari a laudato
  viro 931
laudator 935
  — temporis acti
    past 122
    habit 613
  discontent 832
  detractor 936
laudatory 931
laugh 838
  make one — 853
  raise a — 840
  — at ridicule 856
  sneer 929
    (undervalue 483)
  — to scorn defy 715
    despise 930
  — in one's sleeve
    latent 526
    ridicule 856
    disrespect 929
    contempt 930
  — on the wrong
    side of one's
    mouth
    disappointed 509
    dejected 837
    in disrepute 874
laughable 853
laughing:
  no — matter 642
  — gas 376
laughing-stock 857
laughter-loving 836
launch begin 66
  boat 273
  propel 284
  — forth 676
  — into 676
  — into eternity
    360, 361
  — out 573
  — out against 716
laundress 652, 746
laundry room 191
  heat 386
  clean 652
  — maid 746
  — man 652
laureate 875
  poet — 597
laurel trophy 733
  glory 873
  decoration 877
  repose on one's —s
    265
lava excretion 299

semiliquid 352
lavatory 652
lave water 337
  clean 652
lavender colour 437
laver la tête 932
lavish profuse 641
  give 784
  squander 818
  — of praise 931
law regularity 80
  statue 697
  permission 760
  legality 963
  court of — 966
  give the — 737
  go to — 969
  Jewish — 985
  lay down the —
    certainty 474
    affirm 535
    command 741
  learned in the —
    968
  set the — at
    defiance 964
  take the — into
    one's own
    hands 722, 742
  — of the Medes
    and Persians
    80, 148
  take the — of 969
law-abiding 743
lawful
  permitted 760
  due 924
  legal 963
lawgiver 694
lawless 59
  irregular 83
  mutinous 742
  non-observant 773
  vicious 945
  arbitrary 964
lawn plain 344
  grass 367
  agriculture 371
  — sleeves 999
  — tennis 840
lawsuit 969
lawyer 968
lax incoherent 47
  soft 324
  error 495
  - style 575
  remiss 738
  non-observance
    773
  dishonorable 940
  licentious 945
  irreligious 989
laxity 738
lay moderate 174
  place 184
  ley 344
  music 415
  poetry 597
  bet 621
  secular 997
  — about one
    active 682
    exertion 686
    attack 716
    contend 720
    punish 972
  — one's account for

484
- apart
  exclude 55
  relinquish 782
- aside
  neglect 460
  reject 610
  disuse 678
  give up 782
- on the table 133
- the axe at the root of tree 162
- bare 529
- before 527
- brother 996
- by *store* 636
  sickness 655
  disuse 678
- to one's charge 938
- claim to 924
- in the dust 162
- eggs 161
- at the door of 155
- down [*see* below]
- at one's feet 763
- figure *nonentity* 4
  model 22
  representation 554
- one's finger upon 480a
- the first stone 66
- the flattering unction to one's soul 831, 834
- the foundations 153, 673
- ghosts 992
- hands on
  use 677
  take 789
  rite 998
- under hatches 751
- one's head on the block 942
- heads together 695, 709
- in *eat* 298
  store 636
  provide 637
- on 972
open *divest* 226
  opening 260
  show 525
  disclose 529
- oneself open to 177
- out
  horizontal 213
  corpse 363
  plan 626
  expend 809
- oneself out for 673
- over 133
- reader 996
- under restraint 751
- in ruins 162
- siege to 716
- stress on 642
- to *attribute* 155
  rest 265
- it on thick

cover 223
too much 641
flatter 933
- together 43
- train 626
- up *store* 636
  sickness 655
  disuse 678
- waste 162
lay down *locate* 184
  horizontal 213
  assert 535
  renounce 757
  relinquish 782
  pay 807
- one's arms
  pacification 723
  submission 725
- the law
  certain 474
  assert 535
  command 741
  insolence 885
- one's life 360
- a plan 626
layer 204
layette 225
layman 699, 997
laystall 653
lazaret 662
lazar-house 662
lazy 683, 927
lazzarone 683
lb. 319
lea *land* 342
  plain 344
leach 335
lead *superiority* 33
  in order 62
  pioneer 64
  influence 175
  tend 176
  soundings 208
- *in motion* 280
  heavy 319
  rôle 599
  induce 615
  direct 693
  authority 737
heave the - 466
red - 434
take the -
  influence 175
  importance 642
  authority 737
white - 420
- to the altar 903
- astray 495
- captive
  subject 749
  restraint 751
- a merry chase 623
- the choir 990
- a dance
  run away 623
  circuit 629
  difficulty 704
  disrespect 929
- the dance 280
- one to expect 511
- a life 692
- on 693
- to no end 645
- by the nose 737
- off 62

- the way
  precedence 62
  begin 66
  precession 280
  importance 642
  direction 693
  repute 873
leaden *dim* 422
  colorless 429
  grey 432
  inactive 683
leader
  precursor 64
  dissertation 595
  director 694
  counsel 968
- writer 593
leading
  beginning 66
  important 642
- article 595
- lady 599
- note *music* 413
- part 175
- question 461
- seaman 745
- strings
  childhood 127
  child 129
  pupil 541
  subject 749
  restraint 751, 752
leads 223
leaf *part* 51
  layer 204
  plant 367
- of a book 593
turn over a new - 658
- green 435
leafless 226
leaflet 531
leafy 256
league *length* 200
  co-operation 709
  party 712
- of Nations 696
leak *crack* 198
  dribble 295
  waste 638
spring a -
  injury 659
- out
  disclosure 529
leaky *imperfect* 651
leal 743
lean *thin* 203
  oblique 217
- on 215
- to *shed* 191
  willing 602
- towards 923
- upon *belief* 484
  subjection 749
  hope 858
leaning
  tendency 176
  willingness 602
  desire 865
  friendship 888
  favoritism 923
leap
  sudden change 146
  ascent 305
  jump 309
-s and bounds 274

make a - at 622
- in the dark
  experiment 463
  uncertain 475
  chance 621
  rash 863
- with joy 838
- year 138
leap-frog 840
learn 490, 539
- by experience 950
- by heart 505
learned 490
learner 541
learning 490, 539
lease *property* 780
  lending 787
grant a - 771
take a new - of life 654
- and release 783
leasehold 780
leash *lie* 43
  three 92
hold in - 751
least
- *in quantity* 34
- *in size* 193
at the - 32
leather *skin* 223
  tough 327
  beat 972
nothing like - 481
- bottle 191
- or prunello 643
leave *remainder* 40
  part company 44
  relinquish 624
  permission 760
  bequeathe 784
French - 623
take - *depart* 293
  freedom 748
- alone
  inaction 681
  freedom 748
  permit 760
- the beaten track 83
- to chance 621
- an inference 526
- a loophole 705
- in the lurch
  pass 303
  decisive 545
- no trace
  be no more 2
  disappear 449
  obliterate 552
- it to one 76
- to oneself 748
- off *cease* 142
  desuetude 614
  relinquish 624
  disuse 678
- out 55
- out of one's calculation 460
- a place 293
- ad referendum 605
give me - to say 535
- undecided 609a
- undone 730
- a void *regret* 833

- word 527
leaven
  component 56
  cause 153
  lighten 320
  qualify 469
  unclean 653
  deterioration 659
  bane 663
leavings
  remainder 40
  useless 645
lecher 962
lechery 961
lectern 1000
lection *special* 79
  interpretation 522
lectionary 998
lecture *teach* 537
  speak 582
  dissertation 595
  censure 932
  sermon 998
- room 542
lecturer
  teacher 540
  preacher 996
lectureship 542
led - captain
  follower 746
  servile 886
  favorite 899
- by the nose 749
ledge *height* 206
  horizontal 213
  shelf 215
  projection 250
ledger *list* 86
  record 551
  accounts 811
lee 236
leech 662, 695
leef 829
leek eat the -
  recant 607
  submit 725
Lee-Metford
  rifle 727
leer *stare* 441
  dumb-show 550
leery 702, 864
lees 653
lee-shore 665, 667
leet, court - 936
lee-wall 666
leeward 236
lee-way *space* 180
  tardy 133
  navigation 267
  deviation 279
  progression 282
  shortcoming 304
left *residuary* 40
  sinistral 239
over the - 545
- alone 748
- in the lurch 732
- to shift for oneself 893
pay over the - shoulder 808
left-handed
  clumsy 699
- compliment 932
- marriage 903
leg *support* 215
  walker 266

thief 792
best – foremost 686
fast as –s will carry 274
have a – to stand on 470
keep on one's –s 654
last –s *spoiled* 659
  fatigue 688
light on one's –s 734
make a – 894
not a – to stand on
  illogical 477
  confuted 479
  failure 732
off one's –s
  propulsion 284
on one's –s
  upright 212
  elevation 307
  speaking 582
  in health 654
  active 682
  free 748
set on one's –s 660
– bail 623
legacy 270, 780, 784
legal *permitted* 760
  legitimate 924
  relating to law 963
– adviser 968
– estate 780
legality 963
legate 534
legatee 779, 785
legation 755
legato 415
legend 551, 594
legendary
  imaginary 515
legerdemain 146, 545
légèreté 605
leggings 225
leghorn hat 225
legible 518
– hand 590
legion
  multitude 102
  army 726
legionary 726
legislation 693, 963
legislative assembly 696
legislator 694
legislature 693, 696
legist 968
legitimate *true* 494
  permitted 760
  right 922
  due 924
  legal 963
legume 367
lei 847
leisure 685
at one's – *late* 133
leisurely 275
leman 897
lemma 476
lemon *color* 436
Lemprière 979
lemures 980
lend 787

– aid 707
– countenance 707
– a hand 680
– oneself to
  assent 488
  co-operate 709
– on security 789
– wings to 707
lender *creditor* 805
lending 787
length 200
go all –s
  resolution 604
  activity 682
  exertion 686
at – *in time* 133
full – *portrait* 556
go great –s 549
– and breadth of 50
– and breadth of the land
  space 180
  publication 531
– of time 110
lengthen 35, 200
– out
-*diuturnity* 110
late 133
lengthwise 200
lengthy *long* 200
  diffuse 573
lenient
  moderate 174
  mild 740
  compassionate 914
lenify 174
lenitive
  moderating 174
  remedy 662
  relieving 834
lenity 740
lens 445
Lent 956, 998
lenten 956
lenticular 245, 250
lentor *slowness* 275
  spissitude 352
  inactivity 683
lentous 352
leonem, ex ungue – 550
leonine verses 597
leopard
  variegated 440
  –'s spots *unchanging* 150
leprechaune 980
leprosy 655
lerret 273
lèse-majesté 742
less *inferior* 34
  subduction 38
– than no time 113
lessee
  possessor 779
  receiver 785
lessen
– in quantity or degree 36
– in size 195
– an evil 658
lesson *teaching* 537
  warning 668
give a – to

punish 972
read a – to
  censure 932
say one's –
  memory 505
lessor 805
lest 623
let *hindrance* 706
  permit 760
  lease 771
  lend 787
  sell 796
apartments to –
  fool 499
to – 763
– alone *besides* 37
  permanence 141
  quiescence 265
  avoid 623
  disuse 678
  inaction 681
  not complete 730
  free 748
– be
  permanence 141
  continuance 143
  inaction 681
– blood 297
– 'I dare not' wait upon 'I would' 605
– down
  depress 308
  humble 879
– down easily
  forgive 918
– fall *drop* 308
  inform 527
  speak 582
– fly *violence* 173
  propel 284
– fly at 716
– go *neglect* 460
  liberate 750
  relinquish 782
  restitution 790
– in *interpose* 228
  admit 296
  trick 545
– into *inform* 490
  disclose 529
– one know 527
– off *violent* 173
  propel 284
  permit 760
  forgive 918
  exempt 927a
  acquit 970
– out *disperse* 73
  lengthen 200
  eject 297
  disclose 529
  liberate 750
– out at 716
– pass 460
– slip
  miss an opportunity 135
  neglect 460
  not complete 730
  lose 776
  relinquish 782
– the matter stand over 133
– things take their course 143
– well alone

content 831
caution 864
lethal 361
– chamber 975
lethalis arundo, haeret lateri – 900
lethargy 683, 823
Lethe 982
waters of – 506
lethiferous 361
letter *mark* 550
  character **561**
  epistle 592
to the – 494
– card 524
– of credit 805
– of the law 494
– writer 592
letter-bag 534
letter-carrier 534
lettered 490
letterpress 591
letters
  knowledge 490
  language 560
  description 594
in large – 642
man of – 492
– of marque 791
lettres de cachet 751
leucophlegmatic 823
leucorrhœa 299
Levant *east* 236
levant *abscond* 623
levanter *wind* 349
  defaulter 808
levée *assemblage* 72
  sociality 892
– en masse 719
level *uniform* 16
  equal 27
  destroy 162
  horizontal 213
  instrument 213, 217
  flat 251
  smooth 255
  lower 308
– at *direct* 278
  intend 620
  attack 716
– best 686
– headed 826
– off 27
– with the ground 207
lever *cause* 153
  instrument 633
– de rideau 599
leverage 175
leviathan 192
levigate 255, 330
levitate 320
Levite 996
levity *lightness* **320**
  irresolution 605
  trifle 643
  jocularity 836
  rashness 863
levy *muster* 72
  military 726
  distrain 789
  demand 812
lewd 961

Lewis gun 727
lex – mercatoria 963
– scripta 697
– scripta et non-scripta 963
– talionis *retaliation* 718
  right 922
lexicography 562
lexicology 562
lexicon 86, 562
ley 344
liability 177
  debt 806
  duty 926
liaison 961
liar 548
libation
  potation 298
  drunkenness 959
  worship 990
libel 934, 938
libelant 989
libeller 936
liberal *ample* 639
– party 712
  generous 816
  disinterested 942
over – 818
– education *knowledge* 490
  teaching 537
liberalism *freedom* 748
liberality
  giving 784
  generosity **816**
liberate 672
liberation 750
liberavi animam meam 703
libertinage 961
libertine 962
libertinism 961
liberty *freedom* 748
  permission 760
  right 924
  exemption 927a
gain one's – 750
set at – *free* 750
  exempt 927a
take a –
  arrogate 739
  make free 748
  insolence 885
  discourtesy 895
libidinous 961
libitum, ad –
  at will 600
  enough 639
  freely 748
librarian 593, 694
library *room* 191, 593
  books 593
  storehouse 636
librate 314
libretto 593, 599
licence *laxity* 738
  permission 760
  right 924
  exemption 927a
– to plunder 791
licentiate 492
licentious *lax* 738
  dissolute 954

lion
courage 861
prodigy 872
repute 873
come in like a –
  183
as dewdrops from
  the –'s mane
  483
in the –'s den 665
– lies down with
  the lamb 721
put one's head in
  the –'s mouth
  665
– in the path 706
–'s share *more* 33
chief part 50
too much 641
undue 925
lioness 374
lion-hearted 861
lionize 455, 873
lip *beginning* 66
edge 231
side 236
prominence 250
between cup and
  – 111
finger on the –s
silent 581
speechless 585
hang on the –s of
  418
open one's –s
speak 582
seal the –s 585
smack the –
taste 390
savory 394
– homage
flattery 933
– service
falsehood 544
hypocrisy 988
– wisdom 499
lip salve 847
lipstick 847
lipothymy 688
lippitude 443
liquefaction 335,
  384
liquescence 335
liqueur 298, 396
liquid
fluid 333
sound 405
letter 561
liquidate 807, 812
liquidator 801
liquor *potable* 298
fluid 333
in – 959
– up 959
liquorice 396
liquorish [*see*
  lickerish]
lisp 583
lissom 324
list *catalogue* **86**
strip 205
leaning 217
fringe 231
hear 418
record 551
will 600
choose 609

arena 728
desire 865
enter the –s
attack 716
contend 720
listed 440
listel 847
listen 418
– in 455
– to 457
be –ed to 175
– to reason 498
listless
inattentive 458
inactive 683
indifferent 866
litany 990, 998
lite, pendente – 969
literae scriptae 590
literal
imitated 19
exact 494
manifest 525
letter 561
word 562
orthodox 983a
– meaning 516
– translation 522
literarum
homo multarum –
  492
homo trium – 792
literary 560
– hack 593
– man 492
– power 569
literati 492
literatim [*see*
  literal]
literature 490, 560
lithe 324
lithic 323
lithograph 558
lithology 358
lithomancy 511
lithotint 558
litigant
litigious 713
combatant 726
accusation 938
litigation
quarrel 713
contention 730
lawsuit 969
litigious 713
litter *disorder* 59
derange 61
multitude 102
brood 167
support 215
vehicle 272
useless 645
littéraire, la
  morgue – 569
littérateur 492, 593
little
– *in degree* 32
– *in size* 193
darling 897
mean 940
– cost – 815
do – 683
make – of 483
signify – 643
think – of 458
– did one think
  508

– by little
degree 26
slowly 275
– Mary 191
– one 129
to – purpose
useless 645
failure 732
littleness 193
littoral 342
liturgy 978
live *exist* 1
continue 141
energetic 171
dwell 186
life 359
repute 873
– apart 905
– to fight again
  110
– from hand to
  mouth 674
– hard 954
– in hope 858
– and let live
inaction 681
freedom 748
inexcitability 826
– in the memory
  505
– upon nothing
  819
– on 298
– separately 905
– by one's wits
  545
livelihood 803
livelong 110
lively *keen* 375
– *style* 574
active 682
acute 821
sensitive 822
sprightly 836
– imagination 515
– pace 274
liver 83; hard –
  954a
white – 862
liver-colored 433
livery *suit* 225
color 428
badge 550
decoration 877
– servant 746
liveryman 748
live wire 171
livid *dark* 431
grey 432
purple 437
living *life* 359
business 625
benefice 995
good – 957
– beings 357
–room 191
– soul 372
– thing 366
livraison 593
livret 593
lixiviate 335, 652
lixivium 335
llama 271
lo! 457, 870
load *quantity* 31
fill 52
lade 184

cargo 190
weight 319
store 636
redundance 641
hindrance 706
adversity 735
anxiety 828
oppress 830
prime and – 673
take off a – of care
  834
– the memory 505
– with 706
– with reproaches
  932
loads 102
loadstar [*see* lode-
  star]
loaf *mass* 192
do nothing 681
dawdle 683
loafer
stroller 268
inactive 683
neglect 927
bad man 949
loam 342
loan 787
loathe 867, 898
loathing
[*see* loathe]
weariness 841
hate 898
loathsome
unsavory 395
painful 830
dislike 867
loaves and fishes
prosperity 734
acquisition 775
wealth 803
Lob's pound, in –
  751
lobby 191, 615, 627
lobbying 615
lobe 51
local
– habitation 184,
  189
– board 966
locale 183
locality 182, 183
localize 184
location 184
loch 343
loci, genius – 664
lock *fasten* 43
fastening 45
tuft 256
canal 350
hindrance 706
prison 752
dead – 265
in the –up 938
under – and key
safe 664
restraint 751
prisoner 754
– hospital 662
–out 55, 719
– the stable door
too late 135
useless 645
unskilful 699
–, stock and
  barrel 50
– up *hide* 528

imprison 751
locker 191
locket 847
lock-up *prison* 752
loco, in –
agreeing 23
situation 183
expedience 646
locofoco 388
locomotion 264
– by air 267
– by land 266
– by water 267
locomotive 266, 271
locular 191
locum tenens
substitute 147
inhabitant 188
deputy 759
locus:
– *poenitentiae* 937
– standi
support 215
plea 617
social rank 873
locust *prodigal* 818
evil-doer 913
swarm like –s 102
locution 582
lode 636
lodestar
attraction 288
indication 550
direction 693
lodestone 288, 615
lodge *place* 184
presence 186
dwelling 189
– a complaint 938
lodgement 184
lodger
inhabitant 188
possessor 779
lodging 189
loft 191, 210
lofty *high* 206
– *style* 574
proud 878
insolent 885
magnanimous
  942
log *velocity* 274
fuel 388
record 551
heave the – 466
sleep like a – 683
logarithm 84
loggerhead 501
at –s *discord* 713
contention 720
enmity 889
loggia 191
logic 476
– of facts 467
logician 476
logical acuteness
  570
logography 590
logogriph 533
logolept 562
logomachy
discussion 476
words 588
dispute 720
logometer 85
logometric 84
log-rolling 709

loin 235, 236
gird up one's –s
  strong 159
  prepare 673
  – cloth 225
loisir, impromptu
  fait à – 673
loiter tardy 133
  slow 275
  inactive 683
loll sprawl 213
  recline 215
  inactive 683
lollop 682
lollipop 396
Lombard Street to
  a China orange
  472
lone 87
lonesome 893
long - in time 110
  – in space 200
  diffuse 573
go to one's – ac-
  count 360
  – ago 122
make a – arm
  exertion 686
  seize 789
  –boat 273
draw the – bow
  549
take a – breath
  refreshment 689
  relief 834
  – clothes 129
  – drawn out 573
  – duration 110
  –expected 507
  – face 832, 837
  – for 865
  –headed wise 498
  – life to glory 873
  approval 931
  –lived 110
  – odds chance 156
  improbability 473
  difficulty 704
  – pending 110
  – primer 591
  – pull and strong
  pull 285
  – range 196
  – robe 968
  – run average 29
  whole 50
  destiny 152
  – sea 348
  – and the short
  whole 50
  concise 572
  –sighted
  dim-sighted 443
  wise 498
  foresight 518
  – since 122
  – spun 573
  – standing
  diuturnal 110
  old 124
  –suffering
  lenient 740
  inexcitable 826
  pity 914
  – time 110
  –winded 573
longanimity

inexcitable 826
  forgiving 918
longevity 110, 128
longhead 500
longing 865
  – lingering look
  behind 833
longinquity 196
longitude
  situation 183
  length 200
  measurement 466
longitudinal 200
longo intervallo
  discontinuity 70
  diuturnity 110
  distance 196
  interval 198
longshore-man
  waterman 269
  plebeian 876
longways 217
loo 840
looby fool 501
  bungler 701
  clown 876
look small degree 32
  see 441
  appearance 448
  attend to 457
  – about 459, 461
  – after 459, 693
  – ahead 510
  – alive 457, 684
  – another way 442
  – back 122
  – beyond 510
  – black or blue
  feeling 821
  discontent 832
  dejection 837
  – down upon 930
  – in the face
  sincerity 703
  courage 861
  pride 878
  – foolish 874
  – for 461, 507
  – forwards 121,
  510
  – here 457
  – into 457, 461
  – before one leaps
  864
  – like 17, 448
  – on 186
  – out view 448
  attention 457
  care 459
  seek 461
  expect 507
  intention 620
  business 625
  danger 665
  warning 668
  caution 864
  – over examine
  461
  – round seek 461
  – sharp 682
  – to 459, 926
  – through 461
  – up prosper 734
  high price 814
  hope 858
  visit 892
  – up to repute 873

respect 928
  approbation 931
  – upon as 480, 484
looker-on 444
looking-glass 445
loom destiny 152
  dim 422
  dim sight 443
  come in sight 446
  weave 691
  – of the land 342
  – up 31
loon fool 501
  clown 876
  rascal 949
loop 245, 247, 629
  – the loop 245
loop-hole
  opening 260
  vista 441
  plea 617
  device 626
  escape 671
  fortification 717
loose detach 44
  incoherent 47
  pendent 214
  desultory 279
  illogical 477
  vague 519
  – style 575
  lax 738
  free 748
  liberate 750
  debauched 961
  give a – to
  – imagination 515
  laxity 738
  permit 760
  indulgence 954
let – 750
  on the – 961
  screw – 713
  – character 961
  at a – end 685
  – fish 949, 962
  – morals 945
  – rein 738
  – suggestion 514
  – thread 495
  leave a – 460
  take up a – 664
loosen 47, 750
loot 791, 793
lop 201
  – and top 371
lopped
  incomplete 53
loppet 699
lop-eared 53
lop-sided 28
loquacity 584
loquendi
  cacoëthes – 584
  jus et norma – 567
  usus – 582
lorcha 273
Lord, lord
  ruler 745
  nobleman 875
  God 976
  O – worship 990
  – Chancellor 967
  – of the creation
  372
  –'s day 687
  –s Justices 966,
  967

the – knows 491
  – lieutenant 965
  – of Lords 976
  – of the manor
  779
  – it over 737, 885
  –'s prayer 990
  –'s supper 998
  –'s table 1000
lordling 875
lordly 873, 878
Lord Mayor 745,
  965
  –'s show 883
lordship
  authority 737
  property 780
  title 877
  judge 967
lore 490, 539
Lorelei 980
lorette 962
lorgnette 445
loricated
  clothed 223
lorication
  armor 717
lorn 893
lorry 272
lose forget 506
  unintelligible 519
  fail 732
  loss 776
  no time to – 684
  – one's balance
  732
  – breath 688
  – caste 874, 940
  – the clew 475,
  519
  – color 429
  – one's cunning
  699
  – the day 732
  – flesh 195
  – ground
  slow 275
  regression 283
  shortcoming 304
  – one's head
  bewildered 475
  – heart 837
  – one's heart 897
  – hope 859
  – interest in 624
  – labor 732
  – one's life 360
  – no time 682, 684
  – oneself 475
  – an opportunity
  135
  – one's reason 503
  – sight of
  blind 442
  disappear 449
  neglect 460
  oblivion 506
  not complete 730
  – one's temper 900
  – time 683
  – one's way
  wander 279
  uncertainty 475
  unskilful 699
  difficulty 704
losel 818
losing game 732,

735
loss decrement 40a
  death 360
  evil 619
  deterioration 659
  privation 776
  at a –
  uncertain 475
  at a – for
  desiring 865
  – of fortune 804
  – of health 655
  – of life 360
  – of right 925
  – of strength 160
lost non-existing 2
  absent 187
  invisible 449
  abstracted 458
  uncertain 475
  failure 732
  loss 776
  over-excited 824
  pain 828
  dejection 837
  impenitent 951
  – in admiration
  931
  – in astonishment
  870
  – in iniquity 945
  – labor 645
  – to shame
  insolent 885
  improbity 940
  bad man 949
  – to sight 449
  – in thought 458
  – to virtue 945
lot state 7
  quantity 25
  group 72
  multitude 102
  necessity 601
  chance 621
  sufficient 639
  allotment 786
be one's – 151
  cast – 621
  cast in one's –
  with 609, 709
  fall to one's – 156
  in –s 51
  where one's – is
  cast 189
loth 603, 867
Lothario 897, 962
lotion liquid 337
  clean 652
  remedy 662
loto 840
lottery 156, 840
  put into a – 621
lotus-eater 683
loud 404, 525
  vulgar 851
lough 343
lounge 191, 683
  – suit 225
loup
  hurler avec les –s
  714
  –garou 980
louse 653
lout 501, 701, 876
louvre 351
lovable 897

love *desire* 865
  courtesy 894
  affection **897**
  favorite 899
  abode of – 897
  labor of –
    willing 602
  inexpensive 815
  amusement 840
  disinterested 942
  God's – 906
  make – 902
  no – lost 713
  – affair 897
  – of country 910
  – lock 256
  not for – or money
    640, 814
love-knot *token* 550
love-lorn 898
lovely 845, 897
love-making 902
love-pot 959
love-potion 865
lover [*see* love]
love-sick 897, 902
love-story 897, 902
love-token 897, 902
loving-cup 892, 894
loving-kindness
  906 .
low *small* 32
  not high 207
  - *sound* 405
  moo 412
  vulgar 851
  disreputable 874
  common 876
  base 940
  bring – 308
  – condition 876
  – comedy 599
  at a – ebb
    small 32
  inferior 34
  depressed 308
  waste 638
  deteriorated 659
  – fellow 876
  – life 851
  – note 408
  – origin 876
  – price 815
  – spirits 837
  – tide 207
  – tone *black* 431
  mutter 581
  – water *low* 207
  dry 340
  insufficient 640
  poor 804
low-born 876
low-brow 491
low-lands 207
low-minded 876,
  940
lower *inferior* 34
  decrease 36
  overhang 214
  depress 308
  dark 421
  dim 422
  predict 511
  sad 837
  irate 900
  sulky 901a
  – one's flag 725

– one's note 879
– orders 876
lowering 668, 859
lowly 879
lown 501, 949
lowness [*see* low]
  207
  humility 879
loy 272
loyal *obedient* 743
  observant 772
  honourable 939
lozenge 244, 662
L. s. d. 800
lubbard [*see* lubber]
lubber 683, 701
lubberly 192, 699
lubricant 332
lubrication 255, **332**
lubricity
  slippery 255
  unctuous 355
  impure 961
lucent 420
lucid
  luminous 420
  transparent 425
  intelligible 518
  - *style* 570
  – *interval* 502
lucidus ordo 58
lucifer 388
Lucifer 423, 978
lucimeter 445
luck *chance* 156, 621
  prosperity 734
  good – 858
luckless 735
lucky 134, 731
lucrative 775
lucre 775, 803
Lucretia 960
luctation 720
luculent 420
lucubration 451
lucus a non lucendo
  18, 565
lud! O – 839
ludibrious 840
ludicrous 853
luff 267
lug *pull* 285
  ear 418
luge 272
luggage 270, 780
  – van 272
lugger 273
lugubrious 837
lukewarm
  temperate 382
  irresolute 605
  torpid 823
  indifferent 866
lull *cessation* 142
  mitigate 174
  silence 403
  – to sleep 265
lullaby
  moderate 174
  song 415
  verses 597
  - *inactivity* 683
  relief 834
lumbago 378
lumbar 235
lumbar *disorder* 59
  slow 275.

store 636
  useless 645
  hindrance 706
lumbering 647, 846
lumber-room 191
lumbriciform 249
luminary *star* 318
  light **423**
  sage 500
luminescence 420
luminous *light* 420
  intelligible 518
  – *paint* 423
lump *whole* 50
  chief part 51
  amass 72
  mass 192
  projection 250
  weight 319
  density 321
  in the – 50
  - of affectation
    855
  – sum 800
  - together *join* 43
  combine 48
  assemble 72
lumpish [*see* lump]
  inactive 683
  ugly 846
Luna 318
lunacy 503
lunar 318
  – *caustic* 384
lunatic 503, 504
luncheon 298
lune avec les dents,
  prendre la –
  158, 471
lunette 717
lunge 276, 716
lungs *wind* 349
  loudness 404
  shout 411
  voice 580
luniform &c. 245
lupanar 961
lurch *incline* 217
  sink 306
  oscillation 314
  failure 732
  leave in the –
    outstrip 303
  deceive 545
  relinquish 624
  left in the –
    defeated 732
lure *attraction* 288,
  865
  deceive 545
  entice 615
lurid *dark* 421
  dim 422
  red 434
lurk *unseen* 447
  latent 526
  hidden 528
lurking-place 530
luscious 394, 829
lush *vegetation* 365
  drunkenness 959
lushy 959
lusk 683
lusory 840
lust 865, 961
  – *after* 921
luster

brightness 420
  chandelier 423
  glory 873
lustily 404, 686
  cry out – 839
lustless 158
lustration 652, 952
lustrum 108
lusty 159, 192
lusus naturæ 80
lute *cement* 45, 46
  guitar 417
luteous 436
Lutheran 984
luxation 44
luxuriant 168, 639
luxuriate in 377,
  827
luxurious
  pleasant 377
  delightful 829
  intemperate 954
luxury
  physical - 377
  redundance 641
  enjoyment 827
  sensuality 954
lycanthropy 503
Lyceum 542
Lydford law 964
Lydian measure
  415
lyddite 727
lying
  decumbent 213
  deceptive 544
  faithless 986
Ly-king 986
lymph *fluid* 333
  water 337
  transparent 425
lymphatic 337
lynch 972
  – *law* 964
lyncher 975
lynching 361
lynx-eyed 441, 498
lyre 417
lyric 415
  – *poetry* 597
lyrist 597

M

Mab 979
macadamize 255,
  635
Macaire, Robert –
  792
macaroni 854
macaronic
  absurdity 497
  neology 563
  verses 597
Macchiavel [*see*
  Machiavelism]
mace
  weapon 727
  scepter 747
mace-bearer 965
maceration
  saturation 337
  atonement 952
  asceticism 955
  rite 998

Macheath 792
Machiavelism
  falsehood 544
  cunning 702
  dishonesty 940
machicolation 257,
  717
machination
  trick 545
  plan 626
  cunning 702
  –s of the devil 619
machinator 626
machine 633
  like a – 698
  – gun 407, 727
  be a mere – 749
machinist
  theatrical - 599
  workman 690
macilent 203
mackerel
  mottled 440
  procuress 962
  – sky 349, 353
mackintosh 225
macrobiotic 110
macrocosm 318
macrography 441
macrology 577
mac Sycophant,
  Sir Pertinax –
  886, 935
mactation 991
macte virtute 931
macula 848
maculate
  unclean 653
maculation 440, 848
mad *insane* 503
  excited 824
  drive one – 900
  go – 825
  – after 865
  – with rage 900
madam 374
mad-brained 503
madcap
  violent 173
  lunatic 504
  excitable 825
  buffoon 844
  rash 863
madder *color* 434
made
  – to one's hand
    673
  – man 734
  – to order 673
madefaction 339
madman **504**
Madonna
  good 948
  angel 977
  pious 987
madrigal *music* 415
  verses 597
Maecenas 492, 890
Maelstrom
  whirl 312
  water 348
  pitfall 667
maestro 415
maffick 883
magazine
  periodical 53
  record 551

serve – 989
mammoth 192
man *adult* 131
  mankind 372
  male **373**
  prepare 673
  workman 690
  servant 746
  courage 861
  husband 903
make a – of 648,
  861
Son of – 976
straight – 599
to a – 488
– -at-arms 726
one's – of business
  758
– 's estate 131
– in office 745
– in the street 876
– of-war 273, 726
– of-war's man 269
– at the wheel 694
– and wife 903
manacle 751, 752
manage 693
– to *succeed* 731
manageable 705
management
  conduct 692
  skill 698
manager
  stage – 599
  director 694
managery 693
manche après la
  cognée, jeter le
  – 859
mancible 637
mancipation 751
mandamus 741
mandarin 745
mandate 630, 741
mandible 298
mandolin 417
mandragora 174
mandrel 312
manduction 298
mane 256
man-eater 361
manége 266, 370
manes 362
manet: – altámente
  repostum 505
  – cicatrix 919
maneuver 680, 702
manful *strong* 159
  resolute 604
  brave 861
manger 191
manger:
  cela se laisse – 394
  – son blé en herbe
  818
mangle
  separate 44
  smooth 255
  injure 659
mangled 53
mangy 655
man-hater 911
manhood 131, 861
mania *insanity* 503
  desire 865
maniac 504
manibus pedibus–

que 686
manic 503
manic-depressive
  503
manicure 847
manicheism 978
manichord 417
manie 865
maniéré 855
manifest
  list 86
  visible 446
  obvious 525
  disclose 529
manifestation **525**
manifesto 531
manifold 81, 102
manikin *dwarf* 193
  image 554
maniple 103
manipulate
  handle 379
  use 677
  conduct 692
manipulator 621
mankind **372**
manly
  adolescent 131
  strong 159
  male 373
  brave 861
  honest 939
manna *food* 396
  – in the wilderness
  aid 707
  pleasing 829
manner *kind* 75
  style 569
  way 627
  conduct 692
  in a – 32
  by all – of means
  536
  by no – of means
  602
  to the – born 5
mannered 579
mannerism
  special 79
  unconformity 83
  affectation 855
  vanity 880
mannerly 894
manners 852, 894
manor 780
  lord of the – 779
  – house 189
manorial 780
Mansard roof 223
manse 1000
mansion 189
manslaughter 361
mansuetude 894
mantelpiece 215
mantilla 225
mantle *spread* 194
  dress 225
  foam 353
  shade 424
  redden 434
  robes 747
  flush 821, 824
  anger 900
mantlet *cloak* 225
  defence 717
Mantology 511
manual *guide* 527

schoolbook 542
  book 593
  advice 695
  – labor 686
manubial 793
manufactory 691
manufacture 161,
  680
manufacturer 690
manumission 750
manure
  agriculture 371
  dirt 653
  aid 707
manuscript 22, 590
many 102
  the – 876
  – for – a day 110
  – irons in the fire
  682
  – men many
    minds 489
  – times
  repeated 104
  frequent 136
many-colored 440
many-sided 81, 236
many-tóngued 532
map 234, 527, 554
  – out 626
mar 659, 706
marabou 83
marabout 1000
maranatha 908
marasmus
  shrinking 195
  atrophy 655
  deterioration 659
maraud 791
marauder 792
marble *ball* 249
  hard 323
  sculpture 557
  tablet 590
  insensible 823
marble 440
marble-hearted 907
march *region* 181
  journey 266
  progression 282
  music 415
  dead – 363
  forced – 684
  on the – 264
  steal a –
  advance 280
  go beyond 303
  deceive 545
  active 682
  cunning 702
  – against 716
  – of events 151
  – of intellect
  knowledge 490
  improvement 658
  – off 293
  – on a point 278
  – past 882
  – of time 109
  – with 199
March, Ides of – 601
marches 233
marchioness 875
marcid 203
marconigram 523
marcor 203
mare *horse* 271

female 374
– 's nest 497, 546
– 's tail *wind* 349
  cloud 353
marechal 745
margarine 356
margin *space* 180
  edge 231
  redundance 641
  latitude 748
margravate 780
margrave 745, 875
marimba 417
marine *fleet* 273
  sailor 269
  oceanic 341
  soldier 726
  tell it to the –s
  489, 497
  – painter 559
  – painting 556
mariner **269**
Mariolatry 991
marionnette
  representation
  554
  drama 599
  amusement 840
marish 345
marital 903
maritime 267, 341
mark *degree* 26
  term 71
  take cognizance
    of 450
  attend to 457
  indication 550
  record 551
  writing 590
  object 620
  importance 642
  repute 873
  beyond the – 303
  leave one's – 873
  man of – 873, 875
  near the – 197
  overshoot the –
  699
  put a – upon 457
  save the – 870
  up to the –
  enough 639
  good 648
  skill 698
  due 924
  wide of the – 196,
  495
  within the – 304
  – down 813
  – off 551
  – out *choose* 609
  plan 626
  command 741
  – of recognition
  894
  – with a red letter
  883
  – time
  chronometry 114
  halt 265
  wait 507
  – with a white
    stone 931
marked [*see* mark]
  great 31
  affirmed 535
  well– 446

in a – degree 31
play with – cards
  545
  – down 815
marker 550
market *buy* 795
  mart 799
  bring to – 796
  buy in the cheap-
    est &c. – 794
  in the –
  offered 763
  barter 794
  sale 796
  rig the – 794
  – garden 371
  – overt
  manifest 525
  mart 799
  – place *street* 189
  mart 799
  – price 812
  – woman 797
marketable 794,
  796
marksman 700
marksmanship 698
marl 342
marmalade 396
marmot 683
maroon
  color 433, 434
  abandon 782, 893
marplot
  bungler 701
  obstacle 706
  malicious 913
marque, letters of –
  791
marquee 223
marquetry 440
marquis 875
marriage 903
  companiable –
  903
  ill-assorted – 904
  – bells 836
  – portion 780
marriageable 131,
  903
marrow *essence* 5
  interior 221
  central 222
  chill to the – 385
marrow-bones, on
  one's –
  submit 725
  beg 765
  humble 879
  servile 886
  atonement 952
marrowless 158
marry *combine* 48
  assertion 535
  wed 903
  – come up
  defiance 715
  anger 900
  censure 932
Mars 722, 979
  – orange 439
marsh **345**
marshal
  arrange 60
  messenger 534
  auxiliary 711
  officer 745

merged 228

meridian
region 181
room 125
summit 210
light 420
– of life 131

merit
goodness 648
due 924
virtue 944
make a – of 884
– notice 642

merito, e – 944

meritorious 931

Merlin 994

mermaid 341
monster 83
mythology 979, 980

merman 341

mero motu, ex – 600

merriment
cheerful 836
amusement 840

merry *cheerful* 836
drunk 959
make – *sport* 840
make – with
wit 842
ridicule 856
wish a – Christmas &c. 896
– and wise 842

merry-andrew 844

merry-go-round 312, 840

merry-making 827, 840, 892

merry-thought 842

mersion 337

meruit ferat, palmam qui – 873

merveille, à – 731

mesa 344

mésalliance 24, 903

meseems 484

mesh 198, 219

meshes *trap* 545
difficulty 704
– of sophistry 477

meshwork 219

mesial
middle 68

mesmerism 992

mesmerist 994

mesne lord 779

mess *mixture* 41
disorder 59
barracks 191
meal 298
difficulty 704
portion 786
make a –
unskilful 699
fail 732

message
intelligence 532
command 741

Messalina 962

messenger 271
envoy 534
servant 746
– balloon 463

Messiah 976

messianic 976

messmate 890

messuage 189

messy 59

metabolism 140

metacenter 222

metachronism 115

metage 466

metagenesis 140

metagrammatism 561

metal 635
Brittania – 545

metallic *sound* 410

metalepsis 521

metallurgy 358

metamorphosis 140

metaphor
comparison 464
figure 521
(*analogy* 17)

metaphrase 522

metaphrast 524

metaphrastic 516

metaphysics 450

metastasis, metathesis
change 140
inversion 218
displacement 270

mete *measure* 466
distribute 786
– out *give* 784

metempsychosis 140

meteor 318, 423

meteoric 173, 420

meteorology 338

meteoromancy 466

meter 466

meter
length 200
poetry 597

metheglin 396

methinks 484

method *order* 58
way 627
want of – 59

methodical 60

Methodist 984

methodist
journalist 988

methodize 60

Methuselah 130
old as – 12
since the days of – 124

meticulous 772

métier 625

métis 83

metonymy 521

metoposcopy
front 234
appearance 44
interpret 522

metrical
measured 466
verse 597

metrology 466
moderation 174
mid-course 628

metropolis 189

metropolitan
archbishop 996

mettle *spirit* 820
courage 861

man of – 861
on one's –
resolved 604
put on one's –
excite 824
encourage 861

mettlesome
energetic 171
sensitive 822
excitable 825
brave 861

mettre de l'eau
dans son vin 160

meum et tuum 780
disregard distinction between – 791

mew *moult* 226
cry 412
– up 751

mewed up 229

mewl 412

mews 189

mezzanine floor 191, 599

mezzo rilievo
convex 250
sculpture 557

mezzo termine
middle 68
mid-course 628
compromise 774

Mezzofanti 492

mezzosoprano 416

mezzotint 420, 558

miasm 663

mica 425

micaceous 204

mi-carême 840

Micawber 460

Michael 977

Michaelmas 998

Micomicon 515

microbe 163, 193

microcosm 193

micrography 193, 441

micrometer 193

micro-organism 193

microphone 418

microscope 193, 445

microscopic 32, 193

mid 68

Midas 803

mid-course 628

mid-day 125

midden 653

middle – *in degree* 29
– *in order* 68
– *in space* 222, 228
– classes 736
– constriction 203
– course 29, 628
– man *director* 694
agent 758
– point 29
– term 68
compromise 774

middlemost 222

middling 29, 32, 68, 651

middy 225, 269

midge 193

midget 193

midland 342

midnight *night* 126
dark 421
– oil 539, 689

mid-progress 282

midriff 68, 228

midshipman 269, 745

midships 68

midst - *in order* 68
central 222
interjacent 228
in the – of
mixed with 41
doing 680

midsummer 125
– day 138

midway 68

midwife
instrument 631
remedy 662
auxiliary 711

midwifery 161, 662

mien 448, 692

miff 900

might *power* 157
violence 173
energy 686

mightily 31

mighty *much* 31
strong 159
large 192
haughty 878

migraine 378

migrate 266, 295

mikado 745

milch cow
productive 168
animal 366
store 636

mild *moderate* 174
warm 382
insipid 391
lenient 740
calm 826
courteous 894

mildew 653, 663

mildewed
spoiled 659

mile 200

milestone 550
whistle jigs to a – 645

milieu, juste – 174, 628

militant 722
church – 983a

military
warfare 722
soldiers 726
– authorities 745
– band 417
– power 737
– time 132
– train 726

militate against 708

militia 726

milk *moderate* 174
semiliquid 352
cows &c. 370
white 430
mild 740
– a he-goat into a sieve 471
flow with – and honey *plenty* 639

prosperity 734
pleasant 829
– of human kindness 906
– the ram 645
– and water
weak 160
insipid 391
unimportant 643
imperfect 651

milk-livered 862

milksop
incapable 158
fool 501
coward 862

milky [*see* milk]
semitransparent 427
whiteness 430
– way 318

mill 330
notch 257
machine 633
workshop 691
fight 720
like a horse in a – 312

millennium
number 98
period 108
futurity 121
utopia 515
hope 858

millesimal 99

millet seed 193

milliard 98

milliner 225
man – 854

millinery *dress* 225
ornament 847
display 882
man – 855

million 98
multitude 102
people 372
populace 876
for the –
intelligible 518
easy 705
–s *money* 800

millionaire 803

mill-pond *level* 213
pond 343
store 636

mime 19, 599, 844

mimeograph 19

mimeotype 19

mimic 19

mimodrama 599

minacity 909

minaret 206

minatory 668

minauderie 855

mince *cut up* 44
slow 275
food 298
stammer 583
affected
extenuate 937
– the matter 868
not – the matter
affirm 525
artless 703
– the truth 544

mincemeat of
make – 162

mincing 855

- steps 275
mind *intellect* 450
  attend to 457
  take care 459
  believe 484
  remember 505
  will 600
  willing 602
  purpose 620
  warning 668
  desire 865
  dislike 867
  bear in - 451, 457
  bit of one's - 527
  food for the - 454
  give the - to 457
  have a - 602, 865
  in the -
    thought 451
    topic 454
    willing 602
  make up one's -
    484, 604
  never - *neglect* 460
    unimportant 643
  not - 866
  out of - 506
  set one's - upon
    604
  speak one's - 582, 703
  to one's - *taste* 850
    love 897
  willing - 602
  - one's book 539
  - one's business
    456, 457
  - at ease 827
  make one's - easy
    826
  -'s eye 515
  - what one is
    about 864
minded 602, 620
mindful 457, 505
mindless
  inattentive 458
  imbecile 499
  forgetful 506
  insensible 823
mine
  sap 162
  hollow 252
  open 260
  snare 545
  store 636
  abundance 639
  damage 659
  attack 716
  defence 717
  explosive 727
  dig a - *plan* 626
    prepare 673
  spring a -
    unexpected 508
    attack 716
  - of information
    700
  -layer 726
  -sweeper 726
  -thrower 727
  - of wealth 803
miner 252
  sapper and - 726
mineral 358
  - oil 356
mineralogy 358

Minerva 979
  - invita 603, 709
  - press 577, 594
mingle 41
miniature *small* 193
  portrait 556
  - painter 559
Minié rifle 727
minikin 193
minim *small* 32
  music 413
minimize 36, 483, 934
minimum *small* 32
  inferior 34
minion 899
  type 591
minister *instru-*
  mentality 631
  remedy 662
  director 694
  aid 707
  deputy 759
  give 784
  clergy 996
  rites 998
  - to 746
ministerial
  clerical 995
ministering spirit
  977
ministration
  direction 693
  aid 707
  rite 998
ministry
  direction 693
  aid 707
  church 995
  clergy 996
miniver 223
minnesinger 597
minnow 193
minor *inferior* 34
  infant 129
  - key 413
Minorites 996
minority *few* 103
  youth 127
Minos 694
minotaur 83
minster 1000
minstrel 416, 597
minstrelsy 415
mint *mold* 22
  workshop 691
  wealth 803
  - of money 800
minuend 38
minuet 415, 840
minus *less* 34
  subtracted 38
  absent 187
  deficient 304
  loss 776
  in debt 806
  non-payment 808
minusculae 561
minute
  - *in degree* 32
  - *of time* 108
  instant 113
  - *in size* 193
  record 551
  compendium 596
  to the - 132
  - account 594

- attention 457
minuteness
  care 459
minutiae 32, 79, 643
minx 887, 962
mirabile
  - dictu &c. 870
mirabilis, annus -
  872
miracle 83, 872
  - play 599
miraculous 870
mirage 443
mire 653
mirror *imitate* 19
  reflector 445
  perfection 650
  glory 873
  hold up the - 525
  hold the - up to
    nature 554
  magic - 443
mirth 836
misacceptation 235
misadventure 735
misadvised 699
misanthropy 911
misapply
  misinterpret 523
  misuse 679
  mismanage 699
misapprehend 495,
  523
misappropriate 679
misarrange 61
misbecome 925
misbegotten 243,
  945
misbehave 851, 945
misbehavior 895,
  947
misbelief 485
misbeliever 487,
  984
miscalculate
  misjudge 481
  err 495
  disappoint 509
miscall 565
miscarry 732
miscegenation 41
miscellany
  mixture 41
  collection 72
  generality 78
  compendium 596
mischance 619, 735
mischief 619
  do - 649
  make - 649
mischief-maker
  913, 941
miscible 41
miscite 544
miscompute 481,
  495
misconceive 495,
  523
misconduct 699,
  947
  - oneself 945
misconjecture 481
misconstrue 523
miscorrect 538
miscount 495
miscreance 485
miscreant 949

miscreated 945
misdate 115
misdeed 947
misdemean 945
misdemeanant 949
misdemeanor 947
misdevotion 988
misdirect 538, 699
misdo 945
misdoing 947
misdoubt 485, 523
mise en scène
  appearance 448
  drama 599
  display 882
misemploy 679
miser 819
  -'s hoard 800
miserabile dictu 839
miserable *small* 32
  contemptible 943
  unhappy 828
miserably *very* 31
miserere 215
  sing - 950
misericordiam,
  argumentum ad
  - 914
miseries of human
  life 828
miseris succurrere
  disco 914
miserly 819
misery 828
  put out of one's -
    914
misestimate
  misjudge 481
misfeasance 699,
  947
misfit 24
misfortune
  adversity 735
  unhappiness 830
misgiving 485, 860
misgovern 699
misguide 495, 538
misguided 699
mishap *evil* 619
  failure 732
misinform 538
misinformed 491
misinstruct 538
misintelligence 538
misinterpretation
  523
misjoined 24
misjudgment
  sophistry 477
  misjudge **481**
  misinterpretation
    523
mislay *derange* 61
  lose 776
mislead *error* 495
  misteach 538
  deceive 545
mislike 867
mismanage 699
mismatch 15, 24
misname 565
misnomer **565**
misogamist 904,
  911

misogyny 904
mispersuasion 538
misplace
  derange 61
misplaced
  intrusive 24
  unconformable 83
  displaced 185
misprint 495
misprision
  concealment 528
  guilt 947
  - of treason 742
misprize 483, 929
mispronounce 583
misproportioned
  243, 846
misquote 544
misreckon 481, 495
misrelish 867
misreport 495, 544
misrepresent
  misinterpret 523
  misteach 538
  lie 544
misrepresentation
  555
  untruth 544, 546
misrule
  misconduct 699
  laxity 738
  Lord of - 701
miss *girl* 19
  neglect 460
  error 495
  unintelligible 519
  fail 732
  lose 776
  want 865
  courtesan 962
  - one's aim 732
  - fire 732
  - stays 304
  - one's way
    uncertain 475
    unskilful 699
missa cantata 998
missal 998
missay 563, 583
missend 699
misshapen 243, 846
missile 727
missing
  non-existent 2
  absent 187
  disappear 449
  - link 53, 83, 729
mission 625, 755
missionary 540, 996
missive 592
misspell 523
misspend 818
misstate 495, 544
misstatement 495,
  546
mist 353, 424
  in a - 528
  seen through a -
    519
  -s of error 495
  - before the eyes
    443
mistake *error* 495
  misconstrue 523
  mismanage 699
  failure 732
  never was a

greater – 536
misteaching **538**
mister 373
misterm 565
misthink 481
mistime 135
mistral 349
mistranslate 523
mistress *lady* 374
  master 745
  possessor 779
  title 877
  love 897
  concubine 962
mistrust 485
misty [*see* mist]
  semi-transparent
  427 .
misunderstand
  misinterpret 523
misunderstanding
  495, 713
misuse **679**
mite *bit* 32
  small 193
  insufficiency 649
  money 800
  little – 129
miter *junction* 43
  angle 244
  crown 747, 999
Mithridate 662
mitigate *abate* 174
  improve 658
  relieve 834
mitigation
  [*see* mitigate]
  extenuation 937
mitraille 727
mitrailleur 727
mitten 225
mittimus 741
mix 41
  – oneself up with
  meddle 682
  co-operate 709
  – with 720
mixen 653
mixture 41
  mere – 59
mix-up 59
mizzen 235
mizzle 348
mnemonics 505
Mnemosyne 505
moa 366
moan 405
  cry 411
  lament 839
moat *enclosure* 232
  ditch 259
  canal 350
  defence 717
mob *crowd* 72
  multitude 102
  vulgar 876
  hustle 929
  scold 932
  king – 876
  – cap 225
  – law
  authority 737
  illegality 964
mobile
  inconstant 149
  movable 264
  sensitive 822

mobility, the – 876
mobilize
  assemblage 72
  render movable
  264
  – troops 722
mobocracy 737
mobster 361
moccasin 225
mock *imitate* 17, 19
  repeat 104
  erroneous 495
  deceptive 545
  chuckle 838
  ridicule 856
  disrespect 929
  – danger 861
  – modesty 855
  – sun 423
mockery
  [*see* mock]
  unsubstantial 4
solemn – 882
  – delusion and
  snare
  sophistry 477
  deception 545
mocking-bird 19
modal 6, 7, 8
mode *state* 7
  music 413
  habit 613
  method 627
  fashion 852
  – of expression 569
mode, à la – 852
model *copy* 21
  prototype 22
  rule 80
  form 240
  representation
  554
  sculpture 557
  perfection 650
  good man 948
new – 658
  – after 19
  – condition 80
modeller 559
moderate
  average 29
  small 32
  allay 174
  slow 275
  sufficient 639
  cheap 815
  temperate 953
  – circumstances
  mediocrity 736
moderately
  imperfect 651
moderation [*see*
  moderate] **174**
  mid-course 628
  inexcitability 826
moderato *music*
  415
moderator 174
  lamp 423
  director 694
  mediator 724
  judge 967
modern 123
  music 415
  art 556
modest *small* 32
modesty

humility **881**
  purity 960
mock – 855
modicum *little* 32
  allotment 786
modification
  difference 15
  variation 20a
  change 140
  qualification 469
modish 852
modulation
  variation 20a
  change 140
  music 413
module 22
modulus 84
modus: – operandi
  method 627
  conduct 692
  – in rebus 174
  – vivendi 723
mogul 745
Mohammedan 984
Mohawk
  – *swaggerer* 887
  evil-doer 913
moiety 51, 91
moil *active* 682, 686
  exertion 686
moisture *wet* 337
  humid **339**
mokes 219
molar 330
molasses 396
mole *mound* 206
mold *condition* 7
  matrix 22
  convert 144
  form 240
  structure 329
  earth 342
  vegetation 367
  model 554
  carve 557
  decay 653
  turn to account
  677
molded 820
  – on 19
molder 653, 659
molding 847
moldy 653, 659
  prominence 250
  color 432
  refuge 666
  defence 717
  spot 848
molecular 32
molecule 193
molehill *little* 193
  low 207
  trifling 643
molest *trouble* 830
molestation
  damage 649
  malevolence 907
mollia tempora 134
  – fandi 588
mollify *allay* 174
  soften 324
mollusk 366
mollycoddle 158
Molly Maguire 548
Moloch
  slaughter 361
  demon 980

heathen deity 986
molten 384
moment
  – *of time* 113
  importance 642
  for the – 111
  lose not a – 684
  not have a – 682
  on the spur of the
  – 612
momentous 152
momentum 276
Momus 838
monachism 995
monad 193
monarch 745
monarchy 737
monastery 1000
monastic 995
monasticism 984
monetary 800
  – arithmetic 11
money **800**
  wealth 803
  bad – 800
  command of – 803
  for one's – 609
  made of – 803
  make – 775
  raise – 788
  save – 817
  throw away one's
  – 818
  – to burn 641, 803
  – burning one's
  pocket 818
  – coming in 810
  – down 807
  – going out 809
  – market 800
  – matters 811
  – paid 809
  – 's worth
  useful 644
  price 812
  cheap 815
money-bag 800,
  802
money-belt 800
money-broker 797
money-changer
  797, 801
moneyed 803
moneyer 797
money-grubbing
  775
moneyless 804
monger 797
mongrel
  mixture 41
  anomalous 83
  dog 366
  base 949
moniker 565
moniliform 249
monism 984
monition 527, 668
  information 527
  warning 668
monitor *hear* 418
  oracle 513
  pupil-teacher 540
  director 694
  adviser 695
  war-ship 726
  inward – 926
monitory

prediction 511
  dissuasion 616
  warning 668
monk 996
monkey
  imitative 19
  support 215
  catapult 276
  ridiculous 857
  play the – 499
  –jacket 225
  – trick
  absurdity 497
  sport 840
  – up 900
monkhood 995
monkish Latin 563
monochord 417
monochrome 429,
  556
monocracy 737
monoculous 443
monode 445
monodrame 599
monody 597, 839
monogamist 904
monogamy 903
monogram
  sign 550
  cipher 533
  diagram 554
  letter 561
monograph
  publication 531
  writing 590
  book 593
  description 594
monolith 551
monolithic 983*a*
monologue
  soliloquy 589
  drama 599
monomachy 720
monomania 503
  obstinacy 606
  fanaticism 825
monomaniac 504
monomark 550
monoplane 273
monopolist 943
monopoly
  restraint 751
  possession 777
monostich 572
monosyllable 561
monotheism 983
monotonous
  uniform 16
  equal 27
  repetition 104
  permanent 141
  – style 575
  weary 841
  dull 843
monotype 591
monsoon 349
monsieur 370
monster
  exception 83
  large 192
  ugly 846
  prodigy 872
  evil-doer 913
  ruffian 949
monstrance 998
monstrosity
  [*see* monster]

nihil – ad rem 10
– tetigit quod non
  ornavit 850
nihilism 989
nihilist 165
nihility 2, 4
nil 2, 4
– admirari
  insensible 823
  no wonder 871
  disapproval 932
– conscire sibi
  nullâ pallescere
  culpâ 946
– desperandum
  858
nill *unwilling* 604
  refuse 764
nim 791
nimble 274, 682
nimble-witted 498,
  842
nimbus
  cloud 353
  halo 420
  glory 873
nimiety 641
nimis, ne quid –
  817
nimium ne crede
  colori 485
n'importe 643
Nimrod 361, 622
nincompoop 501
nine 98
  tuneful –
    music 416
    poetry 597
  – days' wonder
    transient 111
    unimportant 643
    no wonder 871
  – lives 359
  – men's morris 840
  – points of the
    law 777
ninefold 98
ninepins 840
ninety 98
ninny 501
Niobe 839
nip *cut* 44
  destroy 162
  shorten 201
  dram 298
  freeze 385
  pungent 392
  drink 959
  – in the bud
    check 201
    kill 361
    hinder 706
  – up 789
nipperkin 191
nippers 781
nipple 250
Nirwana 981
nis 980
nisi prius 741, 969
Nisus and Euryalus
  890
nisus formativus
  161
nitency 420
niter 392
nitor in adversum
  708

---

nitrous oxide 376
nit-wit 499, 501
niveous *cold* 383
  white 430
nixe *demon* 980
nixie *fairy* 979
nizam 745
nizy 501
N or M 78
no *zero* 101
  dissent 489
  negation 536
  refusal 764
  unable to say –
    605
  on – account 761
  have – business
    there 83
  – chicken 128, 131
  – choice 601, 609a
  – conjuror 501,
    701
  – consequence 643
  in – degree 32
  at – great distance
    197
  – doubt 474, 488
  have – end 112
  – end of *great* 31
    multitude 102
    length 200
  – fear 473
  – go 304, 732
  at – hand 32
  matter of – import
    4
  with – interval
    199
  – one knows who
    876
  – less 639
  – longer 122
  – love lost be-
    tween them 898
  – man's land 187,
    778
  – matter
    neglect 460
    unimportant 643
  and – mistake 474
  – more
    inexistent 2
    past 122
    dead 360
  – more than 32
  have – notion of
    489
  – object 643
  – one 4, 187
  – other 13, 87
  to – purpose
    shortcoming 304
    useless 645
    failure 732
  give – quarter 361
  – scholar 493
  make – scruple of
    602
  – great shakes
    small 32
    trifling 643
    imperfect 651
  – sooner said than
    done 113, 132
  – stranger to 490
  – such thing
    non-existent 2

---

unsubstantial 4
  contrary 14
  dissimilar 18
  – surrender 606,
    717
  – thank you 764
  at – time 107
  – wonder 871
Noah's ark 41, 72
nob 210
nobilitate 873
nobility 875
noble *great* 31
  important 642
  rank 873
  peer 875
  disinterested 942
  virtuous 944
noblesse 875
nobody
  unsubstantial 4
  zero 101
  absence 187
  low-born 876
  – knows
    ignorance 491
  – knows where
    distance 196
  – present 187
  – would think 508
noctambulation 266
noctivagant
  travel 266
  dark 421
noctograph 421
noctuary 421, 551
nocturnal
  night 126
  dark 421
  black 431
nocturne 415
nocuous 649
nod *wag* 314
  assent 488
  signal 550
  sleep 683
  command 741
  bow 894
  – of approbation
    931
  – of assent 488
  nodding to its fall
    162, 306
noddle 210, 450
noddy 501
node 250
nodosity 250, 256
nods and becks and
  wreathed smiles
  894
nodule 250.
nodular 256
nodus, dignus vin-
  dice – 704
Noel 998
noggin 191
noise 402, 404
  – abroad 531
  make a – in the
    world 873
noiseless 403
noisome
  fetid 401
  bad 649
  unhealthy 657
nolens volens 601
noli me tangere

---

defiance 715
excitable 825
fastidious 868
nolition 603
nolle prosequi 624
nolumus leges
  Angliae mutari
  permanence 141
  continuance 143
  preservation 670
nom de: – guerre
  565
  – plume 565
nomad 268
nomadic 266
Nomancy 511
nomenclature 564
nominal
  unsubstantial 4
  word 562
  name 564
  – price 815
nomination 564,
  755
nominee 758
nominis umbra 4
Nomology 963
non:
  – compos mentis
    503
  – constat 477
  – deficit alter 100
  – est in ventus 187
  – haec in foedera
    536, 610
  – nobis Domine
    990
  – obstante 707
  – placet 489
  – possumus
    impossible 471
    obstinate 606
    refusal 764
  – nostrum tantas
    componere lites
    471, 713
  – scripta 963
  – semper erit
    aestas 111
  – sequitur 477
  – sum qualis eram
    140, 160
non-addition 38
non-admission 55
nonage 127
nonagenarian 98
non-appearance
  447
non-assemblage 73
non-attendance 187
nonce 118
  for the – 118, 134
nonchalance
  neglect 460
  insensibility 823
  indifference 866
non-coincidence 14
non-cohesive 47
non-com. 726
non-commissioned
  officer 745
non-committal 528,
  864
non-completion 736
non-compliance
  742, 764
nonconformity

---

difference 15
exception 83
dissent 489
sectarianism 984
non-content 489
non-cooperation
  489, 927
nondescript 83
none 101
  – else 87
  – to spare 640
  – such
    superior 33
    exceptional 83
    very good 648
  – in the world 4
  – the worse 660
non-endurance 825
nonentity
  inexistence 2
  unsubstantial 4
  unimportant 643
non esse 2
non-essential 6,
  643
non-existence 2
non-expectance 508
non-extension 180a
non-fulfilment 730,
  732
  – of one's hopes
    509
non-imitation 20
non-interference
  inaction 681
  freedom 748
nonius 466
non-juror 489, 984
non-naturals 657
nonny 501
non-observance
  inattention 458
  desuetude 614
  infraction 773
  dereliction 927
nonpareil 648
  type 591
non-payment 808
non-performance
  non-completion
    730
  dereliction 927
non-plus
  uncertain 475
  difficulty 704
  conquer 731
non-preparation
  674
non-prevalence 614
non-residence 187
non-resistance 725,
  743
non-resonance
  408a
nonsense
  absurdity 497
  unmeaning 517
  trash 643
  talk – *folly* 499
non-subsistence 2
non-success 732
nonsuch [see none]
nonsuit *defeat* 731
  fail 732
  condemn 971
nonum prematur in
  annum 133

non-uniformity 16a
noodle 501
nook *place* 182
  receptacle 191
  corner 244
noology 450
noon *mid-day* 125
noon—day *light* 420
  clear as —
    intelligible 518
  manifest 525
nooscopic 450
noose *ligature* 45
  loop 247
  snare 545
  gallows 975
norma loquendi 567
normal
  intrinsic 5
  mean 29
  regular 82
  perpendicular 212
  – condition
    rule 80
normality 80, 502
Normand, répon-
  dre en – 544
Norns 601
North 278
  – and South 237
Northern 237
  – light 423
  – star
    constant 939
North-west
  passage 311
nose *prominence*
  250
  smell 398
  with one's – in
    the air 878
  lead by the – 615,
    737
  led by the – 749
  not see beyond
    one's –
    misjudge 481
    folly 499
    unskilful 699
  speak through
    the – 583
  thrust one's – in
    interjacence 228
    busy 682
  under one's –
    present 186
    near 197
    manifest 525
    defy 715
  put one's – out of
    joint *defeat* 731
    disrepute 874
  – ring 847
nose-dive 306
nosegay 400, 847
nosey 455
Nosology 655
nostalgia 833
nostril 351
  breath of one's –s
    359
  stink in the –s 401
nostrum 626, 662
not *negation* 536
  what is – 546
  what ought – 923
  – at all 32

– allowed 964
– amiss 618, 651,
  845
– any 101
– bad 651
– bargain for 508
– a bit 536
– to be borne 830
– a Chinaman's
  chance 471
– come up to 34
– cricket 923
– to be despised
  642
it will – do 923
– of the earth 987
– expect 508
– fail 939
– far from 197
– a few 102
– fit to be seen 846
– following 477
– grant 764
– guilty 946
– to be had 471,
  640
– having 187, 777a
– hardened 950
– hear of 764
– included 55
– know what to
  make of 519
– a leg to stand
  on 158
– likely 473
– a little 31
– matter 643
– to mention 37
– mind 823, 930
– often 137
– on your life 489
– one 101
– a particle 4
– particular 831
– pay 808
– a pin to choose
  27
– playing the
  game 923
– within previous
  experience 137
– to be put down
  604
– quite 32
– reach 304
– right 503
– sorry 827
– a soul 101
– on speaking
  terms 889
– the thing 925
– to be thought of
  incogitancy 452
  impossible 471
  refusal 764
  hopeless 859
  undue 925
  disapprobation
  932
– trouble oneself
  about 460
– understand 519
– vote 609a
– wonder 871
– for the world
  603, 764
– worth

trifling 643
  useless 645
nota bene 457
notabilia 642
notabilities 875
notable
  manifest 525
  important 642
  active 682
  distinguished 873
notables 875
notably 31
notary 553, 968
notation 85
notch 198, **257**, 550
note *cry* 412
  music 413
  take cognizance
    450
  remark 457
  explanation 522
  sign 550
  record 551
  printing 591
  epistle 592
  minute 596
  money 800
  fame 873
  change one's – 607
  make a – of 551
  of – 873
  take – of 457
  – of admiration
    870
  – of alarm 669
  – of preparation
    673
note-book
  memorandum 505
  record 551
  compendium 569
  writing 590
noted 490, 873
noteworthy
  great 31
  exceptional 83
  important 642
nothing *nihility* 4
  zero 101
  trifle 643
  come to – 304, 732
  do – 681
  for – 815
  go for – 643
  good for – 646
  make – of
    under-estimate
    483
    fail 732
  take – by 732
  think of – 930
  worse than – 808
  – comes amiss 831
  – to do 681
  – to do with 764
  – doing 681
  – to go upon 471
  – in it 4
  – of the kind 18,
    536
  – loth 602
  – on 226
  – more to be said
    478
  – to signify 643
nothingness 2
notice *intellect* 450

observe 457
  review 480
  information 527
  warning 668
  bring into – 525
  deserve – 642
  give –
    manifest 525
    inform 527
    indicate 550
  short – 111
  take – of 450
  this is to give –
    457
  worthy of – 642
  – is hereby given
    publication 531
  – to quit 782
noticeable 31
notification 527
notion *idea* 453
notional 515
notoriety 531, 873
notorious
  known 490
  public 531
  famous 873
  infamous 874
notturno 415
notwithstanding 30
nought
  [*see* naught]
noun 564
nourish 707
nourishment
  food 298
nous 498
nous avons changé
  tout cela 140
nouveau riche 123,
  734, 876
Nova Zembla 383
novation 609
novel
  dissimilar 18
  new 123
  unknown 491
  tale 594
novelette 594
novelist 594
novice
  ignoramus 493
  learner 541
  bungler 701
  religious 996
novitiate 539, 673
novocaine 376, 381
novus homo 57,
  876
now 118
  – and then 136
  – or never 134
noways 32
nowhere 187
nowise 32, 536
noxious 649, 657
noyade 361, 972
noyerait dans une
  goutte d'eau, il
  se – 699
nozzle
  projection 250
  opening 260
  air-pipe 351
nuance 15, 465
nubibus, in – 2, 515
nubiferous 353, 426

nubile 131, 903
nucleus *middle* 68
  cause 153
  centre 222
  kernel 642
nuda veritas 494
nude 226, 849
nudge 550
nudity 226
nugacity 499, 645
nugae canorae 517,
  842
nugas, magno co-
  natu magnas –
  643
nugatory 158
  unimportant 643
nuggar 273
nugget *mass* 192
  money 800
nuisance 619, 830
null 4
  – and void
    inexistence 2
    powerless 158
    unproductive 169
    illegal 964
  declare – and void
    abrogation 756
    non-observance
    773
nulla dies sine
  lineâ 682
nullah 198
nullâ pallescere
  culpâ, nil con-
  scire sibi – 946
nulli secundus 33
nullibiety 187
nullify *inexistence* 2
  compensate 30
  destroy 162
  abrogate 756
  not observe 773
  not pay 808
nullity 2, 4
nullius jurare in
  verba magistri
  487
numb
  physically insen-
    sible 376, 381
  morally insensible
    823
  –skull 493
number
  part 51
  abstract – **84**
  count 85
  plural 100
  – of a magazine
    &c. 593
  – among 76
  take care of – one
    943
  – of times 104
numbered: days –
  kill 361
  necessity 601
  hopeless 859
  – with the dead
    360
numberless 105
numbers *many* 102
  verse 597
numbness 375, **381**
numerable 85

ocean 341
plough the – 267
oceanography 341
ocher 433, 439
  yellow – 436
ochlocracy 737
o'clock 114
  know what's –
  698
octagon 244
octahedron 244
Octateuch 895
octave
  eight 98
  music 413
  period 108
octavo 593
octet 98
octifid 99
octodecimo 593
octogenarian 98,
  130
octoroon 41
octroi 812
octuple 98
ocular 441
  – demonstration
  see 441
  visible 446
  – inspection 441
oculis subjecta
  fidelibus 446
oculist 662
od force 992
odalisque 746
odd remaining 40
  exception 83
  single 87
  insane 503
  vulgar 851
  ridiculous 853
  – fellows 712
  – fish 857
oddity 857
oddments 51
odds inequality 28
  superiority 33
  chance 156
  discord 713
  at, – 24, 713
  long – 704
  what's the – 643
  – against one 665
  the – are 472
  – and ends
  remainder 40
  mixture 41
  part 51
  useless 645
ode 597
odi profanum
  vulgus 878
Odin 979
odious
  disagreeable 830
  ugly 846
  hateful 898
odium disgrace 874
  hatred 898
  blame 932
odium theologicum
  481, 988
  church 995
odograph 200
odometer 200
odontoid 250, 253
odor 398

in bad – 932
  – of sanctity 897
odylic force 992
odzookens 870
Oedipus 462, 524
  – complex 897
  Davus sum non –
  703
oeil de maitre 459
o'er [see over]
oeuvre 161
of: – all things 33
  – course 82, 154
  – late 123
  – one mind 23
  – no effect 169
  – old 122
  – a piece
  uniform 16
  similar 17
  agreeing 23
off 196
  be – 623
  keep – 623
  make – with 791
  move – 287
  sheer – 287
  stand – 287
  start – 293
  – one's balance
  605
  throw – one's
  center 874
  – one's guard 260,
  508
  – one's hands 776
  take – one's hands
  785
  – one's head 503
  – one's legs 284,
  309
  – one's mind 452
  – and on
  periodical 138
  changeable 149
  irresolute 605
  throw – the scent
  uncertain 475
  avoid 623
  – side 238
  – with you 297
offal 653
offence attack 716
  anger 900
  guilt 947
offend 830, 945
  – against the law
  964
offensive
  unsavory 395
  fetid 401
  foul 653
  aggressive 716
  displeasing 830
  distasteful 867
  obnoxious 898
  – and defensive
  alliance 712
  – to ears polite 579
offer proposal 763
  – the alternative
  609
  – a choice 609
  – of marriage 902
  – oneself 763
  – up prayers 990
  – sacrifice 990

– for sale 796
offering gift 784
  burnt – 990
  sin – 952
offertory gift 784
  worship 990
  rite 998
off-hand soon 132
  inattentive 458
  careless 460
  spontaneous 612
office doing 170
  room 191
  business 625
  mart 799
  worship 900
  do one's – 772
  good –s 724, 906
  hold – 693
  kind –s 906
  do an ill – 907
  man in – 694
officer director 694
  commander 745
  constable 965
offices
  kitchen &c. 191
official certain 474
  true 494
  business 625
  man in office 694
  authoritative 737
  master 745
  servant 746
officialism 739
officiate
  business 625
  act 680
  conduct 692
  religious 998
officio ex –
  officer 694
  authority 737
  duty 924
officinal 613
officious 682
offing 196, 341
offscourings 645,
  653
offset
  compensation 30
  offspring 167
offshoot adjunct 39
  part 51
  effect 154
  offspring 167
offspring effect 154
  posterity 167
offuscate 121, 426
often repeated 104
  frequent 136
  most – 613
  – to be met with
  136
ogee 847
Ogham 590
ogive 215
ogle look 441
  desire 865
  rude 895
  endearment 902
ogpu 696
ogre bugbear 860
  evil-doer 913
  demon 980
oil lubricate 332
  grease 355, 356

pour – on
  relieve 834
  – on the troubled
  waters 174, 714
  – lamp 423
  – stove 386
oiled drunk 959
oilcloth 223
oilskin 386
oil-painting 556
oily smooth 255
  greasy 355
  servile 886
  courteous 894
  flattery 933
oinomania 959
ointment
  grease 356
  remedy 662
O.K. 58
old 124
  of – 122
  – age 128
  die of – age 729
  – bachelor 904
  – clothes 225
  – fashioned 851
  – fogey 501, 857
  – joke 842
  – maid cards 840
  spinster 904
  – man veteran 130
  husband 903
  – man of the sea
  706
  – Nick 978
  – school 124
  obstinate 606
  habit 613
  pay off – scores
  718
  – song
  repetition 104
  trifle 643
  cheap 815
  – stager
  veteran 130
  actor 599
  proficient 700
  – story
  repetition 104
  stale news 532
  love 897
  – times 122
  one's – way 613
  – woman fool 501
  wife 903
Oldbuck 122
olden 124
older 128
oldest inhabitant
  not in memory of
  – 137
old-fashioned 124,
  851
oldness 128
oleagine 356
oleaginous 355
oleomargarine 356
oleum addere
  camino 35, 173
olfactory 398
olid 401
oligarch 745
oligarchy 737
olio 41
olive-branch

infant 129
  offspring 167
  pacification 723
olive-green 435
olla podrida 41
Olympiad 720
Olympus 981
omber 840
ombres chinoises
  448
omega end 67
omelet 298
omen 512
ominate 511
ominous
  predicting 511
  indicating 550
  danger 665
  hopeless 859
omission
  incomplete 53
  exclusion 55
  neglect 460
  failure 732
  non-observance
  773
  guilt 947
omitted 2, 187
omne tulit
  punctum 731
omnibus 272
omnifarious 81
omniform 81
omnigenous 81
omnipotence 157,
  976
omnipresence 186,
  976
omniscience 490,
  976
omnium gatherum
  mixture 41
  confusion 59
  assemblage 72
omnivorous
  eating 298
  desire 865
  gluttony 957
omphalos 68
on forwards 282
  – account of 155
  – all accounts 52
  – that account 155
  – approval 463
  – an average 29
  – the brink of 32
  – the cards 152
  – foot duration 106
  event 151
  doing 170
  – the fire 730
  – all fours 13, 23
  – the other hand
  30
  – one's head 218
  – the increase 35
  – a large scale 31
  – these lines 627
  – the move 264
  – the nail 118
  – no account 32
  – no occasion 107
  – a par 27
  – the part of 9
  – the point of 111
  – the present oc-

overmatch
 unequal 28
 superior 33
 strength 159
 conquer 731
over-measure 641
overmuch 641
over-night 122
 – bag 191
over-officious 682
overpaid 816
overpass
 exceed 33
 transgress 303
overpersuade 615
overplay 855
overplus 40, 641
overpoise 179
overpower
 subdue 731
 emotion 824
overpowering
 strong 159
overpraise
 over-rate 482
 exaggerate 549
 flatter 933
overprize 482
overrate 482
overreach *pass* 303
 deceive 545
 baffle 731
overreckon 482
over-refinement 477
over-religious 955
override
 superior 33
 influence 175
 pass 303
 hinder 706
 defeat 731
 authority 737
 severity 739
 abrogate 756
over-righteous 988
overrule 737, 756
overruling
 important 642
overrun
 presence 186
 spread 194
 redundance 641
 despoil 659
over-running
 printing 591
over-scrupulous 939
overseas 57
oversee 693
overseer 694
over-sensitive 822
overset *invert* 218
 level 308
 subvert 731
overshadow
 darken 421
 repute 873
 disrepute 874
overshoes 225
overshoot the mark
 go beyond 303
 exaggerate 549
 overdo 682
 clumsy 699
oversight
 inattention 458

error 495
 superintendence 693
 failure 732
overskip 303
oversleep 683
overspent 688
overspread
 disperse 73
 be present 186
 cover 233
overstate 549
overstep 303
overstock 641
overstrain
 extol 482
 fatigue 688
oversupply 641
overt 525
 – act 680
overtake 292
overtaken
 tipsy 959
overtask }679, 688
overtax }
overthrow
 undo 145
 destroy 162
 level 308
 confute 479
 vanquish 731
overthrown
 vanquished 732
overthwart 708
overtired 688
overtone 413
overtop 31, 33, 206
overture
 precursor 64
 music 415
 peace 723
 offer 763
 request 765
overturn
 destroy 162
 invert 218
 level 308
 confute 479
overvalue 482
overweening
 excess 641
 rash 863
 pride 878
 conceit 880
 insolence 885
overweigh
 exceed 33
 influence 175
 overrate 482
overwhelm
 ruin 162
 redundant 641
 affect 824
overwhelmed
 defeated 732
 subjection 749
overwhelming
 strong 159
 wonderful 870
over-wise 880
overwork 679, 688
overwrought
 exaggerated 549
 emotion 824
 affectation 855
over-zealous 825
oviform 249

ovo, in – 153
ovoid 247, 249
ovule 247
owe 806
 – it to oneself 926
owing *debt* 806
 – to effect 154
 attribution 155
owl *fool* 501
 –'s light 422
 –s to Athens 641
own *assent* 488
 divulge 529
 possess 777
 property 780
come by one's – 775
condemned out of one's – mouth 479
consult one's – pleasure 943
hold one's – 737
know one's – mind 604
not know one's – interest 699
not know one's – mind 605
will of one's – 604
of one's – accord 600, 602
pay in one's – coin 718
look with one's – eyes 459
– flesh and blood 11
throw a stone in one's – garden *clumsy* 699
 retaliation 718
take the law into one's – hands 722, 964
out of one's – head 600
after one's – heart 897
look after one's – interest 943
stand in one's – light 699
act on one's – responsibility 738
at one's – risk 526
have one's – way *will* 600
 easy 705
 succeed 731
 authority 737
 freedom 748
 – oneself in the wrong 950
owner *possessor* 779
 without an – 777a
ownership
 property 780
ox 366, 373
hot enough to roast an – 382
oxidation 659
oxymoron 24
oyer and terminer, court of – 966
O yes 531

Oyez! *hear* 418
 publication 531

P

P:
 mind one's –'s and Q's
 care 459
 polite 894
 duty 926
pabulum 298, 316
 mental – 454
pace *walk* 264
 journey 266
 measure 466
 permission 760
keep – with
 concur 178
 velocity 274
put through one's –s 525
show one's –s
 ostentation 882
 – tanti nominis 928
 – up and down 266
pachydermatous 376, 823
pacific 172, 721
pacification 723
pacificism 721
pacify 174
pack *arrange* 60
 assemblage 72
 locate 184
 squeeze 195
 prepare 673
 burden 706
send –ing 297
 – of nonsense 643
 – off *depart* 293
 eject 297
 – up 229
package
 assemblage 72
 location 184
packer 673
packet
 assemblage 72
 ship 273
pack-horse 271
pack-saddle 215
pack-thread 205
pact 23, 769
Pactolus 803
pad *thicken* 194
 line 224
 horse 271
 soft 324
 expatiate 577
 tablet 590
padding *lining* 224
 stopper 263
 soft 324
 words 573
paddle *walk* 260
 row 267
 oar 633
 – one's own canoe *conduct* 692
 free 748
 – steamer 273
paddock 232
padishah 745
padlock 45, 752

put a – on one's lips 585
padre 996
padrone 745
paean
 rejoicing 838
 celebration 883
 gratitude 916
 approbation 931
 worship 990
paganism 984
page
 numeration 85
 printing 591
 book 393
 attendant 746
 wedding 903
 – proof 591
pageant 448, 882
paginate 85
pagoda 206, 1000
pah 717
pail 191
paillard 962
paillasse 215
pain *physical* – **378**
 moral – **828**
 penalty 974
painfulness **830**
painfully *very* 31
painim 984
painless 827
pains 686
get for one's – 973
 take – 686
 – and penalties 974
painstaking
 active 682
 laborious 686
paint *coat* 223
 color 428
 deceive 545
 delineate 556
 ornament 847
 – the lily 641
paintable 845
painter *rope* 45
 artist 559
painting **556**
pair *similar* 17
 combine 48
 couple 89
 – off *average* 29
 marry 903
pair-oar 273
pairs *cards* 840
pal 711, 890
palace 189
 bishop's – 1000
 floating – 273
Paladin 717, 726
 hero 861
palaestra
 school 542
 arena 728
palais de vérité 703
palanquin 272
palatable 394, 829
palatal *letter* 561
palate 390
 tickle the – 394
palatial *palace* 189
 ostentatious 882
palatinate 181
palatine 745
Palatine Court 966

palaver
  unmeaning 517
  speech 582
  loquacity 584
  colloquy 588
  council 696
pale *stake* 45
  region 181
  inclosure 232
  limit 233
  dim 422
  colourless 429
  emotion 821
  frightened 860
  turn –
    lose color 429
    emotion 821
    fear 860
  – of the church
    995
  – its ineffectual
    fire
    dim 422
    out of repute 874
pale-faced 429
paleocrystic 124
paleography
  past 122
  philology 560
paleology *past* 122
  language 160
paleontology 368
paleozoic 124
palestric 686, 720
paletot 225
palette 556
palfrey 271
palimpsest 147, 528
palindrone
  inversion 218
  neology 563
paling 232, 752
palingenesia 163
palingenesis 660
palinode 597
palinody 607
palisade
  wall 212
  defence 717
  prison 752
pall *covering* 223
  mantle 225
  funeral 363
  disgust 395
  insignia 747
  weary 841
  dislike 867
  satiety 869
  canonicals 999
palladium
  safety 664
Pallas 979
pall-bearer 363
pallet *support* 215
  painter's - 556
palliament 225
palliate
  moderate 174
  mind 658
  relieve 834
  extenuate 937
palliative 174
  remedy 662
pallid 429
pallium 999
pall-mall 840
pallone 840

pallor 429
palm
  measure of length
    200
  trophy 733
  steal 791
  laurel 877
  bear the – 873
  grease the –
    induce 615
  give 784
  itching – 865
  win the – 731
  – off, – upon 545
  – tree 367
palmated 257
palmer
  traveller 268
  clergy 996
palmist 513
palmistry 511
palmy
  prosperous 734
  pleasant 829
  – days
  prosperous 734
  pleasure 827
palpable
  material 316
  tactile 379
  obvious 446
  manifest 525
  – *obscure* 421
palpation 379
palpitate
  tremble 315
  color 440
  emotion 821
  fear 860
palsy
  impotence 158
  physical insensi-
    bility 376
  disease 655
  mental insensi-
    bility 823
palter
  falsehood 544
  shift 605
  elude 773
paltry *small* 32
  unimportant 643
  mean 940
paludal 345
pampas 344
pamper 902, 954,
  957
pamphlet 531, 593
pamphleteer 595
Pan 979
pan 191
panacea 662
panache 256, 847
panama *hat* 225
panary 636
pancake 298
pandar [see pander]
Pandean pipes 417
pandect
  knowledge 490
  dissertation 595
  compendium 596
  code 963
pandemonium 59,
  404, 982
  inhabitants of –
    978

pandemic 657
pander *pimp* 962
  – to *instrument*
    631
  help 707
  flatter 933
pandiculation
  expansion 194
  opening 260
  sleepy 683
Pandoor 726
Pandora's box 619
  bottom of 858
paned 440
panegyric 931
panegyrize 482
panel *list* 86
  layer 204
  partition 228
  accused 938
  jury 967
  sliding – 545
panelling 847
pang 378, 828
Pangloss 492
panguid 355
panhandle 765, 767,
  876
panic 860
panier 225
Panjandrum 875
pannel 213
pannikin 191
pannier 191
panoply 717, 727
panopticon 752
panorama 448, 556
panoramic 78, 446
  – view 441
pansophy 490
pant *heat* 382
  fatigue 688
  emotion 821
  – for 865
pantaloon
  old man 130
  pantomimist 599
  buffoon 844
pantaloons 225
pantechnicon 272,
  636
pantheism 984
Pantheon 979, 1000
panther 861
pantile 223, 350
pantologist 492, 700
pantology 490
pantomime 550, 599
pantry 191, 636
pants 225
panurgy 698
pap 250, 354
papa *father* 166
Papa *pope* 996
papacy 984, 995
papal 995
paper *cover* 223
  white 430
  writing 590
  book 593
  security 771
  exist only on – 4
  – credit 805
  – money 800
  – pellet 643
  – war 476, 720
Paphian 954, 961

papilla 250
papistry 984
papoose 129
pappous 256
papula 250
papulose 250
papyrus 590
par 27
  above – 648
  below – *low* 207
  imperfect 651
  – excellence 33
  – nobile fratrum
    alike 17
    friends 890
  de – le roi 737
  – parenthèse 134
  – pari refero 718
  – value 812
parable
  metaphor 521
  teaching 537
  description 594
parabola *curve* 245
parabolic
  metaphorical 521
paracentesis 297
parachronism 115
parachute
  balloon 273
  means of safety
    666
  – *light* 423
Paraclete 976
parade *procession*
  69, 266
  walk 189
  ostentation 882
paradigm 22, 567
Paradise *bliss* 827
  heaven 981
  in – 827
parados 717
paradox
  absurdity 497
  obscurity 519
  difficulty 704
paradoxical 475,
  519
paraffin 356
paragon
  perfect 650
  glory 873
  good man 948
paragram
  ambiguous 520
  neology 563
paragraph *part* 51
  phrase 566
  article 593
paraleipsis 460
parallax 196
parallel
  similarity 17
  imitate 19
  harmonious 178
  – *position* 216
  symmetry 242
  draw a – 464
  none but himself
    can be his – 873
  run – 178
parallelism 216
  agreement 23
parallelogram 244
parallelopiped 244
paralogism 477

paralogize 477
paralysis
  impotence 158
  physical insensi-
    bility 376
  disease 655
  moral insensi-
    bility 823
paralyze 158, 376,
  823
paramount
  supreme 33
  important 642
  authority 737
  lord – *master* 745
  possessor 779
  – *estate* 780
paramour 897
paranoia 503, 504
parapet 717
paraph 550
paraphernalia
  machinery 633
  belonging 780
paraphrase
  imitation 19
  copy 21
  synonym 522
  phrase 566
paraphrast 524
paraphrastic 19,
  522
parasite *auxiliary*
  711
  servile 886
  flatterer 935
parasitic
  subjection 749
  grasping 789
  servile 886
parasol *covering* 223
  shade 424
paratus:
  in utrumque –
    resolved 604
    ready 673
  semper – 673
parboil 384
parbuckle 633
Parcae 601
parcel *part* 51
  group 72
  part and – 56
  – out *arrange* 60
  allot 786
parcels
  property 780
parcere subjectis
  740, 914
parch *dry* 340
  heat 382
  bake 384
parched with thirst
  865
parchment
  writing 590
  security 771
parcity 819
pardi 535
pardon 506, 918
  beg – 952
  – me 489
pardonable 937
pare *cut* 38
  reduce 195
  peel 204
  divest 226

– down
  shorten 201
paregoric 662
parenchyma 316, 329
parent 166
  – ship 726
parentage 11, 166
parenthesis
  discontinuity 70
  inversion 218
  interjacence 228
  by way of – 134
parenthetical
  irrelative 10
pargeting 847
parhelion 423
pari passu 27, 120
Pariah
  outlaw 83
  commonalty 876
  outcast 893
parian
  sculpture 557
parietal 236
parietes 224
paring 32
parish 181
  bring to the – 804
  come upon the – 804
  – council 696
parishioner 997
paritor 965
parity 17, 27
park house 189
  plain 344
  trees 367
  artillery 727
  pleasure ground 840
  – paling 232
parkway 627
parlance 582
  in common – 576
parlante 415
parlementaire 534, 723
parler:
  façon de – 521
  – a tort et à travers
  illogical 477
  nonsense 497
parley talk 588
  conference 695
  mediation 724
parliament 696
parliamentary
  securities 802
parlor 191
parlor-maid 746
parlous 665
Parnassus 597
parochial 181, 189
  prejudiced 48
parody
  imitation 19
  copy 21
  misinterpret 523
  misrepresent 555
  travesty 865
parole speech 582
  on – restraint 751
  prisoner 754
  promise 763
Parolles 887

paronomasia
  neology 563
  ornament 577
paronymous 562
paroxysm
  violence 173
  agitation 315
  emotion 825
  anger 900
parquetry 440
Parr, Old – 130
parricide 361
parrot
  imitation 19
  repetition 104
  loquacity 584
  repeat as a – 505
  avert 623
  defend 717
pars magna fui, quorum – 690
parse 461, 567
Parsee 984
parsimony 819
parson 996
parsonage 1000
part divide 44
  portion 51
  diverge 291
  music 413
  book 593
  rôle 599
  function 625
  duty 926
  act a – action 680
  take an active – 682
  bear – in 709
  component – 56
  fractional – 100a
  in – a little 32
  for my – 79
  on the – of 707
  play a – in 175
  principal – 642
  take the – of 709
  take – with 709
  take a – in 680
  take no – in 623
  – company
  disjunction 44
  avoid 623
  quarrel 713
  – and parcel 56
  – by part 51
  – song 415
  – of speech 567
  – with 782, 784
partake 778
  – of the sacrament 998
parte, ex – 481
parterre level 213
  cultivation 371
Parthis mendacior 544
parti pris 611
partial unequal 28
  incomplete 51
  special 79
  misjudging 481
  unjust 923
  – shadow 422
partiality
  preponderance 33
  desire 865

friendship 888
  love 897
partially 32, 51
partible 44
particeps criminis 690, 711
participate 709, 778
  – in be a doer 680
participation 778
participator 690
particle 32, 330
parti-colored 440
particular item 51
  event 151
  attentive 457
  careful 459
  exact 494
  capricious 608
  odd 851
  fastidious 868
  in – 79
  – account 594
  – estate 780
particularize
  special 79
  describe 594
particularly 31, 33
particulars 79, 594
partie carrée 892
parting 44
partisan
  auxiliary 711
  weapon 727
  friend 890
  sympathizer 914
partisanship
  warped judgment 481
  co-operation 709
  partiality 923
partition wall 228
  allot 786
partlet 366
partly 51
partner
  companion 88
  auxiliary 711
  sharer 778
  friend 890
  spouse 903
  sleeping – 683
partnership
  party 712
  join – with 709
parts intellect 450
  skill 698
  wisdom 498
parturition 161
parturiunt montes 482, 509
party assemblage 72
  special 79
  person 372
  association 712
  sociality 892
  – spirit
  warped judgment 481
  cooperation 709
  wrong 923
  – to action 680
  agent 690
  co-operate 709
  – to a suit 969
  – wall 228
parva componere magnis 464

parvenu
  new 123
  successful 734
  vulgar 851
  low-born 876
parvitude 193
pas precedence 62
  term 71
  precession 280
  rank 873
  – de quatre 840
  – seul 840
pas si bête 498
paschal 998
pasha 875
pashalic 737
pashaw 745
pasigraphie 560
pasigraphy 590
pasquinade 934
pass conjuncture 8
  be superior 33
  course 109
  lapse 122
  happen 151
  interval 198
  defile 203
  move 264
  transfer 270
  move through 302
  exceed 303
  vanish 449
  way 627
  difficulty 704
  thrust 716
  passport 760
  gratuity 815
  – as property 783, 784
  barely – 651
  let it – 460
  make a – at 716
  pretty – 704
  – away
  cease to exist 2
  end 67
  transient 111
  past 122
  cease 142
  die 360
  – by course 109
  inattention 458
  neglect 460
  disrespect 929
  – comprehension 519
  – current 484
  – an examination 648, 873
  – the eyes over 457
  – the fingers over 379
  – into one's hand 785
  – through one's hands 625
  – into 144
  – judgment 480
  – a law 963
  – in the mind 451
  – muster
  conform to 82
  sufficient 639
  good 648
  approbation 931
  barely – muster

651
  – under the name of 564
  – off be past 122
  egress 295
  – off for 544
  – on 282
  – an opinion 480
  – to the order of the day 624
  – out of 295
  – over
  exclude 55
  cross 302
  give 784
  forgive 918
  exemption 927a
  – over to 709
  – and repass 302, 314
  – in review 457, 461
  – the Rubicon 609
  – sentence on 971
  – time exist 1
  time 106
  do nothing 681
  – one's time in 625
  – to 144
  – through
  event 151
  motion 302
  – one's word 768
passable small 32
  unimportant 643
  imperfect 651
  pretty 845
passado 716
passage [see pass]
  part 51
  conversion 144
  street 189
  corridor 191
  opening 260
  navigation 267
  moving through 302
  music 413
  – in a book 593
  action 680
  cut a – 260
  force a – 302
  – of arms 720
passant, en –
  transit 270
  incidentally 621
pass-book 811
passe: mot de – 550
passé
  antiquated 124
  aged 128
  spoiled 659
passed away 122
passementerie 847
passenger 268
  – train 272
passe-partout
  key 260
  instrument 631
passer by 444
passer le temps, pour – 681
passerout pas, il ne 717
passe-temps 840

peripharse 566, 573
periplus 267
periscope 441, 445
periscopic 446
– lens 445
perish
  cease to exist 2
  be destroyed 162
  die 360
  decay 659
  – with cold 383
  – with hunger 956
perishable 111
perissology 573
peristaltic 248
peristyle 189
periwig 225
perjured 940
perjurer 548
perjury 544
perk *dress* 225
– up *elevate* 307
  revive 689
perked up
  proud 878
perky 880
perlustration 441
permanence
  durability 110
  unchanging 141
  unchangeable 150
permanent
  habitual 613
permeable 260
permeate
  insinuate 228
  pervade 186
  pass through 302
  –d with 613
permissible 760
permission 760
permissive 760
permit 760
permitting
  weather &c. – 469,
    470
permutation
  numerical - 84
  change 140
  interchange 148
pernicious 649
pernicity 274
perorate
  diffuse style 573
peroration
  sequel 65
  end 67
  speech 582
perpend *think* 451
perpendicular 212
perpension
  attention 457
perpetrate 680
  – a pun &c. 842
perpetrator 690
perpetua, esto –
    928, 931
perpetual 112
  frequent 136
  – curate 996
  – motion 467
perpetuate 112
  continue 143
  establish 150
perpetuity 69, **112**
perplex *derange* 61
  distract 458

uncertainty 475
  bother 830
perplexed 59, 248
perplexity
  disorder 59
  uncertainty 475
  unintelligibility
    519
  difficulty 704
perquisite 775, 973
perquisition 461
perron 627
perscrutation 461
persecute
  oppress 649
  annoy 830
  malevolence 907
perseverance 143,
    604a
Persides 215
persiflage 842, 856
persifleur 844
persist *duration* 106
  permanence 141
  continue 143
  persevere 604a
persistence
  diuturnity 110
person 3, 372
  without distinc-
    tion of –s 922
persona grata 890,
    899
personable 845
personae, dramatis
  – 599, 690
personage 372
personal
  [*see person*]
  special 79
  subjective 317
  – narrative 594
  – property 780
  – remarks 932
  – security 771
personality
  [*see personal*]
  discourtesy 895
  disrespect 929
  censure 932
  detraction 934
personalty 780
personate 19, 554
personify 521, 554
personnel 56, 590
perspective
  view 448
  expectation 507
  painting 556
  aerial – 428
  in – 200
perspicacity
  sight 441
  intelligence 498
  fastidiousness 868
perspicuity
  intelligibility 518
  style **570**
perspiration 295,
    299
  in a – 382
perstringe 457
persuadable 602
persuade *belief* 484
  induce 615
persuasibility
  willingness 602

persuasion
  class 75
  opinion 484
  teaching 537
  inducement 615
  religious – 983
persuasive
  reasoning 476
pert
  vain 880
  insolent 885
  discourteous 895
pertain to
  relate to 9
  included under 76
  power 157
  belong 777
  property 780
  duty 926
perte de vue, à –
    196, 447
pertinacity 604a
pertinent 9, 23
pertingent 199
perturbation
  derange 61
  ferment 171
  agitation 315
  emotion 821
  excitation 824,
    825
  fear 860
pertusion 260
peruke 225
peruse 539
pervade
  influence 175
  extend 186
  affect 821
  – the soul 824
pervading spirit 820
perverse
  obstinate 606
  difficult 704
  churlish 895
  sulky 901a
perversion
  sophistry 477
  misinterpretation
    523
  misteaching 538
  falsehood 544
  untruth 546
  injury 659
  impiety 988
pervert 144, 607
  [*see perversion*]
perverted 495
pervestigation 461
pervicacious 606
pervigilium 682
pervious 260
pessimism
  overrate 482
  underrate 483
  dejection 837
  hopeless 859
pessimist
  [*see pessimism*]
  coward 862
pessomancy 511
pessoribus orti 876
pest 663, 830
pester 830
pest-house 662
pestiferous 657
pestilence 655

pestle 330
pet *love* 897
  favorite 899
  anger 900
  fondle 902
  flatter 933
  – lamb 266
petal 367
petard 727
  hoist on one's own
    – 718, 732
Peter to pay Paul:
  borrow of – 788
  rob – *steal* 791
    wrong 923
  –'s pence 784, 809
  peter out 142
petit-maître 854
petite dame 962
petitio principii 477
petition 765, 969,
    990
petitioner 767
petrel *warning* 668
petrify *dense* 321
  hard 323
  freeze 385
  thrill 824
  affright 860
  astonish 870
petrol 388
petroleum 356
pétroleuse 384
petronel 727
petticoat *dress* 225
  woman 374
  – government
    authority 737
pettifogger 968
pettifogging
  sophistry 477
  deception 545
  litigious 713
  dishonorable 940
pettish 901
petto, in –
  mental 450
  thought of 454
  concealed 528
  intention 620
petty *little* 32, 193
  unimportant 643
  – cash 800, 811
  – jury 967
  – larceny 791
  – officer 745
  – sessions 966
  – treason 742
petulance 885, 901
petulant
  – *language* 574
peu de chose 643
peu s'en faut 32
pew *cell* 191
  church 1000
pewter 41
phaeton 272
Phaethon 423
phalanx 712, 726
phantasm
  unsubstantiality 4
  illusion 443
  appearance 448
  imagination 515
phantasmagoria
    448
phantasy 453, 515

phantom *unreal* 4
  fallacy of vision
    443
  imaginary 515
pharisaical 544, 988
Pharisee 548, 988
pharmacy 662
pharos 550
phase *aspect* 8
  transition 144
  form 240
  appearance 448
  have many –s 149
  assume a new –
    144
  view in all its –s
    461
phasis 448
phasma 443
phenomenon
  event 151
  appearance 448
  prodigy 872
phial 191
Phidias 559
philander 902
philanthropy 784,
    906, 910
Philip drunk to
  Philip sober,
  appeal from –
    658
philippic 932
Philistine 491, 876
philologist 492
philology 560
philomath 492
philomel 416
philosopher 492,
    500
  –'s stone
    impossibility 471
    perfect 650
    remedy 662
    wealth 803
philosophical
  thoughtful 451
  calm 826
philosophy
  calmness 826
  knowledge 490
  Moral – 450
  – of the Mind 450
philter 993
phiz *face* 234
  look 448
phlebotomy
  ejection 297
  remedy 662
Phlegethon 982
phlegm *viscid* 352
  insensibility 823
phlegmatic
  indifferent 866
phlogiston 382
pho! 497
Phoebus *sun* 318
  luminary 423
phoenix
  exception 83
  reproduction 163
  paragon 650
  restoration 660
phonate 402
phonetic
  sound 402
  voice 580

speech 582
– spelling 561
phonics 402
phonograph 417,
   418
phonography
   sound 402
   letter 361
   writing 590
phonology 562
Phosphor 423
phosphorescence
   420, 423
phosphorus 423
photo-engraving
   558
photograph *like* 17
photographer 559
photography 445
   light 420
   representation
   554
photogravure 558
photolysis 49
photometer 445
photosphere 318
photostat 553
phrase *part* 51
   music 413
   language 566
phrasemonger 577
phraseology 569
phrenetic 503
phrenitis 503
phrenology 450
phrenotypics 505
Phryne 962
phthisozoics 361
phylacteric
   sorcery 992
phylactery
   maxim 496
   spell 993
physic
   cure 660
   remedy 662
physical 316
– education
   material 316
   teaching 537
– force
   strength 159
   compulsion 744
– nature 3
– pleasure 377
– pain 378
– science 316
physician
   remedy 662
   advice 695
Physics 316
physiognomy
   face 234
   appearance 448
   interpret 522
Physiology
   organization 357
   life 359
   Vegetable – 369
physique
   strength 159
   animality 364
phytivorous 298
Phytology 369
pi 591
piacere, al – 600
piacular 952

pianino 417
pianissimo 415
pianist 416
piano *gentle* 174
   music 415
– organ 417
– player 417
pianoforte 417
pianola 417
piazza 189, 191
pibroch *music* 415
   war 722
pica 591
picaresco, gusto –
   945
picaroon 792
piccolo 410, 417
pick *axe* 253
   eat 298
   select 609
   best 648
   clean 652
   gain 775
– a-back 215
– the brains of 461
– holes
   censure 932, 934
– the lock 480a
– me up 662
– out *extract* 301
   select 609
– to pieces
   separate 44
   destroy 162
   find fault 932
– a quarrel 713
– one's steps 459
– up *learn* 539
   get better 658
   gain 775
– one's way 675
pickaninny 129
pickaxe 253
picked 648
– men 700
pickeer 791
pickeerer 792
pickelhaube
   armor 717
picket *join* 43
   locate 184
   fence 229
   guard 668
   defence 717
   soldiers 726
   restrain 751
   imprison 752
   torture 972
– boat 273
pickings 775, 793
pickle *condition* 7
   macerate 337
   pungent 392
   condiment 393
   preserve 670
   difficulty 704
   have a rod in –673
pickle-herring 844
pickpocket 792
   abuse like a – 932
pickthank *busy* 682
   servile 886
   flatterer 937
picnic *food* 298
   participation 778
   amusement 840
picquet 840

pictorial
   painting 556
   beauty 845
picture
   appearance 448
   representation
   554
   painting 556
   description 594
– to oneself 515
picture-gallery 556
picture-theater 599
picturesque
   painting 556
   beauty 845
piddle *dawdle* 683
piddling *trivial* 643
pidgin English 563
pie *food* 298
   sweet 396
   printing 591
piebald 440
piece *adjunct* 59
   bit 31
   painting 556
   drama 599
   cannon 727
   coin 800
   courtesan 962
   fall to –s 162
   go to –s 162
   in –s 330
   of a – 42
   pull to –s 162
   give a – of advice
   695
   – of good fortune
   618
   – of music 415
   – of news 532
   – out 52
   – together 43
   – of work 713
   make a – of work
   about 642
pièce
   – justificative 467
   – de résistance 298
piecemeal 51
pied *variegated* 440
pied de la lettre,
   au – 494
pie-poudre, court
   of – 966
pier 189, 666
pierce
   perforate 260
   bodily pain 378
   chill 385
   hurt 649
   wound 659
   affect 824
   mental pain 830
   – the head 410
   – the heart 830
piercer 262
piercing *cold* 383
   loud 404
   shrill 410
   intelligent 498
   feeling 821
   – eye 441
   – pain 378
pier-glass 445
Pierian spring 597
pierre fendre, à –
   383

Pierrot 599
pietas 998
piété, mont de –
   787
pietism 988
pietist 987, 988
piety 987
pig *animal* 366
   sensual 954a
– in a poke
   uncertain 475
– together 72
pigeon
   dupe 547
gorge de – 440
pigeon-hearted 862
pigeon-hole 191,
   260
piggin 191
piggish 954
pig-headed 499, 606
pigment 428
pigmy 193
pignoration 771
pignus 771
pig-sticking 361
pigsty 653
pigtail 214
pigwidgeon 193,
   980
pike *hill* 206
   sharp 253
   highway 627
   weapon 727
pikeman 726
pikestaff *tall* 206
   plain 525
pilaster
   support 215
   projection 250
   ornament 847
pile *stake* 45
   heap 72
   edifice 161
   post 215
   velvet 256
   money 800
   funeral – 363
   – up 549, 641
pile-driver 276
pilfer *steal* 791
pilferer 792
pilgarlic
   outcast 893
pilgrim 268, 996
pilgrimage 266, 676
pill *sphere* 249
   medicine 662
   bitter – 735
pillage 659, 791
pillager 792
pillar *stable* 150
   lofty 206
   support 215
   monument 551
   tablet 590
   –s of Hercules 550
   – of the state &c.
   873
   from – to post
   transfer 270
   agitation 315
   irresolute 505
   circuit 629

pillion 215
pillory 975
pillow
   support 215
   soft 324
   consult one's –
   temporize 133
   reflect 451
pilot *mariner* 269
   inform 527
   guide 693
   director 694
pilot-balloon 463
pilot-boat 273
pilot-officer 745
pilot-jacket 225
pilous 256
pimp 962
pimple 250, 848
pin *fasten* 43
   fastening 45
   locate 184
   sharp 253
   axis 312
   trifle 643
   might hear a –
   drop 403
   point of a – 193
   not a – to choose
   27, 609a
   – down 744, 751
   – one's faith upon
   484
   – oneself upon
   746, 886
pinafore 225
pince-nez 445
pincers 781
pinch *emergency* 8
   contract 195
   pain 378
   chill 385
   need 630
   difficulty 704
   adversity 735
   grudge 819
   hurt morally 830
   at a – 630, 704
   jack at a – 711
   where the shoe –s
   830
   – of snuff 643
pinchbeck 545, 847
pinched [see pinch]
   thin 203
   poor 804
   – with hunger 865
pinching 383, 819
Pindaric 597
ping-pong 840
pine *disease* 655
   dejection 837
   suffer in mind
   828
   – away 837
   – for 865
pinery 371
pinguid 355
pin-hole 260
pinion *fasten* 43
   wing 267
   instrument 633
   restrain 751
   fetter 752
pink *notch* 257
   pierce 260
   thrust 276

color 434
perfection 650
glory 873
pink of beauty 845
- fashion 852
- perfection 650
- politeness 894
pinnace 273
pinnacle 210
pinocle 840
pin-prick 180a
pins *legs* 266
- and needles
  bodily pain 378
  numb 381
  mental pain 828
pinscher 366
Pinto, Fernam
  Mendez – 548
pioneer
  precursor 64
  leader 234
  teacher 540
  prepare 673
pious 987
- fraud 546, 988
pip 747
pipe *tube* 260
  conduit 350
  vent 351
  tobacco 392
  sound 410
  cry 411
  music 416, 417
  weep 839
  no – no dance 812
- one's eye 839
- of peace 721, 723
pipeclay *habit* 613
  strictness 739
piper 416
  pay the – 707, 807
piping – hot 382
- time 721, 734
pipkin 191
piquant
  pungent 392
- style 574
  impressive 821
piquante, sauce –
  393, 829
pique *fly* 267
  excite 824
  pain 830
  hate 898
  anger 900
- oneself
  pride 878
piqueerer 792
piquet 717, 726
pirate 773, 791, 792
piroque 273
pirouette 218, 312
  turn a – 607
Pisa, tower of – 217
pis-aller 147
piscatorial 366
pisces natare
  docere 538, 641
pisciculture 370
piscina 350, 1000
pish! *absurd* 497
  trifling 643
  excitable 825
  irascible 901
piste 551

Pistol 887
pistol 727
pistol-shot 197
piston 263
pit *deep* 208
  hole 252
  opening 260
  extract 301
  grave 363
  theater 599
  danger 667
  bottomless – 982
- of Acheron 982
- against 708, 713
- against one
  another 464
pit-a-pat
  agitation 315
  rattle 407
  feeling 821
  excitation 824
pitch *degree* 26
  term 71
  location 184
  height 206
  summit 210
  erect 212
  throw 284
  descent 306
  depression 308
  reel 314
  resin 356a
  musical - 413
  black 431
  absolute – 416
- of one's breath
  411
- dark 421
- into attack 716
  contend 720
  punish 972
- overboard 782
- one's tent 292
- and toss 621
- upon reach 292
  discover 480a
  choose 609
  get 775
pitched battle 720
pitcher 191
pitchfork 273, 284
  rain -s 348
pitch-pipe 417
piteous 830
piteously *much* 31
pitfall 545, 667
pith *gist* 5
  strength 159
  interior 221
  center 222
  meaning 516
  important part
  642
pithless 158
pithy *meaning* 516
  concise 572
  vigorous 574
pitiable *bad* 649
  painful 830
  contemptible 930
pitied, to be – 828
pitiful
  unimportant 643
  bad 649
  disrepute 874
  pity 914
pitiless 914a

revengeful 919
pittance
  quantity 25
  dole 640
  allotment 786
  income 810
pitted 848
pituitous 352
pity 914
  express – 915
  what a –
  regret 833
  lament 839
  for -'s sake 914
pivot *junction* 43
  cause 153
  support 215
  axis 222, 312
pix *box* 191, 998
  assay 463
pixy 980
pizzicato 415
placable 918
placard 531
placate 723, 918
place
  circumstances 8
  order 58
  arrange 60
  term 71
  situation **182**, 183
  locate 184
  abode 189
  office 625
  rank 873
  give – to 623
  have – 1
  in – 183
  in – of 147
  make a – for 184
  out of – 185
  take – 151
- to one's credit
  805
- itself 58
- in order 60
- upon record 551
- under
  include 76
**placebit, decies re-
  petita** – 829
placebo 933
place-hunter 767
placeman 758
placet 488, 741
placid 826
placket 260
plagiarism
  imitation 19
  borrowing 788
  theft 791
plagiarist 792
Plagiary, Sir
  Fretful – 901
plagiedral 217
plague *disease* 655
  pain 828
  worry 830
plague-spot 657
plaguy 704, 830
plaid *shawl* 225
  variegation 440
plaidoyer 476
plain
  horizontal 213
  country **344**
  obvious 446

meaning 518
manifest 525
style 576
artless 703
ugly 846
simple 849
sneak -ly 576
tell one -ly 527
- English 576
- dealing 543
- interpretation
  522
- question 461
- sailing 705
- sense 498
- speaking 525,
  703
- terms
  intelligible 518
  interpreted 522
  language 576
- truth 494
- words 703
plainness 576
plainsong 990
plain-spoken 525,
  703
plaint 411, 839
plaintiff 938
plaintive 839
plaisance
  [*see* pleasance]
plaisanterie 842
plaister 223
plait 219, 258
plan *itinerary* 266
  information 527
  representation
  554
  scheme 626
  according to – 82
planchette 992
plane *horizontal* 213
  flat 251
  smooth 255
  fly 267
  aeroplane 273
  soar 305
  inclined – 633
planet *world* 318
  luminary 423
  fate 601
planet-struck
  adversity 735
  wonder 870
planimeter 466
planish 255
plank *board* 204
  program 626
  path 627
  safety 666
plant *place* 184
  insert 300
  vegetable 367
  agriculture 371
  trick 545
  tools 633
  property 780
- a battery 716
- a dagger in the
  breast 830
- oneself 184
- a thorn in the
  side 830
plantation
  location 184
  agriculture 371

estate 780
planter 188
planter ses choux,
  aller – 893
plaque 204
plash *lake* 343
  stream 348
  sound 405, 408
plashy 345
plasm 22
plasma 847
plasmic 240
plaster *cement* 45
  covering 223
  remedy 662
- up repair 660
plastered 959
plastic *alterable* 149
  form 240
  soft 324
- arts 557
plastron 717
plat *weave* 219
  ground 344
plate *dish* 191
  layer 204
  covering 223
  flat 251
  food 298
  engraving 558
- layer 690
- printing 558,
  591
plateau 213, 344
plated 545
platform
  horizontal 213
  support 215
  stage 542
  scheme 626
  arena 728
- orator 582
platinum-blond 430
platitude 517, 843
Platonic
  contemplative 451
  inexcitable 826
  chaste 960
- bodies 244
Platonism 451
platoon 726
- fire 716
platter 191
  layer 204
  flat 251
  clean the outside
  of the – 544
plaudit 931
plausible
  probable 472
  sophistical 477
  false 544
  approbation 931
  flattery 933
  vindication 937
play *operation* 170
  influence 175
  scope 180
  oscillation 314
  music 416
  drama 599
  use 677
  action 680
  freedom 748
  amusement 840
  at – 840
  bring into – 677

full – 175
full of – 836
in – 842
– along with 709
– one's best card
  686, 698
– of colors 440
– at cross pur-
  poses 59, 523
– a deep game 702
– the deuce 825
– the devil 907
– one false
  disappoint 509
  falsehood 544
  deception 545
– fast and loose
  falsehood 544
  irresolute 605
  tergiversation 607
  caprice 608
– on the feelings
  824
– first fiddle 642,
  873
– the fool
  folly 499
  clumsy 699
  amusement 840
  ridiculous 853
  ridicule 856
– for *chance* 621
– a game.
  pursue 622
  conduct 692
  pastime 840
– the game 939
– into the hands
  of 709
– havoc 659
– hide and seek
  528, 623
– a joke 853
give – to the im-
  agination 515
– of light 420
– the monkey 499
– off 545
– a part
  false 544
  drama 599
  action 680
– one's part 625,
  692
– second fiddle
  34, 749
– one a trick 509,
  545
– tricks with 699,
  702
– truant 623
– upon 545, 856
– with 460
– upon words
  misinterpret 523
  neology 563
  wit 842
play-boy 818
play-day 840
played out
  end 67
  fatigue 688
  completion 729
  failure 732
player
  musician 416
  actor 599

– piano 417
playfellow 890
playful 836
– imagination 515
playground 728,
  840
play-house 599
playmate 890
playsome 836
plaything
  trifle 643
  toy 840
make a – of 749
playwright 599
plea
  defence 462
  argument 476
  excuse 617
  vindication 937
  lawsuit 969
plead *argue* 467
  plea 617
  beg 765
– one's cause 937
– guilty 950
pleader *lawyer* 968
pleading, special –
  477
pleadings 969
pleasance 189, 840
pleasant
  agreeable 829
  amusing 840
  witty 842
make things –
  deceive 545
  induce 615
  please 829
  flatter 933
pleasantry 840, 842
please 829
as you – 743
do what one –s
  748
if you –
  obedience 743
  consent 762
  request 765
– oneself 943
pleasurableness
  829
pleasure
  physical - 377
  will 600
  moral - 827
  dissipation 954
at – 600
at one's – 737
during – 108a
give – 829
man of – 954a
make a toil of –
  682
take one's – 840
will and – 600
with –
  willingly 602
pleasure-giving 829
pleasure-ground
  demesne 189
  amusement 840
pleat 258
plebeian 851, 876
plébiscite 480, 609
plectrum 417
plectuntur Achivi
  739

pledge *affirmation*
  535
  promise 768
  security 771
  borrow 788
  drink to 883, 894
hold in – 771
take the – 771, 958
– oneself 768
– one's word 768
pledget 263, 662
Pleiades 72, 318
plenary 31, 52
plenipotent 157
plenipotentiary
  consignee 758
  deputy 759
plentitude 639
in the – of power
  159
plenty
  multitude 102
  sufficient 639
– to do 682
plenum *substance* 3
  matter 316
pleonasm
  repetition 104
  diffuseness 573
  redundance 641
plerophory 484
plethora 64˙
plexal 219
plexus 219
pliable 324
pliant *soft* 324
  irresolute 605
  facile 705
  servile 886
plicature 258
pliers 301, 781
plight *state* 7
  promise 768
  security 771
evil – 735
– one's faith 902
– one's troth 768,
  902
plighted love 897,
  902
Plimsoll mark 466
plinth 211, 215
plod *journey* 266
  slow 275
  persevere 604a
  work 682
– along 143
plodding 604a, 682
  dull 843
plot - *of ground* 181
  plain 344
  story 594
  plan 626
  realty 780
the – thickens
  assemblage 72
plough *furrow* 259
  agriculture 371
– the ground 673
– in 228
– the waves 267
– one's way 266
ploughboy
  commonalty 876
ploughman 371
ploughshare 253
pluck *cheat* 545

resolution 604
persevere 604a
reject 610
take 789
steal 791
courage 861
– up courage 861
– a crow with 932
– out 301
plug 261, 263
– along 143
plum *number* 98
  sweet 396
  money 800
plumage 256
plumb *vertical* 212
  close 261
  measure 466
plumber 690
plumb-line 212
plum-colored 437
plume *feather* 256
  ornament 847
borrowed –s 788
– oneself 878
plume
coup de – 590
nom de – 565
plumigerous 256
plummet 208, 212
plumose 256
plump
  instantaneous 113
  fat 192
  plunge 310
  unexpected 508
– down 306
– upon 292
plumper
  expansion 194
  vote 609
plunder 791, 793
plunderer 792
plunge
  revolution 146
  insert 300
  dive 306, **310**
  immerse 337
  hurry 684
– into difficulties
  704
– into dissipation
  954
– headlong 684
– into 676
– in medias res
  576, 604
– into sorrow 830
plunged
– in debt 806
– in grief 828
plunger 621
plurality **100**
plus 37
plus fours 225
plush 256
Pluto 979, 982
realms of – 982
Plutocracy 803
plutonic 382
Plutus 803
pluvial 348
ply *layer* 204
  fold 258
  use 677
  exert 686
  request 765

– one's task 680
– one's trade 625
– a trade 794
Plymouth Brother
  984
p.m. 114, 126
pneumatics 334,
  338
pneumatology 450
pneumatoscopic
  317
poach 791, 964
poacher 792
poachy 345
pock 250
pocket *place* 184
  pouch 191
  diminutive 193
  receive 785
  take 789
  money 800
  treasury 802
  brook 826
button up one's –
  808
out of – 776, 806
touch the – 800
– the affront 725,
  918
pocket-book 551
pocket-handker-
  chief 225
pocket-money 800
pocket-pistol
  bottle 191
pococurante 823,
  866
pocula, inter – 959
pod 191, 223
podestà 967
podgy 201
poem 597
book of –s 593
poenitentiae, locus–
  pity 914
  forgive 918
  vindicate 937
  repent 950
poesy 597
poet 597
poetaster 597, 855
poetic *style* 574
poetic frenzy 515
poetry **597**
poignancy
  physical energy
  171
  pain 378
  pungency 392
  feeling 821
pogrom 361
point *condition* 8
  degree 26
  small 32
  end 67
  term 71
  poignancy 171
  no magnitude
  180a
  place 182
  speck 193
  sharp 253
  topic 454
  mark 550
  vigor 574
  intention 620
  wit 842

vegetation 367
praise *thanks* 916
  commendation
  931
  worship 990
praiseworthy 931,
  944
prame 273
prance 266, 315
prandial 298
prank *caprice* 608
  amusement 840
  adorn 847
prate 584
prattle 582, 584
pravity 945
praxis
  grammar 567
  action 680
Praxiteles 559
pray 765, 990
prayer 765, 990
  house of – 1000
prayer-book 998
preach *teach* 537
  speak 582
  predication 998
  – to the winds 645
  – to the wise 538
preacher
  teacher 540
  priest 996
preachment 998
preadamite 124,
  130
preamble 64
preapprehension
  481
prebend 995
prebendary 996
precarious
  transient 111
  uncertain 475
  dangerous 665
precatory 765
precaution
  care 459
  expedient 626
  safety 664
  preparation 673
precede
  superior 33
  – *in order* 62
  – *in time* 116
  – *in motion* 280
precedence 873
precedent
  [see precede]
  prototype 22
  precursor 64
  habit 613
  legal decision 969
  follow –s 82
precentor 694, 996
precept *adage* 496
  maxim 697
  order 641
  permit 760
preceptor 540
precession 62, 280
précieuse ridicule
  855
precinct *region* 181
  place 182
  environs 227
  boundary 233
precious *great* 31

excellent 648
  valuable 814
  beloved 897
  – *metals* 800
  – *stone* 648, 847
precipice
  vertical 212
  slope 217
  dangerous 667
  on the verge of
  a – 665
precipitancy 684,
  863
precipitate
  early 132
  sink 308
  consolidate 321
  refuse 653
  haste 684
  rash 863
  – oneself 306
precipitous 217
précis 596
precise *exact* 494
preciosity 578
precisely
  literally 19
  assent 488
precisianism
  affectation 855
  heterodoxy 984
  over-religious 988
preclude 55, 706
precocious
  early 132
  immature 674
  pert 885
  rude 895
precognition
  forethought 490
  knowledge 510
preconceived idea
  481
preconception 481
preconcert 611, 626
preconcertation 673
precursor
  – *in order* 62, **64**
  – *in time* 116
  predict 511
predatory 789, 791
predecessor 64
predeliberation
  510, 611
predella 215
predesigned 611
predestination
  fate 152
  necessity 601
  predetermination
  611
  Deity 976
predetermination
  611
predial
  land 342
  agriculture 371
  manorial 780
predicament 8, 75
predicate
  affirm 535
  preach 998
prediction **511**
predilection
  bias 481
  affection 820
  desire 865

predispose 615, 673
predisposed
  willing 602
predisposition 176,
  820
predominant 175,
  737
predominate 33
pre-eminent 33, 873
pre-emption 795
preen 847
pre-engage 132
pre-engagement
  768
pre-establish 626
pre-examine 461
pre-exist 1, 116
preface 62, 64
prefect 745, 759
prefecture 737
prefer *choose* 609
  – a claim 969
  – a petition 765
preference 62
preferment
  improvement 658
  ecclesiastical –
  995
prefigure 511
prefix 62, 64
  letter 561
pre-glacial 124
pregnable 158
pregnant
  producing 161
  productive 168
  predicting 511
  – *style* 572
  important 642
  – with meaning
  516
prehensile 789
prehension 789
pre-historic 124
pre-instruct 537
prejudge 481
prejudicate 481
prejudice
  misjudge 481
  evil 619
  detriment 659
prejudicial 481, 649
prelacy 995
prelate 996
prelation 609
prelection 537, 582
prelector 540
preliminaries:
  settle – 673
  – of peace 723
preliminary 62, 64
prelude 62, 64
  beginning 66
  music 415
premature 132, 674
premeditate 611,
  620
prémices 154
premier 694, 759
  – pas 66
premiership 693
premise *prefix* 62
  precede 116
  announce 511
premises
  precursor 64
  prior 116

ground 182
  evidence 467
  logic 476
premium
  debt 805
  receipt 810
  reward 783
  at a – 814
premonish 668
premonitory 511,
  668
Premonstratensian
  996
premonstration
  appearance 448
  prediction 511
  manifestation 525
premunire 742, 974
prendre la balle au
  bond 134
prenotion
  misjudgment 481
  foresight 510
prensation 789
prentice 541
prenticeship 539
preoccupancy
  possession 777
preoccupation
  inattention 458
preoption 609
preordain 152, 601
preparation **673**
  music 413
  instruction 537
  in – 730
  in course of – 626
preparatory
  preceding 62
prepare the way
  facilitate 705
prepared *expectant*
  507
  ready 698
preparing
  destined 152
prepense
  spontaneous 600
  predetermined
  611
  intended 620
  malice – 907
prepollence 157
preponderance
  superiority 33
  influence 175
  dominance 737
prepossessed
  obstinate 606
prepossessing 829
prepossession
  prejudice 481
  possession 777
preposterous
  great 31
  absurd 497
  exaggerated 549
  ridiculous 853
  undue 925
prepotency 157
pre-Raphaelite 122,
  124, 556
pre-require 630
pre-resolve 611
prerogative 737,924

presage 511, 512
presbyopia 443
presbyter 996
Presbyterian 984
presbytery 995,
  996, 1000
prescience 510
prescious 511
prescribe *direct* 693
  advice 695
  order 741
  entitle 924
  enjoin 926
prescript 697, 741
prescription
  remedy 662
prescriptive *old* 124
  unchanged 141
  habitual 613
  due 924
presence
  in space **186**
  appearance 448
  breeding 894
  in the – of
  near 197
  real – 998
  saving one's – 928
  – of God 981
  – of mind 826,
  864
presence-chamber
  191
present
  – *in time* 118
  – *in space* 186
  offer 763
  give 784
  church prefer-
  ment 995
  at – 118
  these –s 590, 592
  – arms 894, 928
  – a bold front 861
  – a front 719
  – itself *event* 151
  visible 446
  thought 451
  – oneself
  presence 186
  offer 763 •
  courtesy 894
  – to the mind
  457, 505
  – *time* **118**
  instant 113
  – to the view 448
presentable 852
presentation 883,
  894
presentiment
  instinct 477
  prejudgment 481
  foresight 510
presently 132
presentment
  information 527
  law proceeding
  969
preservation
  continuance 141
  conservation **670**
  Divine attributes
  976
preserve *sweets* 396
preserver 664
preshow 511

– against
strong 159
resolute 604
safe 664
defence 717
resistance 719
insensible 823
prop 215, 707
propaedeutics 537
propagable 168
propaganda 537, 542
propagandism 537
propagandist 540, 996
propagate
produce 161
be productive 168
publish 531
propel 284
propellant 727
propeller 267, 312
propend 602
propendency
predetermination 611
inclination 820
propense 602
propension 820
propensity 176, 820
proper special 79
expedient 646
handsome 845
due 924
– name 564
in its – place 58
show a – spirit 939
the – thing 926
– time 134
properties
theatrical – 225, 599
property power 157
possessions 780
wealth 803
property-man 599
prophecy 511
prophet 513, 996
false –s 986
in the name of the – figs! 497
prophetic 511, 985
Prophets, the – 985
prophylactic
healthful 656
remedy 662
preservative 670
hindrance 706
prophylaxis 670
propinquity 197
propitiate
pacify 723, 724
calm 826
content 831
love 897
pity 914
forgive 918
atone 952
worship 990
propitious
timely 134
beneficial 648
helping 707
prosperous 734
auspicious 858
proplasm 22

proportion
relation 9
degree 26
mathematical 84
symmetry 242
style 578
allotment 786
proportionate
agreeing 23
proportions 180, 192
proposal plan 626
propose
suggest 514
broach 535
intend 620
offer 763
offer marriage 912
– a question 461
proposition
supposition 454
reasoning 476
project 626
suggestion 514
offer 763
propound 514, 535
– a question 461
propriâ personâ
in – speciality 79
presence 186
proprietary 779
proprietor 779
proprietorship 780
propriety
agreement 23
elegance 578
expedience 646
fashion 852
right 922
duty 926
proprio motu 600
props 599
propter hoc 155
propugn
resist 717
vindicate 937
propulsion 284
propylon 66
prore 234
prorogue 133
proruption 295
prosaic usual 82
– style 575, 576
dull 843
prosaism prose 598
proscenium
front 234
theatre 599
proscribe
interdict 761
banish 893
curse 908
condemn 971
prose
diffuse style 573
prate 584
not verse 598
– run mad 517, 597
– writer 598
prosecute
pursue 622
act 680
accuse 938
arraign 969
– an inquiry 461
prosecutor 938

proselyte
convert 144, 607
learner 541
proselytism 537
proser 841
prosody 597
prosopopoeia 521
prospect
futurity 121
view 448
probability 472
expectation 507
landscape paint-
ing 556
good – 858
in – intended 620
prospective 121
prospector 463
prospectus list 86
foresight 510
compendium 596
scheme 626
prosper 618
prosperity 734
prospicience 510
prosternation
dejection 837
servility 886
prostitute
corrupt 659
misuse 679
impure 961
courtesan 962
prostrate
powerless 158
destroyed 162
low 207
horizontal 213
depress 308
laid up 655
exhausted 688
dejected 837
servile 886
fall.– 306
– oneself
servile 886
obeisance 928
worship 990, 991
prostration
[see prostrate]
submission 725
pain 828
prosy 841, 843
prosyllogism 476
protagonist
actor 599
proficient 700
protasis
precursor 64
beginning 66
maxim 496
protean 149
protect safe 664
protective 717
protection
influence 175
defence 717
restrain 751
protected cruiser
726
protector 664, 717
master 745
keeper 753
protectorate 737, 780
protégé servant 746
friend 890

proteiform 149
protein 298
semiliquid 352
organic 357
protervity 901
protest dissent 489
assert 535
deny 536
refuse 764
deprecate 766
not observe 773
not pay 808
counter – 468
enter a – 766
under – 603, 744
– against 708, 932
protestant 489, 764
Protestant 984
protested bills 808
Proteus 149
prothesis 1000
prothonotary 553
protocol scheme 626
compact 769
protogram 572
protoplasm
prototype 22
material 316
organization 357
protoplast 22
prototype 22
prediction 511
prototypal 20
protozoon 366
protract time 110
late 133
lengthen 200
diffuse style 573
protreptical 615
protrude 250
protuberance 250
protypify 511
proud 873, 878
– flesh 250
prove
arithmetic 85
turn out 151
try 463
demonstrate 478
affect 821
– one's case
vindication 937
– true 494
provender 298, 637
proverb 496
proverbe acting 599
proverbial 490
provide
furnish 637
– against
prepare 673
– against a rainy
day 817
provided
conditionally 8
qualification 469
supposition 514
well – 639
– for 803
providence
foresight 510
preparation 673
divine govern-
ment 976
Providence 976
special – 711
waiter on – 683,

831
provident
careful 459
wise 498
prepared 673
providential
opportune 134
fortunate 734
province
department 75
region 181
abode 189
office 625
provincial
[see province]
prejudiced 481
vulgar 851
provincialism
neology 563
provision food 298
supply 637
preparation 673
wealth 803
– merchant 637
provisional
uncertain 475
circumstances 8
temporary 111
preparing 673
provisions
conditions 770
proviso 469, 770
provisory 111
provoke cause 153
incite 615
excite 824
vex 830
anger 900
– desire 865
– hatred 898
provoquant 824
provost master 745
deputy 759
prow 234
prowess 861
prowl walk 266
lurk 528
– after 622
proximate
next 63
near 197
– cause 153
proximity near 197
adjacent 199
proximo 121
proximus ardet
danger 665, 667
proxy 634, 759
prude affected 855
chaste 960
prudent
careful 459
wise 498
economical 817
cautious 864
prudery 855, 868
prudish 739
prune
take away 38
lop 201, 371
repair 658
prunes and prisms
855
prunello, leather
or – 643
prurience 865, 961
Prussian blue 438

radically 31
radication 613
radio 532
radio-active 171
    316
radio-activity 420
radio-graph 421,
    554
radiogram
    wireless 532
    X-ray 554
radiometer 420, 445
radiomicrometer
    389
radiophone 418
radio star 899
radiotelegraph 534
radiotelephone 534
radium 423
radius 200, 202
radix 153
radoter 499
radoteur 501
raff 653, 876
raffle 156
Raffles
    thief 792
raft 273
rafter 215
rag 32
    lease 830, 856,
    929
ragamuffin 876
rage violence 173
    influence 175
    excitement 824,
    825
    fashion 852
    desire 865
    wrath 900
    the battle –s 722
ragged 226
ragoût 41, 298
rag-picker 876
rags clothes 225
    useless 645
    do to – 384
    tear to – 162
    worn to – 659
ragtime 415, 473
raid 716, 791
rail inclosure 232
    prison 752
    – at 932
    – in
    circumscribe 229
    restrain 751
railing 232
raillerie, ne pas en-
    tendre – 900
raillery 856
railway 627
    – speed 274
    – station 292
raiment 225
rain stream 348
    sufficient 639
    – or shine 474,
    604
rainbow 440
raincoat 225
rainless 340
rains but it pours,
    never – 641
rainy day 735
    provide against
    a – 673, 817

rainy season 348
raise increase 35
    produce 161
    erect 212
    elevate 307
    excite 824
    – alarm 860
    – anger 900
    – one's banner
    722
    – a cry 531
    – a dust 682
    – expectations 858
    – the finger 550
    – funds 775
    – one's head
    improve 658
    refresh 689
    prosperity 734
    repute 873
    – ghosts 992
    – hope 511
    – a hue and cry
    against 932
    – a laugh 840
    – the mask 529
    – money 788
    – a question 461,
    485
    – a report 531
    – a siege 723
    – the spirits 836
    – spirits from the
    dead 992
    – a storm 173
    – troops 722
    – up 212, 824
    – the voice 441
    – one's voice 535,
    932
    – the wind 775,
    778
raised convex 250
raison:
    – d'être 620
    – de plus 467
raj 737
rajah 745
rajpoot 726
rake drag 285
    gardening 371
    clean 652
    profligate 949
    intemperance 954
    libertine 962
    – out 301
    – up collect 72
    extract 301
    recall 505
    excite 824
    – up evidence 467
rake-hell 949, 962
raking-fire 716
rakish
    intemperate 954
    licentious 961
rallentando 415
rally arrange 60
    improve 658
    restore 660
    ridicule 856
    encourage 861
    – round order 58
    co-operate 709
rallying: – cry 550,
    861
    – point 74

ram impulse 276
    sheep 366
    male 373
    man-of-war 726
    milk the – 645
    – down 261, 321
    – in 300
Ramadan 956, 993
ramage 367
ramble stroll 266
    wander 279
    folly 499
    delirium 503
    digress 573
rambler 269
rambling 139
ramification part 51
    bisection 91
    posterity 167
    filament 205
    symmetry 242
    divergence 291
rammer 263, 276
ramose 242
ramp slope 217
    climb 305
    leap 309
rampage 173
rampant
    violent 173
    prevalent 175
    vertical 212
    raised 307
    free 748
    vehement 825
    licentious 961
rampart 717
ramrod 263
ramshackle 665
ranch 780
rancid 401, 653
rancor 907, 919
randan 273
random casual 156
    carriage 272
    uncertain 475
    aimless 621
    talk at –
    sophistry 477
    exaggerate 549
    loquacity 584
    - experiment 463
    chance 621
range extent 26
    collocate 60
    series 69
    term 71
    class 75
    space 180
    distance 196
    roam 266
    direction 278
    stove 386
    freedom 748
    out– 196
    long – 196
    within – 197
    –finder 200
    – itself 58
    – under, – with 76
ranger
    director 694
    keeper 753
    thief 792
rank have place 1
    degree 26
    thorough 31

    collocate 60
    row 69
    term 71
    vegetation 365
    fetid 401
    estimate 480
    bad 649
    soldiers 726
    glory 873
    nobility 875
    man of – 875
    – and file
    continuity 69
    soldiers 726
    commonalty 876
    – marks 745
rankle unclean 653
    corrupt 659
    painful 830
    animosity 900
    malevolence 907
    revenge 919
ranks
    fill up the – 660
    risen from the –
    876
ransack seek 461
    deliver 672
    plunder 791
    price 812
    atonement 952
    – one's brains
    451, 515
ransom 672
rant
    unmeaning 517
    exaggeration 549
    diffuse style 573
    turgescence 577
    speech 582
    acting 599
    excitement 825
    boasting 884
ranter talker 584
    false piety 988
rantipole 458
rap blow 276
    sound 406
    trifle 643
    money 800
    not worth a – 804
    – on the knuckles
    angry 900
    censure 932
    punish 972
    – out affirm 535
    voice 580
    speak 582
    – out oaths 885,
    908
rapacity
    taking 789
    stealing 791
    avarice 819
    greed 865
rape 791, 961
    – oil 356
rapid 274
    – slope 217
    – strides
    progress 282
    velocity 274
    – succession 136
rapids 348
rapier 727
rapine 791
rapparee 792

rappel 722
rapping, spirit –
    992
rapport 9
rapports, sous tous
    les – 494
rapprochement
    714, 888
rapscallion 949
rapt attention 457
    inattention 458
    emotion 821
    – in thought 451
raptorial 789, 791
rapture 827, 897
rapturous 827
rara avis
    exceptional 83
    good 648
    famous 873
rare exceptional 83
    few 103
    infrequent 137
    light 322
    excellent 648
raree show 448, 840
rarefaction 194, 322
rari nantes 103
rarity 322
rasa, tabula – 552
rascal 941, 949
rascality 940
rase obliterate 552
rash
    skin disease 655
    reckless 863
rasher 204
rashness 863
rasp 330, 331
rasper difficult 704
rasure 552
rat recant 607
    smell a –
    discover 480a
    doubt 485
rataplan 407
rat-a-tat 407
ratchet 253
rate degree 26
    motion 264
    measure 466
    estimation 480
    price, tax 812
    abuse 932
    at a great – 274
rath early 132
    fort 717
rather 32, 643
    have – 609
    – good 651
    have – not 867
ratification
    confirm 467
    affirm 488
    consent 762
    compact 769
ratio relation 9
    degree 26
    proportion 84
    apportionment
    786
ratiocination 476
ration quantity 25
    food 298
    provisions 637
    allotment 786
    short –s 956

remainder 40
corpse 362
vestige 551
organic – 357
remand *defer* 133
order 741
remanet 40
remark *observe* 457
affirmation 535
worthy of – 642
remarkable
great 31
exceptional 83
important 642
remarry 903
Rembrandtesque
160
remediable, remedial 660, 662
remediless 859
remedy 660, **662**
remembrance 505
remembrances 894
remembrances 894
rememoration 505
remigration
regression 283
arrival 292
egress 295
remind 505
that –s me 134
reminiscence 505
remise 927*a*
remiss
neglectful 460
reluctant 603
idle 683
lax 738
remission
cessation 142
moderation 174
laxity 738
forgiveness 918
exemption 927*a*
remit
[*see* remission]
– one's efforts 681
remittance 807
remittent
periodic 138
remitter 790
remnant 40
remodel
convert 144
revolutionize 146
improve 658
remonstrance 615,
766, 932
remora *cohere* 46
hindrance 706
remorse 950
remorseless 919
remote 10, 196
– age 122
– cause 153
– future 121
remotest idea, not
have – 491
remotion 270
remount 147
remove *subduct* 38
term 71
displace 185
transfer 270
recede 287
depart 293
dinner 298
extract 301

school 541
– the mask 529
removedness
distance 196
remugient 412
remunerate 973
remunerative 644,
775
renaissance 660
renascence 660
renascent 163
rencounter
contact 199
meeting 292
fight 720
rend 44
– the air 404, 411,
839
– the heart-strings
830
render *convert* 144
interpret 522
give 784
restore 790
– an account
inform 527
describe 594
– *hors de combat* 645
– a service 644
rendering
covering 223
rendezvous 72, 74
rendition
interpretation 522
restore 790
renegade
convert 144
turncoat 607
fugitive 623
apostate 941
renew *twice* 90
repeat 104
reproduce 163
recollect 505
improve 658
restore 660
– one's strength
689
reniform 245
renitence
counteraction 179
hardness 323
elasticity 325
unwillingness 603
resistance 719
renitency
light 420
renounce
recant 607
relinquish 624
resign 757
abnegate 764
– *property* 782
repudiate 927
renovare dolorem,
infandum – 833
renovate 160, 660
renovated *new* 123
renown 873
renownless 874
rent *tear* 44
fissure 198
hire 788
purchase 795
rental 810
renter 188, 779
rent-free 815

rent-roll 780, 810
rents *houses* 189
renunciation
[*see* renounce]
exemption 927*a*
reorganize
order 60
convert 144
improve 658
restore 660
repair
mend 658
make good 660
refresh 689
out of – 659
– to 266
reparation
[*see* repair]
compensation 30
restitution 790
atonement 952
reward 973
repartee 462, 842
reparteeist 844
repartition 786
repass, pass and –
314
repast 298
repatriation 790
repay 790, 807, 973
repeal 756
repeat *imitate* 19
duplication 90
iterate 104
reproduce 163
affirm 535
– by rote 505
repeated 104, 136
repeater
watch 114
fire-arm 727
repel *repulse* 289
deter 616
defend 717
resist 719
refuse 764
give pain 830
disincline 867
banish 893
excite hate 898
repent 950
repercussion 277
répertoire 399
repertory 636
repetend
arithmetical 84
iteration 104
repetition 19, **104**
repine
pain 828
discontent 832
regret 833
– *sad* 837
replace
substitute 147
locate 184
restore 660
replenish 52, 637
repletion
filling 639
redundance 641
satiety 869
replevin
recovery 775
borrow 788
restore 790
replica 21

replication
answer 462
law pleadings 969
reply 462, 937
répondre en
Normand 544
report *noise* 406
judgment 480
inform 527
publish 531
news 532
rumor 532
record 551
statement 594
good – 873
through evil re-
port and good –
604*a*
– *progress* 527
reporter
informant 527
messenger 534
recorder 553
journalist 593,
758
reports *law* 969
repose
quiescence 265
leisure 685
rest **687**
– confidence in
484
– on *support* 215
evidence 467
– on one's laurels
142
reposit 184
repository 636
repostum, manet
alta mente –
919
repoussé 250
reprehend 932
reprehensible 945,
947
represent *similar* 17
imitate 19
exhibit 525
intimate 527
declare 535
denote 550
delineate 554
commission 755
deputy 759
– to oneself 515
representation
[*see* represent]
copy 21
portrait **554**
drama 599
representative
typical 79
commissioner 758
deputy 759
– government 737
– of the people 696
– of the press
messenger 534
writer 593
repress 751
– one's feelings
826
– a smile 837
reprieve
respite 133, 970
deliverance 672
release 750
pardon 918

reprimand 932
reprint
copy 21
repetition 104
reproduce 183
reprisal
retaliation 718
resumption 789
reprise 40*a*
reproach
disgrace 874
blame 932
accusation 938
reprobate
disapproved 932
vicious 945
bad man 949
sinner 988
reprobation 932,
988
reproduce
imitate 19
repeat 104
renovate 163
reproduction [*see*
reproduce] 21,
163
reproductive 163
reproof 932
reprover 936
reptile
animal 366
servile 886
knave 941
miscreant 949
republic
country 181
people 372
government 737
– of letters 560
republican
party 712
government 737
commonalty 876
republicanism 737
repudiate
exclude 55
deny 489
reject 610
abrogate 756
violate 773
not pay 808
evade 927
repugn 719
repugnance
incongruity 24
resistance 719
dislike 867
hate 898
repulse *recoil* 277
repel 289
resist 719
failure 732
refusal 764
repulsion 157, **289**
repulsive
[*see* repulse]
unsavory 395
painful 830
ugly 846
disliked 867
discourteous 895
hateful 898
repurchase 795
reputable 873, 939
reputation 873
repute **873**

request **765**
in – 630
– permission 760
requiem 839
requies, nec mora
nec – 682
requiescat in pace
363, 723
require
need 630
insufficient 640
exact 741
compel 744
price 812
due 924
duty 926
– explanation 519
requirement **630**
requisite 630
requisition 741, 765
put in – use 677
order 741
requital
retaliation 918
gratitude 916
punishment 972
reward 973
reredos 1000
res ipsa loquitur
525
rescind cut off 44
abrogate 756
refuse 746
rescission 44, 756
rescript answer 462
transcript 590
letter 592
order 741, 963
rescriptive 761
rescue preserve 670
deliver 672
aid 707
research 461
– student 541
reseat 660
resection 44
reseda 435
resemblance 17, 21
resent 900
resentful 901
resentment **900**
reservation
location 184
concealment 528
mental – 477, 528
equivocation 520
untruth 546
with a – 38, 770
reservatory 191,
636
reserve
concealment 528
silence 585
choose 609
store 636
disuse 678
retain 781
shyness 881
in – destined 152
prepared 673
– forces 726
– oneself 881
reservoir 636
re-shape 140
resiance 189
resiant 186
reside 1, 186

residence 189
resident
consignee 758
present 186
inhabitant 188
residentiary 186,
188
clergy 996
residue 40
residuum
remainder 40
dregs 653
commonalty 876
resign 757, 782
– one's being 364
– one's breath 360
– oneself 725, 826
resignation [see
resign]
submission 725
obedience 743
abdication **757**
renunciation 782
endurance 826
humility 879
resile 277
resilience
regression 283
elasticity 325
resin **356a**
resipiscence 950
resist oppose 179
withstand 719
disobey 742
refuse 764
resistance 719
résistance, pièce de
– 298
resister
passive – 710
resisting
tenacious 327
resistless 159, 601
resolute 604, 861
resolution
decomposition 49
conversion 144
music 413
topic 454
investigation 461
mental energy **604**
intention 620
scheme 626
courage 861
resolvable into 27,
144
resolve change 140
liquefy 335
investigate 461
discover 480a
interpret 522
determine 604
predetermine 611
intend 620
– into elements 49
– into convert 144
resonance 402, **408**
resorb 296
resort assemble 72
focus 74
dwelling 189
converge 290
last – 601
– to be present 186
travel 266
employ 677
resound loud 404

ring 408
– praises 931
resourceful 698
resources
means 632
property 780
wealth 803
respect relation 9
observe 772
fame 873
salutation 894
deference **928**
have – to 9
in no – 536
with – to 9
respectability
mediocrity 736
repute 873
probity 939
respectable
unimportant 643
respectful 928
– distance 623,
864
respective 79, 786
respectless 458
respects 894, 928
resperse 73
respicere finem 510
respire breathe 349
live 359
refresh 689
respite
intermission 106
defer 133
pause 142
deliver 672
repose 687
resplendent
luminous 420
splendid 845
respond accord 23
answer 462
feel 821
respondent 462
accused 938
response
answer 462, **587**
concord 714
feeling 821
friendship 888
worship 990
responsible 177,
926
responsibility
upon one's own –
600
responsive 375
rest remainder 40
pause 141
cessation 142
support 215
quiescence 265
death 360
silence 403
inaction 681
repose 687
at – repose 687
content 831
home of – 189
set at –
answer 462
ascertain 474
complete 729
compact 769

set one's mind at –
calm 826
set the question
at – 478, 480
– assured 484, 858
– on support 215
– on one's oars
142, 687
– satisfied 831
– and be thankful
681, 687
– upon
evidence 467
confide 484
– with duty 926
restaurant 189
– car 272
restaurateur 637
restful 265
resting place
support 215
quiet 265
arrival 292
restitution **790**, 660
restive averse 603
obstinate 606
disobedient 742
refusal 764
perverse 901a
restless
changeable 149
moving 264
agitated 315
active 682
excited 825
fearful 860
restoration **660**
restorative
salubrious 656
remedial 662
relieving 834
restore reinstate
660
refresh 689
return 790
– equilibrium 27
– harmony 723
– to health 654
restrain 616, 706,
751
restrainable 743
restrained 751
restraint 578, **751**
self – 826, 953
restrict hinder 706
restrain 751
prohibit 761
restringency 751
result remainder 40
follow 117
effect 154
conclusion 480
completion 729
resultant 48, 154
resume begin 66
repeat 104
change 140
restore 660
take 789
résumé 596
resupination 213
resurgence 163, 660
resurrection
reproduction 163
restoration 660
heaven 981

resuscitate
reproduce 163
reinstate 660
retable 215
retail distribute 73
inform 527
barter 794
sell 796
retailer 797
retain stand 150
keep 781
– the memory of
505
– one's reason 502
retainer 746
retake 789
retaliation **718**, 919
retard later 133
slower 275
hinder 706
retch 297
retection 529
retention **781**
retentive 781
– memory 505
reticence 528
reticle 219
reticulation 219,
248
reticule 191
retiform 219
retina 441
retinue followers 65
series 69
servants 746
retire move back 283
recede 287
resign 757
modest 881
seclusion 893
– into the shade
inferior 34
decrease 36
– from sight
disappear 449
hide 528
retiring
concave 252
- color 438
retold 104
retort
receptacle 191
vaporizer 336
boiler 386
answer 462
confutation 479
retaliation 718
wit 842
retouch restore 660
retoucher 559
retrace 575
– one's steps 607
retract
recant 607
annul 756
abjure 757
violate 773
retreat
resort 74
withdraw 187
abode 189
regression 283
recede 287
ambush 530
refuge 666
escape 671
give way 725

beat a – 623
retreating
  concave 252
retrench *subduct* 38
  shorten 201
  lose 789
  economize 817
retribution
  retaliation 718
  payment 807
  punishment 972
  reward 973
retrieve *restore* 660
  acquire 775
retriever *dog* 366
retroaction
  counteraction 179
  recoil 277
  regression 283
retroactive
  past 122
retrocession
  regression 283
  recession 287
retrograde
  moving back 283
  deteriorated 659
  relapsing 661
retrogression
  regression 283
  deterioration 659
  relapse 661
retrospection
  past 122
  thought 451
  memory 505
retroussé 245
retroversion 218
retrude 289
return *list* 86
  repeat 104
  periodic 138
  reverse 145
  recoil 277
  regression 283
  arrival 292
  answer 462
  report 551
  relapse 661
  appoint 755
  profit 775
  restore 790
  proceeds 810
  reward 973
  in –
  compensation 30
  – the compliment
  interchange 148
  retaliate 718
  – to the original
  state 660
  –ed prodigal 950
  – thanks 916, 990
return game 104
return match 104
reunion *junction* 43
réunion
  assemblage 72
  concord 714
  lieu de – 74
  point de – 74
  social – 892
revamp 140
revanche, en – 718
reveal 529
  – itself **446**
reveille 550

**réveiller le chat qui
  dort, ne pas** –
  668, 864
revel 840, 954
  – in *enjoy* 377
revelation
  disclosure 480a,
  529
  theological 985
Revelations 985
reveller 840
  drunkard 959
revelling 59, 838
revendicate
  claim 741
  acquisition 775
  due 924
revenge 919
  breathe – 900
**revenons à nos
  moutons** 283,
  660
revenue 632, 810
reverberate 277,
  408
reverberatory 386
revere *love* 897
  respect 928
  piety 987
reverence *title* 877
  respect 928
  piety 987
  clergy 996
reverenced 500
reverend 877, 996
reverent 987, 990
reverential 928
reverie
  train of thought
  451
  inattention 458
  imagination 515
reversal 218, 607
reverse *contrary* 14
  inversion 218
  – of a medal 235
  anteposition 237
  adversity 735
  abrogate 756
  cards 840
  – of the shield 468
reverseless 150
reversible 605
reversion
  [see *reverse*]
  posterity 117
  return **145**
  possession 777
  property 780
  succession 783
  remitter 790
reversioner 779
revert *repeat* 104
  return 145
  turn back 283
revest 790
  – to 457
revest 790
revet 223
reviction 660
review *consider* 457
  inquiry 461
  judge 480
  recall 505
  periodical 531
  dissertation 595
  compendium 596

entertainment 599
revise 658
  parade 882
reviewer 480, 595
revile 932, 988
reviler 936
revise *copy* 21
  consider 457
  printing 591
  plan 626
  improve 658
revising barrister
  967
revision, under –
  673
revisit 186
revival
  reproduction 163
  restoration 660
  worship 990
revivalist 996
revive
  reproduce 163
  improve 658
  resuscitate 660
  excite 824
revivify
  reproduce 163
  life 359
  improve 658
  resuscitate 660
revocable 605
revoir, au – 293
revoke 607, 756
revolt *resist* 719
  disobey 742
  shock 830
  disapproval 932
  – against *hate* 898
  – at the idea
  dissent 489
revolting
  painful 830
revolution
  periodicity 138
  change **146**
  rotation 312
  disobedience 742
revolutionize 140,
  146
revolve
  [see *revolution*]
  – in the mind 451
revolver 727
revue 599
  intimate – 599
revulsion
  reversion 145
  revolution 146
  inversion 218
  recoil 277
reward 973
reword 104
Reynard
  animal 366
  cunning 702
rez-de-chaussée
  191, 207
rhabdology 85
rhabdomancy 511
Rhadamanthus
  967, 982
rhapsodical
  irregular 139
  imaginary 515
rhapsodist
  fanatic 504

rhapsody
  discontinuity 70
  music 415
  nonsense 497
  fancy 515
  poetry 597
rhetoric *speech* 582
  flowers of – 577
rheum
  excretion 299
  fluidity 333
  water 337
rhino 800
rhinoceros hide
  376, 823
rhomb 244
rhumb 278
rhyme
  similarity **17**
  verse 597
  without – or
  reason
  absurd 497
  caprice 608
  motiveless 615a
rhymeless 598
rhymester 597
rhythm
  periodicity 138
  melody 413
  elegance 578
  verse 597
rhythmical
  – *style* 578
rialto 799
rib *support* 215
  ridge 250
  wife 903
ribald *vulgar* 851
  disreputable 874
  impure 961
riband
  [see *ribbon*]
ribbed 259
ribbon *tie* 45
  filament 205
  record 550
  decoration 877
  –s *reins* 152
  handle the – 693
ribroast 972
rich *savory* 394
  color 428
  language 577
  abundant 639
  wealthy 803
  beautiful 845
  ornament 847
  – *man* 803
riches 803
**richesses, embarras
  de** – 641, 803
richly *much* 31
  – *deserve* 924
rick 72, 846
rickety *weak* 160
  ugly 846
  imperfect 651
rickshaw 272
ricochet 277
ricordo, non mi –
  506
rid *deliver* 672
  get – of *eject* 297
  liberation 750
  loose 776
  relinquish 782

riddance 672, 776,
  782
  good – 776
riddle *arrange* 60
  sieve 260
  secret 533
  clean 652
ride *get above* 206
  move 266
  break in 370
  – at anchor 265
  – full tilt at 622,
  716
  – hard 274
  – one's hobby 622
  – rough shod
  violence 173
  severity 739
  insolence 885
  illegality 964
  – out the storm
  664
  – and tie
  periodicity 138
  journey 266
  – the whirlwind
  604, 737
rideau, lever de –
  599
**ridentem dicere
  verum** 836, 842
rider *appendix* 39
  equestrian 268
rideret Heraclitus
  853
ridge *narrow* 203
  height 206
  prominence 250
ridicule 856, 929
ridiculous
  absurd 497
  foolish 499
  trifling 643
  grotesque 853
ridiculousness 853
riding *district* 181
  journey 266
ridotto 840, 892
rifacimento 104,
  660
rife *existence* 1
  general 78
  influence 175
riff-raff *dirt* 653
  commonalty 876
  bad folk 949
rifle *musket* 727
  plunder 791
  – shot 406
rifled cannon 727
rifleman 726
rifler 792
rifles 726
rifle-shooting 840
rift 44, 198
  – within the lute
  651, 713
rig *dress* 225
  prepare 673
  frolic 840
  strumpet 962
  – the market 794
  run the – *upon* 929
rigadoon 840
rigging *ropes* 45
  gear 225
  instrument 633

riggish 961
right *dextral* 238
  straight 246
  true 494
  property 780
  just **922**
  privilege 924
  duty 926
  honor 939
  virtuous 944
  bill of – 969
  by – 924
  have a – to 924
  set – *inform* 527
  disclose 529
  that's – 931
  – about
    [*see below*]
  – ahead 234
  – angle 212
  – ascension 466
  – away 133
  step in the – direc-
    tion 644
  – hand [*see below*]
  – itself 660
  – and left 180,
    227, 236
  – line 246
  – man in the right
    place 23
  in one's – mind
    498, 502
  hit the – nail on
    the head 480a,
    698
  – owner 779
  keep the – path
    944
  in the – place 646
  – thing to do 926
  – as a trivet 650
  – word in the
    right place 578
right about: to
  the – 283
  go to the – 311,
    607
  send to the –
    eject 297
  reject 610
  refuse 764
  turn to the – 218,
    279
right hand
  power 157
  dextrality 238
  help 711
  not let the – know
    what the left is
    doing 528
  – of friendship 888
righteous 944
  the – 987
  – overmuch 988
Righteousness:
  Lord our – 976
  Sun of – 976
rightful 922
  – owner 779
rightly served, be –
  972
right-minded 939,
  944
rights 748
  put to – 660
  set to – 60

stand on one's –
  748
rigid *regular* 82
  hard 323
  exact 494
  severe 739
rigmarole 517, 573
rigor 383
  – mortis 360
rigorous *exact* 494
  severe 739
  revengeful 919
rigor 494, 739
Rigsdag 696
rigueur
  de – 744
rile *annoy* 830
  hate 898
  anger 900
rilievo *convex* 250
  sculpture 557
rill 348
rim 231
rime *chink* 198
  frost 283
rimer 262
rimple 258
rind 223
ring
  fastening 45
  pendency 214
  circle 247
  loud 404
  resonance 408
  test 463
  combination 709
  clique 712
  arena 728, 840
  badge 747
  rub the – 992
  have the true –
    494
  – the changes
    repeat 104
  change 140
  changeable 149
  – in the ear 408
  in a – *fence* 229,
    232
  – with the praises
    of 931
  – the tocsin 669
  – up 527
ringleader
  director 694
  mutineer 742
ringlet 247, 256
rink 840
rinse 652
rinsings 653
riot *confusion* 59
  derangement 61
  violence 173
  discord 713
  resist 719
  mutiny 742
  run – *activity* 682
  excitement 825
  intemperance 954
  – in *pleasure* 742
rioter 742
riotous 173
rip 949, 962
  – open 260
  – up tear 44
  recall the past 505
  excite 824

Rip van Winkle
  130
riparian 342
ripe 673
  – *age old* 128
ripen *perfect* 650
  improve 658
  prepare 673
  complete 729
  – into 144
rippet 713
riposte 462
ripple *ruffle* 256
  shake 315
  water 348
  murmur 405
ripuarian 342
rire, pour – 853
rise *grow* 35
  begin 66
  slope 217
  progress 282
  ascend 305
  stir 682
  revolt 742
  – again 660
  – in arms 722
  – from 154
  – to the occasion
    612
  – in price 814
  – up *elevation* 307
  – in the world 734
risible 838, 853
rising [*see rise*]
  – of the curtain
    66, 448
  – generation 127,
    167
  – ground
    height 206
  slope 217
  worship the – sun
    886
risk *chance* 621
  danger 665
  invest 787
  at any – 604
risqué 961
rissole 298
risum teneatis
  amici? 853
rite 963, **998**
  funeral – 363
ritornello 64, 104
ritual
  ostentation 882
  rite 998
ritualism 984
rival
  emulate 648
  oppose 708
  opponent 710
  compete 720
  combatant 726
  outshine 873
rivalry *envy* 921
rive 44
rivel 258
river **348**
rivet 43, 45
  – the attention
    457, 824
  – the eyes upon
    441
  – in the memory
    505

  – the yoke 739
riveted *firm* 150
rivulet 348
rixation 713
Ro 560
road *street* 189
  direction 278
  way 627
  on the –
    transference 270
  progression 282
  approach 286
  on the high – to
    278
  – to ruin
    destruction 162
  danger 665
  adversity 735
road-book 266
roads *lake* 343
roadstead 154
  abode 189
  refuge 666
roadster 271
roadway 627
roam 266
roan *horse* 271
  color 433
roar *violence* 173
  wind 349
  sound 404, 407
  bellow 411, 412
  laugh 838
  weep 839
roaring *great* 31
  – *trade* 731, 734
roast *heat* 384
  ridicule 856
  rib – 972
  – and boiled 298
  – an ox 883
rob 354, 791
robber 792
robbery 791
robe 225, 999
  robes – of state 747
Robin Goodfellow
  980
Robinson
  say Jack – 132
Robot 554
robust *strong* 159,
  654
roc 83
rocaille 853
rock *firm* 150
  oscillate 314
  hard 323
  land 342
  safety 664
  danger 667
  build on a – 150
  founded on a –
    664
  split upon a – 732
  – ahead 665
  –bound *coast* 342
  – oil 356
rocket *rapid* 274
  rise 305
  light 423
  ship 273
  signal 550
  arms 727
  fireworks 840
  go up like a – and
    come down like

  the stick 732
rocking-chair 215
rococo 124, 853
rod *support* 215
  measure 466
  scourge 975
  divining 993
  kiss the – 725
  sounding – 208
  – of empire 747
  – in pickle
    prepared 673
  accusation 938
  punishment 972
  scourge 975
rodeo 720, 840
rodomontade
  exaggeration 482
  unmeaning 517
  boast 884
roe 366, 374
Roentgen rays 420
rogation
  request 765
  worship 990
rogue *cheat* 548
  knave 941
  scamp 949
  –'s march 297
roguery 940
roguish
  playful 840
Roi le veut, le –
  741
roister 885
roisterer 887
Roland for an
  Oliver
  retaliation 716
  revenge 719
  barter 794
rôle *drama* 599
  business 625
  plan 626
  conduct 692
roll *list* 86
  fillet 205
  convolution 248
  rotundity 249
  make smooth 255
  move 264
  fly 267
  rotate 312
  rock 314
  flow 384
  sound **407**
  record 551
  money 800
  strike off the –
    756, 972
  – along 312
  – in the dust 731
  – on the ground
    839
  – of honour 86
  – in 639, 641
  – on 109
  – into one 43
  – in riches 803
  – up 312
  – up in 225
  – in wealth 803
roll-call 85
roller *fillet* 45
  round 249
  clothing 255
  rotate 312

roller-coaster 840
rollers *billows* 348
rollick 836
rollicker 838
rollicking
  frolicsome 836
  blustering 885
rolling: – pin 249
  – stock 272
  – stone 312
Rolls: Master of
  the –
  recorder 553
  judge 967
  – Court 966
Roman candle 840
Roman Catholic
  984
romance
  music 415
  absurdity 697
  imagination 515
  untruth 546
  fable 594
Romanism 984
romantic
  imaginative 515
  art 556
  sensitive 822
romanticism 515
Romanus sum,
  civis – 924
Romany 563
Rome: Church of
  984
do at – as the
  Romans do 82
romp *violent* 173
  game 840
rondeau *music* 415
  poem 597
rondel 597
rondolette 597
rood *area* 180
  cross 998
  – loft 1000
roof 189, 223
roofless 226
rook 791, 792
rookie 726
rookery *nests* 189
  dirt 653
room *occasion* 134
  space 180
  lodge 186
  chamber 191
  plea 617
  assembly – 840
  in the – of 147
  make – for
  opening 260
  respect 928
roommate 890
rooms
  lodgings 189
roomy 180
roost 189
  rule the – 737
rooster 366
root *algebraic* – 84
  cause 153
  place 184
  abide 186
  base 211
  etymon 562
lie at the – of 642
pluck up by the

  –s 301
strike at the – of
  716
take –
  influence 175
  locate 184
  habit 613
  – and branch 52
cut up – and
  branch 162
  – out *eject* 297
  extract 301
  discover 480a
rooted
  old 124
  firm 150
  located 184
  habit 613
deep – 820
  – antipathy 867
  – belief 484
rope *fastening* 45
  cord 205
  freedom 749
  scourge 975
give – enough 738
  –'s end 975
  – of sand
  incoherence 47
  weakness 160
  impossible 471
  – way 627
rope-dancer 700
rope-dancing 698
ropy 352
roquelaure 225
roric 339
rosâ, sub – 528
rosary 990, 998
Roscius 599
rose *pipe* 350
  fragrant 400
  red 434
  beauty 845
  bed of –s 377, 734
couleur de –
  red 434
  good 648
  prosperity 734
  hope 858
under the – 528
welcome as the –s
  in May 829, 892
roseate *red* 434
  hopeful 858
rose-colored
  hope 858
Rosetta stone 522
rosette 847
rose-water
  moderation 174
  flattery 933
  not made with –
  704
Rosicrucian
  sect 984
  sorcerer 994
rosin *rub* 331
  resin 356a
Rosinante 271
roster 86
rostrum *beak* 234
  pulpit 542
rosy 434
  – wine 959
rosy-cheeked 845
rot *decompose* 49

  absurdity 497
  rubbish 517
  putrefy 653
  disease 655
  decay 659
rota 86, 138
Rotarian 892
rotate 138
rotation 312
  periodicity 138
rote, by – 505
  know – 490
  learn – 539
rôti 298
rôtisserie 189
rotogravure 531,
  558
rotten *weak* 160
  bad 649
  foul 653
  decayed 659
  – at the core
  deceptive 545
  diseased 655
  – borough 893
rotulorum, custos –
  553
rotund 249
rotunda 189
rotundity 249
roturier 876
roué 949
rouge 434, 847
rouge-et-noir 621
rough *violent* 173
  shapeless 241
  uneven 256
  pungent 392
  unsavory 395
  sour 397
  sound 410
  unprepared 674
  fighter 726
  ugly 846
  low fellow 876
  bully 887
  churlish 895
  evil-doer 913
  bad man 949
cut up – 900
  – copy *writing* 590
  unprepared 674
  – diamond
  uncouth 241
  unprepared 674
  artless 703
  vulgar 851
  commonalty 876
  good man 948
  – draft 626
  – guess 514
  – it 686
  – sea 348
  – side of the
  tongue 932
  – and tumble 59
  – weather 173, 349
rough-cast 256
  covering 223
  shape 240
  scheme 626
  unpolished 674
rough-hew 240, 673
roughly
  nearly 197
rough-neck 876,
  887

roughness **256**
rough-rider 268
roughshod over,
  ride – 739
roulade 415
rouleau
  assemblage 72
  cylinder 249
  money 800
roulette 621, 840
round *series* 69
  revolution 138
  – of a ladder 215
  curve 245
  circle 247
  rotund 249
  music 415
  fight 720
  all – 227
  bring – 660
  come –
  periodic 138
  recant 607
  persuade 615
  dizzy – 312
  get – 660
  go – 311
  go one's –s 266
  go the –
  publication 531
  make the – of 311
  run the – of 682
  go the same – 104
  turn – *invert* 218
  retreat 283
  revolve 311
  – assertion 535
  – a corner 311
  – dance 840
  – game 840
  – hand 590
  – like a horse in a
  mill 613
  – of the ladder 71
  – number 84, 102
  in – numbers 29,
  197
  – pace 274
  – of pleasures
  377, 840
  – robin
  information 527
  petition 765
  censure 932
  – and round 138,
  312
  – sum 800
  – terms 566
  – trot 274
  – up 370
  – of visits 892
round about
  circumjacent 227
  deviation 279
  circuit 311
  amusement 840
  – phrases 573
  – way 729
rounded periods
  577, 578
roundelay 597
rounders 840
round-house 752
roundlet 247
round-shouldered
  243
roup 796

rouse 615, 824
  – oneself 682
rousing 171
rout *crowd* 72
  agitation 315
  overcome 731
  discomfit 732
  rabble 876
  assembly 892
  put to the – 731
  – out 652
route 627
  en – 270
  en – for 282
routine
  uniform 16
  order 58
  rule 80
  periodic 138
  custom 613
  business 625
rove *travel* 266
  deviate 279
rover *traveller* 268
  pirate 792
roving commission
  475
row *disorder* 59
  series 69
  violence 173
  street 189
  navigate 267
  discord 713
  – in the same
  boat 88
rowdy *vulgar* 851,
  876
  blusterer 887
  bad man 949
rowel 253, 615
rower 269
rowlock 215
royal 737
  – blue 438
  – highness 877
  – road 627, 705
Royal Academician
  559
royalist 737
royaliste que le roi,
  plus 33
royalty 737
Rt. Hon. 877
ruade *impulse* 276
  attack 716
ruat coelum 908
rub *friction* 331
  touch 379
  difficulty 704
  adversity 735
  painful 830
  – off corners 82
  – down *lessen* 195
  powder 330
  – down with an
  oaken towel 972
  – one's eyes 870
  – one's hands 838
  – up the memory
  505
  – off 552
  – on *slow* 275
  progress 282
  inexcitable 826
  – out 552
  – up 658
  – up the **wrong**

way 713
rubadub 407
rubber 325
  whist 840
rubber boots 225
rubber hose 975
rubber-stamp 82
rubbish
  absurdity 497
  unmeaning 517
  trifling 643
  useless 645
rubble 645
rube 876
rubescence 434
Rubicon *limit* 233
  pass the –
  begin 66
  cross 303
  choose 609
rubicund 434
rubify 434
rubigo 653
rubric 550, 697, 998
rubricate
  redden 434
ruby *red* 434
  gem 648
  ornament 847
ruck 29, 258
  in the – 235
rucksack 191
ructation 297
rudder 273, 693
rudderless 158
ruddle 434
ruddy *red* 434
  beautiful 845
rude *violent* 173
  shapeless 241
  ignorant 491
  inelegant 579
  ugly 846
  vulgar 851
  uncivilized 876
  uncivil 895
  disrespect 929
  – health 654
rudera 645
rudiment 66, 153
rudimental 193, 674
rudimentary 66
rudiments 490, 542
rudis indigestaque moles 59, 241
rue *bitter* 395
  regret 833
  repent 950
rueful 830, 837
ruff 225
ruffian 876
  blusterer 876
  maleficent 913
  scoundrel 949
ruffianism 851, 907
ruffle *disorder* 59
  derange 61
  roughen 259
  fold 258
  feeling 821
  excite 824, 825
  pain 830
  anger 900
rufous 434
rug 215, 223
Rugby

football 840
rugged
  shapeless 241
  rough 256
  difficult 704
  ugly 846
  churlish 895
rugose 256
ruin *destruction* 162
  evil 619
  failure 732
  adversity 735
  poverty 804
ruined
  bankrupt 808
  hopeless 859
ruinous
  painful 830
ruins *remains* 40
rule *mean* 29
  regularity 80
  influence 175
  length 200
  measure 466
  decide 480
  custom 613
  precept 697
  government 737
  law 963
  absence of – 699
  as a – 613
  by – 82
  golden – 697
  obey –s 82
  – of three 85
  – of thumb
  experiment 463
  unreasoning 477
  essay 675
  unskilled 699
ruler 745
ruling 697, 969
  – *passion* 606, 820
rum *liquor* 298
  queer 853
  – *running* 964
rumba 840
rumble 407
ruminate
  chew 298
  think 451
rummage 461
rummer 191
rumor 531, 532
rump 235
rumple
  disorder 59
  derange 61
  roughen 256
  fold 258
rumpus
  confusion 59
  violence 173
  discord 713
run *generality* 78
  repetition 104
  continuance 106, 143
  course 109
  eventuality 151
  motion 264
  speed 274
  sequence 281
  liquefy 335
  flow 348
  habit 613
  smuggle 791

contraband 964
have a – 852, 873
have – of 748
near – 197
ordinary – 29
race is – 729
time –s 106
– abreast 27
– after 622, 873
– against 276, 708, 716
– at 716
– away 623
– away with 789, 791
– away with a notion
  misjudge 481
  credulous 486
– back 283
– a chance
  probable 472
  chance 621
– counter to 468, 708
– its course
  course 109
  complete 729
  past 122
– into danger 665
– into debt 806
– down
  underestimate 483
  pursue 622
  bad 649
  finished 678
  attack 716
  depreciate 932
  detract 934
– dry 638, 640
– the eye over 441, 539
– the fingers over 379
– foul of 276
– the gauntlet 861
– on in a groove 613
– hard *danger* 665
  difficult 704
  success 731
– in the head 451, 505
– high *great* 31
  violent 173
– in *introduce* 228
– into
  conversion 144
  insert 300
– low 36
– of luck 156, 734
– mad 503, 825
– mad after 865
– like mad 274
– of the mill 29
– amuck
  violent 173
  kill 361
  mad 503
  attack 716
– on 143
– out *end* 67
  course 109
  past 122
  antiquated 124
  egress 295
  prodigal 818

– out on 573
– over *count* 85
  - *in the mind* 451
  examine 457
  describe 594
  synopsis 596
  overflow 641
– in pairs 17
– parallel 178
– into port 664
– a race *speed* 274
  conduct 692
  contend 720
  – in a race
  act 680
he that –s may read 525
– a rig 840
  – the rig upon 929
– riot *violent* 173
  exaggerate 549
  redundance 641
  active 682
  disobey 742
  intemperance 954
– a risk 665
– rusty 603
– to seed 128, 659
– smooth 705, 734
– a tilt at 716, 720
– of things 151
– through
  uniform 16
  influence 175
  be present 186
  kill 361
  expend 809
  prodigal 818
– up *increase* 35
  build 161
  – up an account
  credit 805
  debt 806
  charge 812
  – up bills 808
  – upon 630
  – upon a bank 808, 809
  – to waste 638
  – wild 173
run-about 272
runagate
  fugitive 623
  disobey 742
  bad man 949
runaway 623
rundle *circle* 247
  convolution 248
  rotundity 249
rundlet 191
Runes *writing* 590
  poetry 597
  spell 993
rung 215
runnel 348
runner *branch* 51
  courier 268
  messenger 534
running
  continuous 69
  the mind – upon 451
  the mind – upon other things 458
– account 811
– commentary 595
– fight 720

– hand 590
– over 641
– water 348
runnion 949
runt 193
rupture
  disjunction 44
  quarrel 713
rural 189, 371
  – dean 893
ruralist 893
rus in urbe 189, 893
ruse 545, 702
Rush, Friar 980
rush *crowd* 72
  violence 173
  velocity 274
  water 348
  plant 367
  trifle 643
  haste 684
  make a – at 716
  – to a conclusion 481, 486
  – on destruction 863
  – in medias res 604
  – into print 591
  – upon 622
rushlight *dim* 422
  candle 423
rusk 298
Russe, montagne – 480
russet
  brown 433
  red 434
Russian
  – ballet 840
  – bath 386, 652
rust *red* 434
  decay 659
  canker 663
  inaction 683
  moth and – 659
  – of antiquity 122
rustic
  village 189
  agricultural 371
  vulgar 851
  clown 876
rusticate
  punish 972
  seclude 893
rusticity
  impolite 895
rusticus expectat dum defluat amnis 858
rustle 405, 407, 409
rustling 791
rusty *dirty* 653
  decayed 659
  sluggish 683
  unskilful 699
  sulky 901a
  run – *averse* 603
rut *rule* 80
  furrow 259
  habit 613
  in a – 16
ruth 914
ruthless
  savage 907
  pitiless 914a
  revengeful 919

schism *dissent* 489
  discord 713
  heterodoxy 984
schismless 983a
schistose 204
scholar 492, 541
scholarly 539
scholarship
  knowledge 490
  learning 539
  distinction 873
scholastic
  knowledge 490
  teaching 537
  learning 539
  school 542
scholiast 496, 522
scholium 496, 522
school
  herd 72
  multitude 102
  system of
    opinions 484
  knowledge 490
  teaching 537
  academy 542
  . *painting* 556
  go to – 539
  send to – 537
schoolboy 129, 541
  familiar to every –
    490
schooldays 127
schoolfellow 541
schoolgirl 129, 541
schoolman 492, 983
schoolmaster 540
  – abroad 490, 537
schoolroom 191
schooner 273
schottische 840
sciatica 378
science 490, 698
scientific *exact* 494
scientist 476, 492
scimitar 727
scintilla *small* 32
  spark 420, 423
scintillate 446, 873
scintillation
  heat 382
  light 420
  wit 842
scintillula forsan,
  latet – 858
sciolism 491
sciolist 493
sciomachy 497
Sciomancy 511
scion *part* 51
  child 129
  posterity 167
scire: – facias 461
  – quid valeant
    humeri 698
scission 44
scissors 253
  – and paste 609
scissure 198
sclerotics 195
scobs 330
scoff *ridicule* 856
  deride 929
  impiety 988
  – at *despise* 930
  censure 932
scold *shrew* 901

malediction 908
  censure 932
scollop 248, 257
sconce *top* 210
  candlestick 423
  brain 450
  defence 717
  mulct 974
scone 298
scoop
  depression 252
  perforator 262
scooter 272
scope *degree* 26
  opportunity 134
  extent 180
  meaning 516
  freedom 748
scorch
  rush 274
  heat 382, 384
scorching
  violent 173
score
  music 60, 415
  count 85
  list 86
  twenty 98
  notch 257
  furrow 259
  mark 550
  success 731
  credit 805
  debt 806
  accounts 811
  on the – of
    relation 9
    motive 615
scores *many* 102
scoria *ash* 384
  dirt 653
scorify 384
scoring board 551
scorn 930
scorpion
  painful 830
  evil-doer 913
  (*bane* 663)
  chastise with –s
    739
scorse 794
scot *reward* 973
scot free *free* 748
  cheap 815
  exempt 927a
escape –
  escape 671
  let off – 970
scotch *notch* 257
  injure 659
  – the snake
    maim 158
  insufficient 640
  non-completion
    730
  – the wheel 706
Scotsman
  canny 702
Scotticism 563
scotomy 443
scoundrel 913, 949
scour *run* 274
  rub 331
  clean 652
  – the country 266
  – the plain 274
scourge *bane* 663

painful 830
  punish 972
instrument of
    punishment 975
  – of the human
    race 913
scourings 645
scout 234
  observer 444
  feeler 463
  messenger 534
  reject 610
  warship 726
  servant 746
  watch 664
  warning 668
  disrespect 929
  disdain 930
  (*looker* 444)
  (*underrate* 483)
  (*ridicule* 856)
scow 273
scowl
  complain 839
  frown 895
  anger 900
  sullen 901a
  disapprobation
    932
scrabble
  unmeaning 517
  scribble 590
scrag 32, 203
scraggy *lean* 193,
    203
  rough 256
scramble
  confusion 59
  climb 305
  pursue 622
  haste 684
  difficulty 704
  contend 720
  seize 789
scranch 330
scrannel 643
scrap 32, 720
  – of paper 158, 940
scrap-book 596
scrape *subduct* 38
  reduce 195
  pulverize 330
  abrade 331
  mezzotint 558
  difficulty 704
  mischance 732
  bow 894
  – together
    assemble 72
    acquire 775
scraper 652
scratch *groove* 259
  abrade 331
  mark 550
  daub 555
  draw 556
  write 590
  hurt 619
  wound 649
come to the –
    720, 861
mere – 209
old – 978
up to the – 861
without a – 654,
    670
  – the head 461

– out 552
scrawl 590
scrawny 203
screak 411
scream *cry* 411, 839
screech 411, 412
screech owl 412
screed 582, 593
screen *sift* 60
  sieve 260
  shade 424
  cinema 448
  hide 528
  hider 530
  side-scene 599
  clean 562
  safety 664
  shelter 666
  defence 717
  – from sight 442
screw *fasten* 43
  fastening 45
  distort 243
  oar 267
  rotation 312
  instrument 633
  miser 819
  put on the – 739,
    744
  – one's courage to
    the sticking
    place 861
  – loose *insane* 503
  imperfect 651
  unskilful 699
  hindrance 706
  attack 713
  – up *fasten* 43
  strengthen 159
  prepare 673
  – up the eyes 443
screwed
  drunk 959
screw-driver 633
screw-steamer 273
scribble 517, 590
scribbler 593
scribe *recorder* 553
  writer 590, 593
  priest 996
  –s and Pharisees
    988
scribendi, ca-
  coëthes – 580
scrimshanker 603
scrimmage 713, 720
scrimp *short* 201
  insufficient 640
  stingy 819
scrip 191
script 590, 599
scripta, lex – 963
scriptae, literae – 590
scriptural 983a
Scripture
  certain 474
  revelation 985
scrivener *writer* 590
  lawyer 968
scroll 86, 551
scrub *rub* 331
  bush 367
  clean 652
  dirty person 653
  commonalty 876
scrubby *small* 193
  trifling 643

stingy 819
  disreputable 874
  vulgar 876
  shabby 940
scruff 235
scruple
  small quantity 32
  weight 319
  doubt 485
  reluctance 603
  probity 939
scrupulous
  careful 459
  incredulous 487
  exact 494
  reluctant 603
  fastidious 868
  punctilious 939
scrutator 461
scrutiny 457, 461
scrutoire 191
scud *sail* 267
  speed 274
  shower 348
  cloud 353
  – under bare
    poles 704
scuffle 720
scull *row* 267
  brain 450
scull-cap 225
scullery 191
scullion 746
sculpsit 558
sculptor 559
sculpture 240, 557
scum *dirt* 653
  – of the earth 949
  – of society 876
scupper 350
scurf 653
scurrilous
  ridicule 856
  malediction 908
  disrespect 929
  detraction 934
scurry 274, 684
scurvy
  insufficient 640
  unimportant 643
  base 940
  wicked 945
scut 235
scutcheon
  standard 550
  honor 877
scutiform 251
scuttle *destroy* 162
  receptacle 191
  speed 274
  – along *haste* 684
Scylla and Charyb-
  dis, between –
    danger 665
  difficulty 704
Scyllam, incidit
  in – 699
scythe *pointed* 244
  sharp 253
'sdeath! *wonder* 870
  anger 900
  disapprobation
    932
se non e vero e ben
  trovato 546
sea *multitude* 102
  ocean 341

impose 741
lease 771, 787
make a dead – at
716
– about 66, 676
– abroach 73
– one's affections
on 897
– afloat 153, 531
– against
oppose 708
quarrel 713
hate 898
angry 900
– against one
another 464
– agoing
impulse 276
propulsion 284
aid 717
– apart
separate 44
exclude 55
select 609
– aside
displace 185
disregard 458
neglect 460
negative 536
reject 610
disuse 678
annul 756
refuse 764
not observe 773
relinquish 782
dereliction 927
– one's back up
878
– before
inform 527
choice 609
– before oneself
620
– by 636
– one's cap at
897, 902
– on a cast 621
– down [*see* below]
– by the ears 898
– at ease 831
– an example
model 22
motive 615
– the eyes on 441
– one's face
against
oppose 708
refuse 764
disapprove 932
– the fashion
influence 175
authority 737
fashion 852
– fast 704
– on fire
ignite 384
excite 824
– on foot 66
– foot on 294
– forth *show* 525
assert 535
describe 594
– forward 293
– free 750
– going
[*see* – agoing]
– one's hand to

467
– one's heart upon
604, 865
– at hazard 665
– in *begin* 66
rain 348
– on its legs 150
– on one's legs 159,
669
– in motion 264,
677
– to music 416
– at naught
make light of 483
reject 610
oppose 708
defy 715
disobey 742
not observe 773
dereliction 927
– no store by 483,
930
– off
compensation 30
depart 293
improve 658
discount 813
adorn 845
display 882
– on 615
– in order 60
– out *arrange* 60
begin 66
depart 293
decorate 845
display 882
– over 755
– phrase 566
– a price 85, 812
– purpose 620
– at rest *end* 67
answer 462
adjudge 480
complete 729
compact 769
– right
inform 527
disclose 529
teach 537
reinstate 660
vindicate 937
– to rights 60
– sail 293
– the seal on 729
– one's seal to 467
– store by 642
– straight 246, 723
– the table in a
roar 840
– one's teeth 604
– terms
manifest 525
phrase 566
style 574
– a trap for 545
– to 720, 722
– in towards 286
– up
printing 54
originate 153
strengthen 159
produce 161
upright 212
raise 307
successful 731
prosperous 734
– up shop 676

– upon
resolved 604
attack 716
desirous 865
– too high a value
upon 482
– watch 459
– one's wits to
work *think* 451
imagine 515
plan 626
– to work
undertake 676
impose 741
set-back 735
set down
record 551
unseat 756
humiliate 879
slight 929
censure 932
give one a –
confute 479
– as 484
– for 484
– a cause for
hearing 969
– to 155
– in writing 551
setaceous 256
seton 662
setose 256
settee 215
setter 366
settle *regulate* 60
establish 150
be located 184
bench 215
come to rest 265
subside 306
kill 361
decide 480
choose 609
vanquish 731
consent 762
compact 769
pay 807
– accounts 807,
811
– down 133
stability 150
moderate 174
locate oneself 184
– into 144
– matters 723
– preliminaries
673
– property 781
– the question 478
– to sleep 683
– upon *give* 784
– with 807, 992
settled [*see* settle]
characteristic 5
ended 67
account – 811
– opinion 484
– purpose 620
settlement [*see*
settle]
location 184
colony 188
dregs 653
compact 769
deed 771
property 780
strict – 781

settler 188
settlor 784
seven 98
–league boots 274,
992
wake the –
sleepers 404
seventy 98
sever 38, 44
several *special* 79
plural 100
many 102
– times 104
severalize 465
severally 44, 79
severalty 44
severance 38
severe
energetic 171
symmetry 242
exact 494
– *style* 576
harsh 739
painful 830
simple 849
critical 932
severely *very* 31
severity 739
sew 43
sewage 299, 653
sewed up
drunk 959
sewer 350, 653
sewerage 652, 653
sewer-gas 663
sewing-silk 205
sex *kind* 75
women 374
fair – 374
sexagenarian 98,
130
sexagenary 99
sextant 217, 244,
247
sextet 98
sextodecimo 593
sexton 363, 996
sextuple 98
seyyid 745
sforzando 415
shabbiness 34
shabby *trifling* 643
deteriorated 659
stingy 819
mean 874
disgraceful 940
shabby-genteel 851
shack 189
shackle
fastening 45
hinder 706
restrain 751
fetter 752
shade *degree* 26
small quantity 32
manes 362
darkness 421
shadow 424
color 428
conceal 528
screen 530
paint 556
ghost 980
eye – 443
in the – 528, 874
shadow of a – 32,
422

throw into the –
surpass 303
conceal 528
glory 873
throw all else into
the – 642
thrown into the –
34, 874
under the – of 664
without a – of
doubt 474
shades:
– below 982
– of death 360
– of difference 15
– of evening 422
shading 421
– off 26
shadow
unsubstantial 4
copy 21
small 32
accompaniment
88
thin 203
be behind 235
sequence 281
dark 421
shade 424
pursue 461, 622
dream 515
demon 980
fight with a – 699
follow as a – 281
partial – 422
without a – of
turning 141
worn to a –
thin 203
worse for wear
659
– of coming
events 511
– forth *dim* 422
predict 511
metaphor 521
represent 554
may your – never
be less
courtesy 894
respect 928
approbation 931
take the – for the
substance
credulous 486
mistake 495
unskilful 699
under the – of
one's wing 664
shadowy 4, 447
shady 874
shaft *deep* 208
frame 215
pit 260
missile 284
axis 312
air-pipe 351
handle 633
weapon 727
shaggy 256
shagreen 223
shah 745
shake *totter* 149
weak 160
vibrate 314
agitation 315
shiver 383

not believe 487
permit 760
not observe 773
– the gates of
mercy 914a
– in 751
– oneself up 893
– out 55, 761
– up shop *end* 67
cease 142
silence 403
relinquish 624
repose 687
– up *close* 261
confute 479
imprison 751
shutter 424
shuttle 314
shuttlecock 605
shy *deviate* 279
draw back 283
propel 284
avoid 623
fearful 860
cowardly 862
modest 881
fight – of 623
have a – at 716
– of belief 487
– cock 862
– of *doubtful* 485
unwilling 603
cautious 864
dislike 867
Shylock 787
Siamese twins 89
sib 11
Siberia 383
sibi gladio hunc
jugulo, suo – 718
sibilation *hiss* 409
disrespect 929
disapprobation
932
Sibyl *oracle* 513
ugly 846
Sibylline 511
– leaves 513
sic *imitation* 19
exact 494
si – omnes! 948
– transit gloria
mundi 111
– volo sic jubeo
600
– vos non vobis
791
siccity 340
sick *ill* 655
make one – 830,
867
visitation of the –
998
– at heart 837
– of *weary* 841
dislike 867
satiated 869
i.i –ness and in
health 604
sick-chamber 655
sicken *nauseate* 395
disease 655
pain 830
weary 841
disgust 867
sickener
too much 641

sickle 244, 253
sickly *weak* 160
sick-room 655
side
consanguinity 11
edge 231
laterality 236
party 712
ostentation 882
at one's – 197
on every – 227
on one – 243
on one's – 714
look only at one –
of the shield 481
pass from one – to
another 607
take up a – 476
wrong – up 218
– by side
accompaniment
88
near 197
laterality 236
party 712
from – to side 314
– with *aid* 707
co-operate 709
concord 714
side-arms 727
sideboard 191
side-blow 702
side-car 272
side-dish 298
side-drum 417
side-kick 890
side issue 643
sideling 279
sidelong 236
sideration 158
sidereal 318
– time 114
siderite 288
Sideromancy 511
side-saddle 215
side-scene 599
sideslip 267
sidesman 996
side-track 287
sidewalk 627
sideways 217, 236
side-wind
oblique 217
circuit 629
cunning 702
sidle *oblique* 217
lateral 236
deviate 279
siege 716
lay – to 716
state of – 722
siege-train 727
siesta 683
sieve *sort* 60
perforate 260
clean 652
memory like a –
506
pour water into
a – 638, 818
stop one hole in
a – 819
sift *simplify* 42
sort 60
inquire 461
discriminate 465
clean 652

– the chaff from
the wheat 609
sigh 405, 839
– for 865
sighing like
furnace 902
sight *much* 31
multitude 102
vision 441
appearance 448
ugly 846
prodigy 872
dim – 443
in – 446
in – of 197, 441
in plain – 525
keep in – 457
within – of shore
858
sightless
blind 442
invisible 447
ugly 846
sightly 845
sights, see – 455
sightseeing 441
sightseer 444, 455
sigil *seal* 550
evidence 769
sigmoidal 248
sign *attest* 467
omen 512
indication 550
record 551
write 590
compact 769
prodigy 872
give – of 525
make no – 585
– of the cross 998
–s of the times
indication 550
omen 512
warning 668
–s of the zodiac
318
signal *great* 31
sign 550
important 642
give the – 741
– of distress 669
signalize
indicate 550
glory 873
celebrate 883
signally 31
signal oil 356
signal-post 668
signature
mark, identifica-
tion 550
writing 590
compact 769
security 771
sign-board 550
signet
mark, identifica-
tion 550
sign of authority
747
compact 769
writer to the – 968
significant 642
[*see signify*]
evidence 467
important 642

signifies, what –
643
signify
forebode 511
mean 516
inform 527
signior 875
sign-manual 550,
590
signor 373, 877
signora 374
sign-painter 559
sign-painting 555
sign-post 550
signum, ecce – 550
sike 348
silence *disable* 158
no sound 403
confute 479
latency 526
concealment 528
aphony 581
taciturn 585
check 731
silencer 405, 408
silentio, sub –
silent 403
inattention 458
latent 526
silhouette
outline 230, 448
shadow 421
portrait 556
siliquose 191
silk 255, 324
– gown
barrister 968
– hat 225
make a – purse
out of a sow's
ear 471
silken repose 686
silkiness 954
sill 215
silly
credulous 486
imbecile 499
insane 503
silo 636
silt *deposit* 321
dirt 653
silvan 367
silver *bright* 420
white 430
grey 432
money 800
bait with a – hook
615
german – 545
– lining of the
cloud 858
– wedding 883
silver certificate
800
silver-toned 413
silviculture 371
simagrée 855
similarity 17
– of form 240
simile
similarity 17
comparison 464
metaphor 521
similitude 17, 21
simmer
agitation 315
boil 382, 384

excitement 824
simmering 825
simoleon 800
Simon Pure
the real – 494
Simon, Simple –
501, 547
Simon Stylites 893
simony 964
simoon 249, 382
simper *smile* 838
affectation 855
simple *mere* 32
unmixed 42
credulous 486
ignorant 493
silly 499
– *language* 576
herb 662
artless 703
unadorned 849
– *meaning* 516
simple-hearted 543
simpleness **42**
Simple Simon 501,
547
simpleton 501
simplex munditiis
849
simplicity
[*see simple*] **849**
ignorance 491
simplify
[*see simple*]
elucidate 518
simply 32, 87
. more – 522
simulacrum 19
simulate
resemble 17
imitate 19
cheat 544
simultaneous 120
sin 945, 947
sinapism 662
since *under the cir-*
cumstances 8
after 117
cause 155
reason 476
sincere
veracious 543
ingenuous 703
feeling 821
sine 217
sine: – curâ 831
– die 107, 133
– ictu 158
– quâ non
required 630
important 642
condition 770
sinecure 681
no – 682
sinew 159
sinewless 158
sinews of war 800
sinful 945
sing *bird* 412
resonance 408
music 416
voice 580
poetry 597
rejoice 838
– Io triumphe 884
– out 411
– praises

approve 931
worship 990
– in the shrouds 349
– small 879
singe 382, 384
singer 416
single *unmixed* 42
  unit 87
  secluded 893
  unmarried 904
  ride at – *anchor* 863
  – combat 720
  – entry
  – file 69
  – out 609
single-handed
  one 87
  easy 705
  unassisted 706
single-minded 703
singleness
  [*see* single]
  – of heart 703, 939
  – of purpose 604a, 703
single-stick 720
singlet 225
Sing Sing 752
sing-song 414, 892
singular *special* 79
  exceptional 83
  one 87
singularly *very* 31
sinister *left* 239
  bad 649
  vicious 945
  bar –
    imperfect 651
    disrepute 874
sinistrality 239
sinistromanual 239
sinistrous
  left-handed 239
  sullen 901a
sink *disappear* 4
  destroy 162
  descend 306
  lower 308
  submerge 310
  neglect 460
  conceal 528
  cloaca 653
  fatigue 688
  vanquish 731
  fail 732
  adversity 735
  invest 787
  pain 828
  depressed 837
  – back 661
  – of corruption 653
  – into the grave 360
  – of iniquity 945
  – in the mind
    thought 451
    memory 505
    excite 824
  – money 809
  – into oblivion 506
  – or swim
    certainty 474
    perseverance 604a
sinking

heart – 837
  – fund 802
sinless 946
sinned against than sinning, more – 946
sinner 949
Sinn Fein 742
sin-offering 952
sinuous 243, 248
sinus 252
sip *small* 32
  drink 298
siphon 350
sippet 298
sir *man* 373
  title 877
  – Oracle 887
sirdar 745
sire 166
siren
  sea-nymph 341
  loud sound 404
  musician 416
  seducing 615
  warning 668
  alarm 669
  evil-doer 913
  demon 980
  sorcerer 994
  song of the –s 615
  – strains 415
sirene *musical instrument* 417
siriasis 503
sirius 423
sirocco *wind* 349
  heat 382
sirrah! 949
sister *kin* 11
  likeness 17
  nurse 662
  nun 996
sisterhood
  party 712
  frail – 962
sisterly 906
sisters:
  weird – 994
  – three 601
sistrum 417
Sisyphus, task of –
  useless 645
  difficult 704
sit 308
  – down *settle* 184
  lie 213
  stoop 308
  – in judgment
    adjudge 480
    jurisdiction 965
    lawsuit 969
  – on 215
  – on thorns
    annoyance 828
    fear 860
site 183, 780
sith 476
sitting [*see* sit]
  incubation 673
  convocation 696
  – up *late* 133
  work 686
sitting-room 191
situ, in – 183, 265
situation
  circumstances 8

place **183**
location 184
business 625
out of a – 185
Siva 979
six 98
  – of one and half-a-dozen of the other 27
sixes and sevens, at – 59, 713
sixty 98
sizar 746
size *degree* 26
  magnitude 31
  glue 45
  arrange 60
  dimensions **192**
  viscid 352
  – up 480
sizzle 409
sjambok 975
skat 840
skate
  locomotion 266
  vehicle 272
skating 840
skean 727
skedaddle 623
skeel 191
skein 219
  tangled – 59
skeleton
  remains 40
  essential part 30
  thin 203
  support 215
  corpse 362
  plan 626
  reduced to a – 659
  – in the closet 649, 830
  – at the feast 836
skelter 276
skepticism
  doubt 485
  incredulity 487
  irreligion 989
sketch
  form 240
  represent 554
  paint 556
  describe 594
  plan 626
sketcher 559
sketchy
  incomplete 53
  feeble 575
  unfinished 730
skew 217
  –bald 440
skewer 45
ski 266, 272
  –running 840
  –joring 840
  –jumping 840
skiagraphy 421, 554, 556
skid *support* 215
  hindrance 706
skies:
  exalt to the – 873
  praise to the – 933
skiff 273
skill **698**
  acquisition of – 539

game of – 840
skillet 191
skilly 293
skim *move* 266
  navigate 267
  rapid 274
  neglect 460
  summarize 596
skimp 460, 819
skimpy 640
skin *outside* 220
  tegument 223
  peel 226
  swindle 791
  fleece 814
  wet to the – 339
  with a whole – 670
  without – 822
  mere – and bone 203
  – a flint 471, 819
  – over 660
skin-deep
  shallow 32, 209
  external 220
skinned: thick– 376
  thin– 375
skinny 203, 223
skip *jump* 309
  neglect 460
  rejoice 838
skipjack
  prosperous 734
  low-born 876
skipper
  sea captain 269
  captain 745
skippingly 70
skips, by – 70
skirmish 720
skirmisher 726
skirt
  appendix 39
  pendent 214
  dress 225
  surrounding 227
  edge 231
  side 236
  – dance 840
skirting 231
skirts of:
  hang upon the –
    sequence 281
  on the –
    near 197
skit *ridicule* 856
  detraction 934
  prostitute 962
skittish
  capricious 608
  excitable 825
  timid 862
  bashful 881
skittle *sharper* 792
skittles 840
skiver 253
skulk 528, 862
skull 450
skull-cap 225
skunk 401
skurry 684
sky *summit* 210
  world 318
  air 338
  necessity 601
sky-aspiring 865
sky-blue 438

sky-lark 305
sky-larking 840
sky-light 260
sky-line 196
sky-pilot 996
sky-rocket 305
sky-scraper 206, 210
slab *layer* 204
  support 215
  flat 251
  viscous 352
  record 551
slabber *slaver* 297
  unclean 653
slack *loose* 47
  weak 160
  inert 172
  slow 275
  cool 385
  fuel 388
  neglectful 460
  unwilling 603
  insufficient 640
  inactive 683
  lax 738
slacken
  loosen 47
  moderate 174
  repose 687
  hinder 706
  one's pace 275
slacker 460, 603, 623, 927
slag *embers* 384
  inutility 641
  dirt 653
slake *quench* 174
  gratify 829
  satiate 869
  – one's appetite
    intemperance 954
slam 276, 406
  – the door in one's face
    oppose 708
    refuse 764
slammerkin 653
slander 934
slanderer 936
slang 560, 563, 908
slant 217
slap *instantly* 113
  strike 276
  censure 932
  punish 972
  – in the face
    opposition 708
    attack 716
    anger 900
    disrespect 929
    disapprobation 932
  – the forehead 461
slap-dash 684
slash 44, 308
slashing *style* 574
slate
  writing tablet 590
  election 609
  disparage 932
  clean the – 918
  – loose *mad* 503
slate-colored 432
slates *roof* 223
slattern
  disorder 59

smooth *uniform* 16
　calm 174
　flattery 213, 251
　not rough 255
　easy 705
　– the bed of death
　　707, 906
　– down 174
　– over 174
　– the ruffled brow
　　of care 834
　– sailing 705
　– water *easy* 705
　– the way 705
smooth-bore 727
smoothly, go on –
　prosperous 734
smoothness 255
smooth-tongued
　544, 933
smother
　repress 174
　kill 361
　stifle sound 581
　restrain 751
smoulder *inert* 172
　burn 382
　latent 526
smous 796, 797
smudge 431, 653,
　848
smug *affected* 855
smuggle
　introduce 228
　steal 791
　illegal 964
smuggler 792
smut
　dirt 653
　impurity 961
smutch 431
snack
　small quantity 32
　food 298
snacks, go – 778
snaffle 752
snag *projection* 250
　sharp 253
　danger 667
　hindrance 706
snail *slow* 275
snake *undulation*
　248
　serpent 366
　hissing 406
　miscreant 913
　scotch the – 640
　– in the grass
　　hidden 528
　deceiver 548
　bad 649
　source of danger
　　667
　evil-doer 913
　knave 941
snake-like
　convoluted 248
snap *break* 44
　eat 298
　brittle 328
　noise 406
　rude 895
　– at *seize* 789
　bite 830
　censure 932
　– of the fingers
　trifle 643

– one's fingers at
　defy 715
　insolence 885
　despise 930
　– the thread 70
　– up *seize* 789
　– one up
　　censure 932
　–shot 554
snap-dragon 840
snappish 901
snare *deception* 545
snarl *growl* 412
　rude 895
　angry 900
　threaten 909
snatch
　small quantity 32
　seize 789
　– at *pursue* 622
　seize 789
　– a grace beyond
　　the reach of art
　　845
　– from one's grasp
　　789
　– from the jaws of
　　death 662, 672
　– from under
　　one's nose 702
　– a verdict 545,
　　702
snatches, by – 70
sneak *hide* 528
　coward 862
　servile 886
　base 940
　knave 941
　bad man 949
　– off, – out of 623
sneer *disparage* 929
　contempt 930
　blame 932
sneeze *blow* 349
　snuffle 409
　– at *despise* 930
sneezed at, not to
　be – 642
snick 32, 51
snicker 838
sniff *blow* 349
　odor 398
　discovery 480a
sniffle 349
snigger *laugh* 838
　ridicule 856
　disrespect 929
sniggle 545
snip
　small quantity 32
　cut 44
　short 201
　tailor 225
sniping 716
snippet 32
snip-snap 713
snip-snap-snorem
　840
snivel *weep* 839
sniveling
　servile 886
snob *vulgar* 851
　plebeian 876
　servile 886
snobbishness
　flattery 933
snood

headdress 225
　circle 247
snooker 840
Snooks, Mr. – 876
snooze 683
snozzle 250
snore 411, 683
snort 411, 412
snout 250
snow *ship* 273
　ice 383
　white 430
snow-ball 72
snow-blindness 443
snow-drift 72
snow-shoe 272
snow-storm 383
snub *short* 201
　hinder 706
　cast a slur 874
　humiliate 879
　bluster 885
　censure 932
snub-nosed 243
snuff *blow* 349
　pungent 392
　odor 398
　up to – 698, 702
　go out like the –
　　of a candle 360
　– out 162, 421
　– up 296, 398
snuff-color 433
snuffing, want –
　pert 885
snuffle *blow* 349
　hiss 409
　stammer 583
　hypocrisy 988
snuffy 653
snug *closed* 261
　comfortable 377
　safe 664
　prepared 673
　content 831
　secluded 893
　keep – 528, 893
　make all – 673
snuggery 189
snugness 827
so *similar* 17
　very 31
　therefore 476
　method 627
　– be it 488, 762
　– far so good 618
　– let it be 681
　– much the better
　　831, 838
　– much the worse
　　832, 835
　– to speak 17, 521
soak *immerse* 300
　water 337
　moist 339
　drunkenness 959
　– up 340
So-and-so, Mr. –
　neology 563
soap *lubricate* 332
　oil 356
　cleanser 652
soapy *unctuous* 355
　servile 886
　flattery 933
soar *great* 31
　height 206

fly 267
　rise 305
sob 839
sober *moderate* 174
　wise 498
　sane 502
　style 576
　grave 837
　temperate 953
　abstinent 958
　– down 174, 502
　humility 879
　in – sadness
　　affirmation 535
　– senses 502
　– truth *fact* 494
sober-minded 502
　calm 826
　humble 879
sobriety 958
sobriquet 565
sob sister 534
so-called 545, 565
soc *jurisdiction* 965
socage 777
soccer 840
sociable
　carriage 272
　sociality 892
social *mankind* 372
　sociable 892
　– circle 892
　– evil 961
　– gathering 892
　– science 910
socialism
　government 737
　participation 778
　philanthropy 910
socialist 712
sociality 892
society
　mankind 372
　party 712
　fashion 852
　sociality 892
　position in – 873
Socinianism 984
sociology 712
sock *hosiery* 225
　drama 599
socket 191, 252
socle 215
Socratic method
　461
sod 344
　beneath the – 363
sodality 712, 888
sodden 339, 384
sofa 215
Sofi 984, 996
soft *stop!* 142
　weak 160
　moderate 174
　smooth 255
　not hard 324
　moist 339
　marsh 345
　silence! 403
　– sound 405
　dulcet 413
　credulous 486
　silly 499
　lenient 740
　tender 822
　timid 862
　own to the – im-

peachment 529
　– music 415
　– pedal 405
　– sawder 617, 933
　– soap 356, 933
　– tongue, – words
　　894
soften [see soft]
　moderate 174
　relieve 834
　pity 914
　palliate 937
softening of the
　brain 158
softer sex 374
soft-hearted 914
softling 160
softness 324
　persuasibility 615
soft-spoken 894
soggy 339
soho
　attention 457
　parley 586
　hunting 622
soi-disant
　asserting 535
　pretender 548
　misnomer 565
　vain 880
　boastful 884
soil *region* 18
　land 342
　dirt 653
　deface 846
　till the – 371, 673
soirée 892
sojourn 186, 189
sojourner 188
soke 181
solace *relief* 834
　recreation 840
　– oneself with
　　pleasure 827
solar 318
　– system 318
　– time 114
solatium 973
sold to the devil 949
soldan [see sultan]
solder *join* 43
　cement 45
　cohere 46
soldier 726
soldier-like 722,
　861
sole *alone* 87
　base 211
　support 215
　feme – 904
solecism 568
soleil, coup de –
　hot 384
　mad 503
solemn
　affirmation 535
　important 642
　grave 837
　glorious 873
　ostentatious 882
　religious 987
　worship 990
　– mockery 882
　– silence 403
solemnity *rite* 998
solemnization 883
sol-fa 416

sozzled 959
spa *town* 189
  sanatorium 662
space *distribute* 60
  time 106
  extension **180**
  musical 413
  ship 273
  celestial –s 318
  wide open –'s 180
spaddle 272
spade 272
  call a – a spade
  plain language
  576
  straightforward
  703
spade-husbandry
  371
spahi 726
span *join* 43
  link 45
  duality 89
  time 106
  transient 111
  distance 196
  near 196
  length 200
  short 201
  measure 466
  – new 124
spangle *spark* 420
  ornament 847
spaniel *dog* 366
  servile 886
spanish fly 171
spank *swift* 274
  flog 972
spanking *large* 192
  – pace 274
spanner 633
spar *beam* 214
  quarrel 713
  contend 720
spare *extra* 37
  small 193
  meagre 203
  refrain 623
  store 636
  scanty 640
  redundant 641
  disuse 678
  inaction 681
  relinquish 782
  give 784
  economy 817
  exempt 927a
  temperate 953
  enough and to –
  639
  not a moment to –
  682
  to – 641
  – diet 956
  – no expense 816
  – no pains 686
  – room 180
  – time 685
spared: be –
  live 359
  it cannot be – 630
sparge 337
spargefaction
  scatter 73
  wet 337
sparing [*see* spare]
  small 32

economy 817
  parsimony 819
  temperate 953
  with a – hand 819
  with no – hand
  639
  – of praise 932
  – of words 585
spark *small* 32
  heat 382
  light 420
  luminary 423
  wag 844
  fop 854
  as the –s fly up-
  wards *habit* 613
sparkle
  bubble 353
  glisten 420
sparkling
  vigorous 574
  excitement 824
  cheerful 836
  wit 842
  beauty 845
  with – eyes 827
sparse 73
sparsity 103
Spartacus 742
spartan 739
spasm
  sudden change 146
  violence 173
  agitation 315
  pain 378
spasmodic
  discontinuous 70
  irregular 139
  changeable 149
  violent 173
spat 225, 713
spate 348
spathic 204
spatter *dirt* 653
spatterdash 225
spatula 191, 272
spavined 655
spawn *produce* 161
  offspring 167
  dirt 653
spay 38, 158
speak 560, 580, 582
  – one fair 894
  – for 937
  – ill of 932, 934
  – for itself 518,
  528
  – low 581
  – of *meaning* 516
  publish 531
  speak 582
  – out *make*
  manifest 525
  artless 703
  – softly 581
  – to 586
  – up 411
  – up for 937
  – volumes 467
  – well of 931
speakeasy 189, 964
speaker
  interpreter 524
  chairman 694
speakie 964
speaking: much –
  584

way of – 521
  – likeness 554
  on – terms 888
speaking-trumpet
  418
spear 260, 727
  – shaped 253
spearman 726
special 79
  – correspondent
  593
special pleader 968
special pleading
  sophistry 477
speciali gratiâ 760
specialist 662, 700
speciality **79**
specialty
  security 771
specie 800
species *kind* 75
  appearance 448
  human – 372
specific *special* 79
  remedy 662
  – gravity 321
specification 594
specify
  particularize 79
  tell 527
  name 564
specimen 82
specious
  probable 472
  sophistical 477
  beauty 845
  flattering 933
  pardonable 937
speck 32
speckle 440, 848
spectacle
  appearance 448
  prodigy 872
  show 882
  drama 599
spectacles 445
  look through rose
  colored – 523
spectacular 882
spectator **444**
spectral 4, 980
spectre
  fallacy of vision
  443
  ugly 846
  ghost 980
spectroscope
  light 420
  color 428
  optical instru-
  ment 445
spectrum
  color 428
  variegation 440
  optical illusion
  443
speculate
  view 441
  think 451
  suppose 514
  chance 621
  essay 675
  traffic 794
speculation
  experiment 463
  cards 840
speculative 463, 514

speculum 445
  veluti in – 446
sped *completed* 729
speech **582**
  figure of – 521
  parts of – 567
speechify 582
speechless 403, 581
speechmaker 582
speed
  velocity 274
  activity 682
  haste 684
  help 707
  succeed 731
  with breathless –
  684
  God – 731, 906
speedily *soon* 132
speedometer 200,
  274, 553
speedway 840
speer 455, 461
spell *period* 106
  influence 175
  read 539
  letter 561
  necessity 601
  motive 615
  exertion 686
  charm **993**
  cast a – 992
  wonder 870
  knurr and – 840
  – for 865
  – out *interpret* 522
spell-bound 601,
  615
spence 636
spencer 225
spend *effuse* 297
  waste 638
  give 784
  purchase 795
  expend 809
  – freely 816
  – time 106
  – time in 683
  – one's time in
  625
spender 818
spendthrift 818
spent 160, 688
spermaceti 356
spermatic 168
spermatize 168
spero, dum spiro –
  858
spes sibi quisque
  604
spew 297
sphacelus 655
sphere *rank* 26
  domain 74
  space 180
  region 181
  ball 249
  world 318
  business 625
  – of influence 181,
  780
spheroid 249
spherule 249
sphery 318
sphinx *monster* 83
  oracle 513
  ambiguous 520

riddle 533
spial 668
spice
  small quantity 32
  mixture 41
  pungent 392
  condiment 393
spiced 390
spicilegium 72, 596
spick and span 123
spiculate 253
spiculum 253
spicy 400, 824
spigot 263
spike *sharp* 253
  pierce 260
  plug 263
  – guns 158, 645
spikebit 262
spikenard 356
spill *filament* 205
  stopper 263
  shed 297
  splash 348
  match 388
  waste 638
  lavish 818
  – blood 722
  – and pelt 59
spin *flying* 267
  rotate 312
  pluck 610
  – out *protract* 110
  late 133
  prolong 200
  diffuse style 573
  – the wheel 140
  – a long yarn 549
spindle 312
spindling 203
spindle-shanks 203
spindle-shaped 253
spindrift 353
spine 222, 253
spinel 847
spinet *copse* 367
  harpsichord 417
spinney 367
spinner of yarns
  594
spinosity
  unintelligible 519
  discourtesy 895
  sullenness 901a
spinous *prickly* 253
spinster 374, 904
spiracle 351
spiral 248
spire *height* 206
  convolution 248
  peak 253
  soar 305
spirit *essence* 5
  immateriality 317
  fuel 388
  intellect 450
  meaning 516
  vigorous language
  574
  activity 682
  affections 820
  courage 861
  ghost 980
  bad – 980
  keep one's – up
  hope 858
  with life and – 682

unclean – 978
– away 791
– up 615, 824
Spirit, the Holy –
976
spirited
language 574
active 682
sensitive 822
cheerful 836
brave 861
generous 942
spiritless
insensible 823
sad 837
cowardly 862
spirit-level 213
spiritoso *music* 415
spirit-rapping 992
spirits *drink* 298,
959
cheer 836
spirit-stirring 824
spiritual
immaterial 317
psychical 450
heterodoxy 984
divine 976
pious 987
– director 996
– existence 987
spiritualism
immateriality 317
intellect 450
sorcery 992
spiritualize 317
reasoning 476
spirituel 842
spirt *eject* 297
stream 348
haste 684
exertion 686
spirtle *disperse* 73
splash 348
spissitude 321, 352
spit *pointed* 253
perforate 260
eject 297
rotate 312
rain 348
– fire *irascible* 901
spite 907 ·
in – of
disagreement 24
notwithstanding
30
counteraction 179
opposition 708
in – of one's teeth
unwilling 603
compulsion 744
spiteful 898, 907
hating 898
spittle 299
spittoon 191
splanchnology 329
splash *affuse* 337
stream 348
spatter 653
parade 882
make a –
fame 873
display 882
–board 666
splay 291
–footed 243
spleen

melancholy 837
hatred 898
anger 900
sullen 901a
harbor – 907
spleenless 906
splendor
bright 420
beautiful 845
glorious 873
display 882
splenetic 837, 901a
splice *join* 43
cross 219
interjacent 228
repair 660
– the main brace
tipsy 959
spliced, be –
marriage 903
splint 215
splinter
small piece 32
divide 44
filament 205
brittle 328
split *divide* 44
discontinuity 70
bisect 91
brittle 328
divulge 529
quarrel 713
fail 732
portion 786
laugh 838
– the difference
29, 774
– the ears } 404
– the head} 410
– hairs
discriminate 465
sophistry 477
fastidiousness 868
– upon a rock 732
– one's sides 838
splutter *energy* 171
spit 297
stammer 583
haste 684
spoil *vitiate* 659
hinder 706
lenity 740
plunder 791
booty 793
deface 846
satiate 869
– sport 706
– trade 708
spoiled child 869,
899
– of fortune 734
spoiler 792
spoke *radius* 200
tooth 253
obstruct 706
put a – in one's
wheel *render*
powerless 158
hinder 706
spokesman 524,
582
spolia opima 793
spoliate 791
spoliative 793
spondee 597
spondulics 800
sponge *moisten* 339

dry 340
pulp 354
clean 652
despoil 791
hanger on 886
drunkard 959
apply the –
obliterate 552
non-payment 808
– out 552
sponging-house 752
spongy *porous* 252
soft 324
marshy 345
sponsion 771
sponsor
witness 467
security 771
be – for
promise 768
obligation 926
sponsorship 771
spontaneous
voluntary 600
willing 602
impulsive 612
spontoon 727
spoof 545
spook 980
spool 312
spoon
receptacle 191
ladle 272
bill and coo 902
born with a silver
– in one's mouth
734
Spoonerism 218,
853
spoonful 25, 32
spoon-like 252
spoon-meat 298
spoony *foolish* 499
lovesick 902
spoor 551
sporadic 73, 137,
657
spore 330
sport *killing* 361
chase 622
amusement 840
show off 882
in – *pastime* 840
humor 842
the – of 749
– of fortune 735
sporting *killing* 361
contention 720
amusement 840
– dog 366
sportive 836, 840
sports 686
sportsman 361, 622,
840
sportulary 784, 785
sportule 784
sporule 330
spot *place* 182
discover 480a
mark 550
dirt 653
blemish 848
blot 874
on the –
instantly 113
present time 118
soon 132

in one's presence
186
spotless *perfect* 650
clean 652
innocent 946
spot light 423, 599
spots in the sun,
see – *fastidious*
868
spotted
variegated 440
damaged 659
spousal 903
spouse 88, 903
spouseless 904
spout *egress* 295
flow out 348
conduit 350
speak 582
act 599
pawn 771, 787,
788
sprag 215
sprain 158, 160
sprat to catch a:
– herring 794
– whale 699
sprawl *length* 200
horizontal 213
descend 306
spray *sprig* 51
vaporizer 336
foam 353
spread *enlarge* 35
disperse 73
broadcast 78
expanse 180
expand 194
diverge 291
feast 298
publish 531
– abroad 531
– canvas 267
– out 194
– sail 267
– a shade 421
– to 196
– the toils 545
spree 840
spretae injuria
formae *ugly* 846
disrespect 929
detraction 934
sprig *branch* 51
child 129
shillelagh 727
sprightly 836, 842
spring *early* 125
source 153
strength 159
velocity 274
recoil 277
fly 293
leap 309
elasticity 325
rivulet 348
instrument 633
store 636
–s of action 615
– back 277
– to one's feet 307
– from 154
– a leak 651, 659
– a mine
destroy 162
unexpected 508
attack 716

– a project 626
– up *begin* 66
event 151
grow 194
ascend 305
visible 446
hot – 382
– upon 789
spring balance 319
springe 545
spring-gun 545
spring tide
greatness 31
increase 35
completeness 52
youth 127
high 206
low 207
wave 348
water 337
springy 325
sprinkle *add* 37
mix 41
scatter 73
wet 337
rain 348
variegate 440
baptize 998
sprinkler 348, 385
sprinkling
small quantity 32
sprint 274
sprit *sprout* 167
support 215
sprite 979, 980
sprout *grow* 35
germinate 161
offspring 167
expand 194
– from *result* 154
spruce 652, 845
– up 847
sprue 653
sprung 651, 659
spry 682, 836
spud 272
spume 353
spun out 110, 573
spunk 861
spur
pointed 250
sharp 253
incite 615
hasten 684
win –s *succeed* 731
glory 873
on the – of the
moment
instantly 113
now 118
soon 132
opportune 134
impulse 612
– gearing 633
the – of necessity
745
spurious
erroneous 495
false 544
deceptive 545
illegitimate 925
spurlos versenkt 2,
449
spurn *reject* 55
disdain 930
spurred 253
spurt

retract one's – 283
take – plan 626
 prepare 673
 conduct 692
tread in the – of
 281
stercoraceous 653
stereography 591
stereometry 466
stereopticon 445
stereoscope 445
stereoscopic 446
stereotype copy 21
 mark 550
 engraving 558
 printing 591
stereotyped
 uniform 16
 stable 150
 habit 613
sterile 169, 645, 732
sterilize 652
sterling true 494,
 944
 – coin 800
stern rear 235
 severe 739
 discourteous 895
 – necessity 601,
 603
 – truth 494
sternmost 235
sternutation
 sneeze 349
 sound 409
sternway 267
stertorous 402, 580
stet 150
 – pro ratione vo-
 luntas 600
stethoscope 418
stevedore 271, 613,
 690
stew food 298
 heat 382
 cook 384
 difficulty 704
 emotion 821
 excitement 825
 annoyance 828
 bagnio 961
 in a – angry 900
steward 637
 director 694
 agent 758
 treasurer 801
stewardship 692,
 693
stewpan 386
stichomancy 511
stick adhere 46
 cease 142
 staff 215
 stab 260
 remain quiet 265
 fool 501
 bungler 701
 weapon 727
 scourge 975
dirty end of the –
 699
give the – to 972
 – at doubt 485
 averse 603
 – fast firm 150
 difficulty 704
 – in one's gizzard

830, 900
 – in 300
 – law 972
 – in the mud
 304, 732
 – at nothing
 resolve 604
 active 682
 rash 863
 – out 250
 – to 143, 604a
 – in the throat
 hoarse 581
 not say 585
 dislike 867
 –.up 212, 307, 791
 – up for aid 707
 applaud 931
 vindicate 937
stickle 603, 616
 – for 720, 794
stickler 606
 severity 739
sticky
 cohering 46
 viscid 352
stiff rigid 323
 style 579
 severe 739
 coactive 751
 ugly 846
 affected 855
 haughty 878
 pompous 882
 – breeze 349
stiffen 323
stiff-necked 606
stiffness
 stability 150
stifle kill 361
 silence 403
 conceal 528
stifled
 faint sound 405
stifling hot 382
stigmatize 874
 censure 932
 accuse 938
stile way 627
 hindrance 706
help a lame dog
 over a – 707
stiletto 262, 727
still
 on the other hand
 30
 moderate 174
 not moving 265
 vaporization 336
 furnace 386
 silent 403
 – less 467
 – life matter 316
 painting 556
 – more
 superior 33
 evidence 467
 – small voice 405
 in – water 714
 still-born 360, 732
stillroom 636
stillicidium 348
stilted
 elevated 307
 – style 577
 ridiculous 853
 affected 855

boasting 884
stilts support 215
on – high 206
 elevated 307
 hyperbolical 549
 proud 878
 boasting 884
stimulant 662
stimulate
 energy 171
 violence 173
 incite 615
 excite 824
stimulating
 suggestive 514
stimulus 615
sting pain 378
 tingle 380
 poison 663
 excite 824
 mental suffering
 830
 anger 900
stinging
 pungent 392
stingo 298
stingy 819
stink 401
 – in the nostrils
 unpleasant 830
 dislike 867
 hate 898
stink-bomb 727
stink-pot 401
stint degree 26
 limit 233
 scanty 640
 begrudge 819
stintless 639
stipend salary 973
stipendiary
 subject 749
 receiving 785
 magistrate 967
stipple
 variegate 440
 painting 556
 engraving 558
stipulate 769, 770
 – for 720
stipule 51
stir energy 171
 move 264
 agitation 315
 excite 375
 activity 682
 jail 752
 emotion 824
make a – 642, 682
 – about 682
 – the blood 824,
 900
 – up dissension
 713
 – the embers 163,
 824
 – the feelings 824
 – the fire 384
 – a question 461,
 476
 – one's stumps
 266, 682
 – up mix 41
 violent 173
 excite 824
stirps kin 11
 source 153

paternity 166
stirring events 151
 important 642
 active 682
 – news 532
stirrup
 support 215
with a foot in the
 – 293
stirrup-cup 293, 959
stitch junction 43
 .pain 378
 work 680
 – in time 132
 – of work 686
stive 384
stiver 800
stoat 401
stoccado 717
stock kinship 11
 quantity 25
 origin 153
 paternity 166
 collar 225
 soup 298
 fool 501
 habitual 613
 materials 635
 store 636
 property 780
 merchandise 798
 money 800
 in – 777
 laughing – 857
lay in a – 637
take – inspect 457
 accounts 811
 – exchange 799
 – still 265
 – in trade
 means 632
 store 636
 property 780
 merchandise 798
 – with 637
stockade 717
stocked, well – 639
stock exchange 621
stock-farm 370
stocking 225
 hoard 800
stock-jobbing 794
stock operator 621
stocks prison 752
 funds 802
 punishment 975
on the –
 business 625
 preparation 673
 incomplete 730
 – and stones 316,
 823
stocky 201
stodge 957
stoicism
 insensibility 823
 inexcitability 826
 disinterested 942
 temperance 953
stoke 388
stoker 268
stole 999
stolen: – away 671
 – goods 793
stolid 499, 843
stomach pouch 191
 taste 390

brook 826
 desire 865
not have the – to
 603
turn the – 830
 – of an ostrich 957
stomacher 225
stone heavy 319
 dense 321
 hard 323
 kill 361
 lithography 558
 material 635
 attack 716
 weapon 727
 punish 972
corner – 642
go down like a –
 310
cast the first – at
 938
heart of – 823, 907
key– 642
 musical –s 417
no – unturned
 461, 686
 philosopher's –
 662
 precious – 648
stepping – 627
throw a – at
 attack 716
 censure 932
 accuse 938
throw –s at 907
tomb– 363
mark with a
 white – 642
throw a – in one's
 own garden 699
 – dead 360
 – of Sisyphus 645
stone-blind 442
stone-colored 432
stone-deaf 419
stone's throw 197
stoneware 384
stony 323
stony-hearted 907,
 919
stooge 711, 746, 886
stook 72
stool 215
between two –s
 704
 – of repentance
 950
 – pigeon 527, 548
stoop slope 217
 lower 308
 humble 879
 servile 886
 dishonorable 940
 – to conquer 702
stop end 67
 cease 142
 close 261
 rest 265
 silent 403
 danger 665
 inaction 681
 hinder 706
 prohibit 761
put a – to 142
 – the breath 361
 – the ears 419
 – a flow 348

cess 653
sumpter-horse 271
sumptuary 800, 809
sumptuous 882
sum-total 50
sun 318
  luminary 423
  glory 873
bask in the – 377
going down of
  the – 126
farthing candle to
  the – 645
under the – 180,
  318
as the – at noon-
  day *bright* 420
  certain 474
  plain 525
– oneself 384
Sun:
  – of Righteousness
  976
sunbeam 420
  –s from cucumbers
  471
sunburn *heat* 384
sunburnt *brown* 433
Sunday:
  – Monday &c. 138
  –'s best 847, 882
  – school 542
sunder 44
sundial 114
sundown 126
sundry 102
sunk [*see* sink]
  deep 208
  – fence 717
  – in iniquity 945
  – in oblivion 508
sunken rocks 667
sunless 421
sunlight 420
sunny *warm* 382
  luminous 420
  cheerful 836
sunny side 829
  view the – 858
  – of the hedge 734
sun-painting 556
sunrise 125
sunset 126
  at – 133
sunshade 223, 424
sunshine *light* 420
  prosperity 734
  happy 827
  cheerful 836
sunstroke 384, 503
sun-up 125
suo: – *periculo* 926
  – *sibi gladio hunc
  jugulo
  absurdity* 479
  retaliation 718
sup *small quantity*
  32
  feed 298
  – full of horrors
  828
super *theatrical* 599
superable 470
superabound 641
superadd 37
superannuated 128
superb 845

supercargo 694
supercherie 545
supercilious
  proud 878
  insolent 885
  disrespectful 929
  scornful 930
superdreadnought
  726
supereminence
  648, 873
supererogation 641,
  645
superexaltation 873
superexcellence
  648
superfetation 37,
  168
superficial
  shallow 209
  outside 220
  misjudging 481
  ignorant 491
  – *extent* 180
superficies 220
superfine 648
superfluitant 305
superfluity 40, 641
superfluous 645
superhuman 650,
  976
superimpose 233
superimposed 206
superincumbent
  206, 319
superinduce
  change 140
  cause 153
  produce 161
superintend 693
superintendent 694
superior *greater* 33
  – *in size* 194
  important 642
  good 648
  director 694
superiority 33
superjunction 37
superlative 33
superlatively good
  648
superman 33
supernal 206, 210,
  981
supernatant 206,
  305
supernatural 976,
  980
  – *aid* 707
supernumerary
  adjunct 39
  theatrical 599
  reserve 636
  redundant 641
superpose 37, 223
supersaturate 641
superscription 550,
  590
supersede
  substitute 147
  disuse 678
  relinquish 782
supersensible 317
superstition
  credulity 486
  error 495
  religion 984

superstratum 220
superstructure 729
supertax 812
supertonic 413
supervacaneous
  641
supervene
  extrinsic 6
  be added 37
  succeed 117
  happen 151
supervise 693
supervisor 694
supination 213
supine
  horizontal 213
  inverted 218
  sluggish 683
  mentally torpid
  823
suppeditate 637
supper 298
supplant 147
supple *soft* 324
  servile 886
supplement
  addition 37
  adjunct 39
  completion 52
  publication 531
  book 593
suppletory 37
suppliant 765, 767
supplicate *beg* 765
  pity 914
  worship 990
supplies
  materials 635
  aid 707
  money 800
supply *store* 636
  provide 637
  give 784
  – *aid* 707
  – deficiencies 52
  – the place of 147
  – and transport
  726
support *perform* 170
  sustain 215
  evidence 467
  preserve 670
  aid 707
  feel 821
  endure 826
  vindicate 937
  – *life* 359
supporter 711
  –s *heraldic* 550
suppose 514
supposing 469
supposition 514
supposititious 546
suppress
  destroy 162
  conceal 528
  silent 581
  restrain 751
suppression of
  truth 544
suppuration 653
suppute 85
supralapsarian 984
supramundane 939
supremacy 33, 737
supreme 33
  summit 210

authority 737
  in a – *degree* 31
Supreme Being 976
surbate 659
surbated 688
surcease 142
surcharge 641
  – and falsify 811
surcingle 45
surcoat 225
surd *number* 84
  deaf 419
  silent letter 561
sure *certain* 474
  belief 484
  safe 664
  make – against
  673
  make – of
  inquire 461
  take 789
  you may be – 535
  to be – *assent* 488
  on – ground 664
  security 771
sure-footed
  careful 459
  skilful 698
surely 489, 602, 870
sureness 474
surety 474, 664
surf 348, 353
surface *outside* 220
  texture 329
  below the – 526
  lie on the – 518,
  525
  skim the – 460
Surface, Joseph –
  548
surfeit 641, 869
surge *swarm* 72
  swell 305
  rotation 312
  wave 348
surgeon 662
surgery 662
surgit amari
  aliquid 651
surly *gruff* 895
  sullen 901a
  unkind 907
surmise 514
surmount *be
  superior* 33
  tower 206
  transcursion 303
  ascent 305
  – a difficulty
  overcome 731
surmountable 470
surname 564
surpass
  be superior 33
  grow 194
  go beyond 303
  outshine 873
surplice 999
surplus 40, 641
surplusage 641
surprint 550
surprise
  non-expectation
  508
  unprepared 674
  wonder 870

surprisingly 31
surrebutter &c.
  answer 462
  pleadings 969
surrender 725, 782
  – one's life 360
surreptitious
  furtive 528
  deceptive 545
  untrue 546
surrogate 759
surround 227, 229
surroundings
  amidst such and
  such – 183
sursum corda 990
surtax 812
surtout *coat* 225
surveillance
  care 459
  direction 693
  under – 938
survene 151
survey 441, 466
surveyor 85, 694
survive *remain* 40
  long time 110
  permanent 141
susceptibility
  power 157
  tendency 176
  liability 177
  sensibility 375
  motive 615
  impressibility 822
  irascibility 901
suscipient 785
suscitate *cause* 153
  produce 161
  stir up 173
  excite 824
suspect *doubt* 485
  suppose 514
suspected 938
suspectless 484
suspend *defer* 133
  discontinue 142
  hang 214
suspended anima-
  tion 823
suspender 45, 214
suspense
  cessation 142
  uncertainty 475
  expectation 507
  irresolution 605
  in – *inert* 172
suspension
  cessation 142
  hanging 214
  music 413
  – of arms 723
suspicion *doubt* 485
  incredulity 487
  knowledge 490
  supposition 514
  fear 860
  under – 938
suspiration 839
sustain
  continue 143
  strength 159
  perform 170
  support 215
  preserve 670
  aid 707
  endure 821

T

T, to a – 494
tab 39, 550, 747
tabard 225
tabby *mottled* 440
  gossip 588
tabefaction 195
tabernacle 189, 1000
  house 189
  temple 1000
tabid *shrunk* 195
  thin 203
  disease 655
  deteriorated 659
table
  arrangement 60
  list 86
  defer 133
  layer 204
  support 215
  flat 251
  repast 298
  writing 590
on the – 626, 673
turn the –s 218, 468
under the –
  hidden 528
  drunk 959
– of the Lord 1000
– the motion 624
tableau *list* 86
  appearance 448
  painting 556
  theatrical 599
table-cloth 652
table d'hôte 298
table-land 213, 344
tabescent 195
tablet *layer* 204
  flat 251
  record 551
  writing 590
  remedy 662
table-talk 532, 588
tablets of the memory 505
table-turning 992
tabloid 531, 662
taboo 762, 992
tabor 417
tabouret 215
tabret 417
tabula rasa
  inexistence 2
  absence 187
  ignorance 491
  obliterated 552
  facility 705
tabulate 60, 69
tabulation 551
tachometer 274
tachygraphy 590
tachy case 191
tacit 526
taciturnity **585**
Tacitus
  concise style 572
tack *join* 43
  nails 45
  change course 140
  sharp 253
  direction 278
  turn 279
  food 289

way 627
go upon another – 607
wrong – 732
– to *add* 37
tackle
  fastening 45
  gear 633
  try 675
  undertake 676
  manage 693
tacky 352
tact *touch* 379
  discrimination 465
  wisdom 498
  skill 698
  taste 850
  want of – 851
tactful 894
tactician 700
tactics 692, 722
tactless 895
tactile &c. 379
tadpole 129
taedium vitae 837, 841
tag *small* 32
  addition 37
  adjunct 39
  fastening 45
  sequel 65
  end 67
  point 253
  sheep 366
  – after 281
tagrag and bobtail 876
tail *sequel* 65
  end 67
  pendent 214
  back 235
  aircraft 273
  estate – 780
  turn – 623
  – off *decrease* 36
tail-coat 225
tailor 225, 690
tailoring 225, 882
tail-piece *sequel* 65
  rear 235
  engraving 558
  ornament 847
tail-race 350
taint
  imperfection 651
  dirt 653
  decay 659
  disgrace 874
tainted 401, 655
taintless 652
taj 225
take *eat* 298
  believe 484
  know 490
  understand 518
  succeed 731
  receive 785
  appropriate 789
  captivate 829
give and – 718
– a back 508, 870
– an account of 85
– action 680
– advice 695
– after 17
– aside 586

– away
  annihilate 2
  subtract 38
  remove 185
  seize 789
– back again 790
– a back seat 34
– by [*see below*]
– the cake 33
– care 668, 864
– care of 459, 664
– no care of 460
– off 293
– one's chance 621, 675
– one's choice 609
– things as they come 683, 826
– comfort 831, 834
– the consequences 154
– coolly 826
– a course 692
– its course 143, 151
– no denial 606, 744
– a disease 655
– down
  swallow 298
  depress 308
  record 551
  write 590
  dismantle 681
  humiliate 874
  censure 932
– easily 826
– effect 151, 170
– an ell 885
– exception 932
– one's fancy 829, 865
– fire 384
– flight 623
– from 38, 789
– for [*see below*]
– the good the gods provide 831
– heart 831, 836
– to heart 828, 832
– heed 864
– a hint 498
– hold of 46, 789
– hold of the mind 484
– in [*see below*]
– an infection 655
– no interest in 823
– into [*see below*]
– it 484, 514
– the lead 62
– a leaf out of another's book 19
– a lease 788
– leave of 624
– a liberty 748
– away life 361
– a likeness 554
– measures 626
– money 810
– no note of 460
– no note of time 115
– notice 457

– one's oath 535
– off [*see below*]
– oneself off 293
– on [*see below*]
– one with another 29
– out 301, 552
– over 783
– part with 709
– a pattern by 19
– a peep 441
– pen in hand 590
– to pieces 44, 681
– place 151
– the place of 147
– possession of 589
– precedence 33, 62
– its rise 66, 154
– root 150, 184
– the shine out of 33
– ship 267
– steps 673, 680
– stock 85
– time
  duration 106
  late 133
  leisure 685
– time by the forelock 132
– to *habit* 613
  pursuit 622
  use 677
  like 827
  desire 865
  love 897
– on trust 484
– a turn 140
– up [*see below*]
– upon oneself 676, 768
– warning 668
– wing 293
– one at one's word 769
take by
– the button 586
– the hand 707
– surprise 508, 674
take for 484
– better or for worse 609
– gospel 486
– granted 484
take in *include* 54
  shorten 201
  admit 296
  understand 518
  deceive 545
  receive money 785
– good part
  be calm 826
  be pleased 827
  content 831
– hand *teach* 537
  undertake 676
  aid 707
– an idea 498
– sail 275
take into
– account
  include 76
  discriminate 465
  qualify 469
– consideration 451

– custody 751
– one's head 514, 608
take off *mimic* 19
  destroy 162
  remove 185
  divest 226
  depart 293
  discount 813
  ridicule 856
– one's hands 785
– the hat 894
take on
  attempt 675
  discontent 832
  melancholy 837
– credit 484
– trust 484
take up
  elevate 307
  inquire 461
  dissent 595
  choose 609
  undertake 676
  befriend 707
  arrest 751
  borrow 788
  censure 932
– arms 722
– a case 476
– one's abode 184
– the cudgels 716, 720
– an inquiry 461
– money 788
– one's pen 590
– with
  attention 457
  use 677
  content 831
taken, be –
  die 360
  ill 655
  with 897
taker 789
taking **789**
  infectious 657
in a – *pained* 828
  angry 900
talapoin 996
talbotype 556
tale
  counting 85
  narrative 594
  thereby hangs a – 526
twice-told –
  diffuse style 573
  weary 841
tale-bearer 532
talent 698
  bury one's – in a napkin 528
  not put one's – in a napkin 878
talionis, lex – 718, 922
taliped 243
talisman 747, 993
talismanic 992
talk
  unsubstantial 4
  rumor 532
  speak 582
  conversation 588
small – 588
– big *boast* 884

insolent 885
threat 909
– glibly 584
– nonsense 497
– of signify 516
publish 531
intend 620
– to oneself 589
– oneself out of
  breath 584
– over
  confer 588
  persuade 615
– to in private 586
– at random
  illogical 477
  loquacity 584
– together 588
– against time
  time 106
  protract 110
  inaction 681
– of the town
  gossip 588
  fame 873
talkative 582, 584
talked of 873
talkies 599, 840
talking, fine –
  over-estimation
  482
tall 206
– hat 225
– talk 884
tallage 812
tallies 85
tallow 356
– candle 423
tallow-faced 429
tally agree 23
  list 85, 86
  sign 550
  credit 805
– with conform 82
tally-ho 622
tally-man 797
talma 225
Talmud 985
talons
  authority 737
  claws 781
talus 217
tam-o'-shanter 225
tambourine 417
tame inert 172
  moderate 174
  domesticate 370
  teach 537
  feeble 575
  subjugate 749
  insensible 823
  calm 826
tameless
  violent 173
  malevolent 907
Tammany 940
tamp 261, 276
tamper with
  alter 140
  seduce 615
  injure 659
  meddle 682
tan color 433
tandem
  at length 200
  vehicle 272
tang taste 390

bane 663
tangent 199
  angle 217
fly off at a –
  deviate 279
  diverge 291
  excitable 825
tangere ulcus 505
tangible
  material 316
  touch 379
  exact 494
  sufficient 639
  useful 644
tangle 61, 219
tangled 59, 704
  weave a – web 704
tango 840
tank pool 343
  reservoir 636
  armored vehicle
  726
tankard 191
tanker 273
tant: – mieux 838
– s'en faut 489
– soit peu 32
tantaene animis
  coelestibus irae
  900
tantalize balk 509
  induce 615
  desire 865
tantalizing
  exciting 824
Tantalus: torment
  of – 507, 865
tantamount 27, 516
tantara 407
tantas componere
  lites 723
tanti 642
tantivy speed 274
tantrums 900
tap open 260
  plug 263
  hit 276
  let out 295, 297
  sound 406
turn on the – 297
tap-dance 840
tape string 205
  measure 466
– machine 553
taper contract 195
  narrow 203
  candle 423
– to a point 253
tapestry 556, 847
tapinois, en – 528
tapis: on the –
  event 151
  topic 454
  intention 620
  plan 626
tap-root 153
taps 550
tapster 746
tar cover 223
  sailor 269
  pitch 356a
– and feather 929,
  972
taradiddle 546
tarantas 272
tarantella 840
tarboosh 225

tardiloquence 583
tardy 133, 275
tare 40a
– and tret 813
tares 645
targe 717
target 620
  shield 717
tariff 812
tarmac 635
tarn 343
tarnish
  discoloration 429
  soil 653
  deface 848
  disgrace 874
tarpaulin 223
tarry remain 110,
  265
  later 133
  continue 141
– for expect 507
tart pastry 298, 396
  acid 397
  rude 895
  irascible 901
  harlot 962
tartan 440
tartane 273
Tartar choleric 901
  catch a – dupe 547
  unskilful 699
  retaliation 718
tartar dirt 653
– emetic 663
Tartarus 982
Tartufe
  hypocrisy 544
  deceiver 548
  impiety 988
task lesson 537
  business 625
  put to use 677
  fatigue 688
  command 741
hard – 704
set a – 741
take to – 932
– the memory 505
taskmaster 694
tass 191
tassel 847
taste sapidity 390
  experience 821
  good taste 850
man of – 850
to one's – savory
  394
  pleasant 829
  love 897
tasteful 850
tasteless insipid
  391
tasty 394, 850
tâtonner 463
tatter
  small quantity 32
tatterdemalion 876
Tattersalls 799
tatters garments
  225
tear to – 162
tatting 847
tattle 588
tattler 532, 588
tattoo
  drumming 407

mottled 440
  summons 741
taught [see teach]
  fastened 43
taunt 929, 938
tauromachy 720
taut 43
tautology 104, 573
tavern 189
tawdry 851
tawny 433, 436
tax inquire 461
  employ 677
  fatigue 688
  command 741
  compel 744
  request 765
  accounts 811
  impost 812
  discount 813
  accuse 938
– one's energies
  686
– the memory 505
taxi 266
taxi-cab 272
taxi-driver 268
taxidermy 368
taxis 60
taxonomy 60
tazza 191
Te Deum 990
te fabula narratur,
  de – retaliate 718
  condemn 971
tea 298
teach 537
– one's grand-
  mother 641, 885
– one his place 879
teachable 539
teacher 540, 673
teaching 537
false – 538
teacup, storm in a –
  overrate 482, 549
  exaggerate 549
teagown 225
team assemblage
  69, 72
teamster 694
tea-party 892
tea-pot 191
tear separate 44
  violence 173
  move rapidly 274
  excite 825
  weeping 839
– away from 789
– oneself away
  623
– asunder one's
  bonds 750
– one's hair 839
– out 301
– to pieces
  separate 44
  destroy 162
– up destroy 162
tear-gas 663, 727
tearful 839
tearing passion 839
tears: draw – 830
  shed – 839
– in one's eyes
  excited 824
  sad 837

tease annoy 830
  spite 907
teaser difficult 704
teasing 830
teat 250
tea-table talk 588
technic 698
technica, memoria
– 505
technical
  conformable 82
  workmanlike 698
– college 542
– education 537
– knowledge 698
– school 542
– term 564
technicality
  special 79
  cant term 563
  formulary 697
technique 556, 698
technocracy 698
technology 698
techy 901
tedious 841
while away the –
  hours 681
tedium 841
teem
  produce 161
  productive 168
  abound 639
– with multitude
  102
teemful 168
teeming crowd 72
teemless 169
'teens 98
in one's – 127, 129
teeter 314
teeth 330, 781
armed to the –
  673, 717, 722
between the – 405
cast in one's – 938
chattering of – 383
have cut one's eye
  – 698
in the – of 704, 708
grind one's – 900
the run of one's –
  815
set one's – 604
show one's – 900
in spite of one's –
  708, 744
make one's – chat-
  ter 385, 860
set the – on edge
  scrape 331
  saw 397
  stridor 410
  pain the feelings
  830
tee 66
teetotalism 953,
  958
teetotum 312, 840
teg 366
tegument 223
teind 99
teinoscope 445
tekel upharsin 668
telautograph 553
telegram 532
telegraph

velocity 274
messenger 534
signal 550
– boy 534
by – haste 684
telegraphone 553
telegraphy
  publication 531
teleology 620
telemeter 200
telepathy 992
telephone 418
  inform 527
  messenger 534
telescope 445
– word 572
telescopic 196
telesis 658
telesm 993
television 993
tell count 85
  influence 175
  evidence 467
  inform 527
  speak 582
  describe 594
  succeed 731
let me – you 535
who can – 475
– one's beads 990, 998
– the cause of 522
– fortunes 511
– how 155
– a lie 544
– a piece of one's mind 529
– of 467
– off 85
– one plainly 527
– its own tale 518
– tales
  disclose 529
– the truth 543
teller treasurer 801
– of tales 594
telling 175
  graphic 518
  important 642
  exciting 824
with – effect 171, 175
telltale news 532
  indicator 550
  knave 941
telluric 318
telum imbelle 158
temerity 863
temper nature 5
  state 7
  moderate 174
  elasticity 323
  pliability 324
  modify 469
  prepare 673
  affections 820
  irascibility 901
command of – 826
lose one's – 900
out of – 901a
trial of – 824
– the wind to the shorn lamb 834
tempera 556
temperament
  nature 5
  tendency 176

musical 413
affections 820
temperance 174, **953**
temperate
  [see temperance]
  mild 826
temperature 382
  increase of – 384
  reduction of – 385
tempest
  violence 173
  agitation 315
  wind 349
  excitement 825
tempestivity 134
tempest-tossed 824
tempestuous 59
Templar 996
Good – 958
temple house 189
  side 236
  church **1000**
– of the Holy Ghost 983a
templet 22
tempora:
O –! O mores!
  lament 839
  disreputable 874
  disapprobation 932
  improbity 940
  vice 945
– mutantur 140
temporal
  transient 111
  laical 997
lords – and spiritual 875
temporality 997
temporary 111
temporize
  protract 110
  defer 133
  cunning 702
temporizer 943
tempt entice 615
  attempt 675
  desire 865
– fortune 621, 675
– Providence 863, 885
tempter 615
  Satan 978
voice of the – 615
temulency 959
ten 98
– to one 472
– thousand 98
tenable 664
tenacity
  coherence 46
  toughness **327**
  memory 505
  resolution 604
  obstinacy 606
  retention 781
  avarice 819
  courage 861
– of life 357
– of purpose 604a
tenaculum 781
tenancy 777
tenant
  present 186
  occupier 188

possessor 779
tenantless
  absence 187
  seclusion 893
tenax propositi 204, 939
tend conduce 176
– animals 370
  aid 707
  serve 631, 746
– towards 278
tendence 749
tendency 176
tender slight 32
  ship 273
  soft 324
  painful 378
  color 428
  war vessel 726
  offer 763
  susceptible 822
  affectionate 897
  compassionate 914
– age 127
– conscience 926
– heart susceptible 822
  kind 906
  compassionate 914
– mercies [ironical]
  badness 649
  severity 739
  cruelty 907
– passion 897
– one's resignation 757
– to 707
tenderfoot 57, 541
tendon 45
tendril fastening 45
  offshoot 51
  infant 129
  filament 205
  convoluted 248
  plant 367
tenebrious 421
tenebrosity 421
tenement 189, 780
– of clay 362
tenet belief 484
tenner 800
tennis 840
– ground 213
tenor course 7
  degree 26
  direction 278
  high note 410
  singer 416
  violin 417
  meaning 516
pursue the noiseless – of one's way 881
tense hard 323
tensile 325
tension 159, 200
tensure 200
tent abode 189
  covering 223
pitch one's –
  locate 184
  arrive 292
tentacle 781
tentative 463, 675
tente d'abri 223

tented field 722
tenter-hook 214
on –s 507
tenth 99
tenths
  tithe 812
tent-pegging 840
tents, O Israel, to your – 722
tenue, en grande – 847, 882
tenuity
  smallness 32
  thinness 203
  rarity 322
tenuous
  shadowy 4
tenure
  possession 777
  property 780
  due 924
tepee 189
tepefaction 384
Tephramancy 511
tepid 382
tepidarium 386
ter quaterque beatus 827
teratology
  unconformity 83
  distortion 243
  altiloquence 577
  boasting 884
tercentenary 98, 138, 883
terceron 41
terebration 260
teres atque rotundus 249
in seipso – 650
tergiversation 283, **607**
term end 67
  place in series **71**
  period of time 106
  limit 233
  word 562
  name 564
  lease 780
termagant 901
terminal 67, 253, 292
terminate 67, 292
  limit 233
termination 154
termine, mezzo – 628
terminology 562
terminus end 67
  limit 233
  arrival 292
termless 105
terms [see term]
  circumstances **8**
  reasoning 476
  pacification 723
  conditions 770
bring to – 723
come to –
  assent 488
  pacify 723
  submit 725
  consent 762
  compact 769
couch in – 566
on friendly – 888
in no measured –

574
ternary 93
ternion 92
Terpsichore 416, 840
terra: – cotta
  baked 384
  sculpture 557
– firma
  support 215
  land 342
  safety 664
– incognita 491
terrace houses 189
  level 213
terrain 181
terraqueous 318
terre verte 435
terrene 318, 342
terrine 191
terrestrial 318
terrible 860
terribly greatly 31
terrier list 86
  auger 262
  dog 366
terrific 31, 830, 860
terrify 860
territorial land 342
  soldier 726
territory 181, 780
terror 860
King of –s 360
  reign of – 739, 828
terrorem, in – 860, 909
terrorism 860
  insolence 885
terrorist
  coward 862
  blusterer 887
  evil-doer 913
terse 572
tertian periodic 138
tertiary three 92
tertium quid
  dissimilar 18
  mixture 41
  combination 48
  unconformable 83
tesselated 440, 847
tesserae
  mosaic 440
  counters 550
test 463
testa, voce di – 410
testament 771
Testament 985
tester bedstead 215
  sixpence 800
testify 467, 550
testimonial 551
testimony 467
testy 901
tetanus 315
tetchy 901
tête: – baissée 863
– exaltée 503
– montée 503, 825
–à-tête two 89
  near 197
  confer 588
tether fasten 43
  locate 184
  restrain 751
  means of restraint 752

active 682
haste 684
ride full – at 622, 716
run a – at 716
– over 218
– up 307
– with 720
tilth 371, 775
tilting at the ring 840
tilt-yard 728
timber *trees* 367
materials 635
timbre 413
timbrel 417
time 106
instant 113
leisure 685
against – 684
at –s 136
behind the –s 124
course of – 109
doing –
imprisonment 752
employ one's – in 625
glass of – 106
in – *course* 109
early 132
destiny 152
measure – 114
no – *instantly* 113
soon 132
no – to lose 630, 684
no – to spare 684
ravages of – 659
slow – 275
take – *slow* 275
inaction 681
inactive 683
true – 113
waste – 683
– and again 104
– has been 122
– being 118
– to come 121
– of day 113
– drawing on 121
– enough 132
– gone by 135
– hanging on one's hands
inaction 681
leisure 685
weariness 841
– immemorial 122
– of life
duration 106
now 118
age 128
– out of mind 122
– to spare 685
– after time 104
– up 111, 134
– was 122
there being –s when 136
timeful 134
time-honored
old 124
repute 873
respected 928
time-keeper 114
time-recorder 553
timeless 135

timelessness 112
timely 132, 134
timeo Danaos 485, 864
timeous 134
time-piece 114
time-pleaser 607
timetable 605
times *present* 118
events 151
hard – 735
many – 136
– out of number 104
time-serving
tergiversation 607
cunning 702
servility 886
improbity 940
selfishness 943
time-worn *old* 124
age 128
deteriorated 659
timid *fearful* 860
cowardly 862
humble 881
timist 607
Timocracy 803
Timon of Athens
wealth 803
seclusion 893
misanthrope 911
timorous [see timid]
tin *preserve* 670
money 800
– hat 717
tinct 428
tinctorial 428
tincture
small quantity 32
mixture 41
color 428
tinctured
disposition 820
tinder *fuel* 388
irascible 901
tine 253
tinge
small quantity 32
mix 41
colour 428
tingent 428
tingle *pain* 378
touch 380
emotion 821
make the ears – 900
tink 408
tinker
repair 660
tinkle
faint sound 405
resonance 408
tinkling cymbal 517
tinnient 408
tinsel *glitter* 420
sham 545
ornament 847
frippery 851
tinsmith 690
tint 428
tintamarre 404
tintinnabulary 408
tiny 32, 193
– bit 32
tip *end* 67
summit 210

cover 223
give 784
reward 973
on –toe *high* 206
expect 507
– off 527
– the wink 550
tip-cat 840
tippet 214, 225
tipple 298, 959
tippler 959
tipstaff 965
tipsy 959
tip-top 210, 648
tirade 582, 932
tire *dress* 225
fatigue 688
worry 830
weary 841
tiré à quatre épingles 850
tirer d'affaire 672
se – 731
Tiresias 513
tiresome [see tire]
Tisiphone 173, 900
tissue *whole* 50
assemblage 72
matted 219
texture 329
tit *small* 193
pony 271
tit for tat 718
Titan 159, 980
Titania 979
titanic 192
titbit 291, 394, 829
tithe *tenth* 99
tax 812
tithing 181
titillate 840, 865
titillation 377, 380
titivate 847
title
indication 550
name 564
printing 590
right to property 780
distinction **877**
right 924
titled 875
title-deed 771
title-page 66
titter 838
tittle 32
to a – 494
tittle-tattle 532, 588
titubancy 583
titubate 306, 732
titular 562, 564
tmesis 218
T.N.T. 727
to *direction* 278
lie – 681
– all intents and purposes 27, 52
– a certain degree 32
– come 121, 152
– the credit of 805
– crown all 33, 642
– do 59
– the end of the chapter 52
– the end of time 112

– and fro 12, 314
– the full 52
– a great extent 31
– the letter 19
– a man 78
– the point 23
– the purpose 23
– a small extent 32
– some extent 26
– be sure 488
– this day 118
– wit 79
toad 649, 846
– under a harrow 378
toad-eater 886, 935
toad-eating
flattery 933
toadstool 367
toady 886
toast *roast* 384
celebrate 883
tobacco 392
toboggan 272, 840
toby *jug* 191
toccata 415
tocsin 669
tod 319
to-day 118
toddle 266, 275
toddy 298
toe 211
on the light fantastic 309, 840
toes turn up the – *die* 360
toff 854
toffee 396
toga 225, 747
assume the – virilis 131
together 88, 120
come – 290
get – 72
hang – 709
lay heads – 695
– with 37, 88
toggery 225
toil
activity 682
exertion 686
– of a pleasure 682
–s *trap* 545
toilet 225
– water 400
toilette 225
en grande – 847
toilsome 686, 704
toilworn 688
token 550
give – 525
– of remembrance 505
told, do what one is – 743
tolderolloll 838
Toledo 727
tolerable
a little 32
trifling 643
pretty good 648
not perfect 651
satisfactory 831
tolerably, get on – 736
toleration

laxity 738
lenity 740
permission 760
feeling 821
calmness 826
benevolence 906
toll *sound* 407
tax 812
– the knell 363
tollbooth
prison 752
market 799
tomahawk 727
tomb 363
lay in the – 363
– of the Capulets 506
tombé des nues 83, 870
tombola 156
tomboy 129, 851
tombstone 363
tom-cat 373
tome 593
tomentous 256
tomfool 501
tomfoolery
absurdity 497
amusement 840
wit 842
ostentation 882
Tom Noddy 501
Tommy Atkins 726
tommy-gun 727
to-morrow 121
– and to-morrow 104, 109
tompion 263
tomtit 193
Tom Thumb 193
tom-tom 417, 722
ton *weight* 319
fashion 852
–s of money 800
tonality 413, 420
tone *slate* 7
strength 159
tendency 176
sound 402
music 413
color 428
blackness 431
painting 556
method 627
disposition 820
give a – to 852
– down
moderate 174
darken 421
discolor 429
– in with 714
– of voice 580
tone poem 415
toney 852
tongs
fire-irons 386
retention 781
tongue
projection 250
taste 390
language 560
bite the – 392
bridle one's – 585
give – 404, 580
hold one's – 403
slip of the – *error* 495

unemployed 678, 681
unencumbered 705, 927a
unendeared 898
unending 112
unendowed 158
– with reason 450a
unendurable 830
unenjoyed 841
unenlightened 491, 499
unenslaved 748
unenterprising 864
unentertaining 843
unenthralled 748
untitled 925
unenvied 929, 930
unequal 28, 139
inequitable 923
– to 640
unequalled 33
unequipped 674
unequitable 923
unequivocal
great 31
sure 474
clear 518
unerring
certain 474
tone 494
innocent 946
unessayed 678
unessential 643
unestablished 185
uneven diverse 16a
unequal 28
irregular 139
rough 256
uneventful 643
unexact 495
unexaggerated 494
unexamined 460
unexampled 83
unexceptionable
good 648
legitimate 924
innocent 946
unexcitable 826
unexcited 823, 826
unexciting 174
unexecuted 730
unexempt 177
unexercised 674, 678
unexerted 172
unexhausted 159, 639
unexpanded 195, 203
unexpected
exceptional 83
inexpectation 508
unexpensive 815
unexplained
not known 491
unintelligible 519
latent 626
unexplored
neglected 460
ignorant 491
unseen 526
unexposed 526
unexpressed 536
unexpressive 517
unextended 317

unextinguished 173, 382
unfaded 428
unfading 112
unfailing 141
unfair false 544
unjust 923
dishonorable 940
unfaithful 940
unfaltering 604a
unfamiliar 83
unfashionable 83, 851
unfashioned 241, 674
unfasten 44
unfathomable
infinite 105
deep 208
mysterious 519
unfavorable
out of season 135
hindrance 706
obstructive 708
– chance 473
unfeared 861
unfeasible 471
unfed 640, 956
unfeeling 376, 823
unfeigned 543
unfelt 823
unfeminine
manly 373
vulgar 851
unfertile 169
unfetter 750
unfettered 748
unfinished 53, 730
unfit
inappropriate 24
impotence 158
inexpedient 647
unskilful 699
wrong 923
undue 925
unfitted
not prepared 674
unfix 44
unfixed 149
unflagging 604a
unflammable 385
unflattering 494, 703
unfledged
young 127, 129
unprepared 674
unflinching
firm 604
persevering 604a
brave 861
unfold
straighten 246
evolve 313
interpret 522
manifest 525
disclose 529
– a tale 594
unforbidden 760
unforced 602, 748
unforeseen 508
unforfeited 781
unforgettable 505
unforgiving 919
unforgotten 505
unformed 241, 674
unfortified
pure 42

powerless 158
unfortunate
ill-timed 135
failure 732
adversity 735
unhappy 828
– woman 962
unfounded 546
unfrequent 137
unfrequented 893
unfriended
powerless 158
secluded 893
unfriendly
opposed 708
hostile 889
malevolent 907
unfrock 756, 972
unfrozen 382
unfruitful 169
unfulfilled 713, 925
unfurl
unfold 313
– a flag 525, 550
unfurnished 640, 674
ungainly 846, 895
ungallant 895
ungarnished 849
ungathered 678
ungenerous 819, 943
ungenial 657
ungenteel 851, 895
ungentle 173, 895
ungentlemanly
vulgar 851
rude 895
dishonorable 940
ungifted 499
unglorified 874
unglue 47
ungodly 989
ungovernable
violent 173
disobedient 742
passionate 825
ungoverned 748
ungraceful
– language 579
ugly 846
vulgar 851
ungracious 895, 907
ungrammatical 568
ungranted 764
ungrateful 917
ungratified 832
ungrounded
unsubstantial 4
erroneous 495
ungrudging 816
unguarded
neglected 460
spontaneous 612
unprepared 674
in an – moment
unexpectedly 508
unguem, ad – 494, 650
unguent 356
unguibus et rostro 686
unguided
ignorant 491
impulsive 612
unskilled 699
unguilty 946

unhabitable 187
unhabituated 614
unhackneyed 614
unhallowed 988, 989
unhand 750
unhandseled 123
unhandsome 940
unhandy 699
unhappy
adversity 735
pain 828
dejected 837
make – 830
unharbored 185
unhardened
tender 914
innocent 946
penitent 950
unharmonious 24, 414
unharness 750
unhatched 674
unhazarded 664
unhealthy 655, 657
unheard of
exceptional 83
improbable 473
ignorant 491
wonderful 870
unheated 383
unheed, -ed 460
unheeding 458
unhesitating
belief 484
resolved 604
unhewn 241, 674
unhindered 748
unhinge 61, 158
unhinged
impotent 158
insane 503
failure 732
unhitch 44
unholy 989
unhonored 874
unhook (44)
unhoped 508
unhorsed 732
unhostile 888
unhouse 297
unhoused 185
unhurt 670
unicorn
monster 83
carriage 272
unideal existing 1
no thought 452
true 494
unification 48, 87
uniform
homogeneous 16
simple 42
orderly 58
regular 80
dress 225
symmetry 242
livery 550
uniformity 16
unilluminated 421
unimaginable 471, 473
wonderful 870
unimaginative 576, 843, 868
unimagined 1, 494
unimitated 20

unimpaired 670
unimpassioned 826
unimpeachable
certain 474
true 494
due 924
approved 931
innocent 946
unimpeached 931, 946
unimpeded 705, 748
unimportance 643
unimpressed 838
unimpressible 823
unimproved 659
unincreased 36
unincumbered
easy 705
exempt 927a
uninduced 616
uninfected 652
uninfectious 656
uninflammable 385
uninfluenced
obstinate 606
unactuated 616
free 768
uninfluential 172, 175a
uninformed 491
uningenuous 544
uninhabit, -able, -ed 187, 893
uninitiated 491, 699
uninjured
perfect 650
healthy 654
preserved 670
uninjurious 656
uninquisitive 456
uninspired 823
uninstructed 491
unintellectual 452, 499
unintelligent 499
unintelligibility 519
unintelligible 519
- style 571
render – 538
unintentional
necessary 601
undesigned 621
uninterested 456, 841, 843
unintermitting
unbroken 69
durable 110
continuing 143
persevering 604a
uninterrupted
continuous 69
perpetual 112
unremitting 893
unintroduced 893
uninured 614
uninvented 526
uninvestigated 491
uninvited 893
uninviting 830
union
agreement 23
junction 43
combination 48
concurrence 178
workhouse 189
party 712
concord 714

censure 932
detract 934
vilipendency 930
villa 189
village 189
– talk 588
villager 188
villain
  servant 746
  serf 876
  knave 941
  rascal 949
villainous 649, 945
– saltpetre 727
villainy 940
villein [*see* villain]
villenage 749, 777
villi 256
villous 256
vim 171
vin: – d'honneur
  292, 894
not think – ordi-
  naire of oneself
  880
vinaigrette 400
vincible 158
vincture 43
vinculo matrimonii,
  separatio a – 905
vinculum 45
– matrimonii 903
vindicate 467, 937
– a right 924
vindication 937
vindicator 919
vindictive 901, 919
vine 367
– grower 371
vinegar 397
– aspect 846
vinery 191
vineyard 371, 691
vingt et un 840
vintage 371, 636
vintner 637
viol 417
violate
  disobey 742
  non-observance
  773
  undue 925
  dereliction 927
  ravish 961
– a law 83
– the law 964
– a usage 614
violence 173
  arbitrary 964
do – to *bad* 649
  non-observance
  773
  undue 925
violent 173
  excitable 825
– death 360, 361
in a – degree 31
lay – hands on 789
violet 437
violin 417
violinist 416
violoncello 417
viper *snake* 366
  bane 663
  evil-doer 913
  bad man 949
– in one's bosom

667
virago 901
virent 435
vires acquirit
  eundo
  increase 35
  energy 171
  velocity 274
virescence 435
Virgilianae, sortes –
  621
virgin *new* 123
  girl 129
  woman 374
  spinster 904
  good 948
  pure 960
– forest 367
– soil
  ignorance 491
  untilled 674
the – Mary 976
virginals 417
virginibus
  puerisque 960
viribus, totis – 686
viridity 435
virile
  adolescent 131
  strong 159
  manly 373
virtu 850
  article of – 847
virtual 2, 5
– image 443
virtue *power* 157
  courage 861
  goodness **944**
  purity 960
by – of 157, 631
in – of 737
make a – of neces-
  sity *no choice*
  609a
  skill 698
  submit 725
  compromise 774
  bear 826
virtueless 945
virtuoso 416, 850
virtuous 944, 960
virulence
  energy 171
  noxiousness 649
  insalubrity 657
  discourtesy 895
  anger 900
  malevolence 907
virulent 932
virum volitare per
  ora 531
virus 655, 663
vis:
– comica 842
– conservatrix 670
– inertia
  power 157
  inertness 172
  insensibility 823
– medicatrix 660,
  662
– mortua 157
– a tergo 284
– viva 157
visa 488
visage 234, 448
vis-à-vis *front* 234

opposite 237
carriage 272
viscera 221
viscid 352
viscount 875
viscous 352
vise 781
Vishnu 979
visibility 446
visible 446
be – 448
become – 448
  darkness – 421
– radiation 420
vision *sight* 441
  phantasm 443
  dream 515
  specter 980
organ of – 441
visionary
  inexistence 2
  unsubstantial 4
  impossible 471
  imaginary 515
  heterodox 984
visionless 442
visit *arrival* 292
  social 892
  courtesy 894
– upon 972
pay a surprise –
  647
visitation
  disease 655
  adversity 735
  suffering 828
–s of Providence
  976
– of the sick 998
visiting:
– card 550
on – terms 888,
  892
visitor *incomer* 294
  director 694
  friend 890
visor 530
vista
  convergence 260
  sight 441
  appearance 448
  expectation 507
visual 441
– organ 441
vitability 359
vitæ, elixir – 662
vital *life* 359
  important 642
vitality
  stability 150
  strength 159
  life 359
vitalize 359
vitals 221
vitamin impendere
  vero 535, 939
vitamines 298
vitiate 659
vitiated 655
viticulture 371
vitreous 323, 425
vitrify 323
vituperate 908, 932
vituperator 936
viva! 873, 931
vivace *music* 415
vivacious

active 682
sensitive 822
cheerful 836
vivamus, dum
  vivimus – 840
vivandière 797
vivarium 370
vivâ voce 582
vive *glory be to* 873
on the qui – 824
vivendi
  modus – 723
– causa 359
vivid *energetic* 171
  sensibility 375
  light 420
  color 428
  distinct 518
  memory 505
vivify 159, 359
vivisection 378
vixen *fox* 366
  female 374
  shrew 901
viz. [*see* videlicet]
vizier *director* 694
  mask 530
  shield 717
  deputy 759
vizor 530
vobis, sic vos non –
  791
vocable 562
vocabulary 562
vocal 415, 580
– training 537
vocalist 416
vocalize 580
vocation 625
voce, sotto – 581
vociferation
  loud 404
  cry 411
  voice 580
vogue *custom* 613
  fashion 852
  fame 873
vogue la galère
  persevere 604a
  amusement 840
voice *sound* 402
  cry 411
  judgment 480
  promulgate 531
  affirmation 535
  express 566
  human - **580**
  speak 580
  choice 609
give one's – for
  488
raise one's – 411,
  582
still small –
  faint sound 405
  conscience 926
want of – 581
warning – 668
– against 489, 708
– of the charmer
  933
make one's –
  heard 175
– of the tempter
  615
voiced 561
voiceless 581

void *unsubstantial* 4
  absence 187
  emit 297
null and – 964
– of foundation
  546
– of suspicion 484
voidance 297
voiturette 274
voiturier 268
volplaner 267
volant 267
volapük 560
volatile *light* 320
  gaseous 334
  vaporizable 336
  irresolute 605
  capricious 608
volatility 111
vol-au-vent 298
volcanic
  violent 173
  heat 382
  burnt 388
  excitable 825
volcano
  violence 173
  heat 382
  furnace 386
  pitfall 667
on a – 665
volitant 267
volitare per ora,
  virum – 531
volitation 267
volition 600
volley
  collection 72
  violence 173
  report 406
  attack 716
volonté, à – 600
volo sic jubeo, sic –
  600, 741
volt 466
voltaic electricity
  157
volte face 283
voltigeur 726
volto sciolto i pen-
  sieri stretti, il –
  544
voluble 584
volume *great* 31
  part 51
  bulk 192
  book 593
speak –s
  evidence 467
  intelligible 518
  inform 527
– of smoke 330
voluminous 573,
  641
voluntary *overture*
  64, 415
  will 600
  willing 602
  donation 784
voluntas, stet pro
  ratione – 600
volunteer *will* 600
  willing 602
  endeavor 676
  combatant 726
  offer 763
voluptas, sua